FVAND	Future value of an annuity due
FVIF	Future value interest factor
FVIFA	Future value interest factor of an annuity
g	Expected annual growth rate in earnings, dividends, and/or stock price
i	Interest rate per time period
I	Interest payments before taxes
i_{eff}	Annual effective interest rate
i_f	Interest rate in the foreign currency country
IFE	International Fisher effect
i_h	Interest rate in the home currency country
i_{nom}	Annual nominal interest rate
i_R	Real rate of return
IRR	Internal rate of return
k	A percentage required return or cost of capital; discount rate
k_a	Weighted (marginal) cost of capital
k_a^*	Risk-adjusted weighted cost of capital (required return) on an investment
k_d	Required return on a bond; pretax cost of debt; yield to maturity on a bond
k_e	Required return on common stock; cost of internal equity
k'_e	Cost of external equity
k_i	After-tax cost of debt
k_j	Required return from security j
k_p	Required return on preferred stock; Cost of preferred stock financing
LBO	Leveraged buyout
LIBOR	London interbank offer rate
LIFO	Last-in, first-out inventory valuation
m	Frequency of compounding per time period
M	Maturity value of a bond
M_e	Market price of stock ex-rights
M_o	Market price of stock rights-on

CONTEMPORARY FINANCIAL MANAGEMENT

UNIVERSITY OF PHOENIX SPECIAL EDITION SERIES

R. CHARLES MOYER
Babcock Graduate School of Management
Wake Forest University

JAMES R. MCGUIGAN
JRM Investments

WILLIAM J. KRETLOW
University of Houston

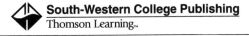
South-Western College Publishing
Thomson Learning™

Australia • Canada • Denmark • Japan • Mexico • New Zealand • Philippines
Puerto Rico • Singapore • South Africa • Spain • United Kingdom • United States

Publisher/Team Director: Jack W. Calhoun
Sponsering Editor: Michael B. Mercier
Developmental Editor: Susan C. Smart
Production Editor: Brenda Owens
Production House: Pre-Press Company, Inc.
Internal Design: Craig Ramsdell
Marketing Manager: Lisa Lysne
Cover Design: Barb Matulionis
Cover Photograph: copyright Greg Girard/The Stock Market

I(T)P®
International Thomson Publishing

South-Western College Publishing is an ITP Company.
The ITP trademark is used under license.

ISBN: 0-324-03701-5

4 5 6 7 WST 2 1 0

Printed in the United States of America

Library of Congress Cataloging-in-Publication Data
Moyer, R. Charles, 1945
  Contemporary financial management / R. Charles Moyer, James R
McGuigan, William J. Kretlow —7th ed.
    p. cm.
    Includes Index
    ISBN 0-324-03701-5
      1. Corporations—Finance. 2. Business enterprises—Finance
I McGuigan, James R.   II Kretlow, William J.   III. Title.
HG4026.M678 1997
  658-15— dc21   97-22789
                                                              CIP

ABOUT THE AUTHORS

R. Charles Moyer holds the Integon Chair in Finance and is Dean of the Babcock Graduate School of Management, Wake Forest University. Prior to assuming his present position, Professor Moyer was a Professor of Finance and Chairman of the Department of Finance at Texas Tech University between 1980 and 1988. Professor Moyer previously taught at the University of Houston, Lehigh University, and the University of New Mexico. Born in Reading, Pennsylvania, he earned his B.A. in economics (*cum laude*) from Howard University, where he was elected to Phi Beta Kappa. He received his M.B.A. and Ph.D. in Business from the University of Pittsburgh. In addition to his teaching career, Professor Moyer has spent a year at the Federal Reserve Bank of Cleveland and a year as a Sears-AACSB Federal Faculty Fellow at the Maritime Administration, U.S. Department of Commerce, serving as a financial and economic analyst. Professor Moyer has taught extensively in executive education programs, including the Stonier Graduate School of Banking. He also frequently is called upon to provide expert testimony in public utility rate cases across the nation.

Professor Moyer has been a productive scholar. In addition to coauthoring *Contemporary Financial Management*, Seventh Edition, he has also coauthored *Managerial Economics*, Seventh Edition (West, 1996), and *Financial Management with Lotus 1-2-3* (West, 1986). Professor Moyer has published extensively in leading finance and economic journals, including *Financial Management, Journal of Financial and Quantitative Analysis, Journal of Finance, Financial Review, Journal of Financial Research, International Journal of Forecasting, Journal of Economics and Business, Journal of Industrial Organization,* and many others. In total, he has published over ninety articles. Professor Moyer has served as a vice president of the Financial Management Association, as a director of the Financial Management Association, the Eastern Finance Association, and the Southern Finance Association, as well as a member of the program committees of those organizations. He is currently Secretary/Treasurer of the Financial Management Association. He is a past president of the Southern Finance Association. He is a frequent reviewer for many finance and economic journals and an associate editor of the *Journal of Financial Research* and of *Financial Practice and Education.*

Professor Moyer has received teaching excellence awards both at the University of New Mexico and at Wake Forest University.

Professor Moyer enjoys athletics and is particularly active as a golfer and tennis player.

James R. McGuigan currently owns and operates his own numismatic investment firm. Prior to this activity, he was Associate Professor of Finance and Business Economics in the School of Business Administration at Wayne State University, where he taught in the undergraduate and masters programs for ten years. He also has taught at the University of Pittsburgh and Point Park College.

Dr. McGuigan received his undergraduate degree from Carnegie-Mellon University. His graduate degrees are from the Graduate Schools of Business at the University of Chicago (M.B.A.) and the University of Pittsburgh (Ph.D.)

He has published articles dealing with his research on options in the *Journal of Financial and Quantitative Analysis*. In addition to his interests in financial management, Dr. McGuigan has coauthored books in managerial economics, including *Managerial Economics*, Seventh Edition (West, 1996), which he coauthored with R. Charles Moyer.

Dr. McGuigan's other interests include running and traveling.

William J. Kretlow is an Associate Professor of Finance at the University of Houston. Born and raised in Chicago, he earned his B.S. from the University of Michigan. He received his M.B.A. from the University of Houston and his Ph.D. from Purdue University, where he was a David Ross Fellow. In addition to teaching at UH, he has been part-time Associate Professor of Economics at Rice University. At UH, he has taught financial management and investments at all levels. He has taught large introductory sections of managerial finance at both Houston and Rice. He has also taught extensively in executive programs, including the UH Executive M.B.A. and Executive Development Programs, and the Stonier Graduate School of Banking of the American Bankers Association.

Professor Kretlow has received several teaching awards, including the University of Houston Teaching Excellence Award and the College of Business Administration Excellence in Teaching Award. He also is recipient of Rice University's *Magna Cum Laude* Teaching Excellence Award.

In the area of academic research, Professor Kretlow has published approximately fifteen articles and given several papers at professional society meetings. His research has dealt with the capital asset pricing model, dividend policy, bond ratings, and financial planning models.

Professor Kretlow's business experience includes a total of five years with Tenneco and Monsanto, and he has advised various small and medium-sized companies on a variety of financial matters. He also has served as an expert witness in a number of financial cases. He is experienced in the valuation of closely held businesses.

CONTENTS

PART II
DETERMINANTS OF VALUATION   123

4 The Time Value of Money   124

PART III
THE CAPITAL INVESTMENT DECISION 309

8 Capital Budgeting and Cash Flow Analysis 310

PART IV
THE COST OF CAPITAL, CAPITAL STRUCTURE, AND DIVIDEND POLICY   413

11 The Cost of Capital   414

12 Capital Structure Concepts   454

13 Capital Structure Management in Practice 484

Appendix 13A
Breakeven Analysis 520

14 Dividend Policy 532

**PART V
WORKING CAPITAL MANAGEMENT
AND FINANCIAL FORECASTING   567**

18 Short- and Intermediate-Term Funding Alternatives   678

PART VI
ADVANCED TOPICS IN
CONTEMPORARY FINANCIAL MANAGEMENT   725

19 Lease Financing   726

Appendix A
Taxes and Depreciation   833

Appendix B
An Overview of the *CFM* Excel Disk   844

Appendix C
An Introduction to the Internet with Applications in Finance   845

PREFACE

The financial management field has recently witnessed an exciting period of change and growth. Financial practitioners are increasingly employing new financial management techniques and sophisticated computer resources to aid in their decision making. "Financial engineers" have created new derivative financial instruments and transactions, such as options, financial futures contracts, options on futures contracts, foreign currency swaps, and interest rate swaps, to help managers manage risk and increase shareholder wealth. Many domestic industries have been restructured because of the pressures of foreign competition. Leveraged buyout transactions also have forced managers to make more careful use of their firm's resources. Corporate reformers have focused attention on the structure of corporate governance relationships and the impact of alternative managerial compensation packages on firm performance. Bankruptcy filings increased dramatically at the end of the 1980s and have remained at high levels in the 1990s. At the same time, financial researchers have made important advances in the areas of valuation, cost of capital, capital structure theory and practice, option valuation (including "real" options associated with capital investments), hedging strategies, and dividend policy. Over the past few years, the access to and content of the Internet have greatly expanded, making timely financial information increasingly available to customers, investors, and financial managers.

The future promises to be an even more exciting time for finance professionals. Spurred on by the activities of "corporate raiders," financial managers have refocused their attention on the basic objective of maximizing shareholder wealth. Managers who act contrary to the interests of shareholders face the prospect of an unfriendly takeover, a corporate restructuring, pressure from foreign competitors, or pressures from shareholder groups and institutional investors. Firms that have been restructured in highly leveraged transactions must now find the operating savings necessary to remain solvent and move toward a sound long-term capital structure. Managers continue to struggle to find the optimal capital structure for their firm. The central importance of cash flows in the financial management of a firm has never been more apparent. Firms that are carrying significantly more debt than in the past will face new challenges during business downturns. With the economic unification of Europe in 1992 and the rise of capitalism in much of Eastern Europe, the former Soviet Union, and China, contemporary financial managers will have to possess greater knowledge of the important aspects of doing business in an international marketplace. In addition, interest in the standards of ethical behavior adopted by managers of business enterprises is growing. Finally, the impact of the Internet on all areas of business practice is sure to be revolutionary as the result of the lifting of barriers to timely information access and the increase of competitive pressures on business managers.

Contemporary Financial Management, Seventh Edition, incorporates these changes—the increased focus on shareholder wealth maximization and cash flow management, an emphasis on the international aspects of financial management, and a concern for the ethical behavior of managers—into a text designed primarily for an introductory course in financial management. Reflecting the increased importance of the Internet, we provide an introduction to the Internet in Appendix C and frequent cites of useful Internet locations throughout the book. The book is also suitable for management development programs and as a reference aid to practicing finance professionals.

We recognize that students enter this course with a wide variety of backgrounds in mathematics, economics, accounting, and statistics. The only presumption we make regarding prior preparation is that all students will have had one course in financial accounting.

DISTINCTIVE FEATURES

Many financial management texts are well written and provide adequate coverage of the basic topics in financial management. In preparing this seventh edition, we continue our commitment to provide a comprehensive, correct, and well-written introduction to the field of financial management. The current edition reflects the many refinements that have been made over the years in subsequent editions. In addition, we have created a text package that fully reflects contemporary financial management developments in the book's organizational design, pedagogical aids to learning, and ancillary materials.

Organizational Design

Contemporary Financial Management (CFM) is organized around the objective of maximizing the value of the firm for its shareholders. This objective is introduced early in the book, and each major financial decision is linked to the impact it has on the value of the firm. The distinctive content features are designed to complement this objective:

1. **Emphasis on the fundamental concepts of cash flow, net present value, risk–return relationships, and market efficiency.** There are four concepts that are central to a complete understanding of most financial management decisions. These concepts are (1) the importance of cash flows as the relevant source of value to a firm, (2) the significance of the net present value rule for valuing cash flows, (3) the relationship between risk and return in the valuation process, (4) the efficiency of the capital markets. These concepts are introduced early in the text. Their central importance in the study of finance is highlighted by specially designated section headings indicating that these are "Foundation Concepts," and hence worthy of extra attention by the student. Other important "Foundation Concepts" are identified throughout the book, including the determinants of the return on equity, the valuation of assets, the valuation of common stock, cash flow estimation principles, capital budgeting decision models, business risk, financial risk, and the weighted cost of capital.
2. **Unique treatment of problems of international financial management.** In a world that is increasingly affected by international trade and capital flows, it is important that finance students be aware of the most important dimensions of international finance. Some texts provide a single chapter dealing with a potpourri of international issues. Unfortunately, most instructors have a difficult time covering this material. Others use a series of

short international topic sections scattered throughout the book. This approach is not suited to providing the in-depth coverage needed for some international finance topics, such as hedging exchange rate risk. In the seventh edition of *CFM*, important international finance relationships, including the operation of foreign currency markets, exchange rate determination, and the role of multinational firms in the global economy, are covered in Chapter 2 ("The Domestic and International Financial Marketplace"). More advanced international topics, such as international parity relationships and the management of foreign exchange risk, are introduced in a new chapter titled "International Financial Management".

To emphasize and reinforce the global nature of financial decision making, we have included "International Issues" sections throughout the book. In these sections, the global issues associated with making financial decisions are illustrated. By covering international finance in this three-tiered manner, we ensure that all students will be exposed to important international dimensions of financial management decisions, as required by the AACSB, and we provide an opportunity for in-depth coverage of some of the more important international finance topics.

3. **Comprehensive and integrated coverage of ethical issues facing financial managers.** Financial managers seeking to maximize shareholder wealth must also confront difficult ethical dilemmas. Integrated throughout the text are fourteen "Ethical Issues" sections that present some of the ethical dilemmas facing financial managers. These sections raise sensitivities to these issues and normally finish with questions and issues for further classroom discussion. This treatment of the ethical dimensions of financial management is consistent with the AACSB's recommendations for coverage of these issues.

4. **Early coverage of institutional characteristics and valuation models for financial instruments.** We have provided separate chapters (Chapters 6 and 7) dealing with the valuation of fixed income securities and common stock. These chapters also define all of the important characteristics of each of these security types and cover the institutional aspects of the markets for these securities, including the reading and understanding of security transaction information from sources like the *Wall Street Journal*. This structure provides students with both an institutional understanding of bonds, preferred stock, and common stock and an understanding of the valuation process for securities in the financial marketplace.

5. **Early coverage of time value of money concepts.** Time value of money concepts are covered in depth in Chapter 4. This treatment provides students with the exposure needed to fully understand the valuation process that is central to the goal of shareholder wealth maximization. In addition, this coverage of the time value of money involves students in useful practical applications early on in the course, setting an early tone of relevance for the course.

6. **The importance of cash flow analysis is introduced early and reemphasized throughout the text.** Chapter 1 introduces students to the importance of the cash flow concept. This concept is then applied extensively in the context of valuation (Chapters 6 and 7), capital budgeting (Chapters 8, 9, and 10), dividend policy (Chapter 14), working capital management and financial forecasting (Chapter 15), and corporate restructuring (Chapter 22).

7. **Attention to unique problems of financial management in entrepreneurial finance.** In recognition of the important and growing role of small and medium-sized firms in the American business environment, we have included seven "Entrepreneurial Finance Issues" sections that appear in appropriate places throughout the book and highlight unique finance-related problems and concerns of entrepreneurs (small businesses).

8. **Extensive development of the cash flow estimation process in capital budgeting.** Perhaps the most important step in the capital budgeting process is the estimation of cash flows for potential projects. *CFM* devotes an entire chapter (Chapter 8) to this topic, with a separate book appendix (Appendix A) detailing the impact of tax laws affecting capital budgeting decisions.

9. **A detailed discussion of real options that are embedded in many capital investment projects.** Finance scholars and practitioners have increasingly focused attention on "embedded options" in capital investment projects, such as the option to abandon, the option to expand, and the option to defer investments. These options add value to an investment project, above that normally identified in a net present value calculation. Chapter 9 includes an extensive, intuitive discussion of real options in capital budgeting.

10. **Coverage of the newest financial analysis and performance appraisal concepts.** The increased attention given to the objective of shareholder wealth maximization has brought about the development of new performance appraisal models that can be used to judge a firm's performance and "incent" managers to create value. The "Market Value Added" and "Economic Value Added" concepts, developed by Stern-Stewart, are covered in detail in Chapter 3 ("Evaluation of Financial Performance").

11. **Broad, integrated treatment of working capital management.** For many small and medium-sized companies, the management of working capital can present more challenges than any other area of financial management. A thorough and up-to-date four-chapter section on working capital management is included.

12. **Emphasis on the impact of inflation.** During the 1970s and 1980s, finance practitioners were forced to learn how to operate in an inflationary environment. These skills are expected to remain important in the 1990s. Therefore, this text contains frequent discussions of the impact of inflation.

13. **Introduction to new financial instruments and strategies.** Financial futures contracts, options, interest rate swaps, corporate restructuring, and leveraged buyouts (LBOs), to name but a few, have become increasingly important to contemporary financial managers. These topics are introduced to the student in an applied context that illustrates their value to financial managers.

14. **Frequent coverage of the impact of agency relationships in financial management.** The impact of principal–agent relationships on decisions in the areas of goal setting, valuation, capital structure, dividend policy, and corporate restructuring are presented throughout the book.

Pedagogical Aids

CFM has been carefully designed to assist the student in learning and to stimulate student interest. Distinctive pedagogical features include:

1. **Financial Challenges.** Each chapter begins with an illustration of a financial management problem faced by a firm or individual. These exciting lead-ins come from real-firm situations including Daimler-Benz AG, AT&T, Citibank, Marriott, Boston Chicken, Ford Motor, Circus Circus, Boeing, Mountain Fuel Supply Company, Florida Power and Light Company, Chrysler, Procter & Gamble, Macy's, Ryder Leasing, and Baring Brothers Bank. These examples focus on financial problems in the topic area of the chapter and highlight the importance of learning sound financial management principles. The "Financial Challenges" have been extensively revised and updated from the sixth edition, including the addition of many totally new examples.

2. **Internet Applications.** New to this edition are numerous references throughout each chapter to interesting Internet applications that can be found on the World Wide Web. These Internet applications provide students with handy references that can be used to explore the Internet for additional information and data dealing with the topic of the chapter.

3. **Thomson Investors Network.** Instructors and students who purchase this text are eligible for a special offer to subscribe to Thomson Investors Network (TIN) at http://www.Thomsoninvest.net. TIN offers pricing and volume information on over 7,000 stocks and 5,000 mutual funds. It also offers stock alerts on expected earnings announcements, earnings surprises, dividend reports, merger activity, and unusual price changes. The service includes links to two-year price-volume charts, company reports, and daily stock tips. Students will be able to conduct in-depth research on individual companies, keep on top of the latest news affecting stocks of interest, and access the Portfolio Tracker to follow real or mock portfolios. Visit the Finance Resource Center (http://finance.swcollege.com) for more details.

4. **Calculator Application Illustrations.** Many chapters have easy-to-follow, step-by-step calculator keystrokes to solve many of the time value of money examples developed in the text. These "Calculator Applications" sections are set up in a generic calculator format and can be used with virtually any financial calculator. In addition to these in-text illustrations, a handy insert card is included with the text that describes the precise keystrokes for many popular calculator brands.

5. **Extensive and fully integrated examples of the financial policies and problems facing real firms.** Throughout the book we have illustrated financial management concepts using problems facing real firms. By minimizing the number of hypothetical firm situations and using data and situations facing actual firms that the students will recognize and can relate to, *CFM* has further enhanced the realism and excitement.

6. **Improved use of notation.** Notation in this edition of the text has been simplified and made more intuitive to aid student learning. Inside the front cover we have provided a handy summary of the key notation used throughout the book.

7. **Expanded problem set.** The end-of-chapter problem set has been expanded with additional, challenging, class-tested problems. Many of the new problems contain a surfeit of information, forcing students to identify the relevant material needed to solve the problem. The expanded problem set provides students and instructors with a greater breadth of problem coverage than is the case in competing texts.

8. **Self-test problems.** Each chapter includes end-of-chapter self-test problems, complete with detailed solutions, that students can use for further practice and enhanced understanding of the concepts developed in the chapter. In addition, selected check answers to some of the regular end-of-chapter problems appear at the end of the text.

9. **Integrative cases.** At the end of appropriate chapters, an expanded set of comprehensive "Integrative Cases" are provided. Many of these cases can be used in conjunction with the Excel templates (available with the book) to demonstrate the power of computers in performing sensitivity analysis.

10. **An exciting four-color design.** The four-color text design provides for a visibly more pleasing and a more understandable presentation of important text material, figures, and tables.

11. **Excel templates.** A set of twenty user-friendly, flexible Excel templates are available to solve a wide range of problems in the text. Problems where these templates can be used are designated with a special logo.

Ancillary Materials

A complete set of ancillary materials is available to adopters to supplement the text, including the following:

■ An *Instructor's Resource Manual* contains detailed solutions to the end-of-chapter questions and problems and documentation for the Excel templates included in the back of the manual. The solutions to text questions and problems have been thoroughly checked to assure their accuracy, and are available on diskette upon request.

■ An expanded *Test Bank,* coauthored by the text authors and Professor John Dunkelberg of Wake Forest University, offers over 1,500 multiple choice questions and problems. This unique test bank is designed with the instructor in mind. Approximately 60 percent of the questions are "fact" questions, taken directly from the discussion in the text. Approximately 20 percent of the questions are "elementary problem" questions that closely parallel problem examples developed in the chapter and easier problems at the end of the chapter. Approximately 20 percent of the questions are "challenging problems" that require the student to apply concepts developed in the chapter to new problem situations.

Following each "fact" question, the instructor is provided with (1) the correct answer and (2) an identification of the question topic (that is, a reference to the major heading and subheading in the text where the correct answer is found).

Following each "elementary problem" and "challenging problem," the instructor is provided with (1) the correct answer, (2) an identification of the question topic (that is, a reference to the major heading and subheading in the text where the procedure for calculating the correct answer is found), and (3) a detailed solution to the problem.

■ A computerized version of the test bank is available to simplify the preparation of quizzes and exams.

■ A *Supplemental Problem Set* that can be assigned to students is available. This problem set contains approximately 400 problems, about 50 percent of which are totally new. The balance are refactored problems from the end-of-chapter problem set in the text. Available both in hard copy and on diskette.

- A set of over 170 *Transparency Acetates* of the most important tables and graphs is available.
- A set of *Demonstration Problems* in transparency master format is available in both hard copy and on diskette. The problems parallel the major examples developed in the text.
- *Excel Templates* are designed to solve a wide variety of financial management problems. Problems in the text that can be solved using these templates are indicated with a small diskette logo next to the problem. The templates require *absolutely no prior knowledge of Excel.* All input and instructions are menu driven in a clear, concise, command menu created by the authors. All of the templates are designed so they can be used to solve actual business financial analysis problems, not just simplified textbook examples. The disk is provided to instructors in the back of the *Instructor's Resource Manual* and may be duplicated or placed on a network for student use.
- A *Study Guide* written by Professor Ramesh Rao of Texas Tech University is available for all students. The *Study Guide* contains detailed chapter outlines, solved true/false questions, and a large number of solved numerical problems.
- *Detailed Chapter Outlines/Lecture Notes* are available as a separate bound manual.
- A *PowerPoint Slide Presentation* package is offered to enhance lecture materials. It presents the key topics in each chapter in an electronic format.
- All of the instructor's supplements are available on CD-ROM upon request, and many can be found on the Web site.
- A Web site that supports *Contemporary Financial Management, seventh edition,* is located at http://moyer.swcollege.com. The site provides teaching resources, learning resources, Internet application links, current updates, and an interactive Ask-the-Author section.

 MAJOR CHANGES IN THE SEVENTH EDITION

The seventh edition of *CFM* has been extensively updated and revised to reflect contemporary developments in finance and the many fine suggestions from sixth edition users and reviewers. Throughout the book, many additional, contemporary examples have been added. In addition, other *major* changes in the text of the seventh edition include:

Chapter 1: The Role and Objective of Financial Management

- Contains new material on careers in finance plus references to WWW locations for more career information.
- Includes a discussion of various business organizational forms.

Chapter 2: The Domestic and International Financial Marketplace

- Provides an overview of the U.S. financial systems and the functioning of U.S. security markets.
- Provides the introductory material needed to understand international financial transactions, including a discussion of foreign currency markets and the determination of exchange rates.

Chapter 3: Evaluation of Financial Performance

■ Provides an updated section on the Stern-Stewart "Market Value Added" and "Economic Value Added" concepts.
■ Includes a new section dealing with dividend policy ratios.

Chapter 4: The Time Value of Money

■ Features an expanded coverage of loan amortization analysis.

Chapter 6: Fixed-Income Securities: Characteristics and Valuation

■ Incorporates material dealing with understanding bond quotations.
■ Provides a new discussion of reinvestment rate risk.
■ Expands and enhances calculator applications.
■ Moves bond refunding analysis to an appendix in this chapter.

Chapter 7: Common Stock: Characteristics, Valuation, and Issuance

■ Incorporates material dealing with understanding stock market data.

Chapter 8: Capital Budgeting and Cash Flow Analysis

■ Adds a new, simplified tabular approach to the determination of net cash flows.

Chapter 9: Capital Budgeting: Decision Criteria and Real Option Considerations

■ Places more emphasis on the role of real options in capital budgeting.

Chapter 10: Capital Budgeting and Risk

■ Adds new material on "scenario analysis."

Chapter 12: Capital Structure Concepts

■ Includes an expanded discussion of the "pecking order" theory of capital structure.

Chapter 13: Capital Structure Management in Practice

■ Includes a new discussion of the effect of leverage on shareholder wealth and the cost of capital.
■ Reviews the breakeven analysis concept in the appendix to this chapter.

Chapter 14: Dividend Policy

■ Provides a new section on "Industry and Company Variations in Dividend Payout Ratios."
■ Includes an expanded discussion of the role of shareholder preferences in the establishment of dividend policy.
■ Presents additional discussion of the share repurchase decision as a dividend policy.

Chapter 15: Financial Forecasting and Working Capital Policy

■ Reorganizes the chapter for a more logical topic flow by moving the financial forecasting material to the beginning.
■ Provides a new section dealing with forecasting financial performance with financial ratios.

Chapter 16: The Management of Cash and Marketable Securities

■ A new chapter that deals with the management of cash and marketable securities.

Chapter 17: Management of Accounts Receivable and Inventories

■ A new chapter that focuses on accounts receivable and inventory management, including the use of inventory control models and other inventory management techniques.

Chapter 18: Short- and Intermediate-Term Funding Alternatives

■ Includes a new discussion of the advantages and disadvantages of various short- and intermediate-term financing alternatives.

Chapter 20: Financing with Derivatives

■ Includes new material on the use of interest rate swaps.

Chapter 21: International Financial Management

■ A new chapter that considers international parity relationships and the management of transaction, translation, and economic exposure.

Chapter 22: Corporate Restructuring

■ Includes a new discussion of antitakeover measures.

Appendix A: Taxes and Depreciation

■ A new book appendix that summarizes in one place the key elements of taxation and depreciation rules as they affect financial decision making.

 ORGANIZATION AND INTENDED USE

CFM is organized into six major parts. Part I defines the finance function, examines the goals of the firm, considers the role of the financial manager, reviews the structure and functioning of the domestic and international financial marketplace, and reviews accounting fundamentals, including the analysis of financial performance. The importance of tax considerations to the practice of financial management also is analyzed. The basic concepts of shareholder wealth maximization, cash flows, net present value, and market efficiency are presented. Part II develops the theory of valuation, including a comprehensive treatment of time value of money concepts, the valuation of fixed income securities, and the valuation of equity securities. The role of investment bankers in the issuance of securities is discussed. Risk-return analysis concepts are presented. Part III presents the capital investment decision, emphasizing both the theoretical and the practical aspects of capital budgeting, including the role played by real options in the capital budgeting process. Part IV deals with the cost of capital, the determinants of an optimal capital structure, and dividend policy. Part V considers working capital management decisions in the areas of cash, marketable securities, accounts receivable, inventories, and sources of short- and intermediate-term financing. Part V also covers financial forecasting techniques. Part VI covers lease financing, financing with derivatives, advanced international finance topics, and corporate restructuring.

Those instructors who wish to cover topics in an order other than that provided in the text will find it easy to make adjustments. The book is designed for use in a three-semester-hour (or the equivalent in the quarter system) course in financial management. Typically, within the constraints of this time limit, it is often not possible to fully cover all topics. Instructors will find it easy to defer more advanced or specialized topics until a later course.

 ACKNOWLEDGMENTS

The authors wish to acknowledge the helpful comments provided by many of our first, second, third, fourth, fifth, and sixth edition users. We are particularly grateful for the careful reviews and suggestions made by the following professors:

Hez A. Aubey	Jerry D. Boswell	Maclyn L. Clouse
Peter W. Bacon	Don Bowlin	David Cox
Richard Bauer	Jay T. Brandi	John Crockett
Carl Beidleman	Peter Brucato	Rudolph D'Souza
Thomas Berry	William Brunsen	Lynn E. Dellenbarger, Jr.
Scott Besley	Robert Chatfield	Shreesh Deshpande
Gordon R. Bonner	Tylor Claggett	William Dukes

John Dunkelberg
Fred Ebeid
John W. Ellis
Holger Engberg
Marilyn Ettinger
Keith W. Fairchild
Edward Farragher
Donald Fehrs
Mike Ferri
Jane Finley
Shifra Fraifeld
Richard Gendreau
James Gentry
Michael Gombola
James Greenleaf
Kamal Haddad
Thomas Hamilton
Charles Harper
Rick Harris
Mahboubul Hassan
Delbert Hastings
Patrick Hays
Shantaram P. Hedge
Robert Hehre
George Hettenhouse
L. Dean Hiebert
K. P. Hill
Shalom Hochman
Barbara Howard
Thomas Howe
Pearson Hunt
Keith B. Johnson
R. Larry Johnson
Charles P. Jones
Raymond G. Jones, Jr.
Kee Kim
Thomas Klaasen

Daniel P. Klein
Timothy Koch
Harry R. Kuniansky
Robert Lamy
Keith Laycock
Thomas D. Legg
Joseph J. Levitzky
Thomas J. Liesz
David Lindsley
Charles Linke
Mike Lockett
Inayat U. Mangla
Wayne M. Marr
Robert McElreath
Z. Lew Melnyk
Richard Meyer
Edward M. Miller
Billy C. Moore
Robert A. Olsen
Coleen G. Pantalone
Ajay Patel
Walter W. Perlick
Susan M. Phillips
Mario Picconi
Pegaret Pichler
Anthony Plath
Alwyn du Plessis
Ralph Pope
Dwight Porter
Robert Porter
Rose Prasad
Dianna Preece
Kelly Price
Dennis Proffitt
Ramesh Rao
Russ Ray
Bruce Resnick

Jesse Reyes
William B. Riley
Charles T. Rini
John T. Rose
Jack H. Rubens
Carolyn J. Ryan
Gary C. Sanger
Richard Sapp
Robert G. Schwebach
Robert Schweitzer
Bernard A. Shinkel
Mark Shrader
Phillip Sisneros
Donald Simonson
John Speltz
Richard F. Sperring
Uma Sridharan
Rolf K. Tedefalk
Richard J. Teweles
Niranjan Tripathy
Anthony M. Tuberose
George Ulseth
David Upton
Howard E. Van Auken
Sue Visscher
John M. Wachowicz, Jr.
Charles Wade
Alan Weatherford
Marsha Weber
Herbert Weinraub
J. Daniel Williams
E. Walter Wilson
Lawrence Wolken
Richard Zock
J. Kenton Zumwalt

and the following business professionals:

Gordon B. Bonfield
Richard H. Brock
Roy V. Campbell
Gary Costley
Norman Dmuchowski
Stephen H. Grace
Samuel C. Hadaway
R. Lee Haney
Raymond A. Hay
Lawrence Ingrassia

Ira G. Kawaller
Carl J. Lange
Martin H. Lange
Lewis Lehr
C. Londa
Paul MacAvoy
Frank Mastrapasqua
John H. Maxheim
John McKinnon
Thomas R. Mongan

Robert B. Morris III
T. Boone Pickens
Jack S. Rader
M. W. Ramsey
William J. Regan
Albert J. Robison
Julie Salamon
Kenneth Schwartz
Terry J. Winders

We are also indebted to Lehigh University, Texas Tech University, the University of Houston, the University of New Mexico, Wayne State University, and Wake Forest University for the considerable support they provided in this or earlier editions. We greatly appreciate the assistance provided by graduate assistant Andrew McPhail.

We owe thanks, as well, to our deans and fellow faculty members at our universities for the encouragement and assistance they provided on a continuing basis during the preparation of the manuscript.

Finally, we wish to express our thanks to the members of the South-Western Publishing Company staff. We are particularly appreciative of the support provided by Chris Will, our editor, Susanna Smart, the developmental editor, and Brenda Owens, the production editor. We also want to acknowledge the assistance provided by Mary Schiller, who was our editor for the previous six editions and was instrumental in the early stages of this revision.

PART I

INTRODUCTION

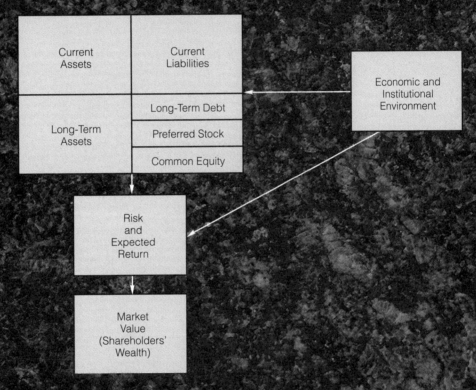

Part I provides an overview of the field of financial management. Chapter 1 discusses the role of financial management in the firm and the alternative forms of business organization and identifies the primary goal of the firm as the maximization of shareholder wealth. The foundation concepts of cash flow and net present value are introduced. The chapter also considers the organization of the financial management function, the relationship between finance and other business disciplines, and various careers that are available in fi- nance. Chapter 2 presents key elements of the U.S. financial marketplace, including the struc- ture of the U.S. financial system and the role of stock exchanges. Also included is an introduc- tion to the various types of financial derivative securities. The last part of the chapter con- tains an introduction to international financial management, including multinational enter- prises and the foreign currency markets and exchange rates. Chapter 3 deals with the tools of financial statement analysis used to evalu- ate a firm's financial performance.

THE ROLE AND OBJECTIVE OF FINANCIAL MANAGEMENT

1

KEY CHAPTER CONCEPTS

1. The most important forms of business organization are the
   a. Sole proprietorship
   b. Partnership—both limited and general
   c. Corporation
2. Corporations have the advantages of limited liability for owners, potentially perpetual life, and the ability to raise large amounts of capital. Even though they account for only 20 percent of U.S. firms, corporations account for over 90 percent of U.S. business revenues.
3. *Shareholder wealth* is defined as the present value of the expected future returns to the owners of the firm. It is measured by the market value of the shareholders' common stock holdings.
4. The primary normative goal of the firm is to maximize shareholder wealth.
5. Achievement of the shareholder wealth maximization goal often is constrained by social responsibility concerns and problems arising out of agency relationships.
6. The market value of a firm's stock is determined by the magnitude, timing, and risk of the cash flows the firm is expected to generate. Managers can take a variety of actions to influence the magnitude, timing, and risk of the firm's cash flows. These actions are often classified as investment, financing, and dividend decisions.

7. Cash flow is a fundamental concept in finance and a focus of financial managers who are concerned with raising cash to invest in assets that will generate future cash flows for the firm and its owners.
8. The net present value rule is the primary decision-making rule used throughout the practice of financial management.
   a. The net present value of an investment is equal to the present value of future returns minus the required initial outlay.
   b. The net present value of an investment made by a firm represents the contribution of that investment to the value of the firm and, accordingly, to the wealth of shareholders.
9. Ethical standards of performance are an increasingly important dimension of the decision-making process of managers.
10. The finance function is usually headed by a vice-president or chief financial officer.
    a. Financial management responsibilities often are divided between the controller and treasurer.
    b. The controller normally has responsibility for all activities related to accounting.
    c. The treasurer normally is concerned with the acquisition, custody, and expenditure of funds.

FINANCIAL MANAGEMENT QUESTIONS

■ In 1989, Kohlberg Kravis Roberts & Co. (KKR) acquired RJR Nabisco, Inc., for $109 per share, nearly twice the price that RJR's stock was selling for prior to the takeover. Why would KKR be willing to pay such a large premium to gain control of RJR Nabisco?

■ In 1990, the bond trading department at Salomon Brothers, a major investment banking firm, submitted a series of illegal bids in connection with U.S. Treasury bond auctions. After details of the scandal became public, the employees involved (down to the clerk who submitted the illegal bids) lost their jobs. Four top Salomon officials, including the president and the chairman of the board, also were forced to resign. The firm paid $290 million in fines and restitution to the U.S. government. Several of the employees involved paid stiff fines and were barred by the government from similar work. One employee received a prison sentence. Furthermore, Salomon's stock lost $1.5 *billion* in market value during the week in August 1991 when news of the scandal broke. How were general business ethics violated, and what was the cost to the firm of those violations?

■ In 1994, Borden, a well-known food company, announced plans to sell off parts of its business in order to raise cash after trying unsuccessfully to find a buyer for the whole company. The financially troubled company had experienced steadily falling revenues and earnings. Borden's food products include such familiar items as Lady Borden ice cream, Lays potato chips, Cracker Jacks, ReaLemon, as well as nonfood items such as Elmer's glue. What financial techniques will the Borden management use to determine a fair price to put on its Cracker Jack business, for example?

■ A complex and fundamental issue in financial management is whether executives should focus on market share

and growth or on profitability. In the case of Ford Motor Company, questions have been raised about whether management is concerned too much with market share and not enough with profitability. Critics claim that the cost of Ford's push for market share has hurt its profit margins. In comparison, Chrysler, which has a smaller market share than Ford, has been leading the industry in profitability. Likewise, GM's efforts to maintain its market share, regardless of the cost, contributed to the company's large losses in the early 1990s. What should be the goal(s) of a company such as Ford?

■ In 1995 Kirk Kerkorian, Chrysler's largest shareholder, made a $20 billion, $55 per share leveraged buyout offer for the company. He claimed that the company's $7.3 billion cash stockpile was more than Chrysler needed for its operations and that some of this hoard should be paid out to stockholders either in the form of cash dividends or share repurchases. Lee Iacocca, a Kerkorian ally and former Chrysler chairman, claimed that the company needed only $2.5 billion in cash (plus an equal amount from credit lines) to handle another economic recession. Chrysler management, on the other hand, with memories of near-bankruptcy a few years ago, believed that the company needed a $7.5 billion cash balance to survive the next cyclical downturn in the automobile business. What is the optimal cash balance for a corporation, such as Chrysler, that is subject to large cyclical swings in sales and cash flows?

■ In 1993, the price of shares of Boston Chicken, a barely profitable restaurant chain, soared by 143 percent on the day of its initial public offering. The initial public offering was priced at $20 per share by Merrill Lynch, the leading investment firm that underwrote the stock. The stock finished its first day of trading at $48.50 a share. Did Merrill Lynch underprice the Boston Chicken

stock and thus deprive Boston Chicken of additional funds, presumably to be used for expansion? Or did investors just pay too much for the Boston Chicken shares? By March 1994, the Boston Chicken stock was trading roughly in the $45 per share range.

■ In 1994, Metallgesellschaft AG, a large German metals and engineering company, announced potential losses of nearly $1 billion resulting from its activities in derivative securities. Derivatives, such as futures and options, are financial contracts whose values are "derived" from, or are dependent upon, the value of some underlying asset, such as crude oil in this instance. Metallgesellschaft is a wholesaler of oil products, and its losses stemmed from unsuccessful attempts by the company to hedge, or protect, itself from changes in the price of oil. In late 1993, as details of the losses emerged, Metallgesellschaft's board of directors fired most of the company's top management. How did Metallgesellschaft allow itself to get into a position to lose such a large amount of money?

Each of these situations have implications for financial decision making. Financial management decisions made within enterprises—small or large, international or local, profit seeking or not for profit—help to determine the kinds of products and services we consume and their prices, availability, and quality. Financial decisions affect the risk of a firm and the success of that firm in maximizing shareholder wealth. In short, financial decision making has impacts that are felt daily throughout the entire economy.

The situations just described pose many important questions for financial managers. The financial concepts and tools needed to deal with problems such as these and to make you a more effective decision maker are the subject matter of this book.

RCM Financial maintains a very comprehensive financial Web site: multimedia presentations, online spreadsheets, financial software, 245 finance and business publications, over 300 search engines, a glossary of over 3,400 financial terms, virtual libraries, 67,000 links to other financial Web sites, and a lot more. It's well worth bookmarking.
http://www.rcmfinancial.com/
index.htm

INTRODUCTION

Financial managers have the primary responsibility for acquiring funds (cash) needed by a firm and for directing those funds into projects that will maximize the value of the firm for its owners. The field of financial management[1] is an exciting and challenging one, with a wide range of rewarding career opportunities in the fields of corporate financial management, investment banking, investment analysis and management, commercial banking, real estate, insurance, and the public sector—to name only a few broad areas.

Articles appear regularly in the major business periodicals, such as the *Wall Street Journal, Business Week, Fortune, Forbes,* and *Dunn's,* describing financial managers' involvement in important and challenging tasks. Consider, for example, the options facing Chrysler when Kirk Kerkorian (and Lee Iacocca, Chrysler's former chairman) made a $20 billion leveraged buyout offer for the company in early 1995. Should Chrysler fight the offer by undertaking a management-led buyout, find an alternative merger partner, such as an alliance with a foreign company, undertake a massive stock-repurchase program, or just reject the offer outright? Think about the challenges facing AT&T in its decision to split itself into three separate, independent companies—AT&T services, network equipment (Lucent Technologies), and global information systems (NCR). How should the former company's assets, liabilities, and personnel be allocated among the three new companies? Put yourself in the position of the managers of Apple Computer as they made choices about whether to sell assets, defer investments, cut dividends, or possibly merge with a stronger company in order to stem the losses and outflow of cash during 1995 and 1996.

Think of being the portfolio manager who bought stock in a newly public firm, Boston Chicken, for $20 per share on Tuesday, November 9, 1993, and saw the shares increase to $48.50 by the end of the day. Should the portfolio manager sell the stock and take the profits or continue to hold the stock in the hope of an even higher price in the future?

Any business has important financial concerns, and its success or failure depends in a large part on the quality of its financial decisions. Every key decision made by a firm's managers has important financial implications. Managers daily face questions like the following:

- Will a particular investment be successful?
- Where will the funds come from to finance the investment?
- Does the firm have adequate cash or access to cash—through bank borrowing agreements, for example—to meet its daily operating needs?
- Which customers should be offered credit, and how much should they be offered?
- How much inventory should be held?
- Is a merger or acquisition advisable?
- How should cash flows be used or distributed? That is, what is the optimal dividend policy?
- In trying to arrive at the best financial management decisions, how should risk and return be balanced?

---

[1]The terms *financial management, managerial finance, corporate finance,* and *business finance* are virtually synonymous and are used interchangeably. Most financial managers, however, seem to prefer either *financial management* or *managerial finance.*

This text presents an introduction to the theory, institutional background, and analytical tools essential for proper decision making in these and related areas. As a prospective manager, you will be introduced to the financial management process of typical firms. By learning how the financial management process works, you establish one of the key building blocks for a successful management career.

 ## FORMS OF BUSINESS ORGANIZATION

Most businesses are organized as either a sole proprietorship, a partnership, or a corporation.

Sole Proprietorship

A **sole proprietorship** is a business owned by one person. One of the major advantages of the sole proprietorship business form is that it is easy and inexpensive to establish. A major disadvantage of a sole proprietorship is that the owner of the firm has *unlimited personal liability* for all debts and other obligations incurred by the firm.

Sole proprietorships have another disadvantage in that their owners often have difficulty raising funds to finance growth. Thus, sole proprietorships generally are small. Although approximately 75 percent of all businesses in the United States are this type, their revenue amounts to less than 6 percent of the total U.S. business revenue.[2] Sole proprietorships are especially important in the retail trade, service, construction, and agriculture industries.

Partnership

A **partnership** is a business organization in which two or more co-owners form a business, normally with the intention of making a profit. Each partner agrees to provide a certain percentage of the funds necessary to run the business and/or agrees to do some portion of the necessary work. In return, the partners share in the profits (or losses) of the business.

Partnerships may be either general or limited. In a **general partnership,** each partner has unlimited liability for all of the obligations of the business. Thus, general partnerships have the same major disadvantage as sole proprietorships. Even so, approximately 90 percent of all partnerships in the United States are of this type.

A **limited partnership** usually involves one or more general partners and one or more limited partners. Although the limited partners may limit their liability, the extent of this liability can vary and is set forth in the partnership agreement. Limited partnerships are common in real estate ventures. During the 1980s some corporations, such as Mesa Petroleum, restructured themselves as *master limited partnerships*, where the partnership units trade just like shares of stock.

The primary motivation for master limited partnerships was to avoid the double taxation of the firm's income that occurs in a corporation. Tax code changes in 1987 largely eliminated the tax motivation for master limited partnerships.[3]

The Small Business Administration offers some very helpful tips and information on running a small business, including financial guidance, local resources, and disaster assistance.
http://www.sba.gov

---

[2]Internal Revenue Service, *Statistics of Income Bulletin,* (Washington, DC: Summer 1996): 137–138, 140–141.
[3]Mesa converted back from a master limited partnership to a corporation at the end of 1991.

Partnerships have been relatively important in the agriculture, mining, oil and gas, finance, insurance, real estate, and services industries. Overall, partnerships account for about 7 percent of all U.S. business firms and less than 5 percent of total business revenues.[4]

Partnerships are relatively easy to form, but they must be reformed when there is a change in the makeup of the general partners. Partnerships have a greater capacity to raise capital than sole proprietorships, but they lack the tremendous capital attraction ability of corporations.

Corporation

Do you know who the 400 richest people in America are? Which are the 200 best-run small companies? The 500 largest private firms? Forbes Magazine *can tell you.*
http://www.forbes.com

A **corporation** is a "legal person" composed of one or more actual individuals or legal entities. It is considered to be separate and distinct from those individuals or entities. Money contributed to start a corporation is called *capital stock* and is divided into *shares*; the owners of the corporation are called *stockholders* or *shareholders*.

Corporations account for less than 20 percent of all U.S. business firms, but about 90 percent of U.S. business revenues, and approximately 70 percent of U.S. business profits.[5]

The corporate form of business organization has four major advantages over both sole proprietorships and partnerships.

- ■ **Limited Liability** Once stockholders have paid for their shares, they are not liable for any obligations or debts the corporation may incur. They are liable only to the extent of their investment in the shares.
- ■ **Permanency** The legal existence of a corporation is not affected by whether stockholders sell their shares, which makes it a more permanent form of business organization.
- ■ **Flexibility** A change of ownership within a corporation is easily accomplished when one individual merely sells shares to another. Even when shares of stock are sold, the corporation continues to exist in its original form.
- ■ **Ability to Raise Capital** Due to the limited liability of its owners and the easy marketability of its shares of ownership, a corporation is able to raise large amounts of capital, which makes large-scale growth possible.

However, the ability to raise capital comes with a cost. In the typical large corporation, ownership is separated from management. This gives rise to potential conflicts of goals and certain costs, called *agency costs*, discussed later. However, the ability to raise large amounts of capital at relatively low cost is such a large advantage of the corporate form over sole proprietorships and partnerships that a certain level of agency costs are tolerated.

As a "legal person," a corporation can purchase and own assets, borrow money, sue, and be sued. Its officers are considered to be *agents* of the corporation and are authorized to act on the corporation's behalf. For example, only an officer, such as the treasurer, can sign an agreement to repay a bank loan for the corporation.

Corporate Organization. In most corporations, the stockholders elect a *board of directors*, which, in theory, is responsible for managing the corporation. In practice, however, the board of directors usually deals only with broad policy matters, leav-

---

[4]Internal Revenue Service, *Statistics of Income Bulletin* (Washington, DC: Summer 1996):137–138, 140–141.
[5]Internal Revenue Service, *Statistics of Income Bulletin* (Washington, DC: Summer 1996): 137–138, 140–141.

ing the day-to-day operations of the business to the *officers*, who are elected by the board. Corporate officers normally include a *chairman of the board, chief executive officer, chief operating officer, president, vice-president(s), treasurer,* and *secretary.* In some corporations, one person holds more than one office; for instance, many small corporations have a person who serves as secretary-treasurer. In most corporations, the president and various other officers are also members of the board of directors. These officers are called "inside" board members, whereas other board members, such as the company's attorney or banker, are called "outside" board members. A corporation's board of directors usually contains at least three members.

Corporate Securities. In return for the use of their funds, investors in a corporation are issued certificates, or *securities.* Corporate securities represent claims against the assets and future earnings of the firm.

There are two types of corporate securities. Investors who lend money to the corporation are issued *debt securities;* these investors expect periodic interest payments, as well as the eventual return of their principal. Owners of the corporation are issued *equity securities.* Equity securities take the form of either *common stock* or *preferred stock.* Common stock is a residual form of ownership; that is, the claims of common stockholders on the firm's earnings and assets are considered only after all other claims—such as those of the government, debtholders, and preferred stockholders—have been met. Common stockholders are considered to be true owners of the corporation. Common stockholders possess certain rights or claims, including dividend rights, asset rights, voting rights, and preemptive rights.[6] In Chapters 6 and 7 we illustrate how to obtain information about a company's common stock and debt securities from such sources as the *Wall Street Journal.*

Preferred stockholders have priority over common stockholders with regard to the firm's earnings and assets. They are paid cash dividends before common stockholders. In addition, if a corporation enters bankruptcy, is reorganized, or is dissolved, preferred stockholders have priority over common stockholders in the distribution of the corporation's assets. However, preferred stockholders are second in line behind the firm's creditors.

Because of the advantages of limited liability, permanency, and flexibility and because ownership shares in corporations tend to be more liquid (and hence relatively more valuable) than ownership interests in proprietorships and partnerships, it is easy to see why the majority of business conducted in the United States is done under the corporate form of organization.

Most major corporations today maintain extensive and superbly illustrated Web sites, displaying their histories, products, services, financial statements, and much more. Usually, a firm's Web site address is "name.com" (such as "Ford.com") or "abbreviation. com" (such as "GM.com" for General Motors). Check out Ford's and GM's Web sites, whose addresses are given below, and explore a few of their many links that lead to some dazzling graphics. If you had to guess, what do you think would be the Web site address of Exxon? The Wall Street Journal? The next time you're cruising the Net, see whether you guessed correctly.
http://www.ford.com
http://www.gm.com

  FOUNDATION CONCEPT
MAXIMIZING SHAREHOLDER
WEALTH AS THE PRIMARY GOAL

Effective financial decision making requires an understanding of the goal(s) of the firm. What objective(s) *should* guide business decision making? That is, what should management try to achieve for the owners of the firm? The most widely accepted objective of the firm is to maximize the value of the firm for its owners; that is, to *maximize shareholder wealth.* **Shareholder wealth** is represented by the market price of a firm's common stock.

[6]Stockholder rights are discussed in greater detail in Chapter 7.

Warren Buffett, CEO of Berkshire Hathaway, an outspoken advocate of the shareholder wealth maximization objective and a premier "value investor," says it this way:

> Our long-term economic goal . . . is to maximize the average annual rate of gain in intrinsic business value on a per-share basis. We do not measure the economic significance or performance of Berkshire by its size; we measure by per-share progress.[7]

The shareholder wealth maximization goal states that management should seek to maximize the present value of the expected future returns to the owners (that is, shareholders) of the firm. These returns can take the form of periodic dividend payments or proceeds from the sale of the common stock. **Present value** is defined as the value today of some future payment or stream of payments, evaluated at an appropriate discount rate. The **discount rate** takes into account the returns that are available from alternative investment opportunities during a specific (future) time period. As we shall see in Chapter 4, the longer it takes to receive a benefit, such as a cash dividend or price appreciation of the firm's stock, the lower the value investors place on that benefit. In addition, the greater the risk associated with receiving a future benefit, the lower the value investors place on that benefit. Stock prices, the measure of shareholder wealth, reflect the *magnitude, timing,* and *risk* associated with future benefits expected to be received by stockholders.

Shareholder wealth is measured by the market value of the shareholders' common stock holdings. **Market value** is defined as the price at which the stock trades in the marketplace, such as on the New York Stock Exchange. Thus, total shareholder wealth equals the number of shares outstanding times the market price per share.

The objective of shareholder wealth maximization has a number of distinct advantages. First, this objective explicitly considers the timing and the risk of the benefits expected to be received from stock ownership. Similarly, managers must consider the elements of timing and risk as they make important financial decisions, such as capital expenditures. In this way, managers can make decisions that will contribute to increasing shareholder wealth.

Second, it is conceptually possible to determine whether a particular financial decision is consistent with this objective. If a decision made by a firm has the effect of increasing the market price of the firm's stock, it is a good decision. If it appears that an action will not achieve this result, the action should not be taken (at least not voluntarily).

Third, shareholder wealth maximization is an impersonal objective. Stockholders who object to a firm's policies are free to sell their shares *under more favorable terms* (that is, at a higher price) *than are available under any other strategy* and invest their funds elsewhere. If an investor has a consumption pattern or risk preference that is not accommodated by the investment, financing, and dividend decisions of that firm, the investor will be able to sell his or her shares in that firm at the best price and purchase shares in companies that more closely meet the investor's needs.

For these reasons, the shareholder wealth maximization objective is the primary goal in financial management. However, concerns for the social responsibilities of business, the existence of other objectives pursued by some managers, and problems that arise from agency relationships may cause some departures from pure wealth-maximizing behavior by owners and managers. (These prob-

[7]Berkshire Hathaway, Inc., *Annual Report* (1995).

lems are discussed later.) Nevertheless, the shareholder wealth maximization goal provides the standard against which actual decisions can be judged and, as such, is the objective assumed in financial management analysis.

Social Responsibility Concerns

Most firms in the 1990s recognize the importance of the interests of all their constituent groups, or **stakeholders**—customers, employees, suppliers, and the communities in which they operate—and not just the interests of stockholders. For example, Tucson Electric Power Company—the public utility providing electric service to the Tucson, Arizona, area—recognizes responsibilities to its various constituencies:[8]

- To sustain an optimum return on investment for *stockholders*.
- To be perceived by *customers* as a provider of quality service.
- To demonstrate that *employees* are our most valuable resource.
- To provide corporate leadership to the *community*.
- To operate compatibly with environmental standards and initiate programs that are sensitive to environmental issues [*community*].

Tucson Electric Power sees no conflict between being a good citizen and running a successful business.

A wide diversity of opinion exists as to what corporate social responsibility actually entails. The concept is somewhat subjective and is neither perceived nor applied uniformly by all firms. As yet, no satisfactory mechanism has been suggested that specifies how these social responsibility commitments can be balanced with the interests of the owners of the firm. However, in most instances, a manager who takes an appropriate long-term perspective in decision making, rather than focusing only on short-term accounting profits, will recognize responsibility to all of a firm's constituencies and will help lead the company to the maximization of value for shareholders.

Divergent Objectives

The goal of shareholder wealth maximization specifies how financial decisions should be made. In practice, however, not all management decisions are consistent with this objective. For example, Bennett Stewart has developed an index of managerial performance that measures the success of managers in achieving a goal of shareholder wealth maximization.[9, 10] Stewart's performance measure, called *Economic Value Added*, is the difference between a firm's annual after-tax operating profit and its total annual cost of capital. Many highly regarded major corporations, including Coca-Cola, AT&T, Quaker Oats, Briggs & Stratton, and CSX, are using the concept. The poor performances of other firms may be due, in part, to a lack of attention to stockholder interests and the pursuit of goals more in the interests of managers.

In other words, there often may be a divergence between the shareholder wealth maximization goal and the *actual* goals pursued by management. The primary reason for this divergence has been attributed to *separation of ownership and control* (management) in corporations.

---

[8]Tucson Electric Power Company, *Annual Report* (1992): 3.
[9]G. Bennett Stewart, III, *The Quest for Value* (New York: Harper & Row, 1990), Chapter 5.
[10]Shawn Tully, "The Real Key to Creating Wealth," *Fortune* (September 20, 1993): 38–50.

Separation of ownership and control has permitted managers to pursue goals more consistent with their own self-interests as long as they satisfy shareholders sufficiently to maintain control of the corporation. Instead of seeking to maximize some objective (such as shareholder wealth), managers "satisfice" or seek acceptable levels of performance, while maximizing their own welfare.

Maximization of their own personal welfare (or utility) may lead managers to be concerned with long-run survival (job security). The concern for long-run survival may lead management to minimize (or limit) the amount of risk incurred by the firm, since unfavorable outcomes can lead to their dismissal or possible bankruptcy for the firm. Likewise, the desire for job security is cited as one reason why management often opposes takeover offers (mergers) by other companies. Giving senior management "golden parachute" contracts to compensate them if they lose their positions as the result of a merger is one approach designed to ensure that they will act in the interests of shareholders in merger decisions, rather than in their own interests.

Other firms, such as Panhandle Eastern and Ford Motor Company, for example, expect top managers and directors to have a significant ownership stake in the firm. Panhandle Eastern's president is paid entirely in the company's common shares, 25,000 per quarter—no severance, no retirement plan, just stock and medical benefits.[11] Ford requires each of its top 80 officers to own common stock in the company at least equal to their annual salary. As the company's chairman, Alex Trotman, explains "I want everyone thinking about the price of Ford stock when they go to work."[12] Many other firms, including Disney, Pepsico, and Anheuser-Busch, provide key managers with significant stock options that increase in value with improvements in the firm's performance in an attempt to align their interests more closely with those of shareholders.

Agency Problems

The existence of divergent objectives between owners and managers is one example of a class of problems arising from agency relationships. **Agency relationships** occur when one or more individuals (the **principals**) hire another individual (the **agent**) to perform a service on behalf of the principals.[13] In an agency relationship, principals often delegate decision-making authority to the agent. In the context of finance, two of the most important agency relationships are the relationship between stockholders (owners) and managers and the relationship between stockholders and creditors.

Stockholders and Managers. Inefficiencies that arise because of agency relationships have been called *agency problems.* These problems occur because each party to a transaction is assumed to act in a manner consistent with maximizing his or her own utility (welfare). The example cited earlier—the concern by management for long-run survival (job security), rather than shareholder wealth maximization—is an agency problem. Another example is the consumption of on-the-job perquisites (such as the use of company airplanes, limousines, and luxurious of-

[11]"Panhandle Eastern Prospects by Hauling Others' Fuel," *Wall Street Journal* (February 2, 1993): B4.
[12]"Alex Trotman's Goal: To Make Ford No. 1 in World Auto Sales," *Wall Street Journal* (July 18, 1995): A1.
[13]See Amir Barnea, R. Haugen, and L. Senbet, *Agency Problems and Financial Contracting* (Englewood Cliffs, NJ: Prentice-Hall, 1985), for an overview of the agency problem issue. See also Michael Jensen and William Meckling, "Theory of the Firm: Managerial Behavior, Agency Costs, and Ownership Structure," *Journal of Financial Economics* (October 1976): 305–360; and Eugene Fama, "Agency Problems and the Theory of the Firm," *Journal of Political Economy* (April 1980): 288–307.

fices) by managers who have no (or only a partial) ownership interest in the firm. Shirking by managers is also an agency-related problem.

These agency problems give rise to a number of *agency costs*, which are incurred by shareholders to minimize agency problems. Examples of agency costs include

1. Expenditures to structure the organization in such a way as to minimize the incentives for management to take actions contrary to shareholder interests, such as providing a portion of management's compensation in the form of stock of the corporation.
2. Expenditures to monitor management's actions, such as paying for audits of managerial performance and internal audits of the firm's expenditures.
3. Bonding expenditures to protect the owners from managerial dishonesty.
4. The opportunity cost of lost profits arising from complex organizational structures that prevent management from making timely responses to opportunities.

Managerial motivations to act in the interests of stockholders include the structure of their compensation package, the threat of dismissal, and the threat of takeover by a new group of owners. Financial theory has shown that agency problems and their associated costs can be reduced greatly if the financial markets operate efficiently. Some agency problems can be reduced by the use of complex financial contracts. Remaining agency problems give rise to costs that show up as a reduction in the value of the firm's shares in the marketplace.

Stockholders and Creditors. Another potential agency conflict arises from the relationship between a company's owners and its creditors. Creditors have a fixed financial claim on the company's resources in the form of long-term debt, bank loans, commercial paper, leases, accounts payable, wages payable, taxes payable, and so on. Because the returns offered to creditors are fixed whereas the returns to stockholders are variable, conflicts may arise between creditors and owners. For example, owners may attempt to increase the riskiness of the company's investments in hopes of receiving greater returns. When this occurs, bondholders suffer because they do not have an opportunity to share in these higher returns. For example, when RJR Nabisco (RJR) was acquired by KKR, the debt of RJR increased from 38 percent of total capital to nearly 90 percent of total capital. This unexpected increase in financial risk caused the value of RJR's bonds to decline by nearly 20 percent. In response to this loss of value, Metropolitan Life Insurance Company and other large bondholders sued RJR for violating the bondholders' rights and protections under the bond covenants. In 1991, RJR and Metropolitan settled the suit to the benefit of Metropolitan. The issue of bondholder rights remains controversial, however.

In order to protect their interests, creditors often insist on certain protective covenants in a company's bond indentures.[14] These covenants take many forms, such as limitations on dividend payments, limitations on the type of investments (and divestitures) the company can undertake, poison puts,[15] and limitations on the issuance of new debt. The constraints on the owner-managers may reduce the potential market value of the firm. In addition to these constraints, bondholders may also demand a higher fixed return to compensate for risks not adequately covered by bond indenture restrictions.

---

[14]Protective covenants are discussed in more detail in Chapters 6 and 18.

[15]A "poison put" is an option contained in a bond indenture that permits the bondholder to sell the bond back to the issuing company at face value under certain circumstances, such as a leveraged buyout that raises the risk for existing debt holders.

MAXIMIZATION OF SHAREHOLDER WEALTH: MANAGERIAL STRATEGIES

If the managers of a firm accept the goal of maximizing shareholder wealth, how should they achieve this objective? One might be tempted to argue that managers will maximize shareholder wealth if they maximize the profits of the firm. After all, profit maximization is the predominant objective that emerges from static microeconomic models of the firm. Unfortunately, the profit maximization objective has too many shortcomings to provide consistent guidance to the practicing manager.

Before discussing some of these shortcomings, it is useful to highlight one important managerial decision rule that emerges from the microeconomic profit maximization model. In order to maximize profits, we learned in microeconomics that a firm should expand output to the point where the marginal (additional) cost (MC) of the last unit produced and sold just equals the marginal revenue (MR) received. To move beyond that output level will result in greater additional costs than additional revenues and hence lower profits. To fail to produce up to the point where MC = MR results in a lower level of total profits than is possible by following the rule. This fundamental rule, that an economic action should be continued up to the point where the marginal revenue (benefit) just equals the marginal cost, offers excellent guidance for financial managers dealing with a wide range of problems. For example, we shall see that the basic capital expenditure analysis model simply is an adaptation of the MC = MR rule. Other applications appear in the working capital management area and the capital structure area.

Despite the insights it offers financial managers, the profit maximization model is not useful as the central decision-making model for the firm for several reasons. First, the standard microeconomic model of profit maximization is *static*; that is, it lacks a time dimension. Profit maximization as a goal offers no explicit basis for comparing long-term and short-term profits. Major decisions made by financial managers *must* reflect the time dimension. For example, capital expenditure decisions, which are central to the finance function, have a long-term impact on the performance of the firm. Financial managers must make trade-offs between short-run and long-run returns in conjunction with capital investment decisions.

The second limitation of the profit maximization objective has to do with the definition of profit. Generally accepted accounting principles (as discussed in Chapter 3) result in literally hundreds of definitions of profit for a firm because of the latitude permitted in recognizing and accounting for costs and revenues. For example, during 1990, Carolina Power & Light Company (CPL) was forced to reduce its earnings by $81.6 million because of an unfavorable regulatory treatment of its Harris nuclear plant. To offset this impact on the firm's earnings, CPL "changed its method of accounting for revenues to accrue unbilled revenues as of the date service is rendered, rather than when billed. The net effect of this accounting change for 1990 is an increase in net income of $77 million, or $0.92 per share."[16] This arbitrary accounting change has *no* impact on the cash flows or economic well-being of CPL and hence has no impact on its value.

---

[16]Carolina Power & Light Company, "Letter to Members of the Financial Community," January 25, 1991.

Even if we could agree on the appropriate accounting definition of profit, it is not clear whether a firm should attempt to maximize total profit, the rate of profit, or earnings per share (EPS).

Consider Columbia Beverages, Inc., a firm with 10 million shares outstanding that currently earns a profit of $10 million after tax. If the firm sells an additional 1 million shares of stock and invests the proceeds to earn $100,000 per year, the total profit of the firm will increase from $10 million to $10.1 million. However, are shareholders better off? Prior to the stock sale, earnings per share are $1 ($10 million profit divided by 10 million shares of stock). After the stock sale, earnings per share decline to $0.92 ($10.1 million in earnings divided by 11 million shares). Although total profit has increased, earnings per share have declined. Stockholders are not better off from this action.

This example might lead one to conclude that managers should seek to maximize earnings per share (for a given number of shares outstanding). This, too, can result in misleading actions. For example, consider a firm with total assets at the start of the year of $10 million. The firm is financed entirely with stock (1 million shares outstanding) and has no debt. After-tax earnings are $1 million, resulting in a return on stockholders' equity of 10 percent ($1 million in earnings divided by $10 million in stockholders' equity), and earnings per share are $1. The company decides to retain one-half of this year's earnings (increasing assets and equity to $10.5 million) and pay out the balance in stockholders' dividends. Next year the company's earnings total $1.029 million, resulting in earnings per share of $1.029. Are shareholders better off because of the decision by managers to reinvest $500,000 in the firm? In this example, a strong argument can be made that the position of shareholders has deteriorated. Although earnings per share have increased from $1 per share to $1.029 per share, the realized return on stockholders' equity actually has declined, from 10 percent to 9.8 percent ($1.029 million divided by $10.5 million of stockholders' equity). In essence, the company's managers have reinvested $500,000 of stockholders' money to earn a return of only 5.8 percent ($0.029 million of additional earnings divided by $0.5 million of additional investment). This type of investment is not likely to result in maximum shareholder wealth. Shareholders could do better by investing in risk-free government bonds yielding more than 5.8 percent.

The third major problem associated with the profit maximization objective is that it provides no direct way for financial managers to consider the risk associated with alternative decisions. For example, two projects generating identical future expected cash flows and requiring identical outlays may be vastly different with respect to the risk of the expected cash flows. Similarly, a firm can often increase its earnings per share by increasing the proportion of debt financing used in the firm's capital structure. However, leverage-induced increases in EPS come at the cost of increased financial risk. The financial marketplace will recognize the increased risk of financial distress that accompanies increases in debt financing and will value the resulting EPS accordingly.

Determinants of Value

If the profit maximization objective does not provide the proper guidance to managers seeking to maximize shareholder wealth, what rules should these managers follow? First, it is important to recognize that the maximization of shareholder wealth is a market concept, not an accounting concept. Managers should attempt to maximize the **market value** of the company's shares, not the accounting or **book value** per share. The book value reflects the historic cost of assets, not the earning capacity of those assets. Also, the book value does not consider the risk associated with the assets.

Three major factors determine the market value of a company's shares of stock: the amount of the cash flows expected to be generated for the benefit of stockholders; the timing of these cash flows; and the risk of the cash flows.

Cash Flow. Throughout the book we stress the importance of cash flows in the practice of financial management. Cash flow relates to the actual cash generated or paid by the firm. Only cash can be used to acquire assets, and only cash can be used to make valuable distributions to investors. In contrast, the accounting system focuses primarily on a matching over time of the historic, cost-based revenues and expenses of a company, resulting in a bottom-line earnings figure. But accounting earnings often are misleading because they do not reflect the actual cash inflows and outflows of the firm. For example, an accountant records depreciation expense on an asset each period over the depreciable life of that asset. Depreciation is designed to reflect the decline in value of that asset over time. However, depreciation itself results in no cash outflow.[17] The entire cash outflow occurred when the asset originally was purchased.

Timing of Cash Flows. The market value of a share of stock is influenced not only by the amount of the cash flows it is expected to produce but also by the timing of those cash flows. If faced with the opportunity of receiving $100 today or $100 three years from today, you would surely choose the $100 today because you could invest that $100 for three years and accumulate the interest. Thus, financial managers must consider both the magnitude of the cash flows they expect to generate and the timing of these cash flows because investors will reflect these dimensions of return in their valuation of the enterprise.

Risk. Finally, the market value of a share of stock is influenced by the perceived risk of the cash flows it is expected to generate. The relationship between risk and required return is an important concept in financial management and is discussed in detail in Chapter 5. In general, *the greater the perceived risk associated with an expected cash flow, the greater is the rate of return required by investors and managers.* Thus, financial managers also must consider the risk of the cash flows expected to be generated by the firm because investors will reflect this risk in their valuation of the enterprise.

Managerial Actions to Influence Value

How can managers influence the magnitude, timing, and risk of the cash flows expected to be generated by the firm in order to maximize shareholder wealth? Many factors ultimately influence the magnitude, timing, and risk of a firm's cash flows and thus the price of the firm's stock. Some of these factors are related to the external economic environment and are largely outside the direct control of managers. Other factors can be directly manipulated by the managers. Figure 1-1 illustrates the factors affecting stock prices. The top panel enumerates some of the factors in the economic environment that have an impact on the strategic decisions managers can make. Even though economic environ-

---

[17]Because depreciation is used in computing a firm's tax liability, it can affect *after-tax* cash flows. This concept is discussed further in Chapters 3 and 8.

FIGURE 1-1
Factors Affecting Stock Prices

Transparency available

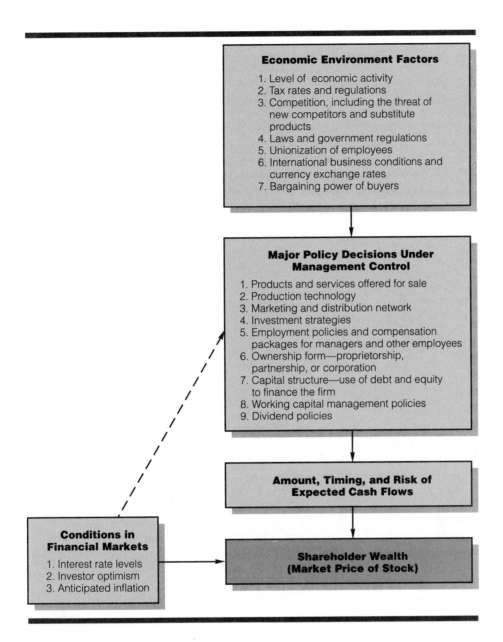

ment factors are largely outside the direct control of managers, managers must be aware of how these factors affect the policy decisions under the control of management.

In this context, it is useful to consider a competitive strategy framework developed initially by Michael E. Porter and developed further by Alfred Rappaport.[18, 19] Porter and Rappaport recommend that managers formulate an overall competitive strategy analyzing five competitive forces that can influence an industry's structure and can thereby, in turn, ultimately affect the market prices of stocks of individual companies in a particular industry. The five competitive forces are

---

[18]Michael E. Porter, *Competitive Advantage* (New York: Free Press, 1985), Chapter 1.
[19]Alfred Rappaport, *Creating Shareholder Value* (New York: Free Press, 1986), Chapter 4.

1. The threat of new entrants.
2. The threat of substitute products.
3. The bargaining power of buyers.
4. The bargaining power of suppliers.
5. The rivalry among current competitors.

By making policy decisions using such a competitive framework, managers can be in a position to create value for shareholders.

The major policy decision areas are listed in the next panel of Figure 1-1. Managers make choices regarding the products to be produced, the technology used to produce them, the marketing effort and distribution channels, and the selection of employees and their compensation. In addition, managers establish investment policies, the ownership structure of the firm, the capital structure (use of debt) of the firm, working capital management policies, and dividend policies. The decisions made in these key policy areas determine the amount, timing, and risk of the firm's expected cash flows. Participants in the financial markets evaluate the cash flows expected by the firm in relation to alternative streams of cash flows expected from other firms and ultimately establish the price of the firm's stock. The value of a firm's stock is influenced at any point in time by general conditions in the financial markets, including the level of interest rates, anticipated inflation rates, and the level of investor optimism regarding the future. Financial market conditions also affect the major policy decisions made by management.

Accordingly, the focus of this book is on making financial decisions that can improve the amount, the timing, or the risk profile of a firm's cash flow stream, thus leading to increases in shareholder wealth and value. Financial managers in the 1990s are not only responsible for *measuring* value, but they also are responsible for *creating* value.

The next section defines the *cash flow concept* and establishes why cash flows are the relevant source of value in finance.

  FOUNDATION CONCEPT
CASH FLOW

The concept of *cash flow* is one of the central elements of financial analysis, planning, and resource allocation decisions. Cash flows are important because the financial health of a firm depends on its ability to generate sufficient amounts of cash to pay its creditors, employees, suppliers, and owners. Only cash can be spent. You cannot spend net income because net income does not reflect the actual cash inflows and outflows of the firm. For example, an accountant records depreciation expense in an attempt to recognize the decline in value of an asset over its life. However, depreciation expense requires no cash outlay, because the entire cash outflow occurred at the time the asset was purchased.

The Cash Flow Generation Process

Financial managers are concerned primarily with raising funds (cash) for use by the firm and investing those funds in assets that can be converted into a stream of cash flows accruing to the firm and its owners. If the value today of the stream of cash flows generated by the assets of a firm exceeds the cost of those assets, the investments undertaken by the firm add value to the firm. When financial managers perform this primary function of acquiring funds and directing the investment of those funds into value-maximizing projects, they must balance the risk (variability) and timing of the expected cash flow stream against the magnitude of the expected returns. The cash flow generation process for a firm is illustrated in Figure 1-2.

A firm can raise funds by issuing different types of financial securities, including both debt and equity types.[20] Financing decisions such as these are summarized on the liabilities and owners' equity side of the balance sheet. In addition to selling securities, a firm can raise cash by borrowing from a lender such as a commercial bank. Funds can also be raised by generating cash flow internally. Internal cash flows include cash generated from operations and cash generated by the sale of assets.

Once cash is available, a decision must be made to invest it in one or more assets. The acquisition of the best long-term assets is crucial, because once acquired, long-term assets impact the firm for a long time. Long-term assets can be sold if necessary but sometimes only at a significant loss. Current assets, or working capital, such as cash, accounts receivable, and inventory, are held for operating purposes and generally offer little or no explicit return. If current asset balances are kept too high, shareholder wealth is sacrificed due to the opportunity cost of funds, that is, the returns that could be earned if these funds had been invested elsewhere. On the other hand, if current asset balances are too low, the risk of the firm increases because the firm may encounter difficulty in meeting its current financial obligations. In addition, low current asset balances (particularly inventories and accounts receivable) may prevent a firm from responding to the needs of prospective customers in a timely and profitable way.

Eventually, all assets are transformed into a cash flow. Plant and equipment generate a product or service. Inventory is gradually sold and generates cash sales or accounts receivable. Cash flow is generated as accounts receivable are collected. Then, the firm must decide how much of its cash flow to use to acquire additional assets, to pay off creditors, and to distribute to its owners.

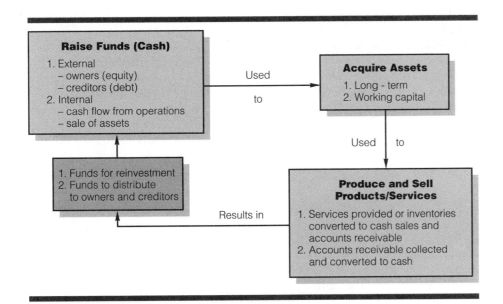

**FIGURE 1-2
A Firm's Cash Flow
Generation Process**

[20]Chapter 6 discusses various types of debt securities, and Chapter 7 discusses various types of equity securities.

Importance of Cash Flows

The valuation of debt and equity securities is based upon the present value of the cash flows that these securities are expected to provide to investors.[21] Similarly, the value of a capital expenditure is equal to the present value of the cash flows that the asset is expected to produce for the firm. In addition, cash flows are central to the prosperity and survival of a firm. For example, rapidly expanding firms often grow faster than their ability to generate internally the cash flows needed to meet operating and financial commitments. As a result, these firms may be faced with difficult financial decisions regarding the external sources of funds needed to sustain rapid growth. On the one hand, increases in debt to support expansion result in an increase in the firm's financial risk. On the other hand, if new shares of stock are sold, ownership in the firm may be diluted more than is desired by the firm's controlling group of owners. Therefore, managers need to pay close attention to the projected cash flows associated with investment and firm expansion strategies.

As you learned in your accounting courses and as is discussed in Chapter 3, generally accepted accounting principles (GAAP) provide considerable latitude in the determination of the net income. As a consequence, GAAP concepts of net income do not provide a clear indication of the economic performance of a firm. Cash flow concepts are unambiguous and provide the necessary insight for managers making a wide range of financial resource allocation decisions. Investors also find that cash flow concepts provide a clear measure of performance. Accordingly, the concept of cash flow assumes great importance in the analysis of a firm's performance and the management of its resources.

Cash Flows and Shareholder Wealth

In spite of the close tie between cash flow concepts and the objective of shareholder wealth maximization, many managers do not seem to place enough emphasis on this concept. Some managers focus on alternative performance measures, including accounting net income, accounting profit ratios (such as the return on equity or the return on assets), the sales growth rate, and market share. The focus on these accounting-based measures of performance may detract from the long-term performance of the company, because performance measures that are not based on cash flows are subject to short-term manipulation by managers.

By emphasizing cash flows rather than accounting-based measures of performance when making decisions, a manager is more likely to achieve the objective of shareholder wealth maximization. A firm that takes actions to maximize the present value of expected future cash flows *will* achieve a record of financial performance that will be reflected both in the company's financial statements and in the market value of its stock.

FOUNDATION CONCEPT
NET PRESENT VALUE RULE

To achieve the objective of shareholder wealth maximization, a set of appropriate decision rules must be specified. Earlier in this chapter we saw that the decision

---

[21]The present value concept is discussed in detail in Chapter 4.

rule of setting *marginal cost equal to marginal revenue* (MC = MR) provides a framework for making many important resource allocation decisions. The MC = MR rule is best suited for situations when the costs and benefits occur at approximately the same time. Many financial decisions, however, require that costs be incurred immediately but result in a stream of benefits over several future time periods. In these cases, the *net present value rule* (NPV) provides appropriate guidance for decision makers. Indeed, the NPV rule is central to the practice of financial management. You will find this rule constantly applied throughout your study of finance.

The **net present value** of an investment is equal to the present value of the expected future cash flows generated by the investment minus the initial outlay of cash, or

$$\text{NPV} = \text{Present value of future cash flows } minus \text{ Initial outlay} \qquad (1.1)$$

For example, as of 1994, Coca-Cola was building 10 plants in China, in addition to the 13 it already had in operation there.[22] In 1993, Coca-Cola sold 100 million cases in China, and the cash flow from its China operations was positive. In deciding whether to invest in the 10 additional plants, financial managers at Coca-Cola had to estimate the amount of future cash flows the plants would generate. Then, using time value of money calculations, the managers determined the present value of those expected cash flows. Finally, they calculated the net present value of the proposed investment by subtracting the initial cost of the plants from the present value of the future cash flows. Coca-Cola apparently determined that the expected net present value was positive and made the decision to invest in the 10 additional China plants.

The net present value of an investment made by a firm represents the contribution of that investment to the value of the firm and, accordingly, to the wealth of shareholders. For example, if the Coca-Cola China project is expected to have a positive net present value of $5 million, the value of Coca-Cola's common stock can be expected to increase by $5 million at the time the investment is made, all other things being equal.

The net present value concept provides a framework for evaluating future *cash flows* from an investment or a firm. Thus, the net present value concept can be viewed as the bridge between cash flows and the goal of shareholder wealth maximization.

 ETHICAL ISSUES
THE PRACTICE OF FINANCIAL MANAGEMENT

During the 1980s and 1990s, interest in the ethical dimensions of business practice has exploded. Front-page stories of the stock trading scandals involving the use of insider information that led to the downfall of Dennis Levine and Ivan Boesky, the Treasury bond trading scandal at Salomon Brothers that severely damaged Salomon's reputation and resulted in its top managers being forced to resign (discussed in the Financial Challenge section of this chapter), and the billions of dollars of questionable loans made by savings and loan executives that caused the collapse of much of the savings and loan industry, have focused attention on the ethical practices followed by business and financial managers.

[22]"Two Reasons Why Coke Is It: China and Russia," *Business Week* (March 7, 1994): 106.

Webster's defines ethics as "the discipline dealing with what is good or bad, right or wrong, or with moral duty and obligation."[23] John J. Casey defines ethics as follows: "At its best, business ethics is excellence in management applied with fairness and dispatch. It involves hard-headed thought, not a sentimental reaction. It also involves articulate, effective communication to all parties. . . ."[24] Casey identifies a number of techniques that managers can keep in mind when addressing the ethical dimensions of a business problem.

- Clarify the parameters of the problem.
- Involve the right team of participants at the outset.
- Collect all the facts bearing on the problem.
- Articulate the harm and benefit that may result from proposed actions.
- Weigh the consequences of alternatives.
- Seek equity for those who may be affected.

Other action guidelines that have been suggested for managers include to

- Ensure that personal interests do not conflict with business decisions being made.
- Respect the confidentiality of information entrusted to you.
- Make decisions based on rational, objective business analysis rather than on inappropriate factors, such as race, sex, or religion.
- Act fairly in dealing with customers while protecting the legitimate interests of the business.[25]

Wouldn't it be handy to be able to obtain Better Business Bureau reports on any company? Actually, such information is easily available on the Internet.
http://www.bbb.org

Ethical considerations impact all kinds of business and financial management decisions. Some financial decisions with important ethical dimensions, such as the loan administration policies apparent in many failed savings and loan institutions, command national attention. However, financial managers encounter day-to-day decisions that have important ethical dimensions. For example, as a new bank loan officer, should you recommend approval of a loan to a longtime friend, even though she does not quite meet the normal loan standards of the bank? As an account executive for a brokerage firm, should you recommend to your clients the securities of firms with poor environmental management records or that deal in such products as alcohol and tobacco? Should you tell your father-in-law that your firm is likely to become a candidate for a takeover before this is publicly announced? As a division manager being evaluated in part on a return-on-assets calculation, should you lease assets to keep them out of the asset base for evaluation purposes and thereby enhance your apparent performance? Should your firm aggressively use allowable accounting practices to mask a fundamentally deteriorating level of performance? Should your firm move its plant from the Northeast to the Southeast in an attempt to break the union and save labor costs?

This brief sampling of the areas of business and financial-management decision making that possess important ethical dimensions provides a feel for the breadth of ethical issues facing financial managers. In most cases, the answers to these questions are not clear-cut. Actual decision making is very complex and involves many trade-offs among parties with competing interests. However, explicitly recognizing the costs and benefits associated with each of these decisions and making the decision in an atmosphere of balanced objectivity and fairness can help financial managers avoid apparent or real breaches of their ethical trust.

---

[23]*Webster's Third New International Dictionary* (Chicago: Merriam Webster, 1981).
[24]John J. Casey, "The New Urgency for Ethics in Banking," *The Bankers Magazine* (March/April 1991): 44–50.
[25]*Ibid.,* 48–49.

An important concern for financial managers, who are entrusted with the resources of stockholders and are expected to maximize the value of these resources, is: How does a concern for ethics in the practice of financial management impact the goal of shareholder wealth maximization? Firms that expect employees to act according to a code of ethics in their business dealings can expect to have reduced litigation and damages expenses. A recent survey concluded that some 90 percent of the Fortune 500 companies have adopted a published code of conduct for their managers and other employees. High ethical standards are respected by customers and valued by investors. One could argue that ethical business dealings build long-term value for investors, whereas breaches of standards of business ethics may provide short-term gains at the expense of future returns. This can be seen clearly in the savings and loan industry, where often unscrupulous managers made decisions promising large short-term profits. In the long run, many of these institutions have failed, and their owners have lost everything.

Throughout the text, we will highlight ethical issues that confront financial managers as they make important financial decisions. Our objective is to raise your consciousness to these issues, rather than to make moral judgments about what is right or wrong in each case. Those judgments are best left to you as the topics of lively discussions with your classmates.

 ENTREPRENEURIAL FINANCE ISSUES
SHAREHOLDER WEALTH MAXIMIZATION

Entrepreneurial finance deals with the financial issues facing small businesses, which constitute an important sector of the U.S. economy. Small business firms may be organized as sole proprietorships, partnerships, or corporations. According to criteria used by the Small Business Administration, over 95 percent of all business firms are considered small. These firms account for the majority of private sector employment and nearly all of the recent net growth in new jobs.

It is difficult to arrive at a precise definition of a small, or entrepreneurial, business; however, the characteristics of small business firms can be identified. In general, small businesses are not the dominant firm in the industries in which they compete, and they tend to grow more rapidly than larger firms. Small firms have limited access to the financial markets, and they often do not have the depth of specialized managerial resources available to larger firms. Small firms also have a high failure rate.

In our discussion of the goals of the firm, we concluded that the predominant goal of financial managers is to maximize shareholder wealth, as measured by the price of the firm's stock. Many entrepreneurial corporations are closely held, and their stock trades infrequently, if ever. Other entrepreneurial firms are organized as sole proprietorships or partnerships. In these cases, there is no readily accessible external measure of performance. Consequently, these firms often rely more heavily on accounting-based measures of performance to track their progress. Accounting-based measures of performance are discussed in Chapter 3. In spite of the lack of an objective, readily available measure of performance, the fundamental decisions made by entrepreneurs are unaltered. That is, the firm should invest resources in projects expected to earn a rate of return *at least* equal to the required return on those projects, considering the project's risk. However, because many entrepreneurs are poorly diversified with respect to their personal wealth (that is, they have a large proportion of their personal wealth tied up in the firm), these owners often are more concerned about avoiding risks that could lead to financial ruin than are managers of public corporations.

As discussed earlier, in the large modern corporation, there is a concern that a firm's managers may not always act in the interests of the owners (the agency problem). This problem is less severe in many entrepreneurial businesses, because managers and owners are one and the same. An entrepreneur who consumes "excessive" perks is merely reducing his or her ability to withdraw profits from the firm. But to the extent that the manager is the owner, there is no owner-manager agency problem. Of course, the potential for agency-related conflicts between entrepreneurs and lenders still exists and may be greater in the closely held firm. As a consequence, many small firms find it difficult to acquire capital from lenders without also giving the lender an option on a part of the ownership in the firm or having the entrepreneur personally guarantee the loan.

In the face of this significant difference in the management-ownership structure of small businesses, it should be kept in mind that entrepreneurs have strong incentives to take actions that will maximize firm value, because the wealth of the entrepreneur is often closely tied to the performance of the firm. Also, a firm that is efficiently run and successful makes a tempting target for acquisition by a larger company. A well-run firm will command a much higher takeover price.

Throughout this book we will identify situations where the entrepreneurial financial management of small businesses poses special challenges. In general, we find that small firms often lack the depth of managerial talent needed to apply sophisticated financial planning techniques. Also, because significant economies of scale often are associated with using sophisticated financial management techniques, these techniques frequently are not justified on a cost-benefit analysis basis in many entrepreneurial companies.

ORGANIZATION OF THE FINANCIAL MANAGEMENT FUNCTION

Many firms divide the decision-making responsibilities of management among several different officers, which often include those in manufacturing, marketing, finance, personnel, and engineering. A sample organization chart emphasizing the finance function is shown in Figure 1-3. The finance function is usually headed by a vice-president of finance or *chief financial officer* (CFO), who reports to the president. In some corporations the CFO may also be a member of the board of directors. In addition to overseeing the accounting, treasury, tax, and audit functions, today's CFO often has responsibility for strategic planning, monitoring and trading foreign currencies, managing the risk from volatile interest rates, and monitoring production and inventory levels. CFOs also must be able to communicate effectively with the investment community concerning the financial performance of the company.

The chief financial officer often distributes the financial management responsibilities between the *controller* and the *treasurer*.[26] The controller normally has responsibility for all accounting-related activities. These include such functions as

---

[26]In smaller companies, the owner may supervise the activities of the controller and treasurer, or the chief financial officer may perform both activities under the title of controller, treasurer, or vice-president of finance.

FIGURE 1-3
Sample Organization Chart

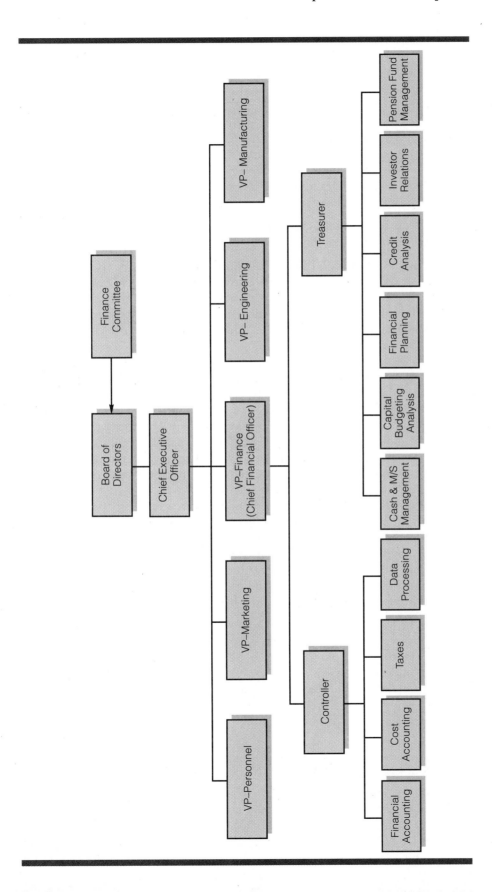

■ **Financial Accounting** This function involves the preparation of the financial statements for the firm, such as the balance sheet, income statement, and the statement of cash flows.

■ **Cost Accounting** This department often has responsibility for preparing the firm's operating budgets and monitoring the performance of the departments and divisions within the firm.

■ **Taxes** This unit prepares the reports that the company must file with the various government (local, state, and federal) agencies.

■ **Data Processing** Given its responsibilities involving corporate accounting and payroll activities, the controller also may have management responsibility for the company's data processing operations.

The treasurer normally is concerned with the acquisition, custody, and expenditure of funds. These duties often include

■ **Cash and Marketable Securities Management** This group monitors the firm's short-term finances—forecasting its cash needs, obtaining funds from bankers and other sources when needed, and investing any excess funds in short-term interest-earning securities.

■ **Capital Budgeting Analysis** This department is responsible for analyzing capital expenditures—that is, the purchase of long-term assets, such as new facilities and equipment.

■ **Financial Planning** This department is responsible for analyzing the alternative sources of long-term funds, such as the issuance of bonds or common stock, that the firm will need to maintain and expand its operations.

■ **Credit Analysis** Most companies have a department that is responsible for determining the amount of credit that the firm will extend to each of its customers. Although this group is responsible for performing financial analysis, it sometimes may be located in the marketing area of the firm because of its close relationship to sales.

■ **Investor Relations** Many large companies have a unit responsible for working with institutional investors (for example, mutual funds), bond rating agencies, stockholders, and the general financial community.

■ **Pension Fund Management** The treasurer also may have responsibility for the investment of employee pension fund contributions. The investment analysis and portfolio management functions may be performed either within the firm or through outside investment advisors.

It should be emphasized that the specific functions of the controller and treasurer shown in Figure 1-3 are illustrative only and that the actual functions performed vary from company to company. For example, in some companies, the treasurer may have responsibility for tax matters. Also, as shown in Figure 1-3, the board of directors of the company may establish a finance committee, consisting of a number of directors and officers of the firm with substantial financial expertise, to make recommendations on broad financial policy issues.

Are you curious about what job opportunities exist for finance majors? What skills are required to be a banker, a stockbroker, a CFO, or some other finance profession? What are the typical starting salaries for these jobs, and what are typical salaries after five or ten years in the same field? To find out, visit the WWW finance virtual library (a terrific financial site!) and then follow the links to "for students" to "MBA Page" to "Finding a Job." The site also offers some excellent job-search tips and career advice for soon-to-be college graduates looking for jobs.
http://www.cob.ohio-state.edu/~fin/overview.htm

FINANCIAL MANAGEMENT AND OTHER DISCIPLINES

As you pursue your study of financial management, you should keep in mind that financial management is not a totally independent area in business administration. Instead, it draws heavily on related disciplines and fields of study. The most important of these are *accounting* and *economics;* in the latter discipline, both *macroeconomics* and *microeconomics* are significant. *Marketing, production,* and the study of *quantitative methods* also have an impact on the financial management field. Each of these is discussed below.

Accounting

Financial managers play the game of managing a firm's financial and real assets and securing the funding needed to support these assets. Accountants are the game's scorekeepers. Financial managers often turn to accounting data to assist them in making decisions. Generally a company's accountants are responsible for developing financial reports and measures that assist its managers in assessing the past performance and future direction of the firm and in meeting certain legal obligations, such as the payment of taxes. The accountant's role includes the development of financial statements, such as the *balance sheet,* the *income statement,* and the *statement of cash flows.*

Financial managers are primarily concerned with a firm's cash flows, because they often determine the feasibility of certain investment and financing decisions. The financial manager refers to accounting data when making future resource allocation decisions concerning long-term investments, when managing current investments in working capital, and when making a number of other financial decisions (for example, determining the most appropriate capital structure and identifying the best and most timely sources of funds needed to support the firm's investment programs).

In many small and medium-sized firms the accounting function and the financial management function may be handled by the same person or group of persons. In such cases, the distinctions just identified may become blurred.

Economics

There are two areas of economics with which the financial manager must be familiar: *microeconomics* and *macroeconomics.* Microeconomics deals with the economic decisions of individuals, households, and firms, whereas macroeconomics looks at the economy as a whole.

The typical firm is heavily influenced by the overall performance of the economy and is dependent upon the money and capital markets for investment funds. Thus, financial managers should recognize and understand how monetary policies affect the cost of funds and the availability of credit. Financial managers should also be versed in fiscal policy and how it affects the economy. What the economy can be expected to do in the future is a crucial factor in generating sales forecasts as well as other types of forecasts.

The financial manager uses microeconomics when developing decision models that are likely to lead to the most efficient and successful modes of operation within the firm. Specifically, financial managers utilize the microeconomic concept of setting marginal cost equal to marginal revenue when making long-term investment decisions (*capital budgeting*) and when managing cash, inventories, and accounts receivable (*working capital management*).

Marketing, Production, and Quantitative Methods

Figure 1-4 depicts the relationship between financial management and its primary supportive disciplines. Marketing, production, and quantitative methods are indirectly related to the key day-to-day decisions made by financial managers.

FIGURE 1-4
Impact of Other Disciplines
on Financial Management

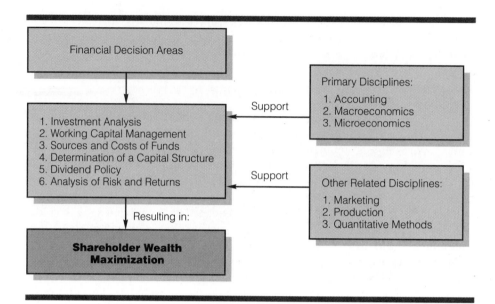

FIGURE 1-4
Impact of Other Disciplines
on Financial Management

For example, financial managers should consider the impact of new product development and promotion plans made in the marketing area, because these plans will require capital outlays and have an impact on the firm's projected cash flows. Similarly, changes in the production process may necessitate capital expenditures, which the firm's financial managers must evaluate and then finance. And, finally, the tools of analysis developed in the quantitative methods area frequently are helpful in analyzing complex financial management problems.

CAREER OPPORTUNITIES IN FINANCE

The finance profession offers a number of exciting career opportunities. As illustrated in the organization chart in Figure 1-3, the corporate finance function encompasses a wide range of activities involved with acquisition and expenditure of the firm's resources. In addition to careers in corporate finance, opportunities are available in the financial services sector. The financial services sector includes such businesses as commercial banks, securities brokers, investment banks, mutual funds, pension funds, real estate companies, and insurance companies.

Detailed job responsibilities and duties are shown in Figure 1-5 for selected positions in the field of finance. These positions span the spectrum from entry-level jobs to leadership roles in corporate finance and financial services. One should keep in mind that organizational structures differ significantly among various companies and that the specific responsibilities and duties for a given position may vary considerably among companies.

PROFESSIONAL FINANCE AFFILIATIONS

There are several professional organizations for practicing financial managers. These include the Financial Executives Institute, the Institute of Chartered

VICE PRESIDENT OF FINANCE

Basic Function: Plan, direct, and execute the long-term financing required to fund corporate capital requirements at the lowest cost.

Primary Responsibilities and Duties

- Plan and execute the financings required to fund corporate capital requirements while maintaining a balanced capital structure
- Direct, support, and review the actions of the department in obtaining long-term financing and maintaining positive relations with lenders and rating agencies
- Provide a capital budgeting and financial projection system
- Integrate projections of capital requirements with the status of credit markets and the company's capital structure
- Coordinate the activities of underwriters, lawyers, and accountants in order to complete financings in a timely manner
- Maintain contact with all company lenders and keep them informed of the company's goals and progress
- Provide financial support for various contractual arrangements
- Monitor pension fund assets and various special projects

DIRECTOR—INVESTOR RELATIONS

Basic Function: Primary work is in investor relations with additional responsibility for pension fund investments and corporate financings.

Primary Responsibilities and Duties

- Keep informed on business conditions of all company operating subsidiaries, strategic planning directions, and financial developments at the corporate level
- Stay abreast of industry matters to help explain external influences on the company as well as to keep up with the operating and financial results of the company and its competitors
- Communicate on a daily basis with the investment community in order to accurately portray company results and general expectations within the guidelines of SEC policy
- Arrange meeting times and places for senior management presentations around the country with investment analyst groups
- Act as host to analysts who visit company
- Establish plans and procedures when company hosts inspection trips or special seminars requiring special coordination among operating subsidiaries
- Select and set up personal meetings with institutional owners in order to develop greater support for our stock by the institution's portfolio managers
- Prepare monthly reports on investor relations matters, review policy and plans, and make recommendations for changes
- Monitor investment results of six investment managers
- Prepare monthly and quarterly reports on results and outlook
- Work with actuary and consultants on long-term strategy, including asset allocation and manager selection

ASSISTANT TREASURER—CASH CONTROL AND RISK MANAGEMENT

Basic Function: Responsible for operations of the Treasury Department involving cash management operations with specific attention

to the effective direction and control of corporate funds internally and through the company's various bank accounts.

Primary Responsibilities and Duties

- Manage, in conjunction with lock box banks retained by company, the processing of over 120,000 customer payments daily
- Disbursement of all company funds, including payrolls, pensions, and vendor payments
- Direct the management staff to assure compliance with our stated objectives and planning in order to assure the effectiveness of the organization
- Sign checks and review and approve various documents such as wire transfer confirmations and investment letters
- Meet with banks and their representatives
- Perform various assignments for senior management
- Also responsible for the risk management/insurance function

MANAGER—INCOME TAX COMPLIANCE

Basic Function: Supervise the income tax compliance activities of the company and its subsidiaries in a way that will meet the statutory requirements of all taxing jurisdictions and protect the company's interest against excessive taxation. The primary responsibility is to control tax costs and compliance costs. This involves developing ways of saving and/or deferring taxes wherever possible.

Primary Responsibilities and Duties

- Supervise the operation and filing of the consolidated Federal income tax and all state and local income tax returns of the company and its affiliates
- Review all returns and make decisions concerning the treatment of all transactions included in the returns
- Establish challenging work performance standards for staff members and develop their professional competence through instruction
- Maintain a good working knowledge of the internal revenue code and related regulations, ruling and cases as well as state income tax laws, etc.
- Analyze various transactions and procedures in order to develop ways of saving or deferring taxes and to reduce or eliminate compliance costs
- Coordinate the efforts of various group, division and subsidiary company controllers to assure proper administration of the income tax function
- Develop the information system necessary to assure proper and timely submission by subsidiaries and divisions of the financial data necessary for preparing tax returns
- Assist the company's independent accountants in their annual audits to assure proper settlement and make recommendations for appeals or possible litigation
- Assist in the preparation of responses to questions from the Internal Revenue Service

FINANCIAL ANALYST—CAPITAL BUDGETS

Basic Function: Review capital and lease appropriate requests that require finance concurrence, coordinate and compile data for the

Continued

FIGURE 1-5 Job Responsibilities and Duties for Selected Positions in Finance*

*Source: Jack S. Rader, *Careers in Finance* (Tampa, FL: Financial Management Association International, College of Business Administration, University of South Florida, 813-974-2084,1995). Reprinted with permission.

annual capital budget, and compile actual and projected capital cash flows for reports.

Primary Responsibilities and Duties

- Check accuracy of financial and accounting treatment for capital and lease requests
- Check for compliance with corporate regulations
- Prepare executive summaries for major capital projects
- Travel to obtain further details on capital projects
- Provide analysis and control prior to authorization of project
- Coordinate and compile data for the annual capital budget
- Analyze all projects submitted for the budget
- Prepare executive summaries on projected authorizations, expenditures, and variances from historical data
- Compile actual and projected capital cash flows for quarterly report

CORPORATE BANKING OFFICER

Basic Function: To maintain and expand existing relationships with clients by marketing all of the bank's services and to develop new client relationships.

Primary Responsibilities and Duties

- Call on Fortune 500 companies headquartered near the bank's offices
- Maintain existing clients in the face of product innovations, constant competition, and the fact that many products have specified terms
- Identify opportunities for all of the services offered by the bank, including credit, cash management, pension management, foreign exchange and interest rate exposure management, tax questions, and merger and acquisition activities
- Perform administrative follow-up on overdrawn deposit accounts, loan documents, rate information, memo writing for credit approvals, credit analysis, etc.
- Bring in the appropriate specialists to discuss technical products with clients
- Stay current with the technical aspects of new products
- Get to know customers better through personal calls
- Review files and annual reports

ACCOUNT EXECUTIVE (SECURITIES BROKER)

Basic Function: Provide advice and counsel to clients concerning potential investments; and execute purchase, sell, and other trade orders on behalf of clients.

Primary Responsibilities and Duties

- Make investment recommendations to clients
- Execute trades on behalf of clients
- Expand market through new contacts and clients
- Learn new investment products
- Serve as a liaison between bookkeeping and clients
- Review research to stay current with several markets

MORTGAGE ANALYST—PRODUCTION

Basic Function: To handle all matters related to the production, analysis, and negotiation of applications for the acquisition of conventional mortgage loans and real estate investments.

Primary Responsibilities and Duties

- Negotiate terms, conditions, interest rates, etc. to obtain a flow of acceptable applications for conventional loans and opportunities to purchase real estate
- Analyze client's financial status and past performance, type of property, nature of offer, property location, facilities and access, and competition.
- Inspect property under consideration
- Prepare detailed analyses of proposed loan or purchase and recommend action on offerings
- Prepare mortgage committee memoranda in conjunction with supervisor and present recommendations to the officer in charge of the mortgage committee
- Prepare commitment letters on those investments which have been approved by the committee
- Assist in the negotiation of the final commitment terms and conditions
- Work with clients to help resolve problems which may jeopardize company's rights under a mortgage
- Prepare correspondence under own signature or for signature by supervisor on all aspect of application processing

FIGURE 1-5 *Continued*

Financial Analysts, and the Financial Management Association. These organizations provide an opportunity for professional interaction and lifelong learning.

The Financial Management Association (FMA) has a goal of serving as a bridge between the academic study of finance and the application of financial principles by financial managers. This goal is achieved through the publication of a quarterly journal, *Financial Management*. The FMA also publishes *Financial Management Collection* three times a year, which reprints and abstracts timely articles of interest to financial practitioners and provides insights into various finance career options. The FMA sponsors student chapters at many universities and sponsors the National Honor Society, the only national honorary organization for students of finance. The FMA also holds an annual meeting featuring the presentation of financial research, panel discussions led by leading academic and financial practitioners, and tutorials on new developments in finance. Additional membership information can be obtained from the Financial Management Association, College of Business Administration, University of South Florida, Tampa, Florida 33620. The FMA can be accessed on the Internet at: www.fma.org

 ## ORGANIZATION OF THE TEXT

This text provides an introduction to both analytical tools and descriptive materials that are useful in financial management. Because this is an introductory-level text, however, it does *not* attempt to make the reader an expert in every aspect of financial decision making. Instead, it is intended to do the following:

■ Acquaint the reader with the types of decisions faced by financial managers.
■ Develop a framework for analyzing these decisions in a systematic manner.
■ Provide the reader with the background necessary to pursue more advanced readings and courses in financial management.

Although the subject matter in this text is divided into distinct parts, in reality and practice, the various types of financial decisions are interrelated and should not be considered in isolation from one another.

Each chapter begins with a summary preview of the key concepts from the chapter. This is followed by a financial challenge faced by a real firm(s) and related to the material in the chapter. At the end of each chapter are a point-by-point summary of the chapter, extensive sets of discussion questions and problems, including "Self-Test Problems" with detailed solutions, which you can use to test your understanding of the text material, and a glossary of new terms used in the chapter. Some chapters also have more complex, integrative case problems. Where appropriate, special *International Financial Management Issues* and *Entrepreneurial Finance Issues* are discussed. The book also has a large number of *Ethical Issues* sections integrated throughout. "Check" answers to selected problems appear at the end of the book. Also, at the end of the book, you will find an overview of the CFM Excel Disk, a set of Excel-based templates that are available for solving many of the complex chapter problems and cases.

Parts of the Text

Part I Introduction. Chapter 2 reviews the major elements of the U.S. and international financial marketplace. It includes a discussion of the structure of the U.S. financial system and the role of stock exchanges. Also included are introductions to various types of derivative securities and international financial management. Chapter 3 considers the financial statements and ratios that can be used to evaluate the financial performance of a firm.

Part II Determinants of Valuation. Valuation is a central theme of the book. Chapter 4 develops the concept of the time value of money. This concept is used in the valuation of securities and the evaluation of investment projects expected to provide benefits over a number of years. Chapter 5 provides a comprehensive introduction to the concept of risk in finance and the relationship between risk, required return, and the shareholder wealth maximization goal of the firm. Chapter 6 applies the basic valuation model to fixed income securities, such as bonds and preferred stock. Chapter 7 deals with the valuation of common stock and the role of investment bankers.

Part III The Capital Investment Decision. This portion of the text focuses on capital expenditures—that is, investments in long-term assets. Chapters 8 and 9 present the fundamentals of capital budgeting, namely, the process of investing in long-term assets. Chapter 8 deals with the measurement of the cash flows (benefits and costs) associated with long-term investment projects. Chapter 9 considers various decision-making criteria that can be used when choosing projects that will maximize the value of the firm. Chapter 10 extends the concepts developed in Chapter 9 by considering some of the decision-making techniques that attempt to deal with the problem of the risk associated with a specific project's cash flow.

Part IV The Cost of Capital, Capital Structure, and Dividend Policy. Chapter 11 illustrates the principles of measuring a firm's cost of capital. The cost of funds to a firm is an important input in the capital budgeting process. Chapters 12 and 13 address the relationship of the cost of capital to the firm's capital structure. Chapter 14 discusses the factors that influence the choice of a dividend policy and the impact of various dividend policies on the value of a firm.

Part V Working Capital Management and Financial Forecasting. Chapters 15 through 18 examine the management of a firm's current asset and liability accounts—that is, net working capital. Chapter 15 provides an overview of working capital management, with emphasis on the risk-return trade-offs involved in working capital decision making. Chapter 15 also covers financial forecasting. Chapter 16 deals with the management of cash and marketable securities, and Chapter 17 focuses on the management of accounts receivable and inventories. Finally, Chapter 18 discusses the management of secured and unsecured short-term and intermediate-term credit.

Part VI Selected Topics in Contemporary Financial Management Chapter 19 deals with lease financing. Chapter 20 focuses on option-related funding alternatives, including convertible securities, warrants, and bond refunding. Chapter 21 discusses the factors that affect exchange rates and foreign exchange risk. Chapter 22 examines corporate restructuring decisions, including mergers and acquisitions, bankruptcy and reorganization.

■ SUMMARY

- The three primary forms of business organization are the *sole proprietorship*, the *partnership*, and the *corporation*. Corporations have certain advantages over the other two forms of business organization, especially for large businesses; as a result, corporations account for about 90 percent of the dollar volume of business activity in the United States.
- A corporation is defined as a "legal person" composed of one or more actual individuals or legal entities. The owners of a corporation are called *stockholders* or *shareholders*. The stockholders elect a *board of directors* that usually deals with broad policy matters, whereas the day-to-day operations are supervised by the corporate *officers*.

- Corporations issue *debt securities* to investors who lend money to the corporation and *equity securities* to investors who become owners.
- The optimal form of organization for a business enterprise is influenced by such factors as cost, complexity, owner liability, business continuity, need for raising capital, the owners' desire to maintain decision-making authority, and tax considerations.
- The primary normative goal of financial management decision making is the *maximization of shareholder wealth* as measured by the price of the firm's stock. This objective permits decision makers to make the needed trade-offs between risk and return and between long-run versus short-run profits.
- *Agency relationships,* such as the relationship between stockholders and managers and the relationship between owners and lenders, give rise to certain agency problems and costs that can have an important impact on firm performance.
- The amount, timing, and risk of the cash flows generated by a firm are, in large part, determined by key financial management decisions, including investment decisions, dividend decisions, financing decisions, and ownership structure decisions. These decisions must be made in the context of factors in the broader economic environment.
- The marginal cost equals marginal revenue rule (MC = MR) from microeconomics provides a framework for structuring many financial management problems.
- The cash flow concept is a fundamental concept in finance. Financial managers focus on raising cash to invest in assets that will, in turn, generate future cash flows for the firm and its owners.
- The net present value (NPV) rule is central to financial analysis. The net present value of an investment is equal to the present value of future returns minus the initial outlay. Future outlays are discounted back to the present at a required rate of return that reflects the perceived risk of the investment.
- The net present value of an investment made by a firm represents the contribution of the investment to the value of the firm and, accordingly, to the wealth of shareholders.
- A primary concern of managers seeking to maximize shareholder wealth is the process by which a firm generates cash flows from its business transactions.
- Financial managers increasingly are giving attention to the ethical dimensions of their business decisions. Ethical decisions and actions are consistent with the goal of shareholder wealth maximization.
- The finance function usually is headed by a vice-president or *chief financial officer.* The financial management responsibilities often are divided between the *controller* and the *treasurer.* The controller normally has responsibility for all accounting-related activities. The treasurer is normally concerned with the acquisition, custody, and expenditure of funds.
- Financial management is closely related to other areas of business decision making, particularly accounting and economics.
- The finance profession offers a number of exciting career opportunities both within the corporate finance function and in the financial services sector.

■ QUESTIONS AND TOPICS FOR DISCUSSION

1. Define *shareholder wealth*. Explain how it is measured.
2. What are the differences between shareholder wealth maximization and profit maximization? If a firm chooses to pursue the objective of shareholder wealth maximization, does this preclude the use of profit maximization decision-making rules? Explain.
3. Which type of corporation is more likely to be a shareholder wealth maximizer—one with wide ownership and no owners directly involved in the firm's management or one that is closely held?
4. Is the shareholder wealth maximization goal a short- or long-term goal? Explain your answer.
5. It has been argued that shareholder wealth maximization is not a realistic normative goal for the firm, given the social responsibility activities that the firm is "expected" to engage in (such as contributing to the arts, education, etc.). Explain why these social responsibility activities are not necessarily inconsistent with shareholder wealth maximization.
6. Explain why management may tend to pursue goals other than shareholder wealth maximization.
7. Explain what is meant by *agency relationships* and *agency costs*.
8. Give some examples of agency costs incurred by shareholders in the agency relationship between the shareholders (owners) and management of a firm.
9. What is the source of potential agency conflicts between owners and bondholders? Who is the agent and who is the principal in this relationship?
10. Explain the differences in the responsibilities of the treasurer and the controller in a large corporation.
11. Explain the relationship between financial management and (a) microeconomics and (b) macroeconomics.
12. Why is earnings per share not a consistently good measure of a firm's performance?
13. Metropolitan Life Insurance Company, Swiss Bank Corporation, and several other holders of RJR Nabisco bonds filed suit against the company to prevent it from completing the leveraged buyout acquisition from Kohlberg Kravis Roberts. Why do you think the bondholders wanted to block this transaction? What arguments can you make for and against the bondholders' case?
14. What are the major factors that determine the value of a firm's stock?
15. What is the relationship between the concepts of net present value and shareholder wealth maximization?
16. Under pressure from outside investors, including corporate raider Carl Icahn, USX Corporation, the parent corporation for U.S. Steel and Marathon Oil, announced a plan to split its stock into separate steel and energy issues. The market response to this action was immediately positive, with the stock price of USX increasing $2.37 to close at $31.25 on the day of the announcement. Why do you think this action by USX was so well received by the stock market?
17. In 1992, retailer R. H. Macy & Co. declared bankruptcy. How can you reconcile a bankruptcy declaration with a management pledged to maximize shareholder wealth?
18. How can the adherence to high standards of ethical business practice contribute to the goal of shareholder wealth maximization?
19. Compare the potential for agency problems in sole proprietorships, partnerships, and corporations. In light of your analysis, why is the corporate form of organization so popular?
20. Assume that your rich uncle gave you $100,000 for safekeeping for 20 days. Instead of stuffing all this money into your mattress, you've decided to invest it for 20 days in the stock market before returning the $100,000 principal to your uncle, hopefully making a sizable profit in the process. Visit the Stock Center at the Thomson Investors Network web site (www.thomsoninvest.net) and choose five stocks whose ini-

tial value is not over $100,000. Twenty days later, close out your portfolio and see how much money you've gained or lost. To receive homework credit for this assignment, prepare a one-page memo to your instructor stating why you chose your particular five stocks, their beginning and ending prices, how much you gained (or lost) from your portfolio, and (hopefully!) what you learned from this experience.

■ GLOSSARY

Agency Relationships Occur when one or more individuals (principals) hire another individual (agent) to perform a service on their behalf. Agency relationships often lead to agency problems and agency costs. Two of the most important agency relationships in finance are the relationship between stockholders (owners) and managers and the relationship between owners and creditors.

Agent The party who acts on behalf of the principal and has a legal responsibility to act in the best interests of the principal in an agency relationship.

Book Value The accounting value of an asset or firm. The book value per share of common stock is equal to a firm's net worth (stockholders' equity) divided by the total number of shares of outstanding common stock.

Corporation A business organization that is created as a "legal person" separate and distinct from the individual or individuals who own the firm's stock. The primary characteristics and advantages of incorporating include limited liability for the firm's owners, permanency, and flexibility with respect to making changes in ownership.

Discount Rate The rate of interest used in the process of finding present values; also called the required rate of return.

Market Value The price at which a stock trades in the financial marketplace.

Net Present Value The present value of expected future cash flows from an investment minus the required initial outlay; the contribution of an investment to shareholder wealth.

Partnership A business organization in which two or more persons form a business with the intention of making a profit. In a *general partnership*, each partner has unlimited liability for the debts of the firm. Limited partnerships allow one or more partners to have limited liability.

Present Value The current value of some future payment or stream of payments, evaluated at an appropriate discount rate.

Principal In an agency relationship, the party who employs someone else, the agent, to perform service on behalf of the principal.

Risk The possibility that actual future returns will deviate from expected returns; the variability of returns.

Shareholder Wealth Present value of the expected future returns to the owners (that is, shareholders) of the firm. It is measured by the market value of the shareholders' common stock holdings—that is, the price per share times the number of shares outstanding.

Sole Proprietorship A business owned by one person. The owner of a sole proprietorship has unlimited liability for debts incurred by the business.

Stakeholders The constituent groups in a firm, including stockholders, bondholders, suppliers, customers, employees, community neighbors, and creditors.

THE DOMESTIC AND INTERNATIONAL FINANCIAL MARKETPLACE

2

1. In the U.S. financial system, funds flow from net savers (such as households) to net investors (such as businesses) through financial middlemen and financial intermediaries.
   a. Financial middlemen include securities brokers and investment bankers.
   b. Financial intermediaries include commercial banks, thrift institutions, investment companies, and finance companies.
2. Financial markets are classified as money or capital markets and primary or secondary markets.
   a. Short-term securities with maturities of one year or less are traded in money markets. Long-term securities have maturities of more than one year and are traded in capital markets.
   b. New securities are traded in the primary markets. Existing securities are traded in the secondary markets, such as the New York Stock Exchange, the American Stock Exchange, and the over-the-counter market.
3. Companies engaged in international financial transactions face such problems as political and exchange rate risk in addition to those risks encountered in domestic transactions.

KEY CHAPTER CONCEPTS

4. The exchange rate is the rate at which a currency can be converted into another currency.
   a. The spot rate is the present exchange rate for immediate delivery.
   b. The forward rate is the present exchange rate for deliveries of currencies in the future.
5. The Eurocurrency market is an important alternative to domestic sources of financing for multinational firms. LIBOR, the London interbank offer rate, is the basic interest rate against which Eurocurrency loans are priced.
6. In efficient capital markets, security prices represent an unbiased estimate of the true economic value of the cash flows expected to be generated for the benefit of that security holder.
7. Holding period returns measure the actual or expected return from holding a security, including price changes and distributions, such as dividends or interest.

DAIMLER-BENZ AG'S DECISION TO LIST ITS SHARES ON THE NEW YORK STOCK EXCHANGE*

On October 5, 1993, the share of Daimler-Benz AG, the parent firm of Germany's maker of Mercedes Benz automobiles, began trading on the New York Stock Exchange. Although this listing attracted considerable attention, it is only one instance of a growing trend of foreign public and private offerings of debt and common stock in the U.S. capital markets. The volume of foreign debt offerings in the United States grew from less than $10 billion in 1985 to nearly $100 billion in 1993. Foreign stock offerings in the United States grew from about $1 billion in 1985 to a figure in excess of $10 billion in 1993.

Foreign firms that want to have their shares listed and traded in the United States must meet strict Security and Exchange Commission (SEC) rules regarding the preparation of financial statements and disclosure of accounting practices. Daimler has a long history of reporting steady profits. Part of this success can be attributed to aggressive manipulation of the financial statements through the use of "off the books" hidden reserves, accumulated from past periods of high but nonreported earnings. In years when product demand declines and actual operating losses are incurred, these reserves are tapped, thus enabling the firm to report profits. To qualify for listing on the New York Exchange, Daimler had to overhaul its accounting practices and eliminate the use of these reserves. As a result, Daimler was forced to report a loss for the first half of 1993 of $592 million: its first loss since the end of World War II. Why would Daimler agree to such radical changes in its financial reporting just to see its shares traded in the United States?

Multinational firms, such as Daimler, are eager to acquire capital in the markets where it is the cheapest. In Daimler's case, the urgent need for additional capital, combined with what it perceived to be a large clientele of over 300,000 rich, happy Mercedes owners who would be potential buyers of its United States shares, was enough to convince management that the benefits were worth the cost of greater financial disclosure. The listing corresponded closely with Daimler's decision to build a plant in Alabama. By raising capital in the United States, Daimler will be able to hedge some of its foreign exchange risk associated with the U.S. venture.

How has this decision benefited Daimler-Benz? Daimler's management believes that its ability to raise capital at the lowest cost will be greatly enhanced by its entry into the U.S. capital markets. Indeed, since the time Daimler announced the plan for the New York Exchange listing, the value of its shares rose more than 30 percent, far exceeding the 11 percent gain recorded by the Dow Jones Equity Market Index for Germany over the same time period. Daimler officials and U.S. investment bankers attribute this gain to increased demand for the shares by U.S. investors who found it difficult to acquire Daimler shares when they traded only on German exchanges. Many other European firms, such as Nestle SA, are now considering the best way for them to tap into the tremendous capital-raising potential of U.S. capital markets.

This chapter develops the underlying principles of the operation of international financial markets and the market for foreign exchange. An understanding of these principles is essential for managers who make resource allocation and capital-raising decisions designed to maximize shareholder wealth.

*For a more complete discussion of foreign firm financing in the United States see "Foreign Firms Raise More and More Money in the U.S. Markets," *Wall Street Journal* (October 5, 1993): A1, A8.

INTRODUCTION

This chapter provides a look at the domestic and international marketplaces within which firms operate. These financial marketplaces serve the role of allocating scarce resources from saving units (such as individuals) to investing units (such as firms). One important element of the financial marketplace is the structure of corporate and personal taxation. The existence of corporate and personal income taxes has important implications for financial managers. Because so many financial decisions are based on after-tax cash flows, finance and business professionals must have a basic understanding of tax matters. (Appendix A at the end of the text contains an overview of important elements of U.S. tax laws.) We provide an overview of the operation of the U.S. and international financial systems, distinguishing between the money and capital markets. The major financial intermediaries are discussed, and the operation and structure of secondary security markets are presented. The concept of an efficient market is developed. This chapter also illustrates how to calculate holding period returns for any investment.

 INCOME TAXES AND FINANCIAL MANAGEMENT

A knowledge of tax laws and regulations is essential in making a wide variety of business decisions that affect shareholder wealth, such as what form of business organization to select, what types of securities to issue, and what investment projects to undertake.

Specific provisions of the federal tax laws applicable to corporations are discussed in Appendix A at the end of the book.

Implications of Income Taxes for Financial Managers

Although the effect of income taxes on financial decisions is discussed in detail where appropriate throughout the book, a brief review of some of the critical areas of concern is provided in this section.

Capital Structure Policy. Taxes have important implications for capital structure policy because the interest payments associated with debt financing are deductible from earnings when computing a company's income tax liability, whereas common stock dividends and preferred stock dividends are not deductible. In other words, for a company with positive pretax earnings and a 40 percent income tax rate, a new debt issue that increases interest expenses by $1,000,000 per year would cost the company (i.e., reduce after-tax income) only $600,000—$1,000,000 interest expense less $400,000 tax savings (= .40 × $1,000,000). This tax advantage of debt is a prime reason for leveraged buyouts and financial restructurings.

Dividend Policy. A firm's dividend policy may be influenced by personal income taxes. When dividends are paid to common stockholders, these dividends are taxed immediately as income to the shareholder. If, instead of paying dividends, a firm retains and reinvests its earnings, the price of the stock can be expected to increase. Personal taxes owed on common stock appreciation are deferred until the stock is sold. The ability to defer personal taxes on retained earnings causes some investors (e.g., those in high marginal tax brackets) to prefer retention and reinvestment and ultimately capital gains rather than immediate dividend payments. This investor preference can have an impact on corporate dividend policy, particularly in small, closely held companies.

Capital Budgeting. Capital expenditure decisions also are influenced by corporate income taxes. Capital expenditures require an outlay of *after-tax* dollars in order to acquire the needed assets. The assets are expected to generate a stream of operating income that is subject to tax. A tax-deductible expense associated with many capital expenditures is depreciation. Depreciation provides a tax deduction equal to a part of the original cost of a depreciable asset such as machinery or buildings. The tax code details the methods that may be used to depreciate assets. Because depreciation is a noncash expense (the cash outlay was made when the asset was purchased), it simply reduces taxable income and hence reduces the amount of taxes that must be paid. Changes in the tax code that speed up (slow down) the depreciation rate increase (decrease) the present value of the cash flows from the investment project and make the project a more (less) desirable investment. Therefore, financial managers must pay close attention to expected tax law changes.

Leasing. The decision to lease or buy an asset is often motivated by its tax effects. If the lessee (asset user) is losing money or not subject to taxation (a nonprofit enterprise), leasing may be advantageous because the lessor (asset owner) can reflect the tax benefits of ownership in the lease rate charged to the lessee.

These and other tax effects of financial decisions will be encountered throughout the text and in the practice of financial management.

Tax Rate Used in the Text

U.S. tax laws impose progressive tax rates on corporate income—the larger the income, the higher the tax rate. As discussed in Appendix A to the book, the largest corporations pay a marginal tax rate (i.e., tax rate on the next dollar of income) of 35 percent. Throughout the text however, we use an *assumed* marginal tax rate of 40 percent rather than the *actual* corporate marginal tax rate of 35 percent. There are two reasons for following this convention. First, it simplifies many of the calculations. Second, most firms also are subject to state-imposed income taxes. A 40 percent rate is an excellent approximation of the *combined* federal and state income tax rates facing most firms.

Wouldn't it be handy to have an all-purpose Web site for taxes? Fortunately, we do. The site listed here can answer virtually any tax question you might have—laws, regulations, procedures, policies, etc. It will even calculate your taxes for you—provided, of course, that you can supply all the necessary information (your income, deductions, etc.). It also has links to the IRS, tax consultants, and other organizations/people involved with taxes.
http://www.tax.org

AN OVERVIEW OF THE U.S. FINANCIAL SYSTEM

The U.S. financial system serves an important function in the efficient operation of the economy. The financial system is the vehicle that channels funds from saving units (savers) to investing units. The rates of return that investing units must pay for the capital supplied by savers are determined competitively in financial markets. As we shall see later in the book, investment activity undertaken by firms is influenced by the rate of return (cost of capital) the firms must pay to attract resources from savers. Accordingly, it is important for financial managers to understand the elements and functioning of the financial marketplace so that capital costs can be minimized for any set of investments a firm undertakes.

In considering any economy as a whole, the actual savings for a given period of time must equal the actual investments. This phenomenon is called the *saving-investment cycle.*

Table 2-1 presents a summary of the saving-investment cycle in the United States for 1995. Total gross savings for that year equaled $1,141.6 billion—$240.8 billion from personal savings by individuals, $821.7 billion from business, and a government surplus of $79.1 billion. (This last figure is a combination of federal, state, and local surpluses.) Gross investment also totaled $1,141.6 billion— $1,287.2 billion in gross private and government domestic investments less $141.1 billion in net foreign investments. This latter figure indicates that investments of foreign entities in the United States exceeded the investments of U.S. entities abroad by $141.1 billion. (Because of estimation errors, there is a statistical discrepancy of $4.5 billion.)

The saving-investment cycle depends on net savers, or *surplus spending units,* and net investors, or *deficit spending units.* The cycle is completed when the surplus spending units transfer funds to the deficit spending units. The main purpose of the U.S. financial system—including the financial markets and all financial institutions—is to facilitate this transfer of funds. Figure 2-1 graphically depicts this continual flow.

Funds flow from surplus spending units, such as households, to deficit spending units, such as businesses, through *financial middlemen* and *financial intermediaries.* Financial middlemen include *brokers,* who bring together buyers and sellers of securities; *dealers,* who sell securities to investors out of an inventory they carry; and *investment bankers,*[1] who assist corporations in selling their securities. These securities are called *primary claims,* because they are sold directly by the borrower and bought directly by the saver (lender).

Financial intermediaries include commercial banks, thrift institutions, investment companies, pension funds, insurance companies, and finance companies. They differ from financial middlemen in that they issue *secondary claims* to the ultimate lender instead of primary claims. (A bank savings account is an example of a secondary claim.) A financial intermediary may lend money to a corporation, even though there is a small chance that the corporation will default on its

TABLE 2-1
U.S. Gross Savings and Investment, 1995 (in Billions of Dollars)

Source: *Federal Reserve Bulletin* (August 1996): A49.

Personal savings		$240.8
Gross business savings:		
Undistributed profits	$142.5	
Depreciation allowances	679.2	821.7
Government surplus or deficit (−)		79.1
Gross savings		$1,141.6
Gross private and government investment		$1,287.2
Net foreign investment		−141.1
Statistical discrepancy		−4.5
Gross investment		$1,141.6

[1]The role of investment bankers in corporate finance is discussed in greater detail in Chapter 8.

FIGURE 2-1
Flow-of-Funds Diagram

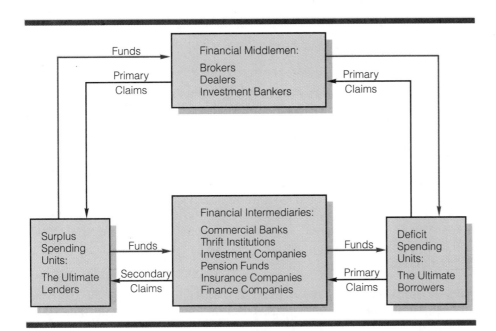

loan. In general, individuals or households are unwilling to lend funds to a corporation under these circumstances, but they will allow a commercial bank to use their funds, because the bank can guarantee them both liquidity and safety.

Thus, financial intermediaries facilitate the transfer of funds. They are compensated for their services by an *interest rate spread*. For example, a bank might loan money to a business at an average of 11 percent interest, pay depositors an average of 8 percent interest, and use the 3 percent difference to pay employee salaries and other expenses, as well as to provide a return to their stockholders. The various financial intermediaries are examined in greater detail later in this section.

Have you ever wondered what a "cyberbank" looks like? What kind of service does it offer, and how exactly can you use cyberbanking services? Check out the cyberbanks maintained by Wells Fargo and Bank of America. Would you do your banking at a cyberbank? Why or why not?
http://www.wellsfargo.com
http://www.bankamerica.com

Financial Assets

Although *money* is the most obvious financial asset, there are others as well, including *debt securities* and *equity securities*. Both debt and equity securities represent claims against the assets and future earnings of the corporation. Debt and equity securities are financial *assets* of the investors who own them, and, at the same time, these securities appear on the *liabilities and stockholder's equity* side of the issuing company's balance sheet.

Financial Markets

Financial markets are the vehicles through which financial assets are bought, sold, and traded. Financial markets generally are classified as money or capital markets and primary or secondary markets.

Money and Capital Markets. Money markets deal in short-term securities having maturities of one year or less. **Capital markets** deal in long-term securities having maturities greater than one year. (In both cases, the one-year breaking point is somewhat arbitrary.)

Most large corporations participate in the money markets, especially when they have more cash on hand than needed to run their businesses. For example, Chrysler Corporation had over $8.1 billion in cash and short-term investments at the end of (fiscal year) 1995—approximately 28 percent of its current assets and 15 percent of its total assets. By investing in money market securities, the company earned interest rather than leaving its funds in non-interest-bearing commercial bank checking accounts.

Corporations enter the capital markets to obtain long-term funds, either debt or equity. Most large U.S. corporations are unable to generate enough funds *internally* to satisfy their needs, so they raise additional funds *externally* in the capital markets. For example, during 1995, Apple South, Inc., a rapidly growing restaurant chain, made capital expenditures and other investments of $172.6 million and paid $630,000 of dividends. During the same year, Apple South generated $51.3 million of operating cash flow internally. As a result, Apple South had to issue substantial amounts of new debt ($46.4 million) and common stock ($59.8 million).

Primary and Secondary Markets. An investor who purchases *new* securities is participating in a **primary** financial market. Net proceeds from the sale of new securities go directly to the issuing company. On virtually any given business day, the *Wall Street Journal* contains announcements about the issuance of new debt and equity securities. (These are called *tombstones* because of their resemblance to epitaphs.) Figure 2-2 shows a tombstone announcement for the sale of new shares of common stock by Panhandle Eastern Corporation, whose shares are traded on the New York Stock Exchange. On May 25, 1993, the company issued 9 million new shares of common stock through an underwriting syndicate of investment bankers, at a price of $21.25 per share. The issue was successful, and during the next 30 days the stock price advanced to over $24 per share. Note that part of the issue (20 percent or 1.8 million shares) was offered to foreign investors through a group of international securities dealers.

An investor who resells existing securities is participating in a **secondary** financial market. Secondary markets are well established in the United States, where stocks can be traded on the "floor" of a security exchange, such as the New York Stock Exchange (NYSE) or the American Stock Exchange (ASE or AMEX) or in the over-the-counter market (OTC). The structure and operation of the secondary markets is discussed in greater detail in the following sections. The operation of the primary markets is examined in Chapter 7.

Financial Intermediaries

A variety of different financial intermediaries exists to facilitate the flow of funds between surplus spending units and deficit spending units. These different financial intermediaries specialize in the types of deposits they accept (sources of funds) and the types of investments they make (uses of funds).

Commercial Banks. Commercial banks accept both demand deposits (in the form of checking accounts) and time deposits (in the form of savings accounts and certificates of deposit). These funds are loaned to individuals, businesses, and governments. Commercial banks are an important source of short-term loans. Seasonal businesses, such as retailers, certain manufacturers (for example, those who deal in leisure products), some food processors, and builders often require short-term financing to help them through peak periods. Many

This announcement is under no circumstances to be construed as an offer to sell or as a solicitation of an offer to buy any of these securities. The offering is made only by the Prospectus Supplement and the Prospectus to which it relates.

New Issue   **May 25, 1993**

9,000,000 Shares

PANHANDLE EASTERN CORPORATION

Common Stock

Price $21.25 Per Share

Copies of the Prospectus Supplement and the Prospectus to which it relates may be obtained in any State or jurisdiction in which this announcement is circulated from only such of the undersigned or other dealers or brokers as may lawfully offer these securities in such State or jurisdiction

7,200,000 Shares

The above shares were underwritten by the following group of U.S. Underwriters.

Merrill Lynch & Co.

Dillon, Read & Co. Inc.

Kidder, Peabody & Co.
Incorporated

The First Boston Corporation   **Alex. Brown & Sons**   **A. G. Edwards & Sons, Inc.**
Incorporated

Goldman, Sachs & Co.   **Howard, Weil, Labouisse, Friedrichs**   **Lazard Frères & Co.**   **Lehman Bros.**
Incorporated

Mabon Securities Corp.   **J.P. Morgan Securities Inc.**   **Oppenheimer & Co., Inc.**

Prudential Securities Incorporated   **Rauscher Pierce Refsnes, Inc.**   **Salomon Brothers Inc.**

Smith Barney, Harris Upham & Co.   **UBS Securities Inc.**   **Dean Witter Reynolds Inc.**
Incorporated

Advest, Inc.   **J.C. Bradford & Co.**   **Cowen & Company**   **Dain Bosworth**   **First Albany Corp.**
Incorporated

First of Michigan Corporation   **Janney Montgomery Scott Inc.**   **Kemper Securities, Inc.**

C. J. Lawrence Inc.   **Legg Mason Wood Walker**   **Piper Jaffray Inc.**
Incorporated

The Principal/Eppler, Guerin & Turner, Inc.   **Raymond James & Associates, Inc.**

The Robinson-Humphrey Company, Inc.   **Stifel, Nicolaus & Company**   **Wheat First Butcher & Singer**
Incorporated   CAPITAL MARKETS

Brean Murray, Foster Securities Inc.   **The Chicago Corporation**   **Johnston, Lemon & Co.**
Incorporated

Parker/Hunter   **Petrie Parkman & Co.**   **Roney & Co.**   **Scott & Stringfellow, Inc.**
Incorporated

1,800,000 Shares

The above shares were underwritten by the following group of International Underwriters.

Merrill Lynch International Limited

Dillon, Read & Co. Inc.

Kidder, Peabody International
Limited

ABC International Bank plc   **Barclays de Zoete Wedd Limited**   **Christiania Fonds AS**

NatWest Securities Limited   **Société Générale**   **UBS Limited**

other types of businesses have a more or less continuing need for short-term financing and make prior arrangements with their banks to borrow on short notice. For example, during 1995, H. J. Heinz Company negotiated confirmed lines of credit with its banks totaling $2 billion. These established lines of credit (prearranged borrowing agreements) give Heinz quick access to substantial funds as they are needed in the operation of the firm. As this example illustrates, banks provide significant amounts of both temporary and more "permanent" short-term financing for businesses.[2]

Banks are also a major source of **term loans,** which have initial maturities between one and 10 years and usually are repaid in installments over the life of the loan.[3] The proceeds from term loans can be used to finance current assets, such as inventory or accounts receivable, and to finance the purchase of fixed plant facilities and equipment, as well as to repay other debts.

Thrift Institutions. Thrift institutions include savings and loan associations, mutual savings banks, and credit unions. These institutions accept both demand and time deposits. Savings and loan associations and mutual savings banks invest most of their funds in home mortgages, whereas credit unions are engaged primarily in consumer loans. Many thrift institutions have been acquired by commercial banks in recent years. The role of thrifts in financing has declined greatly.

Investment Companies. Investment companies, such as mutual funds and real estate investment trusts (REITs), pool the funds of many savers and invest these funds in various types of assets. Mutual funds invest in specific financial assets—such as debt and equity securities of corporations or money market instruments—according to the objectives of the fund. Mutual funds attempt to achieve superior performance through diversification[4] and professional investment management. REITs, as the name suggests, invest their pool of funds in real estate.

Pension Funds. Private pension funds pool the contributions of employees (and/or employers) and invest these funds in various types of financial assets, such as corporate securities, or real assets, such as real estate. Pension funds often are managed by bank trust departments and life insurance companies.

Insurance Companies. Insurance companies receive periodic or lump-sum premium payments from individuals or organizations in exchange for agreeing to make certain future contractual payments. Life insurance companies make payments to a beneficiary based on certain events, such as the death or disability of the insured party. Property and casualty insurance companies make payments when a financial loss occurs due to such events as fire, theft, accident, and illness. The premiums received are used to build reserves to pay future claims. These reserves are invested in various types of assets, such as corporate securities.

Finance Companies. Finance companies obtain funds by issuing their own debt securities and through loans from commercial banks. These funds are used to make loans to individuals and businesses. Some finance companies are formed

[2]Short-term bank credit is discussed further in Chapter 18.
[3]Term loans are examined in Chapter 18.
[4]*Diversification* is the act of investing in a set of securities having different risk-return characteristics. The topic is covered in Chapter 5.

to finance the sale of the parent company's products. A well-known example is General Motors Acceptance Corporation (GMAC).

THE STRUCTURE AND OPERATION OF U.S. SECURITY MARKETS

As discussed above, capital markets usually are classified as either *primary* or *secondary* markets. New securities are issued in the primary markets, and the firms issuing these securities receive the proceeds from their sale, thus raising new capital. Outstanding securities are traded in the secondary markets, where owners of these securities may sell them to other investors. The corporations whose securities are traded in the secondary markets do not share in the proceeds from these sales.

Although primary and secondary markets are separate, they are closely related. Smoothly functioning secondary markets aid the primary markets, because investors tend to be more willing to purchase new securities when they know they can sell them in the secondary market. In fact, the potential liquidity available in the secondary markets may make investors more willing to accept slightly lower returns on their investments, thereby lowering the cost companies have to pay for their funds.

Security Exchanges and Stock Market Indexes

Secondary markets can be classified as either listed security exchanges or over-the-counter (OTC) markets. **Listed security exchanges** operate at designated places of business and have requirements governing the types of securities they can list and trade. The **OTC** security markets do not have centralized places of business but rather exist as networks of security dealers connected by a communications system of telephones and computer terminals that allow the dealers to post the prices at which they are willing to buy and sell various securities.

Listed Security Exchanges. The New York Stock Exchange, sometimes called the *Big Board,* is the oldest and largest stock exchange in the United States. Over 2,000 common and preferred stocks and over 800 bonds are listed on the NYSE. For a company's stock to be listed and traded on the NYSE, the company must meet certain minimum requirements with regard to the number of shares of stock outstanding, the number of shareholders, the geographical distribution of shareholders, the value of assets, the market value of shares, and the net income level. As a result, the NYSE tends to list the stock of larger firms.

The NYSE is composed largely of security firms that purchase memberships, or *seats.* The cost of these seats varies, depending on the securities industry outlook. The other major organized national exchange is the American Stock Exchange, which, like the NYSE, is located in New York City. The companies listed on the AMEX are smaller on average than those listed on the NYSE.

In addition to the national exchanges, there are a number of regional exchanges located around the country. The largest are the Chicago Exchange, the Pacific Exchange, and the Philadelphia, Boston, and Cincinnati exchanges. In general, regional exchanges list stocks of companies located in their geographical areas. Many large companies are listed on both the NYSE and one or more regional exchanges.

Trading activities on the NYSE and the major regional exchanges are listed together and reported in the financial press as the *NYSE Composite Transactions*.

Over-the-Counter Markets. Securities not listed on exchanges are said to be traded "over the counter." In general, these include stocks of small and relatively unknown companies, although a growing number of large companies, such as Microsoft, many bank and insurance company stocks, a majority of corporate bonds and preferred stocks, and most U.S. Treasury and municipal bonds are traded in OTC markets. Security firms that deal in OTC securities and actually carry inventories in certain stocks play an important role in the smooth functioning of OTC markets, and they are said to "make a market" in the securities they inventory.

On each business day, the *Wall Street Journal* contains price quotations on OTC stocks having some national interest. These quotations are from NASDAQ, the automated quotation system of the National Association of Security Dealers. This system has helped to integrate more fully the OTC market at the national level.

Stock Market Indexes. Stock market indexes give a broad indication of how the stock market or a segment of it performed during a particular day. The most frequently quoted stock market index is the Dow Jones Industrial Average (DJIA), which is based on the stock prices of 30 large, well-established industrial corporations.[5] The DJIA is calculated by adding the prices of the 30 stocks and dividing by a number that reflects prior stock dividends and splits. When a radio announcer says, "The market was up five points today," the announcer means the DJIA was up five points.

The Dow Jones Transportation Average is based on 20 major railroad, airline, and trucking stocks, and the Dow Jones Utility Average is derived from 15 major utility stocks. The DJIA is combined with the transportation and the utility averages to form the Dow Jones Composite Average.

The *Standard and Poor's 500* Stock Price Index (S&P 500), another frequently quoted stock market index, is significantly broader than the DJIA. It is compiled from the stock prices of 400 leading industrial firms, 20 transportation firms, 40 utilities, and 40 financial institutions. The S&P 500 is a *market value–weighted index*. This means, for example, that a stock whose total market value is $20 million influences the index twice as much as a stock whose total market value is $10 million.

Figure 2-3 provides a listing and data on major stock market indexes.

Regulation of the Security Markets

Both the individual states and the federal government regulate the securities business. Beginning with Kansas in 1911, each of the fifty states (with the exception of Delaware) has passed so-called blue sky laws. The term *blue sky* came about when some risky securities were called nothing more than "pieces of blue

The United States has two national exchanges (the New York Stock Exchange and the American Stock Exchange), several regional exchanges, and one over-the-counter exchange (NASDAQ). Our national and OTC exchanges support extensive Web sites where they describe themselves, the stocks they trade, how to become listed on their exchanges, and so on. Visit their Web sites and take an inside peak at these cornerstones of our financial system. Using a search engine, try to find out whether a regional exchange exists near you and, if so, whether it has a Web site.
http://www.nyse.com/
http://www.amex.com
http://www.nasdaq.com/

---

[5]Dow Jones and Company is a financial company that publishes the *Wall Street Journal*. Each Monday, the *Wall Street Journal* lists the companies that make up the Dow Jones averages. Every day, the values of all the major stock market indexes are listed in the *Wall Street Journal* and in the financial section of most major newspapers.

FIGURE 2-3
Stock Market Index Data

Source: *Wall Street Journal* (January 3, 1997).

STOCK MARKET DATA BANK

MAJOR INDEXES

†12-MO HIGH	†12-MO LOW		DAILY HIGH	DAILY LOW	CLOSE	NET CHG	% CHG	†12-MO CHG	% CHG	FROM 12/31	% CHG
DOW JONES AVERAGES											
6560.91	5032.94	30 Industrials	6468.54	6352.82	6442.49	− 5.78	− 0.09	+ 1268.65	+ 24.52	+ 1325.37	+ 25.90
2315.47	1882.71	20 Transportation	2256.29	2215.91	2222.07	− 33.60	− 1.49	+ 205.31	+ 10.18	+ 241.07	+ 12.17
238.12	204.86	15 Utilities	233.09	229.53	230.99	− 1.54	− 0.66	+ 3.42	+ 1.50	+ 5.59	+ 2.48
2059.18	1655.55	65 Composite	2030.39	1995.89	2015.04	− 10.79	− 0.53	+ 299.57	+ 17.46	+ 321.83	+ 19.01
714.26	564.39	DJ Global-US	702.24	689.56	696.15	− 4.41	− 0.63	+ 113.48	+ 19.48	+ 114.72	+ 19.73
NEW YORK STOCK EXCHANGE											
398.86	321.41	Composite	392.92	386.36	389.53	− 2.77	− 0.71	+ 58.81	+ 17.78	+ 60.02	+ 18.21
503.23	403.39	Industrials	495.42	487.30	491.53	− 2.85	− 0.58	+ 76.31	+ 18.38	+ 78.24	+ 18.93
266.69	236.63	Utilities	259.94	255.97	258.95	− 0.96	− 0.37	+ 3.47	+ 1.36	+ 6.05	+ 2.39
358.60	294.40	Transportation	352.30	345.24	347.15	− 5.15	− 1.46	+ 40.86	+ 13.34	+ 45.19	+ 14.97
358.18	263.70	Finance	351.70	343.99	346.63	− 4.54	− 1.29	+ 74.12	+ 27.20	+ 72.38	+ 26.39
STANDARD & POOR'S INDEXES											
757.03	598.48	500 Index	742.81	729.55	737.01	− 3.73	− 0.50	+ 119.31	+ 19.32	+ 121.08	+ 19.66
887.95	702.07	Industrials	872.41	857.73	866.92	− 3.05	− 0.35	+ 142.36	+ 19.65	+ 145.73	+ 20.21
213.83	184.66	Utilities	199.21	196.18	197.11	− 1.70	− 0.86	− 7.13	− 3.49	− 5.47	− 2.70
257.41	207.94	400 MidCap	255.66	251.13	252.11	− 3.47	− 1.36	+ 36.69	+ 17.03	+ 34.27	+ 15.73
145.65	115.48	600 SmallCap	145.48	143.42	144.26	− 1.22	− 0.84	+ 25.01	+ 20.97	+ 23.16	+ 19.12
162.77	129.15	1500 Index	160.17	157.41	158.84	− 0.97	− 0.61	+ 25.52	+ 19.14	+ 25.60	+ 19.21
NASDAQ STOCK MARKET											
1316.27	988.57	Composite	1293.63	1272.34	1280.70	− 10.33	− 0.80	+ 250.88	+ 24.36	+ 228.57	+ 21.72
856.64	534.42	Nasdaq 100	826.06	805.83	815.60	− 5.76	− 0.70	+ 252.12	+ 44.74	− 5.76	− 0.70
1193.13	908.41	Industrials	1109.36	1093.85	1098.88	− 10.75	− 0.97	+ 154.99	+ 16.42	+ 134.20	+ 13.91
1465.43	1196.03	Insurance	1465.16	1442.84	1450.10	− 15.33	− 1.05	+ 168.28	+ 13.13	+ 157.46	+ 12.18
1273.46	990.65	Banks	1272.57	1262.79	1265.92	− 7.54	− 0.59	+ 255.99	+ 25.35	+ 256.51	+ 25.41
544.97	329.43	Computer	521.26	509.43	514.96	− 3.83	− 0.74	+ 163.31	+ 46.44	− 3.83	− 0.74
232.57	189.64	Telecommunications	216.68	214.15	215.71	− 0.20	− 0.09	+ 4.98	+ 2.36	− 0.20	− 0.09
OTHERS											
617.61	524.20	Amex Composite*	573.63	567.89	569.16	− 3.18	− 0.56	+ 18.57	+ 3.37	− 3.18	− 0.56
401.21	318.24	Russell 1000	394.58	387.49	391.09	− 2.66	− 0.68	+ 62.18	+ 18.90	+ 62.20	+ 18.91
364.61	301.75	Russell 2000	362.62	357.61	358.96	− 3.65	− 1.01	+ 48.19	+ 15.51	+ 42.99	+ 13.61
425.72	340.20	Russell 3000	420.17	412.88	416.46	− 2.98	− 0.71	+ 65.10	+ 18.53	+ 64.55	+ 18.34
377.41	321.64	Value-Line(geom.)	375.42	370.98	372.50	− 2.82	− 0.75	+ 41.82	+ 12.65	+ 41.46	+ 12.52
7295.57	5850.20	Wilshire 5000	...	...	7147.80	− 50.49	− 0.70	+ 1103.79	+ 18.26	+ 1090.60	+ 18.00

†-Based on comparable trading day in preceding year. *-Replaced previous index eff. 1/02/97.

sky." In spite of these state laws, many investors received incomplete and even fraudulent security information during the 1920s. This fact, combined with the 1929 stock market crash and the general reform spirit of the 1930s, led to the enactment of two principal pieces of security legislation—the Securities Act of 1933 and the Securities Exchange Act of 1934—and the establishment of the **Securities and Exchange Commission (SEC).** This federal legislation has been aimed primarily at ensuring full disclosure of security information.

In addition to regulating the disclosure of information in new security offerings and setting disclosure requirements for nearly all firms whose shares trade publicly, the SEC also regulates "insider" trading. Any time a director, officer, or major stockholder—that is, an "insider"—of a large corporation trades in that corporation's securities, the trade must be reported to the SEC. This information is available to the public and is used by some investors in deciding which stocks to buy or sell. This reporting requirement attempts to prevent insiders from trading securities secretly on the basis of private information.

As we all know, the government is a very important player in our financial markets—from policies, rules, and regulations, to injecting and withdrawing huge amounts of money into our financial system. For one-stop shopping, the following Web address links to scores of government-related Web sites (SEC, Treasury, etc).
http://www.uncle-sam.com

ETHICAL ISSUES
INSIDER TRADING

In 1942, a young lawyer at the Securities and Exchange Commission, reacting to a complaint that a company president had purchased stock after telling shareholders that earnings had declined when he knew earnings were strong, wrote an initially obscure rule, Rule 10b-5. Rule 10b-5 and subsequent SEC rules have since been broadly interpreted and used as the justification for prosecuting insider trading.[6] Insider trading is defined as an individual (the insider) buying or selling securities on the basis of material, nonpublic information.

The story of Dennis Levine, the Drexel Burnham investment banker who spent over two years in federal prison after his conviction on insider trading charges, provides insights into the ethical dilemmas facing young managers. In 1978, the 25-year-old Levine began trading on insider information while working as a trainee at Citibank and earning a salary of $19,000. He began with seemingly innocent trades based on "hot stock tips" from another Citibank employee about pending mergers. His first insider trade earned him no return at all because the rumored merger did not materialize. But in seven years, Levine built his personal wealth from $39,750 to $11.5 million based on insider trades. As his profits grew, his greed grew as well. He stated, "I was confident that the elaborate veils of secrecy I had created . . . would protect me. And Wall Street was crazy in those days. These were the 1980s, remember, the decade of excess, greed, and materialism. . . . In this unbelievable world of billions and billions of dollars, the millions I made trading on nonpublic information seemed almost insignificant."[7]

Levine rationalized his actions with the belief (which is true, at least in part) that insider trading is a victimless crime. Henry Manne, one of the leading legal experts on insider trading, states, "The insiders' gain is not made at the expense of anyone. The occasionally voiced objection to insider trading—that someone must be losing the specific money the insiders make—is not true in any relevant sense."[8] Furthermore, the first criminal prosecution of insider trading did not occur until 1978, the year when Levine first began to use inside information for his private gain.

There is considerable controversy about the criminal status of insider trading. Criminal prosecutions under Rule 10b-5 have been rare. Some of those are under appeal on the grounds that Rule 10b-5 does not permit criminal prosecution of this practice. More general agreement exists regarding the ethics of insider trading for personal gain by individuals who have been entrusted with confidential information. The Levine story illustrates how easy it is for aggressive young managers to step over the bounds of ethical behavior early in their careers.

---

[6]There is considerable controversy whether Rule 10b-5 ever was intended for the purpose of criminally prosecuting insider trading. Indeed, in passing the 1934 Securities Act, Congress considered making insider trading illegal but rejected the idea. It was not until 1961 that the SEC claimed it could use Rule 10b-5 to bring a civil case. Only in 1978 did SEC and federal prosecutors use this rule to bring a criminal case. Only eight insider trading cases had gone to trial by the end of 1990. For a more complete discussion of the evolution and application of Rule 10b-5, see Gordon Crovitz, "The SEC Overstepped When It Made Insider Trading a Crime," *Wall Street Journal* (December 19, 1990): A17.

[7]Dennis B. Levine, "The Inside Story of an Inside Trader," *Fortune* (May 21, 1990): 80–89.

[8]Henry G. Manne, "In Defense of Insider Trading," *Harvard Business Review* (November/December 1966): 113–22.

Do you agree with Manne that insider trading is a victimless crime? Who should be considered an insider for purposes of enforcing the rule? Can you think of any reasons why insider trading should be permitted?

THE GLOBAL ECONOMY AND MULTINATIONAL ENTERPRISES

The importance of understanding the global economy can be seen in the volume of exports and imports in the United States. In 1995, U.S. merchandise exports totaled over $575 billion and merchandise imports totaled over $749 billion. The difference between merchandise exports and imports is the *merchandise trade balance.* In 1995, the United States had a *merchandise trade deficit* of approximately $174 billion, representing a substantial increase from the deficit in 1991 of $74 billion. In 1995, a global recession resulted in reduced demand for export goods from the United States, while at the same time the U.S. economy was in the midst of a strong economic recovery, thus contributing to this growing trade deficit.

Business enterprises participate in the global marketplace in a wide variety of ways. Some firms simply *export* finished goods for sale in another country and/or *import* raw materials or products from another country for use in their domestic operations. At the other end of the spectrum are *multinational enterprises.* A **multinational firm** has direct investments in manufacturing and/or distribution facilities in more than one country. Often, these foreign operations are structured as more or less "free-standing" subsidiaries. Among the largest multinational firms are such U.S. firms as General Motors, Exxon, Ford, IBM, General Electric, and Philip Morris. Large multinational Japanese firms include Toyota, Hitachi, Matsushita, Nissan, and Toshiba. Major European multinationals include Royal Dutch/Shell, Daimler-Benz, British Petroleum, Siemens, Volkswagen, Fiat, Unilever, and Nestlé.

The rise of the multinational firm has drastically changed the way business is done around the world. The multinational organization makes it relatively easy for firms to transfer the key factors of production—land, labor, and capital—to the location where they can be most productive, which represents a dramatic change from the time when the factors of production were thought to be immobile and only goods and services could be moved easily across borders. As a result, the process of resource allocation and business decision making has become more complex. At the same time, multinational firms have the opportunity to benefit from imperfections that arise in various national markets for capital and other factors of production. Furthermore, whether or not a firm is engaged in international transactions, the decline of trade barriers and the increasing ease of moving assets to those countries where they will be the most productive adds a new element of competition for all firms. It is no longer possible for a U.S. manufacturer, such as Ford Motor Company, to worry just about its domestic competitors. Over the past decade, Japanese and German auto companies have built plants in the United States that directly compete with U.S.-based companies.

All firms engaged in international business transactions face unique problems and risks not encountered by firms that operate in only one country. First, there are difficulties associated with doing business in different currencies.

Financial transactions between U.S. firms and firms (or individuals) in foreign countries normally involve foreign currency that ultimately has to be converted into U.S. dollars. Therefore, firms that do business internationally are concerned with the *exchange rate* between U.S. dollars and foreign currencies. Second, problems arise because of different government regulations, tax laws, business practices, and political environments in foreign countries.

FOREIGN CURRENCY MARKETS AND EXCHANGE RATES

Whenever a U.S. firm purchases goods or services from a firm in another country, two currencies normally are involved. For example, when a U.S. company purchases materials from a British supplier, the British firm usually prefers payment in British pounds, whereas the U.S. company prefers to make payment in U.S. dollars. If the sales agreement requires that payment be made in pounds, the U.S. company will have to exchange (that is, *sell*) dollars to obtain the required number of pounds. The exact amount of dollars the U.S. company will have to sell depends on the **exchange rate** between the two currencies.

Suppose, for example, that the exchange rate at the time of the transaction is $1.48 per pound, £. Furthermore, assume that the British supplier and the U.S. firm have agreed on a price of £2 million for the materials. Therefore, the U.S. firm will have to exchange $2.96 million (that is, £2,000,000 x $1.48/pound) to obtain the British currency to pay for the purchase.

Foreign currency needed for international financial transactions can be exchanged for domestic currency in most countries either at large commercial banks or at a central bank operated by the government. The volume of foreign currency transactions is very large. For example, in 1990 the Bank for International Settlements estimated that daily, worldwide foreign currency trading totaled over $640 billion. Of this amount, nearly 60 percent was between international banks; about 25 percent was between banks within a country; and the balance was with foreign currency dealers and other banking customers. The most important foreign currency trading centers are in New York, Tokyo, Hong Kong, Singapore, Bahrain, Frankfurt, Zurich, London, San Francisco, and Los Angeles.

The Eurocurrency Market

LIBOR is a very important interest rate in the world of finance, but so are SIBOR, TIBOR, and a lot of other -IBORs. Can you guess what the S and T in the above terms mean? Using a search engine, see whether you're correct.

A **Eurocurrency** is a currency that is deposited in a bank located outside of the country of origin. Eurocurrencies are created when, for example, a U.S. firm transfers dollars from a bank in the United States to a bank outside of the United States. Also, someone outside of the U.S. may receive dollars in connection with a business transaction or because of a purchase in the foreign exchange market. When these dollars are deposited in a bank outside of the United States they become **Eurodollars**. The bank may either be a foreign bank, such as Deutsche Bank, or a foreign branch of a U.S. bank, such as Chase Manhattan, located in Frankfurt. Other important Eurocurrencies include Euromarks, Euroyen, and Eurosterling (Deutsche marks, Japanese yen, and British pounds), deposited outside of their country of origin. The gross size of the Eurocurrency market is in excess of $5 trillion. About two-thirds of the Eurocurrencies outstanding are U.S. dollar-denominated.

As an illustration, consider the following example. BMW sells a car to an American dealer for $60,000. The American dealer pays BMW with a check for $60,000 drawn on Chase Manhattan Bank. BMW must then decide what to do with this check. BMW could immediately sell the dollars (buy Deutsche marks). However, BMW wants to retain the dollars for use later on (perhaps to pay for goods purchased from U.S. firms), so it buys a Eurodollar deposit by depositing the check in Deutsche Bank in Germany. The typical Eurocurrency deposit is a nonnegotiable time deposit with a fixed term to maturity. Maturities range from overnight to as long as five years.

The Eurocurrency market provides an important alternative to domestic sources of funds for multinational firms. For example, in the United States, large, well-established multinational corporations can borrow funds either in the domestic financial market, or in the international financial marketplace, such as the Eurocurrency market. If General Motors chooses to borrow in the Eurodollar market it would receive a Eurodollar loan from a foreign bank, such as Barclays Bank in London or Deutsche Bank in Frankfurt. The interest rate in the Eurodollar market is usually related to the *London interbank offer rate,* or *LIBOR.* **LIBOR** is the interest rate at which banks in the Eurocurrency market lend to each other. The cost to borrow in the Eurocurrency market is usually stated as a margin above LIBOR. Typically, Eurodollar borrowing rates are between 0.5% and 3% over LIBOR, with a median of about 1.5%. Eurocurrency loans range in maturity up to ten years for the best quality borrowers.

The Euro: A Common European Union Currency

In 1999, a large number of the countries of the European Union are scheduled to create, and begin using, a new, common currency called the **Euro.** This new currency will, in effect, represent a market basket of the participating countries' currencies. During a transition period, both individual country currencies and the Euro would remain in circulation. Ultimately the plan is to have the Euro completely replace the currencies of the participating countries. Although, at present, this plan appears to be on track for implementation in 1999, there are a number of political and economic hurdles that still must be overcome before such a plan is successfully implemented.

Direct and Indirect Quotes

Exchange rates can be expressed either as *direct quotes* or *indirect quotes.* A **direct quote** is the home currency price of one unit of foreign currency. For example, from the perspective of a U.S. firm, a quote of $0.58 per Deutsche mark (DM) would be a direct quote. An **indirect quote** is the foreign currency price of one unit of the home currency. A quote of DM1.7241/$ would be an indirect quote from the perspective of a U.S. firm. Direct quotes and indirect quotes have a reciprocal relationship. Accordingly, the indirect quote was derived by taking the reciprocal (1 ÷ $0.58/DM) of the direct quote.

Spot Rates

Exchange rates between U.S. dollars and the currencies of most countries are reported daily in the *Wall Street Journal.* Table 2-2 lists the (direct quote) exchange rates between U.S. dollars and various currencies as of December 27,

TABLE 2-2
Spot Foreign Exchange Rates

Source: *Wall Street Journal* (December 31, 1996
and December 2, 1993).

		EXCHANGE RATE (U.S. DOLLARS)	
Country	*Currency*	*December 27, 1996*	*December 1, 1993*
Australia	Dollar	$0.7953	$0.6588
Britain	Pound	$1.6945	$1.4775
Canada	Dollar	$0.7311	$0.7500
France	Franc	$0.1907	$0.16829
Germany	Mark	$0.6433	$0.5807
India	Rupee	$0.02790	$0.0312
Italy	Lira	$0.0006536	$0.0005816
Japan	Yen	$0.008673	$0.009191
Netherlands	Guilder	$0.5731	$0.5178
South Africa	Rand	$0.2135	$0.2967
Sweden	Krona	$0.1458	$0.1177
Switzerland	Franc	$0.7416	$0.6658
-	ECU	$1.2415	$1.11620

1996 and December 1, 1993.[9] These quotes are for trades made among banks in amounts of $1 million or more. Smaller, retail transactions usually result in fewer units of a foreign currency per dollar. The quotes in Table 2-2 are known as *spot rates*. **Spot rates** represent the rate of exchange for currencies being bought and sold for immediate delivery.[10]

Banks profit from their foreign currency transactions by buying currencies at one rate (bid) and selling them at another, higher rate (ask or offer). For example, a bank may quote the Deutsche mark at $0.5795 bid, and $0.5807 offer. This quote is often written simply as 0.5795—07. The spread between bid and offer for widely traded currencies is likely to be in the range of 0.1 to 0.5%.

Forward Rates

In addition to spot transactions, currencies can also be bought and sold today for delivery at some future time, usually 30, 90, or 180 days from today. In these cases, **forward rates** are used, rather than spot rates. Forward exchange rates between U.S. dollars and the currencies of several of the major industrial countries also are reported daily in the *Wall Street Journal*. Table 2-3 lists some forward exchange rates as of December 27, 1996.

A comparison of the spot and forward rates in Tables 2-2 and 2-3 shows that the 30-, 90-, and 180-day forward rates for the British pound is below its spot rate, indicating a market expectation that the pound will lose value relative to the dollar over

---

[9]The ECU shown at the bottom of Table 2-2 represents a European Currency Unit. The **ECU** is a composite "currency" that consists of fixed amounts of currencies of the European countries that are part of the Exchange Rate Mechanism, a process by which member countries manage their currencies to maintain exchange rates within predetermined ranges. Each ECU represents a "basket" currency derived from a weighted average of the currencies of all countries participating in the Exchange Rate Mechanism. The weights for each currency depend on each member's proportion of intra-European trade and the size of its economic output as measured by gross national product.
[10]The date at which money must be exchanged among the parties in a spot foreign currency transaction is known as the *value date*. It is customarily set as the second working day after the date on which the transaction is concluded. For example, a spot transaction entered into in Frankfurt on Monday will not normally be settled until the following Wednesday.

TABLE 2-3
Forward Foreign Exchange Rates

Source: *Wall Street Journal*
(December 30, 1996).

EXCHANGE RATE (U.S. DOLLARS) DECEMBER 27, 1996			
Currency	*30-Day Forward*	*90-Day Forward*	*180-Day Forward*
British pound	$1.6938	$1.6912	$1.6863
Canadian dollar	0.7327	0.7354	0.7395
French franc	0.1911	0.1917	0.1928
Japanese yen	0.008713	0.008787	0.008899
Swiss franc	0.7438	0.7478	0.7551
German Mark	0.6446	0.6470	0.6508

this time horizon. In contrast, the forward rates for the other currencies are above their spot rates, indicating an expectation of increasing value relative to the dollar.

The premium or discount between the spot rate, S_0, and a forward rate, F, for a currency (relative to the dollar, for example) can be expressed on an *annualized* percentage basis (using direct quotes) as follows:

$$\text{Annualized forward premium or discount} = \left(\frac{F-S_0}{S_0}\right)\left(\frac{12}{n}\right)(100\%) \qquad (2.1)$$

where n is the number of months in the forward contract. A positive value calculated using Equation 2.1 indicates that a currency is trading at a forward premium relative to the dollar, whereas a negative value indicates a forward discount.

Using the exchange rates from Tables 2-2 and 2-3, the following annualized premium for the 180-day forward quote on the Deutsche mark (DM) can be calculated:

$$\text{Annualized premium} = \left(\frac{\$0.6508 - \$0.6433}{\$0.6433}\right)\left(\frac{12}{6}\right)(100\%)$$
$$= 2.33\%$$

Similarly, the annualized discount for the 180-day forward quote on the British pound can be calculated as

$$\text{Annualized discount} = \left(\frac{\$1.6863 - \$1.6945}{\$1.6945}\right)\left(\frac{12}{6}\right)(100\%)$$
$$= -0.9678\%$$

CALCULATOR SOLUTION

The determination of a forward discount or premium on a currency also can be done with the aid of a financial calculator. Consider the calculation of the forward discount on the British pound as computed above:

Enter: 0.5   −1.6945   1.6863

| n | i | PV | *PMT* | FV |

Solution: −0.9655

which differs slightly from the value computed using Equation 2.1, due to the compounding impacts that are more correctly reflected in the calulator solution.

Thus we can say that the DM is trading at a forward premium relative to the dollar (i.e., the dollar is expected to weaken relative to the DM) and the pound is trading at a forward discount relative to the dollar (i.e., the dollar is expected to strengthen relative to the pound).

As shown later in the book (Chapter 21), firms engaged in international transactions can use the forward foreign exchange market to hedge against the risk of adverse fluctuations in exchange rates.

Foreign Currency Futures

A foreign currency *futures* contract is similar to a forward contract. Both call for the delivery of a specified amount of some item, such as a foreign currency, at a future point in time at a price set at the present time. A **forward contract** is normally a contract between two individuals who are known to each other, such as an importer and a commercial bank. Performance on the contract by the seller and the buyer depends on the character and capacity of the two parties. Because these contracts are negotiated between two individuals, forward contracts can be established for any future time period, and for any quantity of any item that is agreeable to the parties. Forward contracts are not liquid; that is, it is difficult or impossible for either party to transfer their interest in the contract to another party once the contract has been agreed upon. The seller of the contract must deliver the promised item at the time agreed to in the contract, and the buyer must pay for it and accept delivery.

In contrast to a forward contract, a **futures contract** is an *exchange traded agreement* that calls for the delivery of a *standardized amount* of an item (such as DM 125,000) at a *standardized maturity date*. The most important foreign currency futures market in the United States is the Chicago Mercantile Exchange (CME). Contracts traded on the CME mature on the third Wednesday of the contract month, with the last trading day being two days prior to that. Unlike forward contracts, there is virtually no performance risk in a futures contract. Rather than the buyer and seller of the contract dealing directly with each other, the "exchange clearing house" acts as the buyer and seller of all contracts. Buyers and sellers of futures contracts must post collateral (as their performance bond). Each day the value of the contract is "marked to market," with all gains and losses being paid between the parties in cash. If payment is not made, the contract is sold by the clearing house and the performance bond of the defaulting party is charged for any losses. In essence, one can think of a futures contract as a series of forward contracts that are settled each day. Only about five percent of foreign currency futures contracts are settled by means of delivery of the underlying currency from the seller to the buyer. More commonly, the parties will offset their position prior to expiration by making a transaction opposite to the original one. For example, a buyer of a contract for DM125,000 with delivery in March usually sells an identical contract prior to expiration. The sale of an identical contract by an initial buyer of the same contract fully offsets the position from the perspective of the clearing house.

Table 2-4 shows foreign currency futures contract quotations for the German mark (Deutsche mark or DM) as of December 27, 1996. The first line under the headings indicates that the contract is for Deutsche marks, that the contract is traded on the Chicago Mercantile Exchange (CME), that the contract is for 125,000 marks and that the prices are direct quotes ("$ per mark"). The next three lines provide quotes for the contracts maturing on the third Wednesday of March 1997, June 1997, and September 1997. The column numbers indicate

Futures Magazine *(now online) will tell you why coffee prices are surging to record highs while cattle prices are plummeting. They also have free demo software allowing you to chart, analyze, and track futures prices in gold, platinum, pork bellies, British pounds, and virtually any other major commodity, whether you're hedging or speculating.*
http://www.futuresmag.com

CONTRACT DATE	OPEN	HIGH	LOW	SETTLE	CHANGE	LIFETIME HIGH	LIFETIME LOW	OPEN INTEREST
Deutsche Mark (CME)—125,000 marks; $ per mark								
March 97	.6466	.6468	.6443	.6464	–.0001	.6937	.6417	47,694
June	.6492	.6496	.6492	.6503	–.0001	.6947	.6460	4,380
September	....	....	....	.6542	–.0001	.6635	.6510	1,693
Est vol 7,494; vol Th 3,988; open int 53,784, –100.								

TABLE 2-4
Futures Contract Quotation

Source: *Wall Street Journal* (December 39, 1996).

that the opening price of the March 1997 contract was $0.6466/DM, the high price for the day was $0.6468, the low price for the day was $0.6443, and the closing price (settle) was $0.6464. This was a decline of $0.0001 from the previous day. Over the lifetime of this contract, it traded from a high of $0.6937 to a low of $0.6417. Currently, there are 47,694 contracts (open interest) such as this one in existence. As the last trading date approaches, the open interest declines dramatically and only a small minority of the contracts will actually be in existence (and therefore require delivery of DM from the seller to the buyer) at expiration. Also, this table indicates much more trading interest in the near-term contract (March) than in the longer-term contract (September). Finally, the last line in Table 2-4 indicates that 7,494 contracts traded on December 27, compared with 3,988 contracts on the previous day. The number of contracts outstanding declined by 100 contracts on December 27 to a total of 53,784.

Foreign Currency Options

Whereas forward and future currency contracts reflect an *obligation* to either buy or sell a currency at a future date, **options** are contracts that give the option buyer the *right, but not the obligation* to either buy or sell a fixed amount of a foreign currency at a fixed price at a time up to, or at the expiration date of the option. There are two fundamental types of options. A **call** option is an option to buy something, such as foreign currency, and a **put** option is an option to sell (foreign currency). An *American option* gives the holder the right to buy (call options) or sell (put options) the underlying currency at any time prior to expiration. In contrast, a *European option* gives the holder the right to buy or sell the underlying currency only at expiration. Large commercial banks offer customized options for all major currencies with exercise periods of up to a year. In addition, foreign currency options are traded on the Philadelphia Stock Exchange and the Chicago Mercantile Exchange. Foreign currency options provide an alternative to forward and futures contracts for firms seeking to control their foreign exchange risk. Chapter 19 develops the principles of option valuation and illustrates the use of options to hedge foreign currency risk.

A FOUNDATION CONCEPT
MARKET EFFICIENCY

A central theme of much of the academic finance and financial economics research since the 1960s has been the *efficiency* of the capital markets. The more efficient capital markets are, the more likely it is that resources will find their highest (risk-adjusted) return uses. Capital market efficiency is an implicit assumption in many decision models widely used in finance. Consequently, this concept is important to a full understanding of these decision models.

In an **efficient capital market**, *stock prices provide an unbiased estimate of the true value of an enterprise.* Stock prices reflect a *present value* estimate of the firm's *expected cash flows,* evaluated at an appropriate *required rate of return.* The required rate of return is determined by conditions in the financial markets, including the supply of funds from savers, the investment demand for funds, and expectations regarding future inflation rates. The required rate of return on a security also depends on the seniority of the security, the maturity of that security, the business and financial risk of the firm issuing the security, the risk of default, and the marketability of the security. The *efficiency of the capital markets* is the important "glue" that bonds the present value of a firm's net cash flows—discounted at the appropriate risk-adjusted required rate of return—to shareholder wealth as measured by the market value of a company's common stock. Hence, in this section of the chapter, the concept of market efficiency is defined, the evidence regarding the extent of capital market efficiency is reviewed briefly, and some important implications of market efficiency are identified.

Information and Capital Market Efficiency

Capital markets are efficient if security prices instantaneously reflect in an unbiased manner all economically relevant information about a security's prospective returns and the risk of those returns. What is meant by "all economically relevant information"? Information is a message about future events that may occur. "Relevant" information can be used by an individual to take actions that will change the welfare of that individual. Messages that an individual cannot act upon to change his or her welfare have little value. For example, a cotton farmer who grows cotton on irrigated land might be willing to pay for accurate weekly rainfall forecasts, because these forecasts can be used to establish the most efficient irrigation schedule. In contrast, once a dry-land cotton farmer has planted his fields, weekly rainfall forecasts are of little use, because there are no actions the farmer can take on a day-to-day basis using this information.

In addition to being able to act upon the information in a manner that will affect one's welfare, one must be able to correlate the information with the future events when they occur. For example, if your broker always told you that a stock you had identified looked like a "good buy," this message would have little value to you, because you know that some of these stocks will perform well and others will not. In contrast, if your broker recommends stocks to buy and stocks to sell based upon his or her estimate of each security's return prospects and is right more often than he or she is wrong, then this message constitutes economically relevant information.

In security markets, some messages are economically relevant to investors and others are not. If a message has no impact on the future return or risk prospects of a security, it is not relevant to investors and should not be correlated with security performance; that is, it does not constitute information. For example, the news that a company has changed the format of the presentation of its financial reports is not information because this cosmetic change has no impact on the return or risk of that company's securities. In contrast, if the company announces that it has adopted a new accounting convention that will result in significant tax savings, this news is information because it affects the return stream from that company's securities.

Degrees of Market Efficiency

Three levels of market efficiency have been identified based on the information set under consideration: weak-form efficiency, semistrong-form efficiency, and strong-form efficiency.

Weak-Form Efficiency. With weak-form market efficiency, no investor can expect to earn excess returns[11] based on an investment strategy using such information as historical price or return information. All stock market information, including the record of past stock price changes and stock trading volume, is fully reflected in the current price of a stock.

Tests of the weak-form market efficiency hypothesis have included statistical tests of independence of stock price changes from various day-to-day periods.[12] These studies have concluded that stock price changes over time essentially are statistically independent and that a knowledge of past price changes cannot be used to predict future changes. Other tests have looked for the existence of longer-term cycles in stock prices, such as monthly or seasonal cycles.[13] In addition, numerous trading rules based solely on past market price and volume information have been tested. Pinches, in a review of much of this research, has concluded that "with some exceptions, the studies of mechanical trading rules do not indicate that profits can be generated by these rules."[14] In conclusion, the evidence indicates that U.S. capital markets are efficient in a weak-form context.

Semistrong-Form Efficiency. With semistrong-form market efficiency, no investor can expect to earn excess returns based on an investment strategy using *any* publicly available information. Announcements of earnings changes, stock splits, dividend changes, interest rate changes, money supply levels, changes in accounting practices that affect a firm's cash flows, takeover announcements, and so on are quickly and unbiasedly incorporated in the price of a security. A finding of semistrong-form market efficiency implies that the market also is weakly efficient, because the information set considered in the weak-form case also is publicly available. Once information is made public in a semistrong-form efficient capital market, it is impossible for investors to earn excess returns (after considering trading costs) from transactions based upon this information, because the security price already will reflect the value of this information. Studies of stock splits, new issues, stock listing announcements, earnings and dividend announcements, stock acquisition announcements, and announcements of analyst recommendations support the notion of semistrong-form market efficiency, at least after the

---

[11]Excess returns are returns that exceed those that can be expected considering the risk assumed by the investor. In Chapter 5 we formally develop models of the relationship between returns and appropriate measures of risk.

[12]See, for example, Sidney S. Alexander, "Price Movements in Speculative Markets: Trends or Random Walks?" *Industrial Management Review* (May 1961): 7–26; Eugene F. Fama, "The Behavior of Stock Market Prices," *Journal of Business* (January 1965): 34–105; and Eugene F. Fama and James MacBeth, "Risk, Return and Equilibrium: Empirical Tests," *Journal of Political Economy* (May/June 1973): 607–636.

[13]C. W. Granger and O. Morgenstern, *Predictability of Stock Market Prices* (Boston: D. C. Heath, 1970).

[14]George Pinches, "The Random Walk Hypothesis and Technical Analysis," *Financial Analysts Journal* (March/April 1970): 104–110.

cost of commissions on transactions are considered.[15] There have been a few apparent observed violations of semistrong-form market efficiency, but in many cases, alternative explanations for these exceptions have been found. Overall, the evidence on semistrong-form market efficiency tends to support this level of market efficiency.

Strong-Form Efficiency. With strong-form market efficiency, security prices fully reflect *all* information, both public and private. Thus, in a strong-form efficient capital market, no individual or group of individuals should be able to consistently earn above-normal profits, including insiders possessing information about the economic prospects of a firm. The existence of such individuals as Ivan Boesky, who have traded illegally on the basis of inside information and have earned phenomenal profits until they were caught and prosecuted by the Securities and Exchange Commission, provides graphic evidence that strong-form efficiency does not hold.

Implications of Market Efficiency for Financial Managers

In general, we can conclude that capital markets are quite efficient, both in an informational and an operational sense. The observed efficiency of capital markets has some very important implications for financial managers.

Timing or Gambling. In a weak-form efficient capital market, we know there are no detectable patterns in the movement of stock and bond prices. Companies often indicate that they have delayed a stock or bond offering in anticipation of more favorable capital market conditions; that is, a higher stock price or lower interest rates. Since there are no predictable patterns of stock price and interest rate movements over time, financing decisions based upon improved market timing are not likely to be productive, on average. If a stock has traded as high as $30 per share recently but is now trading only at $28, management may delay a proposed new stock issue in anticipation of a higher future price. If this delay is based upon a market timing argument—such as "the market is now temporarily depressed"— rather than on some inside information known only to management that suggests that the stock is currently undervalued, then the strategy is not likely to be successful. In some instances, the stock price will increase in the direction of the target, while in others, it will decline even further. In weak-form efficient capital markets, financial decisions based on timing market cycles are not able consistently to lead to higher returns than are available to managers who do not attempt to time their financial decisions to take advantage of market cycles.

An Expected NPV of Zero. In an efficient capital market, all securities are perfect substitutes for one another, in the sense that each security is priced such

---

[15]See, for example, Eugene Fama, L. Fisher, M. Jensen, and R. Roll, "The Adjustment of Stock Prices to New Information," *International Economic Review* (February 1969): 1–21; Frank K. Reilly, "Further Evidence on Short-Run Results for New Issue Investors," *Journal of Financial and Quantitative Analysis* (March 1974): 165–177; Stanley Block and Marjorie Stanley, "The Financial Characteristics and Price Movement Patterns of Companies Approaching the Unseasoned Securities Market in the Late 1970s," *Financial Management* (Winter 1980): 30–36; Richard W. Furst, "Does Listing Increase the Market Price of Common Stocks?" *Journal of Business* (April 1970): 174–180; R. Richardson Pettit, "Dividend Announcements, Security Performance and Capital Market Efficiency," *Journal of Finance* (December 1972): 993–1007; Michael Firth, "The Information Content of Large Investment Holdings," *Journal of Finance* (December 1975): 1265–1281; and Peter L. Davies and Michael Canes, "Stock Prices and the Publication of Second-Hand Information," *Journal of Business* (January 1978): 43–56.

that its purchase represents a zero net present value investment. This is another way of saying that required returns equal expected returns in efficient capital markets. For example, if you buy one share of Apple Computer stock for $25, the present value of the market expectation of its cash flows is equal to $25. Hence, this purchase has a net present value of zero. If you buy for $35 one share of stock in Duke Power Company, a utility firm with considerably less risk and lower earnings growth prospects than Apple Computer, the present value of the market expectation of its cash flows is equal to $35. The difference between the risk and expected returns of the two companies' stocks is reflected in their market prices and the discount rate used by the market to evaluate the expected future cash flows. Only if an investor possesses information that is not known to the marketplace—for example, insider knowledge of a major new oil strike by an oil firm or of a pending takeover attempt—will the investment in a stock or bond have a positive net present value.

Expensive and Unnecessary Corporate Diversification. If capital markets are efficient and all securities are fairly priced, on average, investors can accomplish much on their own without the help of a firm's financial managers. For example, consider Eastman Kodak's acquisition of Sterling Drug. In 1988, Eastman Kodak paid $89.50 per share to acquire Sterling Drug. During the previous year, Sterling traded for as little as $35.25 per share. As a stockholder of Eastman Kodak, you could have achieved the same diversification in your portfolio simply by buying shares of Sterling Drug in the open market.[16] In spite of this, financial managers of many firms continue to make acquisitions of other companies in order to achieve "the benefits of diversification." In efficient capital markets, this type of activity is better left to individual investors.

Security Price Adjustments. In efficient capital markets, security prices reflect expected cash flows and the risk of those cash flows. If a transaction, such as an accounting change, does not impact the firm's expected *cash flows* or the *risk* of those cash flows, then the transaction should have no impact on security prices. Investors are not fooled by cosmetic accounting or other nonmaterial transactions.

Efficient capital markets research has shown that accounting format changes having no impact on a firm's cash flows do not result in changes in the firm's value. Actions such as including the capitalized value of financial leases on a firm's balance sheet, providing an inflation-adjusted income statement and balance sheet, company name changes, stock splits, and stock dividends unaccompanied by a rise in earnings and/or dividends have no significant impact on stock prices. In contrast, any event impacting actual cash flows—such as a change in inventory valuation designed to reduce tax obligations—or the risk of these cash flows—such as an announcement by Arizona Public Service Company that it will sell all of its nuclear power plants—will be reflected quickly in the stock price.

Prices in efficient capital markets have a story to tell. For example, on December 17, 1986, Republic Bank Corporation of Dallas announced plans to acquire InterFirst Corporation. InterFirst was suffering from severe loan portfolio

---

[16]Eastman Kodak ultimately divested itself of its ownership of Sterling Drug, taking a considerable loss, when it failed to realize the expected benefits from the acquisition.

quality problems at that time due to the energy sector downturn and a real estate glut in its major market areas. On the day following the announcement, the stock price of InterFirst declined from $5 to $4.875 per share. The stock price of Republic declined from $21.75 to $19 per share. The market's assessment of this acquisition was not positive. Indeed, the market's early assessment appears to have been correct. In early 1988, First Republic's stock traded for $1.75 per share. The bank failed shortly thereafter.

 INTERNATIONAL ISSUES
MARKET EFFICIENCY OUTSIDE THE UNITED STATES [17]

As previously mentioned, extensive testing of the efficiency of security markets in the United States has led researchers to conclude that the major capital markets in this country are quite efficient in their operation and the way in which investors process new, economically relevant information. An important question facing the manager of a multinational firm that desires to raise capital outside of the United States is: Are foreign capital markets also efficient with respect to security pricing and the processing of new information?

Extensive tests of the efficiency of capital markets outside of the United States also have been conducted. These studies concluded that the capital markets in the major industrialized countries, such as Japan, Canada, the United Kingdom, and most of Western Europe, are reasonably efficient.

Outside the major industrialized countries, capital markets function without the frequency of trading and liquidity that are necessary for efficient markets. For example, one day in Cairo, the total number of trades on the Cairo Stock Exchange was eight! Transferring shares in Egypt is a complicated, bureaucratized process that requires many signatures, the payment of transfer taxes, and the reissue of stock certificates by the issuing company (a signature is required by two members of the company's board of directors). Overall, it can take between two and three months before the purchaser receives the shares. Brokers in Cairo have an unspoken agreement that prices will not be allowed to move more than 10 percent a day. When someone wants to buy shares from a broker in Egypt, the first question that usually is asked is "Why?" The broker always suspects that the buyer is privy to some inside information. Insider trading is not illegal in Egypt.[18] The inefficiency of the Cairo Exchange holds for the capital markets in many developing countries. Hence, most of the capital that is raised by multinational firms is acquired in countries with well-developed, efficiently functioning capital markets.

Even if the capital markets of the major industrialized countries are relatively efficient, it may still be true that international capital markets, in general, are not efficient. For example, to the extent that there are barriers to the free flow of capital among the major world capital markets, it is possible that a multinational firm can use these barriers to reduce the overall cost of raising capital. Some of the barriers that have been identified include

[17]This section is based, in part, on Bruno Solnick, *International Investments,* 2nd ed. (Reading, MA: Addison-Wesley, 1991).
[18]G. Brooks, "To Play the Market in Egypt Requires a Lot of Patience," *Wall Street Journal* (March 23, 1989): A1

1. *Legal restrictions* limit the amount of foreign investment by some institutional investors. Some countries limit the amount of foreign ownership of domestic industries in an attempt to prevent a loss of local control.
2. High *transactions costs* also may make the free flow of capital difficult across country borders. These high costs include the cost of gathering information, trading costs, fees for managing international investments, and security custodial service fees.
3. *Taxation policies* between nations sometimes discourage the flow of capital across borders.
4. International investments are subject to greater *political risks* than are domestic investments. These political risks range from expropriation to limits on the repatriation of profits and assets.
5. *Foreign exchange risks*, that is, the risks of unfavorable movements in the value of foreign currencies, also act as a deterrent to the flow of capital across national borders.

These factors may lead to somewhat segmented international capital markets. To the extent that international capital markets are not fully integrated, opportunities may exist for multinational firms that are willing to aggressively manage their investment and capital-raising functions to gain some advantage over less internationally integrated firms.

 FOUNDATION CONCEPT
HOLDING PERIOD RETURNS

The return from holding an investment is called the *holding period return, holding period yield,* or *realized rate of return.* The **holding period return** can be defined by the following equation.

$$\text{Holding period return (\%)} = \frac{\text{Ending price} - \text{Beginning price} + \text{Distributions received}}{\text{Beginning price}} \times (100\%) \quad (2.2)$$

Distributions include the interest on debt or the dividends on stock. To illustrate, suppose you purchased one share of Hershey Foods Corporation common stock for $31 a year ago. During the year, you received $0.80 in dividends, and you now sell the share for $46. Your holding period return would be calculated as

$$\text{Holding period return (\%)} = \frac{\$46 - \$31 + \$0.80}{\$31} \times 100\% = 50.97\%$$

Returns are expressed as a percentage or fraction and frequently are quoted on an annual basis. However, holding period returns can be calculated for any time period. But, in order for a calculated holding period return to be a meaningful number, it must be compared to other returns computed using equal time periods.

The returns just computed is called a *realized,* or *ex post* (after the fact), return. Realized returns differ from *expected* or *ex ante* (before the fact), returns. Although ex ante returns are calculated in the same manner as ex post returns, ending prices and distributions for expected returns are *estimated* values, whereas ending prices and distributions for realized returns are *actual* values.

■ SUMMARY

- Tax laws and regulations affect a wide variety of business decisions, including decisions about capital structure, dividend payments, capital expenditures, and leasing.
- The main purpose of an economy's financial system is to facilitate the transfer of funds from *surplus spending units* to *deficit spending units. Financial middlemen,* such as investment bankers, bring together the surplus and deficit spending units in the capital markets so that funds can be transferred. *Financial intermediaries,* such as commercial banks, receive *primary claims* from their borrowers and issue *secondary claims* to their lenders. Secondary claims have different risk and liquidity characteristics than primary claims.
- *Financial assets* consist of *money, debt securities,* and *equity securities.*
- Financial markets are the vehicles through which financial assets are bought and sold. They include *money* or *capital markets* and *primary* or *secondary markets.* Money markets deal in securities with maturities of approximately one year or less, while capital markets deal in securities with maturities greater than one year. Primary markets are those in which *new* securities are issued; secondary markets are those in which *existing* securities are traded.
- *Capital markets* are considered to be *efficient* if security prices instantaneously and fully reflect, in an unbiased way, all economically relevant information about a security's prospective returns and the risk of those returns. U.S. capital markets and the capital markets of most major industrialized nations appear to operate and process relevant information in an efficient manner; however, the capital markets in many developing countries are much less efficient.
- Stocks and bonds are traded both on organized exchanges, such as the New York and the American Stock Exchanges, and in the over-the-counter market, which is a network of securities dealers.
- Firms engaged in international financial transactions face risks and problems not faced in domestic transactions, including difficulties encountered in doing business in different currencies and problems associated with different government regulations, tax laws, business practices, and political environments.
- A *Eurocurrency* is a currency deposited in a bank located outside of the country of origin. The Eurocurrency market is an important alternative to domestic sources of financing for multinational firms. The interest rate charged for Eurocurrency loans is tied to LIBOR, the London interbank offer rate.
- The *exchange rate* is the rate at which one currency can be converted into another. The *spot rate* is the rate of exchange for currencies being bought and sold for *immediate delivery today.* The *forward rate* is the rate of exchange between currencies to be delivered at a future point in time—usually 30, 90, and 180 days from today. The *futures rate* also is a rate of exchange between currencies to be delivered at a future point in time. In contrast to forward contracts, futures contracts are standardized with respect to size and delivery date and are traded on organized exchanges, such as the International Monetary

Market. Foreign currency *options* give the option holder the *right* to buy or sell a foreign currency at a fixed price over some time horizon.

■ QUESTIONS AND TOPICS FOR DISCUSSION

1. Describe and discuss the saving-investment cycle.
2. What roles do financial middlemen and financial intermediaries play in the operation of the U.S. financial system? How do the two differ?
3. How do money and capital markets differ?
4. Describe the various types of financial intermediaries, including the sources of their funds and the types of investments they make.
5. What factors need to be considered when determining the optimal form of organization for a business enterprise?
6. How do primary and secondary financial markets differ?
7. What is the primary distinction between the trading process on the New York Stock Exchange and the over-the-counter markets?
8. Describe the concept of market efficiency. In what sense is this concept an important part of the shareholder wealth maximization objective?
9. If a capital market is not efficient, what is the impact on a firm seeking to raise capital in that market? Why?
10. Define the following terms:
    a. Multinational corporation.
    b. Spot exchange rate.
    c. Forward exchange rate.
    d. Direct quote versus indirect quote.
    e. Letter of credit.
    f. LIBOR.
    g. ECU.

■ SELF-TEST PROBLEMS

ST1. Three months ago, you purchased 100 shares of TCBY Enterprises for $11 per share. The stock has just paid a 10-cent-per-share dividend, and the current price per share is $8.75. What has been your holding period return on this stock?

ST2. What is the premium between the spot rate and the 90-day forward rate for the Swiss franc on December 27, 1996? What does this imply about the future spot rate for Swiss francs (see Tables 2-2 and 2-3.)

ST3. What does the evidence in Table 2-4 indicate about the expected future value of the Deutsche mark (DM) relative to the dollar? How does this compare with the evidence in Table 2-3?

■ PROBLEMS*

1. Using the data contained in Figure 2-3, what rate of return, excluding dividend yields, would an investor have received by purchasing the following portfolios of stocks.
    a. The stocks in the Dow Jones 30 Industrial average?
    b. The stocks in the New York Stock Exchange Industrial average?
    c. The stocks in the NASDAQ Computer Industry average?
    d. The stocks in the Russell 2000 index?

*Color numbers denote problems that have check answers provided at the end of the book.

Assume you purchased the stocks in the various averages in the same proportions that they are in the averages.

2. An investor bought 100 shares of Venus Corporation common stock one year ago for $40 per share. She just sold the shares for $44 each, and during the year, she received four quarterly dividend checks for $40 each. She expects the price of the Venus shares to fall to about $38 over the next year. Calculate the investor's realized percentage holding period return.

3. An investor bought 10 Ellis Industries, Inc. long-term bonds one year ago, when they were first issued by the company. In addition, he bought 200 shares of the company's common stock at the same time for $30 per share. He paid $1,000 each for the bonds, and today, the bonds are selling at $950 each (long-term interest rates have increased slightly over the past year). The bonds have a stated interest rate of 12 percent per year. The investor received an interest payment equaling $60 per bond six months ago and has just received another $60 interest payment per bond. Calculate the investor's percentage holding period return for the one year he has held the bonds.

4. Suppose a U.S. Treasury bill, maturing in 30 days, can be purchased today for $99,500. Assuming that the security is held until maturity, the investor will receive $100,000 (face amount). Determine the percentage holding period return on this investment.

5. Suppose a Midwest Telephone and Telegraph (MTT) Company bond, maturing in one year, can be purchased today for $975. Assuming that the bond is held until maturity, the investor will receive $1,000 (principal) plus 6 percent interest (that is, 0.06 × $1000 = $60). Determine the percentage holding period return on this investment.

6. a. National Telephone and Telegraph (NTT) Company common stock currently sells for $60 per share. NTT is expected to pay a $4 dividend during the coming year, and the price of the stock is expected to increase to $65 a year from now. Determine the *expected* (ex ante) percentage holding period return on NTT common stock.

   b. Suppose that one year later, NTT's common stock is selling for $75 per share. During the one-year period, NTT paid a $4 common stock dividend. Determine the *realized* (ex post) percentage holding period return on NTT common stock.

   c. Repeat Part b given that NTT's common stock is selling for $58 one year later.

   d. Repeat Part b given that NTT's common stock is selling for $50 one year later.

7. One year ago, you purchased a rare Indian head penny for $14,000. Because of the recession and the need to generate current income, you plan to sell the coin and invest in Treasury bills. The Treasury bill yield now stands at 8 percent, although it was 7 percent one year ago. A coin dealer has offered to pay you $12,800 for the coin. Compute the holding period return on this investment.

8. Six months ago, you purchased a tract of land in an area where a new industrial park was rumored to be planned. This land cost you $110,000, and the seller offered you an interest-free loan for 70 percent of the land cost. Today, the industrial park project was formally announced, and an attorney for the developer has just offered you $190,000 for your land. If you accept this offer, what will be your holding period return on this investment?

9. The stock of Tips, Inc., a new firm operating a chain of sports betting parlors, has just been sold in an initial public offering at a price of $25 per share. One week after this offering, the stock has risen in value to $35. You believe the stock will rise to $45 over the coming year. You do not expect Tips to pay any dividends over the year. If you require a rate of return on this stock of 18 percent, do you believe this is a good investment at the current price of $35?

10. Japanese Motors exports cars and trucks to the U.S. market. On December 1, 1993, its most popular model was selling (wholesale) to U.S. dealers for $9,500. What price must Japanese Motors charge for the same model on December 27, 1996, to realize the same amount (of Japanese yen) as it did in 1993? (Refer to Table 2-2.)

11. Valley Stores, a U.S. department store chain, annually negotiates a contract with Alpine Watch Company, located in Switzerland, to purchase a large shipment of

watches. On December 1, 1993, Valley purchased 10,000 watches for a total of 1.26 million Swiss francs. Refer to Table 2-2 and determine the following:

a. The total cost and cost per watch in U.S. dollars.

b. The total cost and cost per watch in U.S. dollars of 12,000 watches purchased on December 27, 1996, assuming that Alpine's price per watch (in Swiss francs) remains unchanged.

12. Determine the percentage change in the value of the following currencies relative to the U.S. dollar between December 1, 1993 and December 27, 1996.

a. India.

b. Britain.

c. Japan.

d. ECU.

e. Germany.

13. Compute the indirect quote for the lira, rupee, krona, and yen as of December 27, 1996. (Refer to Table 2-2.)

14. Over the past 10 years, your $15,000 in gold coins has increased in value by 200 percent. You plan to sell these coins today. You have paid annual storage and insurance costs of $500 per year. Assay expenses at the time of sale are expected to total $400. What is your 10-year (not annualized) holding period return on this investment?

15. Under Market Indices at the Thomson Investors Network site (www.thomsoninvest.net), select "currencies" and look at the pound/dollar exchange rate (GDP/USD), the dollar rates for Swiss francs (C-IF), German deutsche marks (DEM), and the Japanese yen (JPY).

a. Express the Swiss franc, the deutsche mark, and the yen rates in terms of the number of dollars required to buy one unit of each currency.

b. Given the pound/dollar rate and the dollar/yen rate, find the pound/yen rate.

Be sure to show all calculations.

■ SOLUTIONS TO SELF-TEST PROBLEMS

ST1.
$$\text{Holding Period Return (\%)} = \frac{\$8.75 - \$11.00 + \$0.10}{\$11.00} \times 100\%$$

$$= -19.55\%$$

ST2.
$$\text{Annual \% Premium} = \left(\frac{\text{Forward} - \text{Spot}}{\text{Spot}}\right)\left(\frac{12}{n}\right)(100\%)$$

$$= \left(\frac{\$0.7478 - \$0.7416}{\$0.7416}\right)\left(\frac{12}{3}\right)(100\%)$$

$$= 3.34\% \text{ (annualized)}$$

ST3. The evidence in Table 2-4 indicates that the value of DM is expected to increase relative to the dollar. The dollar cost of one DM was $0.6433 as of December 27, 1996 (Table 2-2). From Table 2-4 dollar cost of a DM is expected to be $0.6464 in March 1997 and $0.6503 in June 1997. These values are quite similar to the forward quotes (90 and 180 days) in Table 2-3, the slight differences reflecting primarily timing differences between the March 97 futures quote, for example, and the 90-day forward rate.

■ GLOSSARY

Call Option An option to sell something. See *Option*.

Capital Markets Financial markets in which long-term securities are bought and sold.

Common Stock Shares in the ownership of a company. Common stock represents a residual form of ownership in that dividends are paid out only after more senior financial obligations are fulfilled, such as interest on debt.

Direct Quote The home currency price of one unit of a foreign currency.

Efficient Market A financial market in which new information is quickly reflected in security prices in an unbiased manner.

Euro The new European single currency scheduled to go in circulation in 1999.

Eurobond An international bond issued outside the country in whose currency the bonds are denominated.

Eurocurrency A currency that is deposited in a bank outside of the country of origin.

Eurodollars U.S. dollars deposited in banks outside of the U.S.

European Currency Unit (ECU) A composite "currency" consisting of fixed amounts of currencies of the European countries that are part of the Exchange Rate Mechanism.

Exchange Rate The rate at which a currency can be converted into another currency.

Foreign Bond An international bond denominated in the currency of the country in which it is issued. The issuer, however, is from another country.

Forward Contract A contract calling for the delivery of a specified amount of some item at a future point in time at a price set at the present time. Compared to *futures contracts*, forward contracts are not liquid, can be customized with regard to the date or amount, and carry performance risk.

Forward Rate The rate of exchange between two currencies being bought and sold for delivery at a *future* date.

Futures Contract A contract calling for the delivery of a standardized quantity and quality of some item, such as a foreign currency, crude oil, or government securities, at a future point in time at a price set at the present time.

Holding Period Return The change in price from holding an asset (security) plus distributions received from the asset divided by the initial price at which the asset was acquired.

Indirect Quote The foreign currency price of one unit of the home currency.

International Bond A bond issued outside the country of the borrower.

Listed Security Exchanges Organized secondary security markets that operate at designated places of business. The New York Stock Exchange (NYSE) is an example of a listed security exchange.

London Interbank Offer Rate (LIBOR) The interest rate at which banks in the Eurocurrency market lend to each other.

Money Markets Financial markets in which short-term securities are bought and sold.

Multinational Corporation A firm with direct investments in more than one country.

Nominal Interest Rate A market rate of interest stated in current, not real terms. Nominal interest rates reflect expected inflation rates.

Option A contract that gives the holder the right, but not the obligation, to either buy or sell a fixed amount of a commodity, such as a foreign currency, at a fixed price at a time up to the expiration date of the option.

Over-the-counter (OTC) Securities Markets A network of security dealers connected by a communications system of telephones and computer terminals that provides price quotations on individual securities.

Preferred Stock A type of equity with a claim on earnings and assets of a firm—in the form of a (normally) fixed periodic dividend payment—that takes precedence over the claims of common stockholders.

Primary Markets Financial markets in which *new* securities from an issuing firm are bought and sold for the first time. Investment bankers are active in the primary markets.

Prospectus A document that contains information about a company's legal, operational, and financial position. It is prepared for the benefit of prospective investors in a new security issued by the firm.

Purchasing Syndicate A *group* of investment bankers who agree to underwrite a new security issue in order to spread the risk of underwriting.

Put Option An option to sell something. See *Option*.

Secondary Markets Financial markets in which *existing* securities are offered for resale. The New York Stock Exchange is a secondary market.

Securities and Exchange Commission (SEC) The government regulatory agency responsible for administering federal securities legislation.

Spot Rate The rate of exchange between two currencies being bought and sold for *immediate* delivery.

Term Loan A debt obligation having an initial maturity (i.e., maturity at the time of issue) between one and ten years. Term loans are usually repaid in installments over the life of the loan.

EVALUATION OF FINANCIAL PERFORMANCE

1. The evaluation of financial performance involves a series of techniques that can be used to help identify the strengths and weaknesses of a firm.
2. Financial ratios, which use data from a firm's balance sheet, income statement, statement of cash flows, and certain market data, are often used when evaluating the financial performance of a firm.
   a. *Liquidity ratios* indicate a firm's ability to meet its short-term financial obligations.
   b. *Asset management ratios* indicate how efficiently a firm is using its assets to generate sales.
   c. *Financial leverage management ratios* indicate a firm's capacity to meet short- and long-term debt obligations.
   d. *Profitability ratios* measure how effectively a firm's management generates profits.
   e. *Market-based ratios* reflect the financial market's assessment of a company's performance.
   f. *Dividend policy ratios* indicate the dividend practices of a firm.

KEY CHAPTER CONCEPTS

3. Common-size financial statements express financial items as percentages (rather than dollar amounts) and are useful in evaluating financial performance.
4. Trend analysis evaluates a firm's performance over time, whereas comparative analysis evaluates a firm's performance relative to other firms.
5. When evaluating a firm's performance based on its balance sheet, income statement, and a series of financial ratios, a good financial analyst must be aware of the accounting techniques used by the firm and mindful of the quality of the firm's earnings and its balance sheet.
6. Cash flows are the ultimate source of financial value. Therefore, cash flow analysis and forecasting are important parts of a firm's financial plans.
7. After-tax cash flow is equal to earnings after tax plus noncash charges.
8. The statement of cash flows shows the effects of a firm's operating, investing, and financing activities on its cash balance.

FINANCIAL PERFORMANCE MEASUREMENT AND RESTRUCTURING CHARGES: THE CASE OF AT&T[1]

Generally accepted accounting principles (GAAP) provide firms with a great deal of latitude in the preparation of key financial statements used to measure performance. Some firms take advantage of this latitude and choose financial reporting methods that do not provide a fair reflection of true performance. As a consequence, it is important for financial managers to have a solid understanding of financial statement analysis so that it will be possible to make a balanced assessment of the true performance of a company

In recent years, an increasing number of firms have been making use of "one-time" financial restructuring charges in, as some describe, an attempt to delude investors into thinking that things are better than they really are. Financial restructuring charges have a legitimate role to play in the management and reporting of a firm's financial performance. When a company downsizes, through plant closures and layoffs, or sells off assets that no longer fit in the long-run strategy of the firm, restructuring charges are an appropriate way to "clear the decks" for future earnings gains. Restructuring charges reflect a firm's best estimate of the future costs of these actions. By charging all of these expenses in a single quarter, the company, in effect, has created an account against which all future costs associated with its restructuring actions can be charged. In this way, investors no longer must worry about the future earnings impact of the restructuring.

The problem arises when a company makes frequent use of these charges. For example, between 1988 and 1993, Citicorp took six straight restructuring charges. Between 1989 and 1994, Eastman Kodak took major restructuring charges in five out of six years. Kodak announced a further restructuring charge in early 1997.

AT&T has also been an aggressive user of restructuring charges. On January 2, 1996, AT&T announced that 40,000 employees would be laid off and that a $4 billion restructuring charge would be taken. The market reacted favorably to this action, believing that it

indicated that AT&T was about to become a lean, aggressive competitor in each of its major business lines. In AT&T's case, however, this restructuring was its fourth major restructuring over the past 10 years.

How do these restructuring charges impact performance measures for AT&T? AT&T officials point to a record of nearly 10 percent annual profit growth over the period from 1985 to 1994, *before considering the restructuring charges.* Earnings per share from continuing operations grew from $1.21 to $3.13. However, if one considers AT&T's restructuring charges, the accu-

mulated profit of $10.3 billion over this period is more than wiped out by "one-time" restructuring charges of $14.2 billion. Jack Grubman, a telecommunication's analyst at Salomon Brothers, questions whether AT&T has really made any money at all over the decade.

In cases such as AT&T, many analysts contend that the real measure of corporate performance should be the change in cash flow from operations. For AT&T, that value has increased at an annual rate of 6.2 percent, compared with the reported 10 percent annual profit growth. This difference is extremely important, as we shall see later on, in the process of valuing an enterprise for investment purposes.

This chapter introduces financial statement analysis techniques that can be employed in the evaluation of a firm's true performance. Good financial analysts need to have a strong understanding of the interpretation of financial statements—including their associated notes—which often provide excellent clues regarding potential problems and hidden sources of value. Conclusions about a firm's financial performance that are derived from its financial statements should be regarded with caution and considered only as a sign of a firm's strengths and weaknesses. Some of the shortcomings of financial statement analysis as a performance measure can be overcome by considering alternative measures of performance derived directly from the financial marketplace. These market measures of performance are also discussed in this chapter.

[1]Based on R. Smith and S. Lipin, "Are Companies Using Restructuring Costs to Fudge the Figures?" *Wall Street Journal* (January 30, 1996): A1.

INTRODUCTION

This chapter reviews the basic accounting statements and concepts, and deals with the evaluation of financial performance, using financial statement analysis.[2] A carefully executed financial statement analysis can assist financial managers in assessing the current financial condition of a firm. Trend analysis and common-size financial statements can assist financial managers in detecting changes in a firm's financial performance over time.

Once a firm's current financial condition has been assessed, the financial manager is in a position to plan for the future direction of the firm, given the constraints imposed by, and the strengths of, the current financial condition.

USES OF FINANCIAL ANALYSIS

A *financial analysis* assists in identifying the major strengths and weaknesses of a business enterprise. It indicates whether a firm has enough cash to meet obligations; a reasonable accounts receivable collection period; an efficient inventory management policy; sufficient plant, property, and equipment; and an adequate capital structure—all of which are necessary if a firm is to achieve the goal of maximizing shareholder wealth. Financial analysis can also be used to assess a firm's viability as an ongoing enterprise and to determine whether a satisfactory return is being earned for the risks taken.

When performing a financial analysis, an analyst may discover specific problem areas in time for remedial action. For example, an analyst may find that a firm has unused borrowing power that could finance additional income-producing assets. The results of a financial analysis can indicate certain facts and trends that can aid the financial manager in planning and implementing a course of action consistent with the goal of maximizing shareholder wealth.

Financial analyses are also used by persons other than financial managers. For example, credit managers may examine some basic financial ratios concerning a prospective customer when deciding whether to extend credit. Security analysts use financial analysis to help assess the investment worth of different securities. Bankers use the tools of financial analysis when deciding whether to grant loans. Financial ratios have been used successfully to forecast such financial events as impending bankruptcy. Unions, such as the one that represented American Airlines flight attendants in 1993, refer to them when evaluating the bargaining positions of certain employers. Finally, students and other job hunters may perform financial analyses of potential employers to determine career opportunities.

INTERPRETING FINANCIAL RATIOS

A *financial ratio* is a relationship that indicates something about a firm's activities, such as the ratio between the firm's current assets and current liabilities or between its accounts receivable and its annual sales. Financial ratios enable an analyst to make a comparison of a firm's financial condition over time

[2]See Erich A. Helfert, *Techniques of Financial Analysis*, 9th ed. (Chicago: Irwin, 1997).

or in relation to other firms. Ratios essentially standardize various elements of financial data for differences in the size of a series of financial data when making comparisons over time or between firms. For example, the total profits of IBM normally are many times those of Apple Computer, because IBM is a much larger firm than Apple. By computing a ratio such as net profits divided by total assets, the relative performance of the two firms can be assessed more accurately.

Successful financial ratio analysis requires that an analyst keep in mind the following points:

- Any discussion of financial ratios is likely to include only a representative sample of possible ratios. Many other ratios can be developed to provide additional insights. In some industries, such as banking, the analyst will use special ratios unique to the activities of the firms in those industries.
- Financial ratios are only "flags" indicating potential areas of strength or weakness. A thorough analysis requires the examination of other data as well.
- Frequently a financial ratio must be dissected to discover its true meaning. For example, a low ratio may be caused by either a low numerator or a high denominator. A good financial analyst will examine both the numerator and the denominator before drawing any conclusions.
- A financial ratio is meaningful only when it is compared with some standard, such as an industry ratio trend, a ratio trend for the specific firm being analyzed, or a stated management objective.
- When financial ratios are used to compare one firm with another, it is important to remember that differences in accounting techniques may result in substantial differences in financial ratios. Failure to keep this in mind can lead to incorrect conclusions.

BASIC CLASSIFICATIONS OF FINANCIAL RATIOS

Because different groups inside and outside the firm have varying objectives and expectations, they approach financial analysis from different perspectives. For example, suppliers and short-term creditors are likely to be most concerned with a firm's current liquidity and near-term cash-generating capacity. Bondholders and holders of preferred stock, who have long-term claims on a firm's earnings and assets, focus on the firm's cash-generating ability over the long run and on the claims other investors have on the firm's cash flows. Common stockholders and potential investors are especially interested in measures of profitability and risk, because common stock prices are dependent on the amount and stability of a firm's future earnings and dividends. Management is concerned with all aspects of financial analysis on both a short- and a long-term basis, because it is responsible for conducting the firm's day-to-day operations and earning a competitive rate of return for risks taken.

No single financial ratio could begin to answer all these analytical needs. In fact, five different groups of ratios have been developed:

- *Liquidity ratios* indicate a firm's ability to meet short-term financial obligations.
- *Asset management ratios* indicate how efficiently a firm is using its assets to generate sales.
- *Financial leverage management ratios* indicate a firm's capacity to meet short- and long-term debt obligations.

■ *Profitability ratios* measure how effectively a firm's management generates profits on sales, assets, and stockholders' investments.

■ *Market-based ratios* measure the financial market's evaluation of a company's performance.

■ *Dividend policy ratios* indicate the dividend practices of a firm.

Each type is discussed in detail in this chapter.

Key Financial Statements

The financial statements of the Drake Manufacturing Company, a medium-sized firm that produces various replacement components for the lawn equipment industry, will be examined to illustrate how ratios are used in financial analysis. Data will be used from Drake's *balance sheet* for the years ending December 31, 19X6 and 19X5 and from its *income statement* for the year 19X6.

The Balance Sheet. The balance sheet shown in Table 3-1 contains information on Drake's *assets, liabilities,* and *stockholders' equity.* The figures provide a "snapshot" view of the firm's financial health on December 31, 19X6, and December 31, 19X5. Drake's assets are recorded on the balance sheet at the price the company paid for them (that is, at historic cost). The liabilities are amounts the firm owes its creditors, and the stockholders' equity (also termed *net worth* or *owners' equity*) is the difference between total assets and total liabilities. The

TABLE 3-1
Drake Manufacturing Company
Balance Sheet (in thousands of dollars)

		DECEMBER 31, 19X6		DECEMBER 31, 19X5
ASSETS				
Cash		$ 2,540		$ 2,081
Marketable securities		1,800		1,625
Accounts receivable, net		18,320		16,850
Inventories		27,530		26,470
Total current assets		$50,190		$47,026
Plant and equipment	$43,100		$39,500	
Less: Accumulated depreciation	11,400		9,500	
Net plant and equipment		$31,700		$30,000
Total assets		$81,890		$77,026
LIABILITIES AND STOCKHOLDERS' EQUITY				
Accounts payable		$ 9,721		$ 8,340
Notes payable—bank (10%)		8,500		5,635
Accrued taxes payable		3,200		3,150
Other current liabilities		2,102		1,750
Current portion of long-term debt		2,000		2,000
Total current liabilities		$25,523		$20,875
Long-term debt (9 5/8% mortgage bonds)*		$22,000		$24,000
Total liabilities		$47,523		$44,875
Common stock ($10 par value)	$13,000		$13,000	
Contributed capital in excess of par	10,000		10,000	
Retained earnings	11,367		9,151	
Total stockholders' equity		$34,367		$32,151
Total liabilities and stockholders' equity		$81,890		$77,026

*Mortgage bonds require a $2,000(000) annual payment to a sinking fund.

stockholders' equity accounts in Table 3-1 are (1) common stock ($10 par value), (2) contributed capital in excess of par, and (3) retained earnings.

The Income Statement. The income statement in Table 3-2 indicates Drake's performance during the year ended December 31, 19X6. The *cost of sales, other operating expenses, interest expenses,* and *taxes* are deducted from the revenues generated, or *net sales,* to arrive at the firm's *net income,* or *earnings after taxes (EAT)*. The statement in Table 3-2 also shows how the firm's earnings are distributed between dividend payments to stockholders and earnings reinvested in the firm.

Common-Size Financial Statements. Common-size financial statements also are helpful in financial analysis. A *common-size balance sheet* shows the firm's assets and liabilities and stockholders' equity as a percentage of total assets, rather than in dollar amounts. Table 3-3 shows the Drake Company's common-size balance sheet at December 31, 19X6, and December 31, 19X5. A *common-size income statement* lists the firm's income and expense items as a percentage of net sales, rather than in dollar amounts. Table 3-4 contains Drake's common-size income statement for the year ended December 31, 19X6. Common-size financial statements allow trends in financial performance to be detected and monitored more easily than with financial statements showing only dollar amounts.

The Statement of Cash Flows. The statement of cash flows is useful in financial analysis, too. It indicates how a firm generated cash flows from its operations, how it used cash in investing activities, and how it obtained cash from financing activities. The statement of cash flows is analyzed following the discussion of ratio analysis.

TABLE 3-2
Drake Manufacturing Company Income Statement (in thousands of dollars)

FOR THE YEAR ENDED DECEMBER 31, 19X6		
Net sales		$112,760
Cost of sales		85,300
Gross margin		$ 27,460
Operating expenses:		
Selling	$6,540	
General and administrative*	9,400	
Total operating expenses		15,940
Earnings before interest and taxes (EBIT)		$ 11,520
Interest charges:		
Interest on bank notes	$ 850	
Interest on mortgage bonds	2,310	
Total interest charges		3,160
Earnings before taxes (EBT)		$ 8,360
Federal and state income taxes at a combined 40% rate		3,344
Earnings after taxes (EAT) and available for common stockholders		$ 5,016
OTHER INFORMATION:		
Dividends paid on common stock		$ 2,800
Earnings retained in the firm		$ 2,216
Shares outstanding (000)		1,300
Market price per share		$ 24
Book value per share		$ 26.44
Earnings per share		$ 3.86
Dividends per share		$ 2.15

*Includes $150(000) in annual lease payments.

TABLE 3-3
Drake Manufacturing Company
Common-Size Balance Sheet

	DECEMBER 31, 19X6	DECEMBER 31, 19X5
ASSETS		
Cash	3.1%	2.7%
Marketable securities	2.2	2.1
Accounts receivable, net	22.4	21.9
Inventories	33.6	34.4
Total current assets	61.3%	61.1%
Net Plant and equipment	38.7	38.9
Total assets	100.0%	100.0%
LIABILITIES AND STOCKHOLDERS' EQUITY		
Current liabilities	31.2%	27.1%
Long-term debt (9 5/8% mortgage bonds)	26.8	31.2
Total liabilities	58.0%	58.3%
Stockholders' equity	42.0	41.7
Total liabilities and stockholders' equity	100.0%	100.0%

TABLE 3-4
Drake Manufacturing Company
Common-Size Income Statement

FOR THE YEAR ENDED DECEMBER 31, 19X6	
Net sales	100.0%
Cost of sales	75.7
Gross margin	24.3%
Operating expenses	14.1
Earnings before interest and taxes (EBIT)	10.2%
Interest charges	2.8
Earnings before taxes (EBT)	7.4%
Federal and state income taxes at a combined 40% rate	3.0
Earnings after taxes (EAT) and available for common stockholders	4.4%

Liquidity Ratios

A firm that intends to remain a viable business entity must have enough cash on hand to pay its bills as they come due. In other words, the firm must remain *liquid*. One way to determine whether this is the case is to examine the relationship between a firm's current assets and approaching obligations. Liquidity ratios are quick measures of a firm's ability to provide sufficient cash to conduct business over the next few months. *Cash budgets* provide the best assessment of a firm's liquidity position. They are discussed in Chapter 15.

This section discusses two different liquidity ratios—the *current ratio* and the *quick ratio*.

Current Ratio. The current ratio is defined as follows:

$$\text{Current ratio} = \frac{\text{Current assets}}{\text{Current liabilities}} \tag{3.1}$$

Current assets include the cash a firm already has on hand and in the bank, plus any assets that can be converted into cash within a "normal" operating period of 12 months, such as marketable securities held as short-term investments, accounts receivable, inventories, and prepayments. Current liabilities include any financial obligations expected to fall due within the next year, such as accounts payable, notes payable, the current portion of long-term debt due, other payables, and various accruals such as taxes and wages due.

Using data from Table 3-1, Drake's current ratio at year-end 19X6 can be calculated as $50,190/$25,523 = 1.97, or about 2:1. Or, it can be said that Drake's current assets *cover* its current liabilities about two times.

The ratio is interpreted to mean that to satisfy the claims of short-term creditors exclusively from existing current assets, Drake must be able to convert each dollar of current assets into at least $0.51 of cash ($1.00/1.97 = $0.507, or $0.51). The *industry average* for the current ratio is 2.40 times,[3] meaning that the average firm in the industry must convert only $0.42 ($1.00/2.40 = $0.416, or $0.42) of each dollar of current assets into cash to meet short-term obligations.

The fact that Drake's current ratio is below the industry average does *not* mean that the firm would consider closing its doors voluntarily to meet the demands of short-term creditors. Nor does it mean that Drake's creditors are any less well protected than the creditors of competing firms, because no two firms—even those in the same industry—are identical. In fact, ratios that suggest the presence of a problem in one firm may be quite satisfactory for another firm.[4] Drake's current ratio provides only *one* standard for measuring liquidity. The financial analyst must dissect, or "go behind," the ratio to discover why it differs from the industry average and determine whether a serious problem exists.

Quick Ratio. The quick ratio is defined as follows:

$$\text{Quick Ratio} = \frac{\text{Current assets} - \text{Inventories}}{\text{Current liabilities}} \qquad (3.2)$$

This ratio, sometimes called the "acid test," is a more stringent measure of liquidity than the current ratio. By subtracting inventories from current assets, this ratio recognizes that a firm's inventories are often one of its least-liquid current assets.[5] Inventories, especially work-in-process, are very difficult to liquidate quickly at, or near, their book value. Referring to the figures on Drake's balance sheet (Table 3-1), the firm's quick ratio at year-end 19X6 is calculated as follows:

$$\frac{\$50,190 - \$27,530}{25,523} = \frac{\$22,660}{\$25,523} = 0.89 \text{ times}$$

The industry average is 0.92 times; Drake's quick ratio is nearly equal to that.

The quick ratio is interpreted to mean that Drake's cash and other current assets one step removed from cash—that is, marketable securities and accounts receivable—are equal to 89 percent of the current liabilities. The crucial assumption behind the quick ratio is that a firm's accounts receivable may be converted into cash within the "normal" collection period (and with little "shrinkage") or within the period of time for which credit initially was granted.

[3]Industry averages are obtained from various sources. The Sources of Comparative Financial Data section later in this chapter discusses a number of such sources.

[4]Many practitioners view a current ratio of 1.5 times (1.5) as satisfactory for industrial firms. Public utilities, on the other hand, typically function with considerably lower ratios. However, a financial analyst must be very cautious when using any of these "rules of thumb." The safe level of a current ratio is a function of how fast the firm's current assets and liabilities turn over. In the case of a public utility, the accounts receivable turn over on a monthly basis—much faster than in the typical industrial firm. Thus, public utilities are able to safely sustain lower current ratios than industrial firms.

[5]Some analysts also subtract prepaid expenses from current assets in the calculation of the quick ratio because prepayments are difficult to convert back to cash.

An analyst who doubts the liquidity of a firm's receivables may wish to prepare an *aging schedule.* The following one lists Drake's accounts receivable as of December 31, 19X6:

Days Outstanding	Amount Outstanding (In Thousands Of Dollars)	Percentage Of Total
Less than 30	$ 9,450	51.6%
30–59	5,161	28.2
60–89	2,750	15.0
Over 90	959	5.2
Total accounts receivable	$18,320	100.0%

Unfortunately, the data required to prepare an aging schedule normally are not available to outside analysts. Hence, the aging schedule is useful primarily for internal analysis.

To evaluate the figures contained in an aging schedule, an analyst would need to consider Drake's selling terms. If, for example, Drake's customers are expected to pay within 40 days (which, in fact, they are), then the aging schedule indicates that many accounts are past due. However, because only 5.2 percent of the firm's receivables have been outstanding over 90 days, the major problem appears to be with slow-paying rather than uncollectible accounts. Some analysts adjust the quick ratio *downward* if a significant percentage of a firm's receivables are long past due and have not been written off as losses. Adjusting Drake's quick ratio downward involves the following calculation:

$$\frac{\begin{array}{c}\text{(Current assets – Inventories)}\\ \text{– Accounts outstanding over 90 days}\end{array}}{\text{Current liabilities}} = \frac{\$22{,}660 - \$959}{\$25{,}523} = 0.85 \text{ times}$$

The 0.04 difference between the quick ratio, 0.89 times, and the adjusted ratio, 0.85 times, probably is insignificant. Therefore, even if Drake's accounts over 90 days old were considered uncollectible, this alone would not indicate any real problem for the firm.

Asset Management Ratios

One objective of financial management is to determine how a firm's resources can be best distributed among the various asset accounts. If a proper mix of cash, receivables, inventories, plant, property, and equipment can be achieved, the firm's asset structure will be more effective in generating sales revenue.

Asset management ratios indicate how much a firm has invested in a particular type of asset (or group of assets) relative to the revenue the asset is producing. By comparing asset management ratios for the various asset accounts of a firm with established industry norms, the analyst can determine how efficiently the firm is allocating its resources.

This section discusses several types of asset management ratios, including the *average collection period*, the *inventory turnover ratio*, the *fixed-asset turnover ratio*, and the *total asset turnover ratio*.

Average Collection Period. The average collection period is the average number of days an account receivable remains outstanding. It usually is determined by dividing a firm's year-end receivables balance by the average daily credit sales (based on a 365-day year).[6]

$$\text{Average collection period} = \frac{\text{Accounts receivable}}{\text{Annual credit sales}/365} \qquad (3.3)$$

Using figures from both Drake's balance sheet (Table 3-1) and the income statement (Table 3-2), the average collection period ratio at year-end 19X6 can be calculated as $18,320/($112,760/365) = $18,320/$308.93 = 59.3 days. Because the industry average for this ratio is 47 days, Drake's ratio is substantially above the average.

Drake's credit terms call for payment within 40 days. The ratio calculations show that 59.3 days of sales are tied up in receivables, meaning that a significant portion of Drake's customers are not paying bills on time. (This also is indicated by the aging schedule of the firm's accounts receivable.) The analyst would interpret this ratio to mean that Drake has allocated a greater proportion of total resources to receivables than the average firm in the industry. If the company implemented a more vigorous collection program and reduced the collection period to the industry norm of 47 days, some of these funds would be released for investment elsewhere or debt reduction. The released funds of (59.3 days − 47 days) × $308.93 per day = $3,800 could be invested in other assets that might contribute more significantly to profitability.[7]

An average collection period substantially above the industry norm usually is not desirable and may indicate too liberal a credit policy. Ultimately, a firm's managers must determine if the liberal credit policy generates enough incremental sales and profits to justify the incremental cost.[8] In contrast, an average collection period far *below* the industry norm may indicate that the firm's credit terms are too stringent and are hurting sales by restricting credit only to the very best customers. Although moderate-to-slow paying customers may seem troublesome individually, they can be profitable as a group, and a credit policy that is too tight may drive them to competing firms.

Inventory Turnover Ratio. The inventory turnover ratio is defined as follows:

$$\text{Inventory turnover} = \frac{\text{Costs of sales}}{\text{Average inventory}} \qquad (3.4)$$

Whereas the cost of sales is usually listed on a firm's income statement, the average inventory has to be calculated. This can be done in a number of ways. For example, if a firm has been experiencing a significant and continuing rate of growth in sales, the average inventory may be computed by adding the figures for the beginning and ending inventories for the year and dividing by two. If sales are seasonal or otherwise subject to wide fluctuations, however, it would be better to add the month-end inventory balances for the entire year and divide by twelve.

Some analysts calculate inventory turnover as simply the ratio of annual sales to ending inventory. Although the *sales-to-inventory ratio* is technically inferior and gives different results than more commonly used ratios, it may be satisfactory

---

[6]When credit sales figures are not available (which is frequently the case), total sales figures customarily are used in calculating the ratio, resulting in an *overstatement* of the average daily sales and an *understatement* of the average collection period. When firms have seasonal sales, an analyst should calculate an average of the end-of-month receivables balances. When comparing average collection period ratios with industry norms, the analyst must make sure the industry ratios have been computed in the same manner as the particular firm's ratios.

[7]Recall that the analysis for Drake is being done in terms of thousands of dollars. Hence, the actual released funds total approximately $3.8 million.

[8]Chapter 17 contains an example of this type of incremental analysis.

if used consistently when making comparisons between one firm and the industry as a whole. However, the problem with this ratio is that it tends to differ from one firm to another, depending on policies regarding markups on the cost of sales.

Because Drake's sales are spread evenly over the year and its growth rate has been fairly moderate, the average inventory can be calculated by taking the average of the beginning and ending inventory balances, ($27,530 + $26,470)/2 = $27,000. Dividing the cost of sales by this figure, $85,300/$27,000, gives an inventory turnover ratio of 3.16 times. This is considerably below the industry norm of 3.9 times, indicating that Drake has a larger investment in inventory relative to the sales being generated than the average firm. If the company could increase its inventory turns up to the industry average of 3.9 times, its average inventory investment in 19X6 would be $21,872 ($85,300/3.9). The released funds, $27,000 − $21,872 = $5,128, could be used either for investment in other, potentially more profitable assets or possibly for debt reduction.[9]

Two factors may be responsible for Drake's allocating an excessive amount of resources to inventory:

■ The firm may be attempting to carry all possible types of replacement parts so that every order can be filled immediately. Drake should carefully examine this policy to determine whether the incremental cost of carrying excessive stocks is justified by the incremental profits earned on additional sales.[10]

■ Some of Drake's inventory may be damaged, obsolete, or slow moving. Stock falling into these categories has questionable liquidity and should be recorded at a value more reflective of the realizable market value.

If a firm's inventory turnover ratio is too high, it may mean the firm is frequently running out of certain items in stock and losing sales to competitors. For inventory to contribute fully to profitability, the firm has to maintain a reasonable balance of inventory levels.

Fixed-Asset Turnover Ratio. The fixed-asset turnover ratio is defined as follows:

$$\text{Fixed-asset turnover} = \frac{\text{Sales}}{\text{Net fixed assets}} \tag{3.5}$$

It indicates the extent to which a firm is utilizing existing property, plant, and equipment to generate sales.

The balance sheet figures that indicate how much a firm has invested in property, plant, and equipment are affected by several factors, including the following:

■ The cost of the assets when acquired.
■ The length of time since acquisition.
■ The depreciation policies adopted by the firm.
■ The extent to which fixed assets are leased rather than owned.

Because of these factors, it is possible for firms with virtually identical plants to have significantly different fixed-asset turnover ratios. Thus, the ratio should be used primarily for year-to-year comparisons within the same company, rather than for intercompany comparisons.

Drake's fixed-asset turnover ratio is $112,760/$31,700 = 3.56 times, considerably below the industry average of 4.6 times. However, the financial analyst should

---

[9]Recall that the analysis for Drake is being done in terms of thousands of dollars. Hence, the actual released funds total approximately $5.128 million.
[10]The management of inventory is discussed in Chapter 17.

acknowledge the shortcomings of the ratio and perform further analyses before concluding that the company makes inefficient use of its property, plant, and equipment.

Total Asset Turnover Ratio. The total asset turnover ratio is defined as follows:

$$\text{Total asset turnover} = \frac{\text{Sales}}{\text{Total assets}} \qquad (3.6)$$

It indicates how effectively a firm uses its total resources to generate sales and is a summary measure influenced by each of the asset management ratios previously discussed.

Drake's total asset turnover ratio is $112,760/$81,890 = 1.38 times, whereas the industry average is 1.82 times. In view of Drake's other asset turnover ratios, the firm's relatively poor showing with regard to this ratio is not surprising. Each of Drake's major asset investment programs—accounts receivable, inventory, and property, plant, and equipment—has been found apparently lacking. The analyst could look at these various ratios and conclude that Drake is not generating the same level of sales from its assets as other firms in the industry.

Financial Leverage Management Ratios

Whenever a firm finances a portion of assets with any type of fixed-charge financing—such as debt, preferred stock, or leases—the firm is said to be using *financial leverage*. Financial leverage management ratios measure the degree to which a firm is employing financial leverage and, as such, are of interest to creditors and owners alike.

Both long- and short-term creditors are concerned with the amount of leverage a firm employs, because it indicates the firm's risk exposure in meeting debt service charges (that is, interest and principal repayment). A firm that is heavily financed by debt offers creditors less protection in the event of bankruptcy. For example, if a firm's assets are financed with 85 percent debt, the value of the assets can decline by only 15 percent before creditors' funds are endangered. In contrast, if only 15 percent of a firm's assets are debt financed, asset values can drop by 85 percent before jeopardizing the creditors.

Owners are interested in financial leverage because it influences the rate of return they can expect to realize on their investment and the degree of risk involved. For example, if a firm is able to borrow funds at 9 percent and employ them at 12 percent, the owners earn the 3 percent difference and are likely to view financial leverage favorably. On the other hand, if the firm can earn only 3 percent on the borrowed funds, the –6 percent difference (3% – 9%) will result in a lower rate of return to the owners.[11]

Either balance sheet or income statement data can be used to measure a firm's use of financial leverage. The balance sheet approach gives a *static* measure of financial leverage at a specific point in time and emphasizes *total* amounts of debt, whereas the income statement approach provides a more *dynamic* measure and relates required interest payments on debt to the firm's ability to pay. Both approaches are employed widely in practice.

There are several types of financial leverage management ratios, including the *debt ratio,* the *debt-to-equity ratio,* the *times interest earned ratio,* and the *fixed-charge coverage ratio.*

---

[11]The trade-off between risk and return resulting from the use of financial leverage is discussed in Chapters 12 and 13.

Debt Ratio. The debt ratio is defined as follows:

$$\text{Debt ratio} = \frac{\text{Total debt}}{\text{Total assets}} \qquad (3.7)$$

It measures the proportion of a firm's total assets that is financed with creditors' funds. As used here, the term *debt* encompasses all short-term liabilities and long-term borrowings.

Bondholders and other long-term creditors are among those likely to be interested in a firm's debt ratio. They tend to prefer a low debt ratio, because it provides more protection in the event of liquidation or some other major financial problem. As the debt ratio increases, so do a firm's fixed-interest charges. If the debt ratio becomes too high, the cash flows a firm generates during economic recessions may not be sufficient to meet interest payments. Thus, a firm's ability to market new debt obligations when it needs to raise new funds is crucially affected by the size of the debt ratio and by investors' perceptions about the risk implied by the level of the ratio.

Debt ratios are stated in terms of percentages. Drake's debt ratio as of year-end 19X6 is ($25,523 + $22,000)/$81,890 = $47,523/$81,890 = 0.58, or 58 percent. The ratio is interpreted to mean that Drake's creditors are financing 58 percent of the firm's total assets. This figure is considerably higher than the 47 percent industry average, indicating that Drake has less unused borrowing capacity than the average firm in the industry.

A high debt ratio implies a low *proportionate equity base;* that is, the percentage of assets financed with equity funds. As the proportionate equity base declines, investors are more hesitant to acquire a firm's debt obligations. Whether Drake can continue to finance its assets with 58 percent of "outsider" money largely depends on the growth and stability of future earnings and cash flows.

Because most interest costs are incurred on long-term borrowed funds (greater than one year to maturity) and because long-term borrowing places multiyear, fixed financial obligations on a firm, some analysts also consider the ratio of *long-term debt-to-total assets,* or *long-term debt-to-equity* (discussed in the following section). Another modification that sometimes is made in these ratios is to include the capitalized value of noncancellable financial leases (discussed in Chapter 19) in the numerator. Some analysts also include a firm's preferred stock with its debt when computing these ratios because preferred stock dividends, like interest requirements, are usually fixed.

Debt-to-Equity Ratio. The debt-to-equity ratio is defined as follows:

$$\text{Debt-to-equity} = \frac{\text{Total debt}}{\text{Total equity}} \qquad (3.8)$$

It is similar to the debt ratio and relates the amount of a firm's debt financing to the amount of equity financing. The debt-to-equity ratio, in actuality, is not really a new ratio. It is simply the debt ratio in a different format.

The debt-to-equity ratio also is stated as a percentage. Drake's debt-to-equity ratio at year-end 19X6 is $47,523/$34,367 = 1.383, or 138.3 percent. Because the industry average is 88.7 percent, Drake's ratio indicates that the firm uses more than the usual amount of borrowed funds to finance its activities. Specifically, it raises nearly $1.38 from creditors for each dollar invested by stockholders, which is interpreted to mean that the firm's debt suppliers have a lower margin of safety than is common in the industry. In addition, Drake has a greater potential for financial distress if earnings do not exceed the cost of borrowed funds.

Times Interest Earned Ratio. The times interest earned ratio is defined as follows:

$$\text{Times interest earned} = \frac{\text{Earnings before interest and taxes (EBIT)}}{\text{Interest charges}} \quad (3.9)$$

Often referred to as simply *interest coverage,* this ratio employs income statement data to measure a firm's use of financial leverage. It tells the analyst the extent to which the firm's current earnings are able to meet current interest payments. The EBIT figures are used because the firm makes interest payments out of operating income, or EBIT. When the times interest earned ratio falls below 1.0, the continued viability of the enterprise is threatened because the failure to make interest payments when due can lead to bankruptcy.

Drake's times interest earned ratio is $11,520/$3,160 = 3.65 times. In other words, it covers annual interest payments 3.65 times; this figure is considerably below the industry norm of 6.7 times. This ratio is further evidence that the company makes extensive use of creditors' funds to finance its operations.

Fixed-Charge Coverage Ratio. The fixed-charge coverage ratio is defined as follows:

$$\text{Fixed-charge coverage} = \frac{\text{EBIT} + \text{Lease payments}}{\begin{array}{c}\text{Interest} + \text{Lease payments} + \text{Preferred} \\ \text{dividends before tax} + \text{Before-tax} \\ \text{sinking fund}\end{array}} \quad (3.10)$$

It measures the number of times a firm is able to cover total *fixed charges,* which include (in addition to interest payments) preferred dividends and payments required under long-term lease contracts. Many corporations also are required to make *sinking fund* payments on bond issues, which are annual payments aimed at either retiring a portion of the bond obligation each year or providing for the ultimate redemption of bonds at maturity. Under most sinking fund provisions, the firm either may make these payments to the bondholders' representative (the *trustee*), who determines through a lottery process which of the outstanding bonds will be retired, or may deliver to the trustee the required number of bonds purchased by the firm in the open market. Either way, the firm's outstanding indebtedness is reduced.

In calculating the fixed-charge coverage ratio, an analyst must consider each of the firm's obligations on a *before-tax* basis. However, because sinking fund payments and preferred stock dividends are not tax deductible and therefore must be paid out of after-tax earnings, a mathematical adjustment has to be made. After-tax payments must be divided by $(1 - T)$, where T is the marginal tax rate. This effectively converts such payments to a before-tax basis, or one that is comparable to the EBIT.[12] And, since lease payments are deducted in arriving at the EBIT, they must be added back into the numerator of the ratio, because the fixed charges (in the denominator) also include lease payments.

---

[12]The rationale for this computation is as follows:

$$\text{Earnings after taxes} = \text{Earnings before taxes} - \text{Taxes}$$

$$= \text{Earnings before taxes} - \text{Earnings before taxes} \times T$$

$$= \text{Earnings before taxes} \,(1 - T)$$

$$\frac{\text{Earnings after taxes}}{1 - T} = \text{Earnings before taxes}$$

The fixed-charge coverage ratio is a more severe measure of a firm's ability to meet fixed financial obligations. Using figures from Drake's income statement for 19X6,[13] the fixed-charge coverage ratio can be calculated as follows:

$$\frac{\$11,520 + \$150}{\$3,160 + \$150 + \$2,000/(1 - 0.4)} = \frac{\$11,670}{\$6,643} = 1.76 \text{ times}$$

Because the industry average is 4.5 times, once again it is apparent that Drake provides creditors with a smaller margin of safety—that is, a higher level of risk—than the average firm in the industry. As a result, Drake is probably straining its relations with creditors. If a "tight money" situation developed in the economy, Drake's high debt and low coverage ratios would most likely limit the firm's access to new credit sources, and Drake might be forced to curtail operations or borrow on prohibitively expensive and restrictive terms.

Profitability Ratios

More than any other accounting measure, a firm's *profits*[14] demonstrate how well the firm is making investment and financing decisions. If a firm is unable to provide adequate returns in the form of dividends and share price appreciation to investors, it may be unable to maintain, let alone increase, its asset base. Profitability ratios measure how effectively a firm's management is generating profits on sales, total assets, and, most importantly, stockholders' investment. Therefore, anyone whose economic interests are tied to the long-run survival of a firm will be interested in profitability ratios.

There are several types of profitability ratios, including the *gross profit margin ratio,* the *net profit margin ratio,* the *return on investment ratio,* and the *return on stockholders' equity ratio.*

Gross Profit Margin Ratio. The gross profit margin ratio is defined as follows:

$$\text{Gross profit margin} = \frac{\text{Sales} - \text{Cost of sales}}{\text{Sales}} \tag{3.11}$$

It measures the relative profitability of a firm's sales after the cost of sales has been deducted, thus revealing how effectively the firm's management is making decisions regarding pricing and the control of production costs.

Drake's gross profit margin ratio is $27,460/$112,760 = 24.4%, just slightly below the industry average of 25.6 percent. This percentage indicates that either Drake's pricing policies or production methods are not quite as effective as those of the average firm in the industry. Differences in inventory accounting methods (and, to a lesser extent, depreciation methods) used by Drake and the firms included in the industry average also influence the cost of sales and, by extension, the gross profit margin.

Net Profit Margin Ratio. The net profit margin ratio is defined as follows:

$$\text{Net profit margin} = \frac{\text{Earnings after taxes (EAT)}}{\text{Sales}} \tag{3.12}$$

[13]Some analysts exclude preferred dividend payments when computing the fixed-charge coverage ratio. In the calculation that follows, the $150 represents annual long-term lease payments, and the $2,000 represents sinking fund obligations.

[14]The terms *profits, earnings,* and *net income* are used interchangeably in this discussion.

It measures how profitable a firm's sales are after all expenses, including taxes and interest, have been deducted.

Some analysts also compare an *operating profit margin ratio,* defined as EBIT/sales. It measures the profitability of a firm's operations before considering the effects of financing decisions. Because the operating profit margin is computed before considering interest charges, this ratio often is more suitable for comparing the profit performance of different firms.

Drake's net profit margin ratio is $5,016/$112,760 = 4.45\%$, which is below the industry average of 5.1 percent and is interpreted to mean that the company is earning 0.65 percent less on each dollar of sales than the average firm in the industry. This percentage indicates that Drake may be having difficulty controlling either total expenses (including interest, operating expenses, and the cost of sales) or the prices of its products. In this case, the former probably is more accurate, because Drake's financial structure contains a greater proportion of debt, resulting in more interest charges.

Return on Investment (Total Assets) Ratio. The return on investment ratio is defined as follows:

$$\text{Return on investment} = \frac{\text{Earnings after taxes (EAT)}}{\text{Total assets}} \qquad (3.13)$$

It measures a firm's net income in relation to the total asset investment.

Drake's return on investment ratio, $5,016/$81,890$, is 6.13 percent, which is considerably below the industry average of 9.28 percent and is a direct result of the firm's low asset management ratios and low profit margins.

Some analysts also like to compute the ratio of EBIT/total assets. This measures the operating profit rate of return for a firm. An after-tax version of this ratio is earnings before interest and after tax (**EBIAT**) divided by total assets. These ratios are computed before interest charges and may be more suitable when comparing the operating performance of two or more firms that are financed differently.

Return on Stockholders' Equity Ratio. The return on stockholders' equity ratio is defined as follows:

$$\text{Return on stockholders' equity} = \frac{\text{Earnings after taxes (EAT)}}{\text{Stockholders' equity}} \qquad (3.14)$$

It measures the rate of return that the firm earns on stockholders' equity. Because only the stockholders' equity appears in the denominator, the ratio is influenced directly by the amount of debt a firm is using to finance assets.

Drake's return on stockholders' equity ratio is $5,016/$34,367 = 14.60\%$. Again, Drake's ratio is below the industry average of 17.54 percent. The firm's low asset management ratios and low profit margins result in profitability ratios inferior to the industry norms, even after the effects of debt financing (financial leverage) are considered.

Market-Based Ratios

The financial ratios discussed in the previous four groups are all derived from accounting income statement and balance sheet information provided by the firm. Analysts and investors are also interested in the financial market's assessment of the performance of a firm. The market-based ratios for a firm should parallel the accounting ratios of that firm. For example, if the accounting ratios of a firm suggest that the firm has more risk than the average firm in the industry and has lower profit prospects, this information should be reflected in a lower market price of that firm's stock.

Price-to-Earnings (P/E) Ratio. The price-to-earnings ratio is defined as follows:

$$P/E = \frac{\text{Market price per share}}{\text{Current earnings per share}} \tag{3.15}$$

(Some security analysts use next year's projected earnings per share in the denominator. There is nothing wrong with this alternative definition as long as comparisons between firms are done on the same basis.)

In general, *the lower the firm's risk, the higher its P/E ratio* should be. In addition, *the better the growth prospects of its earnings, the greater is the P/E multiple.* For example, Circus Circus Enterprises, the largest U.S. casino operator, had a P/E ratio of 28.0 in 1997, supported by strong earnings growth and dominant market positions. In contrast, Harrahs, with relatively weak earnings and facing the risk of intense competition in its riverboat gambling markets, had a P/E ratio of only 13.9 times in 1997.

Drake's current (19X6) earnings per share are $3.86 (earnings of $5,016 divided by 1,300 shares). If Drake's current market price is $24 per share, its P/E ratio is 6.22 times. This is below the industry average of 8.0 times, and indicates that Drake has either higher risk than the average firm, lower growth prospects, or both.

As a supplement to the price-to-earnings ratio, financial analysts sometimes also examine a firm's *stock price to free cash flow ratio.* Free cash flow represents the portion of a firm's total cash flow available to service additional debt, to pay common stock dividends, and to invest in other projects (e.g., capital expenditures and/or acquisition of other companies). Free cash flow often is viewed as a better measure than earnings of the financial soundness of a firm. Earnings data sometimes can be misleading because accounting rules give companies discretion in such areas as the recognition of revenues that have not been received and the allocation of costs over different time periods.[15] For example, Integrated Resources and Todd Shipyards had good earnings, but had negative cash flow and were forced to file for bankruptcy.

Market (Price)-to-Book (Value) (P/BV) Ratio. The market-to-book ratio is defined as follows:

$$P/BV = \frac{\text{Market price per share}}{\text{Book value per share}} \tag{3.16}$$

Generally, the higher the rate of return a firm is earning on its common equity relative to the return required by investors (the cost of common equity), the higher will be the P/BV ratio.

The book value per share of common stock is determined by dividing the total common stockholders' equity for a firm by the number of shares outstanding. In the case of Drake at year-end 19X6, the book value per share is equal to $26.44 (stockholders' equity of $34,367 divided by 1,300 shares outstanding). With a market price per share of $24, the market-to-book ratio for Drake is 0.91. This compares unfavorably with the industry average of 1.13.

---

[15]The issue of earnings quality is discussed in more detail later in the chapter.

It should be noted that, because the market-to-book ratio contains the book value of the common stockholders' equity in the denominator (remember that common stockholders' equity is equal to total assets minus total liabilities), it is affected by the accounting treatments used by a firm in such crucial areas as inventory valuation and depreciation. For this reason, comparisons between firms often can be misleading.

Need a quick stock quote? Visit Market-Edge and type in the ticker symbol (IBM, etc.) of any stock. Would such instant information be helpful to you if you were buying and selling stocks?
http://www.thomsoninvest.net

Dividend Policy Ratios

The two primary dividend policy ratios, the payout ratio and the dividend yield, give insights regarding a firm's dividend strategies and its future growth prospects.

Payout Ratio. The payout ratio indicates the percentage of a firm's earnings that are paid out as dividends. It is defined as:

$$\text{Payout ratio} = \frac{\text{Dividend per share}}{\text{Earnings per share}} \tag{3.17}$$

In the case of Drake, the payout ratio is equal to 55.7 percent ($2.15 annual 19X6 dividends ÷ $3.86 annual 19X6 earnings per share). As we shall see in Chapter 14, companies are extremely reluctant to cut their dividends because of the negative signal such an action transmits to the financial marketplace. Accordingly, companies with stable earnings are more likely to pay out a greater proportion of their earnings as dividends than are companies with more volatile earnings. Also, companies with a large, continuing number of high-return investment projects are less likely to pay out a high proportion of earnings as dividends because of their need for the capital to finance these projects.

Dividend Yield. A stock's dividend yield is the expected yearly dividend divided by the current stock price, or:

$$\text{Dividend yield} = \frac{\text{Expected dividend per share}}{\text{Stock price}} \tag{3.18}$$

The current dividend yield for Drake is 8.96 percent ($2.15 dividend divided by the $24 stock price). As we shall see in Chapter 7, the returns received by an investor in common stock are the sum of the dividend yield and expected growth in the company's earnings, dividends, and ultimately its stock price. Stocks with a low dividend yield often indicate high expected future growth. High dividend yields, such as are common for utility companies, frequently are indicators of low future growth prospects. *Very* high dividend yields often signal a company facing financial difficulty that the market expects to be accompanied by future cuts in the dividend amount.

 SUMMARY OF FINANCIAL RATIO ANALYSIS

Table 3-5 lists all the financial ratios calculated for the Drake Manufacturing Company summarizing the comparative financial ratio analysis undertaken for the firm.

TABLE 3-5
Ratio Analysis Summary for the Drake Manufacturing Company

RATIO	DEFINITION
LIQUIDITY	
1. Current ratio	$\dfrac{\text{Current assets}}{\text{Current liabilities}}$
2. Quick ratio (acid test)	$\dfrac{\text{Current assets} - \text{Inventories}}{\text{Current liabilities}}$
ASSET MANAGEMENT	
3. Average collection period	$\dfrac{\text{Accounts receivable}}{\text{Credit sales}/365}$
4. Inventory turnover	$\dfrac{\text{Cost of sales}}{\text{Average inventory}}$
5. Fixed-asset turnover	$\dfrac{\text{Sales}}{\text{Fixed assets}}$
6. Total asset turnover	$\dfrac{\text{Sales}}{\text{Total assets}}$
FINANCIAL LEVERAGE MANAGEMENT	
7. Debt ratio	$\dfrac{\text{Total debt}}{\text{Total assets}}$
8. Debt-to-equity	$\dfrac{\text{Total debt}}{\text{Total equity}}$
9. Times interest earned	$\dfrac{\text{Earnings before interest and taxes (EBIT)}}{\text{Interest charges}}$
10. Times fixed charges earned	$\dfrac{\text{EBIT} + \text{Lease payments}}{\text{Interest} + \text{Lease payments} + \text{Before-tax sinking fund} + \text{Preferred stock dividends before tax}}$
PROFITABILITY	
11. Gross profit margin	$\dfrac{\text{Sales} - \text{Cost of sales}}{\text{Sales}}$
12. Net profit margin	$\dfrac{\text{Earnings after taxes (EAT)}}{\text{Sales}}$
13. Return on investment	$\dfrac{\text{Earnings after taxes (EAT)}}{\text{Total assets}}$
14. Return on stockholders' equity	$\dfrac{\text{Earnings after taxes (EAT)}}{\text{Stockholders' equity}}$
MARKET-BASED	
15. Price-to-earnings ratio	$\dfrac{\text{Market price per share}}{\text{Current earnings per share}}$
16. Market-to-book ratio	$\dfrac{\text{Market price per share}}{\text{Book value per share}}$
DIVIDEND POLICY	
17. Payout ratio	$\dfrac{\text{Dividend per share}}{\text{Earnings per share}}$
18 Dividend yield	$\dfrac{\text{Expected dividend per share}}{\text{Stock price}}$

Continued

TABLE 3-5
Continued

CALCULATION	INDUSTRY AVERAGE	ASSESSMENT
$\dfrac{\$50,190}{\$25,523} = 1.97$ times	2.40 times	Fair
$\dfrac{\$22,660}{\$25,523} = 0.89$ times	0.92 times	Satisfactory
$\dfrac{\$18,320}{\$112,760/365} = 59.3$ days	47 days	Unsatisfactory
$\dfrac{\$85,300}{(\$27,530 + \$26,470)/2} = 3.16$ times	3.9 times	Unsatisfactory
$\dfrac{\$112,760}{\$31,700} = 3.56$ times	4.6 times	Poor
$\dfrac{\$112,760}{\$81,890} = 1.38$ times	1.82 times	Poor
$\dfrac{\$47,523}{\$81,890} = 58$ percent	47 percent	Poor
$\dfrac{\$47,523}{\$34,367} = 138.3$ percent	88.7 percent	Poor
$\dfrac{\$11,520}{\$3,160} = 3.65$ times	6.7 times	Poor
$\dfrac{\$11,520 + \$150}{\$3,160 + \$150 + \$2,000/(1 - 0.4)} = 1.76$ times	4.5 times	Poor
$\dfrac{\$27,460}{\$112,760} = 24.4$ percent	25.6 percent	Fair
$\dfrac{\$5,016}{\$112,760} = 4.45$ percent	5.10 percent	Unsatisfactory
$\dfrac{\$5,016}{\$81,890} = 6.13$ percent	9.28 percent	Poor
$\dfrac{\$5,016}{\$34,367} = 14.60$ percent	17.54 percent	Poor
$\dfrac{\$24}{\$3.86} = 6.22$ times	8.0 times	Poor
$\dfrac{\$24}{\$26.44} = 0.91$	1.13	Poor
$\dfrac{\$2.15}{\$3.86} = 55.7$ percent	28 percent	High, implying low growth prospects or lower earnings risk
$\dfrac{\$2.15}{\$24} = 8.96$ percent	4.2 percent	High, implying low growth prospects

The assessment column to the right of the table contains an evaluation of each of Drake's ratios in comparison with the industry averages. For example, the firm's liquidity position is rated fair to satisfactory. Although its current ratio is somewhat below the industry norm, its quick ratio is satisfactory, indicating that Drake probably has sufficient liquidity to meet maturing obligations. The firm's asset structure is not generating sufficient sales revenues, however. Drake's asset management ratios indicate that the firm is investing too much in receivables and inventories, as well as property, plant, and equipment, relative to the sales volume being generated. Thus, Drake should consider implementing more stringent credit and collection policies as well as better inventory controls. The firm also should evaluate its investment in property, plant, and equipment to determine whether reductions could be made without impairing operations.

Drake's financial leverage ratios indicate that the firm is using significantly more debt to finance operations than the average firm in the industry. Because of its poor coverage ratios, the company may have difficulty obtaining debt financing for further asset additions. In the event of an economic slowdown, Drake's creditors would probably reevaluate the firm's borrowing capacity and make less funds available to it. If Drake wants to restore its borrowing capacity, it should take steps to increase its equity base. The market-based ratios confirm the analysis performed using Drake's financial statements, and the dividend policy ratios indicate that the firm may have low growth prospects.

It should be emphasized that the ratios discussed in this analysis are interrelated. For example, Drake is using more debt and investing more in receivables and inventories than the average firm in the industry. If the company could reduce its investment in receivables and inventories and use the released funds to lower debt, *both* the asset management ratios and the financial leverage ratios would be closer to the industry averages.

TREND ANALYSIS

Thus far, the analysis of the Drake Manufacturing Company has focused solely on the year 19X6. This has provided a fairly complete, if rather static, picture of the company's situation at that particular point in time in comparison with industry standards. To gain insight into the direction the company is moving, however, a trend analysis should be performed. A *trend analysis* indicates a firm's performance *over time* and reveals whether its position is improving or deteriorating relative to other companies in the industry.

A trend analysis requires that a number of different ratios be calculated over several years and plotted to yield a graphic representation of the company's performance. Figure 3-1 depicts a trend analysis for the Drake Company for the years 19X0 to 19X6 and indicates the direction the firm has been taking for the past several years. Each of the four different categories of financial ratios is represented in the figure. For example, it is evident that the firm's liquidity position—as measured by the quick ratio—has declined gradually over the seven-year period, falling to slightly below the industry average in 19X6. Unless this downward trend continues, however, liquidity should not be a major problem for the firm.

The trend analysis tells another story about the firm's leverage and profitability. Drake's use of debt has exceeded the industry average since 19X2. The asset

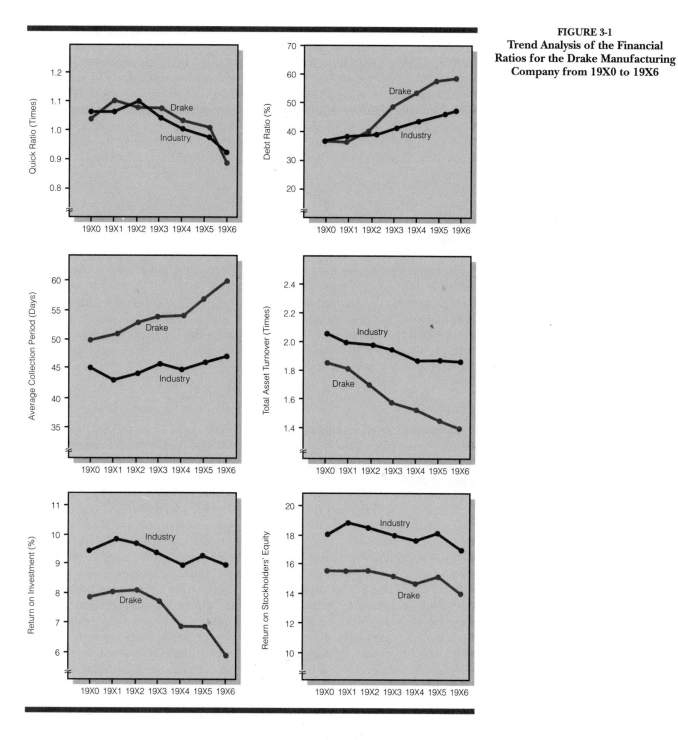

FIGURE 3-1
Trend Analysis of the Financial Ratios for the Drake Manufacturing Company from 19X0 to 19X6

management ratios—the total asset turnover ratio and the average collection period ratio—indicate that the company has used much of this new debt to finance additional assets, including a buildup in receivables. Unfortunately, the new assets have not produced offsetting increases in profits. As a result, returns on investment have dropped below the industry standards by increasing amounts over the past seven years.

In summary, the comparative financial ratio analysis and the trend analysis combined provide the financial analyst with a fairly clear picture of Drake's performance. As is evident from the analysis, the firm has employed excessive debt to finance asset additions, which have not been sufficiently productive in generating sales revenues. The result is returns on investment and stockholders' equity that are significantly lower than the industry average. If the firm intends to reverse these trends, it will have to make more effective use of assets and reduce the use of creditors' funds. These steps will enable the firm to improve relations with creditors and potentially increase profitability and reduce risk for its owners.

ANALYSIS OF PROFITABILITY: RETURN ON INVESTMENT

The preceding discussion on ratios indicates that a firm's return on investment (ROI) is defined as the ratio of earnings after taxes (EAT) to total assets. The ROI ratio can be examined more closely to provide additional insights into its significance.

The ROI also can be viewed as a function of the net profit margin times the total asset turnover, because the net profit margin ratio = EAT/sales and the total asset turnover ratio = sales/total assets:

$$\text{ROI} = \frac{\text{EAT}}{\text{Total assets}} = \frac{\text{EAT}}{\text{Sales}} \times \frac{\text{Sales}}{\text{Total assets}} \qquad (3.19)$$

It is important to examine a firm's ROI in terms of "margin" and "turnover," because each plays a major role in contributing to profitability. "Margin" measures the profit earned per dollar of sales but ignores the amount of assets used to generate sales. The ROI relationship brings these two components together and shows that a deficiency in either one will lower a firm's return on investment.

Using the figures from the net profit margin ratio and total asset turnover ratio calculated previously for the Drake Company, the firm's ROI for 19X6 can be computed as 4.45% x 1.377 = 6.13%. Figure 3-2, called a *modified DuPont chart* because it was developed and is used by the DuPont Corporation, illustrates this relationship. For purposes of comparison, the industry average ROI = 5.10% × 1.82 = 9.28%. The ROI relationship shows Drake to be deficient in both margin and turnover relative to the industry average. Improvement in either area would increase the firm's ROI. To improve its *margin,* for example, Drake must either increase sales revenues more than costs or decrease costs more than sales revenues. To improve its *turnover,* the firm must either increase sales revenue or reduce the asset level required to support the current sales volume. The DuPont chart illustrates the relationship between a firm's ROI and the factors that determine it. By working back through the DuPont chart, an analyst can begin to pinpoint potential areas for improvement that will enhance the firm's ROI.

The relative contributions of the net profit margin and the asset turnover ratio in the ROI relationship differ from industry to industry. Specifically, the turnover ratio is dependent largely on a firm's investment in property, plant, and equipment. Firms with large investments in fixed assets tend to have low turnover ratios; public utilities, railroads, and large industrial firms fall into this category. If these companies are to succeed, their relatively low turnover ratios must be offset by correspondingly high margins to produce competitive ROIs.

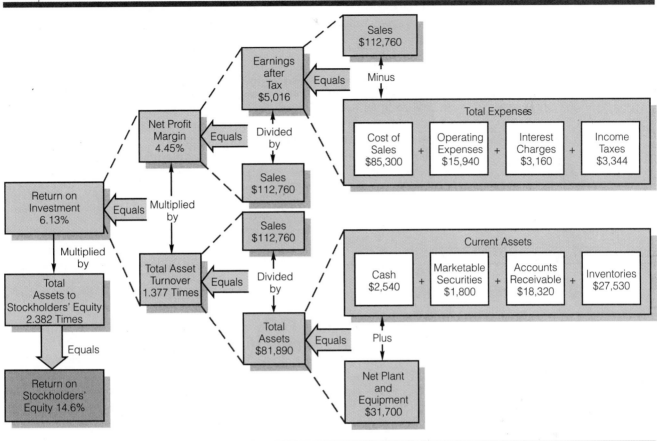

FIGURE 3-2 Modified DuPont Analysis for the Drake Manufacturing Company, 19X6

For example, electric and gas utilities typically have net profit margins of 10 to 15 percent. In contrast, other industries require much lower investments in fixed assets, resulting in higher turnover ratios. A typical example is the retail grocery chain industry, which has margins of only 1 or 2 percent. Firms in this industry often achieve turnovers of 10 times or more. If a grocery chain had a lower turnover, its ROI probably would not be sufficient to attract investors.

FOUNDATION CONCEPT
ANALYZING PROFITABILITY THROUGH RETURN ON STOCKHOLDERS' EQUITY

Figure 3-2 also shows Drake's return on stockholders' equity, which is computed as 14.60 percent. If the firm were financed solely with common equity (stock), the return on stockholders' equity would equal the return on investment. Drake's stockholders have supplied only about 42 percent of the firm's total capital, whereas creditors have supplied the remaining 58 percent. Because the entire 6.13 percent return on investment belongs to the stockholders (even though they only supplied 42 percent of the total capital), Drake's return on common equity is higher than its return on investment.

To clarify how the return on stockholders' equity is determined, a new ratio, the *equity multiplier ratio,* is defined as follows:

$$\text{Equity multiplier} = \frac{\text{Total assets}}{\text{Stockholders' equity}} \qquad (3.20)$$

Drake's equity multiplier ratio is computed from figures found in Table 3-1 as $81,890/$34,367 = 2.382 times. The industry average for the ratio is 1.89 times. Once again, it can be seen that Drake has financed a greater proportion of assets with debt than the average firm in the industry.

The equity multiplier ratio may be used to show how a firm's use of debt to finance assets affects the return on equity, as follows:

$$\begin{array}{l}\text{Return on} \\ \text{stockholders'} \\ \text{equity}\end{array} = \begin{array}{l}\text{Net profit} \\ \text{margin}\end{array} \times \begin{array}{l}\text{Total asset} \\ \text{turnover}\end{array} \times \begin{array}{l}\text{Equity} \\ \text{multiplier}\end{array} \qquad (3.21)$$

$$= \frac{\text{Earning after taxes}}{\text{Sales}} \times \frac{\text{Sales}}{\text{Total assets}} \times \frac{\text{Total assets}}{\text{Stockholders' equity}}$$

In Drake's case the return on stockholders' equity is 4.45 x 1.377 x 2.382 = 14.60%.

Although this figure is the same as the return on equity computed directly by dividing earnings after tax by stockholders' equity, the calculations shown illustrate more clearly how Drake managed to magnify a 6.13 percent return on total investment into a 14.60 percent return on stockholders' equity by making more extensive use of debt financing than did the average firm in the industry. This increased use of debt has improved Drake's return on equity but also has increased its risk—more likely resulting in a decline in Drake's stock price relative to other, similar firms.

 ## SOURCES OF COMPARATIVE FINANCIAL DATA

An analyst may refer to a number of sources of financial data when preparing a comparative financial analysis, including the following:

- **Dun and Bradstreet** Dun and Bradstreet (D&B) prepares a series of fourteen key business ratios for 800 different lines of business. These ratios are based on the financial statements of some 400,000 companies. D&B reports three values for each ratio—the *median,* the *upper quartile,* and the *lower quartile.* The median is the figure that falls in the middle when individual ratios of sampled firms are arranged by size. The figure halfway between the median and the ratio with the highest value is the upper quartile, and the figure halfway between the median and the ratio with the lowest value is the lower quartile. By reporting three values for each ratio, D&B enables the analyst to compare a particular firm with the "average" (median) firm, as well as with the "typical" firms in the top and bottom halves of the sample. The D&B publication containing the data is titled *Industry Norms and Key Business Ratios.*
- **Robert Morris Associates** This national association of bank loan and credit officers uses information provided by loan applications to compile sixteen

ratios for over 250 lines of business. Like D&B, Robert Morris Associates reports the median, upper quartile, and lower quartile for each ratio. Data are presented for four categories of firm size. This source is especially useful to the analyst gathering information about smaller firms. The Robert Morris publication containing the data is titled *Statement Studies*.

■ *Quarterly Financial Report for Manufacturing Companies* The Federal Trade Commission (FTC) and the Securities and Exchange Commission (SEC) cooperate in publishing quarterly reports on balance sheet and income statement data of various manufacturing companies. These include analyses of the firms by industry and asset size, along with presentations of financial statements in ratio form.

■ *Almanac of Business and Industrial Financial Ratios* This annual almanac of business and industrial financial ratios, based on Internal Revenue Service data, reports twenty-two ratios for many industries. It also includes the number of establishments in the sampled industry, the number without net income, and the total dollar receipts for each of the thirteen size groups into which firms in each industry are classified.

■ *Financial Studies of Small Business* This annual publication of Financial Research Associates is particularly valuable for the evaluation of small firms.

■ **Moody's or Standard and Poor's Industrial, Financial, Transportation, and Over-the-Counter Manuals** These contain a large amount of balance sheet and income statement data, as well as other relevant background information about a firm.

■ **Annual reports** Most corporations publish an annual report containing income statement and balance sheet data, along with other information of interest.

■ **10K reports** Every widely held firm is required annually to file a 10K report with the SEC. These reports contain income statement and balance sheet data, plus a wide range of other relevant information dealing with the firm's past and current performance and expected future prospects.

■ **Trade journals** These are published by trade associations and contain a great deal of financial and other types of information on member firms.

■ **Commercial banks** Banks frequently compile financial reports on selected industries. One example is First Chicago's semiannual financial survey of sales finance and consumer finance companies.

■ **Computerized data sources** A number of computerized databases are also available to assist in financial analysis. The *Compustat* database is available from Standard and Poor's. It contains complete balance sheet, income statement, stock price, and dividend information for several thousand companies, covering a period of up to 20 years. The *Compustat* database is available in a form for both mainframe computers and microcomputers. *Value Line* provides summary financial data and forecasts of future performance for over 1,700 firms. The *Value Line* database is available in both hard copy and in a microcomputer-usable format called *Value Screen*. The *Disclosure* database contains complete financial data for over 10,000 firms.

Fortunately, financial data on firms (financial statements, ratio analyses, histories, products, profit projections, etc.) are available at hundreds of different Web sites. Some of these Web sites are completely free, and others charge a small monthly fee. Listed here are a few of the "comprehensive" Web sites for financial information:
http://www.thomsoninvest.net
http://www.hoovers.com
http://www.sec.gov/edgar
http://www.bloomberg.com
http://www.corpfinet.com

Virtually all of these databases are available through on-line services, such as Compuserve and America On-Line. In addition, most of these data sources can be accessed via the Internet, although most nongovernmental sources charge a fee for access.

A WORD OF CAUTION ABOUT FINANCIAL RATIO ANALYSIS

Throughout the analysis of the Drake Manufacturing Company, we emphasized that an analyst must exercise caution when evaluating a firm's financial ratios. Although ratios can provide valuable information, they also can be misleading for a number of reasons.

First, ratios are only as reliable as the accounting data on which they are based. The financial statements of most U.S. companies are prepared in accordance with *generally accepted accounting principles* (GAAP). In the United States, the Financial Accounting Standards Board issues *Statements of Financial Accounting Standards* (SFAS), which describe accounting rules that companies must follow in preparing their financial statements. Even though careful financial analysis can provide excellent insights into the direction and relative strength of the firm, the financial analyst must keep in mind that GAAP gives firms considerable latitude in reporting their financial positions. Different firms follow different accounting procedures for inventory valuation, depreciation, reporting long-term leases, pension fund contributions, and mergers and acquisitions, to name just a few. These, in turn, affect reported earnings, assets, and owners' investments. Unless the analyst makes adjustments for accounting reporting differences, ratio comparisons between individual companies and with various industry norms cannot be viewed as definitive.

Second, with the exception of disclosing upper and lower quartile values, firms that compile industry norms often do not report information about the *dispersion*, or distribution, of the individual values around the mean ratio. If the reported ratios are dispersed widely, the industry average will be of questionable value, because it may not reflect the "typical" firm in the industry. Furthermore, the standard of comparison probably should not be the "typical" firm but rather the better-performing firms in the industry. Without some measure of dispersion, however, ratios for these better-performing firms cannot be determined.

Third, valid comparative analysis depends on the availability of data for appropriately defined industries. Some industry classifications are either too broad or too narrow to be reliable sources of comparative data when an analyst is evaluating a particular firm. Most firms operate in more than one industry, which makes analysis more difficult.

Fourth, it is important to remember that financial ratios provide a *historic* record of the performance and financial condition of a firm. Further analysis is required before this historic record can be used as a basis for future projections.

Finally, comparisons of a firm's ratios with industry norms may not always be what they seem. Ratios comparing unfavorably with industry norms should be construed as "red flags" indicating the need for further investigation—not signals of impending doom. On the other hand, even if a firm's ratios compare favorably with those of the better-performing firms in the industry, it does not necessarily mean the firm is performing adequately. If, for example, the industry itself is experiencing a declining demand for its goods and services, favorable ratio comparisons simply may indicate that a firm is not decaying as rapidly as the typical firm in the industry. Thus, comparisons of selected ratios—particularly those relating to profitability—must be made with *national* industry averages in order to determine whether a particular firm in a particular industry is justified in making further investments.

In summary, ratios should not be viewed as substitutes for sound business judgment. Instead, they are simply tools that can help management make better decisions.

EARNINGS AND BALANCE SHEET QUALITY AND FINANCIAL ANALYSIS

When performing a financial analysis of a firm, an analyst must be mindful of the *quality of the earnings* reported by a firm, as well as the *quality of the firm's balance sheet*. These two dimensions of financial analysis can have a critical impact on the final assessment of the firm's financial condition.

Earnings Quality

When considering the quality of a firm's earnings, two key factors should be kept in mind. First, high-quality earnings tend to be cash earnings. The proportion of a firm's earnings that can be viewed as cash earnings is greatly influenced by the firm's procedures with respect to sales revenue recognition. For example, a firm may recognize a sale at the time a contract is signed, a down payment is made, or when the full proceeds from the sale actually are collected as cash. Generally, the closer the recognition of a sale is to the time the full proceeds from that sale are collected, the higher is the quality of the firm's reported earnings.

Some firms report a large noncash component in their income because of special accounting practices in their industry. For example, utilities generally recognize earnings, for financial reporting purposes, on assets that are under construction but that have not yet been placed in the rate-base of the firm for rate-making purposes. This component of earnings frequently is called *allowance for funds used during construction* (AFUDC), and it recognizes the return that the firm is expected to earn on these assets once they are placed in service by the utility. For utilities with large construction programs, the proportion of noncash to total earnings can be very large. For example, Northeast Utilities reported an AFUDC as a percent of net income ratio of 30.5 percent, indicating that a significant portion of the firm's earnings were not cash income. In contrast, Orange and Rockland Utilities reported an AFUDC to net income ratio of only 0.6 percent, indicating that its earnings were of much higher quality than those of Northeast Utilities.

In the banking industry, an analyst must look to the quality of the loans the bank has made and the adequacy of loan loss reserves to determine if reported net income figures accurately reflect the earnings for the period being reviewed. When loan loss reserves are not adequate, future earnings will be affected adversely if the bank must charge off a significant portion of its bad loans. In the same context, an analyst examining any firm must consider the quality of that firm's accounts receivable. If some receivables are not likely to be collected, then the future earnings of the firm will be reduced.

 Second, a firm's earnings can be viewed as high quality if a greater proportion of those earnings is derived from regularly recurring transactions. To the extent that reported earnings reflect the impact of nonrecurring transactions, the quality of those earnings is reduced. For example, when Tenneco sold its oil and gas businesses, the company was able to recognize a gain of $892 million on the transaction, because these businesses were carried on Tenneco's books at an amount less than the total sales price. This transaction is of a nonrecurring nature and should not be considered when evaluating the earnings capacity of the firm. Other similar nonrecurring gains can emerge when a firm repurchases its debt on the open market at a price lower than the face value of that debt. Also, a firm may change its accounting treatment of inventories and record a significant gain from this transaction. General Motors (GM) did this and reported a one-time gain of $217 million.[16] Another example of a nonrecurring transaction from which gains can occur involves lowering the reported depreciation expense on a company's existing assets. When GM increased the length of time it depreciates auto plants from 35 years to 45 years, it reported a nonrecurring earnings increase of $790 million.[17] Increases or decreases in earnings can also occur as the result of rule changes by the Financial Accounting Standards Board. For example, SFAS No. 96, "Accounting for Income Taxes," issued in December 1987, required a company to follow specific new rules in calculating the income tax liabilities it reports to its stockholders. As a direct result of the Statement of Financial Accounting Standards No. 96 rule changes, General Electric, a company with a reputation of following conservative accounting practices, was required to report a $577 million increase in net income in 1987.[18] A financial analyst reading the *1987 General Electric Annual Report* must understand the reason for the income gain and realize it did not come from increased sales or cost reductions. These are only a few examples of significant nonrecurring transactions. The important point to remember is that the *quality of a firm's earnings decreases* in direct proportion to the increase in the amount of nonrecurring items reported in its earnings figure.

Balance Sheet Quality

The quality of a firm's balance sheet should also be of concern to a financial analyst. If the assets on a firm's balance sheet have a market value equal to or greater than the book value at which they are being carried, this enhances the quality of the firm's balance sheet. In contrast, if a significant portion of the assets of a firm have a market value substantially below book value, the quality of the firm's balance sheet is reduced. Over the last decade, we have seen many firms in the so-called smokestack industries record large losses as significant portions of their assets are abandoned and written off as losses. These firms include Kaiser Aluminum, U.S. Steel (USX), and Bethlehem Steel. Commercial banks regularly write off a portion of their loan portfolios when it becomes clear that particular loans will not be repaid. These actions greatly reduce a firm's equity ratios. Similarly, if a firm has significant amounts of inventory that cannot be moved (such as the Adam computers that Coleco once produced), the quality of the balance sheet is reduced until the firm charges off this low-quality inventory.

In addition to asset quality issues, an analyst should also be aware of hidden liabilities. These liabilities may take the form of such things as long-term lease obligations not appearing on the company's balance sheet or uninsured losses arising from pending lawsuits. When large potential liabilities exist, an analyst must be quite careful before drawing conclusions about the adequacy of a firm's capital structure, based upon an analysis of its reported balance sheet.

In contrast, some firms have significant hidden assets. These assets may be physical assets, such as real property that has appreciated in value but is carried on the firm's books at cost, or securities that are carried on the books at cost even though the market value of these securities has increased above the original cost. These hidden assets also may consist of intangibles, such as valuable patents or brand names. For example, Philip Morris was willing to pay over 10 times the fair value of Kraft's physical assets in order to obtain the brands (e.g., Velveeta cheese and Miracle Whip salad dressing) and consumer loyalty that Kraft had spent decades building up.

---

[16]Gary Hector, "Cute Tricks on the Bottom Line," *Fortune* (April 24, 1989): 193.
[17]Gary Hector, "Cute Tricks on the Bottom Line," *Fortune* (April 24, 1989): 193.
[18]Penelope Lang, "Annual Obfuscation," *Forbes* (May 2, 1988): 71.

This list of balance sheet and earnings quality issues is not all-inclusive, but it does give an indication of the extent to which a surface analysis of a firm's financial statements can lead to misleading conclusions about the financial condition of that firm.

MARKET VALUE ADDED[19]: AN ALTERNATIVE MEASURE OF PERFORMANCE

As already discussed, traditional financial analysis focuses on a set of financial ratios derived primarily from accounting information. Using an approach such as DuPont analysis, a firm's financial performance can be dissected into its component elements. The ultimate measure of firm performance is the return on common equity. Although insights can be gained from this type of analysis, traditional financial analysis suffers from weaknesses inherent in reported accounting information, and it does not directly consider risk in the measure of performance. The greatest shortcoming of traditional financial analysis is the lack of a direct tie between performance, as measured using financial ratios, and shareholder wealth, as measured by the market price of a firm's stock.

A number of alternative performance measures include the *Fortune 500* and the *Business Week 1000* measures. The *Fortune 500* measure is a ranking of the top 500 industrial companies based on annual sales. These rankings have almost no relationship to either accounting financial performance or shareholder wealth. Consequently the *Fortune* rankings are suitable only for identifying the largest firms in terms of sales. In contrast, the *Business Week 1000* rankings are based on the aggregate market value of the outstanding common stock of each of the 1,000 firms considered. This measure looks at the equity component of capital but ignores capital raised from other sources. Furthermore, it includes a bias in favor of large firms when performance is measured by aggregate market value.

The Market Value Added Concept

The *Stern Stewart Performance 1000* is based on the concept of Market Value Added (MVA). MVA is defined as the market value of debt, preferred equity, and common equity capitalization, less capital. Capital is a measure of all the cash raised from investors or retained from earnings to fund new investments in the business, since the company's inception.

$$\text{MVA} = \text{Market value} - \text{Capital} \qquad (3.22)$$

MVA is the capital market's assessment of the accumulated net present value (NPV) of all of the firm's past and projected investment projects. For example, General Motors (GM) had a negative MVA of \$17.8 billion, meaning that GM has destroyed \$17.8 billion of shareholder value by investing in a large number of negative net present value projects.

---

[19]G. Bennett Stewart III, "Announcing the Stern Stewart Performance 1000: A New Way of Viewing Corporate America," *Continental Bank Journal of Applied Corporate Finance* (Summer 1990): 38–59. See also Joel M. Stern, G. Bennett Stewart III, and Donald H. Chew, Jr., "The EVA Financial Management System," *Bank of America Journal of Applied Corporate Finance* (Summer 1995): 32–46, and Irwin Ross, "The Stern Stewart Performance 1000," *Bank of America Journal of Applied Corporate Finance* (Winter 1996).

Consider the performance of General Motors and Merck. These two firms have differed dramatically in their performance rankings over the past decade. Interestingly, General Motors ranked #1 in the *Fortune 500,* #23 in the *Business Week 1000,* but #1000 in the *Stern Stewart Performance 1000,* based on the MVA criterion. In contrast, Merck ranked #55 in the *Fortune 500,* #6 in the *Business Week 1000,* and #4 in the *Stern Stewart Performance 1000* at year-end 1994. See Table 3-6.

Economic Value Added

Economic Value Added (EVA) is a measure of operating performance that indicates how successful a firm has been at increasing the MVA of the enterprise in any given year. EVA is defined as:

TABLE 3-6
Stern Stewart
Performance Measures

Source: *The Stern Stewart Performance 1000: The Definitive Guide to MVA and EVA.* (New York: Stern Stewart, 1996). Used with permission.

MVA RANK					($ mil) MVA 1994	($ mil) EVA 1994	5-Yr Avg Shareholder Return (%)
1994	1989	1984	TIC	Company Name			
1	4	4	KO	Coca-Cola Co.	60846	1884	23.4
2	1	2	GE	General Electric Co.	52071	863	12.7
3	6	7	WMT	Wal-Mart Stores, Inc.	34996	917	14.2
4	3	13	MRK	Merck & Co., Inc.	31467	1124	10.7
5	58		MSFT	Microsoft Corp.	29904	989	44.6
6	8	17	PG	Procter & Gamble Co.	27830	615	14.4
7	2	10	MO	Philip Morris Companies Inc.	27338	2222	10.6
8	9	16	JNJ	Johnson & Johnson	24699	798	15.1
9	7		T	American Telephone & Telegraph Co.	22542	−196	5.2
10	108	46	MOT	Motorola, Inc.	21068	438	32.9
11	16	14	ABT	Abbott Laboratories	20300	973	16.1
12	5	5	BMY	Bristol-Myers Squibb Co.	19686	821	4.8
13	13	993	XON	Exxon Corp.	18907	−1143	8.8
14	106	174	HD	Home Depot (The), Inc.	17333	194	41.7
15	14	110	DIS	Disney (Walt) Co.	17074	519	11.1
16	38	12	PFE	Pfizer Inc.	16851	503	20
17	15	33	PEP	PepsiCo, Inc.	16737	480	12.9
18	70	27	INTC	Intel Corp.	14532	1193	30.1
19	35	995	DD	Du Pont (E.I.) De Nemours & Co.	13892	−1353	10.4
20	54	57	G	Gillette Co.	13799	293	26.6
981	965		CYM	Cyprus AMAX Minerals Co.	−815	−465	3.1
982	979	414	AMR	AMR Corp.	−949	−522	−1.7
983	987	940	CHA	Champion International Corp.	−992	−602	4.1
984	971	474	JR	James River Corp. Of Virginia	−1258	−438	−3.7
985	997	982	CSX	CSX Corp.	−1392	−686	17.3
986	264	937	CGP	Coastal (The) Corp.	−1435	−201	−3.5
987	996	975	S	Sears, Roebuck and Co.	−1534		8.8
988	992	961	MVL	Manville Corp.	−1548	−239	4.4
989	993	880	UIS	Unisys Corp.	−2012	−914	−6.8
990	753		CCE	Coca-Cola Enterprises Inc.	−2099	−409	2.7
991	129	916	OXY	Occidental Petroleum Corp.	−2320	−1306	−1.7
992		908	FD	Federated Department Stores Inc.	−2598	−120	
993	372	104	KM	K Mart Corp.	−2630	−1485	−1
994	42	943	WX	Westinghouse Electric Corp.	−2783	−659	−16.3
995	998	37	C	Chrysler Corp.	−3177	2993	25.6
996	977	26	DEC	Digital Equipment Corp.	−4684	−2992	−16.5
997	172	1	IBM	International Business Machines Corp.	−8864	−3019	−0.4
998		50	RN	RJR Nabisco Holdings Corp.	−11761	−2268	
999	999	997	F	Ford Motor Co.	−13757	985	10.8
1000	1000	996	GM	General Motors Corp.	−17803	−2044	4.3

$$\text{EVA} = [\text{Return on total capital } (r) - \text{Cost of capital } (k)] \times \text{Capital} \quad (3.23)$$

where r = net operating profits after tax divided by beginning of year capital, and k = weighted after-tax cost of capital. Using this relationship it can be seen that a firm's managers can increase EVA by (1) increasing operating efficiency and thereby increasing r, (2) committing new resources to the enterprise that promise a return in excess of the firm's weighted (and risk-adjusted) cost of capital; (3) redirecting resources from projects that do not earn adequate returns (relative to the cost of capital) and show little promise of doing so in the future, to more productive uses, including the payment of dividends and reduction of debt levels if no adequate-return projects are present; and (4) making prudent use of the tax benefits of debt financing to create value, while considering risk versus return trade-offs.

EVA can be thought of as the incremental contribution of a firm's operations to the creation of MVA. MVA is the present value of all expected future EVA. Firms that consistently earn returns in excess of their cost of capital will have positive EVA, thereby enhancing the MVA of the enterprise. For example, in 1994 Wal-Mart's EVA was $917 million, indicating that Wal-Mart was adding to shareholder wealth during that year.

In contrast, firms that earn less than their cost of capital will have negative EVA. Consistent expected negative EVA will result in a decline in a firm's MVA. For example, in 1994 Westinghouse had EVA of *negative* $659 million.

One important implication of the MVA and EVA concepts is that growth in earnings does not necessarily add to the value of an enterprise (MVA), unless it is achieved by making (and managing) investments such that they earn a return in excess of the cost of capital (positive EVA). Another implication is that increasing the rate of return on investment will not necessarily increase MVA, because it is necessary to link the return earned with the market-required rate of return (weighted cost of capital). Finally, a company's dividend policy has no direct impact on MVA since the payment of dividends equally reduces both the book and the market value of capital. Only if dividend payments provide credible signals to the capital markets about future prospects (for EVA), will dividend payment patterns have an impact on value.

The EVA and MVA concepts used in the construction of the *Stern Stewart Performance 1000* index provide a useful alternative way to focus on the performance of an enterprise in the context of the objective of maximizing the value of the enterprise. This way of looking at financial analysis is appealing because it explicitly ties together the investment decisions with measures of firm performance. As such, financial managers and analysts may find this approach to firm performance analysis to be a useful complement to more traditional approaches.

 ## INFLATION AND FINANCIAL STATEMENT ANALYSIS

Inflation can cause a number of problems for a financial analyst who is trying to assess the performance of a firm over time and in comparison with other firms in the industry. In particular, *inventory profits*—short-lived increased profits that occur as a result of the timing of price increases—can make a significant difference in a firm's reported earnings from year to year.

For example, consider a supply company that buys equipment parts wholesale from the manufacturer for $4.00 each and sells them at a retail price of $5.00 each, realizing a profit of $1.00 per unit. Suppose the manufacturer announces a price increase of $0.50 per unit to $4.50, effective on the first of next month. If the supply company passes the increase on to customers and announces a price increase of its own to $5.50, also effective on the first of next month, it will realize a gross profit of $1.50 on every unit sold that originally cost $4.00. In other words, the company will make additional profit on the units already in inventory *prior to the price increase*. Once it begins purchasing parts from the manufacturer at the new price of $4.50 per unit, it will revert to its original $1.00 profit. In the meantime, however, the timing of the price increase will allow the company to enjoy short-lived increased profits, or inventory profits.

Most companies do not want to pay income taxes on inventory profits, preferring to use these funds to replenish inventories—especially in inflationary times. Fortunately, there is a way of avoiding or deferring the necessity of reporting these higher profits. The *last-in, first-out* (LIFO) inventory valuation method assumes that the items a firm uses from inventory are those that were acquired most recently. Thus, they can be *priced out* of the inventory based on the most recent inventory acquisition costs. In contrast, the *first-in, first-out* (FIFO) method of inventory valuation, which assumes that the items a firm uses from inventory are the oldest items in inventory, results in the firm's having to show a higher profit and therefore pay higher income taxes.

During the 1960s, most large U.S. corporations were using the FIFO method. Inflation at that time was low to moderate, and the majority of companies thought it desirable to report their net income as high as possible. By 1974, however, inflation rates had risen to about 12 percent, and companies that were experiencing increasing inventory profits began switching to the LIFO method in an attempt to conserve cash by paying less income taxes.

The accounting method used for inventory will affect a firm's profits and its balance sheet. Hence, any financial ratio that contains balance sheet inventory figures (for example, the total asset turnover ratio) or net income will vary from one firm to another, depending on the firm's accounting treatment of inventory. Another effect of inflation on financial statements is the tendency for the value of fixed assets to be understated. Also, to the extent that inflation causes a rise in interest rates, the value of long-term debt outstanding will decline. Thus, a firm will appear to be more financially leveraged in an inflationary period than is actually the case.

Inventory profits and inflation are only two factors that can affect a firm's reported earnings. Differences in the reporting of earnings, the recognition of sales, and other factors can also make comparisons between firms somewhat misleading. Again, a good financial analyst will always "go behind" the figures stated on a firm's income statement or balance sheet to find out what is actually occurring within a company.

 FOUNDATION CONCEPT
CASH FLOW ANALYSIS

Traditional financial ratio analysis can be a useful tool to an analyst trying to evaluate a firm's performance. However, many of the key performance measures, such as return on sales, assets, and equity, rely on accounting income concepts. Accounting income is not the relevant source of value in a firm—cash flow is. Only cash can be spent. Accounting income, in contrast, does not reflect the actual cash inflows and outflows in a firm. Consequently, in this section we illustrate and define further the cash flow concept you encountered in Chapter 1, and introduce the statement of cash flows.

The Cash Flow Concept

Earlier we encountered the income statement for Drake Manufacturing Company (Table 3-2). The income statement can be modified to provide a quick measure of the after-tax cash flow (ATCF) that is available from current operations to make capital expenditures, pay dividends, and repay debt. Accordingly, the ATCF is generally a more important number than the net income (EAT) figure. One shortcoming of the ATCF is that it does not consider additional cash *problem* tied up in (or released from) net working capital.

Table 3-7 derives ATCF for Drake by taking earnings after tax from Drake's publicly reported income statement and adding back noncash charges:

$$ATCF = EAT + \text{Noncash charges} \tag{3.24}$$

Drake has noncash charges of $2,000 ($1,900 from depreciation and $100 from deferred taxes). Hence, for Drake the ATCF is:

$$ATCF = \$5,016 + \$1,900 + \$100$$
$$= \$7,016$$

Depreciation. *Depreciation* is defined as the systematic allocation of the cost of an asset over more than one year. The annual depreciation expense recorded for a particular asset is an allocation of its original cost and does not represent a cash outlay. As a result, a company's annual depreciation expense is added to earnings after taxes in calculating after-tax cash flow. For example, in 1995, General Electric Company had earnings after taxes of $6,573 million. Its 1995 depreciation expense of $3,594 million must be added to the earnings after taxes amount in calculating General Electric's 1995 ATCF.[20]

Deferred Taxes. After-tax cash flow also differs from earnings after taxes by the amount of a company's *deferred taxes*. In accordance with generally accepted

Net sales	$112,760
Cost of sales	85,300
Gross margin	$ 27,460
Operating expenses	15,940
Earnings before interest and taxes (EBIT)	$ 11,520
Interest charges	3,160
Earnings before taxes (EBT)	$ 8,360
Federal and state income taxes at a combined 40% rate	3,344
Earnings after taxes (EAT) and available for common stockholders	$ 5,016
Plus Noncash expenses	
Depreciation	1,900
Deferred income taxes	100
After-tax cash flow (ATCF)	$ 7,016

TABLE 3-7
Drake Manufacturing Company: After-Tax Cash Flow Calculation (in thousands of dollars) for the Year Ended December 31, 19X6

[20]General Electric Company, *Annual Report* (1995): 53.

accounting principles and specifically in accordance with Statement of Financial Accounting Standards No. 96, a company usually reports a different income tax expense amount to its stockholders than it actually pays in cash during that year. Frequently, the income tax amount shown on the company's income statement is larger than the income tax amount paid. The difference between the tax amount reported to stockholders and the cash amount actually paid is referred to as a *deferred tax*, because it is due to be paid by the company sometime in the future. For example, during 1996, H. J. Heinz reported the following earnings amounts to its stockholders.[21]

Earnings before taxes	$1,024 million
Less Income taxes	364 million
Earnings after taxes	$ 660 million
Income taxes:	
Current portion	$229 million
Deferred	135 million

In calculating Heinz's 1996 after-tax cash flow, the deferred tax amount, $135 million, is added to the earnings after tax, because the deferred taxes were subtracted as an expense in determining earnings but did not constitute a cash payment by Heinz in 1996.

Deferred taxes generally occur because of temporary differences in the stated amounts of assets and liabilities *for financial reporting purposes* and for tax purposes. Specifically, even though deferred taxes can occur for a variety of reasons, some of the more common reasons include differences between financial reporting and tax methods regarding accounting for depreciation, inventories, and pensions. The following example specifically shows how deferred taxes occur as a result of different depreciation methods. Many companies use the straight-line depreciation method to calculate the income they report to their stockholders and an accelerated depreciation method to calculate taxable income. As shown in Table 3-8, this practice usually results in the taxes currently owed being less than they would be if the company used straight-line depreciation methods for tax purposes. Using straight-line depreciation, the company's earnings before taxes are $20 million; using accelerated depreciation, its earnings before taxes are $18 million. Taxes of $6.8 million are calculated assuming a 34 percent tax rate on the taxable earnings figure of $20 million, but only $6.12 million in taxes is currently owed, resulting in $0.68 million in deferred taxes. The company effectively can continue to defer payment of these taxes as long as it continues to purchase a sufficient amount of new fixed assets. When it ceases purchasing such assets or purchases fewer of them, it will have to pay the deferred taxes.

The after-tax cash flow for the company in Table 3-8, $23.88 million, is calculated easily by adding the tax depreciation amount, $12.00 million, to the earnings after taxes (for tax reporting) amount, $11.88 million. If the tax records are not available, the after-tax cash flow is calculated using Equation 3.25, as follows:

$$\text{ATCF} = \text{Earnings after taxes} + \text{Depreciation} + \text{Deferred taxes} \qquad (3.25)$$

$$= \$13.20 \text{ million} + \$10.00 \text{ million} + \$0.68 \text{ million}$$

$$= \$23.88 \text{ million}$$

[21]H. J. Heinz Company, *Annual Report* (1996), 30.

(A) CALCULATION OF TAXES FOR FINANCIAL REPORTING AND TAX PURPOSES (IN MILLIONS OF DOLLARS)

	Financial Reporting Purposes	*Tax Purposes*
Sales	$100.00	$100.00
Expenses, excluding depreciation	70.00	70.00
Depreciation:		
Straight line	10.00	
MACRS*		12.00
Earnings before taxes	$ 20.00	$ 18.00
Taxes (34%)	6.80	6.12
Earnings after taxes	$ 13.20	$ 11.88

(B) Partial Income Statement Reported to Stockholders (in millions of dollars)

Earnings before taxes	$ 20.00
Federal income taxes @ 34%:	
Current	$ 6.12
Deferred	0.68
Total federal income tax	$ 6.80
Earnings after taxes	$ 13.20

*MACRS stands for Modified Accelerated Cost Recovery System and is explained in Appendix A.

The Statement of Cash Flows

The statement of cash flows, together with the balance sheet and the income statement, constitute a major portion of a company's financial statements. The *statement of cash flows* shows the effects of a company's *operating, investing,* and *financing* activities on its cash balance. The principal purpose of the statement of cash flows is to provide relevant information about a company's cash receipts and cash payments during a particular accounting period. The statement of cash flows provides a more complete indication of the sources (and the uses) of a firm's cash resources over time.

The procedures for preparing the statement of cash flows are presented in Statement of Financial Accounting Standards No. 95, issued by the Financial Accounting Standards Board (FASB) in November 1987. It requires companies to include a statement of cash flows when issuing a complete set of financial statements for annual periods ending after July 15, 1988. The FASB encourages companies to prepare their statement of cash flows using the *direct* method of presenting cash flows from operating activities.

Statement of Cash Flows: Direct Method. Table 3-9 shows an example of a statement of cash flows using the direct method for the Summit Furniture Company, a retail furniture store. During the year, Summit's "cash flows from operating activities" totaled $14,600 ($142,000 cash received from customers, plus $600 of interest received, less $120,000 paid to suppliers and employees, less $2,000 interest paid, less $6,000 of income taxes paid). Summit's investing activities used net cash of $18,000. The company spent $19,000 on capital expenditures and received $1,000 in proceeds from the sale of an asset. During the year the net cash provided by financing activities equaled $3,600. The $3,600 is calculated as the

INCREASE (DECREASE) IN CASH AND CASH EQUIVALENTS*

Cash Flows from Operating Activities:

Cash received from customers	$ 142,000	
Cash paid to suppliers and employees	(120,000)	
Interest received	600	
Interest paid (net of amount capitalized)	(2,000)	
Income taxes paid	(6,000)	
Net cash provided (used) by operating activities		$14,600
Cash Flows from Investing Activities:		
Proceeds from sale of asset	1,000	
Capital expenditures	(19,000)	
Net cash provided (used) by investing activities		(18,000)
Cash Flows from Financing Activities:		
Net borrowings under bank line-of-credit agreement	1,000	
Repayments of long-term debt	(2,600)	
Proceeds from issuance of long-term debt	4,000	
Proceeds from issuance of common stock	1,700	
Dividends paid	(500)	
Net cash provided (used) by financing activities		3,600
Net increase (decrease) in cash and cash equivalents		200
Cash and cash equivalents at beginning of year		5,000
Cash and cash equivalents at end of year		$ 5,200

*Cash and cash equivalents include currency on hand, bank deposits and similar accounts, and short-term (maturities less than three months), highly liquid investments.

difference between financing activities that require cash outflows and those that result in cash inflows. Summit had financing cash outflows totaling $3,100 ($2,600 repayment of long-term debt and $500 of dividends paid out) and financing cash inflows totaling $6,700 (bank borrowing of $1,000 plus proceeds from the issuance of long-term debt of $4,000 plus proceeds from the issuance of common stock of $1,700). The overall change in cash is calculated as follows:

$$\text{Net cash increase (decrease)} = \text{Net cash provided (used) by operating activities}$$
$$+ \text{Net cash provided (used) by investing activities} \quad (3.26)$$
$$+ \text{Net cash provided (used) by financing activities}$$

$$\text{Net cash increase (decrease)} = \$14,600 - \$18,000 + \$3,600$$
$$= \$200$$

The statement of cash flows presented in Table 3-9 provides Summit's management, investors, and creditors with a summary of its cash flows for the year. In particular, Summit's operations provided net cash of $14,600; however, the company used a total of $18,000 in its investing activities. As a result, if Summit wanted to keep its cash balance at about $5,000, the company's financing activities would have to provide $3,400 of net cash ($18,000 – $14,600). In fact, Summit's financing activities actually did provide $3,600, causing the ending cash balance to be $5,200, or $200 above the beginning $5,000.

Statement of Cash Flows: Indirect Method. A sampling of recent annual reports shows that very few companies present their statement of cash flows using the direct method. Instead, most companies use the indirect, or reconciliation, method to report the net cash flow from operating activities. The indirect method involves adjusting net income to reconcile it to net cash flow from operating activities. Table 3-10 shows the statements of cash flows using the indirect method for H. J. Heinz Company.

TABLE 3-10
Consolidated Statements
of Cash Flows for H. J. Heinz
Company and Subsidiaries

FISCAL YEAR ENDED (DOLLARS IN THOUSANDS)	MAY 1, 1996 (52 WEEKS)
Operating Activities:	
Net income	$659,319
Adjustments to reconcile net income to cash provided by operating activities:	
Depreciation	254,640
Amortization	89,169
Deferred tax provision	135,235
Gain on sale of confectionery and specialty rice businesses	—
Other items, net	(82,198)
Changes in current assets and liabilities, excluding effects of acquisitions and divestitures:	
Receivables	(222,894)
Inventories	(102,269)
Prepaid expenses and other current assets	(14,361)
Accounts payable	126,596
Accrued liabilities	(114,015)
Income taxes	7,866
Cash provided by operating activities	737,088
Investing Activities:	
Capital expenditures	(334,787)
Acquisitions, net of cash acquired	(156,006)
Proceeds from divestitures	82,061
Purchases of short-term investments	(982,824)
Sales and maturities of short-term investments	1,050,971
Investment in tax benefits	62,081
Other items, net	(11,637)
Cash (used for) investing activities	(290,141)
Financing Activities:	
Proceeds from long-term debt	4,860
Payments on long-term debt	(46,791)
(Payments on) proceeds from short term debt, net	(39,745)
Dividends	(381,927)
Purchase of treasury stock	(155,200)
Proceeds from minority interest	—
Proceeds from borrowings against insurance policies	6,361
Repayments of borrowings against insurance policies	—
Exercise of stock options	95,853
Other items, net	45,788
Cash (used for) provided by financing activities	(470,801)
Effect of exchange rate changes on cash and cash equivalents	(10,420)
Net (decrease) increase in cash and cash equivalents	(34,274)
Cash and cash equivalents at beginning of year	124,338
Cash and cash equivalents at end of year	$ 90,054

Heinz had 1996 net income (EAT) of $659 million. Converting this net income to cash flow requires adding back noncash expenses, including depreciation and deferred taxes. Then Heinz adjusted net income from the accrual method (required by GAAP) to the cash amount by showing increases and decreases in its various current asset and liability accounts. After these adjustments, Heinz had net cash from operations of $737 million. In 1996 Heinz used $290 million in investing activities, primarily for capital expenditures and for acquisitions. Financing activities used $471 million. Finally the cash impact of changes in foreign exchange rates was a reduction of $10 million. The net effect of Heinz's 1996 activities was a decrease in cash and cash equivalents of $34 million.

The Heinz statement of cash flows gives a financial analyst a good feel for the effect Heinz's operating, investing, and financing activities had on its cash position.

INTERNATIONAL ISSUES
FINANCIAL ANALYSIS OF
MULTINATIONAL CORPORATIONS

The tools of financial analysis developed in this chapter are useful in evaluating the financial performance of purely domestic U.S. firms as well as firms with small international operations. However, assessing the financial performance and condition of a firm with sizable international operations is generally more complicated than analyzing a firm whose operations are largely domestic.

Part of the complication involves the translation of foreign operating results from the host country's currency to U.S. dollars. To illustrate, suppose Sara Lee's French operations show net earnings of 100 million French francs. Sara Lee reports its results to stockholders denominated in U.S. dollars. Therefore, the French results must be translated into U.S. dollars. The *dollar* amount of Sara Lee's French earnings depends on the exchange rate between dollars and francs. If, for example, the exchange rate between francs and dollars is 8 French francs per dollar, the earnings of 100 million French francs are reported as $12,500,000 (100 million francs/8 francs per dollar). But, if the exchange rate changes to 10 French francs to the dollar, the earnings of 100 million francs translate into only $10,000,000 U.S. dollars (100 million francs/10 francs per dollar). Thus, the earnings reported by a U.S. company with sizable foreign operations depend not only on the earnings stated in the local currency but on the exchange rates between local currencies and the U.S. dollar. When the U.S. dollar is relatively strong against a foreign currency—that is, when the dollar will "buy" more French francs, for example—foreign earnings translate into fewer dollars than when the dollar is relatively weak.

An additional complication in financial analysis of multinational firms arises because of fluctuating exchange rates. What happens to the *dollar* value on the parent (Sara Lee) balance sheet of Sara Lee's French assets and liabilities as the exchange rate between francs and dollars changes? According to Statement of Accounting Standards No. 52, which deals with international accounting, assets and liabilities normally are translated at the exchange rate in effect on the balance sheet date. However, any gains or losses resulting from the translation of asset and liability accounts are not reflected on the income statement and therefore also are not included in the retained earnings figure on the balance sheet. Instead, gains and losses from foreign translation are reported separately on the balance sheet as a part of stockholders' equity, usually under a heading such as "Cumulative foreign exchange translation adjustment," or "Translation adjustments." For example, during 1995, Sara Lee reported an increase of $173 million in its translation adjustments account. This increase did not affect Sara Lee's 1995 earnings, but it did change stockholders' equity on its balance sheet.

Financial managers and analysts in the 1990s and beyond will have to be knowledgeable about the complex international aspects of financial statement analysis.

ETHICAL ISSUES
ACCURACY OF FINANCIAL STATEMENTS

The financial statements of a company are examined by numerous parties, including shareholders, bondholders, banks, government agencies (e.g., Securities and Exchange Commission), employees, suppliers, and financial analysts. These parties are concerned that the statements present a fair and accurate picture of a company's financial position (i.e., assets, liabilities, earnings, and cash flows). Most companies hire external independent auditors (certified public accountants) to attest that the financial statements reflect the financial position of the company. The external auditor studies the controls that have been built into the company's information-processing system for the purpose of detecting errors and preventing fraud. The auditor also normally performs statistical tests on accounting data to verify the data's reasonableness. A letter from the auditor is included in the company's annual report, stating that the financial information represents fairly the financial position of the company and that these statements were constructed in conformity with generally accepted accounting principles. Any exceptions are supposed to be noted in the auditor's letter.

In spite of these controls on financial reporting practices, generally accepted accounting principles still provide management with considerable latitude to "manipulate" reported earnings for some personal or corporate gain. A senior executive, whose compensation is tied to earnings performance, may direct the corporation's accountants to adopt practices that enhance reported earnings. Earnings enhancement through accounting may also be used when a firm anticipates the sale of securities in the financial markets.

An interesting example of earnings manipulation is the case of Pfizer Inc., one of the nation's largest and healthiest pharmaceutical firms. [22] Under pressure from the Clinton administration regarding high profits earned by drug companies, Pfizer is alleged to have aggressively managed its earnings so as to report declining 1993 profits—thereby hoping to counter the high profit charges. Pfizer boosted R&D spending, took writeoffs for restructuring expenses, and deferred sales from the fourth quarter of 1993 to the first quarter of 1994. Pfizer's management denies the charges of suppressing earnings.

This illustration points out how the choice of accounting reporting procedures has an ethical dimension that managers should confront head-on. What do you think the objective of the choice of accounting practices should be?

[22]"Did Pfizer Doctor its Numbers?" *Business Week* (February 14, 1994): 34.

■ SUMMARY

- *Financial ratios* are statistical yardsticks that relate two numbers generally taken from a firm's income statements and balance sheets.
- Financial ratios fall into five categories:
    1. *Liquidity ratios,* which measure a firm's ability to meet its maturing obligations.
    2. *Asset management ratios,* which measure how efficiently a firm is using resources to generate sales.
    3. *Financial leverage management ratios,* which indicate a firm's capacity to meet short- and long-term debt obligations.
    4. *Profitability ratios,* which measure the firm's ability to generate profits on sales, assets, and owners' investment.
    5. *Market-based ratios,* which measure the market's (investors') perceptions of a firm's performance and risk.
    6. *Dividend policy ratios* indicate the dividend practices of a firm.
- *Common-size financial statements,* which express financial items in percentages, are helpful in detecting and monitoring financial trends.
- *Trend analysis* introduces the element of time into financial ratio analysis. It gives the analyst a more dynamic view of a company's situation than does a pure comparative financial ratio analysis alone.
- The relationship of the return on investment (ROI) to "margin" and "turnover" can be used to determine if one or both of the two is deficient in contributing to the profitability of a firm.
- To gain further insight into the relative financial position of a firm, the analyst must compare the financial ratios with *industry averages.* The more diversified the firm, the more difficult it will be to make such a comparison. Two major sources of industry ratios are Dun and Bradstreet and Robert Morris Associates.
- The quality of a firm's earnings is higher, the greater the proportion of cash earnings to total earnings and the greater the proportion of recurring income to total income.
- The quality of a firm's balance sheet is enhanced as the ratio of the market value of the firm's assets to the book value of those assets increases and as the amount of "hidden liabilities" that appears on the firm's balance sheet decreases.
- Financial ratios have been used in conjunction with sophisticated statistical techniques to forecast such events as bankruptcy of a firm.
- The *market value added* concept is the market's assessment of the *accumulated* value created from a firm's past and projected investment projects.
- *Economic value added* is a *yearly* measure of the operating performance of a firm, considering investor return requirements.
- After-tax cash flow is equal to earnings after tax plus noncash charges. Depreciation and deferred taxes are examples of noncash charges.
- The *statement of cash flows* is a major financial statement showing the effects of a firm's operating, investing, and financing activities on its cash balance.
- *Inflation* can have a significant impact on a firm's reported earnings. For example, it can influence the firm to choose a different inventory valuation

method and cost accounting system. When comparing the performance of two or more firms, the financial analyst should recognize that the firms may use different accounting methods to calculate net income.

■ Financial statements of multinational firms are influenced by fluctuating foreign exchange rates.

■ QUESTIONS AND TOPICS FOR DISCUSSION

1. What are the primary limitations of ratio analysis as a technique of financial statement analysis?
2. What is the major limitation of the current ratio as a measure of a firm's liquidity? How may this limitation be overcome?
3. What problems may be indicated by an average collection period that is substantially above or below the industry average?
4. What problems may be indicated by an inventory turnover ratio that is substantially above or below the industry average?
5. What factors limit the use of the fixed asset turnover ratio in comparative analyses?
6. What are the three most important determinants of a firm's return on stockholders' equity?
7. What specific effects can the use of alternative accounting procedures have on the validity of comparative financial analyses?
8. How can inflation affect the comparability of financial ratios between firms?
9. What is the relationship between a firm's P/E multiple and that firm's risk and growth potential?
10. Discuss the general factors that influence the quality of a company's reported earnings and its balance sheet.
11. Why would you anticipate a lower P/E ratio for a typical natural gas utility than for a computer technology firm, such as Compaq Computer?
12. Recently, many large corporations, such as General Motors, have written off large amounts of their nonperforming (or poorly performing) assets as they have shrunk their operations. What is the impact of these asset writeoffs on the future return on assets, future return on common equity, and future financial leverage ratios? What impact would you expect these writeoffs to have on the market value of the firm's equity securities? Why?
13. The Farmers State Bank recently has been earning an "above average" (compared to the overall banking industry) return on total assets of 1.50 percent. The bank's return on common equity is only 12 percent, compared with an industry average of 15 percent.
    a. What reasons can you give for the bank's low return on common equity?
    b. What impact do you think this performance by the bank is having on the value of its debt and equity securities?
14. What are *deferred taxes*, and how do they come into being?
15. What is the relationship between EVA and MVA?
16. How would you characterize the performance of each of the following firms in creating value for its owners over the period 1984 to 1994? (Refer to Table 3-6.)
    a. Microsoft.
    b. General Electric.
    c. Occidental Petroleum.
    d. General Motors.

■ SELF-TEST PROBLEMS

The following financial data for the Freemont Corporation are to be used in answering the first six self-test problems.

Balance Sheet ($000)

Assets		Liabilities & Stockholders' Equity	
Cash	$ 1,500	Accounts payable	$12,500
Marketable securities	2,500	Notes payable	12,500
Accounts receivable	15,000	Total current liabilities	$25,000
Inventory	33,000	Long-term debt	22,000
Total current assets	$52,000	Total liabilities	$47,000
Fixed assets (net)	35,000	Common stock (par value)	5,000
Total assets	$87,000	Contributed capital in excess of par	18,000
		Retained earnings	17,000
		Total stockholders' equity	$40,000
		Total liabilities and stockholders' equity	$87,000

Income Statement ($000)

Sales (all on credit)	$130,000
Cost of sales	103,000
Gross margin	$ 27,000
Operating expenses*	16,000
Earnings before interest and taxes	$ 11,000
Interest expense	3,000
Earnings before taxes	$ 8,000
Income tax	3,000
Earnings after taxes	$ 5,000

*Includes $200 (000) in lease payments.

Other Information

Stock price	$9.50
Book value/share	$8.00
Number of shares	5,000 (000)

ST1. Calculate the following liquidity ratios:
  a. Current ratio.
  b. Quick ratio.

ST2. Calculate the following asset management ratios:
  a. Average collection period.
  b. Inventory turnover.
  c. Fixed asset turnover.
  d. Total asset turnover.

ST3. Calculate the following financial leverage management ratios:
  a. Debt ratio.
  b. Debt-to-equity ratio.
  c. Times interest earned ratio.
  d. Fixed-charge coverage ratio.

ST4. Calculate the following profitability ratios:
  a. Gross profit margin.
  b. Net profit margin.
  c. Return on investment.
  d. Return on stockholders' equity.

ST5. Calculate the following market-based ratios:
  a. Price-to-earnings ratio.
  b. Market price-to-book value ratio.

ST6. Express the return on stockholders' equity ratio as a function of the net profit margin, total asset turnover, and equity multiplier ratios.

ST7. Jenkins Properties had gross fixed assets of $1,000 at the end of 19X8. By the end of 19X9, these had grown to $1,100. Accumulated depreciation at the end of 19X8 was $500, and it was $575 at the end of 19X9. Jenkins has no interest expenses. Jenkins expected sales during 19X9 to total $500. Operating expenses (exclusive of depreciation) were forecasted to be $125. Jenkins's marginal tax rate is 40 percent.

a. What was Jenkins's 19X9 depreciation expense?
b. What was Jenkins's 19X9 earnings after taxes (EAT)?
c. What was Jenkins's 19X9 after-tax cash flow using Equation 3.24?
d. Show that EAT less the increase in *net* fixed assets is equivalent to after-tax cash flow less the increase in *gross* fixed assets.

■ PROBLEMS*

1. Vanity Press, Inc., has annual credit sales of $1,600,000 and a gross profit margin of 35 percent.
   a. If the firm wishes to maintain an average collection period of 50 days, what level of accounts receivable should it carry? (Assume a 365-day year.)
   b. The inventory turnover for this industry averages 6 times. If all of Vanity's sales are on credit, what average level of inventory should the firm maintain to achieve the same inventory turnover figure as the industry?

2. Pacific Fixtures lists the following accounts as part of its balance sheet.

Total assets	$10,000,000
Accounts payable	$ 2,000,000
Notes payable (8%)	1,000,000
Bonds (10%)	3,000,000
Common stock at par	1,000,000
Contributed capital in excess of par	500,000
Retained earnings	2,500,000
Total liabilities and stockholders' equity	$10,000,000

   Compute the return on stockholders' equity if the company has sales of $20 million and the following net profit margin:
   a. 3 percent.
   b. 5 percent.

3. Clovis Industries had sales in 19X1 of $40 million, 20 percent of which were cash. If Clovis normally carries 45 days of credit sales in accounts receivable, what are its average accounts receivable balances? (Assume a 365-day year.)

4. Williams Oil Company had a return on stockholders' equity of 18 percent during 19X1. Its total asset turnover was 1.0 times, and its equity multiplier was 2.0 times. Calculate the company's net profit margin.

5. Using the data in the following table for a number of firms in the same industry, do the following:
   a. Compute the total asset turnover, the net profit margin, the equity multiplier, and the return on equity for each firm.
   b. Evaluate each firm's performance by comparing the firms with one another. Which firm or firms appear to be having problems? What corrective action would you suggest the poorer performing firms take? Finally, what additional data would you want to have on hand when conducting your analyses?

		Firm		
(in millions of dollars)	A	B	C	D
Sales	$20	$10	$15	$25
Net income after tax	3	0.5	2.25	3
Total assets	15	7.5	15	24
Stockholders' equity	10	5.0	14	10

*Colored numbers denote problems that have check answers provided at the end of the book.

6. Tarheel Furniture Company is planning to establish a wholly owned subsidiary to manufacture upholstery fabrics. Tarheel expects to earn $1 million after taxes on the venture during the first year. The president of Tarheel wants to know what the subsidiary's balance sheet would look like. The president believes that it would be advisable to begin the new venture with ratios that are similar to the industry average.

Tarheel plans to make all sales on credit. All calculations assume a 365-day year. In your computations, you should round all numbers to the nearest $1,000.

Based upon the industry average financial ratios presented here, complete the projected balance sheet for Tarheel's upholstery subsidiary.

	Industry Averages
Current ratio	2:1
Quick ratio	1:1
Net profit margin ratio	5 percent
Average collection period	20 days
Debt ratio	40 percent
Total asset turnover ratio	2 times
Current liabilities/stockholders' equity	20 percent

Forecasted Upholstery Subsidiary Balance Sheet

Cash	____	Total current liabilities	____
Accounts receivable	____	Long-term debt	____
Inventory	____	Total debt	____
Total current assets	____	Stockholders' equity	____
Net fixed assets	____	Total liabilities and stockholders' equity	____
Total assets	____		

7. The Sooner Equipment Company has total assets of $100 million. Of this total, $40 million was financed with common equity and $60 million with debt (both long- and short-term). Its average accounts receivable balance is $20 million, and this represents an 80-day average collection period. Sooner believes it can reduce its average collection period from 80 days to 60 days without affecting sales or the dollar amount of net income after taxes (currently $5 million). What will be the effect of this action on Sooner's return on investment and its return on stockholders' equity if the funds received by reducing the average collection period are used to buy back its common stock at book value? What impact will this action have on Sooner's debt ratio?

8. The Jamesway Printing Corporation has current assets of $3.0 million. Of this total, $1.0 million is inventory, $0.5 million is cash, $1.0 million is accounts receivable, and the balance is marketable securities. Jamesway has $1.5 million in current liabilities.
   a. What are the current and the quick ratios for Jamesway?
   b. If Jamesway takes $0.25 million in cash and pays off $0.25 million of current liabilities, what happens to its current and quick ratios? What happens to its real liquidity?
   c. If Jamesway sells $0.5 million of its accounts receivable to a bank and uses the proceeds to pay off short-term debt obligations, what happens to its current and quick ratios?
   d. If Jamesway sells $1.0 million in new stock and places the proceeds in marketable securities, what happens to its current and quick ratios?
   e. What do these examples illustrate about the current and quick ratios?

9. Gulf Controls, Inc., has a net profit margin of 10 percent and earnings after taxes of $600,000. Its current balance sheet follows:

Current assets	$1,800,000	Current liabilities	$ 600,000
Fixed assets	2,200,000	Long-term debt	1,000,000
Total assets	$4,000,000	Common stock	500,000
		Retained earnings	1,900,000
		Total liabilities and stockholders' equity	$4,000,000

a. Calculate Gulf's return on stockholders' equity.

b. The industry average ratios are as follows:

Net profit margin	6 percent
Total asset turnover	2.5 times
Equity multiplier	1.4 times

Compare Gulf Controls with the average firm in the industry. What is the source of the major differences between the Gulf and the industry average ratios?

10. Using the following data for Jackson Products Company, answer Parts a through g:

e✗cel

Jackson Products Company's Balance Sheet
December 31, 19X1

Cash	$ 240,000	Accounts payable	$ 380,000
Accounts receivable	320,000	Notes payable (9%)	420,000
Inventory	1,040,000	Other current liabilities	50,000
Total current assets	$1,600,000	Total current liabilities	$ 850,000
Net plant and equipment	800,000	Long-term debt (10%)	800,000
Total assets	$2,400,000	Stockholders' equity	750,000
		Total liabilities and	
		stockholders' equity	$2,400,000

Income Statement
for the Year Ended December 31, 19X1

Net sales (all on credit)		$3,000,000
Cost of sales		1,800,000
Gross profit		$1,200,000
Selling, general, and administrative expenses		860,000
Earnings before interest and taxes		$ 340,000
Interest:		
Notes	$37,800	
Long-term debt	80,000	
Total interest charges		117,800
Earnings before taxes		$ 222,200
Federal income tax (40%)		88,880
Earnings after taxes		$ 133,320

Industry Averages

Current ratio	2.5 times ✓
Quick ratio	1.1 times ✓
Average collection period (365-day year)	35 days
Inventory turnover ratio	2.4 times
Total asset turnover ratio	1.4 times
Times interest earned ratio	3.5 times
Net profit margin ratio	4.0 percent
Return on investment ratio	5.6 percent
Total assets/stockholders' equity (equity multiplier) ratio	3.0 times
Return on stockholders' equity ratio	16.8 percent
P/E ratio	9.0 times

Net working capital
2400 000 − 850,000 = 1,550,000

a. Evaluate the liquidity position of Jackson relative to that of the average firm in the industry. Consider the current ratio, the quick ratio, and the net working capital (current assets minus current liabilities) for Jackson. What problems, if any, are suggested by this analysis?

b. Evaluate Jackson's performance by looking at key asset management ratios. Are any problems apparent from this analysis?

c. Evaluate the financial risk of Jackson by examining its times interest earned ratio and its equity multiplier ratio relative to the same industry average ratios.

d. Evaluate the profitability of Jackson relative to that of the average firm in its industry.

e. Give an overall evaluation of the performance of Jackson relative to other firms in its industry.

f. Perform a DuPont analysis for Jackson. What areas appear to have the greatest need for improvement?

g. Jackson's current P/E ratio is 7 times. What factor(s) are most likely to account for this ratio relative to the higher industry average ratio?

11. Given the following data for Profiteers, Inc., and the corresponding industry averages, perform a trend analysis of the return on investment and the return on stockholders' equity. Plot the data and discuss any trends that are apparent. Also, discuss the underlying causes of these trends.

		Years			
	19X1	*19X2*	*19X3*	*19X4*	*19X5*
Profiteers, Inc.					
Net profit margin	14%	12%	11%	9%	10%
Asset turnover	1.26×	1.22×	1.20×	1.19×	1.21×
Equity multiplier	1.34×	1.40×	1.61×	1.65×	1.63×

		Years			
	19X1	*19X2*	*19X3*	*19X4*	*19X5*
Industry Averages					
Net profit margin	12%	11%	11%	10%	10%
Asset turnover	1.25×	1.27×	1.30×	1.31×	1.34×
Equity multiplier	1.42×	1.45×	1.47×	1.51×	1.53×

12. If a company sells additional common stock and uses the proceeds to increase its inventory level and to increase its cash balances, what is the near-term (immediate) impact (increase, decrease, no change) of this transaction on the following ratios?

a. Current ratio.

b. Return on stockholders' equity.

c. Quick ratio.

d. Debt to total assets.

e. Total asset turnover.

13. Lane Enterprises has sales of $20 million and earnings after taxes of $1.6 million. The firm has a total asset turnover of 2.5 times. The industry average is 2.0 times. The equity accounts for Lane are as follows:

Common stock at par	$ 600,000
Contributed capital in excess of par	2,400,000
Retained earnings	3,400,000

The following ratios represent averages for Lane's industry:

Net profit margin	6%
Total asset turnover	2 times
Equity multiplier	2.08 times

a. Use the DuPont analysis to calculate Lane's return on equity.

b. Compare Lane's performance to the industry average.

14. Keystone Resources has a net profit margin of 8 percent and earnings after taxes of $2 million. Its current balance sheet is as follows:

Current assets	$ 6,000,000	Current liabilities	$ 3,500,000
Fixed assets	10,000,000	Long-term debt	5,500,000
Total assets	$16,000,000	Common stock	2,000,000
		Retained earnings	5,000,000
		Total liabilities and stockholders' equity	$16,000,000

a. Calculate Keystone's return on stockholders' equity.

b. Industry average ratios are

Net profit margin	10%
Total asset turnover	2.0 times
Equity multiplier	1.5 times

What does a comparison of Keystone to these averages indicate about the firm's strengths and weaknesses?

c. Keystone has inventories of $3.2 million. Compute the firm's quick ratio.

15. Palmer Chocolates, a maker of chocolates that specializes in Easter candy, had the following inventories over the past year:

Month	Inventory Amount
January	$25,000,000
February	60,000,000
March	90,000,000
April	30,000,000
May	20,000,000
June	22,000,000
July	25,000,000
August	38,000,000
September	50,000,000
October	60,000,000
November	70,000,000
December	30,000,000

Palmer had sales of $290 million over the past year. Cost of sales constituted 50 percent of sales. Calculate Palmer's inventory turnover using beginning of year inventory, end of year inventory, and a monthly average inventory. Which method do you feel is most appropriate? Why?

16. The stock of Jenkins Corporation, a major steel producer, currently is selling for $50 per share. The book value per share is $125. In contrast, the price per share of Dataquest's stock is $40, compared to a book value per share of $10. Dataquest, a leading software developer, has a copyright on the best-selling database management program. Why do these two firms have such dramatically different market-to-book ratios?

17. Using one (or more) of the sources of comparative financial data mentioned in this chapter, evaluate the performance of Bethlehem Steel Corporation versus the performance of Carpenter Technology. In particular, evaluate the total asset turnover, the fixed asset turnover, the net profit margin, the return on investment, and the return on stockholders' equity for each firm. Then do the following:

a. Determine which firm seems to be performing better. What criterion did you use in reaching this conclusion?

b. Point out some problems Bethlehem Steel seems to have had in the past several years.

c. Using the latest five years of data, perform a financial trend analysis on Bethlehem Steel Corporation. Consider such ratios as the current, quick, inventory turnover, average collection period, total asset turnover, net profit margin, return on investment, and return on stockholders' equity ratios. What can you say about the trend in the financial health of Bethlehem Steel?

18. Hoffman Paper Company, a profitable distributor of stationary and office supplies, has an agreement with its banks that allows Hoffman to borrow money on a short-term basis to finance its inventories and accounts receivable. The agreement states that Hoffman must maintain a current ratio of 1.5, or higher, *and* a debt ratio of 50 percent or lower. Given the following balance sheet, determine how much additional money Hoffman could borrow at this time to invest in inventory and accounts receivable without violating the terms of its borrowing agreement.

Cash	$ 50,000	Current liabilities	$ 200,000
Accounts receivable	150,000	Long-term debt	300,000
Inventory	250,000	Stockholders' equity	630,000
Fixed assets (net)	680,000	Total liabilities and	
Total assets	$1,130,000	stockholders' equity	$1,130,000

19. Sun Minerals, Inc., is considering issuing additional long-term debt to finance an expansion. At the present time, the company has $50 million in 10 percent debt outstanding. Its after-tax net income is $12 million, and the company is in the 40 percent tax bracket. The company is required by the debt holders to maintain its times interest earned ratio at 3.5 or greater.
    a. What is the present coverage (times interest earned) ratio?
    b. How much additional 10 percent debt can the company issue now and maintain its times interest earned ratio at 3.5? (Assume for this calculation that earnings before interest and taxes remain at their present level.)
    c. If the interest rate on additional debt is 12 percent, how much unused "debt capacity" does the company have?
20. The balance sheet and income statement of Eastland Products, Inc. are as follows:

Balance Sheet, December 31, 19X1 (in millions of dollars)

Current assets	$ 40	Current liabilities	$ 30
Fixed assets, net	110	Long-term debt	40
		Common stock ($1 par)	5
		Contributed capital in excess of par value	20
		Retained earnings	55
Total assets	$150	Total liabilities and equity	$150

Income Statement for Year Ended December 31, 19X1
(in millions of dollars)

Sales	$120
Cost of sales	80
EBIT	$ 40
Interest	5
EBT	$ 35
Taxes (40%)	14
Net income (EAT)	$ 21

Additional Information

Total dividends	$10 million
Market price of common stock	$32 a share
Number of common shares issued	5 million

Using these data, determine the following:
a. Earnings per share.
b. Price-to-earnings ratio.
c. Book value per share.
d. Market-to-book ratio.
e. How much of the retained earnings total was added during 19X1?
f. Show Eastland's new balance sheet after the company sells 1 million new common shares in early 19X2 to net $30 a share. Part of the proceeds, $10 million, is used to reduce current liabilities, and the remainder is temporarily deposited in the company's bank account. Later, this remaining amount (along with additional long-term debt financing) will be invested in new manufacturing facilities.

21. Jefferson Foods Corporation has the following balance sheet and income statement:

Balance Sheet

Cash	$ 50,000	Current liabilities	$ 200,000
Marketable securities	200,000	Long-term debt	400,000
Other current assets	300,000	Stockholders' equity	800,000
Fixed assets	850,000	Total liabilities and	
Total assets	$1,400,000	stockholders' equity	$1,400,000

Income Statement

Sales and other revenues	$3,000,000
Cost of sales	2,600,000
EBIT	$ 400,000
Interest	50,000
EBT	$ 350,000
Taxes (40%)	140,000
Net income (EAT)	$ 210,000

Additional Information

Shares outstanding	80,000
Market price per share	$20
Interest rate earned on marketable securities	6 percent

a. Calculate Jefferson's present return on stockholders' equity, earnings per share, and debt ratio.

b. Suppose Jefferson's management decides that the company's stock represents a good investment at its present price level. Recalculate the same ratios you calculated in Part a, assuming the company uses a portion of its marketable securities to repurchase 8,000 shares at $20 a share. The repurchased shares will be held as treasury stock.

c. Explain why the ratio values you calculated in Part a changed after the share repurchase.

22. Thompson Electronics, Inc., is presently 100 percent equity financed and has assets of $100 million. Thompson's present net income is $9 million, and the company's marginal and average tax rates are 40 percent. In addition, Thompson has 4 million common shares outstanding, and its current annual dividend is $0.75 a share. At the present time, the company is able to borrow 10 percent *perpetual* debt; that is, debt that has no maturity date. What amount of 10 percent perpetual debt would Thompson have to borrow in order to increase its return on stockholders' equity to 15 percent?

23. Fill in the balance sheet for the Jamestown Company presented below based on the following data (assume a 365-day year):

Sales = $3,650,000
Total asset turnover = 4x
Current ratio = 3:1
Quick ratio = 2:1
Current liabilities to net worth = 30%
Average collection period = 20 days
Total debt to total assets = 0.4

Balance Sheet

Cash	_____	Accounts payable	_____
Accounts receivable	_____	Total current liabilities	_____
Inventory	_____	Long-term debt	_____
Total current assets	_____	Stockholders' equity	_____
Fixed assets	_____		
Total assets	_____	Total liabilities and equity	_____

24. Determine the cost of sales for the Greensburg Company, which has the following financial ratios and data:

$$\text{Current ratio} = 3.0$$
$$\text{Quick ratio} = 2.1$$
$$\text{Current liabilities} = \$500,000$$
$$\text{Inventory turnover} = 6 \text{ times}$$

25. The Southwick Company has the following balance sheet ($000):

Assets		Liabilities & Stockholders' Equity	
Cash	$ 500	Accounts payable	$ 1,750
Marketable securities	750	Notes payable	1,250
Accounts receivable	2,000	Total current liabilities	$ 3,000
Inventory	2,500	Long-term debt	1,750
Total current assets	$ 5,750	Total liabilities	$ 4,750
Plant and equipment (net)	5,000	Common stock ($1 par)	1,000
Total assets	$10,750	Contributed capital in excess of par	2,000
		Retained earnings	3,000
		Total stockholders' equity	$ 6,000
		Total liabilities and stockholders' equity	$ 10,750

Financial Ratios	
Current ratio	1.92
Quick ratio	1.08
Debt-to-equity ratio	0.79

Evaluate the impact of each of the following (independent) financial decisions on Southwick's current, quick, and debt-to-equity ratios:

a. The firm reduces its inventories by $500,000 through more efficient inventory management procedures and invests the proceeds in marketable securities.

b. The firm decides to purchase 20 new delivery trucks for a total of $500,000 and pays for them by selling marketable securities.

c. The firm borrows $500,000 from its bank through a short-term loan (seasonal financing) and invests the proceeds in inventory.

d. Southwick borrows $2,000,000 from its bank through a 5-year loan (interest due annually, principal due at maturity) and uses the proceeds to expand its plant.

e. The firm sells $2,000,000 (net) in common stock and uses the proceeds to expand its plant.

26. Last year, Blue Lake Mines, Inc., had earnings after tax of $650,000. Included in its expenses were depreciation of $400,000 and deferred taxes of $100,000. The company also purchased new capital equipment for $300,000 last year. Calculate Blue Lake's after-tax cash flow for last year.

27. Refer to the Summit Furniture Company example (Table 3-9). Recalculate the cash and cash equivalents at the end of 19X1 assuming that (1) the company had 19X1 capital expenditures of $22,000; (2) it paid dividends of $800; and (3) it did not issue any common stock. Assume that Summit's other cash flows are the same as those shown in Table 3-9.

28. Prepare a statement of cash flows (using the indirect method) for the Midland Manufacturing Corporation for the year ending December 19X2, based on the following comparative balance sheets.

Midland Manufacturing Corporation
*Comparative Balance Sheets (in millions of dollars)**

	DECEMBER 31, 19X1	DECEMBER 31, 19X2
ASSETS		
Current assets:		
Cash	$ 4.9	$ 0.8
Accounts receivable, net	7.2	7.5
Inventories	13.8	14.5
Total current assets	$25.9	$ 22.8
Property and equipment	$80.7	$115.0
Less Accumulated depreciation	16.3	25.8
Net property and equipment	$64.4	$ 89.2
Total assets	$90.3	$112.0
LIABILITIES AND STOCKHOLDERS' EQUITY		
Current liabilities:		
Accounts payable	$ 8.0	$ 9.5
Other current liabilities	6.0	8.2
Total current liabilities	$14.0	$ 17.7
Long-term debt	18.8	31.8
Deferred federal income taxes	$ 1.2	$ 1.4
Stockholders' equity:		
Common stock	$ 3.0	$ 3.0
Additional paid-in capital	29.0	29.0
Retained earnings	24.3	29.1
Total stockholders' equity	$56.3	$ 61.1
Total liabilities and stockholders' equity	$90.3	$112.0

*Net income for the year ended December 31, 19X2 totaled $8.3 million; dividends paid during the same period totaled $3.5 million; $2.0 million of long-term debt was retired in 19X2; and fixed assets were sold during 19X2 for $1.0 million.

29. Canon Manufacturing last year reported earnings after taxes of $1.2 million for financial reporting purposes but only $0.6 million for tax purposes. Depreciation expense, for financial reporting purposes, was $1.0 million. Canon's marginal tax rate is 40 percent.
   a. Calculate Canon's depreciation expense last year for tax purposes, assuming that depreciation is the only difference between Canon's financial statements for financial reporting and tax purposes.
   b. Compute Canon's after-tax cash flow for the year.

30. Armbrust Corporation is the maker of fine fitness equipment. Armbrust's bank has been pressuring the firm to improve its liquidity. Which of the following actions proposed by the CFO do you believe will actually achieve this objective? Why or why not?
   a. Sell new equity and use the proceeds to purchase a new plant site.
   b. Use cash and marketable securities to pay off short-term bank borrowings and accounts payable.
   c. Borrow long-term and use the proceeds to pay off short-term debt.
   d. Sell surplus fixed assets and invest the proceeds in marketable securities.

31. Visit the Stock Center at the Thomson Investors Network site and look (under "Company Reports") at the financial statements and ratios of a Fortune 500 company of your choice. Then look at the consensus buy/sell recommendation by major analysts for that particular company. (The recommendation follows the ratios.) Using the ratios provided, justify the recommendation.
   http://www.thomsoninvest.net

   http://

32. Use the Interactive Tool Box at the following Web site to perform a complete ratio analysis of a company, using one of the hypothetical companies used in this chapter.
   www.edgeonline.com

   http://

■ SOLUTIONS TO SELF-TEST PROBLEMS

ST1. a. Current ratio $= \dfrac{\text{Current assets}}{\text{Current liabilities}}$

$$= \frac{\$52,000}{\$25,000}$$

$$= 2.08$$

b. Quick ratio $= \dfrac{\text{Current assets} - \text{Inventories}}{\text{Current liabilities}}$

$$= \frac{\$52,000 - \$33,000}{\$25,000}$$

$$= 0.76$$

ST2. a. Average collection period $= \dfrac{\text{Accounts receivable}}{\text{Annual credit sales}/365}$

$$= \frac{\$15,000}{\$130,000/365}$$

$$= 42.1 \text{ days}$$

b. Inventory turnover $= \dfrac{\text{Cost of sales}}{\text{Average inventory}}$

$$= \frac{\$103,000}{\$33,000}$$

$$= 3.12$$

c. Fixed asset turnover $= \dfrac{\text{Sales}}{\text{Net fixed assets}}$

$$= \frac{\$130,000}{\$35,000}$$

$$= 3.71$$

d. Total asset turnover $= \dfrac{\text{Sales}}{\text{Total assets}}$

$$= \frac{\$130,000}{\$87,000}$$

$$= 1.49$$

ST3. a. Debt ratio $= \dfrac{\text{Total debt}}{\text{Total assets}}$

$$= \frac{\$47,000}{\$87,000}$$

$$= 0.54$$

b. Debt-to-equity ratio $= \dfrac{\text{Total debt}}{\text{Total equity}}$

$$= \frac{\$47,000}{\$40,000}$$

$$= 1.18$$

c. Times interest earned $= \dfrac{\text{Earnings before interest and taxes (EBIT)}}{\text{Interest charges}}$

$$= \frac{\$11,000}{\$3,000}$$

$$= 3.67$$

d. Fixed charge covered $= \dfrac{\text{EBIT} + \text{lease payments}}{\substack{\text{Interest} + \text{lease payments} + \text{preferred} \\ \text{dividends before tax} + \text{before-tax} \\ \text{sinking fund}}}$

$$= \frac{\$11,000 + \$200}{\$3,000 + \$200}$$

$$= 3.50$$

ST4. a. Gross profit margin $= \dfrac{\text{Sales} - \text{Cost of sales}}{\text{Sales}}$

$$= \frac{\$130,000 - \$103,000}{\$130,000}$$

$$= 20.8\%$$

b. Net profit margin $= \dfrac{\text{Earnings after taxes (EAT)}}{\text{Sales}}$

$$= \frac{\$5,000}{\$130,000}$$

$$= 3.85\%$$

c. Return on investment $= \dfrac{\text{Earnings after taxes (EAT)}}{\text{Total assets}}$

$$= \frac{\$5,000}{\$87,000}$$

$$= 5.75\%$$

d. Return on stockholders' equity $= \dfrac{\text{Earnings after taxes (EAT)}}{\text{Stockholders' equity}}$

$$= \frac{\$5,000}{\$40,000}$$

$$= 12.5\%$$

ST5. a. Price-to-earnings ratio $= \dfrac{\text{Market price per share}}{\text{Current earnings per share}}$

$$= \frac{\$9.50}{\$5,000/5,000}$$

$$= 9.50$$

b. Market-to-book ratio $= \dfrac{\text{Market price per share}}{\text{Book value per share}}$

$$= \frac{\$9.50}{\$8.00}$$

$$= 1.19$$

ST6. Return on stockholders' equity = Net profit margin × Total asset turnover × Equity multiplier

$$= \frac{\$5,000}{\$130,000} \times \frac{\$130,000}{\$87,000} \times \frac{\$87,000}{\$40,000} = 12.5\%$$

ST7. a. Depreciation expense = Increase in accumulated depreciation

$$= \$575 - 500 = \$75$$

b.

Sales	$500
Operating expenses	– 125
Depreciation	– 75
EBT	$300
Taxes	– 120
EAT	$180

c. ATCF = EAT + Depreciation
= $180 + $75
= $255

d. Increase in net fixed assets (NFA):

$100 Increase in gross fixed assets (GFA)
– 75 Increase in accumulated depreciation
$ 25 Increase in net fixed assets

EAT less increase in NFA = ATCF less increase in GFA

$$\$180 - \$25 = \$255 - \$100$$
$$\$155 = \$155$$

■ GLOSSARY

After-tax Cash Flow (ATCF) Earnings after tax plus non-cash charges, such as depreciation and deferred taxes.

Asset Management Ratios Financial ratios that indicate how efficiently a firm is utilizing its assets to generate sales.

Balance Sheet A financial statement that lists a firm's assets, liabilities, and stockholders' equity at a point in time.

Cash Flow The actual amount of cash collected and paid out by a firm.

Common-Size Balance Sheet A balance sheet in which a firm's assets and liabilities are expressed as a percentage of total assets, rather than as dollar amounts.

Common-Size Income Statement An income statement in which a firm's income and expense items are expressed as a percentage of net sales, rather than as dollar amounts.

Comparative Analysis An examination of a firm's performance based on one or more financial ratios, which are compared with the financial ratios of competitive firms or with an industry standard.

Discriminant Analysis A statistical technique designed to classify observations (firms) into two or more predetermined groups based on certain characteristics (such as financial ratios) of the observations.

EAT The acronym for *earnings after taxes*.

EBIT The acronym for *earnings before interest and taxes* (also called *operating earnings*).

EPS The acronym for *earnings per share*.

EVA The acronym for *economic value added*. This measure of operating performance is equal to the difference between operating profits after tax and the cost of capital and indicates a firm's success in creating MVA.

FIFO The acronym for the *first-in, first-out* inventory valuation method. The method assumes that firm uses the oldest items in the inventory first. Thus, they are *priced out* of the inventory based on the oldest inventory acquisition costs rather than the most recent.

Financial Analysis The utilization of a group of analytical techniques, including financial ratio analysis, to determine the strengths, weaknesses, and direction of a company's performance.

Financial Leverage Management Ratios Financial ratios that measure the degree to which a firm is financing its assets with fixed-charge sources of funds such as debt, preferred stock, or leases.

Financial Ratio A statistical yardstick that relates two numbers generally taken from a firm's income statement, balance sheet, or both at a specific point in time.

Generally Accepted Accounting Principles (GAAP) A broad set of accounting rules followed in preparing financial statements.

Income Statement A financial statement that indicates how a firm performed during a period of time.

LIFO The acronym for the *last-in, first-out* inventory valuation method. The method assumes that a firm uses the most recently acquired items in the inventory first. Thus, they are *priced out* of

the inventory based on the most recent inventory acquisition costs rather than the oldest.

Liquidity Ratios Financial ratios that indicate a firm's ability to meet short-term financial obligations.

Market-Based Ratios Financial ratios that measure the market's (investors') assessment of the risk and performance of a firm.

MVA The acronym for *market value added.* The difference between the market value of a firm's debt and equity and the capital that has been invested in the firm.

Profitability Ratios Financial ratios that measure the total effectiveness of a company's management in generating profits.

Statement of Cash Flows A financial statement showing the effects of a firm's operating, investing, and financing activities on its cash balance.

Stockholders' Equity The total of a firm's common stock at par, contributed capital in excess of par, and retained earnings accounts from the balance sheet. It sometimes is called the *book value* of the firm, *owners' equity, shareholders' equity,* or *net worth.*

Trend Analysis An examination of a firm's performance over time. It is frequently based on one or more financial ratios.

DETERMINANTS OF VALUATION

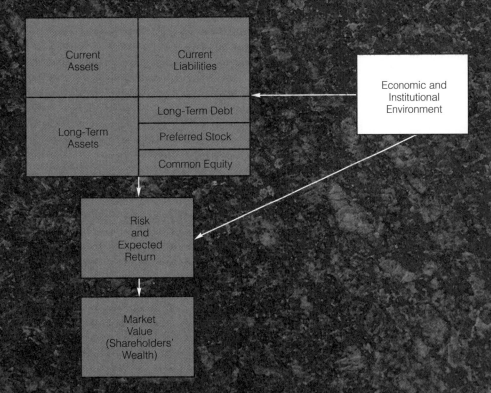

Current Assets

Current Liabilities

Long-Term Assets

Long-Term Debt

Preferred Stock

Common Equity

Economic and Institutional Environment

Risk and Expected Return

Market Value (Shareholders' Wealth)

The primary objective of financial management is to maximize the value of the stock of the firm's shareholders. This part discusses the valuation process in detail. Chapter 4 deals with the time value of money, which is essential for any serious analysis of important financial decisions that have an impact on the firm over a number of years. Chapter 5 explores the determinants of risk and relates risk to the valuation process.

Chapters 6 and 7 build valuation models for a firm's securities. Chapter 6 focuses on the valuation of fixed-income securities—namely, bonds and preferred stock. Chapter 7 deals with the valuation of common stock. These chapters are important because valuation is the dominant theme carried throughout the text and related to all financial decisions. Chapter 7 also discusses the offering process for securities.

THE TIME VALUE OF MONEY

4

1. The concept of interest:
   a. Simple interest is paid on the principal sum only.
   b. Compound interest is paid on both the initial principal amount and on any interest earned but not withdrawn during earlier periods.
2. Future (compound) value calculations determine the value at some point in time in the future of X dollars invested today, earning some compound rate of interest, i, per period.
3. Present value calculations determine the value today (present value) of some amount to be received in the future.
4. An annuity is a series of equal periodic payments.
   a. Ordinary annuity payments are made at the end of each period.
   b. Annuity due payments are made at the beginning of each period.

5. Future value of an annuity calculations determine the future value of an annuity stream of cash flows.
6. Present value of an annuity calculations determine the present value of an annuity stream of cash flows.
7. Other important topics include
   a. Compounding frequency.
   b. Determining the present value of perpetuities.
   c. Determining the present value of uneven cash flow streams.
   d. Determining the present value of deferred annuities.

HOW MUCH IS $1 MILLION WORTH?

A friend of yours recently accepted a marketing position with a major league baseball team in your area. The team has signed several new players and is hoping next season will be a good one, both on the field and at the ticket window. In order to boost attendance, the team is considering rewarding a lucky fan if annual attendance reaches 2,000,000 during the season.

Here are the details of what the team is considering. On the day the team's attendance goes over 2,000,000, a drawing among the fans present that day will be held to determine a winner. The winner will receive $1.0 million, plus a lifetime supply of peanuts and Cracker Jacks. However, the team does not feel it can afford to pay out all of the $1.0 million at once. As a result, the team has asked your friend to determine the cost at the time of the drawing of the following proposed payout schedules to the lucky fan:

1. *$50,000 per year for 20 years, with the first payment occurring the day of the drawing.*
2. *$50,000 per year for 20 years, with the first payment occurring 10 years after the day of the drawing.*
3. *$50,000 per year for 20 years, with the*

first payment occurring 20 years after the day of the drawing.

The team is planning to pay a lump sum of money to an insurance company at the time of the drawing for making the series of annual payments. The insurance company has suggested that the team use an annual discount rate of 8 percent in its calculations.

The team's vice-president of marketing has also asked your friend to determine the present cost of beginning the $50,000 payments 20 years from now, but continuing them *forever* rather than stopping after 20 years. (The vice-president realizes that this total payout amounts to more than $1.0 million.)

Your friend, who didn't do too well in finance courses, has just telephoned and asked if you want some free baseball tickets and if you have access to a fax machine.

This type of problem illustrates the value of having a working knowledge of the time value of money. Later in the chapter we shall provide the solutions to your friend's assignment.

INTRODUCTION

Understanding the time value of money is crucial to effective financial management. In fact, anyone who is involved with money should have some comprehension of the time value of money. Consider the following:

- A banker who makes loans and other investments.
- A financial officer whose job includes the consideration of various alternative sources of funds in terms of their cost.
- A corporate planner who must choose among various alternative investment projects.
- A securities analyst who evaluates the securities that a firm sells to investors.
- An individual who is confronted with a host of daily financial problems ranging from personal credit account management to deciding whether to make certain purchases for the home.

Each of these individuals makes frequent use of the time value of money. Many people fear that a working knowledge of the time value of money concept might be too difficult to master. However, the availability of interest tables and financial calculators makes the subject readily accessible.

Although an understanding of the time value of money is useful in and of itself, it is also a necessary prelude to the following topics:

- Valuation of securities and other assets.
- Capital budgeting (the analysis of investment projects).
- The cost of capital.
- Working capital (short-term asset and liability) management.
- Lease analysis.

This chapter introduces the concepts and skills necessary to understand the time value of money and its applications. The analysis in this chapter assumes that the student will use either a financial calculator or the interest tables (Tables I through IV) at the end of the book to solve problems. Calculator solutions are presented for many of the examples in this chapter. However, we are primarily interested in having students learn the principles of time value of money rather than having them become proficient in the use of financial calculators or interest tables.

A Word About Notation

A brief discussion of financial notation is in order before we begin our time value of money discussion. In finance, as a general rule, lowercase letters are used to denote percentage rates and lengths of time, whereas capital letters are used to denote money, or dollar amounts. For example, we use i to denote the interest rate, n to denote the number of periods, PMT to denote cash payments, PV to denote the present value dollar amount, and FV to denote the future value dollar amount. One important exception in this text is that we use T to denote the tax rate instead of t. Lowercase t denotes time. Our use of i to denote the interest rate is similar to the notation used on most financial calculators. However, later in the text, for example in Chapter 6, when the interest rate becomes a specific required rate of return, we use k to denote required return, as is the custom used by many financial analysts.

CFM Excel Templates

Another feature of *Contemporary Financial Management,* seventh edition, is the availability of a preprogrammed disk containing templates to solve a wide range of complex financial management problems, including the loan amortization problems encountered in this chapter. This disk, the CFM Excel Disk, is designed to be used in conjunction with the Excel electronic spreadsheet program. The CFM Excel Disk requires *no prior knowledge of Excel* and is menu driven. A brief overview of each template is provided in Appendix A at the end of the text. Complete documentation accompanies the disk. As part of the problem section of selected chapters, we have included problems that can be solved using the financial management templates. These problems are identified by a small computer diskette logo printed next to the problem number. The computer template itself is available from your instructor or may have been packaged with your text if it was ordered that way.

 ### INTEREST

Money can be thought of as having a time value. In other words, an amount of money received today is worth more than the same dollar amount would be if it were received a year from now.[1] The primary reason that a dollar today is worth more than a dollar to be received sometime in the future is that the current dollar can be invested to earn a rate of return. (This holds true even if risk and inflation are not considerations.) Suppose, for example, that you had $100 and decided to put it into a savings account for a year. By doing this, you temporarily would give up, or forgo, spending the $100 however you wished, or you might forgo the return that the $100 might earn from some alternative investment, such as U.S. Treasury bonds. Or you might forgo paying an additional $100 on your mortgage. Similarly, a bank that loans money to a firm forgoes the opportunity to earn a return on some alternative investment.

Interest is the return earned by or the amount paid to someone who has forgone current consumption or alternative investment opportunities and "rented" money in a creditor relationship.[2] The **principal** is the amount of money borrowed or invested. The term of a loan is the length of time or number of time periods during which the borrower can use the principal. The **rate of interest** is the percentage on the principal that the borrower pays the lender per time period as compensation for forgoing other investment or consumption opportunities.

 ### SIMPLE INTEREST

Simple interest is the interest paid (in the case of borrowed money) or earned (in the case of invested money) on the principal only. The amount of simple interest is equal to the product of the principal times the rate per time period times the number of time periods:

$$I = PV_0 \times i \times n \tag{4.1}$$

---

[1]The terms *amount of money, cash flow,* and *payment* are used interchangeably throughout the chapter.
[2]Although other forms of returns are dealt with throughout the text, this discussion is limited to borrowing-lending situations.

where $I =$ the simple interest in dollars; $PV_0 =$ the principal amount at time 0, or the present value; $i =$ the interest rate per time period; and $n =$ the number of time periods. The following problems illustrate the use of Equation 4.1.

1. *What is the simple interest on $100 at 10 percent per annum for 6 months?* Substituting $100 for PV_0, 10 percent (0.10) for i, and $\frac{6}{12}$ (0.5) for n yields the following:

$$I = \$100 \times 0.10 \times 0.5$$

$$= \$5$$

2. *If Isaiah Williams bought a house and borrowed $30,000 at a 10 percent annual interest rate, what would be his first month's interest payment?* Substituting $30,000 for PV_0, 10 percent (0.10) for i, and $\frac{1}{12}$ for n yields the following:

$$I = \$30,000 \times 0.10 \times \tfrac{1}{12}$$

$$= \$250$$

3. *Mary Schiller receives $30 every 3 months from a bank account that pays a 6 percent annual interest rate. How much is invested in the account?* Because PV_0 is the unknown in this example, Equation 4.1 is rearranged:

$$PV_0 = \frac{I}{i \times n} \qquad (4.2)$$

Substituting $30 for I, 0.06 for i, and $\frac{1}{4}$ (0.25) for n yields the following:

$$PV_0 = \frac{\$30}{0.06 \times 0.25}$$

$$= \$2,000$$

It also is useful to be able to calculate the amount of funds a person can expect to receive at some point in the future. In financial mathematics, the *terminal,* or *future,* value of an investment is called FV_n and denotes the principal plus interest accumulated at the end of n years. It is written as follows:

$$FV_n = PV_0 + I \qquad (4.3)$$

4. *Raymond Gomez borrows $1,000 for 9 months at a rate of 8 percent per annum. How much will he have to repay at the end of the 9-month period?* Combining Equations 4.1 and 4.3 to solve for FV_n results in the following new equation:

$$FV_n = PV_0 + (PV_0 \times i \times n)$$

or

$$FV_n = PV_0 [1 + (i \times n)] \qquad (4.4)$$

Substituting $1,000 for PV_0, 0.08 for i, and $\frac{3}{4}$ (9 months $= \frac{3}{4}$ of 1 year) for n yields the following:

$$FV_{3/4} = \$1,000[1 + (0.08 \times \tfrac{3}{4})]$$

$$= \$1,000(1 + 0.06)$$

$$= \$1,060$$

This problem can be illustrated using the following time line:

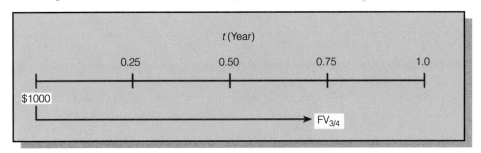

5. *Marie Como agrees to invest $1,000 in a venture that promises to pay 10 percent simple interest each year for 2 years. How much money will she have at the end of the second year?* Using Equation 4.4 and assuming two 10 percent simple interest payments, the future value of Marie's investment at the end of 2 years is computed as follows:

$$FV_2 = PV_0 + (PV_0 \times i \times 2)$$
$$= \$1,000 + (\$1,000 \times 0.10 \times 2)$$
$$= \$1,000 + \$200$$
$$= \$1,200$$

This problem can be illustrated using the following time line:

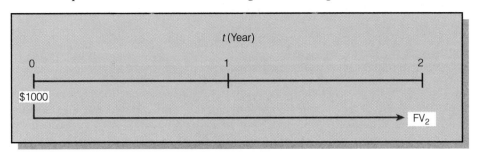

In general, in the case of *simple interest,* the future, or terminal, value (FV_n) at the end of n years is given by Equation 4.4.

 COMPOUND INTEREST AND FUTURE VALUE

Compound interest is interest that is paid not only on the principal but also on any interest earned but not withdrawn during earlier periods. For example, if Jerry Jones deposits $1,000 in a savings account paying 6 percent interest compounded annually, the future (compound) value of his account at the end of 1 year (FV_1) is calculated as follows:

$$FV_1 = PV_0(1 + i) \qquad (4.5)$$
$$= \$1,000(1 + 0.06)$$
$$= \$1,060$$

Is the time value of money an important concept in the world of business? Try typing "present value" (a generic term) into a major search engine, such as Alta Vista, and watch how many millions of hits you obtain. Then take a look at the different kinds of hits (calculators, tutorials, graphs, advisers/consultants, etc.). You'll probably agree that present value is indeed a cornerstone of business theory and practice.
http://www.altavista.com

This problem can be illustrated using the following time line:

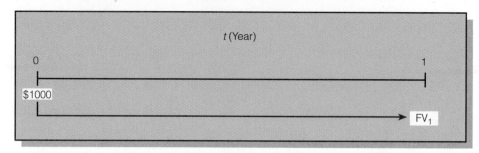

If Jones leaves the $1,000 *plus* the accumulated interest in the account for another year, its worth at the end of the second year is calculated as follows:

$$FV_2 = FV_1(1 + i) \tag{4.6}$$

$$= \$1,060(1 + 0.06)$$

$$= \$1,123.60$$

This problem can be illustrated using the following time line:

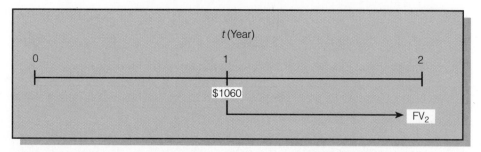

Recall that in the case of compound interest, interest in each period is earned not only on the principal but also on any interest accumulated during previous periods and not withdrawn. As shown in Figure 4-1, if Jones's account paid simple interest instead of compound interest, its value at the end of 2 years would be $1,120 instead of $1,123.60. The $3.60 difference is the interest on the first year's interest, $0.06 \times \$60$.

If Jones makes no withdrawals from the account for another year, it will total the following at the end of the third year:

$$FV_3 = FV_2(1 + i) \tag{4.7}$$

$$= \$1,123.60(1 + 0.06)$$

$$= \$1,191.02$$

This problem can be illustrated using the following time line:

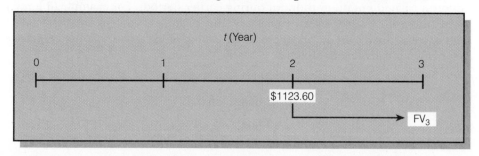

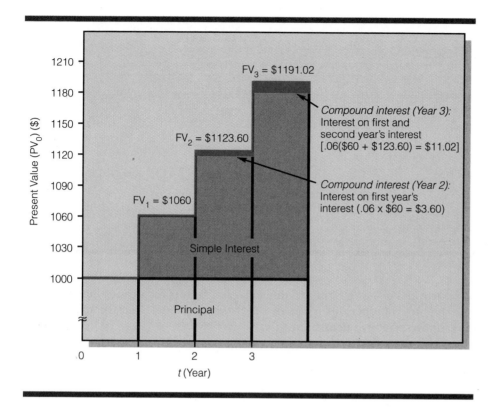

FIGURE 4-1
Simple versus Compound Interest

Figure 4-1 illustrates that if the account paid only simple interest, it would be worth only $1,180 at the end of 3 years. The $11.02 difference (i.e., $1191.02 – $1180) is the interest on the first and second years' interest, $0.06 \times (\$60 + \$123.60)$.

A general formula for computing future values can be developed by combining Equations 4.5, 4.6, and 4.7. Substituting Equation 4.6 into Equation 4.7 yields the following equation:

$$FV_3 = FV_1(1 + i)(1 + i)$$

or

$$FV_3 = FV_1(1 + i)^2 \tag{4.8}$$

Substituting Equation 4.5 into Equation 4.8 yields the following:

$$FV_3 = PV_0(1 + i)(1 + i)^2$$

or

$$FV_3 = PV_0(1 + i)^3 \tag{4.9}$$

This equation can be further generalized to calculate the future value at the end of period n for any payment compounded at interest rate i:

$$FV_n = PV_0(1 + i)^n \tag{4.10}$$

Although Equation 4.10 is useful for solving future value problems involving 1, 2, 3, or even 4 years into the future, it is rather tedious to use this equation for problems involving longer time periods. For example, solving for 20 years into the future would require calculating $(1 + i)^{20}$. *Future value interest factors* (**FVIFs**) commonly are used to simplify such computations. Table I at the end of the

TABLE 4-1
**Future Value Interest Factors
(FVIFs) for $1 at Interest Rate i
for n Periods***

END OF PERIOD(n)	INTEREST RATE (i)				
	1%	*5%*	*6%*	*8%*	*10%*
1	1.010	1.050	1.060	1.080	1.100
2	1.020	1.102	1.124	1.166	1.210
3	1.030	1.158	1.191	1.260	1.331
4	1.041	1.216	1.262	1.360	1.464
5	1.051	1.276	1.338	1.469	1.611
8	1.083	1.477	1.594	1.851	2.144
9	1.094	1.551	1.689	1.999	2.358
10	1.105	1.629	1.791	2.159	2.594
20	1.220	2.653	3.207	4.661	6.728
25	1.282	3.386	4.292	6.848	10.835

*The values in this and similar tables in this text have been rounded off to three places. When large sums of money are involved, more accurate tables or financial calculators should be use.

book provides a listing of future value interest factors for various interest rates covering up to 60 periods (years or other time periods). Because each future value interest factor is defined as

$$\text{FVIF}_{i,n} = (1 + i)^n \tag{4.11}$$

Equation 4.10 may be rewritten as follows:

$$FV_n = PV_0(\text{FVIF}_{i,n}) \tag{4.12}$$

where i = the nominal interest rate per period and n = the number of periods.

To better understand Table I, it is helpful to think of each factor as the result of investing or lending $1 for a given number of periods, n, at interest rate i. The solution for any amount other than $1 is the product of that principal amount times the factor for a $1 principal amount.

A portion of Table I is reproduced as Table 4-1. Table 4-1 can be used to determine the value of $1,000 compounded at 6 percent for 20 years:

$$FV_{20} = PV_0(\text{FVIF}_{0.06,20})$$
$$= \$1,000(3.207)$$
$$= \$3,207$$

CALCULATOR SOLUTION*

The future value amount also can be computed using a financial calculator. For example, the above problem can be solved as follows:

Enter: 20   6   −1,000

| n | i | PV | | PMT | | FV |

Solution: 3,207

Note: When no value appears above a "key box," such as *PMT* in this example, it is not necessary to enter any value to solve the problem.

*Students who are planning to use a financial calculator should become familiar with the keystrokes needed to solve time value of money problems. The manual accompanying your financial calculator and the insert card in this text explain the basic operations required to solve the examples and problems.

The 3.207 figure is arrived at by reading the 6 percent, or 0.06, column down and the 20 row under the "End of Period (n)" heading across to where they meet.

Solving for the Interest Rate

In some compound value problems, the present value (PV_0) and future value (FV_n) are given and the objective is to determine the interest rate (i) that solves Equation 4.10. For example, the future value interest factor for an investment requiring an initial outlay of $1,000 and promising a $1,629 return after 10 years is as follows:

$$FVIF_{i,10} = \frac{FV_{10}}{PV_0}$$

$$= \frac{\$1,629}{\$1,000}$$

$$= 1.629$$

Reading across the 10-year row in Table 4-1, 1.629 is found in the 5 percent column. Thus, the investment yields a 5 percent compound rate of return.

CALCULATOR SOLUTION

The interest rate also can be computed using a financial calculator. For example, the above problem can be solved as follows:

Enter: 10   −1,000   1,629

| n | i | PV | PMT | FV |

Solution: 5.0

Solving for the Number of Compounding Periods

The future value interest factor tables can also be used to determine the number of annual compounding periods (n). For example, to determine how long it would take for $1,000 invested at 8 percent to double, search the 8 percent column to locate a future value interest factor of 2.000. The closest value to this figure is 1.999. Reading to the left of this figure, it can be seen that the original $1,000 would be worth nearly $2,000 in 9 years. This problem can also be solved algebraically:

$$FV_n = PV_0(FVIF_{0.08,n})$$

$$FVIF_{0.08,n} = \frac{FV_n}{PV_0}$$

$$= \frac{\$2,000}{\$1,000}$$

$$= 2.000$$

Referring to Table 4-1, the closest value to FVIF = 2.000 under the 8 percent column is 1.999, which occurs at approximately 9 years.[3]

---

[3]In a shortcut solution to this type of problem known as the "Rule of 72," the number 72 is divided by the interest rate to determine the number of years it would take for a sum of money to double. In this case, 72/8% = 9. The Rule of 72 can also be used to determine the interest rate required for a sum of money to double in a given number of years: 72/9 = 8%. The Rule of 72 does not yield exact figures, but it can be used to calculate good approximations.

FIGURE 4-2
Growth of a $100 Investment at Various Compound Interest Rates

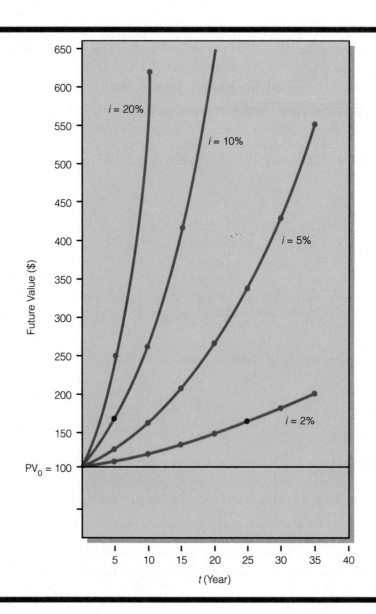

Compounding can also be illustrated graphically. Figure 4-2 shows the effects of time, n, and interest rate, i, on the growth of a $100 investment. As the figure shows, the higher the compound interest rate, the faster the growth rate of the value of the initial principal. The notion that an interest rate may be thought of as a *growth rate* will be useful during later discussions of valuation and cost of capital.

 ## PRESENT VALUE

The compound, or future, value calculations answer the question: What will be the future value of X dollars invested today, compounded at some rate of interest, i? The financial decision maker, however, often is faced with another type of problem: Given some future value, FV_n, what is its equivalent value today? That is, what is its present value, PV_0? The solution requires *present value* calculations, which are used to determine the dollar amount today, PV_0, that is equivalent to some promised *future* dollar amount, FV_n. The equivalence depends upon the rate of interest (return) that can be earned on investments during the time period under consideration.

The relationship between compound value and present value can be shown by rewriting Equation 4.10 to solve for PV_0:

$$FV_n = PV_0(1 + i)^n \qquad (4.10)$$

(handwritten: If no tables or fin. calc.)

or

$$PV_0 = FV_n\left[\frac{1}{(1 + i)^n}\right] \qquad (4.13)$$

where $1/(1 + i)^n$ is the reciprocal of the compound value factor. The process of finding present values frequently is called *discounting*. Equation 4.13 is the basic discounting formula.

To illustrate the use of Equation 4.13, suppose your banker offers to pay you $255.20 in 5 years if you deposit X dollars today at an annual 5 percent interest rate. Whether the investment would be worthwhile depends on how much money you must deposit, or the *present value* of the X dollars. FVIF tables, such as Table 4-1 presented earlier, can be used to solve the problem as follows:

$$PV_0 = FV_5\left(\frac{1}{FVIF_{0.05,5}}\right)$$
$$= \$255.20\left(\frac{1}{1.276}\right)$$
$$= \$200$$

This problem can be illustrated with the following time line:

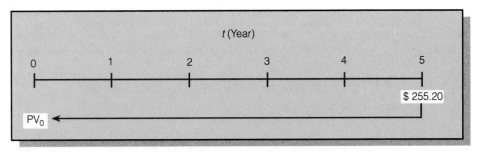

Thus, an investment of $200 today would yield a return of $55.20 in 5 years.

Because determining the reciprocals of the compound value interest factors, $1/(1 + i)^n$, can be a tedious process, *present value interest factors* (PVIFs) commonly are used to simplify such computations. Defining each present value interest factor as

$$PVIF_{i,n} = \frac{1}{(1 + i)^n} \qquad (4.14)$$

Equation 4.13 can be written in the following form:

$$PV_0 = FV_n(PVIF_{i,n}) \qquad (4.15)$$

Table II at the end of the book provides a number of present value interest factors. A portion of Table II is reproduced here as Table 4-2.

For example, Table 4-2 can be used to determine the present value of $1,000 received 20 years in the future discounted at 10 percent:

$$PV_0 = FV_{20} \, (FVIF_{0.10,\,20})$$
$$= \$1,000(0.149)$$
$$= \$149$$

Thus, $149 invested today at 10 percent interest compounded annually for 20 years would be worth $1,000 at the end of the period. Conversely, the promise of $1,000 in 20 years is worth $149 today, given a 10 percent interest rate.

CALCULATOR SOLUTION

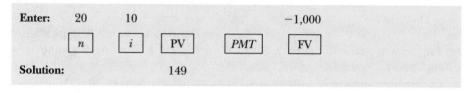

Enter: 20   10   −1,000
        [n] [i] [PV] [PMT] [FV]

Solution: 149

Solving for Interest and Growth Rates

Present value interest factors can also be used to solve for interest rates. For example, suppose you wish to borrow $5,000 today from an associate. The associate is willing to loan you the money if you promise to pay back $6,250 four years from today. The compound interest rate your associate is charging can be determined as follows:

$$PV_0 = FV_4 \, (PVIF_{i,4})$$
$$\$5,000 = \$6,250(PVIF_{i,4})$$
$$(PVIF_{i,4}) = \frac{\$5,000}{\$6,250}$$
$$= 0.800$$

Reading across the 4-year row in Table 4-2, 0.800 is found between the 5 percent (0.823) and 6 percent (0.792) columns. Interpolating between these two values yields

$$i = 5\% + \frac{.823 - .800}{.823 - .792} \, (1\%)$$
$$= 5.74\%$$

TABLE 4-2
Present Value Interest Factors (PVIFs) for $1 at Interest Rate *i* for *n* Periods

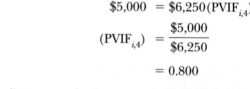

END OF PERIOD (n)	INTEREST RATE (i)					
	1%	5%	6%	8%	10%	13%
1	0.990	0.952	0.943	0.926	0.909	0.885
2	0.980	0.907	0.890	0.857	0.826	0.783
3	0.971	0.864	0.840	0.794	0.751	0.693
4	0.961	0.823	0.792	0.735	0.683	0.613
5	0.951	0.784	0.747	0.681	0.621	0.543
8	0.923	0.677	0.627	0.540	0.467	0.376
10	0.905	0.614	0.558	0.463	0.386	0.295
20	0.820	0.377	0.312	0.215	0.149	0.087
25	0.780	0.295	0.233	0.146	0.092	0.047

Thus, the effective interest rate on the loan is 5.74 percent per year, compounded annually.

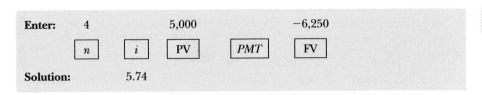

CALCULATOR SOLUTION

Enter:	4		5,000		−6,250
	n	i	PV	PMT	FV
Solution:		5.74			

Another common present value application is the calculation of the compound rate of growth of an earnings or dividend stream. For example, General Motors had earnings of $2.13 per share in 1993. Suppose these earnings grow to $3.92 at the end of 1998. Over this 5-year period, what is the compound annual rate of growth in GM's earnings? The answer to this problem can be obtained by solving for the present value interest factor over the 5-year period as follows:

$$\$2.13 = \$3.92 \ (PVIF_{i,5})$$

$$PVIF_{i,5} = 0.543$$

From Table II or Table 4-2, we find this present value interest factor in the 5-year row under the 13 percent interest, or growth rate, column. Hence the expected compound annual rate of growth in General Motors' earnings per share is 13 percent.

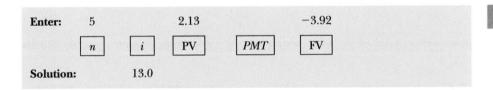

CALCULATOR SOLUTION

Enter:	5		2.13		−3.92
	n	i	PV	PMT	FV
Solution:		13.0			

The discounting process can also be illustrated graphically. Figure 4-3 shows the effects of time, n, and interest rate, i, on the present value of a $100 investment. As the figure shows, the higher the discount rate, the lower the present value of the $100.

What would you do if you needed to calculate present value and future value but didn't have access to a hand-held calculator or a spreadsheet? Handily, many Web sites have built-in time-value calculators, such as the one maintained by salemfive.
http://www.salemfive.com

ANNUITIES

An **annuity** is the payment or receipt of equal cash flows per period for a specified amount of time.[4] An **ordinary annuity** is one in which the payments or receipts occur at the *end* of each period, as shown in Figure 4-4. An **annuity due** is one in which payments or receipts occur at the *beginning* of each period, as shown in Figure 4-5. Most lease payments, such as apartment rentals, as well as life insurance premiums, are annuities due.

In a 4-year ordinary annuity, the last payment is made at the end of the fourth year. In a 4-year annuity due, the last payment is made at the end of the third year (the beginning of the fourth year).

---

[4]This discussion focuses primarily on periods of 1 year.

FIGURE 4-3
Present Value of $100
at Various Discount Rates

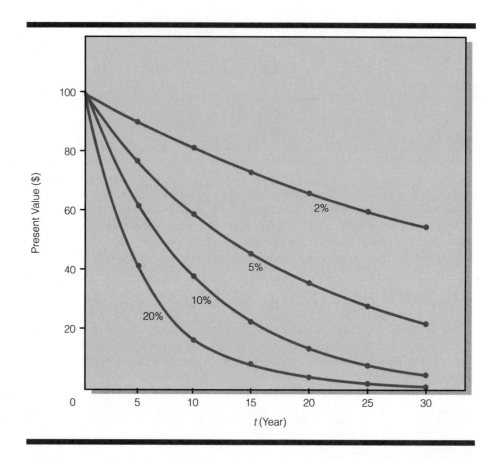

FIGURE 4-4
Time Line of an Ordinary Annuity
of $100 per Period for 4 Periods

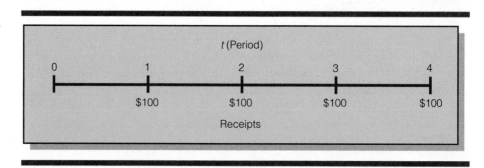

FIGURE 4-5
Time Line of an Annuity Due of
$100 per Period for 4 Periods

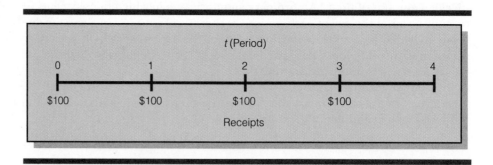

Future Value of an Ordinary Annuity

Future value of an annuity ($FVAN_n$) problems ask the question: If PMT dollars are deposited in an account at the end of each year for n years and if the deposits earn interest rate i compounded annually, what will be the value of the account at the end of n years? To illustrate, suppose Ms. Jefferson receives a 3-year ordinary annuity of $1,000 per year and deposits the money in a savings account at the end of each year. The account earns interest at a rate of 6 percent compounded annually. How much will her account be worth at the end of the 3-year period?

The problem involves the calculation of future values. The last deposit, PMT_3, made at the end of year 3, will earn no interest. Thus, its future value is as follows:

$$FV_{3rd} = PMT_3(1 + 0.06)^0$$
$$= \$1,000(1)$$
$$= \$1,000$$

The second deposit, PMT_2, made at the end of year 2, will be in the account for 1 full year before the end of the 3-year period, and it will earn interest. Thus, its future value is as follows:

$$FV_{2nd} = PMT_2(1 + 0.06)^1$$
$$= \$1,000(1.06)$$
$$= \$1,060$$

The first deposit, PMT_1, made at the end of year 1, will be in the account earning interest for 2 full years before the end of the 3-year period. Therefore its future value is the following:

$$FV_{1st} = PMT_1(1 + 0.06)^2$$
$$= \$1,000(1.124)$$
$$= \$1,124$$

The sum of the three figures is the future value of the annuity:

$$FVAN_3 = FV_{3rd} + FV_{2nd} + FV_{1st}$$
$$= \$1,000 + \$1,060 + \$1,124$$
$$= \$3,184$$

The future value of an annuity interest factor (FVIFA) is the sum of the future value interest factors presented in Table I. In this example, the future value of an annuity interest factor is calculated as

$$FVIFA_{0.06,3} = FVIF_{0.06,2} + FVIF_{0.06,1} + FVIF_{0.06,0}$$
$$= 1.124 + 1.060 + 1.000$$
$$= 3.184$$

Figure 4-6 illustrates this concept.

FIGURE 4-6
Time Line of the Future Value of an
Ordinary Annuity ($PMT = \$1,000$;
$i = 6\%$; $n = 3$)

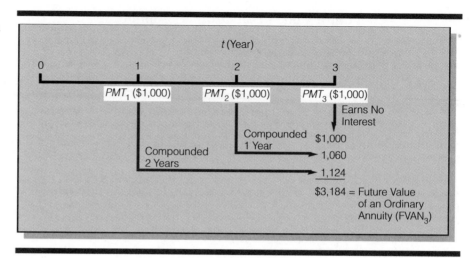

In general, the formula for the future value of an ordinary annuity interest factor is given by

$$\text{FVIFA}_{i,n} = \sum_{t=1}^{n} (1 + i)^{n-t} \qquad (4.16)$$

where i = nominal interest rate and n = number of periods. Tables of the future value of an ordinary annuity interest factors are available to simplify such computations. Table III at the end of the book provides a number of future value of an annuity interest factors. A portion of Table III is reproduced here as Table 4-3. FVIFAs can also be computed as follows:

$$\text{FVIFA}_{i,n} = \frac{(1 + i)^n - 1}{i} \qquad (4.17)$$

This formula is useful when one does not have access to interest tables with the appropriate values of i and n or a financial calculator.

The future value of an ordinary annuity (FVAN_n) may be calculated by multiplying the annuity payment, PMT, by the appropriate interest factor, $\text{FVIFA}_{i,n}$:

$$\text{FVAN}_n = PMT(\text{FVIFA}_{i,n}) \qquad (4.18)$$

TABLE 4-3
Future Value of an Ordinary
Annuity Interest Factors (FVIFA)
for $1 per Period at Interest Rate i
for n Periods

END OF PERIOD (n)	INTEREST RATE (i)			
	1%	**5%**	**6%**	**10%**
1	1.000	1.000	1.000	1.000
2	2.010	2.050	2.060	2.100
3	3.030	3.152	3.184	3.310
4	4.060	4.310	4.375	4.641
5	5.101	5.526	5.637	6.105
10	10.462	12.578	13.181	15.937
20	22.019	33.066	36.786	57.275
25	28.243	47.727	54.865	98.347

Table 4-3 can be used to solve the problem involving Jefferson's annuity. Because PMT = $1,000 and the interest factor for n = 3 years and i = 6% is 3.184, the future value of an ordinary annuity can be calculated as follows:

$$\text{FVAN}_3 = PMT(\text{FVIFA}_{0.06,3})$$

$$= \$1,000(3.184)$$

$$= \$3,184$$

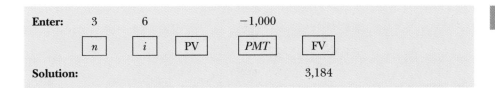

Sinking Fund Problem. Future value of an annuity interest factors also can be used to find the annuity amount that must be invested each year to produce a future value. This type of problem is sometimes called a **sinking fund problem**. Suppose the Omega Graphics Company wishes to set aside an equal, annual, end-of-year amount in a "sinking fund account" earning 10 percent per annum over the next 5 years. The firm wants to have $5 million in the account at the end of 5 years in order to retire (pay off) $5 million in outstanding bonds. How much must be deposited in the account at the end of each year?

This problem can be solved using either Equation 4.18 or a financial calculator. Substituting n = 5, FVAN_5 = $5,000,000, and i = 0.095 into Equation 4.18 yields

$$\$5,000,000 = PMT(\text{FVIFA}_{0.095,5})$$

Since the interest rate of 9.5 percent is not in Table III, one must use Equation 4.17 to determine $\text{FVIFA}_{0.095,5}$.

$$\$5,000,000 = PMT\left(\frac{(1+0.095)^5 - 1}{0.095}\right)$$

$$PMT = \$827,182$$

By depositing approximately $827,182 at the end of each of the next 5 years in the account earning 9.5 percent per annum, Omega will accumulate the $5 million needed to retire the bonds.

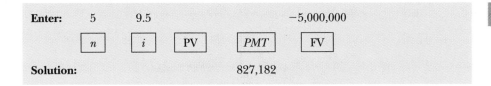

Future Value of an Annuity Due

Table III at the end of the book (future value of an annuity interest factor) assumes *ordinary* (end-of-period) annuities. For an *annuity due*, in which payments are made at the *beginning* of each period, the interest factors in Table III must be modified.

Consider the case of Jefferson cited earlier. If she deposits $1,000 in a savings account at the *beginning* of each year for the next 3 years and the account earns

6 percent interest, compounded annually, how much will be in the account at the end of 3 years? (Recall that when the deposits were made at the *end* of each year, the account totaled $3,184 at the end of 3 years.)

Figure 4-7 illustrates this problem as an *annuity due*. PMT_1 is compounded for 3 years, PMT_2 for 2 years, and PMT_3 for 1 year. The correct *annuity due* interest factor may be obtained from Table III by multiplying the FVIFA for 3 years and 6 percent (3.184) by 1 plus the interest rate (1 + 0.06). This yields a FVIFA for an annuity due of 3.375, and the future value of the annuity due ($FVAND_n$) is calculated as follows:

$$FVAND_n = PMT[FVIFA_{i,n}(1 + i)] \tag{4.19}$$

$$FVAND_3 = \$1,000(3.375)$$

$$= \$3,375$$

CALCULATOR SOLUTION

This problem must be solved with the calculator in the *beginning of period* payment mode.

Enter: 3   6   −1,000

| n | i | PV | PMT | FV |

Solution: 3,375

Note: This amount is larger than the $3,184 obtained in the ordinary annuity example given previously by an amount equal to 1 + *i*, or 1.06 in this particular example.

The next time you win the lottery and can't wait to spend the money, a company named Stonestreet will buy your winning lottery ticket by giving you its present value, that is, cash in hand today. Why wait around to have a good time?
http://www.stonestreet.com

Present Value of an Ordinary Annuity

The present value of an ordinary annuity ($PVAN_0$) is the sum of the present value of a series of equal periodic payments.[5] For example, to find the present value of an ordinary $1,000 annuity received at the end of each year for 5 years

FIGURE 4-7
Time Line of the Future Value of an Annuity Due (PMT = $1,000; i = 6%; n = 3)

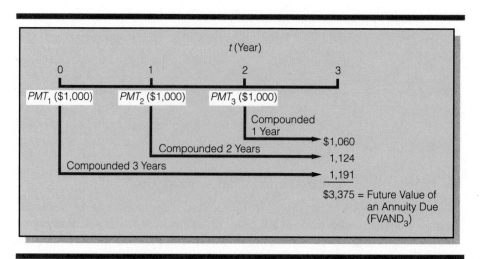

---

[5]This discussion focuses primarily on annual payments.

discounted at a 6 percent rate, the sum of the individual present values would be determined as follows:

$$PVAN_0 = \$1,000\left[\frac{1}{(1+0.06)^1}\right] + \$1,000\left[\frac{1}{(1+0.06)^2}\right]$$

$$+ \$1,000\left[\frac{1}{(1+0.06)^3}\right] + \$1,000\left[\frac{1}{(1+0.06)^4}\right]$$

$$+ \$1,000\left[\frac{1}{(1+0.06)^5}\right]$$

Referring to the interest factors in Table 4-2 yields the following:

$$PVAN_0 = \$1,000(PVIF_{0.06,1}) + \$1,000(PVIF_{0.06,2})$$

$$+ \$1,000(PVIF_{0.06,3}) + \$1,000(PVIF_{0.06,4})$$

$$+ \$1,000(PVIF_{0.06,5})$$

$$= \$1,000(0.943) + \$1,000(0.890) + \$1,000(0.840)$$

$$+ \$1,000(0.792) + \$1,000(0.747)$$

$$= \$1,000(0.943 + 0.890 + 0.840 + 0.792 + 0.747)$$

$$= \$4,212$$

or Table IV

Figure 4-8 illustrates this concept.

In general, the formula for the present value of an ordinary annuity interest factor is given by

$$PVIFA_{i,n} = \sum_{t=1}^{n} \frac{1}{(1+i)^t} \qquad (4.20)$$

where i = nominal interest rate and n = number of periods. Tables of the present value of an ordinary annuity interest factors (**PVIFA**) are available to simplify such computations. Table IV at the end of the book provides a number of the present value of an annuity interest factors. A portion of Table IV is reproduced here as Table 4-4. PVIFAs can also be computed as follows:

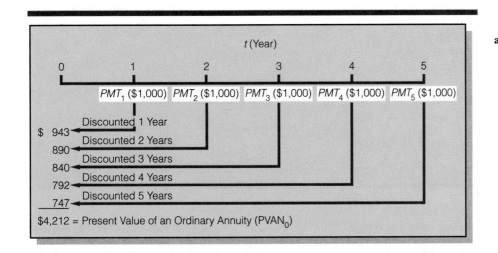

$$PVIFA_{i,n} = \frac{1 - \dfrac{1}{(1 + i)^n}}{i} \qquad (4.21)$$

This formula is useful when one does not have access to interest tables with the appropriate values of i and n or a financial calculator.

The present value of an annuity can be determined by multiplying the annuity payment, PMT, by the appropriate interest factor, $PVIFA_{i,n}$:

$$PVAN_0 = PMT(PVIFA_{i,n}) \qquad (4.22)$$

Referring to Table 4-4 to determine the interest factor for $i = 6\%$ and $n = 5$, the present value of an annuity in the previous problem can be calculated as follows:

$$PVAN_0 = PMT(PVIFA_{0.06,5})$$

$$= \$1{,}000(4.212)$$

$$= \$4{,}212$$

CALCULATOR SOLUTION

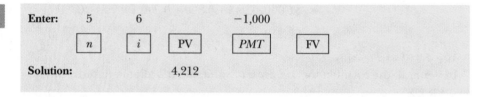

Solving for the Interest Rate. Present value of an annuity interest factors can also be used to solve for the rate of return expected from an investment.[6] Suppose IBM purchases a machine for $100,000. This machine is expected to generate annual cash flows of $23,742 to the firm over the next 5 years. What is the expected rate of return from this investment?

TABLE 4-4
Present Value of an Ordinary Annuity Interest Factors (PVIFA) for $1 per Period at Interest Rate i for n Periods

END OF PERIOD (n)	INTEREST RATE (i)			
	1%	5%	6%	10%
1	0.990	0.952	0.943	0.909
2	1.970	1.859	1.833	1.736
3	2.941	2.723	2.673	2.487
4	3.902	3.546	3.465	3.170
5	4.853	4.329	4.212	3.791
10	9.471	7.722	7.360	6.145
20	18.046	12.462	11.470	8.514
25	22.023	14.094	12.783	9.077

[6]This interest rate, or rate of return, is referred to by various names in finance, depending on the type of "investment" under consideration. When evaluating a bond (fixed-income security), this rate is referred to as the *yield-to-maturity* (YTM) (see Chapter 6). In the analysis of capital expenditure decisions, this rate is known as the *internal rate of return* (IRR) (see Chapter 9). Finally, when calculating the cost of bank loans and other types of credit, this rate is known as the *annual percentage rate* (APR) (see Chapter 18).

Using Equation 4.22, we can determine the expected rate of return in this example as follows:

$$\text{PVAN}_0 = PMT(\text{PVIFA}_{i,5})$$

$$\$100{,}000 = \$23{,}742(\text{PVIFA}_{i,5})$$

$$\text{PVIFA}_{i,5} = 4.212$$

From the 5-year row in Table 4-4 or Table IV, we see that a PVIFA of 4.212 occurs in the 6 percent column.[7] Hence, this investment offers a 6 percent expected rate of return.

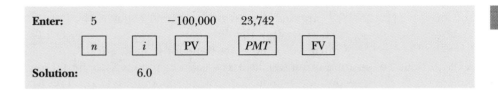

CALCULATOR SOLUTION

Loan Amortization and Capital Recovery Problems. Present value of an annuity interest factors can be used to solve a *loan amortization problem,* where the objective is to determine the payments necessary to pay off, or amortize, a loan.

For example, suppose you borrowed $10,000 from the Whisperwood Bank. The loan is for a period of 4 years at an interest rate of 10.5 percent. It requires that you make four equal, annual, end-of-year payments that include both principal and interest on the outstanding balance.[8] This problem can be solved using either Equation 4.22 or a financial calculator. Substituting $n = 4$, $\text{PVAN}_0 = \$10{,}000$, and $i = 0.105$ into Equation 4.22 yields:

$$\$10{,}000 = PMT(\text{PVIFA}_{0.105,4})$$

Since the interest rate (i) of 10.5 percent is not in Table IV, one must use Equation 4.21 to determine $\text{PVIFA}_{0.105,4}$:

$$\$10{,}000 = PMT\left(\frac{1 - \dfrac{1}{(1 + 0.105)^4}}{0.105}\right)$$

$$PMT = \$3{,}188.92$$

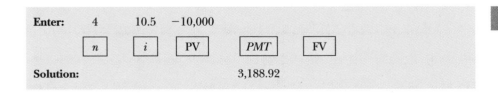

CALCULATOR SOLUTION

By making four annual, end-of-year payments to the bank of $3,188.92 each, you will completely pay off your loan, plus provide the bank with its 10.5 percent interest return. This can be seen in the *loan amortization schedule* developed in

---

[7]Interpolation can be used to find the approximate interest rate when the PVIFA falls between two values in the table. See the examples discussed earlier involving PVIFs for an illustration of this technique.

[8]Loan repayment schedules other than equal periodical payments are discussed in Chapter 18.

TABLE 4-5
Loan Amortization Schedule:
Whisperwood Bank

END OF YEAR	PAYMENT	INTEREST (10%)	PRINCIPAL REDUCTION	REMAINING BALANCE
0	—	—	—	$10,000
1	$3,188.92	$1050	2,138.92	7,861.08
2	3,188.92	825.41	2,363.51	5,497.57
3	3,188.92	577.25	2,611.67	2,885.90
4	3,188.92	303.02	2,885.90	0

You can use the Internet to amortize a loan. Hundreds of Web sites, such as money advisor, contain built-in "calculators" to amortize your loan.
http://www.moneyadvisor.com

Table 4-5. At the end of each year, you pay the bank $3,188.92. During the first year, $1,050 of this payment is interest (0.105 × $10,000 remaining balance), and the rest ($2,138.92) is applied against the principal balance owed at the beginning of the year. Hence, after the first payment, you owe $7,861.08 ($10,000 – $2,138.92). Similar calculations are done for years 2, 3 and 4.

Present value of an annuity interest factors can also be used to find the annuity amount necessary to recover a capital investment, given a required rate of return on that investment. This type of problem is called a **capital recovery problem**.

Present Value of an Annuity Due

Annuity due calculations are also important when dealing with the present value of an annuity problem. In these cases, the interest factors in Table IV must be modified.

Consider the case of a 5-year annuity of $1,000 each year, discounted at 6 percent. What is the present value of this annuity if each payment is received at the *beginning* of each year? (Recall the example presented earlier, illustrating the concept of the present value of an ordinary annuity, in which each payment was received at the *end* of each year and the present value was $4,212.) Figure 4-9 illustrates this problem.

The first payment received at the beginning of year 1 (end of year 0) is already in its present value form and therefore requires no discounting. PMT_2 is discounted for 1 period, PMT_3 is discounted for 2 periods, PMT_4 is discounted for 3 periods, and PMT_5 is discounted for 4 periods.

FIGURE 4-9
Time Line of a Present Value of an Annuity Due ($PMT = $1,000$; $i = 6\%$; $n = 5$)

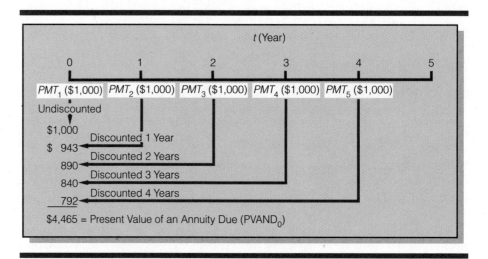

The correct *annuity due* interest factor for this problem may be obtained from Table IV by multiplying the present value of an ordinary annuity interest factor for 5 years and 6 percent (4.212) by 1 plus the interest rate (1 + 0.06). This yields a PVIFA for an annuity due of 4.465, and the present value of this annuity due (PVAND$_0$) is calculated as follows:

$$\text{PVAND}_0 = PMT[\text{PVIFA}_{i,n}(1 + i)]$$

$$\text{PVAND}_0 = \$1,000(4.465)$$

$$= \$4,465$$

0.253

4.212×1.06 (4.23)

This problem must be solved with the calculator in the beginning of period payment mode.

Enter: 5   6   −1,000

    [n]   [i]   [PV]   [*PMT*]   [FV]

Solution: 4,465

Note: This amount is larger than the $4,212 obtained in the ordinary annuity example presented previously by an amount equal to 1 + *i*, or 1.06 in this particular example.

Annuity due calculations are especially important when dealing with rental or lease contracts, because it is common for these contracts to require that payments be made at the beginning of each period.

PRESENT VALUE
SOME ADDITIONAL CASH FLOW PATTERNS

The discussion of present value thus far has focused on two cash flow patterns: single payments and annuities. The present value of three additional types of cash flow streams are examined in this section: namely, *perpetuities, uneven cash flows,* and *deferred annuities.* Examples of these types of cash flows are encountered in many different areas of financial decision making.

As you're learning in this chapter, buying a home, leasing a car, borrowing money, and many other transactions are based on the time value of money. For handy worksheets on mortgages, leases, loans, and so forth, visit financenter:
http://www.financenter.com

Perpetuities

A **perpetuity** is a financial instrument that promises to pay an equal cash flow per period forever; that is, an infinite series of payments. Therefore, a perpetuity may be thought of as an infinite annuity. Some bonds (and some preferred stocks) take the form of a perpetuity because these special securities never mature; that is, there is no obligation on the part of the issuer to redeem these bonds at their face value at any time in the future. A financial instrument such as this provides the holder with a series of equal, periodic payments into the indefinite future.

Consider, for example, a financial instrument that promises to pay an infinite stream of equal, annual payments (cash flows) of $PMT_t = PMT$ for $t = 1, 2, 3, \ldots$ years; that is, $PMT_1 = PMT_2 = PMT_3 = \ldots = PMT$. If we wish to find the present value (PVPER$_0$) of this financial instrument, it can be represented as follows:

$$\text{PVPER}_0 = \frac{PMT}{(1 + i)} + \frac{PMT}{(1 + i)^2} + \frac{PMT}{(1 + i)^3} + \dots$$

or, using summation notation, as

$$\text{PVPER}_0 = \sum_{t=1}^{\infty} \frac{PMT}{(1 + i)^t} \tag{4.24}$$

where i equals the rate of return required by an investor in this financial instrument. It should be apparent that Equation 4.24 represents a special type of annuity where the number of periods for the annuity equals infinity. This type of problem cannot be solved using Table IV.

For example, assume that Baltimore Gas and Electric series B preferred stock promises payments of $4.50 per year forever and that an investor requires a 10 percent rate of return on this type of investment. How much would the investor be willing to pay for this security?

An examination of the PVIFA interest factors for 10 percent (in Table IV) indicates that the value in the 10% column increases as the number of years increases, but at a decreasing rate. For example, the PVIFA factor for 10% and 10 years is 6.145, whereas the factor for 10% and 20 years is only 8.514 (much less than twice the 10-year factor). The limiting value in any column of Table IV is 1 divided by the interest rate of that column, i. In the case of a 10 percent perpetuity, the appropriate interest factor is 1/0.10, or 10. Thus Equation 4.24 can be rewritten as follows:[9]

$$\text{PVPER}_0 = \frac{PMT}{i} \tag{4.25}$$

In this example, the value of a $4.50 perpetuity at a 10 percent required rate of return is given as

$$\text{PVPER}_0 = \frac{\$4.50}{0.10}$$

$$= \$45$$

In Chapter 6 the concept of a perpetuity is examined in more detail in the specific cases of preferred stock and perpetual bonds.

---

[9]Equation 4.24 is the present value of an infinite series and can be simplified to Equation 4.25 in the following manner. Rewrite Equation 4.24 as follows:

$$\text{PVPER}_0 = PMT \left[\frac{1}{(1 + i)^1} + \frac{1}{(1 + i)^2} + \frac{1}{(1 + i)^3} + \dots + \frac{1}{(1 + i)^n} \right] \tag{a}$$

Multiply both sides of Equation a by $(1 + i)$:

$$\text{PVPER}_0 (1 + i) = PMT \left[1 + \frac{1}{(1 + i)^1} + \frac{1}{(1 + i)^2} + \frac{1}{(1 + i)^3} + \dots + \frac{1}{(1 + i)^{n-1}} \right] \tag{b}$$

Subtract Equation a from Equation b:

$$\text{PVPER}_0(1 + i - 1) = PMT \left[1 - \frac{1}{(1 + i)^n} \right] \tag{c}$$

As $n \rightarrow \infty$ then $1/(1 + i)^n \rightarrow 0$ and Equation c approaches the following:

$$\text{PVPER}_0(i) = PMT$$

or

$$\text{PVPER}_0 = \frac{PMT}{i} \tag{d}$$

Present Value of an Uneven Payment Stream

Many problems in finance—particularly in the area of capital budgeting—cannot be solved according to the simplified format of the present value of an annuity because the periodic cash flows are not equal. Consider an investment that is expected to produce a series of *unequal* payments (cash flows), PMT_1, PMT_2, PMT_3, ..., PMT_n, over the next n periods. The present value of this uneven payment stream is equal to the sum of the present values of the individual payments (cash flows). Algebraically, the present value can be represented as

$$PV_0 = \frac{PMT_1}{(1+i)} + \frac{PMT_2}{(1+i)^2} + \frac{PMT_3}{(1+i)^3} + \cdots + \frac{PMT_n}{(1+i)^n}$$

or, using summation notation, as

$$PV_0 = \sum_{t=1}^{n} \frac{PMT_t}{(1+i)^t} \tag{4.26}$$

$$= \sum_{t=1}^{n} PMT_t\,(PVIF_{i,t}) \tag{4.27}$$

where i is the interest rate (that is, required rate of return) on this investment and $PVIF_{i,t}$ is the appropriate interest factor from Table II. It should be noted that the payments can be either positive (cash *in*flows) or negative (*out*flows).

Consider the following example. Suppose Allied Signal Company is evaluating an investment in new equipment that will be used to manufacture a new product it has developed. The equipment is expected to have a useful life of 5 years and yield the following stream of cash flows (payments) over the 5-year period:

End of Year t	Cash Flow PMT_t
1	+ $100,000
2	+ 150,000
3	− 50,000
4	+ 200,000
5	+ 100,000

Note that in year 3, the cash flow is negative. (This is due to a new law that requires the company to purchase and install pollution abatement equipment.) The present value of these cash flows, assuming an interest rate (required rate of return) of 10 percent, is calculated using Equation 4.27 as follows:

$$\begin{aligned} PV_0 &= \$100,000\,(PVIF_{0.10,1}) + \$150,000\,(PVIF_{0.10,2}) \\ &\quad - \$50,000\,(PVIF_{0.10,3}) + \$200,000\,(PVIF_{0.10,4}) \\ &\quad + \$100,000\,(PVIF_{0.10,5}) \\ &= \$100,000\,(0.909) + \$150,000\,(0.826) \\ &\quad - \$50,000\,(0.751) + \$200,000\,(0.683) + \$100,000\,(0.621) \\ &= \$375,950 \end{aligned}$$

Figure 4-10 illustrates a time line for this investment. The present value of the cash flows ($375,950) would be compared with the initial cash outlay (that is,

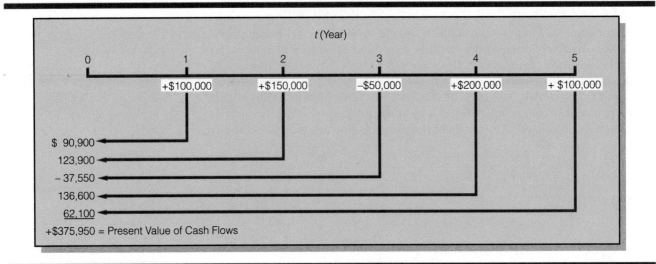

FIGURE 4-10
Time Line of a Present Value
of Unequal Payments
(*i* = 10%, *n* = 5)

net investment in year 0) in deciding whether to purchase the equipment and manufacture the product.

As will be seen later in the text, during the discussion of capital budgeting, calculations of this type are extremely important when making project evaluations.

Present Value of Deferred Annuities

Frequently, in finance, one encounters problems where an annuity begins more than 1 year in the future. For example, suppose that you wish to provide for the college education of your daughter. She will begin college 5 years from now, and you wish to have $15,000 available for her at the beginning of each year in college. How much must be invested today at a 12 percent annual rate of return in order to provide the 4-year, $15,000 annuity for your daughter?

This problem can be illustrated in the time line given in Figure 4-11. Four payments of $15,000 each are required at the end of years 5, 6, 7, and 8. Of course, this problem could be solved by finding the sum of the present values of each of the payments as follows:

Year t	Payment PMT_t	$PVIF_{.12,t}$	Present Value
5	$15,000	0.567	$ 8,505
6	$15,000	0.507	$ 7,605
7	$15,000	0.452	$ 6,780
8	$15,000	0.404	$ 6,060
	Present Value of Deferred Annuity =		$28,950

It should be apparent that this would be an extremely tedious method of calculation in the case of a 10-year-deferred annuity, for example. Figure 4-11 illustrates one alternative means of solving this problem. First, you can calculate the present value of the 4-year annuity, evaluated at the end of year 4 (remember that this is the same as the beginning of year 5). This calculation is made by multiplying the

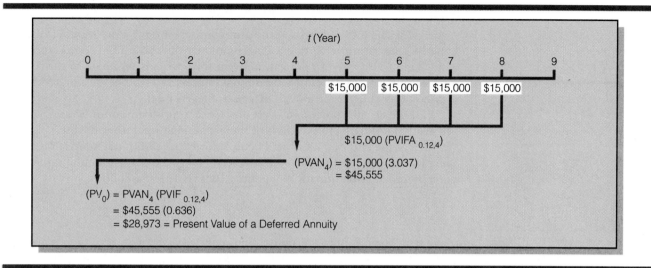

FIGURE 4-11
Time Line of a Deferred
4-Year Annuity ($i = 12\%$)

annuity amount ($15,000) by the PVIFA for a 4-year, 12% annuity. This factor is 3.037 and can be obtained from Table IV. Next the present value of the annuity ($45,555), evaluated at the end of year 4 ($PVAN_4$), must be discounted back to the present time (PV_0). Hence, we multiply $45,555 by a PVIF for 12% and 4 years. This factor, obtained from Table II, is equal to 0.636. The present value of the deferred annuity is $28,973. (This differs from the amount calculated earlier due to rounding in the tables. No difference will exist if this problem is solved with a calculator or tables that are carried out to more decimal places.)[10]

If you have $28,973 today and invest it in an account earning 12% per year, there will be exactly enough money in the account to permit your daughter to withdraw $15,000 at the beginning of each year in college. After the last withdrawal, the account balance will be zero.

COMPOUNDING PERIODS AND EFFECTIVE INTEREST RATES

The frequency with which interest rates are compounded (for example, annually, semiannually, quarterly, and so on) affects both the present and future values of cash flows as well as the effective interest rates being earned or charged.

Effect of Compounding Periods on Present and Future Values

Thus far, it has been assumed that compounding (and discounting) occur annually. Recall the general compound interest equation

---

[10]An alternative way to solve this problem is to multiply the annuity payment ($15,000) by the difference between ($PVIFA_{.12,8}$) and ($PVIFA_{.12,4}$). By subtracting ($PVIFA_{.12,4}$) from ($PVIFA_{.12,8}$) you are viewing this problem as an 8-year annuity that has no payments during the first 4 years. In this case, the calculation yields: $PV_0 = \$15,000(4.968 - 3.037) = \$28,965$. (The slight difference from the amount calculated earlier is due to rounding in Table IV.)

$$FV_n = PV_0(1 + i)^n \tag{4.10}$$

where PV_0 the initial deposit, i the annual interest rate, n the number of years, and FV_n the future value that will accumulate from the annual compounding of PV_0. An interest rate of i percent per year for n years is assumed. In the remainder of this section, this annual **nominal interest rate** will be designated i_{nom} to differentiate it from the annual **effective interest rate, i_{eff}**.

In some circumstances, interest on an account is compounded *semiannually* instead of annually; that is, half of the nominal annual interest rate, $i_{nom}/2$, is earned at the end of 6 months. The investor earns additional interest on the interest earned *before* the end of the year, or $(i_{nom}/2)PV_0$. In calculating interest compounded semiannually, Equation 4.10 is rewritten as follows:

$$FV_n = PV_0\left(1 + \frac{i_{nom}}{2}\right)^{2n}$$

The same logic applies to interest compounded *quarterly*:

$$FV_n = PV_0\left(1 + \frac{i_{nom}}{4}\right)^{4n}$$

In general, the compound interest for any number of periods during a year may be computed by means of the following equation:

$$FV_n = PV_0\left(1 + \frac{i_{nom}}{m}\right)^{mn} \tag{4.28}$$

where m is the number of times during the year the interest is compounded and n is the number of years. (The limiting case of continuous compounding and discounting is discussed in Appendix 4A.)

Table 4-6 contains the future value, FV_1, of $1,000 earning a nominal interest of 10 percent for several different compounding frequencies. For example, the future value (FV_1) of $1,000 compounded *semiannually* ($m = 2$) at a nominal interest rate (i_{nom}) of 10 percent per year by Equation 4.28 is

$$FV_1 = \$1,000\left(1 + \frac{0.10}{2}\right)^{2 \times 1}$$

$$= \$1,102.50$$

CALCULATOR SOLUTION

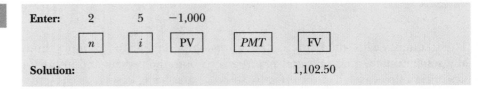

As Table 4-6 shows, the more frequent the compounding, the greater is the future value of the deposit and the greater is the *effective* interest rate. Effective interest, in contrast to *nominal* interest, is the *actual* rate of interest earned by the lender and generally is the most economically relevant definition of interest rates.

The relationship between present values and compound values suggests that present values will also be affected by the frequency of compounding. In general,

TABLE 4-6
Effects of Different Compounding Frequencies on Future Values of $1,000 at a 10 Percent Interest Rate

INITIAL AMOUNT	COMPOUNDING FREQUENCY	FUTURE VALUE, FV_1 (END OF YEAR 1)
$1,000	Yearly	$1,100.00
1,000	Semiannually	1,102.50
1,000	Quarterly	1,103.81
1,000	Monthly	1,104.71
1,000	Daily	1,105.16
1,000	Continuously*	1,105.17

*For advanced applications, it is useful to know that continuous compounding is obtained by letting m approach infinity in $FV_n = PV_0 (1 + i/m)^{mn}$. In this case, $\lim_{m \to \infty} (1 + i/m)^m = e^i$, and the compound value expression becomes $FV_n = PV_0 (e)^{in}$, where e is the exponential number having the approximate value of 2.71828. See Appendix 4A for a complete discussion of continuous compounding and discounting.

the present value of a sum to be received at the end of year n, discounted at the rate of i_{nom} percent and compounded m times per year, is as follows:

$$PV_0 = \frac{FV_n}{\left(1 + \dfrac{i_{nom}}{m}\right)^{mn}} \qquad (4.29)$$

Table 4-7 contains a number of present values, PV_0, for $1,000 received 1 year in the future discounted at a nominal interest rate of 10 percent with several different compounding frequencies. For example, the present value (PV_0) of $1,000 compounded *quarterly* ($m = 4$) at a nominal interest rate (i_{nom}) of 10 percent per year by Equation 4.29 is

$$PV_0 = \frac{\$1,000}{\left(1 + \dfrac{0.10}{4}\right)^{4 \times 1}}$$

$$= \$905.95$$

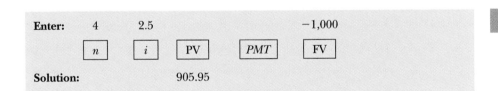

CALCULATOR SOLUTION

Enter:	4	2.5		−1,000
	n	i	PV	PMT	FV
Solution:			905.95		

As shown in Table 4-7, the more frequent the compounding, the smaller the present value of a future amount.

Throughout the text, much of the analysis assumes annual compounding instead of compounding for more frequent periods, because it simplifies matters and because the differences between the two are small. Similarly, unless otherwise stated, cash flows from a security or investment project are assumed to be received in a lump sum at the beginning or end of each period. More frequent compounding periods require more extensive tables or the use of a financial calculator.

TABLE 4-7
Effects of Different Compounding Frequencies on Present Values of $1,000 at a 10 Percent Interest Rate

AMOUNT	COMPOUNDING FREQUENCY	PRESENT VALUE, PV_0
$1,000	Yearly	$909.09
1,000	Semiannually	907.03
1,000	Quarterly	905.95
1,000	Monthly	905.21
1,000	Daily	904.85
1,000	Continuously	904.84

Regardless of the frequency of compounding, it is important to recognize that *effective* rates of interest are the relevant rates to use for financial and economic analysis. The next section considers the calculation of effective interest rates in more detail for those cases where compounding is done more than one time a year.

Effective Rate Calculations

The previous section illustrated the fact that the more frequently an annual *nominal* rate of interest is compounded, the greater is the *effective* rate of interest being earned or charged. Thus, if you were given the choice of receiving (1) interest on an investment, where the interest is compounded annually at a 10 percent rate, or (2) interest on an investment, where the interest is compounded semiannually at a 5 percent rate every six months, you would choose the second alternative, because it would yield a higher effective rate of interest.

Given the annual *nominal* rate of interest (i_{nom}), the *effective* annual rate of interest (i_{eff}) can be calculated as follows:

$$i_{eff} = \left(1 + \frac{i_{nom}}{m}\right)^m - 1 \tag{4.30}$$

where *m* is the number of compounding intervals per year.[11]

For example, suppose a bank offers you a loan at an annual nominal interest rate of 12 percent compounded quarterly. What effective annual interest rate is the bank charging you? Substituting $i_{nom} = 0.12$ and *m* = 4 into Equation 4.30 yields

$$i_{eff} = \left(1 + \frac{0.12}{4}\right)^4 - 1 \tag{4.30}$$

$$= 0.1255$$

or 12.55 percent.

---

[11]Note that annual effective interest rates are eqivalent to annual nominal interest rates in the case where compounding occurs only one time per year, at year end. This can be shown by substituting *m* = 1 into Equation 4.30:

$$i_{eff} = \left(1 + \frac{i_{nom}}{1}\right)^1 - 1$$

$$= 1 + i_{nom} - 1$$

$$= i_{nom}$$

There also are situations in finance where one is interested in determining the interest rate during each compounding period that will provide a given annual effective rate of interest. For example, if the annual effective rate is 20 percent and compounding is done quarterly, you may wish to know what quarterly rate of interest will result in an *effective* annual rate of interest of 20 percent.

In general, the rate of interest per period (where there is more than one compounding period per year), i_m, which will result in an effective annual rate of interest, i_{eff}, if compounding occurs m times per year, can be computed as follows:

$$i_m = (1 + i_{eff})^{1/m} - 1 \qquad (4.31)$$

In this example, the quarterly rate of interest that will yield an annual effective rate of interest of 20 percent is[12]

$$
\begin{aligned}
i_m &= (1 + 0.20)^{0.25} - 1 \\
&= (1.04664) - 1 \\
&= 0.04664 \text{ or } 4.664\%
\end{aligned}
$$

Thus, if you earn 4.664 percent per period and compounding occurs four times per year, the effective annual rate earned will be 20 percent. This concept is encountered in Chapter 6 in the discussion of the valuation of bonds that pay interest semiannually.

For the current rates on mortgages, leases, car loans, home equity loans, savings, educational loans, etc., in your area of the country, as well as a lot of good advice on all these matters, visit the National Financial Services Network:
http:/www.nfsn.com

SOLVING THE FINANCIAL CHALLENGE

Recall from the Financial Challenge at the beginning of this chapter that your friend has been asked to calculate the present value of the following annuities:

1. The present value of an annuity due of $50,000 per year for 20 years, discounted at 8 percent a year.
2. The present value of a deferred annuity of $50,000 per year for 20 years, with the first payment occurring 10 years from now, discounted at 8 percent a year.
3. The present value of a deferred annuity of $50,000 per year for 20 years, with the first payment occurring 20 years from now, discounted at 8 percent a year.

The present value of making annual $50,000 payments *forever* beginning 20 years from now is determined by subtracting the present value of the 20-year annuity due, $530,180, from the present value of a perpetuity due. The present value of a perpetuity due, $PVPERD_0$, is calculated by adding the amount of one annual payment to the present value of an ordinary perpetuity.

---

[12]Finding the ¼ or 0.25 root of (1 + 0.20) can be done easily with any financial or scientific calculator using the root function on the calculator.

For Annuity #1:

$$PVAND_0 = \$50,000[PVIFA_{0.08,20}(1.08)]$$
$$= \$530,180$$

This problem must be solved with the calculator in the beginning of period payment mode.

Enter: 20   8   −50,000

| n | i | PV | PMT | FV |

Solution: 530,180

For Annuity #2:

$$PV_0 = PVAND_{10}(PVIF_{0.08,10})$$
$$= \$530,180(PVIF_{0.08,10})$$
$$= \$245,576$$

Enter: 10   8   −530,180

| n | i | PV | PMT | FV |

Solution: 245,576

Note: The present value of the annuity due in #1 of this problem becomes a *future* value in this part of the problem.

For Annuity #3:

$$PV_0 = PVAND_{20}(PVIF_{0.08,20})$$
$$= \$530,180(PVIF_{0.08,20})$$
$$= \$113,749$$

Enter: 20   8   −530,180

| n | i | PV | PMT | FV |

Solution: 113,749

Note: The present value of the annuity due in #1 of this problem becomes a "future" value in this part of the problem.

$$PVPERD_0 = \frac{PMT}{i} + PMT \tag{4.32}$$

$$PVPERD_0 = \frac{\$50,000}{0.08} + \$50,000$$

$$= \$675,000$$

Thus, the present value of making the annual $50,000 payments forever beginning 20 years from now is equal to the present value of the perpetuity due, $675,000, less the present value of the 20-year annuity due, $530,180, or $144,820.

In summary, by spreading out payment of the $1.0 million over time, the cost to the team in today's dollars, and also the present value of the $1.0 million to the winner, is considerably less than $1.0 million.

■ SUMMARY

- ■ The time value of money plays an important role in many areas of financial decision making.
- ■ An understanding of *interest* is crucial to sound financial management. *Simple interest* is interest earned or paid on the principal only. *Compound interest* is interest paid not only on the principal but also on any interest earned but not withdrawn during earlier periods.
- ■ An *annuity* is the payment or receipt of a series of equal cash flows per period for a specified number of periods. In an *ordinary annuity*, the cash flows occur at the *end* of each period. In an *annuity due,* the cash flows occur at the *beginning* of each period.
- ■ Table 4-8 summarizes the equations used to compute the future and present values of the various cash flow streams.
- ■ In solving financial mathematics problems, it is necessary to answer two questions:
  1. Do we need a future value or a present value?
  2. Are we dealing with a single payment or an annuity?
  Once these questions have been successfully answered, the following table can be used to select the appropriate table of interest factors:

	Future Value	*Present Value*
Single Payment	Table I	Table II
Annuity	Table III	Table IV

- ■ *Sinking fund problems* determine the annuity amount that must be invested each year to produce a future value.
- ■ *Capital recovery problems* determine the annuity amount necessary to recover some initial investment.
- ■ A *loan amortization schedule* shows the dollar amount and total number of periodic payments owed on a debt obligation. It also shows the loan balance after each payment and gives the breakdown of interest and principal of each payment.
- ■ The more frequently compounding occurs during a given period, the higher is the *effective* interest rate on an investment. More frequent compounding results in higher future values and lower present values than less frequent compounding at the same interest rate.
- ■ The appropriate compounding or discount rate to use in a particular problem depends upon the general level of interest rates in the economy, the time frame used for analysis, and the risk of the investment being considered.

TABLE 4-8
Summary of Future and Present Value Equations

TYPE OF CALCULATION	EQUATION	INTEREST FACTOR TABLE	EQUATION NUMBER
Future value of a single payment	$FV_n = PV_0(FVIF_{i,n})$	Table I	4.12
Future value of an (ordinary) annuity	$FVAN_n = PMT(FVIFA_{i,n})$	Table III	4.18
Future value of an annuity due	$FVAND_n = PMT[FVIFA_{i,n}(1 + i)]$	Table III	4.19
Present value of a single payment	$PV_0 = FV_n(PVIF_{i,n})$	Table II	4.15
Present value of an (ordinary) annuity	$PVAN_0 = PMT(PVIFA_{i,n})$	Table IV	4.22
Present value of an annuity due	$PVAND_0 = PMT[PVIFA_{i,n}(1 + i)]$	Table IV	4.23
Present value of an uneven payment stream	$PV_0 = \sum_{t=1}^{n} PMT_t(PVIF_{i,t})$	Table II	4.27
Present value of a (ordinary) perpetuity	$PVPER_0 = \dfrac{PMT}{i}$	—	4.25
Present value of a perpetuity due	$PVPERD_0 = \dfrac{PMT}{i} + PMT$	—	4.32

Definitions:
n = number of time periods of discounting or compounding (usually years).
i = annual rate of interest (i.e., annual nominal interest rate).
PMT = annuity cash flow (i.e., amount of cash flow paid or received for a specified number of years or forever in the case of a perpetuity). In an ordinary annuity, the cash flows are received at the end of each year. In an annuity due, the cash flows are received at the beginning of each year.
PMT_t = payment (cash flow) in period t.

■ QUESTIONS AND TOPICS FOR DISCUSSION

1. Which would you rather receive: the proceeds from a 2-year investment paying 5 percent simple interest per year or from one paying 5 percent compound interest? Why?
2. Which is greater: the future value interest factor (FVIF) for 10 percent and 2 years or the present value interest factor (PVIF) for 10 percent and 2 years?
3. What happens to the present value of an annuity as the interest rate increases? What happens to the future value of an annuity as the interest rate increases?
4. Which would you prefer to invest in: a savings account paying 6 percent compounded annually or a savings account paying 6 percent compounded daily? Why?
5. What type of contract might require the use of annuity due computations?
6. What effect does more frequent compounding have on present values?
7. Why should each of the following be familiar with compounding and present value concepts?
   a. A marketing manager.
   b. A personnel manager.
8. Explain what is meant by the "Rule of 72." How can it be used in finance applications? (See Footnote 3.)
9. What is the relationship between present value and future value?
10. What is the difference between an ordinary annuity and an annuity due? Give examples of each.

11. If the required rate of return increases, what is the impact on the following?
    a. A present value of an annuity.
    b. A future value of an annuity.
12. Explain how future value of an annuity interest factors can be used to solve a sinking fund problem.
13. Describe how to set up a loan amortization schedule.
14. November 21, 1980, was the day of a tragic fire in the MGM Grand Hotel in Las Vegas. At the time of the fire, the hotel had only $30 million of liability insurance. One month after the fire, the hotel bought an extra $170 million of liability coverage for a premium of $37.5 million, retroactive to November 1, 1980 (before the fire). Based on your knowledge of present value concepts, why would insurers be willing to issue insurance to MGM under these conditions?
15. A savings account advertises that "interest is compounded continuously and paid quarterly." What does this mean?
16. Give an example of a perpetuity. How does a perpetuity differ from an annuity?
17. Explain how to determine the present value of an uneven cash flow stream.
18. Evaluate the following statement: "The development of powerful, inexpensive microcomputers have made the hand calculator as obsolete as the slide rule."

■ SELF-TEST PROBLEMS

ST1. Calculate the value in 5 years of $1,000 deposited in a savings account today if the account pays interest at a rate of:
    a. 8 percent per year, compounded annually.
    b. 8 percent per year, compounded quarterly.
ST2. A business is considering purchasing a machine that is projected to yield cash savings of $1,000 per year over a 10-year period. Using a 12 percent discount rate, calculate the present value of the savings. (Assume that the cash savings occur at the end of each year.)
ST3. Simpson Peripherals earned $0.90 per share in 1989 and $1.52 in 1994. Calculate the annual growth rate in earnings per share over this period.
ST4. You own a small business that is for sale. You have been offered $2,000 per year for 5 years, with the first receipt at the end of 4 years. Calculate the present value of this offer, using a 14 percent discount rate.
ST5. Yolanda Williams is 35 years old today and is beginning to plan for her retirement. She wants to set aside an equal amount at the *end* of each of the next 25 years so that she can retire at age 60. She expects to live to an age of 80 and wants to be able to withdraw $50,000 per year from the account on her sixty-first through eightieth birthdays. The account is expected to earn 10 percent per year for the entire period of time. Determine the size of the annual deposits that she must make.

■ PROBLEMS*

1. How much will $1,000 deposited in a savings account earning a compound annual interest rate of 6 percent be worth at the end of the following number of years?
    a. 3 years.
    b. 5 years.
    c. 10 years.

*Color numbers denote problems that have check answers provided at the end of the book.

2. If you require a 9 percent return on your investments, which would you prefer?
   a. $5,000 today.
   b. $15,000 five years from today.
   c. $1,000 per year for 15 years.

3. The Lancer Leasing Company has agreed to lease a hydraulic trencher to the Chavez Excavation Company for $20,000 a year over the next 8 years. Lease payments are to be made at the beginning of each year. Assuming that Lancer invests these payments at an annual rate of 9 percent, how much will it have accumulated by the end of the eighth year?

4. The Mutual Assurance and Life Company is offering an insurance policy under either of the following two terms:
   a. Make a series of twelve $1,200 payments at the beginning of each of the next 12 years (the first payment being made today).
   b. Make a single lump-sum payment today of $10,000 and receive coverage for the next 12 years.

   If you had investment opportunities offering an 8 percent annual return, which alternative would you prefer?

5. How much must you deposit at the end of each year in an account that pays a nominal annual rate of 20 percent, if at the end of 5 years you want $10,000 in the account?

6. A leading broker has advertised money multiplier certificates that will triple your money in 9 years; that is, if you buy one for $333.33 today, it will pay you $1,000 at the end of 9 years. What rate of return will you earn on these money multiplier certificates?

7. You have $10,000 to invest. Assuming annual compounding, how long will it take for the $10,000 to double if it is invested at the following rates?
   a. 8 percent.
   b. 10 percent.
   c. 14 percent.
   d. 20 percent.

8. The Tried and True Corporation had earnings of $0.20 per share in 1978. By 1995, a period of 17 years, its earnings had grown to $1.01 per share. What has been the compound annual rate of growth in the company's earnings?

9. What is the present value of $800 to be received at the end of 8 years, assuming the following annual interest rate?
   a. 4 percent, discounted annually.
   b. 8 percent, discounted annually.
   c. 20 percent, discounted quarterly.
   d. 0 percent.

10. Mr. Jones bought a building for $60,000, payable on the following terms: a $10,000 down payment and 25 equal annual installment payments to include principal and interest of 10 percent per annum. Calculate the amount of the installment payments. How much of the first year's payment goes toward reducing the principal amount?

11. A firm purchases 100 acres of land for $200,000 and agrees to remit 20 equal annual end-of-year installments of $41,067 each. What is the true annual interest rate on this loan?

12. Thirty years ago, Jesse Jones bought 10 acres of land for $1,000 per acre in what is now downtown Houston. If this land grew in value at an 8 percent per annum rate, what is it worth today?

13. Susan Robinson is planning for her retirement. She is 30 years old today and would like to have $600,000 when she turns 55. She estimates that she will be able to earn a 9 percent rate of return on her retirement investments over time; she wants to set aside a constant amount of money every year (at the end of the year) to help achieve

her objective. How much money must Robinson invest at the end of each of the next 25 years to realize her goal of $600,000 at the end of that time?

14. What would you be willing to pay for a $1,000 bond paying $70 interest at the end of each year and maturing in 25 years if you wanted the bond to yield the following rates of return?

   a. 5 percent.
   b. 7 percent.
   c. 12 percent.
      (Note: At maturity, the bond will be retired and the holder will receive $1,000 in cash. Bonds typically are issued with $1,000 face, or par, values. The actual market value at any point in time will tend to rise as interest rates fall and fall as interest rates rise.)

15. A life insurance company offers loans to its policyholders against the cash value of their policies at a (nominal) annual interest rate of 8 percent, compounded quarterly. Determine the effective annual percentage interest rate on these loans.

16. Two investment opportunities are open to you: Investment 1 and Investment 2. Each has an initial cost of $10,000. Assuming that you desire a 10 percent return on your initial investment, compute the net present value of the two alternatives and evaluate their relative attractiveness:

Investment 1		Investment 2	
Cash Flows	Year	Cash Flows	Year
$5,000	1	$8,000	1
6,000	2	7,000	2
7,000	3	6,000	3
8,000	4	5,000	4

17. Your great-uncle Claude is 82 years old. Over the years, he has accumulated savings of $80,000. He estimates that he will live another 10 years at the most and wants to spend his savings by then. (If he lives longer than that, he figures you will be happy to take care of him.)

   Uncle Claude places his $80,000 into an account earning 10 percent annually and sets it up in such a way that he will be making 10 equal annual withdrawals—the first one occurring 1 year from now—such that his account balance will be zero at the end of 10 years. How much will he be able to withdraw each year?

18. You decide to purchase a building for $30,000 by paying $5,000 down and assuming a mortgage of $25,000. The bank offers you a 15-year mortgage requiring annual end-of-year payments of $3,188 each. The bank also requires you to pay a 3 percent loan origination fee, which will reduce the effective amount the bank lends to you. Compute the annual percentage rate of interest on this loan.

19. You purchase a 5-acre vacation property for $10,000. Five years from now, you expect to sell the property for $22,550. Your anticipated annual end-of-year tax payments will be $500 for each of the next 5 years. Compute the annual rate of return on this investment.

20. An investment promises to pay $6,000 at the end of each year for the next 5 years and $4,000 at the end of each year for years 6 through 10.

   a. If you require a 12 percent rate of return on an investment of this sort, what is the maximum amount you would pay for this investment?
   b. Assuming that the payments are received at the *beginning* of each year, what is the maximum amount you would pay for this investment, given a 12 percent required rate of return?

21. You are considering investing in a bond that matures 20 years from now. It pays an annual end-of-year coupon rate of interest of 8.75 percent, or $87.50 per year. The

bond currently sells for $919. Your marginal income tax rate (applied to interest payments) is 28 percent. Capital gains are taxed at the same rate as ordinary income. What is your *after-tax* rate of return if you buy this bond today and hold it until maturity?

22. Your parents have discovered a $1,000 bond at the bottom of their safe deposit box. The bond was given to you by your late great-aunt Hilda on your second birthday. The bond pays interest at a rate of 5 percent per annum, compounded annually. Interest accumulates and is paid at the time the bond is redeemed. You are now 27 years old. What is the current worth of the bond (principal plus interest)?

23. Suppose that a local savings and loan association advertises a 6 percent annual (nominal) rate of interest on regular accounts, compounded monthly. What is the effective annual percentage rate of interest paid by the savings and loan association?

24. Your mother is planning to retire this year. Her firm has offered her a lump sum retirement payment of $50,000 or a $6,000 lifetime annuity—whichever she chooses. Your mother is in reasonably good health and expects to live for at least 15 more years. Which option should she choose, assuming that an 8 percent interest rate is appropriate to evaluate the annuity?

25. A life insurance company has offered you a new "cash grower" policy that will be fully paid up when you turn 45. At that time, it will have a cash surrender value of $18,000. When you turn 65, the policy will have a cash surrender value of $37,728. What rate of interest is the insurance company promising you on your investment?

26. Your aunt would like to help you set up your new medical practice when you complete your medical training in 6 years. She wishes to have $250,000 available for your use at that time. How much must she invest in an account at the end of each of the next 6 years in order to reach her goal, if the account offers a 12 percent annual rate of return?

27. Strikler, Inc. has issued a $10 million, 10-year bond issue. The bonds require Strikler to establish a sinking fund and make 10 equal, end-of-year deposits into the fund. These deposits will earn 8 percent annually, and the sinking fund should have enough accumulated in it at the end of 10 years to retire the bonds. What are the annual sinking fund payments?

28. Construct a loan amortization schedule for a 3-year, 11 percent loan of $30,000. The loan requires 3 equal, end-of-year payments.

29. a. What payments are due on a 5-year, 10 percent loan, with an initial outstanding balance of $100,000? (At the end of 5 years, the loan will be paid off. All loan payments are equal and occur at the end of the year.)

   b. What portion of the year 2 payment is principal? Interest?

30. The Nucleo-Robotics Corporation has just issued $10,000,000 of first mortgage bonds, each having a par value of $1,000 and a coupon interest rate of 15 percent. The bonds have a 25-year maturity and require that the firm establish a sinking fund sufficient to retire *80 percent* of the bonds by the time the bonds are scheduled to mature. The first deposit into the sinking fund will occur at the end of year 6. The firm will make 20 end-of-year deposits. Money deposited into the sinking fund is expected to earn a 12 percent rate of return over the 20-year life of the fund. How much must the firm deposit into the fund each year in order to meet its sinking fund obligations?

31. Mitchell Investments has offered you the following investment opportunity:

   • $6,000 at the end of each year for the first 5 years, plus
   • $3,000 at the end of each year from years 6 through 10, plus
   • $2,000 at the end of each year from years 11 through 20.

   a. How much would you be willing to pay for this investment if you required a 12 percent rate of return?

b. If the payments were received at the beginning of each year, what would you be willing to pay for this investment?

32. Upon retirement, your goal is to spend 5 years traveling around the world. To travel in the style to which you are accustomed will require $250,000 per year at the beginning of each year. If you plan to retire in 30 years, what are the equal, annual, end-of-year payments necessary to achieve this goal? The funds in the retirement account will compound at 10 percent annually.

33. A Baldwin United Company agent has just presented the following offer. If you deposit $25,000 with the firm today, it will pay you $10,000 per year at the end of years 8 through 15. If you require a 15 percent rate of return on this type of investment, would you make this investment?

34. You deposit $4,500 per year at the end of each of the next 25 years into an account that pays 10 percent compounded annually. How much could you withdraw at the end of each of the 20 years following your last deposit? (The twenty-fifth and last deposit is made at the beginning of the 20-year period. The first withdrawal is made at the end of the first year in the 20-year period.)

35. Upon retirement, you are offered a choice between a $250,000 lump sum payment or a lifetime annuity of $51,300, with annuity payments being made at the end of each year. If you expect to live for 15 years after retirement, at what required rate of return would you be indifferent between the two alternatives (to the nearest whole percent)?

36. You deposit $10,000 at the end of each of the next 4 years into an account that pays 12 percent annually. What is the account balance at the end of 10 years?

37. Determine the value at the end of 3 years of a $10,000 investment (today) in a bank certificate of deposit (CD) that pays a nominal annual interest rate of 8 percent, compounded
  a. Semiannually.
  b. Quarterly.
  c. Monthly.

38. A bank offers an *effective* annual interest rate of 15 percent, compounded quarterly. What rate of interest is being paid quarterly by the bank?

39. An investment requires an outlay of $100,000 today. Cash inflows from the investment are expected to be $40,000 per year at the end of years 4, 5, 6, 7, and 8. If you require a 20 percent rate of return on this type of investment, should the investment be undertaken?

40. An investment of $100,000 is expected to generate cash inflows of $60,000 in 1 year and $79,350 in 2 years. Calculate the expected rate of return on this investment to the nearest whole pecent.

41. An investment offers the following year-end cash flows:

End of Year	Cash Flow
1	$20,000
2	$30,000
3	$15,000

Using a 15 percent interest rate, convert this series of irregular cash flows to an equivalent (in present value terms) 3-year annuity.

42. Congratulations! You have just won the Publishers Corporation Sweepstakes. You have been offered a lump sum of $1,000,000, or a lifetime (end-of-year) annuity of $100,000 per year. If you expect to live for 20 years and can earn 15 percent on your investments, which alternative should you choose (ignoring tax consequences)? If you expect to earn only 7 percent on your investments, how does your answer change?

43. James Street's son, Harold, is 10 years old today. Harold, a studious young fellow, already is making plans to go to college on his eighteenth birthday, and his father wants to start putting money away now for that purpose. Street estimates that Harold will need $18,000, $19,000, $20,000, and $21,000 for his freshman, sophomore, junior, and senior years, respectively. He plans on making these amounts available to Harold at the beginning of each of these years.

    Street would like to make 8 annual deposits (the first of which would be made on Harold's eleventh birthday, 1 year from now, and the last on his eighteenth birthday, the day he leaves for college) in an account earning 10 percent annually. He wants the account to eventually be worth enough to *just* pay for Harold's college expenses. Any balances remaining in the account will continue to earn the 10 percent.

    How much will Street have to deposit in this "planning" account each year to provide for Harold's education?

44. How much must you deposit at the end of each quarter in an account that pays a nominal interest rate of 20 percent, compounded quarterly, if at the end of 5 years you want $10,000 in the account? (HINT: In working with the compound interest tables when solving this problem, you need to adjust the interest rate and the number of compounding periods to reflect quarterly, rather than annual, compounding.)

45. IRA Investments develops retirement programs for individuals. You are 30 years old and plan to retire on your sixtieth birthday. You want to establish a plan with IRA that will require a series of equal, annual, end-of-year deposits into the retirement account. The first deposit will be made 1 year from today on your thirty-first birthday. The final payment on the account will be made on your sixtieth birthday. The retirement plan will allow you to withdraw $120,000 per year for 15 years, with the first withdrawal on your sixty-first birthday. Also at the end of the fifteenth year, you wish to withdraw an additional $250,000. The retirement account promises to earn 12 percent annually.

    What periodic payment must be made into the account to achieve your retirement objective?

46. If you deposit $1,000 a year (at the end of each of the next 5 years) in an account paying a nominal 12 percent per year, compounded semiannually, how much will you have in the account at the end of 10 years?

47. Your child will go to college 12 years from now and will require $20,000, $21,000, $22,000, and $23,000 at the beginning of each year in school. In addition, you and your spouse plan to retire in 20 years. You want to have $75,000 available for each of your expected 15 years of blissful retirement. These funds will need to be available at the *beginning* of each year. If you now have $15,000 that can be used to meet these obligations, how much must you invest at the end of each of the next 20 years (if all funds earn an 11 percent rate of return) in order to meet your financial objectives?

48. You have just had your thirtieth birthday. You have two children. One will go to college 10 years from now and require four beginning-of-year payments for college expenses of $10,000, $11,000, $12,000, and $13,000. The second child will go to college in 15 years from now and require 4 beginning-of-year payments for college expenses of $15,000, $16,000, $17,000, and $18,000. In addition, you plan to retire in 30 years. You want to be able to withdraw $50,000 per year (at the end of each year) from an account throughout your retirement. You expect to live 20 years beyond retirement. The first withdrawal will occur on your sixty-first birthday.

    What equal, annual, end-of-year amount must you save for each of the next 30 years to meet these goals, if all savings earn a 13 percent annual rate of return?

49. You are currently 30 years of age. You intend to retire at age 60 and you want to be able to receive a 20-year, $100,000 beginning-of-year annuity with the first payment to be received on your sixtieth birthday. You would like to save enough money over

the next 15 years to achieve your objective; that is, you want to accumulate the necessary funds by your forty-fifth birthday.

a. If you expect your investments to earn 12 percent per year over the next 15 years and 10 percent per year thereafter, how much must you accumulate by the time you reach age 45?

b. What equal, annual amount must you save at the end of each of the next 15 years to achieve your objective, assuming that you currently have $10,000 available to meet your goal? Assume the conditions stated in Part a.

50. Calculate the present value of a perpetuity bond that is expected to pay $50 of interest per year if the investor requires an annual return of 8 percent.

51. Maxine Johnson is 35 years old today and has saved $10,000 toward retirement. Johnson also expects to save $3,000 per year at the end of each of the next 15 years and $5,000 per year at the end of each of the *following* 15 years. Johnson plans to retire at age 65. Assuming a life expectancy of 15 years beyond retirement, how much money can Johnson withdraw at the beginning of each year from the retirement fund and still leave an estate of $100,000 to her heirs. Assume a 10 percent annual interest rate throughout the entire period of time.

52. Suppose today is October 1, 19X1, and you deposit $1,000 today into an account paying 8 percent compounded annually. Suppose also that you continue to deposit $1,000 annually on each succeeding October 1, until your last payment is made on October 1, 19X6. What is the balance in the account at the close of business on October 1, 19X6?

53. Steven White is considering taking early retirement, having saved $400,000. White desires to determine how many years the savings will last if $40,000 per year is withdrawn at the end of each year. White feels the savings can earn 10 percent per year.

54. Suppose today is July 1, 1995, and you deposit $2,000 into an account today. Then you deposit $1,000 into the same account on *each* July 1, beginning in 1996 and continuing until the last $1,000 deposit is made on July 1, 2001. Also, assume that you withdraw $3,000 on July 1, 2003. Assuming a 7 percent annual compound interest rate, what will be the balance in the account at the close of business on July 1, 2005?

55. Cousin Drisilla has just turned 15. Drisilla plans to go to law school on her twenty-second birthday. Law school is expected to cost Drisilla $25,000, $26,000, and $27,000 for each of her 3 years in school. You plan to provide for Drisilla's education and want the needed funds to be available to Drisilla at the beginning of each year in law school. In addition, you want to give Drisilla a $10,000 per year, 10-year annuity as a graduation gift. The first annuity payment will be received by Drisilla on her twenty-seventh birthday.

You currently have $8,000 to meet these obligations. You want to save an equal amount at the end of each of the next 10 years to meet the remaining obligations. If your investments earn 10 percent pretax and your (and Drisilla's) marginal tax rate is 30 percent, how much must you save at the end of each of the next 10 years?

56. If you were to place $4,000 in a savings account today that paid 8 percent compounded quarterly, how much could be withdrawn every 6 months starting 6 months from now so that the savings account balance would be zero 2 years from now?

57. What is the present value of $1,000,000 received 10 years from now at a discount rate of 300 percent per year?

58. Your son, Charlie, has just turned 15. Charlie plans to go to college to study electronics on his eighteenth birthday. College is expected to cost Charlie $15,000, $16,000, $17,000 and $18,000 for each of his 4 years in school. You want these funds to be available to him at the beginning of each year in college. In addition, you want to give Charlie a $25,000 graduation gift on his twenty-second birthday so that he can get a start on his career or on graduate school.

You currently have $8,000 to meet these obligations. You want to save an equal amount at the end of each of the next 6 years to meet the remaining obligations. If your investments earn 10 percent pretax and your marginal tax rate is 30 percent, how much must you save at the end of each of the next 6 years?

59. You have decided to start planning for your retirement by analyzing different retirement plans. The plan offered by IRA Managers requires you to deposit $5,000 at the beginning of each of the next 30 years. The retirement plan guarantees a 10 percent annual compounding rate over the 30-year time period. When you retire at the end of the thirtieth year, the interest earned on the money in the account is guaranteed to increase to a 12 percent annual rate. If you plan on making 20 equal withdrawals at the beginning of each year from the account (with the first withdrawal made at the end of the 30th year—the first year of retirement), how much can you withdraw?

60. Frank Chang is planning for the day when his child, Laura, will go to college. Laura has just turned 8 and plans to enter college on her eighteenth birthday. She will need $25,000 at the beginning of each year in school. Frank plans to give Laura a Mercedes-Benz as a combination graduation and twenty-second birthday present. The Mercedes is expected to cost $55,000. Frank currently has $10,000 saved for Laura. Also, Frank expects to inherit $25,000 nine years from now that will be used for Laura's education. Frank expects to be able to earn 7 percent after tax on any investments. How much must Frank save at the end of each of the next 10 years in order to provide for Laura's education and the Mercedes?

61. Linda and Paul Chavez are each 35 years of age. They have a son, Mike, who is 15 and plans to go to college 4 years from now. Mike's college expenses are expected to be $30,000 per year, payable at the beginning of each year of school. Mike expects to finish school in 4 years. If he does, his parents have offered to purchase him an auto at the end of his fourth year in college, with an expected cost of $19,000. Linda and Paul have accumulated a total of $55,000 that can be used to pay these college expenses. They want to know what equal amount they must save (at the beginning of each of the next 6 years) in order to meet their commitments to Mike. Assume that the savings of Linda and Paul will earn a pretax rate of return of 10 percent and that their marginal tax rate is 30 percent. This tax rate and rate of return are assumed to remain unchanged for the next 8 years.

62. What is the monthly rate of interest that will yield an annual effective rate of interest of 12 percent?

63. Ted Gardiner has just turned 30 years old. He currently has accumulated $35,000 toward his planned retirement at age 60. He wants to accumulate enough money over the next 30 years to provide for a 20-year retirement annuity of $100,000 at the beginning of each year, starting with his 60th birthday. He plans to save $5,000 at the end of each of the next 10 years. What equal amount must he save at the end of years 11 through 30 to meet this objective? The interest rate for the first 10 years will be 5 percent. After that time, the interest rate is expected to be 7 percent.

64. Torbet Fish Packing Company wants to accumulate enough money over the next 10 years to pay for the expected replacement of its digitalized, automated scaling machine. The new machine is expected to cost $200,000 in 10 years. Torbet currently has $10,000 that it plans to invest over the next 10 years to help pay for the new machine. Torbet wants to put away an equal, end-of-year amount into a sinking fund investment account at the end of each of the next 10 years. Earnings on all of the investments are expected to be 7% for the first 5 years and 9% thereafter. What equal, end-of-year amount must Torbet save each year over the next 10 years to meet these needs?

65. Allstate Industries wants to set aside annual, end-of-year payments into a sinking fund account earning 8.25 percent over the next 6 years in order to retire $25 million in outstanding bonds. Determine the annual payment required to meet this obligation.

66. Crab State Bank has offered you a $1,000,000 5-year loan at an interest rate of 11.25 percent, requiring equal annual end-of-year payments that include both principal and interest on the unpaid balance. Develop an amortization schedule for this loan.

67. You can buy a piece of property today for $10,000 that you feel will be worth $20,000 10 years from now. Ignoring real estate and income (capital gains) taxes, determine the expected rate of return on this investment (to the nearest tenth of one percent) using
   a. Present value formulas and tables.
   b. Future value formulas and tables.

68. Determine the present value of an ordinary annuity of $10,000 per year for 3 years discounted of an interest rate of 8 percent using
   a. The definitional formula for $PVIFA_{i,n}$ (Equation 4.20).
   b. The computational formula for $PVIFA_{i,n}$ (Equation 4.21).
   c. The $PVIFA_{i,n}$ table.
   d. Your financial calculator.

69. Determine the future value of an ordinary annuity of $10,000 per year for 3 years at an interest rate of 8 percent using
   a. The definitional formula for $FVIFA_{i,n}$ (Equation 4.16).
   b. The computational formula for $FVIFA_{i,n}$ (Equation 4.17).
   c. The $FVIFA_{i,n}$ table.
   d. Your financial calculator.

70. Garrett Erdle has just turned 26 years of age. Although Garrett currently has a negative net worth, he expects to pay off all of his financial obligations within 4 years and then to embark on an aggressive plan to save for retirement. He wishes to be able to withdraw $100,000 per year during the first 10 years of retirement (the first withdrawal coming on his sixty-first birthday) and $150,000 during the next 10 years of retirement. As a precaution against unexpected longevity, he would like to have a net worth of $500,000 after the withdrawal on his eightieth birthday. Garrett expects the after-tax return on his investments to be 6 percent until he turns age 50, and 7 percent thereafter. What equal annual amount must Garrett save at the end of each year (the first deposit will occur on his thirty-first birthday and the last deposit will occur on his sixtieth birthday) to meet these retirement goals?

71. Bobbi Proctor does not want to "gamble" on Social Security taking care of her in her old age. Hence she wants to begin now to plan for retirement. She has enlisted the services of Hackney Financial Planning to assist her in meeting her goals. Proctor has determined that she would like to have a retirement annuity of $200,000 per year, with the first payment to be received 36 years from now at the end of her first year of retirement. She plans a long, enjoyable retirement of about 25 years. Proctor wishes to save $5,000 at the end of each of the next 15 years, and an unknown, equal end-of-period amount for the remaining 20 years before she begins her retirement. Hackney has advised Proctor that she can safely assume that all savings will earn 12 percent per annum until she retires, but only 8 percent thereafter. How much must Proctor save per year during the 20 years preceding retirement?

72. Try using one of the many Internet calculators, such as the one at Salem Five, to calculate your time-value problems.
   a. Suppose you wanted to borrow $100,000 for 25 years at 8 percent. Using Salem Five's calculator, find your monthly payment.
   b. Using Salem Five's "Savings and Investment Planner," find how much $2000 saved at the end of each of the next 30 years will grow to be, assuming it earns a constant 10 percent per year.
   http://www.salemfive.com

73. Using the amortization calculator at the following Web site, amortize a $100,000 loan over 10 years at 9 percent. What is the remaining balance after the fifth payment?
   www.moneyadvisor.com

■ SOLUTIONS TO SELF-TEST PROBLEMS*

ST1. $FV_n = PV_0(1 + i)^n$

a. $FV_5 = \$1,000(1.08)^5 = \$1,000(FVIF_{0.08,5}) = \$1,000(1.469)$

$= \$1,469$

Enter:	5	8	−1,000		
	n	i	PV	*PMT*	FV

Solution: 1,469.33

b. $FV_5 = \$1,000(1.02)^{20} = \$1,000(FVIF_{0.02,20}) = \$1,000(1.486)$

$= \$1,486$

Enter:	20	2	−1,000		
	n	i	PV	*PMT*	FV

Solution: 1,485.95

ST2. $PVAN_0 = PMT(PVIFA_{0.12,10})$

$= \$1,000(5.650)$

$= \$5,650$

Enter:	10	12		−1,000	
	n	i	PV	*PMT*	FV

Solution: 5,650.22

ST3. $FV_n = PV_0(FVIF_{i,n})$

$1.52 = 0.90(FVIF_{i,5})$

$FVIF_{i,5} = 1.689$

Using Table I and reading across the 5-year row, 1.685 is found in the 11 percent column. Thus, the growth rate is approximately 11 percent per year.

Enter:	5		−.90		1.52
	n	i	PV	*PMT*	FV

Solution: 11.05

ST4. $PVAN_3 = \$2,000(PVIFA_{0.14,5})$

$= \$2,000(3.433)$

$= \$6,866$

*Note: Differences between the financial calculator solution and the solution obtained using the present value tables is due to roundoff errors (3 decimal places) in the tables.

This step calculates the present value of the 5-year *ordinary* annuity at the beginning of year 4, i.e., the end of year 3. Next, $PVAN_3$ must be discounted to the present:

$$PVAN_0 = PVAN_3(PVIF_{0.14,3})$$

$$= \$6,866(0.675)$$

$$= \$4,635$$

Enter: 5　　14　　　　　　−2,000

| n | i | PV | PMT | FV |

Solution:　　　　　　6,866.16

Enter: 3　　14　　　　　　　　　　−6,866.16

| n | i | PV | PMT | FV |

Solution:　　　　　　4,634.46

ST5. $PVAN_0 = \$50,000(PVIF_{0.10,20})$

$$= \$50,000(8.514)$$

$$= \$425,700 \text{ (amount needed in account on sixtieth birthday)}$$

$$FVAN_{25} = PMT(FVIFA_{0.10,25})$$

$$\$425,700 = PMT(98.347)$$

$$PMT = \$4,329$$

Enter: 20　　10　　　　　　−50,000

| n | i | PV | PMT | FV |

Solution:　　　　　　425,678.19

Enter: 25　　10　　　　　　　　　　−425,678.19

| n | i | PV | PMT | FV |

Solution:　　　　　　4,328.33

■ GLOSSARY

Annuity The payment or receipt of a series of equal cash flows per period for a specified amount of time. In an *ordinary annuity*, payments are made at the end of each period; in an *annuity due*, payments are made at the beginning of each period.

Capital Recovery Problem An annuity amount necessary to recover a capital investment.

Compound Interest Interest that is paid not only on the principal but also on any interest earned but not withdrawn during earlier periods.

Discount Rate The rate of interest used in the process of finding present values (discounting).

Effective Interest Rate The actual rate of interest paid by the borrower or earned by the lender.

Future Value (or Terminal Value) The value at some future point in time of a present payment (or a series of payments) evaluated at the appropriate interest (growth) rate.

Interest The return earned by or the amount paid to an individual who forgoes current consumption or alternative investments and "rents" money to a business, bank, the government, some other form of institution, or another individual.

Loan Amortization Schedule A schedule of periodic payments of interest and principal owed on a debt obligations.

Nominal Interest Rate The period rate of interest that is stated in a loan agreement or security. Frequently, the *effective interest rate* is greater than the nominal rate because of such factors as the frequency of compounding and the deduction of interest in advance.

Perpetuity A financial instrument that pays an equal cash flow per period into the indefinite future (that is, infinity).

Present Value The value today of a future payment (or a series of future payments) evaluated at the appropriate discount rate.

Principal An amount of money that has been borrowed or invested.

Simple Interest Interest paid or earned on the principal only.

Sinking Fund Problem An annuity amount that must be invested each period (year) to produce a future value.

AN INTEGRATIVE CASE PROBLEM
TIME VALUE OF MONEY

Assume that you are 30 years old today and expect to retire when you reach age 65. If you were to retire *today*, you would like a fixed (pretax) income of $60,000 per year (in addition to Social Security) for a period of 15 years (your approximate life expectancy at age 65). However, you realize that price inflation will erode the purchasing power of the dollar over the next 35 years and want to adjust your desired retirement income at age 65 to reflect the decline in the purchasing power of the dollar. In addition to the fixed annual income, payable at the *beginning* of each year starting at age 65, you want to have assets (i.e., securities investments) of $1,000,000, either for your own needs or to donate to heirs, when you reach 80 years old.

Empirical studies have estimated the average compound rate of price inflation and returns on stocks and bonds over the past 70 years to be approximately

	Compound Rate
Inflation	3%
Common stocks	11
Corporate bonds	6
Equally weighted portfolio (50% common stocks, 50% bonds)	8.5

Assume that these rates will remain the same over the next 50 years and that you can earn these rates of return, after transactions costs, by investing in stock and/or bond index mutual funds. Also assume that contributions to your retirement fund are made at the *end* of each year. Finally, assume that income taxes on the returns from any retirement investments (e.g., IRAs or 401(k) plans) can be deferred until you withdraw the funds beginning at age 65.

1. Determine your required inflation-adjusted annual (pretax) income at age 65. Assume that this annual amount remains constant from age 65 to age 80.
2. Determine the amount you must accumulate by age 65 to meet your retirement goal, assuming that you invest in
   a. Common stocks.
   b. Corporate bonds.
   c. Equally weighted portfolio (50% common stocks, 50% bonds).
3. Determine the annual investment in *common stocks* required to accumulate the funds determined in Question 2, assuming that the first payment is made at age
   a. 30.
   b. 40.
   c. 50.

171

4. Determine the annual investment in *corporate bonds* required to accumulate the funds determined in Question 2, assuming that the first payment is made at age
   a. 30.
   b. 40.
   c. 50.

5.* Determine the annual investment in an *equally weighted portfolio* (50 percent common stocks, 50 percent bonds) required to accumulate the funds determined in Question 2, assuming that the first payment is made at age
   a. 30.
   b. 40.
   c. 50.

6. What conclusions can be drawn from the answers to Questions 3, 4 and 5?

---

*Note: This question requires the use of present value formulas or a financial calculator. It cannot be solved using the tables at the end of the book.

APPENDIX 4A
CONTINUOUS COMPOUNDING
AND DISCOUNTING

In Chapter 4 we assumed that interest was received (or growth in a stream of payments occurred) at discrete points in time, such as at the end of each year, semiannually, quarterly, and so forth. It was shown that a nominal rate of i_{nom} percent per year results in a greater than i_{nom} percent effective rate per year if compounding occurs more frequently than one time at the end of the year. Specifically, the future value (FV_n) of some initial amount (PV_0) is given by Equation 4.28:

$$FV_n = PV_0 \left(1 + \frac{i_{nom}}{m} \right)^{mn}$$

where i_{nom} is the nominal annual rate of interest or growth, m is the number of times per year that compounding occurs, and n is the number of years compounding occurs. (Recall from Footnote 11 in Chapter 4 that an annual nominal interest rate is equivalent to an effective annual rate in the case where compounding occurs once a year at the end of the year.)

As is shown in Table 4-6, the more often the compounding takes place each year, the greater will be the future value of some present amount. Another way of looking at this is to indicate that the more often that compounding takes place each year, the greater is the *effective* rate of interest (or growth) compared to the stated, annual *nominal* rate.

At the limit, we could accrue, or compound, interest *continuously*. In this limiting case, the future value equation for continuous compounding becomes:

$$FV_n = PV_0(e)^{i_{nom}n} \tag{4A.1}$$

where e is approximately equal to the value 2.71828. (This value is the base number in natural logarithms.) If you have a financial or scientific calculator, the value of $e^{i_{nom}n}$ normally can be found by multiplying the nominal rate i by the number of years n and then punching the e^x key.

For example, if $1,000 is invested for 1 year at a nominal rate of 10 percent compounded continuously, the future value at the end of that year is given as follows:

$$FV_1 = \$1,000(e)^{0.10(1)} = \$1,000(2.71828)^{0.10}$$

$$= \$1,105.17$$

In the case where the $1,000 is invested at a nominal rate of 10 percent for 3 years, the future value, assuming continuous compounding, is equal to

$$FV_3 = \$1000(e)^{0.10(3)} = \$1,000(2.71828)^{0.30}$$

$$= \$1,349.86$$

CONTINUOUS DISCOUNTING

Equation 4A.1 also can be modified to reflect continuous discounting. At the limit where compounding takes place continuously, present values can be computed as follows:

$$PV_0 = \frac{FV_n}{(e)^{i_{nom}n}} \tag{4A.2}$$

or equivalently

$$PV_0 = FV_n(e)^{-i_{nom}n} \tag{4A.3}$$

For example, if $1,349.86 is to be received 3 years from now at the continuously compounded rate of 10 percent, the present value can be computed as follows:

$$PV_0 = \frac{\$1,349.86}{(2.71828)^{0.10(3)}}$$

$$= \$1,000$$

EFFECTIVE RATE CALCULATIONS

When a *nominal* annual rate, i_{nom}, of interest (or growth) is known and compounding occurs continuously, it is easy to compute the *effective* annual rate using the following expression:[13]

$$i_{eff} = e^{i_{nom}} - 1 \tag{4A.4}$$

For example, if the nominal annual rate is 20 percent and compounding occurs continuously, the effective annual rate is computed as follows:

$$i_{eff} = 2.71828^{(0.2)} - 1$$

$$= 1.2214 - 1$$

$$= 0.2214 \text{ or } 22.14\%$$

The effective rate is higher than the nominal rate because, with continuous compounding, the money is working harder; that is, interest is being accumulated more frequently (continuously), and this accumulated interest is available to earn its own interest on an ongoing (continuous) basis.

■ SELF-TEST PROBLEMS

ST1. What is the future value of $1,000 invested for 7 years at a nominal interest rate of 10 percent compounded continuously?

ST2. What is the present value of receiving $5,000, 8 years from now if the nominal discount rate is 9 percent, discounted continuously?

---

[13]Equation 4A.4 is obtained from Equation 4.30 by letting m approach infinity:

$$i_{eff} = \lim_{m \to \infty} \left(1 + \frac{i_{nom}}{m}\right)^m - 1 = e^{i_{nom}} - 1$$

ST3. Calculate the effective annual rate if the nominal annual rate is 12 percent, compounded continuously.

■ PROBLEMS*

1. What is the future value of $10,000 invested for 2 years at a nominal interest rate of 12 percent compounded continuously?

2. You expect to receive $5,000 in 5 years. What is the present value of this future receipt at the continuously discounted rate of 12 percent?

3. The nominal rate of interest on a bank CD is 8 percent. If compounding occurs continuously, what is the effective annual rate?

4. Given a nominal annual interest rate of 20 percent, determine the effective annual rate with
   a. Annual compounding.
   b. Quarterly compounding.
   c. Monthly compounding.
   d. Continuous compounding.

5. What is the future value of $1,000 invested for 10 years at a nominal interest rate of 10 percent compounded continuously? How much higher is this value than the value obtained with annual compounding for 10 years at 10 percent?

6. What is the present value of receiving $1,500 25 years from now if the nominal interest rate is 10 percent, discounted continuously?

■ SOLUTIONS TO SELF-TEST PROBLEMS

ST1. $FV_7 = \$1,000(e)^{0.10(7)}$

$\qquad = \$2,013.75$

ST2. $PV_0 = \$5,000(e)^{-0.09(8)}$

$\qquad = \$2,433.76$

ST3. $i_{eff} = e^{0.12} - 1.0$

$\qquad = 1.1275 - 1.0$

$\qquad = 0.1275 \text{ or } 12.75\%$

---

*Colored numbers denote problems that have check answers provided at the end of the book.

ANALYSIS OF RISK AND RETURN

5

1. Risk represents the variability of possible future returns from an investment. Risk tends to increase as one looks farther into the future.
2. A *probability distribution* indicates the percentage chance of occurrence of each of the possible outcomes.
   a. The *expected value* is a measure of mean or average value of the possible outcomes, each having an associated probability of occurrence.
   b. The *standard deviation* is an important measure of the total risk or variability of possible outcomes, each having an associated probability of occurrence.
   c. The *coefficient of variation* is a useful total risk measure when comparing two investments with different expected returns.
3. The *required rate of return* on an investment—financial asset (security) or physical asset—is equal to the risk-free rate of return plus a risk premium.
   a. The risk-free rate of return refers to the return available on a short-term investment with no risk of default.
   b. The *risk premium* is a function of maturity risk, default risk, seniority risk, and marketability risk.
4. The required rate of return on an investment and the perceived risk of the returns expected from the investment have a positive relationship.

5. Portfolios are composed of two or more assets.
   a. The risk of a portfolio of assets depends on the risk of the individual assets in the portfolio and the correlation of returns between the pairs of assets in the portfolio.
   b. By combining assets that are less than perfectly positively correlated, portfolio risk can be *reduced* below the level of the weighted average risk of the individual assets.
6. The *Capital Asset Pricing Model (CAPM)* is a theory that can be used to determine required rates of return on investments in financial assets (securities) or physical assets.
   a. The *systematic* risk of a security refers to that portion of the variability of an individual security's returns caused by factors affecting the security market as a whole, such as interest rate changes.
   b. *Beta*, measured as the slope of a regression line between market returns and a security's returns, is used commonly as a measure of systematic risk.
   c. The *unsystematic* risk of a security refers to the portion of the variability of a security's returns caused by factors unique to that security.
   d. The *security market line* expresses the relationship between the required returns from a security and the systematic risk of that security.

APPLICATION OF PORTFOLIO MANAGEMENT TECHNIQUES TO CITIBANK'S CORPORATE LOAN BUSINESS*

Prudent Wall Street investors and money managers know that it makes sense to spread their investments among different companies and industries and "not put all of your eggs in one basket." Modern portfolio theory has developed techniques that help to quantify the benefits of such risk management strategies and to apply them in a systematic manner.

Banks are beginning to apply these same concepts to the management of their loan portfolios. In the past, large banks incurred sizeable losses when they invested large proportions of their assets in one particular type of loan and subsequently suffered high default rates with these loans. Examples include loans to Latin American countries, followed later by loans to U.S. real estate developers, and still later by loans to highly leveraged companies. Many large banks have implemented lending strategies that limit the amount of funds they are willing to lend to any single industry

or to any single region of the country. For example, Citibank adopted a system in 1992 that allows the bank to actively manage its $26 billion U.S. corporate loan portfolio. It began to make more

triple-A rated (low risk) loans and increased lending to less risky industries,

such as telephone companies, while cutting back on loans to more risky industries, such as financial services. Rod Ballek, manager of Citibank's debt portfolio, observed, "The point of portfolio management is to match the overall market performance rather than outdo and run the risk of failing, thus falling short of market returns." With this more analytical approach, banks hope to avoid the wild swings in profits and losses that have characterized bank lending over the past 20 years.

This chapter develops various techniques for measuring and managing risk that can be used by financial decision makers, such as mutual fund managers, securities brokers, and corporate treasurers, as well as by yourself in your own personal investing and retirement planning.

*Steven Lipin, "Portfolio Management Catches on For Bank Loans," *Wall Street Journal* (January 4, 1995): C1.

INTRODUCTION

Chapter 1 provided a brief introduction to risk and the relationship between risk and return. Recall that the required rate of return on an investment—financial asset (security) or physical asset—was represented as an increasing function of that investment's perceived risk; that is, the greater the risk, the greater is the required rate of return.[1]

This chapter develops the relationship between risk and return in more detail and presents methods for measuring risk. Later sections of the chapter focus on investment diversification and portfolio risk analysis.

MEANING AND MEASUREMENT OF RISK

Recall in Chapter 1 that **risk** was defined as the possibility that actual future returns will deviate from expected returns. In other words, it represents the variability of returns. Hence, risk implies that there is a chance for some unfavorable event to occur. From the perspective of security analysis or the analysis of an investment in some project (such as the development of a new product line), risk is the *possibility that actual cash flows (returns) will be different than forecasted cash flows (returns)*.

An investment is said to be *risk-free* if the dollar returns from the initial investment are known with certainty. Some of the best examples of risk-free investments are U.S. Treasury securities. There is virtually no chance that the Treasury will fail to redeem these securities at maturity or that the Treasury will default on any interest payments owed. As a last resort, the Treasury can always print more money.[2]

In contrast, RJR-Nabisco bonds constitute a *risky* investment because it is possible that the company will default on one or more interest payments and will lack sufficient funds to redeem the bonds at face value at maturity. In other words, the possible returns from this investment are *variable*, and each potential outcome can be assigned a *probability*.

If, for example, you were considering investing in RJR-Nabisco bonds, you might assign the probabilities shown in Table 5-1 to the three possible outcomes of this investment. These probabilities are interpreted to mean that an 80 percent

TABLE 5-1
Probability of Default
on RJR-Nabisco Bonds

OUTCOME	PROBABILITY
No default, bonds redeemed at maturity	0.80
Default on interest for one or more periods	0.15
No interest default, but bonds not redeemed at maturity	0.05
	1.00

[1]The terms *asset* and *security* will be used interchangeably throughout the chapter to refer to investments in either financial assets (securities) or physical assets.

[2]Note that this discussion of risk deals with *dollar returns* and ignores other considerations, such as potential losses in purchasing power. In addition, it assumes that securities are held until maturity, which is not always the case. Sometimes a security must be sold prior to maturity for less than face value because of changes in the level of interest rates.

chance exists that the bonds will not be in default over their life and will be redeemed at maturity, a 15 percent chance of interest default during the life of the bonds, and a 5 percent chance that the bonds will not be redeemed at maturity.

Hence, from an investment perspective, risk refers to the chance that returns from an investment will be different than expected. We can define risk more precisely, however, by introducing some probability concepts.

Using the Alta Vista search engine, type in the search term risk analysis *(almost one million hits!) and look at the vast wealth of internet information available for analyzing risk of any kind for any assets. Some of the hits may surprise you.* http://www.altavista.digital.com

Probability Distributions

The *probability* that a particular outcome will occur is defined as the *percentage chance* (or likelihood) of its occurrence. A *probability distribution* indicates the percentage chance of occurrence of each of the possible outcomes. Probabilities may be determined either objectively or subjectively. An objective determination is based on past occurrences of similar outcomes, whereas a subjective one is merely an opinion made by an individual about the likelihood that a given outcome will occur. In the case of projects that are frequently repeated—such as the drilling of developmental oil wells in an established oil field—reasonably good objective estimates can be made about the success of a new well. Similarly, good objective estimates can often be made about the expected returns of an AT&T bond. However, the expected returns from securities of new, small firms are often much more difficult to estimate objectively. Hence, highly subjective estimates regarding the likelihood of various returns are necessary. The fact that many probability estimates in business are at least partially subjective does not diminish their usefulness.

Summary of Notation

Before examining specific measures of risk and return, it is useful to summarize the basic elements of notation used throughout the chapter.

r = single rate of return on a given security; a subscript denotes the rate of return on a particular security (or portfolio of securities), such as r_f, described next, and a hat ($\wedge$) symbol denotes an *expected* rate of return.

r_f = riskless (risk-free) rate of return; the return offered on short-term U.S. Treasury securities.

r_p = rate of return on a portfolio of securities.

r_m = rate of return on the Market Portfolio; a broad-based security market index, such as the Standard and Poor's 500 Market Index or the New York Stock Exchange Index, normally is used as a measure of total market returns.

p = probability of occurrence of a specific rate of return.

σ = standard deviation of the rate of return on a security (or portfolio of securities).

σ_p = standard deviation of the rate of return on a portfolio of securities.

σ_m = standard deviation of the rate of return on the Market Portfolio.

v = coefficient of variation.

z = number of standard deviations that a particular value of a random variable (such as rate of return) is from its expected value.

ρ = correlation coefficient between the returns on two securities.

w = portion (weight) of funds invested in a given security within a portfolio.

k_j = *required* rate of return on a given security.

θ_j = risk premium required by investors on a given security.

β_j = measure of the volatility (or risk) of a security's returns relative to the returns on the Market Portfolio.

β_p = measure of risk of a portfolio of securities.

Expected Value

Suppose an investor is considering an investment of $100,000 in the stock of either Wisconsin Public Service (WPS), a public utility firm, or Texas Instruments (TI), a maker of electronic equipment. By investing in the stock of either of these firms, an investor expects to receive dividend payments plus stock price appreciation. We will assume that the investor plans to hold the stock for one year and then sell it. Over the coming year, the investor feels there is a 20 percent chance for an economic *boom*, a 60 percent chance for a *normal* economic environment, and a 20 percent chance for a *recession*. Given this assessment of the economic environment *over the next year,* the investor estimates the probability distribution of returns from the investment in WPS and TI as shown in Table 5-2.

From this information, the *expected value* of returns (or expected return) from investing in the stock of WPS and TI can be calculated. The **expected value** is a statistical measure of the mean or average value of the possible outcomes. Operationally, it is defined as the weighted average of possible outcomes, with the weights being the probabilities of occurrence.

Algebraically, the expected value of the returns from a security or project may be defined as follows:

$$\hat{r} = \sum_{j=1}^{n} r_j\, p_j \tag{5.1}$$

where $\hat{r}$ is the expected return; r_j is the outcome for the jth case, where there are n possible outcomes; and p_j is the probability that the jth outcome will occur. The expected returns for WPS and TI are computed in Table 5-3. The expected return is 18 percent for both WPS and TI.

**TABLE 5-2
Probability Distribution of
Returns from WPS and TI**

STATE OF THE ECONOMY	Probability	RATE OF RETURN ANTICIPATED UNDER EACH STATE OF THE ECONOMY*	
		WPS	TI
Recession	0.2	10%	– 4%
Normal year	0.6	18	18
Boom	0.2	26	40
	1.0		

*For example, a 10 percent rate of return for WPS means that the stock value plus dividends total $110,000 at the end of one year. Working with a *discrete* probability distribution, as this example does, indicates that there is no probability of a loss by investing in WPS. This, of course, is unrealistic. In the following discussion of continuous distributions, this assumption is relaxed.

TABLE 5-3
Expected Return Calculation for
Investment in WPS and TI

	WPS			TI	
r_j	p_j	$r_j \times p_j$	r_j	p_j	$r_j \times p_j$
10%	0.2	2.0%	−4%	0.2	−0.8%
18	0.6	10.8	18	0.6	10.8
26	0.2	5.2	40	0.2	8.0
	Expected return $= \hat{r} = 18.0\%$			Expected return $= \hat{r} = 18.0\%$	

Standard Deviation: An Absolute Measure of Risk

The **standard deviation** is a statistical measure of the dispersion of possible outcomes about the expected value. It is defined as the *square root of the weighted average squared deviations of possible outcomes from the expected value* and computed as follows:

$$\sigma = \sqrt{\sum_{j=1}^{n} (r_j - \hat{r})^2 p_j} \tag{5.2}$$

where σ is the standard deviation.

The standard deviation can be used to measure the variability of returns from an investment. As such, it gives an indication of the *risk* involved in the asset or security. The larger the standard deviation, the more variable is an investment's returns and the riskier is the investment. A standard deviation of zero indicates no variability and thus no risk. Table 5-4 shows the calculation of the standard deviations for the investments in WPS and TI.

As shown in the calculations in Table 5-4, TI appears riskier than WPS, because possible returns from TI are more variable, measured by its standard deviation of 13.91 percent, than those from WPS, which have a standard deviation of only 5.06 percent.

	j	r_j	$\hat{r}$	$r_j - \hat{r}$	$(r_j - \hat{r})^2$	p_j	$(r_j - \hat{r})^2 p_j$
WPS	1 (Recession)	10%	18%	−8%	64	0.2	12.8
	2 (Normal)	18	18	0	0	0.6	0
	3 (Boom)	26	18	+8	64	0.2	12.8

$$\sum_{j=1}^{3} (r_j - \hat{r})^2 p_j = 25.6$$

$$\sigma = \sqrt{\sum_{j=1}^{n} (r_j - \hat{r})^2 p_j} = \sqrt{25.6} = 5.06\%$$

	j	r_j	$\hat{r}$	$r_j - \hat{r}$	$(r_j - \hat{r})^2$	p_j	$(r_j - \hat{r})^2 p_j$
TI	1 (Recession)	−4%	18%	−22%	484	0.2	96.8
	2 (Normal)	18	18	0	0	0.6	0
	3 (Boom)	40	18	+22	484	0.2	96.8

$$\sum_{j=1}^{3} (r_j - \hat{r})^2 p_j = 193.6$$

$$\sigma = \sqrt{\sum_{j=1}^{n} (r_j - \hat{r})^2 p_j} = \sqrt{193.6} = 13.91\%$$

This example deals with a *discrete* probability distribution of outcomes (returns) for each firm; that is, a *limited* number of possible outcomes are identified, and probabilities are assigned to them. In reality, however, many different outcomes are possible for the investment in the stock of each firm—ranging from losses during the year to returns in excess of TI's 40 percent return. To indicate the probability of *all* possible outcomes for these investments, it is necessary to construct a *continuous* probability distribution. This is done by developing a table similar to Table 5-2, except that it would have many more possible outcomes and their associated probabilities. The detailed table of outcomes and probabilities can be used to develop the expected value of returns from WPS and TI, and a continuous curve would be constructed to approximate the probabilities associated with each outcome. Figure 5-1 illustrates continuous probability distributions of returns for investments in the stock of WPS and TI.

As seen in this figure, the WPS possible returns have a tighter probability distribution, indicating a lower variability of returns, whereas the TI possible returns have a flatter distribution, indicating higher variability and, by extension, more risk.

Normal Probability Distribution

The possible returns from many investments tend to follow a *normal* probability distribution. The normal probability distribution is characterized by a symmetrical, bell-like curve. If the expected continuous probability distribution of returns is approximately normal, a table of the *standard normal probability distribution* (that is, a normal distribution with a mean equal to 0.0 and a standard deviation equal to 1.0, such as Table V at the end of the text) can be used to compute the probability of occurrence of any particular outcome. From this table, for example, it is apparent that the actual outcome should be between plus or minus 1 standard deviation from the expected value 68.26 percent of the time,[3] between plus or mi-

FIGURE 5-1
Continuous Probability Distributions for the Expected Returns from Investments in the WPS and TI stocks

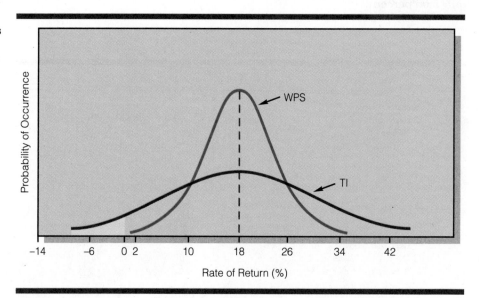

---

[3]For example, Table V indicates that here is a probability of 0.1587 of a value occurring that is greater than +1σ from the mean *and* a probability of 0.1587 of a value occurring that is less than −1σ from the mean. Hence, the probability of a value *between* +1σ and −1σ is 68.26 percent; that is, 1.00 − (2 × 0.1587).

nus 2 standard deviations 95.44 percent of the time, and between plus or minus 3 standard deviations 99.74 percent of the time. This is illustrated in Figure 5-2.

The number of standard deviations, z, that a particular value of r is from the expected value, $\hat{r}$, can be computed as follows:

$$z = \frac{r - \hat{r}}{\sigma} \qquad (5.3)$$

Equation 5.3, along with Table V, can be used to compute the probability of a return from an investment being less than (or greater than) some particular value.

For example, as part of the analysis of the risk of an investment in TI stock, suppose we are interested in determining the probability of earning a negative rate of return; that is, a return less than 0 percent. This probability is represented graphically in Figure 5-1 as the area to the left of 0 (that is, the shaded area) under the TI probability distribution. The number of standard deviations that 0 percent is from the expected return (18 percent) must be calculated. Substituting the expected return and the standard deviation from Tables 5-3 and 5-4 into Equation 5.3 yields the following:

$$z = \frac{0\% - 18\%}{13.91\%}$$

$$= -1.29$$

In other words, the return of 0 percent is 1.29 standard deviations *below* the mean. From Table V, the probability associated with 1.29 standard deviations is 0.0985. Therefore, there is a 9.85 percent chance that TI will have returns below 0 percent. Conversely, there is a 90.15 percent (100 − 9.85) chance that the return will be greater than 0 percent.

Coefficient of Variation: A Relative Measure of Risk

The standard deviation is an appropriate measure of total risk when the investments being compared are approximately equal in expected returns and the

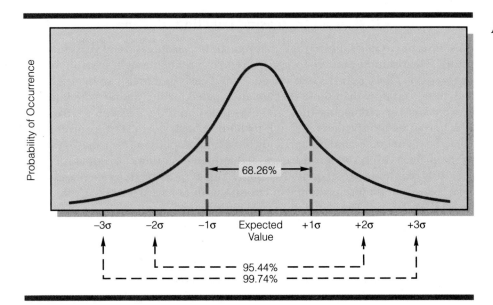

FIGURE 5-2
Areas under the Normal Probability Distribution

returns are estimated to have symmetrical probability distributions. Because the standard deviation is an *absolute* measure of variability, it generally is *not* suitable for comparing investments with different expected returns. In these cases, the **coefficient of variation** provides a better measure of risk. It is defined as the ratio of the standard deviation, σ, to the expected return, $\hat{r}$:

$$v = \frac{\sigma}{\hat{r}} \tag{5.4}$$

The coefficient of variation is a *relative* measure of variability, since it measures the risk per unit of expected return. As the coefficient of variation increases, so does the risk of an asset.

Consider, for example, two assets, T and S. Asset T has expected annual returns of 25 percent and a standard deviation of 20 percent, whereas Asset S has expected annual returns of 10 percent and a standard deviation of 18 percent. Although Asset T has a higher standard deviation than Asset S, intuition tells us that Asset T is less risky, because its *relative* variation is smaller. The coefficients of variation for Assets T and S are computed as follows using Equation 5.4:

$$\text{Asset T:} \quad v = \frac{20\%}{25\%}$$
$$= 0.8$$

$$\text{Asset S:} \quad v = \frac{18\%}{10\%}$$
$$= 1.8$$

Asset T's returns have a lower coefficient of variation than Asset S's, and therefore, Asset T is the less risky of the two investments.

In general, when comparing two equal-sized investments, the standard deviation is an appropriate measure of total risk. When comparing two investments with different expected returns, the coefficient of variation is the more appropriate measure of total risk.[4]

Risk as an Increasing Function of Time

Most investment decisions require that returns be *forecasted* several years into the future. The riskiness of these forecasted returns may be thought of as an *increasing function of time*. Returns that are generated early generally can be predicted with more certainty than those that are anticipated further out into the future.

Consider the risk facing the Tandy Corporation in its decision to market a new line of stereo speakers through its Radio Shack stores. This project is expected to generate cash flows to Tandy of $2 million per year over the 7-year life of the project. Even though the expected annual cash flows are equal for each year, it is reasonable to assume that the riskiness of these flows increases over time as more and more presently unknown variables have a chance to affect the project's cash flows. Figure 5-3 illustrates this situation.

[4]The relationship between the coefficient of variation and several other measures of risk (including the standard deviation) is developed in John M. Wachowicz, Jr., and Ronald E. Shrieves, "An Argument for Generalized Mean-Coefficient of Variation Analysis," *Financial Management* (Winter 1980): 51–58.

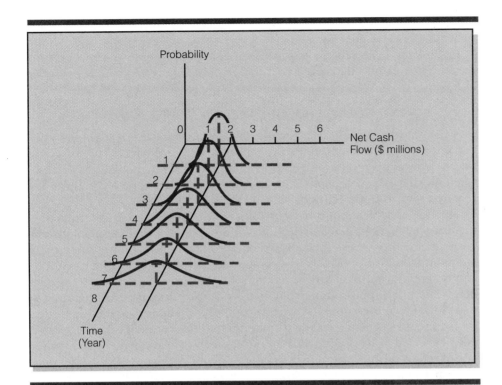

FIGURE 5-3
Risk of a Project over Time:
Tandy Corporation

The distribution is relatively tight in year 1, because the factors affecting that year's cash flows (e.g., demand and costs) are reasonably well known. By year 7, however, the distribution has become relatively flat, indicating a considerable increase in the standard deviation, caused by increased uncertainty about the factors that affect cash flows. For example, competitors may introduce similar (or improved) products, which causes demand to decline for the Tandy speakers.

Some types of cash flows are not subject to increasing variability. These include, for example, contractual arrangements, such as lease payments, in which the expected cash flows remain constant (or change at some predefined rate) over the life of the contract. In spite of the exceptions, it is reasonable to conclude that the riskiness of the cash flows from most investment projects gradually increases over time. Similarly, the riskiness of returns from most securities increases the further into the future these returns are being considered. For instance, the interest return from the purchase of Chrysler Corporation bonds is nearly guaranteed for the next year. However, projecting the interest returns to be received 10 years in the future is much more difficult due to the potential impact of competition, new technology, and other factors.

 FOUNDATION CONCEPT
RELATIONSHIP BETWEEN RISK AND RETURN

The trade-off between risk and return is a key element of effective financial decision making. This includes both decisions by individuals (and financial institutions) to invest in financial assets, such as common stocks, bonds, and other securities, and decisions by a firm's managers to invest in physical assets, such as new plants and equipment.

In Chapter 1 the relationship between risk and required return was introduced. The relationship between risk and *required rate of return* can be expressed as follows:

$$\text{Required rate of return} = \text{Risk-free rate of return} + \text{Risk premium} \quad (5.5)$$

A *risk premium* is a potential "reward" that an investor expects to receive when making a risky investment. Investors generally are considered to be *risk averse;* that is, they expect, on average, to be compensated for the risk they assume when making an investment. Thus, over the long term, expected returns and required returns from securities will tend to be equal.

The rate of return required by investors in financial assets is determined in the financial marketplace and depends on the supply of funds available as well as the demand for these funds. Investors who buy bonds receive interest payments and a return of principal as compensation for postponing consumption and accepting risk. Similarly, common stock investors expect to receive dividends and price appreciation from their stock. The rate of return required by these investors represents a *cost of capital* to the firm. This required rate of return is used by a firm's managers when computing the net present value of the cash flows expected to be generated from the company's investments. The required rate of return on a security also is an important determinant of the market value of financial securities, including common stock, preferred stock, and bonds.

The following sections focus on the two components of the required rate of return—the risk-free return and the risk premium—and also look at the historical relationship between risk and rates of return on various types of securities.

Risk-Free Rate of Return

The concept of a **risk-free rate of return** refers to the return available on a security with no risk of default. In the case of debt securities, no default risk means that promised interest and principal payments are guaranteed to be made. Short-term U.S. government securities, such as Treasury bills, generally are considered to be risk-free investments.[5]

The risk-free rate of return, r_f, is equal to the sum of a real rate of return and an expected inflation premium:

$$r_f = \text{Real rate of return} + \text{Expected inflation premium} \quad (5.6)$$

The *real rate of return* is the return that investors would require from a security having no risk of default in a period of no expected inflation. It is the return necessary to convince investors to postpone current, *real,* consumption opportunities. The real rate of return is determined by the interaction of the supply of funds made available by savers and the demand for funds for investment. Historically, the real rate of return has been estimated to average in the range of 2 to 4 percent.

---

[5]Securities issued by the U.S. Treasury are used to finance the national debt and government operations. During the 1995–96 budget impass between Congress and the President, with the national debt close to its $4.9 trillion authorized ceiling, the issue of a possible default on U.S. government securities was raised. See "What if Uncle Sam Defaults?" *Business Week* (November 13, 1995): 44 and "What Is the Fuss About a U.S. Default?" *Wall Street Journal* (January 24, 1996): A2 for a discussion of the possible consequences of a default.

The second component of the risk-free rate of return is an *inflation premium* or *purchasing power loss premium*. Investors require compensation for expected losses in purchasing power when they postpone current consumption and lend funds. Consequently, a premium for expected inflation is included in the required return on any security. The inflation premium is normally equal to investors' expectations about future purchasing power changes. If, for example, inflation is expected to average 4 percent over some future period, the risk-free rate of return on U.S. Treasury bills (assuming a real rate of return of 3 percent) should be approximately equal to 3 percent + 4 percent = 7 percent by Equation 5.6. By extension, if inflation expectations suddenly increase from 4 to 6 percent, the risk-free rate should increase from 7 to 9 percent (3 percent real return plus 6 percent inflation premium).

At any point in time, the required risk-free rate of return on any security can be estimated from the yields on short-term U.S. government securities, such as 90-day Treasury bills.

When considering return requirements on all types of securities, it is important to remember that *increases in expected inflation rates normally lead to increases in the required rates of return on all securities.*

Risk Premium

The **risk premium** assigned by an investor to a given security in determining the required rate of return (Equation 5.5) is a function of several different risk elements. These risk elements (and premiums) include

- Maturity risk premium
- Default risk premium
- Seniority risk premium
- Marketability risk premium

Each of these risk elements is examined below.

Maturity Risk Premium. The return required on a security is influenced by the maturity of that security. The **term structure of interest rates** is the pattern of interest rate yields (required returns) for securities that differ only in the length of time to maturity. Plotting interest rate yields (percent) on the vertical axis and the length of time to maturity (years) on the horizontal axis results in a yield curve. Three yield curves for U.S. government securities are shown in Figure 5-4.[6] Note the different shapes of the three yield curves. The yield curve for August 1981 is *downward sloping,* indicating that the longer the time to maturity, the lower is the required return on the security. The yield curve for August 1996 is *upward sloping,* indicating that the longer the time to maturity, the higher is the required return on the security.[7]

[6]The primary reason for examining U.S. government securities is that we are able to hold many of the factors affecting yields, such as default risk, constant. Corporate debt security issues, even for the same company, often differ significantly with respect to their key provisions, including sinking fund, call, conversion, subordination, and mortgage features. Hence, these bond issues differ with respect to risk. Consequently, it is difficult to use corporate debt securities to make yield versus time-to-maturity comparisons. However, the same general conclusions concerning the term structure of interest rates apply to these securities.

[7]Upward- and downward-sloping yield curves are not the only possible shapes. At various times in the past, the yield curve has been relatively flat and also has been hump-shaped; that is, high intermediate-term yields and low short-term and long-term yields. In February 1989, the curve was hump-shaped, as shown in Figure 5-4.

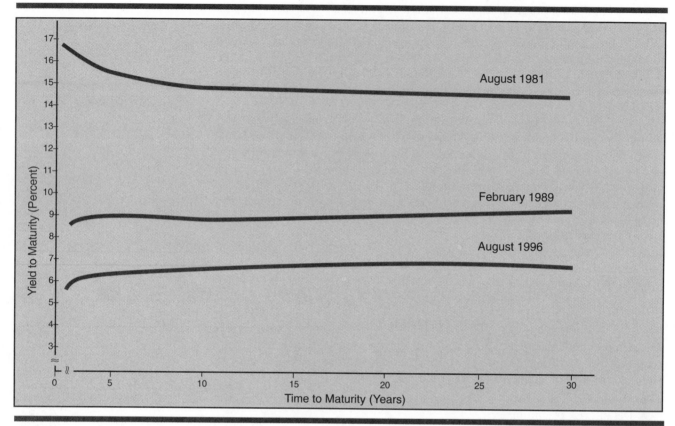

FIGURE 5-4
Yield Curves Showing the
Term Structure of Interest Rates
for U.S. Treasury Securities

Source: *Federal Reserve Bulletin* (October 1981, May 1989, and November 1996).

In general, the yield curve has been upward sloping more often than it has been downward sloping. For example, during the years 1993–1995, the yield on 3-month U.S. government Treasury bills has averaged approximately 4.25 percent. In contrast, the yield on 10-year U.S. government bonds averaged 6.51 percent, and the yield on 30-year U.S. government bonds averaged 6.95 percent.[8]

A number of theories have been advanced to explain the shape of the yield curve, including the expectations theory, liquidity (or maturity) premium theory, and market segmentation theory.

According to the *expectations theory*, long-term interest rates are a function of expected future (that is, forward) short-term interest rates. If future short-term interest rates are expected to rise, the yield curve will tend to be upward sloping. In contrast, a downward-sloping yield curve reflects an expectation of declining future short-term interest rates. According to the expectations theory, current and expected future interest rates are dependent on expectations about future rates of inflation. Many economic and political conditions can cause expected future inflation and interest rates to rise or fall. These conditions include expected future government deficits (or surpluses), changes in Federal Reserve monetary policy (that is, the rate of growth of the money supply), and cyclical business conditions.

[8]*Federal Reserve Bulletin* (November 1996).

The *liquidity (or maturity) premium theory* of the yield curve holds that required returns on long-term securities tend to be greater the longer the time to maturity. The maturity premium reflects a preference by many lenders for shorter maturities, because the *interest rate risk* associated with these securities is less than with longer-term securities. As we shall see in Chapter 6, the value of a bond tends to vary more as interest rates change, the longer the term to maturity. Thus, if interest rates rise, the holder of a long-term bond will find that the value of the investment has declined substantially more than that of the holder of a short-term bond. In addition, the short-term bond holder has the option of holding the bond for the short time remaining to maturity and then reinvesting the proceeds from that bond at the new higher interest rate. The long-term bond holder must wait much longer before this opportunity is available. Accordingly, it is argued that whatever the shape of the yield curve, a liquidity (or maturity) premium is reflected in it. The liquidity premium is larger for long-term bonds than for short-term bonds.

Finally, according to the *market segmentation theory*, the securities markets are segmented by maturity. Furthermore, interest rates within each maturity segment are determined to a certain extent by the supply and demand interactions of the segment's borrowers and lenders. If strong borrower demand exists for long-term funds and these funds are in short supply, the yield curve will be upward sloping. Conversely, if strong borrower demand exists for short-term funds and these funds are in short supply, the yield curve will be downward sloping.

Several factors limit the choice of maturities by lenders. One such restriction is the legal regulations that limit the types of investments commercial banks, savings and loan associations, insurance companies, and other financial institutions are permitted to make. Another limitation faced by lenders is the desire (or need) to match the maturity structure of their liabilities with assets of equivalent maturity. For example, insurance companies and pension funds, because of the long-term nature of their contractual obligations to clients, are interested primarily in making long-term investments. Commercial banks and money market funds, in contrast, are primarily short-term lenders, because a large proportion of their liabilities are in the form of deposits that can be withdrawn on demand.

At any point in time, the term structure of interest rates is the result of the interaction of the factors just described. All three theories are useful in explaining the shape of the yield curve.

The Default Risk Premium. U.S. government securities generally are considered to be free of default risk; that is, the risk that interest and principal will not be paid as promised in the bond indenture. In contrast, corporate bonds are subject to varying degrees of default risk. Investors require higher rates of return on securities subject to default risk. Bond rating agencies, such as Moody's, Standard and Poor's, Duff and Phelps, and Fitch, provide evaluations of the default risk of many corporate bonds in the form of bond ratings. Moody's, for example, rates bonds on a 9-point scale from Aaa through C, where Aaa-rated bonds have the lowest expected default risk.[9] As seen in Table 5-5, the yields on bonds increase as the risk of default increases, reflecting the positive relationship between risk and required return. Over time, the spread between the required returns on bonds having various levels of default risk varies,

TABLE 5-5
Relationship Between Default Risk and Required Returns

Source: *Federal Reserve Bulletin* (November 1996): 1–35.

SECURITY	YIELD
U.S. Treasury Bonds (30 year)	6.84%
Aaa-rated Corporate Bonds	7.46
Aa-rated Corporate Bonds	7.63
A-rated Corporate Bonds	7.77
Baa-rated Corporate Bonds	8.18

[9]A more detailed discussion of the bond rating process is contained in Chapter 6.

reflecting the economic prospects and the resulting probability of default. For example, during the relative prosperity of 1989, the yield on Baa-rated corporate bonds was 0.44 percentage points greater than the yield on higher-quality (lower default risk) A-rated bonds. By late 1990, as the U.S. economy weakened and headed toward a recession, this spread had increased to 0.70 percentage points.

Seniority Risk Premium. Corporations issue many different types of securities. These securities differ with respect to their claim on the cash flows generated by the company and the claim on the company's assets in the case of default. A partial listing of these securities, from the least senior (that is, from the security having the lowest priority claim on cash flows and assets) to the most senior, includes the following: common stock, preferred stock, income bonds, subordinated debentures, debentures, second mortgage bonds, and first mortgage bonds.[10] Generally, the less senior are the claims of the security holder, the greater is the required rate of return demanded by investors in that security. For example, the holders of bonds issued by Exxon are assured that they will receive interest and principal payments on these bonds except in the highly unlikely event that the company faces bankruptcy. In contrast, common stockholders have no such assurance regarding dividend payments. Also, in the case of bankruptcy, all senior claimholders must be paid before common stockholders receive any proceeds from the liquidation of the firm. Accordingly, common stockholders require a higher rate of return on their investment in Exxon stock than do Exxon bond holders.

Marketability Risk Premium. Marketability risk refers to the ability of an investor to buy and sell a company's securities quickly and without a significant loss of value. For example, there is very little marketability risk for the shares of stock of most companies that are traded on the New York or American Stock Exchange or listed on the NASDAQ system for over-the-counter stocks. For these securities, there is an active market. Trades can be executed almost instantaneously with low transactions costs at the current market price. In contrast, if you own shares in a rural Nebraska bank, you might find it difficult to locate a buyer for those shares (unless you owned a controlling interest in the bank). When a buyer is found, that buyer may not be willing to pay the price that you could get for similar shares of a larger bank listed on the New York Stock Exchange. The marketability risk premium can be significant for securities that are not regularly traded, such as the shares of many small and medium-size firms.

Business and Financial Risk[11]

Within individual security classes, one observes significant differences in required rates of return between firms. For example, the required rate of return on the common stock of US Airways is considerably higher than the required rate of return on the common stock of American Airlines. The difference in the required rate of return on the securities of these two companies reflects differences in their business and financial risk. The **business risk** of a firm refers to the variability in the firm's operating earnings over time. Business risk is influenced by many factors, including the variability in sales and operating costs over

---

[10]These various forms of debt (i.e., debentures and bonds) are described in Chapter 6.
[11]Business and financial risk are examined in more detail in Chapter 12.

a business cycle, the diversity of a firm's product line, the market power of the firm, and the choice of production technology. As a larger, more powerful, and diverse firm, American Airlines can be expected to have a lower perceived level of business risk and a resulting lower required return on its common stock (all other things held constant).

Financial risk refers to the additional variability in a company's earnings per share that results from the use of fixed-cost sources of funds, such as debt and preferred stock. In addition, as debt financing increases, the risk of bankruptcy increases. For example, US Airways had a long-term debt to net worth ratio of 66.9 in 1995. In comparison, the long-term debt to net worth ratio was approximately 1.90 for American Airlines in 1995. This difference in financial risk will lead to lower required returns on the common stock of American Airlines compared to the common stock of US Airways, all other things being equal.

Business and financial risk are reflected in the default risk premium applied by investors to a firm's securities. The higher are these risks, the higher are the risk premium and required rate of return on the firm's securities.

Systematic and Unsystematic Risk

As we will learn in more detail later in the chapter, much of the risk facing investors in a firm's securities can be decomposed into *systematic* (undiversifiable) and *unsystematic* (diversifiable) risk components. The **systematic risk** of a security refers to that portion of the return variability caused by factors affecting the security market as a whole, such as a change in the general business outlook. Systematic risk often is measured by a security's **beta,** a measure of the volatility of a security's returns relative to the returns of the overall security market. **Unsystematic risk** refers to the portion of the variability of an individual security's returns caused by factors unique to that security. Unsystematic risk can be greatly reduced or even totally eliminated by investors who hold a broad (diversified) collection (portfolio) of securities. Systematic risk cannot be diversified away. Business and financial risk are components of both systematic and unsystematic risk.

Risk and Required Returns for Various Types of Securities

Figure 5-5 illustrates the relationship between required rates of return and risk, as represented by the various risk premiums just discussed. As shown in Figure 5-5, the lowest risk security is represented by short-term U.S. Treasury bills. All other securities have one or more elements of additional risk, resulting in increasing required returns by investors. The order illustrated in this figure is indicative of the general relationship between risk and required returns of various security types. There will be situations that result in differences in the ordering of risk and required returns. For example, it is possible that the risk of some junk (high risk) bonds may be so great that investors require a higher rate of return on these bonds than they require on high-grade common stocks.

The relationship between risk and return can be observed by examining the returns actually earned by investors in various types of securities over long periods of time. Finance professionals believe that investor expectations of the relative returns anticipated from various types of securities are heavily influenced by the returns that have been earned on these securities over long periods in the past. Table 5-6 shows the returns that have been earned by investors over long periods of time on selected types of securities. All the rates of return are before taxes

FIGURE 5-5
Conceptual Risk-
Return Relationship

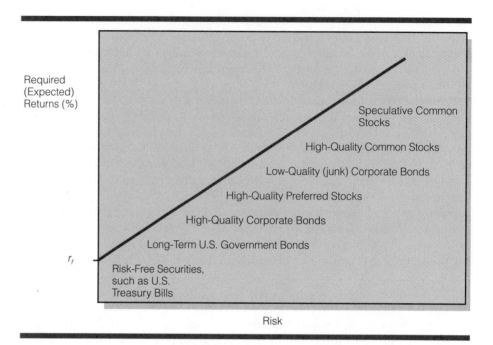

and assume reinvestment of dividends on common stocks or interest on bonds. This table confirms the general positive nature of the relationship between risk, as measured by the standard deviation, and mean return.

TABLE 5-6
Annual Historical Rates of Return:
1926–1995

Source: *Stocks, Bonds, Bills and Inflation: 1996 Yearbook* (Chicago: Ibbotson Associates, Inc., 1996), Table 2-1, 33. Annually updates work by Roger G. Ibbotson and Rex A. Sinquefield. Data reproduced with permission of Ibbotson Associates. All rights reserved.

SERIES	ARITHMETIC MEAN	STANDARD DEVIATION	DISTRIBUTION
Large Company Stocks	12.5%	20.4%	
Small Company Stocks	17.7	34.4	*
Long-Term Corporate Bonds	6.0	8.7	
Long-Term Government Bonds	5.5	9.2	
Intermediate-Term Government Bonds	5.4	5.8	
U.S. Treasury Bills	3.8	3.3	
Inflation	3.2	4.6	

–90%   0%   90%

*The 1993 Small Company Stock Total Return was 12.9 percent.

INVESTMENT DIVERSIFICATION AND PORTFOLIO RISK ANALYSIS[12]

The preceding sections examined the risk and returns associated with investments in single assets—either financial assets (securities) or physical assets. However, most individuals and institutions invest in a **portfolio** of assets, that is, a collection of two or more assets. Commercial banks invest in many different types of financial assets when they make loans to consumers and businesses; individuals invest in many different types of financial assets when they buy securities, such as bank certificates of deposit and corporate bonds and stocks; and corporations invest in many different kinds of physical assets when they acquire production and distribution facilities (i.e., plants and equipment). Consequently, it is important to know how the returns from portfolios of investments behave over time—not just how the returns from individual assets in the portfolio behave. *Portfolio risk,* the risk associated with collections of financial and physical assets, is considered in this and the following two sections. The questions of importance are as follows:

■ What return can be expected to be earned from the portfolio?
■ What is the risk of the portfolio?

Consider the following example. Suppose that Alcoa (the aluminum industry's largest producer) is considering diversifying into gold mining and refining. During economic boom periods, aluminum sales tend to be brisk; gold, on the other hand, tends to be most in demand during periods of economic uncertainty.[13] Therefore, let us assume that the returns from the aluminum business and the gold mining business are inversely, or *negatively,* related. If Alcoa expands into gold mining and refining, its overall return will tend to be less variable than individual returns from these businesses.

This effect is illustrated in Figure 5-6. Panel (a) shows the variation of rates of return in the aluminum industry over time; panel (b) shows the corresponding variation of returns from gold mining over the same time frame; and panel (c) shows the combined rate of return for both lines of business. As can be seen from this figure, when the return from aluminum operations is high, the return from gold mining tends to be low and vice versa. The *combined* returns are more stable and therefore less risky.

This *portfolio effect* of reduced variability results because a *negative correlation* exists between the returns from aluminum operations and the returns from gold mining. The *correlation* between any two variables—such as rates of return or net cash flows—is a relative statistical measure of the degree to which these variables tend to move together. The **correlation coefficient** (ρ) measures the extent to which high (or low) values of one variable are associated with high (or low) values

---

[12]Two economists, Harry M. Markowitz and William F. Sharpe, were co-recipients (along with Merton H. Miller) of the 1990 Nobel Prize for Economics for their pioneering work in portfolio theory (discussed in this section) and the Capital Asset Pricing Model (discussed in the following section). See Harry M. Markowitz, "Portfolio Selection," *Journal of Finance* 7 (March 1952): 77–91, and *Portfolio Selection: Efficient Diversification of Investments* (New York: John Wiley, 1959); William F. Sharpe, "A Simplified Model for Portfolio Analysis," *Management Science* (January 1963): 277–291, and "Capital Asset Prices: A Theory of Market Equilibrium under Conditions of Risk," *Journal of Finance* (September 1964): 425–442.

[13]As investors lose confidence in the economy's performance, many of them turn to gold as an investment. This drives the price of gold up and increases returns to gold mining firms, whose costs of operation are not related directly to the demand for gold.

FIGURE 5-6
Illustration of Diversification
and Risk Reduction: Alcoa

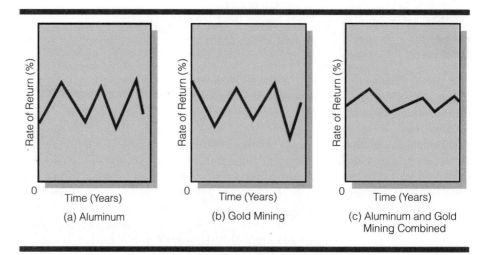

(a) Aluminum

(b) Gold Mining

(c) Aluminum and Gold Mining Combined

of another. Values of the correlation coefficient can range from +1.0 for *perfectly positively correlated* variables to −1.0 for *perfectly negatively correlated* variables. If two variables are unrelated (that is, uncorrelated), the correlation coefficient between these two variables will be 0.

Figure 5-7 illustrates perfect positive correlation, perfect negative correlation, and zero correlation for different pairs of common stock investments. For perfect positive correlation, panel (a), high rates of return from Stock L are always associated with high rates of return from Stock M; conversely, low rates of return from L are always associated with low rates of return from M. For perfect negative correlation, panel (b), however, the opposite is true; high rates of return from Stock P are associated with low rates of return from Stock Q and vice versa. For zero correlation, panel (c), no perceptible pattern or relationship exists between the rates of return on Stocks V and W.

FIGURE 5-7
Illustration of (a) Perfect Positive,
(b) Perfect Negative, and (c) Zero
Correlation for Two Investments

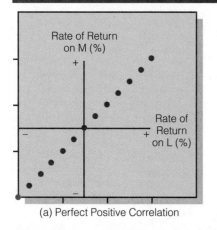

(a) Perfect Positive Correlation

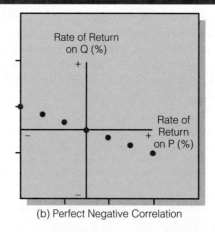

(b) Perfect Negative Correlation

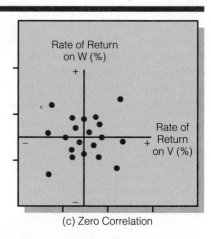

(c) Zero Correlation

In practice, the returns from most investments a firm or individual considers are positively correlated with other investments held by the firm or individual. For example, returns from projects that are closely related to the firm's primary line of business have a high positive correlation with returns from projects already being carried out and thus provide limited opportunities to reduce risk. In the Alcoa example, if Alcoa were to build a new smelter, it would not realize the risk reduction possibilities that investing in gold mining and refining would produce. Similarly, the returns from most common stocks are positively correlated, because these returns are influenced by such common factors as the general state of the economy, the level of interest rates, and so on.

In order to explore further the concepts of diversification and portfolio risk, it is necessary to develop more precise measures of portfolio returns and risk.

Expected Returns from a Portfolio

When two or more securities are combined into a portfolio, the expected return of the portfolio is equal to the weighted average of the expected returns from the individual securities. If a portion, w_A, of the available funds (wealth) is invested in Security A, and the remaining portion, w_B, is invested in Security B, the expected return of the portfolio, $\hat{r}_p$, is as follows:

$$\hat{r}_p = w_A \hat{r}_A + w_B \hat{r}_B \qquad (5.7)$$

where $\hat{r}_A$ and $\hat{r}_B$ are the expected returns for Securities A and B, respectively. Furthermore, $w_A + w_B = 1$, indicating that all funds are invested in either Security A or Security B.

For example, consider a portfolio consisting of the common stock of American Electric Power (A), a public utility company, and Bethlehem Steel (B), an integrated steel producer. The expected returns on the two stocks are 12 percent $(\hat{r}_A)$ and 16 percent $(\hat{r}_B)$, respectively. A portfolio consisting of 75 percent (w_A) invested in American Electric Power and the remainder or 25 percent (w_B) invested in Bethlehem Steel would yield an expected return, by Equation 5.7, of

$$\hat{r}_p = 0.75(12\%) + 0.25(16\%)$$
$$= 13.0\%$$

Table 5-7 (columns w_A and $\hat{r}_p$) and Figure 5-8 illustrate the relationship between the expected return for a portfolio containing Securities A and B and the proportion of the total portfolio invested in each security. For example, when $w_A = 1.0$ (100%) and $w_B = 0$ (because $w_A + w_B = 1.0$), the expected portfolio return is 12 percent, the same as the return for A. When $w_A = 0.5$ (50 percent) and $w_B = 0.5$ (50 percent), the expected portfolio return is 14 percent. As shown earlier, when $w_B = 0.75$ and $w_B = 0.25$, the expected portfolio return is 13 percent. Thus, it can be seen that the expected return from a portfolio of securities is simply equal to the weighted average of the individual security returns, where the weights represent the proportion of the total portfolio invested in each security. This results in the linear relationship shown in Figure 5-8.

TABLE 5-7
Expected Returns and Portfolio Risk from a Portfolio of the Stocks of American Electric Power (A) and Bethlehem Steel (B)

PROPORTION INVESTED IN SECURITY A	EXPECTED RETURN ON PORTFOLIO	PORTFOLIO RISK σ_p (%)		
$w_A(\%)$	$\hat{r}_p(\%)$	$\rho_{AB} = +1.0$	$\rho_{AB} = 0.0$	$\rho_{AB} = -1.0$
0.0%	16.0%	20.0%	20.0%	20.0%
25.0	15.0	17.5	15.0	12.5
33.333	14.67	16.67	13.74	10.0
50.0	14.0	15.0	11.2	5.0
66.667	13.33	13.33	9.43	0.0
75.0	13.0	12.5	9.01	2.5
100.0	12.0	10.0	10.0	10.0

Note: $\hat{r}_A = 12\%$; $\hat{r}_B = 16\%$; $\sigma_A = 10\%$; $\sigma_B = 20\%$.

In general, the expected return from any portfolio of n securities or assets is equal to the sum of the expected returns from each security times the proportion of the total portfolio invested in that security:

$$\hat{r}_p = \sum_{i=1}^{n} w_i \hat{r}_i \qquad (5.8)$$

where $\Sigma w_i = 1$ and $0 \leq w_i \leq 1$.

FIGURE 5-8
Expected Return from a Portfolio of the Stocks of American Electric Power (A) and Bethlehem Steel (B)

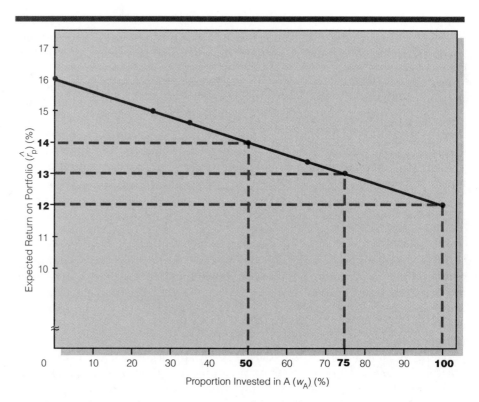

Note: $\hat{r}_A = 12\%$; $\hat{r}_B = 16\%$; $w_A + w_B = 1.0$ (100%). Data points in graph are from Table 5-7.

Portfolio Risk

Although the expected returns from a portfolio of two or more securities can be computed as a weighted average of the expected returns from the individual securities, it generally is not sufficient merely to calculate a weighted average of the risk of each individual security to arrive at a measure of the portfolio's risk. Whenever the returns from the individual securities are not perfectly positively correlated, the risk of any portfolio of these securities may be reduced through the effects of diversification. Thus, **diversification** can be achieved by investing in a set of securities that have different risk-return characteristics. The amount of risk reduction achieved through diversification depends on the degree of correlation between the returns of the individual securities in the portfolio. The lower the correlations among the individual securities, the greater the possibilities of risk reduction.

The risk for a two-security portfolio, measured by the standard deviation of portfolio returns, is computed as follows:

$$\sigma_p = \sqrt{w_A^2 \sigma_A^2 + w_B^2 \sigma_B^2 + 2 w_A w_B \rho_{AB} \sigma_A \sigma_B} \tag{5.9}$$

where w_A is the proportion of funds invested in Security A; w_B is the proportion of funds invested in Security B; $w_A + w_B = 1$; σ_A^2 is the variance of returns from Security A (or the square of the standard deviation for Security A, σ_A); σ_B^2 is the variance of returns from Security B (or the square of the standard deviation for Security B, σ_B); and ρ_{AB} is the correlation coefficient of returns between Securities A and B.[14]

Consider, for example, the portfolio discussed earlier consisting of the common stock of American Electric Power (A) and Bethlehem Steel (B). The standard deviation of returns for these two securities are 10 percent (σ_A) and 20 percent (σ_B), respectively. Furthermore, suppose that the correlation coefficient (ρ_{AB}) between the returns on these securities is equal to +0.50. Using Equation 5.9, a portfolio consisting of 75 percent (w_A) invested in American Electric Power and 25 percent (w_B) in Bethlehem Steel would yield a standard deviation of portfolio returns of

$$\sigma_p = \sqrt{(.75)^2(10)^2 + (.25)^2(20)^2 + 2(.75)(.25)(+.50)(10)(20)}$$
$$= 10.90\%$$

With the techniques just described for calculating expected portfolio return and risk, we can now examine in more detail the risk versus return trade-offs associated with investment diversification. The following three special cases illustrate how the correlation coefficient can affect portfolio risk.

---

[14]In general, the risk of a portfolio containing n securities, as measured by the standard deviation of portfolio returns, is computed as follows.

$$\sigma_p = \sqrt{\sum_{i=1}^{n} \sum_{j=1}^{n} w_i w_j \rho_{ij} \sigma_i \sigma_j}$$

The double summation sign ($\Sigma\Sigma$) indicates that all possible combinations of i and j should be included in calculating the total value. Problem 23 at the end of the chapter examines the case of a three-security portfolio.

Case I: Perfect Positive Correlation (ρ = +1.0). Table 5-7 (columns $\hat{r}_p$ and ρ_{AB} = + 1.0) and panel (a) of Figure 5-9 illustrate the risk-return trade-offs associated with portfolios consisting of various combinations of American Electric Power (A) and Bethlehem Steel (B) stock when ρ_{AB} = +1.0. *When the returns from the two securities are perfectly positively correlated, the risk of the portfolio is equal to the weighted average of the risk of the individual securities* (10 and 20 percent in this example). *Therefore, no risk reduction is achieved when perfectly positively correlated securities are combined in a portfolio.*

Case II: Zero Correlation (ρ = 0.0). Table 5-7 (columns $\hat{r}_p$ and ρ_{AB} = 0.0) and panel (b) of Figure 5-9 illustrate the possible trade-offs when ρ_{AB} = 0.0. In this case, we see that diversification can reduce portfolio risk below the risk of either of the securities that make up the portfolio. For example, an investment consisting of 75 percent in American Electric Power (A) stock and 25 percent in Bethlehem Steel (B) stock has a portfolio standard deviation of only 9.01 percent, which is less than the standard deviations of either of the two securities (10 and 20 percent, respectively) in the portfolio. In general, *when the correlation coefficient between the returns on two securities is less than 1.0, diversification can reduce the risk of a portfolio below the weighted average of the total risk of the individual securities. The less positively correlated are the returns from two securities, the greater will be the portfolio effects of risk reduction.* For example, the expected returns from an investment in two firms in different industries, such as Exxon and Delta Airlines, generally should be less positively correlated than the expected returns between two firms in the same industry, such as Exxon and Mobil.

Case III: Perfect Negative Correlation (ρ = –1.0). Table 5-7 (columns $\hat{r}_p$ and ρ_{AB} = – 1.0) and panel (c) of Figure 5-9 show the risk-return relationship when ρ_{AB} = – 1.0. As illustrated, with perfectly negatively correlated returns, portfolio risk can be reduced to zero. In other words, *with a perfect negative correlation of returns between two securities, there always will be some proportion of the securities that will result in the complete elimination of portfolio risk.*

In summary, these three special cases serve to illustrate the effect that the correlation coefficient has on portfolio risk, as measured by the standard deviation. For any given pair of securities, the correlation coefficient is given (or can be estimated) and this number determines how much risk reduction can be achieved with various weighted combinations of the two securities.

Efficient Portfolios and the Capital Market Line

The risk-return relationships just discussed can be extended to analyze portfolios involving more than two securities. For example, consider the graph shown in Figure 5-10. Each dot within the shaded area represents the risk (standard deviation) and expected return for an individual security available for possible investment. The shaded area (or opportunity set) represents all the possible portfolios found by combining the given securities in different proportions. The curved segment from A to B on the boundary of the shaded area represents the set of **efficient portfolios,** or the **efficient frontier.** A portfolio is efficient if, for a given standard deviation, there is no other

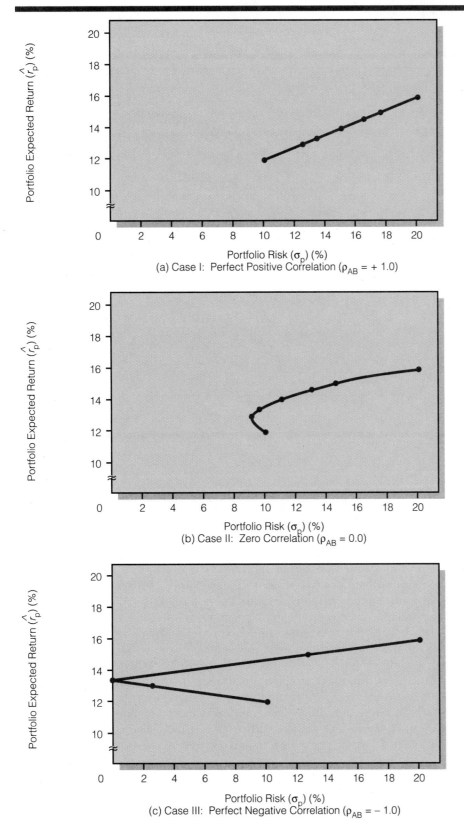

Note: $\hat{r}_A$ = 12%; $\hat{r}_B$ = 16%; σ_A = 10%; σ_B = 20%; $w_A + w_B$ = 1.0 (100%). Data points in graphs are from Table 5-7.

FIGURE 5-10
Portfolio Opportunity Set

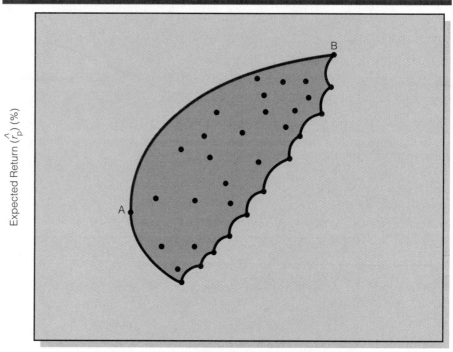

Standard Deviation (σ_p) (%)

portfolio with a higher expected return, or for a given expected return, there is no other portfolio with a lower standard deviation.

Risk-averse investors, in choosing their optimal portfolios, need only consider those portfolios on the efficient frontier. The choice of an optimal portfolio, whether portfolio A that minimizes risk or portfolio B that maximizes expected return or some other portfolio on the efficient frontier, depends on the investor's attitude toward risk (that is, risk aversion). More conservative investors will tend to choose lower-risk portfolios (closer to A); more aggressive investors will tend to select higher-risk portfolios (closer to B).

If investors are able to borrow and lend money at the risk-free rate (r_f), they can obtain any combination of risk and expected return on the straight-line joining r_f and portfolio m as shown in Figure 5-11.[15] When the market is in equilibrium, portfolio m represents the Market Portfolio, which consists of all available securities, weighted by their respective market values. The line joining r_f and m is known as the *capital market line*.[16] The capital market line has an *intercept* of r_f and a *slope* of $(r_m - r_f)/(\sigma_m - 0) = (r_m - r_f)/\sigma_m$. The slope of the capital market line measures the equilibrium market price of risk or the additional ex-

[15] See Thomas E. Copeland and J. Fred Weston, *Financial Theory and Corporate Policy*, 3rd ed. (Reading, MA: Addison-Wesley, 1988): 173–184.

[16] In constructing the capital market line, it is assumed that all investors have homogeneous (i.e., identical) expectations about the distributions of returns offered by securities. As a result of this assumption, all investors will perceive the same set of efficient portfolios.

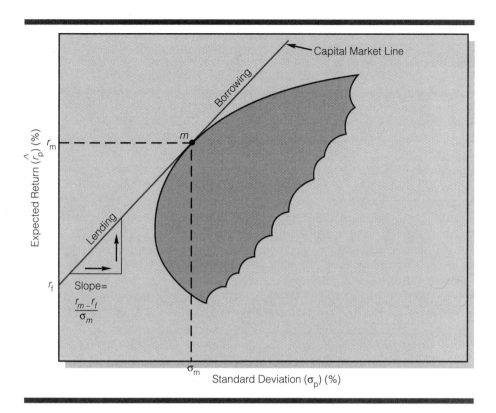

FIGURE 5-11
Capital Market Line

pected return that can be obtained by incurring one additional unit of risk (one additional percentage point of standard deviation). Therefore, the equation of the capital market line is

$$\hat{r}_p = r_f + \left(\frac{r_m - r_f}{\sigma_m} \right) \sigma_p \qquad (5.10)$$

and indicates that the expected return for an efficient portfolio is equal to the risk-free rate plus the market price of risk $[(r_m - r_f)/\sigma_m]$ times the amount of risk (σ_p) of the portfolio under consideration.

Any risk-return combination on this line *between* r_f and m can be obtained by investing (i.e., *lending*) part of the initial funds in the risk-free security (such as U.S. Treasury bills) and investing the remainder in portfolio m. Any combination *beyond* m on this line can be obtained by *borrowing* money at the risk-free rate and investing the borrowed funds (as well as the initial funds) in portfolio m (that is, purchasing securities on margin).

With the ability to borrow and lend at the risk-free rate, the choice of an optimal portfolio for risk-averse investors involves determining the proportion of funds to invest in the Market Portfolio (m) with the remaining proportion being invested in the risk-free security. More conservative investors will tend to choose investments nearer to the r_f point on the capital market line. More aggressive investors will tend to select investments closer to, or possibly beyond, point m on the capital market line.

Analyzing risk is no easy job. Visit MATLAB's Web site and preview some of the quantitative tools used to evaluate risk. Besides such standard tools as time-series analysis and Monte Carlo simulations, MATLAB's products can construct mean/variance efficient frontiers, neural networks, fuzzy logic, and even "wavelets."

http://finprod.mathworks.com

PORTFOLIO RISK AND THE CAPITAL ASSET PRICING MODEL

The preceding analysis illustrates the possibilities for portfolio risk reduction when two or more securities are combined to form a portfolio. Unfortunately, when more than two securities are involved—as is usually the case—the number of calculations required to compute the portfolio risk increases geometrically. For example, whereas 45 correlation coefficients are needed for a portfolio containing 10 securities, 4,950 correlation coefficients must be computed for a portfolio containing 100 securities. In other words, a 10-fold increase in securities causes a greater than 100-fold increase in the required calculations.[17] In addition, a substantial computational undertaking is required to find the particular portfolio of securities that minimizes portfolio risk for a given level of return or maximizes return for a given level of risk, even for a portfolio that contains only a few securities. Obviously, a more workable method is needed to assess the effects of diversification on a portfolio of assets.

One method that has gained widespread use in analyzing the relationship between portfolio risk and return is the **Capital Asset Pricing Model** (**CAPM**). This model provides a strong analytical basis for evaluating risk-return relationships—both in the context of financial management and securities investment decisions. The remainder of this section discusses the development and application of the CAPM.

Systematic and Unsystematic Risk

As illustrated in the previous section, whenever the individual securities in a portfolio are less than perfectly positively correlated, diversification can reduce the portfolio's risk below the weighted average of the total risk (measured by the standard deviation) of the individual securities. Because most securities are positively correlated with returns in the securities market in general, it usually is not possible to eliminate all risk in a portfolio of securities. As the economic outlook improves, returns on most individual securities tend to increase; as the economic outlook deteriorates, individual security returns tend to decline. In spite of this positive "comovement" among the returns of individual securities, each security experiences some "unique" variation in its returns that is unrelated to the underlying economic factors that influence all securities. In other words, there are two types of risk inherent in each security:

- Systematic, or nondiversifiable, risk.
- Unsystematic, or diversifiable, risk.

The sum of these two types of risk equal the total risk of the security:

$$\text{Total risk} = \begin{array}{c}\text{Systematic risk}\\\text{(Nondiversifiable risk)}\end{array} + \begin{array}{c}\text{Unsystematic risk}\\\text{(Diversifiable risk)}\end{array} \quad (5.11)$$

Systematic risk refers to that portion of the variability of an individual security's returns caused by factors affecting the market as a whole; as such, it can be thought of as being nondiversifiable. Systematic risk accounts for 25 to 50 percent of the total risk of any security. Some of the sources of systematic risk,

---

[17]The number of correlation coefficients needed to evaluate an n-security portfolio is computed as $(n^2 - n)/2$.

which cause the returns from all securities to vary more or less together, include the following:

- Interest rate changes.
- Changes in purchasing power (inflation).
- Changes in investor expectations about the overall performance of the economy.

Because diversification cannot eliminate systematic risk, this type of risk is the predominant determinant of individual security risk premiums.

Unsystematic risk is risk that is unique to the firm. It is the variability in a security's returns caused by such factors as the following:

- Management capabilities and decisions.
- Strikes.
- The availability of raw materials.
- The unique effects of government regulation, such as pollution control.
- The effects of foreign competition.
- The particular levels of financial and operating leverage the firm employs.

Since unsystematic risk is unique to each firm, an efficiently diversified portfolio of securities can successfully eliminate most of the unsystematic risk inherent in individual securities, as is shown in Figure 5-12. To eliminate effectively the unsystematic risk inherent in a portfolio's individual securities, it is not necessary for the portfolio to include a large number of securities. In fact, randomly constructed portfolios of as few as ten to fifteen securities on average can successfully diversify away a large portion of the unsystematic risk of the individual securities.[18] The risk remaining *after* diversification is market-related risk, or systematic risk, and it cannot be eliminated through diversification. Because unsystematic risk commonly accounts for 50 percent or more of the total risk of most individual securities, it should be obvious that the risk-reducing benefits of efficient diversification are well worth the effort.

Given the small number of securities required for efficient diversification by an individual investor, as well as the dominance of the securities markets by many large institutional investors who hold widely diversified portfolios, it is safe to conclude that the most relevant risk that must be considered for any widely traded individual security is its systematic risk. The unsystematic portion of total risk is relatively easy to diversify away.

Security Market Line (SML)

As discussed earlier in the chapter (see Equation 5.5), the return required of any risky asset is determined by the prevailing level of risk-free interest rates plus a risk premium. The greater the level of risk an investor perceives about a security's return, the greater the required risk premium will be. In other words, investors require returns that are commensurate with the risk level they perceive. In algebraic terms, the required return from any Security j, k_j, is equal to the following:

$$k_j = r_f + \theta_j \qquad (5.12)$$

where r_f is the risk-free rate and θ_j is the risk premium required by investors.

[18]H Wagner and S. C. Lau, "The Effect of Diversification on Risk," *Financial Analysts Journal* (November -December 1971): 48–53.

FIGURE 5-12
Unsystematic Risk and
Portfolio Diversification

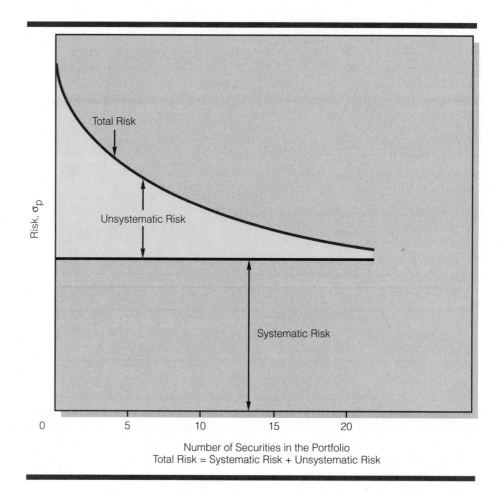

Total Risk = Systematic Risk + Unsystematic Risk

The **security market line (SML)** indicates the "going" required rate of return (k_j) on a security in the market for a given amount of *systematic risk* and is illustrated in Figure 5-13. The SML intersects the vertical axis at the risk-free rate, r_f, indicating that any security with an expected risk premium equal to zero should be required to earn a return equal to the risk-free rate. As systematic risk increases, so do the risk premium and the required rate of return. According to Figure 5-13, for example, a security having a risk level of a' should be required to earn a 10 percent rate of return.

Beta: A Measure of Systematic Risk

Thus far, we have not addressed the question of the appropriate risk measure to use when considering the risk-return trade-offs illustrated by the SML. The previous discussion of risk in a portfolio context suggests that a measure of systematic risk is an appropriate starting point.

The systematic risk of a security is a function of the total risk of a security as measured by the standard deviation of the security's returns, the standard deviation of the returns from the market portfolio, and the correlation of the security's returns with those of all other securities in the market. A broad-based security market index, such as the *Standard and Poor's 500 Market Index* or the

FIGURE 5-13
The Security Market Line (SML)

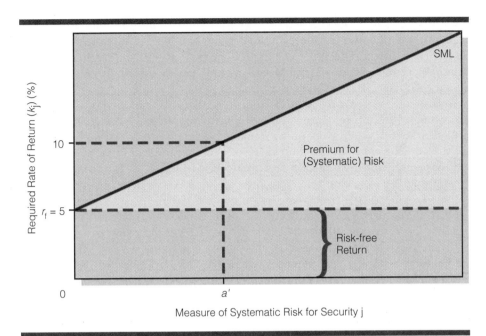

New York Stock Exchange Index, normally is used as a measure of total market returns.

One useful measure of the systematic risk of a Security j is the value called **beta**. Beta is a measure of the volatility of a security's returns relative to the returns of a broad-based Market Portfolio m. It is defined as the ratio of the *covariance* (or comovement) of returns on Security j and Market Portfolio m to the variance of returns on the Market Portfolio:

$$\beta_j = \frac{\text{Covariance}_{j,m}}{\text{Variance}_m}$$

$$\beta_j = \frac{\rho_{jm}\sigma_j\sigma_m}{\sigma_m^2} \qquad (5.13)$$

where β_j is the measure of systematic risk for Security j; σ_j is the standard deviation of returns for Security j; σ_m is the standard deviation of returns for Market Portfolio m; σ_m^2 is the variance of returns for Market Portfolio m; and ρ_{jm} is the correlation coefficient between returns for Security j and Market Portfolio m.

In practice, beta may be computed as the slope of a regression line between periodic (usually yearly, quarterly, or monthly) rates of return on the Market Portfolio (as measured by a market index, such as the *Standard and Poor's 500 Market Index*) and the periodic rates of return for Security j, as follows:

$$k_j = a_j + \beta_j r_m + e_j \qquad (5.14)$$

where k_j is the periodic percentage holding period rate of return for Security j; a_j is a constant term determined by the regression; β_j *is the computed historical beta for Security j;* r_m is the periodic percentage holding period rate of return for the market index; and e_j is a random error term. This equation describes a line called Security j's **characteristic line.**

Figure 5-14 shows the characteristic line for General Motors. The slope (and intercept) of this line can be estimated using the least-squares technique of regression analysis. The slope of this line, or beta, is 0.97, indicating that the systematic returns from General Motors common stock are slightly less variable than the returns for the market as a whole.

A beta of 1.0 for any security indicates that the security is of average systematic risk; that is, a security with a beta of 1.0 has the same risk characteristics as the market as a whole when only systematic risk is considered. When beta equals 1.0, a 1 percent increase (decline) in market returns indicates that the *systematic* returns for the individual security should increase (decline) by 1 percent.[19] A beta greater than 1.0—for example, 2.0—indicates that the security has greater than average systematic risk. In this case, when market returns increase (decline) by 1 percent, the security's systematic returns can be expected to increase (decline) by 2 percent. A beta of less than 1.0—for example, 0.5—is indicative of a security of less than average systematic risk. In this case, a 1 percent increase (decline) in market returns implies a 0.5 percent increase (decline) in the security's systematic returns. Table 5-8 summarizes the interpretation of selected betas.

FIGURE 5-14
Characteristic Line for General Motors

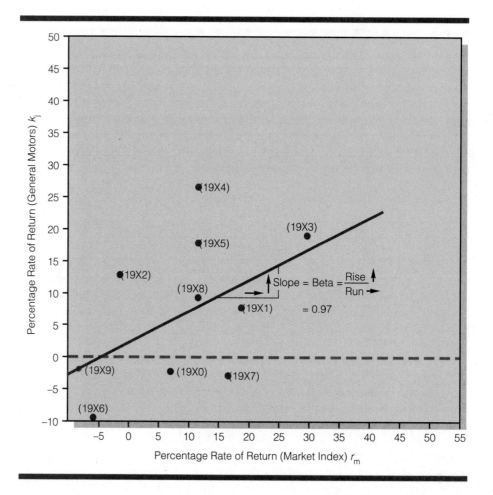

[19]Of course, there also will be *unsystematic* components to a security's returns at any point in time. We assume these are diversified away in the portfolio.

TABLE 5-8
Interpretation of Selected Beta Coefficients

BETA VALUE	DIRECTION OF MOVEMENT IN RETURNS	INTERPRETATION
2.0	Same as market	Twice as risky (responsive) as market
1.0	Same as market	Risk equal to that of market
0.5	Same as market	Half as risky as market
0	Uncorrelated with market movements	No market-related risk
−0.5	Opposite of market	Half as responsive as market but in the opposite direction

The beta for the Market Portfolio as measured by a broad-based market index equals 1.0. This can be seen in Equation 5.13. Because the correlation of the market with itself is 1.0, the beta of the Market Portfolio must also be 1.0.

Finally, the beta of any portfolio of n securities or assets is simply the weighted average of the individual security betas:

$$\beta_p = \sum_{j=1}^{n} w_j \beta_j \qquad (5.15)$$

This concept is useful particularly when evaluating the effects of capital investment projects or mergers on a firm's systematic risk.

Fortunately for financial managers, it is not necessary to compute the beta for each security every time a security's systematic risk measure is needed. Several investment advisory services, including the *Value Line Investment Survey* and Merrill Lynch, regularly compute and publish individual security beta estimates, and these are readily available. Table 5-9 lists the Value Line computed betas for selected stocks.

Security Market Line and Beta

Given the information presented thus far, it is possible to compute risk premiums θ, that are applicable to individual securities. The SML may also be defined in terms of beta. The risk premium for any Security j is equal to the difference between the investor's required return, k_j, and the risk-free rate, r_f:

$$\theta_j = k_j - r_j \qquad (5.16)$$

If we let $\hat{r}_m$ be the expected rate of return on the overall Market Portfolio and $\hat{r}_f$ be the expected (short-term) risk-free rate (that is, the rate of return on Treasury bills), then the market risk premium is equal to

$$\hat{\theta}_m = \hat{r}_m - \hat{r}_f$$

Based on historic stock market data over the time period from 1926 through 1995, the average market risk premium has been 8.8 percent.[20]

[20]*Stocks, Bonds, Bills and Inflation;* 1996 Yearbook™ (Chicago: Ibbotson Associates, 1996): 161. Note that this market risk premium value, 8.8 percent, is slightly higher than the difference between the returns on large-company stocks (12.5 percent) and U.S. Treasury bills (3.8 percent) as shown in Table 5-6. The difference of 0.1 percent is due to rounding.

TABLE 5-9
Betas for Selected Stocks

Source: *The Value Line Investment Survey* (New York: Value Line Publishing, Inc., December 13, 1996). © 1996 by Value Line Publishing, Inc. Used by permission. All rights reserved.

COMPANY	VALUE LINE BETA
America Online	2.15
American Electric Power	.70
Apple Computer	1.15
Boeing	.95
Boston Chicken	1.50
Charles Schwab	2.25
Chrysler	1.25
Coca-Cola	1.05
Connecticut Natural Gas	.50
Delta Air Lines	1.30
Dupont	.95
Exxon	.65
Federal Express	1.40
Ford	1.10
General Electric	1.15
General Motors	1.10
Harley-Davidson	1.50
Homestake Mining	.50
Honeywell	1.00
IBM	1.05
Intel	1.15
K-Mart	1.10
Lone Star Steakhouse	2.20
Merrill Lynch	1.80
Microsoft	1.20
Texaco	.70
Toys 'R' Us	1.25
United Air Lines	1.60
USAirways	1.40
Wal-Mart Stores	1.05
Whirlpool	1.35
Wisconsin Public Energy	.70

For a security with average risk (β_j equal to 1.0), the risk premium should be equal to the market risk premium, or 8.8 percent. A security whose beta is 2.0, however, is twice as risky as the average security, so its risk premium should be twice the market risk premium:

$$\hat{\theta}_j = \beta_j \, (\hat{r}_m - \hat{r}_f)$$
$$= 2.0 \, (8.8\%)$$
$$= 17.6\%$$

The required return for any Security j may be defined in terms of its systematic risk, β_j, the expected market return, $\hat{r}_m$, and the expected risk-free rate, $\hat{r}_f$, as follows:

$$k_j = \hat{r}_f + \hat{\theta}_j$$

or

$$k_j = \hat{r}_f + \beta_j \, (\hat{r}_m - \hat{r}_f) \qquad (5.17)$$

For example, if the risk-free rate is 7 percent and $(\hat{r}_m - \hat{r}_f)$ is 8.8 percent, then the required return for Chrysler, which has a beta of 1.25, is computed as follows:

$$k_j = 7\% + 1.25(8.8\%)$$
$$= 18.0\%$$

Equation 5.17 provides an explicit definition of the SML in terms of the systematic risk of individual securities. Figure 5-15 illustrates the SML for Equation 5-17. The slope of the SML is shown as being constant throughout. When measured between a beta of 0 and a beta of 1.0, it is equal to $(\hat{r}_m - \hat{r}_f)/(1 - 0)$, or simply $\hat{r}_m - \hat{r}_f$. This slope represents the risk premium on an average risk security. Assuming a risk-free rate of 7 percent and a market risk premium of 8.8 percent, the return required on a low-risk stock (for example, a security with a beta equal to 0.50) is 11.4 percent. The return required on a high-risk stock (for example, a security with a beta equal to 1.50) is 20.2 percent, and the return required on a stock of average risk (such as Honeywell, with a beta equal to 1.0) is 15.8 percent, the same as the market required return.

Also, from Figure 5-15 we can determine what securities (assets) are attractive investments by comparing the *expected* return from a security with the return *required* for that security, given its beta. For example, Security A with a beta of 1.0 and an expected return of 17 percent would be an attractive investment because the expected return *exceeds* the 15.8 percent required return. In contrast, Security B with a beta of 1.50 is not an acceptable investment because its expected return (18 percent) *is less than* its required return (20.2 percent).

Inflation and the Security Market Line

As discussed earlier in the chapter, the risk-free rate of return, r_f, consists of the real rate of return and the expected inflation premium. Because the required return on any risky security, k_j, is equal to the risk-free rate plus the risk premium, an increase in inflationary expectations effectively increases the required return on all securities. This is shown in Figure 5-16. In the figure,

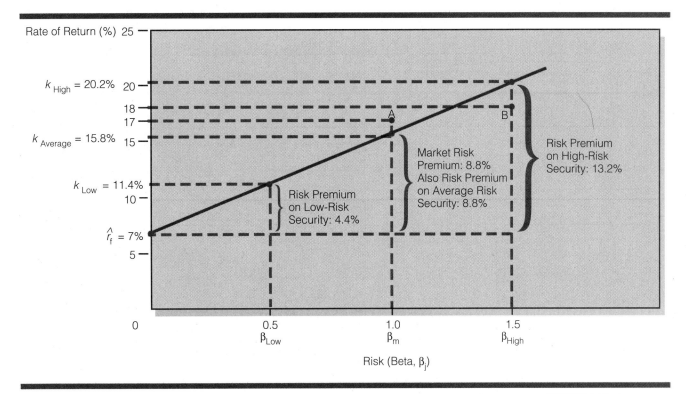

FIGURE 5-15
The Security Market Line
in Terms of Beta

SML' represents the returns required on all securities following a 2 percentage point increase in the expected future inflation rate. The required returns of all securities increase by 2 percentage points—the change in expected inflation. For example, the required rate of return on a security of average risk (that is, beta equal to 1.0) would increase from 15.8 to 17.8 percent. When investors increase their required returns, they become unwilling to purchase securities at existing prices, causing prices to decline. It should come as no surprise, then, that security analysts and investors take a dim view of increased inflation.

Risk Aversion and the Security Market Line

If the average risk premium (measured by the slope of the SML) increases because of an increase in uncertainty regarding the future economic outlook or because investors as a group have tended to become more averse to risk and therefore require a higher rate of return for any level of risk, the slope of the SML will increase. This, in turn, will increase the risk premium on stocks with greater than average risk (beta greater than 1.0) more than on stocks with less than average risk (beta less than 1.0). This is shown in Figure 5-17. In the figure, SML" represents the returns required on all securities following a one percentage point increase in the market risk premium from 8.8 to 9.8 percent. For example, the required risk premium on a security with a beta of 0.5 increases by only 0.5 percentage points [0.5 × (9.8% − 8.8%)], or an increase in the required return from 11.4 to 11.9 percent. In contrast, the risk premium on a security with a beta of 1.50 experiences a rise in its required risk premium of 1.5 percentage points (1.50 × 1.0%), or an increase in the required rate of return from 20.2 to 21.7 percent.

FIGURE 5-16
Inflation and the
Security Market Line

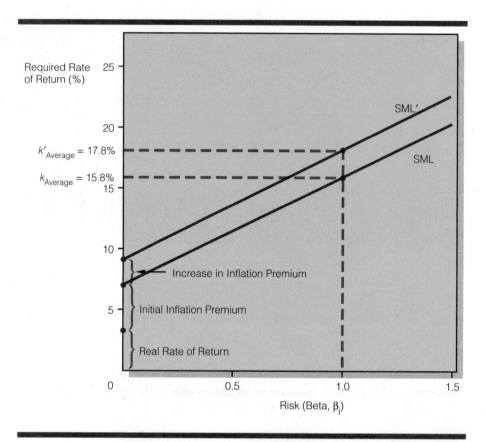

FIGURE 5-17
Risk Aversion and the
Security Market Line

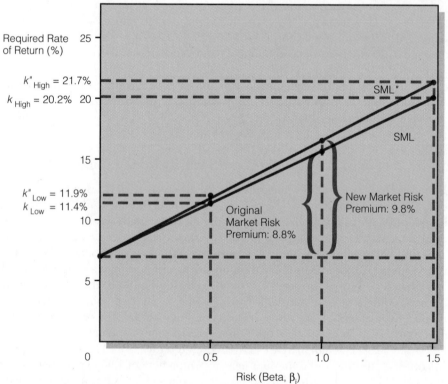

Uses of the CAPM and Portfolio Risk Concepts

The concepts of portfolio risk and the Capital Asset Pricing Model (CAPM), which relates required returns to systematic risk (beta), are powerful pedagogical tools to explain the nature of risk and its relationship to required returns on securities and physical assets. In Chapter 11, the CAPM is discussed as one technique that can be used to estimate the cost of equity capital. Chapter 11 also considers where the necessary data may be obtained to apply the model. Chapter 10 considers the use of CAPM-determined required rates of return as a technique to adjust for risk in the capital budgeting process.

Assumptions and Limitations of the CAPM

The theoretical CAPM and its applications are based upon a number of crucial assumptions about the securities markets and investors' attitudes, including the following:

- Investors hold well-diversified portfolios of securities. Hence, their return requirements are influenced primarily by the systematic (rather than total) risk of each security.
- Securities are traded actively in a competitive market, where information about a given firm and its future prospects is freely available.
- Investors can borrow and lend at the risk-free rate, which remains constant over time.
- There are no brokerage charges for buying and selling securities.
- There are no taxes.
- All investors prefer the security that provides the highest return for a given level of risk or the lowest amount of risk for a given level of return.
- All investors have common (homogeneous) expectations regarding the expected returns, variances, and correlations of returns among all securities.

While these assumptions may seem fairly limiting at first glance, extensions of the basic theory presented in this chapter, which relax the assumptions, generally have yielded results consistent with the fundamental theory.

Empirical studies of the CAPM have produced mixed results. Some researchers have found positive relationships between systematic (beta) risk and return. However, depending on the time period under examination, the results sometimes do not meet the standard tests of statistical significance.[21] Other investigators, using different stock price data, have found that variables other than systematic risk are better predictors of the performance of common stocks.[22] Their results suggest that differences in company size and the ratio of book-to-market values explain the differences in stock returns. Still other researchers have argued that the results of statistical tests of the relationship between systematic risk and return may be flawed because of the difficulty of obtaining accurate estimates of beta.[23] Their studies suggest that the use of market indexes, such as the *Standard and Poor's 500 Market Index,* to measure returns on the true Market Portfolio can introduce significant errors into the process for estimating betas.

[21]Louis K. C. Chan and Josef Lakonishok, "Are the Reports of Beta's Death Premature?" *Journal of Portfolio Management* (Summer 1993): 51–62.
[22]Eugene F. Fama and Kenneth R. French, "The Cross-Section of Expected Returns, " *Journal of Finance* 47 (June 1992): 427–465.
[23]Richard Roll, "A Critique of the Asset Pricing Theory's Tests. Part I: On Past and Present Testability of Theory," *Journal of Financial Economics* 4 (1977): 129–176.

Despite the controversy concerning the validity of the CAPM, the model has been used extensively, both practically and conceptually, to consider the risk-return trade-off required by investors in the securities markets. For example, the CAPM (or a modification thereof) has been used in regulated public utility rate case testimony aimed at determining a reasonable allowed rate of return for the utility's investors.

However, users of this approach also should be aware of some of the major problems encountered in practical applications, which include the following:

- Estimating expected future market returns.
- Determining the most appropriate estimate of the risk-free rate.
- Determining the best estimate of an asset's *future* beta.
- Reconciling the fact that some empirical tests have shown that investors do not totally ignore unsystematic risk, as the theory suggests.
- Recognizing that measures of beta have been shown to be quite unstable over time, making it difficult to measure confidently the beta expected by investors.
- Recognizing the growing body of evidence that suggests that required returns on most securities are determined by macroeconomic factors, such as interest rates and inflation, in addition to the risk-free rate of interest and the systematic risk of the security.[24]

INTERNATIONAL ISSUES
DIVERSIFICATION AND MULTINATIONAL CORPORATIONS

As we discussed earlier in the chapter, the degree to which diversification can reduce risk depends on the correlation among security returns. The returns from domestic companies (DMCs)—companies that are based and operate within a given country—tend to be positively related to the overall level of economic activity within the given country. Hence, these companies tend to have a relatively high degree of systematic risk. Since overall economic activity in different countries is not perfectly correlated, the returns from multinational companies (MNCs)—companies that operate in a number of different countries—may tend to have less systematic risk than those of DMCs. This suggests that further risk reduction benefits may be achieved by either

1. Investing in MNCs, or
2. Investing directly in DMCs located in countries in which the MNC would otherwise operate.

If securities are traded in perfect financial markets, there should be no systematic advantage to holding shares in MNCs (Strategy 1), compared with owning shares directly in DMCs located in different countries (Strategy 2).

---

[24] A model known as the *Arbitrage Pricing Theory (APT)*, developed by Ross in the mid-1970s, uses multiple risk factors to explain security returns. The APT postulates that the expected (and in equilibrium, the required) rate of return on a security is equal to the risk-free rate plus the sum of several risk premiums. See Stephen A. Ross, "Arbitrage Pricing Theory," *Journal of Economic Theory* (December 1976): 341–360; Richard Roll and Stephen A. Ross, "An Empirical Investigation of the Arbitrage Pricing Theory," *Journal of Finance* (December 1980): 1073–1104; and "The Arbitrage Pricing Theory Approach to Strategic Portfolio Planning," *Financial Analysts Journal* (May–June 1984): 14–26.

However, if market imperfections exist, such as controls on capital flows, differential trading costs, and different tax structures, then MNCs may be able to provide diversification benefits to investors.

The empirical evidence suggests that MNCs tend to have lower systematic risk (as measured by beta), as well as lower unsystematic risk, than DMCs.[25] Overall, MNCs tend to have a lower total risk (as measured by the standard deviation of rates of return on equity) than DMCs. Hence, MNCs appear to provide investors with substantial diversification benefits.

OTHER DIMENSIONS OF RISK

This chapter has focused on various measures of variability in returns—either total variability, measured by the *standard deviation* and the *coefficient of variation,* or systematic variability, measured by *beta.* Although variability of returns is very important, it does not consider adequately another important risk dimension that is, the risk of failure. In the case of an individual investment project, failure is a situation in which a project generates a *negative* rate of return. In the case of the entire firm, failure is the situation in which a firm loses money and ultimately is forced into bankruptcy.

For risk-averse investors, the risk of failure may play a large role in determining the types of investments undertaken. For example, the management of a firm is not likely to be eager to invest in a project that has a high risk of failure and that ultimately may cause the firm to fail if it proves to be unsuccessful. After all, the continued survival of the firm is tied closely to the economic well-being of management.

From a shareholder wealth maximization perspective, failure is a particularly undesirable occurrence. The direct and indirect costs of bankruptcy can be very high. Consequently, this failure risk often is an important determinant of investment risk. The risk and cost of failure can explain, in large part, the desire of many firms to diversify. In addition to reducing the overall risk of a firm, diversification can result in a lower probability of bankruptcy and thus lower *expected* costs incurred during bankruptcy. These costs include the following:

- The loss of funds that occur when assets are sold at distressed prices during liquidation.
- The legal fees and selling costs incurred when a firm enters bankruptcy proceedings.
- The opportunity costs of the funds that are unavailable to investors during the bankruptcy proceedings (for example, it took over eight years to settle the Penn-Central bankruptcy).

Lower expected bankruptcy costs should increase shareholder wealth, all other things being equal.[26]

Diversification also may reduce a firm's cost of capital. By reducing the overall risk of the firm, diversification will lower the default risk of the firm's debt securities, and the firm's bonds will receive higher ratings and require lower interest payments. In addition, the firm may be able to increase the

---

[25]See Israel Shaked, "Are Multinational Corporations Safer?" *Journal of International Business Studies* (Spring 1986): 83–101.
[26]The effects of bankruptcy costs on shareholder wealth (that is, market value of the firm) are examined in Chapter 12.

proportion of low-cost debt relative to equity in its optimal capital structure, further reducing the cost of capital and increasing shareholder wealth.[27]

Although we will focus primarily on return variability as our measure of risk in this book, the risk and cost of failure should also be kept in mind.

 ETHICAL ISSUES
HIGH-RISK SECURITIES

The decade of the 1980s experienced a dramatic growth in high-risk, so-called junk bonds. These are bonds with credit ratings below investment grade (BBB from Standard & Poor's and Baa3 from Moody's).[28] The lure of these securities was their high returns relative to the returns available from investment grade corporate and U.S. government-issued debt securities. Junk bonds appeared to offer an easy way to increase quickly the yield on the portfolios of assets held by many financial institutions.

Although there are many complex reasons for the financial collapse of the savings and loan industry, at least in some cases the failure of large institutions can be traced to their over investment in high-risk debt securities. In the early 1990s, similar problems have come to light in parts of the insurance industry. For example, in April 1991, insurance regulators in California seized control of Executive Life Insurance Company. The bond portfolio of Executive Life's parent company, First Executive Corporation, had a market value of $3 billion less than its $9.85 billion book value at the end of 1990. During the first quarter of 1991, the insurance company lost $465.9 million. The potential collapse of Executive Life placed in jeopardy the private pensions of thousands of workers whose employers had purchased retirement annuity contracts through the firm.

The problems caused by the savings and loan industry failure and the failure of large life insurance companies, such as First Executive, which had invested heavily in junk bonds, raises interesting issues of ethics and good business practice. Both savings and loan institutions and First Executive made a conscious decision to accept additional risk in the investment securities they purchased in exchange for additional expected return.

What standards of prudent business practice should be followed by firms when they attempt to improve their investment earnings performance? It is well known that in the financial markets, higher returns usually can be achieved only by assuming greater risks. If this is true, should insurance companies completely avoid high-risk securities? How can these risks be managed effectively? What standards of voluntary disclosure of information to depositors and policyholders about the risk and return characteristics of the assets held by the institution do you believe are appropriate?

http

Could you personally become rich by trading stocks? To find out, set up a simulated portfolio at the PC Financial Network maintained by Thomson Investors Network. Choose the securities you want to trade (IBM? AT&T? Mobil?...), the number of shares you want of each stock, and when you want to purchase them (or sell them short). Thomson Investors Network will thereafter create your "model portfolio" and track its performance for you. Try it for a month and see how well you do.
http://www.thomsoninvest.net

■ SUMMARY

■ The *risk* of a security or an investment project generally is defined in terms of the potential *variability* of its returns. When only one return is possible—

---

[27]The concept of optimal capital structure is discussed in Chapter 12.
[28]See Chapter 6 for a discussion of bond credit ratings.

for example, as with U.S. government securities held to maturity—there is no risk. When more than one return is possible for a particular project, it is risky.

■ The *standard deviation, σ,* of the returns from an investment is an *absolute* measure of risk. It is computed as the square root of the weighted average squared deviations of possible outcomes from the expected value.

■ When investments with unequal expected returns are being compared, the *coefficient of variation, v,* is a more appropriate measure of risk. The coefficient of variation is the ratio of the standard deviation to the expected value.

■ Because cash flow projections and expected returns can be estimated with less certainty further into the future, risk generally is thought to *increase over time.*

■ The *expected rate of return* from a security reflects the distributions an investor *anticipates* receiving from an investment. The *required rate of return* reflects the return an investor *demands* as compensation for postponing consumption and assuming risk. In efficient financial markets, required rates of return and expected rates of return should be approximately equal.

■ The required rate of return on a security is a function of the general level of interest rates, as reflected in the risk-free rate of return, the maturity risk of the security, the default risk of the security, the business and financial risk of the firm that issues the security, the seniority risk of the security, and the marketability risk of the security.

■ The greater the risk associated with the returns from a security or an investment in a physical asset, the greater will be the required rate of return on that investment.

■ Risk is also influenced by the possibility of investment *diversification.* For example, if a proposed project's returns are not *perfectly correlated* with the returns from the firm's other investments, the total risk of the firm may be reduced by accepting the proposed project. This is known as the *portfolio effect.*

■ The *expected return from a portfolio* of two or more securities is equal to the weighted average of the expected returns from the individual securities.

■ The *risk of a portfolio* is a function of both the risk of the individual securities in the portfolio and the correlation among the individual securities' returns.

■ The *Capital Asset Pricing Model* (CAPM) is a theory that can be used to determine required rates of return on financial and physical assets.

■ The *unsystematic* portion of the total risk in a security's return is that portion of return variability unique to the firm. Efficient diversification of a portfolio of securities can eliminate most unsystematic risk.

■ *Systematic risk* refers to the portion of total risk in a security's return caused by overall market forces. This risk cannot be diversified away in a portfolio. Systematic risk forms the basis for the risk premium required by investors in any risky security.

■ The *security market line* (SML) provides an algebraic or graphic representation of the risk-return trade-off required in the marketplace for risky securities. It measures risk in terms of systematic risk.

■ An index of systematic risk for a security is the security's *beta.* Beta is determined from the slope of a regression line, the *characteristic line,* between the market return and the individual security's return. It is a measure of the volatility of a security's returns relative to the returns of the market as a whole.

■ The required return on common stock consists of the risk-free rate plus a risk premium. This risk premium is equal to a security's beta times the market risk premium, and the market risk premium is equal to the difference between the expected market return and the risk-free rate.

■ QUESTIONS AND TOPICS FOR DISCUSSION

1. Define the following terms:

   a. Risk.
   b. Probability distribution.
   c. Standard deviation.
   d. Required rate of return.
   e. Coefficient of variation.
   f. Efficient portfolio.

   g. Efficient frontier.
   h. Capital market line.
   i. Beta coefficient.
   j. CAPM.
   k. Correlation coefficient.
   l. Portfolio.

   m. Characteristic line.
   n. Security market line.
   o. Covariance.
   p. Systematic risk.
   q. Unsystematic risk.

2. If the returns from a security were known with certainty, what shape would the probability distribution of returns graph have?

3. What is the nature of the risk associated with "risk-free" U.S. government bonds?

4. If inflation expectations increase, what would you expect to happen to the returns required by investors in bonds? What would happen to bond prices?

5. Under what circumstances will the coefficient of variation of a security's returns and the standard deviation of that security's returns give the same relative measure of risk when compared with the risk of another security?

6. Explain how diversification can reduce the risk of a portfolio of assets to below the weighted average of the risk of the individual assets.

7. What are the primary variables that influence the risk of a portfolio of assets?

8. Distinguish between unsystematic and systematic risk. Under what circumstances are investors likely to ignore the unsystematic risk characteristics of a security?

9. What effect do increasing inflation expectations have on the required returns of investors in common stock?

10. The stock of Amrep Corporation has a *beta* value estimated to be 1.4. How would you interpret this beta value? How would you evaluate the firm's systematic risk?

11. How is a security's beta value computed?

12. Under what circumstances can the beta concept be used to estimate the rate of return required by investors in a stock? What problems are encountered when using the CAPM?

13. The enclosed area in the graph below shows all the possible portfolios obtained by combining the given securities in different proportions (i.e., the opportunity set).

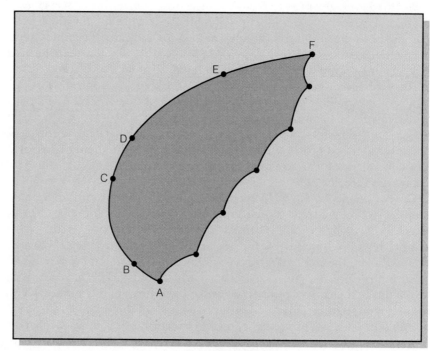

a. Which of the portfolios (A, B, C, D, E, or F) is (are) on the efficient frontier?

b. If an investor is interested in maximizing expected returns, which portfolio should be chosen?

c. If an investor is interested in minimizing risk (as measured by standard deviation), which portfolio should be chosen?

14. What is the *term structure* of interest rates?

15. What is the *risk structure* of interest rates?

16. How is *risk* defined in a financial sense?

17. Discuss the general relationship between risk and expected return.

18. What factors determine investors' required rates of return on corporate bonds? Common stocks? U.S. government bonds?

19. Why do yield curves sometimes have a downward slope and at other times have an upward slope?

20. What is the primary difference between 20-year bonds issued by the U.S. government and 20-year bonds issued by IBM?

21. Is it possible for investors ever to require a lower rate of return on a company's equity than on its debt, assuming the debt is in a junk-bond category of quality?

■ SELF-TEST PROBLEMS

ST1. Given are the following possible returns (dividends plus capital gains) over the coming year from a $10,000 investment in General Motors common stock:

State of Economy	Probability	Return
Recession	0.20	$-1,000
Normal year	0.60	1,500
Boom	0.20	2,500

Determine the

a. Expected return.

b. Standard deviation of returns.

c. Coefficient of variation.

ST2. Given that the rate of return on General Electric common stock over the coming year is normally distributed with an expected value of 15 percent and a standard deviation of 12 percent, determine the probability of earning a negative rate of return.

ST3. Two common stocks, Consolidated Edison and Apple Computer, have the following expected return and standard deviation of return over the next year:

Common Stock	Expected Rate of Return	Standard Deviation
Consolidated Edison	12%	6%
Apple Computer	20	15

Additionally, assume that the correlation coefficient of returns on the two securities is +0.50. For a portfolio consisting of 75 percent of the funds invested in Consolidated Edison and the remainder in Apple Computer, determine the

a. Expected rate of return on the portfolio.

b. Standard deviation of the rate of return.

ST4. Determine the beta of a portfolio consisting of equal investments in the following common stocks:

Security	Beta
Boeing	.95
Chrysler	1.25
Intel	1.15
Wal-Mart Stores	1.05

ST5. The risk-free rate of return is 6 percent, based on an expected inflation premium of 3 percent. The expected rate of return on the market portfolio is 15 percent.

    a. Determine the required rate of return on Wisconsin Public Service (WPS) common stock whose beta is 0.60.

    b. Assume that the expected rate of return on the Market Portfolio remains constant but that the expected inflation premium increases from a current level of 3 percent to 4 percent. Determine the required rate of return on WPS common stock.

    c. Assume that the expected inflation premium remains at 3 percent but that the expected return on the Market Portfolio increases to 16 percent. Determine the required rate of return on WPS common stock.

ST6. The yield to maturity on Xerox Corporation bonds maturing in 1998 is 8.40 percent. The yield to maturity on a similar maturity U.S. government Treasury bond is 7.55 percent. The yield to maturity on 90-day Treasury bills is 6.11 percent.

    a. What is the maturity risk premium between the Treasury bill and the Xerox bond?

    b. What is the default risk premium on the Xerox bond?

■ PROBLEMS*

1. You have estimated the following probability distributions of expected future returns for Stocks X and Y:

	Stock X		Stock Y
Probability	**Return**	**Probability**	**Return**
0.1	−10%	0.2	2%
0.2	10	0.2	7
0.4	15	0.3	12
0.2	20	0.2	15
0.1	40	0.1	16

    a. What is the expected rate of return for Stock X? Stock Y?

    b. What is the standard deviation of expected returns for Stock X? For Stock Y?

    c. Which stock would you consider to be riskier? Why?

2. The return expected from Project No. 542 is 22 percent. The standard deviation of these returns is 11 percent. If returns from the project are normally distributed, what is the chance that the project will result in a rate of return above 33 percent? What is the probability that the project will result in losses (negative rates of return)?

3. The expected rate of return for the stock of Cornhusker Enterprises is 20 percent, with a standard deviation of 15 percent. The expected rate of return for the stock of Mustang Associates is 10 percent, with a standard deviation of 9 percent.

    a. Which stock would you consider to be riskier? Why?

    b. If you knew that the beta coefficient of Cornhusker stock is 1.5 and the beta of Mustang is 0.9, how would your answer to Part a change?

4. An investor currently has all of his wealth in Treasury bills. He is considering investing one-third of his funds in Delta Airlines, whose beta is 1.30, with the remainder left in Treasury bills. The expected risk-free rate (Treasury bills) is 6 percent and the market risk premium is 8.8 percent. Determine the beta and the expected return on the proposed portfolio.

5. You are considering purchasing a portfolio of securities. The securities available to you have the following expected returns:

---

*Colored numbers denote problems that have check answers provided at the end of the book.

Security	Expected Return (%)
A	14
B	9
C	15
D	11

a. If you invest 20 percent of your funds in Security A, 40 percent in B, 20 percent in C, and 20 percent in D, what is the expected return of the portfolio?

b. How does the expected return of the portfolio change if you invest 40 percent in A, 10 percent in B, 40 percent in C, and 10 percent in D?

c. In addition to the portfolio in Part b having a different expected return than the portfolio in Part a, how would you expect the two portfolios to differ with respect to risk?

6. You are considering investing in two securities, X and Y. The following data are available for the two securities:

	Security X	Security Y
Expected return	0.10	0.07
Standard deviation of returns	0.08	0.04
Beta	1.10	0.75

a. If you invest 40 percent of your funds in Security X and 60 percent in Security Y and if the correlation of returns between X and Y is +0.5, compute the following:
   i. The expected return from the portfolio.
   ii. The standard deviation of returns from the portfolio.

b. What happens to the expected return and standard deviation of returns of the portfolio in Part a if 70 percent of your funds are invested in Security X and 30 percent of your funds are invested in Security Y?

c. What happens to the expected return and standard deviation of returns of the portfolio in Part a if the following conditions exist?
   i. The correlation of returns between Securities X and Y is +1.0.
   ii. The correlation of returns between Securities X and Y is 0.
   iii. The correlation of returns between Securities X and Y is −0.7.

7. You have the following information on two securities in which you have invested:

Security	Expected Return	Standard Deviation	Beta	% Invested (w)
Xerox	15%	4.5%	1.20	35%
Kodak	12%	3.8%	0.98	65%

a. Which stock is riskier in a portfolio context? Which stock is riskier if you are considering them as individual assets (not part of a portfolio)?

b. Compute the expected return on the portfolio.

c. If the securities have a correlation of +0.60, compute the standard deviation of the portfolio.

d. Compute the beta of the portfolio.

8. Realizing the benefits of diversification you have invested in the following securities:

	United	Chubb	Chase
Expected return	12%	14%	9%
Standard deviation of return	3%	5%	3%
Beta	1.65	1.2	0.89
Amount invested in each security	$50,000	$125,000	$75,000

a. Compute the expected rate of return on the portfolio.

b. Compute the beta of the portfolio.

9. Given a risk-free rate $(\hat{r}_f)$ of 6 percent and a market risk premium $(\hat{r}_m - \hat{r}_f)$ of 8.8 percent, calculate the required rate of return on each of the following stocks, based on the betas given in Table 5-9:
   a. American Electric Power.
   b. Apple Computer.
   c. Boeing.
   d. USAirways.

10. The SML has been estimated as follows:

$$k_j = 0.06 + 0.088\beta_j$$

This estimate assumes an expected rate of inflation of 4 percent. If inflation expectations increase from 4 to 6 percent, determine the equation of the new SML.

11. The stock of Pizza Hot, Inc., a Mexican pizza chain, has an estimated beta of 1.5. Calculate the required rate of return on Pizza Hot's stock if the SML is estimated as follows:

$$k_j = 0.06 + 0.088\beta_j$$

based on
   a. An initial inflation expectation of 4 percent.
   b. A new inflation expectation of 6 percent.

12. The SML has been estimated as follows:

$$k_j = 0.06 + 0.088\beta_j$$

Suppose that the market risk premium $(\hat{r}_m - \hat{r}_f)$ increases by 1.2 percentage points (i.e., 0.012) as the result of an increase in uncertainty about the future economic outlook.
   a. Determine the equation of the new SML.
   b. Calculate the required rate of return on Meditek stock (whose estimated beta is 1.25) before and after the change in the market risk premium.

13. a. Suppose a U.S. Treasury bill, maturing in 1 year, can be purchased today for $92,500. Assuming that the security is held until maturity, the investor will receive $100,000 (face amount). Determine the rate of return on this investment.
   b. Suppose a National Telephone and Telegraph (NTT) Company bond, maturing in 1 year, can be purchased today for $975. Assuming that the bond is held until maturity, the investor will receive $1,000 (principal) plus 7 percent interest (that is, 0.07 x $1000 = $70). Determine the rate of return on this investment.
   c. Determine the implied risk premium on NTT bonds.

14. The real rate of interest has been estimated to be 3 percent, and the expected long-term annual inflation rate is 7 percent.
   a. What is the current risk-free rate of return on 1-year Treasury bond?
   b. If the yield on 10-year U.S. Treasury bonds is 12 percent, what is the maturity risk premium between a 10-year bond and a 1-year bond?
   c. If American Airlines bonds, scheduled to mature in 10 years, currently sell to yield 13 percent, what is the default risk premium on these bonds?
   d. If investors in the common stock of American Airlines require a 16 percent rate of return, what is the seniority risk premium on American's common stock?

15. Determine beta for a portfolio containing equal investments in each of the following stocks, based on the betas given in Table 5-9:
   a. American Electric Power, Coca-Cola, K-Mart, and Wisconsin Public Energy.
   b. Apple Computer, Chrysler, Intel, Merrill Lynch, and USAirways.

16. Using Equation 5.17, suppose you have computed the required rate of return for the stock of Bulldog Trucking to be 16.6 percent. Given the current stock price, the current dividend rate, and analysts' projections for future dividend growth, you expect to earn a rate of return of 18 percent.
   a. Would you recommend buying or selling this stock? Why?
   b. If your expected rate of return from the stock of Bulldog is 15 percent, what would you expect to happen to Bulldog's stock price?

17. You want to construct a portfolio with a 20 percent expected return. The portfolio is to consist of some combination of Security A and Security B:

Security	Expected Return	Standard Deviation	Beta
A	15%	10%	0.82
B	28	20	1.75

   a. What percentage of your portfolio should consist of Security A? Security B?
   b. What is the beta of the portfolio?
18. The stock of Koch Brickyard, Inc., is expected to return 14 percent with a standard deviation of 5 percent. Uptown Potbelly Stove Works' stock is expected to return 16 percent with a standard deviation of 9 percent.
   a. If you invest 30 percent of your funds in Koch stock and 70 percent in Uptown stock, what is the expected return on your portfolio?
   b. What is the expected risk of this portfolio if the returns for the two stocks have
      i. A perfect positive correlation (+1.0)?
      ii. A slightly negative correlation (−0.2)?
19. Security A offers an expected return of 15 percent with a standard deviation of 7 percent. Security B offers an expected return of 9 percent with a standard deviation of 4 percent. The correlation between the returns of A and B is +0.6. If an investor puts one-fourth of his wealth in A and three-fourths in B, what is the expected return and risk (standard deviation) of this portfolio?
20. The beta of MacDrive is estimated to be 1.3. The beta of MacWalk is estimated to be 1.1. If these two firms merge, to form MacRun, what will be the beta of the new firm, assuming that MacWalk is two times as large as MacDrive?
21. The return on the Tarheel Corporation stock is expected to be 14 percent with a standard deviation of 8 percent. The beta of Tarheel is 0.8. The risk-free rate is 7 percent, and the expected return on the market portfolio is 15 percent. What is the probability that an investor in Tarheel will earn a rate of return less than the required rate of return? Assume that returns are normally distributed.
22. The stock of Jones Trucking is expected to return 13 percent annually with a standard deviation of 8 percent. The stock of Bush Steel Mills is expected to return 17 percent annually with a standard deviation of 14 percent. The correlation between the returns from the two securities has been estimated to be +0.3. The beta of the Jones' stock is 0.9, and the beta of the Bush stock is 1.2. The risk-free rate of return is expected to be 8 percent, and the expected return on the market portfolio is 15 percent. The current dividend for Jones is $4. The current dividend for Bush is $6.
   a. What is the expected return from a portfolio containing the two securities if 40 percent of your wealth is invested in Jones and 60 percent is invested in Bush?
   b. What is the expected standard deviation of the portfolio of the two stocks?
   c. Which stock is the better buy in the current market? Why?
23. Equation 5.9 can be modified to compute the risk of a three-security portfolio as follows:

$$\sigma_p = \sqrt{w_A^2\sigma_A^2 + w_B^2\sigma_B^2 + w_C^2\sigma_C^2 + 2w_Aw_B\rho_{AB}\sigma_A\sigma_B + 2w_Aw_C\rho_{AC}\sigma_A\sigma_C + 2w_Bw_C\rho_{BC}\sigma_B\sigma_C}$$

You have decided to invest 40 percent of your wealth in Security A, 30 percent in Security B, and 30 percent in Security C. The following information is available about the possible returns from the three securities:

Security A		Security B		Security C	
Return	Probability	Return	Probability	Return	Probability
10%	0.25	13%	0.30	14%	0.40
12	0.50	16	0.35	18	0.30
14	0.25	19	0.35	22	0.30

Compute the expected return of the portfolio and the risk of the portfolio if the correlations between returns from the three securities are $\rho_{AB} = 0.70$; $\rho_{AC} = 0.60$; and $\rho_{BC} = 0.85$.

24. A major investment advisory service issued forecasts of the expected rates of return for the following securities:

Security	Expected Return
Boeing	20%
Coca-Cola	25
Dupont	12
Exxon	10
Toys 'R' Us	30

Based on the Capital Asset Pricing Model, with a risk-free rate $(\hat{r}_f)$ of 7 percent, a market risk premium $(\hat{r}_m - \hat{r}_f)$ of 8.8 percent, and the betas shown in Table 5.9, which of the securities (if any) appear to be attractive investments, i.e., expected return exceeds required return?

25. The expected return and standard deviation of returns of General Mills common stock over the next year are estimated to be 20 percent and 12 percent, respectively. Assume that the returns are approximately normally distributed.
    a. Determine the probability of incurring a loss (negative rate of return) from investing in this stock.
    b. Determine the probability of earning a rate of return less than the risk-free rate of 6 percent.

26. Three Rivers Investment Company desires to construct a portfolio with a 20 percent expected return. The portfolio is to consist of some combination of Security X and Security Y, which have the following expected returns, standard deviations of returns, and betas:

	Security X	Security Y
Expected return	15%	26%
Standard deviation	10%	20%
Beta	0.94	1.33

Determine the expected beta of the portfolio.

27. The current (time zero) price of one share of Farrell Corporation's common stock is $25. The price is expected to increase by $5 over the coming year. The company is not expected to pay a dividend during the year. The standard deviation of the expected price change is $3. The distribution of the end-of-year possible prices is approximately normal. Determine the probability of earning a return greater than 30 percent over the coming year from your investment in Farrell common stock.

28. a. Estimate beta for each of the following securities assuming that the standard deviation of returns for the Market Portfolio (m) is 8.0%.

Security	Expected Return	Standard Deviation	Correlation Coefficient Between Returns for the Security and Market Portolio
P	12%	10%	.80
Q	18	20	.60
R	15	15	.40

b. Based on the Capital Asset Pricing Model, with a risk-free rate $(\hat{r}_f)$ of 7 percent and a market risk premium $(\hat{r}_m - \hat{r}_f)$ of 8.8 percent, which of the securities, P, Q, R (if any) appear to be attractive investments?

29. Two securities have the following characteristics:

	Security A	Security B
Expected return	15%	12%
Standard deviation	4%	6%
Beta	0.90	− 0.25

Furthermore, the correlation of returns between the securities is −1.0. Determine the risk (standard deviation) of a portfolio consisting of equal proportions of Securities A and B.

30. New Castle Company common stock has a beta of 1.50. The stock currently pays a dividend of $3 per share. The risk-free rate is 8 percent, and the market risk premium is expected to be 8.0 percent. The returns from New Castle stock are normally distributed with an expected value of 24 percent and a standard deviation of 3 percent.

a. Determine the required rate of return for New Castle's common stock.

b. Determine the probability that the stock of New Castle is undervalued at its current market price of $25 per share.

31. The real rate of return has been estimated to be 2 percent under current economic conditions. The 30-day risk-free rate (annualized) is 5 percent. Twenty-year U.S. government bonds currently yield 8 percent. The yield on 20-year bonds issued by the Forester Hoop Company is 14 percent. Investors require an 18 percent return on Forester's common stock. The common stock of Brown's Forensic Products has a required return of 20 percent. Compute and identify all meaningful risk premiums. What might account for the difference in the required returns for Brown versus Forester?

32. Boston Market's stock has an estimated beta of 1.5. The stock pays no dividend and is not expected to pay one for the foreseeable future. The current price of the stock is $50. You expect this price to rise to $60 by the end of the coming year. You believe that the distribution of possible year-end prices is approximately normal with a standard deviation of $2.50. The risk-free rate of return is currently 4 percent and the market risk premium is 8.8 percent. What is the probability that Boston Market's stock is currently overvalued?

33. Suppose that a portfolio consists of the following stocks:

Stock	Amount	Beta
Texaco	$20,000	70
Delta Air Lines	40,000	1.30
Ford	40,000	1.10

The risk-free rate $(\hat{r}_f)$ is 5 percent and the market risk premium $(\hat{r}_m - \hat{r}_f)$ is 8.8 percent.

a. Determine the beta for the portfolio.

b. Determine how much Delta Air Lines stock one must sell and reinvest in Texaco stock in order to reduce the beta of the portfolio to 1.00.

c. Determine the expected return on the portfolio in parts a and b.

34. International Manyfoods, Inc.'s common stock has a beta of 0.9. The stock does not currently pay a dividend, but is expected to appreciate in value from a current price of $15 to $25 in the next 5 years. The risk-free rate is 6 percent and the market risk premium is 7.4 percent. If the standard deviation of the expected return from this stock is 2 percentage points, what is the probability that it is overvalued?

35. Visit the "Mutual Fund Center" at the Thomson Investors Network site. Pick out some low-risk funds based first on the measure of standard deviation and then beta. Then look at the 1-, 3- and 5-year returns of these funds. Now do the same thing with high-risk funds. Show, using your findings, how return is a function of risk. (Or is it?!?) www.thomsoninvest.net

http://

■ SOLUTIONS TO SELF-TEST PROBLEMS

ST1. a. $\hat{r} = \sum\limits_{j=1}^{n} r_j p_j$

$\qquad = \$1,000(0.20) + \$1,500(0.60) + \$2,500(0.20)$

$\qquad = \$1,200$

b. $\sigma = \sqrt{\sum\limits_{j=1}^{n} (r_j - \hat{r})^2 p_j}$

$\qquad = [(-\$1,000 - \$1,200)^2(0.20) + (\$1,500 - \$1,200)^2(0.60)$

$\qquad + (\$2,500 - \$1,200)^2(0.20)]^{0.50} = \$1,166$

c. $v = \dfrac{\sigma}{\hat{r}}$

$\qquad = \dfrac{\$1166}{\$1200}$

$\qquad = 0.97$

ST2. $z = \dfrac{r - \hat{r}}{\sigma}$

$\qquad = \dfrac{0 - 15}{12} = -1.25$

$\qquad p = 0.1056 \text{ (or } 10.56\%)$

ST3. a. $\hat{r}_p = w_A \hat{r}_A + w_B \hat{r}_B$

$\qquad = 0.75(12) + 0.25(20)$

$\qquad = 14\%$

b. $\sigma_P = \sqrt{w_A^2 \sigma_A^2 + w_B^2 \sigma_B^2 + 2w_A w_B \rho_{AB} \sigma_A \sigma_B}$

$\qquad = [(0.75)^2(6)^2 + (0.25)^2(15)^2 + 2(0.75)(0.25)(.50)(6)(15)]^{0.50}$

$\qquad = 7.15\%$

ST4. $\beta_p = \sum\limits_{j=1}^{n} w_j \beta_j$

$\qquad = 0.25(.95) + 0.25(1.25) + 0.25(1.15) + 0.25(1.05)$

$\qquad = 1.10$

ST5. a. $k_j = \hat{r}_f + \beta_j (\hat{r}_m - \hat{r}_f)$

$\qquad = 6 + 0.60 (15 - 6)$

$\qquad = 11.4\%$

b. $k_j = 7 + 0.60(15 - 7)$

$\qquad = 11.8\%$

c. $k_j = 6 + 0.60(16 - 6)$

$\qquad = 12.0\%$

ST6. a. Maturity risk premium: $7.55\% - 6.11\% = 1.44\%$. The maturity risk premium on the Xerox bond will be the same as on the Treasury bonds.

b. Default risk premium: $8.40\% - 7.55\% = 0.85\%$

■ GLOSSARY

Beta A measure of systematic risk. It indicates the volatility of a security's returns relative to the returns of a broad-based market portfolio of securities.

Business Risk The variability in a firm's operating earnings over time.

Capital Asset Pricing Model (CAPM) A theory that formally describes the nature of the risk-required rate of return relationship on investments in financial assets (securities) or physical assets.

Characteristics Line A regression line relating the periodic returns for a specific security to the periodic returns on the market portfolio. The slope of this regression line is an estimate of the beta of the security—a measure of its systematic risk.

Coefficient of Variation The ratio of the standard deviation to the expected value. It provides a relative measure of risk.

Correlation A relative statistical measure of the degree to which two series of numbers, such as the returns from two assets, tend to move or vary together.

Covariance An absolute statistical measure of how closely two variances (such as securities' returns) move together. It measures the degree to which increases (decreases) in the level of one variable tend to be associated with increases (decreases) in the level of another variable over time.

Diversification The act of investing in a set of financial (securities) or physical assets having different risk-return characteristics.

Efficient Frontier The set of efficient portfolios.

Efficient Portfolio A portfolio that, for a given standard deviation, has the highest expected return, or, for a given expected return, has the lowest standard deviation.

Expected Return The benefits (price appreciation and distributions) an individual anticipates receiving from an investment.

Expected Value A statistical measure of the mean or average value of the possible outcomes. Operationally, it is defined as the weighted average of the possible outcomes with the weights being the probability of occurrence.

Financial Risk The additional variability in a company's earnings per share caused by the use of fixed-cost sources of funds, such as debt and preferred stock.

Market Portfolio The portfolio of securities consisting of all available securities weighted by their respective market values.

Portfolio A collection of two or more financial (securities) or physical assets.

Required Rate of Return The return (yield) an individual demands from an investment as compensation for postponing consumption and assuming risk.

Risk The possibility that actual future returns will deviate from expected returns; the variability of returns.

Risk-free Rate of Return The return required by an investor in a security having no risk of default; equal to the sum of the real rate of return and an inflation risk premium.

Risk Premium The difference between the required rate of return on a risky investment and the rate of return on a risk-free asset, such as U.S. Treasury bills. Components include maturity risk, default risk, seniority risk, and marketability risk.

Security Market Line (SML) The relationship between systematic risk and required rates of return for individual securities.

Standard Deviation A statistical measure of the dispersion, or variability, of possible outcomes around the expected value, or mean. Operationally, it is defined as the square root of the weighted average squared deviations of possible outcomes from the expected value. The standard deviation provides an absolute measure of risk.

Systematic Risk That portion of the variability of an individual security's returns that is caused by the factors affecting the market as a whole. This also is called nondiversifiable risk.

Term Structure of Interest Rates The pattern of interest rate yields for debt securities that are similar in all respects except for their length of time to maturity. The term structure of interest rates usually is represented by a graphic plot called a yield curve.

Unsystematic Risk Risk that is unique to a firm. This also is called diversifiable risk.

FIXED-INCOME SECURITIES: CHARACTERISTICS AND VALUATION

6

1. The characteristics of fixed-income (debt and preferred stock) securities are examined, including
   a. Types of each form of security
   b. Features
   c. Users
   d. Advantages and disadvantages
2. Reading and interpreting financial market data, including stock and bond price quotations, is an essential skill for an effective financial manager.
3. In the capitalization of cash flow method, the value of an asset is equal to the present value of the expected future cash flows discounted at the appropriate required rate of return.
4. The required rate of return is a function of the risk or uncertainty associated with the cash flows from the asset, as well as the risk-free rate.
5. The value of a bond with a finite maturity date is equal to the present value of the interest payments and principal payment (at maturity) discounted at the investor's required rate of return.

KEY CHAPTER CONCEPTS

6. The yield to maturity of a bond is equal to the rate of return that equates the price of the bond to the present value of the interest and principal payments.
7. The value of a perpetual bond, or perpetuity, is determined by dividing the fixed interest rate per period by the required rate of return, since no calculation for payback of principal is needed in the valuation.
8. Preferred stocks are often treated as *perpetuities* with a value equal to the annual dividend divided by the required rate of return.
9. The market value or market price of an asset is the value placed on the asset by the marginally satisfied buyer and seller, who exchange assets in the marketplace.
10. Market equilibrium occurs when the price of an asset is such that the expected rate of return is equal to the required rate of return.
11. Bond refunding occurs when a firm redeems a callable bond issue and replaces it with a lower (interest) cost issue.

Marriott Corporation: Corporate Restructuring and Bond Valuation*

During the late 1980s, a number of large publicly held U.S. companies, such as RJR-Nabisco, restructured themselves through leveraged buyout transactions. More recently, a number of large companies have begun using spinoffs to restructure themselves. In a spinoff, a company distributes stock in a subsidiary to its shareholders. While spinoffs can be beneficial to a company's stockholders, these transactions can be quite detrimental to the interests of bondholders.

For example, consider the case of the Marriott Corporation. In late 1992 the company announced that it was planning to split itself into two new units. The healthier unit, Marriott International, Inc., would operate hotels, manage facilities and food services for various health care and educational institutions, and operate retirement communities. This unit would have very little long-term debt (less than $20 million). The other unit, Host Marriott Corp., would own 141 Marriott hotels and motels and 16 retirement communities, as well as manage airport and toll road concessions. This unit would retain almost all of Marriott's $2.9 billion in long-term debt. The stock market reacted positively to this announce-

ment—Marriott's stock price rose 12 percent on the day the spinoff was announced. Conversely, the prices of the company's bonds plummeted over 30

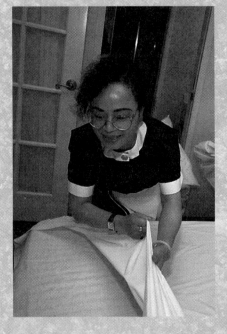

percent—one issue fell from 110 to 80, or a loss of $300 for a bond with a $1,000 principal. The bonds, which had previously been rated investment grade (i.e., high quality) by the bond rating services were downgraded to junk-bond status (i.e., low quality).

Marriott was aware that this spinoff would have a negative impact on bondholders. However, as a Marriott

spokesman noted, "We have a fiduciary obligation to stockholders, and this transaction is in the best interests of stockholders. Our obligation to bondholders is to make all the bond payments on time and to pay off the principal on time. We plan to fulfill that obligation."[1] Bondholders sued Marriott seeking to block the reorganization. This action forced the company to alter the terms of the spinoff, reducing the amount of debt assumed by Host Marriott and swapping higher coupon rate bonds for the existing bonds.

The obligations a company has to its bondholders are spelled out in the bond indenture, or contract, between the firm and the owners of the debt securities. As discussed in the chapter, bondholders can seek to protect themselves against the adverse effects of corporate restructurings, such as spinoffs, through appropriate covenants in the bond indenture.

*Based on Robin Blumenthal, "Marriott to Split Its Businesses into 2 Entities," *Wall Street Journal* (October 6, 1992): A3; Constance Mitchell, "Marriott Plan Enrages Holders of Its Bonds," *Wall Street Journal* (October 7, 1992): C1; and Ann Newman, "Marriott Corp. Modifies Plan to Split in Two," *Wall Street Journal* (March 12, 1993): A2.

[1]Constance Mitchell, "Marriott Plan Enrages Holders of Its Bonds," *Wall Street Journal* (October 7, 1992): C1.

INTRODUCTION

Firms issue various types of long-term securities to help meet their needs for funds. These include long-term debt (bonds),[2] preferred stock, and common stock. Long-term debt and preferred stock are sometimes referred to as *fixed-income securities*. Holders of these types of securities receive relatively constant distributions of interest or dividend payments over time and have a fixed claim on the assets of the firm in the event of bankruptcy.[3] For example, American Telephone and Telegraph sold $250 million of bonds in 1966, at which time it agreed to pay its lenders an interest rate of 5⅛ percent or $51.25 per year until 2001 for each $1,000 of debt outstanding. Since then, the company has continued to pay this interest rate, even though market interest rates have fluctuated. Similarly, duPont issued $70 million of preferred stock in 1947. Investors paid $102 per share, and the company agreed to pay an annual dividend of $3.50 per share. Since then duPont has continued to pay this amount, even though common stock dividends have been increased numerous times.

Common stock, on the other hand, is a *variable-income security*. Common stockholders are said to participate in a firm's earnings, because they may receive a larger dividend if earnings increase in the future, or their dividend may be cut if earnings drop. Investors in common stock have a residual claim on the earnings (and assets) of the firm since they receive dividends only after the claims of bondholders and other creditors, as well as preferred stockholders, have been met.

Fixed-income securities—long-term debt and preferred stock—differ from each other in several ways. For example, the interest paid to bondholders is a tax-deductible expense for the borrowing company, whereas dividends paid to preferred stockholders are not. Legally, long-term debtholders are considered creditors, whereas preferred stockholders are considered owners. Thus, a firm is not legally required to pay dividends to its preferred stockholders, and the failure to do so has less serious consequences than the failure to meet interest payment and principal repayment obligations on long-term debt. In addition, long-term debt normally has a specific maturity, whereas preferred stock is often perpetual.

A knowledge of the characteristics of the various types of long-term securities is necessary in developing valuation models for these securities. The valuation of long-term securities is important to a firm's financial managers, as well as to current owners, prospective investors, and security analysts. For example, financial managers should understand how the price or value of the firm's securities (particularly common stock) is affected by its investment, financing, and dividend decisions. Similarly, both current owners and prospective investors should be able to compare their own valuations of the firm's securities with actual market prices to make rational security purchase and sale decisions. Likewise, security analysts use valuation techniques in evaluating long-term corporate securities when making investment recommendations.

This chapter focuses on the characteristics and valuation of fixed-income securities; namely, long-term debt and preferred stock. The next chapter contains a similar discussion of variable-income securities; namely, common stock.

---

[2]The terms *long-term debt securities, debt,* and *bonds* are used interchangeably throughout the chapter.
[3]While floating rate debt and adjustable rate preferred stock have interest and dividend distributions that can fluctuate over time (as described later in the chapter), they are still classified as fixed-income securities.

CHARACTERISTICS OF LONG-TERM DEBT

When a company borrows money in the capital markets, it issues long-term debt securities to investors. These bonds are usually sold in denominations of $1,000 and constitute a promise by the issuing company to repay a certain amount of money (the $1,000 principal) on a particular date (the maturity date) and to pay a specified amount of interest at fixed intervals (usually twice a year). Most debt has a *par value* of $1,000, and debt prices are often expressed as a percentage of that value. For example, a market price listing of "87" indicates that a $1,000 par value bond may be purchased for $870.

There are many different types of long-term debt. The type or types a company chooses to use will depend on its own particular financial situation and the characteristics of the industry as a whole.

Types of Long-Term Debt

Long-term debt is generally classified according to whether it is secured by specific physical assets of the issuing company. Secured debt issues are usually called **mortgage bonds,** and issues not secured by specific assets are called **debentures** or, occasionally, *debenture bonds*. The term **bond** is often used to denote any type of long-term debt security.

At the present time, utility companies are the largest users of mortgage bonds. In recent years, the use of mortgage bonds relative to other forms of long-term debt has declined, whereas the use of debentures has increased. Because debentures are unsecured, their quality depends on the general creditworthiness of the issuing company. As a result, they are usually issued by large, financially strong firms.

The yield differential between the mortgage bond and debenture alternatives is another example of the risk-return trade-off that occurs throughout finance. For example, suppose Midstates Oil Company could issue either mortgage bonds or debentures. If the mortgage bonds could be sold with a 10 percent interest rate, the debentures would have to be sold at a higher rate—for example, 10¼ percent— to attract investors. This is due to the fact that investors require a higher return on debentures, which are backed only by the unmortgaged assets of the company and the company's earning power, than they do on mortgage bonds, which are secured by specific physical assets as well as the company's earning power.

Debt issues are also classified according to whether they are *senior* or *junior*.[4] **Senior debt** has a higher priority claim to a firm's earnings and/or assets than junior debt. Occasionally, the actual name of the debt issue will contain a "junior" or "senior" qualifier. In most instances, however, identification of how a particular company's debt issues are ranked requires an analysis of the restrictions placed on the company by the purchasers of the issue.

Unsecured debt may also be classified according to whether it is *subordinated* to other types of debt. In the event of a liquidation or reorganization, the claims of *subordinated debenture holders* are considered only *after* the claims of *unsubordinated debenture holders*. In general, **subordinated debentures** are junior to other types of debt, including bank loans, and may even be junior to *all* of a firm's other debt.

---

[4]The senior–junior classification scheme is also used in connection with preferred and common stock. Preferred stock is junior to long-term debt and senior to common stock.

Equipment trust certificates are used largely by railroad and trucking companies. The proceeds from these certificates are used to purchase specific assets, such as railroad rolling stock. The certificate holders own the equipment and lease it to the company. Technically, equipment trust certificates are not true bonds, even though they are guaranteed by the issuing company, because the interest and principal are paid by the **trustee** (the financial institution responsible for looking after the investors' interests). Even so, they are classified as debt because they have all of the characteristics of debt.

Collateral trust bonds are backed by stocks or bonds of other corporations. This type of financing is principally of historic interest; it is used today primarily by holding companies. A holding company, for example, may raise needed funds by pledging the stocks and/or bonds of its subsidiaries as collateral. In this arrangement, the holding company serves as the *parent* company. The *subsidiary* borrows from the parent, and the parent borrows from the capital markets. This makes good sense, because the parent company generally can get more favorable terms for its debt in the capital markets than the subsidiary.

Income bonds also are largely of historic interest, although they still are used occasionally today. **Income bonds** promise to pay interest only if the issuing firm earns sufficient income; if it does not, no interest obligation exists. These securities are rarely issued directly. Instead, they are often created in reorganizations following bankruptcy and normally issued in exchange for junior or subordinated issues. Thus, unsecured income bonds are generally considered to be "weak" securities.

Banks and finance companies often issue bonds backed by a stream of payments from consumer and commercial obligations, known as receivables. Credit card and automobile loan payments are the two primary types of receivables used in the market for *asset-backed securities.*

Pollution control bonds and *industrial revenue bonds* are issued by local governments rather than corporations. The interest paid to purchasers of municipal bonds is tax exempt, and the interest rate typically is less than what a corporation would have to pay. The interest payments are guaranteed by the corporation for whose benefit the bonds are issued.

Features of Long-Term Debt

Long-term debt has a number of unique features. Several of these are discussed in the following paragraphs.[5]

Indenture. An **indenture** is a contract between a firm that issues long-term debt securities and the lenders. In general, an indenture does the following:

- It thoroughly details the nature of the debt issue.
- It carefully specifies the manner in which the principal must be repaid.
- It lists any restrictions placed on the firm by the lenders. These restrictions are called *covenants,* and the firm must satisfy them to keep from defaulting on its obligations.[6] Typical restrictive covenants include the following:

---

[5]See Douglas R. Emery and John D. Finnerty, "A Review of Recent Research Concerning Corporate Debt Provisions," *Financial Markets, Institutions and Instruments* 1, no. 5 (December 1992): 23–39.

[6]A company defaults on its debt when it does not pay interest or required principal on time or when it violates one or more of the bond's restrictive covenants. When default occurs, the debt is often said to be "triggered," meaning that the entire principal amount comes due immediately. This could result in bankruptcy.

1. A minimum coverage, or times interest earned, ratio the firm must maintain.
2. A minimum level of working capital[7] the firm must maintain.
3. A maximum amount of dividends the firm can pay on its preferred and common stock.
4. Other restrictions that effectively limit how much leasing and issuing of additional debt the firm may do.

Debt covenants are used to resolve agency problems among debtholders, stockholders, and managers.[8] Restrictive covenants, such as those listed, can be used to protect debtholders by prohibiting certain actions by shareholders or managers that might be detrimental to the market value of the debt securities and the ability of the firm to repay the debt at maturity. Debt covenants can also be used to alter the terms of a debt issue if a future significant corporate event should lower the market value of the debt issue. One such example of "event risk language" is a "poison put" covenant,[9] which allows bondholders to sell their debt back to the company at par value in the event of a leveraged buyout (LBO) transaction[10] and a downgrade in the credit rating of the debt issue to below investment grade.[11] Marriott International's 1993 issue of 6¾ percent notes, due 2003, contain an option allowing holders to redeem the bonds at par (plus accrued interest) in the event of a change of control of the company or a ratings decline.

Strong debt covenants can reduce managerial flexibility and thus impose opportunity costs on the firm. At the same time, strong covenants can result in higher credit ratings and lower borrowing costs to the firm by limiting transfers of wealth from bondholders to stockholders and placing limits on the bargaining power of management in any future debt renegotiations. The optimal package of covenants minimizes the sum of these costs.

Trustee. Because the holders of a large firm's long-term debt issue are likely to be scattered widely geographically, the Trust Indenture Act of 1939 requires that a trustee represent the debt holders in dealings with the issuing company. A trustee is usually a commercial bank or trust company that is responsible for ensuring that all the terms and covenants set forth in the indenture agreement are adhered to by the issuing company. The issuing company must pay the trustee's expenses.

Call Feature and Bond Refunding. A **call feature** is an optional retirement provision that permits the issuing company to redeem, or *call*, a debt issue prior to its maturity date at a specified price termed the *redemption*, or **call, price.** Many firms use the call feature because it provides them with the potential flexibility to retire debt prior to maturity if, for example, interest rates decline.

The call price is greater than the par value of the debt, and the difference between the two is the **call premium.** During the early years of an issue, the call premium is usually equal to about one year's interest. Some debt issues specify

---

[7] *Working capital*, defined as the firm's investment in current assets less its current liabilities, is discussed in Chapter 15.
[8] Agency problems are discussed in Chapter 1.
[9] A put option is an option to sell an asset at a set price. Put options are discussed in Chapter 20.
[10] In a leveraged buyout (LBO), the buyer of a company borrows a large portion of the purchase price, using the purchased assets as collateral for the loan.
[11] Credit ratings are discussed later in this section.

fixed call premiums, whereas others specify *declining* call premiums. For example, in 1987 Chrysler issued $300 million of 10.95 percent, 30-year sinking fund debentures. Beginning on August 1, 1997, the company can retire all or part of this issue at 105.475 percent of par value, and the following year the redemption price drops to 104.928 percent of par. Similar reductions in the redemption price are scheduled for each year up to the year 2007. Many bonds are not callable at all for several years after the initial date. For example, the Chrysler debentures are not callable until 1997—ten years after the issue date. This situation is referred to as a *deferred call.*

Details of the call feature are worked out in the negotiations between the underwriters and the issuing company before the debt is sold. Because a call feature gives the company significant flexibility in its financing plans, while at the same time potentially depriving the lenders of the advantages they would gain from holding the debt until maturity, the issuing company has to offer the investors compensation in the form of the call premium in exchange for the call privilege. In addition, the interest rate on a callable debt issue is usually slightly higher than the interest rate on a similar noncallable issue.

Because of the interest savings that can be achieved, a firm is most likely to call a debt issue when prevailing interest rates are appreciably lower than those that existed at the time of the original issue. When a company calls a relatively high interest rate issue and replaces it with a lower interest rate issue, the procedure is called **bond refunding.** This topic is discussed in the appendix to this chapter.

Sinking Fund. Often lenders require that a borrowing company gradually reduce the outstanding balance of a debt issue over its life instead of having the entire principal amount come due on a particular date twenty or thirty years into the future. The usual method of providing for a gradual retirement is a sinking fund, so called because a certain amount of money is put aside annually, or "sunk," into a *sinking fund account.* For example, with the Chrysler 10.95 percent debentures described earlier, the company is required to redeem $15 million of the bonds annually between 1998 and 2017, thus retiring 95 percent of the debt issue prior to maturity. In practice, however, a company can satisfy its sinking fund requirements either by purchasing a portion of the debt each year in the open market or, if the debt is callable, by using a lottery technique to determine which actual numbered certificates will be called and retired within a given year. The alternative chosen depends on the current market price of the debt issue. In general, if current interest rates are above the issue's coupon rate, the current market price of the debt will be less than $1,000, and the company should meet its sinking fund obligation by purchasing the debt in the open market. If, on the other hand, market interest rates are lower than the issue's coupon rate, and if the market price of the debt is above the call price, the company should use the call procedure.

Equity-Linked Debt. Some debt issues (and some preferred stock issues) are linked to the equity (common stock) of the firm through a conversion feature that allows the holder to exchange the security for the company's common stock at the option of the holder. Interest costs of a convertible debt issue are usually less than a similar debt issue without the conversion option, because investors are willing to accept the value of the conversion privilege as part of their overall return. Another form of equity-linked debt is the issuance of warrants with debt securities. A **warrant** is an option to purchase shares of a company's common stock at a specified price during a given time period. Convertible securities and warrants are discussed in Chapter 20.

Typical Sizes of Debt Issues. Debt issues sold to the public through underwriters are usually in the $25 to $200 million range, although very large firms occasionally borrow up to $500 million or more at one time. Because the use of an underwriting group in a public offering involves considerable expense, it is usually uneconomical for a company to make a public offering of this nature for debt issues less than about $25 million. *Private placements,* however, frequently involve lesser amounts of money—for example, $5 to $10 million—because the entire debt issue is purchased by a single investor, such as an insurance company.

Coupon Rates. The coupon rates on new bonds are normally fixed and set equal to market interest rates on bonds of comparable quality and maturity so that the bonds sell at or near par value. However, during the inflationary period of the early 1980s, when interest rates reached record levels and bond prices were quite volatile, highly rated companies began issuing bonds with *floating* coupon rates.

An example of a floating rate bond is BankAmerica's 1993 floating rate subordinated notes, due 2003. Interest is paid quarterly at an annual rate equal to the greater of (1) the three month U.S. dollar London Interbank Offer Rate (LIBOR) plus 0.05 percent or (2) 4.20 percent. Such a bond protects investors against a rise in interest rates because the market price of the bond does not fluctuate as much as for fixed interest rate bonds.

Another type of bond that was issued in the early 1980s, when inflation and interest rates were relatively high, was *original issue deep discount* (OID) bonds. These bonds have coupon rates below prevailing market interest rates at the time of issue and hence sell at a discount from par value. Some OID bond issues pay no interest and are known as *zero coupon* bonds. The Allied Signal Corporation zero coupon bond issue of October 1, 1983, maturing on August 1, 2009, is one such example. One of the advantages to the issuing firm of these types of bonds is the reduction in (or elimination of) interest payments (a cash outflow) during the life of the bonds. Another advantage is the slightly lower cost (yield to maturity) of these issues compared with bonds that are issued at or near par value. The primary disadvantage of these types of bonds is the large cash outflow required by the firm at maturity. OID bonds have decreased in popularity in the last few years, due to changes in the tax laws, which eliminated the tax advantages to companies of these issues over debt issued at par, and the issuance by several brokerage firms of lower-risk substitutes. One such substitute is Merrill Lynch's TIGRs—Treasury Investment Growth Receipts—which are backed by U.S. Treasury bonds. The U.S. Treasury also has issued its own zero coupon bonds. These securities, which pay no interest, are purchased at a discount from face value and then can be redeemed for the full face value at maturity.

Maturity. The typical maturity on long-term debt is about 20 to 30 years. Occasionally, companies borrow money for as long as 40 years. (In 1993, Walt Disney and Coca-Cola sold *100-year* bonds, the first such bond issues since 1954.) On the other end of the scale, companies in need of financing are often willing to borrow for as few as 10 years, especially if they feel that interest rates are temporarily high, as was true in the environment of the early 1980s—an environment characterized by high rates of inflation and historically high interest rates. But during the 1990s, a period of generally low inflation and moderate interest rates, many large companies were issuing fixed-rate debt securities with 25- and 30-year maturities.

Like the floating rate bonds described earlier, which protect investors against interest rate risk, firms also have been issuing bonds that are redeemable at par *at the option of the holder.* These are known as *extendable notes* or *put bonds.* If interest rates rise and the market price of the bond falls, the holder can redeem them at par and reinvest the proceeds in higher-yielding securities. An example of a put bond is Chrysler Financial Corporation's putable extendable note issue of 1988 that matures in 2018. The notes are redeemable for the full principal amount plus interest at the option of the holder on February 1, 1992, 1996, and 2000 and on each February 1 thereafter.

When performing bond valuation and yield to maturity calculations (described later in the chapter), bond investors should keep in mind that the realized maturity of a debt issue may differ from its stated maturity. This can occur for a variety of reasons. The bond indenture may include early repayment provisions through the exercise of a call option, required sinking fund payments, open market purchases, or tender offers. Also, maturity extensions or contractions may occur as the result of reorganization, merger, leveraged buyout (LBO), default, or liquidation.

Information on Debt Financing Activities

Every business day, financial newspapers contain information on debt financing activities. For example, the *Wall Street Journal* devotes at least one page to financing activities in the bond market. This page contains announcements by underwriters concerning the characteristics of the new issues presently being offered.

The *Wall Street Journal* also contains information on the secondary debt markets, including price quotations for the widely traded corporate debt issues listed on the New York and American Exchanges and U.S. government debt securities. In this section we illustrate the information that can be obtained from corporate and government bond quotations.

Corporate Bonds. The majority of existing debt issues (bonds) of U.S. corporations are traded in the over-the-counter market. The OTC market is a network of security dealers who buy and sell bonds and stock from each other, either for their own account or for their retail clients. Price information on bonds that are traded over-the-counter is not reported in the *WSJ.* However, some larger issues of corporate bonds are listed and traded on the New York Exchange. Price quotations for these listed bonds are published daily in the *WSJ.* Table 6-1 shows a selected list of bond quotations.

TABLE 6-1
Selected Bond Quotations from the New York Exchange

Source: *Wall Street Journal* (November 25, 1996).

BONDS	CUR YLD	VOL	CLOSE	NET CHG
ATT 7s05	6.8	19	102⅝	−⅛
AlldC zr99	—	65	84½	+1½
DukePw 7s05	6.7	5	104	+1½
UtdAir 10.67s04	8.7	5	122	+1½
Zenith 6¼ 11	cv	35	81⅞	+1⅞

Bond prices are quoted as a percentage of their par value (usually $1,000). For example, the closing price for the Duke Power issue was $1040. The "7s05" after the DukePw name means the bond offers a contract, or coupon, interest rate of 7 percent. Thus, a holder of the issue receives $35 in interest per bond every six months, for a total of $70 (.07 × $1,000) each year. This debt issue, or series (the *s* stands for "series"), matures in the year 2005, hence the 05 after the coupon interest rate. The *current yield* is calculated by dividing the annual interest by the day's closing price; for example, $70/104 = 6.7 percent. However, this current yield is only an approximation of the true promised yield on the bond, called the *yield to maturity*, which is discussed later in the chapter.

A *cv* in the current yield column, which appears for the Zenith bonds, indicates that the bond issue is convertible into common stock under certain conditions. Convertible securities are discussed in Chapter 20. Also, note that the Allied Signal Corporation bond issue (AlldC) has a *zr* before the expiration date of the bond (1999), which indicates that this is a zero coupon bond—a bond that pays no interest. Rather, it is initially sold at a discount from par value ($1,000), and the purchaser receives a return by holding the bond to maturity, at which point it is redeemed for $1,000. You will note that this bond is currently selling for only 84.5 percent of its par value, or $845.

Government Debt Securities. The U.S. government raises funds by selling debt securities. These securities take the form of short-term Treasury bills, intermediate-term Treasury notes, and long-term Treasury bonds. U.S. Treasury bills have an initial maturity of 13, 26, or 52 weeks and pay $10,000 per bill to the holder at maturity. Treasury bills pay no explicit interest; rather, they are sold at a discount from maturity value. An investor who buys a bill at a discount and holds it to maturity will receive as interest the difference between the price paid and $10,000. The quote for a typical Treasury bill follows:

Maturity	Days to Mat.	Bid	Asked	Chg.	Ask Yld.
Jan. 23 '97	59	5.00	4.96	−0.01	5.07

The bill shown above matures in 59 days, the "bid" and "asked" prices indicate the *annualized* percentage discount from maturity value.[12] An *Asked discount* of 4.96 percent translates into a cash discount from $10,000 of approximately $80.18 [=(4.96 ÷ 100) ÷ (365/59) × $10,000], or an asked price of $10,000 − $80.18 = $9,919.82. The *Ask Yld.* is the annualized yield an investor will receive by purchasing this bill and holding it to maturity.

Longer-term government debt is issued in the form of Treasury notes and bonds. Treasury notes typically have an initial maturity ranging from one to 10 years. Treasury bonds typically have initial maturities ranging from 10 to 30 years. Like corporate bonds, Treasury notes and bonds pay a stated coupon rate of interest semiannually. They are issued in denominations of multiples of $1,000. There are two major differences between the price quotations of corporate bonds and the price quotations of Treasury notes and bonds. First, Treasury note and bond prices vary in units of $\frac{1}{32}$nd of 1 percent of par value. Thus, a price quote of 94:17 means that the bond will sell for $94\frac{17}{32}$ percent of par, or $945.31.

---

[12]A "bid" price is the price at which buyers are willing to purchase, and the "asked" price is the price at which sellers wish to sell. For Treasury bills, the "bid" and "asked" quotes represent discounts from face value.

The second difference is that Treasury note and bond quotations indicate the yield to maturity (or the yield to the first call date in the case of bonds that can be called for redemption prior to the maturity date) for the bond at its current price, rather than the current yield shown in the *WSJ* for corporate bonds.

Bond Ratings

Debt issues are rated according to their relative degree of risk by various financial companies, including Moody's Investors Services and Standard and Poor's (S&P) Corporation. These agencies consider a variety of factors when rating a firm's securities, including earnings stability, coverage ratios, the relative amount of debt in the firm's capital structure, and the degree of subordination, as well as past experience. According to Moody's rating scale, the highest-quality, lowest-risk issues are rated Aaa, and the scale continues down through Aa, A, Baa, Ba, B, Caa, Ca, and C. On the Standard and Poor's ratings scale, AAA denotes the highest-quality issues, and this rating is followed by AA, A, BBB, BB, B, and so on. S&P also has various C and D classifications for high-risk issues; the majority of debt issues, however, fall into one of the A or B categories. Figure 6-1 shows Moody's and S&P's bond-rating definitions.

Table 6-2 shows the median profitability and leverage ratios in Standard & Poor's debt rating categories for U.S. industrial companies. In general, firms with the most favorable profitability and leverage ratios tend to have the highest credit ratings. Table 6-3 gives leverage ratios and credit ratings for the debt securities of selected companies. Like the data in the previous table, this table also shows that firms with the lowest debt ratios and highest interest coverage ratios tend to have the best credit ratings.

Companies with weak financial positions (e.g., highly leveraged balance sheets or low earnings) often issue high-yield debt securities to obtain capital needed for internal expansion or for corporate acquisitions and buyouts. Such debt, also known as **junk bonds,** is rated Ba or lower by Moody's (or BB or lower by Standard and Poor's) and typically yields 3 percentage points or more than the highest quality corporate debt. For example, Campeau Corporation had to pay over 17 percent in November 1988 to obtain some of the funds it needed to pay for the acquisition of Federated Department Stores. These bonds were rated CCC+ by Standard and Poor's. At the time, the highest-quality (AAA-rated) corporate debt was yielding less than 10 percent. Two years later Federated filed for bankruptcy when it was unable to meet the required debt payments. Junk bonds constituted an important segment of all corporate debt outstanding during the later half of the 1980s, rising from 13 percent in 1983 to 25 percent in 1988.[13] However, by 1990, new issues of junk bonds were virtually nonexistent, and during 1990, previous issuers *repurchased* $15 billion of junk bonds.[14] A number of developments contributed to this reduced interest by investors in junk bonds, including

1. Economic recession.
2. Failure of a number of banks and savings and loan associations, many of which had invested in junk bonds.
3. Increased government regulation of financial institutions.
4. Collapse of the investment banking firm of Drexel Burnham Lambert, the largest underwriter of junk bonds.

[13] *Business Week* (February 6, 1989): 83.
[14] *Wall Street Journal* (March 4, 1991): C16.

FIGURE 6-1
Moody's and Standard & Poor's
Bond-Rating Definitions

Source: *Moody's Bond Record* (November 1996).
Reprinted by permission of Moody's Investors
Service, Inc. *Standard & Poor's Bond Guide*
(December 1996). Reprinted by permission
of Standard and Poor's, a division of
the McGraw-Hill Companies

KEY TO MOODY'S CORPORATE RATINGS

Aaa

Bonds which are rated **Aaa** are judged to be of the best quality. They carry the smallest degree of investment risk and are generally referred to as "gilt edged." Interest payments are protected by a large or by an exceptionally stable margin and principal is secure. While the various protective elements are likely to change, such changes as can be visualized are most unlikely to impair the fundamentally strong position of such issues.

Aa

Bonds which are rated **Aa** are judged to be of high quality by all standards. Together with the **Aaa** group they comprise what are generally known as high grade bonds. They are rated lower than the best bonds because margins of protection may not be as large as in **Aaa** securities or fluctuation of protective elements may be of greater amplitude or there may be other elements present which make the long-term risk appear somewhat larger than the **Aaa** securities.

A

Bonds which are rated **A** possess many favorable investment attributes and are to be considered as upper-medium-grade obligations. Factors giving security to principal and interest are considered adequate, but elements may be present which suggest a susceptibility to impairment some time in the future.

Baa

Bonds which are rated **Baa** are considered as medium-grade obligations, (i.e., they are neither highly protected nor poorly secured). Interest payments and principal security appear adequate for the present but certain protective elements may be lacking or may be characteristically unreliable over any great length of time. Such bonds lack outstanding investment characteristics and in fact have speculative characteristics as well.

Ba

Bonds which are rated **Ba** are judged to have speculative elements; their future cannot be considered as well-assured. Often the protection of interest and principal payments may be very moderate, and thereby not well safeguarded during both good and bad times over the future. Uncertainty of position characterizes bonds in this class.

B

Bonds which are rated **B** generally lack characteristics of the desirable investment. Assurance of interest and principal payments or of maintenance of other terms of the contract over any long period of time may be small.

Caa

Bonds which are rated **Caa** are of poor standing. Such issues may be in default or there may be present elements of danger with respect to principal or interest.

Ca

Bonds which are rated **Ca** represent obligations which are speculative in a high degree. Such issues are often in default or have other marked shortcomings.

C

Bonds which are rated **C** are the lowest rated class of bonds, and issues so rated can be regarded as having extremely poor prospects of ever attaining any real investment standing.

Note: Moody's applies numerical modifiers, **1, 2** and **3** in each generic rating classification from **Aa** to **B**. The modifier **1** indicates that the company ranks in the higher end of its generic rating category; the modifier **2** indicates a mid-range ranking; and the modifier **3** indicates that the company ranks in the lower end of its generic rating category.

Continued

5. Financial difficulties encountered by some firms that had used junk bonds to finance mergers and acquisitions (leveraged buyouts) and other corporate restructurings, which led to default rates in excess of 10 percent during 1990 and 1991.

With improvement in the economy and lower default rates, the value of new issues of junk bonds again rose to record levels in 1992 and 1993.

FIGURE 6-1
Moody's and Standard & Poor's
Bond-Rating Definitions
(Continued)

STANDARD & POOR'S CORPORATE AND MUNICIPAL DEBT RATINGS

AAA Debt rated 'AAA' has the highest rating assigned by Standard & Poor's. Capacity to pay interest and repay principal is extremely strong.

AA Debt rated 'AA' has a very strong capacity to pay interest and repay principal and differs from the higher rated issues only in small degree.

A Debt rated 'A' has a strong capacity to pay interest and repay principal although it is somewhat more susceptible to the adverse effects of changes in circumstances and economic conditions than debt in higher rated categories.

BBB Debt rated 'BBB' is regarded as having an adequate capacity to pay interest and repay principal. Whereas it normally exhibits adequate protection parameters, adverse economic conditions or changing circumstances are more likely to lead to a weakened capacity to pay interest and repay principal for debt in this category than in higher rated categories.

BB, B, CCC, CC, C Debt rated 'BB', 'B', 'CCC', 'CC' and 'C' is regarded, on balance, as predominantly speculative with respect to capacity to pay interest and repay principal in accordance with the terms of the obligation. 'BB' indicates the lowest degree of speculation and 'C' the highest degree of speculation. While such debt will likely have some quality and protective characteristics, these are outweighed by large uncertainties or major risk exposure to adverse conditions.

BB Debt rated 'BB' has less near-term vulnerability to default than other speculative issues. However, it faces major ongoing uncertainties or exposure to adverse business, financial, or economic conditions which could lead to inadequate capacity to meet timely interest and principal payments. The 'BB' rating category is also used for debt subordinated to senior debt that is assigned an actual or implied 'BBB−' rating.

B Debt rated 'B' has a greater vulnerability to default but currently has the capacity to meet interest payments and principal repayments. Adverse business, financial, or economic conditions will likely impair capacity or willingness to pay interest and repay principal. The 'B' rating category is also used for debt subordinated to senior debt that is assigned an actual or implied 'BB' or 'BB−' rating.

CCC Debt rated 'CCC' has a currently identifiable vulnerability to default, and is dependent upon favorable business, financial, and economic conditions to meet timely payment of interest and repayment of principal. In the event of adverse business, financial, or economic conditions, it is not likely to have the capacity to pay interest and repay principal. The 'CCC' rating category is also used for debt subordinated to senior debt that is assigned an actual or implied 'B' or 'B−' rating.

CC The rating 'CC' is typically applied to debt subordinated to senior debt that is assigned an actual or implied 'CCC' rating.

C The rating 'C' is typically applied to debt subordinated to senior debt which is assigned an actual or implied 'CCC−' debt rating. The 'C' rating may be used to cover a situation where a bankruptcy petition has been filed, but debt service payments are continued.

CI The rating 'CI' is reserved for income bonds on which no interest is being paid.

D Debt rated 'D' is in payment default. The 'D' rating category is used when interest payments or principal payments are not made on the date due even if the applicable grace period has not expired, unless S&P believes that such payments will be made during such grace period. The 'D' rating also will be used upon the filing of a bankruptcy petition if debt service payments are jeopardized.

Plus (+) or Minus (−) The ratings from 'AA' to 'CCC' may be modified by the addition of a plus or minus sign to show relative standing within the major categories.

r The 'r' is attached to highlight derivative, hybrid, and certain other obligations that S&P believes may experience high volatility or high variability in expected returns due to noncredit risks. Examples of such obligations are: securities whose principal or interest return is indexed to equities, commodities, or currencies; certain swaps and options; and interest only and principal only mortgage securities.

The absence of an 'r' symbol should not be taken as an indication that an obligation will exhibit no volatility or variability in total return.

Debt Rating	—PROFITABILITY RATIOS—		—LEVERAGE RATIOS—	
	Operating Income as a Percent of Sales	Pretax Return on Permanent Capital	Pretax Interest Coverage (times)	Long-Term Debt as a Percent of Capitalization
AAA	21.6%	28.2%	16.70×	11.1%
AA	16.0	19.2	9.31	17.0
A	13.9	14.9	4.41	29.7
BBB	12.3	9.8	2.30	40.4
BB	10.3	10.0	1.31	53.0
B	9.7	6.1	0.77	56.8
C	9.8	−0.4	−0.06	74.8

TABLE 6-2
Median Profitability and Leverage Ratios for U.S. Industrial Companies in the Various Standard & Poor's Debt Rating Categories

Source: Standard & Poor's *CreditWeek* (November 8, 1993): 39–42.

COMPANY	STANDARD AND POOR'S DEBT RATING*	MOODY'S DEBT RATING**	TOTAL DEBT TO TOTAL CAPITALIZATION*	TIMES FIXED CHARGES EARNED*
Johnson & Johnson	AAA	Aaa	17.3%	16.24
Shell Oil	AAA	Aa1	21.1	10.46
Northern Illinois Gas	AA	Aa1	38.8	4.52
Coca-Cola	AA	Aa3	43.0	16.02
Campbell Soup	AA–	Aa3	36.2	10.01
Rockwell International	AA–	A3	37.0	8.21
J. C. Penney	A+	A1	50.4	4.48
Phillip Morris	A	A2	53.0	8.43
IBM	A	A1	51.7	11.41
Ryder Systems	A–	Aa3	66.7	2.39
B. F. Goodrich	BBB+	Baa1	37.4	4.33
Black & Decker	BBB–	Baa3	54.0	2.17
Public Service Company of New Mexico	BB+	Ba1	51.9	3.18
American Standard	BB–	Ba3	132.0	2.06
Armco	B	B2	246.0	.82
Nextel Communications	CCC-	B3	45.6	−3.62
Claridge Hotel & Casino	CC	Caa	101.0	.89

*Standard & Poor's Bond Guide (December 1996). Reprinted by permission of Standard and Poor's, a division of McGraw-Hill, Inc.

**Moody's Bond Record (November 1996).

TABLE 6-3
Selected Examples of Capital Structure and Coverage Ratios for Various Debt Ratings

Users of Long-Term Debt

Most large and medium-sized companies finance some portion of their fixed assets with long-term debt. This debt may be in the form of either secured bonds or unsecured debentures. Utilities rely on debt capital to a large degree and, as a group, are the largest users of secured bonds; the *first mortgage bonds* of a utility are typically a safe, low-risk investment. Manufacturing companies, in contrast, rely on debt capital to varying degrees and generally use unsecured debt more often then secured debt.

Many large companies have virtually continuous capital expenditure programs. Usually, a company will plan to finance at least partially any new assets with long-term debt. Because it is generally uneconomical to borrow small amounts of long-term capital, however, companies that have ongoing construction programs often gradually "draw down" on their short-term revolving credit agreements. Then, once every couple of years or so, a firm of this type will enter the capital markets and sell long-term debt. At that time, a portion of the proceeds is used to repay the short-term borrowings, and the cycle begins again. This procedure is called *funding* short-term debt; as a result, long-term debt sometimes is referred to as *funded debt*.

Most established companies attempt to maintain reasonably constant proportions of long-term debt and common equity in their capital structures. During the course of a company's normal profitable operations, though, long-term debt is gradually retired as it matures, and the retained earnings portion of common equity is increased. This in turn decreases the debt-to-equity ratio. Thus, to maintain their desired capital structures, companies have to raise long-term debt capital periodically. This gradual refunding of debt, along with the tax deductibility of interest, accounts for the fact that about 85 to 90 percent of the external long-term capital raised in the United States is in the form of debt.

Advantages and Disadvantages of Long-Term Debt Financing

From the issuing firm's perspective, the major advantages of long-term debt include the following:

- Its relatively low after-tax cost due to the tax deductibility of interest.
- The increased earnings per share possible through financial leverage.
- The ability of the firm's owners to maintain greater control over the firm.

The following are the major disadvantages of long-term debt financing, from the firm's perspective:

- The increased financial risk of the firm resulting from the use of debt.
- The restrictions placed on the firm by the lenders.

From the investors' viewpoint, in general, debt securities offer stable returns and therefore are considered relatively low-risk investments compared with common stock investments. Because debt holders are creditors, however, they do not participate in any increased earnings the firm may experience. In fact, during periods of relatively high inflation, holders of existing debt find that their *real* interest payments decrease, because the nominal interest payments remain constant.

 INTERNATIONAL ISSUES
THE INTERNATIONAL BOND MARKET[15]

In addition to raising capital in the U.S. financial markets, many U.S. firms go to other countries to raise capital. International bonds are sold initially to investors outside the home country of the borrower. There are two major types of long-term instruments in the international bond market—Eurobonds and foreign bonds.

---

[15]This section is based on D. K. Eiteman and A. I. Stonehill, *Multinational Business Finance,* 5th ed. (Reading, MA: Addison-Wesley, 1989), Chapter 10.

Eurobonds are bonds issued by a U.S. corporation, for example, denominated in U.S. dollars but sold to investors outside of the United States, such as in Europe and Japan. The bond offering is often underwritten by an international syndicate of investment bankers. For example, IBM could sell dollar-denominated bonds to investors in Europe or Japan. The Eurobond market has been used because there is less regulatory interference than in the issuing country and, in some cases, less stringent disclosure requirements. Eurobonds also are bearer bonds (the name and country of the bond owner is not on the bond), providing the bondholder with tax anonymity and an opportunity, perhaps, to avoid the payment of taxes. For these reasons, the cost of Eurobond financing may be below that of domestic financing.

Foreign bonds, in contrast, are underwritten by an investment banking syndicate from a single country. Foreign bonds are normally denominated in the currency of the country of sale. The bond issuer, however, is from a country other than the country in which the bonds are being issued. For example, Crown Cork and Seal Company, Inc., with 65 plants outside of the United States, might enter the foreign bond market to raise capital for a new plant to be built in France. These bonds could be sold in France and be denominated in French francs, or they could be sold in another country and denominated in that country's currency.

The international bond market grew rapidly during the 1980s, and it continues to provide firms with additional alternative sources of funds that are, in some cases, lower in cost than purely domestic financing.

 FOUNDATION CONCEPT
VALUATION OF ASSETS

The value of any asset is based on the *expected future benefits,* or *cash flows,* the owner will receive over the life of the asset. For example, the value of a *physical asset,* such as a new piece of equipment or production plant, is based on the expected cash flows the asset will generate for the firm over its useful life. These cash flows are derived from increased revenues and/or reduced costs plus any salvage value received from the sale of the asset.[16]

Similarly, the value of a *financial asset,* such as a stock or bond, is based on the expected cash flows the asset will generate for the owner during the *holding period.* These cash flows take the form of interest or dividend payments over the holding period plus the amount the owner receives when the security is sold.

It is assumed throughout this and the following chapter that the firms under discussion are *going concerns;* that is, their organization and assets will remain intact and be used to generate future cash flows. Techniques other than the ones described here must be used to value long-term securities of firms faced with the possibility of bankruptcy. In such cases, the **liquidation value** of the firm's assets is the primary determinant of the value of the various types of long-term securities.[17]

Visit Spreadware's Web site and look at some of the many methods their software programs use to find the value of a company (discounting cash flows, income, or dividends; using P/E, sales, profit, and other kinds of multiples; calculating liquidation values or replacement values; "quick values"; and more. Which method is correct?
http://spreadware.com

---

[16]Chapters 8 through 10 contain a detailed discussion of capital budgeting.
[17]This topic is discussed in Chapter 22.

Capitalization of Cash Flow Method

One way of determining the value of an asset is to calculate the present value of the stream of expected future cash flows discounted at an appropriate *required rate of return*. This is known as the **capitalization of cash flow** method of valuation and is represented algebraically as follows:

$$V_0 = \frac{CF_1}{(1+i)^1} + \frac{CF_2}{(1+i)^2} + \ldots + \frac{CF_n}{(1+i)^n} \tag{6.1}$$

or, using summation notation, as follows:

$$V_0 = \sum_{t=1}^{n} \frac{CF_t}{(1+i)^t} \tag{6.2}$$

where V_0 is the value of the asset at time zero, CF_t the expected cash flow in period t, i the required rate of return or discount rate, and n the length of the holding period.

For example, assume that the cash flows, CF_t, of an investment are expected to be an annuity of $1,000 per year for $n = 6$ years, and the required rate of return, i, is 8 percent. Using the capitalization of cash flow method, the value of this investment is

$$V_0 = \sum_{t=1}^{6} \frac{\$1,000}{(1+0.08)^t}$$

Recognizing this expression as the present value of an annuity ($PVAN_0$), the value of the investment is computed using Equation 4.22 of Chapter 4:

$$V_0 = \$1,000 \, (PVIFA_{0.08,6})$$
$$= \$1,000 (4.623)$$
$$= \$4,623$$

Finding the values of bonds and certain other assets is rather straightforward. But how do you find the value of intellectual property such as books, songs, plays, and software programs? Visit the IPC Group's Web site and examine some of the thorny issues involved in putting a price tag on intellectual properly.
http://www.ipcgroup.com

Enter:	6	8.00		−1,000	
	n	i	PV	*PMT*	FV

Solution: 4622.88

This solution is identical (rounded to the nearest dollar, $4,623) as calculated earlier.

The *required rate of return*, i, on an asset is a function of the uncertainty, or risk, associated with the returns from the asset as well as the risk-free interest rate.[18] As indicated in the discussion of the determinants of discount rates in the previous chapter, this function is upward sloping, indicating that the higher the risk, the greater is the investor's required rate of return.

Market Value of Assets and Market Equilibrium

From Equation 6.1, it can be seen that the value of an asset depends on both the expected cash flows, CF_t, and the owner's (or prospective buyer's) required rate

---

[18]Recall that risk was defined in Chapter 5 as the possibility that actual future returns will deviate from expected returns.

of return, *i*. However, potential buyers and sellers can have different opinions of an asset's value based on their individual assessments of the potential cash flows from the asset and individual required rates of return.

The *market price,* or *market value,* of an asset (such as shares of common stock) is determined in much the same way as the price of most goods and services in a market-oriented economy; namely, by the interaction of supply and demand. This interaction is shown in Figure 6-2. Potential buyers are represented by a *demand* schedule showing the maximum prices they are willing to pay for given quantities of an asset, and potential sellers are represented by a *supply* schedule showing the minimum prices at which they are willing to sell given quantities of the asset. The transaction price, the price at which an asset is sold, occurs at the intersection of the demand and supply schedules. The intersection represents the *market value,* or *market price,* of the asset, P_m, in Figure 6-2.

The market price of an asset is the value placed on the asset by the *marginally satisfied buyer and seller* who exchange assets in the marketplace. A marginally satisfied buyer is one who paid his or her maximum acceptable price for the asset, and a marginally satisfied seller is one who received his or her minimum acceptable price for the asset. Clearly, many owners (potential sellers) will place a higher value on the asset than the current market price; likewise, many investors (potential buyers) will place a lower value on the asset than the current market price.

Market equilibrium exists whenever there is no tendency for the price of the asset to move higher or lower. At this point, the *expected* rate of return on the asset is equal to the marginal investor's *required* rate of return. *Market disequilibrium* occurs when investors' required rates of return, *i,* and/or the expected

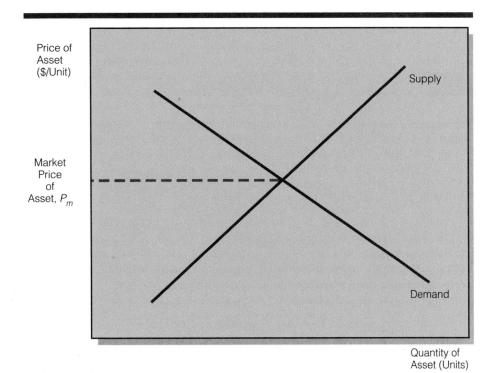

FIGURE 6-2
Market Price of an Asset

cash flows, CF_t, from the asset change. The market price adjusts over time—that is, it moves upward or downward—to reflect changing conditions, and a new market equilibrium is established.

Most financial assets are bought and sold in organized markets. The bonds, preferred stock, and common stock of many small, as well as most medium and large, firms are traded in one or more national or regional exchanges or in the over-the-counter market. Because large numbers of competing buyers and sellers operate in the markets, the market price of a security represents a *consensus* judgment as to the security's value or worth. Although no such market-determined measure of value exists for securities of firms that are not publicly traded, their market values can be approximated using the market price of publicly traded securities of firms having similar operating and financial characteristics.

Book Value of an Asset

The **book value** of an asset represents the *accounting* value, or the historic acquisition cost minus any accumulated depreciation or other write-offs. Because market value is normally related to expected future cash flows and book value is based on historic cost, the market value of an asset does not necessarily bear any relationship to the book value. In fact, the market value may be either greater or less than the book value, depending on the changes over time in the market capitalization rate and the asset's expected future cash flows. For example, prior to the leveraged buyout of RJR Nabisco in 1988 by the investment firm Kohlberg Kravis Roberts & Co., RJR Nabisco common stock was selling for about $56 per share—more than twice its book value of $24 per share. After a bidding war among potential buyers, Kohlberg Kravis Roberts & Co. agreed to purchase RJR Nabisco for $109 per share, which was over four times its book value per share and almost twice its pretakeover stock price.

BOND VALUATION

The valuation of bonds is a relatively straightforward process, because future cash flows to the bondholder always are specified ahead of time in a contract. The firm issuing the bonds must meet the interest and principal payments as they come due, or the bonds will go into default. Defaulting on bond payments can have disastrous consequences for the firm and its stockholders, such as possible bankruptcy, reorganization, or both.

Due to default risk, investors normally require a higher rate of return than the risk-free rate before agreeing to hold a firm's bonds. The required rate of return varies among bond issues of different firms, depending on their relative risks of default. All other things being equal, the greater the default risk on a given bond issue, the higher the required rate of return.

Bonds Having Finite Maturity Dates

Bonds that mature within finite periods of time pay the investor two types of returns: interest payments ($I_1, I_2, \ldots, I_n$) during each of the next n periods and a principal payment (M) in period n. Period n is defined as the bond's *maturity date*, or the time at which the principal must be repaid and the bond issue retired.

The value of a bond can be computed by applying the capitalization of cash flow method to the series of cash flows:

$$P_0 = \frac{I_1}{(1 + k_d)^1} + \frac{I_2}{(1 + k_d)^1} + \cdots + \frac{I_{n-1}}{(1 + k_d)^{n-1}} + \frac{I_n + M}{(1 + k_d)^n} \qquad (6.3)$$

where P_0 is the present value of the bond at time zero, or its purchase date, and k_d is the investor's required rate of return on this particular bond issue.

Because all of the interest payments on a bond normally are equal (that is $I_1 = I_2 = \ldots = I_{n-1} = I_n = I$), Equation 6.3 can be simplified as follows:

$$P_0 = \sum_{t=1}^{n} \frac{I}{(1 + k_d)^t} + \frac{M}{(1 + k_d)^n} \qquad (6.4)$$

The first term in Equation 6.4 represents the present value of an *annuity* of I per period for n periods; the second term represents the present value of a *single payment* of M in period n. Equation 6.4 can be further simplified as follows:

$$P_0 = I(\text{PVIFA}_{k_d,n}) + M(\text{PVIF}_{k_d,n}) \qquad (6.5)$$

To illustrate the use of Equation 6.5, consider the following example. Dole Food Company issued $300 million of 7 percent bonds maturing on May 15, 2003. The bonds were issued in $1,000 denominations (par value). For purposes of simplifying this example, assume that the bonds pay interest on May 15 each year.[19]

An investor who wishes to purchase one of these Dole bonds on May 15, 1996 and requires an 8 percent rate of return on this particular bond issue would compute the value of the bond as follows. These calculations assume that the investor will hold the bond until maturity and receive seven annual ($n = 7$) interest payments of $70 each ($I = \$1,000 \times 0.07$) plus a principal payment, M, of $1,000 at the end of the seventh year, May 15, 2003. The expected cash flows from this bond are shown in Figure 6-3. Substituting these values along with $k_d = 8\%$ (0.08) into Equation 6.4 gives the following value for the bond:

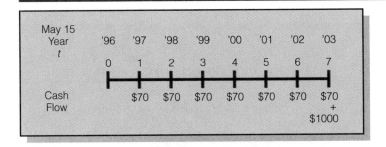

FIGURE 6-3
Cash Flows from a Dole Food Company Bond

[19]This particular bond issue actually pays interest *semiannually* on May 15 and November 15 each year.

$$P_0 = \sum_{t=1}^{7} \frac{\$70}{(1+0.08)^t} + \frac{\$1,000}{(1+0.08)^7}$$

$$= \$70(\text{PVIFA}_{0.08,7}) + \$1,000(\text{PVIF}_{0.08,7})$$

$$= \$70(5.206) + \$1,000(0.583)$$

$$= \$364.42 + \$583$$

$$= \$947.42 \text{ (or } \$947)$$

CALCULATOR SOLUTION

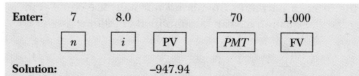

Enter: 7   8.0   70   1,000

          [n]   [i]   [PV]   [PMT]   [FV]

Solution: –947.94

Note: The financial calculator solution and the solution obtained using Equation 6.4 and the interest tables differ slightly due to the use of interest tables with 3 decimal places of accuracy. Using more accurate interest tables gives an answer closer to $947.94, the true answer to this problem.

In other words, an investor requiring an 8 percent return on this Dole bond would be willing to pay approximately $948 for it on May 15, 1996.

A question often arises as to why investors would require an 8 percent rate of return on bonds that pay only 7 percent interest. The answer is that the required rate of return has increased since the bonds originally were issued. At the time of issue, the prevailing rate of interest (that is, the required rate of return) on bonds of this maturity and quality was approximately 7 percent. Hence, the coupon rate was set at 7 percent. Because of such factors as tight credit market conditions, higher inflation, increased firm risk, and so on, investors now require a higher rate of return to induce them to purchase these bonds.

An investor who desires more than an 8 percent rate of return on this bond would value it at a price less than $948. Similarly, an investor who requires less than an 8 percent rate of return would value it at a price greater than $948. This *inverse relationship* between the required rate of return and the corresponding value of a bond to the investor is illustrated for bonds with 3-year and 15-year maturities in Table 6-4 and Figure 6-4. In other words, as the required rate of return increases, the value of the bond decreases, and vice versa.

TABLE 6-4
Value of 7 Percent Coupon Rate Bonds at Various Required Rates of Return

REQUIRED RATE OF RETURN, k_d	VALUE OF 15-YEAR BOND	VALUE OF 3-YEAR BOND	BOND VALUE RELATIVE TO PAR VALUE
3%	$1,478	$1,113	Premium
5	1,208	1,055	Premium
6	1,097	1,027	Premium
7	1,000	1,000	At Par
8	914	974	Discount
9	839	949	Discount
11	712	902	Discount

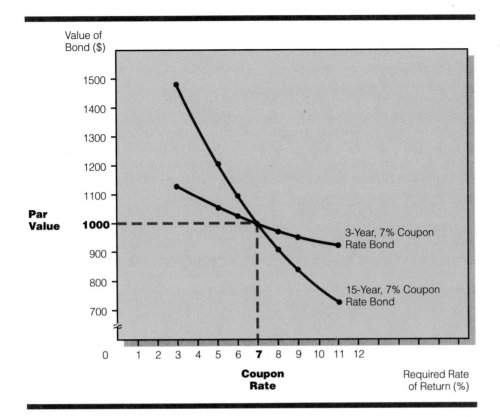

The relationship between a bond's value and the investor's required rate of return depends on the time remaining before maturity. All other things being equal, the value of a longer-term bond is affected more by changes in required rates of return than the value of a shorter-term bond. As Table 6-3 and Figure 6-4 show, the variation in the value of the 15-year bond is considerably greater than the variation of the 3-year bond over the given range of required rates of return (3 to 11 percent).

Also, as can be seen in Table 6-3, when the required rate of return (prevailing market interest rate) is less than the coupon rate, the bond is valued at a *premium* over its par value of $1,000. Conversely, when the required rate of return is greater than the coupon rate, the bond is valued at a *discount* under its par value.

Investors who purchase a bond at the price determined by Equation 6.4 and *hold it until maturity* will realize their required rate of return, regardless of any changes in the market price of the bond.[20] However, if the market price of the bond declines due to a rise in prevailing interest rates and if the bond is sold *prior to maturity,* the investors will earn less than their required rate of return and may even incur a loss on the bond. This variation in the market price (and hence in the realized rate of return) of a bond (or any fixed income security) is known as **interest rate risk.**

In addition to interest rate risk, bond investors are subject to reinvestment rate risk. **Reinvestment rate risk** occurs when a bond issue matures (or is called) and, because of a decline in interest rates, the investor has to reinvest the principal at

[20]This assumes that the investor reinvests all interest received from the bond at a rate equal to the required rate of return on the bond. Otherwise, the realized return will differ slightly from the required return.

a lower coupon rate. For example, the owner of Chrysler's 30-year, 10.95 percent debentures, purchased at the time of issue in 1987, is receiving $109.5 annual interest per bond. However, as noted earlier, this bond issue is callable beginning in 1997. If Chrysler decides to call the bonds because of a decline in interest rates since the time of issue, the bondholder probably will be unable to reinvest the principal in another bond, of comparable risk, that is yielding a 10.95 percent (or higher) rate of return. Reinvestment rate risk also refers to the rate at which interest cash flows can be reinvested over the life of the bond. When the reinvestment rate of interest cash flows is different from the yield to maturity on the bond, the return actually realized by a bond investor will be greater than (less than) the yield to maturity if the reinvestment rate is greater than (less than) the promised yield to maturity.

Semiannual Interest Payments. Most bonds, such as the Dole bonds, pay interest *semiannually.* Recall from the discussion of "Effect of Compounding Periods on Present and Future Values" in Chapter 4, the required rate of return (k_d) is divided by 2 and the number of periods (n) is multiplied by 2. Therefore, with semiannual interest payments and compounding, the bond valuation formula (Equation 6.4) becomes:

$$P_0 = \sum_{t=1}^{2n} \frac{I/2}{(1 + k_d/2)^t} + \frac{M}{(1 + k_d/2)^{2n}} \qquad (6.6)$$

With semiannual interest and compounding, the value for the Dole bond is calculated as follows:

$$P_0 = \sum_{t=1}^{14} \frac{\$35}{(1 + 0.04)^t} + \frac{\$1,000}{(1 + 0.04)^{14}}$$

$$= \$35(\text{PVIFA}_{0.04,14}) + \$1,000(\text{PVIF}_{0.04,14})$$

$$= \$35(10.563) + \$1,000(0.577)$$

$$= \$369.71 + \$577$$

$$= \$946.71 \text{ (or } \$947)$$

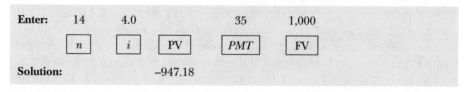

Enter:	14	4.0		35	1,000
	n	i	PV	PMT	FV
Solution:			−947.18		

In this problem, the annual required rate of return $(k_d = .08)$ is divided by 2 $(.08/2 = .04)$ and the number of periods $(n = 7)$ is multiplied by 2 $(7 \times 2 = 14)$.[21] These bond values differ only slightly from the solutions obtained above for annual interest payments and compounding.

---

[21]It also should be noted that the use of a semiannual discount rate of 4 percent will result in a slightly greater than 8 percent effective annual discount rate. Based on the discussion of "Effective Rate Calculations" in Chapter 4, a semiannual discount rate of (see Equation 4.31):

$$i_2 = (1 + 0.08)^{1/2} - 1$$

$$= 0.03923$$

or 3.923 percent should be used in the bond valuation calculation. However, we will ignore this complication in the remainder of this chapter.

Perpetual Bonds

A **perpetual bond,** or perpetuity, is a bond issued without a finite maturity date.[22] Perpetual bonds promise to pay interest indefinitely, and there is no contractual obligation to repay the principal; that is, $M = 0$.

The valuation of a perpetual bond is simpler than the valuation of a bond having a finite maturity date. Assuming that the bond pays a fixed amount of interest, I, per period forever, the value is as follows:

$$P_0 = \sum_{t=1}^{\infty} \frac{I}{(1 + k_d)^t} \tag{6.7}$$

where k_d is the required rate of return. Equation 6.7 can be simplified to obtain the following expression:[23]

$$P_0 = \frac{I}{k_d} \tag{6.8}$$

Consider, for example, the Canadian Pacific Limited Railroad's perpetual 4 percent debentures. What is the value of a $1,000 bond to an investor who requires an 8 percent rate of return on these Canadian Pacific bonds? Because $I = 0.04 \times \$1,000$, or $40, and $k_d = 8\%$, Equation 6.8 can be used to compute the answer as follows:

$$P_0 = \frac{\$40}{0.08}$$

$$= \$500$$

Thus, the investor would be willing to pay up to $500 for this bond.

Yield to Maturity of a Bond

The **yield to maturity** of a bond is the discount rate that equates the present value of all expected interest payments and the repayment of principal from a bond with the present bond price.[24] (In contrast, the current yield, which is equal to the annual interest payment divided by the current price, ignores the repayment of the principal.) If the current price of a bond, P_0, the uniform annual interest payments, I, and the maturity value, or principal, M, are known, the yield to maturity of a bond having a finite maturity date can be calculated by solving Equation 6.4 presented earlier for k_d:

$$P_0 = \sum_{t=1}^{n} \frac{I}{(1 + k_d)^t} + \frac{M}{(1 + k_d)^n}$$

Given values for any three of the four variables in this equation, one can solve for the value of the fourth variable. In the bond valuation calculation illustrated earlier in this section, this equation was used to determine the value of a bond (P_0) when the value of k_d is known (along with the values of I and M). In the yield to maturity calculation, which follows, the equation is used to determine k_d when the value of P_0 is known (along with the values of I and M).

---

[22]Perpetual bonds, also referred to as *consuls*, are rare. Some countries, such as Great Britain, and some railroads, such as the Canadian Pacific and the Canadian National, have issued perpetual bonds.

[23]Footnote 10 in Chapter 4 shows how Equation 6.8 is derived from Equation 6.7.

[24]The yield to maturity calculation assumes that cash flows from the bond occurring prior to maturity are reinvested at a rate equal to the yield to maturity.

For bonds with a call feature, one also can compute the expected *yield to call.* This is done by replacing the maturity value (M) by the call price and the number of years until maturity (n) by the number of years until the company can call the bond. If present interest rates are significantly below the coupon rate on the (callable) bond, then it is likely that the bond will be called in the future. In such a case, the relevant expected rate of return on the bond is the yield to call rather than the yield to maturity.

There are a number of ways to compute the yield to maturity of a bond. Most financial calculators are programmed to compute the yield to maturity, given P_0, I, and M. Also, special bond tables can be used to identify the yield to maturity for any particular bond. In the absence of these aids, a trial-and-error approach, in conjunction with present value tables such as the ones at the end of the text, can be used to find an *approximate* yield to maturity.[25]

Consider again the Dole Food Company 7 percent bonds discussed earlier. Again, assume that interest is paid annually on May 15 each year. Suppose that the bonds are selling for $980 on May 15, 1996 (7 years prior to maturity). Determine the bond's exact yield to maturity. Given $n = 7$, $I = 70$, $P_0 = \$980$, and $M = \$1,000$, we can compute k_d.

CALCULATOR SOLUTION

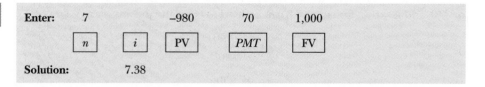

Therefore, the yield to maturity is 7.38 percent.[26]

The yield to maturity (or yield to call) can be used to compare the risk of two or more bonds that are similar *in all other respects* including time to maturity. The bond with the higher yield to maturity is the one perceived to be the riskier by investors. Also, the yield to maturity on existing bonds can be used as an estimate of the required returns of investors on any new (and similar) bonds the firm may issue.

---

[25]The steps in the trial and error procedure as follows:

Step 1.   Make an approximate estimate of the yield to maturity. Note that if the current price (P_0) of the bond is above (below) the maturity value (M)—i.e., if the bond is selling at a premium (discount)—then the trial rate should be less than (greater than) the coupon rate.

Step 2.   Use this rate to compute the present value of the bond's cash flows (that is, interest payments and principal payment).

Step 3.   Try a *higher* (*lower*) rate if the present value of the bond's cash flows are *greater* (*less*) than the current bond price.

Step 4.   Repeat the process (attempting to "bracket" the yield to maturity). Interpolate between the closest higher and lower values of k_d to obtain an approximate yield to maturity.

[26]Trial-and-error procedure:

At $k_d = 7\%$

$$\sum_{t=1}^{7} \frac{\$70}{(1+.07)^t} + \frac{\$1,000}{(1+.07)^7} = \$1,000 > \$980 = P_0$$

Therefore, try a higher rate, $k_d = 8\%$

$$\sum_{t=1}^{7} \frac{\$70}{(1+.08)^t} + \frac{\$1,000}{(1+.08)^7} = \$70(5.206) + \$1,000(.583) = \$947.42 < \$980 = P_0$$

Thus the yield to maturity is between 7% and 8%. By interpolation, the yield to maturity is approximately

$$k_d \approx 7\% + \frac{\$1,000 - \$980}{\$1,000 - \$947.42} \, (1\%) \approx 7.38\%$$

Zero Coupon Bonds. For zero coupon bonds that pay no interest over their life, the only payment to holders is the principal payment at maturity. Therefore, it is not necessary to use the trial-and-error approach just discussed in determining the yield to maturity of zero coupon bonds. To illustrate the calculation of the yield to maturity for such a bond, consider the Allied Signal Corporation zero coupon money multiplier notes that mature on August 15, 2000. Suppose these bonds (having a par value of $1,000) were purchased for $760 on August 15,1996 (4 years prior to maturity). Determine the yield to maturity on these bonds.

Figure 6-5 shows cash flows from the purchase of an AlliedSignal Corporation zero coupon bond. Because there are no interest payments, the yield to maturity equation (Equation 6.4) can be simplified to

$$P_0 = \frac{M}{(1 + k_d)^n}$$
(6.9)
$$= M(\text{PVIF}_{k_d, n})$$

Substituting $n = 4$, $P_0 = \$760$, and $M = \$1,000$ into this expression yields

$$\$760 = \$1,000(\text{PVIF}_{k_d, 4})$$

$$(\text{PVIF}_{k_d, 4}) = 0.760$$

From Table II at the back of the book, we find this present value interest factor in the 4-year row between the 7 percent (0.763) and 8 percent (0.735) interest rate columns. Hence by interpolation the yield to maturity (k_d) on this zero coupon bond is approximately

$$k_d = 7\% + \frac{.763 - .760}{.763 - .735} (1\%)$$

$$= 7.11\%$$

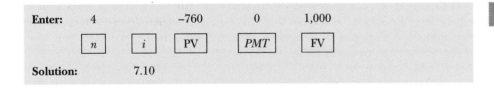

Enter:	4		−760	0	1,000
	n	i	PV	PMT	FV
Solution:		7.10			

Perpetual Bonds. The rate of return, or yield to maturity, on a *perpetual* bond can be found by solving the perpetual bond valuation equation presented earlier (Equation 6.8) for k_d:

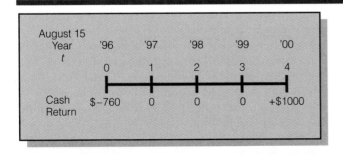

FIGURE 6-5
Cash Flows from the Purchase of an Allied Corporation Zero Coupon Bond

$$P_0 = \frac{I}{k_d}$$

which gives

$$k_d = \frac{I}{P_0} \tag{6.10}$$

It is not necessary to employ the trial-and-error method (or interpolation) to determine the yield for a perpetual bond.

For example, recall the 4 percent Canadian Pacific Limited Railroad debentures described earlier. If the current price of a bond is $640, what is the yield on the bond? Substituting $P_0 = \$640$ and $I = \$40$ (or 4 percent of $1,000) into Equation 6.10 gives the following:

$$k_d = \frac{\$40}{\$640}$$

$$= 0.0625 \text{ (or 6.25 percent)}$$

 ETHICAL ISSUES
LEVERAGED BUYOUTS AND BOND VALUES

During the 1980s and early 1990s, many firms were acquired or financially restructured in a transaction called a leveraged buyout (LBO). In a typical LBO, the buyer of the firm borrows a large amount of the purchase price, using the purchased assets as collateral for a large portion of the borrowings. Debt ratios (debt to total capital) of 90 percent or more have not been uncommon in LBOs.

LBOs have led to enormous wealth increases for the common stockholders of the acquired firm. For example, RJR Nabisco (RJR) shareholders saw the value of their common stock increase from the mid-fifties price range to over $100 when the firm was acquired by Kohlberg Kravis Roberts in an LBO. Bondholders generally have not fared quite so well. The impact of most LBOs has been a decline in the bond ratings of the acquired or restructured firm because of the substantial increase in perceived risk. Declines in the market value of bonds for firms acquired in LBO transactions have averaged about 7 percent. In the case of the RJR transaction, these bondholder losses initially exceeded 20 percent.

In the RJR case, several large bondholders, notably Metropolitan Life Insurance and Hartford Insurance, sued RJR, claiming among other things that RJR management had the duty to disclose that it was considering the possibility of an LBO at the time it issued bonds six months prior to the announcement of the LBO. Metropolitan Life sought compensation for its bond losses not just on the recent bond issue but also on earlier bond issues of RJR that it held.

Do you think that RJR bondholders and the bondholders in many other firms that were restructured with LBOs have a right to compensation from the firm's owners to offset bondholder losses in these transactions? What role do you think bond covenants should play in an analysis of the rights of bondholders and the obligations of management? How can bondholders protect themselves from losses arising out of LBOs?

CHARACTERISTICS OF PREFERRED STOCK

As a source of capital for a firm, preferred stock occupies an intermediate position between long-term debt and common stock. Like common stock, preferred stock is part of the stockholders' equity. Like long-term debt, it is considered a fixed-income security, although preferred stockholders receive dividends instead of interest payments. Because the issuing firm often does not promise repayment at a specific date, preferred stock tends to be a more permanent form of financing than long-term debt. Dividends on preferred stock, like interest payments on long-term debt, normally remain constant over time.

The popularity of preferred stock financing has declined in recent decades. Dividends cannot be deducted from income for corporate income tax purposes, whereas interest payments are tax deductible. This means that for a company paying more than one-third of its income in taxes, the after-tax cost of preferred stock is greater than that of long-term debt, assuming that the pretax preferred stock and long-term debt rates are about the same and that the company makes no change in its capital structure.[27]

Preferred stock bears its name because it usually has preference, or priority, over common stock with regard to the company's dividends and assets. For example, if a company's earnings in a given year are insufficient to pay dividends on preferred stock, the company is not permitted to pay dividends on its common stock. In the event of a liquidation following bankruptcy, the claims on the firm's assets by preferred stockholders are subordinate to those of creditors but have priority over those of common stockholders.

Features of Preferred Stock

Like long-term debt, preferred stock has its own unique distinguishing characteristics. A number are discussed here.

Selling Price and Par Value. The selling price, or issue price, is the per-share price at which preferred stock shares are sold to the public. Preferred stocks typically are issued at prices of $25, $50, or $100 per share.

The **par value** is the value assigned to the stock by the issuing company, and it is frequently the same as the initial selling price. No relationship necessarily exists between the two, however. A preferred stock sold at $25 per share may have a $25 par value, $1 par value, or no par value at all. Regardless of what a preferred stock's actual par value is, however, the preferred stockholders are entitled to their issue price plus dividends in the event of liquidation after the claims of creditors have been paid in full.

Preferred stock usually is designated by its dividend amount rather than its dividend percentage. For example, suppose Intermountain Power Company has a series of preferred stock that pays an annual dividend of $2.20, has a $1 par value, and was initially sold to the public at $25 per share. An investor would most likely refer to the stock as "Intermountain Power's $2.20 preferred."

---

[27]For a given company at a particular time, preferred stock will often cost slightly more than long-term debt, even on a pretax basis, because investors require a higher return to compensate them for the greater risk involved with preferred stock. (See Chapter 11 for a further discussion of this topic.) In contrast, preferred dividends received by corporate investors qualify for a 70 percent intercompany dividend exclusion, whereas interest income does not. Thus, a preferred stock offering that largely is purchased by other corporations may have a lower yield than similar debt offerings.

Adjustable Rate Preferred Stock. This type of preferred stock became popular in the early 1980s. With these issues, dividends are reset periodically and offer returns that vary with interest rates. For example, Citicorp ("Citibank") issued 4 million shares of adjustable rate preferred stock on February 18, 1983, with an initial dividend rate of 9.75 percent per annum until August 31, 1983. The annual dividend rate thereafter was to be set quarterly at 4.125 percentage points below the highest of (1) the three month U.S. Treasury Bill Rate, (2) the U.S. Treasury 10-year Constant Maturity Rate, and (3) the U.S. Treasury 20-year Constant Maturity Rate prior to each quarterly dividend period, with upper and lower limits of 12 percent and 6 percent, respectively.

Cumulative Feature. Most preferred stock is cumulative. This means that if, for some reason, a firm fails to pay its preferred dividend, it cannot pay dividends on its common stock until it has satisfied all or a prespecified amount of preferred dividends in arrears. The principal reason for this feature is that investors are generally unwilling to purchase preferred stock that is not cumulative.

Participation. Stock is said to be *participating* if the holders share in any increased earnings the company might experience. Virtually all preferred stock, however, is *nonparticipating;* that is, the preferred dividend remains constant, even if the company's earnings increase. Any dividend increases resulting from higher earnings accrue directly to the common stockholders.

Maturity. Preferred stock technically is part of a firm's equity capital. As such, some firms issue preferred stock that is intended to be *perpetual,* that is, a permanent portion of the stockholders' equity having no specific maturity date. Many preferred stock investors, however, desire sinking fund provisions, which guarantee that the issue will be retired over a specified time period.

Call Feature. Like long-term debt, preferred stock can sometimes be redeemed, or *called,* at the issuing firm's option at some specified price. For example, the Citicorp adjustable rate preferred stock discussed above is callable (deferred call) from February 28, 1988 to February 28, 1993 at $103 per share and thereafter at $100 per share.

Whereas the call feature allows the issuing company a measure of flexibility in its financing plans, the call feature is generally not attractive to investors. Thus, a firm usually must also provide investors with a *call premium,* or the difference between the call price and the original selling price, should it decide to attach a call feature to its preferred stock.

The probability that a firm will exercise the call privilege is likely to increase during times when market interest rates have decreased below those that existed at the time of issue. After calling the original issue, the firm can replace it with a lower-cost issue.

Voting Rights. As a general rule, preferred stockholders are not entitled to vote for the company's board of directors. However, special voting procedures frequently take effect if the company omits its preferred dividends or incurs losses for a period of time. In such a case, the preferred stockholders often vote as a separate group to elect one or more members of the company's board of directors. This ensures that the preferred holders will have direct representation on the board.

Trading of Preferred Shares

Following the initial sale of preferred stock by a firm, investors who purchase the shares may decide to sell them in the secondary markets. Large issues of actively traded preferred stock are listed on the major stock exchanges, such as the New York and the American stock exchanges. However, a majority of preferred stock issues are traded rather thinly, and these are traded over-the-counter.

Users of Preferred Stock

Utility companies are the most frequent users of preferred stock financing, largely because of the regulatory treatment of preferred stock dividend payments. Utilities are permitted by their regulatory agencies to consider preferred dividends as an expense for rate-making purposes, thus reducing the after-tax cost disadvantage of preferred stock that deters nonutility firms from making extensive use of this form of financing.

Within the last twenty-five years or so, preferred stock (usually convertible) has been used rather widely in mergers and acquisitions. Frequently, acquiring companies issue preferred stock in exchange for the common stock of acquired companies. For example, Chrysler issued (convertible) preferred stock in August 1987 when it acquired American Motors. This, in effect, is another example of financial leverage, and it can cause an increase in the earnings per common share of the acquiring company.[28]

Other occasional users of preferred stock financing are capital-intensive companies undertaking expansion programs. These companies may choose preferred stock as a means of securing long-term financing for the following reasons:

■ Their capital structures and various other restrictions prevent the judicious use of additional long-term debt.
■ Depressed common stock prices and the potential dilution of per-share earnings may cause them to decide against external common equity financing.

Often these same companies have relatively low marginal tax rates (because of losses and accelerated depreciation) that make the after-tax cost of preferred stock not appreciably different from that of long-term debt. For example, USX (formerly U.S. Steel) and Armco have issued preferred stock during the past decade.

Large commercial banks were another group of preferred stock users during the 1980s. These banks, including BankAmerica, Citicorp, and Mellon, issued variable-rate preferred stock, partly to get additional equity into their capital structures.

Advantages and Disadvantages of Preferred Stock Financing

From the issuing company's perspective, the principal advantage of preferred stock is that preferred dividend payments are potentially flexible. Omitting a preferred dividend in difficult times usually results in less severe consequences than omitting an interest payment on long-term debt.

---

[28]Chapter 22 contains a more detailed discussion of the use of preferred stock in mergers.

In addition, preferred stock financing can increase a firm's degree of financial leverage. However, financial analysts may regard the issuance of preferred stock as equivalent to debt. In this case, the company is viewed as having used up a portion of its "debt capacity." Or, in effect, the company has leveraged with preferred stock rather than long-term debt—at a greater after-tax cost.

From the investors' perspective, companies who purchase the preferred stock of other companies accrue certain tax advantages resulting from the 70 percent exclusion of intercompany dividends from federal income taxes. For example, an insurance company in the 35 percent tax bracket can invest in the preferred stock of another company and pay taxes equal to only about 10.5 percent of the preferred dividend income.[29] In contrast, the same insurance company would be required to include all the interest received in its taxable income.

The principal disadvantage of preferred stock financing is its high after-tax cost as compared with long-term debt, because dividends cannot be deducted for income tax purposes. Thus the after-tax cost to the firm for preferred stock is greater than the after-tax cost of long-term debt, assuming that the firm's capital structure remains constant. As a result, most companies considering long-term financing with fixed-income securities choose long-term debt over preferred stock. A complete discussion of the cost of debt and preferred stock is in Chapter 11.

VALUATION OF PREFERRED STOCK

Most preferred stock pays regular, fixed dividends. Preferred dividends per share are normally not increased when the earnings of a firm increase, nor are they cut or suspended unless the firm faces serious financial problems. If preferred stock dividends are cut or suspended for a period of time for whatever reason, the firm is usually required to make up the past-due payments before paying any common stock dividends. Thus, the investor's expected cash return from holding most preferred stocks can be treated as a fixed, constant amount per period.

The investor's required rate of return on a preferred stock issue is a function of the risk that the firm will be unable to meet its dividend payments. The higher the risk, the higher the required rate of return. Because bondholders have a prior claim over preferred stockholders on the income and assets of a firm, it is more risky to hold a firm's preferred stock than to hold its bonds. As a result, investors normally require a higher rate of return on preferred stock than on bonds.

Because many preferred stock issues do not have maturity dates, the cash flows from holding no-maturity preferred stock can be treated as a perpetual stream of payments, or a *perpetuity*. Capitalizing the perpetual stream of dividend payments gives the following valuation expression:

$$P_0 = \sum_{t=1}^{\infty} \frac{D_p}{(1 + k_p)^t} \tag{6.11}$$

[29]This 10.5 percent figure is calculated by multiplying the portion of dividends that is subject to taxes, namely, 30 percent, by 35 percent.

where D_p is the dividend per period, and k_p is the investor's required rate of return.[30]

Equation 6.11 is similar to Equation 6.7 for a perpetual bond. Like the perpetual bond valuation model, this equation can be simplified into the following valuation model:

$$P_0 = \frac{D_p}{k_p} \qquad (6.12)$$

To illustrate the use of Equation 6.12, assume that Baltimore Gas & Electric pays annual end-of-year dividends on a series B, 4½ percent cumulative preferred stock issue (par value of $100). What is the value of this stock to an investor who requires an 8 percent annual rate of return on the investment? Assume that the issue will not be called for the forseeable future. Substituting $4.50 ($0.045 \times 100) for D_p and 0.08 for k_p yields the following:

$$P_0 = \frac{\$4.50}{0.08}$$

$$= \$56.25$$

■ SUMMARY

■ The value of a long-term security is based on the *expected future cash flows* the owner will receive in the period during which the asset is held.

■ The *capitalization of cash flow* method of valuation can be used to determine the value of a security to an investor. This involves calculating the present value of the stream of expected future cash flows discounted at the investor's required rate of return. The required rate of return is a function of the *risk* associated with the cash flows from the asset, as well as the risk-free rate.

■ The *market price* of a security represents the value placed on it by marginally satisfied buyers and sellers.

■ Long-term debt and preferred stock are classified as *fixed-income securities*, because interest (on long-term debt) and dividends (on preferred stock) tend to remain constant over time. Common stock, on the other hand, is a *variable-income security*, because the dividends paid on common stock tend to fluctuate over time.

■ Long-term debt generally is classified according to whether it is *secured* by specific physical assets of the issuing company. Secured debt issues are *mortgage bonds*, whereas debt issues backed only by unmortgaged assets and the company's earning power are *debentures*.

■ Long-term debt usually has the following features:
1. The *indenture*, or the contract between the issuing company and the debtholders.
2. The *trustee*, who represents the debtholders in dealings with the company.
3. The *call feature*, which gives the issuing company the option to retire the debt prior to maturity.

---

[30]If an investor is considering purchasing a preferred stock issue that is expected to be called in the future, its value is calculated by capitalizing (that is, discounting) the call price plus the dividend payments to be received before the issue is called.

4. The *sinking fund requirement,* which, in practice, means the company must gradually reduce the outstanding balance of the debt issue over its life.

■ Bond *refunding* occurs when a company redeems a callable issue and sells a lower-cost issue to take its place.

■ The value of a *perpetual bond* is equal to the interest payment divided by the investor's required rate of return.

■ The major disadvantage of long-term debt financing is the increased financial risk of the firm.

■ The value of a *bond having a finite maturity date* is equal to the present value of the stream of interest and principal payments discounted at the investor's required rate of return.

■ The *yield to maturity* on a bond is the rate of return the investor expects to earn if the bond is purchased at a given price and held until maturity.

■ Preferred stock occupies an intermediate position between long-term debt and common stock as a source of capital. Like common stock, preferred stock is part of the stockholders' equity, and preferred stockholders receive returns in the form of dividends. Preferred stock is also similar to long-term debt in that preferred dividends, like the interest on long-term debt, usually remain constant over time.

■ Preferred stock usually has the following features:
  1. The *selling price,* or *issue price,* is the per-share price at which the shares are sold to the public.
  2. The *par value* is an arbitrary value assigned to the stock by the issuing company.
  3. Most preferred stock is *cumulative;* that is, dividends on common stock cannot be paid as long as any past or present preferred dividends remain unpaid.
  4. Virtually all preferred stock is *nonparticipating;* that is, preferred stock does not share in any increased earnings of the firm.
  5. Some preferred stock is *perpetual,* whereas other preferred stock is gradually retired by the firm.
  6. Preferred stock is often *callable.*

■ From the issuing company's perspective, preferred stock financing is advantageous due to the potential flexibility of preferred dividend payments.

■ The principal disadvantage of preferred stock financing is that dividends are not tax deductible, which causes the after-tax cost of preferred stock to the firm to be higher than the cost of long-term debt, all other things being equal.

■ The cash flows from most preferred stocks can be treated as perpetuities. Therefore, the value of a preferred stock is equal to the annual preferred dividend divided by the investor's required rate of return.

■ QUESTIONS AND TOPICS FOR DISCUSSION

1. Define the following terms associated with long-term debt:
   a. Indenture.
   b. Trustee.
   c. Call feature.
   d. Sinking fund.
   e. Conversion feature.
   f. Coupon rate.

2. Describe the basic features of each of the following types of bonds:
   a. Mortgage bonds.
   b. Debentures.
   c. Subordinated debentures.
   d. Equipment trust certificates.
   e. Collateral trust bonds.
   f. Income bonds.
3. Suppose a company simultaneously sold two long-term debt issues at par: 9⅛ percent senior debentures and 9⅜ percent subordinated debentures. What risk-return trade-off would an investor face who was considering one of these issues?
4. What is the relationship between par value, market value, and book value for the following?
   a. Long-term debt.
   b. Preferred stock.
5. Define the following terms associated with preferred stock:
   a. Cumulative feature.
   b. Participation.
   c. Call feature.
6. What variables must be known (or estimated) in applying the capitalization of cash flow method of valuation to a physical or financial asset?
7. Define the following:
   a. The market value of an asset.
   b. Market equilibrium.
8. What is the primary difference between the book value and the market value of an asset?
9. Describe the relationship between the coupon rate and the required rate of return that will result in a bond selling at
   a. A discount.
   b. Par value.
   c. A premium.
10. How does the yield to maturity on a bond differ from the coupon yield or current yield?
11. Under what conditions will a bond's current yield be equal to its yield to maturity?
12. In what ways is preferred stock similar to long-term debt? In what ways is it similar to common stock?
13. Explain why bondholders often prefer a sinking fund provision in a bond issue.
14. Explain what is meant by *interest rate risk*.
15. Explain how a bond can be classified as a fixed-income security when the yield to maturity can fluctuate significantly over time, depending on the market price of the bond.
16. Describe the basic features of each of the following types of bonds:
   a. Floating-rate bonds.
   b. Original issue deep discount bonds.
   c. Zero coupon bonds.
   d. Extendable notes (put bonds).
17. Explain what is meant by reinvestment rate risk.
18. Compare the debt and preferred stock outstanding for USAirways and Southwest Airlines. Use the S & P *Bond Guide* from your library to determine the bond rating of each of these firms. What reasons can you cite for the differences in bond ratings between the firms?

■ SELF-TEST PROBLEMS

ST1. What is the current value of a $1,000 par value perpetual bond to an investor who requires a 10 percent annual rate of return? The perpetual bond pays interest at the rate of 8 percent per year.

ST2. AlliedSignal Corporation has a series of zero coupon bonds outstanding that mature on August 1, 2007. Calculate the yield to maturity if an investor purchases one of these bonds on August 1, 1996 at a price of $2,250. The bond is expected to pay $5,000 at maturity.

ST3. Bankers Trust has bonds outstanding ($1,000 par value) that mature 10 years from today and have a coupon interest rate of 9 percent. Calculate the maximum price an investor should be willing to pay if the investor desires a 10 percent yield to maturity.

ST4. What is the value of a share of duPont $4.50 cumulative, perpetual preferred stock to an investor who requires a 6 percent annual rate of return on this security? This preferred stock was originally issued at $100 a share.

ST5. The following corporate bond quotations recently were reported in the *Wall Street Journal*:

Boise C	7s16	cv	10	95	−½
Motrla	zr09	…	1	91½	−1½
Sou Bell	4¾00	4.9	20	97½	−¼
USAir	12⅞00	12.3	160	104⅜	−¼

a. What is the coupon rate and year to maturity for the Southern Bell bonds?

b. If you purchased one US Airways bond, what price would you have to pay at the closing trade?

c. Why do you think the yield is so much greater for the USAirways bond than the Southern Bell bond?

d. What does the "cv" indicator tell you about the Boise Cascade bond?

ST6. A U.S. government bond was quoted as :

Rate	Maturity Mo/Yr	Bid	Asked	Chg*	Ask Yld
11¾	Feb 01	140:07	140:11	−10	5.11

*Chg is in 32nds of a percent.

a. How much would you have to pay for one of these $1,000 face value bonds?

b. What was the dollar amount of the price change on this bond?

■ PROBLEMS*

1. Determine the value of a $1,000 Canadian Pacific Limited perpetual 4 percent debenture (bond) at the following required rates of return:
   a. 4 percent.
   b. 5 percent.
   c. 6 percent.

2. During 1996, the high and low market prices of Canadian Pacific Limited's debentures (see Problem 1) were $790 and $475, respectively. Determine the yield to maturity of one of these debentures if it was purchased under the following conditions:
   a. At the high 1996 market price.
   b. At the low 1996 market price.

3. Consider AlliedSignal Corporation's 9⅞ percent bonds that mature on June 1, 2002. Assume that the interest on these bonds is paid and compounded annually. Determine the value of a $1,000 denomination AlliedSignal Corporation bond as of June 1, 1996, to an investor who holds the bond until maturity and whose required rate of return is
   a. 7 percent.
   b. 9 percent.
   c. 11 percent.
   d. What would be the value of the AlliedSignal Corporation bonds at an 8 percent required rate of return if the interest were paid and compounded *semiannually*?

eXcel

---

*Colored numbers denote problems that have check answers provided at the end of the book.

4. Creative Financing, Inc., is planning to offer a $1,000 par value 15-year maturity bond with a coupon interest rate that changes every 5 years. The coupon rate for the first 5 years is 10 percent, 10.75 percent for the next 5 years, and 11.5 percent for the final 5 years. If you require an 11 percent rate of return on a bond of this quality and maturity, what is the maximum price you would pay for the bond? (Assume interest is paid annually at the end of each year.)

5.† Southern Bell has issued 4⅜ percent bonds that mature on August 1, 2003. The bonds are callable at $1,000 beginning on August 1, 1999. Assume that interest is paid and compounded annually. Determine the yield to maturity (to the nearest tenth of 1 percent) if an investor purchases a $1,000 denomination bond for $853.75 on August 1, 1996.

6.† American Telephone & Telegraph has issued 8⅛ percent debentures that will mature on July 15, 2024. Assume that interest is paid and compounded annually. If an investor purchases a $1,000 denomination bond for $1,025 on July 15, 1996, determine the bond's yield to maturity. Explain why an investor would be willing to pay $1,025 for a bond that it going to be worth only $1,000 at maturity.

7. Consider the AlliedSignal Corporation zero coupon money multiplier notes of 2000. The bonds were issued in 1982 for $100. Determine the yield to maturity (to the nearest tenth of 1 percent) if the bonds are purchased at the
   a. Issue price in 1982. (Note: To avoid a fractional year holding period, assume that the issue and maturity dates are at the midpoint—July 1—of the respective years.)
   b. Market price as of July 1, 1996, of $750.
   c. Explain why the returns calculated in Parts a and b are different.

8. If you purchase a zero coupon bond today for $225 and it matures at $1,000 in 11 years, what rate of return will you earn on that bond (to the nearest tenth of 1 percent)?

9.† In 1987, Chrysler issued 10.95 percent debentures that will mature on August 1, 2017.
   a. If an investor purchased one of these bonds ($1,000 denomination) on August 1, 1996, for $1,086.25, determine the yield to maturity. Explain why an investor would be willing to pay $1,086.25 in 1996 for one of these bonds when he or she is going to receive only $1,000 when the bond matures in 2017.
   b. The Chrysler 10.95 percent debentures are callable by the company any time on or after August 1, 1998, at $1,054.75. Determine the *yield to call* as of August 1, 1996, assuming that Chrysler calls the bonds on August 1, 1998.

10. Determine the value of a share of Litton Industries Series B $2.00 cumulative preferred stock to an investor who requires the following rates of return:
    a. 9 percent.
    b. 10 percent.
    c. 12 percent.

11. Determine the value of a share of Baltimore Gas and Electric 4½ percent cumulative preferred stock, series B, par value $100 to an investor who requires a 9 percent rate of return on this security. The issue is callable at $110 per share plus accrued dividends. However, the issue is not expected to be called at any time in the foreseeable future.

12.† Consider again the American Telephone & Telegraph 8⅛ percent debentures that mature on July 15, 2024 (see Problem 6). Determine the yield to call if the bonds are callable beginning on July 15, 2003 at $1,039.71.

13.† American Telephone & Telegraph has bonds that trade frequently and commonly are listed in the financial press as ATT 5⅛ 01. The bonds mature on April 1 in the maturity year. Suppose an investor buys this bond on April 1, 1996, and assume interest is paid annually on April 1. Calculate the yield to maturity assuming the investor buys the bond at the following price, as quoted in the financial press:
    a. 100
    b. 90
    c. 105

†Requires use of financial calculator or trial-and-error procedure described in Footnotes 25 and 26.

14. Hooks Athletics, Inc., has outstanding a preferred stock with a par value of $30 that pays a dividend of $2.50. The preferred stock is redeemable at the option of the stockholder in 10 years at a price equal to $30. The stock may be called for redemption by the company in 15 years at a price of $32.50. (Any stock that is not redeemed at the end of 10 years can be expected to be called by the company in 15 years.) If you knew that investors require a 15 percent pretax rate of return on this preferred stock, what is the current market value of this preferred stock?

e✗cel   15. Dooley, Inc., has outstanding $100 million (par value) bonds that pay an annual coupon rate of interest of 10.5 percent. Par value of each bond is $1,000. The bonds are scheduled to mature in 20 years. Because of Dooley's increased risk, investors now require a 14 percent rate of return on bonds of similar quality with 20 years remaining until maturity. The bonds are callable at 110 percent of par at the end of 10 years.
    a. What price would the bonds sell for assuming investors *do not expect* them to be called?
    b. What price would the bonds sell for assuming investors *expect* them to be called at the end of 10 years?

e✗cel   16. Zabberer Corporation bonds pay a coupon rate of interest of 12 percent annually and have a maturity value of $1,000. The bonds are scheduled to mature at the end of 14 years. The company has the option to call the bonds in 8 years at a premium of 12 percent above the maturity value. You believe the company will exercise its option to call the bonds at that time. If you require a pretax return of 10 percent on bonds of this risk, how much would you pay for one of these bonds today?

e✗cel   17. Waters, Inc., has outstanding a $100 million (face value) issue of bonds. The bonds pay a coupon rate of interest of 8 percent per annum. At the time the bonds were first issued, they sold at face value of $1,000 per bond. The bonds have 12 years remaining until maturity. They are "puttable" at the option of the bondholder at face value in 5 years. The bonds are not callable by the company. If you require a 9 percent return on bonds such as these with 5 years remaining until maturity and 8.2 percent on bonds such as these with 12 years remaining until maturity, how much would you pay for one of these bonds?

e✗cel   18. RJR Nabisco has issued preferred stock ($10 par value) that pays an annual dividend of $0.84. The preferred stock matures in 5 years. At that time, holders of the stock will receive, at their option, either $10 or one share of common stock with a value up to $14. If the common stock is trading at a price above $14, the preferred stock holders will receive a fractional share of common stock worth $14. The current common stock price is $8.875. The common stock pays a 10 cent per share dividend. This dividend is expected to grow at a 10 percent rate per year for the next 5 years. If you require a 12 percent rate of return on a stock of this risk and maturity, what is the *maximum* value for which this share can be expected to trade?

19. Determine the annual dividend rate for Citicorp's adjustable rate preferred stock issue of 1983 (see the section "Features of Preferred Stock") for the following quarter under each of the following combinations of interest rates:

	Treasury Bill Rate	10-Year Constant Maturity Rate	20-Year Constant Maturity Rate
a.	5.0%	6.0%	6.5%
b.	8.5	10.5	11.5
c.	16.0	14.5	14.0

20. The following bond quotations recently appeared in the *Wall Street Journal*:

ATT 7⅛ 02	6.9	7	103¾	+¼
AlskAr 6⅞ 14	cv	81	99	—
Chryslr 10.4s99	10.0	55	104	–⅜
MGM Grd 12s02	11.1	25	108⅛	–⅝
US West zr11	—	12	36	—

a. What is the coupon rate and year of maturity for each bond?
b. How much would you have had to pay to buy one US West bond at the closing trade?
c. Why is the yield on the MGM Grand bond so much higher than the yield on the AT&T bond?
d. How much did the price of one Chrysler bond change from the prior day's closing price?

21. The "asked" discount on a six-month Treasury bill recently was quoted as 3.02 percent. Approximately how much would you have to pay to buy one of these Treasury bills ($10,000 maturity value)?
22. How much would you have to pay for a U.S. government bond ($1,000 maturity value) scheduled to mature in November 2015 and quoted at 143:15 "asked"? The coupon rate on the bond is 9⅞ percent.
23. The following price quote for Pep Boys bonds appeared in the *Wall Street Journal*:

PepBoys zr11	—	82	57	+⅛

a. Why is there no yield quoted for the bonds?
b. How do bondholders get a return when they buy these bonds?

24. The bonds of Columbia Gas currently (late 1993) paid no interest because the firm has declared bankruptcy. One issue of these bonds, the 8¼ percent coupon bonds due in 1996, is selling at 109 percent of par value, or for approximately $1090. Why would someone pay $1090 for the bonds of a bankrupt firm?
25. Chock Full O'Nuts has a 7 percent coupon rate bond issue outstanding that matures in 2012. The *Wall Street Journal* reports a bond price of 83½ ($835). However, no yield is given in the current yield column. Rather, a "cv" is indicated. What does this "cv" mean about the bond? Why do you think a company would issue this type of bond?
26. Visit Money Advisors Web site and use their Human Life Value Calculator to find the monetary value of your life. According to their calculations, what is your life worth? Do you agree? Why or why not? http://
www.moneyadvisor.com

■ SOLUTIONS TO SELF-TEST PROBLEMS

ST1. $$P_0 = \frac{I}{k_d} = \frac{\$80}{0.10} = \$800$$

ST2. $$P_0 = \frac{M}{(1 + k_d)^n}$$

$$= M(\text{PVIF}_{k_d,n})$$

$n = 11$ $M = \$5{,}000$ $P_0 = \$2{,}250$

$$\$2{,}250 = \$5{,}000\ (\text{PVIF}_{k_d,11})$$

$$(\text{PVIF}_{k_d,11}) = 0.450$$

Using Table II and reading across the 11-year row, 0.450 is found between the 7%(0.475) and 8% (0.429) interest rate columns. Interpolation between these two values gives an approximate yield to maturity (k_d) of

$$k_d = 7\% + \frac{.475 - .450}{.475 - .429}\,(1\%)$$

$$= 7.54\%$$

CALCULATOR SOLUTION

Enter:	11		−450	0	1,000
	n	i	PV	PMT	FV
Solution:		7.53			

ST3. $P_0 = \sum_{t=1}^{n} \dfrac{I}{(1 + k_d)^t} + \dfrac{M}{(1 + k_d)^n}$

$n = 10$ $I = .09(\$1,000) = \$90$ $M = \$1,000$ $k_d = 0.10$

$P_0 = \sum_{t=1}^{10} \dfrac{\$90}{(1.10)^t} + \dfrac{\$1,000}{(1.10)^{10}}$

$= \$90(\text{PVIFA}_{0.10,10}) + \$1,000(\text{PVIF}_{0.10,10})$

$= \$90(6.145) + \$1,000(0.386)$

$= \$939.05 \ (\text{or } \$939)$

CALCULATOR SOLUTION

Enter:	10	10.0		90	1,000
	n	i	PV	PMT	FV
Solution:			−938.55		

If the investor pays $938.55, the expected yield to maturity is 10 percent. If the investor pays more than $938.55, the expected yield to maturity is less than 10 percent. Therefore, the maximum price the investor should be willing to pay is $938.55.

ST4. $P_0 = \dfrac{D_p}{k_p} = \dfrac{\$4.50}{0.06} = \$75$

ST5.   a. Coupon rate: 4¾ percent
Year of maturity: 2000
b. $1046.25 (104⅝% of $1000)
c. USAirways is perceived to be *much* riskier than Southern Bell.
d. The Boise Cascade bonds can be converted to common stock under certain circumstances.

ST6.   a. 140¹¹⁄₃₂ percent of $1000, or $1,403.44
b. −¹⁰⁄₃₂ of 1% ($1,000) = −$3.125

■ GLOSSARY

Bond A long-term debt instrument that promises to pay the lender a series of periodic interest payments in addition to returning the principal at maturity. Most corporate bonds are offered in $1,000 principal amounts (par value).

Bond Rating An evaluation of a bond's probability of default. This is peformed by an outside rating agency, such as Standard and Poor's or Moody's.

Bond Refunding The redemption of a callable bond issue and replacement at a lower-interest cost issue.

Book Value The accounting value of an asset or a corporation. The book value per share of common stock is equal to the total book value of the company, or stockholders' equity, divided by the total number of shares of common stock outstanding.

Call Feature A provision that permits an issuer of bonds (and sometimes preferred stock) to retire the obligation prior to its maturity.

Call Premium The difference between a bond's call price and its par value.

Call Price The price at which a bond may be retired, or called, prior to its maturity.

Capitalization of Cash Flow A method of determining the present value of an asset that is expected to produce a stream of future cash flows. This involves discounting the stream of expected future cash flows at an appropriate rate.

Convertible Bond A bond that may be exchanged for common stock at the holder's option.

Coupon Rate of Interest The interest rate stated on a bond. The coupon rate of interest times the par, or principal, value of a bond determines the periodic dollar interest payment received by the bondholder.

Cumulative Dividends A typical feature of preferred stock that requires past-due preferred stock dividends to be paid before any common stock dividends can be paid.

Current Yield The annual interest payment divided by the current (market) price of a bond.

Debenture A bond that is not secured by a mortgage on any specific asset but instead by the general credit and earning power of the issuing firm.

Going-Concern Value The value of a firm, assuming that the firm's organization and assets remain intact and are used to generate future income and cash flows.

Income Bond A bond that pays interest only if the firm earns sufficient income.

Indenture The contract between the issuing firm and the lenders in a debt obligation.

Interest Rate Risk The variation in the market price (and hence in the realized rate of return or yield) of a security that arises from changes in interest rates.

Junk Bond A high-yield debt security issued by a company with a low credit rating.

Liquidation Value The value of a firm, assuming that it sells all its assets and stops using them to generate future income and cash flows.

Mortgage Bond A bond secured by a pledge of a specific asset or group of assets.

Par Value (Bond) Represents the amount of principal borrowed (usually $1,000) and due at maturity.

Par Value (Preferred Stock) An arbitrary value assigned by the issuing firm.

Perpetual Bond A bond that has no maturity date.

Reinvestment Rate Risk Risk that occurs when a bond issue matures (or is called) and because of a decline in interest rates, the owner has to reinvest the principal at a lower coupon rate.

Required Rate of Return The rate used to value a stream of expected cash flows from an asset (also called the discount rate). The riskier the expected cash flows from the asset, the higher the required rate of return.

Senior Debt Debt that has a higher claim on a firm's earnings and/or assets than junior debt.

Subordinated Debenture A bond with a claim on the issuing firm's assets that is junior to other forms of debt in the event of a liquidation. The claims of subordinated debenture holders can be met only after all the claims of senior creditors have been met.

Trustee The bondholder's representative in a public debt offering. The trustee is responsible for monitoring the borrower's compliance with the term of the indenture.

Warrant A company-issued long-term option to purchase a specified number of shares of the firm's stock at a particular price during a specified time period.

Yield to Maturity The discount rate that equates the present value of all expected interest payments and the repayment of principal from a bond with the present bond price.

Appendix 6A
Bond Refunding Analysis

 ## THE BOND REFUNDING PROCESS

Bond refunding occurs when a company exercises its option to redeem a callable issue and sells a lower-cost issue to take its place.[31] The decision of whether to refund a particular debt issue is usually based on a capital budgeting (present value) analysis. The principal benefit, or cash inflow, is the present value of the after-tax interest savings over the life of the issue. The principal investment, or cash outflow at the time of refunding, consist primarily of the call premium and the issuance (flotation) cost of the new debt.

Bond refunding differs from other capital expenditure projects in one very important way: the cash inflows are known with considerably more certainty than the cash flows from a typical capital expenditure project and thus are less risky. As a result, the weighted cost of capital is not used. Instead, the *after-tax cost of the new debt* is believed to be a more appropriate discount rate for bond refunding analysis.[32]

Bond refunding becomes an important decision facing many firms whenever interest rates decline substantially from earlier levels. For example, firms that had issued bonds with coupon rates of 13 percent or more during the period of high inflation and high interest rates in the early 1980s found that they could refund these issues at rates under 9 percent during the early 1990s.

As an illustration of bond refunding, consider the following example. The APCO Company issued $100 million of 30-year, 13 percent debt 5 years ago. In the meantime, interest rates have declined, and the firm's management feels the decline has bottomed out. The debt issue is now callable at 107 percent of par. The company could refund the old issue with a new 25-year, 10 percent, $100 million issue. Issuance costs on the new issue would be 0.5 percent, or $500,000, whereas the unamortized issuance costs on the old issue are $450,000. If APCO decided to call the old issue and refund it, both issues would be outstanding for a 3-week period, resulting in overlapping interest payments. The company's marginal tax rate is 40 percent. For purposes of discounting, the after-tax cost of new debt is $0.10 \times (1 - 0.4) = 0.06$.

To determine whether APCO should refund the old issue, a bond refunding analysis is carried out.

■ Step 1: Calculate the interest savings (cash inflows).[33]

$$\text{Annual interest, after tax} = \text{Issue size} \times \text{Interest rate} \times (1 - \text{Tax rate}) \qquad (6A.1)$$

Annual interest, old issue = $100 million $\times$ 13% $\times$ 0.6 = $7.8 million
Annual interest, new issue = $100 million $\times$ 10% $\times$ 0.6 = $6.0 million
Annual after-tax interest savings $1.8 million

---

[31]Callable preferred stock can also be refunded. The same consideration and analysis apply to both debt and preferred stock.
[32]See Chapter 11 for a discussion of the cost of capital.
[33]This calculation assumes that interest is received once a year at year-end. Actually, interest is paid every 6 months. However, the two results are not materially different.

$$\text{Present value of interest savings} = \text{Annual after-tax interest savings}$$
$$\times \text{PVIFA}_{0.06,25}$$
$$= \$1.8 \text{ million} \times 12.783$$
$$= \$23.009 \text{ million}$$

■ **Step 2: Calculate the net investment (net cash outflow at time 0).** This involves computing the after-tax call premium, the issuance cost of the new issue, the issuance cost of the old issue, and the overlapping interest.

The after-tax call premium is calculated as follows:

$$\text{Call premium, after-tax} = \text{Call premium} \times (1 - \text{Tax rate}) \qquad (6A.2)$$
$$= \$7 \text{ million} \times (1 - 0.4)$$
$$= \$4.2 \text{ million}$$

The call premium is a cash outflow.

The issuance cost on the new issue is 0.5 percent, or \$500,000. This amount cannot be deducted from APCO's current period income for tax purposes. Instead, it must be capitalized and amortized over the life of the debt issue, because the benefits that accrue to a firm as a result of an issuance cost expenditure occur over the life of the issue. Thus,

$$\begin{array}{l} \text{Present value of} \\ \text{issuance cost} \\ \text{of new issue} \end{array} = \text{Issuance cost} - \text{Present value tax effect} \qquad (6A.3)$$

$$= \text{Issuance cost} - \left(\begin{array}{c} \text{Annual after-tax} \\ \text{savings from} \\ \text{amortization} \end{array} \times \text{PVIFA}_{0.06,25} \right)$$

$$= \text{Issuance cost} - \left(\frac{\text{Issuance cost}}{\text{Number of years}} \times \text{Tax rate} \right.$$

$$\left. \times \text{PVIFA}_{0.06,25} \right)$$

$$= \$500,000 - \left(\frac{\$500,000}{25} \times 0.4 \times 12.783 \right)$$

$$= \$500,000 - \$102,264$$

$$= \$397,736$$

The present value of the issuance cost of the *new* issue is a net cash outflow.

APCO has been amortizing the issuance cost of the old issue over its life. If it refunded the issue, the company no longer would receive the benefits from the old issue's issuance cost and therefore could write off the remaining unamortized issuance cost at the time of refunding. Because of the write-off, however, APCO would lose the benefits of the old issuance cost over the remaining life of the issue. Thus,

$$\begin{array}{c} \text{Present value of} \\ \text{issuance cost of} \\ \text{old issue} \end{array} = \begin{array}{c} \text{Present value,} \\ \text{lost benefits,} \\ \text{old issuance cost,} \\ \text{after tax} \end{array} - \begin{array}{c} \text{Present value,} \\ \text{write-off old} \\ \text{issuance cost,} \\ \text{after tax} \end{array} \qquad (6A.4)$$

$$= \left(\frac{\text{Old issuance cost}}{\text{Number of years}} \times \text{Tax rate} \times \text{PVIFA}_{0.06,25} \right)$$

$$- (\text{Old issuance cost} \times \text{Tax rate})$$

$$= \left(\frac{\$450,000}{25} \times 0.4 \times 12.783 \right) - (450,000 \times 0.4)$$

$$= \$92,038 - \$180,000$$

$$= -\$87,962$$

The issuance cost effect of the old issue is a net cash inflow at the time of refunding.

In most bond refundings, it is necessary for a firm to sell the new issue and receive the proceeds before paying off the old lenders. Both issues are usually outstanding for less than a month. Thus, the interest expense on the old issue during the overlapping period is considered a cost, or part of the refunding investment. In APCO's case, this expense is calculated as follows:

$$\begin{array}{c} \text{Overlapping} \\ \text{interest} \end{array} = \begin{array}{c} \text{Size of} \\ \text{issue} \end{array} \times \begin{array}{c} \text{Annual interest rate} \\ \text{of old issue,} \\ \text{after tax} \end{array} \times \begin{array}{c} \text{Fraction of year} \\ \text{both issues} \\ \text{outstanding} \end{array} \qquad (6A.5)$$

$$= \$100 \text{ million} \times 0.078 \times \frac{3}{52}$$

$$= \$450,000$$

The overlapping interest is a cash outflow.[34]

In summary, the net investment is calculated as follows:

Call premium	$4,200,000
Present value of issuance cost, new issue	397,736
Present value of issuance cost, old issue	–87,962
Overlapping interest	450,000
Net investment (cash outflow)	$4,959,774

■ **Step 3: Finally, calculate the net present value of refunding.**

$$\begin{array}{c} \text{Net present value} \\ \text{of refunding} \end{array} = \begin{array}{c} \text{Present value,} \\ \text{interest savings} \end{array} - \begin{array}{c} \text{Present value,} \\ \text{net investment} \end{array} \qquad (6A.6)$$

$$= \$23.009 \text{ million} - \$4.960 \text{ million}$$

$$= \$18.049 \text{ million}$$

Because the net present value is positive, APCO should call its old issue and refund it with the new one.[35]

---

[34]Normally, during the period of the overlap, the proceeds from the sale of the new issue are temporarily invested in short-term securities. The interest earned will offset part of the overlapping interest expense. For simplification, this offset against the overlapping interest expense has not been considered in this example.

[35]Financial analysts normally can determine the *approximate* net present value of refunding by comparing the present value of the interest savings with the after-tax cost of the call premium. However, as is true with any shortcut method, caution should be exercised.

■ SUMMARY

- *Bond refunding* occurs when a firm exercises its option to redeem a callable bond issue and replaces it with a lower (interest) cost issue.
- Bond refunding decisions are analyzed in a capital budgeting (present value) framework. A bond issue should be redeemed and replaced with a lower-cost issue if the present value of the after-tax interest savings over the life of the issue exceeds the present value of cash outflows at the time of refunding. The cash outflows consist primarily of the call (option) premium and issuance costs of the new debt issue.

■ QUESTIONS AND TOPICS FOR DISCUSSION

1. What is *bond refunding*? At what relative level of interest rates is bond refunding most likely to occur? Explain.

■ SELF-TEST PROBLEM

ST1. The Warren Electric Company is considering refunding its $150 million, 12 percent debt issue with a 10 percent, 20-year debt issue. The existing (old) issue also matures in 20 years and now is callable at 105 percent of par. The unamortized issuance cost on the old issue is $600,000, and the issuance cost of the new issue is 0.4 percent. Both the new and old debt issues will be outstanding for 4 weeks, resulting in overlapping interest. Warren Electric's weighted cost of capital is 10 percent and its marginal tax rate is 40 percent. The company's treasurer feels that the decline in interest rates has bottomed out. Determine the net present value of refunding the old bond issue.

■ PROBLEMS

eXcel   1. The Springfield Gas and Electric Company is considering refunding $50 million of 11 percent debt with an 8 percent, 20-year debt issue. The existing, or old, issue also matures in 20 years and now is callable at 108 percent of par. The unamortized issuance cost on the old issue is $400,000, and the issuance cost of the new issue is 0.875 percent. The company estimates that both issues will be outstanding for 4 weeks, resulting in overlapping interest. The company has a weighted cost of capital of 10 percent and a 40 percent marginal tax rate. In addition, the company's financial management feels as though the present interest rate decline has nearly bottomed out. Calculate the net present value of the refunding and make a recommendation to management on whether to refund the bonds. (Note: $PVIFA_{0.048,20}$ can be determined using Equation 4.21 from Chapter 4.)

eXcel   2. The Phillipsburg Power Company is considering refunding its $250 million, 11.5 percent debt issue with a 10 percent, 15-year debt issue. The existing (old) issue also matures in 15 years and now is callable at 103.5 percent of par. The unamortized issuance cost on the old issue is $937,500, and the issuance cost of the new issue is 0.5 percent. Both the new and old debt issues will be outstanding for 3 weeks, resulting in overlapping interest. Phillipsburg's weighted cost of capital is 10 percent, and its marginal tax rate is 40 percent. The company's chief financial officer feels that the decline in interest rates has bottomed out. Determine the net present value of refunding the old bond issue.

eXcel   3. The Altoona Electric Company is considering refunding its $200 million, 12.5 percent debt issue with a 10 percent, 10-year debt issue. The existing (old) issue also matures in 10 years and now is callable at 104 percent of par. The unamortized issuance cost on the old issue is $666,667, and the issuance cost of the new issue is 0.4 percent. Both the new and old debt issues will be outstanding for 4 weeks, resulting in overlapping interest. Altoona Electric's weighted cost of capital is 10 percent, and its marginal tax rate is 40 percent. The company's treasurer feels that the decline in interest rates has bottomed out. Determine the net present value of refunding the old bond issue.

■ SOLUTION TO SELF-TEST PROBLEM

ST1. *Step 1*: Interest savings (cash inflow)

Annual interest, after tax = Issue size × Interest rate × (1 – Tax rate)

Annual interest, old issue = $150 million × 12% × (1 – 0.40) = $10,800,000

Annual interest, new issue = $150 million × 10% × (1 – 0.40) = $\underline{\$\ 9,000,000}$

Annual after-tax interest savings $ 1,800,000

Present value of interest savings = Annual after-tax interest savings × $PVIFA_{0.06,20}$

$$= \$1,800,000 \times 11.470 = \$20,646,000$$

Step 2: Calculate the net investment

Call premium, after-tax = $150 million × (0.05) (1 – 0.40)

$$= \$4,500,000$$

Present value of issuance cost of new issue = Issuance cost – Present value tax effect

$$= \$600,000 - \left(\frac{\$600,000}{20} \times 0.40 \times 11.470 \right)$$

$$= \$462,360$$

Present value of issuance cost of old issue = Present value, lost benefits, old issuance cost, after tax – Present value, write-off of old issuance cost, after tax

$$= \left(\frac{\$600,000}{20} \times 0.40 \times 11.470 \right) - (\$600,000 \times 0.40)$$

$$= -\$102,360$$

Overlapping interest = Annual interest rate of old issue, after tax × Fraction of year both issues outstanding

$$= \$150 \text{ million} \times (0.12)(1 - 0.40) \left(\frac{4}{52} \right)$$

$$= \$830,769$$

In summary

Call premium	$4,500,000
Present value of issuance cost, new issue	462,360
Present value of issuance cost, old issue	–102,360
Overlapping interest	830,769
Net investment (cash outflow)	$5,690,769

Step 3: Calculate NPV

NPV of refunding = Present value, interest savings – Present value, net investment

$$= \$20,646,000 - \$5,690,769$$

$$= \$14,955,231$$

COMMON STOCK: CHARACTERISTICS, VALUATION, AND ISSUANCE

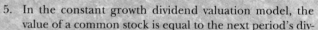

1. The characteristics of variable income (common stock) securities include
   a. Accounting aspects.
   b. Stockholder rights.
   c. Features.
   d. Advantages and disadvantages.
2. Investment bankers provide a number of important services within the operation of the capital markets.
3. Methods of selling securities in the primary capital markets include
   a. Public cash offering.
   b. Direct placement.
   c. Rights offering to shareholders.
4. In the general dividend valuation model, the value of a common stock is equal to the present value of all future dividend payments discounted at the investor's required rate of return.

KEY CHAPTER CONCEPTS

5. In the constant growth dividend valuation model, the value of a common stock is equal to the next period's dividend divided by the difference between the investor's required rate of return and the dividend growth rate.
6. A zero growth dividend valuation model can be used when a firm's future dividend payments are expected to remain constant forever, as in a perpetuity.
7. A nonconstant growth dividend valuation model uses the present value of yearly dividends plus the present value of the expected stock price at the end of the period of nonconstant growth.
8. The valuation of small firm stock requires an explicit consideration of the marketability of that stock, whether the stock represents minority or majority ownership, and whether the stock is voting or nonvoting.

BOSTON CHICKEN'S INITIAL PUBLIC OFFERING

In the mid-1980s, Scott Beck helped to guide the small movie-rental company, Blockbuster Video, into a position as a powerful and profitable national chain. In 1989, Blockbuster purchased Beck's limited partnership units in Blockbuster for $120 million. In 1991, Beck and two other partners invested $27 million to gain control of Boston Chicken, a small franchise operation that roasts its chickens whole on a rotisserie. Sales of Boston Chicken were estimated to be $44 million in 1993. Profits were expected to total $2 million in 1993. (Actual 1993 sales were $42.5 million and profit was $1.6 million, or 13 cents a share.)

In late 1993, Boston Chicken's management approached Merrill Lynch about underwriting a public offering of the stock in order to raise capital to support an aggressive expansion strategy. As the underwriter of the offering, Merrill Lynch's investment bankers faced the challenge of establishing a fair price for the stock. If the price they set was too high, Merrill Lynch would be unable to sell the 1.9 million shares planned for the offering, leaving it stuck either with the shares or with losses when it attempted to sell the shares at a lower market-determined price. On the other hand, if the price was set too low, Boston Chicken's managers would be giving up control of a greater percentage of the company than necessary in order to raise a fixed amount of capital.

The pricing of initial public stock offerings (IPOs) is a difficult task, because an underwriter often has no direct market evidence regarding the value of the shares to be sold. In Boston Chicken's case, the past performance of the company was unspectacular.

Sales in 1991 were $5.2 million, with a loss of $2.6 million. In 1991, the company owned only five stores and franchised 29 others. In 1992, sales reached $8.3 million and the company's losses expanded to $5.9 million. A total of 19 company-owned stores were in operation and there were 64 franchised outlets. This past record of performance, the market valuation of other rapidly growing companies, and the record of Beck while at Blockbuster, were important pieces of evidence available to Merrill Lynch when establishing a valuation

for the Boston Chicken shares. As in other public offerings, Merrill Lynch prepared a preliminary prospectus of the company (often called a "red herring" prospectus) that was distributed through various brokerage houses to potential investors in the Boston Chicken shares. On the basis of estimated retail demand and the factors discussed above, Merrill Lynch set the price for the new offering at $20 per share.

On November 9, 1993, the public offering was made. With the new shares priced to investors at $20 by Merrill Lynch, the demand far exceeded the available supply. The opening price of the stock among NASDAQ traders was $45. The stock traded as high as $51 on the opening day, and closed at $48. Many in the investment community were incredulous, saying "I'd say Wall Street flew the coop," and "I wouldn't touch it with a 10-foot rotisserie spit."[1] In early February 1994, however, the stock continued to trade at around $48 per share. Adjusted for a two-for-one stock split, the stock traded at $76 per share in early 1997, or about 33 times earnings per share.

In one sense, this IPO was a rousing success. Merrill Lynch successfully sold all of the shares being offered. Boston Chicken received the funds needed for expansion. However, from the perspective of the efficiency of raising capital for Boston Chicken's initial owners, this IPO was a disaster. Merrill Lynch had underestimated demand, forcing the company to sell to the public more than twice as many shares as would have been necessary if the initial offering value had been closer to the value established in the marketplace shortly after the IPO. Indeed, if the offering had been priced closer to its "true" value and the same number of shares had been sold, Boston Chicken would have been able to defer a $130 million convertible note offering that was made in early 1994. When asked about their pricing of the issue, Merrill Lynch declined comment except to say that there was "strong demand in the aftermarket."

As this example illustrates, the valuation of common stocks is a challenging undertaking, even for professionals like the investment bankers at Merrill Lynch. The principles and methods used in the valuation of common stocks are discussed in this chapter.

[1]"Boston Chicken Soars by 143% on its IPO Day," *Wall Street Journal* (November 10, 1993): C1.

INTRODUCTION

Unlike long-term debt and preferred stock, which are normally fixed-income securities, common stock is a variable-income security. Common stockholders are said to participate in a firm's earnings, because they may receive a larger dividend if earnings increase in the future or their dividends may be cut if earnings drop. For example, in 1974, Tucson Electric Power Company sold new common stock when annual dividends were $0.84 per share. By 1989, the annual rate was $3.90 per share, having been raised several times during the intervening years. However, during 1990, the company suffered substantial losses and cut its dividend to zero. Its common stock price dropped from about $65 a share in 1986 and 1987 to $3⅞ a share by early 1994. In 1996 the stock had a 1 for 5 reverse stock split and the stock traded at $16⅝ in early 1997.

Common stock also differs from long-term debt and preferred stock in that the market price tends to fluctuate more than the price of bonds and preferred stock, thus causing returns on common stock investments to vary more widely over time than returns on long-term debt or preferred stock.

This chapter describes the characteristics of common stock. The process by which securities are offered for sale and the role of the investment banker in this process are discussed. Finally, valuation models for common stock are developed.

Understanding Stock Quotations

Table 7-1 shows selected stock quotations for stocks traded on the New York Stock Exchange. Beginning at the left-hand side, the first two columns show the stock's price range during the previous 52 weeks. For example, the per-share price of E. I. du Pont de Nemours & Company common stock ranged between $70⅛ and $109¾. The column immediately to the right of the stock name shows the ticker symbol used to identify this stock on the exchange's ticker tape, DD for du Pont. The next column shows the current annual dividend rate; for example, the du Pont Company's current annual dividend rate is $2.28 per share of common stock. Dividends are normally paid in four quarterly install-ments throughout the year. The next column shows the dividend (percentage) yield. For du Pont the figure is 2.0 (calculated as the annual dividend divided by the closing price, or $2.28/$111⅝ = 2.0%).

The price-to-earnings or P/E ratio (the closing price divided by the sum of the latest four quarters of earnings per share) is shown next. The P/E ratio (18) indicates how much investors are willing to pay for $1 of current earnings from the firm. Generally, the greater the risk of the firm, the lower will be its P/E multiple. Similarly, the P/E ratio will tend to be higher the more rapid the

TABLE 7-1
Selected Stock Quotations from the New York Stock Exchange

Source: *Wall Street Journal* (January 20, 1997).

52 WEEKS		STOCK	SYM	DIV	YLD %	PE	VOL 100S	HI	LO	CLOSE	NET CHG
HI	LO										
109¾	70⅛	DuPont	DD	2.28	2.0	18	29428	112⅝	108⅝	111⅝	+2⅞
60¼	51⅝	DuPont	pfA	3.50	6.4	...	2	55	55	55	–½
76	65	DuPont	pfB	4.50	6.3	...	2	72	71½	72	+1

expected growth rate in future earnings. The next figure is the sales volume in hundreds of shares; on this day, 2,942,800 shares of du Pont common stock were traded. The next three columns list the high, low, and closing prices for the day. The final column shows the net change in price per share for the day, or the difference between this day's closing price and the closing price on the previous business day (or the last day on which a trade took place). For the day, the common stock of du Pont gained $2⅞ per share.

When a company has preferred stock outstanding that is also traded on a securities exchange, the different classes of preferred stocks will be listed below the common stock. As can be seen in Table 7-1, du Pont has one preferred stock issue (A) outstanding that pays a dividend of $3.50 per share and another issue (B) that pays $4.50. Unlike common stock dividends, the preferred stock dividend rate normally will not change over the time the issue is outstanding.

CHARACTERISTICS OF COMMON STOCK

A firm's common stockholders are its true owners. Common stock is a *residual form of ownership* in that the claims of common stockholders on the firm's earnings and assets are considered only *after* the claims of governments, debt holders, and preferred stockholders have been met. Common stock is considered a *permanent* form of long-term financing, because, unlike debt and some preferred stock, common stock has no maturity date.

The American Association of Individual Investors will help you obtain all the information you need to make good investing decisions. It's a good lifetime resource for your investing needs.
http://www.aaii.com

Common Stock and Accounting

Common stock appears on the right-hand side of a firm's balance sheet as part of the stockholder's equity. This is shown for the Lawrence Company in Table 7-2.

Stockholders' equity includes both preferred stock (if any exists) and common stock. The total equity attributable to the common stock of the Lawrence Company is equal to the total stockholders' equity less the preferred stock:

$$\$117,820,000 - \$37,500,000 = \$80,320,000$$

In other words, the sum of the common stock account, contributed capital in excess of par value account, and retained earnings account equals the total common stockholders' equity.

TABLE 7-2
Lawrence Company Stockholders' Equity, December 31, 19X5 (in thousands of dollars)

STOCKHOLDERS' EQUITY	
Preferred stock; $25 par value; authorized, 2,000,000 shares; issued and outstanding, 1,500,000 shares	$37,500
Common stock; $2 par value; authorized, 10,000,000 shares; issued and outstanding, 6,675,000 shares	13,350
Contributed capital in excess of par value*	28,713
Retained earnings	38,257
Total stockholders' equity	$117,820

*The *contributed capital in excess of par* account has several other frequently used names, including *capital surplus* and *additional paid-in capital*. Many accountants feel that the expression *capital surplus* is misleading, because it incorrectly implies that a firm has excess capital.

The **book value per share** of common stock is calculated as follows:

$$\text{Book value per share} = \frac{\text{Total common stockholders' equity}}{\text{Number of shares outstanding}} \quad (7.1)$$

In the case of the Lawrence Company,

$$\text{Book value per share} = \frac{\$80,320,000}{6,675,000}$$

$$= \$12.03$$

A common stock's book value is calculated on the basis of balance sheet figures and does not necessarily have any relationship to the common stock's *market value*, which is based primarily on expectations concerning general economic conditions and the firm's future earnings.

The amount shown in the common stock account is calculated by multiplying the number of shares actually outstanding by the **par value,** an arbitrary value assigned to shares of common stock.[2] To continue with this example, the Lawrence Company has 6.675 million shares outstanding and a $2 par value, resulting in a balance of $13.35 million.

To illustrate the nature of the contributed capital in excess of par value account, suppose Lawrence decides to raise an additional $12 million in external equity capital by selling 600,000 common shares at $20 each. The amount credited to the common stock account is $1.2 million (600,000 shares times the $2 par value). The remainder of the $12 million is added to the contributed capital in excess of par value account. In other words, this account represents capital that is paid into the firm in excess of the par value when common stock is issued.

Additions to the retained earnings account occur as a result of earnings retained in the business, as opposed to earnings paid out to the stockholders as dividends. Retained earnings, which are internally generated funds, are one of the most important sources of capital for business.

Stockholder Rights

Common stockholders have a number of general rights, including the following:

- **Dividend rights.** Stockholders have the right to share equally on a per-share basis in any distribution of corporate earnings in the form of dividends.
- **Asset rights.** In the event of a liquidation, stockholders have the right to assets that remain after the obligations to the government (taxes), employees, and debtholders have been satisfied.
- **Preemptive rights.** Stockholders may have the right to share proportionately in any new stock sold. For example, a stockholder who owns 20 percent of a corporation's stock may be entitled to purchase 20 percent of any new issue.
- **Voting rights.** Stockholders have the right to vote on stockholder matters, such as the selection of the board of directors.

[2]At one time, par value was considered important for any possible liquidation proceedings, but today it has little, if any, real significance. Par value is normally a low figure and tends to be less than $5 per share. Occasionally, companies issue stock with no par value. In these instances, the balance in the common stock account is a "stated value."

Whereas all stockholders have dividend and liquidation rights, in addition to voting rights (unless the stock is specifically nonvoting), preemptive rights exist in a relatively small minority of firms at the present time. (Preemptive rights are discussed in detail in Chapter 20.)

Stockholder Voting Rights. A firm's stockholders elect its board of directors by means of either a *majority* or a *cumulative* voting procedure. Majority voting is similar to the voting that takes place in political elections; namely, if two slates of people are running for the board, the one that receives more than 50 percent of the votes wins. With majority voting, it is possible that a group of stockholders with a minority viewpoint will have no representation on the board.

Cumulative voting, in contrast, makes it easier for stockholders with minority views to elect sympathetic board members. Because of this, cumulative voting is rare among major corporations and is frequently opposed by management. For example, in response to a shareholder proposal to adopt cumulative voting, General Mills' management recommended a vote against the proposal, arguing that it would result in dysfunctional partisanship on the board. In **cumulative voting**, each share of stock represents as many votes as there are directors to be elected. For example, if a firm is electing seven directors, a particular holder of 100 shares would have 700 votes and could cast all of them for *one* candidate, thereby increasing that candidate's chances for being elected to the board. The following formula can be used to determine the number of shares necessary to elect a certain number of directors:

$$\text{Number of shares} = \frac{\text{Number of directors desired} \times \text{Number of shares outstanding}}{\text{Number of directors being elected} + 1} + 1 \qquad (7.2)$$

Of course, it is possible that not all the shareholders will vote their shares. In this case, the calculation is based on the number of shares actually voting rather than the number of shares outstanding.

Consider the following example. The Markham Company has eleven members on its board and 1 million shares of common stock outstanding. If seven members were up for reelection in a given year and all the shares were voted, the number of shares necessary to elect one director would be as follows:

$$\frac{1 \times 1,000,000}{7 + 1} + 1 = 125,001$$

In addition to electing the board of directors, a firm's stockholders may vote from time to time on various other matters, such as whether to retain a particular auditing firm or increase the number of shares authorized.

The election of directors and other voting normally occurs at the annual stockholders' meeting. Because it usually is not possible for all stockholders to attend, management—or anyone else—can solicit votes by *proxy.* Normally, a stockholder can expect to receive a single proxy statement from the firm's management requesting that stockholders follow management's recommendations. In the rather unlikely event that another group of stockholders sends out its own proxy statement, a *proxy fight* is said to occur. Proxy fights are most common when a company is performing poorly.

Stockholders often are asked to vote (either directly or by tendering, i.e., offering, their shares to competing parties) in a takeover battle. For example, in late 1993 and early 1994, QVC and Viacom were locked in a battle for control of Paramount Communications, and shareholders were asked to choose between the competing bids.

Other Features of Common Stock

This section covers other topics related to the ownership of common stock, including *common stock classes, stock splits, stock dividends,* and *stock repurchases.*

Common Stock Classes. Occasionally, a firm may decide to create more than one class of common stock. The reason for this may be that the firm wishes to raise additional equity capital by selling a portion of the existing owners' stock while maintaining control of the firm. This can be accomplished by creating a separate class of *nonvoting stock.* Typically so-called Class A common stock is nonvoting, whereas Class B has voting rights; normally, the classes are otherwise equal. The Ford Motor Company is an example of a large, widely held company that has more than one class of common stock. Ford's 37.7 million shares of "Class B stock" are held entirely by Ford family interests. This class has 40 percent of the total voting power. Ford's 469.8 million shares of "common stock" are held by the public and have 60 percent of the total voting power. The two classes are otherwise equal. In recent years, General Motors has had two classes of common stock, its regular common stock and its "H" class, which it used in the acquisition of Hughes Aircraft Company.

Stock Splits. If management feels that the firm's common stock should sell at a lower price to attract more purchasers, it can effect a **stock split.** There seems to be a feeling among some in the finance community that the optimum price range for a share of common stock should be roughly $15 to $60. Consequently, if a stock rises above this range, management may decide on a stock split to get the price back to a more desirable trading level.

For example, the per-share price of Colgate-Palmolive common stock rose to the $150 range in early 1997, at which time the board of directors declared a two-for-one stock split.

Frequently companies choose to raise their dividend levels at the time of a split. At the time IBM announced its split, many analysts forecasted an increase in IBM's dividend to coincide with the effective date of the stock split.

Many investors believe stock splits are an indication of good financial health. The mere splitting of a stock, however, should not be taken in and of itself as evidence that the stock will necessarily perform well in the future.

From an accounting standpoint, when a stock is split, its par value is changed accordingly. For example, when the split is two for one, the par value is reduced by one-half, and the number of shares is doubled. No changes occur in the firm's account balances or capital structure.

Reverse Stock Splits. Reverse stock splits are stock splits in which the number of shares is decreased. They are used to bring low-priced shares up to more desirable trading levels. For example, in mid-1996 Tucson Electric Power Corporation, the troubled electric utility, declared a 1-for-5 reverse stock split. After the split, Tucson's stock traded in the range of $16 per share. In addition to the negative image accorded low-priced stocks, Tucson's management was concerned that potential investors would be unwilling to buy the stock due to the higher (percentage-wise) commissions on low-priced stocks.

Many investors feel reverse stock splits indicate poor corporate health. For this reason, such splits are relatively uncommon.

Stock Dividends. A **stock dividend** is a dividend to stockholders that consists of additional shares of stock instead of cash. Normally, stock dividends are in the 2 to 10 percent range—that is, the number of shares outstanding is increased by 2 to 10 percent. From an accounting (but not a cash flow) standpoint, stock dividends involve a transfer from the retained earnings account to the common stock and additional paid-in capital accounts.[3]

Stock Repurchases. From time to time, companies repurchase some of their own shares (known as **treasury stock**). Figure 7-1 contains an announcement of such a share repurchase by TRW. In addition to undertaking share repurchases as an alternative to the payment of cash dividends, which is discussed in Chapter 14, a company may have a number of other reasons for repurchasing its own stock. These include

■ **Disposition of excess cash.** The company may want to dispose of excess cash that it has accumulated from operations or the sale of assets. These funds are expendable because management may not feel that they can be invested profitably within the company in the foreseeable future.

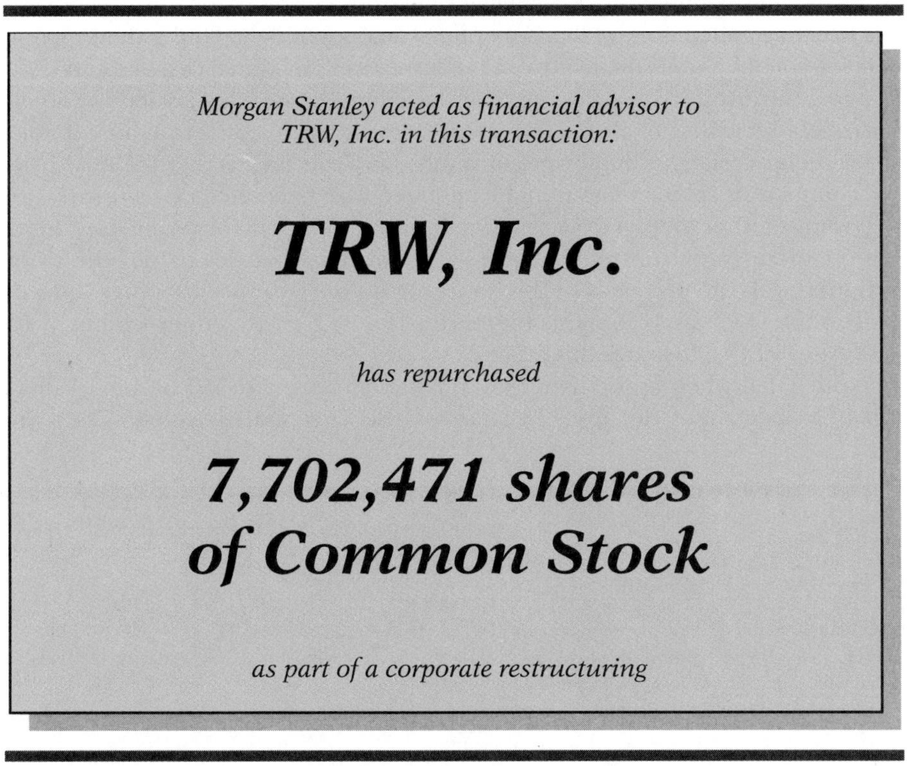

FIGURE 7-1
Share Repurchase Announcement

Morgan Stanley acted as financial advisor to TRW, Inc. in this transaction:

TRW, Inc.

has repurchased

7,702,471 shares of Common Stock

as part of a corporate restructuring

---

[3]Chapter 14 contains a more detailed discussion of stock dividends.

■ **Financial restructuring.** By issuing debt and using the proceeds to repurchase its common stock, the firm can alter its capital structure to gain the benefits of increased financial leverage.

■ **Future corporate needs.** Stock can be repurchased for use in future acquisitions of other companies, stock option plans for executives, conversion of convertible securities, and the exercise of warrants.[4]

■ **Reduction of takeover risk.** Share repurchases can be used to increase the price of a firm's stock and reduce a firm's cash balance (or increase its debt proportion in the capital structure) and thereby reduce returns to investors who might be considering an acquisition of the firm.

These reasons are not mutually exclusive—a firm may repurchase shares for a combination of reasons.

Advantages and Disadvantages of Common Stock Financing

One of the major advantages of common stock financing is that no fixed-dividend obligation exists, at least in principle. In practice, however, dividend cuts are relatively uncommon for companies paying a "regular" dividend, a fact that implies that corporate management generally views a firm's current level of dividends as a minimum for the future.[5] Nevertheless, common stock financing does allow firms a greater degree of flexibility in their financing plans than fixed-income securities. Thus, common stock is less risky to the firm than fixed-income securities. Limits on additional debt and the maintenance of working capital levels are only two of the constraints imposed on a firm when fixed-income security financing is employed.

In addition, common stock financing can be advantageous for a firm whose capital structure contains more than an optimal amount of debt. Under these circumstances, common stock financing can lower the firm's weighted cost of capital.[6]

From the investors' perspective, however, common stock is a riskier investment than debt securities or preferred stock. Because of this, investors in common stock require relatively high rates of return, and this means that the firm's cost for common stock financing is high compared with fixed-income securities.

From another perspective, external common stock financing frequently results in an initial dilution of per-share earnings, particularly if the assets acquired with the proceeds of the financing do not produce earnings immediately. Table 7-3, which contains figures for Desert Electric Power Company for 19X6 and 19X5, illustrates this point.

Notice that whereas the firm's net income increased in 19X6 over 19X5, its earnings per share declined because of the new shares issued. Thus, the

TABLE 7-3
Example of Diluted Per-Share Earnings as a Result of Common Stock Financing: Desert Electric Power Company

	YEAR ENDED SEPTEMBER 30	
	19X6	*19X5*
Net income available for common stock	$25,821,000	$20,673,000
Average number of common shares outstanding	15,600,000	12,122,007
Earnings per average share of common stock	$1.66	$1.71

[4]Warrants and convertible securities are examined in Chapter 20.
[5]See Chapter 14 for a discussion of dividend policy.
[6]Chapters 11–13 for a discussion of the measurement of and the effect of capital structure on the firm's weighted cost of capital.

additional issue of common shares can dilute the original owners' claims on the firm's earnings. If, on the other hand, the new assets earn a higher rate of return than the existing assets, the original owners will benefit from the increased earnings. Also, the problem of diluted earnings should be only temporary if the firm is investing wisely and should have no adverse consequences in a well-informed market.

A final disadvantage of external equity financing involves the relatively high issuance costs associated with common stock sold to the public.[7]

THE SECURITY OFFERING PROCESS: ROLE OF THE INVESTMENT BANKER

Investment bankers are financial middlemen who bring together suppliers and users of long-term funds in the capital markets and thereby play a key role in the security offering process. Whenever a large corporation is considering raising funds in the capital markets, it almost always enlists the services of an investment banker. In fact, most large industrial corporations have ongoing relationships with their investment bankers.

Investment bankers assist client corporations in the offering process in a variety of ways, including the following:

- Long-range financial planning.
- The timing of security issues.
- The purchase of securities.
- The marketing of securities.
- The arrangement of private loans and leases.
- The negotiation of mergers.

In summary, the investment banker is an important source of financial market expertise and an important part of the security offering process.

How Securities Are Sold

Firms can sell securities in the primary capital markets in one of three ways:

- By selling securities through investment bankers to the public in a *public cash offering.*
- By placing a debt or stock issue with one or more large investors in a *private,* or *direct, placement.*
- By selling common stock to existing stockholders through a *rights offering.*

Investment bankers usually assist firms in all three methods of sale. Figure 7-2 is a flowchart that outlines the various methods and steps for the sale of corporate securities.

Public Cash Offerings. Normally, when a corporation wishes to issue new securities and sell them to the public, it makes an arrangement with an investment banker whereby the investment banker agrees to purchase the entire issue at a set price. This is called a firm commitment **underwriting.** The investment banker then resells the issue to the public at a higher price.

Founded by the folks at Spring Street Brewery, WitCapital is a New York City start-up company that first persuaded the SEC to allow an Internet IPO. It has since grown into a very active cyber investment bank.
http://www.witcap.com

Capital Markets, Inc., is a good example of the newly emerging cybercompanies, which exist almost entirely in cyberspace. Capital Markets' specialty niche is IPOs. Virtually anything you want to know about IPOs is available at their Web site, including how to do a complete IPO over the Internet. (The first Internet IPO was by Spring Street Brewery, which makes a pretty good beer.)
http://capmarkets.com/index.html

---

[7]Issuance costs for various sources of capital are discussed in the following sections of this chapter.

FIGURE 7-2
How Securities Are Sold:
A Flowchart

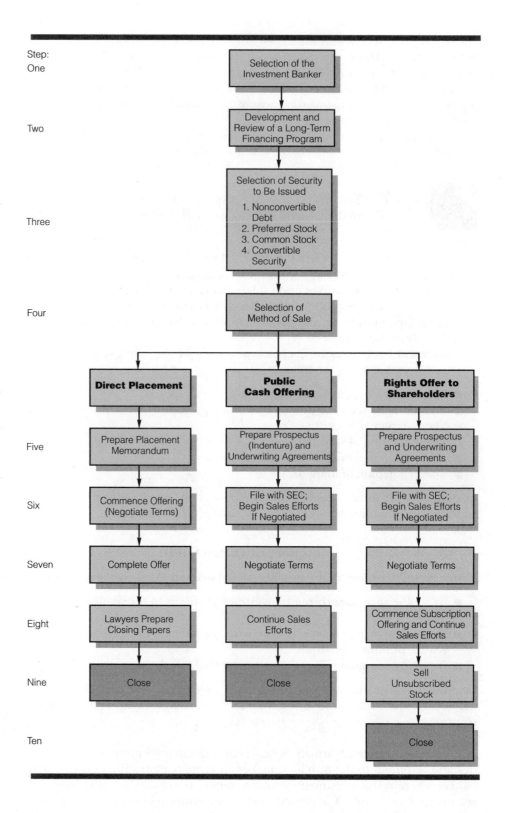

Underwriting can be accomplished either through *negotiations* between the underwriter and the issuing company or by *competitive bidding*. A **negotiated underwriting** is simply an arrangement between the issuing firm and its investment bankers. Most large industrial corporations turn to investment bankers with whom they have had ongoing relationships. In competitive bidding, the firm sells the securities to the underwriter (usually a group) that bids the highest price. Many regulated companies, such as utilities and railroads, are required by their regulatory commissions (for example, the Federal Energy Regulatory Commission, the Interstate Commerce Commission, and state regulatory bodies) to sell new security issues in this way.

Security issues sold to the public through underwriters normally exceed $25 million in size; amounts totaling $250 million are not uncommon. Due to the size of these issues, individual investment bankers usually do not want to underwrite an entire issue by themselves. Normally, a group of underwriters, called a *purchasing syndicate,* agrees to underwrite the issue in order to spread the risk.[8] Sometimes the purchasing syndicate can sell an entire issue to large institutional investors;[9] this often is true with high-quality debt issues. On other occasions—particularly with large debt issues or equity issues—the underwriters organize a *selling group* of security firms to market the issue to the public. It is not uncommon for a selling group responsible for marketing a large issue to number over 100 security firms. Figure 2-2 in Chapter 2 shows the underwriting syndicate for a Panhandle Eastern Corporation common stock offering.

An important part of the negotiations between the issuing firm and the investment banker is the determination of the security's selling price. It is in the best interests of both the issuing firm and the underwriter to have the security "fairly priced." If the security is underpriced, the issuing firm will not raise the amount of capital it could have, and the underwriter may lose a customer. If the security is overpriced, the underwriter may have difficulty selling the issue, and investors who discover that they paid too much may choose not to purchase the next issue offered by either the corporation or the underwriter.

Occasionally, with smaller company issues, the investment banker agrees to help market the issue on a "best efforts" basis rather than underwriting it. Under this type of arrangement, the investment banker has no further obligation to the issuing company if some of the securities cannot be sold. The investment banker functions as a *dealer* in an underwriting situation and as a *broker* in a best-efforts situation. In a best-efforts offering, the investment banker does not assume the risk that the securities will not be sold at a favorable price.

Private Placements. Many industrial companies choose to *directly,* or *privately, place* debt or preferred stock issues with one or more institutional investors instead of having them underwritten and sold to the public. In these cases, investment bankers who act on behalf of the issuing company receive a "finder's fee" for finding a buyer and negotiating the terms of the agreement. The private market is an important source of long-term debt capital, especially for smaller corporations.

---

[8]In most cases, one to three underwriters agree to manage an issue, handling all legal matters, advertising, and so on. These firms are the *managing underwriters.*

[9]Institutional investors include life insurance companies, pension funds, mutual funds, and commercial banks.

Private security placements have a number of advantages:

■ They can save on flotation costs by eliminating underwriting costs.
■ They can avoid the time delays associated with the preparation of registration statements and with the waiting period.
■ They can offer greater flexibility in the writing of the terms of the contract (called the *indenture*) between the borrower and the lender.

An offsetting disadvantage is that, as a very general rule, interest rates for private placements are about one-eighth of a percentage point *higher* than they are for debt and preferred issues sold through underwriters. For small-sized debt and preferred stock issues—that is, those that are less than about $20 million—the percentage cost of underwriting becomes fairly large. Because of this, these smaller-sized issues frequently are placed privately with institutional investors.

Rights Offerings and Standby Underwritings. Firms may sell their common stock directly to their existing stockholders through the issuance of **rights,** which entitle the stockholders to purchase new shares of the firm's stock at a *subscription price* below the market price. (**Rights offerings** also are called *privileged subscriptions*.) Each stockholder receives one right for each share owned; in other words, if a firm has 100 million shares outstanding and wishes to sell an additional 10 million shares through a rights offering, each right entitles the holder to purchase 0.1 shares, and it takes 10 rights to purchase 1 share.[10]

When selling stock through a rights offering, firms usually enlist the services of investment bankers, who urge rights holders to purchase the stock. In an arrangement called a *standby underwriting*, the investment banker agrees to purchase—at the subscription price—any shares that are not sold to rights holders. The investment banker then resells the shares. In a standby underwriting, the investment banker bears risk and is compensated by an underwriting fee.

Rights offerings have declined in popularity as a method of raising equity capital in the United States. However, in Britain, rights offerings are more common. In October 1992, British Aerospace attempted an underwritten rights offering totaling $732 million (£432 million). The offering price was 380 pence per share. Unfortunately, the price of British Aerospace stock declined to 363 pence during the period of the offering and only a small portion (4.9%) of the offering was purchased by rights holders. The underwriters were forced to take large losses on the offering when they were stuck with the balance of the issue.[11]

Direct Issuance Costs. An investment banker who agrees to underwrite a security issue assumes a certain amount of risk and, in turn, requires compensation in the form of an *underwriting discount* or **underwriting spread,** computed as follows:

$$\text{Underwriting spread} = \text{Selling price to public} - \text{Proceeds to company} \quad (7.3)$$

Examples of underwriting spread amounts are shown in Table 7-4.

---

[10]Rights and rights offerings are discussed in greater detail in Chapter 20.
[11]"British Aerospace Lesson: How Not to Sell Issues," *Wall Street Journal* (October 30, 1992): C1.

It is difficult to compare underwriting spreads for negotiated and competitive offerings, because rarely are two offerings brought to market at the same time that differ only in the ways in which they are underwritten. Generally, underwriters receive lower spreads for competitively bid utility issues than for negotiated industrial offers. This is primarily because utilities have tended to have a lower level of risk than industrial companies.

In addition to the underwriting spread, other direct costs of security offerings include legal and accounting fees, taxes, the cost of registration with the Securities and Exchange Commission, and printing costs. For small equity offerings of less than $10 million, these direct costs may exceed 10 percent of the gross proceeds from the offering, on average. For offerings with gross proceeds in the $20 million to $50 million range, direct costs averaged slightly less than 5 percent of gross proceeds. For large equity offerings (greater than $200 million), the direct issuance costs have averaged about 3.3 percent of gross proceeds.[12] A recent offering of 1.35 million shares of common equity by Service Corporation International had an underwriting spread of $2,160,000 and other direct issue expenses of $280,564. Direct costs of underwritten debt offerings are much lower than direct equity issuance costs, often ranging from 0.5 percent to 4.0 percent.

Generally, direct issuance costs are higher for common stock than for preferred stock issues, and direct issuance costs of preferred stock are higher than those of debt issues. One reason for this is the amount of risk each type of issue involves. Common stocks usually involve more risk for underwriters than preferred stock, and preferred stock involves more risk than debt. Stock prices are subject to wider price movements than debt prices. Another reason for these differences in direct issuance costs is that investment bankers usually incur greater marketing expenses for common stock than for preferred stock or debt issues. Common stock is customarily sold to a large number of individual investors, whereas debt securities frequently are purchased by a much smaller number of institutional investors.

TABLE 7-4
Sample Underwriting Spreads for Selected Issues

COMPANY	ISSUE SIZE (IN MILLIONS OF DOLLARS)	UNDER-WRITING SPREAD (%)	S&P RATING*
Debt Issues			
First Interstate Bancorp.	$100	0.63	AA
CIGNA Corporation[†]	100	1.00	AA
Corning Glass Works[†]	100	1.00	A
U.S. Leasing International[†]	30	2.00	BBB
Jerrico, Inc.	40	1.88	BB
Petro-Lewis	85	3.35	B
Sunshine Mining Company	30	3.68	B
Common Stock Issues			
El Paso Electric Company	$57.5	3.26	
Ryder System, Inc.	83.4	3.88	
Southwest Airlines	34.7	3.89	
Service Corporation International	48.26	4.48	
Adage, Inc.	10.0	6.26	
Atlantic Southeast Airlines	5.2	8.00	

*Standard and Poor's (S&P) bond-rating scale is AAA (for the highest quality issues), AA, A, BBB, BB, B, CCC, CC, C.
[†]Convertible issues.

[12]Robert Hansen, "Evaluating the Costs of a New Equity Issue," *Midland Corporate Finance Journal* (Spring 1986): 42–55.

Direct issuance costs also depend on the quality of the issue. Low-quality debt issues, for example, tend to have higher percentage direct issuance costs than high-quality issues, because underwriters bear more risk with low-quality issues and therefore require greater compensation. And, finally, direct issuance costs are dependent on the size of the issue—costs tend to be a higher percentage of small-sized issues, all other things being equal, because underwriters have various fixed expenses (such as advertising expenses, legal fees, registration statement costs, and so on) that are incurred regardless of the issue's size.

Other Issuance Costs. In addition to direct costs, there are significant other costs associated with new security offerings, including

1. The *cost of management time* in preparing the offering.
2. The *cost of underpricing* a new (initial) equity offering below the correct market value. Underpricing occurs because of the uncertainty associated with the value of initial public offerings and a desire to ensure that the offering is a success. For example, the initial public offering for Duracell, the well-known battery manufacturer, was priced at $15. After the first day of trading it closed at $20¾, or a gain of 38.3%. Examples such as this and Boston Chicken, discussed earlier, are extreme, although not uncommon examples of the underpricing associated with many initial public offerings.
3. The *cost of stock price declines* for stock offerings by firms whose shares are already outstanding—so-called *seasoned* offerings. The announcement of new stock issues by a firm whose shares are already outstanding causes a price decline averaging about 3 percent for the outstanding shares.
4. The *cost of other incentives* provided to the investment banker, including the overallotment or "Green Shoe" option. This option, often contained in underwriting contracts, gives the investment bankers the right to buy up to 15 percent more new shares than the initial offering amount at a price equal to the offering price. The option is designed to allow investment bankers to handle oversubscriptions. This option normally lasts for 30 days.

These indirect costs can, in aggregate, constitute a very significant expense associated with security offerings (especially for common equity). Ritter has estimated that the sum of direct issue costs and underpricing for new equity offerings averages over 31 percent for best efforts offerings and over 21 percent for firm commitment underwritings.[13]

Registration Requirements. The Securities Act of 1933 requires any firm offering *new* securities to the public to make a complete disclosure of all pertinent facts regarding these securities; the Securities Exchange Act of 1934 expanded the coverage to include trading in *existing* securities. The 1934 act also created the Securities and Exchange Commission (SEC), which is responsible for administering the federal securities legislation. These federal laws make no judgments regarding the quality of securities issues; they simply require full disclosure of the facts.[14]

---

[13]See J. R. Ritter, "The Costs of Going Public," *Journal of Financial Economics* (December 1987): 269–281.
[14]In recent years, some states have prohibited the sale of certain securities on the grounds of poor quality rather than any problems associated with the disclosure of information.

Any company that plans to sell an interstate security issue totaling over $1.5 million and having a maturity greater than 270 days is required to register the issue with the SEC.[15] The procedure involves the preparation of a *registration statement* and a *prospectus.* The registration statement contains a vast amount of information about the company's legal, operational, and financial position; the prospectus summarizes the information contained in the registration statement and is intended for the use of potential investors.

After a company has filed a registration statement and prospectus, there normally is a waiting period of 20 days before the SEC approves the issue and the company can begin selling the securities. During the waiting period, the company may use a preliminary prospectus in connection with the anticipated sale of securities. This preliminary prospectus is often called a "red herring" because it contains a statement, usually marked in red, saying that the prospectus is "not an offer to sell." When the registration statement is approved by the SEC, the new securities can be offered formally for sale. All buyers of the new securities must be provided with a final copy of the prospectus.

Shelf Registration. In November 1983, the SEC permanently adopted a new registration option that it had allowed experimentally for the prior one-and-a-half years. Rule 415 permits the *shelf registration* of debt and equity securities. The shelf registration option is available only to larger firms (the market value of outstanding equity must exceed $150 million) with a high (*investment grade*) rating. Under the shelf registration procedure, a firm files a *master registration* statement with the SEC. The company then is free to sell small increments of the offering over an extended time period (two years) merely by filing a brief *short-form statement* with the SEC only hours before the actual offering. By placing its new securities "on the shelf" awaiting an opportune time for issuance, the company has the capability to time their issuance with the specific financing needs of the firm and to take advantage of perceived favorable pricing windows in the market. There is some evidence that the shelf registration procedure is less costly than traditional underwriting for equity offerings.[16] In spite of this apparent cost advantage, shelf registrations of new equity offerings have not been popular.

The New York Stock Exchange has an excellent tutorial on stocks. It truly covers everything: the history of stocks; how stocks are bought and sold; how a stock exchange works; why stock prices "go up and down"; regulation; strategies; lots of pictures; and much more. It also has a comprehensive glossary of financial terms.
http://www.nyse.com/public

INTERNATIONAL ISSUES
GLOBAL EQUITY MARKETS

Large multinational corporations increasingly have been turning to international markets to raise both equity and debt capital. Large, non–U.S.-domiciled corporations may sell equity in the United States because of the size and liquidity of the market for new issues in this country. For example, during 1993 Daimler-Benz, the large German conglomerate best known for its Mercedes-Benz automobiles, offered its equity in the U.S. capital market. By selling its stock in multiple country capital markets, Daimler hopes to reach more potential investors and perhaps realize some capital cost savings.

---

[15]Security issues of the federal government and nonprofit organizations do not have to be registered with the SEC. Bank and railroad issues are also exempt, because these industries are regulated by other government agencies.
[16]S. Bhagat, M. W. Marr, and G. R. Thompson, "The Rule 415 Experiment: Equity Markets," *Journal of Finance* (December 1985): 1385–1401.

By dealing in global equity markets, multinational firms can take advantage of institutional differences from one country to another that may temporarily disadvantage a firm that is limited to selling its shares in a single capital market. Many multinational firms now have their shares trading in the United States, Japan, and Western European markets, such as London and Paris. The existence of these markets permits nearly 24-hour per day trading in the stock of large multinational firms. Around-the-clock trading provides investors with opportunities to buy and sell shares at almost any time they wish. In addition, multinational firms can increase their name and product recognition abroad, to the benefit, it is hoped, of the firm's bottom-line performance.

As a truly global capital market emerges, it is clear that national borders will be less important in determining where, and in what form, capital will be acquired by a firm. Rather, firms can be expected to sell their shares in those markets with the greatest demand (and hence the lowest cost to the firm).

FOUNDATION CONCEPT
VALUATION OF COMMON STOCK

In principle, the valuation of common stock is no different than the valuation of other types of securities, such as bonds and preferred stock. The basic procedure involves capitalizing (that is, discounting) the expected stream of cash flows to be received from holding the common stock. This is complicated by several factors, however.

First, the expected cash flows from holding a common stock take two forms: the cash dividend payments made during the holding period and/or changes in the price of the stock (capital gains or losses) over the holding period. All the cash flows received by the common stockholder are derived from the firm's earnings and can either be paid to shareholders in the current period as cash dividends or reinvested in the firm to (it is hoped) provide higher future dividends and a higher stock price.

Second, because common stock dividends normally are expected to grow rather than remain constant, the relatively simple annuity and perpetuity formulas used in the valuation of bonds and preferred stock generally are not applicable, and more complicated models must be used.

Finally, the expected cash flows from common stock are more uncertain than the cash flows from bonds and preferred stock. Common stock dividend payments are related to the firm's earnings in some manner, and it can be difficult to forecast future long-term earnings and dividend payments with a high degree of accuracy.

To better understand the application of the capitalization of cash flow valuation method to common stock, it is best to begin by considering a *one*-period dividend valuation model and then move on to consider multiple-period valuation models.

One-Period Dividend Valuation Model

Assume that an investor plans to purchase a common stock and hold it for *one* period. At the end of that period, the investor expects to receive a cash dividend, D_1, and sell the stock for a price, P_1. What is the value of this stock to the investor *today* (time 0), given a required rate of return on the investment, k_e?

In the capitalization of cash flow valuation method, the discounted present value of the expected cash flows from the stock is calculated as follows:

$$P_0 = \frac{D_1}{1 + k_e} + \frac{P_1}{1 + k_e} \qquad (7.4)$$

For example, if Ohio Engineering Company common stock is expected to pay a $1.00 dividend and sell for $27.50 at the end of one period, what is the value of this stock to an investor who requires a 14 percent rate of return? The answer is computed as follows:

$$
\begin{aligned}
P_0 &= \frac{\$1.00}{(1 + 0.14)} + \frac{\$27.50}{(1 + 0.14)} \\
&= \$1.00(\text{PVIF}_{0.14,1}) + \$27.50\,(\text{PVIF}_{0.14,1}) \\
&= \$1.00(0.877) + \$27.50(0.877) \\
&= \$24.99 \text{ (or } \$25)
\end{aligned}
$$

Thus, the investor who purchases the stock for $25, collects the $1 dividend, and sells the stock for $27.50 at the end of one period will earn the 14 percent required rate of return.

CALCULATOR SOLUTION

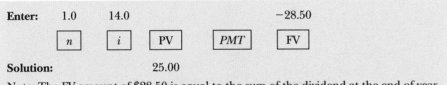

Enter:	1.0	14.0		−28.50
	n	i	PV	PMT	FV

Solution: 25.00

Note: The FV amount of $28.50 is equal to the sum of the dividend at the end of year 1 and the stock price at the end of year 1.

Multiple-Period Dividend Valuation Model

The dividend valuation process just described can be generalized to a multiple-period case. The expected cash flows to the investor who purchases a share of common stock and holds it for n periods consist of dividend payments during each of the next n periods $(D_1, D_2, \ldots, D_n)$ plus an amount, P_n, from the sale of the stock at the end of the nth period. Capitalizing these expected cash flows at the investor's required rate of return, k_e, gives the following valuation equation:

$$P_0 = \frac{D_1}{(1 + k_e)^1} + \frac{D_2}{(1 + k_e)^2} + \ldots + \frac{D_n}{(1 + k_e)^n} + \frac{P_n}{(1 + k_e)^n} \qquad (7.5)$$

Consider again the Ohio Engineering Company common stock. Suppose that the investor is considering purchasing a share of this stock and holding it for 5 years. Assume that the investor's required rate of return is still 14 percent. Dividends from the stock are expected to be $1 in the first year, $1 in the second year, $1 in the third year, $1.25 in the fourth year, and $1.25 in the fifth year. The expected selling price of the stock at the end of 5 years is $41.

Using Equation 7.5, the value of the stock to the investor is computed as follows:

$$P_0 = \frac{\$1.00}{(1 + 0.14)^1} + \frac{\$1.00}{(1 + 0.14)^2} + \frac{\$1.00}{(1 + 0.14)^3}$$

$$+ \frac{\$1.25}{(1 + 0.14)^4} + \frac{\$1.25}{(1 + 0.14)^5} + \frac{\$41.00}{(1 + 0.14)^5}$$

$$= \$1.00(\text{PVIF}_{0.14,1}) + \$1.00 (\text{PVIF}_{0.14,2})$$

$$+ \$1.00(\text{PVIF}_{0.14,3}) + \$1.25 (\text{PVIF}_{0.14,4})$$

$$+ \$1.25(\text{PVIF}_{0.14,5}) + \$41.00 (\text{PVIF}_{0.14,5})$$

$$= \$1.00(0.877) + \$1.00(0.769) + \$1.00(0.675)$$

$$+ \$1.25(0.592) + \$1.25(0.519) + \$41.00(0.519)$$

$$= \$24.99 \text{ (or } \$25)$$

Note that the *current* value of a share of Ohio Engineering common stock is the same (that is, $P_0 = \$25.00$) regardless of whether the investor plans to hold it for 1, 5, or any other number of years.[17]

CALCULATOR SOLUTION

In order to solve this problem with the aid of your calculator, it is necessary to use the cash flow function/keys (CF) on your calculator

Enter: 14.0   1.00   1.00   1.00   1.25   42.25

   | i | | CF$_1$ | | CF$_2$ | | CF$_3$ | | CF$_4$ | | CF$_5$ | | NPV |

Solution: 25.00

A General Dividend Valuation Model

In each of the valuation models described, the current value of the stock, P_0, is dependent upon the expected price of the stock at the end of the expected holding period. Although this seems straightforward, providing accurate forecasts of stock prices when applying the models to specific stocks can be difficult. A final generalization permits the elimination of P_n from the model while showing that the dividend valuation models discussed are consistent with one another.

First, the value of the stock at the end of the nth period, P_n, must be redefined. Using the capitalization of cash flow approach, it can be shown that P_n is a function of all expected *future* dividends that the investor will receive in periods $n + 1$, $n + 2$, and so on. Discounting the stream of dividends at the required rate of return, k_e, gives the value of the stock at the end of the nth period:

$$P_n = \sum_{t = n + 1}^{\infty} \frac{D_t}{(1 + k_e)^{t - n}} \tag{7.6}$$

Substituting Equation 7.6 into Equation 7.5 and simplifying yields the following *general dividend valuation model:*

$$P_0 = \sum_{t = 1}^{\infty} \frac{D_t}{(1 + k_e)^t} \tag{7.7}$$

---

[17]The value of a stock at *any* point in time is simply the present value of all dividends expected to be paid from that time forward. Hence, the price P_5, of $41 reflects the present value of dividends expected in years 6 through infinity.

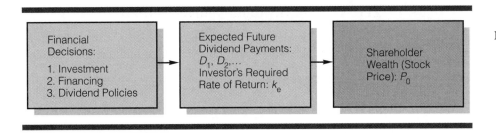

Thus, *the value of a firm's common stock to the investor is equal to the discounted present value of the expected future dividend stream.* As was shown, the valuation of a firm's common stock given by the multiple-period model (Equation 7.5) is equivalent to the valuation given by the general model (Equation 7.7). The general dividend valuation model is applicable regardless of whether the stream of dividends over time is fluctuating or constant, increasing or decreasing.

Note that the general dividend valuation model treats the stream of dividends as a *perpetuity* having no finite termination date. Whereas this assumption is reasonable for firms that are going concerns, shorter time horizons must be used when considering firms that might be either acquired by other firms or liquidated in the foreseeable future.

Some profitable firms (such as Compaq Computer and Federal Express) reinvest all their earnings and do not pay current cash dividends. In fact, some profitable firms have *never* paid cash dividends for as long as they have been in existence and are not expected to do so in the near future. How can the general dividend valuation model be applied to the common stock of a firm such as this? It must be assumed that the firm will be able to start making regular, periodic cash dividend payments to its shareholders *at some time in the future*. Or, these returns could consist of the *proceeds from the sale of the firm's outstanding common stock,* should the firm be acquired by another company, or a final liquidating dividend (distribution), should the firm be liquidated.

As stated in Chapter 1, the primary goal of firms should be the *maximization of shareholder wealth*. The general dividend valuation model (Equation 7.7) indicates that shareholder wealth, as measured by the value of the firm's common stock, P_0, is a function of the expected stream of future dividend payments and the investor's required rate of return. Thus, when making financial decisions that are consistent with the goal of maximizing shareholder wealth, management should be concerned with how these decisions affect both the expected future dividend stream and the discount rate that investors apply to the dividend stream. The relationship between financial decision making and shareholder wealth is illustrated in Figure 7-3. A primary emphasis of the financial management function is attempting to define and measure this relationship.

APPLICATIONS OF THE
GENERAL DIVIDEND VALUATION MODEL

The general dividend valuation model can be simplified if a firm's dividend payments over time are expected to follow one of several different patterns, including *zero growth, constant growth,* and *nonconstant growth.*

Zero Growth Dividend Valuation Model

If a firm's future dividend payments are expected to remain constant *forever,* then D_t in Equation 7.7, the general dividend valuation model, can be replaced by a constant value D to yield the following:

$$P_0 = \sum_{t=1}^{\infty} \frac{D}{(1 + k_e)^t} \tag{7.8}$$

This equation represents the value of a perpetuity and is analogous to those used for valuing a perpetual bond (Equation 6.7) and a preferred stock (Equation 6.11) developed in the previous chapter. It can be simplified to obtain

$$P_0 = \frac{D}{k_e} \tag{7.9}$$

This model is valid only when a firm's dividend payments are expected to remain constant *forever.* Although there are few common stocks that strictly satisfy these conditions, the model still can be used to approximate the value of a stock for which dividend payments are expected to remain constant for a relatively long period into the future. Figure 7-4 shows a zero growth dividend payment pattern.

To illustrate the zero growth dividend valuation model, assume that the Mountaineer Railroad common stock pays an annual dividend of $1.50 per share, which is expected to remain constant for the foreseeable future. What is the value of the stock to an investor who requires a 12 percent rate of return? Substituting $1.50 for D and 12 percent (0.12) for k_e in Equation 7.9 yields the following:

FIGURE 7-4
Dividend Growth Patterns

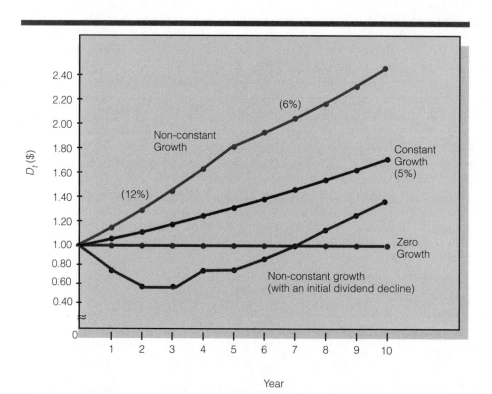

$$P_0 = \frac{\$1.50}{0.12}$$

$$= \$12.50$$

Constant Growth Dividend Valuation Model

If a firm's future dividend payments per share are expected to grow at a *constant* rate, g, per period forever, then the dividend at any future time period t can be forecasted as follows:

$$D_t = D_0(1 + g)^t \tag{7.10}$$

where D_0 is the dividend in the current period ($t = 0$). The expected dividend in period 1 is $D_1 = D_0(1 + g)^1$, the expected dividend in period 2 is $D_2 = D_0(1 + g)^2$, and so on. The constant-growth curve in Figure 7-4 illustrates such a dividend pattern.

Substituting Equation 7.10 for D_t in the general dividend valuation model (Equation 7.7) yields the following:

$$P_0 = \sum_{t=1}^{\infty} \frac{D_0(1 + g)^t}{(1 + k_e)^t} \tag{7.11}$$

Assuming that the required rate of return, k_e, is greater than the dividend growth rate,[18] *g, Equation 7.11 can be transformed algebraically to obtain the following simplified common stock valuation model:*[19]

---

[18]If this assumption is not satisfied—that is, if the growth rate (g) is greater than or equal to the required rate of return (k_e)—then the market price (P_0) would be infinite.

[19]Equation 7.12 is often referred to in finance literature as the *Gordon model*, for Myron J. Gordon, who pioneered its use. See Myron J. Gordon, *The Investment, Financing, and Valuation of the Corporation.* (Homewood, IL: Irwin, 1962). Equation 7.12 can be derived from Equation 7.11 in the following manner. Rewrite Equation 7.11 as follows:

$$P_0 = \frac{D_0(1 + g)^1}{(1 + k_e)^1} + \frac{D_0(1 + g)^2}{(1 + k_e)^2} + \ldots + \frac{D_0(1 + g)^n}{(1 + k_e)^n} \tag{a}$$

Multiply both sides of Equation (a) by $(1 + k_e)/(1 + g)$:

$$\frac{P_0(1 + k_e)}{(1 + g)} = D_0 + \frac{D_0(1 + g)^1}{(1 + k_e)^1} + \ldots + \frac{D_0(1 + g)^{n-1}}{(1 + k_e)^{n-1}} \tag{b}$$

Subtract Equation (a) from Equation (b):

$$\frac{P_0(1 + k_e)}{(1 + g)} - P_0 = D_0 - \frac{D_0(1 + g)^n}{(1 + k_e)^n} \tag{c}$$

Given that k_e is greater than g, as the number of time periods (n) approaches infinity, the second term on the right-hand side of Equation (c) approaches zero. Hence,

$$\frac{P_0(1 + k_e)}{(1 + g)} - P_0 = D_0 \tag{d}$$

or

$$P_0 \left[\frac{1 + k_e - (1+g)}{(1 + g)} \right] = D_0 \tag{e}$$

Multiplying both sides of Equation (e) by $(1 + g)$ yields

$$P_0 (k_e - g) = D_0(1 + g) \tag{f}$$

Solving Equation (f) for P_0 and recognizing that $D_1 = D_0(1 + g)$ gives

$$P_0 = \frac{D_1}{k_e - g}$$

$$P_0 = \frac{D_1}{k_e - g} \tag{7.12}$$

Note that in the constant growth valuation model (Equation 7.12), the dividend value in the numerator is D_1, that is, the dividend expected to be received one year from now. The model assumes that D_0, the current dividend, has just been paid and does not enter the (forward-looking) valuation process.

The constant growth valuation model (Equation 7.12) assumes that a firm's *earnings, dividends and stock price are expected to grow at a constant rate, g, into the future.* Hence to apply this model to a specific common stock, it is necessary to estimate the expected future growth rate, *g.* Considerable research evidence indicates that (1) the most accurate estimates of future growth are those provided by security analysts, and (2) consensus analyst forecasts of growth are an excellent proxy for growth expectations of investors. Sources of analyst growth rate forecasts include:

1. *Value Line Investment Survey.* Value Line reports, even though they represent only one analyst's forecast for each company, are readily available at most public and university libraries and have been shown to be reasonably accurate and closely related to investor expectations.
2. *Institutional Brokers Estimate System, Inc.* (IBES). It provides summaries of long-term (five years) and short-term earnings growth expectations from more than 2,100 analysts covering more than 3,500 companies. IBES forecast summaries can be accessed through popular on-line networks such as *Compuserve* or via the Internet.
3. *Zacks Earnings Estimates.* This service is similar to IBES. Forecasts from Zacks are available through the Internet.

The constant growth dividend valuation model can be used to illustrate the two forms of returns an investor can expect to receive from holding a common stock. Solving Equation 7.12 for k_e yields the following:

$$k_e = \frac{D_1}{P_0} + g \tag{7.13}$$

The investor's required rate of return is equal to the expected dividend yield, D_1/P_0, plus the price appreciation yield, *g*—the expected increase in dividends and, ultimately, in the price of the stock.

To illustrate the application of the constant growth valuation model, consider Duke Power Company. Dividends for Duke Power are expected to be $2.23 per share *next year.* According to estimates from *Value Line,* earnings and dividends are expected to grow at about 5.0 percent annually. To determine the value of a share of this stock to an investor who requires a 10 percent rate of return, substituting $2.23 for D_1, 5.0 percent (0.05) for *g*, and 10 percent (0.10) for k_e in Equation 7.12 yields the following value for a share of Duke Power's common stock:

$$P_0 = \frac{\$2.23}{0.10 - 0.05}$$

$$= \$44.60$$

Thus, the investor's 10 percent required return consists of a 5 percent dividend yield ($D_1/P_0 = \$2.23/\$44.60$) plus a growth return of 5 percent annually.

Nonconstant Growth Dividend Valuation Model

Many firms experience growth rates in sales, earnings, and dividends that are *not* constant. Typically, many firms experience a period of above-normal growth as they exploit new technologies, new markets, or both; this generally occurs relatively early in a firm's life cycle. Following this period of rapid growth, earnings and dividends tend to stabilize or grow at a more normal rate comparable to the overall average rate of growth in the economy. The reduction in the growth rate occurs as the firm reaches maturity and has fewer sizable growth opportunities. The upper curve in Figure 7-4 illustrates a nonconstant growth pattern.[20]

Nonconstant growth models can also be applied to the valuation of firms that are experiencing temporary periods of poor performance, after which a normal pattern of growth is expected to emerge. (The lower nonconstant growth line in Figure 7-4 illustrates this type of pattern.) For example, during 1992 IBM paid a dividend of $4.84 per share. This dividend was cut to $1.58 in 1993 and $1 in 1994. As IBM's restructuring efforts bear fruit, earnings and dividend growth are expected to resume. *Value Line,* for example, projects per share dividends to grow to $2.00 by 1997 and $3.50 by 2000. An investor attempting to value IBM's stock at the beginning of 1993 should have reflected the declining, then increasing pattern of dividend growth for the firm.

There is no single model or equation that can be applied when nonconstant growth is anticipated. In general the value of a stock that is expected to experience a nonconstant growth rate pattern of dividends is equal to the present value of expected yearly dividends during the period of nonconstant growth plus the present value of the expected stock price at the end of the nonconstant growth period, or:

$$P_0 = \begin{array}{c} \text{Present value of} \\ \text{expected dividends} \\ \text{during period of} \\ \text{nonconstant growth} \end{array} + \begin{array}{c} \text{Present value of the} \\ \text{expected stock price} \\ \text{at the end of the} \\ \text{nonconstant growth period} \end{array} \qquad (7.14)$$

The stock price at the end of a nonconstant growth rate period can be estimated in a number of ways:

1. Security analysts such as *Value Line* provide an estimated (5-year) future price range for the stocks they follow.
2. *Value Line, IBES,* and *Zacks* all provide earnings growth rate estimates for five years into the future. These growth rate estimates can be used to derive earnings per share (EPS) forecasts for five years in the future. The EPS forecasts can be multiplied by the expected price-to-earnings (P/E) multiple, estimated by looking at current P/E multiples for similar firms, to get an expected price in five years.
3. At the end of the period of nonconstant growth, an estimate of the value of the stock can be derived by applying the constant growth rate valuation model (Equation 7.12). For example, consider a firm expected to experience dividend growth at a nonconstant rate for m periods. Beginning in period $m + 1$, dividends are expected to grow at rate g_2 forever. The value of the stock, P_m, at the end of period m is equal to

---

[20]The transition between the periods of above-normal and normal, or average, growth usually is not as pronounced as Figure 7-4 indicates. Typically, a firm's growth rate *declines gradually* over time from the above-normal rate to the normal rate. Growth models similar to Equation 7.14 can be developed to handle cases like this.

$$P_m = \frac{D_{m+1}}{k_e - g_2} \qquad (7.15)$$

To demonstrate how this model works, suppose investors expect the earnings and common stock dividends of NICOR, Inc. (a diversified holding company engaged in the exploration, production, marketing and distribution of natural gas) to grow at a rate of 12 percent per annum for the next 5 years. Following the period of above-normal growth, dividends are expected to grow at the slower rate of 6 percent for the foreseeable future. The firm currently pays a dividend, D_0, of $2 per share. What is the value of NICOR common stock to an investor who requires a 15 percent rate of return?

Table 7-5 illustrates the step-by-step solution to this problem. First, compute the sum of the present values of the dividends received during the nonconstant

TABLE 7-5
Value of the NICOR Common Stock

YEAR, t	DIVIDEND $D_t = \$2.00(1 + 0.12)^t$	PRESENT VALUE INTEREST FACTOR, $PVIF_{0.15,t}$	PRESENT VALUE, D_t
Present Value of First 5 Years' Dividends			
1	$2.00(1 + 0.12)^1 = \$2.24$	0.870	$1.95
2	$2.00(1 + 0.12)^2 = 2.51$	0.756	$1.90
3	$2.00(1 + 0.12)^3 = 2.81$	0.658	$1.85
4	$2.00(1 + 0.12)^4 = 3.15$	0.572	$1.80
5	$2.00(1 + 0.12)^5 = 3.53$	0.497	$1.75
			$9.25

Value of Stock at End of Year 5, $P_5 = \dfrac{D_6}{k_e - g_2}$

$$P_5 = \frac{D_6}{0.15 - 0.06}$$

$$D_6 = D_5(1 + g_2)$$

$$= \$3.53(1 + 0.06)$$

$$= 3.74$$

$$P_5 = \frac{\$3.74}{0.15 - 0.06}$$

$$= \$41.56$$

Present Value of P_5, $PV(P_5) = \dfrac{P_5}{(1 + k_e)^5}$

$$PV(P_5) = \frac{\$41.56}{(1 + 0.15)^5}$$

$$= \$41.56(PVIF_{0.15,5})$$

$$= \$41.56(0.497)$$

$$= \$20.66$$

Value of Common Stock, $P_0 = PV$ (first 5 years' dividends) $+ PV(P_5)$

$$P_0 = \$9.25 + \$20.66$$

$$= \$29.91$$

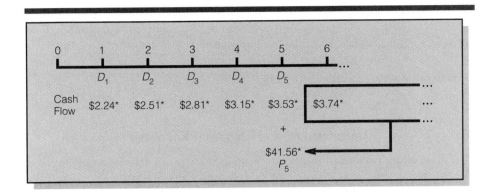

FIGURE 7-5
**Cash Flows from NICOR
Common Stock**

*Values as computed in Table 7-5

growth period (years 1 through 5 in this problem). This equals $9.25. Second, use the constant growth model to determine the value of NICOR common stock at the end of year 5; namely, P_5 equals $41.56. Next, determine the present value of P_5, which is $20.66. Finally, add the present value of the dividends received during the first 5 years ($9.25) to the present value of P_5 ($20.66) to obtain the total value of the common stock of $29.91 per share. A time line showing the expected cash flows from the purchase of NICOR common stock is given in Figure 7-5.

 ENTREPRENEURIAL FINANCE
VALUATION OF CLOSELY HELD FIRMS

The ownership of many small firms is closely held. An active market for shares of closely held companies normally does not exist. As a result, entrepreneurs occasionally need to have the value of their enterprises estimated by independent appraisers. The reasons for these valuations include mergers and acquisitions, divestitures and liquidations, initial public offerings, estate and gift tax returns, leveraged buyouts, recapitalizations, employee stock ownership plans, divorce settlements, estate valuation, and various other litigation matters.

The principles of valuation developed in this chapter and applied to large publicly traded firms also apply to the valuation of small firms. Small firm valuation poses several unique challenges. When valuing the shares of a closely held corporation, many factors are considered, including the nature and history of the business, the general economic outlook and the condition and outlook of the firm's industry, earnings capacity, dividend paying capacity, the book value of the company, and the company's financial condition, whether the shares represent a majority or minority (less than 50 percent) interest, and whether the stock is voting or nonvoting.

Specifically, however, in valuing a company that sells products and services, earnings capacity usually is the most important factor to be considered. Typically, the company as a whole is valued by determining a normal earnings level and multiplying that figure by an appropriate price-earnings multiple. This approach is known as the "capitalization of earnings" approach and results in a "going concern value." If the shares represent a minority interest in the corporation, a discount is taken for the lack of marketability of these shares.

Determination of Normal Earnings

The determination of an average, or "normal," earnings figure usually involves either a simple average or some type of weighted average of roughly the last five years of operations. For example, if the earnings of the company have been growing, some type of weighted average figure that places greater emphasis on more recent results is often used.

In some cases, the reported earnings of the company may not be an appropriate figure for valuation purposes. For example, suppose a portion of the salary paid to the president (and principal stockholder) really constitutes dividends paid as salary to avoid the payment of income taxes. In this situation, it is appropriate to adjust the reported earnings to account for these dividends.

Determination of an Appropriate Price-Earnings Multiple

The next step in the valuation process is to determine an appropriate rate at which to capitalize the normal earnings level. This is equivalent to multiplying the earnings by a price-earnings multiple. Had there been recent arms-length transactions in the stock, the price-earnings multiple would be known and observable in the financial marketplace. However, this situation rarely exists for closely held corporations. As a consequence, the analyst must examine the price-earnings multiple for widely held companies in the same industry as the firm being valued in an attempt to find firms that are similar to the firm of interest. The price-earnings multiple for these comparable firms is used to capitalize the normal earnings level.

Minority Interest Discount

The owner of a minority interest in a closely held corporation has an investment that lacks control and often marketability. There usually is either no market for the shares or the only buyer is either the other owners or the corporation itself. In addition, the owner of minority interest shares generally receives little, if any, dividends. The minority interest shareholder lacks control and is not able to change his or her inferior position. As a result of these problems, it is a widely practiced and accepted principle of valuation that the value of minority interest shares should be discounted.

The usual procedure in valuing minority interest shares is to value the corporation as a whole. Next, this value is divided by the number of shares outstanding to obtain a per-share value. Finally, a discount is applied to this per-share value to obtain the minority interest share value. These discounts have ranged from a low of 6 percent to more than 50 percent.[21]

In conclusion, the basic valuation concepts are the same for small and large firms. However, the lack of marketability of shares for many small firms and the problem of minority interest positions pose special problems for the analyst.

ETHICAL ISSUES
AT&T VERSUS NCR

In late 1990, AT&T offered to purchase NCR Corporation for $90 a share, a premium of nearly 88 percent over the preoffer price of NCR's stock. NCR's board of directors rejected the "friendly" offer by AT&T, saying they believed that this amount was inadequate and did not reflect the value of NCR Corporation. Prior to the AT&T offering, the stock of NCR was trading in the high forties. Presumably, this preoffer price reflected the present value of the expected future cash flows to stockholders in this large business information processing concern, assuming the firm continued under its current management team. AT&T countered with a hostile takeover offer.

The reluctance of NCR's board of directors and its managers to permit an AT&T takeover of the firm raises many interesting questions. Why would AT&T be willing to offer to purchase NCR for such a large premium? If stock prices reflect (in an unbiased way) the present value of expected future cash flows, why would the price of NCR's stock before the takeover be so much less than the takeover price offered by AT&T? The board of directors at NCR had earlier approved elaborate takeover defenses, such as requiring an 80 percent vote to oust NCR's board. In the context of a goal of maximizing shareholder wealth, what role do you feel antitakeover defenses, such as a supermajority voting provision for changing the composition of the board of directors, play in contributing to this goal? Under what circumstances do you feel that takeover resistance, such as that displayed by NCR, can contribute to the goal of shareholder wealth maximization?

■ SUMMARY

■ The common stockholders are the true owners of the firm; and, as such, common stock is a permanent form of financing. Common stockholders participate in the firm's earnings, potentially receiving larger dividends if earnings rise or smaller dividends if earnings drop.

[21]See George S. Arneson, "Minority Discounts Beyond Fifty Percent Can Be Supported," *Taxes: The Tax Magazine* (February 1981): 97–102; and Ruth R. Longenecker, "A Practical Guide to Valuation of Closely Held Stock," *Trusts and Estates* (January 1983): 32–41.

- Stockholder rights include the following:
  1. The right to dividends.
  2. The right to any assets remaining after senior claims are satisfied in a liquidation.
  3. Voting rights.
  4. The *preemptive right,* or the right to share proportionately in any new stock sold. This right is available in some firms but not in others.
- If a company's common stock price rises above the price range considered optimal, the company's management can effect a *stock split* to get the price back to a more desirable trading level.
- A firm may decide to repurchase its own shares for various reasons, including financial restructuring, future corporate needs, disposition of excess cash, and reduction of takeover risk.
- Common stock permits a firm more flexibility in its financing plans than fixed-income securities, because, in principle, no fixed-dividend obligation exists.
- Investment bankers assist firms in the security offering process by providing advice on a wide range of corporate financial transactions, including the timing and structure of new security offerings. New corporate securities are sold through *public cash offerings, private placements,* and *rights offerings.*
- Issuance costs for sales of common equity are normally significantly greater than for corporate debt or preferred stock. There are significant economies of scale associated with security offerings.
- The valuation of *common stock* is considerably more complicated than the valuation of either bonds or preferred stock for the following reasons:
  1. The cash flows can take two forms, cash dividend payments and price appreciation.
  2. Common stock dividends normally are expected to grow and not remain constant.
  3. The cash flows from common stocks generally are more uncertain than the cash flows from other types of securities.
- In the *general dividend valuation model,* the value of a common stock is equal to the present value of all the expected future dividends discounted at the investor's required rate of return. Simpler common stock valuation models can be derived from assumptions concerning the expected growth of future dividend payments.
- Assuming that dividends continue to grow at a *constant* rate, g, indefinitely, the value of a common stock is equal to the next year's dividend, D_1, divided by the difference between the investor's required rate of return, k_e, and the growth rate, g.
- The valuation of stock in small corporations poses special challenges because of its limited marketability, lack of liquidity, and the difference between minority interest and controlling interest shares.

■ QUESTIONS AND TOPICS FOR DISCUSSION

1. Define the following terms associated with common stock:
   a. Nonvoting stock.
   b. Stock split.

    c. Reverse stock split.

    d. Stock dividend.

    e. Book value.

    f. Treasury stock.

2. Does the retained earnings figure on a company's balance sheet indicate the amount of funds the company has available for current dividends or capital expenditures? Explain fully.

3. Discuss the reasons why a firm may repurchase its own common stock.

4. Explain the differences between par value, book value, and market value per share of common stock.

5. Discuss the various stockholder rights.

6. What factor or factors make the valuation of common stocks more complicated than the valuation of bonds and preferred stocks?

7. According to the general dividend valuation model, a firm that reinvests all its earnings and pays no cash dividends still can have a common stock value greater than zero. How is this possible?

8. Explain the relationship between financial decisions and shareholders' wealth.

9. Explain how *each* of the following factors would affect the valuation of a firm's common stock, assuming that all other factors remain constant:

    a. The general level of interest rates shifts upward, causing investors to require a higher rate of return on securities in general.

    b. Increased foreign competition reduces the future growth potential of the firm's earnings and dividends.

    c. Investors reevaluate upward their assessment of the risk of the firm's common stock as the result of increased South American investments by the firm.

10. In the context of the constant growth dividend valuation model, explain what is meant by

    a. Dividend yield.

    b. Price appreciation yield.

11. Explain why the valuation models for a perpetual bond, preferred stock, and common stock with constant dividend payments (zero growth) are virtually identical.

12. Explain how the book value per share of common stock can change over time.

13. What is the difference between majority voting and cumulative voting?

14. What are the primary functions served by investment bankers?

15. What are the differences between a *direct placement*, a *public cash offering*, and a *rights offering* of securities?

16. Which do you think is more risky for a firm trying to raise capital—an *underwritten offering* or a *best-efforts offering*?

17. Identify the major issuance costs associated with a security offering by a corporation.

18. How does a *shelf registration* differ from other public security offerings?

■ SELF-TEST PROBLEMS

ST1. What is the current value of a share of Commonwealth Edison common stock to an investor who requires a 12 percent annual rate of return, if *next* year's dividend, D_1, is expected to be $3 per share and dividends are expected to grow at an annual rate of 4 percent for the foreseeable future?

ST2. The Edgar Corporation currently (D_0) pays a $2 per share dividend. This dividend is expected to grow at a 20 percent annual rate over the next 3 years and then to grow at 6 percent per year for the foreseeable future. What would you pay for a share of this stock if you demand a 20 percent rate of return?

■ PROBLEMS*

eXcel **1.** General Cereal common stock dividends have been growing at an annual rate of 7 percent per year over the past 10 years. Current dividends are $1.70 per share. What is the current value of a share of this stock to an investor who requires a 12 percent rate of return if the following conditions exist?

   a. Dividends are expected to continue growing at the historic rate for the foreseeable future.

   b. The dividend growth rate is expected to *increase* to 9 percent per year.

   c. The dividend growth rate is expected to *decrease* to 6.5 percent per year.

eXcel **2.** The Foreman Company's earnings and common stock dividends have been growing at an annual rate of 6 percent over the past 10 years and are expected to continue growing at this rate for the foreseeable future. The firm currently (that is, as of year 0) pays an annual dividend of $5 per share. Determine the current value of a share of Foreman common stock to investors with each of the following required rates of return:

   a. 12 percent.

   b. 14 percent.

   c. 16 percent.

   d. 6 percent.

   e. 4 percent.

3. The common stock of General Land Development Company (GLDC) is expected to pay a dividend of $1.25 next year and currently sells for $25. Assume that the firm's future dividend payments are expected to grow at a constant rate for the foreseeable future. Determine the implied growth rate of GLDC's dividends (and earnings), assuming that the required rate of return of investors is 12 percent.

eXcel **4.** Cascade Mining Company expects its earnings and dividends to increase by 7 percent per year over the next 6 years and then to remain relatively constant thereafter. The firm currently (that is, as of year 0) pays a dividend of $5 per share. Determine the value of a share of Cascade stock to an investor with a 12 percent required rate of return.

eXcel **5.** Over the past 5 years, the dividends of the Gamma Corporation have grown from $0.70 per share to the current level of $1.30 per share ($D_0$). This growth rate (computed to one tenth of 1 percent accuracy) is expected to continue for the foreseeable future. What is the value of a share of Gamma Corporation common stock to an investor who requires a 20 percent return on her investment?

eXcel **6.** Simtek currently pays a $2.50 dividend ($D_0$) per share. Next year's dividend is expected to be $3 per share. After next year, dividends are expected to increase at a 9 percent annual rate for 3 years and a 6 percent annual rate thereafter.

   a. What is the current value of a share of Simtek stock to an investor who requires a 15 percent return on his or her investment?

   b. If the dividend in year 1 is expected to be $3 and the growth rate over the following 3 years is expected to be only 7 percent and then 6 percent thereafter, what will the new stock price be?

7. What is the current per-share value of JRM Corporation to an investor who requires a 16 percent annual rate of return, if JRM's current per-share dividend is $2 and is expected to remain at $2 for the foreseeable future?

eXcel **8.** The Seneca Maintenance Company currently (that is, as of year 0) pays a common stock dividend of $1.50 per share. Dividends are expected to grow at a rate of 11 percent per year for the next 4 years and then to continue growing thereafter at a rate of 5 percent per year. What is the current value of a share of Seneca common stock to an investor who requires a 14 percent rate of return?

eXcel **9.** Ten years ago, Video Toys began manufacturing and selling coin-operated arcade games. Dividends are currently $1.50 per share, having grown at a 15 percent compound annual rate over the past 5 years. That growth rate is expected to be main-

*Colored numbers denote problems that have check answers provided at the end of the book.

tained for the next 3 years, after which dividends are expected to grow at half that rate for 3 years. Beyond that time, Video Toys's dividends are expected to grow at 5 percent per year. What is the current value of a share of Video Toys common stock if your required rate of return is 18 percent?

10. During the previous 4 years, Spiro Company's common stock dividends have grown from $1 (year 0) to $1.36 (year 4) per share.

   a. Determine the compound annual dividend growth rate over the 4-year period.

   b. Forecast Spiro's dividends for the next 5 years, assuming that dividends continue to grow at the rate determined in Part a.

   c. Determine the current value of a share of Spiro common stock to an investor who plans to hold it for 5 years, assuming that the stock price *increases at the same rate* as the dividends. The investor's required rate of return is 12 percent.

11. The chairman of Heller Industries told a meeting of financial analysts that he expects the firm's earnings and dividends to double over the next 6 years. The firm's current (that is, as of year 0) earnings and dividends per share are $4 and $2, respectively.

   a. Estimate the compound annual dividend growth rate over the 6-year period (to the nearest whole percent).

   b. Forecast Heller's earnings and dividends per share for each of the next 6 years, assuming that they grow at the rate determined in Part a.

   c. Based on the constant growth dividend valuation model, determine the current value of a share of Heller Industries common stock to an investor who requires an 18 percent rate of return.

   d. Why might the stock price calculated in Part c not represent an accurate valuation to an investor with an 18 percent required rate of return?

   e. Determine the current value of a share of Heller Industries common stock to an investor (with an 18 percent required rate of return) who plans to hold it for 6 years, assuming that earnings and dividends per share grow at the rate determined in Part a for the next 6 years and then at 6 percent thereafter.

12. Kruger Associates is considering a substantial investment in the stock of McIntyre Enterprises. McIntyre currently (time 0) pays a dividend of $1.50 per share. This dividend is expected to grow at 15 percent per year for the next 3 years and 10 percent per year for the following three years. McIntyre's marginal tax rate is 40 percent. Kruger expects the value of the McIntyre stock to increase by 50 percent between now and the *beginning* of year 5. If Kruger requires a 12 percent rate of return on investments of this type, what value would Kruger place on the McIntyre stock?

13. Piedmont Enterprises currently pays a dividend (D_0) of $1 per share. This dividend is expected to grow at a 20 percent per year rate for the next two years, after which it is expected to grow at 6 percent per year for the foreseeable future. If you require a 15 percent rate of return on an investment of this type, what price do you expect the stock to sell for *at the beginning of year 5*?

14. Over the past 10 years, the dividends of Party Time, Inc. have grown at an annual rate of 15 percent. The current (D_0) dividend is $3 per share. This dividend is expected to grow to $3.40 next year, then grow at an annual rate of 10 percent for the following 2 years and 6 percent per year thereafter. You require a 15 percent rate of return on this stock.

   a. What would you be willing to pay for a share of Party Time stock today?

   b. What price would you anticipate the stock selling for at the beginning of year 3?

   c. If you anticipated selling the stock at the end of 2 years, how much would you pay for it today?

15. Canadian National Railway sold 10 million shares of stock to the public at $30 per share. The company received net proceeds from its underwriters of $287,506,114. What was the underwriting spread from this stock offering?

16. Suppose you have accumulated a sizable investment (100,000 common shares) in Alpine Land and Development Company. You are dissatisfied with the performance

of the present management and are considering running for the board of directors. The company has a nine-member board and a total of 1.5 million common shares outstanding. Assume that all shares will be voted in the upcoming election and that four of the nine board members are up for reelection.

   a. If the voting procedure is cumulative, what number of shares is necessary to ensure your election to the board? Is it possible for you to be elected with fewer votes? Explain.

   b. Suppose a close friend of yours also owns a good deal of Alpine and shares your feelings about the present management. If the voting procedure is cumulative, how many shares are necessary to elect both you and your friend to the board?

   c. If the voting procedure is majority, how many votes are necessary for election in Parts a and b of this problem? Explain your answer.

17. Suppose General Electric common stock currently is selling at $68 a share, and its present dividend, D_0, is $2 a share. If investors are requiring a 14 percent annual return, what annual growth rate are they expecting, assuming a constant growth valuation model is appropriate for General Electric?

18. The stock of Carroll's Bowling Equipment currently pays a dividend (D_0) of $3. This dividend is expected to grow at an annual rate of 15 percent for the next three years. The dividend is expected to increase by $1 in year 4 and to grow at a constant annual rate of 6 percent thereafter. If you require a 24 percent rate of return on an investment such as this, how much would you be willing to pay per share?

19. The stock of Dravo Corporation currently pays a dividend (D_0) at the rate of $2 per share. This dividend is expected to increase at a 9 percent annual rate for the next three years, at a 7 percent annual rate for the following 2 years, and then at 4 percent per year thereafter. What is the value of a share of stock of Dravo to an investor who demands a 24 percent rate of return on this stock?

20. Excel Corporation has recently witnessed a period of depressed earnings performance. As a result, cash dividend payments have been suspended. Investors do not anticipate a resumption of dividends until two years from today, when a yearly dividend of $0.25 will be paid. That yearly dividend is expected to be increased to $0.75 in the following year and $1.50 in the year after that. Beyond the time when the $1.50 dividend is paid, investors expect Excel's dividends to grow at an annual rate of 5 percent into perpetuity. All dividends are assumed to be paid at the end of each year. If you require an 18 percent rate of return on Excel's stock, what is the value of one share of this stock to you today?

21. The Cremmins Coat Company recently has completed a period of extraordinary growth, due to the popularity of its yellow jackets. Earnings per share have grown at an average compound annual rate of 15 percent, while dividends have grown at a 20 percent annual rate over the past 10 years. The current dividend (D_0) rate is $2 per share. Current earnings are $3.25 per share. Earnings are expected to grow at an annual rate of 15 percent for the next 3 years and 6 percent per annum thereafter. Dividends are expected to grow by 25 percent during the coming year, by 15 percent per annum for the following 2 years, and by 6 percent per annum thereafter.

   a. What price do you expect the stock to sell for today, if your required rate of return on equity for a firm of this risk level is 16 percent?

   b. What price do you expect the stock to sell for at the beginning of year 2?

22. The VSE Corporation currently pays no dividend because of depressed earnings. A recent change in management promises a brighter future. Investors expect VSE to pay a dividend of $1 next year (the end of year 1). This dividend is expected to increase to $2 the following year and to grow at a rate of 10 percent per annum for the following two years (years 3 and 4). Chuck Brown, a new investor, expects the price of the stock to increase 50 percent in value between now (time zero) and the end of year 3. If Brown plans to hold the stock for two years and requires a rate of return of 20 percent on his investment, what value would he place on the stock today?

23. Sports Novelties, Inc. has experienced an explosion in demand for its feathered football novelties. The firm currently (time 0) pays a dividend of $0.25 per share. This dividend is expected to increase to $0.75 per share one year from now. It is expected to grow at a rate of 15 percent per year for the following 7 years. Coley, a naive investor, seeks your advice regarding the current value of this stock. Coley plans to purchase this stock today, if the price is right, and to hold it for 3 years. He believes that the stock will increase in value to $30 at the end of 4 years. What is the current value of this stock to Coley if he requires a 20 percent rate of return on stocks of this risk level?

24. The Blinkelman Corporation has just announced that it plans to introduce a new solar panel that will greatly reduce the cost of solar energy. As a result, analysts now expect the company's earnings, currently (year 0) $1 per share to grow by 50 percent per year for the next 3 years, by 25 percent per year for the following 3 years, and by 8 percent per year, thereafter. Blinkelman does not currently pay a dividend, but it expects to pay out 20 percent of its earnings beginning two years from now. The payout ratio is expected to become 50 percent in 5 years and to remain at that level. The company's marginal tax rate is 40 percent. If you require a 20 percent rate of return on a stock such as this, how much would you be willing to pay for it today?

25. Watkins, Inc. has experienced an explosion in demand for its ram football novelties. The firm currently (time 0) pays a dividend of $0.50 per share. This dividend is expected to increase to $1.00 per share one year from now. It is expected to grow at a rate of 20 percent per year for the next 7 years. Susan seeks your advice regarding the current value of this stock. Susan plans to purchase this stock today, if the price is right, and to hold it for 3 years. She believes that the stock will increase in value to $40 at the end of 5 years. What is the current value of this stock to Susan if she requires a 20 percent rate of return on stocks of this risk level?

26. Whitehurst Associates is considering a substantial investment in the stock of Ivanhoe Enterprises. Ivanhoe currently (time 0) pays a dividend of $3 per share. This dividend is expected to grow at 15 percent per year for the next 3 years and 10 percent per year for the following 3 years. Ivanhoe's marginal tax rate is 40 percent. Whitehurst expects the value of the Ivanhoe stock to increase by 40 percent between now and the *beginning* of year 5. If Whitehurst requires a 12 percent rate of return on investments of this type, what value would Whitehurst place on the Ivanhoe stock?

27. The Alpha Tool Corporation has never paid a dividend, but the new company president has announced that the firm would pay its first dividend exactly 2 years from now. That dividend is expected to be $2 per share. It is anticipated that this dividend will grow by 15 percent for the following three years, and by 10 percent for the two years after that. No explicit dividend forecast is available beyond that point in time, although the firm is expected to continue to pay some dividends every year. The stock's current price to earnings (P/E) multiple is 15 times. The company (and investigators) expect the P/E multiple to remain constant for the foreseeable future. Earnings per share at the end of year 6 are expected to be $7. The company's marginal tax rate is 40 percent and the firm has a capital structure consisting of 40 percent debt (at a pretax cost of 20 percent) and 60 percent common equity. If you require a 15 percent rate of return on this stock, how much would you pay for one share of stock today.

28. Bragg's Fort Corporation has experienced rapidly growing earnings per share at a rate of 20 percent per annum over the past 15 years. The price of the stock of Bragg's is $50 per share. Earnings per share are $3. The current dividend rate is $2 per share. Bragg's has a beta of 1.3. The long-term risk-free rate is 6.9 percent and the expected return on the overall market is 14 percent. The company's bonds are rated Aa by Moody's and currently sell to yield 9 percent. The average tax rate of Bragg's is 30 percent, but it marginal rate is 40 percent. A new financial analyst has suggested that Bragg's can be valued using a constant growth dividend valuation model. What

constant growth rate would that analyst recommend using if she believes in capital market efficiency and the capital asset pricing model? Do you agree with her valuation recommendation? Why or why not?

29. The following stock quotations were recently reported in the *Wall Street Journal*:

25⅝	12⅞	Offc Depot	ODP		...	26	9083	21¼	20½	21¼	+¾
39½	32⅜	PubSvcCol	PSR	2.10	5.4	14	366	39	38¾	39	+¼
40½	30	SaraLee	SLE	.84	2.2	20	14280	37⅞	37⅛	37⅞	+⅞
28⅞	27¼	Gen Motor pfG		2.28	8.1	...	22	28⅛	27⅞	28	+⅛

a. What are the dividend yields on the common stock of Office Depot, Public Service Company of Colorado, and Sara Lee?

b. What possible explanation can you give for the differences in the common stock dividend yields observed in Part a?

c. What is the current price-earnings ratio for Public Service Company of Colorado and for Office Depot?

d. What possible explanation can you give for the differences in the price-earnings ratios observed in Part c?

e. Why do you think the dividend yield on General Motors' preferred stock is so much larger than the divided yield on Sara Lee's common stock?

f. What was the previous day's closing price for Sara Lee's common stock?

30. The American Association of Individual Investors has put together a list of stock-picking techniques that "stand the test of time." Given what you learned in the last chapter about valuation, coupled with what you now know about stock, do you agree or disagree with their techniques? Why or why not?
http://www.aaii.com

■ SOLUTIONS TO SELF-TEST PROBLEMS

ST1. $P_0 = \dfrac{\$3.00}{0.12 - 0.04} = \$37.50$

ST2. Present Value of First 3 Years' Dividends

$$D_0 = \$22.00 \qquad g_1 = 0.20 \qquad k_e = 0.20$$

Year	Dividend	PV Interest Factor	Present Value
t	$D_t = \$2.00(1 + 0.20)^t$	$\text{PVIF}_{0.20,t} = 1/(1 + 0.20)^t$	$D_t \times \text{PVIF}_{0.20,t}$
1	$\$2.00(1 + 0.20)^1 = \$2.400$	0.833	$\$2.00$
2	$2.00(1 + 0.20)^2 = \$2.880$	0.694	2.00
3	$2.00(1 + 0.20)^3 = \$3.456$	0.579	2.00
PV (First 3 Years' Dividends)			$\$6.00$

Value of Stock at End of Year 3

$$P_3 = \frac{D_4}{(k_e - g_2)} \qquad g_2 = 0.06$$

$$D_4 = D_3 (1 + g_2) = \$3.456(1 + 0.06) = \$3.663$$

$$P_3 = \frac{\$3.663}{(0.20 - 0.06)} = \$26.164$$

Present Value of P_3

$$PV(P_3) = \frac{P_3}{(1 + k_e)^3} = \frac{\$26.164}{(1 + 0.20)^3}$$

$$= \$26.164(PVIF_{0.20,t}) = \$26.164(0.579) = \$15.15$$

Value of Common Stock

$$P_0 = PV(\text{First 3 Years' Dividends}) + PV(P_3)$$

$$= \$6.00 + \$15.15 = \$21.15$$

■ GLOSSARY

Book Value (per share) The total book value of the company divided by the total number of shares of common stock outstanding.

Capital Gains Yield The expected percentage increase in the price of the stock.

Capitalization of Cash Flow Method of Valuation A method of determining the present value of an asset that is expected to produce a stream of future cash flows. This involves discounting the stream of expected cash flows at an appropriate rate.

Competitive Bidding The process of selling a new security offering to the highest bidding underwriting syndicate.

Cumulative Voting A voting procedure by which stockholders may cast multiple votes for a single board of directors candidate. Cumulative voting makes it easier for stockholders with minority views to elect sympathetic board members.

Direct Placement The sale of an entire security offering to one or more institutional investors rather than the general public. This also is termed a private placement.

Dividend Yield The annual dividend payment divided by the price of the stock.

Flotation Cost The cost of issuing new securities. This includes both underwriting expenses and other issue expenses, such as printing and legal fees.

Investment Banker A financial institution that underwrites and sells new securities. In general, investment bankers assist firms in obtaining new financing.

Negotiated Underwriting A process whereby a firm wishing to sell new securities to the public negotiates the terms of the underwriting with the investment banker or bankers.

Par Value (Common Stock) An arbitrary value assigned to common stock by the issuing firm.

Preemptive Right A provision contained in some corporate charters that gives common stockholders the right to buy on a pro rata basis any new common shares sold by the firm.

Required Rate of Return The rate used to value a stream of expected cash flows from an asset (also called the discount rate). The riskier the expected cash flows from an asset, the higher is the required rate of return.

Reverse Stock Split A stock split in which the number of outstanding shares is reduced.

Right A short-term option issued by a firm that permits an existing stockholder to buy a specified number of shares of common stock at a specified price (the subscription price) below the current market price.

Rights Offering The sale of new shares of common stock by distributing stock purchase rights to a firm's existing shareholders. This also is termed a *privileged subscription.*

Shareholder Wealth Present value of the expected future cash flows to the owners (that is, shareholders) of the firm. It is measured by the market value of the shareholders' common stock holdings.

Stock Dividend A payment of additional shares of common stock to stockholders.

Stockholders' (Common) Equity The total of a firm's common stock at par, contributed capital in excess of par, and retained earnings accounts from the balance sheet. It sometimes is called the *owners' equity*, or *net worth*.

Stock Split The issuance of a number of new shares in exchange for each old share held by a stockholder.

Treasury Stock Common stock that has been reacquired by the issuing company.

Underwriting A process whereby a group of investment bankers agrees to purchase a new security issue at a set price and then offers it for sale to investors.

Underwriting Spread The difference between the selling price to the public of a new security offering and the proceeds received by the offering firm. This also is termed an underwriting discount.

PART III

THE CAPITAL INVESTMENT DECISION

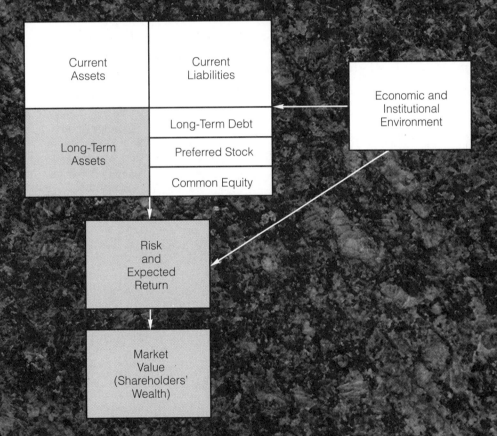

This part of the text looks at the financial management of the long-term asset portion of a firm's balance sheet. Investments in these assets (for example, property, plant, and equipment) have a major impact on a firm's future stream of cash flows and the risk of those cash flows. As such, the long-term investment (capital budgeting) decision has a significant effect on the value of the firm. Chapter 8 deals with the measurement of cash flows from the long-term investments. Chapter 9 analyzes various investment decision criteria in light of the wealth maximization objective of the firm. Chapter 10 extends the analysis to consider techniques to account for differential levels of risk among projects.

CAPITAL BUDGETING
AND CASH FLOW ANALYSIS

1. *Capital budgeting* is the process of planning for purchases of assets whose cash flows are expected to continue beyond one year.
2. The *cost of capital* is defined as the cost of funds supplied to a firm. It represents the required rate of return a firm must earn on its investments and thus is an important input in the capital budgeting process.
3. There are four key steps in the capital budgeting process:
    a. Generating investment project proposals.
    b. Estimating cash flows.
    c. Evaluating alternatives and selecting projects to be implemented.
    d. Reviewing a project's performance after it has been implemented, and postauditing its performance after termination.
4. Investment projects can be generated by growth opportunities, by cost reduction opportunities, and to meet legal requirements and health and safety standards.
5. The initial outlay required to implement a project is called the *net investment*. It includes

KEY CHAPTER CONCEPTS

a. The installed cost of the assets,
b. Plus any initial net working capital requirements,
    c. Less any cash inflows from the sale of replacement assets,
    d. Plus or minus the tax consequences associated with the sale of existing assets and/or the purchase of new assets.
6. The *net operating cash flow* from a project is equal to the change in net operating earnings after tax plus the change in depreciation minus the change in net working capital investment requirements associated with the adoption of a project. In the last year of a project's life, this net cash flow definition may have to modified to reflect the recapture of the accumulated net working capital investment and any after-tax salvage value received.
7. The economic viability of a project can be affected by special tax considerations, such as the use of accelerated depreciation methods like the Modified Accelerated Cost Recovery System (MACRS) of depreciation.

FORD MOTOR COMPANY'S INVESTMENT IN JAGUAR CARS, LTD.*

Ford purchased Jaguar for $2.5 billion in 1990 in order to compete with such companies as Mercedes-Benz, BMW, and Lexus in the American luxury car market. Over the next 4 years, Ford incurred an additional $1.2 billion in operating losses and restructuring charges. Included in the nearly $4 billion in investment costs were replacement of the 40-year-old assembly line in Coventry, England, with a line that can produce 25 percent more cars, as well as the redesign of the XJ sedan, Jaguar's most popular model. The more efficient assembly plant lowered the break even point at Jaguar from 50,000 to about 35,000 cars per year. The redesign of the XJ sedan was done in an attempt to boost sales, which auto analysts felt should rise by 7,000 units to 35,000 in the next year.

The objective of Ford's investment in production facilities and redesigned products was to return Jaguar to profitability and to begin earning a return on its investment. However, many financial analysts felt that even if the new XJ model sells well, Ford will not realize a decent return on its investment in Jaguar until the year 2000—at the earliest. The chairman of another automobile company even questioned whether Ford would ever earn its money back on its Jaguar investment.

Despite these lackluster returns, Ford also was considering whether to add another model to Jaguar's lineup, which consisted of the XJ sedan and XJ sports car. A new model could require an investment between $500 million and $1 billion. Another invest-

ment decision facing Ford management was whether to continue manufacturing future Jaguar models in England or to move production to another country, such as the United States—its key market. Two of its major competitors, Mercedes-Benz and BMW, had already decided to build assembly plants in the United States in order to lower their costs and be closer to their primary market. A United States assembly plant, with its lower production costs, could generate higher cash inflows and returns to Ford, but also could result in increased risk, particularly if consumers perceive this decision as cheapening the Jaguar brand. The decisions by Ford of whether to build a new model and, if so, where to manufacture the car, require careful analysis of the factors that determine the cash inflows and outflows of the proposed investments.

The analysis of capital investments (that is, projects having economic lives extending beyond one year in time) is a key financial management function. Each year, large and small firms spend hundreds of billions of dollars on capital investments. These investments chart the course of a company's future for many years to come. Therefore, it is imperative that capital investment analysis be performed correctly. This chapter develops the principles of capital investment analysis—with emphasis on the estimation of cash flows from a project. Chapter 9 considers appropriate decision criteria in the capital budgeting process that will maximize shareholder wealth.

*Based on "Is the Jinx Finally Off Jaguar?" *Business Week* (October 10, 1994): 62 and "Ford Set to See Profit from Jaguar, Ponders New Line Outside England," *Wall Street Journal* (October 6, 1994): A13.

INTRODUCTION

This is the first of several chapters that explicitly deal with the financial management of the assets on a firm's balance sheet. In this and the following two chapters, we consider the management of long-term assets. Later in the book (Chapters 15 to 17), the emphasis shifts to the management of short-term assets; that is, the working capital decision.

Capital budgeting is the process of planning for purchases of assets whose returns are expected to continue beyond one year. A **capital expenditure** is a cash outlay that is expected to generate a flow of future cash benefits lasting longer than one year. It is distinguished from a normal operating expenditure, which is expected to result in cash benefits during the coming one-year period. (The choice of a one-year period is arbitrary, but it does serve as a useful guideline.)

Several different types of outlays may be classified as capital expenditures and evaluated using the framework of capital budgeting models, including the following:

- The purchase of a new piece of equipment, real estate, or a building in order to expand an existing product or service line or enter a new line of business.
- The replacement of an existing capital asset, such as a drill press.
- Expenditures for an advertising campaign.
- Expenditures for a research and development program.
- Investments in permanent increases of target inventory levels or levels of accounts receivable.
- Investments in employee education and training.
- The refunding of an old bond issue with a new, lower interest issue.
- Lease-versus-buy analysis.
- Merger and acquisition evaluation.

Capital expenditures are important to a firm both because they require sizable cash outlays and because they have a long-range impact on the firm's performance. Table 8-1 summarizes the capital expenditures made by U.S. firms during 1995 and plans for 1996. Total capital expenditures of all industries in the United States during 1995 exceeded 594 *billion* dollars. During 1995 Exxon earned about $6.5 billion after taxes and made capital and exploration expenditures of $9.0 billion. Unisys had 1995 losses of $625 million, yet it made $727 million in capital expenditures that year, which included engineering, research and development, software, and plants and equipment.

A firm's capital expenditures affect its future profitability and, when taken together, essentially plot the company's future direction by determining which products will be produced, which markets will be entered, where production facilities will be located, and what type of technology will be used. Capital expenditure decision making is important for another reason as well. Specifically, it is often difficult, if not impossible, to reverse a major capital expenditure without incurring considerable additional expense. For example, if a firm acquires highly specialized production facilities and equipment, it must recognize that there may be no ready used-equipment market in which to dispose of them if they do not generate the desired future cash flows. For these reasons, a firm's management should establish a number of definite procedures to follow when analyzing capital expenditure projects. Choosing from among such projects is the objective of capital budgeting models.

TABLE 8-1
Capital Expenditures Made by U.S. Firms (in billions of dollars)

Source: U.S. Bureau of the Census, *Annual Capital Expenditures Survey.* Reprinted in 1996 *Statistical Abstract of the United States.*

INDUSTRY	1995		1996 PLANS	
Mining and construction		36.0		33.6
Manufacturing		172.3		184.8
Durable goods	91.4		100.1	
Nondurable goods	80.9		84.7	
Transportation		37.0		35.2
Communications		46.0		46.3
Utilities		42.8		40.6
Electric	21.4		18.9	
Gas transmission, distribution, and other utilities	21.4		21.7	
Wholesale and retail trade		75.1		71.9
Wholesale trade	21.9		19.7	
Retail trade	53.2		52.2	
Finance, insurance, and real estate		57.3		57.7
Finance	31.0		34.6	
Insurance and real estate	26.3		23.1	
Services		123.7		129.4
Personal and business services, including agriculture	68.4		67.4	
Health services	31.3		34.8	
Social, educational, and other professional services	24.0		27.2	
Expenditures serving multiple industries		1.5		1.3
Not distributed by industry		2.8		2.7
TOTAL		594.5		603.5

KEY TERMS AND CONCEPTS IN CAPITAL BUDGETING

Before proceeding with the discussion of the capital budgeting process, it is necessary to introduce a number of terms and concepts encountered in subsequent chapters.

Cost of Capital

A firm's *cost of capital* is defined as the cost of the funds supplied to it. It also is termed the *required rate of return,* because it specifies the minimum necessary rate of return required by the firm's investors. In this context, the cost of capital provides the firm with a basis for choosing among various capital investment projects. In this and the following two chapters, it is assumed that the cost of capital is a known value. Chapter 11 explores the methods used to determine the cost of capital.

How Projects Are Classified

A firm usually encounters several different types of projects when making capital expenditure decisions, including *independent projects, mutually exclusive projects,* and *contingent projects.* As is demonstrated in Chapter 9, project classification can influence the investment decision process.

Independent Projects. An **independent project** is one whose acceptance or rejection does not directly eliminate other projects from consideration. For example, a firm may want to install a new telephone communications system in its headquarters and replace a drill press during approximately the same time. In the absence of a constraint on the availability of funds, both projects could be adopted if they meet minimum investment criteria.

Mutually Exclusive Projects. A **mutually exclusive project** is one whose acceptance precludes the acceptance of one or more alternative proposals. Because two mutually exclusive projects have the capacity to perform the same function for a firm, only one should be chosen. For example, General Motors was faced with deciding whether it should locate its Saturn manufacturing complex in Kalamazoo, Michigan, or Spring Hill, Tennessee. It ultimately chose the Spring Hill site, and this precluded the Kalamazoo alternative.

Contingent Projects. A **contingent project** is one whose acceptance is dependent on the adoption of one or more other projects. For example, the decision by RJR Nabisco to build a new bakery in North Carolina was contingent upon RJR Nabisco investing in suitable air and water pollution control equipment. When a firm is considering contingent projects, it is best to consider together all projects that are dependent on one another and treat them as a single project for purposes of evaluation.

Availability of Funds

When a firm has adequate funds to invest in all projects that meet some capital budgeting selection criterion, such as has been true for Phillip Morris in recent years, the firm is said to be operating without a *funds constraint.* Frequently, however, the total initial cost of the acceptable projects in the absence of a funds constraint is greater than the total funds the firm has available to invest in capital projects.[1] This necessitates **capital rationing,** or setting limits on capital expenditures, and results in some special capital budgeting problems.[2]

BASIC FRAMEWORK FOR CAPITAL BUDGETING

According to economic theory, a firm should operate at the point where the marginal cost of an additional unit of output just equals the marginal revenue derived from the output. Following this rule leads to *profit maximization.* This principle also may be applied to capital budgeting decisions. In this context, a firm's marginal revenue is the rates of return earned on succeeding investments, and marginal cost may be defined as the firm's *marginal cost of capital* (MCC); that is, the cost of successive increments of capital acquired by the firm.

Figure 8-1 illustrates a simplified capital budgeting model. This model assumes that all projects have the same risk. The projects under consideration are indicated by lettered bars on the graph.

[1]Many times firms limit their capital expenditures, not because of a fund's constraint, but because of limited managerial resources needed to manage the project effectively.
[2]These are treated in Chapter 9.

FIGURE 8-1
Simplified Capital Budgeting Model

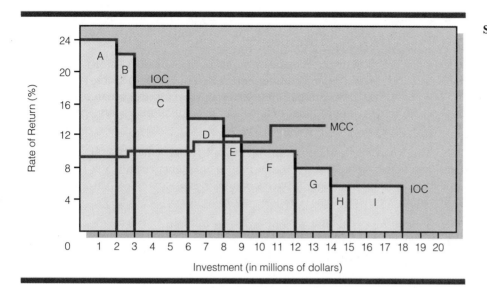

Project A requires an investment of $2 million and is expected to generate a 24 percent rate of return. Project B will cost $1 million ($3 million minus $2 million on the horizontal axis) and is expected to generate a 22 percent rate of return, and so on. The projects are arranged in descending order according to their expected rates of return, in recognition of the fact that no firm has an inexhaustible supply of projects offering high expected rates of return. This schedule of projects is often called the firm's *investment opportunity curve* (IOC). Typically, a firm will invest in its best projects first—such as Project A—before moving on to less-attractive alternatives.

The MCC schedule represents the marginal cost of capital to the firm. Note that the schedule increases as more funds are sought in the capital markets. The reasons for this include the following:

■ Investors' expectations about the firm's ability to successfully undertake a large number of new projects.

■ The business risk to which the firm is exposed because of its particular line of business.

■ The firm's financial risk, which is due to its capital structure.

■ The supply and demand for investment capital in the capital market.

■ The cost of selling new stock, which is greater than the cost of retained earnings.

MCC ↑

The basic capital budgeting model indicates that, in principle, the firm should undertake Projects A, B, C, D, and E, because the expected returns from each project exceed the firm's marginal cost of capital. Unfortunately, however, in practice financial decision making is not this simple. Some practical problems are encountered in trying to apply this model, including the following:

■ At any point in time, a firm probably will not know all of the capital projects available to it. In most firms, capital expenditures are proposed continually, based on results of research and development programs, changing market conditions, new technologies, corporate planning efforts, and so on. Thus, a schedule of projects similar to Figure 8-1 probably will be incomplete at the time the firm makes its capital expenditure decisions.

■ The shape of the MCC schedule itself may be difficult to determine. (The problems and techniques involved in estimating a firm's cost of capital are discussed in Chapter 11.)

■ In most cases, a firm can make only uncertain estimates of a project's future costs and revenues (and, consequently, its rate of return). Some projects will be more risky than others. The riskier a project is, the greater the rate of return that is required before it will be acceptable. (This concept is considered in more detail in Chapter 10.)

In spite of these and other problems, all firms make capital investment decisions. This chapter and the following two chapters provide tools that may be applied to the capital budgeting decision-making process.

Briefly, that process consists of four important steps:

1. Generating capital investment project proposals.
2. Estimating cash flows.
3. Evaluating alternatives and selecting projects to be implemented.
4. Reviewing a project's performance after it has been implemented, and postauditing its performance after its termination.

The remainder of this chapter is devoted to a discussion of the first two steps.

GENERATING CAPITAL INVESTMENT PROJECT PROPOSALS

Ideas for new capital investments can come from many sources, both inside and outside a firm. Proposals may originate at all levels of the organization—from factory workers up to the board of directors. Most large and medium-sized firms allocate the responsibility for identifying and analyzing capital expenditures to specific staff groups. These groups can include cost accounting, industrial engineering, marketing research, research and development, and corporate planning. In most firms, systematic procedures are established to assist in the search and analysis steps. For example, many firms provide detailed forms that the originator of a capital expenditure proposal must complete. These forms normally request information on the project's initial cost, the revenues it is expected to generate, and how it will affect the firm's overall operating expenses. These data then are channeled to a reviewer or group of reviewers at a higher level in the firm for analysis and possible acceptance or rejection.

Where a proposal goes for review often depends on how the particular project is *classified*.

Classifying Investment Projects

As noted earlier, there are several types of capital expenditures. These can be grouped into *projects generated by growth opportunities, projects generated by cost reduction opportunities,* and *projects generated to meet legal requirements and health and safety standards.*

Projects Generated by Growth Opportunities. Assume that a firm produces a particular product that is expected to experience increased demand during the upcoming years. If the firm's existing facilities are inadequate to handle the demand, proposals should be developed for expanding the firm's capacity.

These proposals may come from the corporate planning staff group, from a divisional staff group, or from some other source.

Because most existing products eventually become obsolete, a firm's growth is also dependent on the development and marketing of new products. This involves the generation of research and development investment proposals, marketing research investments, test marketing investments, and perhaps even investments in new plants, property, and equipment. For example, in order for the mineral extraction industries to keep growing, they must continually make investments in exploration and development. In 1995, Amoco's capital and exploration expenditures were $4.1 billion. Of that amount, $2.7 billion was in the exploration and production area. Similarly, firms in high technology industries—such as electronics and pharmaceuticals—must undertake continuing programs of research and development to compete successfully. For example, in 1995 Merck spent $1.331 billion on research and development, or about 8 cents out of each sales dollar.

Projects Generated by Cost Reduction Opportunities. Just as products become obsolete over time, so do plants, property, equipment, and production processes. Normal use makes older plants more expensive to operate because of the higher cost of maintenance and down time (idle time). In addition, new technological developments may render existing equipment economically obsolete. These factors create opportunities for cost reduction investments, which include replacing old, obsolete capital equipment with newer, more efficient equipment.

Projects Generated to Meet Legal Requirements and Health and Safety Standards. These projects include investment proposals for such things as pollution control, ventilation, and fire protection equipment. In terms of analysis, this group of projects is best considered as contingent upon other projects.

To illustrate, suppose Bethlehem Steel wishes to build a new steel plant in Cleveland, Ohio. The decision will be contingent upon the investment in the amount of pollution abatement equipment required by state and local laws. Thus, the decision to invest in the new plant must be based upon the *total* cost of the plant, including the pollution abatement equipment, and not just the operating equipment alone. In the case of existing facilities, this type of decision making is sometimes more complex. For example, suppose a firm is told it must install new pollution abatement equipment in a plant that has been in operation for some time. The firm first needs to determine the lowest cost alternative that will meet these legal requirements. "Lowest cost" is normally measured by the smallest present value of net cash outflows from the project. Then management must decide whether the remaining stream of cash flows from the plant is sufficient to justify the expenditure. If it appears as though it will not be, the firm may consider building a new facility, or it may decide simply to close down the original plant.

Project Size and the Decision-Making Process

The classification of a proposed project influences the capital investment decision-making process. However, there are other factors to consider—in particular, the size of the expenditure required to carry out the project.

Most firms *decentralize* the decision-making function. For example, whereas the approval of the president and the board of directors may be needed for especially large outlays, a divisional vice-president may be the final decision maker in the case of medium-sized outlays. A plant manager may have responsibility for deciding on smaller outlays, and a department head in a particular plant may be authorized to approve small outlays. For example, at Hershey Foods, a corporate-level review is required for all projects of more than $500,000. Projects below this amount are evaluated at the operating division level only. Hershey is moving toward a system that will require a corporate-level review for all projects of $50,000 or more. This "chain of command" varies with individual companies. In large firms, however, it is impossible for any one person to make every decision regarding proposed capital expenditures, and a decentralized system is usually employed.

   FOUNDATION CONCEPT
PRINCIPLES OF ESTIMATING CASH FLOWS

The capital budgeting process is concerned primarily with the estimation of the *cash flows* associated with a project, not just the project's contribution to accounting profits. Typically, a capital expenditure requires an initial *cash outflow*, termed the **net investment.** Thus, it is important to measure a project's performance in terms of the *net (operating) cash flows* it is expected to generate over a number of future years.

Figure 8-2 shows the estimated cash flows for a particular project. After an initial net investment of $100,000, the project is expected to generate a stream of net cash inflows over its anticipated 5-year life of $50,000 in year 1; $40,000 in year 2; $30,000 in year 3; $25,000 in year 4; and $5,000 in year 5. This type of project is called a **normal** or **conventional project.**

Nonnormal or nonconventional projects have cash flow patterns with more than one sign change. Table 8-2 illustrates the cash flow patterns for three sample projects. Projects X, Y, and Z can cause some analytical problems, as we shall see. Project X might require that certain equipment be shut down and rebuilt in year 3, and Project Y could be an investment in a mining property, with the negative cash flow in year 5 representing abandonment costs associated with closing down the mine after its mineral wealth has been depleted. Finally, Project Z might represent the investment in some pollution control equipment.

Regardless of whether a project's cash flows are expected to be normal or nonnormal, certain basic principles should be applied during their estimation, including the following:

FIGURE 8-2
Illustration of Estimated Cash Flows for a Normal Capital Investment Project

■ **Cash flows should be measured on an incremental basis.** In other words, the cash flow stream for a particular project should be estimated from the

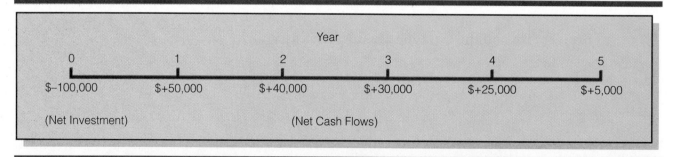

TABLE 8-2
Sample Cash Flow Patterns
for Nonnormal Projects

| | **YEAR** | | | | | |
Project	0	1	2	3	4	5
X	−100,000	+ 80,000	+60,000	−50,000	+75,000	+60,000
Y	−200,000	+150,000	+50,000	+40,000	+30,000	−20,000
Z	−150,000	− 20,000	−20,000	−25,000	−25,000	−30,000

perspective of how the entire cash flow stream of the firm will be affected if the project is adopted as compared with how the stream will be affected if the project is not adopted. Therefore, *all* changes in the firm's revenue stream, cost stream, and tax stream that would result from the acceptance of the project should be included in the analysis. In contrast, cash flows that would not be changed by the investment should be disregarded.

■ **Cash flows should be measured on an after-tax basis.** Because the initial investment made on a project requires the outlay of after-tax cash dollars, the returns from the project should be measured in the same units; namely, after-tax cash flows.

■ **All the indirect effects of a project should be included in the cash flow calculations.** For example, if a proposed plant expansion requires that working capital be increased for the firm as a whole—perhaps in the form of larger cash balances, inventories, or accounts receivable—the increase in working capital should be included in the *net investment* required for the project. As another example, assume that one division of a firm introduces a new product that competes directly with a product produced by another division. The first division may consider this product desirable, but when the impact on the second division's sales are considered, the project may be much less attractive.

■ **Sunk costs should not be considered when evaluating a project.** A *sunk cost* is an outlay that already has been made (or committed to be made). Because sunk costs cannot be recovered, they should not be considered in the decision to accept or reject a project. For example, in 1994, the Chemtron Corporation was considering constructing a new chemical disposal facility. Two years earlier, the firm had hired the R.O.E. Consulting Group to do an environmental impact analysis of the proposed site at a cost of $500,000. Because this $500,000 cost cannot be recovered whether the project is undertaken or not, it should not be considered in the accept-reject analysis taking place in 1994. The only relevant costs are the incremental outlays that will be made from this point forward if the project is undertaken.

■ **The value of resources used in a project should be measured in terms of their opportunity costs.** *Opportunity costs* of resources (assets) are the cash flows those resources could generate if they are not used in the project under consideration. For example, suppose that the site Chemtron is considering to use for its disposal facility has been owned by the firm for some time. The property originally cost $50,000, but a recent appraisal indicates that the property could be sold for $1 million. Because Chemtron must forego the receipt of $1 million from the sale of the site if the disposal facility is constructed, the appropriate opportunity cost of this piece of land is $1 million, not the original cost of $50,000.

These five principles of cash flow estimation may be applied to the specific problem of defining and calculating a project's *net investment* and *net cash flows*.

NET INVESTMENT (NINV)

The *net investment* (NINV) in a project is defined as the project's initial net cash outlay, that is, the outlay at time (period) 0. It is calculated using the following steps:

Step 1. The new project cost plus any installation and shipping costs associated with acquiring the asset and putting it into service[3]

PLUS

Step 2. Any increases in net working capital *initially* required as a result of the new investment

MINUS

Step 3. The net proceeds from the sale of existing assets when the investment is a replacement decision[4]

PLUS or MINUS

Step 4. The taxes associated with the sale of the existing assets and/or the purchase of the new assets[5]

EQUALS

The net investment (NINV).

The calculation of the net investment for two example projects is illustrated in later sections of the chapter dealing with asset expansion and asset replacement projects. Also discussed are some of the tax consequences that can influence the net investment of a project. These tax effects are the treatment of gains and losses from asset sales in the case of replacement decisions.

If a project generates additional revenues and the company extends credit to its customers, an additional initial investment in accounts receivable is required. Moreover, if additional inventories are necessary to generate the increased revenues, then an additional initial investment in inventory is required, too. This increase in initial working capital—that is, cash, accounts receivable, and inventories—should be calculated *net* of any automatic increases in current liabilities, such as accounts payable or wages and taxes payable, that occur because of the project. As a general rule, replacement projects require little or no net working capital increase. Expansion projects, on the other hand, normally require investments in additional net working capital.

Some projects require outlays over more than one year before positive cash inflows are generated. It may take several years to design and construct a new production facility, such as an automobile assembly plant. In these cases, the NINV for that project will be equal to the present value (at time 0) of this series of outlays, discounted at the firm's cost of capital. For example, consider a project requiring outlays of $100,000 in year 0, $30,000 in year 1, and $20,000 in year 2, with a cost of capital equal to 10 percent. The NINV or present value of the cash outlays is calculated as follows:[6]

---

[3]The asset cost plus installation and shipping costs form the basis upon which depreciation is computed.

[4]This normally is computed as the actual salvage value of the asset being replaced less any costs associated with physically removing or selling it.

[5]These taxes include any taxes associated with disposal of the old asset. The total tax effect may be either positive or negative; this is why it is either added to or subtracted from the new project cost.

[6]For tax purposes, the installed cost of this asset would be $150,000—the actual cash outlays required to put the plant or equipment in service.

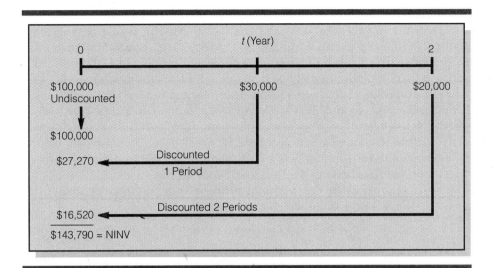

Year t	Cash Outlay	$PVIF_{0.10,t}$	Present Value of Cash Outlay
0	$100,000	1.000	$100,000
1	30,000	0.909	27,270
2	20,000	0.826	16,520
			NINV = $143,790

Figure 8-3 illustrates this concept.

NET (OPERATING) CASH FLOWS

Capital investment projects are expected to generate after-tax cash flow streams after the initial net investment has been made. The process of estimating incremental cash flows associated with a specific project is an important part of the capital budgeting process.

Capital budgeting is concerned primarily with the after-tax **net (operating) cash flows** (NCF) of a particular project, or change in cash inflows minus change in cash outflows. For any year during the life of a project, these may be defined as the change in operating earnings after taxes, ΔOEAT,[7] plus the change in depreciation, ΔDep, minus the change in the net working capital investment required by the firm to support the project, ΔNWC:[8]

$$NCF = \Delta OEAT + \Delta Dep - \Delta NWC \qquad (8.1)$$

[7]Operating earnings after tax, OEAT, differs from earnings after tax, EAT, because OEAT *does not* consider interest expenses in its calculation. Net cash flows, NCF, as used for capital budgeting purposes, normally do not consider financing charges, such as interest, because these financing charges will be reflected in the cost of capital that is used to discount a project's cash flows. To include financing charges in NCF would result in double counting of these costs.

[8]In years when a firm must increase its investment in net working capital (NWC) associated with a particular project, this increased investment in NWC *reduces* NCF. Normally, however, at the end of the life of a project, the NWC investment accumulated over the life of the project is recovered (for example, as inventories are sold and accounts receivable are collected). Thus, ΔNWC is negative (a reduction). Because of the minus sign before ΔNWC in Equation 8.1, the effect of a decline in the net working capital investments is an *increase* in NCF.

Depreciation is the systematic allocation of the cost of an asset with an economic life in excess of one year.[9] Depreciation reduces reported earnings and it also reduces taxes paid by a firm. If a firm's depreciation increases in a particular year as a result of adopting a project, after-tax net cash flow in that year will increase, all other things being equal. In addition, after-tax net cash flow also considers changes in a firm's investment in net working capital.[10] If a firm increases its accounts receivable, for example, in a particular year without increasing its current liabilities as a result of adopting a specific project, after-tax net cash flow in that year will decrease, all other things being equal. On the other hand, a reduction in a firm's investment in net working capital during a year results in an increase in the firm's NCF for that year.

ΔOEAT is equal to the change in operating earnings before taxes (ΔOEBT) times $(1 - T)$, where T is the marginal tax rate:

$$\Delta\text{OEAT} = \Delta\text{OEBT}(1 - T) \qquad (8.2)$$

ΔOEBT is defined as the change in revenues, ΔR, minus the changes in operating costs, ΔO, and depreciation, ΔDep:

$$\Delta\text{OEBT} = \Delta R - \Delta O - \Delta Dep \qquad (8.3)$$

Substituting Equation 8.3 into Equation 8.2 yields the following:

$$\Delta\text{OEAT} = (\Delta R - \Delta O - \Delta Dep)(1 - T) \qquad (8.4)$$

Substituting this Equation 8.4 into Equation 8.1 yields the following definition of net cash flow:

$$\text{NCF} = (\Delta R - \Delta O - \Delta Dep)(1 - T) + \Delta Dep - \Delta\text{NWC} \qquad (8.5)$$

These calculations and equations are summarized in Table 8-3. Equation 8.5 can be further extended into an *operational* definition of NCF by defining ΔR as $R_w - R_{wo}$, ΔO as $O_w - O_{wo}$, and ΔDep as $Dep_w - Dep_{wo}$ where

R_{wo} = Revenues of the firm *without* the project.

R_w = Revenues of the firm *with* the project.

O_{wo} = Operating costs exclusive of depreciation for the firm *without* the project.

O_w = Operating costs exclusive of depreciation for the firm *with* the project.

Dep_{wo} = Depreciation charges for the firm *without* the project.

Dep_w = Depreciation charges for the firm *with* the project.

The definition given in Equation 8.5 can be rewritten as follows:

$$\text{NCF} = [(R_w - R_{wo}) - (O_w - O_{wo}) - (Dep_w - Dep_{wo})](1 - T) \qquad (8.6)$$
$$+ (Dep_w - Dep_{wo}) - \Delta\text{NWC}$$

In the final year of a project's economic life, Equation 8.6 must be modified to reflect recovery of the incremental after-tax salvage value of the asset(s).

The following two sections illustrate the calculation of net cash flows using these equations.

---

[9]Depreciation *itself* is not a cash flow. Rather, it reduces earnings before taxes (EBT) and thus reduces income tax payments (a cash outflow). Equation 8.1 provides an easy procedure for reflecting the cash flow impact of depreciation.

[10]Changes in net working capital can occur as part of the net investment at time 0 or at any time during the life of the project.

TABLE 8-3
Summary of Net Cash Flow
Calculations and Equations

CALCULAT	VARIABLE	EQUATION
Change in revenue	ΔR	
Less: Change in operating costs	$-\Delta O$	
Less: Change in depreciation	$-\Delta Dep$	
Equals: Change in operating ear... taxes	ΔOEBT	8.3
Less: Taxes	$-T(\Delta\text{OEBT})$	
Equals: Change in operating earnings after taxes	ΔOEAT	8.2 & 8.4
Plus: Change in depreciation	$+\Delta Dep$	
Less: Change in net working capital	$-\Delta$NWC	
Equals: Net cash flow	NCF	8.1 & 8.5

Recovery of After-Tax Salvage Value

Whenever an asset is sold that has been depreciated, there are potential tax consequences that may affect the after-tax net proceeds received from the asset sale. These tax consequences are important when estimating the after-tax salvage value to be received at the end of the economic life of any project. As discussed earlier, the tax consequences of asset sales are also important when calculating the net investment required in a replacement investment project. There are four cases that need to be considered.

Case 1: Sale of an Asset for Its Book Value. If a company disposes of an asset for an amount exactly equal to the asset's tax book value, there is neither a gain nor a loss on the sale and thus there are no tax consequences. For example, if Burlington Textile sells for $50,000 an asset with a book value for tax purposes of $50,000, no taxes are associated with this disposal. (In general, the tax book value of an asset equals the installed cost of the asset less accumulated tax depreciation.)

Case 2: Sale of an Asset for Less Than Its Book Value. If Burlington Textile sells for $20,000 an asset having a tax book value of $50,000, Burlington Textile incurs a $30,000 pretax loss. Assuming that this asset is used in business or trade (an essential criterion for this tax treatment), this loss may be treated as an operating loss or an offset to operating income. This operating loss effectively reduces the company's taxes by an amount equal to the loss times the company's marginal tax rate.

Assume that the company's earnings before taxes is $100,000 (before consideration of the operating loss from the disposal of the asset). Taxes on these earnings are $100,000 times the company's marginal (40 percent) tax rate, or $40,000. (We use a 40 percent marginal tax rate throughout the book for ease of calculation. Actual current corporate marginal tax rates are discussed in Appendix A at the back of the book.) Because of the operating loss incurred by selling the asset for $20,000, the company's taxable income is reduced to $70,000, and the taxes decline to $28,000 (40 percent of $70,000). The $12,000 difference in taxes is equal to the tax loss on the sale of the old asset times the company's marginal tax rate ($30,000 × 40%).

Case 3: Sale of an Asset for More Than Its Book Value But Less Than Its Original Cost. If Burlington Textile sells the asset for $60,000—$10,000 more than the current tax book value—$50,000 of this amount constitutes a tax-free cash inflow, and the remaining $10,000 is taxed as operating income. As a result, the firm's taxes increase by $4,000, or the amount of the gain times the firm's marginal tax rate ($10,000 × 40%). (The IRS treats this gain as a recapture of depreciation.)

Case 4: Sale of an Asset for More Than Its Original Cost. If Burlington Textile sells the asset for $120,000 (assuming an original asset cost of $110,000), part of the gain from the sale is treated as ordinary income, and part is treated as a long-term *capital gain*. The gain receiving ordinary income treatment is equal to the difference between the original asset cost and the current tax book value, or $60,000 ($110,000 – $50,000). The capital gain portion is the amount in excess of the original asset cost, or $10,000. Under the Revenue Reconciliation Act of 1993, both ordinary income and capital gains are taxed at the same corporate rate (35 percent).

Recovery of Net Working Capital

In the last year of a project that, over its economic life, has required incremental net working capital investments, this net working capital is assumed to be liquidated and returned to the firm as cash. At the end of a project's life, all net working capital additions required over the project's life are recovered—not just the initial net working capital outlay occurring at time 0. Hence, the total accumulated net working capital is normally recovered in the last year of the project. This *decrease* in net working capital in the last year of the project *increases* the net cash flow for that year, all other things being equal. Of course, no tax consequences are associated with the recovery of NWC.

Interest Charges and Net Cash Flows

Often the purchase of a particular asset is tied closely to the creation of some debt obligation, such as the sale of mortgage bonds or a bank loan. Nevertheless, it is generally considered *incorrect* to deduct the interest charges associated with a particular project from the estimated cash flows. This is true for two reasons.

First, the decision about how a firm should be financed can—and should—be made independently of the decision to accept or reject one or more projects. Instead, the firm should seek some combination of debt, equity (common stock), and preferred stock capital that is consistent with management's wishes concerning the trade-off between financial risk and the cost of capital. In many cases, this will result in a capital structure with the cost of capital at or near its minimum. Because investment and financing decisions normally should be made independently of one another, each new project can be viewed as being financed with the same proportions of the various sources of capital funds used to finance the firm as a whole.

Second, when a discounting framework is used for project evaluation, the discount rate, or cost of capital, already incorporates the cost of funds used to finance a project. Thus, including interest charges in cash flow calculations essentially would result in a double counting of costs.

Depreciation

Depreciation is defined as the systematic allocation of the cost of an asset over more than one year. It allows a firm to spread the costs of fixed assets over a period of years to better match costs and revenues in each accounting period. The annual depreciation expense recorded for a particular asset is simply an allocation of historic costs and does not necessarily indicate a declining market value. For example, a company that is depreciating an office building may find the building's market value *appreciating* each year.

There are a number of alternative methods of recording the depreciation of an asset for *financial reporting* purposes. These include straight-line depreciation and various accelerated depreciation methods. Under the straight-line depreciation method, the annual amount of an asset's depreciation is calculated as follows:

$$\text{Annual depreciation amount} = \frac{\text{Installed cost}}{\text{number of years over which the asset is depreciated}} \qquad (8.7)$$

For *tax* purposes, the depreciation rate a firm uses has a significant impact on the cash flows of the firm. This is so because depreciation represents a *noncash* expense that is deductible for tax purposes. Hence, the greater the amount of depreciation charged in a period, the lower will be the firm's taxable income. With a lower reported taxable income, the firm's tax obligation (a cash outflow) is reduced, and the cash inflows for the firm are increased.

For example, if the Badger Company in a given year has revenues of $1,000, operating expenses exclusive of depreciation of $500, straight-line depreciation of $100, and a marginal tax rate of 40 percent, its operating cash flow will be:[11]

Revenues		$1,000
Less Operating expenses	$500	
Depreciation	100	
Total		600
Operating earnings before taxes		$ 400
Less Taxes (40%)		160
Operating earnings after taxes		$ 240
Plus Depreciation		100
Operating cash flow (CF)		$ 340

Now suppose Badger opts to use an accelerated depreciation method for tax purposes, rather than the straight-line method. As a result, its depreciation expense is recorded as $150 instead of $100. Its new operating cash flow will be as follows:

Revenues		$1,000
Less Operating expenses	$500	
Depreciation	150	
Total		650
Operating earnings before taxes		$ 350
Less Taxes (40%)		140
Operating earnings after taxes		$ 210
Plus Depreciation		150
Operating cash flow (CF)		$ 360

[11]This example assumes net working capital remains constant.

A comparison of the two cash flow statements shows that the use of accelerated depreciation reduces operating earnings after taxes from $240 to $210 and reduces taxes from $160 to $140 but increases operating cash flow to $360 from $340. Hence, the use of accelerated depreciation for tax purposes is desirable for the firm, because it reduces tax outlays and thereby increases cash flow. In general, a profitable firm will depreciate its assets as quickly as the tax law allows, and it should use whatever allowable method permits the highest percentage depreciation in the early years of an asset's life. The tax method currently used in the United States is the **Modified Accelerated Cost Recovery System** (MACRS) method; it is explained in Appendix A at the back of the book.

The cash flow examples discussed in this chapter use straight-line depreciation to keep the calculations simple. In actual practice, companies today should use the MACRS method when computing the NCFs from a project. *The relevant depreciation number that should be used when computing the after-tax net cash flows expected from a capital expenditure project is the tax depreciation amount.*

ASSET EXPANSION PROJECTS

A project that requires a firm to invest funds in additional assets in order to increase sales (or reduce costs) is called an *asset expansion project*. For example, suppose the TLC Yogurt Company has decided to capitalize on the exercise fad and plans to open an exercise facility in conjunction with its main yogurt and health foods store. To get the project underway, the company will rent additional space adjacent to its current store. The equipment required for the facility will cost $50,000. Shipping and installation charges for the equipment is expected to total $5,000. This equipment will be depreciated on a straight-line basis over its 5-year economic life to an estimated salvage value of $0. In order to open the exercise facility, TLC estimates that it will have to add about $7,000 initially to its net working capital in the form of additional inventories of exercise supplies, cash, and accounts receivable for its exercise customers (less accounts payable).

During the first year of operations, TLC expects its total revenues (from yogurt sales and exercise services) to increase by $50,000 above the level that would have prevailed without the exercise facility addition. These incremental revenues are expected to grow to $60,000 in year 2, $75,000 in year 3, decline to $60,000 in year 4, and decline again to $45,000 during the fifth and final year of the project's life. The company's incremental operating costs associated with the exercise facility, including the rental of the facility, are expected to total $25,000 during the first year and increase at a rate of 6 percent per year over the 5-year project life. Depreciation will be $11,000 per year ($55,000 installed cost, assuming no salvage value, divided by the 5-year economic life). TLC has a marginal tax rate of 40 percent. In addition, TLC expects that it will have to add about $5,000 per year to its net working capital in years 1, 2, and 3 and nothing in years 4 and 5. At the end of the project, the total accumulated net working capital required by the project will be recovered.

Calculating the Net Investment

First, we determine the net investment required for the exercise facility expansion. TLC must make a cash outlay of $50,000 to pay for the facility equipment. In addition, it must pay $5,000 in cash to cover the costs of shipping and installation of the equipment. Finally, TLC must invest $7,000 in initial net working capital to get the project underway. The four-step procedure discussed earlier for calculating the net investment yields the NINV required at time 0:

Purchase price of exercise equipment	$50,000
Plus Shipping and installation	5,000
Plus Initial net working capital required	7,000
Equals Net investment	$62,000

Note that steps 3 and 4 are not required in this problem since this is an asset expansion decision and no existing assets are being sold.

Calculating Annual Net Cash Flows

Next, we need to calculate the annual net cash flows associated with the project. Using Equation 8.5, these cash flows can be computed as shown in Table 8-4.

The cash flows associated with the exercise facility project can be summarized as follows:

Year	Net Investment and Net Cash Flows
0	−$62,000
1	14,400
2	19,500
3	27,546
4	22,535
5	34,463

TABLE 8-4
Calculation of Annual Net Cash Flows for TLC Exercise Facility

	YEAR 1	YEAR 2	YEAR 3	YEAR 4	YEAR 5
Incremental revenues (ΔR)	$50,000	$60,000	$75,000	$60,000	$45,000
Minus Incremental operating costs (ΔO)	25,000	26,500	28,090	29,775	31,562
Minus Incremental depreciation (ΔDep)	11,000	11,000	11,000	11,000	11,000
Equals Incremental operating earnings before tax (ΔOEBT)	$14,000	$22,500	$35,910	$19,225	$ 2,438
Minus Incremental taxes (40%) (T)	5,600	9,000	14,364	7,690	975
Equals Incremental operating earnings after tax (ΔOEAT)	$ 8,400	$13,500	$21,546	$11,535	$ 1,463
Plus Incremental depreciation (ΔDep)	11,000	11,000	11,000	11,000	11,000
Minus Incremental net working capital (ΔNWC)	5,000	5,000	5,000	0	−22,000
Plus After-tax salvage	—	—	—	—	0
Equals Net cash flow (NCF)	$14,400	$19,500	$27,546	$22,535	$34,463

In Chapter 9, several different capital budgeting decision models are applied to cash flows such as these to determine the desirability of capital investment projects.

 ## ASSET REPLACEMENT PROJECTS

The previous example of an asset expansion project illustrated the key elements of the calculation of a project's net investment and its annual net cash flows. In this section, we consider an *asset replacement* project. Asset replacements involve retiring one asset and replacing it with a more efficient asset.

Suppose Briggs & Stratton purchased an automated drill press 10 years ago that had an estimated economic life of 20 years. The drill press originally cost $150,000 and has been fully depreciated, leaving a current book value of $0. The actual market value of this drill press is $40,000. The company is considering replacing the drill press with a new one costing $190,000. Shipping and installation charges will add an additional $10,000 to the cost. The new machine would be depreciated to zero on a straight-line basis. The new machine is expected to have a 10-year economic life, and its actual salvage value at the end of the 10-year period is estimated to be $25,000. Briggs & Stratton's current marginal tax rate is 40 percent.

Calculating the Net Investment

Steps 1 and 2 of the net investment calculation are easy; the new project cost ($190,000) plus shipping and installation ($10,000) is $200,000. In this case, no initial incremental net working capital is required.

In steps 3 and 4, the net proceeds received from the sale of the old drill press have to be adjusted for taxes.

Because the old drill press is sold for $40,000, the gain from this sale is treated as a recapture of depreciation and thus taxed as ordinary income. Table 8-5 summarizes the NINV calculation for Briggs & Stratton. As can be seen in this table, the NINV is equal to $176,000.

Calculating Annual Net Cash Flows

Suppose Briggs & Stratton expects annual revenues during the project's first year to increase from $70,000 to $85,000 if the new drill press is purchased. (This might occur because the new press is faster than the old one and can meet the increasing demands for more work.) After the first year, revenues from the new project are expected to increase at a rate of $2,000 a year for the remainder of the project life.[12]

Assume further that while the old drill press required two operators, the new drill press is more automated and needs only one, thereby reducing annual operating costs from $40,000 to $20,000 during the project's first year. After the first year, annual operating costs of the new drill press are expected to increase by $1,000 a year over the remaining life of the project.[13] The old machine is fully depreciated, whereas the new machine will be depreciated on a straight-line

---

[12]For simplicity, we have assumed that the revenue figure of $70,000 without the project remains constant over the life of the project.

[13]For simplicity, we have assumed that the operating cost figure of $40,000 without the project remains constant over the life of the project.

TABLE 8-5
Net Investment Calculation
for Briggs & Stratton

Cost of new drill press	$190,000
Plus Shipping and installation charges	10,000
Equals Installed cost	$200,000
Plus Increase in initial net working capital	0
Minus Proceeds from sale of old drill press	40,000
Equals Net investment before taxes	$160,000
Plus Tax on gain from sale of old drill press (40% × $40,000)	16,000
Equals Net investment	$176,000

basis. The marginal tax rate of 40 percent applies. Assume also that the company's net working capital does not change as a result of replacing the drill press.

The first-year net cash flow resulting from the purchase of the new drill press can be computed by substituting R_w = $85,000, R_{wo} = $70,000, O_w = $20,000, O_{wo} = $40,000, Dep_w = $20,000, Dep_{wo} = $0, T = 0.40, and ΔNWC = $0 into Equation 8.6 as follows:

$$NCF = [(R_w - R_{wo}) - (O_w - O_{wo}) - (Dep_w - Dep_{wo})](1 - T) + (Dep_w - Dep_{wo}) - \Delta NWC$$

Year 1:

$$NCF_1 = [(\$85,000 - \$70,000) - (\$20,000 - \$40,000) - (\$20,000 - \$0)](1 - 0.4) + (\$20,000 - \$0) - \$0 = \$29,000$$

Using the different expected values for new revenues, R_w, and new operating costs, O_w, the remaining annual net cash flows can be computed as follows:

Year 2:

$$NCF_2 = [(\$87,000 - \$70,000) - (\$21,000 - \$40,000) - (\$20,000 - \$0)](1 - 0.4) + (\$20,000 - \$0) - \$0 = \$29,600$$

Year 3:

$$NCF_3 = [(\$89,000 - \$70,000) - (\$22,000 - \$40,000) - (\$20,000 - \$0)](1 - 0.4) + (\$20,000 - \$0) - \$0 = \$30,200$$

Year 4:

$$NCF_4 = [(\$91,000 - \$70,000) - (\$23,000 - \$40,000) - (\$20,000 - \$0)](1 - 0.4) + (\$20,000 - \$0) - \$0 = \$30,800$$

Year 5:

$$NCF_5 = [(\$93,000 - \$70,000) - (\$24,000 - \$40,000) - (\$20,000 - \$0)](1 - 0.4) + (\$20,000 - \$0) - \$0 = \$31,400$$

Year 6:

$$NCF_6 = [(\$95,000 - \$70,000) - (\$25,000 - \$40,000) - (\$20,000 - \$0)](1 - 0.4) + (\$20,000 - \$0) - \$0 = \$32,000$$

Year 7:

$$NCF_7 = [(\$97,000 - \$70,000) - (\$26,000 - \$40,000)$$
$$- (\$20,000 - \$0)](1 - 0.4) + (\$20,000 - \$0) - \$0$$
$$= \$32,600$$

Year 8:

$$NCF_8 = [(\$99,000 - \$70,000) - (\$27,000 - \$40,000)$$
$$- (\$20,000 - \$0)](1 - 0.4) + (\$20,000 - \$0) - \$0$$
$$= \$33,200$$

Year 9:

$$NCF_9 = [(\$101,000 - \$70,000) - (\$28,000 - \$40,000)$$
$$- (\$20,000 - \$0)](1 - 0.4) + (\$20,000 - \$0) - \$0$$
$$= \$33,800$$

In this example, in year 10, the $25,000 estimated salvage from the new drill press must be added along with its associated tax effects. This $25,000 salvage is treated as ordinary income because it represents a recapture of depreciation for tax purposes.

$$NCF_{10} = [(\$103,000 - \$70,000) - (\$29,000 - \$40,000)$$
$$- (\$20,000 - \$0)](1 - 0.4) + (\$20,000 - \$0) - \$0$$
$$+ \$25,000 \text{ salvage} - \text{tax on salvage } (0.4 \times \$25,000)$$
$$= \$34,400 + \$25,000 - \$10,000$$
$$= \$49,400$$

Table 8-6 is a summary worksheet for computing the net cash flows for Briggs & Stratton during the 10-year estimated economic life of the new drill press.

Table 8-7 summarizes the net cash flows for the entire project. This schedule of net cash flows plus the NINV computed in the preceding section form the basis for further analysis. In Chapter 9, several different capital budgeting decision models are applied to similar cash flow streams from other projects to determine the investment desirability of these projects. The cash flows developed in this chapter are an essential input in the capital budgeting decision process.

 PROBLEMS IN CASH FLOW ESTIMATION

Because project cash flows occur in the future, there are varying degrees of *uncertainty* about the value of these flows. Therefore, it is difficult to predict the actual cash flows of a project. The capital budgeting process assumes the decision maker is able to estimate cash flows accurately enough that these estimates can be used in project evaluation and selection. For this assumption to be realistic, a project proposal should be based on inputs from marketing managers regarding revenue estimates and inputs from the production and engineering staffs regarding costs and achievable levels of performance. Objective inputs from these sources can help reduce the uncertainty associated with cash flow estimation.

In addition, cash flow estimates for different projects may have varying degrees of uncertainty. For example, the returns from asset replacement projects generally are easier to forecast than the returns from new product introduction projects. Chapter 10 discusses some of the techniques used to incorporate risk analysis into capital budgeting decision models.

	YEAR									
	1	2	3	4	5	6	7	8	9	10
Change in revenues $(R_w - R_{wo})$*	$15,000	$17,000	$19,000	$21,000	$23,000	$25,000	$27,000	$29,000	$31,000	$33,000
Minus Change in operating costs $(O_w - O_{wo})$†	−20,000	−19,000	−18,000	−17,000	−16,000	−15,000	−14,000	−13,000	−12,000	−11,000
Minus Change in depreciation $(Dep_w - Dep_{wo})$‡	20,000	20,000	20,000	20,000	20,000	20,000	20,000	20,000	20,000	20,000
Equals Change in operating earnings before taxes (ΔOEBT)	$15,000	$16,000	$17,000	$18,000	$19,000	$20,000	$21,000	$22,000	$23,000	$24,000
Minus Tax (40%)	6,000	6,400	6,800	7,200	7,600	8,000	8,400	8,800	9,200	9,600
Equals Change in operating earnings after taxes (ΔOEAT)	$ 9,000	$ 9,600	$10,200	$10,800	$11,400	$12,000	$12,600	$13,200	$13,800	$14,400
Plus Change in depreciation $(Dep_w - Dep_{wo})$	20,000	20,000	20,000	20,000	20,000	20,000	20,000	20,000	20,000	20,000
Minus Change in net working capital (ΔNWC)	0	0	0	0	0	0	0	0	0	0
Equals Net cash flow before salvage	$29,000	$29,600	$30,200	$30,800	$31,400	$32,000	$32,600	$33,200	$33,800	$34,400
Plus Salvage	0	0	0	0	0	0	0	0	0	25,000
Minus Tax on salvage (0.4 × salvage)	0	0	0	0	0	0	0	0	0	10,000
Equals Net cash flow	$29,000	$29,600	$30,200	$30,800	$31,400	$32,000	$32,600	$33,200	$33,800	$49,400

*The change in revenues from undertaking a project may be either positive or negative.

†The change in operating costs may be either positive or negative. In this case, the firm's operating costs *decline* by $20,000 in year 1, for example; that is, the change in operating costs is *negative*, indicating a cost saving. This cost saving is *added* to the change in revenues (subtracting a negative number is the same as adding a positive number). If, in another situation, operating costs were to *increase* as a result of a project, the increased costs would be *subtracted* from the change in revenues.

‡The change in depreciation may be either positive or negative. In this case, it is *positive* and has the effect of reducing the amount of taxable earnings, thus reducing the amount of taxes paid. Hence, this *increases* the cash flow from the project. If the change in depreciation were *negative*, it would have the effect of increasing the taxable earnings, increasing taxes paid, and *reducing* the cash flows from the project.

TABLE 8-6
Annual Net Cash Flow Worksheet for the Briggs & Stratton Drill Press Acquisition

THE PRACTICE OF CASH FLOW ESTIMATION FOR CAPITAL BUDGETING

The analysis presented in this chapter and throughout the book suggests that generating accurate estimates of the cash flows from investment projects is extremely important to the success of the firm. A recent survey supports this conclusion and provides considerable insight regarding the cash flow estimation procedures used by larger firms (Fortune 500).[14]

The majority of the firms responding to the survey had annual capital budgets of more than $100 million. Nearly 67 percent of the firms prepared formal cash flow estimates for over 60 percent of their annual capital outlays, and a majority produced detailed cash flow projections for capital investments requiring an initial outlay of $40,000 or more. Firms with high capital intensity

[14]Randolph A. Pohlman, E. S. Santiago, and F. L. Markel, "Cash Flow Estimation Practices of Large Firms," *Financial Management* (Summer 1988): 71–79.

TABLE 8-7
Summary Project Cash Flows
for Briggs & Stratton

YEAR	NET INVESTMENT AND NET CASH FLOWS
0	–$176,000
1	29,000
2	29,600
3	30,200
4	30,800
5	31,400
6	32,000
7	32,600
8	33,200
9	33,800
10	49,400

and high leverage were more likely to have one or more persons, such as a financial analyst, treasurer, controller, or department manager, designated to oversee the process of cash flow estimation. This reflects the larger number of projects associated with capital intensive firms and the need to effectively manage the risk associated with high leverage.

When asked about the type of cash flow estimates that were generated, 56 percent indicated that they used single dollar estimates, 8 percent used a range of estimates, and 36 percent used both single-dollar estimates and a range of estimates. There was a significant positive correlation between firms that use both types of estimates and measures of operating and financial risk, suggesting that the use of a range of estimates is one procedure for managing high risk.

Forecasting methods employed by the respondent firms included subjective estimates from management, sensitivity analysis, consensus analysis of expert opinions, and computer simulation. Many firms used multiple cash flow forecasting techniques. The longer the forecasting horizon—that is, the longer the economic life of the project—the more likely is a firm to use multiple methods for forecasting future cash flows.

Financial factors considered to be important in generating cash flow estimates include working capital requirements, project risk, tax considerations, the project's impact on the firm's liquidity, the anticipated rate of inflation, and expected salvage value. Important marketing factors considered include sales forecasts, the competitive advantages and disadvantages of the product, and product life. Important production factors include operating expenses, material and supply costs, overhead and expenses for manufacturing, capacity utilization, and start-up costs.

Three-fourths of the companies surveyed make comparisons between actual and projected cash flows, with nearly all the firms comparing actual versus projected initial outlays and operating cash flows over the project life; and about two-thirds of these firms make comparisons of actual versus projected salvage values. The most accurate cash flow estimates are reported to be the initial outlay estimates, and the least accurate element of cash flow estimates is the annual operating cash flows. Cash flow forecasts were more accurate for equipment replacement investments, compared with expansion and modernization investments, and acquisitions of ongoing businesses. Firms with the information system in place to generate cash flow forecasts tend to produce more accurate forecasts than firms with less sophisticated capital project evaluation procedures.

 ETHICAL ISSUES
CASH FLOW ESTIMATION BIASES

The estimation of the cash flows associated with an investment project is the most important step in the capital expenditure evaluation process. If the cash flow estimates associated with a project are intentionally or unintentionally biased, a firm's resources are unlikely to be allocated to the set of investment projects that will maximize shareholder wealth.

There are several reasons why managers might produce biased cash flow estimates when preparing capital expenditure project proposals. First, a manager might be tempted to overestimate the revenues or underestimate the costs associated with a project if the manager is attempting to expand the resource base over which he or she has control. By biasing the estimates of a project's cash flows upward, a manager is likely to receive a larger share of the investment resources of the firm. Because managerial compensation is sometimes tied to the span of job responsibilities, managers may be tempted to expand this span of control at the expense of other areas in the firm.

Second, some firms tie employee compensation to performance relative to stated objectives—a compensation scheme often called *management by objective*. If a manager is confident that the best estimate of the cash flows from a proposed project are sufficiently large to guarantee project acceptance, the manager may be tempted to reduce these cash flow estimates to a level below the "most likely outcome" level, confident that the project will continue to be viewed as an acceptable investment and that it will be funded. However, once the project is underway, the project manager will feel less pressure to meet projected performance standards. The downward bias in the cash flow estimates provides a cushion that permits suboptimal management of the project while achieving the objectives enunciated when the project was first proposed.

What impact does intentionally biasing cash flow estimates for investment projects have on achieving the goal of shareholder wealth maximization?

■ SUMMARY

- *Capital budgeting* is the process of planning for purchases of assets whose returns are expected to continue beyond one year.
- Capital investments have a long-term impact on the performance of a firm. The proper forecasting of capital needs can help to ensure that a firm's productive capacity will meet future requirements.
- Ideally, a firm should invest in new projects up to the point at which the rate of return from the last project is equal to the marginal cost of capital.
- Projects may be classified as *independent, mutually exclusive,* or *contingent.* The acceptance of an independent project does not directly eliminate other projects from consideration; the acceptance of a mutually exclusive project precludes other alternatives; and the acceptance of a contingent project depends on the adoption of one or more other projects.
- The *cost of capital* is the cost of funds supplied to a firm. It is often used in conjunction with capital project evaluation techniques as a basis for choosing among various investment alternatives.
- There are four basic steps in the capital budgeting process: *the generation of proposals, the estimation of cash flows, the evaluation and selection of alternatives,* and *the postaudit or review.* The first two steps are detailed in this chapter.
- New projects may be generated by *growth opportunities, cost reduction opportunities,* or *the need to meet legal requirements and health and safety standards.*
- Project cash flows should be measured on an *incremental after-tax* basis and should include all the indirect effects the project will have on the firm.
- Resources of a firm used in an investment project should be valued at their *opportunity cost* based upon the cash flows these resources could generate in their next-best alternative use.

■ *Sunk costs* represent outlays that already have been made or committed and that cannot be recovered. Sunk costs should not be considered when evaluating an investment project.

■ The *net investment* (NINV) in a project is the net cash outlay required to place the project in service. It includes the project cost *plus* any necessary increases in initial net working capital *minus* any proceeds from the sale of the old asset(s) (in the case of replacement decisions) *plus or minus* the taxes associated with the sale of the old asset(s) and/or the purchase of the new asset(s).

■ The *net (operating) cash flows* (NCF) from a project are the incremental changes in a firm's operating cash flows that result from investing in the project. These flows include the changes in the firm's revenues, operating costs, depreciation, taxes, and net working capital with and without the project.

■ An *asset expansion* project requires a firm to invest funds in additional assets to increase sales or reduce costs. *Asset replacements,* in contrast, involve retiring one asset and replacing it with a more efficient one.

■ Two problems that complicate the estimation of cash flows are the element of *uncertainty* associated with cash flows and the intentional or unintentional introduction of *bias* into the estimation procedure.

■ QUESTIONS AND TOPICS FOR DISCUSSION

1. Discuss how capital budgeting procedures might be used by each of the following:
   a. Personnel managers.
   b. Research and development staffs.
   c. Advertising executives.
2. What is a mutually exclusive investment project? An independent project? A contingent project? Give an example of each.
3. What effect does capital rationing have on a firm's ability to maximize shareholder wealth?
4. What are the primary types of capital investment projects? Does a project's type influence how it is analyzed?
5. Cash flows for a particular project should be measured on an incremental basis and should consider all the indirect effects of the project. What does this involve?
6. What factors should be considered when estimating a project's NINV?
7. Because depreciation is a noncash expense, why is it considered when estimating a project's net cash flows?
8. What are the potential tax consequences of selling an old asset in an asset replacement investment decision?
9. Why is it generally incorrect to consider interest charges when computing a project's net cash flows?
10. Distinguish between asset expansion and asset replacement projects. How does this distinction affect the capital expenditure analysis process?
11. How is the opportunity cost concept used in the capital budgeting process?

■ SELF-TEST PROBLEMS

ST1. The Fleming Company, a food distributor, is considering replacing a filling line at its Oklahoma City warehouse. The existing line was purchased several years ago for $600,000. The line's book value is $200,000, and Fleming management feels it could be sold at this time for $150,000. A new, increased capacity line can be purchased for $1,200,000. Delivery and installation of the new line are expected to cost an additional $100,000. Assuming Fleming's marginal tax rate is 40 percent, calculate the net investment for the new line.

ST2. International Foods Corporation (IFC) currently processes seafood with a unit it purchased several years ago. The unit, which originally cost $500,000, currently has a book value of $250,000. IFC is considering replacing the existing unit with a newer, more efficient one. The new unit will cost $700,000 and will require an additional $50,000 for delivery and installation. The new unit also will require IFC to increase its investment in initial net working capital by $40,000. The new unit will be depreciated on a straight-line basis over 5 years to a zero balance. IFC expects to sell the existing unit for $275,000. IFC's marginal tax rate is 40 percent.

If IFC purchases the new unit, annual revenues are expected to increase by $100,000 (due to increased processing capacity), and annual operating costs (exclusive of depreciation) are expected to decrease by $20,000. Annual revenues and operating costs are expected to remain constant at this new level over the 5-year life of the project. IFC estimates that its net working capital investment will increase by $10,000 per year over the life of the project. After 5 years, the new unit will be completely depreciated and is expected to be sold for $70,000. (Assume that the existing unit is being depreciated at a rate of $50,000 per year.)

a. Calculate the project's net investment.
b. Calculate the annual net cash flows for the project.

■ PROBLEMS*

1. The MacCauley Company has sales of $200 million and total expenses (excluding depreciation) of $130 million. Straight-line depreciation on the company's assets is $15 million, and the maximum accelerated depreciation allowed by law is $25 million. Assume that all taxable income is taxed at 40 percent. Assume also that net working capital remains constant.

   a. Calculate the MacCauley Company's after-tax operating cash flow using both straight-line and accelerated depreciation.
   b. Assuming the company uses straight-line depreciation for book purposes and accelerated depreciation for tax purposes, show the income statement reported to the stockholders. What is the after-tax operating cash flow under these circumstances?

2. Calculate the annual straight-line depreciation for a machine that costs $50,000 and has installation and shipping costs that total $1,000. The machine will be depreciated over a period of 10 years. The company's marginal tax rate is 40 percent.

3. The Cooper Electronics Company has developed the following schedule of potential investment projects that may be undertaken during the next 6 months:

Project	Cost (in millions of dollars)	Expected Rate of Return
A	$ 3.0	20%
B	1.5	22
C	7.0	7
D	14.0	10
E	50.0	12
F	12.0	9
G	1.0	44

*Colored numbers denote problems that have check answers provided at the end of the book.

a. If Cooper requires a minimum rate of return of 10 percent on all investments, which projects should be adopted?

b. In general, how would a capital budgeting constraint on the available amount of investment funds influence these decisions?

c. How would differing levels of project risk influence these decisions?

4. Johnson Products is considering purchasing a new milling machine that costs $100,000. The machine's installation and shipping costs will total $2,500. If accepted, the milling machine project will require an initial net working capital investment of $20,000. Johnson plans to depreciate the machine on a straight-line basis over a period of 8 years. About a year ago, Johnson paid $10,000 to a consulting firm to conduct a feasibility study of the new milling machine. Johnson's marginal tax rate is 40 percent.

a. Calculate the project's net investment (NINV).

b. Calculate the annual straight-line depreciation for the project.

e✗cel
5. A new machine costing $100,000 is expected to save the McKaig Brick Company $15,000 per year for 12 years before depreciation and taxes. The machine will be depreciated on a straight-line basis for a 12-year period to an estimated salvage value of $0. The firm's marginal tax rate is 40 percent. What are the annual net cash flows associated with the purchase of this machine? Also compute the net investment (NINV) for this project.

6. The Jacobs Chemical Company is considering building a new potassium sulfate plant. The following cash outlays are required to complete the plant:

Year	Cash Outlay
0	$4,000,000
1	2,000,000
2	500,000

Jacob's cost of capital is 12 percent, and its marginal tax rate is 40 percent.

a. Calculate the plant's net investment (NINV).

b. What is the installed cost of the plant for tax purposes?

e✗cel
7. The Taylor Mountain Uranium Company currently has annual cash revenues of $1.2 million and annual cash expenses of $700,000. Depreciation amounts to $200,000 per year. These figures are expected to remain constant for the foreseeable future (at least 15 years). The firm's marginal tax rate is 40 percent.

A new high-speed processing unit costing $1.2 million is being considered as a potential investment designed to increase the firm's output capacity. This new piece of equipment will have an estimated usable life of 10 years and a $0 estimated salvage value. If the processing unit is bought, Taylor's annual revenues are expected to increase to $1.6 million and annual expenses (exclusive of depreciation) will increase to $900,000. Annual depreciation will increase to $320,000. Assume that no increase in net working capital will be required as a result of this project. Compute the project's annual net cash flows for the next 10 years, assuming that the new processing unit is purchased. Also compute the net investment (NINV) for this project.

8. A firm has an opportunity to invest in a new device that will replace two of the firm's older machines. The new device costs $570,000 and requires an additional outlay of $30,000 to cover installation and shipping. The new device will cause the firm to increase its net working capital by $20,000. Both the old machines can be sold—the first for $100,000 (book value equals $95,000) and the second for $150,000 (book value equals $75,000). The original cost of the first machine was $200,000, and the original cost of the second machine was $140,000. The firm's marginal tax bracket is 40 percent. Compute the net investment for this project.

e✗cel
9. Five years ago, the Mori Foods Company acquired a bean processing machine. The machine cost $30,000 and is being depreciated using the straight-line method over a

10-year period to an estimated salvage value of $0. A new, improved processor is now available, and the firm is considering making a switch. The firm's marginal tax rate is 40 percent. What are the after-tax cash flow effects of selling the old processing unit if it can be sold for the following prices?

a. $15,000

b. $5,000

c. $26,000

d. $32,000

10. Nguyen, Inc. is considering the purchase of a new computer system (ICX) for $130,000. The system will require an additional $30,000 for installation. If the new computer is purchased it will replace an old system that has been fully depreciated. The new system will be depreciated over a period of 10 years using straight-line depreciation. If the ICX is purchased, the old system will be sold for $20,000. The ICX system, which has a useful life of 10 years, is expected to increase revenues by $32,000 *per year* over its useful life. Operating costs are expected to decrease by $2,000 *per year* over the life of the system. The firm is taxed at a 40 percent marginal rate.

a. What net investment is required to acquire the ICX system and replace the old system?

b. Compute the annual net cash flows associated with the purchase of the ICX system.

11. Two years ago, Agro, Inc. purchased an ACE generator that cost $250,000. Agro had to pay an additional $50,000 for delivery and installation, and the investment in the generator required the firm to increase its net working capital position by $25,000. The generator, which is being depreciated over a period of 5 years using straight-line depreciation, has a current market value of $79,550. The firm's marginal tax rate is 40 percent. If the firm liquidates the asset for its current market value, compute the after-tax proceeds from the sale of the asset.

12. Benford, Inc. is planning to open a new sporting goods store in a suburban mall. Benford will lease the needed space in the mall. Equipment and fixtures for the store will cost $200,000 and be depreciated over a 5-year period on a straight-line basis to $0. The new store will require Benford to increase its net working capital by $200,000 at time 0. First-year sales are expected to be $1 million and to increase at an annual rate of 8 percent over the expected 10-year life of the store. Operating expenses (including lease payments and excluding depreciation) are projected to be $700,000 during the first year and increase at a 7 percent annual rate. The salvage value of the store's equipment and fixtures is anticipated to be $10,000 at the end of 10 years. Benford's marginal tax rate is 40 percent.

a. Compute the net investment required for Benford.

b. Compute the annual net cash flows for the 10-year projected life of the store.

13. A new machine costing $100,000 is expected to save the McKaig Brick Company $15,000 per year for 12 years before depreciation and taxes. The machine will be depreciated as a 7-year class MACRS asset. The firm's marginal tax rate is 40 percent. What are the annual net cash flows associated with the purchase of this machine? Also compute the net investment (NINV) for this project. (Hint: See Appendix A at the back of the book for information on MACRS depreciation. This problem is the same as Problem 5 except for depreciation method.)

14. Nguyen, Inc. is considering the purchase of a new computer system (ICX) for $130,000. The system will require an additional $30,000 for installation. If the new computer is purchased, it will replace an old system that has been fully depreciated. The new system will be depreciated under the MACRS rules applicable to 7-year class assets. If the ICX is purchased, the old system will be sold for $20,000. The ICX system, which has a useful life of 10 years, is expected to increase revenues by

$32,000 *per year* over its useful life. Operating costs are expected to decrease by $2,000 *per year* over the life of the system. The firm is taxed at a 40 percent marginal rate. (Hint: See Appendix A at the back of the book for information on MACRS depreciation. Except for the depreciation method, this problem is the same as Problem 10.)

  a. What net investment is required to acquire the ICX system and replace the old system?

  b. Compute the annual net cash flows associated with the purchase of the ICX system.

15. Argyl Manufacturing is evaluating the possibility of expanding its operations. This expansion will require the purchase of land at a cost of $100,000. A new building will cost $100,000 and be depreciated on a straight-line basis over 20 years to a salvage value of $0. Actual land salvage at the end of 20 years is expected to be $200,000. Actual building salvage at the end of 20 years is expected to be $150,000. Equipment for the facility is expected to cost $250,000. Installation costs will be an additional $40,000 and shipping costs will be $10,000. This equipment will be depreciated as a 7-year MACRS asset. Actual estimated salvage at the end of 20 years is $0. The project will require net working capital of $70,000 initially (year 0), an additional $40,000 at the end of year 1, and an additional $40,000 at the end of year 2. The project is expected to generate increased EBIT (operating income) for the firm of $100,000 during year 1. Annual EBIT is expected to grow at a rate of 4 percent per year until the project terminates at the end of year 20. The marginal tax rate is 40 percent. Compute the initial net investment and the annual net cash flow from the project in year 20.

16. Homecraft Stores (HSI), which operates a chain of retail warehouse-type stores, is considering opening a new store in the Tampa area. The store itself will cost $7,000,000 to build. In addition, fixtures for the store are expected to cost $700,000 and installation of the fixtures is estimated to cost another $50,000. Initial net working capital (primarily due to inventory) is expected to be $600,000. HSI plans to build the Tampa store on land it purchased 5 years ago for $200,000. The land presently is worth $500,000 and is expected to remain at $500,000 while the store is being built. Calculate the net investment for the proposed Tampa store.

17. Ralph's Bow Works (RBW) is planning to add a new line of bow ties that will require the acquisition of a new knitting and tying machine. The machine will cost $1,000,000. It is classified as a 7-year MACRS asset and will be depreciated as such. Interest costs associated with financing the equipment purchase are estimated to be $50,000 per year. The expected salvage value of the machine at the end of 10 years is $50,000. The decision to add the new line of bow ties will require additional net working capital of $50,000 immediately, $25,000 at the end of year 1, and $10,000 at the end of year 2. RBW expects to sell $300,000 worth of the bow ties during each of the 10 years of product life. RBW expects the sales of its other ties to decline by $25,000 (in year 1) as a result of adding this new line of ties. The lost sales level will remain constant at $25,000 over the 10-year life of the proposed project. The cost of producing and selling the ties is estimated to be $50,000 per year. RBW will realize savings of $5,000 each year because of lost sales on its other tie lines. The marginal tax rate is 40 percent. Compute the net investment (year 0) and the net cash flows for years 1 and 10 for this project.

18. Bratton Stone Works is considering an expansion proposal that will require an outlay of $1 million for land and $5 million for equipment. The equipment will be depreciated under MACRS rules as a 7-year class asset. The salvage value of the equipment at the end of 10 years is expected to be $1 million. The actual life of the project is expected to be 10 years. At the end of 10 years, Bratton hopes to sell the land for $1,800,000. Revenues from the project are expected to be $700,000 per

year. Operating costs are expected to be $200,000 per year. The ordinary and capital gains tax rate for Bratton is 40 percent. The project will require an additional investment in working capital of $250,000 in year 0 and $150,000 at the end of year 1. What net cash flow will this project produce in year 10?

19. Locus Quintatus, Inc., a highly profitable maker of customized chariots, is planning to introduce a new model shortly. The firm must purchase equipment immediately at a cost of $900,000. Freight and installation costs for this equipment will be $100,000. The equipment will be depreciated as a 7-year class asset under MACRS. During the first year, Locus will have incremental operating expenses of $300,000 that are attributable to this project. Locus expects to be able to sell 1,000 chariots during year 2 at an average price of $800 each and to incur operating expenses of $300,000. Also, Locus expects its net working capital investment will increase by $50,000 during year 2. (Assume all operating costs and revenues are incurred at the end of each year.) The marginal tax rate for Locus is 40 percent. What is the required net investment, and what are the year 1 and year 2 net cash flows?

20. Clyne Industries wants to market its new Slammin Jammin Basketball Goal Set. To bring this product to the market will require the purchase of equipment costing $650,000. Shipping and installation expenses associated with the equipment are estimated to be $50,000. In addition, Clyne will incur incremental employee training and recruiting expenses of $100,000, all of which will be incurred at time 0. Additional net working capital investments of $50,000 will be required at time 0, $25,000 in year 1, and $10,000 in year 2. Revenues are expected to be $250,000 in year 1 and grow at a rate of $25,000 per year through year 5, and then decline by $25,000 per year until the project is terminated at the end of year 10. Annual operating expenses are expected to be $80,000 in year 1 and to grow at a rate of $10,000 per year until the end of the project life. Depreciation will be under MACRS for a 7-year class asset. The salvage value of the equipment at the end of 10 years is expected to be $50,000. The marginal, ordinary tax rate is 40 percent and the capital gains tax rate is 30 percent. Compute the expected net cash flow for year 10, the last year in the life of the project.

21. Steber Packaging, Inc. expects sales next year of $50 million. Of this total, 40 percent are expected to be for cash and the balance will be on credit, payable in 30 days. Operating expenses are expected to total $25 million. Accelerated depreciation is expected to total $10 million, although the company will only report $6 million of depreciation on its public financial reports. The marginal tax rate for Steber is 34 percent. Current assets now total $25 million and current liabilities total $15 million. Current assets are expected to increase to $30 million over the coming year. Current liabilities are expected to increase to $17 million. Compute the projected after-tax operating cash flow for Steber during the coming year.

22. Hurley's Winery is planning to acquire a new grape masher. The masher will cost $100,000 including shipping and installation and will be depreciated as a 7-year MACRS asset. At the time the masher is purchased, Hurley will have to invest $5,000 in net working capital. Additional investments in net working capital are required at the end of year 1 ($3,000) and year 2 ($2,000). Net revenues attributable to the masher are expected to total $25,000 during year 1 and to grow by 5 percent per annum through the end of year 6. After that time, revenues are expected to decline by 10 percent per annum. Annual year 1 cash operating expenses are expected to total $10,000 and grow at an annual rate of 10 percent per annum. Hurley expects to sell the masher at one second after midnight on the first day of year 8 for $10,000. The marginal tax rate for Hurley is 40 percent for ordinary income and 28 percent for capital gains. Compute the expected net cash flows for year 7. Include in your year 7 calculations the proceeds from the salvage value of the masher and recovery of net working capital at the beginning of year 8. For the purposes of present value calculations, you may assume that the end of year 7 is the same as the beginning of year 8.

http://

23. Visit *Fortune Magazine*'s Web site and find the top ten companies on their list of the *Fortune 500* (as ranked by total revenue). Then visit the Thomson Investors Network site and find the cash flow of these companies for the past four years. Do you see a relationship between revenues and cash flows for these companies? Based on what you know, what *should be* the long-term relationship between revenues and cash flow?
http://www.fortune.com
http://www.thomsoninvest.net

■ SOLUTIONS TO SELF-TEST PROBLEMS

ST1. Net investment calculation:

Asset cost	$1,200,000
Plus Delivery and installation	100,000
Installed cost	$1,300,000
Minus Proceeds from sale of old asset	150,000
Minus Tax savings on loss from sale of old asset	
($50,000 (loss) × 0.4)	20,000
Net investment	$1,130,000

ST2. a. Net investment calculation:

Asset cost	$700,000
Plus Delivery and installation	50,000
Installed cost	$750,000
Minus Proceeds from sale of old asset	275,000
Plus Tax on sale of old asset ($275,000 − $250,000) (0.4)	10,000
Plus Net working capital	40,000
Net investment	$525,000

b. Net cash flow calculation:

$$NCF_{1-4} = [\$100,000 - (-\$20,000) - (\$150,000 - \$50,000)]$$

$$(1 - 0.40) + (\$150,000 - \$50,000) - \$10,000$$

$$= \$102,000$$

$$NCF_5 = NCF_{1-4} + \text{recovery of accumulated net working capital}$$
$$\text{investment} + \text{after-tax cash flow from sale of new unit}$$

$$= \$102,000 + \$90,000 + \$70,000 (1 - 0.4)$$

$$= \$234,000$$

■ GLOSSARY

Capital Budgeting The process of planning for purchases of assets whose cash flows are expected to continue beyond one year.

Capital Expenditure The amount of money spent to purchase a long-term asset, such as a piece of equipment. This cash outlay generally is expected to result in a flow of future cash benefits extending beyond one year in time. (Also called *capital investment*.)

Capital Rationing The process of limiting the number of capital expenditure projects because of insufficient funds to finance all projects that otherwise meet the firm's criteria for acceptability or because of a lack of sufficient managerial resources to undertake all otherwise acceptable projects.

Contingent Project A project whose acceptance depends on the adoption of one or more other projects.

Depreciation The systematic allocation of the cost of an asset over its expected economic life or some other period of time for financial reporting purposes, tax purposes, or both.

Independent Project A project whose acceptance or rejection does not result directly in the elimination of other projects from consideration.

MACRS Depreciation The Modified Accelerated Cost Recovery System of depreciation, established in 1986.

Mutually Exclusive Project A project whose acceptance precludes the acceptance of one or more alternative projects.

Net (Operating) Cash Flow Cash inflow minus cash outflow. It is measured as the change in net operating earnings after taxes plus the change in depreciation minus the change in net working capital requirements associated with a particular investment project.

Net Investment The net cash outlay required at the beginning of an investment project.

Normal Project A project whose cash flow stream requires an initial outlay of funds followed by a series of positive net cash inflows. This sometimes is called a conventional project.

CAPITAL BUDGETING: DECISION CRITERIA AND REAL OPTION CONSIDERATIONS

9

1. The *net present value* of an investment project is defined as the present value of the stream of expected net cash flows from the project minus the project's net investment.
   a. A project is acceptable if its NPV is greater than or equal to zero.
   b. By maximizing the net present value of accepted projects, a firm will also maximize shareholder wealth.
2. The *internal rate of return* (IRR) is defined as the discount rate that equates the present value of the expected net cash flows from a project with the present value of the net investment.
   a. A project is acceptable if it has an internal rate of return that is greater than or equal to the firm's cost of capital.
   b. The net present value and internal rate of return approaches give the same accept-reject signals for independent projects, although the two may be in conflict in the case of mutually exclusive investment alternatives. In these cases, using the net present value is preferable.
   c. Another disadvantage of the IRR approach is that it can lead to multiple internal rates of return in some cases. In these cases, the net present value technique should be used.
3. The *profitability index* (PI) is the ratio of the preset value of expected net cash flows over the life of the project to the net investment.
   a. If the project has a PI equal to or greater than 1.0, it is acceptable.

KEY CHAPTER CONCEPTS

   b. The PI can be used as a guide to resource allocation in a situation of capital rationing.
4. The *payback period* of an investment is the period of time required for the cumulative cash inflows (net cash flows) from a project to equal the initial cash outlay.
   a. Weaknesses of the payback method include that it ignores the timing of cash flows; it ignores cash flows beyond the payback period; and it has no explicit tie to the goal of shareholder wealth maximization.
   b. The payback technique can be used as a project liquidity measure and as a crude risk-screening technique.
5. Project postaudits and reviews can assist management in uncovering biases in the project analysis procedure of a firm. Project reviews can also assist management in making abandonment decisions for projects that are not performing up to expectations.
6. The use of conventional discounted cash flow techniques in capital budgeting without considering "real" options may result in a downward-biased estimate of the true value of a project's net present value.
7. For international capital budgeting projects, the present value of a project's net cash flows to the parent company is equal to the present value of the project's net cash flows from the foreign viewpoint converted into the home country currency at the current spot exchange rate, given that an efficient capital market exists in the foreign country.

A NEW CASINO FOR CIRCUS CIRCUS*

Circus Circus Enterprises, Inc. is the largest casino operator that targets the broad gambling market. In 1996 it had approximately 600,000 square feet of casino space and over 13,000 hotel rooms. Its major properties in Las Vegas include Circus Circus, Excalibur, and Luxor. The company caters to the lower end of the casino gambling markets, largely ignoring the traditional "high rollers" who may lose six-figure amounts on a single visit to Las Vegas. This strategy has been largely successful because of the lower promotional costs and the greater stability in its gambling win rate. Over the past 10 years, earnings have grown at a rate of about 17.5 percent per year.

In early 1997, Circus Circus unveiled plans for its largest-ever casino project—a 4,000 room resort in Las Vegas with a cost expected to approach $1 billion. This new gambling resort property will break tradition for Circus Circus and court the high-roller segment of the gambling market, including the big-stakes—mostly foreign—baccarat players.

This new, 10-acre property will follow a South Seas Island theme. It will have a surfing beach, a tropical reef stocked with tropical fish for customers to view while snorkeling, and an enclosed, clear shark tank where viewers will experi-

ence a close mingling with the tank's sharks.

Circus Circus will face plenty of competition in this new high-end Las Vegas gambling venture. For example, Mirage Resorts, Inc. is currently building a

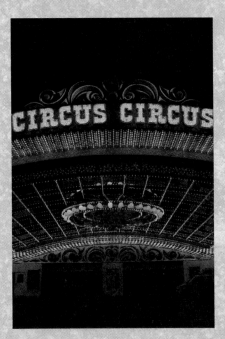

$1.25 billion theme gambling resort named Bellagio. ITT is investing $900 million into refurbishing its Caesar's Palace casino. Others including MGM Grand, Inc. and Marriott International plan other large-scale projects.

This new project represents a bold step by Circus Circus to dominate the south portion of the famed Las Vegas Strip. With the new resort casino, Circus Circus will control 12,500 rooms

in that area, and it has plans to add an additional 8,000 rooms by 2004. Circus Circus is attempting to develop a portfolio of gambling properties that will appeal to all segments of the gambling public.

This chapter considers a number of techniques that are of value when analyzing the cash flows anticipated from capital expenditures, such as this new gambling resort. In principle, the capital budgeting process is quite simple—if the present value of a project's net cash flows exceeds its net investment, the project is acceptable and should be undertaken. In practice, it is often difficult to generate confident estimates of a project's cash flows, due to the risk inherent in many capital investments. The problems that have been experienced by such showcase projects as Euro Disney in France and the Channel Tunnel project between London and Paris provide strong evidence of these difficulties. However, by following sound, disciplined capital budgeting practices, it is possible to reduce the risk inherent in these projects and to achieve a result that will enhance shareholder wealth.

*Based on *Value Line Investment Survey*, "Circus Circus" (New York: Value Line Publishing Company, November 29, 1996):1788, and "Circus Circus to Announce Plans for Casino Costing Up to $1 Billion," *Wall Street Journal* (December 31, 1996).

INTRODUCTION

This chapter looks at some widely used capital budgeting decision models, discussing and illustrating their relative strengths and weaknesses. When combined with the cash flow procedures developed in Chapter 8 and the time value of money procedures developed in Chapter 4, these models provide the basis for making capital expenditure decisions.

This chapter also examines project review and postaudit procedures and concludes by tracing a sample project through the capital budgeting analysis process.

 FOUNDATION CONCEPT
DECISION MODELS FOR EVALUATING ALTERNATIVES

As mentioned in Chapter 8, there are four basic steps in the capital budgeting process: the generation of proposals, the estimation of cash flows, the evaluation and selection of alternatives, and the project postaudit and review. This chapter discusses the final two steps in that process.

Four criteria are commonly used for evaluating and selecting investment projects.[1]

- Net present value (NPV)
- Internal rate of return (IRR)
- Profitability index (PI)
- Payback (PB) period

Net Present Value

Recall from Chapter 1 that the net present value rule is the primary decision-making rule used throughout the practice of financial management. The net present value—that is, the present value of the expected future cash flows minus the initial outlay—of an investment made by a firm represents the contribution of that investment to the value of the firm and, accordingly, to the wealth of the firm's shareholders. In this chapter, we consider the net present value of capital expenditure projects.

The **net present value (NPV)** of a capital expenditure project is defined as the present value of the stream of net (operating) cash flows from the project minus the project's net investment. The net present value method is also sometimes called the *discounted cash flow* (DCF) technique. The cash flows are discounted at the firm's required rate of return; that is, its *cost of capital*. A firm's cost of capital is defined as its minimum acceptable rate of return for projects of average risk.

The net present value of a project may be expressed as follows:

$$NPV = PVNCF - NINV \tag{9.1}$$

where NPV is the net present value; PVNCF, the present value of net (operating) cash flows; and NINV, the net investment.

Assuming a cost of capital, k, the net present value for a project with a 5-year expected life would be the following:

---

[1]Another procedure sometimes used is the accounting rate of return (also called the *average rate of return*). It is computed as the ratio of average annual profits after taxes to the average investment in the project. Because this approach has been shown generally to be incorrect as a project selection criterion, it is not discussed here.

$$NPV = \frac{NCF_1}{(1 + k)^1} + \frac{NCF_2}{(1 + k)^2} + \frac{NCF_3}{(1 + k)^3} \qquad (9.2)$$

$$+ \frac{NCF_4}{(1 + k)^4} + \frac{NCF_5}{(1 + k)^5} - NINV$$

where $NCF_1 \ldots NCF_5$ are the net (operating) cash flows occurring in years 1 through 5. NCF_5 may be assumed to include any salvage value remaining at the end of the project's life.

As mentioned in Chapter 8, the annual net cash flows for normal projects are usually positive after the initial net investment. Occasionally, however, one or more of the expected net cash flows over the life of a project may be negative. When this occurs, positive numbers are used for years having positive net cash flows (net inflows), and negative numbers are used for years having negative net cash flows (net outflows).

In general, the net present value of a project may be defined as follows:

$$NPV = \sum_{t=1}^{n} \frac{NCF_t}{(1 + k)^t} - NINV$$

$$= \sum_{t=1}^{n} NCF_t \times PVIF_{k,t} - NINV \qquad (9.3)$$

where n is the expected project life and $\sum_{t=1}^{n} [NCF_t / (1 + k)^t]$ is the arithmetic sum of the discounted net cash flows for each year t over the life of the project (n years); that is, the present value of the net cash flows.

To illustrate net present value calculations, suppose a firm is considering two projects, A and B, having net investments and net cash flows as shown in Table 9-1. The net present value computations for the two projects are presented in Table 9-2. These calculations assume a 14 percent cost of capital. The calculations in these tables also assume that cash flows are received at the end of each year, rather than as a flow during the year. This assumption, although a normal one, tends to slightly understate a project's net present value or internal rate of return. Project A is shown in Table 9-2 to have a negative net present value and Project B has a positive net present value.

CALCULATOR SOLUTION

In order to calculate NPVs for these projects with the aid of your calculator, it is necessary to use the cash flow function/keys (CF) on your calculator

Project A

Enter:	−50,000	12,500	14	
	CF$_0$	CF$_{1-6}$	i	NPV

Solution: −1,392

Project B

Enter:	−50,000	5,000	10,000	15,000	15,000	25,000	30,000	14	
	CF$_0$	CF$_1$	CF$_2$	CF$_3$	CF$_4$	CF$_5$	CF$_6$	i	NPV

Solution: 7,738

Note: The calculator solutions and the solutions obtained using interest tables with 3 decimal places differ slightly. Using more accurate interest tables gives answers closer to the answers obtained using the calculator.

TABLE 9-1
Sample Project Cash Flows

YEAR	PROJECT A NET CASH FLOW AFTER TAXES	PROJECT B NET CASH FLOW AFTER TAXES
1	$12,500	$ 5,000
2	12,500	10,000
3	12,500	15,000
4	12,500	15,000
5	12,500	25,000
6	12,500	30,000
	Net investment = $50,000	Net investment = $50,000

Decision Rule. In general, a project should be accepted if its net present value is greater than or equal to zero and rejected if its net present value is less than zero. This is so because a positive net present value in principle translates directly into increases in stock prices and increases in shareholders' wealth. In the previous example, Project A would be rejected because it has a negative net present value, and Project B would be accepted because it has a positive net present value.

If two or more *mutually exclusive* investments have positive net present values, the project having the largest net present value is the one selected. Assume, for example, that a firm has three mutually exclusive investment opportunities, G, H, and I, each requiring a net investment of $10,000 and each having a 5-year expected economic life.[2] Project G has a net present value of $2,000; H has a net present value of $4,000; and I has a net present value of $3,500. Of the three, H would be preferred over the other two because it has the highest net present value and therefore is expected to make the largest contribution to the objective of shareholder wealth maximization.

TABLE 9-2
Sample Net Present Value Calculations

PROJECT A	PROJECT B			
	Year	NCF	$PVIF_{0.14,t}$*	PV of NCF
Present value of an annuity of $12,500 for 6 years at 14 percent:				
PV of NCF = $12,500(PVIFA$_{0.14,6}$)	1	$ 5,000	0.877	$ 4,385
= $12,500(3.889)†	2	10,000	0.769	7,690
= $48,613	3	15,000	0.675	10,125
	4	15,000	0.592	8,880
	5	25,000	0.519	12,975
Less Net investment 50,000	6	30,000	0.456	13,680
				57,735
Net present value $−1,387	*Less* Net investment			50,000
	Net present value			$ 7,735

*From the PVIF table (Table II).
†From the PVIFA table (Table IV).

[2]Appendix 9A discusses procedures to use in evaluating mutually exclusive projects having unequal lives.

Sources of Positive Net Present Value Projects. What causes some projects to have a positive net present value and others to have a negative net present value? When product and factor markets are other than perfectly competitive, it is possible for a firm to earn above-normal profits (economic rents) that result in positive net present value projects. The reasons why these above-normal profits may be available arise from conditions that define each type of product and factor market and distinguish it from a perfectly competitive market. These reasons include the following barriers to entry and other factors:[3]

1. Buyer preferences for established brand names.
2. Ownership or control of favored distribution systems (such as exclusive auto dealerships).
3. Patent control of superior product designs or production techniques.
4. Exclusive ownership of superior natural resource deposits.
5. Inability of new firms to acquire necessary factors of production (management, labor, equipment).
6. Superior access to financial resources at lower costs (economies of scale in attracting capital).
7. Economies of large-scale production and distribution arising from
   a. Capital-intensive production processes.
   b. High initial start-up costs.
8. Access to superior labor or managerial talents at costs that are not fully reflective of their value.

These factors can permit a firm to identify positive net present value projects for internal investment. If the barriers to entry are sufficiently high (such as a patent on key technology) so as to prevent any new competition or if the start-up period for competitive ventures is sufficiently long, then it is possible that a project may have a positive net present value. However, in assessing the viability of such a project, it is important that the manager or analyst consider the likely period of time when above-normal returns can be earned before new competitors emerge and force cash flows back to a more normal level. It is generally unrealistic to expect to be able to earn above-normal returns over the entire life of an investment project.

Thus, it may be possible for a firm to identify investment projects with positive net present values. However, if capital markets are efficient, the securities of the firm making these investments will reflect the value of these projects. Recall that the net present value of a project can be thought of as the *contribution to the value of a firm resulting from undertaking that particular project.* Therefore, even though a firm may be able to identify projects having expected positive net present values, efficient capital markets will quickly reflect these positive net present value projects in the market value of the firm's securities.

Suppose Project B in the preceding example is a new baby care product from Johnson & Johnson. Its positive net present value could be the result of buyer preferences due to Johnson & Johnson's established baby care business. Suppose Project A, on the other hand, involves a new soap product to compete with Procter & Gamble's Tide. Consumers' brand preferences for Tide, as well as Procter & Gamble's economies of scale for production and distribution, could easily cause Project A to have a negative net present value.

---

[3]D. Vickers, "Disequilibrium Structures and Financing Decisions in the Firm," *Journal of Business Finance and Accounting* (Autumn 1974): 375.

Advantages and Disadvantages of the Net Present Value Method. The net present value of a project is the expected number of dollars by which the present value of the firm is increased as a result of adopting the project. Therefore, as we have pointed out, the net present value method is consistent with the goal of shareholder wealth maximization. The net present value approach considers both the magnitude and the timing of cash flows over a project's entire expected life.

A firm can be thought of as a series of projects, and the firm's total value is the sum of the net present values of all the independent projects that make it up. Therefore, when the firm undertakes a new project, the firm's value is increased by the net present value of the new project. The additivity of net present values of independent projects is referred to in finance as the *value additivity principle.*

The net present value approach also indicates whether a proposed project will yield the rate of return required by the firm's investors. The cost of capital represents this rate of return; when a project's net present value is greater than or equal to zero, the firm's investors can expect to earn at least their required rate of return.

The net present value criterion has a weakness in that many people find it difficult to work with a present value dollar return rather than a percentage return. As a result, many firms use another present value based method that is interpreted more easily; namely, the internal rate of return method.

Internal Rate of Return

The **internal rate of return** is defined as the discount rate that equates the present value of the net cash flows from a project with the present value of the net investment.[4] It is the discount rate that causes a project's net present value to equal zero. The internal rate of return for a capital expenditure project is identical to the yield to maturity for a bond investment.

A project's internal rate of return can be determined by means of the following equation:

$$\sum_{t=1}^{n} \frac{\text{NCF}_t}{(1+r)^t} = \text{NINV} \tag{9.4}$$

where $\text{NCF}_t/(1+r)^t$ is the present value of net (operating) cash flows in period t discounted at the rate r; NINV is the net investment in the project, and r is the internal rate of return.

For a project having a 5-year life, this basic formula can be rewritten as follows:

$$\frac{\text{NCF}_1}{(1+r)^1} + \frac{\text{NCF}_2}{(1+r)^2} + \frac{\text{NCF}_3}{(1+r)^3} + \frac{\text{NCF}_4}{(1+r)^4} + \frac{\text{NCF}_5}{(1+r)^5} = \text{NINV} \tag{9.5}$$

Subtracting the net investment, NINV, from both sides of Equation 9.5 yields the following:

$$\frac{\text{NCF}_1}{(1+r)^1} + \frac{\text{NCF}_2}{(1+r)^2} + \frac{\text{NCF}_3}{(1+r)^3} + \frac{\text{NCF}_4}{(1+r)^4} + \frac{\text{NCF}_5}{(1+r)^5} - \text{NINV} = 0 \tag{9.6}$$

[4]This also is called the *discounted cash flow (DCF)* rate of return.

This is essentially the same equation as that used in the net present value method. The only difference is that in the net present value approach a discount rate, k, is specified and the net present value is computed, whereas in the internal rate of return method the discount rate, r, which causes the project net present value to equal zero, is the unknown.

Figure 9-1 illustrates the relationship between net present value and internal rate of return. The figure plots the net present value of Project B (from Table 9-1) against the discount rate used to evaluate its cash flows. Note that at a 14 percent cost of capital, the net present value of B is $7,735—the same figure that resulted from the computations performed in Table 9-2. The internal rate of return for Project B is approximately equal to 18.2 percent. Thus, the internal rate of return is a special case of the net present value computation.

The internal rate of return for Projects A and B now can be calculated. Because Project A is an annuity of $12,500 for 6 years requiring a net investment of $50,000, its internal rate of return may be computed directly with the aid of a PVIFA table, such as Table IV, or with a financial calculator.

In this case, the present value of the annuity, $PVAN_0$, is $50,000, the annuity payment, PMT, is $12,500, and $n = 6$ years. The following equation,

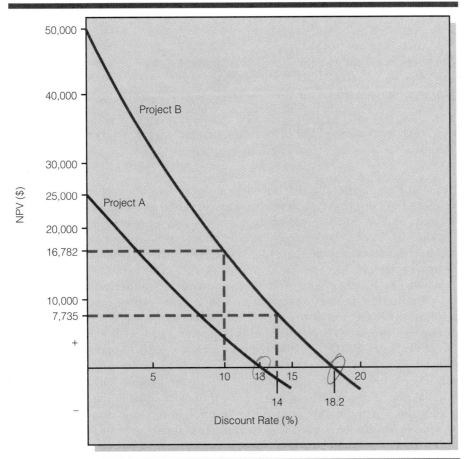

FIGURE 9-1
NPV Profiles: Relationship Between the Net Present Value and the Internal Rate of Return for Projects A and B

$$\text{PVAN}_0 = PMT(\text{PVIFA}_{r,n})$$

can be rewritten to solve for the PVIFA:

$$\text{PVIFA}_{r,n} = \frac{\text{PVAN}_0}{PMT}$$

In this case, PVIFA = \$50,000/\$12,500 = 4.000. Referring to Table IV and reading across the table for $n = 6$, it can be seen that the interest factor of 4.000 occurs near 13 percent, where it is 3.998. Thus, the internal rate of return for Project A is about 13 percent.

CALCULATOR SOLUTION

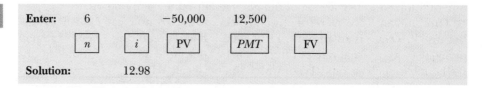

Enter:	6		−50,000	12,500	
	n	i	PV	PMT	FV

Solution: 12.98

The internal rate of return for Project B is more difficult to calculate because the project is expected to yield uneven cash flows. In this case, the internal rate of return is computed with the help of a financial calculator or by using capital budgeting spreadsheet programs, such as the one available with this text.

CALCULATOR SOLUTION

In order to solve this problem with the aid of your calculator, it is necessary to use the cash flow function/keys (CF) on your calculator.

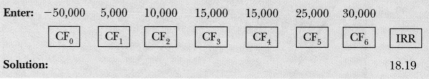

Enter:	−50,000	5,000	10,000	15,000	15,000	25,000	30,000	
	CF_0	CF_1	CF_2	CF_3	CF_4	CF_5	CF_6	IRR

Solution: 18.19

Decision Rule. Generally, the internal rate of return method indicates that a project whose internal rate of return is greater than or equal to the firm's cost of capital should be accepted, whereas a project whose internal rate of return is less than the firm's cost of capital should be rejected. In the case of Projects A and B, if the cost of capital were 14 percent, B would be acceptable and A would be unacceptable.

When two independent projects are considered under conditions of no capital rationing, the net present value and internal rate of return techniques result in the same accept-reject decision. This can be seen in Figure 9-1. For example, if the firm's cost of capital is 10 percent, Project B has a positive net present value (\$16,782). Its internal rate of return is 18.19 percent, exceeding the cost of capital. When two or more mutually exclusive projects are being considered, it *generally* is preferable to accept the project having the highest internal rate of return as long as it is greater than or equal to the cost of capital. In this case, if A and B were mutually exclusive, B would be chosen over A, as can be seen in Figure 9-1. Exceptions to this general rule are considered later in the chapter.

Advantages and Disadvantages of the Internal Rate of Return Method. The internal rate of return method is used widely in industry by firms that employ present value based capital budgeting techniques. In fact, in a 1992 survey of 74 of the 100 largest firms in the *Fortune 500* Industrial Firm listing, 99 percent of the firms (all except one) used internal rate of return compared to 63 of the firms (85 percent) using net present value.[5] The greater popularity of the internal rate of return method may be due to the fact that some people feel more comfortable dealing with the concept of a project's percentage rate of return than with its dollar amount of net present value. Like the net present value approach, the internal rate of return technique takes into account both the magnitude and the timing of cash flows over the entire life of a project in measuring the project's economic desirability.

However, some potential problems are involved in using the internal rate of return technique. The possible existence of **multiple internal rates of return** is one such problem. Whereas equating the net present value of a project to zero will yield only one internal rate of return, *r*, for *normal* investments, there are times when two or more rates may be obtained. Recall that a normal project has an initial cash outlay or outlays (net investment) followed by a stream of positive net cash flows. If for some reason—such as large abandonment costs at the end of a project's life or a major shutdown and rebuilding of a facility sometime during its life—the initial net investment is followed by one or more positive net cash flows (inflows) that then are followed by a negative cash flow,[6] it is possible to obtain more than one internal rate of return.

Whenever a project has multiple internal rates of return, the pattern of cash flows over the project's life contains more than one sign change, for example, $- \uparrow + + \uparrow -$. In this case, there are two sign changes (indicated by the arrows) —from minus to plus and again from plus to minus.

Consider the following investment, which has three internal rates of return—0, 100, and 200 percent:

Year	Net Cash Flows
0	$ –1,000
1	+6,000
2	–11,000
3	+6,000

Unfortunately, none of these rates can be compared to the firm's cost of capital to determine the project's acceptability.

Although several techniques have been proposed for dealing with the multiple internal rate of return problem, none provide a simple, complete, and generally satisfactory solution. The best approach is to use the net present value criterion. If a project's net present value is positive, it is acceptable; if it is negative, it is not acceptable. Many financial calculators and software packages are available that compute internal rates of return, and they usually will warn the user when a potential multiple internal rate of return problem exists. Whenever this is a possibility, the use of the net present value method is preferred.

---

[5]Harold Bierman, Jr., "Capital Budgeting in 1992: A Survey," *Financial Management* (Autumn 1993): 24. (Many firms reported using both techniques.)
[6]Table 8-2 in Chapter 8 illustrates two such projects, X and Y.

Profitability Index

The **profitability index (PI)**, or benefit-cost ratio, is the ratio of the present value of expected net cash flows over the life of a project to the net investment. It is expressed as follows:

$$PI = \frac{\sum_{t=1}^{n} NCF_t / (1 + k)^t}{NINV} \qquad (9.7)$$

Assuming a 14 percent cost of capital, k, and using the data from Table 9-2, the profitability index for Projects A and B can be calculated as follows:

$$PI_A = \frac{\$48,613}{\$50,000}$$

$$= 0.97$$

$$PI_B = \frac{\$57,735}{\$50,000}$$

$$= 1.15$$

The profitability index is interpreted as the present value return *for each dollar of initial investment.* In comparison, the net present value approach measures the total present value dollar return.

Decision Rule. A project whose profitability index is greater than or equal to 1 is considered acceptable, whereas a project having a profitability index less than 1 is considered unacceptable.[7] In this case, Project B is acceptable, whereas Project A is not. When two or more *independent* projects with normal cash flows are considered, the profitability index, net present value, and internal rate of return approaches all will yield identical accept-reject signals; this is true, for example, with Projects A and B.

When dealing with mutually exclusive investments, conflicts may arise between the net present value and the profitability index criteria. This is most likely to occur if the alternative projects require significantly different net investments.

Consider, for example, the following information on Projects J and K. According to the net present value criterion, Project J would be preferred because of its larger net present value. According to the profitability index criterion, Project K would be preferred.

	Project J	Project K
Present value of net cash flows	$25,000	$14,000
Less Net investment	20,000	10,000
Net present value	$ 5,000	$ 4,000
$PI = \dfrac{\text{Present value of net cash flows}}{\text{Net investment}}$	1.25	1.40

When a conflict arises, the final decision must be made on the basis of other factors. For example, if a firm has no constraint on the funds available to it for cap-

---

[7]When a project has a profitability index equal to 1, the present value of the net cash flows is exactly equal to the net investment. Thus, the project has a net present value of zero, meaning that it is expected to earn the investors' required rate of return and nothing more.

ital investment—that is, no capital rationing—the net present value approach is preferred, because it will select the projects that are expected to generate the largest *total dollar* increase in the firm's wealth and, by extension, maximize shareholder wealth. If, however, the firm is in a capital rationing situation and capital budgeting is being done for only one period,[8] the profitability index approach may be preferred, because it will indicate which projects will maximize the returns *per dollar of investment*—an appropriate objective when a funds constraint exists.

Net Present Value Versus Internal Rate of Return: The Reinvestment Rate Assumption

As was indicated, both the net present value and the internal rate of return methods result in identical decisions to either accept or reject an *independent* project. This is true because the net present value is greater than (less than) zero if and only if the internal rate of return is greater than (less than) the required rate of return, *k*. In the case of *mutually exclusive* projects, however, the two methods may yield contradictory results; one project may have a *higher* internal rate of return than another and, at the same time, a *lower* net present value.

Consider, for example, *mutually exclusive* projects L and M described in the following table. Both require a net investment of $1,000. Using the internal rate of return approach, Project L is preferred, with an IRR of 21.5 percent compared with Project M's IRR of 18.3 percent. Using the net present value approach with a discount rate of 5 percent, Project M is preferred to Project L. Hence, it is necessary to determine which technique is the correct one to use in this situation.

	Project L	*Project M*
Net investment	$1,000	$1000
Net cash flows		
Year 1	$ 667	$ 0
Year 2	$ 667	$1,400
Net present value at 5%	$ 240	$ 270
Internal rate of return	21.5%	18.3%

The outcome depends on what *assumptions* the decision maker chooses to make about the *implied reinvestment rate* for the net cash flows generated from each project. This can be seen in Figure 9-2. For discount (reinvestment) rates below 10 percent, Project M has a higher net present value than Project L and therefore is preferred. For discount rates greater than 10 percent, Project L is preferred using both the net present value and internal rate of return approaches. Hence, a conflict only occurs in this case for discount (cost-of-capital) rates below 10 percent. The net present value method assumes that cash flows are *reinvested at the firm's cost of capital,* whereas the internal rate of return method assumes that these cash flows are *reinvested at the computed internal rate of return.*[9] Generally, the cost of capital is considered to be a more realistic reinvestment rate than the computed internal rate of return, because the cost of capital is the

Did you know that the U.S. Department of Agriculture has a special office that ensures that the USDA's policies and regulations are based on sound scientific and economic principles? ORACBA (it's Office of Risk Assessment and Cost-Benefit Analysis) assesses the risks and then calculates the costs and benefits of major USDA policies affecting our health, safety, and environment. Actually, most major government bodies (the U.S. Department of Defense, the World Bank, etc.) do extensive cost-benefit analyses (of weapons systems, foreign aid, etc.) to make sure that their money is being well spent.
http://www.usda.gov/agency/oce/oracba/oracba.htm

---

[8]If the firm makes capital budgeting decisions for more than one period in the future, it usually is necessary to use some kind of programming model. Footnote 10 lists a number of references for some of these techniques.

[9]A more complete discussion of this problem and the underlying assumptions is found in early articles by J. Hirshleifer, "On the Theory of the Optimal Investment Decision," *Journal of Political Economy* 66 (August 1958): 95–103; and James H. Lorie and Leonard J. Savage, "Three Problems in Rationing Capital," *Journal of Business* 23 (October 1955): 229–239.

FIGURE 9-2
NPV Profiles: Net Present Value
versus Internal Rate of Return for
Mutually Exclusive Alternatives

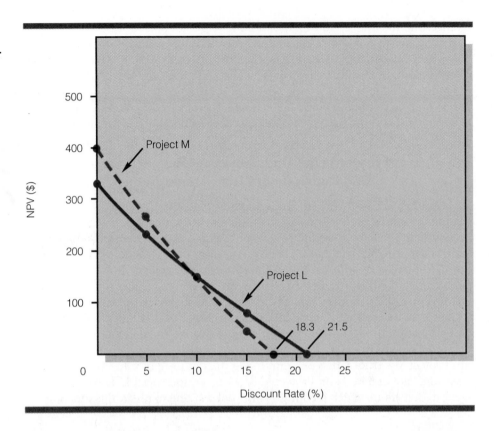

FIGURE 9-2
NPV Profiles: Net Present Value versus Internal Rate of Return for Mutually Exclusive Alternatives

rate the next (marginal) investment project can be assumed to earn. This can be seen in Figure 8-1 in Chapter 8, where the last acceptable project, Project E, offers a rate of return nearly equal to the firm's marginal cost of capital.

Consequently, in the absence of capital rationing, the net present value approach is normally superior to both the profitability index and the internal rate of return when choosing among mutually exclusive investments.

Payback (PB) Period

The **payback (PB) period** of an investment is the period of time required for the cumulative cash inflows (net cash flows) from a project to equal the initial cash outlay (net investment).

To illustrate, suppose a firm is considering Project A again (that requires a net investment of $50,000 and is expected to generate 6 years of net cash inflows of $12,500 a year). Because the expected net cash inflows are *equal* in each year, the payback period is the ratio of the net investment to the annual net cash inflows:

$$PB = \frac{\text{Net Investment}}{\text{Annual net cash inflows}} \tag{9.8}$$

The payback (PB) period for the preceding example is computed as follows:

$$PB = \frac{\$50,000}{\$12,500}$$

$$= 4 \text{ years}$$

When annual cash flows are not equal each year, Equation 9.8 cannot be used to compute the PB period. Rather, the analyst must add up the yearly net cash flows until the total equals the net investment amount. The number of years it takes for this to occur is the project's PB period.

Decision Rule. Because the payback method has a number of serious shortcomings, it should not be used in deciding whether to accept or reject an investment project.

Advantages and Disadvantages of the Payback Method. The payback method suffers from the following serious disadvantages. First, the payback method gives equal weight to all cash inflows within the payback period, regardless of when they occur during the period. In other words, the technique ignores the *time value of money*.

Assume, for example, that a firm is considering two projects, E and F, each costing $10,000. Project E is expected to yield cash flows over a 3-year period of $6,000 during the first year, $4,000 during the second year, and $3,000 during the third year. Project F is expected to yield cash flows of $4,000 during the first year, $6,000 during the second year, and $3,000 during the third year. Viewed from the payback perspective, these projects are equally attractive, yet the net present value technique clearly indicates that Project E increases the value of the firm more than Project F.

Second, payback essentially ignores cash flows occurring after the payback period. Thus, payback figures can be misleading. For example, suppose a firm is considering two projects, C and D, each costing $10,000. It is expected that Project C will generate net cash inflows of $5,000 per year for three years and that Project D will generate net cash inflows of $4,500 per year forever. The payback period for Project C is two years ($10,000/$5,000), whereas the payback period for Project D is 2.2 years ($10,000/$4,500). If these projects were mutually exclusive, payback would favor C, because it has the lower payback period. Yet Project D clearly has a higher net present value than Project C.

Third, payback provides no *objective* criterion for decision making that is consistent with shareholder wealth maximization. The choice of an acceptable payback period is largely a *subjective* one, and different people using essentially identical data may make different accept-reject decisions about a project.

The payback method is sometimes justified on the basis that it provides a measure of the *risk* associated with a project. Although it is true that less risk may be associated with a shorter payback period than with a longer one, risk is thought of best in terms of the *variability* of project returns. Because payback ignores this dimension, it is at best a crude tool for risk analysis.

A more valid justification for the use of the payback method is that it gives some indication of a project's desirability from a *liquidity* perspective because it measures the time required for a firm to recover its initial investment in a project. A company that is very concerned about the early recovery of investment funds—such as one investing overseas in a politically unstable area or one expecting a cash shortage in the future—might find this method useful.

In summary, payback is not a satisfactory criterion for investment decision making because it may lead to a selection of projects that do not make the largest possible contribution to a firm's value. It can be useful as a supplementary decision-making tool, however.

Table 9-3 presents a summary of the four capital budgeting methods discussed in the chapter.

MODEL	PROJECT ACCEPTANCE CRITERION	STRENGTHS	WEAKNESSES
Net present value (NPV)	Accept project if project has a positive or zero NPV; that is, if the present value of net cash flows, evaluated at the firm's cost of capital, equals or exceeds the net investment required.	Considers the timing of cash flows. Provides an objective, return-based criterion for acceptance or rejection. Most conceptually correct approach.	Difficulty in working with a dollar return value, rather than percentage returns.
Internal rate of return (IRR)	Accept project if IRR equals or exceeds the firm's cost of capital.	Same benefits as the NPV. Easy to interpret the meaning of IRR.	Multiple rates of return problem. Sometimes gives decision that conflicts with NPV.
Profitability index (PI)	Accept project if PI is greater than or equal to 1.0	Same benefits as the NPV. Useful to guide decisions in capital rationing problems.	Sometimes gives decision that conflicts with NPV.
Payback (PB)	PB should not be used in deciding whether to accept or reject an investment project.	Easy and inexpensive to use. Provides a crude measure of project risk. Provides a measure of project liquidity.	No objective decision criterion. Fails to consider timing of cash flows.

TABLE 9-3
Summary of the Capital Budgeting Methods

CAPITAL RATIONING AND THE CAPITAL BUDGETING DECISION

For each of the selection criteria previously discussed, the decision rule is to undertake *all* independent investment projects that meet the acceptance standard. This rule places no restrictions on the total amount of acceptable capital projects a company may undertake in any particular period.

However, many firms do not have unlimited funds available for investment. Rather than letting the size of their capital budget be determined by the number of profitable investment opportunities available, many companies choose to place an upper limit, or *constraint,* on the amount of funds allocated to capital investments. This constraint may be either *self-imposed* by the firm's management or *externally imposed* by conditions in the capital markets.

 example

For example, a very conservative firm may be reluctant to use debt or external equity to finance capital expenditures. Instead, it would limit capital expenditures to cash flows from continuing operations minus any dividends paid. Another firm may feel that it lacks the managerial resources to undertake successfully all acceptable projects in a given year and may choose to limit capital expenditures for this reason.

A number of externally imposed constraints might limit a firm's capital expenditures. For example, a firm's loan agreements may contain restrictive covenants that limit future borrowing. Similarly, a weak financial position, conditions in the securities markets, or both may make the flotation of a new bond or stock issue by the firm impossible or prohibitively expensive. Examples of such market-imposed constraints include depressed stock market prices, unusually high interest rates due to a "tight money" policy on the part of the Federal Reserve, and a reluctance on the part of investors to purchase new securities if the firm has a large percentage of debt in its capital structure.

Several different methods can be used in making capital budgeting decisions under capital rationing. When the initial outlays occur in two (or more) periods, the methods are quite elaborate and require the use of linear, integer, or goal programming.[10] However, when there is a single-period capital budgeting constraint, a relatively simple approach employing the profitability index can be used. Briefly, the approach consists of the following steps:

Step 1: Calculate the profitability index for each of a series of investment projects.

Step 2: Rank the projects according to their profitability indexes (from highest to lowest).

Step 3: Beginning with the project having the highest profitability index, proceed down through the list, and accept projects having profitability indexes greater than or equal to 1 until the entire capital budget has been utilized.

At times, a firm may not be able to utilize its entire capital budget because the next acceptable project on its list is too large, given the remaining available funds. In this case, the firm's management should choose among the following three alternatives:

Alternative 1: Search for another combination of projects, perhaps including some smaller, less profitable ones that will allow for a more complete utilization of available funds *and* increase the net present value of the combination of projects.

Alternative 2: Attempt to relax the funds constraint so that sufficient resources are available to accept the last project for which funds were not fully available.

Alternative 3: Accept as many projects as possible and either invest any excess funds in short-term securities until the next period,[11] pay out the excess funds to shareholders as dividends, use the funds to reduce outstanding debt, or do a combination of the above.

The following example illustrates how these alternatives can be applied to an actual capital budgeting decision. Suppose that management of the Old Mexico Tile Company has decided to limit next year's capital expenditures to $550,000. Eight capital expenditure projects have been proposed—P, R, S, U, T, V, Q, and W—and ranked according to their profitability indexes, as shown in Table 9-4. Given the $550,000 ceiling, the firm's management proceeds down the list of projects, selecting P, R, S, and U, in that order. Project T cannot be accepted, because this would require a capital outlay of $25,000 in excess of the $550,000

---

[10]The following references contain information on the use of these more advanced models: James R. McGuigan and R. Charles Moyer, *Managerial Economics,* 7th ed. (St. Paul: West Publishing, 1996): 367–395; or H. Martin Weingartner, *Mathematical Programming and the Analysis of Capital Budgeting Problems* (Englewood Cliffs, NJ: Prentice-Hall, 1963). See also Sang M. Lee and A. J. Lerro, "Capital Budgeting for Multiple Objectives," *Financial Management* 3 (Spring 1974): 58–66; and Richard H. Bernhard, "Mathematical Programming Models for Capital Budgeting: A Survey, Generalization, and Critique," *Journal of Financial and Quantitative Analysis* 4 (June 1969): 111–158.

[11]If a firm does not invest a portion of its available capital resources in projects earning a rate of return at least equal to the cost of capital, an implicit opportunity cost of lost earnings is incurred. However, as long as profitable investment alternatives exist, the firm should seek ways to utilize fully all available capital funds.

PROJECT (1)	NET INVESTMENT (2)	NET PRESENT VALUE (3)	PRESENT VALUE OF NET CASH FLOWS (4)	PI = (4) ÷ (2)	CUMULATIVE NET INVESTMENT	CUMULATIVE NET PRESENT VALUE
P	$100,000	$25,000	$125,000	1.25	$100,000	$ 25,000
R	150,000	33,000	183,000	1.22	250,000	58,000
S	175,000	36,750	211,750	1.21	425,000	94,750
U	100,000	20,000	120,000	1.20	525,000	114,750
T	50,000	9,000	59,000	1.18	575,000	123,750
V	75,000	12,500	87,500	1.17	650,000	136,250
Q	200,000	30,000	230,000	1.15	850,000	166,250
W	50,000	–10,000	40,000	0.80	900,000	156,250

TABLE 9-4
Sample Ranking of Proposed Projects According to Their Profitability Indexes

limit. Projects P, R, S, and U together yield a net present value of $114,750 but require a total investment outlay of only $525,000, leaving $25,000 from the capital budget that is not invested in projects. Management is considering the following three alternatives:

Alternative 1: It could attempt to find another combination of projects, perhaps including some smaller ones, that would allow for a more complete utilization of available funds and increase the cumulative net present value. In this case, a likely combination would be Projects P, R, S, T, and V. This combination would fully utilize the $550,000 available and create a net present value of $116,250—an increase of $1,500 over the net present value of $114,750 from projects P, R, S, and U.

Alternative 2: It could attempt to increase the capital budget by another $25,000 to allow Project T to be added to the list of adopted projects.

Alternative 3: It could merely accept the first four projects—P, R, S, and U—and invest the remaining $25,000 in a short-term security until the next period. This alternative would result in an NPV of $114,750, assuming that the risk-adjusted required return on the short-term security is equal to its yield.

In this case, *Alternative 1* seems to be the most desirable of the three. In rearranging the capital budget, however, the firm should never accept a project, such as W, that does not meet the minimum acceptance criterion of a positive or zero net present value (a profitability index greater than or equal to 1).

 REVIEWING AND POSTAUDITING AN ACCEPTED PROJECT

A final important step in the capital budgeting process is the review of investment projects after they have been implemented. This can provide useful information on the effectiveness of the company's selection process. The **postaudit** procedure consists of comparing *actual* cash flows from an accepted project with *projected* cash flows that were estimated when the project was adopted. Because projected cash flows contain an element of uncertainty, actual values would not be expected to match estimated values exactly. Instead, a project review should be concerned with identifying systematic biases or errors in cash flow estimation on the part of individuals, departments, plants, or divisions and attempting to determine *why* these biases or errors exist. This type of analysis, when properly performed, can help a company's decision makers better evaluate investment proposals submitted in the future.

The importance of the postaudit process has been highlighted in research by Brown and Miller.[12] They observed that in the common situation where bad projects outnumber good ones, the simple procedure of making unbiased cash flow estimates and choosing projects with positive net present values will result in an upwardly biased acceptance rate for proposed projects (and returns that are, on average, below those that are expected) if there is uncertainty regarding future cash flows. In a situation such as this, the firm needs to correct for this potential bias when projects are being reviewed. The information needed to make this necessary bias-eliminating correction can be gathered from careful project postaudits.

The importance of a good project review and tracking system is illustrated in the following example from Ameritech, a holding company consisting of five telephone companies in the Midwest and several other subsidiaries. Ameritech has a sophisticated tracking system that permits the company to identify the individual responsible for each estimate in a capital project proposal. When the tracking system was announced and initiated, budgets had already been submitted for the coming year. Divisions were permitted to take back their budgets and resubmit them in light of the new tracking system. Seven hundred projects disappeared from the new budgets, and many others had reduced estimates of benefits![13]

Another objective of the project review process involves determining whether a project that has not lived up to expectations should be continued or abandoned. The decision to abandon a project requires the company to compare the cost of abandonment with any future cash flows that are expected over the project's remaining life. These estimates of future cash flows usually will be more accurate after the project has been in service for a period of time.[14]

A COMPREHENSIVE EXAMPLE OF CAPITAL BUDGETING: OPENING A NEW BANK BRANCH

The First National Bank and Trust Company has a single banking office located in the downtown business district of a medium-sized town. As the population moved to the suburbs, First National has seen its share of both local banking

[12]Keith C. Brown, "A Note on the Apparent Bias of Net Revenue Estimates for Capital Investment Projects," *Journal of Finance* (September 1974): 1215–1216; K. C. Brown, "The Rate of Return on Selected Investment Projects," *Journal of Finance* (September 1978): 1250–1253; Edward M. Miller, "Uncertainty Induced Bias in Capital Budgeting," *Financial Management* (Autumn 1978): 12–18; E. M. Miller, "The Competitive Market Assumption and Capital Budgeting Criteria," *Financial Management* (Winter 1987): 22–28.

[13]"Capital Budgeting: A Panel Discussion," *Financial Management* (Spring 1989): 10–17.

[14]A further discussion of the abandonment question may be found in Gordon Shillinglaw's two articles, "Profit Analysis for Abandonment Decision" and "Residual Values in Investment Analysis," reprinted in Ezra Solomon, ed., *The Management of Corporate Capital* (New York: Free Press, 1959): 269–281 and 259–268, respectively. See also Alexander Robichek and James C. Van Horne, "Abandonment Value and Capital Budgeting," *Journal of Finance* 22 (December 1967): 577–589.

deposits and profits decline. Two of the bank's vice-presidents have proposed that First National try to reverse this trend by building a branch in a new, affluent suburban community. They have presented the bank's executive committee with the following information.

The initial cost of the bank building and equipment is $1 million. This facility is expected to have a useful life of 20 years. Also, in 20 years at the end of the project the branch building and its equipment are expected to be sold for a $200,000 salvage value. The branch building and its equipment will be depreciated over their 20-year life using straight-line depreciation to a zero balance. We have assumed straight-line depreciation for simplicity. As discussed in Appendix A, in actual practice the bank would use MACRS depreciation with a 39-year life on the building and a 7-year life on the equipment. The annual straight-line depreciation will be $1,000,000/20 = $50,000. The bank building is to be constructed on land leased for $20,000 per year. In addition to the $1 million investment for the building and equipment, the parent bank's net working capital must be increased by $100,000 to accommodate the new branch.

Based on customer surveys, population trends, the location of competitor banks, and the experience other area banks have had with their branches, it is estimated that the annual revenues from the new branch will be $400,000. Of this $400,000 in revenues, $50,000 will be drawn away from the bank's main office. (Assume that the main office will not attempt to cut its expenses because of this loss in revenues.)

In addition to the $20,000 annual expense for the land lease, the new branch will incur about $130,000 per year in other expenses, including personnel costs, utilities, and interest paid on accounts. Both expenses and revenues are expected to remain approximately constant over the branch's 20-year life.

The bank's marginal tax rate is 40 percent and its cost of capital (required rate of return) is 9 percent after taxes.

Step 1: Computing the Net Investment

New project cost	$1,000,000
Plus Increase in net working capital	100,000
Net investment	$1,100,000

The net investment equals the new project cost ($1 million) plus the increase in net working capital ($100,000)

Step 2: Computing Net Cash Flows

Net increase in revenues ($400,000 – $50,000)	$350,000
Less Operating costs of branch ($130,000 + $20,000)	150,000
Less Depreciation	50,000
Operating earnings before taxes	$150,000
Less Tax (40%)	60,000
Operating earnings after taxes	$ 90,000
Plus Depreciation	50,000
Net cash flow	$140,000

Net cash flows are calculated for years 1 through 19 by subtracting branch operating costs and depreciation from the incremental revenues of $350,000. This yields operating earnings before taxes from which taxes (at the 40 percent rate) are deducted to arrive at operating earnings after taxes. By adding back depreciation, the net cash flow equals $140,000 for each year from 1 through

19. Net cash flows in year 20 are computed by adding the $120,000 estimated after-tax salvage and the $100,000 return of working capital to the annual net cash flow of $140,000 to equal $360,000.[15]

The $100,000 working capital requirement is added back to the year 20 cash flows because at the end of 20 years, when the project is terminated, there no longer will be a need for this incremental working capital, and thus the working capital of $100,000 can be liquidated and made available to the bank for other uses.

Step 3: Arraying Project Cash Flows and Evaluating Alternatives

Net investment	$1,100,000
Net cash flows:	
Years 1–19	140,000
Year 20	360,000

After the project cash flows have been computed and arrayed, the decision of whether to accept or reject the new branch project must be made. Next, the project is evaluated using the decision criteria discussed in this chapter; namely, net present value, internal rate of return, and profitability index.

■ **Criterion 1: Net Present Value**

$$NPV = PVNCF - NINV$$

$$= \sum_{t=1}^{19} \frac{\$140,000}{(1 + 0.09)^t} + \frac{\$360,000}{(1 + 0.09)^{20}} - \$1,100,000$$

$$= (\$140,000 \times PVIFA_{0.09,19})$$
$$+ (\$360,000 \times PVIF_{0.09,20}) - \$1,100,000$$

The first term in the net present value equation is the present value of an annuity of $140,000 for 19 years at 9 percent, the bank's cost of capital. Using the present value of an annuity table (Table IV), an interest factor of 8.950 may be found. The second term is the present value of $360,000 received in 20 years at 9 percent. From the present value table (Table II), an interest factor of 0.178 is found. Thus, the net present value of this project at a 9 percent cost of capital is as follows:

$$NPV = \$140,000(8.950) + \$360,000(0.178) - \$1,100,000$$

$$= \$1,253,000 + \$64,080 - \$1,100,000$$

$$= \$217,080$$

Using the net present value criterion and a cost of capital of 9 percent, this project would be acceptable, because it has a positive net present value.

■ **Criterion 2: Internal Rate of Return**

According to this method, a discount rate that makes the net present value of the project equal to zero must be found:

$$Present\ value\ of\ net\ cash\ flows - Net\ investment = 0$$

---

[15]The $200,000 salvage value is taxable as ordinary income because the branch building and its equipment are fully depreciated at the end of the project. Therefore, the after-tax salvage cash flow is $200,000 minus 40 percent tax, or $120,000.

or

$$\sum_{t=1}^{19} \frac{\$140,000}{(1+r)^t} + \frac{\$360,000}{(1+r)^{20}} - \$1,100,000 = 0$$

where r is the internal rate of return.

CALCULATOR SOLUTION

In order to solve this problem with the aid of your calculator, it is necessary to use the cash flow function/keys (CF) on your calculator.

Enter: −1,100,000   140,000   360,000

| CF_0 | | CF_{1-19} | | CF_{20} | | IRR |

Solution: 11.56

Given that the internal rate of return equals 11.56 percent, which is greater than the cost of capital, the project is acceptable by this criterion.

■ Criterion 3: Profitability Index

The profitability index is the ratio of the present value of future net cash flows to the net investment. From the previous net present value calculation, we know that the present value of net cash flows at a 9 percent cost of capital is $1,317,080 ($1,253,000 + $64,080). Thus, the profitability index is computed as follows:

$$PI = \frac{\$1,317,080}{\$1,100,000}$$

$$= 1.20$$

Because the profitability index is greater than 1, the new branch bank project is acceptable according to this criterion.

Based on these calculations, it appears that the new branch proposal will increase shareholder wealth and therefore should be undertaken. The only step remaining is to monitor the performance of the project to see if it meets, falls short of, or exceeds its projected cash flow estimates. Based on the actual results of this project, the bank's management will be able to evaluate other new branch bank proposals in a more knowledgeable manner.

INFLATION AND CAPITAL EXPENDITURES

To see a "CBA Walk-Through," that is, a graphic walk-through Cost-Benefit Analysis, go to the following Web site. http://www.gis.uiuc.edu/gems/ CBA/CBA.html

During inflationary periods the level of capital expenditures made by firms tends to decrease. For example, suppose the Apple Manufacturing Company has an investment opportunity that is expected to generate 10 years of cash inflows of $300 per year. The net investment is $2,000. If the company's cost of capital is relatively low—say, 7 percent—the net present value is positive:

$$NPV = PVNCF - NINV$$

$$= \$300(PVIFA_{0.07,10}) - \$2,000$$

$$= \$300(7.024) - \$2,000$$

$$= \$107.2$$

According to the net present value decision rule, this project is acceptable.

Suppose, however, that inflation expectations increase and the overall cost of the firm's capital rises to say, 10 percent. The net present value of the project then would be negative:

$$NPV = PVNCF - NINV$$

$$= \$300(PVIFA_{0.10,10}) - \$2,000$$

$$= \$300(6.145) - \$2,000$$

$$= -\$156.5$$

Under these conditions, the project would not be acceptable.

The example assumes that expected cash inflows are not affected by inflation. Admittedly, project revenues usually will increase with rising inflation, but so will expenses. As a result, it is somewhat difficult to generalize about net cash inflows. The experience of recent years, however, seems to indicate that cash flow increases often are not sufficient to offset the increased cost of capital. Thus, capital expenditure levels tend to be lower (in real terms) during periods of relatively high inflation than during low inflation times.

Fortunately, it is quite easy to adjust the capital budgeting procedure to take inflationary effects into account. The cost of capital already includes the effects of expected inflation.[16] As the expected future inflation rate increases, the cost of capital also tends to increase. Thus, the financial manager has to estimate future cash flows (revenues and expenses) that reflect the expected inflationary rate. For example, if prices are expected to increase at a rate of 5 percent per year over the life of a project, the revenue estimates made for the project should reflect this rising price trend. Cost or expense estimates also should be adjusted to reflect anticipated inflationary increases, such as labor wage rate increases and raw material price increases.

If these steps are taken, the capital budgeting procedure outlined in this and the preceding chapter will assist the financial manager even in an inflationary environment.

REAL OPTIONS IN CAPITAL BUDGETING[17]

In our discussion of capital budgeting we have used so-called conventional discounted cash flow techniques; that is, we determine a project's net present value by discounting the expected net cash flows at an applicable cost of capital, minus the net investment. This type of analysis does not consider the value of any operating (real) options that may be embedded in the project or the value of any options, or flexibilities, that the firm may choose to incorporate into the project's design. An option gives its holder the right, but not the obligation, to buy, sell, or otherwise transform an asset at a set price during a specified time period.

---

[16]The cost of capital is discussed in Chapter 11.

[17]This section is based on Nalin Kulatilaka and Alan J. Marcus, "Project Valuation Under Uncertainty: When Does DCF Fail?" *Journal of Applied Corporate Finance* (Fall 1992): 92–100. See also A. K. Dixit and R. S. Pindyck, "The Options Approach to Capital Investment," *Harvard Business Review*, (May–June 1995): 105–119.

To illustrate how an embedded option may influence the net present value of a project, consider a manufacturing firm that calculates a negative net present value on a proposed project to purchase a new lathe to make a series of industrial parts for a particular application. The project's negative net present value is based on a cash flow analysis that assumes that the lathe will produce the parts for the entire economic life of the project. This cash flow analysis does not take into consideration the option of the company to abandon the project and sell the lathe in the active secondary market that exists for lathes and other manufacturing equipment. Or the company could simply choose to switch from making the specific parts to another potentially more profitable product. The abandonment option is embedded in the project; its existence may limit the downside risk of the project.

To illustrate a designed-in option, consider an electric power plant project that is evaluating whether to use a gas burner or an oil burner to fire the turbines. The designed-in option in this instance would be a flexible dual-fuel boiler that can switch back and forth between gas and oil, depending on which energy source is cheaper to acquire and use. It may be, under certain conditions, that the flexible boiler project has a higher net present value than either of the projects using the gas-fired boiler or the oil-fired boiler, even though the initial cost of the flexible boiler is higher than the cost of either of the two single-fuel boilers. In other words, the value of the designed-in option may be greater than the additional cost of the flexible boiler.[18]

While option valuation in actual capital budgeting projects is complicated, financial managers should recognize the presence of options in projects and should consider including designed-in options when possible in planning projects.

Real options in capital budgeting can be classified in the following manner:

1. *Investment timing options.* Delaying investment in a project, say for a year or so, may allow a firm to evaluate additional information regarding demand for outputs and costs of inputs, for example. Investing in a project today or waiting one year to invest in the same project is an example of two mutually exclusive projects. In this example the firm should select the project with the higher net present value, assuming at least one project has a positive net present value. The "waiting-to-invest" option is a common real option.

2. *Abandonment option.* The option to discontinue a project is an important real option in capital budgeting. A project may be discontinued either by shutting it down completely and selling the equipment or by switching its use to an alternative product. Generally, the existence of an abandonment option reduces the downside risk of a project and should be considered in project analysis.

3. *Shutdown options.* A firm may have the option of *temporarily* shutting down a project in order to avoid negative cash flows. Consider a mining or manufacturing operation characterized by relatively high variable costs. If output prices drop below variable costs, a business has the option to shut down until output prices recover and rise above variable costs. The shutdown option also reduces the downside risk of a project.

4. *Growth options.* A firm may have an opportunity to undertake a research program, build a small manufacturing facility to serve a new market, or make a small strategic acquisition in a new line of business. Each of these

---

[18]See Nalin Kulatilaka, "The Value of Flexibility: The Case of a Dual-Fuel Industrial Steam Boiler," *Financial Management* (Autumn 1993): 271–280 for a further discussion of the flexible boiler option.

examples may be a negative net present value project, but each project can be viewed as having generated a growth option for the company which, if exercised, may lead ultimately to a large positive net present value project.

5. *Designed-in options.* In addition to options that can occur naturally in projects, managers have the opportunity to include options in projects in order to increase net present value. These designed-in options are classified either as input flexibility options, output flexibility options, or expansion options.

Input flexibility options allow a firm to design into a project the capability of switching between alternative inputs because of input cost differences. The dual-fuel boiler project discussed earlier in this section is an example of an input flexibility option.

Output flexibility options allow a firm to design into a project the capability of shifting the product mix of the project if relative product prices dictate such a shift. Oil refineries normally have output flexibility options.

Expansion options give project managers the ability to add future capacity to a project at a relatively low marginal cost. For example, consider a company that presently needs a manufacturing facility totalling 50,000 square feet. If instead, it builds a facility now with 70,000 square feet of space, the cost to the company to expand by 20,000 square feet in the future may be less than if it has to build a separate 20,000 square-foot facility later. Even if the need for the additional capacity never materializes, the value of the expansion option may justify the cost of the larger initial facility beforehand, particularly if significant uncertainty about future product demand exists.

Using conventional discounted cash flow analyses in capital budgeting without considering real options results in a downward-biased estimate of the true value of a project's net present value. Some operating options, such as an option to expand, may increase a project's upside potential, while other operating options, such as an option to abandon, may reduce a project's downside risk.

A large amount of advanced work on real options has been done and more is being done.[19] Financial managers should attempt to incorporate options analyses in project evaluations whenever possible.

INTERNATIONAL ISSUES
A FRAMEWORK FOR INTERNATIONAL CAPITAL EXPENDITURE DECISIONS[20]

The capital budgeting decision criteria discussed earlier in this chapter can also be used to evaluate international capital expenditure projects. To illustrate, suppose McCormick & Company, a U.S. spice company based in Maryland, is considering expanding its German spice operations.

---

[19]The Autumn 1993 issue of *Financial Management* contains a section of six articles devoted to "Topics in Real Options and Applications." See Lenos Trigeorgis, "Real Options and Interactions with Financial Flexibility," *Financial Management* (Autumn 1993): 202–224 for an extensive review of the real options literature.

[20]This section is based on James S. Ang and Tsong-Yue Lai, "A Simple Rule for Multinational Capital Budgeting," *The Global Finance Journal* 1, no. 1 (1989): 71–75. See also the special issue of *Managerial Finance*, "Capital Budgeting for the Multinational Enterprise," vol. 22, no. 1, 1996.

The company plans to invest \$5 million in additional German facilities. Based on this level of investment, McCormick estimates that its proposed German expansion project will generate annual net cash inflows of DM1.5 million for a period of 10 years and nothing thereafter. Also, based upon its analysis of present German capital market conditions, McCormick has determined that the applicable German cost of capital, k, for the expansion project is 15 percent. The present value of the expected net cash flows from the project, denominated in the *foreign* currency, is calculated as follows:

$$PVNCF_f = \sum_{t=1}^{n} \frac{NCF_t}{(1+k)^t} \qquad (9.9)$$

Using Equation 9.9, a present value of approximately DM7.5 million is obtained for the net cash flows of McCormick's proposed German expansion:

$$PVNCF_f = \sum_{t=1}^{10} \frac{1.5 \text{ million}}{(1.15)^t}$$

$$= DM7.5 \text{ million}$$

CALCULATOR SOLUTION

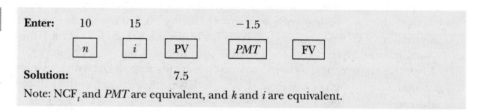

Enter: 10　15　　　−1.5

n　i　PV　PMT　FV

Solution:　　　　7.5

Note: NCF_t and *PMT* are equivalent, and k and i are equivalent.

The present value of the project's net cash flows from the foreign viewpoint, $PVNCF_f$, is used to calculate the present value of the project's net cash flows to the parent company in the *home* country, $PVNCF_h$, as follows:

$$PVNCF_h = PVNCF_f \times S_0 \qquad (9.10)$$

where S_0 is the spot exchange rate expressed in units of home country currency per unit of foreign currency. Using a spot exchange rate of \$0.60 per DM, the present value of the net cash flows to the parent company for McCormick's proposed expansion project is approximately \$4.5 million.

$$PVNCF_h = DM7.5 \text{ million} \times \$0.60/DM$$

$$= \$4.5 \text{ million}$$

The project's net present value is calculated by subtracting the parent company's net investment in the project from $PVNCF_h$, the parent company's present value of the net cash flows:

$$NPV = PVNCF_h - NINV \qquad (9.11)$$

A net present value of approximately −\$0.5 million is obtained for the McCormick project.

$$NPV = \$4.5 \text{ million} - \$5.0 \text{ million}$$

$$= -\$0.5 \text{ million}$$

Based on this analysis, McCormick's proposed German expansion is an unacceptable project.

The McCormick example assumes that an efficient capital market exists in the foreign country, as it does in Germany and other developed countries. Assets can be bought and sold and the required rates of return for projects can be determined from prices of other comparable assets in the foreign capital market.

The McCormick example also assumes that the amount and timing of the expected net cash flows to the foreign subsidiary are the same as for the parent company. If the amount and timing of the net cash inflows to the foreign subsidiary and the parent company are not the same, the evaluation of the capital expenditure project is more complex than the example presented in this section. Some of the reasons that the amount and timing of the net cash flows to the foreign subsidiary and parent may differ include the following:

- Differential tax rates for foreign and domestic companies in the country in which the project is planned.
- Legal and political constraints on cash remittances from the foreign country to the home country.
- Subsidized loans.

The example presented in this section shows that the present value of a project's net cash flows to the parent company is simply the present value of the project's net cash flows from the foreign viewpoint converted into the home country currency at the current spot exchange rate.

 ENTREPRENURIAL FINANCE ISSUES
CAPITAL BUDGETING

The capital budgeting techniques discussed in this chapter are appropriate for use when evaluating proposed investment projects in both small, or entrepreneurial, and large firms. Conceptually, there is no difference between the value-maximizing capital investment techniques used by large and entrepreneurial firms. In practice, however, there often are significant differences between the capital budgeting procedures used by entrepreneurial firms and larger firms.

As we have seen, larger firms tend to use the net present value and the internal rate of return approaches to evaluate proposed capital expenditures. A study by Runyon of firms with a net worth under $1 million found that nearly 70 percent used payback or another technically incorrect procedure, such as the accounting rate of return, to evaluate capital expenditures.[21] Several of the firms surveyed reported that they performed no formal analysis of proposed capital expenditures.

Several reasons have been advanced to explain the dramatic differences in the practice of capital expenditure analysis between large and entrepreneurial firms. First, many entrepreneurs simply may lack the expertise needed to implement formal analysis procedures. Or managerial talent may tend to be stretched to its limits in many entrepreneurial firms, such that the managers simply cannot find the time to implement better project evaluation techniques. Also, one must recognize that implementing and maintaining a sophisticated capital budgeting system is expensive. Large fixed costs are associated with

[21]L. R. Runyon. "Capital Expenditure Decision Making in Small Firms," *Journal of Business Research* (September 1983): 389–397. Also, see Footnote 1 in this chapter for more detail on the accounting rate of return method.

putting a formal system in place, and continuing costs are associated with collecting the data necessary for the system to function effectively. In entrepreneurial firms, investment projects tend to be small, and they may not justify the cost of a complete, formal analysis.

The emphasis on the use of payback techniques by entrepreneurial firms also may reflect the critical cash shortages that face many small and rapidly expanding firms. Because of their limited access to the capital markets for additional funds, these firms may be more concerned with the speed of cash generation from a project than with the profitability of the project.

Regardless of these impediments to the use of value-maximizing capital budgeting techniques, entrepreneurs have an excellent opportunity to improve their competitive position by implementing effective managerial control techniques. Entrepreneurs who rely on incorrect techniques, such as payback, to make their project accept-reject decisions are more likely to make poor investment decisions than managers who analyze their investment projects correctly.

ETHICAL ISSUES
THE USE OF SHAREHOLDER RESOURCES

Managers are employed by the owners of a firm with the objective of maximizing wealth for the shareholders. As we have learned, this objective can be accomplished by investing in the set of projects possessing the maximum expected net present value. As discussed in Chapter 1, the managers of some firms, such as Berkshire Hathaway, have focused intently on this objective and have had good success in achieving their objective. Other managers, however, seem to have strayed frequently from this objective.

Investing in projects with negative net present values is most likely to occur in firms possessing large discretionary cash flows. Usually these are firms in mature industries with few true growth opportunities. Mature firms tend to generate substantial cash flows over which managers have considerable control. Marginal projects may be accepted, often with little analysis, because of their "strategic" importance to the firm. Managers may be reluctant to pay these "excess" cash flows out to shareholders as increased dividends because that will cause the firm to grow at a slower rate in the future.

As discussed in Chapter 3, Stern Stewart's *Performance 1000* is a corporate performance measuring system designed to consider how effective managers have been in adding to their shareholders' investment.[22] Their "Market Value Added" (MVA) measure can be viewed as the "net present value of all a company's past and projected capital investment projects." For example, as shown in Table 3-6, Coca Cola has an MVA of more than $60 billion; General Electric has more than $52 billion of MVA; and Merck has about $31 billion. In contrast, IBM has an MVA of $–8.8 billion; General Motors has an MVA of –$17.8 billion; Ford's is –$13.7 billion; and Digital Equipment's is –$4.6 billion.

What factors might cause managers consistently to adopt investment projects with negative net present values? What are the consequences of these decisions for shareholders? What are the consequences of these decisions for the U.S. economy?

[22]G. Bennett Stewart, III, "Announcing the Stern Stewart Performance 1000: A New Way of Viewing Corporate America," *Continental Bank: Journal of Applied Corporate Finance* (Summer 1990): 38–59.

■ SUMMARY

■ The *net present value rule* is the primary decision-making rule used throughout the practice of financial management.

■ The net present value of an investment made by a firm represents the contribution of the investment to the value of the firm and, accordingly, to the wealth of shareholders.

■ The net present value is calculated by subtracting a project's net investment from the expected net cash flows discounted at the firm's cost of capital.

■ The *internal rate of return* of a project is the discount rate that gives the project a net present value equal to zero.

■ The *profitability index* is the ratio of the present value of net cash flows to the net investment. It gives a measure of the relative present value return per dollar of initial investment. The profitability index is useful when choosing among projects in a *capital rationing* situation.

■ The *payback period* is the number of years required for the cumulative net cash flows from a project to equal the net investment. The payback method has serious weaknesses, including the failure to account for the time value of money or to consider cash flows after the payback period.

■ The net present value and internal rate of return approaches normally yield the same accept-reject decisions for a particular project. However, conflicts may arise when dealing with *mutually exclusive* projects. The reinvestment rate assumption embodied in the net present value approach—namely, that cash flows from a project are reinvested at the cost of capital—generally is more realistic than that underlying the internal rate of return method. For this reason, the net present value method is preferred to the internal rate of return method.

■ Project postaudit reviews provide useful information regarding the effectiveness of a company's capital budgeting analysis and selection procedures. If a postaudit uncovers systematic biases in these procedures, corrective action should be taken. Project reviews may also identify whether a project should be abandoned prior to, at, or after its scheduled termination.

■ In general, relatively high levels of inflation tend to reduce the level of capital expenditures in the economy. The general capital budgeting procedures discussed in this text can be applied with equal validity in an inflationary environment as long as the estimates of revenues and costs used in the capital budgeting process include expected price and cost increases.

■ Financial managers must be aware that using conventional discounted cash flow techniques in capital budgeting without considering real options results in a downward-biased estimate of the true value of a project's net present value.

■ For international capital budgeting projects, the present value of a project's net cash flows to the parent company is equal to the present value of the project's net cash flows from the foreign viewpoint converted into the home country currency at the current spot exchange rate, given that an efficient capital market exists in the foreign country.

■ QUESTIONS AND TOPICS FOR DISCUSSION

1. How does the net present value model complement the objective of maximizing shareholder wealth?

2. When is it possible for the net present value and the internal rate of return approaches to give conflicting rankings of mutually exclusive investment projects?

3. When are multiple rates of return likely to occur in an internal rate of return computation? What should be done when a multiple rate of return problem arises?

4. Describe how the profitability index approach may be used by a firm faced with a capital rationing investment funds constraint.

5. What are the primary strengths and weaknesses of the payback approach in capital budgeting.

6. What are the primary objectives of the investment project postaudit review?

7. What is the likely effect of inflation on the level of capital expenditures made by private firms? What must the financial manager do to ensure that a firm's capital budgeting procedures will be effective in an inflationary environment?

8. What major problems can you foresee in applying capital budgeting techniques to investments made by public sector and not-for-profit enterprises or organizations?

9. What effect would you expect the use of MACRS depreciation rules to have on the acceptability of a project having a 10-year economic life but a 7-year MACRS classification?

■ SELF-TEST PROBLEMS

ST1. Calculate the net present value of a project with a net investment of $20,000 for equipment and an additional net working capital investment of $5,000 at time 0. The project is expected to generate net cash flows of $7,000 per year over a 10-year estimated economic life. In addition, the net working capital will be recovered at the end of the project. The required return on the project is 11 percent and the company has a marginal tax rate of 40 percent. What is the meaning of the computed net present value figure?

ST2. Calculate the internal rate of return and profitability index for a project that is expected to generate 8 years of annual net cash flows of $75,000. The project has a net investment of $360,000 and the required return on the project is 12 percent.

ST3. Two mutually exclusive projects have the following expected cash flows:

Year	G	H
0	−$10,000	−$10,000
1	5,000	0
2	5,000	0
3	5,000	17,000

a. Calculate the internal rate of return for each project.
b. Calculate the net present value for each project, assuming the firm's weighted cost of capital is 12 percent.
c. Which project should be adopted? Why?

■ PROBLEMS*

1. Calculate the net present value and profitability index of a project with a net investment of $20,000 and expected net cash inflows of $3,000 a year for 10 years if the project's required return is 12 percent. Is the project acceptable?

2. A firm wishes to bid on a contract that is expected to yield the following after-tax net cash flows at the end of each year:

*Colored numbers denote problems that have check answers provided at the end of the book.

Year	Net Cash Flow
1	$ 5,000
2	8,000
3	9,000
4	8,000
5	8,000
6	5,000
7	3,000
8	−1,500

To secure the contract, the firm must spend $30,000 to retool its plant. This retooling will have no salvage value at the end of the 8 years. Comparable investment alternatives are available to the firm that earn 12 percent compounded annually. The depreciation tax benefit from the retooling is reflected in the net cash flows in the table.

a. Compute the project's net present value.

b. Should the project be adopted?

c. What is the meaning of the computed net present value figure?

3. A machine that costs $8,000 is expected to operate for 10 years. The estimated salvage value at the end of 10 years is $0. The machine is expected to save the company $1,554 per year before taxes and depreciation. The company depreciates its assets on a straight-line basis and has a marginal tax rate of 40 percent. What is the internal rate of return on this investment?

4. Jefferson Products, Inc., is considering purchasing a new automatic press brake, which costs $300,000 including installation and shipping. The machine is expected to generate net cash inflows of $80,000 per year for 10 years. At the end of 10 years, the book value of the machine will be $0, and it is anticipated that the machine will be sold for $100,000. If the press brake project is undertaken, Jefferson will have to increase its net working capital by $75,000. When the project is terminated in 10 years, there no longer will be a need for this incremental working capital, and it can be liquidated and made available to Jefferson for other uses. Jefferson requires a 12 percent annual return on this type of project and its marginal tax rate is 40 percent.

a. Calculate the press brake's net present value.

b. Is the project acceptable?

c. What is the meaning of the computed net present value figure?

d. What is the project's internal rate of return?

e. For the press brake project, at what annual rates of return do the net present value and internal rate of return methods assume that the net cash inflows are being reinvested?

5. An acre planted with walnut trees is estimated to be worth $12,000 in 25 years. If you want to realize a 15 percent rate of return on your investment, how much can you afford to invest per acre? (Ignore all taxes and assume that annual cash outlays to maintain your stand of walnut trees are nil.)

6. A company is planning to invest $100,000 (before tax) in a personnel training program. The $100,000 outlay will be charged off as an expense by the firm this year (year 0). The returns from the program in the form of greater productivity and a reduction in employee turnover are estimated as follows (on an after-tax basis):

Years 1–10:	$10,000 per year
Years 11–20:	$22,000 per year

The company has estimated its cost of capital to be 12 percent. Assume that the entire $100,000 is paid at time 0 (the beginning of the project). The marginal tax rate for the firm is 40 percent. Should the firm undertake the training program? Why or why not?

7. Two mutually exclusive investment projects have the following forecasted cash flows:

Year	A	B
0	−$ 20,000	−$ 20,000
1	+10,000	0
2	+10,000	0
3	+10,000	0
4	+10,000	+60,000

a. Compute the internal rate of return for each project.

b. Compute the net present value for each project if the firm has a 10 percent cost of capital.

c. Which project should be adopted? Why?

8. Show that the internal rate of return of the following investment is 0, 100, and 200 percent:

Net investment	−$1,000	Year 0
Net cash flows	+6,000	Year 1
	−11,000	Year 2
	+6,000	Year 3

9. Commercial Hydronics is considering replacing one of its larger control devices. A new unit sells for $29,000 (delivered). An additional $3,000 will be needed to install the device. The new device has an estimated 20-year service life. The estimated salvage value at the end of 20 years will be $2,000. The new control device will be depreciated over 20 years on a straight-line basis to $0. The existing control device (original cost = $15,000) has been in use for 12 years, and it has been fully depreciated (that is, its book value equals zero). Its scrap value is estimated to be $1,000. The existing device could be used indefinitely, assuming the firm is willing to pay for its very high maintenance costs. The firm's marginal tax rate is 40 percent. The new control device requires lower maintenance costs and frees up personnel who normally would have to monitor the system. Estimated annual cash savings from the new device will be $9,000. The firm's cost of capital is 12 percent.

Using this information, evaluate the relative merits of replacing the old control device using the net present value approach.

10. A $1,230 investment has the following expected cash returns:

Year	Net Cash Flow
1	$800
2	200
3	400

8%

Compute the internal rate of return for this project.

11. Imperial Systems has $1 million available for capital investments during the current year. A list of possible investment projects, together with their net investments and net present values, is provided in the following table:

Project	Net Investment	Net Present Value
1	$200,000	$ 20,000
2	500,000	41,000
3	275,000	60,000
4	150,000	5,000
5	250,000	20,000
6	100,000	4,000
7	275,000	22,000
8	200,000	−18,000

a. Rank the various investment projects in terms of their profitability indexes (computed to three decimal places).

b. In the order of decreasing profitability index values and considering the capital constraints, which projects should be adopted? Are all capital funds expended?

c. Is there another combination that produces a higher aggregate net present value than the one developed in Part b?

d. If less than the entire amount of available funds is invested, what is the opportunity cost of the unused funds?

12. A junior executive is fed up with the operating policies of his boss. Before leaving the office of his angered superior, the young man suggests that a well-trained monkey could handle the trivia assigned to him. Pausing a moment to consider the import of this closing statement, the boss is seized by the thought that this must have been in the back of her own mind ever since she hired the junior executive. She decides to consider seriously replacing the executive with a bright young baboon. She figures that she could argue strongly to the board that such "capital deepening" is necessary for the cost-conscious firm. Two days later, a feasibility study is completed, and the following data are presented to the president:

- It would cost $12,000 to purchase and train a reasonably alert baboon with a life expectancy of 20 years.
- Annual expenses of feeding and housing the baboon would be $4,000.
- The junior executive's annual salary is $7,000 (a potential saving if the baboon is hired).
- The baboon will be depreciated on a straight-line basis over 20 years to a zero balance.
- The firm's marginal tax rate is 40 percent.
- The firm's current cost of capital is estimated to be 11 percent.

On the basis of the net present value criterion, should the monkey be hired (and the junior executive fired)?

13. The L-S Mining Company is planning to open a new strip mine in western Pennsylvania. The net investment required to open the mine is $10 million. Net cash flows are expected to be +$20 million at the end of year 1 and +$5 million at the end of year 2. At the end of year 3, L-S will have a net cash *outflow* of $17 million to cover the cost of closing the mine and reclaiming the land.

a. Calculate the net present value of the strip mine if the cost of capital is 5, 10, 15, 30, 71, and 80 percent.

b. What is unique about this project?

c. Should the project be accepted if L-S's cost of capital is 10 percent? 20 percent?

14. Fred and Frieda have always wanted to enter the blueberry business. They locate a 50-acre piece of hillside in Maine that is covered with blueberry bushes. They figure that the annual yield from the bushes will be 200 crates. Each crate is estimated to sell for $400 for the next 10 years. This price is expected to rise to $500 per crate for all sales from years 11 through 20).

In order to get started, Fred and Frieda must pay $150,000 for the land plus $20,000 for packing equipment. The packing equipment will be depreciated on a straight-line basis to a zero estimated salvage value at the end of 20 years. Fred and Frieda believe that at the end of 20 years, they will want to retire to Florida and sell their property.

Annual operating expenses, including salaries to Fred and Frieda and exclusive of depreciation, are estimated to be $50,000 per year for the first 10 years and $60,000 thereafter. The land is expected to appreciate in value at a rate of 5 percent per year. The couple's marginal tax rate is 30 percent for both ordinary income and capital gains and losses.

a. If the couple requires at least a 13 percent return on their investment, should they enter the blueberry business?

b. Assume that the land can be sold for only $50,000 at the end of 20 years (a capital loss of $100,000). Should the couple invest in the land and blueberry business? (Assume that the couple may claim the full amount of their capital loss in the year it occurs—year 20).

e✕cel 15. The Sisneros Company is considering building a chili processing plant in Hatch, New Mexico. The plant is expected to produce 50,000 pounds of processed chili peppers each year for the next 10 years. During the first year, Sisneros expects to sell the processed peppers for $2 per pound. The price is expected to increase at a 7 percent rate per year over the 10-year economic life of the plant. The costs of operating the plant, exclusive of depreciation, including the cost of fresh peppers, are estimated to be $50,000 during the first year. These costs are expected to increase at an 8 percent rate per year over the next 10 years.

The plant will cost $80,000 to build. It will be depreciated as a 7-year MACRS asset. The estimated salvage at the end of 10 years is zero. The firm's marginal tax rate is 40 percent.

a. Calculate the net investment required to build the plant.
b. Calculate the annual net cash flows from the project.
c. If Sisneros uses a 20 percent cost of capital to evaluate projects of this type, should the plant be built?
d. Calculate the payback period for this project.
e. How many internal rates of return does this project have? Why?

16. Note the following information on two mutually exclusive projects under consideration by Wang Food Markets, Inc.

Annual Cash Flows

Year	A	B
0	-$30,000	-$60,000
1	10,000	20,000
2	10,000	20,000
3	10,000	20,000
4	10,000	20,000
5	10,000	20,000

Wang requires a 14 percent rate of return on projects of this nature.
a. Compute the NPV of both projects.
b. Compute the internal rate of return on both projects.
c. Compute the profitability index of both projects.
d. Compute the payback period on both projects.
e. Which of the two projects, if either, should Wang accept? Why?

17. Channel Tunnel, Inc., plans to build a new 23-mile long tunnel under the English Channel for added train service. The cost (NINV) of the tunnel is expected to be $3.3 billion. Net cash inflows are expected to equal $651 million per year. How many years must the firm generate this cash inflow stream for investors to earn their required 19 percent rate of return?

e✕cel 18. Commercial Hydronics is considering replacing one of its larger control devices. A new unit sells for $29,000 (delivered). An additional $3,000 will be needed to install the device. The new device has an estimated 20-year service life. The estimated salvage value at the end of 20 years will be $2,000. The new control device will be depreciated as a 7-year MACRS asset. The existing control device (original cost = $15,000) has been in use for 12 years, and it has been fully depreciated (that is, its book value equals zero). Its scrap value is estimated to be $1,000. The existing device could be used indefinitely, assuming the firm is willing to pay for its very high maintenance costs. The firm's marginal tax rate is 40 percent. The new control device requires lower maintenance costs and frees up personnel who normally would have to monitor the system. Estimated annual cash savings from the new device will be $9,000. The firm's cost of capital is 12 percent.

Using this information, evaluate the relative merits of replacing the old control device using the net present value approach. (This problem is the same as Problem 9 except for depreciation method. Comparing the answers you get to Problems 9 and 18, what effect does the use of MACRS depreciation have on the economic desirability of the project?)

19. The Taylor Mountain Uranium Company currently has annual revenues of $1.2 million and annual expenses exclusive of depreciation of $700,000. Depreciation amounts to $200,000 per year. These figures are expected to remain constant for the foreseeable future (at least 15 years). The firm's marginal tax rate is 40 percent.

eXcel

A new high-speed processing unit costing $1.2 million is being considered as a potential investment designed to increase the firm's output capacity. This new piece of equipment will have an estimated usable life of 10 years and a $0 estimated salvage value. If the processing unit is bought, Taylor's annual revenues are expected to increase to $1.6 million, and annual expenses exclusive of depreciation will increase to $900,000. Annual depreciation will increase to $320,000. Assume that no increase in net working capital will be required as a result of this project. (Note: This problem is the same as Problem 7 in Chapter 8, except for the following questions.)

a. Calculate the processing unit's net present value, using a 12 percent required return.

b. Should Taylor accept the project?

c. How many internal rates of return does the processing unit project have? Why?

d. Calculate the processing unit's internal rate of return.

20. Benford, Inc., is planning to open a new sporting goods store in a suburban mall. Benford will lease the needed space in the mall. Equipment and fixtures for the store will cost $200,000 and be depreciated to $0 over a 5-year period on a straight-line basis. The new store will require Benford to increase its net working capital by $200,000 at time 0.

eXcel

First-year sales are expected to be $1 million and to increase at an annual rate of 8 percent over the expected 10-year life of the store. Operating expenses (including lease payments but excluding depreciation) are projected to be $700,000 during the first year and to increase at a 7 percent annual rate. The salvage value of the store's equipment and fixtures is anticipated to be $10,000 at the end of 10 years.

Benford's marginal tax rate is 40 percent. (Note: This problem is the same as Problem 12 in Chapter 8, except for the following questions.)

a. Calculate the store's net present value, using an 18 percent required return.

b. Should Benford accept the project?

c. Calculate the store's internal rate of return.

d. Calculate the store's profitability index.

21. Seco Dame Enterprises (SDE) acquired a robotic saw 6 years ago at a cost of $10 million. The saw was depreciated under the old ACRS rules to its current book value of $0. Actual salvage value today is estimated to be $2 million. SDE's average tax rate is 30 percent, and its marginal tax rate is 40 percent. The weighted cost of capital for SDE is 15 percent.

eXcel

A new robotic saw will cost $15 million. It will be depreciated under MACRS rules for a 7-year class asset. If SDE acquires the new saw, it estimates that its net working capital investment will decline, due to the reduced need to carry inventories of spare parts for this more reliable machine. Net working capital should decline from a current level of $1 million to a new level of $500,000 as a result of this purchase.

a. Calculate the net investment required to acquire the new saw.

b. The new saw is expected to reduce operating costs (exclusive of depreciation) for SDE by $800,000 per year over the asset's expected 10-year life. Also, the increased productivity of the new saw is expected to increase SDE's revenue by $2 million per year. Salvage value at the end of 10 years is expected to be $0. Calculate the annual net cash flows for this investment.

c. Compute the NPV for this project.

22. Project Alpha requires an outlay of $10,000 immediately. Project Alpha has a 1-year life and is expected to produce a net cash flow at the end of one year of $20,000. Project Beta, a mutually exclusive alternative to Alpha, requires an outlay of $20,000 immediately. It too is expected to have a 1-year life and to produce a net cash flow at the end of one year of $35,000.
    a. Compute the internal rate of return for both projects. Compute the NPV for both projects, using a cost of capital of 10 percent.
    b. Which project should be undertaken?

23. International Foods Corporation, a U.S.-based food company, is considering expanding its soup-processing operations in France. The company plans a net investment of $8 million in the project. The current spot exchange rate is FF6.25 per $ (FF = french francs). Net cash flows for the expansion project are estimated to be FF5 million for 10 years and nothing thereafter. Based on its analysis of current conditions in France's capital markets, International Foods has determined that the applicable cost of capital for the project is 16 percent. Calculate the net present value of the proposed expansion project.

24. You have just been named the Chief Financial Officer of Fabco, a large metal fabricator located in Chama, New Mexico. The company has long been a user of the net present value method for evaluating its investment projects. The firm undertakes all projects offering a positive net present value, based upon data submitted by the project proposer. Fabco's weighted cost of capital has been estimated to be 15 percent. This capital cost has remained approximately constant over the past 5 years.

   Over the past 5 years Fabco has earned a return on assets averaging 8 percent. You are concerned about the apparent disagreement between Fabco's cost of capital and its earned returns. The CEO has asked you to prepare a report on the situation. What factors (both within and outside of the firm) might account for this *apparent* discrepancy in performance?

■ SOLUTIONS TO SELF-TEST PROBLEMS

STI. $NPV = -(\$20,000 + \$5,000) + \$7,000(PVIFA_{0.11,10}) + \$5,000(PVIF_{0.11,10})$

$= \$17,983$

The value of the firm, and therefore the shareholders' wealth, is increased by $17,983 as a result of undertaking the project. The project is acceptable, because its NPV is positive.

ST2. $NPV = PV \text{ cash inflows} - \text{Net investment}$

$0 = \$75,000(PVIFA_{r,8}) - \$360,000$

$(PVIFA_{r,8}) = 4.80$

$r \approx 13 \text{ percent (from Table IV)}$

$$PI = \frac{\$75,000(PVIFA_{0.12,8})}{\$360,000}$$

$= 1.035$

ST3. a. Project G: $\$10,000 = \$5,000 \, (PVIFA_{r,3})$

$PVIFA_{r,3} = 2.0$

$r \approx 23.4 \text{ percent (from Table IV)}$

Project H: $\$10,000 = \$17,000(PVIF_{r,3})$

$PVIF_{r,3} = 0.588$

$r \approx 19.3 \text{ percent (from Table II)}$

   b. $\text{NPV}_G = -\$10,000 + \$5,000(\text{PVIFA}_{0.12,3})$

         $= \$2,010$

     $\text{NPV}_H = -\$10,000 + \$17,000(\text{PVIF}_{0.12,3})$

         $= \$2,104$

   c. Project H should be adopted, because it has the higher NPV. It is assumed that the firm's reinvestment opportunities are represented more accurately by the firm's cost of capital than by the unique internal rate of return of either project.

■ GLOSSARY

Capital Rationing The process of limiting the number of capital expenditure projects because of insufficient funds to finance all projects that otherwise meet the firm's criteria for acceptability or because of a lack of sufficient managerial resources to undertake all otherwise acceptable projects.

Contingent Project A project whose acceptance depends on the adoption of one or more other projects.

Independent Project A project whose acceptance or rejection does not result directly in the elimination of other projects from consideration.

Internal Rate of Return (IRR) The discount rate that equates the present value of net cash flows from a project with the present value of the net investment. It is the discount rate that gives the project a net present value equal to zero. The IRR is used to evaluate, rank, and select from among various investment projects.

Multiple Rates of Return Two or more internal rates of return from the same project. This situation sometimes arises when the IRR method is being used for project selection. It occurs only with nonnormal projects or those whose cash flow patterns contain more than one sign change.

Mutually Exclusive Project A project whose acceptance precludes the acceptance of one or more alternative projects.

Net Present Value (NPV) The present value of the stream of net cash flows resulting from a project, discounted at the firm's cost of capital, minus the project's net investment. It is used to evaluate, rank, and select from among various investment projects.

Normal Project A project whose cash flow stream requires an initial outlay of funds followed by a series of positive net cash inflows. This also sometimes is called a *conventional project*.

Opportunity Cost The rate of return that can be earned on funds if they are invested in the *next best* alternative investment.

Payback (PB) Period The period of time required for the cumulative cash inflows from a project to equal the initial cash outlay.

Profitability Index (PI) The ratio of the present value of net cash flows over the life of a project to the net investment. It is used to evaluate, rank, and select from among various investment projects. Frequently it is used in conjunction with resource allocation decisions in capital rationing situations.

Project Postaudit A review of a project that assesses its progress and evaluates its performance after termination.

Real Option Managerial opportunities to make decisions that will impact the expected cash flows of a project, their timing, or the future acceptability of the project. Real options include the option to abandon, the option to defer investment, flexibility options, and growth options.

Reinvestment Rate The rate of return at which cash flows from an investment project are assumed to be reinvested from year to year. The reinvestment rate may vary, depending on the investment opportunities available to the firm.

An Integrative Case Problem
Capital Budgeting

e✗cel First Republic Bancorp is considering the acquisition of a new data processing and management information system. The system, including computer hardware and software, will cost $1 million. Delivery and installation of the system is expected to add $100,000 to this cost. To put this new system in place, the bank expects to have to make an investment of $50,000 in net working capital immediately and an additional net working capital investment of $25,000 at the end of year 1. The system has an expected economic life of 10 years. It will be depreciated as a 7-year asset under MACRS rules. Actual salvage value at the end of 10 years is expected to be $100,000, and the bank plans to sell the system for its salvage value at that time.

The new data processing system will save the bank the $190,000 fee per year that it currently pays to a computer time-sharing company. Operating, maintenance, and insurance costs for the system are estimated to total $50,000 during the first year. These costs are expected to increase at a rate of 7 percent per year over the 10-year period.

First Republic plans to sell excess computer time to a number of local firms. The demand function for this service during year 1 is estimated to be

$$Q = 20,000 - 200P$$

where Q = number of units of computer time sold, and P = price per unit of computer time sold.

Based on an analysis of the local market for computer time, the bank feels that it can charge $14 per unit of computer time. Although the bank does not anticipate changing this charge over the 10-year period, it expects the quantity demanded to decline by 5 percent per year after year 1. It is expected that these outside sales of computer time will cost the bank an *additional $40,000 per year* in computer operating costs (including the salary of a computer services representative to handle the new customers). These additional operating costs are expected to increase at a rate of 7 percent annually over the 10-year period.

The bank has a marginal ordinary tax rate of 34 percent. This rate is expected to remain in effect over the life of the project. First Republic uses an after-tax cost of capital of 15 percent to evaluate projects of this risk. This cost of capital was computed based upon the current after-tax cost of equity and debt funds in the bank's capital structure.

Based on the information contained in the case, use the NPV approach to determine if First Republic should acquire the new data processing system.

APPENDIX 9A
MUTUALLY EXCLUSIVE INVESTMENTS HAVING UNEQUAL LIVES

 REPLACEMENT CHAINS

Chapter 9 discusses a number of capital budgeting decision models. When mutually exclusive investments are considered, it is assumed implicitly that the alternative projects have *equal* lives. In actual practice, however, this may not be the case. When two or more mutually exclusive alternatives have *unequal* lives, neither the net present value nor the internal rate of return method yields reliable accept-reject information unless the projects are evaluated for an equal period of time. If, for example, a firm adopts the longer-lived of two projects simply on the basis of net present value or internal rate of return data, it essentially ignores any alternative investment opportunities that might have been available at the end of the shorter-lived project.

Suppose a firm is considering two mutually exclusive investments, I and II. Project I requires an initial outlay of $2,000 and is expected to generate a 5-year stream of net cash flows of $600 per year. Project II also requires an initial outlay of $2,000 but is expected to generate a 10-year stream of net cash flows of $375 per year. The firm has a 10 percent cost of capital.

Table 9A-1 shows that the net present value of Project I is $274.60 and the net present value of Project II is $304.37. Therefore, the net present value criterion suggests that Project II should be chosen over Project I.

The expected life of Project II is twice as long as that of Project I. Therefore, the two net present values calculated in Table 9A-1 are not really comparable. At this point, the firm also must consider what might happen if Project I were

TABLE 9A-1
Cash Flows for Projects I and II

	PROJECT I		PROJECT II	
Year	Net Investment	Net Cash Flow	Net Investment	Net Cash Flow
0	$2,000	—	$2,000	—
1		$600		$375
2		600		375
3		600		375
4		600		375
5		600		375
6		—		375
7		—		375
8		—		375
9		—		375
10		—		375

$$NPV_I = -\$2,000 + \$600\,(3.791)$$
$$= \$274.60$$

$$NPV_{II} = -\$2,000 + \$375\,(6.145)$$
$$= 304.37$$

	PROJECT I WITH REPLACEMENT		PROJECT II	
Year	Net Investment	Net Cash Flow	Net Investment	Net Cash Flow
0	$2,000	—	$2,000	—
1		$600		$375
2		600		375
3		600		375
4		600		375
5	2,100	600		375
6		600		375
7		600		375
8		600		375
9		600		375
10		600		375

$$NPV_I = -\$2,000 + \$600(6.145) - \$2,100(0.621)$$
$$= \$382.80$$

$$NPV_{II} = -\$2,000 + \$375(6.145)$$
$$= 304.37$$

replaced with a similar 5-year life project at the end of 5 years. In other words, it would create a *replacement chain* for the shorter-lived project. Suppose, for example, the firm estimates that replacing Project I with a similar project at the end of 5 years would cost $2,100 and, like Project I, would generate annual net cash flows of $600. This results in a new stream of cash flows for Project I, as shown in Table 9A-2. The new net present value for Project I is higher than that for Project II, thus indicating—correctly—that Project I should be chosen over Project II.

Many times it is not possible to get a series of projects (such as Project I with its replacement at the end of 5 years) that will have an identical time duration to that of the longer-lived project (II). For example, one project might have a life of 15 years, whereas an alternative requires replacement every 8 years. Hence, the shorter-lived project together with its replacement have a 16-year life, whereas the longer-lived project has a 15-year life. Such a comparison normally will be acceptable, because the discrepancy occurs for only 1 year that is 15 years in the future. In present value terms, this will not have much impact.

The importance of time discrepancies such as these depends on the following:

■ The number of years of the discrepancy. The fewer the years of the discrepancy, the less important it is.
■ The number of years into the future the discrepancy occurs. The further into the future, the less important the discrepancy is.
■ The relationship between the rate of return on future investments and the cost of capital. When the rate of return on future investments is equal to the cost of capital, these investments have an NPV = 0. Under these circumstances, the discrepancy can be ignored.

 EQUIVALENT ANNUAL ANNUITIES

An alternative approach for dealing with the problem of mutually exclusive investments having unequal lives is to use the equivalent annual annuity approach. This technique can solve the problem of time discrepancies often encountered when using the replacement chain approach.

For example, consider the case of a firm that needs to replace an aging piece of machinery. One alternative would be to buy new Machine A having a 9-year life. Another alternative would be to buy new Machine B with a 5-year life. In this case, the time discrepancy between A and B is significant—4 years. Commonly, this problem is dealt with by developing a string of replacement chains out to a year when both machines would need replacement. The common denominator year in this case is 45 years—indicating nine investments in B and five investments in A.

In cases like this, the equivalent annual annuity approach is often easier to use. In our example, assume the new Machine A will require a net investment of $34,500 and generate net cash flows of $7,000 per year for 9 years. Machine B will require a net investment of $25,000 and generate net cash flows of $8,000 per year for 5 years. The firm's cost of capital is 10 percent. To make our decision on the basis of the equivalent annual annuity criterion, we use the following three steps:

1. First, compute the net present value of each machine over its original expected economic life:

$$NPV_A = -\$34,500 + \$7,000(PVIFA_{0.10,9})$$

$$= -\$34,500 + \$7,000(5.759)$$

$$= \$5,813$$

$$NPV_B = -\$25,000 + \$8,000(PVIFA_{0.10,5})$$

$$= -\$25,000 + \$8,000(3.791)$$

$$= \$5,328$$

As these calculations indicate, if the possibility of the replacement of Machine B at the end of 5 years is not considered, Machine A would appear to be the better alternative because of its greater net present value.

2. Next, divide the net present value for each machine computed in Step 1 by the PVIFA factor for the project's original life. This gives the *equivalent annual annuity:*

$$\text{Equivalent annual annuity (A)} = \frac{\$5,813}{PVIFA_{0.10,9}}$$

$$= \frac{\$5,813}{5.759}$$

$$= \$1,009.38$$

$$\text{Equivalent annual annuity (B)} = \frac{\$5,328}{PVIFA_{0.10,5}}$$

$$= \frac{\$5,328}{3.791}$$

$$= \$1,405.43$$

3. The equivalent annual annuity method assumes that each machine will be replaced an infinite number of times into the future and therefore will provide these annual annuities in perpetuity. As perpetuities, these equivalent

annual annuities can be valued (at present) by dividing the annuity amount by the cost of capital:

$$NPV_A \text{(assuming infinite replacement)} = \frac{\$1,009.38}{0.10}$$

$$= \$10,093.80$$

$$NPV_B \text{(assuming infinite replacement)} = \frac{\$1,405.43}{0.10}$$

$$= \$14,054.30$$

Machine B should be acquired, because it has the higher net present value when evaluated over an infinite replacement horizon.

In general, the equivalent annual annuity method will give the same decision as the replacement chain technique. Its advantage is that it often is computationally simpler, and it simplifies the handling of the time discrepancies that frequently arise in the replacement chain method.

■ SELF-TEST PROBLEM

ST1. Turbomachinery Parts, Inc. is considering two mutually exclusive equipment investments that would increase its production capacity. The firm uses a 14 percent required rate of return to evaluate capital expenditure projects. The two investments have the following costs and expected cash flow streams:

Year	Investment D	Investment E	Year	Investment D	Investment E
0	-$50,000	-$50,000	4	—	15,000
1	24,000	15,000	5	—	15,000
2	24,000	15,000	6	—	15,000
3	24,000	15,000			

a. Calculate the net present value for Investments D and E, using the above data.

b. Create a replacement chain for Investment D. Assume that the cost of replacing D remains at $50,000 and that the replacement project will generate cash inflows of $24,000 for years 4 through 6. Using these figures, recompute the net present value for Investment D.

c. Which of the two investments should be chosen, D or E? Why?

d. Use the equivalent annual annuity method to solve this problem. How does your answer compare with the one obtained in Part b?

■ PROBLEMS*

1. The Smith Pie Company is considering two mutually exclusive investments that would increase its capacity to make strawberry tarts. The firm uses a 12 percent cost of capital to evaluate potential investments. The two projects have the following costs and expected cash flow streams:

Year	Alternative A	Alternative B	Year	Alternative A	Alternative B
0	-$30,000	-$30,000	5	—	6,500
1	10,500	6,500	6	—	6,500
2	10,500	6,500	7	—	6,500
3	10,500	6,500	8	—	6,500
4	10,500	6,500			

*Colored numbers denote problems that have check answers provided at the end of the book.

  a. Using this data, calculate the net present value for Projects A and B.

  b. Create a replacement chain for Alternative A. Assume that the cost of replacing A will be $30,000 and that the replacement project will generate cash flows of $10,500 for years 5 through 8. Using these figures, recompute the net present value for Alternative A.

  c. Which of the two alternatives should be chosen, A or B? Why?

  d. Use the equivalent annual annuity method to solve this problem. How does your answer compare with the one obtained in Part b?

2. BC Minerals is considering a new production process. Two alternative pieces of equipment are available. Alternative P costs $100,000, has a 10-year life, and is expected to generate annual cash inflows of $22,000 in each of the 10 years. Alternative R costs $85,000, has an 8-year life, and is expected to generate annual cash inflows of $18,000 in each of the 8 years. BC Minerals's weighted cost of capital is 12 percent. Using the equivalent annual annuity method, which alternative should be chosen?

3. Germania Corporation is considering replacing its plant cooling unit. The existing unit has recently "died" and has no salvage value. Of the two competing cooling units, B has a long life but a higher initial cost than the cheaper unit A. The following data are available:

Year	NCF_A	NCF_B	Year	NCF_A	NCF_B
0	−$50,000	−$79,000	3	25,000	28,000
1	25,000	28,000	4	—	28,000
2	25,000	28,000	5	—	28,000

The marginal cost of capital is 19 percent. Which cooling unit should be purchased? Why?

■ SOLUTION TO SELF-TEST PROBLEM

ST1. a. $NPV_D = -$50,000 + $24,000(2.322)$

      $= $5,728$

    $NPV_E = -$50,000 + $15,000(3.889)$

      $= $8,335$

  b. NPV_D (replacement chain)

      $= $5,728 - $50,000(PVIF_{0.14,3}) + $24,000(PVIFA_{0.14,3})(PVIF_{0.14,3})$

      $= $9,594$

  c. Investment D should be chosen because it has the higher positive net present value when the two investments are compared for an equal period of time.

  d. $NPV_D = $5,728$ (from Part a)

    $NPV_E = $8,335$ (from Part a)

    Equivalent annual annuity (D) $= \dfrac{$5,728}{PVIFA_{0.14,3}}$

        $= $2,467$

    Equivalent annual annuity (E) $= \dfrac{$8,335}{PVIFA_{0.14,6}}$

        $= $2,143$

    NPV_D (assuming infinite replacement) $= \dfrac{$2,467}{0.14} = $17,621$

    NPV_E (assuming infinite replacement) $= \dfrac{$2,143}{0.14} = $15,307$

    Investment D should be selected because it has the higher net present value when evaluated over an infinite replacement horizon.

CAPITAL BUDGETING AND RISK

10

KEY CHAPTER CONCEPTS

1. *Total project risk* refers to the chance that a project will not perform up to expectations. It is often measured by either the standard deviation or the coefficient of variation of cash flows from a project.

2. The *portfolio*, or *beta, risk* of a project refers to the contribution a project makes to the risk of the firm when the interactions between the cash flows of the project are considered in conjunction with the other cash flows of the firm.

3. When considering the systematic risk of individual projects, the *beta* concept can be used to determine risk-adjusted discount rates for individual projects.

4. A number of techniques can be used to analyze total project risk. These techniques include
   a. The *net present value/payback approach*.
   b. The *simulation analysis approach*.
   c. The *sensitivity analysis approach*.
   d. The *scenario analysis approach*.
   e. The *risk-adjusted discount rate approach*.
   f. The *certainty equivalent approach*.

THE BOEING 747 SUPERJUMBO JET*

The capital budgeting process discussed in the previous two chapters is quite simple, in reality. If the present value of a project's net cash flows (including the value of any embedded real options) exceeds the outlays required (the net investment), a project is acceptable and should be undertaken. The major difficulty is developing realistic estimates of the costs and benefits from a project. The problems a firm may encounter can stem from an incomplete analysis of a project or from a lack of sufficient concern for the profitability of the firm. In addition to these problems, it must be recognized that nearly all projects have some element of risk—the chance that the actual cash flows will differ from the forecasted ones.

In early 1997, Boeing Company announced that it was canceling plans for a pair of superjumbo 747 models. One model would have a range of 10,000 miles and carry 500 or more passengers. This project would have cost Boeing an additional $5 billion to $7 billion. As Boeing proceeded with the development of these new models, it became increasingly concerned about the risk inherent in its forecasts of final de-

mand. Furthermore, the advanced technology that Boeing planned to incorporate into the new models increased the risk of higher-than-expected development costs. At the same time, Boeing's primary competitor, Airbus, confirmed that it planned to move ahead with its new superjumbo airliner, designed to carry 550 passengers. Airbus projected final demand for a plane of this size at about 1,300, whereas Boeing's estimates were around 500 planes. The risk inherent in these drastically different demand forecasts were too great for

Boeing to justify proceeding with the project. Airbus also faces development cost risks. It plans to spend about $8 billion on the development and certification of the new plane. Some analysts forecast that the final cost will be closer to $16 billion. The stock market apparently agreed with Boeing's assessment that the risk of the new model was too high. Boeing's stock jumped $7.375 or 6.9 percent on the news of the cancellation of the new 747 models.

In this case, Boeing determined that the risks associated with the project were too great to justify the substantial outlays required. Although risk cannot be eliminated, a capable financial manager should try to determine at the outset what risks are being assumed when a project is undertaken, just as Boeing did in this case. What is the worst-case outcome? How likely is this outcome? What actions can be taken to reduce this risk? How will investors react to this risk? Given the answers to these questions, risky projects can be evaluated properly. This chapter examines these important questions.

*Based on "Boeing's 747 Decision Shifts Rivalry With Airbus," *Wall Street Journal* (January 22, 1997): A3.

INTRODUCTION

In Chapter 5 we discussed the nature of risk and its influence on financial decision making. The greater the risk associated with an investment, the greater the return required. This basic principle also applies in the capital budgeting area.

In the previous chapter, investment projects were evaluated using the firm's weighted cost of capital (required rate of return). This approach implicitly assumes that all projects being considered are of equal risk and that this risk is the same as that for the firm as a whole. When a project has more or less than an average risk level, it is necessary to adjust the analysis to account for this risk level.

TOTAL PROJECT RISK VERSUS PORTFOLIO RISK

When analyzing the risk associated with a capital expenditure, it is important to distinguish between the *total project risk* and the *portfolio, or beta, risk* of that investment. By total project risk we mean the chance that a project will perform below expectations—possibly resulting in losses from the project and for the firm. In the worst case, these losses could be so severe as to cause the firm to fail.

In contrast, a project that has a high level of total project risk may not affect the portfolio risk of the firm at all. Consider the case of oil and gas exploration companies. The firms know that any wildcat well they drill will cost about $2 million and have only a 10 percent chance of success. Successful wells produce profits of $24 million. Unsuccessful wells produce no profits at all, and the entire investment will be a loss. If each firm only drilled one well, there would be a 90 percent chance the firm would fail (the total project risk would be very high). In contrast, if one firm drilled 100 wildcat wells, the risk of failure from all wells would be very low because of the portfolio risk reduction that results from drilling many wells. In this case, the expected return of the firm would be as follows:

$$\text{Expected return} = \frac{\text{Expected profit per well}}{\text{Investment required per well}}$$

$$= \frac{\left(\begin{array}{c}\text{Probability of}\\\text{success}\end{array}\right)\left(\text{Profit}\right) + \left(\begin{array}{c}\text{Probability of}\\\text{failure}\end{array}\right)\left(\text{Loss}\right)}{\text{Investment required per well}}$$

$$= \frac{0.10(\$24 \text{ million}) + 0.90(-\$2 \text{ million})}{\$2 \text{ million}}$$

$$= \frac{\$2.4 \text{ million} - \$1.8 \text{ million}}{\$2 \text{ million}}$$

$$= 0.30, \text{ or } 30\%$$

This return is achieved with very little risk relative to that facing a firm drilling a single well. As this example illustrates, the risk of drilling any individual well can be diversified away very effectively. Consequently, these risks are not market related, and they should have little, if any, impact on the beta risk of the firm. That risk remains unchanged and approximately equal to the market risk facing other oil and gas exploration companies.

This example has shown that an investment with high total project risk does not necessarily have to possess high beta (systematic) risk. Of course, it is possible for a project to have both high total project risk and high beta risk. For example, a grocery store chain (which typically has low beta risk) might decide to develop and market a new line of small business computers. Because of the large number of competitors in this business and because of the grocery chain's lack of expertise, this investment can be expected to have a high level of total project risk. At the same time, the beta risk of this investment is likely to be high relative to that of the grocery chain, because business computer sales expand rapidly during boom periods and slow down dramatically during recessions.

From a capital budgeting perspective, the beta risk of a project certainly is important, because the beta of a firm influences the returns required by investors in that firm and hence the value of the firm's shares.

Total project risk is also important to consider in most cases for several reasons. There are a number of relatively undiversified investors, including the owners of small firms, for whom total project and total firm risk are important. Also, the total risk of the firm—not just the beta risk—determines the risk of firm failure and potential bankruptcy. Stockholders, creditors, managers, and other employees all are interested in preventing the tragedy (and avoiding the costs) of total firm failure.

Consequently, in the evaluation of an investment, it is important to consider both the total project risk and the impact of the project on the beta risk of the firm. We continue the chapter with a discussion of techniques to use when evaluating the beta risk of a project. In the final section, we examine a number of techniques that can be used to account for total project risk in the capital budgeting process.

ADJUSTING FOR BETA RISK IN CAPITAL BUDGETING

The *beta* concept introduced in Chapter 5 for security risk analysis also can be used to determine risk-adjusted discount rates (RADR) for individual capital budgeting projects. This approach is appropriate for a firm whose stock is widely traded and for which there is very little chance of bankruptcy. (The probability of bankruptcy is a function of total risk, not just systematic risk.)

Just as the beta (systematic risk) of a portfolio of securities can be computed as the weighted average of the individual security betas, a firm may be considered as a portfolio of assets, each having its own beta. From this perspective, the systematic risk of the firm is simply the weighted average of the systematic risk of the individual assets.

For a great glossary of terms describing financial risks of any type, visit the following Web site. You've probably already heard about beta, arbitrage, CAPM, systematic risk, and the efficient frontier. But do you know what deltas, collars, leptokurtosis, swaptions, and inverse floaters are?
http://www.contingencyanalysis.com/glossary.htm#

The All-Equity Case

For example, consider the security market line shown in Figure 10-1. The firm has a beta of 1.2 and is financed exclusively with internally generated equity capital. The market risk premium is 7 percent. When considering projects of average risk—that is, projects that are highly correlated with the firm's returns on its existing assets and that have a beta similar to the firm's beta (1.2)—the firm should use the computed 13.4 percent cost of equity from Figure 10-1. When considering projects having estimated betas different from 1.2, it should use an equity discount rate equal to the required return calculated from the security

FIGURE 10-1
Risk-Adjusted Discount Rates
and the SML

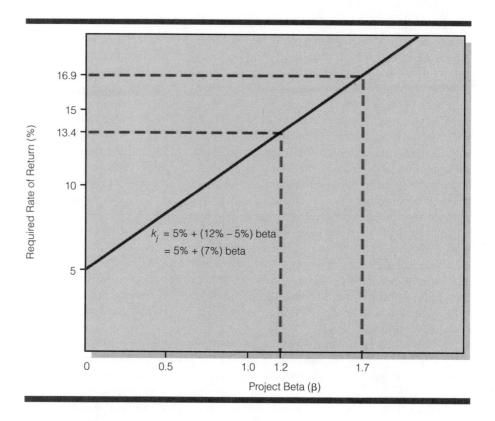

market line. For example, if a project's estimated beta is 1.7 and the risk-free rate is 5 percent, the project's required equity return would be 16.9 percent, or 5% +1.7 (7%), and this would be used as the risk-adjusted discount rate for that project, assuming the project is financed with 100 percent equity.

The Equity and Debt Case

Next, we develop a procedure for computing the risk-adjusted discount rate for projects financed with both debt and equity. To better understand the material in this section, we briefly introduce the concept of a weighted cost of capital, which is developed more extensively in Chapter 11. At this point, it is necessary only to recognize that the required return on the project discussed in this section reflects the project's equity return requirement and the debt return requirement for the funds expected to be used to finance the project.

Consider the example of Vulcan Industries, with a current capital structure consisting of 50 percent debt and 50 percent equity. Vulcan is considering expanding into a new line of business and wants to compute the rate of return that will be required on projects in this area. Vulcan has determined that the debt capacity associated with projects in its new business line is such that a capital structure consisting of 40 percent debt and 60 percent common equity is appropriate to finance these new projects. Vulcan's company beta has been estimated to be 1.3, but the Vulcan management does not believe that this beta risk is appropriate for the new business line. Vulcan's managers must estimate the beta risk appropriate for projects in this new line of business and then determine the risk-adjusted return requirement on these projects.

Because the beta risk of projects in this new business line is not directly observable, Vulcan's managers have decided to rely on surrogate market information. They have identified a firm, Olympic Materials, that competes exclusively in the line of business into which Vulcan proposes expanding. The beta of Olympic has been estimated to be 1.50.

Recall from Chapter 5 that a firm's beta is computed as the slope of its characteristic line and that actual security returns are used in the computations. Accordingly, a firm's computed beta is a measure of both its business risk *and* its financial risk. When a beta is computed for a firm such as Olympic, it reflects both the business and financial risk of that firm. To determine the beta associated with Vulcan's proposed new line of business using the observed beta from another firm (Olympic) that competes exclusively in that business line, it is necessary to convert the observed beta, often called a *leveraged beta*, β_l, into an *unleveraged*, or pure project beta, β_u. This unleveraged beta then can be releveraged to reflect the amount of debt capacity appropriate for this type of project and that will be used by Vulcan to finance it. The following equation can be used to convert a leveraged beta into an unleveraged, or pure project, beta:[1]

$$\beta_u = \frac{\beta_l}{1 + (1 - T)(B/E)} \tag{10.1}$$

where β_u is the unleveraged beta for a project or firm, β_l is the leveraged beta for a project or firm, B is the market value of the firm's debt, E is the market value of the firm's equity, and T is the firm's marginal tax rate.

The use of this equation can be illustrated for the Vulcan Materials example. The beta, β_l, for Olympic has been computed to be 1.50. Olympic has a capital structure consisting of 20 percent debt and 80 percent common equity and a tax rate of 35 percent. Substituting these values into Equation 10.1 yields

$$\beta_u = \frac{1.50}{1 + (1 - 0.35)(0.25)} = 1.29$$

The unleveraged, or pure project beta for the proposed new line of business of Vulcan is estimated to be 1.29. Vulcan intends to finance this new line of business with a capital structure consisting of 40 percent debt and 60 percent common equity. In addition, Vulcan's tax rate is 40 percent. Equation 10.2 can be used to compute the leveraged beta associated with this new line of business, given Vulcan's proposed target capital structure for the project.

$$\beta_l = \beta_u[1 + (1 - T)(B/E)] \tag{10.2}$$

$$= 1.29[1 + (1 - 0.4)(0.667)]$$

$$= 1.81$$

With a risk-free rate of 5 percent and a market risk premium of 7 percent, the required return on the equity portion of the proposed new line of business is computed from the security market line as

$$k_e = 5\% + 1.81(7\%)$$

$$= 17.7\%$$

[1]Robert Hamada, "The Effect of the Firm's Capital Structure on the Systematic Risk of Common Stocks," *Journal of Finance* (May 1972): 435–452.

If the after-tax cost of debt, k_i, used to finance the new line of business is 8 percent, the risk-adjusted required return, k_a^*, on the new line of business, given the proposed capital structure of 40 percent debt and 60 percent equity, is a weighted average of the marginal, after-tax debt and equity costs, or

$$k_a^* = 0.4(8\%) + 0.6(17.7\%)$$

$$= 13.8\%$$

Therefore, the risk-adjusted required rate of return on the proposed new line of business for Vulcan is 13.8 percent. This number reflects both the pure project risk and the financial risk associated with the project as Vulcan anticipates financing it.

Equations 10.1 and 10.2 provide only an approximation of the effect of leverage on beta. Capital market imperfections, such as the existence of risky debt and uncertainty regarding future levels of debt, introduce error into the beta adjustments just presented. Hence, this procedure should be used with caution. This general procedure is used by many different firms, including Digital Equipment and Southwestern Bell Corporation.[2]

Computing the Risk-Adjusted Net Present Value

The net present value (NPV) of a project using the RADR approach is defined as follows:

$$\text{NPV} = \sum_{t=1}^{n} \frac{\text{NCF}_t}{(1 + k_a^*)^t} - \text{NINV} \tag{10.3}$$

where k_a^* is the risk-adjusted weighted cost of capital (required return), NCF_t is the net cash flow in period t, and NINV is the net investment. Suppose a company's weighted cost of capital is 12 percent and the risk-adjusted discount rate for a new product project the company is considering is 16 percent. If the project's net investment is $50,000 and its expected cash inflows are $10,000 a year for 10 years, the project's NPV is −$1,670 ($10,000 × 4.833 − $50,000), using a 16 percent discount rate, and $6,500 ($10,000 × 5.650 − $50,000), using a 12 percent discount rate. Assuming the 16 percent RADR figure has been determined correctly by using the security market line with an accurate beta value, the project should not be accepted even though its NPV, calculated using the company's weighted cost of capital, is positive. This new product project is similar to Project 4 in Figure 10-2.

The new product project discussed in the previous paragraph has an internal rate of return of about 15 percent, compared to its 16 percent required return. Therefore, the project should be rejected, according to the IRR decision rule. When the IRR technique is used, the RADR given by the SML frequently is called the **hurdle rate.** Some finance practitioners use the term *hurdle rate* to describe any risk-adjusted discount rate.

Figure 10-2 illustrates the difference between the use of a single discount rate, the weighted cost of capital,[3] for all projects regardless of risk level and a dis-

---

[2]"Divisional Hurdle Rates and the Cost of Capital," *Financial Management* (Spring 1989): 18–25.

[3]The weighted cost of capital for a firm is defined in more detail in Chapter 11. It is equal to the marginal cost of equity times the proportion of a common equity in the firm's target capital structure, plus the after-tax marginal cost of debt times the debt proportion in the firm's target capital structure, plus the after-tax marginal cost of preferred stock times its proportion in the firm's target capital structure. In general, the weighted cost of capital is the appropriate discount rate to use when evaluating projects of average risk.

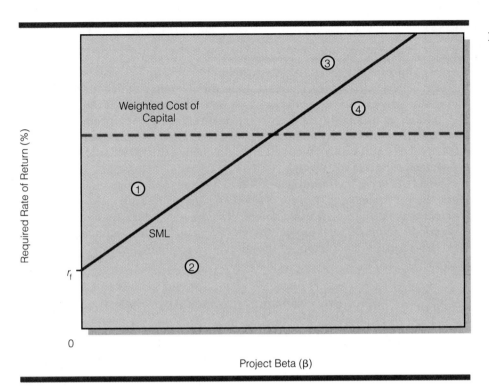

count rate based on the security market line for each project. In the example shown in Figure 10-2, Projects 1, 2, 3, and 4 are being evaluated by the firm. Using the weighted cost of capital approach, the firm would adopt Projects 3 and 4. However, if the firm considered the differential levels of systematic risk for the four alternatives, it would accept Projects 1 and 3 and reject Projects 2 and 4. In general, *the risk-adjusted discount rate approach is considered preferable to the weighted cost of capital approach when the projects under consideration differ significantly in their risk characteristics.*

The one problem remaining with this suggested procedure involves the determination of beta values for individual projects. Thus far, the most workable approach available is the use of *surrogate market information,* as illustrated in the Vulcan Materials example. For example, if an aluminum firm is considering investing in the leisure-time product industry, the beta for this new project could be computed using the average beta for a sample of firms engaged principally in the leisure product industry. Although the beta for the aluminum firm might be 1.3—resulting in a required equity return on projects of average risk of 14.1 percent, or $5\% + (1.3 \times 7\%)$, according to Figure 10-1—this would not be the appropriate rate for leisure product projects. Assuming a beta of 0.9 for leisure product firms, the leisure product projects would be required to earn an equity return of only 11.3 percent, or $5\% + (0.9 \times 7\%)$, because of the lower average level of systematic risk associated with leisure product projects. This assumes that the leisure product projects are financed in the same manner as the firms used to generate the surrogate betas. Otherwise, the beta adjustment procedure in Equations 10.1 and 10.2 must be used.

ADJUSTING FOR TOTAL PROJECT RISK

The risk adjustment procedures discussed in this section are appropriate when the firm believes that a project's total risk is the relevant risk to consider in evaluating the project and when it is assumed that the returns from the project being considered are highly positively correlated with the returns from the firm as a whole. Therefore, these methods are appropriate only in the absence of internal firm diversification benefits, which might change the firm's total risk (or the systematic portion of total risk).

Several different techniques are used to analyze total project risk. These include the *net present value/payback approach, simulation analysis, sensitivity analysis, scenario analysis,* the *risk-adjusted discount rate approach,* and the *certainty equivalent approach.* In addition, total project risk can be measured by calculating the standard deviation and coefficient of variation. These calculations are discussed in Chapter 5.

Net Present Value/Payback Approach

Many firms combine net present value (NPV) with payback (PB) when analyzing project risk. As noted in Chapter 9, the project payback period is the length of time required to recover the net investment. Because cash flow estimates tend to become more uncertain further into the future, applying a payback cutoff point can help reduce this degree of uncertainty. For example, a firm may decide not to accept projects unless they have positive net present values *and* paybacks of less than some stated number of years.

The net present value/payback method is both simple and inexpensive but it suffers from some notable weaknesses. First, the choice of which payback criterion should be applied is purely subjective and not directly related to the variability of returns from a project. Some investments may have relatively certain cash flows far into the future, whereas others may not. The use of a single payback cutoff point fails to allow for this. Second, some projects are more risky than others during their start-up periods; the payback criterion also fails to recognize this. Finally, this approach may cause a firm to reject some actually acceptable projects. In spite of these weaknesses, however, some firms feel this approach is helpful when screening investment alternatives, particularly international investments in politically unstable countries and investments in products characterized by rapid technological advances. Also, firms that have difficulty raising external capital and thus are concerned about the timing of internally generated cash flows often find a consideration of a project's payback period to be useful.

Simulation Analysis

Computers have made it both feasible and relatively inexpensive to apply simulation techniques to capital budgeting decisions. The simulation approach generally is more appropriate for analyzing larger projects. A **simulation** is a financial planning tool that models some event. When simulation is used in capital budgeting, it requires that estimates be made of the probability distribution of each cash flow element (revenues, expenses, and so on). If, for example, a firm is considering introducing a new product, the elements of a simulation might include the number of units sold, market price, unit production costs, unit selling costs, the purchase price of the machinery needed to produce the new product, and the cost of capital. These probability distributions then are entered into the simulation model to compute the project's net present value probability distribution.

Recall that net present value is defined as follows:

$$NPV = \sum_{t=1}^{n} \frac{NCF_t}{(1+k)^t} - NINV$$

where NCF_t is the net cash flow in period t, and NINV is the net investment. In any period, NCF_t may be computed as follows:

$$NCF_t = [q(p) - q(c+s) - Dep](1-T) + Dep - \Delta NWC \qquad (10.4)$$

where q is the number of units sold; p, the price per unit; c, the unit production cost (excluding depreciation); s, the unit selling cost; Dep, the annual depreciation; ΔNWC, the change in net working capital; and T, the firm's marginal tax rate. Using Equation 10.4, it is possible to simulate the net present value of the project. Based on the probability distribution of each of the elements that influence the net present value, one value for each element is selected at random.

Assume, for example, that the following values for the input variables are randomly chosen: $q = 2,000$; $p = \$10$; $c = \$2$; $s = \$1$; $Dep = \$2,000$; $\Delta NWC = \$1,200$; and $T = 40\%$, or 0.40. Inserting these values into Equation 10.4 gives the following calculations:

$$NCF_t = [2,000(\$10) - 2,000(\$2 + \$1) - \$2,000](1 - 0.40) + \$2,000 - \$1,200$$

$$= (\$20,000 - \$6,000 - \$2,000)0.60 + \$2,000 - \$1,200$$

$$= \$8,000$$

Assuming that the net investment is equal to the purchase price of the machinery (\$10,000, in this example), that the net cash flows in each year of the project's life are identical, except for year 5, when \$6,000 of NWC is recovered, that $k = 10\%$,[4] and that the project has a 5-year life, the net present value of this particular iteration of the simulation can be computed as follows:

$$NPV = \frac{\$8,000}{(1+0.10)^1} + \frac{\$8,000}{(1+0.10)^2} + \frac{\$8,000}{(1+0.10)^3} + \frac{\$8,000}{(1+0.10)^4}$$

$$+ \frac{\$14,000}{(1+0.10)^5} - \$10,000$$

$$= \$8,000 \times 3.170 + \$14,000 \times 0.621 - \$10,000$$

$$= \$24,054$$

In an actual simulation, the computer program is run a number of different times, using different randomly selected input variables in each instance. Thus, the program can be said to be repeated, or iterated, and each run is termed an *iteration*.[5] In each iteration, the net present value for the project would be computed accordingly. Figure 10-3 illustrates a typical simulation approach.

---

[4]A strong case can be made for using a risk-free rate to discount the cash flows generated in a simulation analysis, because the simulation technique directly considers risk by generating a probability distribution of the project's NPV or IRR. To use the cost of capital as the discount rate will result in a double counting of risk. Although this is correct, when a risk-free rate is used as the discount rate, the NPV that results is difficult to interpret. For this reason, many practitioners prefer to use the cost of capital when performing simulation analyses.

[5]Often 100 or more iterations of a simulation model are performed.

FIGURE 10-3
An Illustration of the
Simulation Approach

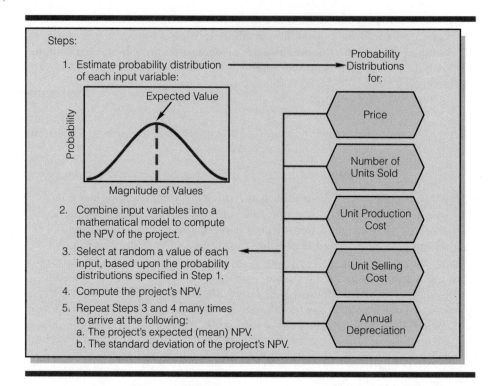

The results of these iterations then are used to plot a probability distribution of the project's net present values and to compute a mean and a standard deviation of returns.[6] This information provides the decision maker with an estimate of a project's expected returns, as well as its risk. Given this information, it is possible to compute the probability of achieving a net present value that is greater or less than any particular value.

For example, assume that the simulation for the project previously illustrated results in an expected net present value of $12,000, with a standard deviation of $6,000. The probability of the project's having a net present value of $0 or less now can be found. The value of $0 is −2.0 standard deviations below the mean:

$$z = \frac{\$0 - \$12,000}{\$6,000}$$

$$= -2.0$$

where z = the number of standard deviations.

It can be seen from Table V at the back of the book that the probability of a value less than −2.0 standard deviations from the mean is 2.28 percent. Thus, there is a 2.28 percent chance that the actual net present value for this project will be negative. Figure 10-4 shows the probability distribution of this project's net present value. The shaded area under the curve represents the probability that the project will have a net present value of $0 or less.

The simulation approach is a powerful one because it explicitly recognizes all of the interactions among the variables that influence a project's net present

---

[6]Regardless of the shape of the probability distribution for the individual variables used in the simulation, the net present value probability distribution often will be normally, or near normally, distributed.

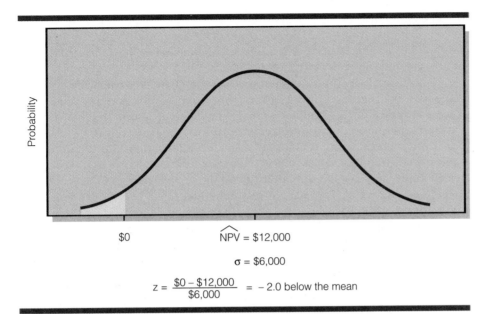

FIGURE 10-4
A Sample Illustration of the Probability That a Project's Returns Will Be Less than $0

$0 $\widehat{NPV} = \$12,000$

$\sigma = \$6,000$

$$z = \frac{\$0 - \$12,000}{\$6,000} = -2.0 \text{ below the mean}$$

value. It provides both a mean net present value and a standard deviation that can help the decision maker analyze trade-offs between risk and expected return.[7] Unfortunately, it can take considerable time and effort to gather the information necessary for each of the input variables and to correctly formulate the model. This limits the feasibility of simulation to very large projects. In addition, the simulation examples illustrated assume that the values of the input variables are independent of one another. If this is not true—if, for example, the price of a product has a large influence on the number sold—then this interaction must be incorporated into the model, introducing even more complexity.

Sensitivity Analysis

Sensitivity analysis is a procedure that calculates the change in net present value given a change in one of the cash flow elements, such as product price. In other words, a decision maker can determine *how sensitive* a project's return is to changes in a particular variable.

Because sensitivity analysis is derived from the simulation approach, it also requires the definition of all relevant variables that influence the net present value of a project. The appropriate mathematical relationships between these variables must be defined, too, in order to estimate the cash flow from the project and compute the net present value. Rather than dealing with the entire probability distribution for each of the input variables, however, sensitivity analysis allows the decision maker to use only the "best estimate" of each variable to compute the net present value.

The decision maker then can ask various "what if" questions in which the project's net present value is recomputed under various conditions. For example, the best estimate of a product's price might be $10. The net present value of the project could be computed using this input together with best estimates of all

---

[7]Simulation also may be applied to other decision models, such as the internal rate of return or payback approaches. In these cases, the mathematical relationships involved in the simulation have to be respecified.

the other variables. The next step would involve asking a question like "What if we cannot charge more than $8 per unit?" The net present value could be re-computed using the $8 price and the best estimates for each of the other input variables to determine the effect of the $8 price on the NPV.

Sensitivity analysis can be applied to any variable to determine the effect of changes in one or more of the inputs on a project's net present value. This process provides the decision maker with a formal mechanism for assessing the possible consequences of various scenarios.

It is often useful to construct sensitivity curves to summarize the impact of changes in different variables on the net present value of a project. A sensitivity curve has the project's net present value on the vertical axis and the variable of interest on the horizontal axis. For example, Figure 10-5 shows the sensitivity curves for two variables, sales price and cost of capital for a project.

The steep slope of the price–NPV curve indicates that the net present value is very sensitive to changes in the price for which the product can be sold. If the product price is approximately 10 percent below the base case (or initial analysis) estimate, the net present value of the project drops to $0, and the project be-comes unacceptable for further price declines.[8] In contrast, the relatively flat cost of capital–NPV curve indicates that the net present value is not very sensi-tive to changes in the firm's cost of capital. Similar curves could be constructed for project life, salvage value, units sold, operating costs, and other important variables.

Using Spreadsheets for Sensitivity Analysis. Spreadsheets, such as Excel, have made the application of sensitivity analysis techniques simple and inexpensive. Once the base case has been defined and entered in the spreadsheet, it is easy to ask hundreds of "what if" questions. For example, assume that revenues from a project are expected to be $20,000 in year 1 and to grow by 10 percent annu-ally over the 5-year life of the project. This relationship would be entered into the spreadsheet along with similar relationships for all other factors that go into the determination of the annual net cash flows from the project. The net pres-ent value of the base case is computed by the spreadsheet. Now, what if the rev-enues are estimated to grow only 5 percent annually, instead of 10 percent? Only one change must be made on the spreadsheet (redefine the growth rate to 5 percent), and it automatically recomputes each period's net cash flows and the net present value of the project. This process can be repeated rapidly, liter-ally hundreds of times, to develop a profile of how sensitive the project is to changes in the individual components of the project's cash flows. This allows the decision maker to focus his or her analysis on the key variables that are crit-ical to the project's success. (The CFM Excel Disk available with this text can be used effectively to illustrate the power of spreadsheets in performing sensitivity analyses.)

Scenario Analysis

Scenario analysis is another technique that has been used to assess the risk of an investment project. Sensitivity analysis considers the impact of changes in key

---

[8]Notice that sensitivity analysis does not tell the decision maker the actual probability of NPV being negative. The reason for this is that sensitivity analysis uses only the "best estimate" of each variable and not the entire probability distribution.

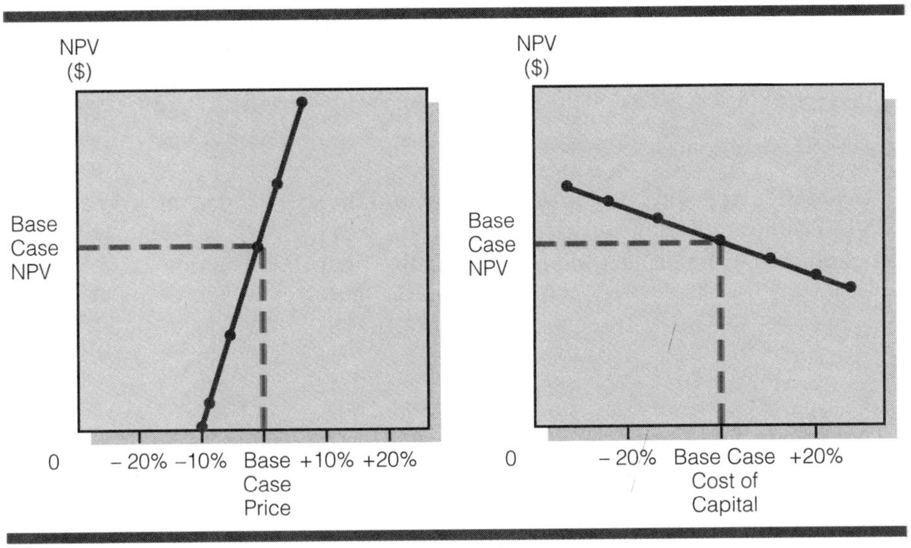

FIGURE 10-5
Illustrative Sensitivity Curves

variables, one at a time, on the desirability of an investment project. In contrast, **scenario analysis** considers the impact of simultaneous changes in key variables on the desirability of an investment project.

For example, consider the case of Boeing's decision to invest in new, larger, longer-range versions of its 747 plane (as discussed in the Financial Challenge at the beginning of this chapter). The success of this proposed investment project depends on many factors, including the price of the plane, the number of units likely to be demanded, the cost of development, the time of development, and the cost of production. When using the scenario analysis technique, the financial analyst might ask the project director to provide various estimates of the project's expected net present value. In addition to what is perceived to be the most-likely scenario, the project director might be asked to provide both optimistic and pessimistic estimates. An *optimistic scenario* might be defined by the most optimistic values of each of the most input variables—for example, low development costs, low production costs, high prices, and strong demand. A *pessimistic scenario* would be defined by low prices, soft demand, high development costs, and high production costs. The project manager could also be asked to provide estimates of the probability that the optimistic scenario will result and the probability that the pessimistic scenario will result. With these probability estimates, the financial manager can compute an estimate of the standard deviation of the NPV of the project.

Assume, for example, that the following estimates of the NPV of the 747 project for Boeing have been developed using scenario analysis:

Pessimistic outcome	−$11.4 billion	0.20
Most likely outcome	$1.3 billion	0.60
Optimistic outcome	$10.1 billion	0.20

The expected NPV of this project would be

$$\overline{\text{NPV}} = 0.20(-\$11.4) + 0.60(\$1.3) + 0.20(\$10.1) = \$0.52 \text{ billion}$$

Using Equation 5.2 from Chapter 5, the standard deviation of this NPV estimate can be computed as

$$\sigma_{NPV} = [(-\$11.4 - \$0.52)^2 0.20 + (\$1.3 - \$0.52)^2 0.60 + (\$10.1 - \$0.52)^2 0.20]^{0.5}$$

$$= \$6.87 \text{ billion}$$

Given the expected NPV of $0.52 billion and the expected standard deviation of $6.87 billion, it is now possible to compute, with the help of Equation 5.3, the probability that the project will have a negative net present value:

$$z = \frac{0 - \overline{NPV}}{\sigma_{NPV}}$$

$$= \frac{0 - \$0.52}{\$6.87}$$

$$= -0.08$$

From Table V it can be seen that the probability of a value less than -0.08 standard deviations from the mean ($0.52 billion) is about 46.8 percent. This means that there is a 46.8 percent chance that this project will have a negative NPV.

This example illustrates both the value of scenario analysis and some of its shortcomings. With the aid of spreadsheet programs such as Excel, it is possible to easily estimate the impact of various scenarios on the expected performance of a project. However, scenario analysis techniques normally look only at a limited number of alternative scenarios. Furthermore, the process of assigning probabilities to the outcomes expected from alternative scenarios is difficult and largely subjective.

Risk-Adjusted Discount Rate Approach

The risk-adjusted discount rate approach (RADR), as discussed in the section on beta risk, adjusts for risk by varying the rate at which the expected net cash flows are discounted when determining a project's net present value. The RADR approach can also be used in the analysis of projects for which total project risk is the applicable risk measure, rather than beta risk.

In the risk-adjusted discount rate approach, net cash flows for each project are discounted at a risk-adjusted rate, k_a^*. The magnitude of k_a^* depends on the relationship between the total risk of the individual project and the overall risk of the firm. To compute k_a^*, the *risk-free rate*, r_f—that is, a required rate of return associated with investment projects characterized by certain cash flow streams—is used. U.S. Treasury securities are good examples of risk-free investments, because there is no chance that investors will not get the dollar amount of interest and the principal repayment on schedule. Thus, the yield on U.S. government securities, such as 90-day Treasury bills, is used as the risk-free rate.

Most companies are not in business to invest in risk-free securities; individual investors can do that just as well. Instead, companies assume some amount of risk, expecting to earn higher returns than those available on risk-free securities. The difference between the risk-free rate and the firm's required rate of return (cost of capital) is an *average risk premium* to compensate investors for the fact that the company's assets are risky. This relationship is expressed algebraically as follows:

$$\theta = k_a - r_f \tag{10.5}$$

where θ is the average risk premium for the firm; r_f, the risk-free rate; and k_a, the required rate of return for projects of average risk, that is, the firm's cost of capital.

The cash flows from a project having greater than average risk are discounted at a higher rate, k_a^*—that is, a risk-adjusted discount rate—to reflect the increased riskiness. Total project risk premiums applied to individual projects are commonly established *subjectively*. For example, some firms establish a small number of *risk classes* and then apply a different *risk premium* to each class. Below-average-risk projects, such as straightforward equipment replacement decisions, might be evaluated at 2 percent *below* the firm's cost of capital (a risk discount). Average-risk projects, such as equipment modification decisions, might be evaluated at the firm's cost of capital; above-average-risk projects, such as facility expansions, might be assigned a risk premium of 3 percent *above* the firm's cost of capital; and high-risk projects, such as investments in totally new lines of business or the introduction of new products, might be assigned a risk premium of 8 percent *above* the firm's cost of capital.

Although the risk-class approach saves time in the analysis stage, it can lead to suboptimal decisions, because the risk premiums themselves are usually determined subjectively and no explicit consideration is given to the variation in returns of the projects assigned to individual classes. In short, the risk-class approach is most useful when evaluating relatively small projects that are repeated frequently. In these cases, much is known about the projects' potential returns, and it is probably not worth the effort to try to compute more "precise" risk premiums.

Certainty Equivalent Approach

Another approach that can be used to deal with total project risk uses certainty equivalents. The **certainty equivalent** approach adjusts the net cash flows in the *numerator* of the NPV equation, in contrast to the RADR approach, which involves adjustments to the *denominator* of the NPV equation. A certainty equivalent factor is the ratio of the amount of cash someone would require with certainty at a point in time in order to make him or her indifferent between that certain amount and an amount expected to be received with risk at the same point in time. The project is adjusted for risk by converting the expected risky cash flows to their certainty equivalents and then computing the net present value of the project. The risk-free rate, r_f—not the firm's cost of capital, k—is used as the discount rate for computing the net present value. This is done because the cost of capital is a *risky* rate, reflecting the firm's average risk, and using it would result in a double counting of risk.

Certainty equivalent factors range from 0 to 1.0. The higher the factor, the more certain the expected cash flow. For example, one project might offer expected cash flows over its 5-year life as follows:

Year	Expected NCF	Certainty Equivalent Factor (α)	Certainty Equivalent Cash Flows
0	$-10,000	1.0	$-10,000
1	+5,000	0.9	+4,500
2	+6,000	0.8	+4,800
3	+7,000	0.7	+4,900
4	+4,000	0.6	+2,400
5	+3,000	0.4	+1,200

The initial outlay of $10,000 is known with certainty. It might be for the purchase price of a piece of equipment. Hence, the certainty equivalent factor for year 0 is 1.0, and the certainty equivalent cash flow is $-$10,000 ($-$10,000 $\times$ 1.0). The $5,000 cash inflow in year 1 is viewed as being somewhat risky. Consequently, the decision maker has assigned a certainty equivalent factor of 0.9 to the net cash flow in year 1. Multiplying $5,000 times the 0.9 certainty equivalent factor yields a certainty equivalent cash flow of $4,500. This means that the decision maker would be indifferent between receiving the promised, risky $5,000 a year from now or receiving $4,500 with certainty at the same time. A similar interpretation is given to the certainty equivalent factors and certainty equivalent cash flows for years 2 through 5.

Algebraically, the certainty equivalent factors, α, for the cash flows expected to be received during each time period, t, are expressed as follows:

$$\alpha_t = \frac{\text{Certain return}}{\text{Risky return}} \tag{10.6}$$

The certainty equivalent factors are used to compute a certainty equivalent net present value as follows:

$$\text{NPV} = -\text{NINV}(\alpha_0) + \sum_{t=1}^{n} \frac{\text{NCF}_t \alpha_t}{(1 + r_f)^t} \tag{10.7}$$

where

α_0 = Certainty equivalent factor associated with the net investment (NINV) at time 0.

n = Expected economic life of the project.

α_t = Certainty equivalent factor associated with the net cash flows (NCF) in each period, t.

r_f = Risk-free rate.

Note in this example that the certainty equivalent factors decline into the future. This reflects the fact that *most* cash flows are viewed as being more risky the further into the future they are projected to occur.[9] This point is discussed in more detail in Chapter 5. In Table 10-1, we have computed the certainty equivalent net present value for this project assuming an 8 percent risk-free rate. It equals $4,753, and the project therefore is acceptable.

The certainty equivalent approach of considering risk is viewed as conceptually sound for the following reasons:

■ The decision maker can adjust separately each period's cash flows to account for the specific risk of those cash flows. This normally is not done when the risk-adjusted discount rate approach is applied.[10]

■ Decision makers must introduce their own risk preferences directly into the analysis. Consequently, the certainty equivalent net present value pro-

---

[9]Different individuals may have different certainty equivalent factors, depending on each individual's relative risk aversion. Risk aversion is a function of many factors, including wealth, age, and the nature of a firm's reward structure.

[10]It is possible, however, to find a risk-adjusted discount rate that will provide results identical (that is, with the same risk-adjusted net present value) to those obtained from the certainty equivalent approach.

YEAR	EXPECTED NCF	CERTAINTY EQUIVALENT FACTOR (α)	CERTAINTY EQUIVALENT CASH FLOW	$PVIF_{0.08,t}$	PRESENT VALUE OF CASH FLOWS
0	$-10,000	1.0	$-10,000	1.000	$-10,000
1	+5,000	0.9	+4,500	0.926	+4,167
2	+6,000	0.8	+4,800	0.857	+4,114
3	+7,000	0.7	+4,900	0.794	+3,891
4	+4,000	0.6	+2,400	0.735	+1,764
5	+3,000	0.4	+1,200	0.681	+817
			Certainty Equivalent NPV =		+ $4,753

TABLE 10-1
Calculation of Certainty Equivalent Net Present Value

vides an unambiguous basis for making a decision. A positive net present value means the project is acceptable to that decision maker, and a negative net present value indicates it should be rejected.

INTERNATIONAL ISSUES
SPECIAL ELEMENTS OF CAPITAL BUDGETING RISK

The techniques of risk analysis presented in this chapter will serve a firm well whether it operates only in the United States or multinationally. However, managers of multinational firms need to be aware of special elements of risk when investing abroad.

When evaluating a capital expenditure to be made in another country, the parent firm must be concerned with the cash flows that can be expected to be received by the parent—not the cash flows that will accrue to the overseas subsidiary making the investment. There are several reasons for focusing on cash flows to the parent. First, the host country might block the subsidiary from remitting funds back to the parent. Hence, these "captive" funds are not available to the parent for reinvestment in projects offering the highest rate of return. Second, the parent needs to be concerned with the prospect that its assets in foreign subsidiaries could be taken by the host government with inadequate or no compensation. Third, the parent must consider exchange-rate risk between the host country's currency and the dollar. (Exchange-rate risk and procedures for managing it are discussed in detail in Chapters 2 and 21). Related to exchange rate risk is the higher risk of inflation in many countries, particularly developing countries. The risk of highly volatile inflation and the ability of a firm to protect itself from this risk adds additional uncertainty to investments made abroad. Finally, more uncertainty may be associated with tax rates in the host country than is typical in the United States.

Each of these factors affects the risk of the cash flows that can be expected from investments in other countries. Although multinational firms predominantly use standard capital budgeting procedures, such as NPV and IRR, to evaluate their investments abroad, there is evidence that many multinational firms also use the risk analysis techniques discussed in this chapter. A recent study of the capital budgeting practices of affiliates of U.S.-based multinational firms found that sensitivity analysis and simulation are widely used for

What do you suppose would be the certainty equivalent of playing the lottery? Visit the following Web site to see how the lottery's CE is calculated and graphed. Skip through the rocket-scientist math and look at the answer: a large negative number. What does this tell you about whether you should play the lottery?
http://www.isor.vuw.ac.nz/~vignaux/teaching/utility/utility/node13.html

assessing project risk.[11] In addition, some financial managers reported that they relied more heavily on their own personal feelings about political and economic events in the host country than on quantitative methods to evaluate project risk.

ETHICAL ISSUES
JOHNSON & JOHNSON AND PROPRIETARY COMPETITIVE INFORMATION[12]

During the 1970s Johnson & Johnson's (J&J) plaster bandage roll dominated the market for casting materials. In 1980, 3M Company introduced a stronger and lighter fiberglass cast. The early version of this product had some initial problems that 3M resolved by 1985. At that time, 3M was set to mount a major challenge to J&J's leadership in the casting market.

In 1985 a disgruntled contract employee at 3M, Philip Stegora, sent samples of the new casting tape to four rival firms, including J&J. He offered to explain the new technology to anyone who contacted him through a Minneapolis post office box and agreed to pay him $20,000. None of the competitors accepted the offer (nor did they report it to 3M). However, Skip Klintworth, Jr., then the CEO of a small castmaker in Tulsa, heard about the offer from colleagues at one of the four firms that were contacted. He tipped off the FBI. By 1987 Stegora was tracked down and convicted of mail fraud and transporting stolen property across state lines.

The story does not end with Stegora's conviction. Although none of the competitors accepted Stegora's offer, J&J did perform chemical tests on the samples it received and used this information in developing its own competitive products. Although the evidence indicates that J&J's use of this information was largely unintentional, in 1991 J&J was ordered to pay 3M $116.3 million for infringing on its patents and misappropriating trade secrets. This case raises questions about the appropriate response of a firm when it is offered stolen trade secrets. What actions do you think J&J and the other three firms should have taken when they received the stolen property from Stegora?

■ SUMMARY

- The *risk* of an investment project is defined in terms of the potential *variability* of its returns. When only one return is possible—for example, as with U.S. government securities held to maturity—there is no risk. When more than one return is possible for a particular project, it is risky.
- Risk is also influenced by the possibility of investment *diversification*. If a proposed project's returns are not *perfectly correlated* with the returns from the firm's other investments, the total risk of the firm may be reduced by accepting the proposed project. This is known as the *portfolio effect*.

---

[11]Lawrence P. Shao, "Capital Investment Evaluation Procedures Utilized by North and Latin American Affiliates," *Multinational Business Review* (Spring 1994): 11–18.

[12]Adapted from "When a Rival's Trade Secret Crosses Your Desk," *Business Week* (May 20, 1991): 48.

■ When a project differs significantly in its systematic risk profile (as measured by *beta*) from the systematic risk of the total firm, a risk-adjusted discount rate appropriate for that project can be computed using the security market line relationship between risk and required return from the capital asset pricing model.

■ A decision maker can adjust for total project risk in capital budgeting several different ways, including the *net present value/payback approach, simulation analysis, sensitivity analysis, scenario analysis,* the *risk-adjusted discount rate approach,* and the *certainty equivalent approach.*

■ The simulation approach is the most expensive of the techniques discussed in this chapter; it normally is applied only when large projects are being analyzed. The widespread availability of inexpensive and powerful computer software, such as electronic spreadsheets, has made the use of sensitivity analysis far more accessible to small and medium-sized firms than was previously possible.

■ The risk-adjusted discount rate approach is widely used by firms that attempt to consider differential project risk in their capital budgeting procedures. It requires that a *risk premium* be computed for each project or group of projects so that an appropriate risk-adjusted discount rate can be applied when evaluating a project's cash flows.

■ The decision to employ some risk analysis technique to evaluate an investment project depends on the project's size and the additional cost of applying such a technique as compared with the perceived benefits. For small projects, only the simpler risk adjustment techniques should be used; for major projects that have above- or below-normal risk, it is worthwhile to analyze the project's risk as precisely as possible. Failure to fully analyze the risk of a large project could result in bad investment decisions and even substantial losses.

■ Multinational firms must be concerned with additional risk elements when investing abroad, such as inflation risk, exchange rate risk, and the risk of expropriation.

■ QUESTIONS AND TOPICS FOR DISCUSSION

1. How does the basic net present value model of capital budgeting deal with the problem of project risk? What are the shortcomings of this approach?
2. How would you define *risk* as it is used in a capital budgeting analysis context?
3. Recalling the discussion in Chapter 5, when is the standard deviation of a project's cash flows an appropriate measure of project risk? When is the coefficient of variation an appropriate measure?
4. How does the basic net present value capital budgeting model deal with the phenomenon of increasing risk of project cash flows over time?
5. When should a firm consider the portfolio effects of a new project?
6. What are the primary advantages and disadvantages of applying *simulation* to capital budgeting risk analysis?
7. Computer simulation is used to generate a large number of possible outcomes for an investment project. Most firms invest in a particular project only once, however. How can a computer simulation model be helpful to the typical decision maker who is making a one-time-only investment decision?
8. On average, the expected value of returns from each $1 of premiums paid on an insurance policy is less than $1; this is due to the insurance company's administrative costs and profits. In spite of this fact, why do so many individuals and organizations purchase insurance policies?
9. Describe how certainty equivalent cash flow estimates can be derived for individual project cash flows.

10. Will all individuals apply the same certainty equivalent estimates to the cash flows from a project? Why or why not?

■ SELF-TEST PROBLEMS

ST1. Lehigh Products Company is considering the purchase of new automated equipment. The project has an expected net present value of $250,000 with a standard deviation of $100,000. What is the probability that the project will have a net present value less than $50,000, assuming that net present value is normally distributed?

ST2. The Jacobs Company is financed entirely with equity. The beta for Jacobs has been estimated to be 1.0. The current risk-free rate is 10 percent and the expected market return is 15 percent.

   a. What rate of return should Jacobs require on a project of average risk?

   b. If a new venture is expected to have a beta of 1.6, what rate of return should Jacobs demand on this project?

   c. The project in question requires an initial outlay of $9 million and is expected to generate a 10-year stream of annual net cash flows of $1.9 million. Calculate the NPV of the project using Jacobs's required return for projects of average risk.

   d. Calculate the NPV of the project using the risk-adjusted rate computed in Part b.

ST3. Homer Stores is considering a new location that is expected to yield the following net cash flows following an initial (year 0), certain outlay (NINV) of $75,000:

Year	Net Cash Flows	Certainty Equivalent Factor
1	$30,000	0.90
2	30,000	0.80
3	30,000	0.65
4	20,000	0.50

   a. Compute the NPV of this project at a 15 percent cost of capital.

   b. If the risk-free rate is 8 percent, what is the certainty equivalent NPV for the new location?

■ PROBLEMS*

1. Mitchell Auto Parts, Inc. has estimated the probability distribution of its annual net cash flows as follows:

Probability	Cash Flows (in Thousands of Dollars)
0.10	$1,000
0.20	1,500
0.40	2,000
0.20	2,500
0.10	3,000

   a. Compute the expected annual cash flow.

   b. Compute the standard deviation of annual cash flows.

   c. Compute the coefficient of variation of annual cash flows.

2. A new project has expected annual net cash flows of $400,000 with a standard deviation of $250,000. The distribution of annual net cash flows is approximately normal.

   a. What is the probability of the project having negative annual net cash flows?

   b. What is the probability that annual net cash flows will be greater than $575,000?

*Colored numbers denote problems that have check answers provided at the end of the book.

3. A proposed factory expansion project has an expected net present value of $100,000 with a standard deviation of $50,000. What is the probability that the project will have a negative net present value, assuming that net present value is normally distributed?

4. Two projects have the following expected net present values and standard deviations of net present values:

Project	Expected Net Present Value	Standard Deviation
A	$50,000	$20,000
B	10,000	7,000

   a. Using the standard deviation criterion, which project is riskier?
   b. Using the coefficient of variation criterion, which project is riskier?
   c. Which criterion do you think is appropriate to use in this case? Why?

5. American Steel Corporation is considering two investments. One is the purchase of a new continuous caster costing $100 million. The expected net present value of this project is $20 million. The other alternative is the purchase of a supermarket chain, also costing $100 million. It, too, has an expected net present value of $20 million. The firm's management is interested in reducing the variability of its earnings.
   a. Which project should the company invest in?
   b. What assumptions did you make to arrive at this decision?

6. Gamma Biosciences is financed entirely with equity. Its beta is 1.5, and its price-earnings ratio is 16. The current risk-free rate is 8 percent, and the expected return on the market is 14 percent.
   a. What rate of return should the company require on projects of average risk?
   b. If a new project has a beta of 2.0, what rate of return should the company require?

7. Advanced Systems Company is financed one-third with debt and two-thirds with equity. Its market beta has been estimated to be 1.5. The current risk-free rate is 8 percent, and the expected market return is 15 percent. Advanced Systems' tax rate is 40 percent. Advanced Systems is planning a major research and development (R&D) investment program. Advanced Systems' management believes that these types of projects should be financed conservatively. Specifically, the company plans to finance all R&D investments with 90 percent equity and 10 percent debt.
   a. If the pure project beta for the R&D investment is the same as the pure project beta for Advanced Systems' other assets, what rate of return is required on the equity-financed portion of the R&D investment, assuming it is financed 90 percent with equity and 10 percent with debt?
   b. Advanced Systems' managers believe this project may have more risk than their other investments. Another firm that invests very heavily in R&D similar to the type proposed by Advanced has been identified. Its capital structure is 80 percent equity and 20 percent debt. Its tax rate is 35 percent, and its market beta is 1.6. Using this information, determine the required return on the equity-financed portion of Advanced Systems' R&D project, assuming it is financed 90 percent with equity and 10 percent with debt.

8. Valley Products, Inc. is considering two independent investments having the following cash flow streams:

Year	Project A	Project B
0	-$50,000	-$40,000
1	+20,000	+20,000
2	+20,000	+10,000
3	+10,000	+5,000
4	+5,000	+5,000
5	+5,000	+40,000

Valley uses a combination of the net present value approach and the payback approach to evaluate investment alternatives. It requires that all projects have a positive net present value when cash flows are discounted at 10 percent and that all projects have a payback no longer than 3 years. Which project or projects should the firm accept? Why?

9. Fox Enterprises is considering expanding into the growing laser copier business. Fox estimates that this expansion will cost $1.8 million and will generate a 20-year stream of expected net cash flows amounting to $400,000 per year. The company's weighted cost of capital is 15 percent.

   a. Compute the net present value of the laser copier project using the company's weighted cost of capital and the expected cash flows from the project.

   b. Using the risk-adjusted discount rate approach, management has decided that this project has substantially more risk than average and has decided that it requires a 24 percent expected rate of return on projects like this. Recompute the risk-adjusted net present value of this project.

10. Apple Jacks, Inc. produces wine. The firm is considering expanding into the snack food business. This expansion will require an initial investment in new equipment of $200,000. The equipment will be depreciated on a straight-line basis over a 10-year period to zero. At the end of the project the equipment is estimated to have a salvage value of $50,000. The expansion will also require an increase in working capital for the firm of $40,000. Revenues from the new venture are forecasted at $200,000 per year for the first 5 years and $210,000 per year for years 6 through 10. Operating costs exclusive of depreciation from the new venture are estimated at $90,000 for the first 5 years and $105,000 for years 6 through 10. It is assumed that at the end of year 10, the snack food equipment will be sold for its estimated salvage value. The firm's marginal tax rate is 40 percent. The required return for projects of average risk has been estimated at 15 percent.

   a. Compute the project's net present value, assuming that it is an average-risk investment.

   b. If management decides that all product line expansions have above-average risk and therefore should be evaluated at a 24 percent required rate of return, what will be the risk-adjusted net present value of the project?

11. The Seminole Production Company is analyzing the investment in a new line of business machines. The initial outlay required is $35 million. The net cash flows expected from the investment are as follows:

Year	Net Cash Flow
1	$ 5 million
2	8 million
3	15 million
4	20 million
5	15 million
6	10 million
7	4 million

The firm's cost of capital (used for projects of average risk) is 15 percent.

   a. Compute the net present value of this project assuming it possesses average risk.

   b. Because of the risk inherent in this type of investment, Seminole has decided to employ the certainty equivalent approach. After considerable discussion, management has agreed to apply the following certainty equivalents to the project's cash flows:

Year	α_t
0	1.00
1	0.95
2	0.90
3	0.80
4	0.60
5	0.40
6	0.35
7	0.30

If the risk-free rate is 9 percent, compute the project's certainty equivalent net present value.

c. On the basis of the certainty equivalent analysis, should the project be accepted?

12. A simulation model similar to the one described in this chapter has been constructed by the Great Basin Corporation to evaluate the largest of its new investment proposals. After many iterations of the model, Great Basin's management has arrived at an expected net present value for Project A of $1.0 million. The standard deviation of the net present value has been estimated from the simulation model results to be $0.8 million.

a. What is the probability that the project will have a negative net present value?

b. What is the probability that the project will have a net present value greater than $2.2 million?

13. The Buffalo Snow Shoe Company is considering manufacturing radial snow shoes, which are more durable and offer better traction. Buffalo estimates that the investment in manufacturing equipment will cost $250,000 and will have a 10-year economic life. Buffalo will depreciate the equipment on a straight-line basis to a $0 estimated salvage value over a 10-year period. The estimated selling price of each pair of shoes will be $50. Buffalo anticipates that it can sell 5,000 pairs a year at this price. Unit production and selling costs (exclusive of depreciation) will be about $25. The firm's marginal tax rate is 40 percent. A cost of capital of 12 percent is thought to be appropriate to analyze a project of this type. Buffalo has decided to perform a sensitivity analysis of the project before making a decision.

a. Compute the expected net present value of this project.

b. Buffalo's president does not believe that 5,000 pairs of the new snow shoes can be sold at a $50 price. He estimates that a maximum of 3,000 pairs will be sold at this price. How does the change in the estimated sales volume influence the net present value of the project?

14. Project Alpha offers the following net cash flows following an initial (year 0), certain outlay (NINV) of $70,000:

Year	Net Cash Flows	Certainty Equivalent Factor
1	$30,000	0.91
2	30,000	0.79
3	30,000	0.65
4	20,000	0.52
5	20,000	0.40
6	10,000	0.30

a. Compute the NPV of this project at a 17 percent cost of capital.

b. If the risk-free rate is 8 percent, what is the certainty equivalent NPV for Project Alpha?

15. A new project is expected to have an 8-year economic life. The project will have an initial cost of $100,000. Installation and shipping charges for the equipment are estimated at $10,000. The equipment will be depreciated as a 7-year asset under MACRS rules. A working capital investment of $15,000 is required to undertake the project. The revenues from the project in year 1 are expected to be $60,000. These are expected to increase at a compound annual rate of 6 percent. Operating costs exclusive of depreciation are $15,000. These costs are expected to increase at an 8 percent compound annual rate. The firm's marginal tax rate is 40 percent. The expected salvage value of the equipment at the end of year 8 is $20,000.

a. Compute the project's net investment.

b. Compute the annual net cash flows for the project.

c. If the firm's cost of capital is 19 percent, should the project be undertaken?

d. The managers of the firm have also decided to evaluate this project using the certainty equivalent approach. They have established the following certainty equivalent factors for the cash flows forecasted in each year:

Year	α_t
0	1.00
1	0.95
2	0.90
3	0.80
4	0.60
5	0.50
6	0.45
7	0.40
8	0.35

The risk-free rate is 8 percent. Compute the certainty equivalent NPV for this project.

16. The managers of U.S. Rubber have analyzed a proposed investment project. The expected net present value (NPV) of the project, evaluated at the firm's weighted cost of capital of 18 percent, has been estimated to be $100,000. The company's managers have determined that the most optimistic NPV estimate of the project is $175,000 and the most pessimistic estimate is $25,000. The most optimistic estimate is a value that is not expected to be exceeded more than 10 percent of the time. The most pessimistic estimate represents a value that the project's NPV is not expected to fall below more than 10 percent of the time. What is the probability that this project will have a negative NPV?

17. U.S. Robotics (USR) has a current (and target) capital structure of 70 percent common equity and 30 percent debt. The beta for USR is 1.4. USR is evaluating an investment in a totally new line of business. The new investment has an expected internal rate of return of 15 percent.

USR wishes to evaluate this investment proposal. If the investment is made, USR intends to finance the project with the same capital structure as its current business. USR's marginal tax rate is 34 percent. USR has identified three firms that are primarily in the line of business into which USR proposes expanding. Their average beta is 1.7, and their average capital structure is 40 percent common equity and 60 percent debt. The marginal tax rate for these three firms averages 40 percent. The risk-free rate is 8 percent, and the expected market risk premium is 8.3 percent. Should USR undertake the project?

18. Essex Chemical Company is considering an expansion into a new product line that is more risky than its existing product mix. The new product line requires an investment, NINV, of $10 million and is expected to generate annual net cash inflows of $2.0 million over a 10-year estimated economic life. Essex Chemical's weighted cost of capital is 12 percent, and the new product line requires an estimated risk-adjusted discount rate of 17 percent, based upon the security market line and betas for comparable companies engaged in the contemplated new line of business.
    a. What is the project's NPV, using the company's weighted cost of capital?
    b. What is the project's NPV, using the risk-adjusted discount rate?
    c. Should Essex Chemical adopt the project?

19. The 3Z Company has estimated that a major project has an expected internal rate of return (IRR) of 18 percent. The most optimistic estimate of the project's IRR is 24 percent, and the most pessimistic estimate is 12 percent. The company expects that its most optimistic estimate of the project's achieved IRR will not be exceeded more than 10 percent of the time. Similarly, 3Z managers do not expect an achieved IRR that is below 12 percent more than 10 percent of the time. The weighted cost of capital is 14 percent. What is the probability that this project will generate returns less than 3Z's weighted cost of capital?

20. An investment your firm is considering will cost you $5 million today. You expect to receive $7 million one year from now from the sale of the investment. You also expect to receive $500,000 in income from the investment at the end of one year. The expected sales price of $7 million is normally distributed with a standard deviation of $1 million. If you require a 10 percent rate of return on risk-free projects and a 15

percent rate of return on projects such as this, what contribution will this project make to your firm's value, after considering the riskiness of the projected returns?

21. You have estimated the expected NPV from a project to be $3,000,000 with a standard deviation of $4,000,000. The distribution of the possible NPVs is approximately normal. If you are willing to accept a 25 percent chance of incurring a negative NPV on the project, should it be undertaken?

22. Albright Properties, Inc. (API) has 3 divisions:

Division	Beta	Proportion of Firm's Assets
Property management	1.1	40%
Land resources	1.6	30%
Financial services	—	30%

The leveraged beta for API is 1.2. API has a consolidated capital structure consisting of 50 percent debt and 50 percent equity. The Financial Services Division's capital structure is 80 percent debt and 20 percent equity. API is planning to finance new projects in that division with a capital structure of 90 percent debt and 10 percent equity. The risk-free rate is 9 percent, and the market risk premium is 8.3 percent. The pretax cost of debt to API is 19 percent. The tax rate is 40 percent. What discount rate should API apply to the cash flows from "new" projects in the Financial Services Division?

23. The management of Greensboro Products has been evaluating the risk of the cash flows associated with a proposed new project. The expected net cash flow for year 1 is $50,000. The most optimistic estimate (not expected to be exceeded more than 10 percent of the time) of the year 1 net cash flow is $110,000, and the most pessimistic net cash flow estimate for year 1 is –$10,000 (no greater than a 10 percent chance of a value this low or lower). What is the probability that year 1 net cash flows will be negative?

24. The Carthage Sceptre Corporation is evaluating a possible investment in a new regional distribution warehouse. A careful evaluation of the anticipated net cash flows and net investment expected from the project indicates that the expected net present value (NPV) of this project is $4.5 million. The anticipated standard deviation of this expected NPV is $3 million, and the distribution of the project's NPV is approximately normal. What is the chance that this project will have a positive NPV at least equal to $1,000,000?

25. The Super Muench Cookie Company is considering a diversification effort that would move it into small retail outlets at major malls around the country. Currently, Super Muench has a capital structure consisting of 30 percent debt and 70 percent equity. Super Muench believes that for the riskier retail outlet portion of its business, a more conservative capital structure of 20 percent debt and 80 percent equity is more appropriate. Super Muench's current pretax cost of debt is 12 percent. The firm's average tax rate is 30 percent, and its marginal tax rate is 40 percent.

Another retail cookie company, Dietz's Dessertery, has been identified. Dietz has a beta (leveraged) of 1.2. Dietz's current capital structure consists of 40 percent debt and 60 percent equity. Dietz's tax rate is 40 percent. The risk-free rate is 7 percent and the market risk premium is 7.4 percent.

Super Muench wants to know what risk-adjusted rate of return is appropriate for investments in its retail outlets.

26. Worrall's Wahoo Novelties is considering a new venture that would produce golden Wahoo commemorative coins. Worrall has estimated that the net investment required will be $15,000, including a $2,000 investment in net working capital. The project is expected to have a 4-year life. Annual net operating cash flows are estimated to be $10,000 in year 1, $8,000 in year 2, $7,000 in year 3, and $6,000 in year 4. The cost of capital is 12 percent. Worrall's marginal tax rate is 40 percent. The standard deviation of the project's *net present value* is $3,000.

What is the probability that this project will be an acceptable investment?

■ SOLUTIONS TO SELF-TEST PROBLEMS

ST1. $z = \dfrac{\$50,000 - \$250,000}{\$100,000}$

$= -2.0$

It can be seen from Table V at the back of the book that the probability of a value less than –2.0 standard deviations from the mean is 2.28 percent. Thus, there is a 2.28 percent chance that the actual net present value for the project will be less than $50,000.

ST2. a. $k_e = 10\% + 1.0(15\% - 10\%) = 15\%$

b. $k_a^* = 10\% + 1.6(15\% - 10\%) = 18\%$

c. NPV @ 15% = $-\$9 + \$1.9(5.019) = \$0.54$ million

d. NPV @ 18% = $-\$9 + \$1.9(4.494) = -\$0.46$ million

The project is acceptable using the required return for average risk projects, but it is unacceptable using the risk-adjusted rate.

ST3. a. NPV calculation:

$$NPV = -\$75,000 + \$30,000(0.870) + \$30,000(0.756)$$
$$+ \$30,000(0.658) + \$20,000(0.572)$$
$$= \$4,960$$

b. Certainty equivalent NPV:

$$NPV = -\$75,000 + \$30,000(0.90)(0.926) + \$30,000(0.80)(0.857)$$
$$+ \$30,000(0.65)(0.794) + \$20,000(0.5)(0.735)$$
$$= -\$6,597$$

■ GLOSSARY

Beta Risk (Project) The risk contribution of a project to the systematic risk of the firm.

Certainty Equivalent The amount of cash someone would require with certainty in order to make him or her indifferent between that certain amount and an amount expected to be received with risk at the same point in time.

Hurdle Rate The minimum acceptable rate of return from an investment project. For projects of average risk, it usually is equal to the firm's cost of capital.

Risk-Adjusted Discount Rate A discount rate that reflects the risk associated with a particular project. In capital budgeting, a higher risk-adjusted rate is used to discount cash flows for riskier projects, whereas a lower risk-adjusted rate is used to discount cash flows for less risky projects.

Scenario Analysis A procedure used to evaluate the change in some objective, such as net present value, to simultaneous changes in several variables influencing that objective, such as price, unit sales volume, and operating costs.

Sensitivity Analysis A procedure used to evaluate the change in some objective, such as net present value, to changes in a variable influencing that objective, such as product price, one of the cash flow elements.

Simulation A financial planning tool that models some event, such as the cash flows from an investment project. A computerized simulation is one technique used to assess the risk associated with a particular project.

AN INTEGRATIVE CASE PROBLEM
CAPITAL BUDGETING
AND RISK ANALYSIS

ZeeBancorp is considering the establishment of a contract collection service subsidiary that would provide collection services to small and medium-sized firms. Compensation would be in the form of a percentage of the amount collected. For amounts collected up to $100, the fee is 55 percent of the amount collected. For amounts collected between $100 and $500, the fee would be 40 percent of the total amount collected on the account. For amounts collected over $500, ZeeBancorp would receive 35 percent of the total amount collected on the account.

ZeeBancorp expects to generate the following amount of business during the first year of operation of the new subsidiary:

Account Class	Number of Collections	Average Amount Collected for Each Account
Up to $100	4,800	$ 75
Between $100 and $500	2,100	$325
Over $500	1,250	$850

Over the projected 10-year life of this collection venture, the number of accounts in each group is expected to grow at 6 percent per annum. The average amount collected from each account is expected to remain constant.

To establish the collection subsidiary, ZeeBancorp will have to rent office space at a cost of $250,000 for the first year. (Assume the rent is payable at the *end* of each year.) This amount is expected to grow at a rate of 11 percent per year. Other operating expenses (excluding depreciation) are expected to total $350,000 during the first year and grow at an 11 percent annual rate.

ZeeBancorp will have to invest $150,000 in net working capital if it undertakes this venture. In addition, required new equipment will cost $275,000 to purchase and an additional $25,000 to install. This equipment will be depreciated using the MACRS schedule for a 7-year asset. The salvage value for the equipment is estimated to be $50,000 at the end of 10 years.

The firm's *marginal* tax rate is estimated to be 40 percent over the project's life, and its *average* tax rate is projected to be 35 percent over the project's life. The firm requires a 15 percent rate of return on projects of average risk.

1. Compute the net investment required to establish the collection subsidiary.
2. Compute the annual net cash flows over the 10-year life of the project.
3. Compute the net present value of this project assuming it is an average-risk investment.
4. Should ZeeBancorp invest in the new subsidiary?
5. ZeeBancorp requires all expansion projects such as this to have a payback of four years or less. Under these conditions, should ZeeBancorp invest in the new subsidiary?

6. If management decides that this project has above-average risk and hence the required return is 20 percent, should the investment be made?
7. If collections are only 80 percent of projections and the required return is 20 percent, should the investment be made?
8. If operating (excluding depreciation) and lease expenses are expected to increase at an annual rate of 13 percent, should the collection subsidiary be established, assuming a required return of 20 percent and the original revenue projections?

THE COST OF CAPITAL, CAPITAL STRUCTURE, AND DIVIDEND POLICY

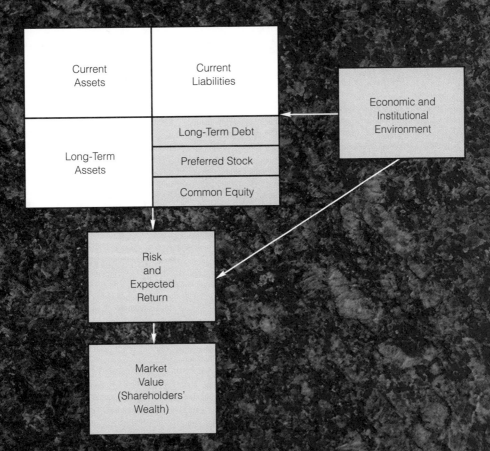

This section considers three closely related topics: the cost of capital (Chapter 11), capital structure (Chapters 12 and 13), and dividend policy (Chapter 14). The cost of capital is an important input in the capital budgeting decision process. This market-determined cost of funds also directly influences the value of a firm's securities. The cost of capital cannot be considered in isolation. The capital structure of a firm directly affects its cost of capital. A more debt-laden capital structure at some point will increase the risk of the firm's securities and increase the overall cost of capital in the firm. This results in a reduction in the value of the firm. Chapters 12 and 13 look at the determinants of an "optimal" capital structure—one that is consistent with the objective of shareholder wealth maximization. Finally, from the dividend policy of a firm discussed in Chapter 14, investors gain important information that ultimately may affect the firm's risk and cost of capital as perceived by those investors.

THE COST OF CAPITAL

11

KEY CHAPTER CONCEPTS

1. The cost of capital is the rate of return required by investors in the firm's securities. The cost of capital determines the rate of return that the firm must earn on its new investments (of average risk) to maximize its value.
2. The required return on any security consists of a risk-free rate of return plus a premium for the risk of that security.
   a. The risk-free rate varies over time and is influenced by the expected rate of inflation and the supply and demand of funds in the overall economy.
   b. The risk premium on a specific security is influenced by the business risk of the firm, the financial risk of the firm, the marketability risk of the security, and the time to maturity of the security.
3. The weighted cost of capital is equal to the after-tax cost of debt times its proportion in the optimal capital structure, plus the after-tax costs of preferred stock times its proportion in the optimal capital structure, plus the cost of common equity times its proportion in the optimal capital structure.
4. The weighted cost of capital is appropriate for determining the return required on projects of average risk.
5. For capital budgeting purposes, the marginal cost of each capital source needs to be calculated.

   a. The after-tax cost of debt is equal to the pretax cost of new debt times one minus the firm's marginal tax rate.
   b. The after-tax cost of a perpetual preferred stock is equal to the annual dividend divided by the net proceeds to the firm from the sale of preferred stock.
   c. The cost of internal equity capital can be computed using a version of the dividend valuation model, the capital asset pricing model, or a risk-premium-on-debt approach.
   d. The cost of external equity capital exceeds the cost of internal equity capital by the amount of the issuance costs.
6. The beta concept also can be used to compute divisional costs of capital for firms with several operating divisions that differ substantially with respect to the risks of investments that are made.
7. The optimal capital budget can be determined by comparing the expected project returns to the company's marginal cost of capital schedule.
8. The cost of depreciation-generated funds is equal to the firm's weighted (marginal) cost of capital, before considering new stock issuance costs.

COST OF EQUITY CAPITAL FOR MOUNTAIN FUEL SUPPLY COMPANY

In 1923, the U.S. Supreme Court issued a landmark decision in the *Bluefield Water Works and Improvement Company v. Public Service Commission of the State of West Virginia* (262 U.S. 679). Among other things, this ruling set judicial standards regarding the rate of return a public utility is allowed to earn on its invested capital. The Court stated:

A public utility is entitled to such rates as will permit it to earn a return on the value of the property which it employs for the convenience of the public equal to that generally being made at the same time . . . in other business undertakings which are attended by corresponding risks and uncertainties; . . . The return should be reasonably sufficient to assure confidence in the financial soundness of the utility and should be adequate, under efficient and economical management, to maintain and support its credit and enable it to raise the money necessary for the proper discharge of its public duties. A rate of return may be reasonable at one time and become too high or too low by changes affecting opportunities for investment, the money market and business conditions generally.

This opinion has been affirmed in many subsequent cases, the most notable one being *Federal Power Commission et al. v. Hope Natural Gas Company* (320 U.S. 591) in 1944.

These decisions establish a number of basic principles that are used when a public utility commission decides on the rate of return a public utility is allowed an opportunity to earn on its equity capital. First, it has been established that the return on equity should be consistent with the opportunity cost principle; that is, the company should be permitted to earn a return equal to that being earned by other companies with similar risks. Second, the return should be sufficient to maintain the financial integrity of the company, maintain its credit, and give it access to the capital markets. Finally, it is recognized that the cost of capital changes depending on business conditions and conditions in the financial markets. The decisions, however, do not establish a methodology for determining the allowed rate of return

on common equity to a public utility. In a typical rate case, there normally is extensive controversy regarding the cost of common equity.

Mountain Fuel Supply Company is the largest natural gas utility operating in Utah. It is a wholly owned division of Questar Corporation, which also has an

interstate gas pipeline and engages in exploration, production, gathering, and processing of natural gas. During 1995, Mountain Fuel brought a major rate case before the Utah Public Service Commission. In that case, three witnesses submitted testimony on the cost of equity capital. Their recommendations follow:

■ A *company witness* recommended a 12.5 percent cost of equity capital as determined by using a constant-growth dividend valuation model, with long-term growth rates provided from Value Line and consensus analyst forecasts supplied by IBES (Institutional Brokers Estimate System, Inc.). The company

witness also considered returns projected to be earned by comparable natural gas companies, used the risk premium over debt approach, and used the capital asset pricing model approach.

■ A witness from the *Committee of Consumer Services* quoted the cost of equity capital at 11 percent as determined from a constant-growth dividend valuation model with long-term growth rates provided by Value Line and historical average growth rates. This witness also used the capital asset pricing model approach, and a comparable returns analysis approach.

■ A witness from the staff of the *Division of Public Utilities* stated that the cost of equity capital was 11.0 percent as determined by using a two-stage growth dividend valuation model with growth rates derived from Value Line and IBES, although somewhat different criteria were employed than those used by the company witness.

Having considered volumes of conflicting testimony on the issues and having heard two days of live testimony on the question of the cost of equity capital, the Utah Public Service Commission faced the challenge of making a final recommendation. In late 1995, the Commission issued its final order. The Commission found that the range of reasonable equity costs extends from 11.3 percent to 11.5 percent and authorized the company to earn returns in that range.

This chapter develops the principles and models that can be used to compute a firm's cost of debt, preferred stock, and common equity capital. All of the models require the use of some judgment by the analyst. This is particularly true in the case of the cost of common equity. The cost of common equity cannot be computed with the same precision as is possible with debt and preferred stock. However, an analyst who is knowledgeable of the basic principles contained in this chapter can make reasonable estimates of the cost of equity capital for any company.

INTRODUCTION

Chapters 8 through 10 considered the capital budgeting decisions of a firm. One of the key variables in capital expenditure analysis is the cost of capital. This chapter discusses the concept of the cost of capital and develops approaches that can be used to measure this important variable.

The **cost of capital** is concerned with what a firm has to pay for the capital—that is, the debt, preferred stock, retained earnings, and common stock—it uses to finance new investments. It also can be thought of as the rate of return required by investors in the firm's securities. As such, the firm's cost of capital is determined in the capital markets and is closely related to the degree of risk associated with new investments, existing assets, and the firm's capital structure. In general, the greater the risk of a firm as perceived by investors, the greater the return investors will require and the greater will be the cost of capital.

The cost of capital can also be thought of as the minimum rate of return required on new investments undertaken by the firm.[1] If a new investment earns an internal rate of return that is greater than the cost of capital, the value of the firm increases. Correspondingly, if a new investment earns a return less than the firm's cost of capital, the firm's value decreases.

This chapter discusses the weighted cost of capital and its use in the capital budgeting process. The nature of the risk versus required return trade-off made by investors in a firm's securities and the measurement of the cost of individual capital components (debt, common equity, and preferred stock) are also presented. Chapters 12 and 13 continue by considering the relationship between capital structure and the cost of capital.

SUMMARY OF NOTATION

Before beginning the discussion of the cost of capital, it is helpful to summarize the important elements of notation used throughout this chapter.

r_f = riskless (risk-free) rate of return; the return offered on short-term U.S. Treasury securities

k_d = pretax cost of debt

k_i = after-tax cost of debt

k_p = cost of preferred stock

k_e = cost of internal common equity

k_e' = cost of external common equity

k_a = weighted (marginal) cost of capital

P_0 = the current market price of a security

P_{net} = the net proceeds to the firm from the sale of a security

P_f = market value of a firm's preferred stock

E = market value of a firm's common equity

---

[1]Technically, this statement assumes that the risk of the new investments is equal to the risk of the existing assets. Also, when used in this context, the cost of capital refers to a weighted cost of the various so used by the firm. The computation of the weighted cost of capital is considered in this chapter.

B = market value of a firm's debt in its capital structure

r_m = expected return on the "market" portfolio

ß = the beta (systematic risk) of a company's stock.

FOUNDATION CONCEPT
WEIGHTED COST OF CAPITAL

The *weighted cost of capital* is an extremely important input in the capital budgeting decision process. The **weighted cost of capital** is the discount rate used when computing the net present value (NPV) of a project of *average* risk. Similarly, the weighted cost of capital is the hurdle rate used in conjunction with the internal rate of return (IRR) approach to project evaluation (for a project of average risk).

Thus, the appropriate after-tax cost of capital figure to be used in capital budgeting not only is based on the next (marginal) capital to be raised but also is weighted by the proportions of the capital components in the firm's long-range target capital structure. Therefore, this figure is called the *weighted, or overall, cost of capital.*

The general expression for calculating the weighted cost of capital, k_a, follows:

$$k_a = \begin{pmatrix} \text{Equity} \\ \text{fraction} \\ \text{of} \\ \text{capital} \\ \text{structure} \end{pmatrix} \begin{pmatrix} \text{Marginal} \\ \text{cost} \\ \text{of} \\ \text{equity} \end{pmatrix} + \begin{pmatrix} \text{Debt} \\ \text{fraction} \\ \text{of} \\ \text{capital} \\ \text{structure} \end{pmatrix} \begin{pmatrix} \text{Marginal} \\ \text{cost} \\ \text{of} \\ \text{debt} \end{pmatrix} \quad (11.1)$$

$$+ \begin{pmatrix} \text{Preferred} \\ \text{fraction} \\ \text{of} \\ \text{capital} \\ \text{structure} \end{pmatrix} \begin{pmatrix} \text{Marginal} \\ \text{cost} \\ \text{of} \\ \text{preferred} \\ \text{stock} \end{pmatrix}$$

$$= \left(\frac{E}{E + B + P_f} \right) (k_e) + \left(\frac{B}{E + B + P_f} \right) (k_d)(1 - T) + \left(\frac{P_f}{E + B + P_f} \right) (k_p)$$

where B is debt, P_f is preferred stock, E is common equity in the target capital structure, k_e is the marginal cost of equity capital, k_d is the marginal pretax cost of debt capital, and k_p is the marginal cost of preferred stock capital.

KN Energy's Weighted Cost of Capital

KN Energy, Inc., a Denver-based natural gas company, has a target capital structure consisting of 47 percent common equity, 51 percent debt, and 2 percent preferred stock. The company plans to finance future capital investments in these proportions. All common equity is expected to be derived internally from additions to retained earnings.

The marginal cost of internal common equity has been estimated to be 13.2 percent. The marginal cost of preferred stock is 8.1 percent and the pretax marginal cost of debt is 8 percent. The marginal tax rate is 40 percent. Using these figures, the weighted cost of capital for KN Energy can be computed using Equation 11.1 as follows:

$$k_a = 0.47 \times 13.2\% + 0.51 \times 8.0\%(1 - 0.4)$$

$$+ 0.02 \times 8.1\%$$

$$= 8.81\%$$

This is the rate that KN Energy should use to evaluate investment projects of average risk over the coming year. Table 11-1 illustrates the weighted cost of capital calculation for KN Energy.

In the following sections, the techniques used to compute each of the component capital costs are presented and illustrated. Then more complex weighted cost of capital schedule calculations are presented.

The Problem of "Lumpy" Capital

Firms usually raise funds in "lumpy" amounts; for example, a firm may sell $50 million in bonds to finance capital expenditures at one point in time, and it may use retained earnings or proceeds from the sale of stock to finance capital expenditures later on. In spite of this tendency to raise funds in lumpy amounts from various sources at different points in time, the weighted (or composite) cost of funds, not the cost of any particular component of funds, is the cost we are interested in for capital budgeting purposes. Another way of saying this is that *it generally is incorrect to associate any particular source of financing with a particular project;* that is, the investment and the financing decisions should be separate.[2]

Consider, for example, the case of a firm that is financed 50 percent with debt and 50 percent with equity. The after-tax cost of equity is 16 percent, and the after-tax cost of debt is 10 percent. The firm has two plants, A and B, which are identical in every respect. The manager of Plant A proposes to acquire a new automated packaging machine costing $10 million. A bank has offered to loan the firm the needed $10 million at a rate that will give the firm a 10 percent after-tax cost. The internal rate of return for this project has been estimated to be 12 percent. Because the rate of return exceeds the cost of funds (debt) used to finance the machine, the manager of Plant A argues that the investment should be made.

The manager of Plant B now argues that she, too, should be allowed to make a similar investment. Unfortunately, she is reminded that the firm has a target capital structure of 50 percent debt and 50 percent equity and that her investment will have to be financed with equity in order for the firm to maintain

TABLE 11-1
Weighted Cost of Capital for KN Energy, Inc.

SOURCE OF CAPITAL	AFTER-TAX COST	TARGET PROPORTION OF CAPITAL	WEIGHTED COST
Internal common equity	13.2%	0.47	6.2 %
Debt	4.8	0.51	2.45
Preferred stock	8.1	0.02	0.16
		1.00	8.81%

[2]This statement generally is true; however, there are exceptions. For example, some projects may possess a higher "debt capacity" than is present for the firm as a whole. This may be due to a different level of business risk. The evaluation of mergers frequently considers the debt capacity of the to-be-acquired firm. Hence, the financing of the project may be considered along with the investment decision itself.

its target capital structure. Because the cost of equity is 16 percent and the project only offers a 12 percent return, the investment is denied for Plant B.

The point of this illustration is that two economically identical projects were treated very differently, simply because the method of financing the projects was tied to the accept-reject decision. To avoid problems of this type, the capital expenditure decision is usually based on a composite capital cost—that is, each project is assumed to be financed with debt and equity in the proportion in which it appears in the target capital structure. In this example, the composite cost of capital is 13 percent, computed as follows:

Source of Capital	After-Tax Cost	Proportion	Composite Cost
Debt	10%	0.5	5%
Equity	16	0.5	8
		Weighted cost of capital =	13%

In this example, neither project should be accepted, because the company's weighted cost of capital exceeds the projects' expected rates of return.

Accordingly, as a firm evaluates proposed capital expenditure projects, it normally does not specify the proportions of debt, preferred stock, and common equity financing for each individual project. Instead, each project is presumed to be financed with the same proportion of debt, preferred stock, and equity contained in the company's target capital structure.

NATURE OF RISK PREMIUMS

Throughout finance, numerous trade-offs must be made between risk and required return. In capital budgeting, for example, companies require higher returns on projects perceived as "high risk" than on projects considered to be "low risk." The following discussion focuses on the relationship between the risk and the required return on a firm's securities.

The required return on any security may be thought of as the riskless, or risk-free, rate of return, r_f, plus a premium for the risk inherent in that security:

$$\text{Required return} = r_f + \text{Risk premium} \qquad (11.2)$$

The riskless rate of return normally is measured by the rate of return on risk-free securities, such as short-term U.S. Treasury securities. This rate varies over time and, as discussed in Chapter 5, consists of two key components:

■ A *real* rate of return that is free from the effects of any inflationary expectations, determined by the supply and demand for funds in the overall economy.
■ A *premium* that is equal to the effects of expected inflation.

These two factors are the primary determinants of returns on risk-free securities. The returns required on all other securities are also influenced by the risk of those securities.

The risk premium on a specific security (as discussed in greater detail in Chapter 5) is determined by many factors, including the length of *maturity* (in the case of various bonds and preferred stocks), the ability of an investor to buy and sell a security quickly and without loss of value (called **marketability risk**), and the *seniority* position of the security in a firm's capital structure.

Investors are also concerned about the variability of expected returns from a security and the chance of default. Variability and default risk are determined by

- The business risk of the firm.
- The financial risk of the firm.

The **business risk** of a firm refers to the variability in the firm's operating earnings (EBIT). It is determined by the variability in the firm's sales revenues and operating costs and by the amount of operating leverage the firm uses in producing sales. The determinants of business risk are discussed in Chapter 12.

Financial risk refers to the additional variability in a company's earnings per share that results from the use of fixed-cost sources of funds, such as debt and preferred stock. In addition, the financial risk premium includes a premium to compensate for the increased potential risk of bankruptcy that arises from the use of debt financing. The determinants of financial risk are also discussed in Chapter 12.

Finally, a firm's cost of funds may increase at any point in time with increases in the amount of needed financing. For example, a company might be able to sell 1 million new shares of common stock at $25 per share. If the firm sought to sell an additional 1 million shares, however, it may have to offer them at a lower price in order to attract enough buyers. This would, of course, increase the cost of the funds raised by the firm. In addition, as a firm seeks increasing amounts of capital from investors, there is a point at which the investors begin to question the firm's ability to effectively manage the large number of investment projects to be financed with these funds.

Figure 11-1 illustrates the relationship between the riskless rate of return, the risk premium, and the required rate of return on any security.

FIGURE 11-1
Determinants of the Required Return of Any Security

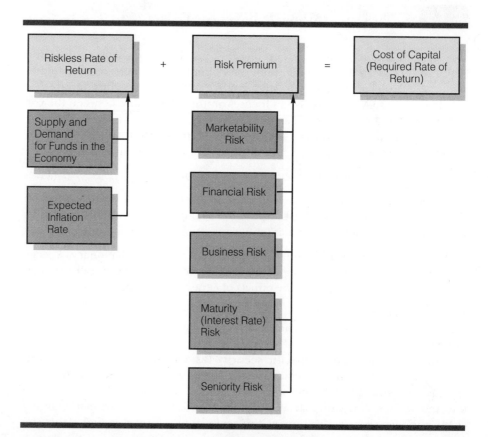

Although the foregoing concepts provide a useful background for analyzing the cost of a firm's capital, they are not directly applicable to measuring the cost of capital for specific sources of funds. Before considering how the cost of capital may be estimated, it is necessary to examine the relationship between the costs of various sources of capital.

RELATIVE COSTS OF CAPITAL

Figure 11-2 illustrates the general risk-return trade-off between investors' required rates of return and various sources of funds. As was noted, the risk-free rate, r_f, is usually measured as the rate of return on short-term U.S. Treasury securities. Longer-term U.S. government bonds normally command a higher rate than shorter-term debt, because bond prices vary more than prices of shorter-term debt securities over time for equal changes in interest rates. Thus, if interest rates rise, the price of long-term bonds falls, resulting in losses for any investor who must sell the security prior to maturity. Investors normally require a premium to compensate for this **interest rate risk.**

Long-term debt securities of the U.S. government are always less risky than corporate long-term debt securities of the same maturity. The reason, of course, is the finite probability, however small, that the company will default on its obligation to pay interest and principal. Because the government controls the money supply, it can always meet its nominal financial obligations by printing more money. The actual difference in returns, or yields, between government debt and high-quality corporate debt (Aaa rated) is usually less than 1 percent and sometimes less than 0.5 percent. For example, in early 1997, the average yield on Aaa corporate bonds was 7.29 percent, and the average yield on long-term U.S. Treasury bonds was 6.7 percent. Companies with high default risk must offer high coupon interest rates

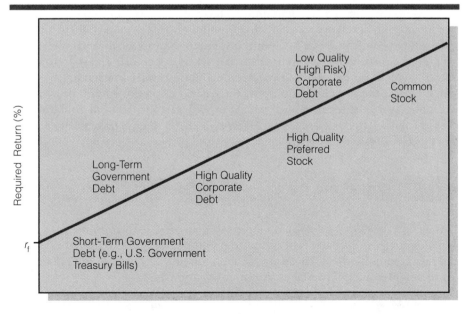

FIGURE 11-2
General Risk-Required Return Trade-off

to investors in order to sell their debt issues, because the market recognizes that these high default risk companies are more likely to have difficulty meeting their obligations than low default risk companies. For example, the yield in early 1997 on Weirton Steel bonds, rated B by Standard & Poor's, was 10.56 percent.

Recently, another element of risk (event risk) has become apparent to owners of corporate bonds. This is the risk that a recapitalization of the firm, such as may occur in a leveraged buyout, may greatly increase the financial risk of the firm. For example, in late 1988 when RJR Nabisco was acquired in a leveraged buyout by a group headed by Kohlberg Kravis Roberts (KKR), the holders of the RJR Nabisco bonds experienced a loss of 20 percent or more in the value of their bonds. The KKR takeover increased the debt ratio of RJR Nabisco substantially. Accordingly, buyers of corporate bonds now require relatively higher returns when the risk of a leveraged buyout is present. (By early 1991, however, the RJR bonds had regained much of their lost value.)

Preferred stock is normally riskier than debt. The claims of preferred stockholders on the firm's assets and earnings are junior to those of debtholders. Also, dividends on preferred stock are more likely to be cut or omitted than interest on debt. Consequently, investors usually demand a higher return on a company's preferred stock than on its debt.

Common stock is the riskiest type of security considered here, because dividends paid to common stockholders are made from cash remaining after interest and preferred dividends have been paid. Thus, the common stock dividends are the first to be cut when the firm encounters difficulties. Because there is a greater degree of uncertainty associated with common stock dividends than with the interest on debt or preferred stock dividends, common stock dividends are judged riskier. In addition, the market price fluctuations of common stocks tend to be wider than those of preferred stocks or long-term debt. As a result of this higher risk, investors' required returns on common stock are higher relative to preferred stock and debt. Over the years, the differences between returns realized from long-term corporate debt and common stock of large companies have averaged 6.5 percent.[3]

So far, this section has shown that a particular security's risk affects the return required by investors. The analysis must be taken one important step further, however. If capital markets are to clear (that is, supply equals demand), the firm must offer returns consistent with investor requirements. Suppose, for example, that a firm offers a security for sale in the capital markets at a return that is less than investors generally require. Obviously, not enough buyers will come forth. Unless the firm increases the return (by dropping the price, raising the interest or dividend rate, and so on), the securities will remain unsold, and the firm will not be able to raise its capital. Therefore, *the cost of capital to the firm is equal to the equilibrium rate of return demanded by investors in the capital markets for securities with that degree of risk.*

COMPUTING THE COMPONENT COSTS OF CAPITAL

This section develops and applies methods a firm can use to compute the cost of its major component sources of capital: debt, preferred stock, retained earnings, and new common equity. These are the component costs used in the calculation of the weighted cost of capital as shown in Equation 11.1.

[3] *Stocks, Bonds, Bills, and Inflation: 1996 Yearbook*™ (Chicago: Ibbotson Associates, 1996). Annual updates of work by Roger G. Ibbotson and Rex A. Sinquefield. All rights reserved.

Marginal Costs

Firms calculate their cost of capital in order to determine a discount rate to use for evaluating proposed capital expenditure projects. Recall that the purpose of capital expenditure analysis is to determine which *proposed* projects the firm should *actually* undertake. Therefore, it is logical that *the capital whose cost is measured and compared with the expected benefits from the proposed projects should be the next or marginal capital the firm raises.*

As we saw in Chapter 8, the capital budgeting process involves an extension of the marginal analysis principle from economics. The marginal revenue (internal rate of return) from a project is compared with the marginal cost of funds needed to finance the project. The marginal cost of funds is the cost of the next increments of capital raised by the firm. Hence, the costs of the various capital funding components (debt, preferred stock, and common equity) must be their marginal costs. Historic *average* capital costs are not relevant for making new (marginal) resource allocation decisions.

When computing the marginal cost of the various component capital sources, companies typically estimate the component costs they anticipate encountering (paying) during the coming year. If capital costs change significantly during the year, it may be necessary to recompute the new capital costs and use the new estimates when evaluating projects from that time forward. Under most circumstances, a semiannual or annual computation of marginal capital costs is sufficient.

Cost of Debt

The cost of debt capital to the firm is the rate of return required by a firm's creditors. For a debt issue, this rate of return, k_d, equates the present value of all expected future receipts—interest, I, and principal repayment, M—with the net proceeds, P_{net}, of the debt security (as discussed earlier in Chapter 6):

$$P_{net} = \sum_{t=1}^{n} \frac{I}{(1 + k_d)^t} + \frac{M}{(1 + k_d)^n}$$

or

$$P_{net} = I(\text{PVIFA}_{k_d,n}) + M(\text{PVIF}_{k_d,n}) \qquad (11.3)$$

The pretax cost of debt, k_d, is calculated in the same way as the yield to maturity, shown in Chapter 6. The only difference in the calculation is that when making yield-to-maturity calculations, the price of the bond is the current market price. When computing the pretax cost of debt to a company, the price of the bond is the net proceeds the company receives after considering all issuance costs.

Interest payments made to investors are deductible from the firm's taxable income. Therefore, the *after-tax* cost of debt, k_i, is computed by multiplying the coupon interest rate by one minus the firm's marginal tax rate, T.[4]

$$k_i = k_d(1 - T) \qquad (11.4)$$

To illustrate the cost-of-debt calculation for KN Energy, assume that the firm sells $100 million of 20-year 7.8 percent coupon rate bonds. The net proceeds

---

[4]The conversion from a pretax to an after-tax cost of debt is accurate when there are no bond issuance costs. When a bond offering entails issuance costs and the bond is sold either at a discount or premium over face value, there will be a small, insignificant error when using Equation 11.4.

to KN Energy after issuance costs are $980 for each $1,000 bond. To compute the pretax cost, k_d, of this debt offering, the relationship in Equation 11.3 can be used as follows:

$$\text{Net proceeds} = P_{net} = \$78(\text{PVIFA}_{k_d,20}) + \$1,000(\text{PVIF}_{k_d,20})$$

The calculation of k_d can be done either by trial and error using Tables IV and II at the end of the book or with the aid of a financial calculator.

By trial and error, try 8 percent:

$$\$980 = \$78(9.818) + \$1000(0.215)$$

$$\approx \$980$$

Therefore, the pretax cost of debt is 8 percent.

CALCULATOR SOLUTION

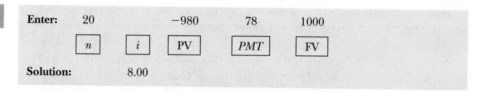

Enter:	20		−980	78	1000
	n	i	PV	PMT	FV

Solution: 8.00

Assuming a 40 percent marginal tax rate, the after-tax cost of debt is computed using Equation 11.4:

$$k_i = k_d(1 - T)$$

$$= 8\%(1 - 0.4)$$

$$= 4.80\%$$

The tax benefits of interest deductibility are available only to firms that are making profits. For a firm losing money, the tax rate in Equation 11.4 is *zero*, and the after-tax cost, k_i, is the same as the pretax cost, k_d.

This procedure works well when a firm is in the process of selling, or has just sold, bonds at the time the cost of capital is being computed. However, in most instances, trips to the capital markets are sporadic. How can the marginal cost of debt be computed in these cases? That is, how can one determine what it would cost a firm to sell debt today (at the time of the cost-of-capital calculation)? This problem has two solutions:

1. If a firm has bonds that are currently outstanding and are being traded in the marketplace, the firm can observe the current market price for those bonds. Given a current price, the maturity of the bonds, and the coupon rate of interest, the yield to maturity on the bond can be computed. This yield to maturity may be used as an estimate of the marginal pretax cost of debt, k_d, for the firm.[5]

2. If a firm's outstanding bonds are not traded frequently or are privately held, then the best estimate of the marginal pretax cost of debt can be derived by looking at the pretax cost of debt recently sold by other firms having risk similar to the firm under consideration. For these purposes, having similar risk is normally interpreted to mean that firms have equivalent bond ratings (according to Moody's or Standard and Poor's).

[5]This computed yield to maturity likely will understate slightly the pretax marginal cost of debt because it does not consider issuance costs.

Cost of Preferred Stock

The cost of preferred stock to the firm is the rate of return required by investors on preferred stock issued by the company. Because many preferred stocks are perpetuities, it is possible to use the simplified preferred stock valuation model developed in Chapter 6:

$$P_0 = \frac{D_p}{k_p} \qquad (11.5)$$

where P_0 is the preferred stock price; D_p, the annual preferred dividend; and k_p, the investors' required rate of return. The cost of preferred stock, k_p, is given by the following equation:

$$k_p = \frac{D_p}{P_{net}} \qquad (11.6)$$

In calculating preferred stock cost, the price that should be used, P_{net}, is the net proceeds to the firm; that is, the proceeds from the sale of the stock after subtracting *issuance costs*.

To illustrate, KN Energy has just issued 3 million shares of a preferred stock that pay an annual dividend of $4.05. The preferred stock was sold to the public at a price of $52 per share. With issuance costs of $2 per share, the marginal cost of preferred stock is calculated as follows:

$$k_p = \frac{\$4.05}{\$52 - \$2}$$

$$= 0.081 \text{ or } 8.1\%$$

Because payments by the firm to preferred stockholders are in the form of dividends, they are not tax deductible; therefore, the after-tax cost of preferred stock is equal to the pretax rate.

An increasing number of preferred stock issues are callable, have a sinking fund redemption provision, or have a fixed maturity. In these cases, the computation of the cost of preferred stock financing is similar to that for bonds. For example, Carolina Power plans an offering of $50 par value preferred stock that will pay a $5.00 dividend per year. The preferred stock is expected to yield Carolina net proceeds of $46.40 per share after all issue costs. The preferred stock must be retired at its par value in 15 years. The cost of this preferred stock issue can be computed by solving for k_p in the following valuation model:

$$P_{net} = \$46.40 = \$5(\text{PVIFA}_{k_p,15}) + \$50(\text{PVIF}_{k_p,15})$$

Try:

$$k_p = 11 \text{ percent}$$

$$\$46.40 = \$5(7.191) + \$50(0.209)$$

$$= \$35.95 + \$10.45$$

$$\$46.40 = \$46.40$$

Therefore, k_p equals 11 percent for Carolina's anticipated preferred stock offering.

CALCULATOR SOLUTION

Enter:	15		−46.50	5	50
	n	i	PV	PMT	FV

Solution: 11.00

Cost of Internal Equity Capital

Like the cost of debt and preferred stock, the cost of equity capital to the firm is the equilibrium rate of return required by the firm's common stock investors.

Firms raise equity capital in two primary ways:

■ *Internally,* through retained earnings.
■ *Externally,* through the sale of new common stock.

Some analysts and managers incorrectly assume that the cost of internal equity is zero. The opportunity cost concept makes it clear that this is an erroneous assumption. When funds are generated through the earnings of the firm, managers can either pay out these funds as dividends to common stockholders or the funds can be retained and reinvested in the firm. If the funds were paid out to stockholders, they could reinvest the funds elsewhere to earn an appropriate return, given the risk of the investment. Therefore, if managers decide to retain earnings and reinvest them in the firm, there must be investment opportunities in the firm offering a return equivalent to the returns available to common stockholders, on a risk-adjusted basis, in alternative investments.

The cost of internal equity to the firm is less than the cost of new common stock because the sale of new stock requires the payment of issuance costs. The concept of the cost of internal equity (or simply equity, as it is commonly called) can be developed using several different approaches. The first considered here is based on the dividend valuation model.

Dividend Valuation Model Approach

Briefly reviewing from Chapter 7, the general dividend valuation model (or the dividend capitalization model, as it is often referred to) for common stock valuation is as follows:

$$P_0 = \sum_{t=1}^{\infty} \frac{D_t}{(1 + k_e)^t} \tag{11.7}$$

where P_0 is the stock's present value or current market price; D_t, the dividend received in period t; and k_e, the return required by investors. This equation shows that in efficient capital markets, k_e, the required return and thus the cost of equity capital, equates the present value of all expected future dividends with the current market price of the stock. In principle, the cost of equity capital can be calculated by solving Equation 11.7 for k_e. In practice, however, the expected future dividends are not known and cannot be estimated with the same degree of confidence as preferred stock dividends and debt interest. As a result, the general form of the dividend valuation model is not directly useful in calculating the cost of equity capital.

As shown in Chapter 7, if the firm's future per-share dividends are expected to grow each period perpetually at a constant rate, g, the dividend valuation model can be written as follows:

$$P_0 = \frac{D_1}{k_e - g} \tag{11.8}$$

where $D_1 = D_0(1 + g)$ and D_0 is the current period dividend ($t = 0$). Note that in Equation 11.8, k_e must be greater than g, the expected growth rate. As discussed in Chapter 7, the *constant growth valuation model* assumes that a firm's earnings, dividends, *and* stock price will grow at rate g. Thus, g equates to the yearly price appreciation (capital gain). But the total return to stockholders, k_e, is composed of both the price appreciation *and* the dividend yield. Therefore, g cannot be greater than or equal to k_e because it is only one of two components making up k_e.

Equation 11.8 can be rearranged to obtain an expression for calculating the cost of equity, assuming that dividends are expected to grow perpetually at a rate g per year:[6]

$$k_e = \frac{D_1}{P_0} + g \tag{11.9}$$

To illustrate the use of Equation 11.9, suppose KN Energy's common stock is currently selling for $22 a share. Its present dividend, D_0, is $0.96 a share, and the expected long-term dividend growth rate is 8.5 percent. The cost of internal equity capital, k_e, is calculated as follows:

$$k_e = \frac{\$0.96(1 + 0.085)}{\$22} + 0.085$$

$$= 0.132 \text{ or } 13.2\%$$

Nonconstant Dividend Growth and the Cost of Common Equity.[7] The dividend valuation model can also be used to compute the cost of equity for common stocks expected to pay dividends that grow at variable rates in the future. An approach similar to the nonconstant growth dividend valuation model illustrated in Chapter 7 (Equation 7.14) can be used.

For example, Avtec Corporation is a rapidly growing producer of microcircuit boards used in the aerospace industry. Its stock is selling currently for $10.95 per share. Current dividends, D_0, are $1.00 per share and are expected to grow at a rate of 10 percent per year over the next 4 years and 6 percent annually thereafter. Avtec's cost of internal equity, k_e, can be found as follows:

$$\$10.95 = \frac{\$1.10}{(1 + k_e)^1} + \frac{\$1.21}{(1 + k_e)^2} + \frac{\$1.33}{(1 + k_e)^3} + \frac{\$1.46}{(1 + k_e)^4} + \frac{1}{(1 + k_e)^4} \times \frac{\$1.55}{k_e - 0.06}$$

$$= \$1.10(\text{PVIF}_{k_e,1}) + \$1.21(\text{PVIF}_{k_e,2}) + \$1.33(\text{PVIF}_{k_e,3})$$

$$+ \$1.46(\text{PVIF}_{k_e,4}) + (\text{PVIF}_{k_e,4}) \frac{\$1.55}{k_e - 0.06}$$

Note that the last term in this expression, $\$1.55/(k_e - 0.06)$, is equal to the expected stock price at the beginning of year 5 (which is the same as the end of year 4 in time-value terms). Hence it must be discounted back four periods.

---

[6]The relevant growth rate is the rate expected by investors. This normally is estimated by examining projected future growth rates provided by security analysts, such as Value Line, Merrill Lynch, and IBES. A further discussion of this issue is presented at the end of this section.

[7]This section may be omitted without loss of continuity.

The valuation expression above must be solved for k_e, the cost of equity capital, using a trial-and-error procedure. A trial value of 17 percent for k_e yields the following:

$$\$10.95 = \$1.10(0.855) + \$1.21(0.731) + \$1.33(0.624)$$

$$+ \$1.46(0.534) + 0.534\left(\frac{\$1.55}{0.17 - 0.06}\right)$$

$$= \$10.95$$

Thus, Avtec's cost of equity is 17 percent.

In principle, the general dividend valuation model approach can be used to estimate the cost of equity capital for any expected dividend pattern. In practice, many stocks not only have exhibited rather constant growth rates in the past but look as though they will continue to do so in the future. For these stocks, the constant growth form of the dividend capitalization model is appropriate, and the expected growth rate often can be estimated in the manner discussed in the next section.

Issues in Implementation

Dividend valuation models (sometimes also referred to as DCF models) are frequently used in the calculation of a firm's cost of equity capital. In implementing these models, the analyst must obtain an estimate of the growth rate(s) in earnings and dividends (and stock price) expected by investors. Where can these investor expectations be obtained?

Investors form expectations about future growth rates based upon past realized growth, current earnings and retention rates, expected future earnings rates (such as the return on equity), and conditions in the markets that the firm serves. These factors are often well summarized in the form of analysts' estimates of future growth rates. Analysts' forecasts may be viewed as the best market- and investor-available summary of all of the factors that determine future growth rates. There are two reasons for this. First, a growing body of research supports the conclusion that analysts' estimates of future earnings growth rates are very accurate—consistently more accurate than estimates provided from any other forecasting model.[8] Second, another body of research has confirmed that analysts' forecasts outperform extrapolative forecasts in explaining share prices.[9]

Analyst forecasts are available from a number of sources. As discussed in more detail in Chapter 7, they can be obtained from individual brokerage houses and investment advisory services, such as Merrill Lynch, Salomon Brothers, Shearson Lehman Bros., Goldman Sachs, and Value Line. In addition, the **Institutional Brokers Estimate System (IBES)** summarizes the short- and long-term earnings forecasts made by analysts from major investment firms throughout the United States. IBES covers the stocks of more than 3,500 firms. Similar growth rate consensus forecasts are available from *Zacks Earnings Estimates*.

---

[8]See, for example, L. D. Brown and M. S. Rozeff, "The Superiority of Analyst Forecasts as Measures of Expectations: Evidence from Earnings," *Journal of Finance* (March 1978): 1–16; M. S. Rozeff, "Predicting Long-Term Earnings Growth: Comparisons of Expected Return Models, Submartingales and Value Line Analysts," *Journal of Forecasting* (December 1983): 425–435; R. C. Moyer, R. E. Chatfield, and G. D. Kelley, "The Accuracy of Long-Term Earnings Forecasts in the Electric Utility Industry," *International Journal of Forecasting*, no. 3 (1985): 241–252; and R. C. Moyer, R. E. Chatfield, and P. Sisneros, "The Accuracy of Long-Term Earnings Forecasts for Industrial Firms," *Quarterly Journal of Business and Economics* (Summer 1989): 91–104.

[9]See, for example, J. G. Cragg and B. G. Malkiel, *Expectations and the Structure of Share Prices* (Chicago: University of Chicago Press, 1982); and R. Harris, "Using Analysts' Growth Forecasts to Estimate Shareholder Required Rates of Return," *Financial Management* (Spring 1986): 58–67.

Capital Asset Pricing Model (CAPM) Approach

Many firms, including Pepsico, use the **Capital Asset Pricing Model (CAPM),** discussed in Chapter 5, to compute their cost of common equity. The CAPM formally describes the risk-required return trade-off for securities. Equation 11.2 illustrates that the rate of return required by investors consists of a risk-free return, r_f, plus a premium compensating the investor for bearing the risk. This risk premium varies from stock to stock.

Less risk is associated with an investment in a stable stock, such as AT&T, than in the stock of Western Digital Corp., a medium-sized computer components firm. As a result, an investor in Western's stock, W, requires a higher return than the AT&T investor. Figure 11-3 illustrates the difference in required rates of return (or the cost of internal equity) for the two securities. The relationship illustrated in this figure is the **security market line (SML).** The SML depicts the risk-required return relationship in the market for all securities.

Recall from Chapter 5 that the security market line is defined as follows:[10]

$$k_j = r_f + \beta_j(r_m - r_f) \tag{11.10}$$

where k_j = the required rate of return on any security j; r_f = the expected risk-free rate; β_j = the beta (systematic risk) measure for security j; and r_m = the

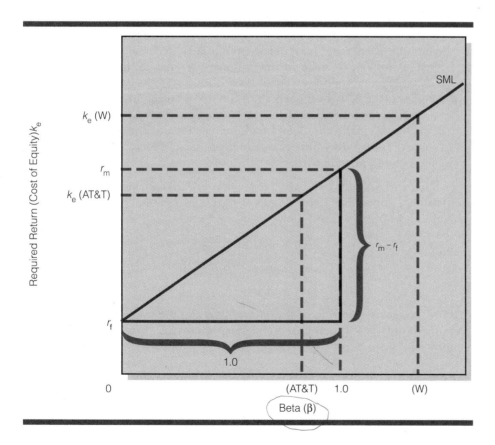

FIGURE 11-3
Security Market Line (SML)

[10]In Chapter 5, we used a hat (^) over the r_f and r_m variables to indicate these are *expected* values. For simplicity, the hats are dropped here, but it should be kept in mind that we are still dealing with expected values for these variables.

expected return on the market portfolio. Hence, the value $(r_m - r_f)$ equals the market risk premium (the slope of the SML), or the risk premium applicable to a stock of average (beta = 1.0) risk.

The SML concept is based on investors' expectations regarding a security's risk and return characteristics. Required returns for any individual security are also dependent on expected future levels of interest rates and the expected return on the market as a whole. These expected values are determined as follows:

■ *The risk-free rate* (r_f). The value for r_f that is most frequently used in computing the required return for a security is the 3- or 6-month U.S. Treasury bill rate. (Some practitioners prefer to use a long-term government bond rate instead.)

■ *The expected market return* (r_m). The expected market return is the return investors expect to earn in the future on stocks with an average beta of 1.0. The average holding period return for stocks during the time period from 1926 to 1995 was about 12.5 percent per year. These actual returns have varied substantially, depending on the holding periods assumed. The average market risk premium measured relative to Treasury bill rates has been 8.8 percent over the past 70 years. The average market risk premium measured relative to long-term government bond yields has been 7.3 percent over the same period.[11] These risk premiums may be used for the market risk premium $(r_m - r_f)$ in Equation 11.10. Remember that if the 8.8 percent market risk premium is used, then the risk-free rate (the first term on the right-hand side of Equation 11.10) must be the short-term Treasury bill rate. When the 7.3 percent market risk premium is used, then the risk-free rate must be the long-term government bond rate, such as the yield on 20-year U.S. government bonds.

■ *The firm's beta,* β_j. Beta is normally estimated by using historic values of the relationship between a security's returns and the market returns. In Chapter 5, we illustrated the computation of the beta for General Motors. The *Value Line Investment Survey* and brokerage firms, such as Merrill Lynch, regularly compute and provide betas.[12]

To illustrate, KN Energy's *Value Line* beta is 0.75. If short-term Treasury bills are yielding 5.5 percent, KN Energy's cost of equity capital may be computed using the short-term SML as follows:

$$k_e = r_f + \beta_j(r_m - r_f)$$
$$= 5.5\% + 0.75(8.8\%)$$
$$= 12.1\%$$

If the longer-term version of the SML is used and the yield on long-term U.S. Treasury bonds is 7.1 percent, KN Energy's cost of equity capital may be computed as

$$k_e = r_f + \beta_j(r_m - r_f)$$
$$= 7.1\% + 0.75(7.3\%)$$
$$= 12.6\%$$

---

[11] *Stock, Bonds, Bills and Inflation: 1996 Yearbook*, p. 118.

[12] Because of statistical biases inherent in the historic computation of betas, these reported betas are often adjusted to provide a better estimate of future betas.

Note the variation between the two SML estimates of KN Energy's cost of equity and also the variation between these estimates and the 13.2 percent figure derived using the constant growth dividend valuation model earlier in the chapter. Such variation is normal and highlights the fact that estimates of the cost of equity capital are subject to some error.

The SML concept is one more tool that may be used in computing the firm's cost of equity capital, k_e. If all the parameters required of the model are correctly estimated (r_f, $r_m - r_f$, and β_j), the model should give a reasonably accurate estimate of k_e. Many analysts find it useful to compute k_e in more than one way to arrive at a consensus about the rate of return investors require on a security.

Recall from Chapter 5 that the beta measure of risk considers only the systematic risk or market risk of a stock. Poorly diversified investors may be more interested in total risk than in systematic risk. When this is true, the CAPM may understate returns required by those investors.

Did you know that Ibbotson (one of the leading suppliers of high-quality financial information) will sell their "Beta Book" to you for $1,250? Alternatively, you can visit their Web site and see some sample pages of how Ibbotson actually uses CAPM and beta to enable calculations of a firm's cost of equity.
http://www.ibbotson.com/research/cost.htm

Risk Premium on Debt and Other Approaches for Estimating the Cost of Equity Capital

This section begins by considering a shortcut method of estimating the cost of equity capital based on actual historic returns and ends by discussing non-dividend-paying stocks.

Studies analyzing the historical returns earned by common stock investors have found that the holding period returns from average risk common stock investments over the past 70 years have averaged 6.5 percentage points higher than holding period returns on corporate debt issues.[13] Therefore, the cost of equity capital for an average risk company (a firm with a beta of about 1.0) can be estimated by adding approximately 6.5 percentage points to the company's current cost of debt. For companies with a less-than-average level of systematic risk, such as electric utilities (electric utility betas average about 0.7), a risk premium over the company's current cost of long-term debt of 3 to 5 percentage points has been found to be approximately correct. For companies with a higher-than-average level of systematic risk, a risk premium in excess of 6.5 percentage points is warranted. Studies have shown that equity risk premiums over a company's debt yields tend to be higher when interest rates are relatively low and lower when interest rates are relatively high. Many analysts use this shortcut method as a reference. Whenever possible, however, the other more precise methods should be used.

For stocks that do not pay dividends, the dividend capitalization model is obviously an inappropriate valuation model and therefore cannot be used to determine an accurate cost of equity capital. Investors in non-dividend-paying stocks expect to sell the stock in the future at a higher price than the present price, realizing a capital gain. Investors' expectations about the future price are incorporated into the following valuation model:[14]

$$P_0 = \frac{P_t}{(1 + k_e)^t} \tag{11.11}$$

[13] *Stock, Bonds, Bills and Inflation: 1996 Yearbook*, p. 118.
[14] If investors in a non-dividend-paying stock expected the company to begin paying dividends at some future date, a form of the dividend capitalization model could be constructed to reflect these expectations.

where P_t is the expected stock price at time t. In principle, a firm could use this valuation model to determine its cost of equity capital. In practice, however, this would be difficult to do, because the company probably has no way of confidently determining the P_t expectations of investors. Instead, the cost of equity capital for non-dividend-paying stocks normally is determined either by using the Capital Asset Pricing Model, the risk premium on debt approach, or by estimating k_e for comparable dividend-paying stocks in their industry.

Cost of External Equity Capital

The cost of external equity is greater than the cost of internal equity for the following reasons:

- Issuance (flotation) costs associated with new shares are usually high enough that they cannot realistically be ignored.
- The selling price of the new shares to the public is normally set less than the market price of the stock before the announcement of the new issue. Before any announcement, the current market price of a stock usually represents an equilibrium between supply and demand. If supply is increased (all other things being equal), the new equilibrium price will be lower.

In addition, Masulis and Trueman have argued that retained earnings are a cheaper source of funds than the sale of new equity because retention defers the payment of taxable dividends to shareholders and, therefore, reduces the present value of taxes that must be paid by shareholders.[15]

When a firm's future dividend payments are expected to grow at a constant rate of g per period forever, the cost of external equity, k_e', is defined as follows:

$$k_e' = \frac{D_1}{P_{net}} + g \tag{11.12}$$

where P_{net} is the net proceeds to the firm on a per-share basis.[16] To illustrate, consider the KN Energy example used in the constant growth dividend valuation model example earlier in the chapter. KN Energy's projected dividend for next year was \$1.04 (\$0.96 × 1.085); its stock price was \$22; and the long-term growth rate in earnings and dividends was projected to be 8.5 percent per annum. Assuming that new common stock can be sold at \$21 to net the company \$20 after issuance expenses, k_e' is calculated as follows:

$$k_e' = \frac{D_1}{P_{net}} + g$$

$$= \frac{\$1.04}{\$20} + 0.085$$

$$= 0.137 \text{ or } 13.7\%$$

[15]R. W. Masulis and B. Trueman, "Corporate Investment and Dividend Decisions under Differential Personal Taxation," *Journal of Financial and Quantitative Analysis* 23 (1988): 369–386.

[16]An alternative approach to the treatment of issuance costs is to allocate the dollar amount of these costs to individual projects, thus increasing the project cost. When this procedure is used, no adjustment to capital costs is required. This procedure may be superior (from a theoretical perspective) to the cost of capital adjustment procedure, but it is difficult to implement and not widely used.

Because of the relatively high cost of newly issued equity, many companies try to avoid this means of raising capital. The question of whether a firm should raise capital with newly issued common stock depends on its investment opportunities.[17]

Table 11-2 summarizes the cost of capital formulas developed in the preceding sections.

 DIVISIONAL COSTS OF CAPITAL

The approaches already discussed provide an estimate of the return required by equity investors on investment projects of "average" risk. When some divisions of a company have lower (higher) systematic risk than others, the discount rates for projects adopted by these divisions should be lower (higher) than the discount rate for the firm as a whole.

For example, West Coast Power is an electric utility that has a calculated beta of 0.91. The firm has three divisions: the electric power generation and distribution division, which has 70 percent of the firm's assets; an oil and gas exploration division, which has 20 percent of the assets; and a transportation and barge division, which has 10 percent of the assets. Using surrogate market information—that is, estimating the beta for one or more firms that are purely

TABLE 11-2
Formulas for Computing Component Costs

Cost of Debt	$k_i = k_d(1 - T)$ where: k_d = pretax cost of debt = yield to maturity on a new bond issue when the current price of the bond is set equal to the net proceeds to the issuing company
Cost of Preferred Stock	$k_p = \dfrac{\text{Annual preferred dividend}}{\text{Net proceeds to the company}}$ (for perpetual preferred stock) $= \dfrac{D_p}{P_{net}}$
Cost of Internal Common Equity	1. Dividend capitalization model approach, used when dividends grow at a perpetual constant rate: $k_e = \dfrac{\text{Next year's expected dividend}}{\text{Common stock price}} + \text{Expected dividend growth rate}$ $= \dfrac{D_1}{P_0} + g$ 2. Capital Asset Pricing Model approach: k_e = Risk-free return + Risk premium $= r_f + \beta_j(r_m - r_f)$
Cost of External Common Equity	$k'_e = \dfrac{\text{Next year's expected dividend}}{\text{Net proceeds per share to the company}} + \text{Expected dividend growth rate}$ $= \dfrac{D_1}{P_{net}} + g$

[17]This discussion is continued in the section on determining the optimal capital budget.

(or nearly so) engaged in the business of each of West Coast's major divisions and using these surrogate betas (after adjusting for leverage differentials using Equations 10.1 and 10.2)—the beta for each division is estimated as shown here:

	Estimated Divisional Beta	Proportion of Firm's Assets	Weighted Average Beta
Electric power	0.75	0.70	0.53
Exploration	1.30	0.20	0.26
Transportation	1.20	0.10	0.12
		Weighted average firm beta =	0.91

Note that the weighted average of the divisional betas is equal to the firm's overall beta—in this case, 0.91.

Conglomerate firms that compete in many different product and geographical markets, such as Pacificorp, Litton, or General Electric, often estimate separate divisional costs of capital. These divisional costs of capital reflect both the differential required returns of equity investors, estimated from the security market line, and the differential debt-carrying capacity of each division. For example, the parent company may have a debt-to-total-assets ratio of 60 percent. Individual divisions within the firm may compete against other firms that typically have higher or lower debt-to-total-assets ratios. In computing each divisional cost of capital, many firms try to reflect both the differential divisional risks and the differential normal debt ratios for each division.

DETERMINING THE WEIGHTED (MARGINAL) COST OF CAPITAL SCHEDULE

In the beginning of the chapter, the computation of the weighted (marginal) cost of capital was based on the assumption that the firm would get equity funds only from internal sources, that all debt had a single cost, and that all preferred stock had a single cost. The procedure illustrated in that earlier discussion must be modified if the firm anticipates selling new common stock (having a higher component cost) or issuing additional increments of debt securities at successively higher costs to finance its capital budget.

To illustrate, suppose the Major Foods Corporation is developing its capital expenditure plans for the coming year. The company's schedule of potential capital expenditure projects for next year is as follows:

Project	Amount (in millions of dollars)	Internal Rate of Return
A	$4.0	13.8%
B	8.0	13.5
C	6.0	12.5
D	5.0	12.0
E	8.0	11.0
F	4.0	10.0

These projects are closely related to the company's present business and have the same degree of risk as its existing assets.

The firm's current capital structure (as well as its targeted future capital structure) consists of 40 percent debt, 10 percent preferred stock, and 50 percent common equity measured on the basis of the current market value of debt, preferred stock, and equity in the capital structure. Table 11-3 shows the current balance sheet for Major Foods. Major Foods can raise up to $5 million in debt funds at a pretax cost of 9 percent; debt amounts exceeding $5 million will cost 10 percent. Preferred stock can be sold at an after-tax cost of 10 percent. Major Foods' marginal tax rate is 40 percent.

Major Foods expects to generate $10 million of retained earnings over the coming year. Its present dividend rate, D_0, is $2 per share. The firm's common stock is now selling at $25 per share, and new common stock can be sold to net the firm $24 per share.[18]

Over the past several years, Major Foods' earnings and dividends have grown at an average of 7 percent per year, and this growth rate is expected to continue for the foreseeable future. The company's dividend payout ratio has been, and is expected to remain, more or less constant.

Given this information, Major Foods' weighted (marginal) cost of capital can be calculated for the coming year:

■ **Step 1: Calculate the cost of capital for each individual component**—the cost of debt, the cost of preferred stock, and the cost of equity.

Cost of debt:

$$k_i = k_d (1 - T) = \ \ 9.0 \times 0.6 = 5.4\% \text{ for the first \$5 million of debt}$$
$$k_i = k_d (1 - T) = 10.0 \times 0.6 = 6.0\% \text{ for debt exceeding \$5 million}$$

Cost of preferred stock:

$$k_p = 10\% \text{ (given)}$$

Cost of common equity:
Internal (for amounts of retained earnings up to $10 million):

$$k_e = \frac{D_0(1 + g)}{P_0} + g$$

$$= \frac{\$2(1.07)}{\$25} + 0.07 = 0.156, \text{ or } 15.6\%$$

ASSETS		LIABILITIES AND EQUITY	
Current assets	$100	Current liabilities	$ 50
Fixed assets	30	Long-term debt	32(40%)
Total assets	$130	Preferred stock	8(10%)
		Common equity	40(50%)
		Total liabilities and equity	$130

TABLE 11-3
Balance Sheet for Major Foods (in millions of dollars)

[18] The net proceeds per share depend on the number of shares sold. As a very general rule, underwriters are reluctant to sell new shares in an amount that exceeds 10 to 15 percent of a company's existing shares.

External (for amounts of new common stock greater than $10 million):

$$k_e' = \frac{\$2(1.07)}{\$24} + 0.07 = 0.159, \text{ or } 15.9\%$$

■ **Step 2: Compute the weighted (marginal) cost of capital for each increment of capital raised.**

Major Foods should raise funds in proportion to its target capital structure from its lowest cost sources first. In this case, these sources are retained earnings (15.6 percent after-tax cost), preferred stock (10 percent after-tax cost), and the first $5 million in debt (5.4 percent after-tax cost). When these sources are exhausted, the company should consider using the higher cost sources—external equity (15.9 percent after-tax cost) and additional debt (6.0 percent after-tax cost)—together with preferred stock.

How much total financing through combining retained earnings, preferred stock, and debt can be done before the $5 million in low-cost debt is exhausted and Major must acquire additional debt funds at the higher cost? Because we know that the target capital structure consists of 40 percent debt, the total financing, *X*, that this will support is equal to the amount of low-cost debt available divided by the debt fraction in the capital structure:

$$X = \frac{\text{Amount of low-cost debt available}}{\text{Debt fraction of capital structure}}$$

$$= \frac{\$5 \text{ million}}{0.40}$$

$$= \$12.5 \text{ million}$$

This $12.5 million level represents a break point in the marginal cost of capital schedule. *Break points* delineate the levels of financing where the weighted cost of capital increases due to an increase in the cost of one component source of capital; that is, debt, preferred stock, or common equity.

Break points can be determined by dividing the amount of funds available from each financing source at a fixed cost by the target capital structure proportion for that financing source. Thus, we saw in the Major Foods example that the $5 million of debt, with an after-tax cost of 5.4 percent, would support total financing of $12.5 million. Beyond $12.5 million in total financing, the weighted (marginal) cost of capital will rise, because higher-cost debt (6.0 percent) now must be used. Of this $12.5 million in total financing, $5 million will be debt, $1.25 million (10 percent of the total) will be preferred stock, and $6.25 million will be retained earnings. The cost of this first block of funds using Equation 12.1 is as follows:

$$k_a = 0.50 \times 15.6\% + 0.40 \times 5.4\% + 0.10 \times 10\%$$

$$= 10.96\%$$

The amount of available retained earnings also determines a break point. The $10 million of retained earnings will support total financing of $20 million ($10 million/0.5). Therefore, a new break point occurs at a total financing level of $20 million. Beyond that point, the weighted cost of capital increases due to the higher cost (15.9 percent) of external equity. Thus, the second block of financing totals $7.5 million ($20 million equity break point minus $12.5 million debt financing break point).

This $7.5 million block of funds represents the size of the second lowest-cost block of funds. Of this $7.5 million in financing, $3.75 million will be retained earnings, $0.75 million will be preferred stock, and $3 million will be debt. The cost of this second block of funds will be as follows:

$$k_a = 0.50 \times 15.6\% + 0.40 \times 6.0\% + 0.10 \times 10\%$$
$$= 11.20\%$$

Beyond the second block, all additional funds raised will be with high-cost debt, new common stock, and preferred stock. The weighted cost of these funds is as follows:

$$k_a = 0.50 \times 15.9\% + 0.40 \times 6.0\% + 0.10 \times 10\%$$
$$= 11.35\%$$

Figure 11-4 provides a graph of the weighted (marginal) cost of capital schedule for Major Foods.

The weighted (marginal) cost of capital schedule now can be used to determine the optimal capital budget for Major Foods. This procedure is illustrated in the next section.

DETERMINING THE OPTIMAL CAPITAL BUDGET

The **optimal capital budget** can be determined by comparing the expected project returns to the company's marginal cost of capital schedule. This is accomplished by first plotting the returns expected from the proposed capital expenditure

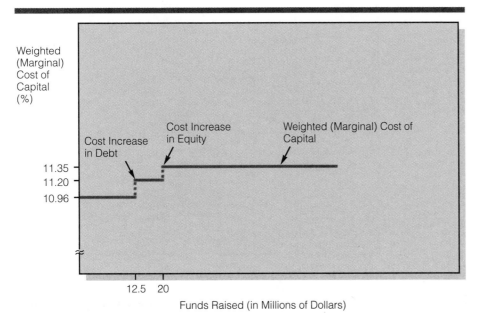

FIGURE 11-4
Weighted (Marginal) Cost of Capital Schedule for Major Foods

projects against the cumulative funds required. The resulting graph is called an **investment opportunity curve.** Next, the previously calculated k_a for the three capital "packages" are combined to determine the company's *marginal cost of capital curve.* The optimal capital budget is indicated by the point at which the investment opportunity curve and the marginal cost of capital curve intersect, as shown in Figure 11-5.

Specifically, the Major Foods Corporation's optimal capital budget totals $23 million and includes Projects A, B, C, and D. Projects E and F are excluded, because their returns are expected to be below the 11.35 percent cost of funds. Acceptance of Projects E and F would result in a decrease in the firm's value. In principle, the optimal capital budget maximizes the value of the firm.

The procedure for determining the optimal capital budget discussed in this section assumes that all projects being considered are equal in risk to the average risk of the firm. Indeed, whenever the weighted cost of capital is used for capital project evaluation, the assumption is being made that the capital project has a level of risk equal to the average risk of the firm. If this is not the case, one of the capital budgeting under risk techniques discussed in Chapter 10 must be incorporated into the procedure described.

FIGURE 11-5
Determining the Optimal
Capital Budget

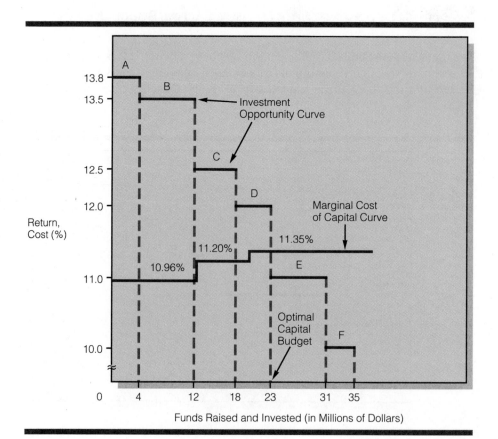

COST OF DEPRECIATION-GENERATED FUNDS

One large source of funds for many firms is funds generated from depreciation. Of course, depreciation per se does not generate cash. Rather, depreciation simply is a noncash expense charged against income. Therefore, a firm's reported net income normally will understate the amount of cash flow generated by the firm during a given time period. To adjust net income for the cash flow effect of depreciation, the amount of depreciation must be added to net income after taxes. It is in this sense that depreciation represents a source of funds. Also, some firms may generate funds from the sale of assets from time to time. What is the cost of these funds? Because the firm always has the option to either reinvest these funds in the firm or to return them to the stockholders as dividends and to retire outstanding debt, the appropriate opportunity cost of these funds is the firm's weighted (marginal) cost of capital, before considering new stock issuance costs.

With respect to the marginal cost of capital schedule in Figure 11-5, it is generally agreed that these funds have an opportunity cost equal to the first "block" of funds; that is, 10.96 percent. If $10 million in depreciation-generated funds were available, the first block of funds would increase from $12.5 million to $22.5 million, and all other blocks also would be shifted to the right by $10 million.

INTERNATIONAL ISSUES
THE COST OF CAPITAL FOR
MULTINATIONAL COMPANIES

Multinational companies face a more complex cost of capital problem than purely domestic firms. However, the increased complexity of the problem also offers opportunities to reduce capital costs.

Multinational companies have an opportunity to raise capital in other countries' capital markets, as well as at home, whenever these firms have major operations in foreign countries. One opportunity open to multinational firms is that a host country's government may offer preferential (subsidized) financing terms as an incentive for a firm to locate some of its operations in that country.

Evidence also indicates significant, persistent real differences in the cost of capital between countries. For example, studies of the relative real costs of capital for U.S. and Japanese firms have concluded that during the 1980s, the cost of capital for U.S. firms averaged about 3.3 percentage points higher than for Japanese firms.[19] However, as global capital markets become more integrated and barriers to international capital flows are reduced, opportunities to take advantage of country-to-country differences in capital costs have diminished. Recent evidence suggests that differences in capital costs between U.S. and Japanese firms have all but disappeared.[20]

[19]Robert E. Lippens, "The Cost of Capital: A Summary of Results for the U.S. and Japan in the 1980s," *Business Economics* (April 1991): 19–24.
[20]Jeffrey A. Frankel, "The Cost of Capital in Japan: Update," *Business Economics* (April 1991): 25–31.

Most multinational companies raise all or the vast majority of their equity capital in their home country. However, multinational firms commonly raise a substantial portion of their debt capital in the countries in which they maintain significant operations. By doing so, a multinational firm effectively hedges much of the balance sheet risk associated with changes in the value of assets in place due to changes in exchange rates. For example, if Sara Lee builds a plant in France, the accounting value of this investment will decline with decreases in the value of the French franc against the U.S. dollar.[21] Offsetting this decline in the accounting value of the French subsidiary's assets is a decline in the value of the debt obligations (when converted to dollars) of the subsidiary. Another advantage of raising a significant portion of a multinational firm's capital in the countries in which it operates is the fact that this insulates the firm from much of the risk of expropriation.

In summary, multinational firms have an opportunity to shop the world for the lowest available capital costs.

 ENTREPRENEURIAL FINANCE ISSUES
THE COST OF CAPITAL

Small firms have a difficult time attracting capital to support their investment programs. Owners of small firms are reluctant to sell common stock because they do not want to lose voting control in the company. When shares are sold, many small firms create two classes of stock, such as Class A and Class B. The Class A stock is the one that is traded most extensively in the capital markets. Class A stock usually receives a higher dividend than Class B. In contrast, Class B stock, often held by the company's founders, has greater voting power than Class A stock. In this way, capital can be raised without losing voting control.

Many firms are so small that it is nearly impossible to raise funds by selling common stock. If stock can be sold, investors often will pay much less for these shares than they would for similar firms that are larger and have their stock traded regularly on an organized exchange or over-the-counter. Issuance costs for common stock sales of small firms may exceed 20 percent of the issue size. As a consequence, the cost of equity capital tends to be significantly higher for small firms than it is for larger firms. Because of the limited access to the capital markets for new equity, small firms tend to retain a much larger portion of their earnings to fund future growth than larger firms.

Similarly, the sources of debt capital to small firms are also limited. Bonds and debentures cannot be sold publicly until a firm has grown to a relatively large size. Before reaching a size that will permit it to sell securities publicly, the small firm will have to rely upon the following sources for debt funds:

■ The owners' own funds and loans from friends.
■ Loans from commercial banks and savings and loan associations.
■ Small Business Administration loans.

---

[21]The value references made here are limited to the accounting value of the assets. The market value of the French assets may actually increase with declines in the value of the franc, because the goods produced by the plant will be relatively cheaper when sold for export.

- Commercial finance company loans.
- Leasing companies.
- Venture capital firms that normally demand some equity interest in the firm through conversion features or warrants (discussed in Chapter 20).
- Private placements of debt issues with insurance companies and large corporations, often with a conversion feature or warrants.

Generally, the cost of both debt and equity capital is significantly higher for small firms than larger firms. The high cost of capital puts small firms at a competitive disadvantage relative to large firms in raising funds needed for expansion.

Conceptually, computing the cost of capital for a small, closely held firm is no different than for a large, publicly traded firm. The same models of valuation apply to small firms as for large firms. In practice, however, there often are serious difficulties in developing confident estimates of the cost of capital for small firms. Computing the cost of straight debt and preferred stock (nonconvertible and without attached warrants) is relatively easy. However, when debt and preferred stock securities are convertible or have attached warrants, an analyst must make an estimate about the time and conditions under which these securities will be converted into common stock or when the warrants to purchase common stock will be exercised.

In the case of common stock, there often is no ready market for the stock. Hence, it may not be possible to make confident estimates of the stock price when computing the cost of equity. Also, because many small firms pay little or no dividends, applying the dividend valuation model is more difficult. As a consequence, when computing the cost of equity for small firms, analysts often must compute the cost of equity for a group of larger, publicly traded companies in the same line of business and with a similar financial risk (as measured by the capital structure) and then add an additional risk premium reflective of the perceived increased risk due to reduced marketability and liquidity of the small firm's stock and any differential in business and financial risk.

■ SUMMARY

- A firm's *cost of capital* is defined as the rate the firm has to pay for the debt, preferred stock, common stock, and/or retained earnings it uses to finance its new investments in assets. The cost of capital is the rate of return required by investors in the firm's securities. Cost of capital can also be thought of as the minimum rate of return required on new investments of average risk undertaken by the firm.
- The higher the risk of a security, the higher is the return required by investors. In general, common stock is more risky than preferred stock; preferred stock is more risky than corporate debt securities; and corporate debt securities are more risky than government debt securities. Investors' required returns generally decrease in the same order.
- Firms normally use an after-tax *weighted cost of capital* to evaluate proposed capital expenditure projects. Each project is presumed to be financed with the same proportion of debt, preferred stock, and common equity contained

in the company's target capital structure. The general formula for calculating the weighted cost of capital, k_a, is as follows:

$$k_a = \begin{pmatrix} \text{Equity} \\ \text{fraction} \\ \text{of} \\ \text{capital} \\ \text{structure} \end{pmatrix} \begin{pmatrix} \text{Marginal} \\ \text{cost} \\ \text{of} \\ \text{equity} \end{pmatrix} + \begin{pmatrix} \text{Debt} \\ \text{fraction} \\ \text{of} \\ \text{capital} \\ \text{structure} \end{pmatrix} \begin{pmatrix} \text{Marginal} \\ \text{cost} \\ \text{of} \\ \text{debt} \end{pmatrix}$$

$$+ \begin{pmatrix} \text{Preferred} \\ \text{fraction} \\ \text{of} \\ \text{capital} \\ \text{structure} \end{pmatrix} \begin{pmatrix} \text{Marginal} \\ \text{cost} \\ \text{of} \\ \text{preferred} \\ \text{stock} \end{pmatrix}$$

■ A firm's pretax *cost of debt capital*, k_d, is the rate of return required by investors. The after-tax cost of debt, k_i, is calculated as follows:

$$k_i = k_d(1 - T) = \text{Coupon interest rate } (1 - T)$$

where T is the firm's marginal tax rate.

■ A firm's *cost of preferred stock*, k_p, is the rate of return required by the preferred stock investors. In the case of perpetual preferred stock, the cost is calculated as follows:

$$k_p = \frac{D_p}{P_{\text{net}}}$$

where D_p is the annual preferred dividend, and P_{net} is the preferred stock price net of issuance costs on new issues. Preferred stock is used relatively infrequently as a source of capital, because its after-tax cost normally is significantly greater than that of debt. This is because interest on debt is a tax-deductible expense for the firm, whereas dividends on stock are not.

■ A firm's *cost of equity capital* is defined as the rate of return required by its common stock investors. Equity capital can be raised *internally* through retained earnings and *externally* through the sale of new common stock.

■ A firm's cost of *internal equity* can be determined by the dividend valuation model, the Capital Asset Pricing Model (CAPM), using the security market line (SML), or the risk premium on debt approach. Using the dividend valuation model and assuming that dividends grow perpetually at a rate of g per year, the following equation for calculating the cost of equity capital, k_e, is obtained:

$$k_e = \frac{D_1}{P_0} + g$$

More complex calculations are required if the constant growth assumption does not hold. Using the CAPM, the cost of equity capital can be calculated as follows:

$$k_e = r_f + \beta(r_m - r_f)$$

where r_f is the risk-free rate; β (beta) is the relative measure of the stock's return volatility; and $(r_m - r_f)$ is the market risk premium.

■ A firm's *cost of external equity*, k_e', when dividends are expected to grow perpetually at a constant rate, is as follows:

$$k'_e = \frac{D_1}{P_{net}} + g$$

where P_{net} is the net proceeds to the firm on a per-share basis.

- The *optimal capital budget* maximizes the value of the firm and occurs at the point where the firm's *investment opportunity curve* and *weighted marginal cost of capital curve* intersect. The investment opportunity curve is obtained by plotting the returns expected from proposed capital expenditure projects against the cumulative funds required.
- The cost of depreciation-generated funds is equal to the weighted cost of the firm's first "block" of funds.

■ QUESTIONS AND TOPICS FOR DISCUSSION

1. How do retained earnings differ from other sources of financing?
2. Does the retained earnings figure shown on a firm's balance sheet necessarily have any relationship to the amount of retained earnings the firm can generate in the coming year? Explain.
3. Why is corporate long-term debt riskier than government long-term debt?
4. Why do investors generally consider common stock to be riskier than preferred stock?
5. Should a firm pay cash dividends in a year in which it raises external common equity?
6. Discuss the meaning of an *optimal* capital budget.
7. Evaluate the statement "Depreciation-generated funds have no explicit cost and therefore should be assigned a zero cost in computing a firm's cost of capital."
8. Describe how to derive the break points in the marginal cost of capital schedule.
9. Discuss the pros and cons of various sources of estimates of future earnings and dividend growth rates for a company.
10. What market risk premium should be used when applying the CAPM to compute the cost of equity capital for a firm if
    a. the risk-free rate is the 90-day Treasury bill rate?
    b. the risk-free rate is the 20-year government bond rate?
11. What factors determine the required rate of return for any security?
12. What are the similarities and differences in preferred stock and debt as sources of financing for a firm?
13. Why is the marginal cost of capital the relevant concept for evaluating investment projects, rather than a firm's actual, historic cost of capital?

■ SELF-TEST PROBLEMS

ST1. Scherr Enterprises has a series of 8 percent coupon bonds outstanding with a $1,000 par value. The bonds mature in 10 years and currently sell for $946. If new bonds are issued, the issuance cost is expected to be $11 per bond. Scherr's marginal tax rate is 40 percent. What is the marginal after-tax cost of debt for Scherr? (Assume annual interest payments.)

ST2. Clarke Equipment currently pays a common stock dividend of $3.50 per share. The common stock price is $60. Analysts have forecast that earnings and dividends will grow at an average annual rate of 6.8 percent for the foreseeable future.
    a. What is the marginal cost of retained earnings?
    b. What is the marginal cost of new equity if the issuance costs per share are $3?

ST3. Vargo, Inc. has a beta estimated by Value Line of 1.3. The current risk-free rate (short-term) is 7.5 percent and the market risk premium is 8.6 percent. What is the cost of equity capital for Vargo?

ST4. Walther Enterprises has a capital structure target of 60 percent common equity, 15 percent preferred stock, and 25 percent long-term debt. Walther's financial analysts have estimated the marginal, after-tax cost of debt, preferred stock, and common equity to be 9 percent, 15 percent, and 18 percent, respectively. What is the weighted marginal cost of capital for Walther?

■ PROBLEMS*

1. Calculate the after-tax cost of a $25 million debt issue that Pullman Manufacturing Corporation (40 percent marginal tax rate) is planning to place privately with a large insurance company. This long-term issue will yield 9⅞ percent to the insurance company.

2. Husky Enterprises recently sold an issue of 10-year maturity bonds. The bonds were sold at a deep discount price of $615 each. After flotation costs, Husky received $604.50 each. The bonds have a $1,000 maturity value and pay $50 interest at the end of each year. Compute the after-tax cost of debt for these bonds if Husky's marginal tax rate is 40 percent.

3. Calculate the after-tax cost of preferred stock for Bozeman-Western Airlines, Inc., which is planning to sell $10 million of $6.50 cumulative preferred stock to the public at a price of $50 a share. Issuance costs are estimated to be $2 a share. The company has a marginal tax rate of 40 percent.

4. St. Joe Trucking has sold an issue of $6 cumulative preferred stock to the public at a price of $60 per share. After issuance costs, St. Joe netted $57 per share. The company has a marginal tax rate of 40 percent.

   a. Calculate the after-tax cost of this preferred stock offering assuming this stock is a perpetuity.

   b. If the stock is callable in 5 years at $66 per share and investors expect it to be called at that time, what is the after-tax cost of this preferred stock offering? (Compute to the nearest whole percent.)

5. The following financial information is available on Fargo Fabrics, Inc.:

Current per-share market price	$20.25
Current per-share dividend	$ 1.12
Current per-share earnings	$ 2.48
Beta	0.90
Expected market risk premium	8.3%
Risk-free rate (Treasury bills)	5.2%

   Past 10 years earnings per share:

19X1	$1.39	19X6	$ 1.95
19X2	1.48	19X7	2.12
19X3	1.60	19X8	2.26
19X4	1.68	19X9	2.40
19X5	1.79	19Y0	2.48

   This past earnings growth trend is expected to continue for the foreseeable future. The dividend payout ratio has remained approximately constant over the past 9 years and is expected to remain at current levels for the foreseeable future.

   Calculate the cost of equity capital using the following methods:

   a. The dividend capitalization model approach.

   b. The Capital Asset Pricing Model approach.

6. The stock of Alpha Tool sells for $10.25 per share. Its current dividend rate D_0, is $1 per share. Analysts and investors expect Alpha to increase its dividends at a 10 percent rate for each of the next 2 years. This annual dividend growth rate is

*Colored numbers denote problems that have check answers provided at the end of this book.

expected to decline to 8 percent for years 3 and 4 and then to settle down to 4 percent per year forever. Calculate the cost of internal equity for Alpha Tool.

7. The Hartley Hotel Corporation is planning a major expansion. Hartley is financed 100 percent with equity and intends to maintain this capital structure after the expansion. Hartley's beta is 0.9. The expected market return is 16 percent and the risk-free rate is 10 percent. If the expansion is expected to produce an internal rate of return of 17 percent, should Hartley make the investment?

8. Wentworth Industries is 100 percent equity financed. Its current beta is 0.9. The expected market rate of return is 14 percent and the risk-free rate is 8 percent.
   a. Calculate Wentworth's cost of equity.
   b. If Wentworth changes its capital structure to 30 percent debt, it estimates that its beta will increase to 1.1. The after-tax cost of debt will be 7 percent. Should Wentworth make the capital structure change?

9. The Ewing Distribution Company is planning a $100 million expansion of its chain of discount service stations to several neighboring states. This expansion will be financed, in part, with debt issued with a coupon interest rate of 15 percent. The bonds have a 10-year maturity and a $1,000 face value, and they will be sold to net Ewing $990 after issue costs. Ewing's marginal tax rate is 40 percent.

   Preferred stock will cost Ewing 14 percent after taxes. Ewing's common stock pays a dividend of $2 per share. The current market price per share is $15, and new shares can be sold to net $14 per share. Ewing's dividends are expected to increase at an annual rate of 5 percent for the foreseeable future. Ewing expects to have $20 million of retained earnings available to finance the expansion.

   Ewing's target capital structure is as follows:

Debt	20%
Preferred stock	5
Common equity	75

   Calculate the weighted cost of capital that is appropriate to use in evaluating this expansion program.

10. Pacific Intermountain Utilities Company has a present capital structure (which the company feels is optimal) of 50 percent long-term debt, 10 percent preferred stock, and 40 percent common equity. For the coming year, the company has determined that its optimal capital budget can be externally financed with $70 million of 10 percent first-mortgage bonds sold at par and $14 million of preferred stock costing the company 11 percent. The remainder of the capital budget will be financed with retained earnings. The company's common stock is presently selling at $25 a share, and next year's common dividend, D_1, is expected to be $2 a share. The company has 25 million common shares outstanding. Next year's net income available to common stock (including net income from next year's capital budget) is expected to be $106 million. The company's past annual growth rate in dividends and earnings has been 6 percent. However, a 5 percent annual growth in earnings and dividends is expected for the foreseeable future. The company's marginal tax rate is 40 percent.

    Calculate the company's weighted cost of capital for the coming year.

11. Panhandle Industries, Inc., currently pays an annual common stock dividend of $2.20 per share. The company's dividend has grown steadily over the past 9 years from $1.10 to its present level; this growth trend is expected to continue. The company's present dividend payout ratio, also expected to continue, is 40 percent. In addition, the stock presently sells at 8 times current earnings (that is, its P/E multiple is 8).

    Panhandle Industries stock has a beta of 1.15, as computed by a leading investment service. The present risk-free rate is 7.0 percent, and the expected return on the stock market is 13.0 percent.
    a. Suppose an individual investor feels that 12 percent is an appropriate required rate of return for the level of risk this investor perceives for Panhandle Industries.

eXcel

Using the dividend capitalization model and the Capital Asset Pricing Model approaches, determine whether this investor should purchase Panhandle Industries stock.

b. Calculate the company's cost of equity capital using both the dividend capitalization model approach and the Capital Asset Pricing Model approach.

eXcel

12. Colbyco Industries has a target capital structure of 60 percent common equity, 30 percent debt, and 10 percent preferred stock. The cost of retained earnings is 15 percent, and the cost of new equity (external) is 16 percent. Colbyco anticipates having $20 million of new retained earnings available over the coming year. Colbyco can sell $15 million of first-mortgage bonds with an after-tax cost of 9 percent. Its investment bankers feel the company could sell $10 million of debentures with a 9.5 percent after-tax cost. Additional debt would cost 10 percent after tax and be in the form of subordinated debentures. The after-tax cost of preferred stock financing is estimated to be 14 percent.

Compute the marginal cost of capital schedule for Colbyco, and determine the break points in the schedule.

eXcel

13. The White Corporation makes small Bozo replicas for sale in the growing Austin market. The firm's capital structure consists of 60 percent common equity, 10 percent preferred stock, and 30 percent long-term debt. This capital structure is believed to be optimal. White is planning to raise funds over the coming year to finance expansion plans. The firm expects to have $40 million of retained earnings available. The cost of retained earnings is 18 percent. Additional common equity can be obtained by selling new common stock at a cost of 19.6 percent. The firm can sell a maximum amount of $20 million of preferred stock at a cost of 15 percent. First-mortgage bonds totaling $25 million can be sold at a pretax cost of 14 percent. Beyond $25 million, the firm would have to sell debentures at a pretax cost of 15 percent. The firm's marginal tax rate is 40 percent.

Identify the size of each block of funds and the cost of the funds in each block. Be sure to identify the *maximum* amount of funds White can acquire.

eXcel

14. Owens Enterprises is in the process of determining its capital budget for the next fiscal year. The firm's current capital structure, which it considers to be optimal, is contained in the following balance sheet:

Balance Sheet

Current assets	$ 40,000,000	Accounts Payable	$ 20,000,000
Fixed assets	400,000,000	Other current liabilities	10,000,000
Total assets	$440,000,000	Long-term debt	123,000,000
		Common stock at par	15,500,000
		Paid in capital in excess of par	51,000,000
		Retained earnings	220,500,000
		Total liabilities and stockholders' equity	$440,000,000

Through discussions with the firm's investment bankers, lead bank, and financial officers, the following information has been obtained:

■ The firm expects net income from this year to total $80 million. The firm intends to maintain its dividend policy of paying 42.25 percent of earnings to stockholders.

■ The firm can borrow $18 million from its bank at a 13 percent annual rate.

■ Any additional debt can be obtained through the issuance of debentures (at par) that carry a 15 percent coupon rate.

■ The firm currently pays $4.40 per share in dividends (D_0). Dividends have grown at a 5 percent rate in the past. This growth is expected to continue.

■ The firm's common stock currently trades at $44 per share. If the firm were to raise any external equity, the newly issued shares would net the company $40 per share.

■ The firm is in the 40 percent marginal tax bracket.

Compute Owens' marginal cost of capital schedule.

15. Matsumoto Limited (ML), a large conglomerate firm, has a capital structure that currently consists of 20 percent long-term debt, 10 percent preferred stock, and 70 percent common equity. ML has determined that it will raise funds in the future using 40 percent long-term debt, 10 percent preferred stock, and 50 percent common equity.

excel

ML can raise up to $50 million in the long-term debt market at a pretax cost of 18 percent. Beyond $50 million, the pretax cost of long-term debt is expected to increase to 20 percent. Preferred stock can be raised at a cost of 19 percent. The limited demand for this security permits ML to sell only $20 million of preferred stock. ML's marginal tax rate is 40 percent.

ML's stock currently sells for $40 per share and has a beta of 1.5. ML pays no dividends and is not expected to pay any dividends for the foreseeable future. Investment advisory services expect the stock price to increase from its current level of $40 per share to a level of $99.50 per share at the end of 5 years. New shares can be sold to net the company $38.35. ML expects earnings after taxes and available for common stockholders to be $60 million.

Compute the marginal cost of capital schedule for ML and determine the break points in the schedule.

16. Rolodex, Inc. is in the process of determining its capital budget for the next fiscal year. The firm's current capital structure, which it considers to be optimal, is contained in the following balance sheet:

excel

Rolodex, Inc. Balance Sheet (in millions of dollars)

Current assets	$110	Accounts payable	$ 30
Fixed assets	260	Other current liabilities	20
Total assets	$370	Long-term debt	128
		Preferred stock	32
		Common stock (20 million shares at par)	20
		Contributed capital in excess of par	30
		Retained earnings	110
		Total liabilities and equity	$370

Discussions between the firm's financial officers and the firm's investment and commercial bankers have yielded the following information:

- Rolodex can borrow $40 million from its bank at a pretax cost of 13 percent.
- Rolodex can borrow $80 million by issuing bonds at a net price of $687 per bond. The bonds would carry a 10 percent coupon rate and mature in 20 years.
- Additional debt can be issued at a 16 percent pretax cost.
- Preferred stock can be issued at a pretax cost of 16.5 percent.
- Rolodex expects to generate $140 million in net income and pay $2 per share in dividends.
- The $2 per share dividend ($D_1$) represents a growth of 5.5 percent over the previous year's dividend. This growth rate is expected to continue for the foreseeable future. The firm's stock currently is trading at $16 per share.
- Rolodex can raise external equity by selling common stock at a net price of $15 per share.
- Rolodex's marginal tax rate is 40 percent.

a. Compute Rolodex's marginal cost of capital schedule.

b. Given the following investment opportunity schedule, determine Rolodex's optimal capital budget.

Project	Required Investment	Expected Return on Project
A	$140,000,000	17.0%
B	130,000,000	16.0
C	100,000,000	15.0
D	80,000,000	14.2
E	24,000,000	13.0
F	16,000,000	10.9

17. The Folske Fan Corporation has four divisions:

Division	Proportion of Firm's Assets
Consumer products	50%
Consulting	10%
Industrial products	30%
Financial services	10%

The (leveraged) beta for Folske has been estimated to be 1.25. The company believes that the (leveraged) beta for consumer products is 1.2; for consulting, 1.3; and for financial services, 1.5. The appropriate capital structure for the industrial products division is 70 percent equity and 30 percent debt (and all projects in that division are currently financed in those proportions). The firm's consolidated capital structure consists of 60 percent equity and 40 percent debt. The risk-free rate is 9 percent, and the market risk premium is 8.6 percent. Folske's marginal tax rate is 40 percent. What is the minimum rate of return that Folske should demand on the equity-financed portion of investments in its industrial products division, assuming these investments continue to be financed with 70 percent equity and 30 percent debt?

18. Jenkins Resources, Inc. has the following capital structure:

Financing Source	Proportion of Capital Structure
Debentures (9% coupon, $1,000 par value, 12 year maturity)	27%
Preferred stock ($2 dividend, $25 par value)	8
Common equity	65
Total	100%

Jenkins expects to raise future capital in the proportions currently indicated on the balance sheet. The current market price for Jenkins debentures is $1,075. If new debentures were sold, the issuance cost would be $20 per bond. The current market price for the preferred stock is $19. Issuance costs on new preferred stock would be $1 per share for a $25 par value issue. Issuance costs on new equity would be $2.50 per share. The current market price for Jenkins common stock is $40. The stock pays a current (D_0) dividend of $3. This dividend is expected to grow at an annual rate of 7 percent.

What is the weighted (marginal) cost of capital for Jenkins Resources, assuming new capital is raised in the proportions shown above and that all new equity comes from the sale of new shares, new debt comes from the sale of debentures, and new preferred comes from the sale of preferred stock? The firm's marginal tax rate is 40 percent.

19. Intermountain Resources is a multidivisional company. It has three divisions with the following betas and proportion of the firm's total assets:

Division	Beta	Proportion of Assets
Natural gas pipelines	0.70	50%
Oil and gas production	1.20	30%
Oil and gas exploration	1.50	20%

The risk-free rate is 7 percent and the market risk premium is 8 percent.
a. What is the firm's weighted average beta?
b. What required equity rate of return should the firm use for average-risk projects in its natural gas pipeline division?
c. What required equity rate of return should the firm use for average-risk projects in its oil and gas exploration division?

 20. The current dividend, D_0, of the stock of Sun Devil Corporation is $3 per share. Under present conditions, this dividend is expected to grow at a rate of 6 percent

annually for the foreseeable future. The beta of Sun Devil's stock is 1.5. The risk-free rate of return is 7 percent and the expected market rate of return is 14 percent.

a. At what price would you expect Sun Devil's common stock to sell?

b. If the risk-free rate of return declines to 6 percent, what will happen to Sun Devil's stock price? (Assume the expected market rate of return remains at 14 percent.)

c. Sun Devil's management is considering acquisitions in the machine tool industry. Management expects the firm's beta to increase to 1.6 as a result of these acquisitions. The dividend growth rate is expected to increase to 7 percent annually. Would you recommend this acquisition program to management? (Assume the same initial conditions that existed in Part a.)

21. Caledonia Minerals has an estimated beta of 1.6. The company is considering the acquisition of another firm that has a beta of 1.2. Both companies are exactly the same size.

a. What is the expected new beta value for the combined firm?

b. The risk-free rate of return is estimated at 7 percent and the market return is estimated as 12 percent. What is your estimate of the required return of investors in Caledonia before and after the merger?

Caledonia Minerals is expected to pay a $1 dividend next year ($D_1$ = $1). This dividend is expected to grow at a rate of 6 percent per year for the foreseeable future if the merger is not completed. The merger is not expected to change the current dividend rate, but future dividends are expected to grow at a 7 percent rate as a result of the merger.

c. What is the value of a share of stock in Caledonia Minerals prior to the merger?

d. What is the new value of a share of stock, assuming that the merger is completed?

e. Would you recommend that Caledonia go ahead with the merger?

22. Globe Steel has decided to diversify into the home improvement field. As a result of this expansion, Globe's beta value drops from 1.3 to 0.9, and the expected future, long-term growth rate in the firm's dividends drops from 8 to 7 percent. The expected market return is 14 percent; the risk-free rate is 7 percent; and the current dividends per share, D_0, are $3. Should Globe undertake the planned diversification?

23. Tucker Manufacturing Company has a beta estimated at 1.0. The risk-free rate is 6 percent and the expected market return is 12 percent. Tucker expects to pay a $4 dividend next year ($D_1$ = $4). This dividend is expected to grow at 3 percent per year for the foreseeable future. The current market price for Tucker is $40.

a. Is the current stock price an equilibrium price, based upon the SML calculation of k_e for Tucker?

b. What do you think the appropriate equilibrium price is? How will that price be achieved?

24. Highland Pet Supplies Company forecasts earnings per share of $2.50 during the coming year. Highland has always paid a dividend equal to 40 percent of its earnings, and it anticipates continuing this practice. Earnings are expected to increase at a rate of 20 percent per year in years 2 and 3, 15 percent in year 4, and 6 percent per year thereafter. The beta of Highland stock is 1.5, the risk-free rate is 7 percent, and the market risk premium has been estimated to be 8 percent.

a. What is the current (time 0) value of a share of Highland stock?

b. What value would you project for a share of stock at the beginning of year 3?

25. The Super Muench Cookie Company is considering a diversification effort that would move it into small outlets at major malls around the country. Currently, Super Muench has a capital structure consisting of 30 percent debt and 70 percent equity. Super Muench believes that for the riskier retail outlet portion of its business, a more conservative capital structure of 20 percent debt and 80 percent equity is more appropriate. Super Muench's current pretax cost of debt is 12 percent. The firm's average tax rate is 30 percent, and its marginal tax rate is 40 percent.

Another retail cookie company, Dietz's Dessertery, has been identified. Dietz has a beta (leveraged) of 1.2. Dietz's current capital structure consists of 40 percent debt and 60 percent equity. Dietz's tax rate is 40 percent. The risk-free rate is 7 percent and the market risk premium is 7.4 percent.

Super Muench wants to know what risk-adjusted rate of return is appropriate for investments in its retail outlets.

26. Del Sarto's Minuteman Novelties, Inc. (DSMN) expects its earnings to grow from a current (time 0) level of $2 per share to $4 per share over the coming year. After that, earnings are expected to grow at 10 percent per year for five years. The current price of the stock of DSMN is $20 per share. The stock is expected to increase in value by 50 percent over the next 3 years. DSMN's dividend policy is to pay out 50 percent of each year's earnings as dividends. DSMN's marginal tax rate is 40 percent and its average tax rate is 35 percent. Compute DSMN's cost of internal equity capital.

27. Bragg's Fort Corporation has experienced rapidly growing earnings per share at a rate of 20 percent per annum over the past 15 years. The price of the stock of Bragg's is $50 per share. Earnings per share are $3. The current dividend rate is $2 per share. Bragg's has a beta of 1.3. The long-term risk-free rate is 6.9 percent and the expected return on the overall market is 14 percent. The company's bonds are rated Aa by Moody's and currently sell to yield 9 percent. The average tax rate of Bragg's is 30 percent, but its marginal rate is 40 percent.

A new financial analyst has suggested that Bragg's can be valued using a constant growth dividend valuation model. What constant growth rate would that analyst recommend using if she believes in capital market efficiency and the capital asset pricing model? Do you agree with her valuation recommendation? Why or why not?

http:// 28. Visit Ibbotson's Web site and see how they've fit CAPM to the stock prices of five different companies. Compare each company's "adjusted beta" to its "peer group" beta. What factors would account for the differences?
http://www.ibbotson.com/research/fama/page0002.asp

http:// 29. Read the sample issue of the *Cost of Capital Quarterly* at Ibbotson's Web site. Find and report the median cost of equity capital for normal-size firms and then compare it to the cost for small-cap firms. Does the difference seem excessive to you? Why? Justify the difference in terms of risk.
http://www.ibbotson.com/research/size_premium/page0000.asp

■ SOLUTIONS TO SELF-TEST PROBLEMS

ST1. Net proceeds = $946 − $11 = $935

$$\$935 = \$80(\text{PVIFA}_{k_d,10}) + \$1,000(\text{PVIF}_{k_d,10})$$

Try $k_d = 9\%$

$$\$935 = \$80(6.418) + \$1,000(0.422)$$

$$\$935 \approx \$935.44$$

Therefore, $k_i = 9\%(1 − 0.4) = 5.4\%$

ST2. a. $k_e = \dfrac{D_1}{P_0} + g$

$$= \frac{\$3.50(1 + 0.068)}{\$60} + 0.068$$

$$= 0.13 \text{ or } 13\%$$

b. $k'_e = \dfrac{\$3.50(1 + 0.068)}{\$60 − \$3} + 0.068$

$$= 0.134 \text{ or } 13.4\%$$

ST3. $k_e = r_f + \beta(r_m - r_f)$

$\qquad = 7.5\% + 1.3(8.6\%)$

$\qquad = 18.7\%$

ST4. $k_a = 0.60(k_e) + 0.15(k_p) + 0.25(k_i)$

$\qquad = 0.60(18\%) + 0.15(15\%) + 0.25(9\%)$

$\qquad = 15.3\%$

■ GLOSSARY

Beta A measure of systematic risk. It is a measure of the volatility of a security's returns relative to the returns of a broad-based market portfolio of securities.

Business Risk The variability in a firm's operating earnings (EBIT).

Capital Asset Pricing Model (CAPM) A theory that formally describes the nature of the risk-required return trade-off in finance. It provides one method of computing a firm's cost of equity capital.

Cost of Capital The equilibrium rate of return demanded by investors in the securities issued by a firm.

Divisional Cost of Capital A risk-adjusted discount rate for investments being evaluated by a firm's various divisions. It reflects both the differential required returns of equity investors, estimated from the security market line, and a division's differential debt capacity.

Expected Market Return The return investors expect to earn on stocks with an average beta of 1.0.

Financial Risk The additional variability in a company's earnings per share that results from the use of fixed-cost sources of funds, such as debt and preferred stock.

IBES Institutional Brokers Estimate System, a service providing summaries of the earnings growth rate forecasts of security analysts.

Interest Rate Risk The variability in the rate of return or yield on securities that arises from changes in interest rates.

Investment Opportunity Curve A graph or listing showing a firm's investment opportunities (projects) ranked from highest to lowest expected rate of return.

Marginal Cost of Capital The weighted after-tax cost of the next dollar of capital the firm expects to raise to finance a new investment project.

Marketability Risk The ability of an investor to buy and sell an asset (security) quickly and without a significant loss of value.

Optimal Capital Budget The level of capital spending at which a firm's investment opportunity curve just intersects its marginal cost of capital curve.

Risk-Free Rate The rate of return on securities that are free of default risk, such as U.S. Treasury bills.

Security Market Line (SML) A line depicting the risk-required return relationship in the market for all securities.

Weighted Cost of Capital The weighted average of the marginal costs of debt, equity, and preferred stock in proportion to their inclusion in the firm's target capital structure.

An Integrative Case Problem
Cost of Capital

The Marietta Corporation, a large manufacturer of mufflers, tail pipes, and shock absorbers, is presently carrying out its financial planning for next year. In about two weeks, at the next meeting of the firm's board of directors, Frank Bosworth, vice-president of finance, is scheduled to present his recommendations for next year's overall financial plan. He has asked Donna Botello, manager of financial planning, to gather the necessary information and perform the calculations for the financial plan.

The company's divisional staffs, together with corporate finance department personnel, have analyzed several proposed capital expenditure projects. The following is a summary schedule of acceptable projects (defined by the company as projects having internal rates of return greater than 8 percent):

Project	Investment Amount (in millions of dollars)	Internal Rate of Return
A	$10.0	25%
B	20.0	21
C	30.0	18
D	35.0	15
E	40.0	12.4
F	40.0	11.3
G	40.0	10
H	20.0	9

All projects are expected to have one year of negative cash flow followed by positive cash flows over the remaining years. In addition, next year's projects involve modifications and expansion of the company's existing facilities and products. As a result, these projects are considered to have approximately the same degree of risk as the company's existing assets.

Botello feels that this summary schedule and detailed supporting documents provide her with the necessary information concerning the possible capital expenditure projects for next year. She now can direct her attention to obtaining the data necessary to determine the cost of the capital required to finance next year's proposed projects.

The company's investment bankers indicated to Bosworth in a recent meeting that they feel the company could issue up to $50 million of 9 percent first-mortgage bonds at par next year. The investment bankers also feel that any additional debt would have to be subordinated debentures with a coupon of 10 percent, also to be sold at par. The investment bankers rendered this opinion after Bosworth gave an approximate estimate of the size of next year's capital budget, and after he estimated that approximately $100 million of retained earnings would be available next year.

Both the company's financial managers and its investment bankers consider the present capital structure of the company, shown in the following table, to be optimal (assume that book and market values are equal):

Debt	$ 400,000,000
Stockholders' equity:	
Common stock	150,000,000
Retained earnings	450,000,000
	$1,000,000,000

Botello has assembled additional information, as follows:

■ Marietta common stock is presently selling at $21 per share.
■ The investment bankers also have indicated that an additional $75 million in new common stock could be issued to net the company $19 per share.
■ The company's present annual dividend is $1.32 per share. However, Bosworth feels fairly certain that the board will increase it to $1.415 per share next year.
■ The company's earnings and dividends have doubled over the past 10 years. Growth has been fairly steady, and this rate is expected to continue for the foreseeable future. The company's marginal tax rate is 40 percent.

Using the information provided, answer the following questions. (Note: Disregard depreciation in this case.)

1. Calculate the after-tax cost of each component source of capital.
2. Calculate the marginal cost of capital for the various intervals, or "packages," of capital the company can raise next year. Plot the marginal cost of capital curve.
3. Using the marginal cost of capital curve from Question 2, and plotting the investment opportunity curve, determine the company's optimal capital budget for next year.
4. Should Project G be accepted or rejected? Why?
5. What factors do you feel might cause Bosworth to recommend a different capital budget than the one obtained in Question 3?
6. Assume that a sudden rise in interest rates has caused the cost of various capital components to increase. The pretax cost of first-mortgage bonds has increased to 11 percent; the pretax cost of subordinated debentures has increased to 12.5 percent; the company's common stock price has declined to $18; and new stock could be sold to net Marietta $16 per share.
   a. Recompute the after-tax cost of the individual component sources of capital.
   b. Recompute the marginal cost of capital for the various intervals of capital Marietta can raise next year.
   c. Determine the optimal capital budget for next year at the higher cost of capital.
   d. How does the interest rate surge affect Marietta's optimal capital budget?

e✗cel

e✗cel

CAPITAL STRUCTURE CONCEPTS

12

1. Capital structure is defined as the relative amount of permanent short-term debt, long-term debt, preferred stock, and common equity used to finance a firm. The optimal capital structure occurs at the point at which the cost of capital is minimized and firm value is maximized.

2. Leverage involves the use of fixed operating costs or fixed capital costs by a firm.

3. Business risk is the inherent variability or uncertainty of a firm's operating income. Business risk is caused by many factors, including sales variability and the use of operating leverage.

4. Financial risk is the additional variability of earnings per share and the increased probability of insolvency resulting from the use of fixed cost sources of capital, such as debt and preferred stock.

5. The value of the firm is independent of capital structure given perfect capital markets and no corporate income taxes.

KEY CHAPTER CONCEPTS

6. The optimal capital structure consists entirely of debt if a corporate income tax exists and there are no financial distress costs or agency costs.

7. Given a corporate income tax, financial distress costs, and agency costs, an optimal capital structure consists of some combination of both debt and equity.

8. Changes in the capital structure often serve as a signal to outside investors about management's expectations concerning future earnings prospects for the company.

9. According to the pecking order theory, companies prefer internal financing to external financing and, given that external financing is necessary, they prefer to issue debt securities first and then issue equity securities as a last resort.

CORPORATE DELEVERAGING*

The decade of the 1980s witnessed a large number and variety of corporate restructurings, including changes in the ownership, asset structure, and/or capital structure of companies. Mergers and acquisitions (takeovers), asset divestitures, and stock buybacks are all examples of corporate restructurings. Many corporate restructurings significantly alter the capital structure of the firm.

Over the period from 1983 to 1990, leveraged restructurings took more than $500 billion of equity out of the stock market. Among nonfinancial corporations, debt as a percentage of total capitalization rose from 34.2% at the end of 1983 to 46.8% at the end of 1990.

The following examples indicate some of the types of leveraged restructurings and their impact on the firm's balance sheet:

■ In 1988 the investment firm of Kohlberg Kravis Roberts & Co. (KKR) purchased RJR Nabisco for $25 billion in an LBO transaction. This represented the largest corporate takeover in history. The buyout price of $109 per share of common stock was approximately twice the pretakeover share price. Upon completion of this LBO transaction, *RJR Nabisco had a debt-to-equity ratio of 25 to 1.*

■ During the late 1980s the Gillette Company borrowed $1.5 billion to buy back some of its common stock in order to avoid a takeover attempt by Coniston Partners (an investment firm) and investor Ronald Perelman. As a result of these transactions, *Gillette had a negative shareholders' equity at the end of 1988.*

■ In 1988 Campeau Corporation (a Canadian corporation controlled by financier Robert Campeau) purchased

Federated Department Stores, a large department store chain, for $7.67 billion, and *financed 97% of the purchase price with debt* (including assumed Federated debt). Two years later Federated filed for bankruptcy when it was unable to meet the required debt payments.

Along with a significant decrease in merger and acquisition activity in the early 1990s, the trend has been toward deleveraging—that is, the use of more equity and less debt in the capital structures of corporations. For example, 1991 was the first year since 1983 during which a decrease in aggregate debt-equity ratios and a positive net issuance of equity securities occurred (i.e., new equity issues less equity retired by stock buy-backs and acquisitions).

The companies in the examples given—RJR Nabisco, Gillette, and Fed-

erated Department Stores—used various methods to deleverage their balance sheets:

■ KKR sold new issues of preferred and common stock and used cash flows from operations and asset sales to retire some of the debt it incurred in financing the purchase of RJR Nabisco. These actions reduced its debt-to-equity ratio to 2.8 to 1 at the end of 1992.

■ Gillette used strong cash flows from operations and the proceeds from the purchase of $600 million in convertible preferred stock by Warren Buffett's Berkshire Hathaway Company to reduce its former debt level of nearly $1.7 billion to less than $750 million in 1991.

■ Federated Department Stores emerged from bankruptcy in 1992 with much less debt in its capital structure by getting its creditors (i.e., banks and bondholders) to exchange their debt (i.e., loans and bonds) for a combination of cash, new debt securities, and equity in the reorganized company.

By deleveraging, companies are able to price their products more competitively in order to win new markets, to invest in new technology for improvements in productivity, and to pay lower interest rates on future borrowings. This chapter focuses on some theoretical aspects of the relationship between a firm's capital structure and its valuation and cost of capital. The practice of capital structure decision making is covered in the following chapter.

*Fred R. Bleakley, "A Decade of Debt Is Now Giving Way to the Age of Equity," *Wall Street Journal* (December 16, 1991): A1.

INTRODUCTION

Capital structure is defined as the amount of permanent short-term debt,[1] long-term debt, preferred stock, and common equity used to finance a firm. In contrast, *financial structure* refers to the amount of total current liabilities, long-term debt, preferred stock, and common equity used to finance a firm. Thus, capital structure is part of the financial structure, representing the permanent sources of the firm's financing. This chapter deals only with the total permanent sources of a firm's financing; the decision about what proportions of debt should be long-term and short-term is considered in Chapter 15.

To illustrate the capital structure concept, suppose that Baker Oil Company currently has $10 million in permanent short-term debt, $40 million in long-term debt outstanding, $10 million in preferred stock, and $40 million in common equity (common stock and retained earnings). In this case, Baker's current capital structure is said to be "50 percent debt, 10 percent preferred stock, and 40 percent common equity."[2] Thus, the capital structure pertains to the permanent debt, preferred stock, and common equity portion of the balance sheet.

The emphasis of capital structure analysis is on the firm's long-range **target capital structure,** that is, the capital structure at which the firm ultimately plans to operate. For most companies, the current and target capital structures are virtually identical, and calculating the target structure is a straightforward process. Occasionally, however, companies find it necessary to change from their current capital structure to a different target. The reasons for such a change may involve a change in the company's asset mix (and a resulting change in its risk) or an increase in competition that may imply more risk. For example, in response to increased risk and competition in the electric utility industry, Standard and Poor's, a bond rating agency, reduced the desired proportion of debt in the capital structure of an AA-rated utility from a range of 42 to 47 percent to a range of 39 to 46 percent. As a consequence many utilities have moved toward more conservative capital structures.

This chapter examines some of the basic concepts used in determining a firm's optimal capital structure. The following chapter develops a number of tools of analysis that can assist managers in making actual capital structure decisions.

CAPITAL STRUCTURE DECISIONS AND MAXIMIZATION OF SHAREHOLDER WEALTH

What is meant by a firm's optimal capital structure? The **optimal capital structure** is the mix of debt, preferred stock, and common equity that *minimizes* the *weighted cost* to the firm *of* its employed *capital.* At the capital structure where the weighted cost of capital is minimized, the total value of the firm's securities (and, hence, the value of the firm) is maximized. As a result, the minimum-cost capital structure is called the *optimal* capital structure.

---

[1]*Permanent* short-term debt is contrasted with *seasonal* short-term debt. Short-term debt financing policy is discussed in Chapter 15.

[2]Companies normally do not distinguish in their capital structure between whether common equity is obtained by retained earnings or new common stock. In other words, only the *total* common shareholders' equity is considered, not the *relative* amounts in the common stock, contributed capital in excess of par, and retained earnings accounts.

The amount of debt contained in a firm's optimal capital structure is often referred to as the firm's **debt capacity.** The optimal capital structure and, accordingly, the debt capacity of a firm are determined by factors including the business risk of the firm, the tax structure, the extent of potential financial distress (e.g., bankruptcy) and agency costs, and the role played by capital structure policy in providing signals to the capital markets regarding the firm's performance. Each of these factors is considered in the sections below.

Assumptions of Capital Structure Analysis

The analysis that follows is based on some important assumptions. First, it is assumed that a firm's investment policy is held constant when we examine the effects of capital structure changes on firm value and particularly on the value of common stock. This assumption means that the level and variability of operating income (EBIT) is not expected to change as changes in capital structure are contemplated. Therefore, capital structure changes affect only the distribution of the operating income between the claims of debtholders, preferred stockholders, and common stockholders.

By assuming a constant investment policy, we also assume that the investments undertaken by the firm do not materially change the debt capacity of the firm. This assumption does not always hold in practice, but for the overwhelming majority of investment projects, it is a realistic assumption that also helps us focus on the key determinants of an optimal capital structure.

FOUNDATION CONCEPT
BUSINESS RISK

Two elements of risk are primary considerations in the capital structure decision: the business risk and the financial risk of a firm. Financial risk is discussed in the following section. **Business risk** refers to the variability or uncertainty of a firm's operating income (EBIT).

Business risk is often measured by the coefficient of variation of EBIT over time. For example, between 1986 and 1995, the mean level of EBIT for American Brands, a cigarette manufacturer and consumer products firm, was $1.285 billion with a standard deviation of $252.5 million, resulting in a coefficient of variation of 0.20 ($252.5 million/$1.285 billion).[3,4] In comparison, the mean level of EBIT for Delta Airlines over the same period was $54.8 million with a standard deviation of $541.9 million, or a coefficient of variation of 9.89. Delta Airlines had operating losses in four of the ten years under consideration, whereas American Brands did not have operating losses in any of the years.

Many factors influence a firm's business risk (holding constant the effects of all other important factors) including

1. *The variability of sales volumes over the business cycle.* Firms, such as Delta Airlines, whose sales tend to fluctuate greatly over the business cycle have more business risk than firms such as American Brands. For example,

---

[3]A better measure of the coefficient of variation would be the ratio of the standard error of the estimate of a regression line relating EBIT to time divided by the mean value of EBIT from the regression line. This would eliminate much of the bias that results when the simple measure of the coefficient of variation, defined earlier, is computed for a growing firm.

[4]Recall from Chapter 5 that the coefficient of variation is defined as the ratio of the standard deviation to the expected value (mean) and is a measure of relative risk.

during the recession of 1991, financial analysts were forecasting that American Brands would have record high sales and earnings. In contrast, analysts were expecting Delta Airlines to have lower sales and losses during 1991.

2. *The variability of selling prices.* In some industries, prices are quite stable from year to year, or the firm may be able to increase prices regularly over time. This is true for many consumer products, such as brand name prepared food items (e.g., Kraft cheese, Nabisco cookies). In contrast, in other industries, price stability is much less certain. For example, over the past two decades, the oil companies, such as Exxon, Shell Oil, and Mobil, have learned important lessons about the instability of prices as the price of crude oil declined from more than $30 a barrel to less than $10 a barrel. Generally, the more price competitive an industry is, the greater is the business risk for firms in that industry.

3. *The variability of costs.* The more variability there is in the cost of the inputs used to produce a firm's output, the greater is the business risk of that firm. For example, airline companies, such as Delta, American, and United, have been affected significantly by the volatility in the price of jet fuel.

4. *Existence of market power.* Firms that have greater market power, such as General Electric, because of their size or the structure of the industries in which they compete, often have a greater ability to control their costs and the price of their outputs than firms operating in a more competitive market environment. Therefore, the greater is a firm's market power, the less its business risk. When evaluating a firm's market power, it often is useful to consider not only the current competition facing the firm but also potential future competition, especially competition that might develop from abroad.

5. *The extent of product diversification.* All other things held constant, the more diversified a firm's product line, the less variable its operating income is likely to be. For example, IBM has an extensive product line, ranging from computer chip production to personal computers, mid-range computers, and large mainframe computers. When demand for one of its product lines falters, this can be somewhat offset by sales in its other lines. In contrast, Applied Magnetics Corporation primarily produces magnetic recording heads for the computer industry. It has experienced great volatility in operating earnings over time as demand for its limited product line has fluctuated.

6. *The level and rate of growth.* Rapidly growing firms, such as Compaq Computer, often experience great variability in their operating earnings. Rapid growth causes many stresses on the operations of a firm. New facilities must be constructed, often possessing uncertain operating cost characteristics, internal control systems must be expanded and updated, the pool of managerial talent must be increased rapidly, and new products require expensive research and development outlays. These factors often combine to result in high variability of operating income.

7. *The degree of operating leverage (DOL).* Operating leverage involves the use of assets having fixed costs. The more a firm makes use of operating leverage, the more sensitive EBIT will be to changes in sales. The degree of operating leverage is the multiplier effect resulting from a firm's use of fixed operating costs. The DOL is defined as the *percentage change in EBIT* resulting from (divided by) a given *percentage change in sales (output).*[5] Thus, if a firm is subject to considerable sales volatility over the business cycle, the variability

---

[5]The degree of operating leverage is discussed in greater detail in the following chapter.

of EBIT (business risk) can be reduced by limiting the use of assets having fixed costs in the production process. Similarly, if a firm's sales tend to be stable over the business cycle, using a high percentage of fixed-cost assets in the production process will have little impact on the variability of EBIT.

In a sense, the business risk of a firm is determined by the accumulated investments the firm makes over time. These investments determine the industries in which a firm will compete, the amount of market power the firm will possess, and the extent of fixed costs in the production process. Firms in consumer products industries, such as grocery retailing (Albertsons, for example), brewing (Anheuser Busch), food processing (RJR Nabisco), and electric (Duke Power) and natural gas distribution (Atlanta Gas Light) utilities, tend to have low levels of business risk. In contrast, firms in durable goods manufacturing (Chrysler), industrial goods manufacturing (Bethlehem Steel), and airlines (Delta Airlines) tend to have higher levels of business risk.

Business Risk: Systematic or Unsystematic Risk?

Business risk possesses elements of both systematic risk and unsystematic risk. Some of the variability in operating income that results from business risk cannot be diversified away by investors who hold a broad-based portfolio of securities. For example, the variability attributable to business cycle behavior is clearly systematic. In contrast, the variability attributable to specific managerial decisions, such as product line diversity, is primarily unsystematic. When analysts attempt to assess the specific total risk of a firm, they must consider both systematic and unsystematic components of that risk. A firm may encounter operating (and financial) difficulty because of both economywide factors that impact its operations and because of unique decisions made by its management.

  FOUNDATION CONCEPT
FINANCIAL RISK AND FINANCIAL LEVERAGE

Financial risk refers to the additional variability of earnings per share *and* the increased probability of insolvency that arises when a firm uses fixed-cost sources of funds, such as debt and preferred stock, in its capital structure.[6] (Insolvency occurs when a firm is unable to meet contractual financial obligations—such as interest and principal payments on debt, payments on accounts payable, and income taxes—as they come due.) Fixed capital costs represent contractual obligations a company must meet regardless of the EBIT level.[7] The use of increasing amounts of debt and preferred stock raises the firm's fixed financial costs; this, in turn, increases the level of EBIT that the firm must earn in order to meet its financial obligations and remain in business. The reason a firm accepts the risk of fixed-cost financing is to increase the possible returns to stockholders.

---

[6]Long-term, noncancelable leases (often called *financial leases*) also represent a significant source of fixed-cost financing for many firms. They are not discussed in this chapter in order to simplify the analysis. See Chapter 19 for a discussion of lease financing.

[7]In financial emergencies, firms are able to omit preferred dividends. Omitting preferred dividends has many undesirable consequences for the firm, however (see Chapter 6). Therefore, the payment of preferred dividends is treated here as if it were a contractual obligation similar to interest.

The use of fixed-cost financing sources is referred to as the use of **financial leverage.** Financial leverage causes a firm's earnings per share (EPS) to change at a rate greater than the change in operating income (EBIT). For example, if a firm is 100 percent equity financed and EBIT increases (decreases) by 10 percent, EPS also will increase (decrease) by 10 percent. When financial leverage, such as long-term debt, is used, a 10 percent change in EBIT will result in a greater than 10 percent change in EPS. Figure 12-1 illustrates the concept of financial leverage. Line A represents the financial leverage used by a firm financed *entirely with common stock.* A given percentage change in EBIT results in the *same* percentage change in EPS.

Line B represents a firm that uses debt (or other sources of fixed-cost funds) in its capital structure. As a result, the *slope* of the EPS-EBIT line is increased, thus increasing the responsiveness of EPS to changes in EBIT. As can be seen in Figure 12-1, a given change in EBIT yields a larger change in EPS if the firm is using debt financing (ΔEPS_B) than if the firm is financed entirely with common stock (ΔEPS_A).

It is also clear from Figure 12-1 that the use of financial leverage magnifies the returns—both positive and negative—to the shareholder. When EBIT is at a relatively high level, such as $EBIT_2$, Firm B's use of financial leverage *increases*

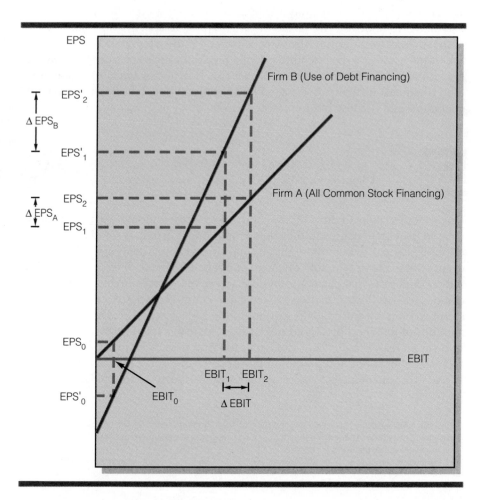

EPS above the level attained by Firm A, which is not using financial leverage. On the other hand, when EBIT is relatively low—for example, at $EBIT_0$—the use of financial leverage *decreases* EPS below the level that would be obtained otherwise; that is, $EPS'_0 < EPS_0$. At $EBIT_0$, the use of financial leverage results in negative EPS for Firm B.

Financial Risk: Systematic or Unsystematic Risk?

Financial risk, like business risk, contributes to both the systematic and unsystematic risk of a firm's securities. To the extent that the use of *financial leverage* magnifies variations in operating income that come about because of unsystematic risk factors, financial leverage contributes to the unsystematic risk of a firm's securities.

Financial researchers also have studied the contribution that financial leverage makes to the systematic risk of a firm's securities.[8] It is well established that systematic risk is a function both of financial risk *and* operating risk. Hence, security analysts and investors find the measurement of a company's financial risk to be an important element of good financial analysis.

Effect of Financial Leverage on Stockholder Returns and Risk

Firms employ financial leverage to increase the returns to common stockholders. These increased returns are achieved at the expense of increased risk. The objective of capital structure management is to find the capital mix that leads to shareholder wealth maximization.

To illustrate the effects of financial leverage on stockholder returns and risk, consider the following example of KMI Technology, Inc. As can be seen in Table 12-1, KMI has total assets of $1 million. Suppose KMI expects an operating income (EBIT) of $200,000. If KMI uses debt in its capital structure, the cost of this debt will be 10 percent per annum.[9] Table 12-1 shows the effect of an increase in the debt to total assets ratio (debt ratio) from 0 percent to 40 percent and to 80 percent on the return on stockholders' equity. With an all-equity capital structure, the return on equity is 12 percent. At a debt ratio of 40 percent, the return on equity increases to 16 percent, and at a debt ratio of 80 percent, the return on equity is 36 percent. KMI is earning 20 percent (pretax) on its assets. The cost of debt is 10 percent pretax. Thus, when KMI uses debt in its capital structure, the difference between the return on its assets and the cost of debt accrues to the benefit of equity holders.

However, this increased equity return is achieved only at the cost of higher risk. For example, if EBIT declines by 25 percent to $150,000, the return on equity for the all-equity capital structure also declines by 25 percent to 9.0 percent. In contrast, at a 40 percent debt ratio, the return on equity declines by 31.25 percent to 11 percent. At an 80 percent debt ratio, the return on equity declines by 41.67 percent to 21 percent. The effects of a 60 percent reduction in

[8]An excellent review of the relationship between business risk and financial risk on one hand and systematic risk on the other can be found in C. M. Callahan and R. M. Mohr, "The Determinants of Systematic Risk: A Synthesis," *The Financial Review* (May 1989): 157–181. See also J. M. Gahlon and James A. Gentry, "On the Relationship between Systematic Risk and the Degrees of Operating and Financial Leverage," *Financial Management* (Summer 1982): 15–23.

[9]In this simplified example, we hold the cost of debt constant as the ratio of debt to total assets increases from 0 percent to 80 percent. In reality, as the debt ratio increases, the cost of debt can also be expected to increase.

TABLE 12-1
Effect of Financial Leverage on
Stockholder Returns and Risk at
KMI Technology, Inc.

LEVERAGE FACTOR (DEBT/TOTAL ASSETS)	0%	40%	80%
Total assets	$1,000,000	$1,000,000	$1,000,000
Debt (at 10% interest)	$ 0	$ 400,000	$ 800,000
Equity	1,000,000	600,000	200,000
Total liabilities and equity	$1,000,000	$1,000,000	$1,000,000
Expected operating income (EBIT)	200,000	$ 200,000	$ 200,000
Interest (at 10%)	0	40,000	80,000
Earnings before tax	$ 200,000	160,000	$ 120,000
Income tax at 40%	80,000	64,000	48,000
Earnings after tax	$ 120,000	$ 96,000	$ 72,000
Return on equity	12.0%	16.0%	36.0%
Effect of a 25 Percent Reduction in EBIT to $150,000			
Expected operating income (EBIT)	$ 150,000	$ 150,000	$ 150,000
Interest (at 10%)	0	40,000	80,000
Earnings before tax	$ 150,000	$ 110,000	$ 70,000
Income tax at 40%	60,000	44,000	28,000
Earnings after tax	$ 90,000	$ 66,000	$ 42,000
Return on equity	9.0%	11.0%	21.0%
Effect of a 60 Percent Reduction in EBIT to $80,000			
Expected operating income (EBIT)	$ 80,000	$ 80,000	$ 80,000
Interest (at 10%)	0	40,000	80,000
Earnings before tax	$ 80,000	$ 40,000	$ 0
Income tax at 40%	32,000	16,000	0
Earnings after tax	$ 48,000	$ 24,000	$ 0
Return on equity	4.8%	4.0%	0.0%

EBIT to $80,000 are even more dramatic. In this case, the pretax return on assets is *less than* the pretax cost of debt. To pay the prior claims of the debtholders, the equity returns are reduced to a level below those that prevail under the all-equity capital structure. In the case of a 40 percent debt ratio, the return on equity is only 4.0 percent, and in the case of an 80 percent debt ratio, the return on equity is 0 percent. Thus, it can be seen that the use of financial leverage both increases the potential returns to common stockholders and the risk, or variability, of those returns.

Generally, *the greater is a firm's business risk, the less the amount of financial leverage that will be used in the optimal capital structure,* holding constant all other relevant factors.

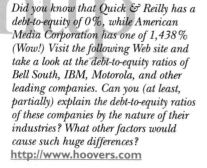

Did you know that Quick & Reilly has a debt-to-equity of 0%, while American Media Corporation has one of 1,438% (Wow!) Visit the following Web site and take a look at the debt-to-equity ratios of Bell South, IBM, Motorola, and other leading companies. Can you (at least, partially) explain the debt-to-equity ratios of these companies by the nature of their industries? What other factors would cause such huge differences?
http://www.hoovers.com

CAPITAL STRUCTURE THEORY

In this section, we develop some simplified models of the relationship between capital structure, as measured by the ratio of debt to total assets, and the cost of capital (and the value of the firm). These models help isolate the impact of personal and corporate taxes, financial distress costs, and agency costs on the determination of an optimal capital structure. In this section we also consider some other factors that influence the choice of long-term financing instruments, including the impact of signaling and information asymmetries. We conclude with a brief review of the market reaction to various capital structure altering transactions that firms undertake.

Capital Structure without a Corporate Income Tax

In 1958, two prominent financial researchers, Franco Modigliani and Merton Miller (MM), showed that, under certain assumptions, a firm's overall cost of capital, and therefore its value, is *independent* of capital structure.[10] In particular, assume that the following *perfect* capital market conditions exist:

- There are no transaction costs for buying and selling securities.
- A sufficient number of buyers and sellers exists in the market, so no single investor can have a significant influence on security prices.
- Relevant information is readily available to all investors and is costless to obtain.
- All investors can borrow or lend at the same rate.

MM also assumed that all investors are rational and have homogeneous expectations of a firm's earnings. Additionally, firms operating under similar conditions are assumed to face the same degree of business risk. This assumption is called the *homogeneous risk class assumption*. Finally, MM assumed that there are no income taxes. MM later relaxed this no-tax assumption. The results of the tax case follow after the no-tax case discussion.

In the no-tax MM case, the cost of debt and the overall cost of capital are constant regardless of a firm's financial leverage position, measured as the firm's debt-to-equity ratio, B/E. As a firm increases its relative debt level, the cost of equity capital, k_e, increases, reflecting the higher return requirement of stockholders due to the increased risk imposed by the additional debt. The increased cost of equity capital exactly offsets the benefit of the lower cost of debt, k_d, so that the overall cost of capital does not change with changes in capital structure. This is illustrated in Figure 12-2. Because the firm's market value is calculated by discounting its expected future operating income by the weighted (marginal) cost of capital, k_a, the market value of the firm is independent of capital structure.

MM support their theory by arguing that a process of arbitrage will prevent otherwise equivalent firms from having different market values simply because of capital structure differences. **Arbitrage** is the process of simultaneously buying and selling the same or equivalent securities in different markets to take advantage of price differences and make a profit. Arbitrage transactions are risk-free. For example, suppose two firms in the same industry differed only in that one was *levered* (that is, it had some debt in its capital structure) and the other was *unlevered* (that is, it had no debt in its capital structure). If the MM theory did not hold, the unlevered firm could increase its market value by simply adding debt to its capital structure. However, in a perfect capital market without transactions costs, MM argue that investors would not reward the firm for increasing its debt. Stockholders could change *their* own financial debt-equity structure without cost to receive an equal return. Therefore, stockholders would not increase their opinion of the market value of an unlevered firm just because it took on some debt.

The MM argument is based on the *arbitrage* process. If one of two unlevered firms with identical business risk took on some debt and the MM theory did not hold, its value should increase and, therefore, so would the value of its stock. MM suggest that under these circumstances, investors will sell the overpriced

---

[10]Merton H. Miller (along with Harry M. Markowitz and William F. Sharpe) was a recipient of the 1990 Nobel Prize for Economics for his pioneering work on the cost of capital and capital structure. See Franco Modigliani and Merton Miller, "The Cost of Capital, Corporation Finance, and the Theory of Investment," *American Economic Review* 48 (June 1958): 261–296.

FIGURE 12-2
Weighted Cost of Capital: Miller and Modigliani (No Taxes)

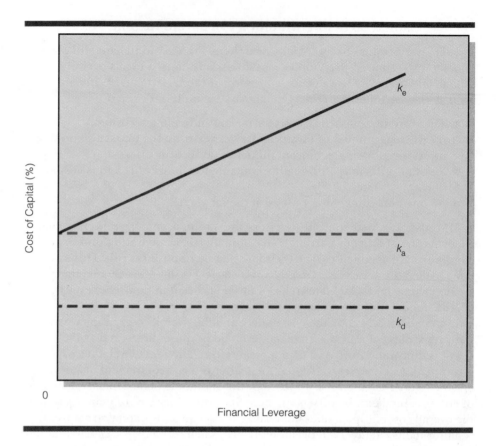

stock of the levered firm. They then can use an arbitrage process of borrowing, buying the unlevered firm's stock, and investing the excess funds elsewhere. Through these costless transactions, investors can increase their return without increasing their risk. Hence, they have substituted their own personal financial leverage for corporate leverage. MM argue that this arbitrage process will continue until the selling of the levered firm's stock drives down its price to the point where it is equal to the unlevered firm's stock price, which has been driven up due to increased buying.

The arbitrage process occurs so rapidly that the market values of the levered and unlevered firms are equal. Therefore, MM conclude that *the market value of a firm is independent of its capital structure in perfect capital markets with no income taxes.*

The MM no-tax theory is illustrated in the example shown in Table 12-2. The table contains financial data on two firms, U and L, that have equal levels of operating risk and differ only in their capital structure. Firm U is unlevered, and firm L is levered, with a perpetual debt, *B*, of $2,000 in its capital structure. For simplicity, we assume that the income of both firms available for stockholders is paid out as dividends. As a result, the expected growth rate of both firms is zero, because no income is available for the firms to reinvest.

The present value of both firms is calculated using the following perpetuity valuation equation:[11]

[11]Recall from Chapter 6 that the value of a perpetual bond (Equation 6.8) is equal to the annual interest payment (*I*) divided by the required rate of return (k_d). Also, in Chapter 7, the value of a common stock that pays a constant dividend in perpetuity (Equation 7.9) is equal to the annual dividend payment (*D*) divided by the required rate of return (k_e).

	FIRM U	FIRM L
Equity amount in capital structure, E	$10,000	$8,000
Cost of equity, k_e	10%	11.25%
Debt amount in capital structure, B	—	$2,000
Cost of debt, k_d	—	5%
Net operating income (EBIT)	$ 1,000	$1,000
Less Interest payments to debtholders	—	100
Income available to stockholders (dividend)	$ 1,000	$ 900
Total income available to security holders	$ 1,000	$1,000

TABLE 12-2
Capital Structure without a Corporate Income Tax: Financial Data on Firms U and L

Market value of firm = Market value of equity

+ Market value of debt

$$= \frac{D}{k_e} + \frac{I}{k_d} \qquad (12.1)$$

where D is the annual amount of dividends paid to the firm's stockholders; I is the interest paid on the firm's debt; k_e is the return required on common equity; and k_d is the return required on debt. The required return on debt, k_d, is assumed to equal the coupon rate on the debt, i. For firm U, the present value of the expected future cash flows is $10,000, calculated as follows:

$$\text{Market value of firm U} = \frac{\$1,000}{0.10}$$

$$= \$10,000$$

For firm L, the present value is also $10,000, calculated as follows:

$$\text{Market value of firm L} = \frac{\$900}{0.1125} + \frac{\$100}{0.05}$$

$$= \$8,000 + \$2,000$$

$$= \$10,000$$

Thus, the market values of firms U and L are equal. This example shows that the market value of the firm is independent of capital structure, assuming that the MM theory holds and no corporate income tax exists.

Capital Structure with a Corporate Income Tax

Next, the relationship between capital structure and firm market value is considered, assuming that a corporate income tax exists. Table 12-3 shows financial data for an unlevered firm, U, and a levered firm, L. The total income available to the security holders of firm U is $600, and assuming a cost of equity capital equal to 10 percent, the value of firm U is calculated using Equation 12.1 to be $6,000.

Because interest paid to debtholders is a tax-deductible expense, the total income available to the debt and equity security holders of firm L, shown in Table 12-3, is $640. This amount is greater than the $600 available to the firm U equity security holders by $40. The $40 amount is the **tax shield** caused by the tax

	FIRM U	FIRM L
Equity amount in capital structure, E	$6,000	$4,000
Cost of equity, k_e	10%	11.25%
Debt amount in capital structure, B	—	$2,000
Cost of debt, k_d	—	5%
Net operating income (EBIT)	$1,000	$1,000
Less Interest payments to debtholders	—	100
Income before taxes	$1,000	$ 900
Corporate tax, $T = 40\%$	$ 400	$ 360
Income available to stockholders (dividend)	$ 600	$ 540
Total income available to security holders	$ 600	$ 640

deductibility of the interest payments.[12] The annual tax shield amount is calculated using the following equation:

$$\text{Tax shield amount} = i \times B \times T \qquad (12.2)$$

$$= (0.05) \times (\$2,000) \times (0.40)$$

$$= \$40$$

The total market value of firm L is obtained using Equation 12.1:

$$\text{Market value of firm L} = \frac{D}{k_e} + \frac{I}{k_d}$$

$$= \frac{\$540}{0.1125} + \frac{\$100}{0.05}$$

$$= \$4,800 + \$2,000$$

$$= \$6,800$$

In this example, the value of firm L is greater than firm U's value by an amount equal to $800. This difference in value is caused by the tax shield. In fact, the difference in value between the levered and unlevered firm is equal to the present value of the tax shield from the perpetual debt:

$$\text{Present value of tax shield} = \frac{i \times B \times T}{i}$$

$$= B \times T \qquad (12.3)$$

In this equation, the annual tax shield amount, iBT, is discounted at a rate, $i(i = k_d)$. In the case of firm L, the present value of the tax shield is $800, calculated as follows:

$$\text{Present value of tax shield} = \$2,000 \times 0.40$$

$$= \$800$$

We can now state that the market value of the levered firm is equal to the market value of the unlevered firm plus the present value of the tax shield:

---

[12]Calculation of the tax shield assumes that a company can take full advantage of the deductibility of interest payments in computing its tax liability. Firms with substantial accumulated losses or firms that can shield income with depreciation may not be able to realize the full amount of the tax savings associated with debt financing.

$$\begin{array}{ccc} \text{Market value of} & = & \text{Market value of} & + & \text{Present value of} \\ \text{levered firm} & & \text{unlevered firm} & & \text{tax shield} \end{array} \quad (12.4)$$

From this equation, we can conclude that the value of the firm increases linearly as the amount of debt in the capital structure increases, as shown in Panel (a) of Figure 12-3. This result implies that a firm should increase its level of debt to the point at which the capital structure consists entirely of debt. In other words, the market value of the firm is maximized and its optimal capital structure is achieved when capital structure is all debt. As shown in Panel (b) of Figure 12-3, the weighted cost of capital k_a declines with increases in financial leverage.

In practice, we *normally* do not observe companies with extremely high levels of debt in their capital structures. (The large volume of financial restructurings and leveraged buyouts during the 1980s, such as the KKR takeover of RJR Nabisco, which have resulted in debt ratios of 80 to more than 90 percent, suggest that many managers are paying closer attention to the advantages of debt financing.) Even in the face of leveraged buyouts, however, we still do not observe many companies that approach a 100 percent debt-financed capital structure. Hence, other factors must be influencing the determination of an optimal capital structure. Two of the most important factors are financial distress costs and agency costs. These are considered in the following section.

Capital Structure with a Corporate Income Tax, Financial Distress Costs, and Agency Costs

This section examines the effect of capital structure on the market value of the firm given the existence of a corporate income tax and financial distress and agency costs.

Financial Distress Costs. From a practical viewpoint, a firm cannot expect to gain the benefits associated with the tax deductibility of interest payments without also increasing certain costs. One significant cost category is the costs of financial distress. Financial distress costs include the costs incurred to avoid bankruptcy as well as the direct and indirect costs incurred if the firm files for bankruptcy protection.[13] As a firm increases its debt level, lenders may demand higher interest rates to compensate for the increased financial risk taken on by the firm. The higher interest payments constitute a cost to the firm. In the extreme, lenders may choose not to lend at all. Under these conditions, the firm may have to forgo acceptable projects. Thus, the firm incurs an opportunity cost. In addition, some customers and potential customers may lose confidence in the firm's ability to continue in existence and instead buy from other companies more likely to remain in business. This loss of customer confidence is another financial distress cost. A company that experiences cash flow, or insolvency, problems, which leads to bankruptcy, must incur legal and accounting costs as it attempts to restructure itself financially. Finally, if the firm is forced to liquidate, assets may have to be sold at less than their market values. These costs are also bankruptcy costs.

Altman has measured the size of bankruptcy costs for industrial firms.[14] He defines *bankruptcy costs* to consist of direct costs (costs paid by debtors in the bankruptcy and restructuring process) and indirect costs (costs associated with

---

[13]Bankruptcy is discussed in more detail in Chapter 22.
[14]Edward Altman, "A Further Empirical Investigation of the Bankruptcy Cost Question," *Journal of Finance* 39 (1984): 1067–1089.

FIGURE 12-3
Market Value of the Firm and
Cost of Capital as a Function of
Capital Structure (with Corporate
Income Tax)

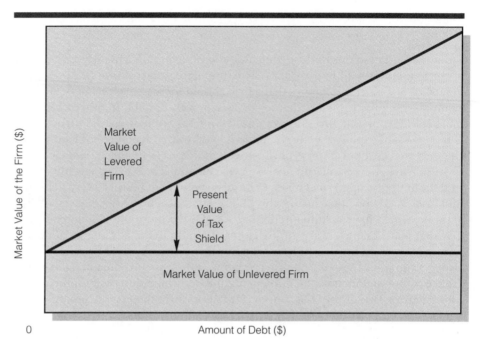

(a) Market Value of the Firm as a Function of Capital Structure

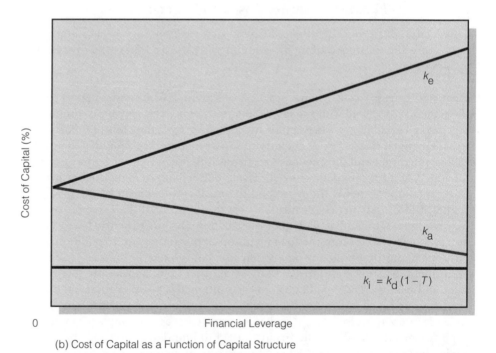

(b) Cost of Capital as a Function of Capital Structure

the loss of customers, suppliers, and key employees plus the managerial effort expended to manage the firm in its distressed condition). Altman found evidence that the direct costs of bankruptcy average about 6 percent of firm value at the time of filing for bankruptcy. Direct plus indirect costs as a percent of firm value averaged 12.1 percent three years prior to filing and 16.7 percent at the time of filing. Thus, it appears that bankruptcy costs are significant, even if one adjusts for the expected time of occurrence and the probability of occurrence. Castanias offers evidence that supports this conclusion when he finds that small firms in industries with high failure rates tend to use less financial leverage.[15]

The likelihood of bankruptcy is not a linear function of a firm's debt ratio. Rather, there is evidence that it increases at an increasing rate beyond some threshold level. Accordingly, bankruptcy costs also become more important beyond this threshold debt ratio.

Agency Costs. As discussed in Chapter 1, in most large firms, the security holders (often referred to as the *principals*), both debtholders and common stockholders, are not in a position to actively manage the firm's investment, financing, and daily operational activities. Security holders employ "agents" to carry out these important activities. Under these circumstances, conflicts can develop between the interests of the principal and those of the agent. In the case of the choice between debt and common equity financing, the debtholders can be viewed as the principal and the common stockholders can be viewed as the agents. The common stockholders are in a position to direct the investment and financing decisions of the firm through the elected board of directors and the managers hired by the board.

When debt is used in the capital structure of a firm, common stockholders have incentives to undertake actions that may be detrimental to the interests of the debtholders. These actions include investing in extremely risky projects. The higher expected returns from risky investments accrue to the benefit of stockholders. Also, in the absence of restraints, stockholders are inclined to increase the proportions of debt in the capital structure, thus diminishing the protection afforded the earlier bondholders. The higher risk resulting from these actions may lead to a reduction in a firm's bond ratings. Lower bond ratings translate into lower bond values in the marketplace and thus a loss in wealth to the bondholders.

Not surprisingly, bondholders will want to take actions that reduce the prospect of this wealth transfer to stockholders. Agency theory argues that expected agency costs will be borne by the agent. Therefore, debtholders can be expected to demand a higher interest rate on the bonds they purchase in order to compensate them for the expected wealth losses. As an alternative, monitoring and bonding expenses can be incurred to reduce the incidence of these agency problems and thereby reduce the interest rate that will be demanded by bondholders. In the case of bonds, monitoring and bonding expenses take the form of protective covenants in the bond indenture.

Typical protective covenants place restrictions on the payment of dividends, limit the issuance of additional debt, limit the sale of assets, and limit the type of assets that may be acquired. (Protective covenants are discussed in greater detail in Chapters 6 and 18.) However, the more extensive are the protective covenants, the more costly it is to monitor compliance. In addition, increasingly extensive covenants may restrict the operating freedom and efficiency of managers, to the detriment of both stockholders and bondholders.

Thus, the firm can be viewed as having a choice along a continuum. At one extreme, there would be no protective covenants, resulting in high interest rates, low or no monitoring costs, and no restrictions placed on the operating freedom of managers. At the other extreme, all decisions of the firm would be subject to review by the debtholders. This is obviously not feasible. *Monitoring*

---

[15]Richard Castanias, "Bankruptcy Risk and Optimal Capital Structure," *Journal of Finance* 38 (1983): 1617–1635.

and bonding activities should be carried out by the firm up to the point that the reduction in the interest rate charged by debtholders is balanced against the cost of additional monitoring and bonding activities.

At low debt levels, bondholders do not demand extensive protective covenants and monitoring arrangements, because the risk exposure for the bondholders is viewed as being quite limited.[16] Also, at low debt levels, the interest cost of debt financing will be low. As the amount of debt increases as a proportion of the total capital structure, bondholders find themselves subject to increased risk that managers (acting on behalf of stockholders) may make investments or take financing actions that could harm the current bondholders. Accordingly, monitoring costs are assumed to increase with increases in a firm's financial leverage, resulting in an increase in the *implicit* cost of debt, including the cost of monitoring and lost operating efficiency. This increase in the cost of debt has the effect of reducing the total value of the firm's securities.

In summary, the agency costs of debt are an increasing function of the proportion of debt in the capital structure of a firm. Because of this, agency costs represent another powerful reason why, in addition to the increased probability of financial distress or bankruptcy at higher debt ratios, a firm will choose a value-maximizing capital structure that is less than the 100 percent debt corner solution implied by the MM analysis.

Value-Maximizing Capital Structure. The preceding discussion of the impact of taxes, bankruptcy costs, and agency costs indicates that the market value of a levered firm can be represented by the following equation:

$$\text{Market value of levered firm} = \left(\begin{array}{c} \text{Market value} \\ \text{of unlevered} \\ \text{firm} \end{array}\right) + \left(\begin{array}{c} \text{Present} \\ \text{value of} \\ \text{tax shield} \end{array}\right)$$

$$- \left(\begin{array}{c} \text{Present value} \\ \text{of financial} \\ \text{distress costs} \end{array}\right) - \left(\begin{array}{c} \text{Present} \\ \text{value of} \\ \text{agency} \\ \text{costs} \end{array}\right) \quad (12.5)$$

Figure 12-4 illustrates this relationship graphically. As indicated in this figure and in Equation 12.5, the present value of expected financial distress costs and the agency costs associated with debt financing offset the present value of the tax shield accruing from debt—resulting in an optimal (value-maximizing) amount of debt, B^*, and an optimal capital structure, B^*/E. This approach to determining the optimal capital structure is sometimes referred to as the *static tradeoff theory.*[17]

The Cost of Capital and the Optimal Capital Structure

In this section, we examine the relationship between the cost of capital and the firm's capital structure when corporate taxes, financial distress costs, and agency

---

[16]The takeover of RJR Nabisco by KKR appears to have altered this market perception somewhat. RJR's bondholders experienced a wealth loss of 20 percent or more as a result of the high leverage used in the takeover by KKR. This transaction had a significant impact on the corporate bond market as investors in the bonds of the most creditworthy U.S. firms demanded higher returns to compensate them for this heretofore unexpected risk.

[17]Stewart C. Myers, "The Capital Structure Puzzle," *Journal of Finance* 39 (July 1984): 575–592; and Stewart C. Myers, "Still Searching for Optimal Capital Structure," *Journal of Applied Corporate Finance* 6 (Spring 1993): 4–14.

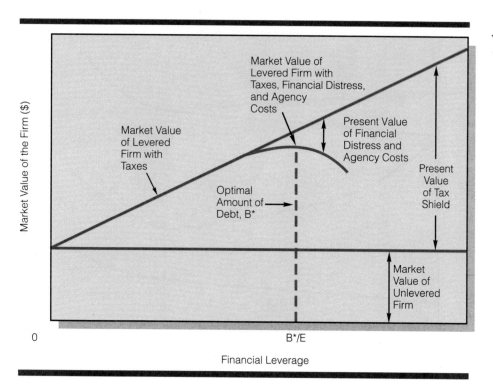

costs are considered. In the following analysis, we assume that capital structure contains only permanent debt and common equity; that is, we assume, for simplicity, that no preferred stock financing is used.

The first step in the analysis considers the relationship between the cost of debt and capital structure. All other things being equal, investors in debt consider the debt less risky if the firm has a low, rather than high, proportion of debt in its capital structure. As the proportion of debt in the capital structure increases, investors require a higher return on the more risky debt. And because the firm's cost of capital is the investor's required return, the cost of debt increases as the proportion of debt increases.

The precise relationship between the cost of debt and the debt ratio is difficult to determine, because it is impossible to observe the cost of debt at two different capital structures (at the same time) for a single firm. Nevertheless, as discussed earlier, evidence suggests that the cost of debt increases rather slowly for moderate amounts of debt. There is a point at which the capital markets begin to consider any new debt "excessive" and therefore much more risky. The cost of debt curve, k_i, in Figure 12-5 illustrates such a relationship. The actual region where the cost of debt begins to increase more rapidly varies by firm and industry, depending on the firm's level of business risk.

The next step in this analysis focuses on the relationship between the cost of equity capital and capital structure. When a firm has low financial leverage, that is, a low debt-to-equity ratio, any equity employed is less risky than equity used when the firm is financed with a relatively high proportion of debt. Earlier in this chapter, it was shown that the greater the fraction of debt used, the greater is the variability in earnings per common share. In addition, the greater the fraction of

FIGURE 12-5
Overall Cost of Capital as a
Function of Capital Structure

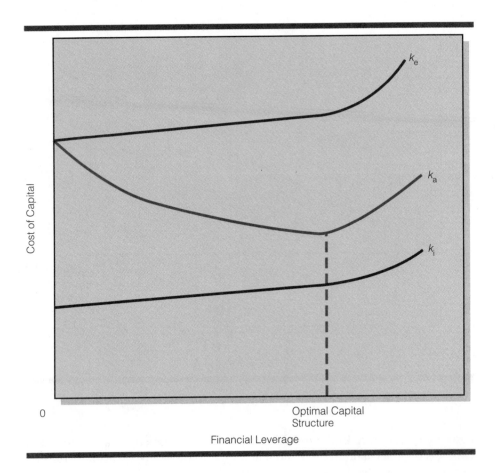

debt used, the greater is the risk of financial distress. Because the returns expected by stockholders in the form of present and future dividends depend partly on current earnings, it can be concluded that variability in earnings per common share can result in variability of the returns to investors; that is, greater risk. Therefore, it can be stated that investors' required returns and the cost of equity capital increase as the relative amount of debt used to finance the firm increases.

Once again, the exact nature of the relationship between the cost of equity and financial leverage is difficult to determine in practice. However, there is agreement that the cost of equity capital increases at a relatively slow rate as the debt proportion increases up to moderate amounts. Then, in the range where additional debt begins to be viewed as excessive and more risky, the cost of equity increases more rapidly. This is shown in Figure 12-5. As is true in the debt illustration, the region where the cost of equity capital, k_e, begins to increase more rapidly varies by firm and industry.

The relationship between the weighted cost of capital, k_a, and financial leverage now can be considered. The following equation (which is a modified version, without preferred stock in the capital structure, of Equation 11.1 from Chapter 11):

$$k_a = \left(\frac{E}{B + E}\right)(k_e) + \left(\frac{B}{B + E}\right)(k_i) \qquad (12.6)$$

can be used to calculate k_a for any level of financial leverage, provided that the values of k_e and k_i at the level of financial leverage are known. (B is the market value of debt, and E is the market value of equity in the firm's capital structure.) Because the relationships between financial leverage and k_i and k_e have been developed, the relationship between k_a and financial leverage follows accordingly. The k_a curve, shown in Figure 12-5, begins at $k_a = k_e$, because, by definition, the weighted cost of capital for an all-equity firm equals the cost of equity. As even small increments of debt are used, k_a becomes lower; as the debt proportion continues to increase from moderate to excessive, k_a "bottoms out" and then begins to increase. The resulting saucer-shaped curve contains a point at which the firm's overall cost of capital is minimized and its value maximized. This point is the firm's *optimal capital structure*. If the firm is thought of as a cash-flow generator, then the lower the discount rate (the weighted cost of capital), the higher is the firm's value.

Other Considerations in the Capital Structure Decision

In this section, we briefly discuss some other factors that have an impact on the determination of an optimal capital structure. These factors include personal tax effects, industry effects, signaling effects, and managerial preference effects.

Personal Tax Effects. The MM tax case led to the conclusion that, in the absence of financial distress costs and agency costs, the firm should attempt to minimize its taxes by employing the maximum amount of debt. The MM tax case did not consider the effect of personal income taxes, however. Miller has extended the tax case analysis to include both corporate and personal income taxes.[18] Miller argued that although a firm can save taxes by increasing its debt ratio, individual investors would pay greater taxes on their returns from the firm if these returns were predominantly interest, rather than dividends and capital appreciation on common stock. Historically, the tax code has favored capital gains income from stock over interest income, because capital gains generally have been taxed at a lower rate than ordinary income (including interest income) and because taxes on capital gains are deferred until the capital gain is realized.

Miller concluded that when both personal and corporate income taxes are considered, there is no optimal debt ratio for an individual firm, although there is an optimal amount of total debt in the marketplace, reflecting the difference in corporate and personal tax rates. The Tax Reform Act of 1986, which removed much of the personal tax advantage associated with equity financing, has raised questions about the validity of the Miller model. Under the current tax law, corporate borrowing probably has some associated tax advantage as long as a firm is confident it can use the full amount of the interest tax shield. This debt advantage depends upon corporate tax rates being higher than the tax rates of bondholders. The debt advantage disappears as the probability of being able to use the full amount of the interest tax shield declines.

Industry Effects. A number of studies have found significant capital structure differences among industries. For example, a study by Kester shows a debt-to-equity ratio for firms in the paper industry of 1.36 times, compared with 0.079

---

[18]M. H. Miller, "Debt and Taxes," *Journal of Finance* 32 (May 1977): 261–276.

for firms in the pharmaceutical industry.[19] Kester found that the more profitable are firms, the less debt they tend to use. Other studies have found that leverage ratios are negatively related to the frequency of bankruptcy in the industry. Also, some evidence indicates that firms generating stable cash flows over the business cycle tend to have higher debt ratios. In general, the studies of industry effects in capital structure tend to conclude that there is an optimal capital structure for individual firms. The market rewards firms that achieve this capital structure.

Signaling Effects. The preceding discussion assumed that all investors have access to relevant information concerning a firm's future earnings prospects. However, this assumption may not be valid in many cases. Instead one can argue that the officers and managers of a company, as insiders, have access to information about the expected future earnings and cash flows of the firm that is not available to outside investors. This situation is referred to as **asymmetric information.** Given that managers know more about the firm than do outside investors, changes in a company's investment, financing, or dividend decisions can represent a *signal* to investors concerning management's assessment of the expected future returns, and hence market value, of the company.

Thus, when a firm issues new securities, this event can be viewed as providing a signal to the financial marketplace regarding the future prospects of the firm or the future actions planned by the firm's managers.[20] Ross argues that signals provided by capital structure changes are credible because of the potential bankruptcy cost penalty incurred if the implied future cash flows do not occur. In general, studies of capital structure changes have found that new common equity offerings tend to yield *negative* stock price responses and new debt offerings tend to yield no significant stock price responses.[21] Repurchases of common stock have led to large *positive* announcement returns on the company's common stock. Actions that increase leverage generally have been associated with *positive* stock returns, and actions that decrease leverage are associated with negative stock returns. The results of many studies of capital structure changes are consistent both with direct effects of the change, such as the benefits of greater tax shields, and with indirect information effects. Therefore, when a firm makes capital structure changes it must be mindful of the potential signal that the proposed transaction will transmit to the marketplace regarding the firm's current and future earnings prospects and the intentions of its managers.[22]

Managerial Preference Effects: The Pecking Order Theory. According to the **pecking order theory**, as developed by Myers, a firm may not have a particular

---

[19]W. C. Kester, "Capital and Ownership Structure: A Comparison of United States and Japanese Manufacturing Corporations," *Financial Management* (Spring 1986): 5–16.

[20]Stephen Ross, "The Determination of Financial Structure: The Incentive-Signaling Approach," *Bell Journal of Economics* 8 (1977): 23–40.

[21]See Thomas E. Copeland and J. Fred Weston, *Financial Theory and Corporate Policy,* 3rd ed. (Reading, MA: Addison-Wesley, 1988): 519–523 for a summary of empirical evidence concerning the effects of capital structure changes on security prices.

[22]See Ronald W. Masulis, *The Debt/Equity Choice* (Cambridge, MA: Ballinger Publishing, 1988) for an excellent discussion and review of the signaling literature as it relates to capital structure decisions.

target or optimal capital structure.[23] Instead, a company's capital structure changes when an imbalance between internal cash flows, net of cash dividend payments, and acceptable (i.e., NPV > 0) investment opportunities occurs. Firms whose investment opportunities exceed internally generated funds tend to issue more debt securities and hence have higher debt ratios. Conversely, highly profitable firms with limited needs for investment funds will tend to have lower debt ratios. In this situation, the firm builds up **financial slack** in the form of highly liquid assets (i.e., cash and marketable securities) and unused debt capacity. Financial slack allows a firm to take advantage of any attractive investment opportunities that may occur in the future.

The pecking order theory indicates that firms prefer internal financing (retained earnings) to external financing (new security issues). This preference for internal financing is based on two considerations. First, because of flotation costs of new security issues, internal financing is less costly than external financing. Second, internal financing avoids the discipline and monitoring that occurs when new securities are sold publicly. Also, according to the pecking order theory, dividends are "sticky," that is, many firms are reluctant to make major changes in dividend payments and only gradually adjust dividend payout ratios to reflect their investment opportunities, and thereby avoid the issuance of new securities.[24]

If external financing is required, the "safest" securities, namely debt, are issued first. As discussed in Chapter 7, the flotation costs of debt securities are generally lower than the costs of equity securities. Also, as noted in the discussion of asymmetric information above, the stock market tends to react negatively to announcements of new common stock offerings, whereas debt security announcements tend to have little impact on stock prices. As additional external financing is needed, the firm will work down the pecking order—from safe to more risky debt, then possibly to convertible debt, and finally to common equity as a last resort.

A survey of large (Fortune 500) firms suggests that the pecking order theory is more descriptive of how financing decisions are made in practice compared with optimal capital structure theories based on financial distress costs or agency costs.[25] Furthermore, among the respondents expressing a preference for the pecking order theory, approximately 85 percent, ranked internal equity (retained earnings) as their first choice for financing new investments. Among external financing sources, straight (i.e., nonconvertible) debt was ranked highest (most preferred) and external equity (i.e., new common stock) was ranked lowest (least preferred) by the respondents. Given a list of principles that govern their financing decisions, maintaining financial flexibility and ensuring long-term survivability ranked highest among respondents. Of lesser importance were such considerations as maintaining a predictable source of funds, maximizing security prices, and maintaining financial independence. Finally, principles such as maintaining a high debt rating and maintaining comparability with other firms in the industry were ranked relatively unimportant by the respondents.

---

[23]See Myers, "The Capital Structure Puzzle," *Journal of Finance* 39 (July 1984): 575–592; and Myers, "Still Searching for Optimal Capital Structure," *Journal of Applied Corporate Finance* 6 (Spring 1993): 4–14.

[24]This is referred to as a *stable dollar dividend policy*. See Chapter 14.

[25]J. Michael Pinegar and Lisa Wilbricht, "What Managers Think of Capital Structure Theory: A Survey," *Financial Management* 18, no. 4 (Winter 1989): 82–91.

Managerial Implications of Capital Structure Theory

The rich body of theoretical and empirical capital structure studies provides important insights for financial managers. First, it is clear that the capital structure decision is one of the centrally important decisions facing financial managers. There is little doubt that changes in capital structure result in changes in the market value of the firm. Second, the benefits of the tax shield from debt lead to increased firm value, at least up to the point that increased financial distress and agency costs begin to offset the debt advantage. Third, the optimal capital structure is influenced heavily by the business risk facing the firm. Fourth, when managers make explicit changes in a firm's capital structure, these actions transmit important information to investors about expected future returns and the market value of a company.

 ETHICAL ISSUES
LBO STAKEHOLDER IMPACTS

The rapid pace of mergers and acquisitions during the 1980s has raised many interesting issues regarding the rights of the various corporate stakeholders in these transactions. Leveraged buyouts result in dramatic increases in the amount of debt used to finance a firm—up to 95 percent of the capital structure in some cases. The use of this large amount of debt permits a small group of investors to acquire ownership and control of a large firm with a relatively small equity investment. By concentrating ownership and control, the equity agency problems associated with separation of ownership from control are largely eliminated. Also, the heavy burden of fixed charges from the debt financing forces managers to increase dramatically the efficiency of operations of the acquired firm. These benefits from LBOs are well documented.[26]

However, these benefits do not come without significant costs. For example, increased operating efficiency is often achieved by eliminating jobs, reducing other payroll expenses, and closing inefficient plants. The LBO of Safeway resulted in 63,000 managers and workers losing their jobs through store sales and closings. Those employees who were reemployed by the new owners of sold stores received significantly lower wages. Many communities lost the substantial civic contributions and support of a formerly generous Safeway.[27]

Bondholders of acquired firms typically experience a loss in the value of their bonds when an LBO is announced.[28] In the RJR Nabisco acquisition, Metropolitan Life Insurance Company and other bondholders sued KKR because of the loss the RJR bondholders experienced at the time of the takeover.

LBOs raise important ethical questions. How are the competing interests of stakeholders to be resolved in LBOs and other significant financial transactions?

---

[26]See, for example, G. P. Baker and K. H. Wruck, "Organization Changes and Value Creation in Leveraged Buyouts: The Case of O. M. Scott & Sons Company," *Journal of Financial Economics* 25 (1989): 163–190.

[27]A Pulitzer Prize-winning discussion of the impact of the Safeway LBO can be found in Susan C. Faludi, "Safeway LBO Yields Vast Profits But Exacts a Heavy Human Toll," *Wall Street Journal* (May 16, 1990): 1.

[28]For example, see P. Asquith and T. A. Wizman, "Event Risk, Wealth Redistribution and the Return to Existing Bondholders in Corporate Buyouts," *Journal of Financial Economics* (September 1990): 195–214.

These questions rarely have simple answers, however. Some issues to consider when debating the ethics of LBOs are

1. Is it in the long-run interest of employees to maintain staffing levels and operate facilities that are inefficient and reduce the company's ability to compete with other enterprises?
2. Are bondholders truly harmed in LBO transactions, considering the bond covenants for which they contracted when they purchased the bonds and the relationship between bond yields and covenant protection?

INTERNATIONAL ISSUES
CAPITAL STRUCTURE

Multinational firms have a more complex capital structure decision than purely domestic firms. Should each foreign subsidiary maintain the same capital structure as the parent's consolidated structure, or should separate capital structures be established for each foreign subsidiary? Most firms tend to pay relatively little attention to establishing uniquely optimal capital structures for their foreign subsidiaries. Rather, the approach normally is one of establishing an optimal capital structure for the multinational firm as a whole and then adjusting foreign subsidiary capital structures to take advantage of local financing opportunities. The object is to minimize the multinational firm's overall cost of capital.

Factors that determine the specific capital structure that will prevail for each subsidiary include

1. *Exchange rate risk in the host country.* When exchange rate risk is high, there will be a preference to raise more of the subsidiary's capital in the financial markets of the host country.
2. *Local industry standards.* In some countries, it may be common for firms to have higher debt ratios than in others. Subsidiary capital structures normally reflect these traditions.[29]
3. *Host country requirements.* Some governments place restrictions on the capital structure of multinational firms operating in their country.
4. *Risk of expropriation.* The greater is the risk that a multinational firm's subsidiary assets may be expropriated without adequate compensation, the greater will be the incentive for the multinational firm to finance that subsidiary with debt capital, especially debt capital raised in the host country and not guaranteed by the parent firm.
5. *Availability of special, low-cost financing in a host country.* Some host countries make low-cost financing available to multinational firms to stimulate additional investment. When this low-cost financing is available, firms normally take advantage of it.

Other factors that determine the optimal capital structure for a multinational firm as a whole include the increased capital market access for firms operating in several different countries and the extent to which political and economic country risk is diversified by the firm. The diversification of political and

---

[29] J. M. Collins and W. S. Sekely, "The Relationship of Headquarters Country and Industry Classification to Financial Structure," *Financial Management* (Autumn 1983): 45–51.

economic country risk is largely a function of the number and location of foreign subsidiaries of the multinational firm.

■ SUMMARY

- *Capital structure* is defined as the relative amount of permanent short-term debt, long-term debt, preferred stock, and common stock used to finance a firm. The capital structure decision is important to the firm, because there exists in practice a capital structure at which the *cost of capital* is minimized. This minimum-cost capital structure is the *optimal* capital structure, because the value of the firm is maximized at this point.
- The *business risk* of a firm refers to the variability of a firm's operating income. It is influenced by the variability of sales volumes, prices, and costs over the business cycle. Business risk is also influenced by a firm's market power and its use of operating leverage.
- The *financial risk* of a firm is the additional variability of earnings per share and the increased probability of insolvency that arises when a firm uses fixed-cost sources of funds, such as debt and preferred stock, in its capital structure.
- The use of financial leverage results in an increase in perceived risk to the suppliers of a firm's capital. To offset this increased risk, higher returns are required.
- Modigliani and Miller show that the value of the firm is *independent* of capital structure given perfect capital markets and no corporate income taxes. MM also show that the optimal capital structure consists entirely of debt if a corporate income tax exists.
- Given a corporate income tax, financial distress costs, and agency costs, an optimal capital structure consisting of both debt and equity is shown to exist. Determination of the optimal capital structure involves balancing the present value of the tax shield accruing from debt financing against the present value of the expected financial distress costs and the agency costs associated with debt financing.
- Given that managers have access to better information about a firm's future prospects than do outside investors (*asymmetric information*), capital structure changes often *signal* important information to investors about a firm's future prospects.
- According to the *pecking order theory*, there is no particular optimal capital structure for a firm. Companies prefer internal financing to external financing and, given that external financing is necessary, they prefer to issue debt securities first and then equity securities only as a last resort.

■ QUESTIONS AND TOPICS FOR DISCUSSION

1. Explain the research results of Modigliani and Miller in the area of capital structure.
2. What is the relationship between the value of a firm and its capital structure without a corporate income tax? With a corporate income tax?
3. What is the relationship between the value of a firm and its capital structure, given the existence of a corporate income tax, bankruptcy costs, and agency costs?

4. What is the *asymmetric information* concept? What role does this concept play in a company's decision to change its financial structure or issue new securities?
5. According to the pecking order theory, if additional external financing is required, what type of securities should a firm issue first? Last?
6. Explain why, according to the pecking order theory, firms prefer internal financing to external financing.
7. What assumptions are required in deriving the proposition that a firm's cost of capital is independent of its capital structure?
8. What role does *signaling* play in the establishment of a firm's capital structure?
9. What is arbitrage? How is it used in deriving the proposition that the value of a firm is independent of its capital structure?
10. Explain the difference between business risk and financial risk.
11. What other factors besides operating leverage can affect a firm's business risk?

■ SELF-TEST PROBLEM

ST1. Ogden Optical Company has estimated the following costs of debt and equity capital (with bankruptcy and agency costs) for various proportions of debt in its capital structure:

Proportion of Debt $\left(\dfrac{B}{B+E}\right)$	Cost of Debt, k_i	Cost of Equity, k_e
0.00	—	10.0%
0.10	4.0%	10.1
0.20	4.2	10.3
0.30	4.4	10.8
0.40	4.8	11.4
0.50	5.5	12.5
0.60	6.6	14.5
0.70	8.0	18.0

Determine the firm's optimal capital structure.

■ PROBLEMS*

1. Referring back to Table 12-2, calculate the value of firm L (without a corporate income tax) if the equity amount in its capital structure decreases to $5,000 and the debt amount increases to $5,000. At this capital structure, the cost of equity is 15 percent.
2. **a.** Referring back to Table 12-3, calculate the value of firm L (with a corporate income tax) if the equity amount in its capital structure decreases to $3,000 and the debt amount increases to $3,000.
   b. For firm L (with equity = $3,000 and debt = $3,000), calculate the income available to the stockholders and the cost of equity.
3. Two firms, No Leverage, Inc. and High Leverage, Inc., have equal levels of operating risk and differ only in their capital structure. No Leverage is unlevered and High Leverage has $500,000 of perpetual debt in its capital structure. Assume that the perpetual annual income of both firms available for stockholders is paid out as dividends. Hence, the growth rate for both firms is zero. The income tax rate for both

*Colored numbers denote problems that have check answers provided at the end of the book.

firms is 40 percent. Assume that there are no financial distress costs or agency costs. Given the following data:

	No Leverage, Inc.	High Leverage, Inc.
Equity in capital structure	$1,000,000	$500,000
Cost of equity, k_e	10%	13%
Debt in capital structure	—	$500,000
Pretax cost of debt, k_d	—	7%
Net operating income (EBIT)	$ 100,000	$100,000

determine the
a. Market value of No Leverage, Inc.
b. Market value of High Leverage, Inc.
c. Present value of the tax shield to High Leverage, Inc.
4. Jersey Computer Company has estimated the costs of debt and equity capital (with bankruptcy and agency costs) for various proportions of debt in its capital structure:

Proportion of Debt	Cost of Debt, k_i	Cost of Equity, k_e
0.00	—	12.0%
0.10	4.7%	12.1
0.20	4.9	12.5
0.30	5.1	13.0
0.40	5.5	13.9
0.50	6.1	15.0
0.60	7.5	17.0

a. Determine the firm's optimal capital structure.
b. Suppose that the firm's current capital structure consists of 30 percent debt (and 70 percent equity). How much higher is its weighted cost of capital than at the optimal capital structure?
5. Piedmont Instruments Corporation has estimated the following costs of debt and equity capital for various fractions of debt in its capital structure.

Debt Fraction	k_i	k_e with Financial Distress Costs and without Agency Costs	k_e with Financial Distress Costs and Agency Costs
0.00	—	12.00%	12.00%
0.10	4.8%	12.05	12.05
0.30	4.9	12.10	12.20
0.40	5.0	12.20	12.60
0.45	5.2	12.40	13.40
0.50	5.7	12.80	14.80
0.60	7.0	15.00	18.00

a. Based on these data, determine the company's optimal capital structure (i) with financial distress costs and without agency costs and (ii) with financial distress and agency costs.
b. Suppose the company's actual capital structure is 50 percent debt and 50 percent equity. How much higher is k_a at this capital structure than at the optimal value of k_a, with financial distress and agency costs?
c. Is it necessary in practice for the company to know precisely its optimal capital structure? Why?

6. Arrow Technology, Inc. (ATI) has total assets of $10,000,000 and expected operating income (EBIT) of $2,500,000. If ATI uses debt in its capital structure, the cost of this debt will be 12 percent per annum.

   a. Complete the following table:

	Leverage Ratio (Debt/Total Assets)		
	0%	25%	50%
Total assets	═════	═════	═════
Debt (at 12% interest)	─────	─────	─────
Equity	─────	─────	─────
Total liabilities and equity	═════	═════	═════
Expected operating income (EBIT)	─────	─────	─────
Less: Interest (at 12%)	─────	─────	─────
Earnings before tax	─────	─────	─────
Less: Income tax at 40%	─────	─────	─────
Earnings after tax	═════	═════	═════
Return on equity	─────	─────	─────

Effect of a 20% Decrease in EBIT to $2,000,000

	0%	25%	50%
Expected operating income (EBIT)			
Less: Interest (at 12%)	─────	─────	─────
Earnings before tax	─────	─────	─────
Less: Income tax at 40%	─────	─────	─────
Earnings after tax	═════	═════	═════
Return on equity	─────	─────	─────

Effect of a 20% Increase in EBIT to $3,000,000

	0%	25%	50%
Expected operating income (EBIT)			
Less: Interest (at 12%)	─────	─────	─────
Earnings before tax	─────	─────	─────
Less: Income tax at 40%	─────	─────	─────
Earnings after tax	═════	═════	═════
Return on equity	─────	─────	─────

   b. Determine the percentage change in return on equity of a 20 percent decrease in expected EBIT from a base level of $2,500,000 with a debt/total assets ratio of
      i. 0%
      ii. 25%
      iii. 50%
   c. Determine the percentage change in return on equity of a 20 percent increase in expected EBIT from a base level of $2,500,000 with a debt/total assets ratio of
      i. 0%
      ii. 25%
      iii. 50%
   d. Which leverage ratio yields the highest expected return on equity?
   e. Which leverage ratio yields the highest variability (risk) in expected return on equity?
   f. What assumption was made about the cost of debt (i.e., interest rate) under the various capital structures (i.e., leverage ratios)? How realistic is this assumption?

7. Visit the Stock Center at Thomson Investors Network and calculate the debt ratio of a major auto manufacturer, such as General Motors. Then calculate the debt ratio of a major service company, such as Merrill Lynch. Based on what you learned about leverage in this chapter, what would account for the difference in their debt ratios?
http://www.thomsoninvest.net

http://

http://

8. Visit the following Web site and compare the ten companies with the highest debt-to-equity ratios of the ten companies with the lowest. What conclusions can you derive from your comparison?
http://www.hoovers.com

SOLUTION TO SELF-TEST PROBLEM

ST1.

Proportion of Debt $\left(\dfrac{B}{B+E}\right)$	Cost of Debt, k_i	Cost of Equity, k_e	Weighted Cost of Capital, k_a
0.00	—	10.0%	10.00%
0.10	4.0%	10.1	9.49
0.20	4.2	10.3	9.08
0.30	4.4	10.8	8.88
0.40	4.8	11.4	8.76
0.50	5.5	12.5	9.00
0.60	6.6	14.5	9.76
0.70	8.0	18.0	11.00

Note: $k_a = \left(\dfrac{E}{B+E}\right)k_e + \left(\dfrac{B}{B+E}\right)k_i$

The optimal capital structure consists of 40 percent debt and 60 percent equity since this minimizes the firm's cost of capital.

■ GLOSSARY

Agency Costs Costs incurred by owners of a firm when the firm is managed by others; includes monitoring costs, bonding costs, and any losses that cannot be eliminated economically by monitoring and bonding.

Arbitrage The process of simultaneously buying and selling the same or equivalent securities in different markets to take advantage of temporary price differences.

Asymmetric Information The assumption that managers of a company, as insiders, have access to information about expected future earnings and cash flows that is not available to outside investors.

Business Risk The inherent variability or uncertainty of a firm's operating earnings (EBIT).

Capital Structure The amount of permanent short-term debt, long-term debt, preferred stock, and common equity used to finance a firm.

Debt Capacity The amount of debt contained in a firm's optimal capital structure.

Financial Distress Costs The costs incurred to avoid bankruptcy plus the direct and indirect costs incurred if a firm files for bankruptcy protection.

Financial Leverage The extent to which a firm is financed by securities having fixed costs or charges, such as debt and preferred stock.

Financial Risk The additional variability of a company's earnings per share and the increased probability of insolvency that result from the use of fixed-cost sources of funds, such as debt and preferred stock. In general, the more financial leverage a firm uses, the greater is its financial risk.

Financial Slack Highly liquid assets (i.e., cash and marketable securities) plus unused debt capacity which allows a firm to take advantage of any attractive investment opportunities.

Financial Structure The amount of current liabilities, long-term debt, preferred stock, and common equity used to finance a firm.

Operating Leverage The extent to which a firm uses assets having fixed costs.

Optimal Capital Structure The capital structure that minimizes a firm's weighted cost of capital and, therefore, maximizes the value of the firm.

Pecking Order Theory A capital structure theory indicating that firms prefer internal financing (retained earnings) to external financing (new security issues) and that, if external financing is required, debt is preferred to new common stock.

Signal Changes in investment, financing, or dividend policies that convey information to outside investors concerning management's assessment of the expected future returns of the company.

Target Capital Structure The proportions of permanent short-term debt, long-term debt, preferred stock, and common equity that a firm desires to have in its capital structure.

Tax Shield The amount of tax savings from the deductibility of interest payments on debt in computing corporate income taxes.

CAPITAL STRUCTURE MANAGEMENT IN PRACTICE

1. The degree of operating leverage (DOL) is defined as the percentage change in EBIT resulting from a 1 percent change in sales.
   a. The degree of operating leverage approaches a maximum as the firm comes closer to operating at its breakeven level of output.
   b. All other things being equal, the higher a firm's DOL, the greater is its business risk.
   c. Business risk, the inherent variability of a firm's EBIT, is also influenced by the variability of sales and operating costs over time.

2. The degree of financial leverage (DFL) is defined as the percentage change in earnings per share (EPS) resulting from a 1 percent change in EBIT.
   a. The degree of financial leverage approaches a maximum as the firm comes closer to operating at its loss level, the level where EPS = $0.
   b. All other things being equal, the higher a firm's DFL, the greater is its financial risk.
   c. Financial risk, the additional variability of a firm's EPS that resuls from the use of financial leverage, also can be measured by various financial ratios, such as the debt to total assets ratio and the times interest earned ratio.

KEY CHAPTER CONCEPTS

3. The degree of combined leverage (DCL) is defined as the percentage change in earnings per share resulting from a 1 percent change in sales. It also is equal to the DOL for a company times that company's DFL. The degree of combined leverage used by a firm is a measure of the overall variability of EPS due to the use of fixed operating and capital costs, as sales levels change.

4. EBIT-EPS analysis is an analytical technique that can be used to help determine the circumstances under which a firm should employ financial leverage. The indifference point in EBIT-EPS analysis is that level of EBIT where earnings per share are the same regardless of which of two alternative capital structures is used.

5. Cash insolvency analysis can be used to evaluate the impact of a proposed capital structure on the cash position of a firm during a major business downturn.

6. Other factors that are considered when establishing a capital structure policy are industry standards, profitability and need for funds, lender requirements, managerial risk aversion, and the desire of owners to retain control of the firm.

DEREGULATION AND BUSINESS RISK OF ELECTRIC UTILITIES*

A number of industries in the United States, such as investor-owned electric power companies, operate as "regulated monopolies." Electric power is made available to the consumer through a production process characterized by three distinct stages. First, the power is generated in generating plants. Next, in the transmission stage, the power is transmitted at high voltage from the generating site to the locality where it is used. Finally, in the distribution stage, the power is distributed to the individual users. The complete process may take place as part of the operations of a single firm, or the producing firm may sell power at wholesale rates to a second enterprise that carries out the distribution function. In the latter case, the distribution firm is often a department within the municipal government serving the locality or a consumers' cooperative.

Firms producing electric power are subject to regulation at several levels. Integrated firms carrying out all three stages of production are usually regulated by state public utility commissions. These commissions set the rates to be charged to the final consumers. The firms normally receive exclusive rights to serve individual localities through franchises granted by local governing bodies. As a consequence of their franchises, electric power companies have well-defined markets within which they are the sole provider of output. Finally, the Federal Energy Regulatory Commission (FERC) has the authority to set rates on power that crosses state lines and on wholesale power sales.

Despite operating as regulated monopolies, electric utilities have always been subject to some degree of competition. For example, electric utilities compete with gas companies in supplying energy for heating and cooling. Also, regions of the country compete with each other to attract additional industrial demand for electricity by offering economic development rates or tax

breaks. Likewise, self-generation of electricity is always an option for large industrial users.

More recently, deregulation has subjected electric utility companies to additional competition. The National Energy Policy Act (NEPA) of 1992 mandated a more open transmission system, which will provide more power supply options to wholesale customers who are not locked into long-term contracts. Additionally, the prospect of increased competition at the wholesale level may lead retail customers to pressure utilities

and state regulators to reduce prices or allow them to choose suppliers.

Recall from the previous chapter that business risk refers to the uncertainty of a firm's EBIT, which is caused by a number of factors, including variability of revenues, selling prices, and costs, as well as a firm's market power, product diversification, growth, and degree of operating leverage. In the future, under deregulation, the business risk of electric utility firms will tend to increase since prices and revenues will be more variable as rate structures (i.e., prices) become deregulated and subject to market-driven forces. Standard & Poor's, a major credit-rating company, believes that this environment of increased competition will have negative effects on the credit quality of the securities of such firms. Deregulation could be particularly detrimental to electric utility companies in regions of the country that have excess reserves of power, high costs, and that have experienced decreases in demand, such as the Northeast and parts of the Southwest.

The increased business risk associated with deregulation and the resulting lower credit ratings may raise the cost of capital that electric utility companies pay for debt and equity funds. As noted in the previous chapter, this has led some utility companies to adopt more conservative (i.e., less leveraged) capital structures. This chapter focuses on the practical aspects of capital structure decisions, such as those faced by electric utilities.

*Deborah Goldsmith and Debra Bromberg, "Competition Raises Business Risk for Electric Utilities," *Standard & Poor's Creditweek* (June 7, 1993): 37–39.

INTRODUCTION

This chapter focuses on various tools of analysis that can assist managers in making capital structure decisions that will lead to a maximization of shareholder wealth. The following section develops techniques, derived from accounting data, for measuring operating and financial leverage. As discussed in the previous chapter, operating leverage and financial leverage are important components of a firm's business risk and financial risk. Other techniques, namely, *EBIT-EPS analysis* and *cash insolvency analysis,* can aid management in assessing the risk versus return trade-offs associated with the use of debt in a firm's capital structure. The appendix to the chapter discusses *breakeven analysis*—an analytical tool that can provide insights into the business risk facing a firm.

OPERATING AND FINANCIAL LEVERAGE

The concepts of operating and financial leverage were introduced in the previous chapter. In finance, *leverage* is defined as a firm's use of assets and liabilities having fixed costs in an attempt to increase potential returns to stockholders. Specifically, operating leverage involves the use of *assets* having fixed costs, whereas financial leverage involves the use of *liabilities* (and *preferred stock*) having fixed costs.

A firm utilizes operating and financial leverage in the hope of earning returns in excess of the fixed costs of its assets and liabilities, thereby increasing the returns to common stockholders. Leverage is a double-edged sword, however, because it also increases the *variability* or risk of these returns. If, for example, a firm earns returns that are *less* than the fixed costs of its assets and liabilities, then the use of leverage can actually *decrease* the returns to common stockholders. Thus, leverage magnifies shareholders' potential losses as well as potential gains. Leverage concepts are particularly revealing to the financial analyst in that they highlight the *risk-return trade-offs* of various types of financial decisions, such as those involving the capital structure of the firm.

Leverage and the Income Statement

Financial statements of the Allegan Manufacturing Company are referred to throughout this section for purposes of illustration. Table 13-1 contains two types of statements for the firm—a traditional format and a revised format. The traditional format shows various categories of costs as separate entries. *Operating costs* include such items as the cost of sales and general, administrative, and selling expenses. Interest charges and preferred dividends, which represent *capital costs*, are listed separately, as are income taxes.

The revised format is more useful in leverage analysis, because it divides the firm's operating costs into two categories, *fixed* and *variable*.

Short-Run Costs Over the short-run, certain operating costs within a firm vary directly with the level of sales whereas other costs remain constant, regardless of changes in the sales level. Costs that move in close relationship to changes in sales are called **variable costs**. They are tied to the number of units produced

TRADITIONAL INCOME STATEMENT FORMAT

	Sales		$5,000,000
Operating	*Less* Cost of sales	$2,500,000	
leverage	Selling, administrative, and general expenses	1,500,000	
	Total operating costs		4,000,000
	Earnings before interest and taxes (EBIT)		1,000,000
	Less Interest expense		250,000
	Earnings before taxes (EBT)		750,000
Financial	*Less* Income taxes (40% rate)		300,000
leverage	Earnings after taxes (EAT)		450,000
	Less Preferred stock dividends		150,000
	Earnings available to common stockholders		$ 300,000
	Earnings per share (EPS)—100,000 shares		$3.00

REVISED INCOME STATEMENT FORMAT

	Sales		$5,000,000
Operating	*Less Variable* operating costs	$3,000,000	
leverage	*Fixed* operating costs	1,000,000	
	Total operating costs		4,000,000
	Earnings before interest and taxes (EBIT)		1,000,000
	Less Fixed capital costs (interest)		250,000
	Earnings before taxes (EBT)		750,000
Financial	*Less* Income taxes (*variable*), 40% rate		300,000
leverage	Earnings after taxes (EAT)		450,000
	Less Fixed capital costs (preferred stock dividends)		150,000
	Earnings available to common stockholders		$ 300,000
	Earnings per share (EPS)—100,000 shares		$3.00

and sold by the firm, rather than to the passage of time. They include raw material and direct labor costs, as well as sales commissions.

Over the short run, certain other operating costs are independent of sales or output levels. These, termed **fixed costs,** are primarily related to the passage of time. Depreciation on property, plant, and equipment; rent; insurance; lighting and heating bills; property taxes; and the salaries of management all usually are considered fixed costs. If a firm expects to keep functioning, it must continue to pay these costs, regardless of the sales level.

A third category, *semivariable costs,* also can be considered. Semivariable costs are costs that increase in a *stepwise* manner as output is increased. One cost that sometimes behaves in a stepwise manner is management salaries. Whereas these costs generally are considered fixed, this assumption is not always valid. A firm faced with declining sales and profits during an economic downturn often may cut the size of its managerial staff.

Panels (a), (b), and (c) of Figure 13-1 show the behavior of variable, fixed, and semivariable costs, respectively, over the firm's output range.

Not all costs can be classified as either completely fixed or variable; some have both fixed and variable components. Costs for utilities, such as water and electricity, frequently fall into this category. Whereas part of a firm's utility costs (such as electricity) are fixed and must be paid regardless of the level of sales or output, another part is variable in that it is tied directly to sales or production

FIGURE 13-1
Behavior of (a) Variable, (b) Fixed,
and (c) Semivariable Costs

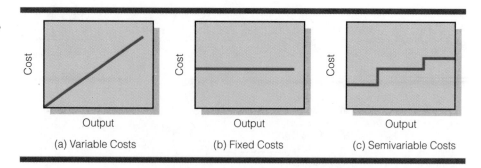

levels. In the revised format of Allegan's income statement, these are divided into their fixed and variable components and included in their respective categories of operating costs.

Note that in the revised income statement format, both interest charges and preferred dividends represent fixed capital costs. These costs are contractual in nature and thus are independent of a firm's level of sales or earnings. Also, note that income taxes represent a variable cost that is a function of earnings before taxes.

Long-Run Costs Over the *long run,* all costs are variable. In time, a firm can change the size of its physical facilities and number of management personnel in response to changes in the level of sales. Fixed capital costs can also be changed in the long run.

Measurement of Operating and Financial Leverage

Fixed obligations allow a firm to magnify small changes into larger ones—just as a small push on one end of an actual lever results in a large "lift" at the other end.

Operating leverage has fixed operating costs for its "fulcrum." When a firm incurs fixed operating costs, a change in sales revenue is magnified into a relatively larger change in earnings before interest and taxes (EBIT). The multiplier effect resulting from the use of fixed operating costs is known as the **degree of operating leverage**.

Financial leverage has fixed capital costs for its "fulcrum." When a firm incurs fixed capital costs, a change in EBIT is magnified into a larger change in earnings per share (EPS). The multiplier effect resulting from the use of fixed capital costs is known as the **degree of financial leverage**.

Degree of Operating Leverage

A firm's *degree of operating leverage* (DOL) is defined as the multiplier effect resulting from the firm's use of fixed operating costs. More specifically, DOL can be computed as the *percentage change* in earnings before interest and taxes (EBIT) resulting from a given *percentage change* in sales (output):

$$\text{DOL at } X = \frac{\text{Percentage change in EBIT}}{\text{Percentage change in sales}}$$

This can be rewritten as follows:

$$\text{DOL at } X = \frac{\frac{\Delta\text{EBIT}}{\text{EBIT}}}{\frac{\Delta\text{Sales}}{\text{Sales}}} \qquad (13.1)$$

where ΔEBIT and ΔSales are the changes in the firm's EBIT and sales, respectively. Because a firm's DOL differs at each sales (output) level, it is necessary to indicate the sales (units of output or dollar sales) point X, at which operating leverage is measured. The degree of operating leverage is analogous to the elasticity concept of economics (for example, price and income elasticity) in that it relates percentage changes in one variable (EBIT) to percentage changes in another variable (sales).

The calculation of the DOL can be illustrated using the Allegan Manufacturing Company example discussed earlier. From Table 13-1, recall that Allegan's variable operating costs were $3 million at the current sales level of $5 million. Therefore, the firm's *variable operating cost ratio* is $3 million/$5 million = 0.60, or 60 percent.

Suppose the firm increased sales by 10 percent to $5.5 million while keeping fixed operating costs constant at $1 million and the variable (operating) cost ratio at 60 percent. As can be seen in Table 13-2, this would increase the firm's earnings before interest and taxes (EBIT) to $1.2 million. Substituting the two sales figures ($5 million and $5.5 million) and associated EBIT figures ($1 million and $1.2 million) into Equation 13.1 yields the following:

$$\text{DOL at } \$5,000,000 = \frac{\frac{(\$1,200,000 - \$1,000,000)}{\$1,000,000}}{\frac{(\$5,500,000 - \$5,000,000)}{\$5,000,000}}$$

$$= \frac{\$200,000}{\$1,000,000} \times \frac{\$5,000,000}{\$500,000}$$

$$= 2.0$$

A DOL of 2.0 is interpreted to mean that each 1 percent change in sales from a base sales level of $5 million results in a 2 percent change in EBIT *in the same*

TABLE 13-2
Effect on Earnings per Share of a 10 Percent Increase in Sales, Allegan Manufacturing Company, Year Ending December 31, 19X1

	(1)		(2)	% CHANGE [(2) − (1)] ÷ (1)
Sales		$5,000,000	$5,500,000	+10%
Less Variable operating costs (0.60 × Sales)	$3,000,000		$3,300,000	+10%
Fixed operating costs	1,000,000		$1,000,000	0%
Total operating costs		4,000,000	4,300,000	+8%
Earnings before interest and taxes		$1,000,000	$1,200,000	+20%
Less Interest payments (fixed capital cost)		250,000	250,000	0%
Earnings before taxes		$ 750,000	$ 950,000	+27%
Less Income taxes (variable), 40%		300,000	380,000	+27%
Earnings after taxes		$ 450,000	$ 570,000	+27%
Less Preferred dividends (fixed capital cost)		150,000	150,000	0%
Earnings available to common stockholders		$ 300,000	$ 420,000	+40%
Earnings per share (100,000 shares)		$ 3.00	$ 4.20	+40%

TABLE 13-3
DOL at Various Sales Levels,
Allegan Manufacturing Company

SALES, TR = $P \times Q$*	DEGREE OF OPERATING LEVERAGE, DOL
$ 500,000	−0.25
1,000,000	−0.67
1,500,000	−1.50
2,000,000	−4.00
2,500,000**	(Undefined)
3,000,000	+6.00
3,500,000	+3.50
4,000,000	+2.67
4,500,000	+2.25
5,000,000	+2.00
5,500,000	+1.83
6,000,000	+1.71

*Total Revenue = Price × Quantity. (See Appendix 13A.)
**Breakeven sales level.

direction as the sales change. In other words, a sales *increase* of 10 percent results in a 10% × 2.0 = 20% *increase* in EBIT. Similarly, a 10 percent *decrease* in sales produces a 10% × 2.0 = 20% *decrease* in EBIT. The greater a firm's DOL, the greater the magnification of sales changes into EBIT changes.

Equation 13.1 requires the use of two different values of sales and EBIT. Another equation that can be used to compute a firm's DOL more easily is as follows:[1]

$$\text{DOL at } X = \frac{\text{Sales} - \text{Variable costs}}{\text{EBIT}} \tag{13.2}$$

Inserting data from Table 13-1 on the Allegan Manufacturing Company into Equation 13.2 gives the following:

$$\text{DOL at \$5 million} = \frac{\$5 \text{ million} - \$3 \text{ million}}{\$1 \text{ million}}$$

$$= 2.0$$

This result is the same as that obtained using the more complex Equation 13.1.

Table 13-3 shows the DOL at various sales levels for Allegan Manufacturing Company. Note that Allegan's DOL is largest (in absolute value terms) when the firm is operating at the breakeven sales point [that is, where Sales = $2,500,000 and EBIT = Sales − Variable Operating Costs − Fixed Operating Costs = $2,500,000 − 0.60($2,500,000) − $1,000,000 = $0]. Note also that the firm's DOL is negative below the breakeven sales level. A negative DOL indicates the percentage *reduction* in operating *losses* that occurs as the result of a 1 percent increase in output. For example, the DOL of −1.50 at a sales level of $1,500,000 indicates that, from a base sales level of $1,500,000, the firm's operating *losses* are *reduced* by 1.5 percent for each 1 percent *increase* in output.

A firm's DOL is a function of the nature of the production process. If the firm employs large amounts of labor-saving equipment in its operations, it tends to have relatively high fixed operating costs and relatively low variable operating costs. Such a cost structure yields a high DOL, which results in large operating profits (positive EBIT) if sales are high and large operating losses (negative EBIT) if sales are depressed.

Degree of Financial Leverage

A firm's degree of financial leverage (DFL) is computed as the *percentage change in earnings per share (EPS)* resulting from a given *percentage change* in earnings before interest and taxes (EBIT):

$$\text{DFL at } X = \frac{\text{Percentage change in EPS}}{\text{Percentage change in EBIT}}$$

This can also be written as follows:

$$\text{DFL at } X = \frac{\dfrac{\Delta \text{EPS}}{\text{EPS}}}{\dfrac{\Delta \text{EBIT}}{\text{EBIT}}} \tag{13.3}$$

where ΔEPS and ΔEBIT are the changes in EPS and EBIT, respectively. Because a firm's DFL is different at each EBIT level, it is necessary to indicate the EBIT point, *X*, at which financial leverage is being measured.

[1]Equation 13.2 is derived from Equation 13.1. See Problem 4 at the end of this chapter.

EBIT	$ 400,000	$800,000	$1,000,000	$1,200,000	$1,600,000
Less Interest expenses	250,000	250,000	250,000	250,000	250,000
Earnings before taxes	$ 150,000	$550,000	$ 750,000	$ 950,000	$1,350,000
Less Income taxes	60,000	220,000	300,000	380,000	540,000
Earnings after taxes	$ 90,000	$330,000	$ 450,000	$ 570,000	$ 810,000
Less Preferred dividends	150,000	150,000	150,000	150,000	150,000
Earnings available to common stockholders	$−60,000	$180,000	$ 300,000	$ 420,000	$ 660,000
Earnings per share (EPS)	$ −0.60	$ 1.80	$ 3.00	$ 4.20	$ 6.60

TABLE 13-4
Earnings per Share for Alternative Levels of EBIT, Allegan Manufacturing Company, Year Ending December 31, 19X1

Using the information contained in Table 13-4 and shown in Figure 13-2, the degree of financial leverage used by the Allegan Manufacturing Company can be calculated. The firm's EPS level is $3.00 at an EBIT level of $1 million. At an EBIT level of $1.2 million, EPS equals $4.20. Substituting these quantities into Equation 13.3 yields the following:

$$\text{DFL at } \$1,000,000 = \frac{\dfrac{(\$4.20 - \$3.00)}{\$3.00}}{\dfrac{(\$1,200,000 - \$1,000,000)}{\$1,000,000}}$$

$$= \frac{\$1.20}{\$3.00} \times \frac{\$1,000,000}{\$200,000}$$

$$= 2.0$$

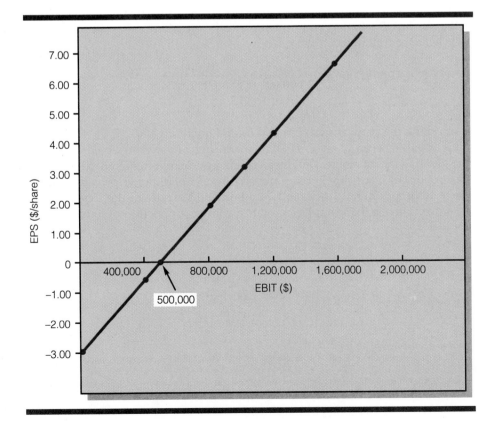

FIGURE 13-2
EPS-EBIT Graph for the Allegan Manufacturing Company

A DFL of 2.0 indicates that each 1 percent change in EBIT from a base EBIT level of $1 million results in a 2 percent change in EPS *in the same direction as the EBIT change*. In other words, a 10 percent *increase* in EBIT results in a 10% × 2.0 = 20% *increase* in EPS. Similarly, a 10 percent *decrease* in EBIT produces a 20 percent *decrease* in EPS. The larger the firm's DFL, the greater is the magnification of EBIT changes into EPS changes.

Measuring a firm's DFL using Equation 13.3 is somewhat cumbersome, because it necessitates using two EBIT and EPS projections. Computation is simplified when Equation 13.3 is rewritten as follows:[2]

$$\text{DFL at } X = \frac{\text{EBIT}}{\text{EBIT} - I - D_p/(1 - T)} \tag{13.4}$$

where I is the firm's interest payments, D_p the firm's preferred dividend payments, T the firm's marginal income tax rate, and X the level of EBIT at which the firm's DFL is being measured.

Unlike interest payments, preferred dividend payments are not tax deductible. Therefore, on a comparable tax basis, a dollar of preferred dividends costs the firm more than a dollar of interest payments. Dividing preferred dividends in Equation 13.4 by $(1 - T)$ puts interest and preferred dividends on an equivalent, *pretax* basis.

As shown in Figure 13-2, Allegan will have EPS = $0 at an EBIT level of $500,000. With this level of EBIT, there is just enough operating earnings to pay interest ($250,000) and preferred dividends (after-tax).[3] Using Equation 13.4, it can be seen that DFL will be maximized at that level of EBIT where EPS = $0.

Consider again the data presented in Table 13-1 on the Allegan Manufacturing Company. According to that table, EBIT = $1 million, I = $250,000, D_p = $150,000, and T = 40 percent, or 0.40. Substituting these values into Equation 13.4 yields the following:

$$\text{DFL at } \$1,000,000 = \frac{\$1,000,000}{\$1,000,000 - \$250,000 - \$150,000/(1 - 0.40)}$$

$$= 2.0$$

This result is the same as that obtained using Equation 13.3.

Just as a firm can change its DOL by raising or lowering fixed operating costs, it also can change its DFL by increasing or decreasing fixed capital costs. The amount of fixed capital costs incurred by a firm depends primarily on the mix of debt, preferred stock, and common stock equity in the firm's capital structure. Thus, a firm that has a relatively large proportion of debt and pre-

---

[2]For the firm with no preferred stock, Equation 13.4 becomes the following:

$$\text{DFL at } X = \frac{\text{EBIT}}{\text{EBIT} - I}$$

$$= \frac{\text{EBIT}}{\text{EBT}}$$

where EBT represents earnings before taxes.

[3]Recall that preferred dividends are paid from after-tax earnings. Hence, EBIT must be large enough to cover preferred dividends ($150,000) and the tax ($100,000) on the pretax earnings needed to pay preferred dividends. For example, if Allegan has EBIT of $500,000, interest of $250,000 can be paid (before any taxes are paid), leaving $250,000 of taxable income. At a 40 percent rate, the tax is $100,000 leaving $150,000 for preferred dividends.

ferred stock in its capital structure will have relatively large fixed capital costs and a high DFL.

Degree of Combined Leverage

Combined leverage occurs whenever a firm employs *both* operating leverage and financial leverage in an effort to increase the returns to common stockholders. It represents the magnification of sales increases (or decreases) into relatively larger earnings per share increases (or decreases), resulting from the firm's use of both types of leverage. The joint multiplier effect is known as the **degree of combined leverage**.

A firm's degree of combined leverage (DCL) is computed as the percentage change in earnings per share resulting from a given percentage change in sales:

$$\text{DCL at } X = \frac{\text{Percentage change in EPS}}{\text{Percentage change in sales}}$$

This can be rewritten as follows:

$$\text{DCL at } X = \frac{\dfrac{\Delta \text{EPS}}{\text{EPS}}}{\dfrac{\Delta \text{Sales}}{\text{Sales}}} \tag{13.5}$$

where ΔEPS and ΔSales are the changes in a firm's EPS and sales, respectively, and X represents the level of sales at which the firm's combined leverage is measured. The degree of combined leverage is also equal to the product of the degree of operating leverage and the degree of financial leverage.[4]

$$\text{DCL at } X = \text{DOL} \times \text{DFL} \tag{13.6}$$

To simplify matters, Equations 13.2 and 13.4 can be substituted into Equation 13.6 to obtain a new formula for determining the DCL in terms of basic income statement quantities:

$$\text{DCL at } X = \frac{\text{Sales} - \text{Variable costs}}{\text{EBIT}} \times \frac{\text{EBIT}}{\text{EBIT} - I - D_{\text{p}}/(1 - T)}$$

or

$$\text{DCL at } X = \frac{\text{Sales} - \text{Variable costs}}{\text{EBIT} - I - D_{\text{p}}/(1 - T)} \tag{13.7}$$

These three formulas for calculating DCL can be illustrated using the Allegan Manufacturing Company example. Equation 13.5 can be used to calculate Allegan's DCL with the data from Tables 13-1 and 13-2. The EPS level was $3.00 at a sales level of $5 million and $4.20 at a sales level of $5.5 million. Substituting these values into Equation 13.5 yields the following:

---

[4]This follows logically from the definitions of DCL, DOL, and DFL:

$$\frac{\text{Percentage change in EPS}}{\text{Percentage change in sales}} = \frac{\text{Percentage change in EBIT}}{\text{Percentage change in sales}} \times \frac{\text{Percentage change in EPS}}{\text{Percentage change in EBIT}}$$

$$\text{DCL at } \$5,000,000 = \frac{\dfrac{(\$4.20 - \$3.00)}{\$3.00}}{\dfrac{(\$5,500,000 - \$5,000,000)}{\$5,000,000}}$$

$$= \frac{\$1.20}{\$3.00} \times \frac{\$5,000,000}{\$500,000}$$

$$= 4.0$$

Substituting Sales = \$5,000,000; Variable costs = \$3,000,000; EBIT = \$1,000,000; I = \$250,000; D_p = \$150,000; and T = 40% (0.40) into Equation 13.7 gives the same value for Allegan's DCL:

$$\text{DCL at } \$5,000,000 = \frac{\$5,000,000 - \$3,000,000}{\$1,000,000 - \$250,000 - \$150,000/(1 - 0.40)}$$

$$= 4.0$$

Also, recall from the earlier discussion of operating and financial leverage for Allegan that DOL = 2.0 and DFL = 2.0. Substituting these values into Equation 13.6 yields a DCL value identical to that just calculated:

$$\text{DCL at } \$5,000,000 = 2.0 \times 2.0$$

$$= 4.0$$

This DCL is interpreted to mean that each 1 percent change in sales from a base sales level of \$5 million results in a 4 percent change in Allegan's EPS.

The degree of combined leverage used by a firm is a measure of the overall variability of EPS due to fixed operating and capital costs as sales levels vary. Fixed operating and capital costs can be combined in many different ways to achieve a desired DCL. In other words, a number of possible trade-offs can be made between operating and financial leverage.

Equation 13.6 shows that DCL is a function of DOL and DFL. If a firm has a relatively high DOL, for example, and wishes to achieve a certain DCL, it can offset this high DOL with a lower DFL. Or it may have a high DFL, in which case it would aim for a lower DOL. To illustrate, assume that a firm is considering purchasing assets that will increase fixed operating costs. To offset this high DOL, the firm may want to decrease the proportion of debt in its capital structure, thereby reducing fixed financial costs and the DFL.

Effect of Leverage on Shareholder Wealth and the Cost of Capital

Firms are limited in the amount of combined (i.e., operating and financial) leverage that can be used in seeking to increase EPS and shareholder wealth. Recall from Chapter 12 (see Figures 12-4 and 12-5) that the use of "excessive" amounts of *financial* leverage caused the market value of the firm (i.e., shareholder wealth) to decline and the cost of capital to rise. Like financial leverage, the use of increasing amounts of combined leverage increases the risk of financial distress. As this risk increases, investors will require higher rates of return on the funds supplied to the firm in the form of preferred and common equity and debt. In other words, because of the financial distress costs and agency costs associated with "excessive" combined leverage, the firm will have to pay higher costs for its funds. These higher costs will tend to offset the returns gained from the combined leverage, resulting in a decline in the market value of the firm and a rise in its cost of capital.

 ## OTHER FINANCIAL RISK MEASURES

In addition to using various financial ratios and the degree of combined leverage as measures of the financial risk facing a firm, it is possible to make more formal statements about the financial risk facing a company if the probability distribution of future operating income (EBIT) is approximately normal and the mean and standard deviation can be estimated. The number of standard deviations, z, that a particular value of EBIT is from the expected value, $\widehat{EBIT}$, can be computed using an expression similar to Equation 5.3 in Chapter 5:

$$z = \frac{EBIT - \widehat{EBIT}}{\sigma} \qquad (13.8)$$

where σ is the standard deviation of EBIT. Equation 13.8, along with the probability values from Table V in the back of the book, can be used to compute the probability that EBIT will be less than (or greater than) some particular value.

For example, consider the case of the Travco Manufacturing Corporation. Given the current capital structure of Travco, the company has interest payment obligations of $500,000 for the coming year. The company has no preferred stock. The $500,000 in interest represents the *loss level* for Travco. If EBIT falls below $500,000, losses will be incurred (EPS will be negative). At EBIT levels above $500,000, Travco will have positive earnings per share. Based upon past experience, Travco's managers have estimated that the expected value of EBIT over the coming year is $700,000 with a standard deviation of $200,000 and that the distribution of operating income is approximately normal, as illustrated in Figure 13-3. With this information, it is possible to compute the probability of Travco having negative earnings per share over the coming year (or, conversely, the probability of having positive earnings per share).

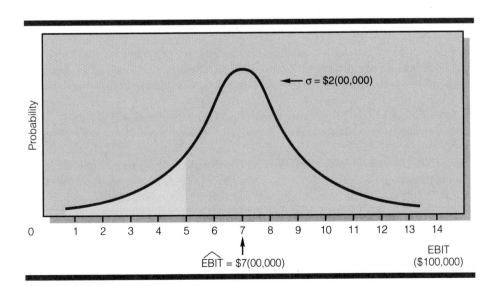

FIGURE 13-3
Probability Distribution of EBIT, Travco Manufacturing Company

Using Equation 13.8, the probability of Travco having negative EPS is equal to the probability of having EBIT below the loss level of $500,000, or

$$z = \frac{\$500,000 - \$700,000}{\$200,000} = -1.0$$

In other words, a level of EBIT of $500,000 is 1.0 standard deviation below the mean. From Table V, it can be seen that the probability associated with a value that is less than or equal to 1.0 standard deviation below the mean is 15.87 percent. Thus, there is a 15.87 percent chance that Travco will have negative earnings per share (i.e., the shaded area in Figure 13-3) with its current capital structure. Conversely, there is an 84.13 percent chance (100 percent less 15.87 percent chance of losses) of having positive earnings per share.

This type of analysis can give a financial manager a better feel for the level of financial risk facing a firm. As we shall see later in the chapter, when a financial manager is considering two or more alternative capital structures, this same kind of analysis can be used to help select the most desirable capital structure.

 EBIT-EPS Analysis

An analytical technique called *EBIT-EPS analysis*[5] can be used to help determine when debt financing is advantageous and when equity financing is advantageous.

Consider the Yuma Corporation with a present capital structure consisting only of common stock (35 million shares). Assume that Yuma is considering an expansion and evaluating two alternative financing plans.[6] Plan 1, equity financing, would involve the sale of an additional 15 million shares of common stock at $20 each. Plan 2, debt financing, would involve the sale of $300 million of 10 percent long-term debt.

If the firm adopts Plan 1, it remains totally equity financed. If, however, the firm adopts Plan 2, it becomes partially debt financed. Because Plan 2 involves the use of financial leverage, this financing issue basically is one of whether it is in the best interests of the firm's existing stockholders to employ financial leverage.

Table 13-5 illustrates the calculation of EPS at two different assumed levels of EBIT for both financing plans. Because the relationship between EBIT and EPS is linear, the two points calculated in Table 13-5 can be used to graph the relationship for each financing plan, as shown in Figure 13-4.

In this example, earnings per share at EBIT levels less than $100 million are higher using the equity financing alternative. Correspondingly, at EBIT levels greater than $100 million, earnings per share are higher with debt financing. The $100 million figure is called the **EBIT-EPS indifference point.** By definition, the earnings per share for the debt and equity financing alternatives are equal at the EBIT-EPS indifference point:

$$\text{EPS (debt financing)} = \text{EPS (equity financing)} \qquad (13.9)$$

---

[5]To review briefly, EBIT is earnings before interest and taxes, or operating earnings; EPS is earnings per share.
[6]Preferred stock is not included in this example because it merely complicates the matter. Because preferred stock is a fixed-income security, it would be treated much like debt in this example.

TABLE 13-5
**EBIT-EPS Analysis, Yuma
Corporation (all dollar figures
except per-share amounts are
in millions of dollars)***

	EBIT = $75	EBIT = $125
Equity Financing (Plan 1)		
EBIT	$ 75	$ 125
Interest	—	—
EBT	$ 75	$ 125
Taxes @ 40%	30	50
EAT	$ 45	$ 75
Shares outstanding	50	50
EPS	$0.90	$1.50
% change in EBIT		+66.67%
% change in EPS		+66.67%
DFL		1.00
Debt Financing (Plan 2)		
EBIT	$ 75	$ 125
Interest	30	30
EBT	$ 45	$ 95
Taxes @ 40%	18	38
EAT	$ 27	$ 57
Shares outstanding	35	35
EPS	$0.77	$1.63
% change in EBIT		+66.67%
% change in EPS		+111.69%
DFL		1.68

*EBIT = earnings before interest and taxes; EBT = earnings before taxes; EAT = earnings after taxes; EPS = earnings per share.

This equation may be rewritten as follows:

$$\frac{(\text{EBIT} - I_\text{d})(1 - T) - D_\text{p}}{N_\text{d}} = \frac{(\text{EBIT} - I_\text{e})(1 - T) - D_\text{p}}{N_\text{e}} \quad (13.10)$$

where EBIT is earnings before interest and taxes; I_d is the firm's total interest payments if the debt alternative is chosen; I_e is the firm's total interest payments if the equity alternative is chosen; and N_d and N_e represent the number of common shares outstanding for the debt and equity alternatives, respectively. The firm's effective tax rate is indicated as T, and D_p is the amount of preferred dividends for the firm. This equation may be used to calculate directly the EBIT level at which earnings per share for the two alternatives are equal.[7] The data from the example shown in Table 13-5 yield the EBIT-EPS indifference point:

$$\frac{(\text{EBIT} - \$30)(1 - 0.4) - 0}{35} = \frac{(\text{EBIT} - \$0)(1 - 0.4) - 0}{50}$$

$$50(0.6\ \text{EBIT} - \$18) = 35(0.6\ \text{EBIT})$$

$$30\ \text{EBIT} - \$900 = 21\ \text{EBIT}$$

$$9\ \text{EBIT} = \$900$$

$$\text{EBIT} = \$100\ (\text{million})$$

[7]An alternative indifference point measure is defined in terms of uncommitted earnings per share. *Uncommitted earnings per share* are defined as earnings after tax and preferred dividends *minus sinking fund obligations* (which are not tax deductible) *on outstanding debt* divided by the number of shares outstanding. Uncommitted earnings per share recognizes that sinking fund payments must be made if the firm is to remain solvent. The indifference point based on uncommitted EPS always will be at a higher EBIT level than the indifference point based on EPS.

FIGURE 13-4
EBIT-EPS Analysis,
Yuma Corporation

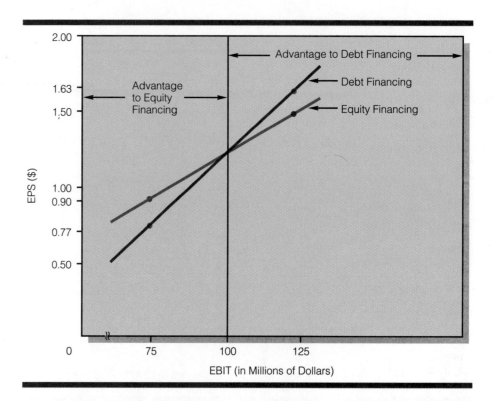

Note that in the equity financing alternative, a 66.67 percent increase in EBIT (from $75 million to $125 million) results in a 66.67 percent increase in earnings per share (from $0.90 to $1.50), or, by Equation 13.3, a degree of financial leverage of

$$DFL = \frac{66.67\%}{66.67\%}$$

$$= 1.00$$

Similarly, in the debt financing alternative, a 66.67 percent increase in EBIT results in a 111.69 percent increase in earnings per share, or a degree of financial leverage of

$$DFL = \frac{111.69\%}{66.67\%}$$

$$= 1.68$$

A comparable magnification of earnings per share will occur if EBIT declines. This wider variation in earnings per share, which occurs with the debt financing alternative, is an illustration of *financial risk,* because *financial risk* is defined as the increased variability in earnings per share due to the firm's use of debt. All other things being equal, an increase in the proportion of debt financing is said to increase the financial risk of the firm.

EBIT-EPS Analysis and Capital Structure Decisions

The tools of EBIT-EPS analysis and the theory of an optimal capital structure can help a firm choose an appropriate capital structure. This section utilizes an example to develop a five-step procedure designed to assist financial managers in making capital structure decisions.

Balboa Department Stores has been 100 percent financed with equity funds since the firm was founded. While analyzing a major expansion program, the firm has decided to consider alternative capital structures. In particular, it has been suggested that the firm should use this expansion program as an opportunity to increase the long-term debt ratio from the current level of 0 percent to a new level of 30 percent. Interest on the proposed new debt will amount to $100,000 per year.

- **Step 1: Compute the expected level of EBIT after the expansion.** Based on Balboa's past operating experience and a projection of the impact of the expansion, it estimates its expected EBIT to be $500,000 per year under normal operating circumstances.
- **Step 2: Estimate the variability of this level of operating earnings.** Based on the past performance of the company over several business cycles, the standard deviation of operating earnings is estimated to be $200,000 per year. (Operating earnings are assumed to be normally distributed, or at least approximately so.)
- **Step 3: Compute the indifference point between the two financing alternatives.** This calculation will determine whether it is preferable to add new debt or to maintain the all-equity capital structure. Using the techniques of EBIT-EPS analysis previously discussed, the indifference point is computed to be $300,000.
- **Step 4: Analyze these estimates in the context of the risk the firm is willing to assume.** After considerable discussion, it has been decided that the firm is willing to accept a 25 percent chance that operating earnings in any year will be below the indifference point and a 5 percent chance that the firm will have to report a loss in any year. To complete this analysis, it is necessary to compute the probability that operating earnings will be below the indifference point; that is, the probability that EBIT will be less than $300,000. This is equivalent on the standard normal curve (using Equation 13.8) to the following:

$$z = \frac{\$300,000 - \$500,000}{\$200,000}$$

$$= -1.0$$

or 1.0 standard deviation below the mean. The probability that EBIT will be less than 1.0 standard deviation below the mean is 15.87 percent; this is determined from Table V at the end of the book. Therefore, on the basis of the indifference point criterion, the proposed new capital structure appears acceptable. The probability of incurring losses now must be analyzed. This is the probability that EBIT will be less than the required interest payments of $100,000. On the standard normal curve, this corresponds to the following:

$$z = \frac{\$100,000 - \$500,000}{\$200,000}$$

$$= -2.0$$

or 2.0 standard deviations below the mean. The probability that EBIT will be less than 2.0 standard deviations below the mean is 2.28 percent, as shown in Table V. According to this criterion, the proposed capital structure also seems acceptable.

If either or both of these tests had shown the proposed capital structure to have an unacceptable level of risk, the analysis would have been repeated for lower levels of debt than the proposed 30 percent rate. Similarly, because the proposed capital structure has exceeded the standards set by the firm, management might want to consider even higher levels of debt than the proposed 30 percent.

■ **Step 5: Examine the market evidence to determine whether the proposed capital structure is too risky.** This evaluation should be made in relation to the following: the firm's level of business risk, industry norms for leverage ratios and coverage ratios, and the recommendations of the firm's investment bankers.

This step is undertaken only after a proposed capital structure has met the "internal" tests for acceptability. Financial leverage is a double-edged sword: it enhances expected returns, but it also increases risk. If the increase in perceived risk is greater than the increase in expected returns, the firm's weighted cost of capital may rise instead of fall, and the firm's stock price and market value will decline.

It is important to note that a firm need not feel constrained by industry standards in setting its own capital structure. If, for example, a firm traditionally has been more profitable than the average firm in the industry, or if a firm's operating income is more stable than the operating income of the average firm, a higher level of financial leverage probably can be tolerated. The final choice of a capital structure involves a careful analysis of expected future returns and risks relative to other firms in the industry.

EBIT-EPS Analysis and Stock Prices

An important question arising from EBIT-EPS analysis is the impact of financial leverage on the firm's common stock price. Specifically, which financing alternative results in the higher stock price? Returning to the Yuma Corporation example discussed earlier (see Table 13-5), suppose the company is able to operate at the $125 million EBIT level. Then, if the company chooses the debt financing alternative, its EPS will equal $1.63, and if it chooses the equity alternative, its EPS will be $1.50. But the stock price depends on the price-earnings (P/E) ratio that the stock market assigns to each alternative. Suppose the stock market assigns a P/E ratio of 16.0 to the company's common stock if the equity alternative is chosen and a P/E ratio of 15.4 if the debt alternative is chosen. Recalling from Chapter 3 that the P/E ratio (Equation 3.15) was defined as the market price per share of common stock (P_0) divided by the current earnings per share (EPS), the common stock price, can be calculated for both alternatives as follows:

$$P_0 = (\text{P/E ratio})(\text{EPS}) \qquad (13.11)$$

Equity alternative:

$$P_0 = (16.0)(\$1.50) = \$24.00$$

Debt alternative:

$$P_0 = (15.4)(\$1.63) = \$25.10$$

These calculations show that in this case the stock market places a higher value on the company's stock if the debt alternative is chosen rather than the equity alternative. Note that the stock market assigned a slightly lower P/E ratio to the debt alternative. The stock market recognized the increased financial risk associated with the debt alternative, but this increased risk was more than offset by the increased EPS possible with the use of debt.

To carry the Yuma Corporation example one important step further, suppose the company, while operating at the $125 million EBIT level, chooses an even higher debt capital structure, which causes its EPS to increase to $2.25. Suppose further that the stock market feels that this high-debt capital structure significantly increases the company's financial risk—to the point where bankruptcy could occur if EBIT levels turned downward in a recession. If the stock market assigns a P/E ratio of 10.0, for example, the stock price would be $22.50 (= $2.25 × 10.0), and it would be clear that this change in capital structure is not desirable.

It is important to emphasize that the P/E ratios in the preceding example simply are assumptions. As an analytical technique, EBIT-EPS analysis does not provide a complete solution to the optimal capital structure question.

In summary, the firm potentially can show increased earnings to its stockholders by increasing its level of financial risk. However, because increases in risk tend to increase the cost of capital (which is analogous to a decrease in the P/E ratio), the firm's management has to assess the trade-off between the higher earnings per share for its stockholders and the higher costs of capital.

 ## CASH INSOLVENCY ANALYSIS

In Chapter 3, the *times interest earned* and *fixed-charge coverage* ratios were introduced. These ratios provide an indicator of the ability of a firm to meet its interest and other fixed charge obligations (including lease payments, sinking fund payments, and preferred dividends) out of current operating income. Also, in that chapter, liquidity ratios, such as the *current ratio* and the *quick ratio,* were introduced. Liquidity ratios provide a simple measure of a firm's ability to meet its obligations, especially in the near term. In that chapter, we also indicated that the best measure of a firm's cash adequacy can be obtained by preparing a detailed cash budget, which is discussed in greater detail in Chapter 15.

Coverage ratios and liquidity ratios do not provide an adequate picture of a firm's solvency position. A firm is said to be technically insolvent if it is unable to meet its current obligations. We need a more comprehensive measure of the ability of a firm to meet its obligations if this information is to be used to assist in capital structure planning. This measure must consider both the cash on hand and the cash expected to be generated in the future. Donaldson has suggested that a firm's level of fixed financial charges (including interest, preferred dividends, sinking fund obligations, and lease payments), and thus its debt carrying capacity, should depend on the cash balances and net cash flows that can be expected to be available in a worst-case (recessionary environment) scenario.[8] This analysis requires the preparation of a detailed cash budget under assumed recessionary conditions.

[8]See Gordon Donaldson, "New Framework for Corporate Debt Policy," *Harvard Business Review* 40 (March–April 1962): 117–131; and Gordon Donaldson, "Strategy for Financial Emergencies," *Harvard Business Review* 47 (November–December 1969): 67–79.

Donaldson defines a firm's net cash balance in a recession, CB_R, to be

$$CB_R = CB_0 + FCF_R \qquad (13.12)$$

where CB_0 is the cash (and marketable securities) balance at the beginning of the recession, and FCF_R is the free cash flows expected to be generated during the recession. *Free cash flow* represents the portion of a firm's total cash flow available to service additional debt, to make dividend payments to common stockholders, and to invest in other projects.

For example, suppose AMAX Corporation, a natural resource company, reported a cash (and marketable securities) balance of approximately $154 million. Suppose also that management anticipates free cash flows of $210 million during a projected one-year recession. These free cash flows reflect both operating cash flows during the recession and current required fixed financial charges. Under the current capital structure, consisting of approximately 32 percent debt, the cash balance at the end of the recession would be $364 million ($154 million plus $210 million). Assume that the management of AMAX is considering a change in its capital structure that would add an additional $280 million of annual after-tax interest and sinking fund payments (i.e., fixed financial charges). The effect would be a cash balance at the end of the recession of

$$CB_R = \$154 \text{ million} + \$210 \text{ million} - \$280 \text{ million} = \$84 \text{ million}$$

The managers of AMAX must decide if this projected cash balance of $84 million leaves them enough of a cushion in a recession.

This analysis can be enhanced if it is possible to specify the probability distribution of expected free cash flows during a recession. For example, if the AMAX managers believe, based upon past experience, that free cash flows are approximately normally distributed [see panel (a) of Figure 13-5] with an expected value during a one-year recession (FCF_R) of $210 million and a standard deviation of $140 million, they can compute the probability of running out of cash if the new debt is added. The probability of running out of cash is equal to the probability of ending the recession with a cash balance of less than $0. The probability distribution of AMAX's *cash balance* [panel (b) of Figure 13-5] will have the same shape (i.e., approximately normal with a standard deviation, σ, of $140 million) as the probability distribution of *free cash flows* [panel (a) of Figure 13-5], except that it will be shifted to the left from a mean (FCF_R) of $210 million to a mean ($CB_R$) of $84 million [i.e., by the beginning cash balance ($154 million) plus expected free cash flows ($210 million) less additional fixed financial charges ($280 million)]. Employing an expression similar to Equation 13.8, where cash balance (CB_R) is the variable of interest rather than EBIT, a cash balance of $0 is equivalent on the standard normal curve to the following:

$$z = \frac{(\$0 - \$84 \text{ million})}{\$140 \text{ million}} = -0.60$$

From Table V, the probability of a z value of -0.60 or less is 27.43 percent. Thus, with an additional $280 million in fixed financial charges, the probability of AMAX running out of cash during a one-year recession is about 27 percent [i.e., shaded area in panel (b) of Figure 13-5].

The AMAX managers may feel that this is too much risk to assume. If they only want to assume a 5 percent risk of running out of cash during a one-year

FIGURE 13-5
Cash Flows and Cash Balance
Probability Distributions,
Amax Corporation

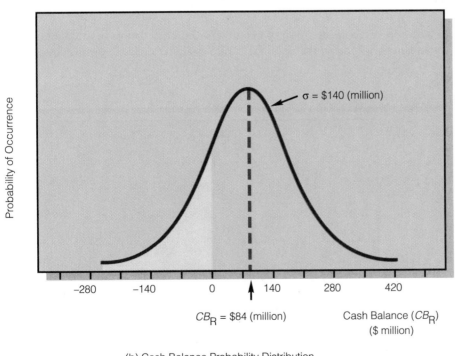

(a) Free Cash Flow Probability Distribution

(b) Cash Balance Probability Distribution

recession, they can determine the amount of additional interest and sinking fund payments (i.e., fixed financial charges) that can be added safely. First, find the number of standard deviations (z) to the left of the mean that gives a 5 percent probability of occurrence in the lower tail of the distribution (i.e., the shaded area in Figure 13-6). From Table V, this value of z is found to be approximately -1.65. Next, we calculate the expected cash balance (CB_R) needed at the end of a one-year recession if the risk of running out of cash is to be held to 5 percent:

$$z = -1.65 = \frac{(\$0 - CB_R)}{\$140 \text{ million}}$$

$$CB_R = \$231 \text{ million}$$

Finally, since AMAX expects to enter the recession with $154 million in cash and to generate $210 million in free cash flow during a one-year recession, it can take on just $133 million (i.e., $154 million + $210 million − $231 million) in additional fixed financial charges.

The willingness of management to assume the risk associated with running out of cash depends on several factors, including funds available from outstanding lines of credit with banks and the sale of new long-term debt, preferred stock, and common stock, and the potential funds realized by cutting back on expenses during a business downturn, reducing dividends, and selling assets.

OTHER FACTORS TO CONSIDER IN MAKING CAPITAL STRUCTURE DECISIONS

In addition to a consideration of tax effects, financial distress costs, agency costs, the business risk facing the firm, EBIT-EPS analysis, and cash insolvency analysis,

FIGURE 13-6
Cash Balance Probability
Distribution, AMAX Corporation

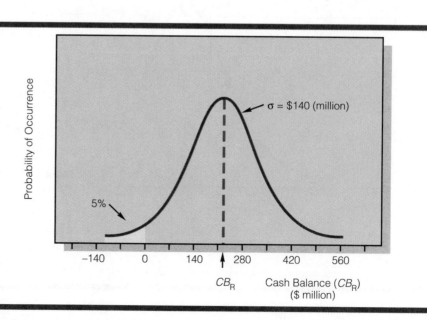

there are additional factors normally considered as a firm makes its capital structure decisions. These factors are discussed briefly in this section.

Industry Standards

Financial analysts, investment bankers, bond rating agencies, common stock investors, and commercial bankers normally compare the financial risk for a firm, as measured by its interest and fixed-charge coverage ratios and its long-term debt ratio, with industry standards or norms. There is considerable evidence that the capital structure of an average firm varies significantly from industry to industry. For example, in 1995, the average long-term debt ratio in the airline industry was about 72 percent. This ratio was 33 percent for the restaurant industry, 49 percent for the natural gas distribution industry, 42 percent for the tobacco industry, and 21 percent for the computer industry.[9] Although there are exceptions, firms generally tend to cluster around the industry debt ratio, probably reflecting the fact that the business risk facing a firm is largely industry determined. A firm adopting a capital structure that differs significantly from the industry norms will have to convince the financial markets that its business risk is sufficiently different than the risk facing the average firm in the industry to warrant this divergent capital structure.

Profitability and Need for Funds

As noted in the previous chapter, highly profitable firms, with limited needs for funds, tend to have lower debt ratios when compared with less profitable firms. Also, firms that undertake highly leveraged restructurings, such as the RJR Nabisco leveraged buyout, may temporarily have debt ratios that are significantly above the optimal level until funds from asset sales, new equity issues, or operations can be generated to pay off the debtholders.

Lender and Bond-Rater Requirements

Lenders and bond-rating agencies often impose restrictions on a firm's capital structure choices as a condition for extending credit or maintaining a bond or preferred stock rating. For example, Standard & Poor's has established the benchmark standards shown in Table 13-6 for rating the debt of electric utilities. These are not the only factors considered when establishing a company's bond rating, but they are very important guidelines that a firm must follow if it wishes to retain or improve its credit rating. A more complete discussion of the factors considered by bond rating agencies is contained in Chapter 6.

TABLE 13-6
Electric Utility Bond Rating Standards

Source: *Standard and Poor's CreditWeek* (November 1, 1993): 41, reprinted by permission of Standard and Poor's, a division of McGraw-Hill Companies

RATING LEVEL	PRETAX INTEREST COVERAGE (TIMES)	DEBT LEVERAGE (%)
AA	Greater than 3.5	Less than 47
A	2.75 to 4.5	41 to 52
BBB	1.75 to 3.5	48 to 59
BB	1.25 to 2.5	54 to 65

[9]*Value Line Investment Survey* (New York: Value Line, 1996–97): various issues.

Managerial Risk Aversion

Management's willingness to assume risk often has a major impact on the capital structure chosen by the firm, although the relative risk aversion of management *does not* influence the firm's optimal capital structure. Some managers adopt unusually risky or unusually low-risk capital structures. When a suboptimal capital structure is chosen, the financial marketplace normally will penalize a firm for this action.

For example, because of an extremely conservative owner-management financing philosophy, Adolph Coors (the third largest U.S. brewer) did not have any long-term debt in its capital structure until 1990, when the company issued its first long-term debt securities. Even after the issuance of these securities, Coors' long-term debt ratio was still well below the industry average. Most financial analysts agree that Coors could safely add a significant amount of debt to its capital structure and thereby lower its overall cost of capital and increase the market value of the firm. Coors has been able to sustain this capital structure because the Coors family controls 100 percent of the company's voting shares. If this owner-management control did not exist, it is very likely that Coors would be acquired by new owners who would significantly modify the company's capital structure.[10] Differences in managerial philosophies regarding the appropriate capital structure for a firm are a major driving force behind many leveraged buyout offers.

Retention of Control

Some firms use debt or preferred stock financing rather than common stock financing to avoid selling new shares of common stock. When new voting common stock is sold, the relative control position of existing stockholders is diluted.

 INTERNATIONAL ISSUES
BALANCING OPERATING AND FINANCIAL
RISKS AT NESTLÉ

Nestlé is a huge, multinational Swiss foods corporation with operations in at least 150 countries. The overwhelming majority of its sales occur outside of Switzerland. Nestlé's various foreign operating subsidiaries enjoy considerable decentralized operational flexibility. Local division managers handle all marketing and production decisions.

In contrast to its decentralized operating policy, Nestlé uses a highly centralized financing strategy. All financing decisions are handled at corporate headquarters. The small corporate finance staff makes all funding decisions for the subsidiaries, establishes the firm's worldwide consolidated capital structure, sets individual subsidiary capital structures, manages worldwide currency exposure risk, and mandates the dividend policy for subsidiaries.

When a subsidiary is first formed, about one-half of the needed financing—the funds used to acquire fixed assets—comes from equity contributions by the parent. The balance of the needed funds, primarily to support working capital

---

[10]The issuance of debt securities in 1990 reflected a new management philosophy that came about as the result of a change in top management.

investments, is acquired in the host country through the banking system or the sale of commercial paper. In some countries, where there is little or no risk of capital expropriation, the parent company may finance working capital needs, depending on the relative cost of funds for the parent compared to the local cost of funds for the subsidiary.

Each subsidiary normally pays a dividend of 100 percent of its profits back to the parent. This guarantees central control over the capital structure of each subsidiary. If additional funds are needed for investment, the parent provides them using the lowest available cost source of capital. Nestlé manages its overall sources of capital with the objective of maintaining a top credit rating and thereby minimizing its capital costs.

Why does Nestlé follow such a conservative financing strategy? Senior vice-president of finance Daniel Regolatti states, "Our basic strategy is that we are an industrial company. We have a lot of risks in a lot of countries, so we should not add high financial risks."[11] This strategy recognizes the trade-offs between business risk and financial risk that have been discussed in this chapter.

■ SUMMARY

- *Leverage* refers to a firm's use of assets and liabilities having fixed costs. A firm uses leverage in an attempt to earn returns in excess of the fixed costs of these assets and liabilities, thus increasing the returns to common stockholders.
- *Operating leverage* occurs when a firm uses assets having fixed operating costs. The *degree of operating leverage* (DOL) measures the percentage change in a firm's EBIT resulting from a 1 percent change in sales (or units of output). As a firm's fixed operating costs rise, its DOL increases.
- *Financial leverage* occurs when a firm makes use of funds (primarily from debt and preferred stock) having fixed capital costs. The *degree of financial leverage* (DFL) measures the percentage change in the firm's EPS resulting from a 1 percent change in EBIT. As a firm's fixed capital costs rise, its DFL increases.
- The *combined leverage* of a firm is equal to the *product* of the degrees of operating and financial leverage. These two types of leverage can be combined in many different ways to achieve a given degree of combined leverage (DCL). The total variability of the firm's EPS is a combination of business risk and financial risk.
- *EBIT-EPS analysis* is an analytical technique that can be used to help determine the circumstances under which a firm should employ financial leverage. Basically, it involves calculating earnings per share at different levels of EBIT for debt and equity financing plans. This information then may be used to graph earnings per share versus EBIT to determine the EBIT levels at which financial leverage is advantageous to the firm.
- The *indifference point* in EBIT-EPS analysis is that level of EBIT where earnings per share are the same, regardless of which of two alternative capital structures is used. At EBIT levels greater than the indifference level, a more financially levered capital structure will produce a higher level of earnings per share; at EBIT levels less than the indifference point, a less financially levered capital structure will produce a higher level of earnings per share.

[11]"The Nestlé Approach to Capital Markets and Innovation," *Business International Money Report* (October 27, 1986): 337; and Alan C. Shapiro, *Multinational Financial Management*, 3d ed. (Needham Heights, MA: Allyn & Bacon, 1989).

■ A firm can analyze its capital structure decision by performing an EBIT-EPS analysis, computing the risk of unfavorable financial leverage at its expected level of operating income, and analyzing financial leverage ratios and coverage ratios for other firms in the industry. A careful evaluation of these facts, together with an analysis of the firm's business risk, can assist in making the final determination regarding the desirability of a proposed capital structure.

■ *Cash insolvency analysis* can provide additional insights about the appropriate capital structure. Cash insolvency analysis evaluates the adequacy of a firm's cash position in a worst-case (recession) scenario.

■ QUESTIONS AND TOPICS FOR DISCUSSION

1. Define *leverage* as it is used in finance.
2. Define and give examples of the following:
   a. Fixed costs.
   b. Variable costs.
3. Define the following:
   a. Operating leverage.
   b. Financial leverage.
4. How is a firm's degree of combined leverage (DCL) related to its degrees of operating and financial leverage?
5. Is it possible for a firm to have a high degree of operating leverage and a low level of business risk? Explain.
6. Is it possible for a firm to have a high degree of combined leverage and a low level of total risk? Explain.
7. What are the major limitations of EBIT-EPS analysis as a technique to determine the optimal capital structure?
8. In practice, how can a firm determine whether it is operating at (or near) its optimal capital structure?
9. Under what circumstances should a firm use *more* debt in its capital structure than is used by the "average" firm in the industry? When should it use *less* debt than the "average" firm?
10. Why do public utilities typically have capital structures with about 50 percent debt, whereas major oil companies average about 25 percent debt in their capital structures?
11. What is *cash insolvency analysis,* and how can it help in the establishment of an optimal capital structure?

■ SELF-TEST PROBLEMS

ST1. Pinches Salt Company has the following income statement for 19X1:

Sales	$5,000,000
Variable operating costs	1,000,000
Fixed operating costs	2,000,000
EBIT	$2,000,000
Interest	500,000
EBT	$1,500,000
Tax (at 40%)	600,000
EAT	$ 900,000
Preferred dividends	100,000
Earnings available to common stockholders	$ 800,000
Shares outstanding	400,000

a. Compute Pinches's DOL, DFL, and DCL.
b. If sales increase to $5,500,000, what is your forecast of EPS?

ST2. Flagstaff Industries, Inc. has determined that its EBIT for the coming year is approximately normally distributed with an expected value of $1.75 million and a standard deviation of $1.2 million. Given its current capital structure, Flagstaff has $250,000 in interest obligations due during the coming year. Determine the probability that Flagstaff will have negative EPS.

ST3. The Euclid Corporation has a present capital structure consisting of 100 million shares of common stock. Euclid is considering an expansion program. Two alternative financing plans are under consideration:

- *Plan 1: Equity financing.* Sale of 10 million additional shares of common stock at $15 per share.
- *Plan 2: Debt financing.* Sale of $150 million of 12 percent long-term debt.

The firm's marginal tax rate is 40 percent.

  a. Determine the indifference level of EBIT between the two financing plans.
  b. Suppose that Euclid's EBIT is normally distributed with an expected value of $250 million and a standard deviation of $200 million. If the debt alternative is chosen, determine the probability that Euclid will have negative EPS.
  c. Determine the probability that the debt financing alternative will produce higher earnings than the equity alternative.

ST4. Buy-Low Distributors has a cash (and marketable securities) balance of $20 million. Free cash flows during a projected one-year recession are expected to be $60 million with a standard deviation of $60 million. (Assume Buy-Low's free cash flows are approximately normally distributed.)

  a. Determine the probability that Buy-Low will run out of cash during the recession.
  b. Buy-Low is considering a change in its capital structure that would increase its annual fixed charges by $10 million. Determine the probability of running out of cash during the recession if the change in capital structure is undertaken.

■ PROBLEMS*

1. The Hurricane Lamp Company forecasts that next year's sales will be $6 million. Fixed operating costs are estimated to be $800,000, and the variable cost ratio (that is, variable costs as a fraction of sales) is estimated to be 0.75. The firm has a $600,000 loan at 10 percent interest. It has 20,000 shares of $3 preferred stock and 60,000 shares of common stock outstanding. Hurricane Lamp is in the 40 percent corporate income tax bracket.

  a. Forecast Hurricane Lamp's earnings per share (EPS) for next year. Develop a complete income statement using the revised format illustrated in Table 13-1. Then determine what Hurricane Lamp's EPS would be if sales were 10 percent above the projected $6 million level.

  b. Calculate Hurricane Lamp's degree of operating leverage (DOL) at a sales level of $6 million using the following:
    i. The definitional formula (Equation 13.1).
    ii. The simpler, computational formula (Equation 13.2).
    iii. What is the economic interpretation of this value?

  c. Calculate Hurricane Lamp's degree of financial leverage (DFL) at the EBIT level corresponding to sales of $6 million using the following:
    i. The definitional formula (Equation 13.3).
    ii. The simpler computational formula (Equation 13.4).
    iii. What is the economic interpretation of this value?

  d. Calculate Hurricane Lamp's degree of combined leverage (DCL) using the following:
    i. The definitional formula (Equation 13.5).
    ii. The simpler computational formula (Equation 13.7).

*Colored numbers denote problems that have check answers provided at the end of the book.

iii. The degree of operating and financial leverage calculated in Parts b and c.

iv. What is the economic interpretation of this value?

2. The Alexander Company reported the following income statement for 19X1:

Sales		$15,000,000
Less Operating expenses		
Wages, salaries, benefits	$6,000,000	
Raw materials	3,000,000	
Depreciation	1,500,000	
General, administrative, and selling expenses	1,500,000	
Total operating expenses		12,000,000
Earnings before interest and taxes (EBIT)		$ 3,000,000
Less Interest expense		750,000
Earnings before taxes		$ 2,250,000
Less Income taxes		1,000,000
Earnings after taxes		$ 1,250,000
Less Preferred dividends		250,000
Earnings available to common stockholders		$ 1,000,000
Earnings per share—250,000 shares outstanding		$4.00

Assume that all depreciation and 75 percent of the firm's general, administrative, and selling expenses are *fixed costs* and that the remainder of the firm's operating expenses are *variable costs*.

a. Determine Alexander's fixed costs, variable costs, and variable cost ratio.

b. Based on its 19X1 sales, calculate the following:
   i. The firm's DOL.
   ii. The firm's DFL.
   iii. The firm's DCL.

c. Assuming that next year's sales increase by 15 percent, fixed operating and financial costs remain constant, and the variable cost ratio and tax rate also remain constant, use the leverage figures just calculated to forecast next year's EPS.

d. Show the validity of this forecast by constructing Alexander's income statement for next year according to the revised format.

e. Construct an EPS-EBIT graph based on Alexander's 19X1 income statement.

3. Gibson Company sales for the year 19X1 were $3 million. The firm's variable operating cost ratio was 0.50, and fixed costs (that is, overhead and depreciation) were $900,000. Its average (and marginal) income tax rate is 40 percent. Currently, the firm has $2.4 million of long-term bank loans outstanding at an average interest rate of 12.5 percent. The remainder of the firm's capital structure consists of common stock (100,000 shares outstanding at the present time).

a. Calculate Gibson's degree of combined leverage for 19X1.

b. Gibson is forecasting a 10 percent increase in sales for next year (19X2). Furthermore, the firm is planning to purchase additional labor-saving equipment, which will increase fixed costs by $150,000 and reduce the variable cost ratio to 0.475. Financing this equipment with debt will require additional bank loans of $500,000 at an interest rate of 12.5 percent. Calculate Gibson's expected degree of combined leverage for 19X2.

c. Determine how much Gibson must reduce its debt in 19X2 (for example, through the sale of common stock) to maintain its DCL at the 19X1 level.

4. Show algebraically that Equation 13.2:

$$\text{DOL at } X = \frac{\text{Sales} - \text{Variable costs}}{\text{EBIT}}$$

is equivalent to Equation 13.1:

$$\text{DOL at } X = \frac{\Delta EBIT/EBIT}{\Delta Sales/Sales}$$

5. Albatross Airline's fixed operating costs are $5.8 million, and its variable cost ratio is 0.20. The firm has $2 million in bonds outstanding with a coupon interest rate of 8 percent. Albatross has 30,000 shares of preferred stock outstanding, which pays a $2.00 annual dividend. There are 100,000 shares of common stock outstanding. Revenues for the firm are $8 million, and the firm is in the 40 percent corporate income tax bracket.
   a. Compute Albatross's degree of operating leverage.
   b. Compute its degree of financial leverage.
   c. Compute its degree of combined leverage and interpret this value.

6. Given the following information for Computech, compute the firm's degree of combined leverage (dollars are in thousands except EPS):

	19X1	19X2
Sales	$500,000	$570,000
Fixed costs	120,000	120,000
Variable costs	300,000	342,000
Earnings before interest and taxes	80,000	108,000
Interest	30,000	30,000
Earnings per share (EPS)	$ 1.00	$ 1.56

7. McGee Corporation has fixed operating costs of $10 million and a variable cost ratio of 0.65. The firm has a $20 million, 10 percent bank loan and a $6 million, 12 percent bond issue outstanding. The firm has 1 million shares of $5 (dividend) preferred stock and 2 million shares of common stock ($1 par). McGee's marginal tax rate is 40 percent. Sales are expected to be $80 million.
   a. Compute McGee's degree of operating leverage at an $80 million sales level.
   b. Compute McGee's degree of financial leverage at an $80 million sales level.
   c. If sales decline to $76 million, forecast McGee's earnings per share.

8. A firm has earnings per share of $2.60 at a sales level of $5 million. If the firm has a degree of operating leverage of 3.0 and a degree of financial leverage of 5.5 (both at a sales level of $5 million), forecast earnings per share for a 2 percent sales decline.

9. Blums, Inc. expects its operating income over the coming year to equal $1.5 million, with a standard deviation of $300,000. Its coefficient of variation is equal to 0.20. Blums must pay interest charges of $700,000 next year and preferred stock dividends of $240,000. Blums' marginal tax rate is 40 percent. What is the probability that Blums will have negative earnings per share next year? (Assume operating income is normally distributed.)

10. A firm has sales of $10 million, variable costs of $5 million, EBIT of $2 million, and a degree of combined leverage of 3.0.
   a. If the firm has no preferred stock, what are its annual interest charges?
   b. If the firm wishes to reduce its degree of combined leverage to 2.5 by reducing interest charges, what will be the new level of annual interest charges?

11. Cohen's Bowling Emporium has a degree of financial leverage of 2.0 and a degree of combined leverage of 6.0. The breakeven sales level for Cohen's has been estimated to be $500,000. Fixed costs total $250,000. What effect will a 15 percent increase in sales have on EBIT?

12. Connely, Inc. expects sales of silicon chips to be $30 million this year. Because this is a very capital-intensive business, fixed operating costs are $10 million. The variable cost ratio is 40 percent. The firm's debt obligations consist of a $2 million, 10 percent bank loan and a $10 million bond issue with a 12 percent coupon rate. The firm has 100,000 shares of preferred stock outstanding that pays a $9.60 dividend. Connely has 1 million shares of common stock outstanding and its marginal tax rate is 40 percent.

a. Compute Connely's degree of operating leverage.

b. Compute Connely's degree of financial leverage.

c. Compute Connely's degree of combined leverage.

d. Compute Connely's EPS if sales decline by 5 percent.

13. McGonnigal, Inc. has expected sales of $40 million. Fixed operating costs are $5 million, and the variable cost ratio is 65 percent. McGonnigal has outstanding a $10 million, 10 percent bank loan and $3 million in 12 percent coupon-rate bonds. McGonnigal has outstanding 250,000 shares of a $10 (dividend) preferred stock and 1 million shares of common stock ($1 par value). McGonnigal's average tax rate is 35 percent, and its marginal rate is 40 percent.

   a. What is McGonnigal's degree of operating leverage at a sales level of $40 million?

   b. What is McGonnigal's current degree of financial leverage?

   c. Forecast McGonnigal's EPS if sales drop to $38 million.

14. A firm's operating income is expected to be $1 million at a sales level of $10 million, and interest expenses equal $200,000. Forecast operating income for the firm with a degree of operating leverage of 2.5, assuming sales decline by 4 percent.

15. Earnings per share (EPS) for Valcor, Inc. are $3 at a sales level of $2 million. If Valcor's degree of operating leverage is 2.0 and its degree of combined leverage is 8.0, what will happen to EPS if operating income increases by 3 percent?

16. Walker's Gunnery, a small-arms manufacturer, has current sales of $10 million and operating income (EBIT) of $450,000. The degree of operating leverage for Walker is 2.5. Next year's sales are expected to increase by 5 percent. Walker has found that over time, the standard deviation of operating income is $300,000 and that operating income is approximately normally distributed about its expected value in any year. Walker's current financial structure contains both debt and preferred stock. Interest payments total $200,000, and preferred stock dividends total $60,000. Walker's marginal tax rate is 40 percent. What is the probability that Walker's Gunnery will report negative earnings per share during the coming year?

17. Scherr Corporation's current EPS is $5.00 at a sales level of $10,000,000. At this sales level, EBIT is $2,000,000. Scherr's DCL has been estimated to be 2.0 at the current level of sales. Sales are forecast to have an expected value of $11,000,000 next year, with a standard deviation of $500,000. The coefficient of variation of sales is equal to 0.045. What is the probability that EPS will be less than $5.00 per share next year, assuming that sales are normally distributed?

18. Kaufman Industries expects next year's operating income (EBIT) to equal $4 million, with a standard deviation of $2 million. The coefficient of variation of operating income is equal to 0.50. Interest expenses will be $1 million, and preferred dividends will be $600,000. Debt retirement will require principal payments of $1 million. Kaufman's marginal tax rate is 40 percent. If EBIT is normally distributed, what is the probability that Kaufman will have negative EPS next year?

19. Emco Products has a present capital structure consisting only of common stock (10 million shares). The company is planning a major expansion. At this time, the company is undecided between the following two financing plans (assume a 40 percent marginal tax rate):

   ■ *Plan 1: Equity financing.* Under this plan, an additional 5 million shares of common stock will be sold at $10 each.

   ■ *Plan 2: Debt financing.* Under this plan, $50 million of 10 percent long-term debt will be sold.

   One piece of information the company desires for its decision analysis is an EBIT-EPS analysis.

   a. Calculate the EBIT-EPS indifference point.

   b. Graphically determine the EBIT-EPS indifference point.
      Hint: Use EBIT = $10 million and $25 million.

   c. What happens to the indifference point if the interest rate on debt increases and the common stock sales price remains constant?

d. What happens to the indifference point if the interest rate on debt remains constant and the common stock sales price increases?

20. Two capital goods manufacturing companies, Rock Island and Davenport, are virtually identical in all aspects of their operations—product lines, amount of sales, total size, and so on. The two companies differ only in their capital structures, as shown here:

	Rock Island	Davenport
Debt (8%)	$400 million	$100 million
Common equity	$600 million	$900 million
Number of common shares outstanding	30 million	45 million

Each company has $1,000 million ($1 billion) in total assets.

Capital goods manufacturers typically are subject to cyclical trends in the economy. Suppose that the EBIT level for both companies is $100 million during an expansion and $60 million during a recession. (Assume a 40 percent tax rate for both companies.)

a. Calculate the earnings per share for both companies during expansion and recession.
b. Which stock is riskier? Why?
c. At what EBIT level are the earnings per share of the two companies identical?
d. Calculate the common stock price for both companies during an expansion if the stock market assigns a price-earnings ratio of 10 to Davenport and 9 to Rock Island.

21. Morton Industries is considering opening a new subsidiary in Boston, to be operated as a separate company. The company's financial analysts expect the new facility's average EBIT level to be $6 million per year. At this time, the company is considering the following two financing plans (use a 40 percent marginal tax rate in your analysis):

■ *Plan 1: Equity financing.* Under this plan, 2 million common shares will be sold at $10 each.
■ *Plan 2: Debt-equity financing.* Under this plan, $10 million of 12 percent long-term debt and 1 million common shares at $10 each will be sold.

a. Calculate the EBIT-EPS indifference point.
b. Calculate the expected EPS for both financing plans.
c. What factors should the company consider in deciding which financing plan to adopt?
d. Which plan do you recommend the company adopt?
e. Suppose Morton adopts Plan 2, and the Boston facility initially operates at an annual EBIT level of $6 million. What is the times interest earned ratio?
f. If the lenders require that the new company maintain a times interest earned ratio equal to 3.5 or greater, by how much could the EBIT level drop and the company still be in compliance with the loan agreement if Plan 2 is adopted?
g. Suppose the expected annual EBIT level of $6 million is normally distributed with a standard deviation of $3 million. What is the probability that the EPS will be negative in any given year if Plan 1 is selected?

22. High Sky, Inc., a hot air balloon manufacturing firm, currently has the following simplified balance sheet:

Assets		Liabilities and Capital	
Total assets	$1,100,000	Bonds (10% interest)	$600,000
		Common stock at par ($3), 100,000	
		shares outstanding	300,000
		Contributed capital in excess of par	100,000
		Retained earnings	100,000
		Total liabilities and capital	$1,100,000

The company is planning an expansion that is expected to cost $600,000. The expansion can be financed with new equity (sold to net the company $4 per share) or with the sale of new bonds at an interest rate of 11 percent. (The firm's marginal tax rate is 40 percent.)

a. Compute the indifference point between the two financing alternatives.

b. If the expected level of EBIT for the firm is $240,000 with a standard deviation of $50,000, what is the probability that the debt financing alternative will produce higher earnings than the equity alternative? (EBIT is normally distributed.)

c. If the debt alternative is chosen, what is the probability that the company will have negative earnings per share in any period?

e❌cel   **23.** The Anaya Corporation is a leader in artificial intelligence research. Anaya's present capital structure consists of common stock (30 million shares) and debt ($250 million with an interest rate of 15 percent). The company is planning an expansion and wishes to examine alternative financing plans. The firm's marginal tax rate is 40 percent. Two alternatives under consideration are

■ *Plan 1: Common equity financing.* An additional 3 million shares of common stock will be sold at $20 each.

■ *Plan 2: Debt financing.* The firm would sell $30 million of first-mortgage bonds with a pretax cost of 14 percent and $30 million of debentures with a pretax cost of 15 percent.

a. Compute the indifference point between these two alternatives.

b. One of Anaya's artificially intelligent financial managers has suggested that the firm might be better off to finance with preferred stock rather than common stock. He suggested that the indifference point be computed between the debt financing alternative and a preferred stock financing alternative. Preferred stock ($60 million) will cost 16 percent after tax. Which option should be selected on an EPS basis? (No calculations are necessary if you set the problem up and think about the implications.)

e❌cel   **24.** The Bullock Cafeteria Corporation has computed the indifference point between a debt and common equity financing option to be $4 million of EBIT. EBIT is approximately normally distributed with an expected value of $4.5 million and a standard deviation of $600,000. The coefficient of variation is equal to 0.13.

a. What is the probability that the equity financing option will be superior to the debt option?

b. Under the debt option, Bullock will incur $3 million in interest expenses. What is the chance of Bullock losing money under the debt option?

e❌cel   **25.** Jenkins Products has a current capital structure that consists of $50 million in long-term debt at an interest rate of 10 percent and $40 million in common equity (10 million shares). The firm is considering an expansion program that will cost $10 million. This program can be financed with additional long-term debt at a 13 percent rate of interest, preferred stock at a cost of 14 percent, or the sale of new common stock at $10 per share. The firm's marginal tax rate is 40 percent.

a. Compute the indifference point level of EBIT between the debt financing option and the common stock option.

b. Compute the indifference point level of EBIT between the common stock option and the preferred stock option.

c. Is there an indifference point between the debt and preferred stock options? Why or why not?

26. The Oakland Shirt Company has computed its indifference level of EBIT to be $500,000 between an equity financing option and a debt financing option. Interest expense under the debt option is $200,000 and interest expense under the equity option is $100,000. The EBIT for the firm is approximately normally distributed with an expected value of $620,000 and a standard deviation of $190,000.

a. What is the probability that the equity financing option will be preferred to the debt financing option?

b. What is the probability that the firm will incur losses under the debt option?

27. Lassiter Bakery currently has 3 million shares of common stock outstanding that sell at a price of $25 per share. Lassiter also has $10 million of bank debt outstanding at a pretax interest rate of 12 percent and a private placement of $20 million in bonds at a pretax interest rate of 14 percent. Lassiter's marginal tax rate is 40 percent.

    Lassiter is planning entry into a new market area. This project will require Lassiter to raise $30 million. Two alternatives have been proposed:
    - *Plan 1: Common equity financing.* Sell new stock at a net proceeds price to Lassiter of $20 per share.
    - *Plan 2: Debt-equity financing.* Sell a combination of stock at a net proceeds price to Lassiter of $20 per share and $10 million of long-term debt at a pretax interest rate of 15 percent.
    a. Compute the indifference level of EBIT between these two alternatives.
    b. If Lassiter's EBIT next year is approximately normally distributed with an expected value of $20 million and a standard deviation of $5 million, what is the probability that Plan 2 will result in higher earnings per share than Plan 1?

28. Jackson Asphalt, Inc. (JA) currently has 2 million shares of common stock outstanding and $50 million of 10 percent coupon-rate first-mortgage bonds. JA's marginal tax rate is 40 percent. JA's CFO has made three alternative proposals for financing a planned capital expansion:
    - *Plan 1: Debt financing.* Sell $50 million of debentures at a coupon interest rate of 12 percent.
    - *Plan 2: Preferred stock financing.* Sell $50 million of preferred stock paying a dividend at an 11 percent rate.
    - *Plan 3: Common stock financing.* Sell 1 million shares of new common stock to raise $50 million.

    If JA's only objective is to have the highest possible earnings per share next year, and if EBIT is expected to total $21 million next year, which alternative should be chosen based on an EBIT-EPS indifference point analysis?

29. Bowaite's Manufacturing has a current cash and marketable securities balance of $50 million. The company's economist is forecasting a two-year recession. Free cash flows during the recession, which are normally distributed, are expected to total $70 million, with a standard deviation of $60 million. The company's marginal tax rate is 40 percent.
    a. Under these conditions, what is the probability that Bowaite's will run out of cash during the recession?
    b. Bowaite's is considering a major capital expansion project. If the project is undertaken it will be financed initially with debt totaling $200 million. This debt financing will require after-tax cash outflows for debt service during the two-year recession of $60 million. If Bowaite's is willing to accept a 10 percent chance of running out of cash, should the expansion (with debt financing) be undertaken?

30. Dalton Carpet Company has determined that its EBIT for the coming year is approximately normally distributed with an expected value of $4.0 million and a standard deviation of $2.5 million. The coefficient of variation is equal to 0.625. Given its current capital structure, Dalton has $1 million in interest payments due during the coming year. (There is no preferred stock in its capital structure.) Determine the probability that Dalton will have
    a. Negative EPS.
    b. Positive EPS.

31. Next year's EBIT for the Latrobe Company is approximately normally distributed with an expected value of $8 million and a standard deviation of $5 million. The firm's marginal tax rate is 40 percent. Fixed financial charges (interest payments) next year are $1.5 million. Determine the probability that Latrobe will have
    a. Negative EPS.
    b. Positive EPS.

32. Waco Manufacturing Company has a cash (and marketable securities) balance of $150 million. Free cash flows during a projected one-year recession are expected to

be $200 million with a standard deviation of $200 million. (Assume that free cash flows are approximately normally distributed.)

a. Determine the probability that Waco will run out of cash during the recession.

b. Waco is considering a change in its capital structure that would add $50 million (after-tax) to its fixed financial charges. Determine the probability of running out of cash if the change in capital structure is undertaken.

c. Determine the maximum additional fixed financial charges that Waco can incur if it is willing to tolerate only a 5 percent chance of running out of cash during the recession.

33. Fairfield Electronics has a current capital structure consisting of $250 million in long-term debt at an interest rate of 10 percent and $150 million in common equity (15 million shares). The firm is considering an expansion program that will cost $50 million. The program can be financed using one of the following plans:

■ *Plan 1: Debt financing.* $50 million in long-term debt at a pretax interest rate of 11 percent.

■ *Plan 2: Preferred stock financing.* $50 million in preferred stock at a cost of 13 percent.

■ *Plan 3: Common stock financing.* 5 million shares at $10 per share (net).

The company's marginal tax rate is 40 percent.

a. Determine the EBIT indifference point between Plans 1 and 3.

b. Determine the EBIT indifference point between Plans 2 and 3.

c. Construct an EPS-EBIT graph for the three financing plans.

d. Determine which financing plan should be chosen if EBIT is
   i. $30 million.
   ii. $60 million.
   iii. $90 million.

34. University Technologies, Inc. (UTI) has a current capital structure consisting of 10 million shares of common stock, $200 million of first-mortgage bonds with a coupon interest rate of 13 percent, and $40 million of preferred stock paying a 5 percent dividend. In order to expand into Asia, UTI will have to undertake an aggressive capital outlay campaign, expected to cost $200 million. This expansion can be financed either by selling 4 million new shares of common stock at a price of $50 per share or by the sale of $200 million of subordinated debentures at a pretax interest rate of 15 percent. The company's tax rate is 40 percent.

a. Compute the EBIT-EPS indifference point between the equity and debt financing alternatives.

b. If UTI expects next year's EBIT to be $150 million with a standard deviation of $20 million, what is the probability that the equity financing option will produce higher earnings per share than the debt financing option?

35. EBITDA, Inc., a subsidiary of Robinson Enterprises, is considering the purchase of a fleet of new BMW's for the CEO and other senior managers. Currently the firm has a capital structure that consists of 60 percent debt, 30 percent common equity, and 10 percent preferred stock. The pretax interest rate on currently outstanding debt is 9 percent. The dividend yield on the company's preferred stock is 12 percent. Total capitalization is $20 million. This fleet of new cars will cost $1,000,000 and the company plans to finance the entire purchase with debt, at a pretax interest rate of 10 percent. The firm's marginal tax rate is 40 percent. The expected level of EBIT for the firm over the coming year is $1.7 million with a standard deviation of $200,000.

If the firm acquires the cars and finances them with debt as proposed, what is the *increase* in the probability of the company generating losses during the coming year?

36. Ellington's Cabaret is planning a major expansion that will require $95 million of new financing. Ellington's currently has a capital structure consisting of $400 million of common equity (with a cost of 14 percent and 4 million shares outstanding), $50 million of preferred stock ($50 par, $5 dividend), and $200 million of long-term debt

(with a coupon interest rate of 9 percent). The marginal tax rate is 40 percent and the average tax rate is 30 percent.

In order to finance the expansion, Ellington is considering two possible sources of funding: (1) the sale of new sharers of stock at a net price of $95 per share; or (2) the sale of debentures at a coupon rate of interest of 10 percent.

a. What is the level of EBIT at the indifference point between these two alternatives? What are the earnings per share at this level?

b. If the expected level of EBIT is $100 million with a standard deviation of $20 million, what is the probability of having unfavorable financial leverage if the debt financing alternative is chosen?

■ SOLUTIONS TO SELF-TEST PROBLEMS

ST1. a. $\text{DOL} = \dfrac{\text{Sales} - \text{Variable costs}}{\text{EBIT}}$

$$= \frac{\$5,000,000 - \$1,000,000}{\$2,000,000}$$

$$= 2.0$$

$$\text{DFL} = \frac{\text{EBIT}}{\text{EBIT} - I - D_p/(1 - T)}$$

$$= \frac{\$2,000,000}{\$2,000,000 - \$500,000 - \dfrac{\$100,000}{(1 - 0.4)}}$$

$$= \frac{\$2,000,000}{\$1,333,333}$$

$$= 1.5$$

$$\text{DCL} = \frac{\text{Sales} - \text{Variable Costs}}{\text{EBIT} - I - D_p/(1 - T)}$$

$$= \frac{\$5,000,000 - \$1,000,000}{\$2,000,000 - \$500,000 - \dfrac{\$100,000}{(1 - 0.4)}}$$

$$= 3.0$$

Check: DCL = DOL × DFL

$$= 2.0 \times 1.5$$

$$= 3.0$$

b. Current EPS $= \dfrac{\$800,000}{400,000 \text{ shares}} = \$2.00$

A sales increase to $5.5 million represents a 10 percent increase in sales. Hence, EPS should increase by 30 percent (10% × 3.0), to $2.60.

ST2. $p(\text{EPS} < \$0) = p(\text{EBIT} < \$250,000)$

$$z = \frac{\text{EBIT} - \widehat{\text{EBIT}}}{\sigma}$$

$$= \frac{\$250,000 - \$1,750,000}{\$1,200,000}$$

$$= -1.25$$

$$p = 0.1056 \text{ (or } 10.56\%)$$

ST3. a. $\dfrac{(\text{EBIT} - I_d)(1 - T) - D_p}{N_d} = \dfrac{(\text{EBIT} - I_e)(1 - T) - D_p}{N_e}$

$$\frac{(\text{EBIT} - \$18)(1 - 0.40)}{100} = \frac{(\text{EBIT} - \$0)(1 - 0.40)}{110}$$

$$\text{EBIT} = \$198 \text{ (million)}$$

b. $p(\text{EPS} < \$0) = p(\text{EBIT} < \$18.0)$

$$z = \frac{\text{EBIT} - \widehat{\text{EBIT}}}{\sigma}$$

$$= \frac{\$18.0 - \$250}{\$200}$$

$$= -1.16$$

$$p = 0.1230 \text{ (or } 12.30\%)$$

c. $p(\text{EBIT} > \$198)$

$$z = \frac{\$198 - \$250}{\$200}$$

$$= -0.26$$

$$p = 1 - 0.3974 = 0.6026 \text{ (or } 60.26\%)$$

ST4. a. $CB_0 = \$20$ million; $FCF_R = \$60$ million; $\sigma = \$60$ million

$$CB_R = CB_0 + FCF_R$$

$$= \$20 \text{ million} + \$60 \text{ million}$$

$$= \$80 \text{ million}$$

$$z = \frac{\$0 - CB_R}{\sigma}$$

$$= \frac{\$0 - \$80}{\$60}$$

$$= -1.33$$

$$p = 0.0918 \text{ (or } 9.18\%)$$

b. $CB_R = \$20$ million $+ \$60$ million $- \$10$ million

$$= \$70 \text{ million}$$

$$\sigma = \$60 \text{ million}$$

$$z = \frac{\$0 - \$70}{\$60} = -1.17$$

$$p = 0.1210 \text{ (or } 12.10\%)$$

■ GLOSSARY

Degree of Combined Leverage (DCL) The percentage change in a firm's earnings per share (EPS) resulting from a 1 percent change in sales or output. This also is equal to the degree of operating leverage times the degree of financial leverage used by the firm.

Degree of Financial Leveragel (DFL) The percentage change in a firm's EPS resulting from a 1 percent change in EBIT.

Degree of Operating Leverage (DOL) The percentage change in a firm's EBIT resulting from a 1 percent change in sales or output.

EBIT-EPS Indifference Point That level of EBIT where the earnings per share of a firm are the same, regardless of which of two alternative capital structures is employed.

Fixed Costs Costs that do not vary as the level of a firm's output changes.

Variable Costs Costs that vary in close relationship with changes in a firm's output level.

APPENDIX 13A
BREAKEVEN ANALYSIS

GLOSSARY OF NEW TERMS

Breakeven Analysis A technique used to examine the relationship between a firm's sales, costs, and profits at various levels of output. It sometimes is termed *cost-volume-profit analysis.*

Cash Breakeven Point The output level at which total revenues equal cash operating costs. In the linear breakeven model, the breakeven point is found by dividing fixed cash (operating) costs by the difference between price and variable cost per unit.

Contribution Margin The difference between price and variable cost per unit in breakeven analysis.

INTRODUCTION

To gain an understanding of the role that operating leverage plays in determining the business risk of a firm, it is useful to develop the fundamentals of **breakeven analysis** (also known as *cost-volume-profit analysis*). Breakeven analysis considers the relationships among a firm's sales, fixed and variable operating costs, and EBIT (operating income) at various output levels.

The term *breakeven analysis* is somewhat misleading, because breakeven analysis is used to answer many questions beyond those dealing with the breakeven (EBIT = 0) output level of a firm or division of a firm. Possible uses include:[1]

1. Forecasting the profitability for a firm, division, or product line, given a cost structure and expected sales levels.
2. Analyzing the impact of changes in fixed costs, variable costs, and selling price on operating profits.
3. Analyzing the impact of substituting fixed costs (primarily capital equipment) for variable costs (labor) in a production process.
4. Analyzing the profit impact of a firm's restructuring efforts designed to cut fixed costs.

In addition, we will find that breakeven analysis concepts and an understanding of the relationships between fixed costs, variable costs, prices, and profits are useful when planning the mix of financing sources a firm will use. If a firm, such as United Airlines, already has a high proportion of fixed operating costs that must be covered by sales revenue, it may not be prudent to use large amounts of fixed-cost sources of financing, such as bonds or preferred stock. Airlines that have made this financing error, such as Pan American, Eastern, Continental, TWA, and Braniff either have failed or are operating close to the edge of bankruptcy.

[1]A good illustration of the application of breakeven analysis in finance can be found in U.E. Reinhardt, "Break-Even Analysis for Lockheed's Tri Star: An Application of Financial Theory," *Journal of Finance* 28 (September 1973): 821–838.

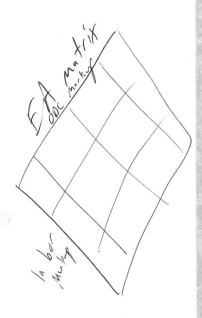

forecasting

GRAPHIC BREAKEVEN ANALYSIS

Breakeven analysis can be developed graphically, algebraically, or as a combination of the two. Figure 13A-1 is an example of a basic linear breakeven analysis chart. Costs and revenues (measured in dollars) are plotted on the vertical axis, and output (measured in units) is plotted on the horizontal axis. The *total revenue* function, TR, represents the total revenue the firm will realize at each output level, given that the firm charges a constant selling price, P, per unit of output. Similarly, the *total (operating) cost* function, TC, represents the total cost the firm will incur at each output level. Total cost is computed as the sum of the firm's fixed costs, F, which are independent of the output level, plus the variable costs, which increase at the constant rate, V, per unit of output.

The assumptions of a constant selling price per unit, P, and a constant variable cost per unit, V, yield *linear* relationships for the total revenue and total cost functions. However, these linear relationships are valid only over some *relevant range* of output values, such as from Q_1 to Q_2 in Figure 13A-1.

The breakeven point occurs at point Q_b in Figure 13A-1, where the total revenue and the total cost functions intersect. If a firm's output level is below this breakeven point—that is, if TR < TC—it incurs *operating losses,* defined as a *negative EBIT.* If the firm's output level is above this breakeven point—that is, if TR > TC—it realizes *operating profits,* defined as a *positive EBIT.*

Determining a firm's breakeven point graphically involves three steps:

1. Drawing a line through the origin with a slope of P to represent the TR function.
2. Drawing a line that intersects the vertical axis at F and has a slope of V to represent the TC function.

3. Determining the point where the TR and TC lines intersect, dropping a perpendicular line to the horizontal axis, and noting the resulting value of Q_b.

ALGEBRAIC BREAKEVEN ANALYSIS

To determine a firm's breakeven point algebraically, it is necessary to set the total revenue and total (operating) cost functions equal to each other and solve the resulting equation for the breakeven volume.

Total revenue is equal to the selling price per unit times the output quantity:

$$TR = P \times Q \tag{13A.1}$$

Total (operating) cost is equal to fixed plus variable costs, where the variable cost is the product of the variable cost per unit times the output quantity:

$$TC = F + (V \times Q) \tag{13A.2}$$

Setting the total revenue and total cost expressions equal to each other (that is, setting EBIT = TR − TC = 0) and substituting the breakeven output Q_b for Q results in the following:

$$TR = TC$$

or

$$PQ_b = F + VQ_b \tag{13A.3}$$

Finally, solving Equations 13A.3 for the breakeven output Q_b yields the following:

$$PQ_b - VQ_b = F$$
$$(P - V)Q_b = F$$
$$Q_b = \frac{F}{P - V} \tag{13A.4}$$

The *difference* between the selling price per unit and the variable cost per unit, $P - V$, is sometimes referred to as the **contribution margin per unit.** It measures how much each unit of output contributes to meeting fixed costs and operating profits. Therefore, it also can be said that the breakeven output is equal to the fixed costs divided by the contribution margin per unit.

Breakeven analysis can also be performed in terms of dollar *sales,* rather than units of output. The breakeven dollar sales volume, S_b, can be determined by the following expression:

$$S_b = \frac{F}{1 - (V/P)} \tag{13A.5}$$

where V/P is the variable cost ratio (that is, the variable cost per dollar of sales).

Occasionally, the analyst is interested in determining the output quantity at which a *target profit* (expressed in dollars) is achieved. An expression similar to Equation 13A.4 can be used to find such a quantity:

$$\text{Target volume} = \frac{\text{Fixed cost} + \text{Target profit}}{\text{Contribution margin per unit}} \tag{13A.6}$$

Examples of Breakeven Analysis

Consider again the Allegan Manufacturing Company discussed in the chapter (see Table 13–1). Assume that the firm manufactures one product, which it sells for $250 per unit. The current output, Q, is obtained by dividing total dollar sales ($5 million) by the selling price per unit ($250) to obtain 20,000 units per year. Its variable (operating) costs per unit, V, are determined by dividing total variable costs ($3 million) by current output (20,000) to obtain $150 per unit.

The firm's fixed costs, F, are $1 million. Substituting these figures into Equation 13A.4 yields the following breakeven output:

$$Q_b = \frac{\$1,000,000}{\$250 - \$150}$$

$$= 10,000 \text{ units}$$

Allegan's breakeven output can also be determined graphically, as shown in Figure 13A-2. The breakeven level of dollar sales also is shown in Figure 13A-2 to be $2,500,000.

Because a firm's breakeven output is dependent upon a number of variables—in particular, the price per unit and variable (operating) costs per unit—managers may wish to analyze the effects of changes in any one of the variables on the breakeven output. For example, they may wish to consider either of the following: (1) changing the selling price or (2) substituting fixed costs for variable costs.

Assume that Allegan increased the selling price per unit by $25, to $275, P'. Substituting this figure into Equation 13A.4 gives a new breakeven output:

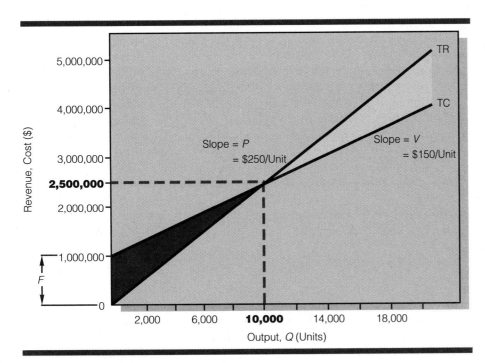

FIGURE 13A-2
Linear Breakeven Analysis Chart for
the Allegan Manufacturing Company

FIGURE 13A-3
Linear Breakeven Analysis Chart for the Allegan Manufacturing Company Showing the Effects of a Price Increase

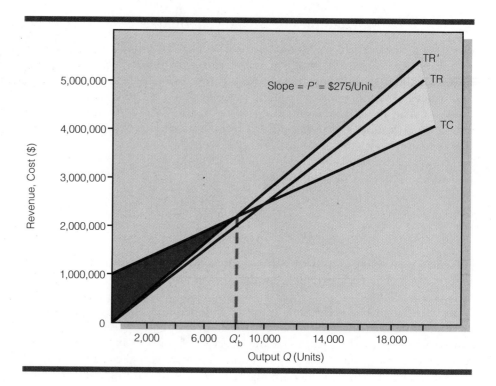

$$Q'_b = \frac{\$1,000,000}{\$275 - \$150}$$

$$= 8,000 \text{ units}$$

Figure 13A-3 graphically shows how an increase in the price per unit increases the slope of the total revenue function, TR', and reduces the breakeven output.

Rather than increasing the selling price per unit, Allegan's management may decide to substitute fixed costs for variable costs in some aspect of the company's operations. For example, as labor wage rates increase over time, many firms seek to reduce operating costs through automation, which in effect represents the substitution of fixed-cost capital equipment for variable-cost labor. Suppose that Allegan determines it can reduce labor costs by $25 per unit by purchasing $1 million in additional equipment. Assume that the new equipment is depreciated over a 10-year life using the straight-line method. Under these conditions, annual depreciation of the new equipment would be $1,000,000/10 = $100,000, and the firm's new level of fixed costs, F', would be $1,000,000 + $100,000 = $1,100,000. Variable costs per unit, V', would be $150 − $25 = $125. Substituting $P = $250 per unit, $V' = $125 per unit, and $F' = $1,100,000 into Equation 13A.4 yields a new breakeven output:

$$Q'_b = \frac{\$1,100,000}{\$250 - \$125}$$

$$= 8,800 \text{ units}$$

As Figure 13A-4 shows, the effect of this change in operations is to raise the intercept on the vertical axis, decrease the slope of the total cost function, TC', and reduce the breakeven output.

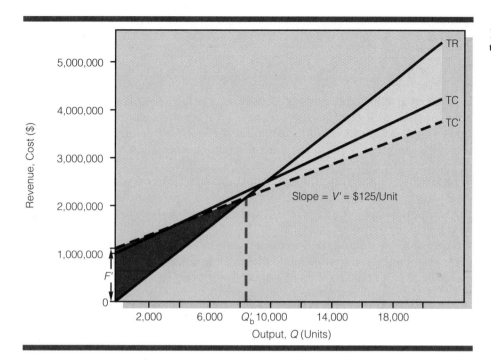

FIGURE 13A-4
**Linear Breakeven Analysis Chart for
the Allegan Manufacturing Company
Showing the Effects of Substituting
Fixed Costs for Variable Costs**

DOL and Breakeven Analysis

The variables defined in the preceding section (TR = total revenue, Q = quantity, P = price per unit, V = variable cost per unit, and F = fixed costs) can also be used to develop a formula for determining a firm's degree of operating leverage, or DOL, at any given output level. Because sales are equivalent to TR (or $P \times Q$), variable cost is equal to $V \times Q$, and EBIT is equal to total revenue (TR) less total (operating) cost, or $(P \times Q) - F - (V \times Q)$, these values can be substituted into Equation 13.2 given in the chapter to obtain the following:

$$\text{DOL at } Q = \frac{(P \times Q) - (V \times Q)}{(P \times Q) - F - (V \times Q)}$$

or

$$\text{DOL at } Q = \frac{(P - V)Q}{(P - V)Q - F} \tag{13A.7}$$

For example, in the case of Allegan Manufacturing Company, where P = \$250/unit, V = \$150/unit, and F = \$1,000,000, the DOL at an output level of Q = 20,000 units is

$$\text{DOL at } 20,000 = \frac{(\$250/\text{unit} - \$150/\text{unit})20,000 \text{ units}}{(\$250/\text{unit} - \$150/\text{unit})20,000 \text{ units} - \$1,000,000}$$

$$= 2.0$$

This is the same value that was obtained in the chapter using Equation 13.1 at a total revenue (TR) of \$5,000,000 (i.e., P = \$250/unit $\times$ Q = 20,000 units).

Are you (or your parents, a neighbor, a friend . . .) thinking of refinancing your home? The correct decision is actually based on a breakeven analysis. Chase Manhattan Mortgage will calculate the amount of time you must live in your home after refinancing in order to break even. (It's a free calculation—just plug in the numbers.)
http://www.chase.com:8009/
noframes/refi-calc-intro.html

BREAKEVEN ANALYSIS AND RISK ASSESSMENT

The information generated from a breakeven analysis can be used to assess the operating risk to which a firm is exposed. Consider the example represented in Figure 13A-2. With fixed costs of $1 million, a price per unit of $250, and variable costs per unit of $150, the breakeven output was computed to be 10,000 units. If we add to this set of information the *expected* (mean) level of sales (in units) for some future period of time, the standard deviation of the distribution of sales, and the assumption that actual sales are approximately normally distributed, it is possible to compute the probability that the firm will have operating losses (that is, sell fewer units than the breakeven level) and the probability that the firm will have operating profits (that is, sell more units than the breakeven level).

For example, suppose that expected unit sales for Allegan are 15,000 units with a standard deviation of 4,000 units. The probability of having operating losses (that is, the probability of selling fewer than 10,000 units) can be computed by determining the number of standard deviations that this value is from the expected value and using the probability values from Reference Table V.

$$z = \frac{10,000 - 15,000}{4,000} = -1.25$$

In other words, a sales level of 10,000 units is 1.25 standard deviations *below* the mean. From Table V it can be seen that the probability associated with -1.25 standard deviations is 10.56 percent. Therefore, there is a 10.56 percent chance that the firm will incur operating losses and an 89.44 percent (100 percent minus 10.56 percent chance of losses) chance that the firm will record operating profits (that is, sell more than the breakeven number of units of output).

SOME LIMITATIONS OF BREAKEVEN ANALYSIS

Breakeven analysis as presented above has a number of limitations. These arise from the *assumptions* that are made in constructing the model and developing the relevant data. The application of breakeven analysis is of value only to the extent that these assumptions are valid.

Constant Selling Price and Variable Cost per Unit

Recall that in the graphic breakeven analysis model, the assumptions of a constant selling price and variable cost per unit yield linear relationships for the total revenue and total cost functions. In practice, these functions tend to be nonlinear. In many cases, a firm can sell additional units of output only by lowering the price per unit. This results in a total revenue function that is curvilinear, as shown in Figure 13A-5, instead of a straight line.

In addition, a firm's total cost function may be nonlinear because variable costs per unit initially decrease and then increase. This is also shown in Figure 13A-5. Decreasing variable costs per unit can occur if, for example, labor specialization results in increased output per labor hour. Increasing variable costs per unit can occur if, for example, a firm uses more costly overtime labor as output approaches production capacity.

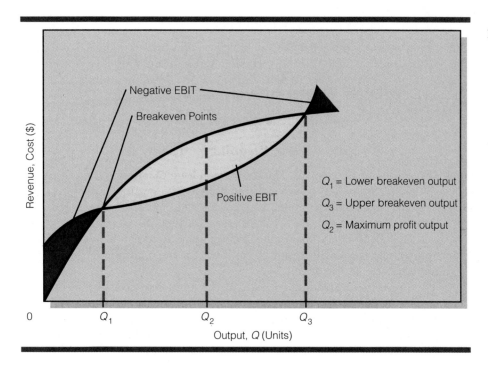

Nonlinear TC and TR functions can result in a firm having more than one breakeven output point. This is shown in Figure 13A-5, where a breakeven situation occurs at both Point Q_1 and Point Q_3. This is interpreted to mean that the firm will incur operating losses *below* an output level of Q_1 and *above* an output level of Q_3. The firm's total operating profits are maximized within the range of $Q_1 - Q_3$ at the point where the vertical distance between the TR and TC curves is greatest; that is, at output level Q_2.

In summary, the assumption of a constant selling price and variable cost per unit is probably valid over some "relevant range" of output levels. However, consideration of output levels outside this range normally will require modifications in the breakeven chart, such as the construction of a new total revenue curve reflecting expected sales levels at each new price.

Composition of Operating Costs

Another assumption of breakeven analysis is that costs can be classified as either fixed or variable. In fact, fixed and variable costs are dependent on both the time period involved and the output range under consideration. All costs are variable in the long run. In addition, some costs are partly fixed and partly variable. Furthermore, some costs increase in a stepwise manner as output is increased (that is, *semivariable costs*) and are constant only over relatively narrow ranges of output.

Multiple Products

The breakeven model also assumes that a firm is producing and selling either a *single* product or a *constant* mix of different products. In many cases, the product mix changes over time, and problems can arise in allocating fixed costs among the various products.

Uncertainty

Still another assumption of breakeven analysis is that the selling price and variable cost per unit, as well as fixed costs, are known at each level of output. In practice, these parameters are subject to uncertainty. Thus, the usefulness of the results of breakeven analysis depends on how accurate the estimates of these parameters are.

Short-Term Planning Horizon

Finally, breakeven analysis normally is performed for a planning period of 1 year or less. However, the benefits received from some costs may not be realized until subsequent periods. For example, research and development costs incurred during a specific period may not result in new products for several years. For breakeven analysis to be a dependable decision-making tool, a firm's operating costs should be matched with resulting revenues for the planning period under consideration.

A related problem associated with the horizon for analysis is the fact that a firm's cost and pricing structure change almost continually. When a significant change occurs in the cost or pricing structure of a firm, a new breakeven point must be computed. Hence, breakeven analysis will tend to be more valuable in industries characterized by relative cost and pricing stability.

 CASH BREAKEVEN POINT

The calculation of a **cash breakeven point** may assist a firm in its financial planning. Some of a firm's fixed operating costs, namely depreciation, are *noncash outlays.* The cash breakeven point is calculated by subtracting the noncash depreciation charges, *Dep,* from the fixed operating costs, *F,* in the numerator of the breakeven equation (Equation 13A.4):

$$\text{Cash breakeven point} = \frac{F - Dep}{P - V} \tag{13A.8}$$

It measures the volume of output (units) required to cover the firm's fixed cash operating outlays, such as management salaries, rent, and utilities.

Cash breakeven analysis can also be performed in terms of dollar sales. The cash breakeven dollar sales volume can be determined with the following expression:

$$\text{Cash breakeven sales} = \frac{F - Dep}{1 - (V/P)} \tag{13A.9}$$

All other things being equal, a firm with a larger proportion of its fixed costs in the form of noncash outlays will have a lower cash breakeven point and be better able to survive during a business downturn than a firm whose fixed costs consist mainly of cash outlays.

Consider the following example. Victor Rodriguez has been offered a new auto dealership, and the manufacturer has provided him with various sales forecasts. As part of a detailed analysis of the proposed dealership, he would like an estimate of the cash breakeven point for new car sales. He estimates that fixed costs will be $2 million a year, including depreciation expense of

$300,000 a year. In addition, the new car sales price is expected to be $13,000 per unit, and the new car variable cost is expected to be $11,000 per unit. The estimated cash breakeven point for new car sales can be calculated using Equation 13A.9:

$$\text{Cash breakeven point} = \frac{\$2,000,000 - \$300,000}{\$13,000 - \$11,000}$$

$$= 850 \text{ units}$$

The cash breakeven sales volume is calculated using Equation 13A.9:

$$\text{Cash breakeven sales} = \frac{\$2,000,000 - \$300,000}{1 - (\$11,000/\$13,000)}$$

$$= \$11,050,000$$

Rodriguez can now analyze the manufacturer's marketing data to determine the likelihood of exceeding the estimated cash breakeven point for new car sales.

■ QUESTIONS AND TOPICS FOR DISCUSSION

1. Explain how a linear breakeven chart is constructed when a firm's selling price, variable costs per unit, and fixed costs are known.
2. What are some of the limitations of breakeven analysis? How can these limitations affect actual financial decision making?
3. Assuming that all other factors remain unchanged, determine how a firm's breakeven point is affected by each of the following:
   a. The firm finds it necessary to reduce the price per unit because of competitive conditions in the market.
   b. The firm's direct labor costs increase as a result of a new labor contract.
   c. The Occupational Safety and Health Administration requires the firm to install new ventilating equipment in its plant. (Assume that this action has no effect on worker productivity.)

■ SELF-TEST PROBLEMS

ST1. Myers Implements is attempting to develop and market a new garden tractor. Fixed costs to develop and produce the new tractor are estimated to be $10,000,000 per year. The variable cost to make each tractor has been estimated at $2,000. The marketing research department has recommended a price of $4,000 per tractor.
   a. What is the breakeven level of output for the new tractor?
   b. If management expects to generate a target profit of $2,000,000 from the tractor each year, how many tractors must be sold?

ST2. Westerfield Enterprises has determined that the breakeven level of output for its snowblower is 20,000 units. The marketing research department has determined that expected sales will be 22,000 units, with a standard deviation of 4,000 units. What is the probability that Westerfield will incur operating losses from the sale of the snowblower?

■ PROBLEMS*

1. East Publishing Company is doing an analysis of a proposed new finance text. Using the following data, answer Parts a through e.

*Colored numbers denote problems that have check answers provided at the end of the book.

Fixed Costs (per edition):

Development (reviews, class testing, and so on)	$18,000
Copyediting	5,000
Selling and promotion	7,000
Typesetting	40,000
Total	$70,000

Variable Costs (per copy):

Printing and binding	$4.20
Administrative costs	1.60
Salespeople's commission (2% of selling price)	.60
Author's royalties (12% of selling price)	3.60
Bookstore discounts (20% of selling price)	6.00
Total	$ 16.00
Projected Selling Price	$ 30.00

The company's marginal tax rate is 40 percent.

  a. Determine the company's breakeven volume for this book
    i. In units.
    ii. In dollar sales.
  b. Develop a breakeven chart for the text.
  c. Determine the number of copies East must sell in order to earn an (operating) profit of $21,000 on this text.
  d. Determine total (operating) profits at the following sales levels:
    i. 3,000 units.
    ii. 5,000 units.
    iii. 10,000 units.
  e. Suppose East feels that $30.00 is too high a price to charge for the new finance text. It has examined the competitive market and determined that $24.00 would be a better selling price. What would the breakeven volume be at this new selling price?

2. Jenkins Appliances produces microwave ovens. Jenkins has computed its breakeven level of sales to be 60,000 units. An analysis of the market has led Jenkins to *expect* sales of 75,000 units with a standard deviation of 10,000 units. Assume that sales are normally distributed.
  a. What is the probability that Jenkins will incur operating losses?
  b. What is the probability that Jenkins will operate above its breakeven point?

3. Vargo Industries has computed its breakeven level of output to be 25,000 units. Based on forecasts from its sales force and past experience, expected unit sales are 32,000, with a standard deviation of 5,200. What is the probability that Vargo will have operating losses? Assume that sales are normally distributed.

4. Logue Lock Company expects its fixed costs next year to be $750,000. The selling price for its lock is $40. Logue is considering the purchase of some new equipment that is expected to reduce unit variable costs from a current level of $25 to a new level of $20. How large could the additional fixed costs from the new equipment be without impacting the breakeven point?

5. Francis Furniture has current fixed costs of $1,000,000. Francis's only product, a roll-top desk, sells for $3,000. Variable operating costs per unit are $1,000. Francis plans to buy a new lathe that will produce a more precise roller for the desk. The lathe will add $100,000 in annual fixed costs. Variable operating costs are not expected to change as a result of the lathe purchase. If Francis wishes to leave its breakeven point unchanged, what action must it take?

6. Rodney Rogers, a recent business school graduate, plans to open a wholesale dairy products firm. Rogers expects first year sales to total $5,500,000. He desires to earn a target pretax profit of $1,000,000 during his first year of operation. Variable costs are 40 percent of sales.
  a. How large can Rogers's fixed costs be if he is to meet his profit target?

    b. What is Rogers's breakeven level of sales at the level of fixed costs determined in Part a?

7. The current price per unit for shock absorbers produced by Leveland Products is $25. The variable cost per unit is $10. Fixed costs are $600,000.

    a. What is the breakeven point in units?

    b. What is the DOL at the breakeven point? Explain what this value means conceptually.

8. The Covington Engine Company is considering opening a new plant facility to build truck engines. As part of a detailed analysis of the proposed facility, Covington's management wants some information on the cash breakeven point. Fixed costs for the facility are expected to be $6 million a year, including depreciation expenses of $800,000 a year. The engines' sales price is expected to be $7,000 per unit, and the variable cost is expected to be $3,000 per unit. Calculate the expected annual cash breakeven point and the expected annual cash breakeven sales.

■ SOLUTIONS TO SELF-TEST PROBLEMS

ST1. a. $Q_b = \dfrac{F}{P - V} = \dfrac{\$10,000,000}{\$4,000 - \$2,000} = 5,000$ units/year

    b. Target volume $= \dfrac{F + \$2,000,000}{P - V}$

$$= \dfrac{\$10,000,000 + \$2,000,000}{\$4,000 - \$2,000} = 6,000 \text{ units/year}$$

ST2. The probability of having operating losses is the probability of selling 20,000 units or less.

$$z = \dfrac{20,000 - 22,000}{4,000} = -0.5$$

The probability of a $z \le 0.5$ (i.e., the probability of selling 20,000 units or less) can be determined from Table V as 0.3085, or 30.85%.

DIVIDEND POLICY 14

1. Dividend policy determines the ultimate distribution of the firm's earnings between retention (that is, reinvestment) and cash dividend payments to shareholders.
2. Factors influencing the firm's choice of a dividend policy are examined, including
   a. Legal constraints.
   b. Restrictive covenants.
   c. Tax considerations.
   d. Liquidity considerations.
   e. Borrowing capacity and access to the capital markets.
   f. Earnings stability.
   g. Growth prospects.

KEY CHAPTER CONCEPTS

   h. Inflation.
   i. Shareholder preferences.
      j. Protection against dilution.
4. Alternative dividend policies include
   a. Passive residual approach.
   b. Stable dollar dividend approach.
   c. Constant payout ratio approach.
   d. Policy of paying a small, regular dividend plus year-end extras.
5. Other important topics include
   a. How dividends are paid.
   b. Stock dividends.
   c. Stock splits.
   d. Share repurchase as a dividend decision.

FLORIDA POWER & LIGHT'S DECISION TO CUT ITS DIVIDEND*

As a matter of policy, many firms pay out a relatively stable amount of their earnings to shareholders in the form of dividends. In general, a firm will increase dividend payments only when it is confident that it can sustain the higher rate through increased earnings and cash flows. Likewise, there is a reluctance to reduce the dollar amount of dividends from one period to the next unless the firm is faced with severe financial problems.

Prior to 1994, FPL (parent company of Florida Power & Light) had a record of 47 years of continuous annual dividend increases—the longest record of any electric utility and the third longest of any company traded on the New York Stock Exchange. However, on May 9, 1994 FPL announced a 32 percent reduction in its quarterly dividend from $.62 per share to $.42. While other utilities faced with financial difficulties had cut their dividends in the past, this was the first time a profitable utility had taken this action. This decision reduced FPL's dividend payout ratio from an average of 90 percent of the previous years' earnings.

The stock market's initial reaction to this decision was negative—FPL's stock price fell 14 percent on the day of the announcement. Since dividend cuts are often associated with reduced future earnings prospects, this price decline was not unexpected. In announcing the dividend cut, FPL explained that the company's high dividend payout ratio

was no longer in the shareholders' long-term interests. Because of deregulation, electric utilities were in the process of shifting from low-risk, regulated monopolies to riskier competitive companies. Faced with greater competition and less predictable future earnings, FPL's dividend decision was designed to increase its long-term financial flexibility and prospects for growth.

At the same time as the dividend cut, FPL also announced a stock repurchase program in which the company would purchase up to 10 million shares of its common stock over the next 3 years. Under present tax laws, capital gains income is taxed at lower rates than dividend income and taxes on

capital gains income can be deferred until the stock is sold. Thus, the substitution of stock repurchases for cash dividends provides a more tax-efficient means for companies to distribute excess capital to shareholders.

Once the reasons for FPL's dividend cut were studied by securities analysts and investors, FPL's stock price began to recover. Approximately one month after the announcement, over 15 major securities brokerage firms had placed FPL's common stock on their "buy" lists. One year later (on May 9, 1995), the rate of return (price increase plus dividends) on FPL's common stock was 23.8 percent—more than twice the rate of return on the Standard & Poor's Index and significantly higher than the 14.2 percent rate of return on the Standard & Poor's Utilities Index.

The decision by FPL to cut its cash dividend and substitute share repurchases for part of its cash dividends illustrates some of the important dividend policy issues that must be considered by management, including shareholder preferences, signaling effects of changes in dividends, taxes, earnings stability, and growth prospects.

This chapter discusses the elements of a sound dividend policy and how this policy can contribute to the overall firm objective of maximizing shareholder wealth.

*Based on Denis Soter, Eugene Brigham, and Paul Evanson, "The Dividend Cut Heard 'Round the World: The Case of FPL," *Journal of Applied Corporate Finance*, vol. 9, no. 1 (Spring 1996): 4–15.

INTRODUCTION

The value of a firm is influenced by three types of financial decisions:

- Investment decisions.
- Financing decisions.
- Dividend decisions.

Although each is presented as a separate topic in this and most financial management textbooks,[1] these three types of financial decisions are interdependent in a number of ways. For example, the investments made by a firm determine the level of future earnings and future potential dividends; capital structure influences the cost of capital, which determines, in part, the number of acceptable investment opportunities; and dividend policy influences the amount of equity capital in a firm's capital structure (via the retained earnings account) and, by extension, influences the cost of capital. In making these interrelated decisions, the goal is to maximize shareholder wealth.

Consider the following dividend decisions:

1. During 1994, Pennzoil paid out $138 million ($3.00 per share) in common stock dividends, despite after-tax losses of $35 million. Only after these losses continued did Pennzoil cut its annual dividend to $2.50 in 1995 and to $1.00 in 1996. During 1995 Pennzoil's stock fell to its lowest level in 10 years.

2. During 1996, Compaq Computer was expected to post record profits of $4.55 per share. The company has *never* paid a dividend. Compaq's stock price is near its all-time high.

3. In February 1994, Utah Medical Products, Inc., suspended its quarterly dividend in favor of repurchasing $3 million of the company's shares.

4. In January 1997, General Motors announced an increase in its quarterly cash dividend by 25 percent from $0.40 to $0.50 per share, along with plans to repurchase up to $2.5 billion of its common stock (or more than 5 percent of the total outstanding) over the next 12 months.

5. During 1992, General Motors paid out approximately $990 million ($1.40 per share) in common stock dividends (a *decrease* in stockholders' equity) while, during the same period, the company sold $2.145 billion in new common stock (an *increase* in stockholders' equity) and incurred $53.625 million in issuance costs.

6. Huntington Bank has paid stock dividends (i.e., additional shares of common stock), in addition to regular cash dividends during 18 of the past 23 years.

These dividend decisions raise a number of important questions, such as

1. Is Pennzoil's dividend policy more consistent with shareholder wealth maximization than is Compaq's dividend policy? Is one dividend policy necessarily optimal for all firms?

2. Why did Pennzoil pay a common stock dividend when it had negative earnings? Alternatively, would not the elimination of its dividend have been a more prudent strategy, because it would conserve cash (i.e., reduce cash outflows) during this period of economic difficulty?

---

[1]In this text, investment decisions are dealt with in Chapters 8 through 10 and 15 through 17, and financing decisions are discussed in Chapters 6, 7, 12, 13, 18, 19, and 20.

3. Why did Utah Medical Products substitute a share repurchase program for its cash dividends, while General Motors chose both to increase its cash dividends and to repurchase some of its shares of common stock?

4. Why did General Motors pay common stock dividends *and* incur the issuance costs of selling new common stock during the same time period? As an alternative to issuing new common stock, why didn't General Motors reduce its common stock dividend temporarily until it accumulated the amount of equity funds it planned to raise externally?

5. Why does Huntington Bank pay stock dividends when the net effect of these transactions is that total stockholders' equity remains unchanged and each shareholder's proportionate claim on the firm's total earnings remains constant?

6. What are the advantages to General Motors and its shareholders of the $2.5 billion stock repurchase program compared with paying shareholders an equivalent amount of cash dividends?

7. Finally, on a more fundamental level, does it really matter, with respect to the maximization of shareholder wealth, what amount (or percentage of earnings) a firm pays out in dividends?

In this chapter, we seek to answer dividend policy questions such as these.

This chapter begins by examining the factors that influence a company's choice of dividend policy. Next, it considers the pros and cons of a number of different dividend policies. And, finally, it discusses the mechanics of dividend payments, along with stock dividends and share repurchase plans.

 ## DETERMINANTS OF DIVIDEND POLICY

Dividend policy determines how the earnings of a company are distributed. Earnings either are retained and reinvested in the company or they are paid out to shareholders. In recent years, the retention of earnings has been a major source of equity financing for private industry. In 1994, corporations retained more than $120 billion in earnings while paying dividends of about $211 billion. Retained earnings are the most important source of equity. Retained earnings can be used to stimulate growth in future earnings and as a result can influence future share values. On the other hand, dividends provide stockholders with tangible current returns.

Industry and Company Variations in Dividend Payout Ratios

Dividend payout policies vary among different industries. As shown in Table 14-1, there is a wide variation in dividend payout ratios among different industries. Likewise, within a given industry, while many firms may have similar dividend payout ratios, there still can be considerable variation. For example, as illustrated in Table 14-2, within the tobacco industry, while most of the dividend payout ratios are in the 57 to 67 percent range, two firms have ratios down in the 40s. Within the basic chemical industry, the variation is even wider—with a range from 5.8 to 80.8 percent. This section examines some of the more important factors that combine to determine the dividend policy of a firm.

**TABLE 14-1
Dividend Payout Ratios
for Selected Industries**

Source: *The Value Line Investment Survey*
(New York: Value Line, Inc., 1996–1997,
various issues). Copyright © 1996–1997
by Value Line Publishing, Inc. Used by
permission. All rights reserved.

INDUSTRY	1995 DIVIDEND PAYOUT RATIO
Telecommunications Equipment	1%
Computer Software & Services	7
Air Transport	14
Restaurant	15
Securities Brokerage	24
Building Materials	24
Chemicals (Basic)	32
Banks	36
Retail Store	36
Food Processing	39
Electrical Equipment	41
Newspaper	41
Drug	45
Tobacco	55
Telecommunications Services	67
Electric Utility	76
Water Utility	79

**TABLE 14-2
Dividend Payout Ratios for
Firms in the Tobacco and Basic
Chemical Industries**

Source: *The Value Line Investment Survey*
(New York: Value Line, Inc., 1996–1997,
various issues). Copyright © 1996–1997
by Value Line Publishing, Inc. Used by
permission. All rights reserved.

TOBACCO INDUSTRY	
Company	Average Dividend Payout Ratio*
American Brands, Inc.	64
B.A.T. Industries, PLC	48.3
Imasco, Ltd.	42
Philip Morris, Inc.	57
RJR Nabisco Holdings Corp.	66.3
UST, Inc.	59.3
Universal Corp.	66.5

BASIC CHEMICAL INDUSTRY	
Company	Average Dividend Payout Ratio*
Arco Chemical	80.8
Dow Chemical	47
DuPont	46.5
Georgia Gulf	5.8
Lyondell Petro	30.8
Monsanto	46.5
Olin Corp.	51.3
Union Carbide	35.3

*Average calculated over four year period from 1993 to 1996.

Legal Constraints

Most states have laws that regulate the dividend payments a firm chartered in that state can make. These laws basically state the following:

- A firm's capital cannot be used to make dividend payments.
- Dividends must be paid out of a firm's present and past *net* earnings.
- Dividends cannot be paid when the firm is insolvent.

The first restriction is termed the *capital impairment restriction*. In some states, *capital* is defined as including only the par value of common stock; in others, *capital* is more broadly defined to also include the contributed capital in excess of par account (sometimes called *capital surplus*).

For example, consider the following capital accounts on the balance sheet of Johnson Tool and Die Company:

Common stock ($5 par; 100,000 shares)	$ 500,000
Contributed capital in excess of par	400,000
Retained earnings	200,000
Total common stockholders' equity	$1,100,000

If the company is chartered in a state that defines capital as the par value of common stock, then it can pay out a total of $600,000 ($1,100,000 − $500,000 par value) in dividends. If, however, the company's home state restricts dividend payments to retained earnings alone, then Johnson Tool and Die could only pay dividends up to $200,000. Regardless of the dividend laws, however, it should be realized that dividends are paid from a firm's *cash* account with an offsetting entry to the *retained earnings* account.

The second restriction, called the *net earnings restriction,* requires that a firm have generated earnings *before* it is permitted to pay any cash dividends. This prevents the equity owners from withdrawing their initial investment in the firm and impairing the security position of any of the firm's creditors.

The third restriction, termed the *insolvency restriction,* states that an insolvent company may not pay cash dividends. When a company is insolvent, its liabilities exceed its assets. Payment of dividends would interfere with the creditors' prior claims on the firm's assets and therefore is prohibited.

These three restrictions affect different types of companies in different ways. New firms, or small firms with a minimum of accumulated retained earnings, are most likely to feel the weight of these legal constraints when determining their dividend policies, whereas well-established companies with histories of profitable performance and large retained earnings accounts are less likely to be influenced by them.

Restrictive Covenants

Restrictive covenants generally have more impact on dividend policy than the legal constraints just discussed. These covenants are contained in bond indentures, term loans, short-term borrowing agreements, lease contracts, and preferred stock agreements.

These restrictions limit the total amount of dividends a firm can pay. Sometimes they may state that dividends cannot be paid at all until a firm's earnings have reached a specified level. For example, the adjustable rate preferred stock issue (Series B) of New York State Electric and Gas limits the amount of common stock dividends that can be paid if common stock equity falls below 25 percent of total capitalization. In a dividend policy study of 80 troubled firms that cut dividends, researchers found that more than half of the firms apparently faced binding debt covenants in the years managers reduced dividends.[2]

In addition, *sinking fund requirements,* which state that a certain portion of a firm's cash flow must be set aside for the retirement of debt, sometimes limit dividend payments. Also, dividends may be prohibited if a firm's net working capital (current assets less current liabilities) or its current ratio does not exceed a certain predetermined level.

Tax Considerations

Prior to the 1986 Tax Reform Act, the personal marginal tax rates (up to 50 percent) on dividend income were higher than the marginal rates (up to 20 percent) on long-term capital gains income. This was an incentive for corporations to keep dividends low so that shareholders could receive a greater proportion of their pretax returns in the form of capital gains and thus increase their portion of pretax returns in the form of capital gains and thereby increase *after-tax* returns. The 1986 Tax Reform Act eliminated this differential by taxing both dividend and capital gains income at the same marginal rate.

However, the Revenue Reconciliation Act of 1993 created a new top marginal tax rate of 39.6 percent for individual taxpayers. In contrast, the maximum individual capital gains tax rate is 28 percent. Although only a small proportion of taxpayers (those in the highest income tax bracket with taxable income in excess of $250,000) will pay taxes at this rate, many other taxpayers will encounter marginal tax rates of 31 and 36 percent. Thus there is a tax benefit for many individuals to receive distributions in the form of capital gains income (that arise when a firm retains and reinvests earnings in the company) rather than as cash dividends.[3]

Another tax disadvantage of dividends versus capital gains is that dividend income is taxed immediately (in the year it is received), but capital gains income (and corresponding taxes) can be deferred into the future. If a corporation decides to retain its earnings in anticipation of providing growth and future capital appreciation for its investors, the investors are not taxed until their shares are sold. Consequently, for most investors, the *present value* of the taxes on future capital gains income is less than the taxes on an equivalent amount of current dividend income.[4] The deferral of taxes on capital gains can be viewed as an interest-free loan to the investor from the government.

Whereas the factors just explained tend to encourage corporations to retain their earnings, the IRS Code—specifically Sections 531 through 537—has the opposite effect. In essence, the code prohibits corporations from retaining an excessive amount of earnings to protect stockholders from paying taxes on dividends received.

If the IRS rules that a corporation has accumulated excess earnings to protect its stockholders from having to pay personal income taxes on dividends, the

---

[2]Harry DeAngelo and Linda DeAngelo, "Dividend Policy and Financial Distress: An Empirical Investigation of Troubled NYSE Firms," *Journal of Finance* (December 1990): 1415–1431.

[3]For taxpayers in the 28 percent and lower tax brackets, the marginal tax rate applied to dividends and capital gains is the same.

[4]The exceptions to this rule are institutional investors (such as pension funds) that pay no income taxes and corporations (such as insurance companies) that pay a lower marginal tax rate on dividend income (10.5 percent) than on capital gains income (35 percent). See the Appendix at the back of the book for a discussion of corporate income taxes.

firm has to pay a heavy penalty tax on those earnings. It is the responsibility of the IRS to prove this allegation, however. Some companies are more likely to raise the suspicions for the IRS than others. For example, small closely held corporations whose shareholders are in high marginal tax brackets, firms that pay consistently low dividends, and those that have large amounts of cash and marketable securities are good candidates for IRS review.

Liquidity and Cash Flow Considerations

Recall from the previous chapter that free cash flow represents the portion of a firm's cash flows available to service debt, *make dividend payments* to shareholders, and to invest in other projects. Since dividend payments represent cash outflows, the more liquid a firm is, the more able it is to pay dividends. Even if a firm has a past record of high earnings that have been reinvested, resulting in a large retained earnings balance, it may not be able to pay dividends unless it has sufficient liquid assets, primarily cash.[5] For example, Unisys Corporation, a computer manufacturer, suspended cash dividend payments in 1991 when faced with declining cash flows. Liquidity is likely to be a problem during a long business downturn, when both earnings and cash flows often decline. Rapidly growing firms with many profitable investment opportunities also often find it difficult to maintain adequate liquidity and pay dividends at the same time.

Borrowing Capacity and Access to the Capital Markets

Liquidity is desirable for a number of reasons. Specifically, it provides protection in the event of a financial crisis. It also provides the flexibility needed to take advantage of unusual financial and investment opportunities. There are other ways of achieving this flexibility and security, however. For example, companies frequently establish lines of credit and revolving credit agreements with banks, allowing them to borrow on short notice.[6] Large well-established firms usually are able to go directly to credit markets with either a bond issue or a sale of commercial paper. The more access a firm has to these external sources of funds, the better able it will be to make dividend payments.

A small firm whose stock is closely held and infrequently traded often finds it difficult (or undesirable) to sell new equity shares in the markets. As a result, retained earnings are the only source of new equity. When a firm of this type is faced with desirable investment opportunities, the payment of dividends is often inconsistent with the objective of maximizing the value of the firm.

Earnings Stability

Most large widely held firms are reluctant to lower their dividend payments, even in times of financial stress. Therefore, a firm with a history of stable earnings is usually more willing to pay a higher dividend than a firm with erratic earnings.

---

[5]For example, John A. Brittain found that corporate dividend payments are positively related to a firm's liquidity. See John A. Brittain, *Corporate Dividend Policy* (Washington, DC: Brookings, 1966): 184–187.
[6]See Chapter 18 for a more detailed discussion of this topic.

A firm whose cash flows have been more or less constant over the years can be fairly confident about its future and frequently reflects this confidence in higher dividend payments.

Growth Prospects

A rapidly growing firm usually has a substantial need for funds to finance the abundance of attractive investment opportunities. Instead of paying large dividends and then attempting to sell new shares to raise the equity investment capital it needs, this type of firm usually retains larger portions of its earnings and avoids the expense and inconvenience of public stock offerings. Table 14-3 illustrates the relationship between earnings growth rates and dividend payout ratios for selected companies. Note that the companies with the highest dividend payout ratios tend to have the lowest growth rates and vice versa.

Inflation

In an inflationary environment, funds generated by depreciation often are not sufficient to replace a firm's assets as they become obsolete. Under these circumstances, a firm may be forced to retain a higher percentage of earnings to maintain the earning power of its asset base.

Inflation also has an impact on a firm's working capital needs. In an atmosphere of rising prices, *actual* dollars invested in inventories and accounts receivable tend to increase to support the same *physical* volume of business.[7] And, because the dollar amounts of accounts payable and other payables requiring cash outlays are higher with rising prices, transaction cash balances normally have to be increased. Thus, inflation can force a firm to retain more earnings as it attempts to maintain its same relative preinflation working capital position.

TABLE 14-3
Recent Dividend Payout Ratios and Growth Rates for Selected Companies

COMPANY	1996 DIVIDEND PAYOUT RATIO	10-YEAR EPS GROWTH RATE
Kansas City Power and Light	96.4	–2.0
Idaho Power	84.2	–2.0
Boston Edison	69.6	0.0
H. J. Heinz	57.9	9.5
Exxon	57.0	3.0
Merck	44.5	20.5
Hershey Foods	38.0	10.0
Maytag	35.0	–1.5
Coca-Cola	35.7	18.0
Dayton Hudson	27.0	5.5
Hewlett-Packard	16.5	13.5
McDonald's	16.5	13.5
Wal-Mart Stores	15.8	25.5
Compaq Computer	0.0	42.5

[7]The ultimate impact of inflation on a firm's liquidity depends on whether the firm is able to pass these higher costs on to its customers in the form of higher prices.

Shareholder Preferences

In a closely held corporation with relatively few stockholders, management may be able to set dividends according to the preferences of its stockholders. For example, assume that the majority of a firm's stockholders are in high marginal tax brackets. They probably favor a policy of high earnings retention, resulting in eventual price appreciation, over a high payout dividend policy. However, high earnings retention implies that the firm has enough acceptable capital investment opportunities to justify the low payout dividend policy. In addition, recall that the IRS does not permit corporations to retain excessive earnings if they have no legitimate investment opportunities. Also, a policy of high retention when investment opportunities are not available is inconsistent with the objective of maximizing shareholder wealth.

In a large corporation whose shares are widely held, it is nearly impossible for a financial manager to take individual shareholders' preferences into account when setting dividend policy. Some wealthy stockholders who are in high marginal income tax brackets may prefer that a company reinvest its earnings (i.e., low payout ratio) to generate long-term capital gains. Other shareholders, such as retired individuals and those living on fixed incomes (i.e., sometimes referred to as "widows and orphans"), may prefer a high dividend rate. These shareholders may be willing to pay a premium for common stock in a company that provides a higher dividend yield. Large institutional investors that are in a zero income tax bracket, such as pension funds, university endowment funds, philanthropic organizations (e.g., Ford Foundation), and trust funds, may prefer a high dividend yield for reasons different from those of private individual stockholders. First, endowment and trust funds sometimes are prohibited from spending the principal and must limit expenditures to the dividend (and/or interest) income generated by their investments. Second, pension and trust funds have a legal obligation to follow conservative investment strategies, which have been interpreted by the courts to mean investments in companies that have a record of regular dividend payments.

It has been argued that firms tend to develop their own "clientele" of investors. This **clientele effect,** originally articulated by Merton Miller and Franco Modigliani, indicates that investors will tend to be attracted to companies that have dividend policies consistent with the investors' objectives.[8] Some companies, such as public utilities, that pay out a large percentage (typically 70 percent or more) of their earnings as dividends traditionally have attracted investors who desire a high dividend yield. In contrast, growth-oriented companies, which pay no (or very low) dividends, have tended to attract investors who prefer earnings retention and greater price appreciation. Empirical studies generally support the existence of a dividend clientele effect.[9]

[8]Merton Miller and Franco Modigliani, "Dividend Policy, Growth and the Valuation of Shares," *Journal of Business* 34 (October 1961): 411–433.

[9]See Edwin J. Elton and Martin J. Gruber, "Marginal Stockholder Tax Rates and the Clientele Effect," *Review of Economics and Statistics* (February 1970): 68–74; Wilbur C. Lewellen, Kenneth L. Stanley, Ronald C. Lease, and Gary C. Schlarbaum, "Some Direct Evidence on the Dividend Clientele Phenomenon," *Journal of Finance* (December 1970): 1385–1399; and R. Richardson Pettit, "Taxes, Transactions Costs and the Clientele Effect of Dividends," *Journal of Financial Economics* (December 1977): 419–436.

Protection Against Dilution

If a firm adopts a policy of paying out a large percentage of its annual earnings as dividends, it may need to sell new shares of stock from time to time to raise the equity capital needed to invest in potentially profitable projects. If existing investors do not or cannot acquire a proportionate share of the new issue, their percentage ownership interest in the firm is *diluted*. Some firms choose to retain more of their earnings and pay out lower dividends rather than risk dilution.

One of the alternatives to high earnings retention, however, involves raising external capital in the form of debt. This increases the financial risk of the firm, ultimately raising the cost of equity capital and at some point lowering share prices.[10] If the firm feels that it already has an optimal capital structure, a policy of obtaining all external capital in the form of debt is likely to be counterproductive, unless sufficient new equity capital is retained or acquired in the capital markets to offset the increased debt.

DIVIDEND POLICY AND FIRM VALUE

There are two major schools of thought among finance scholars regarding the effect dividend policy has on a firm's value. Although Miller and Modigliani argue that dividend policy does not have a significant effect on a firm's value,[11] Myron Gordon, David Durand, and John Lintner have argued that it does.[12] Each viewpoint is discussed in this section.

Arguments for the Irrelevance of Dividends

The group led by Miller and Modigliani (MM) contends that a firm's value is determined solely by its investment decisions and that the dividend payout ratio is a mere detail. They maintain that the effect of any particular dividend policy can be exactly offset by other forms of financing, such as the sale of new common equity shares. This argument depends on a number of key assumptions, however, including the following:

- *No taxes.* Under this assumption, investors are indifferent about whether they receive either dividend income or capital gains income.
- *No transaction costs.* This assumption implies that investors in the securities of firms paying small or no dividends can sell at no cost any number of shares they wish in order to convert capital gains into current income.
- *No issuance costs.* If firms did not have to pay issuance costs on the issue of new securities, they could acquire needed equity capital at the same cost, regardless of whether they retained their past earnings or paid them out as dividends. The payment of dividends sometimes results in the need for periodic sales of new stock.

---

[10]See Chapters 12 and 13.
[11]Miller and Modigliani, "Dividend Policy, Growth, and the Valuation of Shares." (See Footnote 8.)
[12]See Myron Gordon, "The Savings, Investment and Valuation of a Corporation," *Review of Economics and Statistics* (February 1962): 37–51; Gordon, *The Investment, Financing and Valuation of the Corporation* (Homewood, Ill.: Irwin, 1962); David Durand, "Bank Stocks and the Analysis of Covariance," *Econometrica* (January 1955): 30–45; and John Lintner, "Dividends, Earnings, Leverage, Stock Prices and the Supply of Capital to Corporations," *Review of Economics and Statistics* (August 1962): 243–269.

■ *Existence of a fixed investment policy.* According to MM, the firm's investment policy is not affected by its dividend policy. Furthermore, MM claim that it is investment policy, *not* dividend policy, that really determines a firm's value.

Informational Content. MM realize that there is considerable empirical evidence indicating that changes in dividend policy influence stock prices. As discussed later in this chapter, many firms favor a policy of reasonably stable dividends. An increase in dividends conveys a certain type of *information* to the shareholders, such as an expectation of higher future earnings. Similarly, a cut in dividends may be viewed as conveying unfavorable information about the firm's earnings prospects (see the FPL example discussion in the Financial Challenge at the beginning of the chapter.) MM argue that this **informational content** of dividend policy influences share prices, *not* the pattern of dividend payments per se.

Signaling Effects. In effect, changes in dividend payments represent a *signal* to investors concerning management's assessment of the future earnings and cash flows of the company.[13] Management, as an insider, is perceived as having access to more complete information about future profitability than is available to investors outside the company. Dividend changes are thought to provide unambiguous signals about the company's future prospects—information that cannot be conveyed fully through other methods, such as annual reports and management presentations before security analysts. The signaling effect of changes in dividends is similar to the signaling effect of changes in capital structure discussed in Chapter 12.

Clientele Effect. MM also claim that the existence of clienteles of investors favoring a particular firm's dividend policy should have no effect on share value. They recognize that a firm that changes its dividend policy could lose some stockholders to other firms with a more appealing dividend policy. This, in turn, may cause a temporary reduction in the price of the firm's stock. Other investors, however, who prefer the newly adopted dividend policy will view the firm as being undervalued and will purchase more shares. In the MM world, these transactions occur instantaneously and at no cost to the investor, the net result being that a stock's value remains unchanged.

Arguments for the Relevance of Dividends

Scholars belonging to the second school of thought argue that share values are indeed influenced by the division of earnings between dividends and retention. Basically, they contend that the MM propositions are reasonable—given MM's restrictive assumptions—but that dividend policy becomes important once these assumptions are removed.

Risk Aversion. Specifically, Gordon asserts that shareholders who are risk averse may prefer some dividends over the promise of future capital gains, because

[13]Merton H. Miller and Kevin Rock, "Dividend Policy under Asymmetric Information," *Journal of Finance* (September 1985): 1031–1051; and Paul M. Healy and Krishna G. Palepu, "Earnings Information Conveyed by Dividend Initiations and Omissions," *Journal of Financial Economics* 21 (1988): 149–175.

dividends are regular, certain returns, whereas future capital gains are less certain. This is sometimes referred to as the "bird-in-the-hand" theory. According to Gordon, dividends reduce investors' uncertainty, causing them to discount a firm's future earnings at a lower rate, thereby increasing the firm's value. In contrast, failure to pay dividends increases investors' uncertainty, which raises the discount rate and lowers share prices. Although there is some empirical evidence to support this argument, it is difficult to decide which is more valid—the MM informational content (or signaling effect) of dividends approach or the Gordon uncertainty resolution approach.

Transaction Costs. If the assumption of no transaction costs for investors is removed, then investors care whether they are paid cash dividends or receive capital gains. In the MM world, investors who own stock paying low or no dividends could periodically sell a portion of their holdings to satisfy current income requirements. In actuality, however, brokerage charges and odd-lot differentials make such liquidations expensive and imperfect substitutes for regular dividend payments.

Taxes. Removal of the no-tax assumption also makes a difference to shareholders. As discussed earlier, shareholders in high income tax brackets may prefer low (or no) dividends and reinvestment of earnings within the firm because of the lower (marginal) tax rates on capital gains income and the ability to defer taxes into the future (when the stock is sold) on such income. In his study of dividend policy from 1920 to 1960, John A. Brittain found evidence in support of this proposition.[14] In general, he found that rising tax rates tend to reduce dividend payout rates.

Issuance (Floatation) Costs. The existence of issuance costs on new equity sales also tends to make earnings retention more desirable. Given a firm's investment policy, the payout of earnings the firm needs for investments requires it to raise external equity. External equity is more expensive, however, because of issuance costs. Therefore, the use of external equity will raise the firm's cost of capital and reduce the value of the firm. In addition, the cost of selling small issues of equity to meet investment needs is likely to be prohibitively high for most firms. Therefore, firms that have sufficient investment opportunities to profitably utilize their retained funds tend to favor retention.[15]

Agency Costs. It has also been argued that the payment of dividends can reduce *agency costs*[16] between shareholders and management.[17] The payment of dividends reduces the amount of retained earnings available for reinvestment and requires the use of more external equity funds to finance growth. Raising external equity funds in the capital markets subjects the company to the scrutiny of regulators (such as the SEC) and potential investors, thereby serving as a monitoring function of managerial performance.

---

[14]Brittain, *Corporate Dividend Policy,* especially Chapter 4.

[15]This argument provides the basis for the passive residual or marginal theory of dividends discussed later in this chapter.

[16]Agency costs are discussed in Chapter 1.

[17]See M. Rozeff, "Growth, Beta and Agency Costs as Determinants of Dividend Payout Ratios," *Journal of Financial Research* (Fall 1982): 249–259; and Chinmoy Ghosh and J. Randall Woolridge, "An Analysis of Shareholder Reaction to Dividend Cuts and Omissions," *Journal of Financial Research* (Winter 1988): 281–294.

Conclusions Regarding Dividend Relevance. The empirical evidence as to whether dividend policy affects firm valuation is mixed. Some studies have found that, because of tax effects, investors require higher pretax returns on high-dividend payout stocks than on low-dividend payout stocks.[18] Other studies have found that share prices are unaffected by dividend payout policy.[19]

Many practitioners believe that dividends are important, both for their informational content and because external equity capital is more expensive than retained equity.[20] Thus, when establishing an optimal dividend policy, a firm should consider shareholder preferences along with investment opportunities and the relative cost of retained equity versus externally raised equity.

DIVIDEND POLICIES

A number of practical considerations influence a firm's board of directors in determining an "optimal" dividend policy. Next, several alternative dividend strategies are discussed.

Passive Residual Policy

The **passive residual policy** suggests that a firm should retain its earnings as long as it has investment opportunities that promise higher rates of return than the required rate. For example, assume a firm's shareholders could invest their dividends in stocks of similar risk with an expected rate of return (dividends plus capital gains) of 18 percent. This 18 percent figure, then, would constitute the required rate of return on the firm's retained earnings.[21] As long as the firm can invest these earnings to earn this required rate or more, it should not pay dividends (according to the passive residual policy), because such payments would require either that the firm forgo some acceptable investment opportunities or raise necessary equity capital in the more expensive external capital markets.

Interpreted literally, the residual theory implies that dividend payments will vary from year to year, depending on available investment opportunities. There is strong evidence, however, that most firms try to maintain a rather stable dividend payment record over time. Of course, this does not mean that firms ignore the principles of the residual theory in making their dividend decisions,

---

[18]See Robert H. Litzenberger and Krishna Ramaswamy, "The Effect of Personal Taxes and Dividends on Capital Asset Prices: Theory and Empirical Evidence," *Journal of Financial Economics* (June 1979): 163–196; Litzenberger and Ramaswamy, "Dividends, Short-Selling Restrictions, Tax Induced Investor Clienteles and Market Equilibrium," *Journal of Finance* (May 1980); and Litzenberger and Ramaswamy, "The Effects of Dividends on Common Stock Prices: Tax Effects or Information Effects?" *Journal of Finance* (May 1982): 429–444.

[19]See Fischer Black and Myron Scholes, "The Effects of Dividend Yield and Dividend Policy on Common Stock Prices and Returns," *Journal of Financial Economics* (May 1974): 1–22; and Merton H. Miller and Myron S. Scholes, "Dividends and Taxes: Some Empirical Evidence," *Journal of Political Economy* (December 1983): 1118–1141.

[20]For a survey of chief financial officers' attitudes on dividend policy, see H. Kent Baker, Gail E. Farrelly, and Richard B. Edelman, "A Survey of Management Views on Dividend Policy," *Financial Management* (Autumn 1985): 78–84.

[21]This is the rate of return that must be earned on the equity-financed portion of new investments. To earn this return on equity, new investments must earn an overall rate of return equal to the weighted cost of capital—reflecting the fact that all investments are made with a mix of debt and equity funds in the proportions of the target capital structure.

because dividends can be smoothed out from year to year in two ways.[22] First, a firm can choose to retain a larger percentage of earnings during years when funding needs are large. If the firm continues to grow, it can manage to do this without reducing the dollar amount of the dividend. Second, a firm can borrow the funds it needs, temporarily raise its debt-to-equity ratio, and avoid a dividend cut in this way. Because issue costs are lower for large offerings of long-term debt, long-term debt capital tends to be raised in large, lumpy sums. If many good investment opportunities are available to a firm during a particular year, this type of borrowing is preferable to cutting back on dividends. The firm will need to retain earnings in future years to bring its debt-to-equity ratio back in line. A firm that has many good investment opportunities for a number of years eventually may be forced to cut its dividend and/or sell new equity shares to meet financing requirements and maintain an optimal capital structure.

The residual theory also suggests that "growth" firms normally will have lower dividend payout ratios than firms in mature, low-growth industries. As shown earlier in Table 14-3, companies with low growth rates (such as Kansas City Power and Light and Idaho Power) tend to have rather high payout ratios, whereas firms with high growth rates (such as Compaq Computer and Wal-Mart Stores) tend to have rather low payout ratios.

Stable Dollar Dividend Policy

Evidence indicates that most firms—and stockholders—prefer reasonably stable dividend policies. This stability is characterized by a rather strong reluctance to reduce the dollar amount of dividends from one period to the next. Similarly, increases in the dollar dividend rate normally are not made until the firm's management is satisfied that future earnings will be high enough to justify the larger dividend. Thus, although dividend rates tend to follow increases in earnings, they also tend to lag behind them to a certain degree.

Figure 14-1 illustrates the relationship between corporate dividends and profits since 1960. It is apparent from this chart that aggregate dividend payments fluctuate much less than corporate earnings. There has been a strong upward trend in the amount of dividends paid, with very few years showing significant reductions. This is in sharp contrast to the more erratic record of corporate earnings.

More specifically, Figure 14-2 shows the dividend and earnings history of Atlantic-Richfield. Although there has been an upward trend in dividends over time, dividend increases tend to lag earnings increases. Annual dividend payments are also more stable than earnings figures. Note, for instance, the dramatic growth in earnings in 1990, yet dividends were increased only by $.50 per share. Despite a significant earnings decline in 1991, the dividend rate was actually increased by $.50 per share.

Investors prefer stable dividends for a variety of reasons. For instance, many investors feel that dividend changes possess *informational content;* they equate changes in a firm's dividend levels with profitability. A cut in dividends may be interpreted as a signal that the firm's long-run profit potential has declined.

---

[22]Robert C. Higgins, "The Corporate Dividend-Saving Decision," *Journal of Financial and Quantitative Analysis* (March 1972): 1531–1538, provides empirical support for the view that each period's dividends are a function of longer-term trends.

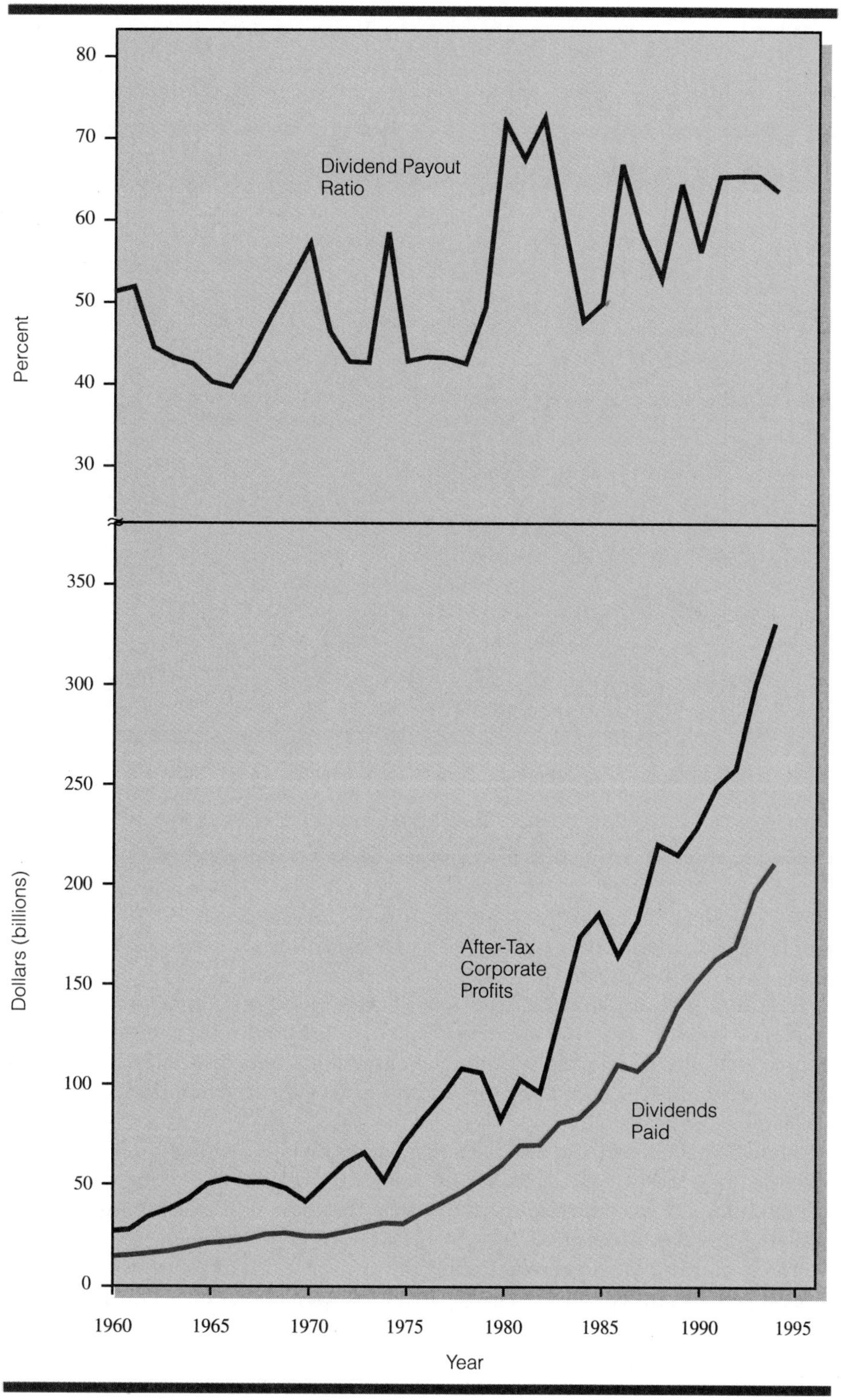

FIGURE 14-1
Historic Pattern of Profits and Dividends for U.S. Corporations

Source: *Economic Report of the President*, 1996.

**FIGURE 14-2
Dividends and Earnings
for Atlantic-Richfield**

Source: *Value Line Investment Survey*
(New York: Value Line, Inc.,
December 27, 1996).

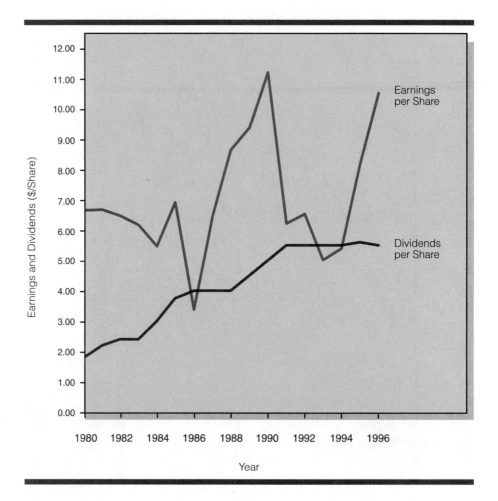

Similarly, a dividend increase is seen as a verification of the expectation that future profits will increase.[23]

In addition, many shareholders need and depend on a constant stream of dividends for their cash income requirements. Although they can sell off some of their shares as an alternative source of current income, associated transaction costs and odd-lot charges make this an imperfect substitute for steady dividend income.

Some managers feel that a stable and growing dividend policy tends to reduce investor uncertainty concerning future dividend streams. They believe investors will pay a higher price for the stock of a firm that pays stable dividends, thereby reducing the firm's cost of equity.

And, finally, stable dividends are legally desirable. Many regulated financial institutions—such as bank trust departments, pension funds, and insurance companies—are limited as to the types of common stock they are allowed to own. To qualify for inclusion in these "legal lists," a firm must have a record of continuous and stable dividends. The failure to pay a dividend or the reduction

---

[23]Sometimes, however, an increase in a firm's dividend payout ratio may be interpreted to mean the firm no longer has a large number of high-return investment opportunities available to it.

of a dividend amount can result in removal from these lists. This, in turn, reduces the potential market for the firm's shares and may lead to price declines. As shown earlier in Figure 14-2, Atlantic-Richfield maintained its per share dividend during the 1993–94 period, even though its earnings per share were less than this amount in each of those years.

③ Other Dividend Payment Policies

Some firms have adopted a *constant payout ratio* dividend policy. A firm that uses this approach pays out a certain percentage of each year's earnings—for example, 40 percent—as dividends. If the firm's earnings vary substantially from year to year, dividends also will fluctuate. (The late Penn Central Company had adopted this type of dividend payout policy at one time.)

As shown earlier in Figure 14-1, the aggregate dividend payout ratio for U.S. corporations generally has ranged between 40 and 70 percent. This finding supports the notion that firms try to maintain fairly constant pay-out ratios over time. On a year-to-year basis, however, these payout ratios vary substantially. For example, the aggregate payout ratio was about 66 percent during 1991, a recession year, and only about 40 percent during 1965, a year of relative prosperity. Because of the reluctance to reduce dividends, payout ratios tend to increase when profits are depressed and decrease as profits increase.

Other firms choose to pay a *small quarterly dividend plus year-end extras*. This policy is especially well suited for a firm with a volatile earnings record, volatile year-to-year cash needs, or both. Even when earnings are low, the firm's investors can count on their regular dividend payments. When earnings are high and no immediate need for these excess funds exists, the firm declares a year-end extra dividend. This policy gives management the flexibility to retain funds as needed and still satisfy investors who desire to receive some "guaranteed" level of dividend payments. U.S. Steel, Du Pont, and General Motors have all followed this policy from time to time. Figure 14-3 shows how this policy has affected General Motors. Although actual dividend payments have varied dramatically from year to year (compare this figure, for example, with Figure 14-2, which shows Atlantic-Richfield's earnings and dividends), only in 1993, after three years of huge losses, were dividends cut below $1.20, the "regular" rate in effect in 1975.

 ENTREPRENEURIAL FINANCE ISSUES
DIVIDEND POLICY

Small firms typically differ significantly from larger, more mature firms in terms of the dividend policies they follow. For example, one study of the financial differences between small and large firms found that the average dividend payout ratio for large firms was in excess of 40 percent, whereas the average dividend payout ratio for small firms was less than 3 percent.[24] The study found that the majority of small firms that were planning an initial public stock offering paid no dividends at all in the year prior to their stock offering.

---

[24]Ernest W. Walker and J. W. Petty, II, "Financial Differences between Large and Small Firms," *Financial Management* (Winter 1978): 61–68.

FIGURE 14-3
Dividends and Earnings per
Share for General Motors

Source: *Value Line Investment Survey*
(New York: Value Line, Inc.,
December 13, 1996).

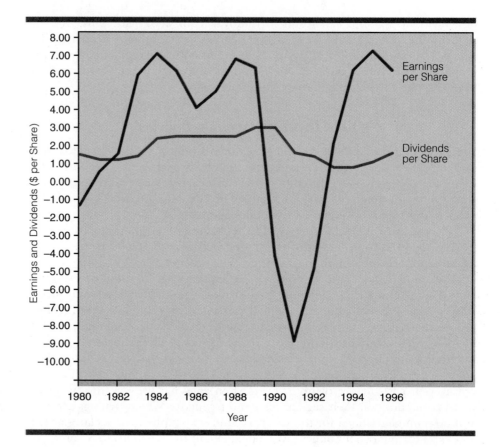

What are the reasons for this dramatic difference in dividend policies between large and small firms? First, it is likely that many small firms are in the rapid growth phase of their business development. During this early phase, the firm is often short of funds needed to finance planned investments and increases in working capital. Another aspect related to the growth phase argument is that small firms typically have restricted access to capital markets, relative to larger firms. A small, closely held firm has no easy way to raise equity capital other than the retention of earnings. If new shares of stock can be sold, the owners risk a loss of control. In addition, stock offerings for small firms are extremely expensive, both in terms of transactions costs and minority interest discounts (as well as marketability) that investors demand.

Another reason dividend policies differ between small and large firms is because many small firms are closely held by only one or a few owners, and the dividend policy of these firms frequently reflects the income preferences of these individuals. If funds are retained in the firm, taxes are postponed until a distribution is made at some time in the future or until the firm is sold.

As firms mature, their need for funds to support rapid growth declines, and their access to capital markets improves. At this point, they show a tendency to begin or increase dividend payouts. For example, in 1978, Apple Computer had sales of $7.9 million and earnings of 2 cents a share. By 1986, sales had grown to over $1.9 billion and earnings per share were

$1.20. During this period of rapid growth, Apple paid no dividends. However, as the company entered the maturing stage of its life cycle, the need for internally generated cash flow to support expansion declined and Apple began paying dividends. In 1987, dividends totalling $0.12 per share were paid equalling a payout ratio of about 7 percent. In 1989, dividends were being paid at the rate of $0.40 per share, and by 1993, dividends had increased to the rate of $0.48 per share, equalling a payout ratio of about 20 percent.

Clearly, the dividend policies of small and large firms differ significantly. Small firms often pay out a smaller percentage of their earnings than larger firms because small firms tend to be growing rapidly and have limited access to the capital markets for other sources of funds to support their growth.

INTERNATIONAL ISSUES
DIVIDEND POLICIES FOR MULTINATIONAL FIRMS

Dividend payments from foreign subsidiaries represent the primary means of transferring funds to the parent company. Many factors determine the dividend payments that are made back to the parent, including tax effects, exchange risk, political risk, the availability of funds, the financing requirements of the foreign subsidiary, and the existence of exchange controls.[25]

Taxes in the host country play a significant role in determining a multinational firm subsidiary's dividend policy. For example, in Germany, the tax rate on earnings paid out as dividends is much lower than the tax rate on retained earnings. When the parent is located in a country with a strong currency and the subsidiary is located in a country with a weak currency, there will be a tendency to rapidly transfer a greater portion of the subsidiary's earnings to the parent to minimize the exchange rate risk. In the face of high political risk, the parent may require the subsidiary to transfer all locally generated funds to the parent except for those funds necessary to meet the working capital and planned capital expenditure needs of the subsidiary. As is true for domestic enterprises, large and more mature foreign subsidiaries tend to remit a greater proportion of their earnings to the parent, reflecting the reduced growth opportunities and needs for funds that exist in larger firms. Also, when the foreign subsidiary has good access to capital within the host country, it tends to pay larger dividends to the parent, because funds needed for future expansion can be obtained locally. Finally, some countries with balance-of-payments problems often restrict the payment of dividends from the subsidiary back to the parent.

Many firms require that the payout ratio for foreign subsidiaries be set equal to the payout ratio of the parent. The argument in favor of this strategy is that it requires each subsidiary to bear an equal proportionate burden of the parent's dividend policy. However, even when this strategy is adopted, it often is modified on a country-by-country basis to reflect the considerations just identified.

[25]A more thorough discussion of these issues is found in Alan C. Shapiro, *Multinational Financial Management,* 4th ed. (Boston: Allyn and Bacon, 1992), Chapter 15.

HOW DIVIDENDS ARE PAID

In most firms, the board of directors holds quarterly or semiannual meetings to evaluate the firm's past performance and decide the level of dividends to be paid during the next period. Changes in the amount of dividends paid tend to be made rather infrequently—especially in firms that follow a stable dividend policy—and only after there is clear evidence that the firm's future earnings are likely to be either permanently higher or permanently lower than previously reported levels.

Most firms follow a dividend declaration and payment procedure similar to that outlined in the following paragraphs. This procedure usually revolves around a *declaration date,* an *ex-dividend date,* a *record date,* and a *payment date.*

Figure 14-4 is a time line that illustrates the Pennzoil Company's dividend payment procedure. The firm's board of directors meets on the **declaration date**—Thursday, February 24—to consider future dividends. They *declare* a dividend on that date, which will be payable to *shareholders of record* on the **record date,** Friday, March 18. On that date, the firm makes a list from its stock transfer books of those shareholders who are eligible to receive the declared dividend.

The major stock exchanges require four *business days* prior to the record date for recording ownership changes. The day that begins this four-day period is called the **ex-dividend date**—in this case, Monday, March 14. Investors who purchase stock prior to March 14 are eligible for the March 18 dividend; investors who purchase stock on or after March 14 are not entitled to the dividend. On March 14, the ex-dividend date, one would expect the stock price to decline by the amount of the dividend, because this much value has been removed from the firm. Empirical evidence indicates that, on average, stock prices decline by less than the amount of the dividend on the ex-dividend day.[26]

The *payment date* is normally two to four weeks after the record date; in this case, April 4. On this date, Pennzoil makes dividend payments to the holders of record.

FIGURE 14-4
Key Dates in the Pennzoil Company's Dividend Payment Procedure

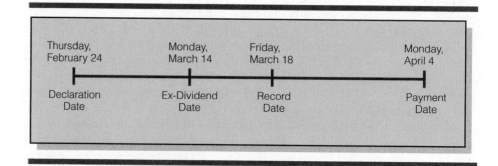

---

[26]See Edwin J. Elton and Martin J. Gruber, "Marginal Stockholder Tax Rates and the Clientele Effect," *Review of Economics and Statistics* (February 1978): 68–74; Avner Kalay, "The Ex-Dividend Behavior of Stock Prices: A Re-examination of the Clientele Effect," *Journal of Finance* (September 1983): 1059–1070; and Kenneth M. Eades, Patrick J. Hess, and E. Han Kim, "On Interpreting Security Returns during the Ex-Dividend Period," *Journal of Financial Economics* (March 1984): 3–34.

Dividend Reinvestment Plans

In recent years, many firms have established **dividend reinvestment plans.** Under these plans, shareholders can have their dividends automatically reinvested in additional shares of the company's common stock. There are two types of dividend reinvestment plans—one type involves the purchase of *existing* stock, and the other type involves the purchase of *newly issued* stock. The first type of plan is executed through a bank that, acting as a trustee, purchases the stock on the open market and then allocates it on a pro rata basis to the participating shareholders. In the second type of plan, the cash dividends of the participants are used to purchase, often at a small discount (up to 5 percent) from the market price, newly issued shares of stock.

This second type of plan enables the firm to raise substantial amounts of new equity capital over time as well as reduce the cash outflows required by dividend payments.[27] The advantage of a dividend reinvestment plan to shareholders is that it represents a convenient method for them to purchase additional shares of the company's common stock while saving brokerage commissions. The primary disadvantage is that shareholders must pay taxes on the cash dividends reinvested in the company, even though they never receive any cash.[28]

You've heard of a dividend reinvestment plan, but do you know how one actually works? CSX Corporation has one and tells you all about it at their Web site.
http://www.csx.com/docs/94annrep/notes6.html

STOCK DIVIDENDS AND STOCK SPLITS

A **stock dividend** is the payment of additional shares of stock to common stockholders. It involves making a transfer from the retained earnings account to the other stockholders' equity accounts.

For example, the Colonial Copies Company has the following common stockholders' equity:

Equity Analytics, Ltd., has a very good tutorial on stock splits, reverse stock splits, cash dividends, stock dividends, and the tax consequences of dividends and splits. They also have some excellent links to software downloads, glossaries, insurance and retirement planning, and very good tutorials on most major financial subjects (stocks, bonds, options, futures, etc.). It's a neat Web site and a handy resource.
http://www.e-analytics.com/index.htm

Pre-Stock Dividend
Common Stockholders' Equity

Common stock ($5 par, 100,000 shares)	$ 500,000
Contributed capital in excess of par	1,000,000
Retained earnings	5,000,000
Total common stockholders' equity	$6,500,000

Suppose the firm declares a 10 percent stock dividend and existing shareholders receive 10,000 (10% × 100,000) new shares. Because stock dividend accounting usually is based on the predividend market price, a total of $200,000 (10,000 shares × an assumed market price of $20 per share) is transferred from the firm's retained earnings account to the other stockholders' equity accounts. Of this $200,000, $50,000 ($5 par × 10,000 shares) is added to the common stock account and the remaining $150,000 is added to the contributed capital in excess of par account. Following the stock dividend, Colonial has the following common stockholders' equity:

[27]See *Moody's Annual Dividend Record* (December 31, 1996) for a list of the New York and American Stock Exchange companies offering dividend reinvestment plans.
[28]See Richard H. Pettway and R. Phil Malone, "Automatic Dividend Reinvestment Plans of Nonfinancial Corporations," *Financial Management* (Winter 1973): 11–18, for a more detailed discussion of these plans.

Post-Stock Dividend
Common Stockholders' Equity

Common stock ($5 par, 110,000 shares)	$ 550,000
Contributed capital in excess of par	1,150,000
Retained earnings	4,800,000
Total common stockholders' equity	$6,500,000

The net effect of this transaction is to increase the number of outstanding shares and to redistribute funds among the firm's capital accounts. The firm's total stockholders' equity remains unchanged, and each shareholder's proportionate claim to the firm's earnings remains constant. For example, if Colonial Copies Company has 100,000 shares outstanding prior to a 10 percent stock dividend and its total earnings are $200,000 ($2 per share), a stockholder who owns 100 shares has a claim on $200 of the firm's earnings. Following the 10 percent stock dividend, earnings per share decline to $1.82 ($200,000/110,000 shares). The stockholder who originally owned 100 shares now has 110 shares but continues to have a claim on only $200 (110 shares × $1.82 per share) of the firm's earnings.

Because each shareholder's proportionate claim on a firm's net worth and earnings remains unchanged in a stock dividend, the market price of each share of stock should decline in proportion to the number of new shares issued. This relationship can be expressed as follows:

$$\text{Post-stock dividend price} = \frac{\text{Pre-stock dividend price}}{1 + \text{Percentage stock dividend rate}} \quad (14.1)$$

In the Colonial Copies example, a $20 pre-stock dividend price should result in a post-stock dividend price of

$$\text{Post-stock dividend price} = \frac{\$20}{1 + 0.10}$$

$$= \$18.18$$

If a stockholder's wealth prior to the dividend is $2,000 (100 shares × $20 per share), post-dividend wealth should also remain at $2,000 (110 shares × $18.18 per share).

In essence, all a stock dividend does is increase the number of pieces of paper in the stockholders' hands. Nevertheless, there are a number of reasons why firms declare stock dividends. First, a stock dividend may have the effect of broadening the ownership of a firm's shares, because existing shareholders often sell their stock dividends.[29] Second, in the case of a firm that already pays a cash dividend, a stock dividend results in an effective increase in cash dividends, providing that the per-share dividend rate is not reduced. (It is rare for a firm to declare a stock dividend and reduce its cash dividend rate at the same time.) And, finally, the declaration of stock dividends effectively lowers the per-share price of a stock, thereby possibly broadening its investment appeal. Investors seem to prefer stocks selling in approximately the $15 to $70 price range, because more investors will be financially able to purchase 100-share round lots.[30] Round lots of 100 shares are more desirable for investors

---

[29]See C. Austin Barker, "Evaluation of Stock Dividends," *Harvard Business Review* (July–August 1958): 99–114, for an empirical confirmation of this point.

to own because lower transactions costs are associated with their purchase and sale.

Stock splits are similar to stock dividends in that they have the effect of increasing the number of shares of stock outstanding and reducing the price of each outstanding share. From an accounting standpoint, stock splits are accomplished by reducing the par value of existing shares of stock and increasing the number of shares outstanding. For example, in a two-for-one stock split, the number of shares would be doubled. Although stock splits have an impact similar to stock dividends, they normally are not considered an element of a firm's dividend policy. They are discussed in greater detail in Chapter 7.

Key in the term stock split *into a search engine such as InfoSeek and you'll literally receive hundreds of thousands of hits. Many of these links are actually companies announcing their stock splits. As you'll see, splitting stocks is a very common corporate practice.*
http://www.guide-p.infoseek.htm

SHARE REPURCHASES AS DIVIDEND DECISIONS

In addition to the reasons discussed in Chapter 7 for repurchasing stock, share repurchases can be undertaken as part of the firm's dividend decision. According to the passive residual dividend policy, a firm that has more funds than it needs for investments should pay a cash dividend to shareholders. In lieu of, or in addition to, cash dividends, some firms also repurchase outstanding shares from time to time.

Share repurchases have become increasingly popular. The volume of announced share repurchases rose to record levels of approximately $70 billion per year during 1994 and 1995—nearly double the yearly average of repurchases during the early 1990s.[31]

Companies engaging in large buyback programs typically have large cash flows and an insufficient number of positive NPV investments in which to invest. For example, Quaker Oats repurchased 20 million shares over a five-year period and is planning the repurchase of an additional 5 million shares. Quaker Oats treasurer, Janet K. Cooper says, "We spend on new products, we make acquisitions, and we raise the dividend, and we still can't soak up all the cash."[32]

Firms that are under threat of a hostile takeover sometimes announce large share repurchase programs designed to drain "excess" cash from the firm, thereby making it a less desirable takeover target.

Procedures for Repurchasing Shares

Firms carry out share repurchase programs in a number of ways. For example, a company may buy directly from its stockholders in what is termed a *tender offer;* it may purchase the stock in the open market, or it may privately negotiate purchases from large holders, such as institutions. When a firm initiates a share repurchase program through a tender offer, it is, in effect, giving shareholders a

---

[30]For an empirical view of the effects of stock dividends and splits on share values, see Barker, "Evaluation of Stock Dividends"; Keith B. Johnson, "Stock Splits and Price Change," *Journal of Finance* (December 1966): 675–686; W. H. Hausman, R. R. West, and J. A. Langay, "Stock Splits, Price Changes and Trading Profits: A Synthesis," *Journal of Business* (January 1971): 69–77; and E. Fama, R. Fisher, M. Jensen, and R. Roll, "The Adjustment of Stock Prices to New Information," *International Economic Review* (February 1969): 1–21.

[31]It should be noted that not all announced share repurchases are completed. For example, if the primary reason for a share buyback program is that the company feels that its shares are underpriced and if the price of the stock subsequently increases, there is less incentive for the company to complete the buyback transaction.

[32]"The Great Buyback Boom of '93," *Business Week* (August 23, 1993): 76.

put option—an option to sell their shares at a fixed price above the current market price for a limited period of time.

Repurchased shares become known as **treasury stock.** Treasury stock is often used to facilitate mergers and acquisitions; to satisfy the conversion provisions of some preferred stock and debentures, as well as the exercise of warrants; and to meet the need for new shares in executive stock options and employee stock purchase plans. From the stockholders' perspective, share repurchases increase earnings per share for the remaining outstanding shares and also increase stock prices, assuming that investors continue to apply the same *price to earnings (P/E) ratio* to the earnings per share before and after repurchase.[33] (Recall from Chapter 3 that the P/E ratio is equal to the price per share divided by the earnings per share.) For example, if a stock sells for $40 per share and earns $8 per share, its P/E multiple is 5 times (40/8). The P/E multiple indicates the value placed by investors on a dollar of a firm's earnings. It is influenced by a number of factors, including earnings prospects and investors' perceptions regarding a firm's risk.

Normally, a firm will announce its intent to buy back some of its own shares so that investors will know why there is sudden additional trading in the stock. An announcement of repurchase is also useful to current shareholders, who may not want to sell their shares before they have had an opportunity to receive any price appreciation expected to result from the repurchase program.

Share Repurchase Example

Suppose that the Hewlett-Packard (H-P) Company (electronic equipment manufacturer) plans to distribute to its shareholders $750 million in the form of either a one-time extra cash dividend or a share repurchase. The company has expected earnings of $625 million during the coming year and approximately 250 million shares currently outstanding. The current (ex-dividend) market price of H-P stock is $50 per share. The company can pay a one-time extra cash dividend of $3 per share ($750 million divided by 250 million shares). Alternatively, it can make a tender offer at $53 per share for 14,150,943 shares ($750 million divided by $53 per share).

If H-P decides to declare a one-time extra cash dividend of $3 per share, shareholder wealth would be $53 per share, consisting of the $50 (ex-dividend) share price plus the $3 dividend. The effect on shareholder wealth before and after the stock repurchase is shown in Table 14-4, assuming that the price-earnings (P/E) ratio remains the same at 20 ($50 stock price per share divided by $2.50 earnings per share). If H-P repurchases $750 million worth of its common stock (at $53 per share), then shareholder wealth is $53 per share, with $3 of this value representing price appreciation. Note that the pretax returns to shareholders are the same under each alternative.

Ignoring taxes, transaction costs, and other market imperfections, shareholders should be indifferent between equivalent returns from cash dividends and share repurchases. In other words, the value of the firm should not be affected by the manner in which returns (cash dividends versus capital gains) are paid to

---

[33]If a stock purchase results in a substantial increase in the debt-to-equity ratio, the new P/E ratio may be lower because of increased financial risk.

TABLE 14-4
Hewlett-Packard Company
Share Repurchase

	BEFORE REPURCHASE	AFTER REPURCHASE
Expected net earnings	$625,000,000	$625,000,000
Shares outstanding	250,000,000	235,849,057
Expected earnings per share	$2.50	$2.65
Price-earnings (P/E) ratio	20×	20×
Expected share price (ex-dividend)	$50	$53
Expected dividend	$3	$0

shareholders. However, empirical studies suggest that share repurchases do increase stock prices (i.e., value of the firm).[34] Some reasons why this occurs are examined next.

Tax Considerations

In the context of dividend decisions, tax considerations historically have been the primary reason why firms decided to repurchase their own stock in lieu of, or in addition to, payment of cash dividends. As discussed earlier in the chapter, prior to passage of the 1986 Tax Reform Act, long-term capital gains income was taxed at lower rates than dividend income. The 1986 law eliminated the tax rate differential between capital gains and dividend income. The 1993 tax law changes have restored a significant tax advantage to capital gains income (taxed at a maximum individual rate of 28 percent) versus dividend income (taxed at a maximum individual rate of 39.6 percent). In addition, because taxes on capital gains can be deferred into the future (when the stock is sold), whereas taxes on an equivalent amount of dividend income have to be paid in the current year, firms now have substantial tax reasons to make distributions in the form of share repurchases.

Although a stock repurchase program seems like a desirable way of distributing a firm's earnings, repurchases may be deterred by the IRS. Specifically, the IRS will not permit a firm to follow a policy of regular stock repurchases as an alternative to cash dividends, because repurchase plans convert cash dividends to capital gains. The IRS looks upon regular repurchases as essentially equivalent to cash dividends and requires that they be taxed accordingly.

Financial Flexibility

Substituting discretionary stock repurchases for all or part of regular cash dividends (i.e., stable dollar dividend policy) provides a company with greater financial flexibility. Under such a strategy, when the company has profitable uses for its funds, it can defer the buyback of its stock (and the corresponding cash outflows) until a more appropriate time in the future. The company thus avoids incurring the costs associated with raising the external equity capital needed to finance investments. Likewise, when the company accumulates excess funds, it can undertake periodic stock repurchases.

[34]See Larry Y. Dann, "Common Stock Repurchases: An Analysis of Returns to Bondholders and Stockholders," *Journal of Financial Economics* (June 1981): 113–138; and Theo Vermaelen, "Common Stock Repurchases and Market Signaling: An Empirical Study," *Journal of Financial Economics* (June 1981): 139–183.

Signaling Effects

Like the signaling effects of cash dividend increases, share repurchases also can have a positive impact on shareholder wealth. A share repurchase may represent a signal to investors that management expects the firm to have higher earnings and cash flows in the future.[35]

Advantages and Disadvantages

Let us summarize the advantages and disadvantages of share repurchases as an addition to, or as a substitute for, cash dividends.

Advantages. Share repurchases effectively convert dividend income into capital gains income. Shareholders in high (marginal) income tax brackets may prefer capital gains income because of the lower (marginal) tax rates on such income and because of the ability to defer taxes into the future (when the stock is sold). Also, share repurchases provide the firm with greater financial flexibility in timing the payment of returns to shareholders. Finally, share repurchases can represent a signal to investors that the company expects to have higher earnings and cash flows in the future.

Disadvantages. A company may overpay for the stock that it repurchases. If the stock price declines, the share repurchase represents an unprofitable use of the company's resources. Also, a share repurchase may trigger IRS scrutiny (and possible tax penalties) if the buyback is viewed as a way for shareholders to avoid taxes on cash dividends. Finally, some current shareholders may be unaware of the share repurchase program and may sell their shares before the expected benefits, (i.e., price appreciation) occurs.

■ SUMMARY

- *Dividend policy* determines the ultimate distribution of a firm's earnings between retention (reinvestment) and cash dividend payments to stockholders. Retained earnings provide investors with a source of potential future earnings growth, whereas dividends provide them with a current distribution.
- A number of factors influence a firm's choice of dividend policy. These include the following:
  1. Legal constraints prohibiting dividends that impair capital.
  2. Restrictive covenants in bond indentures and other financing agreements.
  3. Tax considerations.
  4. The need for liquidity.
  5. Borrowing capacity and access to the capital markets.
  6. Earnings stability.
  7. Capital expansion (growth) opportunities.
  8. Inflation.

[35]See Vermaelen, "Common Stock Repurchases and Market Signaling: An Empirical Study"; and Paul Asquith and David W. Mullins, Jr., "Signaling with Dividends, Stock Repurchases, and Equity Issues," *Financial Management* (Autumn 1986): 27–44.

Shareholders' preferences (*clientele effect*) may also influence a firm's choice of dividend policy. These are determined by stockholders' tax positions and their desire to maintain control of the firm. Some of these factors favor high dividends, whereas others imply a lower payout policy. The board of directors should weigh these factors in each instance and arrive at the best possible dividend policy.

■ Under a restrictive set of assumptions articulated by Miller and Modigliani (MM), the value of the firm is dependent solely on its investment decisions. They claim that any observed changes in firm value as a result of dividend decisions are due only to the *informational content* or *signaling effects* of dividend policy. Under these conditions, dividend policy does not affect the value of the firm. After the MM assumptions are removed, dividend policy may affect firm value because of

1. Risk-averse behavior of investors.
2. Shareholder transaction costs.
3. Personal taxes.
4. Issuance costs.
5. Agency costs.

■ A firm may employ any one of a number of alternative dividend policies, including the following:

1. The passive residual approach.
2. The stable dollar dividend approach.
3. The constant payout ratio approach.
4. The policy of paying a small, regular dividend plus year-end extras.

Ample evidence indicates that many firms favor a stable dollar dividend policy.

■ Small firms tend to pay out a smaller percentage of their earnings as dividends than large firms, reflecting the critical funding needs of many small firms and their limited access to capital markets.

■ Multinational firms establish dividend policies for their subsidiaries reflecting such factors as foreign tax rates, political and exchange rate risk, currency controls, the subsidiary's need for funds, and access to host country capital markets for funds.

■ *Stock dividends* are sometimes used in lieu of (and in conjunction with) cash dividends. The net effect of stock dividends is to leave the total book value of the firm unchanged while increasing the number of shares outstanding and broadening the ownership base.

■ Some firms employ *share repurchase plans* in lieu of (or in addition to) cash dividends. Stock repurchases convert shareholder benefits from ordinary income (dividends) to capital gains income. Theoretically, ignoring taxes, transaction costs, and other market imperfections, share repurchases should have the same effect on shareholder wealth as the payment of cash dividends. However, possibly due to tax considerations (that is, lower tax rates on capital gains income than on dividends and the ability to defer taxes on capital gain income) and signaling effects, share repurchases (via tender offers) are observed to have a positive effect on shareholder wealth.

■ QUESTIONS AND TOPICS FOR DISCUSSION

1. What legal constraints limit the amount of cash dividends that may be paid by a firm?
2. What aspects of U.S. tax laws tend to (a) encourage and (b) discourage large dividend payments by corporations? Explain how.

3. What other "external" factors limit a firm's ability to pay cash dividends?
4. What is the likely impact of a highly inflationary economy on a firm's ability to pay dividends? Would you expect this impact to be greater or smaller for a rapidly expanding firm? Why?
5. Explain what is meant by the *clientele effect.*
6. Explain what is meant by the *informational content* of dividend policy.
7. Explain what is meant by the *signaling effects* of dividend policy.
8. In the theoretical world of Miller and Modigliani, what role does dividend policy play in the determination of share values?
9. What role do most practitioners think dividend policy plays in determining share values?
10. How can the "passive residual" view of dividend policy be reconciled with the tendency of most firms to maintain a constant or steadily growing dividend payment record?
11. Why do many managers prefer a stable dollar dividend policy to a policy of paying out a constant percentage of each year's earnings as dividends?
12. Under what circumstances would it make sense for a firm to borrow money to make its dividend payments?
13. Some people have suggested that it is irrational for a firm to pay dividends and sell new stock in the same year, because the cost of newly issued equity is greater than the cost of retained earnings. Do you agree? Why or why not?
14. What is a *dividend reinvestment plan*? Explain the advantages of a dividend reinvestment plan to the firm and to shareholders.
15. Why do many firms choose to issue stock dividends? What is the value of a stock dividend to a shareholder?
16. What are the tax limitations on the practice of share repurchases as a regular dividend policy?
17. What effect do share repurchases (undertaken as part of the firm's dividend decision) have on the value of the firm?
18. You are the holder of common stock in the G. Lewis Apartment Renovation Company. Historically, the firm has paid generous cash dividends. The firm has recently announced that it would replace its cash dividend with a 20 percent annual stock dividend. Is this good news, bad news, or is it impossible to tell from the information provided? Explain the reason for your answer.
19. What issues of business ethics may be involved in the establishment of a firm's dividend payment amounts?

■ SELF-TEST PROBLEMS

ST1. The board of directors of Complex Computers has decided to declare a 20 percent stock dividend. The company's common stockholders' equity is as follows:

Pre-Stock Dividend Common Stockholders' Equity

Common stock ($1 par, 100,000 shares)	$ 100,000
Contributed capital in excess of par	900,000
Retained earnings	5,000,000
Total common stockholders' equity	$6,000,000

The common stock of Complex Computers currently is trading at $80 a share. The company is growing rapidly and has never paid a cash dividend.

a. Show the company's common stockholder's equity after the stock dividend.
b. Calculate the post-stock dividend price of Complex Computers stock, assuming no other changes occur.

ST2. Sanchez Supermarkets, Inc. (50,000 common shares outstanding) currently has annual earnings before interest and taxes of $1,000,000. Its interest expenses are $200,000 a year, and it pays $100,000 in annual dividends to its stockholders. The company's tax rate is 40 percent, and its common stock's current dividend yield is 2.0 percent.

    a. Calculate the company's earnings per share.

    b. Calculate the company's dividend payout ratio.

    c. Calculate the company's current common stock price.

    d. If Sanchez declares and pays a 100 percent stock dividend and then pays an annual cash dividend of $1.10 per share, what is the effective rate by which the dividend has been increased?

■ PROBLEMS*

1. Jacobs Corporation earned $2 million after tax. The firm has 1.6 million shares of common stock outstanding.

    a. Compute the earnings per share of Jacobs.

    b. If Jacobs' dividend policy calls for a 40 percent payout ratio, what are the dividends per share?

2. Drew Financial Associates currently pays a quarterly dividend of 50 cents per share. This quarter's dividend will be paid to stockholders of record on Friday, February 22, 19X1. Drew has 200,000 common shares outstanding. The retained earnings account has a balance of $15 million before the dividend, and Drew holds $2.5 million in cash.

    a. What is the ex-dividend date for this quarter?

    b. Drew's stock traded for $22 per share the day prior to the ex-dividend date. What would you expect the stock price to open at on the ex-dividend date? Give some reasons why this might not occur.

    c. What is the effect of the dividend payment on Drew's cash, retained earnings, and total assets?

3. Winkie Baking has just announced a 100 percent stock dividend. The annual cash dividend per share was $2.40 before the stock dividend. Winkie intends to pay $1.40 per share on each of the new shares. Compute the percentage increase in the cash dividend rate that will accompany the stock dividend.

4. Wolverine Corporation plans to pay a $3 dividend per share on each of its 300,000 shares next year. Wolverine anticipates earnings of $6.25 per share over the year. If the company has a capital budget requiring an investment of $4 million over the year and it desires to maintain its present debt to total assets (debt ratio) of 0.40, how much external equity must it raise? Assume Wolverine's capital structure includes only common equity and debt, and that debt and equity will be the only sources of funds to finance capital projects over the year.

5. Tulia Dairy pays a $2.50 cash dividend and earns $5 per share. The cash dividend has recently been increased to $2.65 per share, *and* a 3 percent stock dividend has been declared. What is the effective rate of increase in the dividends for Tulia as a result of this action?

6. The Mori Egg Noodle Company has the following equity accounts on its balance sheet:

Common stock ($10 par, 300,000 shares)	$ 3,000,000
Contributed capital in excess of par	1,500,000
Retained earnings	6,000,000
Total common stockholders' equity	$10,500,000

*Colored numbers denote problems that have check answers provided at the end of the book.

a. What is the maximum amount of dividends that may be paid by the Mori Company if the capital impairment provisions of state law are limited to the following?
   i. The par value of common stock.
   ii. The par value and the capital in excess of par accounts.
b. What other factors may limit Mori's ability to pay dividends?

7. Champoux Hair Factory, Inc. has earnings before interest and taxes of $200,000. Annual interest amounts to $80,000, and annual depreciation is $80,000. Taxes are computed at a 40 percent rate. Existing bond obligations require the payment of $40,000 per year into a sinking fund.

Champoux wishes to pay a $2 per-share dividend on the existing 20,000 shares. The firm's bond indenture prohibits the payment of dividends unless the cash flow (before dividends and sinking fund payments) is greater than the total of dividends, interest, and sinking fund obligations.
   a. Can Champoux pay the proposed dividend?
   b. What is the maximum dividend per share that may be paid? $1.60

8. Lenberg Lens Company believes in the "dividends as a residual" philosophy of dividend policy. This year's earnings are expected to total $10 million. A very conservative company, Lenberg is financed solely with common stock. The required rate of return on retained earnings is 12 percent, whereas the cost of newly raised capital is 14 percent because of issuance costs.
   a. If Lenberg has $6 million of investment projects having expected returns greater than 12 percent, what total amount of dividends should Lenberg pay?
   b. If Lenberg has $12 million of investment projects having expected returns greater than 14 percent, what total amount of dividends should Lenberg pay?
   c. What factors, other than its belief in the residual theory of dividends, should Lenberg consider in setting its dividend policy in Part b?

9. Phoenix Tool Company and Denver Tool Company have had a very similar record of earnings performance over the past 8 years. Both firms are in the same industry and, in fact, compete directly with each other. The two firms have nearly identical capital structures. Phoenix has a policy of paying a constant 50 percent of each year's earnings as dividends, whereas Denver has sought to maintain a stable dollar dividend policy, with changes in the dollar dividend payment occurring infrequently. The record of the two companies follows:

	Phoenix			Denver		
Year	EPS	Dividend	Average Market Price	EPS	Dividend	Average Market Price
19X1	$2.00	$1.00	$20	$2.10	$0.75	$18
19X2	2.50	1.25	24	2.40	0.75	22
19X3	1.50	1.25	15	1.60	0.75	17
19X4	1.00	0.50	10	0.90	0.75	14
19X5	0.50	0.25	8	0.50	0.50	10
19X6	−1.25	nil	8	−1.10	0.50	10
19X7	1.00	0.50	10	1.10	0.75	14
19X8	1.50	0.75	14	1.45	0.75	17

The president of Phoenix wonders what accounts for Denver's current (19X8) higher stock price, in spite of the fact that Phoenix currently earns more per share than Denver and frequently has paid a higher dividend.
   a. What factors can you cite that might account for this phenomenon?
   b. What do you suggest as an optimal dividend policy for both Phoenix and Denver that might lead to increases in both of their share prices? What are the limitations of your suggestions?

10. The Emco Steel Company has experienced a slow (3 percent per year) but steady increase in earnings per share. The firm consistently has paid out an average of 75 percent of each year's earnings as dividends. The stock market evaluates Emco primarily on the basis of its dividend payout, because growth prospects are modest.

Emco's management presents a proposal to the board of directors that would require the outlay of $50 million to build a new plant in the rapidly expanding Florida market. The expected annual return on the investment in this plant is estimated to be in excess of 30 percent, more than twice the current company average. To finance this investment, a number of alternatives are being considered. They include the following:

a. Finance the expansion with externally raised equity.

b. Finance the expansion with 50 percent externally generated equity and 50 percent internally generated equity. This alternative would necessitate a dividend cut for this year only.

c. Finance the expansion with a mix of debt and equity similar to their current relative proportions in the capital structure. Under this alternative, dividends would not be cut. Rather, any equity needs in excess of that which could be provided internally would be raised through a sale of new common stock.

Evaluate these various financing alternatives with reference to their effects on the dividend policy and common stock values of the company.

11. The Sweet Times Candy Company has the following equity accounts on its balance sheet:

Common stock ($1 par, 500,000 shares)	$ 500,000
Contributed capital in excess of par	2,000,000
Retained earnings	13,000,000
Total common stockholders' equity	$15,500,000

The current market price of the firm's shares is $50.

a. If the firm declares a 10 percent stock dividend, what will be the impact on the firm's equity accounts?

b. If the firm currently pays no cash dividend, what is the impact of a 10 percent stock dividend on the wealth position of the firm's existing stockholders?

c. If the firm currently pays a cash dividend of $1 per share and this per-share dividend rate does not change after the 10 percent stock dividend, what impact would you expect the stock dividend to have on the wealth position of existing shareholders?

12. Striker's Match Company reports the following financial data:

Net earnings	$3,000,000
Shares outstanding	1,000,000
Earnings per share	$ 3
Market price per share (ex-dividend)	$40
Expected dividend per share	$ 2

Striker is considering distributing $2 million to existing stockholders, either as cash dividends or through the repurchase of outstanding shares. The repurchase plan is favored by some of the company's wealthiest and most influential stockholders.

If the shares are repurchased, the company would make a tender offer for 47,619 shares at a price of $42. Alternatively, the firm could pay a $2 dividend, after the payment of which each share would sell for $40.

a. Ignoring taxes, what impact does the choice of a dividend payment or share repurchase plan have on the wealth position of the firm's shareholders?

b. If most shareholders are in a very high marginal tax bracket, which alternative is favored?

c. What are the limitations on the repurchase alternative as an element of the firm's dividend policy?

13. Concave Systems presently has earnings before interest and taxes of $3,000,000. Its interest expenses are $500,000 a year, and it pays $600,000 in annual dividends to its shareholders. Concave has 300,000 common shares outstanding, and its tax rate is 40 percent. Its annual capital expenditures are $900,000. Concave's present price-earnings ratio is 12.

    a. Calculate the company's earnings per share.
    b. Calculate the company's dividend payout ratio.
    c. Calculate the company's dividend yield.

14. During 1996, *Value Line* projected that Pennzoil would earn about $2.00 per share in 1996 and $2.75 in 1997, a substantial increase from the $0.17 per share *loss* in 1995. Pennzoil's dividend per share was $1.00 in 1996, down from $2.50 in 1995, and $3.00 during 1989–1993. As an investor trying to assess whether Pennzoil will increase its dividend back up to its previous $3.00 per share level, what additional information would you want to gather? (A good source of relevant information is the company's *Value Line* report—available in most libraries.)

15. On Friday, August 6, the Board of Directors of Cisco Industries declares a $0.22 quarterly dividend payable on September 15 to stockholders of record on Tuesday, August 24. When is the ex-dividend date? If you purchase the stock on this date are you entitled to receive the dividend?

16. Clynne Resources expects earnings this year to be $2 per share. Clynne plans to pay a dividend of $0.70 for the year. During the year Clynne expects to borrow $10 million in addition to its already outstanding loan balances. Clynne has 10 million shares of common stock outstanding.

    a. If all capital outlays are funded from retained earnings and new borrowings and if Clynne follows a residual dividend policy, what capital outlays are planned for the coming year?
    b. What is Clynne's target capital structure given these assumptions?

http:// 17. Visit the following Web site and complete the tutorial on cash dividends, stock dividends, stock splits, and reverse stock splits.
http://www.e-analytics.com/index.htm

http:// 18. Visit the Stock Center at Thomson Investors Network and look at the dividends paid over the past few years by major established companies ("blue chip" companies), such as Ford and Exxon. Then look at the dividends paid by relatively new, quickly growing companies, such as Intel. In terms of what you've learned in this chapter, cate-gorize their dividend policy and then justify this policy, given the nature of the company.
http://www.thomsoninvest.net

■ SOLUTIONS TO SELF-TEST PROBLEMS

ST1. a. *Post-Stock Dividend Common Stockholders' Equity*

Common stock ($1 par, 120,000 shares)	$ 120,000
Contributed capital in excess of par	2,480,000
Retained earnings	3,400,000
Total common stockholders' equity	$6,000,000

A total of $1,600,000 (20,000 shares × an assumed market price of $80 per share) is transferred from retained earnings to the other stockholders' equity accounts. Of this $1,600,000, $20,000 ($1 par × 20,000 shares) is added to the common stock account and the remaining $1,580,000 is added to the contributed capital in excess of par account.

b. Post-stock dividend price $= \dfrac{\$80}{1+0.20}$

$= \$66.67$

ST2. a.

EBIT	$1,000,000
Interest	200,000
EBT	$ 800,000
Taxes	320,000
EAT	$ 480,000

$$\text{Earnings per share} = \frac{\$480,000}{50,000 \text{ shares}}$$

$$= \$9.60$$

b.

$$\text{Dividends per share} = \frac{\$100,000}{50,000 \text{ shares}}$$

$$= \$2.00$$

$$\text{Dividend payout ratio} = \frac{\$2.00}{\$9.60}$$

$$= 20.8\%$$

c.

$$\text{Dividend yield} = \frac{\text{Dividend per share}}{\text{Price per share}}$$

$$0.02 = \frac{\$2.00}{\text{Price per share}}$$

$$\text{Price per share} = \$100.00$$

d. Equivalent (pre-stock dividend)
dividend per share: $2.00 ÷ 2 = $1.00

$$\text{Dividend rate increase} = \frac{\$1.10 - \$1.00}{\$1.00}$$

$$= 0.10 \text{ or } 10\%$$

∎ GLOSSARY

Clientele Effect The concept that investors will tend to be attracted to companies that have dividend policies consistent with the investors' objectives.

Declaration Date The day on which the directors of a company declare a dividend.

Dividend Reinvestment Plan An option that allows shareholders to have their cash dividends automatically reinvested in additional shares of the company's stock.

Ex-dividend Date The date on which the right to the most recently declared dividend no longer goes along with the sale of the stock. The ex-divided date is 4 business days prior to the *record date*.

Informational Content The concept that, for a company following a stable dividend policy, changes in dividend payments convey information (i.e., a signal) to investors concerning management's expectations about the future profitability of the company.

Insolvency A situation in which either a firm's liabilities exceed its assets or the firm is unable to pay its creditors as required.

Passive Residual Theory A theory of dividend policy that suggests that a company should retain its earnings as long as there are investment opportunities available promising a rate of return higher than the required rate of return.

Record Date The date on which a company makes a list from its stock transfer books of those shareholders who are eligible to receive the declared dividend.

Stock Dividend A payment of additional shares of common stock to stockholders.

Treasury Stock Common stock that has been reacquired by the issuing company.

P A R T V

WORKING CAPITAL MANAGEMENT AND FINANCIAL FORECASTING

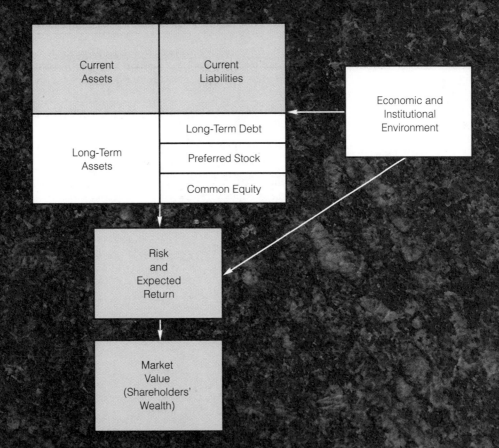

This part of the book considers the financial management of a firm's current assets and current liabilities, called *working capital management*. Chapter 15 deals with financial forecasting and working capital policy, with emphasis on the risk-return tradeoffs that are implied. Chapter 16 covers the management of cash and marketable securities.

Chapter 17 discusses the management of accounts receivable and inventories. Chapter 18 looks at current liabilities and the sources of short-term and intermediate-term credit. Working capital management influences both the risk of a firm and its expected returns. As such, it is an important determinant of firm value.

Financial Forecasting and Working Capital Policy

15

1. The percentage-of-sales forecasting method is used in estimating the amount of additional financing that a firm will need for a given increase in sales, based on certain assumptions about the relationship between sales and the various asset and liability accounts.
2. A cash budget is the projection of a firm's cash receipts and disbursements over a future time period and is useful in determining the amount of short-term funds the firm will need to borrow.
3. Examination of a firm's operating cycle and cash conversion cycle is important in analyzing its liquidity.
4. Working capital policy decisions include
   a. Investment—level of working capital.
   b. Financing—proportions of short-term and long-term debt.
5. Determination of the optimal level of working capital investment involves profitability versus risk trade-off analysis:

   a. Higher levels of working capital generally reduce profitability.
   b. Higher levels of working capital reduce the risk of financial difficulties.
6. Determination of the optimal proportions of short- and long-term debt involves profitability versus risk trade-off analysis:
   a. Higher proportions of short-term debt increase profitability because of generally lower interest costs.
   b. Higher proportions of short-term debt increase the risk of financial difficulties.
7. Overall working capital policy involves analyzing the joint impact of the working capital investment decision and the working capital financing decision on the firm's risk and profitability.
8. Other important topics include
   a. Pro forma statement of cash flows.
   b. Computerized financial planning models.

GOING BROKE WHILE MAKING A PROFIT*

At the beginning of the year, George Mills was in good spirits. He was president of CAM Products, a firm that manufactured computer connectors for $6 each and sold them for $8 each. Demand was strong in this segment of the computer market. Mills kept a 30-day inventory, paid his bills promptly, and billed his customers on terms of net 30 days (that is, payments were due in 30 days). Sales forecasts had been accurate, and a steady increase was anticipated over the next year.

On January 1, the firm's books read as follows:

Cash = $8,000,000
Inventory = $6,000,000
Receivables = $8,000,000

In January, Mills sold 1,000,000 connectors, produced at a cost of $6,000,000, and collected receivables of $8,000,000. January's profits totaled $2,000,000.

On February 1, the firm's books read as follows:

Cash = $10,000,000
Inventory = $6,000,000
Receivables = $8,000,000

February sales increased to an expected 1,500,000 units. To maintain a 30-day inventory, production was increased to 2,000,000 units at a cost of $12,000,000. All January receivables were collected, and profits through February totaled $5,000,000.

On March 1, the account balances were as follows:

Cash = $6,000,000
Inventory = $9,000,000
Receivables = $12,000,000

March sales increased to 2,000,000 units. Collections from February were made on time. Production was in-

creased to 2,500,000 units to maintain a 2,000,000-unit inventory. Profits for the month totaled $4,000,000 ($9,000,000 year to date).

On April 1, the books read as follows:

Cash = $3,000,000
Inventory = $12,000,000
Receivables = $16,000,000

Sales increased to 2,500,000 units in April; Mills was overjoyed. Customers

continued to pay on time. Production was increased to 3,000,000 units to maintain a 2,500,000-unit inventory. Profits for the month totaled $5,000,000 ($14,000,000 year to date). Mills headed for a long-deserved vacation in the islands.

On May 1, the books read as follows:

Cash = $1,000,000
Inventory = $15,000,000
Receivables = $20,000,000

In May, sales exploded to new records—3,000,000 units—and production was increased to 3,500,000. Profits for the first 5 months of the year were $20,000,000. Then Mills got an unexpected call from his accountant, telling him to come home as quickly as possible. The firm was out of cash.

On June 1, CAM Products' accounts had the following balances:

Cash = $0
Inventory = $18,000,000
Receivables = $24,000,000

Mills came home, confused and perplexed, and immediately arranged a meeting with his banker.

This example illustrates the importance of proper planning and management of a firm's working capital. This chapter is the first of three chapters dealing with this important area.

*Adapted from "How to Go Broke. . . While Making a Profit," *Business Week* (April 28, 1956): 46–54.

INTRODUCTION

The first half of this chapter discusses various techniques for forecasting a company's future cash flows and need for funds. Various forecasting methods are developed, including the percentage of sales forecasting method, cash budgets, and the pro forma statement of cash flows. Other techniques, such as computerized financial forecasting and planning models and the use of statistical models (i.e., discriminant analysis) are also briefly outlined. The second half of the chapter deals with the management of working capital, which involves decisions about the optimal overall level of current assets and the optimal mix of short-term and long-term funds used to finance the company's assets. These decisions require an analysis of the risk and expected return trade-offs associated with the various alternative policies.

FINANCIAL FORECASTING

Financial forecasting allows a firm to estimate the amount of additional financing it will require in an upcoming period. The proportions of short-term and long-term debt that make up the additional financing requirements can be determined by analyzing the profitability-risk trade-offs of alternative working capital investment and financing policies.

This section presents an overview of the financial forecasting process, with emphasis on the important role of pro forma financial statements. **Pro forma financial statements,** showing the results of some *assumed* event, rather than an *actual* event, are usually an integral part of a financial forecast. For example, an operating budget that shows the level of net income that can be expected if sales and expenses are at a given assumed level next year is a pro forma income statement. Short-term forecasts, those that deal with one year or less, tend to be rather detailed, whereas long-term forecasts are more general. This section discusses the percentage of sales forecasting method, cash budgets, the pro forma statement of cash flows, computerized financial forecasting and planning models, and using financial ratios to forecast future financial performance.

Percentage of Sales Forecasting Method

The **percentage of sales forecasting method** permits a company to forecast the amount of financing it will need for a given increase in sales. This method is simple and can provide information useful in preparing pro forma financial statements and in estimating future funds needs. The method assumes that (1) present asset levels are optimal with respect to present sales; (2) most items on the balance sheet increase in proportion to sales increases; and (3) the firm's profit margin on sales (EAT/Sales) remains constant. The use of this method is illustrated with the following example of the Industrial Supply Company (ISC).

The present (19X6) ISC balance sheet and income statement are shown in Table 15-1. Management forecasts that sales will increase by 25 percent, or $3,750,000, next year to $18,750,000.

One of management's primary concerns is the amount of funds (cash) needed to finance this sales growth. Until now, the company has financed its

TABLE 15-1
Industrial Supply Company
Financial Statements

BALANCE SHEET AS OF DECEMBER 31, 19X6

Assets		Liabilities and Equity	
Cash	$ 500,000	Accounts payable	$ 1,500,000
Accounts receivable	2,000,000	Notes payable	1,000,000
Inventories	4,000,000	Total current liabilities	$ 2,500,000
Total current assets	$6,500,000	Long-term debt	500,000
Fixed assets, net	1,000,000	Stockholders' equity	4,500,000
Total assets	$7,500,000	Total liabilities and equity	$ 7,500,000

INCOME STATEMENT FOR THE YEAR ENDED DECEMBER 31, 19X6

Sales	$15,000,000
Expenses, including interest and taxes	14,250,000
Earnings after taxes	$ 750,000
Dividends paid	$ 250,000

SELECTED FINANCIAL RATIOS

Current ratio	2.60 times
Debt ratio	40%
Return on stockholders' equity	16.7%
Net profit margin on sales (EAT/Sales)	5.0%

growth by using both internally and externally generated funds. The company has reinvested most of its past earnings, primarily into additional inventory. The company has also used external financing in the form of short-term borrowings from its bank.

To determine the amount of additional financing necessary to reach the expected $18,750,000 annual sales level, the ISC management has made the following observations about the company's various assets and liabilities:

1. **Cash.** Management feels the company's cash balances are generally adequate for the present sales level and would have to increase proportionately as sales increase.
2. **Accounts receivable.** The company's present average collection period is approximately 49 days. Management feels the company's present credit policies are appropriate for its type of business. As a result, they feel that the average collection period will remain approximately constant and that accounts receivable will increase proportionately as sales increase.
3. **Inventory.** Management feels the company's inventory is properly managed at present. Therefore, they feel inventory would have to increase proportionately for sales to increase.
4. **Fixed assets.** The company is a distributor with relatively few fixed assets (delivery trucks, forklifts, office equipment, storage racks, and so forth). Because the company's fixed assets *are being utilized at nearly full capacity,* management feels fixed assets will have to increase as sales grow. For financial planning purposes, management is willing to assume that the *net* fixed asset figure on the balance sheet will increase proportionately as sales increase.
5. **Accounts payable.** The company now maintains good relations with its suppliers. As the company purchases more inventory, its accounts payable balance will increase proportionately as sales increase.

6. Long-term debt. Long-term debt and notes payable do not necessarily have a direct relationship to the sales level. For example, a portion of the company's future cash flows may be used to pay off the present debt.

In summary, as the company's sales increase, its assets will increase proportionately to support the new sales. In addition, the current liabilities that vary directly with sales, namely accounts payable, will also increase. The difference between the forecasted asset increase and the forecasted current liability increase is equal to the total financing the company will need. This relationship can be expressed in equation form as follows:

$$
\begin{pmatrix} \text{Total} \\ \text{financing} \\ \text{needed} \end{pmatrix} = \begin{array}{c} \text{Forecasted} \\ \text{asset} \\ \text{increase} \end{array} - \begin{array}{c} \text{Forecasted} \\ \text{current} \\ \text{liability} \\ \text{increase} \end{array}
$$

$$
= \frac{A}{S}\,(\Delta S) - \frac{CL}{S}\,(\Delta S) \tag{15.1}
$$

where A is the company's present level of assets that vary proportionately with sales, S is the company's present sales, CL is the company's present level of current liabilities that vary proportionately with sales, and ΔS is the forecasted sales increase.

A portion of the total financing needed can be generated internally from increased retained earnings. Specifically, the increased retained earnings generated during the time period when sales increase from S to $S + \Delta S$ can be expressed in equation form as follows:

$$
\begin{pmatrix} \text{Increased} \\ \text{retained} \\ \text{earnings} \end{pmatrix} = \begin{array}{c} \text{Forecasted} \\ \text{earnings after} \\ \text{taxes} \end{array} - \text{Dividends} \tag{15.2}
$$

$$
= \text{EAT} - \text{D}
$$

The additional financing needed can be calculated by subtracting the increased retained earnings from the total financing needed:

$$
\begin{array}{c} \text{Additional} \\ \text{financing} \\ \text{needed} \end{array} = \begin{array}{c} \text{Total} \\ \text{financing} \\ \text{needed} \end{array} - \begin{array}{c} \text{Increased} \\ \text{retained} \\ \text{earnings} \end{array}
$$

$$
= \left[\frac{A}{S}\,(\Delta S) - \frac{CL}{S}\,(\Delta S) \right] - [\text{EAT} - \text{D}] \tag{15.3}
$$

Referring back to the ISC example, the additional financing needed to support a sales increase of $3,750,000 up to the $18,750,000 level now can be calculated. Assume that management forecasts expenses to be $17,750,000 and EAT to be $1,000,000 during the coming year. Assume further that the company plans to maintain its dividend payments at the same level in 19X7 as in 19X6. Substituting this data into Equation 15.3 yields

$$
\begin{array}{c} \text{Additional} \\ \text{financing} \\ \text{needed} \end{array} = \left[\frac{\$7,500,000}{\$15,000,000}\,(\$3,750,000) - \frac{\$1,500,000}{\$15,000,000}\,(\$3,750,000) \right]
$$

$$
- (\$1,000,000 - \$250,000)
$$

$$
= \$750,000
$$

The approximate amount of additional financing that will be needed to finance ISC's forecasted growth in sales from $15,000,000 to $18,750,000 is $750,000.[1] Even though the financing will be needed gradually as sales increase, the ISC management has to decide whether to (1) borrow on a short-term basis, (2) borrow on a long-term basis, (3) sell additional common stock, or (4) cut dividends. The factors that influence the debt versus equity decision are discussed in Chapter 12, the factors that influence the short-term versus long-term debt decision are discussed later in this chapter, and the factors that influence the dividend decision are discussed in Chapter 14. As this example illustrates, *the investment, financing, and dividend decisions of the firm are interdependent.*

Table 15-2 shows ISC's pro forma financial statements for 19X7, *assuming* that all of the additional financing needed is in the form of short-term notes payable. Examination of the selected financial ratios in Tables 15-1 and 15-2 shows that this financing plan will increase the return on stockholders' equity from 16.7 percent in 19X6 to 19.0 percent in 19X7. However, it also reduces the firm's current ratio (measure of liquidity) from 2.60 to 2.24 times and increases its debt ratio (measure of leverage) from 40 percent to 44 percent. ISC management would have to weigh these factors in determining how to obtain the $750,000 of additional financing needed.

The percentage of sales forecasting method for calculating financing needs is a useful and convenient cash flow forecasting technique. However, as with all analytical techniques, the application of this method should be supplemented by any additional factors that are unique to the particular situation.

TABLE 15-2
Industrial Supply Company
Pro Forma Financial Statements

PRO FORMA BALANCE SHEET AS OF DECEMBER 31, 19X7

Assets		Liabilities and Equity	
Cash	$ 625,000	Accounts payable	$ 1,875,000
Accounts receivable	2,500,000	Notes payable	1,750,000
Inventories	5,000,000	Total current liabilities	$ 3,625,000
Total current assets	$8,125,000	Long-term debt	500,000
Fixed assets, net	1,250,000	Stockholders' equity	5,250,000
Total assets	$9,375,000	Total liabilities and equity	$ 9,375,000

PRO FORMA INCOME STATEMENT FOR THE YEAR ENDING DECEMBER 31, 19X7

Sales	$18,750,000
Expenses, including interest and taxes	17,750,000
Earnings after taxes	$ 1,000,000
Dividends	250,000
Retained earnings	$ 750,000

SELECTED PRO FORMA FINANCIAL RATIOS

Current ratio	2.24 times
Debt ratio	44%
Return on stockholders' equity	19.0%

[1]The $750,000 figure assumes that none of the present notes payable or long-term debt will have to be repaid during the year.

may not be strictly proportional

One such factor is *economies of scale.* Economies of scale may result in nonlinear relationships between sales and certain types of assets. In other words, the relationships may not be strictly proportional, as assumed in the model. For example, a 10 percent increase in sales may only require a 5 percent increase in fixed assets or inventories. Another factor in some industries is that capacity can be added only in *discrete* or *"lumpy"* increments. Once output reaches the capacity of an existing production facility, expansion requires building another facility. This causes fixed assets to increase in a stepwise manner as sales are increased, rather than increasing proportionately.

Cash Budgeting

Even though the percentage of sales forecasting method is a useful tool that can provide insights regarding financing needs associated with projected sales increases, *cash budgets* can estimate more precisely *both* the *amount* of financing needed by a firm and the *timing* of those financing needs. Cash budgeting plays an important role in the firm's financial forecasting process. Effective cash budgeting can help management identify potential cash flow problems. Usually, cash flow problems are easier to solve when they are anticipated. In addition to a detailed discussion of cash budgets, this section contains a brief overview of budgeting.

An Overview of Budgeting. *Budgets* are simply pro forma financial statements that detail a firm's financial forecasts. They show how the company's cash will be spent on labor, materials, and capital goods and indicate how cash will be obtained.

Budgets are used to *plan, coordinate,* and *control* a firm's operations. They are essential to *planning* because they represent the company's objectives in numerical terms, such as dollars of sales, units of production, pounds of raw materials, and dollars of financing required from the capital markets. Once a firm has made financial plans, it refers to the budgets when *coordinating* its overall activities. For example, the purchasing department examines the budgets when deciding how best to integrate purchasing activities with monthly production requirements to ensure the availability of sufficient raw materials. The production and marketing departments then work together to guarantee that sufficient finished goods inventories are on hand. Finally, the finance department coordinates the company's need for funds with the requirements of the purchasing, production, and marketing departments.

The projected figures in a firm's budgets are also used as a *control* device against which actual figures are compared; this ensures that the various departments and divisions are functioning properly and working together toward the objectives developed in the planning phase.

A firm's budgets are based on the *assumption* of certain future sales and production levels. As pro forma financial statements, budgets predict *what* a company's financial statements will look like *if* specific plans are realized.

Cash Budgets. A **cash budget** is the projection of a company's cash receipts and disbursements over some future period of time. Typically, a cash budget is prepared on an annual basis and subdivided into months. However, more detailed and refined cash budgeting is done on a weekly or even daily basis by some companies that employ good ongoing cash management procedures.

Entrepreneurial Edge Online bills itself as the "Small Business Solution Source." Take a look at their "Business Builders" (e.g., preparing cash budgets and cash flow statements), "Interactive Toolbox," "Virtual Networks," and other handy tools available to entrepreneurs.
http://www.edgeonline.com

Cash budgets are useful in determining the amount of short-term funds the firm may need to borrow to cover any projected cash shortages. Short-term borrowed funds are almost always easier to obtain when the need for them is anticipated. In addition to planning for any cash shortages, the cash budget also indicates the periods when the firm may have cash surpluses. This information is helpful in managing the firm's marketable securities investments. Thus, the cash budget is one of the most important short-range financial forecasting tools. In addition, cash budgets can be useful for control and coordination purposes.

To explore actual cash budgeting procedures, the Midwestern Manufacturing Company Central Division will be examined. Table 15-3 illustrates a cash budget worksheet for that division for the first quarter of 19X6. Table 15-4 is an actual cash budget for the time period.

The first step in cash budget preparation is the estimation of cash receipts, which results directly from the sales forecast. Midwestern has found that, on the average, about 10 percent of total sales in any given month are cash sales. The remaining 90 percent are credit sales.[2]

About 30 percent of the company's credit sales are collected during the month in which the sale is made, and all of the remaining 70 percent are collected during the following month. Thus, the total accounts receivable the company can expect to collect during January are equal to 70 percent of the forecasted December credit sales plus 30 percent of the forecasted January credit sales.

$$(0.70 \times \$486,000) + (0.30 \times \$450,000) = \$340,200 + \$135,000$$

$$= \$475,200$$

The forecasted cash receipts for February and March are calculated the same way.

TABLE 15-3
Cash Budget Worksheet

MIDWESTERN MANUFACTURING COMPANY—CENTRAL DIVISION
CASH BUDGET WORKSHEET
FIRST QUARTER, 19X6

	December	January	February	March
Budget of Receipts from Sales				
Estimated sales	$540,000	$500,000	$550,000	$620,000
Estimated credit sales	486,000	450,000	495,000	558,000
Estimated receipts:				
Cash sales		$ 50,000	$ 55,000	$ 62,000
Collections of accounts receivable:				
70% of last month's credit sales		$340,200	$315,000	$346,500
30% of current month's credit sales		135,000	148,500	167,400
Total accounts receivable collections *(Cash reciepts)*		$475,200	$463,500	$513,900
Budget of Payments for Purchases				
Estimated purchases*	$275,000	$302,500	$341,000	
Estimated payments of accounts payable†		$275,000	$302,500	$341,000

*Purchases are estimated at 55 percent of next month's sales.   †Payments are estimated to lag purchases by one month.

[2]Estimated December credit sales are 90 percent of estimated December sales; that is, $0.90 \times \$540,000 = \$486,000$.

TABLE 15-4
Cash Budget

	MIDWESTERN MANUFACTURING COMPANY—CENTRAL DIVISION CASH BUDGET* FIRST QUARTER, 19X6			
	December	*January*	*February*	*March*
Sales	$540,000	$500,000	$550,000	$620,000
Projected cash balance, beginning of month		$ 61,000	$ 50,700	$ 50,000
Receipts:				
Cash sales		50,000	55,000	62,000
Collection of accounts receivable		475,200	463,500	513,900
Total cash available		$586,200	$569,200	$625,900
Disbursements:				
Payment of accounts payable		$275,000	$302,500	$341,000
Wages and salaries		158,000	154,500	145,500
Rent		17,000	17,000	17,000
Other expenses		4,500	7,000	8,000
Taxes		81,000	—	—
Dividends on common stock		—	—	30,000
Purchase of new equipment (capital budget)		—	70,000	—
Total disbursements		$535,500	$551,000	$541,500
Excess of available cash over disbursements		$ 50,700	$ 18,200	$ 84,400
Cash loans needed to maintain balance of $50,000		—	31,800	—
Loan repayment		—	—	(31,800)
Projected cash balance, end of month		$ 50,700	$ 50,000	$ 52,600

*Prepared December 15, 19X5.

The next step in cash budgeting is the scheduling of *disbursements,* or payments the firm must make to others. Many of these items remain relatively constant from month to month and thus are relatively easy to budget. Others, however, such as the payment of accounts payable for purchases of merchandise, raw materials, and supplies, are more complicated. The key determinants of a firm's schedule of payables are the level of purchases per period and the terms given by suppliers.

Frequently, accounts payable become due before goods are sold and cash is received; this can lead to temporary cash shortages. In fact, many companies experience cash difficulties immediately after a good sales period. Inventories are depleted and must be replenished, but cash is low because collections from the good sales period have not yet been received. Midwestern's purchases generally are estimated to be 55 percent of next month's sales. This percentage is based on the company's past experience and can vary considerably among industries and companies. (Note that depreciation does not appear as a disbursement in the cash budget, because it is a noncash charge.)

After cash receipts and disbursements have been estimated, the next step in the cash budgeting process is the determination of a desired cash balance at the beginning of each month. This minimum cash balance figure is usually a function of several factors, including the nature of the business, tax laws, and bank requirements. Table 15-4 lists Midwestern's projected cash balances for the beginnings of January, February, and March. In this example, $50,000 is assumed to be the most appropriate minimum cash balance for the first quarter, 19X6.[3]

Table 15-4 shows that Midwestern expects to need a short-term loan of $31,800 in February to maintain a minimum cash balance of $50,000, because the company expects a decrease in the collection of accounts receivable in February, brought about by slightly lower than normal sales expected in January. In addition, the company plans to purchase new equipment in February, which will cost $70,000; this also contributes to the expected need for a short-term loan.

If the company planned to spend much more money than this on new equipment, it might decide to secure longer-term financing at this time, instead of the short-term loan. The proceeds from longer-term financing could be budgeted as a separate cash receipt in February, permitting the company to separate short-term and long-term cash needs.

After projecting the need for a short-term loan in February, the cash budget in Table 15-4 shows that the loan probably can be paid at the end of March, because the available cash balance of $84,400 will still be above $50,000 after repayment of $31,800. The company has indicated the repayment on the cash budget by adding another side caption: Loan repayment.[4]

Most companies follow this same general format for cash budgeting, yet few companies use *exactly* the same format. A company's actual cash budgeting system will depend on its business and its accounting procedures. Computerized financial spreadsheet models are useful in constructing and analyzing cash budgets.

Pro Forma Statement of Cash Flows

The statement of cash flows can also be used to determine how much additional financing a company will need in some future period. Suppose the Summit Furniture Company, whose statement of cash flows for 19X1 was shown earlier in Table 3-9, is preparing a cash flow forecast for 19X2. In the fall of 19X1, the company's management tentatively decides to spend $25,000 in 19X2 for capital expenditures. Also, Summit's financial manager estimates that the company's 19X2 operating activities will *provide* approximately $21,000 of net cash. This forecast is detailed in Summit's pro forma statement of cash flows, which is shown in Table 15-5.

Next, Summit's financial manager must estimate whether the company's financing activities will need to provide cash in order to maintain its desired cash balance. Because the net cash expected to be *used* by investing activities is greater than the net cash expected to be *provided* by operating activities, the company's financing activities will need to *provide* net cash to maintain the present cash balance. In addition, Summit feels that its cash balance needs to be increased by approximately $1,500. As a result, Summit's financing activities in 19X2 must *provide* net cash of $5,500 (– $21,000 + $25,000 + $1,500). The pro forma statement of cash flows details how Summit expects to achieve $5,500 of net cash provided by financing activities.

---

[3]Cash management is discussed further in Chapter 16.

[4]Note that the cash budget does not include any interest payments on this loan (or interest earned on investments of excess cash). These items generally have a relatively small impact on cash flows. However, they can be added to a cash budget if necessary.

TABLE 15-5
Summit Furniture Company
Pro-Forma Statement of Cash
Flows For the Year Ending
December 31, 19X2

INCREASE (DECREASE) IN CASH AND CASH EQUIVALENTS*		
Cash Flows Expected from Operating Activities:		
Cash received from customers	$ 170,000	
Cash paid to suppliers and employees	(140,000)	
Interest received	500	
Interest paid (net of amount capitalized)	(2,500)	
Income taxes paid	(7,000)	
Expected net cash provided (used) by operating activities		$ 21,000
Cash Flows Expected from Investing Activities:		
Proceeds from sale of assets	—	
Capital expenditures	(25,000)	
Expected net cash provided (used) by investing activities		(25,000)
Cash Flows Expected from Financing Activities:		
Net borrowings under bank line-of-credit agreement	2,000	
Repayment of long-term debt	(3,000)	
Proceeds from issuance of long-term debt	7,000	
Proceeds from issuance of common stock	—	
Dividends paid	(500)	
Expected net cash provided (used) by financing activities		5,500
Expected Net Increase (Decrease) in Cash and Cash Equivalents		1,500
Cash and Cash Equivalents at Beginning of Year		5,200
Expected Cash and Cash Equivalents at End of Year		$ 6,700

*Cash and cash equivalents include currency on hand, bank deposits and similar accounts, and short-term (maturities less than 3 months), highly liquid investments.

*Ever thought of starting your own busi-
ness? British Columbia has an excellent
"OnLine Small Business Workshop" in
which they show you how to put together
a good business plan for a new venture,
including cash flow forecasts and pro
formas.*
http://www.sb.gov.bc.ca

Computerized Financial Forecasting and Planning Models

In recent years, many companies have spent considerable amounts of time and money developing models to represent various aspects of their financial planning process, as well as cash flow forecasting. Today, these representations usually are computerized and generally are called **financial planning models.** A detailed discussion of these models is beyond the scope of this text, because it requires a familiarity with a number of quantitative techniques, such as regression analysis and linear programming—topics not covered here. A brief general introduction to the topic is provided for informational purposes, however.

Financial planning models are often classified according to whether they are *deterministic* or *probabilistic* and whether they attempt to *optimize* (that is, achieve the most desirable level of) the value of some objective function, such as net income or stock price.

A **deterministic model** gives a single-number forecast of a financial variable or variables without stating anything about its probability of occurrence. An example of a deterministic model is a computerized representation of a firm's operating budget, or a *budget simulator.* Companies that employ budget simulators enter estimated future revenues and expenses into the computer and receive as output an estimate of various financial variables, such as net income and earnings per share. The model tells the company nothing about the chances of achieving these estimates, nor does it indicate whether the company will be able to manage its resources in such a way as to attain higher levels of these variables.

The main advantage of deterministic models is that they allow the user to perform *sensitivity analyses* quickly and easily. A **sensitivity analysis** essentially consists of rerunning the model to determine the effect on the output variables of changes in the input variables. For example, a company may want to know *what* its net income will be *if* it discontinues some product line. Thus, sensitivity analysis is also called *what if* analysis.

Some companies prepare different budgets to reflect different assumptions about the type of year they expect to have. For instance, a company may compile three separate budgets to reflect *pessimistic, realistic,* and *optimistic* assumptions about the coming year. Whereas these scenario analysis models are essentially deterministic, they represent a first step toward the use of probabilistic models.

Probabilistic models are becoming increasingly popular, because they often provide financial decision makers with more useful information than other models. Whereas deterministic models yield single-point estimates, probabilistic models yield more general probability distributions. To illustrate, suppose a company is planning to build a new plant. Instead of estimating a single sales figure, the company's planners might estimate a 25 percent chance that the firm's sales will be $2 million, a 50 percent chance that they will be $3 million, and a 25 percent chance that they will be $4 million. The use of a probabilistic planning model yields output in the form of a probability distribution, which gives the company's planners more useful information than a deterministic model would. In the case of complex probabilistic models, more input is necessary.[5]

Optimization models determine the values of financial decision variables that optimize (that is, maximize or minimize) some objective function such as profits or costs. For example, consider an oil refinery whose capacity and production costs are known. By combining these known figures with estimates of the sales prices for gasoline and heating fuel, it is possible, with the use of an optimization model, to specify what output product mix will achieve an optimal level of operating income. Optimization models are not used widely in finance, even though various applications have been proposed in the financial literature.

Using Financial Ratios to Forecast Future Financial Performance

Financial ratios have been used in connection with sophisticated statistical techniques to forecast a firm's financial events. Because a detailed discussion of forecasting is beyond the scope of this text, this section will provide a brief overview of one such event: bankruptcy.

One of the primary limitations of traditional financial ratio analysis is that it looks at only one ratio at a time and then relies on the analyst to form a judgment about the overall financial profile of the firm. Recently, more powerful statistical techniques have been applied to assist analysts in making judgments about the financial condition of the firm.

Discriminant analysis is a statistical technique that helps the analyst classify observations (firms) into two or more predetermined groups based on certain characteristics of the observation. In the context of financial statement analysis, the characteristics typically are financial ratios.

One early application of discriminant analysis in finance was a model developed by Edward Altman to predict bankruptcy of firms.[6] Altman identified five financial ratios that contributed significantly to the predictive accuracy of his model:

---

[5]Additional examples of probabilistic models are discussed in Chapter 10.
[6]Edward I. Altman, "Financial Ratios, Discriminant Analysis, and the Prediction of Corporate Bankruptcy," *Journal of Finance* (September 1968): 589–609.

- Net working capital/Total assets
- Retained earnings/Total assets
- EBIT/Total assets
- Market value of total equity (common and preferred)/Book value of total debt
- Sales/Total assets

Altman's basic model was developed from a sample of 66 manufacturing firms—half of which went bankrupt. On the basis of the analysis, he established a guideline score, which could be used to classify firms as either financially sound or headed toward bankruptcy. The lower the score, the greater was the probability of bankruptcy; the higher the score, the lower was the probability of bankruptcy. In other words, the lower the values of the five ratios just listed, in general, the greater was the probability of bankruptcy.

More recent refinements of Altman's bankruptcy forecasting model have made it applicable to retailing as well as manufacturing firms.[7] The newer model is about 70 percent accurate as much as five years prior to bankruptcy.

     ETHICAL ISSUES
USE OF EMPLOYEE RETIREMENT FUNDS[8]

Many firms offer their employees so-called 401(k) retirement savings plans. The employer normally makes a contribution to the plan to match voluntary contributions made by employees. These funds are invested on behalf of the employees.

In March 1990, Black & Decker made an unusual investment decision. It invested $47 million from its 401(k) employee thrift plan in common stock of Black & Decker. At the time the investment was made, Black & Decker was facing serious financial difficulties. It was behind in its schedule to sell businesses needed to reduce the $2.7 billion in debt assumed at the time it purchased Emhart Corporation in 1989. Internal financial forecasts at the firm in 1990 indicated that the company faced serious, near-term financial difficulties.

Furthermore, Black & Decker was getting close to violating a major covenant (the debt-to-equity ratio covenant) in its bank loan agreement. Over the following 10 months, the price of Black & Decker's stock dropped from $18.12 to $8.50. After that, however, the price of Black & Decker's stock increased, and by early 1994, the stock was selling in the $20 a share range.

Using the employer contributions to the 401(k) plan offered a short-term solution to Black & Decker's longer-term problems. Stephen Page, Black & Decker's chief financial officer, defended the transaction because the firm only used company matching funds, saying "We haven't taken their [employees'] money—there was no risk." Indeed, in up to one-third of the 401(k) plans in effect with account balances exceeding $143 billion, the employer contribution has been in the form of company stock.

Under what conditions do you feel it is appropriate for an employer to make 401(k) contributions on behalf of employees in the form of the stock of the

[7]Edward I. Altman, R. G. Haldeman, and P. Narayanan. "Zeta Analysis: A New Model to Identify Bankruptcy Risk of Corporations," *Journal of Banking and Finance* (June 1977): 29–54.
[8]Based, in part, on Dana Wechsler Linden, "We Haven't Taken Their Money," *Forbes* (March 4, 1991): 109.

employer? What ethical concerns are raised by this type of transaction? Do you agree with Page that this was not employees' money that was being invested? Do you feel this type of transaction should be prohibited? Why or why not?

WORKING CAPITAL POLICY

Working capital policy involves decisions about a company's current assets and current liabilities—what they consist of, how they are used, and how their mix affects the risk versus return characteristics of the company. Both the terms **working capital** and **net working capital** normally denote the *difference* between the company's current assets and current liabilities. The two terms are often used interchangeably.

Working capital policies, through their effect on the firm's expected future returns and the risk associated with these returns, ultimately have an impact on shareholder wealth.[9] Effective working capital policies are crucial to a firm's long-run growth and survival. If, for example, a company lacks the working capital needed to expand production and sales, it may lose revenues and profits. A firm needs to maintain high enough working capital levels that it remains **liquid;** that is, it meets its cash obligations as they come due. Otherwise, it may incur the costs associated with a deteriorating credit rating, a potential forced liquidation of assets, and possible bankruptcy.

Working capital management is a continuing process that involves a number of day-to-day operations and decisions that determine the following:

- The firm's level of current assets.
- The proportions of short-term and long-term debt the firm will use to finance its assets.
- The level of investment in each type of current asset.
- The specific sources and mix of short-term credit (current liabilities) the firm should employ.

Working capital differs from *fixed* capital in terms of the time required to recover the investment in a given asset. In the case of fixed capital, or long-term assets (such as land, buildings, and equipment), a company usually needs several years or more to recover the initial investment. In contrast, working capital is turned over, or circulated, at a relatively rapid rate. Investments in inventories and accounts receivable are usually recovered during a firm's normal operating cycle, when inventories are sold and receivables are collected.

Importance of Working Capital

It already has been noted that a firm must have working capital to operate and survive. In many industries, working capital (current assets) constitutes a relatively large percentage of total assets. In the manufacturing sector, for example, current assets comprise about 40 percent of the total assets of all U.S. manufacturing corporations. Among the wholesaling and retailing sectors, the percentages are even higher—in the 50 to 60 percent range.

[9]See James A. Gentry, "State of the Art of Short-Run Financial Management," *Financial Management* 17 (Summer 1988): 41–57, for a review of the literature concerning the management of short-run assets and liabilities.

Table 15-6 shows the distribution of aggregate assets for several large companies. For the six companies shown, current assets as a percentage of total assets range from 19.0 to 50.7 percent. Exxon, with its relatively high percentage of fixed assets, has a relatively low percentage of current assets. In contrast, 3M has a relatively high percentage of current assets. Dayton Hudson, a diversified retailer that owns both Target and Mervyn's stores, has about 24 percent of its assets in inventories. IBM has about 20 percent of its assets in receivables. Because current assets constitute a relatively high percentage of total assets in most businesses, it is important to have effective working capital policies.

In a survey of large industrial corporations, it was found that about 30 percent of the companies have a formal policy for the management of their working capital and another 60 percent have an informal policy.[10] A significantly greater percentage of the larger companies within the sample have a formal policy than do the smaller companies. In almost one-half of the companies that responded to the survey, the financial vice-president has responsibility for establishing the company's overall working capital policy. The president and treasurer are the next most frequently mentioned positions as having responsibility for working capital policy. There is considerable variation in the frequency with which companies review their working capital policy. Annual, quarterly, and monthly reviews are mentioned with about the same relative frequency (approximately 14 to 18 percent), whereas approximately one-half of the companies review working capital policy "whenever necessary."

A firm's net working capital position is not only important from an internal standpoint; it is also widely used as one measure of the firm's risk. *Risk,* as used in this context, deals with the probability that a firm will encounter financial difficulties, such as the inability to pay bills on time. All other things being equal, the more net working capital a firm has, the more likely that it will be able to meet current financial obligations. Because net working capital is one measure of risk, a company's net working capital position affects its ability to obtain debt financing. Many loan agreements with commercial banks and other lending institutions contain a provision requiring the firm to maintain a minimum net working capital position. Likewise, bond indentures also often contain such provisions.

Have you ever heard of a working capital revolver? The KBK Capital Corporation will arrange one for you, from $100,000 (peanuts) to $5 million.
http://www.kbkcapital.com/screen_2_a.html

TABLE 15-6
Distribution of Aggregate Assets in Selected Companies

Source: *Moody's Industrial Manual,* 1996.

	DAYTON HUDSON	EXXON	IBM	MERCK	3M
Cash and marketable securities	1.4%	2.0%	9.0%	14.1%	5.4%
Receivables—net	12.0	9.8	20.5	10.5	16.9
Inventories—net	24.0	6.2	7.9	7.9	15.6
All other current assets	2.0	1.0	13.3	3.8	7.2
Total current assets*	39.4%	19.0%	50.7%	36.2%	45.1%
Fixed assets—net	58.0	71.7	23.7	22.1	32.7
All other noncurrent assets	2.6	9.3	25.7	41.7	22.2
Total assets*	100.0%	100.0%	100.0%	100.0%	100.0%

*Totals may differ from sums of numbers in column because of rounding.

[10]Keith V. Smith and Shirley B. Sell, "Working Capital Management in Practice," in *Readings in the Management of Working Capital,* 2nd ed, Keith V. Smith, ed. (St. Paul: West Publishing Company, 1980).

Operating Cycle Analysis

A company's operating cycle typically consists of three primary activities: purchasing resources, producing the product, and distributing (selling) the product. These activities create cash flows that are both unsynchronized and uncertain. They are unsynchronized because cash disbursements (for example, payments for resource purchases) usually take place before cash receipts (for example, collection of receivables). They are uncertain because future sales and costs, which generate the respective receipts and disbursements, cannot be forecasted with complete accuracy. If the firm is to maintain liquidity and function properly, it has to invest funds in various short-term assets (working capital) during this cycle. It has to maintain a *cash balance* to pay the bills as they come due. In addition, the company must invest in *inventories* to fill customer orders promptly. And, finally, the company invests in *accounts receivable* to extend credit to its customers.

Figure 15-1 illustrates the operating cycle of a typical firm.[11] The **operating cycle** is equal to the length of the inventory and receivables conversion periods:

$$\text{Operating cycle} = \text{Inventory conversion period} \\ + \text{Receivables conversion period} \qquad (15.4)$$

The **inventory conversion period** is the length of time required to produce and sell the product. It is defined as follows:

$$\text{Inventory conversion period} = \frac{\text{Average inventory}}{\text{Cost of sales}/365} \qquad (15.5)$$

The **receivables conversion period,** or average collection period, represents the length of time required to collect the sales receipts. It is calculated as follows:

$$\text{Receivables conversion period} = \frac{\text{Accounts receivable}}{\text{Annual credit sales}/365} \qquad (15.6)$$

The **payables deferral period** is the length of time the firm is able to defer payment on its various resource purchases (for example, materials, wages, and taxes). The following equation is used to calculate the payables deferral period:

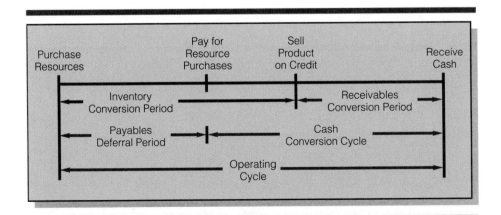

FIGURE 15-1
Operating Cycle of a Typical Company

[11]The following discussion is based on Verlyn D. Richards and Eugene J. Laughlin, "A Cash Conversion Cycle Approach to Liquidity Analysis," *Financial Management* 9 (Spring 1980): 32–38.

$$\begin{pmatrix} \text{Payables} \\ \text{deferral} \\ \text{period} \end{pmatrix} = \frac{\text{Accounts payable} + \begin{array}{c} \text{Salaries, benefits, and} \\ \text{payroll taxes payable} \end{array}}{(\text{Cost of sales} + \text{Selling, general and} \\ \text{administrative expense})/365} \qquad (15.7)$$

Finally, the **cash conversion cycle** represents the net time interval between the collection of cash receipts from product sales and the cash payments for the company's various resource purchases. It is calculated as follows:

$$\text{Cash conversion cycle} = \text{Operating cycle} - \text{Payables deferral period} \qquad (15.8)$$

The cash conversion cycle shows the time interval over which additional nonspontaneous sources of working capital financing must be obtained to carry out the firm's activities.[12] An increase in the length of the operating cycle, without a corresponding increase in the payables deferral period, lengthens the cash conversion cycle and creates further working capital financing needs for the company.

Table 15-7 shows an actual cash conversion cycle analysis for SYSCO Corporation, the largest distributor of food service products in the United States. SYSCO's liquidity, as measured by the current and quick ratios, appears to have deteriorated slightly in 1996 compared to 1995. Analysis of the cash conversion cycle shows that the company's liquidity position remained the same from 1995 to 1996. The decrease in the inventory conversion period from 25 days to 24 days was offset by the decrease in the payables deferral period from 29 days to 28 days. Note that the length of SYSCO's operating cycle remained the same from 1995 to 1996.

LEVELS OF WORKING CAPITAL INVESTMENT

Overall working capital policy considers *both* a firm's level of working capital investment and its financing. In practice, the firm has to determine the *joint* impact of these two decisions upon its profitability and risk. However, to permit a better understanding of working capital policy, the working capital investment

TABLE 15-7
Cash Conversion Cycle Analysis for SYSCO Corporation

Source: SYSCO Corporation, Annual Report (1996).

	1996	1995
Liquidity ratios:		
Current ratio	1.85	1.92
Quick ratio	1.16	1.20
Cash conversion cycle:		
Inventory conversion period	24 days	25 days
Receivables conversion period	28 days	28 days
Operating cycle	52 days	53 days
Less payables deferral period	28 days	29 days
Cash conversion cycle	24 days	24 days

[12]Spontaneous sources of financing (such as trade credit offered by suppliers) automatically expand (contract) as the company's volume of purchases increases (decreases). Nonspontaneous sources of financing (such as bank loans), in contrast, do not automatically expand or contract with the volume of purchases. This concept is discussed further in Chapter 18, which deals with sources of short-term funds.

decision is discussed in this section, and the working capital financing decision is discussed in the following section. The two decisions then are considered together.

The size and nature of a firm's investment in current assets is a function of a number of different factors, including the following:

■ The type of products manufactured.
■ The length of the operating cycle.
■ The sales level (because higher sales require more investment in inventories and receivables).
■ Inventory policies (for example, the amount of safety stocks maintained; that is, inventories needed to meet higher than expected demand or unanticipated delays in obtaining new inventories).
■ Credit policies.
■ How efficiently the firm manages current assets. (Obviously, the more effectively management economizes on the amount of cash, marketable securities, inventories, and receivables employed, the smaller the working capital requirements.)

Variable

For the purposes of discussion and analysis, these factors are held constant for the remainder of this chapter. Instead of focusing on these factors, this section examines the risk-return trade-offs associated with alternative levels of working capital investment.

Profitability Versus Risk Trade-off for Alternative Levels of Working Capital Investment

Before deciding on an appropriate level of working capital investment, a firm's management has to evaluate the trade-off between expected profitability and the risk that it may be unable to meet its financial obligations. Profitability is measured by the rate of (operating) return on total assets; that is, EBIT/total assets. As mentioned earlier in this chapter, the risk that a firm will encounter financial difficulties is related to the firm's net working capital position.

EBIT = rate of return on assets

Figure 15-2 illustrates three alternative working capital policies.[13] Each curve in the figure demonstrates the relationship between the firm's investment in current assets and sales for that particular policy.

Policy C represents a *conservative* approach to working capital management. Under this policy, the company holds a relatively large proportion of its total assets in the form of current assets. Because the rate of return on current assets normally is assumed to be less than the rate of return on fixed assets,[14] this policy results in a *lower expected profitability* as measured by the rate of return on the company's total assets. Assuming that current liabilities remain constant, this type of policy also increases the company's net working capital position, resulting in a *lower risk* that the firm will encounter financial difficulties.

In contrast to Policy C, Policy A represents an *aggressive* approach. Under this policy, the company holds a relatively small proportion of its total assets in the

---

[13]The relationship between current assets and sales is drawn as a concave, *curvilinear* function, because it is assumed that economies of scale exist in the holding of current assets. In other words, increases in sales normally should require less than proportionate increases in current assets, particularly for cash and inventories. The amount of the company's *fixed* assets is held constant in the following discussion.

[14]This assumption is based on the principle that the lower an asset's risk, the lower its expected return. Current assets normally are less risky than fixed assets, because they can be converted into cash more easily and with less potential loss in value. Therefore, current assets should have lower expected returns.

FIGURE 15-2
Three Alternative Working
Capital Investment Policies

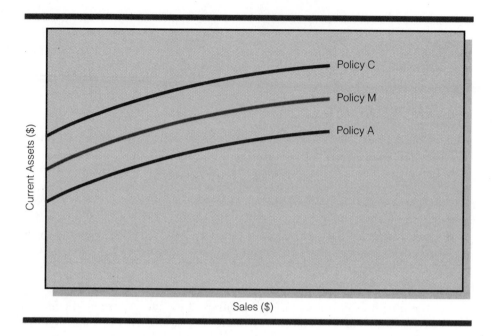

form of lower-yielding current assets and thus has relatively less net working capital. As a result, this policy yields a *higher expected profitability* and a *higher risk* that the company will encounter financial difficulties.

Finally, Policy M represents a *moderate* approach. With this policy, expected profitability and risk levels fall between those of Policy C and Policy A.

These three approaches may be illustrated with the following example. Burlington Northern, Inc., a Seattle-based railroad and natural resources company, recently formed Burlington Resources, Inc., a new subsidiary. Then Burlington Northern sold off a portion of the newly created subsidiary in an initial public offering. The proceeds from the stock offering were added to Burlington Resources's working capital. As a result, the management of Burlington Resources faced working capital decisions of the types discussed in this section. In addition, the numbers used in this section are probably typical of the numbers used by Burlington Resources in its working capital policy discussions. Suppose Burlington Resources has forecasted sales next year to be $100 million and EBIT to be $10 million. The company has fixed assets of $30 million and current liabilities totaling $20 million.

Burlington Resources is considering three alternative working capital investment policies:

■ An *aggressive* policy consisting of $35 million in current assets.
■ A *moderate* policy consisting of $40 million in current assets.
■ A *conservative* policy consisting of $45 million in current assets.

Assume that sales and EBIT remain constant under each policy.[15] Table 15-8 contains the results of the three proposed policies.

[15]In practice, however, this assumption may not be completely realistic, because a firm's sales usually are a function of its inventory and credit policies. Higher levels of finished goods inventories and a more liberal credit extension policy—both of which increase a firm's investment in current assets—also may lead to higher sales. This effect can be incorporated into the analysis by modifying the sales and EBIT projections under the various alternative working capital policies. Although changing these projections would affect the numerical values contained in Table 15-8, it does not affect the general conclusions concerning the profitability versus risk trade-offs.

TABLE 15-8
**Profitability and Risk of Alternative
Working Capital Investment Policies
for Burlington Resources
(in millions of dollars)**

	AGGRESSIVE	**MODERATE**	**CONSERVATIVE**
	Relatively Small Investment in Current Assets	*Moderate Investment in Current Assets*	*Relatively Large Investment in Current Assets*
Current assets (C/A)	$ 35	$ 40	$ 45
Fixed assets (F/A)	30	30	30
Total assets T/A	$ 65	$ 70	$ 75
Current liabilities (C/L)	$ 20	$ 20	$ 20
Forecasted sales	$ 100	$ 100	$ 100
Expected EBIT	$ 10	$ 10	$ 10
Expected rate of return on total assets (EBIT ÷ T/A)	15.38%	14.29%	13.33%
Net working capital position (C/A − C/L)	$ 15	$ 20	$ 25
Current ratio (C/A ÷ C/L)	1.75	2.0	2.25

The aggressive policy would yield the highest expected rate of return on total assets, 15.38 percent, whereas the conservative policy would yield the lowest rate of return, 13.33 percent. The aggressive policy also would result in a lower net working capital position ($15 million) than would the conservative policy ($25 million).

Using net working capital as a measure of risk, the aggressive policy is the riskiest and the conservative policy is the least risky. The current ratio is another measure of a firm's ability to meet financial obligations as they come due. The aggressive policy would yield the lowest current ratio, and the conservative policy would yield the highest current ratio.

Optimal Level of Working Capital Investment

The optimal level of working capital investment is the level expected to maximize shareholder wealth. It is a function of several factors, including the variability of sales and cash flows and the degree of operating and financial leverage employed by the firm. Therefore, no single working capital investment policy is necessarily optimal for all firms.

PROPORTIONS OF SHORT-TERM AND LONG-TERM FINANCING

Not only does a firm have to be concerned about the *level* of current assets; it also has to determine the *proportions* of short- and long-term debt to use in financing these assets. This decision also involves trade-offs between profitability and risk.

Sources of debt financing are classified according to their *maturities*. Specifically, they can be categorized as being either *short-term* or *long-term,* with short-term sources having maturities of one year or less and long-term sources having maturities of greater than one year.[16]

---

[16]In this discussion, the term *long-term financing* includes any *intermediate-term financing.*

Cost of Short-Term Versus Long-Term Debt

Recall from Chapter 5 that the *term structure of interest rates* is defined as the relationship among interest rates of debt securities that differ in their length of time to maturity. Historically, long-term interest rates normally have exceeded short-term rates.

Also, because of the reduced flexibility of long-term borrowing relative to short-term borrowing, the *effective* cost of long-term debt may be higher than the cost of short-term debt, even when short-term interest rates are equal to or greater than long-term rates. With long-term debt, a firm incurs the interest expense even during times when it has no immediate need for the funds, such as during seasonal or cyclical downturns. With short-term debt, in contrast, the firm can avoid the interest costs on unneeded funds by paying off (or not renewing) the debt. In summary, the cost of long-term debt is generally higher than the cost of short-term debt.

Risk of Long-Term Versus Short-Term Debt

Borrowing companies have different attitudes toward the relative risk of long-term versus short-term debt than do lenders. Whereas lenders normally feel that risk increases with maturity, borrowers feel that there is more risk associated with short-term debt. The reasons for this are twofold.

First, there is always the chance that a firm will not be able to refinance its short-term debt. When a firm's debt matures, it either pays off the debt as part of a debt reduction program or arranges new financing. At the time of maturity, however, the firm could be faced with financial problems resulting from such events as strikes, natural disasters, or recessions that cause sales and cash inflows to decline. Under these circumstances the firm may find it very difficult or even impossible to obtain the needed funds. This could lead to operating and financial difficulties. The more frequently a firm must refinance debt, the greater is the risk of its not being able to obtain the necessary financing.

Second, short-term interest rates tend to fluctuate more over time than long-term interest rates. As a result, a firm's interest expenses and expected earnings after interest and taxes are subject to more variation over time with short-term debt than with long-term debt.

Profitability Versus Risk Trade-off for Alternative Financing Plans

A company's need for financing is equal to the sum of its fixed and current assets.[17] Current assets can be divided into the following two categories:

■ *Permanent* current assets.
■ *Fluctuating* current assets.

Fluctuating current assets are those affected by the seasonal or cyclical nature of company sales. For example, a firm must make larger investments in inventories and receivables during peak selling periods than during other periods of the year. **Permanent current assets** are those held to meet the company's minimum long-term needs (for example, "safety stocks" of cash and inventories). Figure 15-3 illustrates a typical firm's financing needs over time. The fixed assets and

---

[17]The following discussion assumes a constant amount of equity financing.

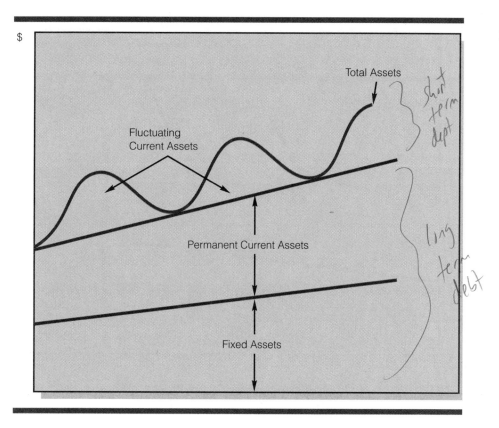

FIGURE 15-3
Financing Needs Over Time

permanent current assets lines are upward sloping, indicating that the investment in these assets and, by extension, financing needs tend to increase over time for a firm whose sales are increasing.

One way in which a firm can meet its financing needs is by using a **matching approach** in which the maturity structure of the firm's liabilities is made to correspond exactly to the life of its assets, as illustrated in Figure 15-4. Fixed and permanent current assets are financed with long-term debt and equity funds, whereas fluctuating current assets are financed with short-term debt.[18] Application of this approach is not as simple as it appears, however. In practice, the uncertainty associated with the lives of individual assets makes the matching approach difficult to implement.

Figures 15-5 and 15-6 illustrate two other financing plans. Figure 15-5 shows a *conservative* approach, which uses a relatively high proportion of long-term debt. The relatively low proportion of short-term debt in this approach reduces the risk that the company will be unable to refund its debt, and it also reduces the risk associated with interest rate fluctuations. At the same time, however, this approach cuts down on the expected returns available to stockholders, because the cost of long-term debt is generally greater than the cost of short-term debt.

[18]This analysis does not consider "spontaneous" sources of short-term credit, such as accounts payable. Because spontaneous short-term credit is virtually cost-free when used within reasonable limits, a company normally will employ this type of credit to the fullest extent possible before using "negotiated" sources of short-term credit, such as bank loans. Because none of the conclusions concerning the trade-off between profitability and risk is affected by ignoring spontaneous sources of short-term credit, it need not be considered here.

FIGURE 15-4
Matching Approach
to Asset Financing

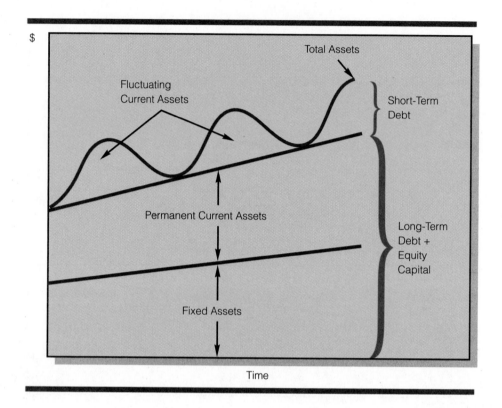

FIGURE 15-5
Conservative Approach
to Asset Financing

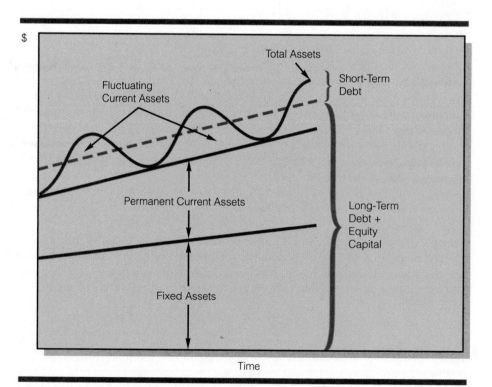

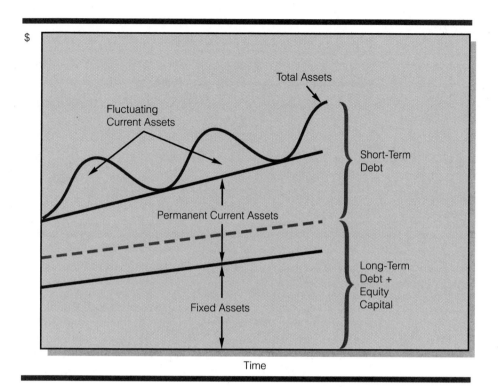

FIGURE 15-6
Aggressive Approach
to Asset Financing

Figure 15-6 illustrates an *aggressive* approach, which uses a relatively high proportion of short-term debt. A firm that uses this particular approach must refinance debt more frequently, and this increases the risk that it will be unable to obtain new financing as needed. In addition, the greater possible fluctuations in interest expenses associated with this financing plan also add to the firm's risk. These higher risks are offset by the higher expected after-tax earnings that result from the normally lower costs of short-term debt.

Table 15-9 shows two years of actual working capital data for the retailer Dayton Hudson. The company's total current assets and inventories fluctuate during the year, peaking during autumn (third quarter) as the holiday shopping season approaches. Its notes payable and accounts payable also fluctuate and peak in autumn, which suggests that the company is using more or less a matching approach to finance its fluctuating current assets.

Consider again Burlington Resources, which has total assets of $70 million and common shareholders' equity of $28 million on its books, thus requiring $42 million in short- or long-term debt financing. Forecasted sales for next year are $100 million and expected EBIT is $10 million. Interest rates on the company's short-term and long-term debt are 8 and 10 percent respectively, due to an upward-sloping yield curve.

Burlington Resources is considering three different combinations of short-term and long-term debt financing:

■ An *aggressive* plan consisting of $30 million in short-term debt (STD) and $12 million in long-term debt (LTD).

■ A *moderate* plan consisting of $20 million in short-term debt and $22 million in long-term debt.

QUARTER	4TH	1ST	2ND	3RD	4TH	1ST	2ND	3RD
Date	February 1, 1992	May 2, 1992	August 1, 1992	October 31, 1992	January 30, 1993	May 1, 1993	July 31, 1993	October 30, 1993
Cash and marketable securities	$ 96	$ 139	$ 128	$ 160	$ 117	$ 156	$ 97	$ 165
Accounts receivable	1,430	1,260	1,171	1,335	1,514	1,280	1,207	1,338
Inventories	2,381	2,412	2,537	3,296	2,618	2,812	2,725	3,346
Total C/A	$4,032	$3,872	$3,952	$4,919	$4,414	$4,355	$4,115	$4,949
Notes payable	$ 265	$ 112	$ 55	$ 630	$ 23	$ 101	$ 121	$ 326
Accounts payable	1,324	1,232	1,395	1,712	1,596	1,450	1,464	1,931
Total C/L	$2,580	$2,366	$2,514	$3,612	$2,964	$2,788	$2,797	$3,567
Net working capital	$1,452	$1,506	$1,438	$1,307	$1,450	$1,567	$1,318	$1,382

*The totals differ from the sums of individual entries because other current assets and other current liabilities are omitted from this table.

TABLE 15-9
Working Capital Data for Dayton Hudson Corporation (in millions of dollars)

Source: Dayton Hudson Corporation, *Annual* and *Quarterly Reports:* 1991, 1992, 1993.

■ A *conservative* plan consisting of $10 million in short-term debt and $32 million in long-term debt.

Table 15-10 shows the data for each of these alternative proposed financing plans. From the standpoint of profitability, the aggressive financing plan would yield the highest expected rate of return to the stockholders—13.6 percent—whereas the conservative plan would yield the lowest rate of return—12.9 percent. In contrast, the aggressive plan would involve a greater degree of risk that the company will be unable to refund its debt, because it assumes $30 million in short-term debt and the conservative plan assumes only $10 million

TABLE 15-10
Profitability and Risk of Alternative Financing Policies for Burlington Resources (in millions of dollars)

	AGGRESSIVE	MODERATE	CONSERVATIVE
	Relatively Large Amount of Short-Term Debt	Moderate Amount of Short-Term Debt	Relatively Small Amount of Short-Term Debt
Current assets (C/A)	$ 40	$ 40	$ 40
Fixed assets (F/A)	30	30	30
Total assets (T/A)	$ 70	$ 70	$ 70
Current liabilities (STD)(C/L) (interest rate, 8%)	$ 30	$ 20	$ 10
Long-term liabilities (LTD) (interest rate, 10%)	12	22	32
Total liabilities (60% of T/A)	$ 42	$ 42	$ 42
Common equity	28	28	28
Total liabilities and common equity	$ 70	$ 70	$ 70
Forecasted sales	$100	$100	$100
Expected EBIT	10	10	10
Less Interest:			
STD, 8%	2.4 ⎱	1.6 ⎱	0.8 ⎱
LTD, 10%	1.2 ⎰ 3.6	2.2 ⎰ 3.8	3.2 ⎰ 4.0
Taxable income	$ 6.4	$ 6.2	$ 6.0
Less Taxes (40%)	2.6	2.5	2.4
Net income after taxes	$ 3.8	$ 3.7	$ 3.6
Expected rate of return on common equity	13.6%	13.2%	12.9%
Net working capital position (C/A − C/L)	$ 10	$ 20	$ 30
Current ratio (C/A ÷ C/L)	1.33	2.0	4.0

0.08 × 30

in short-term debt. This is substantiated further by the fact that the company's net working capital position and current ratio would be lowest under the aggressive plan and highest under the conservative plan—making the degree of risk that the company will be unable to meet financial obligations greater with the aggressive plan. The moderate financing plan represents a middle-of-the-road approach, and the expected rate of return and risk level are between the aggressive and the conservative approaches. In summary, both expected profitability and risk increase as the proportion of short-term debt increases.[19]

Optimal Proportions of Short-Term and Long-Term Debt

As is the case with working capital investment policy, no one combination of short- and long-term debt is necessarily optimal for all firms. In choosing a financing policy that maximizes shareholder wealth, a firm's financial manager must also take into account various other factors, such as the variability of sales and cash flows, that affect the valuation of the firm.

 OVERALL WORKING CAPITAL POLICY

Until now, this chapter has analyzed the working capital investment and financing decisions independent of one another in order to examine the profitability–risk trade-offs associated with each, assuming that all other factors are held constant. Effective working capital policy, however, also requires the consideration of the *joint* impact of these decisions on the firm's profitability and risk.

Referring to Burlington Resources again, assume that the company is 60 percent debt financed (both short-term and long-term) and 40 percent financed with common stock. Also, it is evaluating three alternative working capital investment and financing policies. The *aggressive* policy would require a relatively *small* investment in current assets, $35 million, and a relatively *large* amount of short-term debt, $30 million. The *conservative* policy would require a relatively *large* investment in current assets, $45 million, and a relatively *small* amount of short-term debt, $10 million. The firm is also considering a middle-of-the-road approach, which would involve a *moderate* investment in current assets, $40 million, and a *moderate* amount of short-term debt, $20 million.

Table 15-11 shows the data for each approach. The aggressive working capital policy is expected to yield the highest return on shareholders' equity, 15.4 percent, whereas the conservative policy is expected to yield the lowest return, 11.3 percent. The net working capital and current ratio are lowest under the aggressive policy and highest under the conservative policy, indicating that the aggressive policy is the riskiest. The moderate policy yields an expected return and risk level somewhere between the aggressive and the conservative policies.

---

[19]This example assumes that the costs of short-term and long-term debt would be the same for each of the three financing policies. In practice, however, this would probably not be the case, because lenders generally require higher interest rates before making loans involving higher risks. Thus, a company following an aggressive financing policy probably will have to pay slightly higher interest rates on debt than a company following a conservative policy. This effect can be incorporated into the analysis by modifying the interest rates on short-term and long-term debt under the various financing policies. This would affect the numerical values in the example, but it should not affect the general conclusions concerning the profitability versus risk trade-offs.

	AGGRESSIVE	MODERATE	CONSERVATIVE
	Relatively Small Investment in Current Assets; Relatively Large Amount of Short-Term Debt	Moderate Investment in Current Assets; Moderate Amount of Short-Term Debt	Relatively Large Investment in Current Assets; Relatively Small Amount of Short-Term Debt
Current assets (C/A)	$ 35	$ 40	$ 45
Fixed assets (F/A)	30	30	30
Total assets (T/A)	$ 65	$ 70	$ 75
Current liabilities (STD)(C/L) (interest rate, 8%)	$ 30	$ 20	$ 10
Long-term liabilities (LTD) (interest rate, 10%)	9	22	35
Total liabilities (60% of T/A)	$ 39	$ 42	$ 45
Common equity	26	28	30
Total liabilities and common equity	$ 65	$ 70	$ 75
Forecasted sales	$100	$100	$100
Expected EBIT	10	10	10
Less Interest:			
STD, 8%	2.4	1.6	0.8
LTD, 10%	0.9 ⎵ 3.3	2.2 ⎵ 3.8	3.5 ⎵ 4.3
Taxable income	$ 6.7	$ 6.2	$ 5.7
Less Taxes (40%)	2.7	2.5	2.3
Net income after taxes	$ 4.0	$ 3.7	$ 3.4
Expected rate of return on common equity	15.4%	13.2%	11.3%
Net working capital position (C/A − C/L)	$ 5	$ 20	$ 35
Current ratio (C/A ÷ C/L)	1.17	2.0	4.5

TABLE 15-11
Alternative Working Capital Investment and Financing Policies for Burlington Resources (in millions of dollars)

Whereas this type of analysis will not directly yield the optimal working capital investment and financing policies a company should choose, it can give the financial manager some insight into the profitability–risk trade-offs of alternative policies. With an understanding of these trade-offs, the financial manager should be able to make better decisions concerning the working capital policy that will lead to a maximization of shareholder wealth.

■ SUMMARY

■ A firm's financial manager plays an important role in the financial forecasting process. Basically, the financial forecasting process involves the development of a set of financial plans for the orderly acquisition and expenditure of cash. Pro forma financial statements are usually an integral part of any financial plan. *Pro forma financial statements* show the results of some *assumed* rather than *actual* events.

■ Financial forecasting involves the projection and estimation of a firm's future cash needs. The percentage of sales method, cash budgeting, the pro forma statement of cash flows, and cash breakeven analysis are used in financial forecasting.

■ The *percentage of sales* method is used to estimate the amount of additional financing that will be needed to support a given future sales level.

■ *Budgets* are pro forma financial statements that detail a company's future plans regarding the acquisition and spending of funds. Budgets are used for *planning, coordinating,* and *controlling* the operations of the firm.

■ *Cash budgets* are projections of cash receipts and disbursements over some future time period. The steps involved in preparing a cash budget include the following:

  1. Estimating cash receipts based on historical information about the collection of receivables.

  2. Scheduling disbursements.

  3. Determining a minimum cash balance.

  4. Calculating the amount of loans required to cover any cash shortages.

■ A pro forma statement of cash flows may assist the financial manager in forecasting financial needs.

■ A *financial planning model* is a computerized representation of some aspect of a firm's financial planning process. Financial planning models are usually classified according to whether they are *deterministic* or *probabilistic* and whether they seek to *optimize* the value of some objective function.

■ *Working capital* is the difference between current assets and current liabilities. The term *working capital* is used interchangeably with the term *net working capital.*

■ A firm's *operating cycle* is equal to the sum of the inventory and receivables conversion periods. The *cash conversion cycle* is equal to the operating cycle less the payables deferral period.

■ *Working capital policy* is concerned with determining the *aggregate amount* and *composition* of a firm's current assets and current liabilities.

■ Working capital decisions affect both the *expected profitability* and the *risk* of a firm. In this context, risk refers to the probability that the firm will encounter financial difficulties, such as the inability to meet current financial obligations.

■ When the level of working capital is increased, both the expected profitability and the risk are lowered. Similarly, when the level of working capital is decreased, both the expected profitability and the risk are increased.

■ When the proportion of short-term debt used is increased, both the expected profitability and the risk are increased. Similarly, when the proportion of short-term debt used is decreased, both the expected profitability and the risk are lowered.

■ Effective working capital policy requires that the working capital investment and financing decisions be analyzed simultaneously so that their *joint* impact on the firm's expected profitability and risk can be evaluated.

■ No single working capital investment and financing policy is necessarily *optimal* for all firms. To select the working capital policy that maximizes shareholder wealth, a financial manager should consider additional factors, including the inherent variability in sales and cash flows and the degree of operating and financial leverage employed.

■ QUESTIONS AND TOPICS FOR DISCUSSION

1. Why does the typical firm need to make investments in working capital?

2. Define and describe the difference between the operating cycle and cash conversion cycle for a typical manufacturing company.

3. Discuss the probability versus risk trade-offs associated with alternative levels of working capital investment.

4. Describe the difference between permanent current assets and fluctuating current assets.

5. Why is it possible for the effective cost of long-term debt to exceed the cost of short-term debt, even when short-term interest rates are higher than long-term rates?

6. Describe the matching approach for meeting the financing needs of a company. What is the primary difficulty in implementing this approach?

7. Discuss the probability versus risk trade-offs associated with alternative combinations of short-term and long-term debt used in financing a company's assets.

8. As the difference between the costs of short- and long-term debt becomes smaller, which financing plan, aggressive or conservative, becomes more attractive?

9. Why is no single working capital investment and financing policy necessarily optimal for all firms? What additional factors need to be considered in establishing a working capital policy?

10. a. Which of the following working capital financing policies subjects the firm to a greater risk?
    i. Financing permanent current assets with short-term debt.
    ii. Financing fluctuating current assets with long-term debt.
    b. Which policy will produce the higher expected profitability?

11. What are *pro forma financial statements*?

12. What is the *percentage of sales forecasting method*? What are some of the limitations financial analysts should be aware of in applying this method?

13. What is a *cash budget*? What are the usual steps involved in preparing a cash budget?

14. Illustrate how the statement of cash flows can be used as a financial planning technique.

15. Explain the difference between deterministic and probabilistic financial planning models.

■ SELF-TEST PROBLEMS

ST1. The Stowe Manufacturing Company's balance sheet and income statement for last year are as follows:

Balance Sheet
(in Millions of Dollars)

Assets		Liabilities and Equity	
Cash and marketable securities	$ 887	Accounts payable	$ 724
Accounts receivable	2,075	Accrued liabilities (salaries and benefits)	332
Inventories*	2,120	Other current liabilities	1,665
Other current assets	300	Total current liabilities	2,721
Total current assets	$5,382	Long-term debt and other liabilities	1,677
Plant and equipment (net)	3,707	Common stock	296
Other assets	687	Retained earnings	5,082
Total assets	$9,776	Total stockholders' equity	$5,378
		Total liabilities and equity	$9,776

*Assume that average inventory over the year was $2,120 million, i.e., the same as ending inventory.

Income Statement (in Millions of Dollars)

Net sales*	$11,990
Cost of sales	6,946
Selling, general, and administrative expenses	2,394
Other expenses	581
Total expenses	$ 9,921
Earnings before taxes	2,069
Taxes	825
Earnings after taxes (net income)	$ 1,244

*All sales are credit sales.

Determine the length of Stowe's

a. Inventory conversion period.

b. Receivables conversion period.

c. Operating cycle.

d. Payables deferral period.

e. Cash conversion cycle.

ST2. Cranberry Manufacturing Company is considering the following two alternative working capital investment and financing policies:

	Policy A	Policy B
Current assets ÷ Sales	60%	40%
Short-term debt ÷ Total debt	30%	60%

Forecasted sales next year are $150 million. EBIT is projected to be 20 percent of sales. The company's income tax rate is 40 percent. Fixed assets are $100 million. Cranberry wishes to maintain its current capital structure, which consists of 60 percent debt and 40 percent equity. Interest rates on the company's short-term and long-term debt are 10 and 14 percent, respectively.

a. Determine the expected rate of return on equity under each of the working capital policies.

b. Which working capital policy is riskier? Explain.

ST3. Piedmont Products Inc. (PPI) has current sales of $60 million. Sales are expected to grow to $80 million next year. PPI currently has accounts receivable of $9 million, inventories of $15 million, and net fixed assets of $21 million. These assets are expected to grow at the same rate as sales over the next year. Accounts payable are expected to increase from their current level of $15 million to a new level of $19 million next year. PPI wants to increase its cash balance at the end of next year by $3 million over its current cash balance. Earnings after taxes next year are forecasted to be $12 million. PPI plans to pay a $2 million dividend. PPI's marginal tax rate is 40 percent.

How much external financing is required by PPI next year?

ST4. Use the percentage of sales forecasting method to compute the additional financing needed by Lambrechts Specialty Shops, Inc. (LSS), if sales are expected to increase from a current level of $20 million to a new level of $25 million over the coming year. LSS expects earnings after taxes to equal $1 million over the next year (19X3). LSS intends to pay a $300,000 dividend next year. The current year balance sheet for LSS is as follows:

Lambrechts Specialty Shops, Inc.
Balance Sheet
as of December 31, 19X2

Cash	$1,000,000	Accounts payable	$ 3,000,000
Accounts receivable	1,500,000	Notes payable	3,000,000
Inventories	6,000,000	Long-term debt	2,000,000
Net fixed assets	3,000,000	Stockholders' equity	3,500,000
Total assets	$11,500,000	Total liabilities and equity	$11,500,000

All assets, except "cash," are expected to vary proportionately with sales. Of total liabilities and equity, only "accounts payable" is expected to vary proportionately with sales.

■ PROBLEMS*

1. The Fisher Apparel Company balance sheet for the year ended 19X6 is as follows:

December 31, 19X6
(in Thousands of Dollars)

Assets

Cash		$ 3,810
Marketable securities		2,700
Accounts receivable		27,480
Inventories		41,295
Plant and equipment	$64,650	
Less Accumulated depreciation	17,100	
Net plant and equipment		47,550
Total assets		$122,835

Liabilities and Stockholders' Equity

Accounts payable	$ 14,582
Current portion of long-term debt	3,000
Accrued wages	1,200
Accrued taxes	3,600
Other current liabilities	2,200
Long-term debt	33,000
Common stock ($10 par)	19,500
Capital contributed in excess of par	15,000
Retained earnings	30,753
Total liabilities and stockholders' equity	$122,835

a. What is Fisher's investment in current assets?
b. Determine Fisher's working capital investment.
c. Determine Fisher's current ratio.
d. Determine Fisher's return on stockholders' equity if its 19X6 earnings after tax are $10,000(000).

2. Consider again the comprehensive example involving Burlington Resources (Table 15-11). In this example, it was assumed that forecasted sales and expected EBIT, as well as the interest rates on short-term and long-term debt, were independent of the firm's working capital investment and financing policies. However, these assumptions are not always completely realistic in practice. Sales and EBIT generally are a function of the firm's inventory and receivables policies. Both of these policies, in turn, affect the firm's level of investment in working capital. Likewise, the interest rates on short-term and long-term debt normally are a function of the riskiness of the firm's debt as perceived by lenders and, hence, are affected by the firm's working capital investment and financing decisions. Recompute Burlington's rate of return on common equity under the following set of assumptions concerning sales, EBIT, and interest rates for each of the three different working capital investment and financing policies.

---

*Colored numbers denote problems that have check answers provided at the end of the book.

Policy	Forecasted Sales (in Millions of Dollars)	Expected EBIT (in Millions of Dollars)	Interest Rate STD(%)	LTD(%)
Aggressive	$ 98	$ 9.8	8.5	10.5
Moderate	100	10.0	8.0	10.0
Conservative	102	10.2	7.5	9.5

3. The Garcia Industries balance sheet and income statement for the year ended 19X5 are as follows:

Balance Sheet
(in Millions of Dollars)

Assets		Liabilities and Stockholders' Equity	
Cash	$ 6.0	Accounts payable	$10.0
Accounts receivable	14.0	Salaries, benefits, and	
Inventories*	12.0	payroll taxes payable	2.0
Fixed assets, net	40.0	Other current liabilities	10.0
	$72.0	Long-term debt	12.0
		Stockholders' equity	38.0
			$72.0

*The average inventory over the past two years also equals $12.0 million.

Income Statement
(in Millions of Dollars)

Net sales	$100.0
Cost of sales	60.0
Selling, general, and administrative expenses	20.0
Other expenses	15.0
Earnings after tax	$ 5.0

a. Determine the length of the inventory conversion period.
b. Determine the length of the receivables conversion period.
c. Determine the length of the operating cycle.
d. Determine the length of the payables deferral period.
e. Determine the length of the cash conversion cycle.
f. What is the meaning of the number you calculated in Part e?

4. Wilson Electric Company, a manufacturer of various types of electrical equipment, is examining its working capital investment policy for next year. Projected fixed assets and current liabilities are $20 million and $18 million, respectively. Sales and EBIT are partially a function of the company's investment in working capital—particularly its investment in inventories and receivables. Wilson is considering the following three different working capital investment policies:

Working Capital Investment Policy	Investment in Current Assets (in Millions of Dollars)	Projected Sales (in Millions of Dollars)	EBIT (in Millions of Dollars)
Aggressive (small investment in current assets)	$28	$59	$5.9
Moderate (moderate investment in current assets)	30	60	6.0
Conservative (large investment in current assets)	32	61	6.1

2 4 582

a. Determine the following for each of the working capital investment policies:

   i. Rate of return on total assets (that is, EBIT/total assets).

  ii. Net working capital position.

 iii. Current ratio.

b. Describe the profitability versus risk trade-offs of these three policies.

5. Reynolds Equipment Company is investigating the use of various combinations of short-term and long-term debt in financing its assets. Assume that the company has decided to employ $30 million in current assets, along with $35 million in fixed assets, in its operations next year. Given this level of current assets, anticipated sales and EBIT for next year are $60 million and $6 million, respectively. The company's income tax rate is 40 percent. Stockholders' equity will be used to finance $40 million of its assets, with the remainder being financed by short-term and long-term debt. Reynolds is considering implementing one of the following financing policies:

Financing Policy	Amount of Short-Term Debt (in Millions of Dollars)	Interest Rate	
		LTD(%)	STD(%)
Aggressive (large amount of short-term debt)	$24	8.5	5.5
Moderate (moderate amount of short-term debt)	18	8.0	5.0
Conservative (small amount of short-term debt)	12	7.5	4.5

a. Determine the following for each of the financing policies:

  i. Expected rate of return on stockholders' equity.

  ii. Net working capital position.

 iii. Current ratio.

b. Evaluate the profitability versus risk trade-offs of these three policies.

6. Superior Brands, Inc. wishes to analyze the *joint impact* of its working capital investment and financing policies on shareholder return and risk. The company has $40 million in fixed assets. Also, the firm's financial structure consists of short-term and long-term debt and common equity. Superior wishes to maintain a debt-to-total assets ratio of 50 percent, where debt consists of both short-term and long-term sources. The company's tax rate is 40 percent. The following information was developed for three different policies under consideration:

Working Capital Investment and Financing Policy	Investment in Current Assets (in Millions of Dollars)	Amount of STD (in Millions of Dollars)	Projected Sales (in Millions of Dollars)	EBIT (in Millions of Dollars)	Interest Rate	
					LTD (%)	STD (%)
Aggressive	$56	$48	$118	$11.8	9.5	6.5
Moderate	60	36	120	12.0	9.0	6.0
Conservative	64	24	122	12.2	8.5	5.5

a. Determine the following for each of the three working capital investment and financing policies:

  i. Expected rate of return on stockholders' equity.

  ii. Net working capital position.

 iii. Current ratio.

b. Evaluate the profitability versus risk trade-offs associated with these three policies.

7. Educational Toys, Inc. (ETI) has highly seasonal sales and financing requirements. The company's balance sheet on December 31, 19X0 (*now*) is as follows:

Assets (in Millions of Dollars)		Liabilities and Equity (in Millions of Dollars)	
		Short-term debt	$ x
Current assets	$20	Long-term debt	y
Fixed assets	34	Net worth (equity)	30
Total assets	$54	Total liabilities and equity	$54

ETI has made the following projections of its asset needs and net additions to retained earnings (that is, equity) for the next 3 years:

Year	Quarter	Fixed Assets (in Millions of Dollars)	Current Assets (in Millions of Dollars)	Net Additions to Retained Earnings (in Millions of Dollars)
19X1	1 (March 31)	$36	$20	$0
	2 (June 30)	36	24	0
	3 (Sept. 30)	36	30	1
	4 (Dec. 31)	36	24	1
19X2	1 (March 31)	38	24	0
	2 (June 30)	38	28	0
	3 (Sept. 30)	38	36	1
	4 (Dec. 31)	38	28	2
19X3	1 (March 31)	40	28	0
	2 (June 30)	40	32	0
	3 (Sept. 30)	40	38	1
	4 (Dec. 31)	40	30	2

Assuming that ETI does not plan to sell any preferred or new common stock over the next 3 years:

a. Determine ETI's quarterly total assets and *total* (short-term and long-term) *debt requirements* for the next 3 years.

b. Plot the firm's *fixed, current,* and *total* assets over time on a graph.

c. Assume that ETI follows a *matching* approach in financing its assets. In other words, long-term debt will be used to finance its fixed and permanent current assets, and short-term debt will be used to finance its fluctuating current assets. The costs of short-term and long-term debt to ETI under this plan are 6 and 8 percent per annum (that is, 1.5 and 2 percent per quarter), respectively. Using this information, determine the following:

 i. The amount of short-term and long-term debt outstanding each quarter.

 ii. ETI's total interest costs over the 3-year period under this approach.

d. ETI is also considering other financing plans. One plan under consideration is a *conservative* policy. Under this policy, the company would determine its *maximum* debt requirements for the coming year and finance this entire amount with long-term debt at an interest rate of 8 percent per annum on December 31 of each year. Any funds in excess of its seasonal (quarterly) needs would be invested in short-term interest-bearing securities to yield a 4 percent per annum rate of return. Using this information, determine the following:

 i. The amount of long-term debt ETI would have to borrow each year.

 ii. ETI's *net* interest costs over the 3-year period under this conservative policy.

e. Finally, ETI is also considering an *aggressive* policy. Under this policy, the company would determine its *minimum* debt requirements for the coming year on December 31 of each year and finance one-half of this amount with long-term debt, with the remainder being financed by short-term debt. The costs of short-term and long-term debt under this policy are 6 and 8 percent per annum, respectively.

Using this information, determine the following:

    i. The amount of short-term and long-term debt outstanding each quarter.

    ii. ETI's total interest costs over the 3-year period under this aggressive policy.

8. Greenwich Industries has forecasted its monthly needs for working capital (net of spontaneous sources, such as accounts payable) for 19X3 as follows:

Month	Amount	Month	Amount
January	$7,500,000	July	$6,000,000
February	6,000,000	August	7,500,000
March	3,000,000	September	8,500,000
April	2,500,000	October	9,000,000
May	3,500,000	November	9,500,000
June	4,500,000	December	9,000,000

Short-term borrowing (that is, a bank line of credit) costs the company 10 percent, and long-term borrowing (that is, term loans) costs the company 12 percent. Any funds in excess of its monthly needs can be invested in interest-bearing marketable securities to yield 8 percent per annum.

    a. Suppose the company follows a *conservative* policy by financing the *maximum* amount of its working capital requirements for the coming year with long-term borrowing and investing any excess funds in short-term marketable securities. Determine Greenwich's *net* interest costs during 19X3 under this policy.

    b. Suppose the company follows an *aggressive* policy by financing *all* its working capital requirements for the coming year with short-term borrowing. Determine Greenwich's interest costs during 19X3 under this policy.

    c. Discuss the profitability versus risk trade-offs associated with these conservative and aggressive working capital financing policies.

9. Nguyen Enterprises is considering two alternative working capital investment and financing policies. *Policy A* requires the firm to keep its current assets at 65 percent of forecasted sales and to finance 70 percent of its debt requirements with long-term debt (and 30 percent with short-term debt). *Policy B*, on the other hand, requires the firm to keep its current assets at 40 percent of forecasted sales and to finance 40 percent of its debt requirements with long-term debt (and 60 percent with short-term debt). Forecasted sales for next year are $20 million. Earnings before interest and taxes are projected to be 15 percent of sales. The firm's corporate income tax rate is 40 percent. Its fixed assets total $10 million. The firm desires to maintain its existing financial structure, which consists of 50 percent debt and 50 percent equity. Interest rates on short- and long-term debt are 12 and 15 percent, respectively.

    a. Determine the expected rate of return on equity next year for Nguyen under each of the working capital policies.

    b. Which policy is riskier? Cite specific evidence to support this contention.

10. The Hopewell Pharmaceutical Company's balance sheet and income statement for last year are as follows:

Balance Sheet (in Millions of Dollars)

Assets		Liabilities and Equity	
Cash and marketable securities	$1,100	Accounts payable	$ 900
Accounts receivable	1,300	Accrued liabilities	
Inventories*	800	(salaries and benefits)	300
Other current assets	200	Other current liabilities	700
Total current assets	$3,400	Total current liabilities	$1,900

Continued

Balance Sheet (in Millions of Dollars)

Assets		Liabilities and Equity	
Plant and equipment (net)	2,300	Long-term debt and other	
Other assets	1,000	liabilities	1,000
Total assets	$6,700	Common stock	1,800
		Retained earnings	2,000
		Total stockholders' equity	$3,800
		Total liabilities and equity	$6,700

*Assume that average inventory over the year was $800 million, that is, the same as ending inventory.

Income Statement (in Millions of Dollars)

Net sales	$6,500
Cost of sales	1,500
Selling, general, and administrative expenses	2,500
Other expenses	800
Total expenses	$4,800
Earnings before taxes	1,700
Taxes	680
Earnings after taxes (net income)	$1,020

a. Determine Hopewell's cash conversion cycle.

b. Give an interpretation of the value computed in Part a.

11. Brakenridge Industries is considering the following two alternative working capital investment and financing policies:

	Policy A	Policy B
Current assets ÷ Sales	50%	40%
Short-term debt ÷ Total debt	40%	50%

Forecasted sales next year are $30 million. EBIT is projected at 25 percent of sales. Fixed assets are $30 million. The firm's income tax rate is 40 percent. Brakenridge desires to maintain its current capital structure, which consists of 50 percent debt and 50 percent equity. Interest rates on the company's short-term and long-term debt are 9 and 12 percent, respectively.

a. Determine the expected rate of return on equity capital under each of the working capital policies.

b. Which working capital policy is riskier? Explain.

12. The Butler-Huron Company's balance sheet and income statement for last year are as follows:

Balance Sheet (in Millions of Dollars)

Assets		Liabilities and Equity	
Cash and marketable securities	$ 103	Accounts payable	$1,166
Accounts receivable*	1,138	Accrued liabilities	
Inventories**	1,827	(salaries and benefits)	536
Other current assets	39	Other current liabilities	493
Total current assets	$3,107	Total current liabilities	$2,195
Plant and equipment (net)	3,523	Long-term debt and other	
Other assets	54	liabilities	2,736
Total assets	$6,684	Common stock	105
		Retained earnings	1,648
		Total stockholders' equity	$1,753
		Total liabilities and equity	$6,684

*Assume that all sales are credit sales.

**Assume that average inventory over the year was $1,827 million, that is, the same as ending inventory.

Income Statement (in Millions of Dollars)

Net sales	$13,644
Cost of sales	9,890
Selling, general, and administrative expenses	2,264
Other expenses	812
Total expenses	$12,966
Earnings before taxes	678
Taxes	268
Earnings after taxes (net income)	$ 410

a. Determine Butler-Huron's cash conversion cycle.

b. Determine Butler-Huron's cash conversion cycle assuming that 75 percent of annual sales are credit sales (i.e., 25 percent represent cash sales).

c. Determine Butler-Huron's cash conversion cycle assuming that 50 percent of annual sales are credit sales.

13. Consider the Industrial Supply Company example (Table 15-1) again. Assume that the company plans to maintain its dividend payments at the same level in 19X7 as in 19X6. Also assume that all of the additional financing needed is in the form of short-term notes payable. Determine the amount of additional financing needed and pro forma financial statements (that is, balance sheet, income statement, and selected financial ratios) for 19X7 under each of the following conditions:

	Increase in Sales	Increase in Expenses
a.	$3,750,000	$3,750,000
b.	$3,000,000	$2,800,000
c.	$4,500,000	$4,000,000

14. Prepare a cash budget for Atlas Products, Inc. for the first quarter of 19X2, based on the following information.

The budgeting section of the corporate finance department of Atlas Products has received the following sales estimates from the marketing department:

	Total Sales	Credit Sales
December 19X1	$825,000	$770,000
January 19X2	730,000	690,000
February 19X2	840,000	780,000
March 19X2	920,000	855,000

The company has found that, on average, about 25 percent of its credit sales are collected during the month when the sale is made, and the remaining 75 percent of credit sales are collected during the month following the sale. As a result, the company uses these figures for budgeting.

The company estimates its purchases at 60 percent of next month's sales, and payments for those purchases are budgeted to lag the purchases by 1 month.

Various disbursements have been estimated as follows:

	January	February	March
Wages and salaries	$250,000	$290,000	$290,000
Rent	27,000	27,000	27,000
Other expenses	10,000	12,000	14,000

In addition, a tax payment of $105,000 is due on January 15, and $40,000 in dividends will be declared in January and paid in March. Also, the company has ordered a $75,000 piece of equipment. Delivery is scheduled for early January, and payment will be due in February.

The company's projected cash balance at the beginning of January is $100,000, and the company desires to maintain a balance of $100,000 at the end of each month.

15. Prepare a cash budget for Elmwood Manufacturing Company for the first 3 months of 19X7 based on the following information:

Month	Estimated Sales	Estimated Factory Overhead	Estimated Selling and Administrative Expenses
December	$ 4,600,000	$640,000	$1,250,000
January	6,400,000	650,000	1,275,000
February	11,200,000	670,000	1,285,000
March	8,400,000	670,000	1,310,000
April	7,000,000	680,000	1,300,000

The company has found that approximately 40 percent of sales are collected during the month the sale is made and the remaining 60 percent are collected during the month following the sale. Material purchases are 30 percent of next month's estimated sales, and payments lag these purchases by 1 month. Labor costs are 35 percent of next month's sales and are paid during the month incurred. Factory overhead and selling and administrative expenses are paid during the month incurred. In addition, a payment for new equipment of $1.5 million is due in February. Also, a tax payment of $1.6 million and a dividend payment of $650,000 are due in March.

The company's projected cash balance at the beginning of January is $1.5 million. Furthermore, Elmwood desires to maintain a $750,000 cash balance at the end of each month.

16. The Podrasky Corporation is considering a $200 million expansion (capital expenditure) program next year. The company wants to know approximately how much additional financing (if any) will be required if it decides to go through with the expansion program. The company presently has $400 million in net fixed assets on its books. Next year, the company expects to earn $80 million after interest and taxes. The company also expects to maintain its present level of dividends, which is $15 million. If the expansion program is accepted, the company expects its inventory and accounts receivable each to increase by approximately $20 million next year. Long-term debt retirement obligations total $10 million for next year, and depreciation is expected to be $80 million. The company does not expect to sell any fixed assets next year. The company maintains a cash balance of $5 million, which is sufficient for its present operations. If the expansion is accepted, the company feels it should increase its year-end cash balance to $8 million because of the increased level of activities. For planning purposes, assume no other cash flow changes for next year.

17. Baldwin Products Company anticipates reaching a sales level of $6 million in one year. The company expects earnings after taxes during the next year to equal $400,000. During the past several years, the company has been paying $50,000 in dividends to its stockholders. The company expects to continue this policy for at least the next year. The actual balance sheet and income statement for Baldwin during 19X8 follow.

Baldwin Products Company
Balance Sheet as of December 31, 19X8

Cash	$ 200,000	Accounts payable	$ 600,000
Accounts receivable	400,000	Notes payable	500,000
Inventories	1,200,000	Long-term debt	200,000
Fixed assets, net	500,000	Stockholders' equity	1,000,000
Total assets	$2,300,000	Total liabilities and equity	$2,300,000

Income Statement for the Year Ending December 31, 19X8

Sales	$4,000,000
Expenses, including interest and taxes	$3,700,000
Earnings after taxes	$ 300,000

a. Using the percentage of sales method, calculate the additional financing Baldwin Products will need over the next year at the $6 million sales level. Show the pro forma balance sheet for the company as of December 31, 19X9, assuming a sales level of $6 million is reached. Assume that the additional financing needed is obtained in the form of additional notes payable.

b. Suppose that the Baldwin Products's management feels that the average collection period on its additional sales—that is, sales over $4 million—will be 60 days, instead of the current level. By what amount will this increase in the average collection period increase the financing needed by the company over the next year?

c. If the Baldwin Products's banker requires the company to maintain a current ratio equal to 1.6 or greater, what is the maximum amount of additional financing that can be in the form of bank borrowings (notes payable)? What other potential sources of financing are available to the company?

18. In the Industrial Supply Company example (Table 15-1) it was assumed that the company's fixed assets were being utilized at nearly full capacity and that net fixed assets would have to increase proportionately as sales increased. Alternatively, suppose that the company has excess fixed assets and that *no increase* in net fixed assets is required as sales are increased. Assume that the company plans to maintain its dividend payments at the same level in 19X7 as in 19X6. Determine the amount of additional financing needed for 19X7 under each of the following conditions:

	Increase in Sales	Increase in Expenses
a.	$3,750,000	$3,750,000
b.	$3,000,000	$2,800,000
c.	$4,500,000	$4,000,000

19. Berea Resources is planning a $75 million capital expenditure program for the coming year. Next year, Berea expects to report to the IRS earnings of $40 million after interest and taxes. The company presently has 20 million shares of common stock issued and outstanding. Dividend payments are expected to increase from the present level of $10 million to $12 million. The company expects its current asset needs to increase from a current level of $25 million to $30 million. Current liabilities, excluding short-term bank borrowings, are expected to increase from $15 million to $17 million. Interest payments are $5 million next year, and long-term debt retirement obligations are $8 million next year. Depreciation next year is expected to be $15 million on the company's financial statements, but the company will report depreciation of $18 million for tax purposes.

How much external financing is required by Berea for the coming year?

20. Appalachian Registers, Inc. (ARI) has current sales of $50 million. Sales are expected to grow to $75 million next year. ARI currently has accounts receivable of $10 million, inventories of $15 million, and net fixed assets of $20 million. These assets are expected to grow at the same rate as sales over the next year. Accounts payable are expected to increase from their current level of $10 million to a new

level of $13 million next year. ARI wants to increase its cash balance at the end of next year by $2 million over its current cash balances, which average $4 million. Earnings after taxes next year are forecasted to be $10 million. Next year, ARI plans to pay dividends of $1 million, up from $500,000 this year. ARI's marginal tax rate is 34 percent.

How much external financing is required by ARI next year?

21. Use the Interactive Tool Box at the following Website to set up a cash budget for a real (if you have all the data) or imaginary firm. Then set up a variance budget (variance = budgeted amount less actual amount). Tutorials are also available if you need them.

www.edgeonline.com

http://

22. Examine the Interactive Business Planner at the following Website. How can you use these tools as the manager of an existing company or a new start-up enterprise? Also examine the tutorial Preparing a Cash Flow Forecast. Then look at the cash flow worksheet. Prepare a one-page memo to your instructor summarizing what you found.

www.sb.gov.bc.ca

http://

■ SOLUTIONS TO SELF-TEST PROBLEMS

ST1. a. Inventory conversion period $= \dfrac{\text{Average inventory}}{\text{Cost of sales}/365}$

$= \dfrac{\$2,120}{\$6,946/365}$

$= 111.4$ days

b. Receivables conversion period $= \dfrac{\text{Accounts receivable}}{\text{Annual credit sales}/365}$

$= \dfrac{\$2,075}{\$11,990/365}$

$= 63.2$ days

c. Operating cycle $=$ Inventory conversion period $+$ Receivables conversion period

$= 111.4 + 63.2$

$= 174.6$ days

d. Payables deferral period $=$

$\dfrac{\text{Accounts payable} + \text{Salaries and benefits payable}}{(\text{Cost of sales} + \text{Selling, general, and administrative expenses})/365}$

$= \dfrac{724 + 332}{(6,946 + 2,394)/365}$

$= 41.3$ days

e. Cash conversion cycle $=$ Operating cycle $-$ Payables deferral period

$= 174.6 - 41.3$

$= 133.3$ days

ST2. a.

	Policy A	Policy B
Current assets	$ 90,000,000	$ 60,000,000
Total assets	190,000,000	160,000,000
Total equity	76,000,000	64,000,000
Total debt	114,000,000	96,000,000
Short-term debt	34,200,000	57,600,000
Long-term debt	79,800,000	38,400,000
EBIT	30,000,000	30,000,000
Interest {STD (10%) / LTD (14%)	14,592,000	11,136,000
EBT	15,408,000	18,864,000
Taxes	6,163,200	7,545,600
EAT	9,244,800	11,318,400
Rate of return on equity	12.16%	17.69%

b. Policy B is riskier than policy A since it results in a lower net working capital position ($2,400,000 versus $55,800,000) and a lower current ratio (1.04 versus 2.63). (This answer assumes there are no current liabilities other than short-term debt. If there were, the numbers would differ but the relative magnitudes of both calculated measures of risk would be unchanged.)

ST3. Rate of sales increase is one-third (33.33%; i.e., from $60 million to $80 million).

Accounts receivable	$ 9 million
Inventories	15 million
Net fixed assets	21 million
Assets that vary with sales	$45 million

Increased funds needed for these asset increases = ⅓ × $45 million = $15 million

Funds provided by accounts payable increase = $4 million

Funds required for cash balance increase = $3 million

Increased retained earnings = $12 million − $2 million (dividend)

$$= \$10 \text{ million}$$

Additional financing needed = $3 million (cash) + $15 million (other asset increases)

$$- \$4 \text{ million (accounts payable increase)}$$

$$- \$10 \text{ million (increased retained earnings)}$$

$$= \$4 \text{ million}$$

ST4. Additional financing needed $= \left[\dfrac{\$10,500,000}{\$20,000,000} (\$5,000,000) - \dfrac{\$3,000,000}{\$20,000,000} (\$5,000,000) \right]$

$$- [\$1,000,000 - \$300,000]$$

$$= \$1,175,000$$

Notes: $10,500,000 = assets that vary with sales
$3,000,000 = accounts payable
$5,000,000 = sales increase
$20,000,000 = current sales

■ GLOSSARY

Cash Budget A projection of a company's cash receipts and disbursements over some future period of time.

Cash Conversion Cycle The net time interval between the collection of cash receipts from product sales and the cash payments for the company's various resources. The cash conversion cycle is calculated by subtracting the payables deferral period from the operating cycle.

Cash Flow Forecasting The projection and estimation of a firm's future cash flows.

Deterministic Model A financial planning model that projects single number estimates of a financial variable or variables without specifying their probability of occurrence.

Discriminant Analysis A statistical technique designed to classify observations (firms) into two or more predetermined groups based on certain characteristics (such as financial ratios) of the observations.

Financial Forecasting The projection and estimation of a firm's future financial statements.

Financial Planning Model A computerized representation of some aspect of a firm's financial planning process.

Fluctuating Current Assets Current assets affected by the seasonal or cyclical nature of the company's sales.

Inventory Conversion Period The length of time required to produce and sell the product.

Liquidity The ability of a firm to meet its cash obligations as they come due.

Matching Approach A financing plan in which the maturity structure of a firm's liabilities is made to correspond exactly to the life of its assets.

Net Working Capital The difference between a firm's current assets and current liabilities. The term *net working capital* is used interchangeably with *working capital*.

Operating Cycle For a typical company, the three primary activities of purchasing resources, producing the product, and distributing (selling) the product. The operating cycle is calculated by summing the inventory conversion period and the receivables conversion period.

Optimization Model A financial planning model that determines the values of financial decision variables that maximize (or minimize) some objective function such as profits (or costs).

Payables Deferral Period The length of time a firm is able to deter payment on its resource purchases.

Percentage of Sales Forecasting Method A method of estimating the additional financing that will be needed to support a given future sales level.

Permanent Current Assets Current assets held to meet the company's long-term minimum needs.

Probabilistic Model A financial planning model that uses probability distributions as inputs and generates a probability distribution for financial variables as output.

Pro Forma Financial Statements Financial statements that project the results of some *assumed* event, rather than an *actual* event.

Receivables Conversion Period The length of time required to collect sales receipts. Receivables conversion period is another name for the *average collection period.*

Sensitivity Analysis A method of analysis in which a financial planning model is rerun to determine the effect on the output variable(s) (for example, profit) of given changes in the input variable(s) (for example, sales). Sensitivity analysis is sometimes called *what if* analysis.

Working Capital The difference between a firm's current assets and current liabilities. The term *working capital* is used interchangeably with *net working capital.*

THE MANAGEMENT OF CASH AND MARKETABLE SECURITIES

16

KEY CHAPTER CONCEPTS

1. Companies hold liquid asset balances for several reasons, including:
   a. To conduct transactions.
   b. For precautionary reasons.
   c. To meet future requirements.
   d. For speculative reasons.
   e. To compensate banks for various services provided to the firm.
2. The optimal liquid asset balance reflects risk and return trade-offs and is a function of the following:
   a. Holding costs, which are the opportunity returns the company could earn on these funds in their next best alternative use.
   b. Shortage costs, which include possible lost cash discounts, deterioration of the company's credit rating, higher interest expenses, and financial insolvency.
3. The primary objective in controlling cash collections is to reduce the delay between when the customer mails the payment and when it becomes a collected balance in the firm's bank account.
4. Methods for reducing collection time include
   a. Decentralized collection centers and concentration banks.
   b. Lockboxes.
   c. Wire transfers and depository transfer checks (DTC).
   d. Special handling of large remittances.
   e. Preauthorized checks (PAC).
5. The primary objective in controlling cash disbursements is to slow payments and keep the firm's funds in the bank as long as possible.
6. Methods of slowing disbursements include
   a. Scheduling and centralizing payments (zero-balance systems).
   b. Use of drafts rather than checks.
   c. Maximizing check-clearing float.
   d. Stretching payables.
7. Electronic funds transfer systems, including wire transfers, the use of automated clearinghouses, and customer-directed computer movements of funds from one account to another have the potential to greatly reduce the float in financial transactions.
8. Aggressive financial managers need to avoid overstepping the bounds of legal and ethical behavior.
9. The primary criteria the firm should use in selecting marketable securities include default risk, marketability (or liquidity), maturity date, and rate of return.

CHRYSLER'S $7.3 BILLION CASH HOARD: HOW MUCH IS TOO MUCH?*

In 1995, Kirk Kerkorian, Chrysler's largest shareholder, made a $20 billion, $55 per share leveraged buyout offer for the company. He claimed that the company's $7.3 billion cash stockpile was more than Chrysler needed for its operations and that some of this hoard should be paid out to stockholders— either in the form of cash dividends or share repurchases. As the result of an enduring 5-year economic expansion, many companies, besides Chrysler, had built up sizeable cash balances. Chrysler's cash balance, for example, represented 30 percent of the market value of the firm. At General Dynamics, cash ($1 billion) represented 35 percent of market value; at United Health Care, cash ($2.3 billion) was 33 percent; and at Ford, cash ($6.2 billion) was 22 percent. These large cash balances raised the issue of how much cash a company should hold.

In the case of Chrysler, the company used up more than $4 billion in cash during the most recent recession from the end of 1989 to the end of 1991. Coming out of the recession, Chrysler

decided to build up its cash holdings to $5 billion to meet its needs during the next downturn. However, as the company's revenues increased, manage-

ment expanded its target cash balance to $7.5 billion. With a smaller amount, management felt that it would run a greater risk of having to cut product spending and pension funding during the next recession.

Other automobile industry experts and analysts felt that Chrysler was being too conservative and that the $7.5

billion target cash balance was too high. For example, Frederick Zuckerman, Chrylser's former treasurer, felt that the company needed $5.5 billion in cash to weather another economic downturn. Lee Iacocca, a Kerkorian ally and former Chrysler chairman, claimed that the company needed only $2.5 billion in cash (plus an equal amount from credit lines) to handle another economic recession. Stock market traders noted that the combination of Chrysler's large cash hoard and weak stock price indicated that the company was not managing its finances properly.

Determining a firm's appropriate cash balance involves risk versus return tradeoffs. The factors that must be considered in determining a company's optimal cash and marketable securities (i.e., liquid assets) balance are examined in this chapter.

*Based on Neal Templin and Steven Lipin, "Sides in Chrysler Bid Differ on How Much a Rainy Day Costs," *Wall Street Journal* (April 17, 1995): A3; and David Kansas and Randall Smith, "How Much Cash a Firm Should Keep Is at Issue in Wake of Chrysler Bid," *Wall Street Journal* (April 30, 1995): A1.

INTRODUCTION

Cash and marketable securities are the most liquid of a company's assets. *Cash* is the sum of the currency a company has on hand and the funds on deposit in bank checking accounts. Cash is the medium of exchange that permits management to carry on the various functions of the business organization. In fact, the survival of a company can depend on the availability of cash to meet financial obligations on time. *Marketable securities* consist of short-term investments a firm makes with its temporarily idle cash. Marketable securities can be sold quickly and converted into cash when needed. Unlike cash, however, marketable securities provide a firm with interest income.

Effective cash and marketable securities management is important in contemporary companies, government agencies, and not-for-profit enterprises. Corporate treasurers continually seek ways to increase the yields on their liquid cash and marketable security reserves. Traditionally, these liquid reserves were invested almost exclusively in jumbo certificates of deposit, Treasury bills, commercial paper, and repurchase agreements (short-term loans backed by Treasury securities). However, in recent years many treasurers have shown a willingness to take some additional risks to increase the return on liquid assets. Financial managers constantly face these types of risk-return trade-offs.

Many firms hold significant cash and marketable securities balances. For example, at the beginning of 1996, IBM's cash balances equaled $1.7 billion; General Electric's cash balances exceeded $2.8 billion; Exxon had $1.5 billion; and Philip Morris had over $1.1 billion. These cash balances give the firm a cushion to handle economic downturns and the ability to make investments in other firms when the price is attractive. As illustrated in the Financial Challenge at the beginning of the chapter, large cash balances have also made many firms attractive takeover targets for corporate raiders, who seek to redeploy these surplus funds in more productive ways.

In addition to managing the cash and marketable securities already in the firm's possession, financial managers also aggressively seek to speed up cash collections from customers and to slow down disbursements to suppliers. For example, when Alaska sold its oil leases for $900 million, the state was paid with checks that had to physically reach New York before the state could collect and invest the funds. The state chartered a plane to take the checks to New York, thus saving one day in transit over commercial carriers. The daily interest on these funds at the time was nearly $200,000, and the plane charter cost only $15,000, resulting in $185,000 of additional returns to the state. Cash managers continually look for ways to reduce the collection and clearing time for checks received by the firm so that the funds can be put to work earning a return.

Cash management involves much more than simply paying bills and receiving payments for goods and services. The cash management function is concerned with determining

- The optimal size of a firm's liquid asset balance.
- The most efficient methods of controlling the collection and disbursement of cash.
- The appropriate types and amounts of short-term investments a firm should make.

Cash management decisions require a firm's managers to consider explicitly the *risk versus expected return* trade-offs from alternative policies. Because cash and marketable securities generally earn low rates of return relative to a firm's other assets, a firm can increase its expected return on assets and common equity by minimizing its investment in cash and marketable securities. However, a firm that carries a bare minimum of liquid assets exposes itself to the risk that it will run out of cash needed to keep the business operating. Also, a firm with extremely low cash balances may not be able to take advantage of unique investment opportunities when they arise.

In this chapter, we review the various cash management decisions that must be made by financial managers. Our analysis considers the risk versus expected return trade-offs characteristic of these decisions.

LIQUID ASSET BALANCE

Firms hold liquid asset balances for a number of reasons, including the following:

- First, because cash inflows and outflows of the day-to-day operations of a firm are not perfectly synchronized, liquid asset balances are necessary to serve as a buffer between these flows. This reason is the *transactions motive.* Liquid asset balances help a firm handle seasonal fluctuations in cash flows. For example, a firm may wish to hold a large amount of liquid assets during surplus months and "draw down" on them during deficit months.
- Second, because future cash flows and the ability to borrow additional funds on short notice are often uncertain, liquid asset balances are necessary to meet unexpected requirements for cash. This is the *precautionary motive.*
- Third, liquid asset balances are held to meet *future requirements,* which include fixed outlays required on specific dates, such as quarterly dividend and tax payments, capital expenditures, and repayments of loans or bond issues. A firm also may hold as liquid assets the proceeds from a new debt or equity securities offering prior to using these funds for expansion.
- Fourth, firms often hold liquid assets for *speculative reasons.* Some firms build up large cash balances in preparation for major acquisitions. For example, several years ago Ford Motor Company built up its liquid asset balances to over $9 billion. Security analysts expected Ford to make major future acquisitions, particularly if it could identify one or more attractively priced firms to acquire. In fact, this is just what Ford did; it acquired Jaguar for $2.5 billion. The large cash balances gave Ford timing flexibility in pursuing acquisitions.
- Finally, a firm generally has to hold cash balances to compensate its bank (or banks) for the services provided. These are called **compensating balances.**

The following sections consider the importance of cash from a number of perspectives.

Cash Flows and the Cash Budget

Virtually every activity within a firm generates cash flows. As shown in Figure 16-1, the firm's cash balance is affected by every transaction that involves either a cash inflow or a cash outflow. Cash inflows, or *receipts,* occur when customers pay for their purchases, when a firm obtains bank loans, when it sells new issues of debt and equity securities, and when it sells (or collects interest on)

FIGURE 16-1
Cash Flows within a Typical Firm*

*Arrows indicate the direction of cash flows.

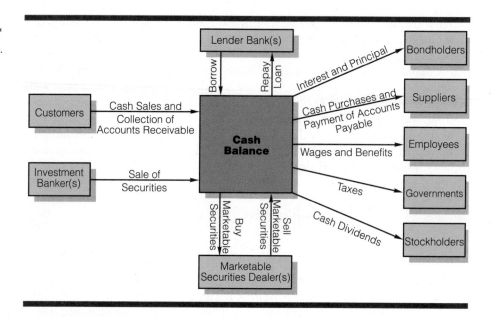

marketable securities. Cash outflows, or disbursements, occur when a firm makes payments to suppliers, when a firm pays wages to employees, taxes to governments, interest and principal to bondholders, and cash dividends to shareholders, and when a firm repays bank loans and purchases marketable securities. Therefore, the cash balance at the end of any given period is the result of many interrelated activities.

Cash flows differ with respect to their degree of *certainty*. In general, future outflows are more certain than future inflows. Most expenditures (outflows) are directly controllable by a firm and, as a result, can be forecasted more easily. For example, outflows for such items as raw materials, labor, dividends, debt repayments, and capital equipment are determined primarily by management decisions and are usually known in advance of their occurrence. Inflows, in contrast, occur partly as a result of decisions made outside a firm and thus are usually more difficult to control and forecast. For example, cash inflows from sales depend primarily on the buying decisions of customers, as well as on when they make their payments.

The first step in efficient cash management is the development of a *cash budget* showing the forecasted cash receipts and disbursements over the planning horizon of the firm.[1] A complete cash budget also contains a forecast of any cumulative cash shortages or surpluses expected during each of the budgeting subperiods—which is the kind of information needed in making cash management decisions. Many larger firms prepare a series of cash budgets, each covering a different time period. For example, a firm may prepare daily cash budgets for the next 5 working days, weekly cash budgets for the next 10 weeks, and monthly cash budgets for the next 12 months. The daily and weekly forecasts are used in making short-term decisions, such as determining the amount of marketable securities the firm should purchase or sell. The monthly projections are used in longer-range planning, such as determining the amount of bank loans the firm

---

[1]Chapter 15 contains a discussion of how cash budgets are developed.

will need. A survey of medium- and large-size companies found that over 80 percent of the respondents relied on cash budgets as a cash forecasting technique.[2]

Knowledge of a potential cash shortage ahead of time gives a financial manager ample opportunity to investigate alternative sources of financing and to choose the least costly one. All other things being equal, lending institutions prefer to make loans to firms that have demonstrated an ability to anticipate their future cash needs. Firms that seem to be faced with frequent cash "emergencies" generally have more difficulty getting loans. Similarly, advance knowledge of a cash surplus allows the financial manager to invest in appropriate marketable securities.

Corporate–Bank Relations

A firm's bank provides a variety of both tangible and intangible services. The most significant tangible services include the following:

- Disbursement, wire transfer, direct deposit, and payroll checking accounts.
- Collection of deposits—including lockbox, automated collections, depository transfers, and vault services.
- Cash management.
- Lines of credit, term loans, or both.
- Handling of dividend payments.
- Registration and transfer of a firm's stock.

The most important intangible banking service is the availability of future credit if and when the need arises. Other intangible services include the following:

- Supplying credit information.
- Providing consultation on such matters as economic conditions, mergers, and international business.

First Union will set up and operate a cash management system for you, including lock boxes, faster collections, efficient disbursements, and much more. They've even introduced "CyberCoin."
http://www.firstunion.com/index.html

A bank is compensated for the services it provides by charging the firm explicit fees and/or requiring the maintenance of a minimum cash balance, or *compensating balance,* in its checking account. The bank can use this compensating balance to make other loans or investments, and the interest income realized is *compensation* for the various services rendered to a firm. Although some banks require firms to maintain *absolute* minimum compensating balances, most stipulate minimum *average* balances.

The monthly account fee that a bank charges a business customer is usually determined by calculating various service charges and then deducting an earnings credit on the account balance. The service charges are computed by multiplying the number of each type of transaction a firm makes per period (such as payroll checks, vendor checks, customer payments, and other deposits) by the bank's charge per item. The earnings credit is computed by multiplying the available balance during the month (which often includes various deductions, such as the bank's reserve requirement) by the earnings credit rate (that is, some specified interest rate). When the total service charges exceed the earnings credit, the bank collects a fee from the customer. Due to competition among banks and differences in the methods used to compute account income and costs, service fees and compensating balance requirements for a given level

[2]R. Kamath, S. Khaksari, H. Meier, and J. Winklepleck, "Management of Excess Cash: Practices and Developments," *Financial Management* (Autumn 1985): 70–77.

of account activity vary from bank to bank. As a result, a firm should occasionally do some "comparison shopping" to determine whether its present bank is offering the best fee schedule, compensating balance requirement, and total package of services currently available.

Optimal Liquid Asset Balance

When a firm holds liquid asset balances, whether in the form of currency, bank demand deposits, or marketable securities, in effect it is investing these funds. To determine the optimal investment in liquid assets, a firm must weigh the benefits and costs of holding these various balances. The determination of an optimal liquid asset balance reflects the classic *risk versus return* trade-off facing financial managers. Because liquid assets earn relatively low rates of return, a firm can increase its profitability in relation to its asset base by minimizing liquid asset balances. However, low liquid asset balances expose a firm to the risk of not being able to meet its obligations as they come due. Effective cash management calls for a careful balancing of the risk and return aspects of cash management.

A minimum compensating balance requirement on the part of a bank essentially imposes a *lower limit* on a firm's optimal level of liquid asset balances. When a firm holds liquid assets in excess of this lower limit, it incurs an *opportunity cost*. The opportunity cost of excess liquid assets, held in the form of bank deposits, is the return the firm could earn on these funds in their next best use, such as in the expansion of other current or fixed assets. The opportunity cost of liquid asset balances, held in the form of marketable securities, is the income that could be earned on these funds in their next best alternative use *less* the interest income received on the marketable securities.

Given the opportunity cost of holding liquid asset balances, why would a firm ever maintain a bank balance exceeding the compensating balance requirements? The answer is that these balances help the firm avoid the "shortage" costs associated with inadequate liquid asset balances.

Shortage costs can take many different forms, including the following:

- Forgone cash discounts.
- Deterioration of the firm's credit rating.
- Higher interest expenses.
- Possible financial insolvency.

Many suppliers offer customers a cash discount for prompt payment. Having to forgo this cash discount can be quite costly to a firm. In addition, the creditworthiness of a firm is determined at least partially by the current and quick ratios—both of which can be affected by an inadequate liquid asset balance. This, in turn, can cause a firm's credit rating to deteriorate and make loans on favorable terms more difficult to secure in the future. The credit rating also can fall if a firm fails to pay bills on time because of inadequate cash. This can make future credit difficult to obtain from suppliers. If a firm has inadequate liquid asset reserves, it may have to meet unforeseen needs for cash by short-term borrowing, and it may be unable to negotiate for the best terms—including the lowest possible interest rate—if its credit rating is questionable. Inadequate liquid asset balances may cause a firm to incur high transactions costs when converting illiquid assets to cash. Finally, an inadequate liquid asset balance increases a firm's risk of insolvency, because a serious recession or natural disaster would be more likely to reduce the firm's cash inflows to the point where it could not meet contractual financial obligations.

An inverse relationship exists between a firm's liquid asset balance and these shortage costs: the larger a firm's liquid asset balance, the smaller its associated shortage costs. The opportunity holding costs, in contrast, increase as a firm's liquid asset balance is increased. As shown in Figure 16-2, the optimal liquid asset balance occurs at the point where the sum of the opportunity holding costs and the shortage costs is minimized. Admittedly, many of these shortage costs are difficult to measure. Nevertheless, a firm should attempt to evaluate the trade-offs among these costs in order to economize on cash holdings.

Gilmer has performed empirical tests to determine if firms actually do face a U-shaped total cost function associated with the maintenance of liquid asset balances. His results were consistent with the concept of an optimal liquid asset balance as shown in Figure 16-2.[3]

The Practice of Liquidity Management

In practice, a wide variety of liquidity policies are found to exist among firms. Table 16-1 offers a sample of the liquidity policies practiced by different firms in several industries. As the table shows, liquidity practices, as measured by the ratio of cash and marketable securities to total assets, vary significantly among industries and among firms within an industry. Utility firms, retailers, and service industry establishments, such as restaurants, tend to hold low liquid asset balances as a proportion of total assets.

Although this table does not provide data on small to medium-sized firms, in general it can be observed that larger firms tend to hold lower liquid asset balances (relative to total assets) than smaller firms. This is because larger firms tend to have better access to "backup" short-term financing should they need it from commercial banks or the ability to sell commercial paper. Because smaller firms have more limited credit access, they tend to hold greater liquid asset balances as a cushion against the unexpected.

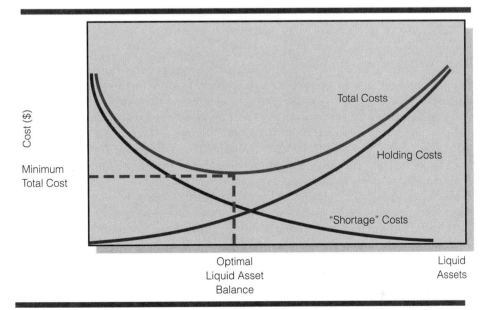

FIGURE 16-2
Optimal Liquid Asset Balance

[3]R. H. Gilmer, Jr., "The Optimal Level of Liquid Assets: An Empirical Test," *Financial Management* (Winter 1985): 39–43.

TABLE 16-1
Ratio of Cash and Marketable Securities to Total Assets

Source: *Moody's Industrial Manual,* 1996.
Moody's Public Utility Manual, 1996.

FIRM	RATIO
Aerospace-defense industry:	
Boeing	16.88%
General Dynamics	34.61
Lockheed Martin	3.70
Automotive industry:	
Chrysler	15.11%
Ford	17.05
General Motors	7.67
Computer industry:	
Digital Equipment	16.11%
Hewlett-Packard	10.71
IBM	9.59
Unisys	15.74
Electric utility industry:	
Duke Power	0.911%
Pennsylvania Power and Light	0.748
Sierra Pacific Resources	0.242
Tucson Electric Power	3.36
Restaurant industry:	
McDonald's	2.17%
Shoney's	1.40
Wendy's	14.17
Retailing industry:	
Dayton Hudson	1.39%
K-Mart	7.11
May Department Stores	1.57
JC Penney	1.01

CONTROLLING THE COLLECTION AND DISBURSEMENT OF CASH

The cash collection and disbursement processes provide a firm two areas in which it can economize on cash holdings. For example, the sales of Briggs and Stratton average about $5 million per business day. If the company can speed up collections by only *one* day, the cash balance will increase by $5 million, and these released funds can be invested in other current assets or in fixed assets. If this additional cash can be invested to yield a 5 percent return, it will generate added income of $250,000 per year (5% × $5 million).

Cash collection and disbursement policies are designed to reduce a firm's liquid asset balances (cash and marketable securities) by exploiting imperfections in the collection and payment process. The objective is to speed up collections and slow down disbursements. Financial managers should be aware that policies designed to speed up collections and slow down disbursements are highly competitive. If all firms were to employ the same procedures, the net benefit would be zero. Thus, incremental benefits associated with procedures designed to control collections and disbursements will accrue only to the most aggressive and progressive firms. Similarly, cash managers who do not do at least as much as the average firm in speeding up collections and slowing disbursements will find their firms at a competitive disadvantage.

The primary objective of cash collection involves expediting collections by reducing the lag between the time customers pay their bills and the time the checks are collected. In contrast, the primary objective of cash disbursement is to slow payments so that the firm can keep the funds invested or in the bank as long as possible. Expediting collections and slowing disbursements help increase a firm's cash balance and provide it with funds to use for other profitable investments. Policies designed to control collections and disbursements take advantage of the *float* present in the payment and disbursement system.

Float

A firm's cash balance as shown on the bank's books generally differs from that shown on the firm's own books. This difference is known as **float** and represents the net effect of the delays in the payment of checks a firm writes and the collection of checks a firm receives. Checks written by a firm result in *disbursement,* or *positive,* float; that is, an excess of bank net collected balances over the balances shown on a firm's books. In contrast, *collection float,* or *negative,* float arises from the delay between the time a customer writes a check to a supplier or other payee and the time the payee actually receives these funds as collected balances (which are spendable). Action being taken by the Federal Reserve System and the rapid progress being made with electronic payment systems means that float will be less important over time. However, until these developments virtually eliminate float, financial managers must understand the sources of float so that they can take legal actions to benefit from it.

There are three primary components, or sources, of float:

1. *Mail float* is the delay between the time a payment is sent to the payee through the mail and the time that payment arrives at the payee's office.

2. *Processing float* represents the delay between receipt of payment from a payer and the deposit of that receipt in the payee's account.
3. *Check-clearing float* is the delay between the time a check is deposited in the payee's account and the time the funds are available to be spent. Checks processed through the Federal Reserve System are "cleared" in 2 days or less, although the depositor's bank may not make the funds available quite that fast.

Expediting Collections

Figure 16-3 illustrates the main steps in the cash collection process. The total time involved in this process is a combination of mailing (float) time, company processing (float) time, and check-clearing (float) time, each of which may vary depending on where the firm's customers and their respective banks are located.[4] Some methods available for reducing the collection float are discussed in the following paragraphs.

Decentralized Collection Centers and Concentration Banks. Cash collection systems can be either *centralized* or *decentralized*. In the centralized system, customers are instructed to send their payments to the firm's headquarters. In the *decentralized* system, customers mail their payments to a nearby collection center, which is strategically located to minimize mail delay. The collection center then deposits the checks in a local bank and reports this information to the firm's headquarters. Because most of the checks are drawn on banks located in the same geographical area as the collection center, check-clearing float is reduced. Each business day, funds in excess of the amount necessary to compensate the local bank for its services are transferred to an account in a **concentration bank,** where the firm maintains a disbursement account upon which checks are written.

A trade-off exists between the number of collection centers and the potential savings realized. The more collection centers used, the less time is required to convert customers' checks into collected balances. However, these savings from faster collections are offset by the direct fees involved, the opportunity costs of the compensating balances the firm must maintain at each local bank, or both.

FIGURE 16-3
Cash Collection Process

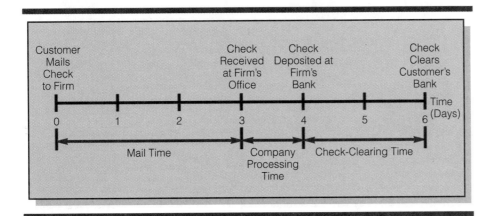

[4]The particular times shown in Figure 16-3 are merely illustrative. Actual times will vary. (This is also true for Figure 16-5.)

Financial managers must weigh the trade-offs involved in both savings and costs in deciding on the appropriate number and location of collection centers.

Lockboxes. Figure 16-4 illustrates a lockbox collection system. A **lockbox** is a post office box maintained by a local bank for the purpose of receiving a firm's remittances. Customers mail payments to this post office box, which is usually no more than a few hundred miles away.[5] The bank empties the box several times each working day, deposits the payments in the firm's account, puts the checks into the clearing system, and sends the firm a list of the payments received each day. Not only does the lockbox reduce mailing time, it also eliminates company processing time, because the checks are deposited and begin the clearing process *before* the company's accounting department processes the payments received, rather than after processing them. The bank normally charges a fee for this service, requires a compensating balance, or both. Funds in excess of the bank's compensating balance requirement are transferred each day to a master collection account in a concentration bank.

The decision to establish a lockbox collection system requires a comparison of the associated benefits and costs. If the earnings on the funds released by the acceleration of collections exceed the forgone returns on the required compensating balances, the service fees charged by the lockbox bank, or both, the establishment of a lockbox collection system is profitable.

If the number of checks handled is small and the dollar amount of each check is large, a lockbox arrangement is very beneficial to the firm. Under these conditions the bank's workload is light, and the associated service fees, compensating balances, or both, are small. However, when large numbers of checks with

FIGURE 16-4
Lockbox Collection System

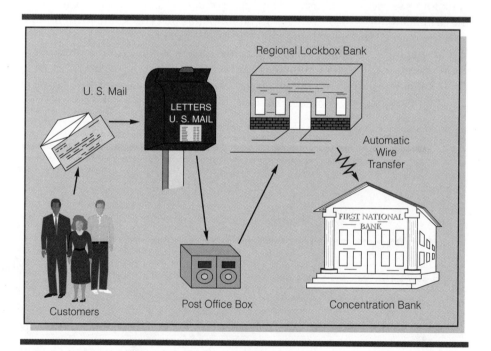

[5]Determining the optimal location of lockboxes is a complex problem. For some solutions, see Ferdinand K. Levy, "An Application of Heuristic Problem Solving to Accounts Receivable Management," *Management Science* 12 (February 1966): B-236–B-244; and Robert M. Nauss and Robert E. Markland, "Solving Lock Box Location Problems," *Financial Management* (Spring 1979): 21–31.

small dollar amounts are involved—for example, in the case of oil company credit cards—a lockbox system may not be profitable. Under these conditions, the opportunity costs on the required compensating balances, the service fees, or both may exceed the earnings the firm realizes from having the funds available a few days earlier.

The lockbox decision can be illustrated with the following example. Suppose that the Transamerica Occidental Life Insurance Company (a subsidiary of Transamerica Corporation), located in Los Angeles, currently receives and processes all customer payments at its corporate headquarters (that is, a *centralized* system). The firm is considering establishing a bank lockbox collection system for seven southeastern states—Florida, North Carolina, South Carolina, Tennessee, Alabama, Georgia, and Mississippi—that would be located in Atlanta. The lockbox would reduce average mailing time for customer payments from 3 days to 1½ days, check-processing time from 2 days to 1 day, and clearing time from 3 days to 1½ days.

Annual collections from the southeastern region are $91.25 million, and the average number of payments received total 550 per day (assume 365 days per year). A bank in Atlanta has agreed to process the payments for an annual fee of $15,000 plus $0.10 per payment received. This bank would not require a compensating balance. Assuming an 8 percent opportunity cost for released funds, should Transamerica use the lockbox collection system?

Table 16-2 shows an analysis of this decision. In Step A, the amount of funds released ($1 million) is found by multiplying average daily collections ($250,000) by the reduction in collection time (4 days). The annual (pretax) earnings on the released funds ($80,000) are found in Step B by multiplying the amount of funds released ($1 million) by the opportunity cost of funds (0.08). The annual bank processing fee ($35,075) is computed in Step C as the sum of fixed costs ($15,000) and variable costs ($20,075). Finally, in Step D, the net (pretax) benefits of establishing a lockbox system ($44,925) are computed by deducting the annual bank processing fee ($35,075) from the earnings on the released funds ($80,000). Because the net (pretax) benefits are positive, Transamerica should employ the lockbox collection system.

Wire Transfers and Depository Transfer Checks. Once deposits enter the firm's banking network, the objective is to transfer surplus funds (that is, funds in excess of any required compensating balances) from its local (collection) bank accounts to its concentration (disbursement) bank account or accounts. Two methods used to perform this task are *wire transfers* and *depository transfer checks*.

With a **wire transfer,** funds are sent from a local bank to a concentration bank electronically through the Federal Reserve System or a private bank wire system. Wire transfers are the fastest way of moving funds between banks, because the transfer takes only a few minutes and the funds become *immediately available* (that is, they can be withdrawn) by the firm upon receipt of the wire notice at the concentration bank. Wire transfers eliminate the mailing and check-clearing times associated with other funds-transfer methods. Some firms leave standing instructions with their local (collection) banks to automatically wire surplus funds on a periodic basis (for example, daily, twice a week, and so on) to their concentration bank. Also, some firms specify in their sales contracts that customers must wire their payments on the due dates.

Wire transfer of funds is available to member banks of the Federal Reserve System and to nonmember banks through their correspondent banks. The cost to corporate customers to send a wire transfer at most banks ranges from $10 to

TABLE 16-2
Transamerica Occidental Life Insurance Company's Analysis of the Decision to Establish a Lockbox Collection System for the Southeastern Region

Step A: Reduction in collection time = Reduction in mailing time + Reduction in processing time + Reduction in check-clearing time

$$= (3 - 1.5) + (2 - 1) + (3 - 1.5)$$

$$= 4 \text{ days}$$

Average daily collections = Annual collections ÷ 365

$$= \$91,250,000 \div 365$$

$$= \$250,000$$

Amount of funds released = Average daily collections × Reduction in collection time

$$= \$250,000 \times 4 \text{ days}$$

$$= \$1,000,000$$

Step B: Annual (pretax) earnings on released funds = Amount of funds released × Interest rate

$$= \$1,000,000 \times 0.08$$

$$= \$80,000$$

Step C: Annual bank processing fee = Fixed cost + Number of payments per year × Variable cost per payment

$$= \$15,000 + (550 \times 365) \times \$0.10$$

$$= \$15,000 + \$20,075$$

$$= \$35,075$$

Step D: Net (pretax) benefits = Annual (pretax) earnings on released funds − Annual bank processing fee

$$= \$80,000 - \$35,075$$

$$= \$44,925$$

$25. A similar charge is made to receive and process a domestic wire transfer. For a firm with multiple collection centers that use wire transfers on a daily basis, the annual costs can be substantial. Consequently, this method of transferring funds should be used only when the incremental value of having the funds immediately available exceeds the additional cost, relative to alternatives, such as depository transfer checks.

A **mail depository transfer check** (DTC) is an unsigned, nonnegotiable check drawn on the local collection bank and payable to the concentration bank. As it deposits customer checks in the local bank each day, the collection center mails a depository transfer check to the concentration bank authorizing it to withdraw the deposited funds from the local bank. Upon receipt of the depository transfer check, the firm's account at the concentration bank is credited for the designated amount. Depository transfer checks are processed through the usual check-clearing process. Although the use of depository transfer checks does not eliminate mailing and check-clearing time, it does ensure the movement of funds from the local collection center banks to the concentration bank in a timely manner. Also, the cost of this method of transferring funds is low; often the only cost involved is postage.

An *electronic depository transfer check* (EDTC) can also be used to move funds from a local bank to a concentration bank. The process of transmitting deposit information to a concentration bank is similar to that for mail DTCs just described, except that the information is sent electronically through an automated clearinghouse, such as the Automated Clearing House (ACH) system of the Federal Reserve (Fedwire) or the Clearing House Interbank Payments System (CHIPS). These systems eliminate the mail float in moving funds from the local bank to a concentration bank. Funds transferred through an automated system are available for use by the firm in 1 day (or less).

Special Handling of Large Remittances. Firms that receive individual remittances in the multimillion-dollar range may find it more profitable to use special courier services to pick up these checks from customers (rather than having their customers mail the checks) and present them for collection to the banks upon which they are drawn.

Use of Preauthorized Checks. A **preauthorized check** (PAC) resembles an ordinary check except that it does not require the signature of the person (or firm) on whose account it is being drawn. This system is especially useful for firms that receive a large volume of payments of a fixed amount each period. Insurance companies, savings and loans, charitable institutions, and leasing firms make extensive use of this collection procedure. When preauthorized checks are used, the payer agrees to allow the payee (the firm that is owed the money) to write a check on the payer's account and deposit that check immediately for collection at an agreed-upon time. Preauthorized checks have the advantages of completely eliminating the mail float, reducing billing and collecting expenses, and making the cash flows for both parties highly predictable. Many payers like preauthorized check systems because they do not have to bother to write a check each month.

Slowing Disbursements

Figure 16-5 illustrates the principal steps involved in the cash disbursement process. Several ways in which a firm can slow disbursements and keep funds in the bank for longer periods of time are discussed in the following paragraphs.

Scheduling and Centralizing Payments. A firm should pay bills *on time*—not before or after they are due. Payments made ahead of time lower the firm's

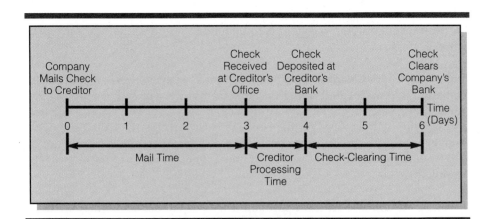

**FIGURE 16-5
Cash Disbursement Process**

average cash balance, whereas late payments can impair the firm's credit rating or fail to qualify for a cash discount.

Centralizing payments from disbursement accounts maintained at a concentration bank helps minimize the amount of idle funds a firm must keep in local field offices and divisional bank accounts. A number of firms have set up *zero-balance* systems to use disbursement float more effectively. In a **zero-balance system,** a *master,* or *concentration, account* is set up to receive all deposits coming into the zero-balance system. As checks clear through the zero-balance accounts on which they are issued, funds are transferred to these accounts from the master account. These disbursement accounts are called *zero-balance accounts* because exactly enough funds are transferred into them daily to cover the checks that have cleared, leaving a zero balance at the end of the day. In general, all disbursements for accounts payable, payroll, and whatever other purposes the firm desires are issued from these zero-balance accounts. For a zero-balance system to operate effectively, a firm must have a well-developed network for reporting deposits and disbursements, as well as a close working relationship with its bank.

Drafts. A **draft** is similar to a check, except that it is not payable on demand. Instead, when a draft is transmitted to a firm's bank for collection, the bank must present the draft to the firm for acceptance before making payment. In practice, individual drafts are considered to be legally paid automatically by the bank on the business day following the day of presentation to the firm, unless the firm returns a draft and explicitly requests that it not be paid. Once the draft has been presented, the firm must immediately deposit the necessary funds to cover the payment.

The use of drafts rather than checks permits a firm to keep smaller balances in its disbursement accounts, because funds do not have to be deposited in them until the drafts are presented for payment. Normally, drafts are more expensive to use than checks. The lower account balances and higher processing costs cause banks to impose service charges on firms using drafts; this cost must be included in the analysis of the benefits and costs of using drafts to pay bills.

Drafts are now used primarily to provide for centralized control over payments authorized in field offices, rather than as a means of slowing disbursements. For example, a claims agent for Nationwide Insurance might issue a draft to provide for quick settlement of an insurance claim. The claims agent does not have the authority to write a check against Nationwide's checking accounts. By issuing a draft, centralized control can be maintained over these disbursements. The Federal Reserve System requires a firm to transfer funds to the bank through which payment is to be made as soon as the drafts are presented to the firm.

Maximizing Check-Clearing Float. Some firms make payments to suppliers from checking accounts located a long distance from the supplier. For example, an East Coast supplier might be paid with checks drawn on a West Coast bank; this increases the time required for the check to clear through the banking system. Some firms maintain an intricate network of disbursing accounts. Checks are issued from the account most distant from the payee, thereby maximizing check-clearing float.

Stretching Payables. Many firms pay their accounts payable before they are due. There is no significant benefit to be received by paying these accounts before they are actually due, unless a cash discount is offered for early payment.[6] For example, if Campbell Soup Company makes payments on its accounts payable averaging $10 million per day, and if Campbell found that it made these payments an average of 3 days early, Campbell could gain substantial benefits by slowing its disbursements by 3 days. This would result in an increase in available cash balances of $30 million, which could be invested by Campbell. In making the decision to put a more efficient cash disbursement system in place, Campbell's financial managers would compare the return that can be earned on the $30 million of released funds against the costs of implementing the system.

ELECTRONIC FUNDS TRANSFER[7]

The previous discussion of methods to speed up collections and slow disbursements assumes that virtually all transactions involve the transfer of paper (checks) between the payer and the payee. These methods to control collections and disbursements are designed to reduce the float involved in financial transactions. In a sense, the total float in the financial system can be viewed as a measure of inefficiency in the financial system. In an idealized world, the total float would be reduced to zero. Payments would be made and received as usable funds instantaneously. Although the financial system has a long way to go before this ideal is realized, in recent years, tremendous progress has been made.

Many consumers now have automatic teller cards that give them access to cash 24 hours a day, 7 days a week. In addition, banking customers can use automatic tellers to transfer funds between accounts. Special credit cards, called "debit cards," are used by some consumers. When a debit card is used, funds are transferred from the consumer's bank account electronically to the account of the retailer. The retailer no longer must be concerned whether a check will be good when it is deposited. Increasingly, small and large businesses are using microcomputer links to manipulate funds between interest-bearing accounts and non-interest-bearing disbursement accounts.

Large payments can be made by wire transfers or through an *automated clearinghouse.* Automated clearinghouse (ACH) systems are computer-based alternatives to the paper-check collection and clearing system. The ACH sorts checklike electronic images and exchanges electronic records of payment and receipt. Although acceptance of electronic checking initially was slow, growth has increased dramatically in recent years. Electronic funds transfer systems account for less than 1 percent of the number of all payments in the U.S., but they account for more than 80 percent of the value of payments.

EFT mechanisms are profoundly changing the nature of the cash management function. Although paper checks, with their associated mail and processing float, will not disappear completely for some time (if ever), as increased volumes of payments are made electronically, the importance of developing elaborate mechanisms to manage float will be reduced greatly. Increased reliance on EFT as the mechanism for payment will free up some of the cash invested in accounts receivable for more productive uses in a firm. Contemporary financial managers

---

[6]The cost of not taking cash discounts is discussed in Chapter 18.
[7]This section is based, in part, on Bernell K. Stone, "Electronic Payment Basics," *Economic Review* (March 1986): 9–18; "The Automated Clearinghouse: How Do We Get There From Here," *Economic Review* (April 1986): entire issue; and George R. Juncker, Bruce J. Summers, and Florence M. Young, "A Primer on the Settlement of Payments in the United States," *Federal Reserve Bulletin* (November 1991): 847–858.

will be challenged in the years ahead to stay current with a fast-changing, high technology system of receiving payments and making disbursements.

ETHICAL ISSUES
CASH MANAGEMENT

Financial managers are confronted with legal and ethical issues as they make cash collection and disbursement decisions. For example, a large firm, such as General Motors (GM) might be tempted to systematically be a few days late in making payments to a small supplier. GM managers may be confident that the small firm will not risk damaging its supply relationship with GM over payment delays of a few days.

Similarly, a cash manager may take advantage of weak control mechanisms in its banks and make short-term investments using uncollected funds. E. F. Hutton's managers got into a lot of trouble with this type of activity. In 1985, E. F. Hutton & Company, a large securities brokerage firm, pleaded guilty to federal fraud charges involving the operation of a massive check-writing scheme to obtain money from many of its 400 banks without paying interest. The firm pleaded guilty to 2,000 counts of mail and wire fraud and agreed to pay more than $10 million in criminal fines and restitution to the banks. According to the Justice Department, Hutton systematically overdrew hundreds of its own accounts in banks throughout the country and intentionally moved money between banks to artificially delay the collection of funds. The scheme involved checks totaling more than $4 billion. By doing this, Hutton was able to use as much as $250 million in interest-free money on some days.

According to Justice Department documents, Hutton officials frequently misused bank accounts of its branches by writing checks for amounts in excess of the volume of customer funds deposited in these accounts. Hutton also pleaded guilty to extending the float time during which checks are cleared by setting up a chain of transfers between branch accounts. These transactions, according to the Justice Department, resembled a check-kiting scheme and were carried out illegally without the prior agreement or consent of the banks involved. Indeed, the banks generally did not realize they were victims until they were told by officials from the government.

A good financial manager should be mindful of the legal and ethical effects of the firm's actions. Legal violations can result in costly fines, embarrassment, and, in some cases, prison terms. Violations of business contracts and the trust built in business transactions may be very costly to a firm's reputation and its future business relationships. In the Hutton case, not only were key employees prosecuted, but also the firm's reputation was so damaged that it was forced to combine with another investment bank to avert failure.

ENTREPRENEURIAL FINANCE ISSUES
CASH MANAGEMENT

Following efficient cash management policies is important for all firms, government agencies, and not-for-profit enterprises. However, effective cash management is particularly important for entrepreneurial firms for several reasons. First, entrepreneurial businesses do not have the same, extensive access to the capital markets as do larger firms. A major source of capital funds to small firms is commercial banks. However, bankers require borrowers to present detailed analyses of their anticipated cash needs. To do this, a firm must have efficient cash management procedures in place. Second, because of an entrepreneurial firm's limited access to capital, a cash shortage problem is both more difficult and more costly for an entrepreneurial firm to rectify than for a large firm. Third, because many entrepreneurial firms are growing rapidly, they have a tendency to run out of cash. Growing sales require increases in inventories and accounts receivable, thereby using up cash resources. This problem is illustrated in the Financial Challenge at the start of Chapter 15. Finally, entrepreneurial firms frequently operate with only a bare minimum of cash resources because of the high cost of, and limited access to, capital. As a result, it is imperative that financial managers of entrepreneurial firms use their firm's scarce cash resources in the most efficient way possible.

 ## INVESTING IN MARKETABLE SECURITIES

Rather than let their cash reserves build up in excess of daily cash requirements, many firms invest in interest-bearing short-term marketable securities. Determining the level of liquid assets that should be invested in marketable securities depends on several factors, including:

- The interest to be earned over the expected holding period.
- The transaction costs involved in buying and selling the securities.
- The variability of the firm's cash flows.

Various quantitative models have been developed for determining the optimal division of a firm's liquid asset balance between cash and marketable securities.[8] These models vary in complexity, depending partly on the assumptions made about the firm's cash flows. The simpler *deterministic* models assume that cash payments occur at a *uniform certain rate* over time. The more complex *probabilistic* or *stochastic* models assume that cash balances fluctuate from day to day in a *random* or unpredictable manner. Although these models provide the financial manager with useful insights into the cost trade-offs involved in effective cash management, they have not been widely implemented in actual decision-making situations.

Choosing Marketable Securities

A firm may choose among many different types of securities when deciding where to invest excess cash reserves. In determining which securities to include in its portfolio, the firm should consider a number of criteria, including the following:[9]

---

[8]Inventory models were first applied to cash management by William J. Baumol in "The Transactions Demand for Cash: An Inventory Theoretic Approach," *Quarterly Journal of Economics* 66 (November 1952): 545–556. See Terry S. Maness and John T. Zietlow, *Short-Term Financial Management* (St. Paul: West Publishing Co., 1993), Chapter 15, for a discussion of the cash and marketable securities allocation decision.

[9]Another criterion is *tax considerations*. Interest received by corporations on municipal securities is exempt from federal (and some state) income taxes. Likewise, a large proportion (70 percent) of intercompany dividends is exempt from federal income taxes. Thus, when comparing yields (or rates of return) on alternative marketable securities, it is important that this be done on an after-tax basis.

- Default risk.
- Marketability.
- Maturity date.
- Rate of return.

Notice that the first three criteria deal with risk and the last one deals with return.

Default Risk. Most firms invest only in marketable securities that have little or no **default risk** (the risk that a borrower will fail to make interest and/or principal payments on a loan). U.S. Treasury securities have the lowest default risk, followed by securities of other U.S. government agencies and, finally, by corporate and municipal securities. Various financial reporting agencies, including Moody's Investors Service and Standard and Poor's, compile and publish information concerning the safety ratings of the various corporate and municipal securities. Given the positive relationship between a security's expected return and risk and the desire to select marketable securities having minimal default risk, a firm has to be willing to accept relatively low expected yields on its marketable securities investments.

Marketability. A firm usually buys marketable securities that can be sold on short notice without a significant price concession. Thus, there are two dimensions to a security's marketability: the time required to sell the security and the price realized from the sale relative to the last quoted price. If a long period of time, a high transaction cost, or a significant price concession is required to dispose of a security, the security has poor marketability and generally is not considered suitable for inclusion in a marketable securities portfolio. Naturally, a trade-off is involved here between risk and return. Generally, a highly marketable security has a small degree of risk that the investor will incur a loss, and consequently, it usually has a lower expected yield than one with limited marketability.

Maturity Date. Firms usually limit their marketable securities purchases to issues that have relatively short maturities. Recall that prices of debt securities decrease when interest rates rise and increase when interest rates fall. For a given change in interest rates, prices of long-term securities fluctuate more widely than prices of short-term securities with equal default risk. Thus, an investor who holds long-term securities is exposed to a greater risk of loss if the securities have to be sold prior to maturity. This is known as *interest rate risk.*[10] For this reason, most firms generally do not buy marketable securities that have more than 180 to 270 days remaining until maturity, and many firms restrict most of their temporary investments to those maturing in less than 90 days. Because the yields on securities with short maturities are often lower than the yields on securities with longer maturities, a firm has to be willing to sacrifice yield to avoid interest rate risk.

Rate of Return. Although the rate of return, or yield, also is given consideration in selecting securities for inclusion in a firm's portfolio, it is less important than the other three criteria just described. The desire to invest in securities that have minimum default and interest rate risk and that are readily marketable usually limits the selection to those having relatively low yields.

[10]Interest rate risk is discussed in Chapter 6.

Types of Marketable Securities

Firms normally confine their marketable securities investments to "money market" instruments; that is, those high-grade (low default risk), short-term debt instruments having original maturities of one year or less. Money market instruments that are suitable for inclusion in a firm's marketable securities portfolio include U.S. Treasury issues, other federal agency issues, municipal securities, negotiable certificates of deposit, commercial paper, repurchase agreements, bankers' acceptances, Eurodollar deposits, auction rate preferred stocks, money market mutual funds, and bank money market accounts. (In some cases, firms will also use long-term bonds having one year or less remaining to maturity as "marketable" securities and treat them as money market instruments.)

Table 16-3 lists the characteristics and yields of various money market instruments. As can be seen in the last three columns of the table, yields on these securities vary considerably over time. Yields are a function of a number of factors, including the state of the economy, the rate of inflation, and government monetary and fiscal policies.

U.S. Treasury Issues. U.S. Treasury bills are the most popular marketable securities. They are sold at weekly auctions through Federal Reserve Banks and their branches and have standard maturities of 91 days, 182 days, and one year. Treasury bills are issued at a discount and then redeemed for the full face amount at maturity. Once they are issued, Treasury bills can be bought and sold in the secondary markets through approximately 40 government securities dealers. There is a large and active market for Treasury bills, which means that a firm can easily dispose of them when it needs cash. The smallest denomination of Treasury bills is $10,000 of maturity value.

The advantages of Treasury issues include short maturities, a virtually default-free status, and ready marketability. Their primary disadvantage lies in the fact that their yields normally are the lowest of any marketable security.

The Treasury also issues notes that have original maturities from 2 to 10 years and bonds that have maturities over 10 years. As these securities approach their maturity dates, they become, in effect, short-term instruments that are then suitable for inclusion in a firm's marketable securities portfolio. Treasury bonds and notes pay interest semiannually. Minimum Treasury bond denominations are $1,000.

Other Federal Agency Issues. A number of federal government-sponsored agencies issue their own securities, including the "big five": the Federal Home Loan Bank, the Federal Land Banks, the Federal Intermediate Credit Bank, the Bank for Cooperatives, and the Federal National Mortgage Association. Although each of these agencies guarantees its own securities, they do not constitute a legal obligation on the part of the U.S. government. Nevertheless, most investors consider them to be very low risk securities, and they sell at yields slightly above U.S. Treasury securities but below other money market instruments. Because these securities are traded in the secondary markets through the same dealers who handle U.S. Treasury securities, they are readily marketable should a firm need to dispose of them before maturity. Minimum denominations generally are $5,000.

Municipal Securities. State and local governments and their agencies issue various types of interest-bearing securities. Short-term issues are suitable for

TABLE 16-3
Characteristics and Yields of Selected Money Market Instruments

*Source: Federal Reserve Bulletin, Table 1.35, various issues.

INSTRUMENT	DENOMINATIONS	MATURITIES	MARKETABILITY	YIELDS* (%) Aug. 1981	Oct. 1993	Dec. 1996
U.S. Treasury bills	Various denominations from $10,000 to $1,000,000	91 days, 182 days, 52 weeks	Highly organized secondary market	(3 months) 15.51 (6 months) 15.52 (1 year) 14.70	3.04 3.13 3.25	4.91 5.04 5.18
Federal agency issues	Various denominations from $5,000 to $1,000,000	Wide variation in maturities, from several days to more than 10 years	Well-established secondary market for short-term securities of "big five" agencies	—		
Short-term municipal securities	$5,000 to $5,000,000	1 month to 1 year	Not as good as U.S. Treasury and federal agency issues	—		
Negotiable certificates of deposit	$100,000 to $1,000,000	7 days to 18 months or more	Fairly good secondary market	(1 month) 17.91 (3 months) 17.96 (6 months) 17.98	3.09 3.24 3.25	5.50 5.44 5.47
Commercial paper	$100,000 or more	2 or 3 days to 270 days	Weak secondary market	(1 month) 17.58 (3 months) 17.23 (6 months) 16.62	3.14 3.26 3.27	5.70 5.51 5.44
Repurchase agreements	Varying amounts; no standard denominations	1 day to several months	Limited, but borrower agrees to repurchase securities at a fixed price on a fixed date			
Bankers' acceptances	Varying amounts, depending on the size of commercial transaction	30 to 180 days	Good, although less extensive than for most other instruments	(3 months) 17.22 (6 months) 16.56	3.19 3.19	5.35 5.33
Eurodollar deposits	$1,000,000	1 day to 6 months (or more)	Developing a secondary market	(3 months) 18.79	3.26	5.43
Auction rate preferred stock	$100,000 to $500,000 depending on issue	—	Saleable at auction every 49 days	—		
Money market mutual funds	Minimum of $1,000 is usually required; no standard denominations	Redeemable at any time	Good, because the fund agrees to redeem shares at any time	Yields vary from fund to fund, but usually exceed the yield available on Treasury bills		
Bank money market accounts	Minimum of $2,500 required	Normally redeemable at any time (by law, banks reserve the right to require 7 days' written notice for withdrawals)	Excellent, but not available to all business firms	Yields vary significantly from bank to bank, but usually are below Treasury bill yields		

inclusion in a firm's marketable securities portfolio. The yields on these securities vary with the creditworthiness of the issuer. The pretax yields on these securities generally are lower than the yields on Treasury bills because the interest is exempt from federal (and some state) income taxes. The secondary market for municipal issues is not as strong as that for Treasury and other federal agency issues. Municipal (tax-exempt) money market mutual funds also are available.

Negotiable Certificates of Deposit. Commercial banks are permitted to issue certificates of deposit (CDs), which entitle the holder to receive the amount deposited plus accrued interest on a specified date. At the time of issue, maturities on these instruments range from 7 days to 18 months or more. Once issued, CDs become *negotiable,* meaning they can be bought and sold in the secondary markets. Because CDs of the largest banks are handled by government securities dealers, they are readily marketable and thus are suitable for inclusion in a firm's marketable securities portfolio. Yields on CDs generally are above the rates on federal agency issues having similar maturities.

Commercial Paper. Commercial paper consists of short-term unsecured promissory notes issued by large, well-known corporations and finance companies. Some finance companies, such as General Motors Acceptance Corporation (GMAC) and C.I.T. Financial Corporation, which issue large amounts of commercial paper regularly, sell it directly to investors. Industrial, utility, and transportation firms and smaller finance companies, which issue commercial paper less frequently and in smaller amounts, sell their commercial paper through commercial paper dealers. Maturities on commercial paper at the time of issue range from 2 or 3 days to 270 days.

The secondary market for commercial paper is weak, although it sometimes is possible to make arrangements with the issuer or commercial paper dealer to repurchase the security prior to maturity. This weak secondary market combined with a somewhat higher default risk results in higher yields on commercial paper than on most other money market instruments.

Repurchase Agreements. A repurchase agreement, or "repo," is an arrangement with a bank or securities dealer in which the investor acquires certain short-term securities subject to a commitment from the bank or dealer to repurchase the securities on a specified date. Securities used in this agreement can be government securities, CDs, or commercial paper. Their maturities tend to be relatively short, ranging from 1 day to several months, and are designed to meet the needs of the investor.

The yield on a repo is slightly less than the rate that can be obtained from outright purchase of the underlying security. The repo rate approximates the rate on federal funds, which is the rate used when banks borrow from other banks. Although repos generally are considered very safe investments, a number of investors did incur losses when several small government securities dealers (which were active in the repo market) failed.

Bankers' Acceptances. A bankers' acceptance is a short-term debt instrument issued by a firm as part of a commercial transaction. Payment is guaranteed by a commercial bank. Bankers' acceptances are commonly used financial instruments in international trade, as well as in certain lines of domestic trade.

These instruments vary in amount, depending on the size of the commercial transactions. A secondary market exists in which these acceptances can be traded should a bank or investor choose not to hold them until maturity, which usually ranges between 30 and 180 days at the time of issue. Bankers' acceptances are relatively safe investments, because both the bank and the borrower are liable for the amount due at maturity. Their yields are comparable to the rates available on CDs.

Eurodollar Deposits. Eurodollar deposits are dollar-denominated deposits in banks or bank branches located outside the United States. These deposits usually have slightly higher yields than on corresponding deposits in domestic banks because of the additional risks. Eurodollar CDs issued by London banks are negotiable, and a secondary market is developing for them.

Auction Rate Preferred Stocks. A number of large investment banks issue, on behalf of their client companies, a type of preferred stock known as **auction rate preferred stock,** which is a suitable short-term investment for excess corporate funds. The dividend yield on this type of security is adjusted every 49 days through an auction process, where investors can exchange their stock for cash. As a result, the price of the stock stays near par. Because 70 percent of the dividends received are exempt from corporate income taxes, the after-tax yields often are above the yields on other marketable securities such as CDs or commercial paper. The stock is sold in minimum denominations of $100,000 to $500,000, depending on the issue.

Money Market Mutual Funds. Many of the higher-yielding marketable securities described earlier are available only in relatively large denominations. For example, negotiable CDs usually come in amounts of $100,000 or more. As a result, a smaller firm that has limited funds to invest at any given time is often unable to obtain the higher yields offered on these securities. An alternative is a *money market mutual fund* that pools the investments of many other small investors and invests in large-denomination money market instruments. By purchasing shares in a money market fund, such as Dreyfus Liquid Assets or Merrill Lynch Ready Assets, a smaller firm can approach the higher yields offered on large-denomination securities. In addition, most of these funds offer check-writing privileges, which provides liquidity and enables firms to earn interest on invested funds until their checks clear.

Bank Money Market Accounts. Banks are permitted to offer checking accounts with yields comparable to those on money market mutual accounts with limited check-writing privileges. These accounts provide yields that are comparable to those on money market mutual funds.

Contingency Analysis maintains a nice glossary that defines and then discusses such financial terms as repos, reverse repos, liquidity, payment netting, reinvestment risk, and much more. It's a handy reference source.
http://www.contingencyanalysis.com

INTERNATIONAL ISSUES
Cash Management

The goals of cash management in a multinational company (MNC) parallel the cash management goals of purely domestic corporations. That is, MNCs attempt to speed up collections, slow disbursements, and make the most efficient use of the firm's cash resources by minimizing excess balances and investing balances to earn the highest possible return, consistent with liquidity and safety constraints. However, there are some unique elements of cash management for an MNC.

First, cash management is complicated by difficulties and costs associated with moving funds from one country (and currency) to another. It is costly to convert cash from one currency to another. Second, there is a general lack of integrated international cash transfer facilities, such as exist in the United States and most other Western nations. The absence of this capability makes it difficult to move funds quickly from one country to another. Third, investment opportunities for temporary excess cash balances are much broader for an MNC than for a domestic firm. MNCs must consider short-term investment options in many different countries—a process further complicated by exchange rate risk. Fourth, the host government may place restrictions on the movement of cash out of the country.

Practicing MNC cash managers have developed a number of techniques designed to optimize the process of international cash management in the face of these difficulties. First, there is general agreement that the cash management function for an MNC should be centralized with respect to the information-gathering and decision-making process. The parent normally maintains an international cash manager who has the expertise and responsibility to keep track of the firm's cash balances around the world and to identify the best sources for short-term borrowing and lending.

Second, many MNCs have instituted a process called multilateral netting. **Multilateral netting** is designed to minimize the cost associated with misdirected funds. **Misdirected funds** are funds that cross an international border unnecessarily. It is costly to convert funds from one currency to another, hence it is desirable to minimize unnecessary transactions. For example, consider an MNC that has subsidiaries operating in Spain, Germany, and Italy. Each subsidiary purchases supplies from the other subsidiaries. If the German unit purchases $10 million from the unit in Spain, and the Spanish unit purchases $8 million from the German unit, the transaction cost associated with transferring funds from the German unit to the Spanish unit can be reduced if these payments are *netted out* against each other. Thus, instead of the German unit converting $10 million in funds to send to the Spanish unit, it will net out the Spanish unit's purchases from the German unit and simply send a $2 million payment. The greater the number of subsidiaries an MNC has, the more complex is the process of managing a multilateral netting system. At the same time, the potential cost savings are greatly increased.

■ SUMMARY

■ A firm holds liquid asset balances for the following primary reasons:
1. To conduct transactions.
2. For precautionary purposes.
3. To meet future requirements.
4. For speculative reasons.
5. To compensate its bank or banks for various services rendered.
■ To manage cash effectively, a firm must first develop a *cash budget* showing all of the forecasted cash inflows and outflows over the planning horizon.

■ A firm's optimal liquid asset balance reflects risk and return trade-offs and depends on both the opportunity cost of holding excess balances and the "shortage" costs associated with not having enough needed cash available.

■ The primary objective in controlling cash collections is to reduce the delay between the time when the customer mails the payment and when it becomes a collected balance. Methods for reducing collection time include decentralized collection centers and concentration banks, lockboxes, wire transfers, depository transfer checks, special handling of large remittances, and the use of preauthorized checks.

■ The primary objective in controlling cash disbursements is to slow payments and keep the firm's funds in the bank as long as possible. Techniques for slowing disbursements include scheduling and centralizing payments (zero-balance systems), using drafts rather than checks, maximizing check-clearing float, and stretching payables.

■ Electronic funds transfer mechanisms, including the use of wire transfers and automated check clearinghouses, increasingly will reduce the importance of float management techniques.

■ The primary criteria a firm should use in selecting *marketable securities* include *default risk, marketability* (or *liquidity*), *maturity date,* and *rate of return.*

■ QUESTIONS AND TOPICS FOR DISCUSSION

1. Define the following terms:
   a. Demand deposits.
   b. Compensating balance.
   c. Disbursement float.
   d. Deposit float.
   e. Lockbox.
   f. Wire transfer.
   g. Depository transfer check.
   h. Zero-balance system.
   i. Draft.
   j. Automated clearinghouse.
2. What are the primary reasons a firm holds a liquid asset balance?
3. Describe the cost trade-offs associated with maintaining the following:
   a. Excessive liquid asset balances.
   b. Inadequate liquid asset balances.
4. Define *float* and describe the difference between *disbursement* float and *deposit* float.
5. Describe the primary services a bank provides to a firm. How is the bank compensated for these services?
6. Describe the methods available to a firm for expediting the collection of cash.
7. Describe the techniques available to a firm for slowing disbursements.
8. Explain the trade-offs involved in determining the number of collection centers that a firm should use.
9. What factors should the firm consider in deciding whether to establish a lockbox collection system?
10. What are the primary criteria in selecting marketable securities for inclusion in a firm's portfolio?
11. What types of marketable securities are most suitable for inclusion in a firm's portfolio? What characteristics of these securities make them desirable investments for temporarily idle cash balances?
12. What is multilateral netting? Give an example of how this would work for a multinational firm.

13. What measures can the board of directors of a corporation take to discourage unethical (and illegal) behavior, such as the mail and wire fraud by E. F. Hutton managers described in the chapter?

■ SELF-TEST PROBLEMS

Note: **When converting from annual data to daily data or vice versa, assume there are 365 days per year.**

ST1. The White Oak Company's annual sales are $219 million. An average of 9 days elapses between when a customer mails its payment and when the funds become usable by the firm.

a. If the company could speed up the collection of funds by 2 days, what would be the increase in the firm's average cash balance?

b. Assuming that these additional funds can be invested in marketable securities that yield 7 percent per year, determine the increase in White Oak's annual (pretax) earnings.

ST2. Builders Circle, a hardware and building supplies company, processes all its customer credit card payments at its Atlanta headquarters. A Boston bank has offered to process the payments from Builders Circle customers located in the New England region for $50,000 per year plus $0.20 per payment. No compensating balance will be required. Under this lockbox arrangement, the average mailing time for payments would be reduced from 3 days to 1.5 days. Check processing and clearing time would be reduced from 5 days to 2. Annual collections from the New England region are $292 million. The total number of payments received annually is 600,000 (an average of 50,000 credit cardholders × 12 payments per year). Assume that any funds released by this lockbox arrangement can be invested by Builders Circle to earn 10 percent per year before taxes. The establishment of a lockbox system for the New England region will reduce payment processing costs at its Atlanta headquarters by $40,000 per year. Using this information, determine

a. The amount of funds released by this lockbox arrangement.

b. The annual (pretax) earnings on the released funds.

c. The annual fee that Builders Circle must pay the Boston bank for processing the payments.

d. The annual *net* (pretax) benefits Builders Circle will receive by establishing this lockbox arrangement with the Boston bank.

■ PROBLEMS*

Note: **When converting annual data to daily data or vice versa in these problems, assume there are 365 days per year.**

1. Dexter Instrument Company's sales average $3 million per day.

a. If Dexter could reduce the time between customers' mailing their payments and the funds' becoming collected balances by 2.5 days, what would be the increase in the firm's average cash balance?

b. Assuming that these additional funds can be invested in marketable securities to yield 8.5 percent per annum, determine the annual increase in Dexter's (pretax) earnings.

2. Exman Company performed a study of its billing and collection procedures and found that an average of 8 days elapses between the time when a customer's payment is received and when the funds become usable by the firm. The firm's *annual* sales are $540 million.

a. Assuming that Exman could reduce the time required to process customer payments by 1.5 days, determine the increase in the firm's average cash balance.

*Colored numbers denote problems that have check answers provided at the end of the book.

b. Assuming that these additional funds could be used to reduce the firm's outstanding bank loans (current interest rate is 8 percent) by an equivalent amount, determine the annual pretax savings in interest expenses.

3. Great Lakes Oil Company currently processes all its credit card payments at its domestic headquarters in Chicago. The firm is considering establishing a lockbox arrangement with a Los Angeles bank to process its payments from ten western states (California, Nevada, Arizona, Utah, Oregon, Washington, Montana, Wyoming, Colorado, and Idaho). Under the arrangement, the average mailing time for customer payments from the western region would be reduced from 3 days to 1.5 days, whereas check processing and clearing time would be reduced from 6 days to 2.5 days. Annual collections from the western region are $180 million. The total number of payments received annually is 4.8 million (an average of 400,000 credit card customers × 12 payments per year). The Los Angeles bank will process the payments for an annual fee of $75,000 plus $0.05 per payment. No compensating balance will be required. Assume that the funds released by the lockbox arrangement can be invested elsewhere in the firm to yield 10 percent before taxes. The establishment of a lockbox system for the western region will reduce payment-processing costs at the Chicago office by $50,000 per year. Using this information, determine the following:

a. The amount of funds released by the lockbox arrangement.
b. The annual (pretax) earnings on the released funds.
c. The annual fee Great Lakes Oil must pay to the Los Angeles bank for processing the payments.
d. The annual *net* (pretax) benefits Great Lakes Oil will receive by establishing this lockbox arrangement with the Los Angeles bank.

Great Lakes Oil also has received a proposal from a Salt Lake City bank to set up a lockbox system for the firm. Average mailing time for checks in the western region would be reduced to 2 days under the proposal from the Salt Lake City bank, and check processing and clearing time would average 2.5 days. The Salt Lake City bank would not charge any fees for processing the payments, but it would require Great Lakes Oil to maintain a $1.5 million average compensating balance with the bank—funds that normally would be invested elsewhere in the firm (yielding 10 percent) and not kept in a non-interest-bearing checking account.

e. Determine the annual *net* (pretax) benefits to Great Lakes Oil of establishing a lockbox system with the Salt Lake City bank.
f. Which of the two lockbox systems (if any) should the firm select?

4. Japanese Motors, a major importer of foreign automobiles, has a subsidiary (Japanese Motor Credit Company, or JMCC) that finances dealer inventories, as well as retail installment purchases of the company's cars. With respect to the financing of retail purchases, JMCC currently employs a centralized billing and collection system. Once a customer's credit has been approved at one of the subsidiary's 50 local branch offices, the information is forwarded to JMCC headquarters (located in Los Angeles), and the customer is issued a book of payment coupons. Each month during the life of the installment contract, the customer mails a coupon stub along with the payment to the Los Angeles office. The average mailing, processing, and check-clearing time with the present collection system is 8 days.

In an effort to reduce this collection time, JMCC is considering establishing a decentralized collection system. Under this system, customers would be instructed to mail their payments to the nearest local branch office, which would then deposit the checks in a local bank and report this information to JMCC headquarters in Los Angeles. As the checks clear in the local banks, funds would be sent each day to JMCC's central bank in Los Angeles. This decentralized collection system would reduce both mailing time and check-clearing time and reduce the average collection time to 5 days.

JMCC's annual installment collections are $900 million. Implementation of the decentralized collection system is expected to reduce collection costs at the Los

Angeles headquarters by $100,000 a year compared with the currently employed centralized collection system. However, branch office collection costs are expected to *rise* by $225,000 if the decentralized system is implemented. JMCC's Los Angeles bank currently requires the firm to maintain a $250,000 balance as compensation for depositing customer payments. Compensating balances at the 50 local banks that JMCC would employ with the decentralized collection system are expected to total $500,000. Any funds released under the decentralized collections system would be used to reduce the firm's debt, which currently carries an interest rate of 7.5 percent.

Using this information, determine the annual *net* pretax benefits JMCC would realize by implementing a decentralized collection system.

5. J-Mart, a nationwide department store chain, processes all its credit sales payments at its suburban Detroit headquarters. The firm is considering the implementation of a lockbox collection system with an Atlanta bank to process monthly payments from its southeastern region. Annual credit sales collections from the region are $60 million. The establishment of the lockbox system would reduce mailing, processing, and check-clearing time from 8 days currently to 3.5 days, reduce company processing costs by $25,000 per year, and reduce the compensating balance of its Detroit bank by $200,000. The Atlanta bank would not charge any fee for the lockbox service but would require J-Mart to maintain a $500,000 compensating balance. Funds released by the lockbox arrangement could be invested elsewhere in the firm to earn 15 percent before taxes. Determine the following:
   a. The amount of funds released by the lockbox arrangement.
   b. The annual (pretax) earnings on the released funds.
   c. The annual *net* (pretax) benefits to J-Mart of establishing the lockbox system with the Atlanta bank.
6. Peterson Electronics uses a decentralized collection system whereby customers mail their payments to one of six regional collection centers. The checks are deposited each working day in the collection center's local bank, and a depository transfer check for the amount of the deposit is *mailed* to the firm's concentration bank in New York. An average of 5 days elapse between the time the checks are deposited in the local bank and the time the funds become collected funds (and available for disbursements) at the concentration bank. Peterson is considering using wire transfers instead of depository transfer checks in moving funds from the six collection centers to its concentration bank. Wire transfers would reduce the elapsed time by 3 days. Depository transfer checks cost $0.50 (including postage), and wire transfers cost $10. Assume there are 250 working days per year. Peterson can earn 7 percent before taxes on any funds that are released through more efficient collection techniques. Determine the net (pretax) benefit to Peterson of using wire transfers if annual sales are
   a. $15 million.
   b. $75 million.
   Suppose Peterson is considering using *electronic* depository transfer checks, rather than mail depository transfer checks, to move funds from its six collection centers to its concentration bank. Electronic depository transfer checks would *reduce* collection time by 2 days and would cost $2.50 each. Determine the net (pretax) benefit to Peterson of using electronic depository transfer checks if annual sales are
   c. $15 million.
   d. $75 million.
7. Wisconsin Paper Company is considering establishing a zero-balance system for its payroll account. The firm pays its employees every 2 weeks on Friday (that is, 26 pay periods per year). Currently, the firm deposits the necessary funds in the payroll account on Friday to cover the total amount of the checks written each pay period, which averages $1 million. However, the firm has found that the majority of the checks did not clear the payroll account until the following week. A typical distribution of when the checks clear the payroll account is as follows:

Day	Amount of Funds Clearing Payroll Account
Friday	$ 300,000
Monday	450,000
Tuesday	150,000
Wednesday	100,000
Total	$1,000,000

Assume that the firm can earn 6 percent on any funds released from its payroll account using a zero-balance system.

a. Determine the annual pretax returns the firm would realize from the use of a zero-balance system for its payroll account.

b. What additional information is necessary to make a decision concerning the desirability of establishing such a system?

8. The High-Rise Construction Company, located in Houston, receives large remittances (that is, progress payments) from customers with whom it has contracts. These checks are frequently drawn on New York City banks. If the checks are deposited in High-Rise's Houston bank, the funds will not become collected balances and usable by the firm until 2 *business* days later. In other words, deposits made on Monday become available for use on Wednesday, and deposits made on Friday become available to the firm on the following Tuesday. However, if High-Rise sends an employee to New York with the check and she presents it for payment at the bank upon which it is drawn, the funds will be available immediately (that is, the same day) to the firm. Assuming that High-Rise can earn 6 percent on short-term investments and that the cost of sending an employee to New York to present the check for payment is $350, determine the following:

a. The net (pretax) benefit to the firm of using this special handling procedure for a $1 million check received on the following days:
   i. Monday.
   ii. Friday.
   Why do the answers to Parts i and ii differ?

b. The amount of a check on which the firm just "breaks even" (that is, the net pretax benefit equals zero) using the special handling procedure, assuming that the check is received on the following days:
   i. Monday.
   ii. Friday.

9. Jackson's Thriftway currently processes all of its credit sales at its Seguin, Texas, headquarters. The firm is considering establishing a lockbox arrangement with a Chicago bank to process payments from customers in twelve midwestern states. Average mailing time for customers from this region is currently 4 days. It is expected that the system will reduce this to 2.5 days. Check processing and clearing time would be reduced from 4 days to 1.5 days with the lockbox arrangement. Annual collections from this region are $200 million. The lockbox arrangement would reduce the compensating balance requirement at the firm's Seguin bank by $400,000 and reduce annual payment processing costs at the Seguin office by $25,000. Funds released by the lockbox arrangement can be invested elsewhere in the firm to earn 14 percent before taxes.

a. The Chicago bank has agreed to process Jackson's customer payments for an annual fee of $130,000. Determine the annual net pretax benefits to Jackson's of establishing a lockbox system with the Chicago bank.

b. The Chicago bank has agreed to process Jackson's customer payments "free of charge" if the firm maintains a minimum compensating balance of $2 million in its account at the bank. Determine the annual net pretax benefits to Jackson's of establishing the lockbox system under these conditions.

10. Two banks, First Fidelity Bank and First Union Bank, have offered to process Zack's retail charge card payments. First Fidelity will process the payments for a fee of $0.15

per payment with no compensating balance required. First Union will process the payments "free of charge," provided that Zack's maintains a compensating balance of $3,000,000 at the bank. Zack's averages 125,000 payments per month from its credit cardholders. The company can earn 8 percent before taxes on any available funds.

a. Determine which of the two payment processing proposals Zack's should accept if the objective is to minimize costs.

b. Determine the rate of return (i.e., Zack's opportunity cost of funds) at which the costs of the two proposals would be equal.

c. Determine the number of payments per month at which the costs of the two proposals would be equal, assuming that the processing fees ($0.15) and compensating balances ($3,000,000) remain constant.

11. World Telephone & Telegraph (WTT) is considering the establishment of a zero-balance system for its dividend payment account. The firm pays common stockholders quarterly dividends. Currently, WTT deposits the necessary funds to cover the dividend payments on the day the checks are mailed to shareholders. A typical distribution of when the checks clear the dividend account is as follows:

	Day	Amount of Funds Clearing Dividend Account (in millions of dollars)
Week 1	Friday (checks mailed)	—
	Monday	$ 3
	Tuesday	15
	Wednesday	18
	Thursday	14
	Friday	8
Week 2	Monday	6
	Tuesday	5
	Wednesday	3
	Thursday	1
	Friday	1
	Total	$74

WTT can earn 7.5 percent per annum on any funds released from its dividend payment account using a zero-balance system.

a. Determine the annual pretax returns the firm would earn on the funds released from a zero-balance system.

b. What other considerations need to be examined in making a decision about the desirability of establishing such a system?

12. Tokyo Electric Company (TEC) sells most of its products in the United States through 50 large distributors and retail chains (e.g., Sears, K-Mart, etc.). Currently, TEC's customers mail their payments, which are due monthly, to the company. The company is considering having its customers make payments by wire transfer on the dates payments are due. TEC's financial analysts expect this method of payment would reduce average mailing and check-clearing time by 5 days. Any funds released by this system could be reinvested in the firm to earn 8 percent before taxes. The cost to TEC (including a $15 per payment rebate to customers) would be $30 per payment. Determine the net (pretax) benefits to TEC of using a wire transfer payment system if monthly payments from each customer average:

a. $25,000.

b. $50,000.

13. NationsBank maintains a comprehensive "treasury-management" (i.e., cash-management) service for its clients. Visit its Web site and read about its services. Prepare a one-page memo summarizing their services.

http://www.nationsbank.com/smallbiz/html/treasury.htm

■ SOLUTIONS TO SELF-TEST PROBLEMS

ST1. a. Increase in average cash balance = Average daily sales × Decrease in payment processing time

$$= (\$219,000,000/365) \times 2 = \$1,200,000$$

b. Increase in (pretax) earnings = Increase in average cash balance × Interest rate

$$= \$1,200,000 \times 0.07 = \$84,000$$

ST2. a. Reduction in collection time = Reduction in mailing time + Reduction in processing and clearing time

$$= (3.0 - 1.5) + (5.0 - 2.0) = 4.5 \text{ days}$$

Average daily collections = Annual credit sales/365

$$= \$292,000,000/365 = \$800,000$$

Amount of funds released = Average daily collections × Reduction in collection time

$$= \$800,000 \times 4.5 = \$3,600,000$$

b. Annual (pretax) earnings on released funds = Amount of funds released × Interest rate

$$= \$3,600,000 \times 0.10 = \$360,000$$

c. Annual bank processing fee = Fixed cost + Number of payments per year × Variable cost per payment

$$= \$50,000 + (600,000 \times \$0.20) = \$170,000$$

d. Net (pretax) benefits = Annual (pretax) earnings on released funds + Reduction in firm's payment processing costs − Annual bank processing fee

$$= \$360,000 + \$40,000 - \$170,000 = \$230,000$$

■ GLOSSARY

Auction Rate Preferred Stock A form of preferred stock where the dividend yield is adjusted every 49 days through an auction process and investors can exchange their stock for cash.

Bank Draft An order to pay, similar to a check, except that it is not payable on demand. Instead, a bank draft is payable when the issuing firm accepts it.

Banker's Acceptance A short-term debt instrument issued by a firm as part of a commercial transaction. Payment is guaranteed by a commercial bank.

Commercial Paper Short-term, unsecured promissory notes. Commercial paper generally is issued by large, well-known corporations and finance companies.

Compensating Balance A minimum (absolute or average) balance that a bank requires a customer to keep in its checking account. This balance, which the bank can invest in interest-earning assets, compensates the bank for the services rendered to the customer.

Concentration Banking The use of decentralized collection centers and local banks to collect customer payments. This speeds up a firm's collections.

Default Risk The risk that a borrower will fail to make interest payments, principal payments, or both on a loan.

Depository Transfer Check (DTC) An unsigned nonnegotiable check used to transfer funds from a local collection bank to a concentration bank.

Float The difference between an account balance as shown on the bank's books and as shown on the firm's books. Float represents the net effect of the delays in the payment of checks the firm writes and the collection of checks the firm receives.

Lockbox A post office box maintained by a bank to speed up the collection of payments from customers.

Misdirected Funds Funds that cross an international border unintentionally.

Multilateral Netting A process of international cash management designed to minimize the cost associated with misdirected funds.

Preauthorized Check (PAC) Similar to an ordinary check except that it does not require the signature of the person (or firm) on whose account it is being drawn. PACs are useful for firms that receive a large volume of payments of a fixed amount each period.

Repurchase Agreement An arrangement with a bank or securities dealer in which an investor acquires certain short-term securities subject to a commitment that the securities will be repurchased by the bank or securities dealer on a specified date.

Wire Transfer The process of electronically sending funds from one bank to another through the Federal Reserve System or private bank wire systems.

Zero-balance System A payment system that uses a master disbursing account that services all other disbursing accounts. A zero balance is maintained in all but the master account until payments must be made.

MANAGEMENT OF ACCOUNTS RECEIVABLE AND INVENTORIES

17

KEY CHAPTER CONCEPTS

1. *Accounts receivable management* refers to the decisions a business makes regarding its overall credit and collection policies and the evaluation of individual credit applicants.

2. In formulating an optimal credit policy, a company's finanical managers must analyze the marginal benefits and costs associated with changes in each of the following variables:
   a. Credit standards.
   b. Credit terms.
   c. Collection effort.

3. The evaluation of individual credit applicants consists of the following three principal steps:
   a. Gathering relevant information on the credit applicant.
   b. Analyzing the information obtained to determine the applicant's creditworthiness.
   c. Deciding whether to extend credit to the applicant and, if so, determining the amount of the line of credit.

4. The determination of the optimal level of inventory investment requires that the benefits and costs associated with alternative levels be measured and compared.

5. Inventory-related costs include
   a. Ordering costs.
   b. Carrying costs.
   c. Stockout costs.

6. The use of inventory control models can aid in efficiently managing a company's level of inventory investment.

7. The economic order quantity model permits determination of the quantity of an inventory item that should be ordered to minimize total inventory costs.

CHANGING CREDIT TERMS AT PROCTER & GAMBLE*

Large consumer goods manufacturers, such as Procter & Gamble, frequently extend trade credit to distributors and retailers of their products. The credit terms under which credit is granted include the length of the credit period and the cash discount (if any) given for prompt payment. In the past, Procter & Gamble offered a 2 percent cash discount with the length of the cash discount period varying among different types of products. The cash discount period for orders of health and beauty aids, such as Pert shampoo and Oil of Olay lotion, was 30 days. For paper goods, such as Puff's facial tissues, the cash discount period was 15 days. For soaps, such as Ivory and Zest, and for food and beverage brands, such as Duncan Hines cake mix and Hawaiian Punch, retailers had only 10 days to qualify for the 2 percent discount.

In order to standardize and streamline the way retailers pay for shipments,

Procter & Gamble was planning to eliminate the variations in the cash discount period. In the future, retailers would have 19 days (from the date that the retailer receives the shipment) to pay

and qualify for the cash discount. The decision to make such a change in payment terms required Procter & Gamble to analyze the effect of the change on the company's cash flows and profits. Some retailers, such as buyers of food and beverage products, will have a longer discount period and will take

longer to pay for their purchases, which will *increase* Procter & Gamble's accounts receivable balance and cost of funds invested in this asset. Conversely, other retailers, such as buyers of health and beauty aids, will have a shorter discount period and will have to pay sooner if they wish to take the 2 percent cash discount, which will *decrease* Procter & Gamble's investment in accounts receivable and associated costs. By changing its payment terms, Procter & Gamble hoped to reduce the number of invoices and associated costs to both itself and its customers.

In this chapter we develop techniques for evaluating the impact of changes in credit terms on the firm's accounts receivable and profits, such as the change in the cash discount period by Procter & Gamble.

*Gabriella Stern, "Retailers of P&G to Get New Plan on Bills, Shipments," *Wall Street Journal* (June 22, 1994): A12.

INTRODUCTION

Accounts receivable and inventories constitute important investments for most companies. As we saw earlier in Table 15-6, these two current assets represent sizeable proportions of the total assets of firms in a wide variety of industries. Among firms engaged in wholesale and retail trade, the proportions for each asset are often 25 percent or more of total assets in many companies. In the next two sections we discuss the management of accounts receivable. We examine inventory management in the remainder of the chapter.

ACCOUNTS RECEIVABLE MANAGEMENT

Accounts receivable consist of the credit a business grants its customers when selling goods or services.[1] They take the form of either *trade credit,* which the company extends to other companies, or *consumer credit,* which the company extends to its ultimate consumers.[2] The effectiveness of a company's credit policies can have a significant impact on its total performance. For example, Monsanto's credit manager has estimated that a reduction of only one day in the average collection period for the company's receivables increases its cash flow by $10 million and improves pretax profits by $1 million.

For a business to grant credit to its customers, it has to do the following:

■ Establish credit and collection policies.
■ Evaluate individual credit applicants.

In this section we develop the establishment of optimal credit and collection policies. In the following section we discuss procedures for evaluating individual credit applicants.

Shareholder Wealth and Optimal Investments in Accounts Receivable

When a company decides to extend credit to customers, it is making an investment decision; namely, an investment in accounts receivable, a *current asset.* As with the decision to invest in *long-term assets,* the primary goal is the maximization of shareholder wealth. Recall from the discussion of the basic framework for capital budgeting decisions in Chapter 8 that the optimal capital budget is determined by accepting all investment projects whose marginal returns, as measured by the internal rate of return, are greater than or equal to the marginal costs of the funds invested in the projects, as measured by the marginal cost of capital. Such a decision rule maximizes shareholder wealth because the projects accepted will earn a return greater than or equal to cost of the funds to the owners of the firm. Following similar reasoning, a company will maximize

---

[1]From the *customer's* perspective, credit represents a form of short-term financing known as *accounts payable.* This is discussed in greater detail in Chapter 18.
[2]Some companies use their accounts receivable to obtain short-term financing. For example, a company that is somewhat weak financially might be unable to borrow short-term funds without putting up collateral for the loan. In such a case, the company might use its accounts receivable as the collateral by *pledging* them to the bank. Alternatively, the company might consider selling, or *factoring,* its accounts receivable to obtain cash. Accounts receivable pledging and factoring are discussed in Chapter 18.

shareholder wealth by investing in accounts receivable as long as the expected marginal returns obtained from each additional dollar of receivables investment exceed the associated expected marginal costs of the investment, *including the cost of the funds invested.*

The establishment of an *optimal credit extension policy* requires the company to examine and attempt to measure the *marginal costs* and *marginal returns* (benefits) associated with alternative policies. What are the marginal returns and costs associated with a more liberal extension of credit to a company's customers? With respect to returns, a more liberal extension presumably stimulates sales and leads to increased gross profits, assuming that all other factors (such as economic conditions, prices, production costs, and advertising expenses) remain constant. Offsetting these increased returns are several types of credit-related marginal costs, including the opportunity costs of the additional capital funds employed to support the higher level of receivables. Checking new credit accounts and collecting the higher level of receivables also results in additional costs. And finally, a more liberal credit policy frequently results in increased bad-debt expenses, because a certain number of new accounts are likely to fail to repay the credit extended to them.

In determining an optimal credit extension policy, a company's financial managers must consider a number of major controllable variables that can be used to alter the level of receivables, including the following:

■ Credit standards.
■ Credit terms.
■ Collection effort.

The remainder of this section discusses each of these variables in more detail.

Credit Standards

Credit standards are the criteria a company uses to screen credit applicants in order to determine which of its customers should be offered credit and how much. The process of setting credit standards allows the firm to exercise a degree of control over the "quality" of accounts accepted.[3] The quality of credit extended to customers is a multidimensional concept involving the following:

■ The time a customer takes to repay the credit obligation, *given that it is repaid.*
■ The probability that a customer will fail to repay the credit extended to it.

The **average collection period** serves as one measure of the promptness with which customers repay their credit obligations. It indicates the average number of days a company must wait after making a credit sale before receiving the customer's cash payment. Obviously, the longer the average collection period, the higher a company's receivables investment and, by extension, its cost of extending credit to customers.

The likelihood that a customer will fail to repay the credit extended to it is sometimes referred to as *default risk.* The **bad-debt loss ratio,** which is the

---

[3]Complete control over the quality of accounts accepted generally is impossible due to uncertainty about future events (for example, a recession or a strike) that could make it difficult or even impossible for a customer to repay its account.

proportion of the total receivables volume a company never collects, serves as an overall, or aggregate, measure of this risk. A business can estimate its loss ratio by examining losses on credit that has been extended to similar types of customers in the past.[4] The higher a firm's loss ratio, the greater is the cost of extending credit.

For example, suppose that Bassett Furniture Industries is considering making a change in its credit standards. Before reaching any decision, the company first must determine whether such a change would be profitable. The first step in making this decision involves an evaluation of the overall creditworthiness of the company's existing and potential customers (retailers) using various sources of information.[5] Table 17-1 illustrates the credit sales, average collection period, and loss ratio data for various credit risk groups of the company's customers in its northwest region.

Under its current credit policy, Bassett extends unlimited credit to all customers in Credit Risk Groups 1, 2, and 3 and no credit to customers in Groups 4 and 5, meaning that the customers in these latter two groups must submit payment along with their orders. As a result of this policy, Bassett estimates that it "loses" $300,000 per year in sales from Group 4 customers and $100,000 per year in sales from Group 5 customers.[6]

Bassett also estimates that its *variable* production, administrative, and marketing costs (including credit department costs) are approximately 75 percent of total sales; that is, the *variable cost ratio* is 0.75.[7] Thus, the profit contribution ratio per dollar of sales is 1.0 − 0.75 = 0.25 or 25 percent. The company's required pretax rate of return (that is, the opportunity cost) on its current assets investment is 20 percent.

One alternative Bassett is considering is to relax credit standards by extending full credit to Group 4 customers. Bassett estimates that an additional

TABLE 17-1
Credit Evaluation Data Compiled by Bassett Furniture Industries

CREDIT RISK GROUP	CREDIT SALES ($)	AVERAGE COLLECTION PERIOD (DAYS)	BAD-DEBT LOSS RATIO (%)
1	900,000	25	—
2	1,100,000	30	0.5
3	400,000	45	3
4	300,000*	60	7
5	100,000*	90	13

*Estimated lost sales due to the fact that no credit is extended to customers in these risk categories.

[4]This estimation procedure assumes that the loss ratio does not change significantly over time because of changing economic conditions. Otherwise, the loss ratio should be adjusted to take account of expected future economic changes. This procedure also assumes that credit extension and repayment information is available on a sufficiently large sample of accounts to provide a company with a reliable estimate of its loss ratio. Without this information, the financial manager simply has to make an "educated guess" as to the size of the loss ratio.
[5]Some of these sources of information are described later in this chapter.
[6]Throughout the chapter, *estimates* of variables, such as sales, the average collection period, and the bad-debt loss ratio, are used in the analysis of credit policy decisions. These estimates are subject to uncertainty. *Sensitivity analysis* (described in Chapter 10) can be performed to determine the effect on profitability of different estimates of one (or more) of these variables.
[7]This analysis assumes that the collection costs for Credit Risk Group 4 customers are the same as for customers in the other groups and are included in credit department costs.

inventory investment (that is, raw materials, work-in-process, and finished goods) of $120,000 is required to expand sales by $300,000. In evaluating this alternative, the financial manager has to analyze how this policy would affect pretax profits. If the marginal returns of this change in credit standards exceed the marginal costs, pretax profits would increase, and the decision to extend full credit to the Group 4 customers would increase shareholder wealth.

Summation

Table 17-2 contains the results of this analysis. In Step A, the marginal profitability of the additional sales, $75,000, is calculated. Next, the cost of the additional investment in receivables, $9,863, is calculated in Step B.[8] In Step C, the additional bad-debt loss, $21,000, is computed. Then, the cost of the additional investment in inventory, $24,000, is calculated in Step D. Finally, in Step E, the net change in pretax profits is determined by deducting the marginal costs computed in Steps B, C, and D from the marginal returns found in Step A. Because this expected net change is a positive $20,137, the analysis indicates that Bassett should relax its credit standards by extending full credit to the Group 4 customers.

Assumptions

This analysis contains a number of explicit and implicit assumptions of which the financial manager must be aware. One assumption is that *the company has excess capacity* and thus could produce the additional output at a *constant variable cost ratio* of 0.75. If the company currently is operating at or near full capacity, and additional output could be obtained only by paying more costly overtime rates and/or investing in new facilities, this analysis would have to be modified to take account of these incremental costs. This analysis also assumes that the average collection period of the customers in Groups 1, 2, and 3 would *not increase* once the company began extending credit to Group 4 customers. If it became known that the Group 4 customers had 60 days or more to pay their bills with no penalty involved, the Group 1, 2, and 3 customers, who normally pay their bills promptly, might also start delaying their payments. If this occurred, the analysis would have to be modified to account for such shifts. It also was assumed that the required rate of return on the investment in receivables and inventories for Group 4 *does not change* as a result of extending credit to these more risky accounts. A case can be made for increasing the required rate of return to compensate for the increased risk of the new

[8]Note that we have chosen to use sales value in determining the (opportunity) cost of the additional receivables investment. Disagreement exists in the finance literature concerning the measurement of the incremental investment in accounts receivable (and its associated opportunity cost) arising from a change in credit standards. Some authors contend that the relevant measure of investment is the dollar *cost* the firm has tied up in the new accounts receivable, rather than the total *sales value*. The rationale for this approach is that the "profit" on the sale—that is, the difference between the amount of the accounts receivable and their associated cost—would be nonexistent without the change in credit standards. Hence, no opportunity cost is incurred on this uncollected "profit." Advocates of this approach use variable cost or total cost as a measure of the amount of funds invested in accounts receivable. Other authors claim that the total sales value of the new accounts receivable is indeed the relevant measure of investment in accounts receivable, because the opportunity cost of the increased level of accounts receivable is the return a company could earn if it reduced accounts receivable back to its original level. In other words, considerations of symmetry require that the opportunity cost of increasing accounts receivable by a given amount should be equal to the returns that could be earned on the funds released from decreasing accounts receivable by the same amount. The interested reader should consult the following references for a more complete discussion of the issues involved: John S. Oh, "Opportunity Cost in the Evaluation of Investment in Accounts Receivable," *Financial Management* 5 (Summer 1976): 32–35; Edward A. Dyl, "Another Look at the Evaluation of Investment in Accounts Receivable," *Financial Management* 6 (Winter 1977): 67–70; Joseph C. Atkins and Yong H. Kim, "Comment and Correction: Opportunity Cost in the Evaluation of Investment in Accounts Receivable," *Financial Management* 6 (Winter 1977): 71–74; Tirlochan S. Walia, "Explicit and Implicit Cost of Changes in the Level of Accounts Receivable and the Credit Policy Decision of the Firm," *Financial Management* 6 (Winter 1977): 75–80; and J. Fred Weston and Pham D. Tuan, "Comment on Analysis of Credit Policy Changes," *Financial Management* 9 (Winter 1980): 59–63.

TABLE 17-2
Bassett Furniture Industries's Analysis of the Decision to Relax Credit Standards by Extending Full Credit to Customers in Credit Risk Group 4

Step A: Additional sales $300,000

Marginal profitability of additional sales

= Profit contribution ratio × Additional sales

= 0.25 × $300,000 $75,000

Step B: Additional investment in receivables

= Additional average daily sales*
× Average collection period

$$= \frac{\text{Additional annual sales}}{365} \times 60$$

$$= \frac{\$300,000}{365} \times 60 \qquad \$49,315$$

Cost of the additional investment in receivables

= Additional investment in receivables
× Required pretax rate of return

= $49,315 × 0.20 $9,863

Step C: Additional bad-debt loss

= Bad-debt loss ratio × Additional sales

= 0.07 × $300,000 $21,000

Step D: Additional investment in inventory $120,000

Cost of the additional investment in inventory

= Additional investment in inventory
× Required pretax rate of return

= $120,000 × 0.20 $24,000

Step E: Net change in pretax profits

= Marginal returns − Marginal costs

= A − (B + C + D)

= $75,000 − ($9,863 + $21,000 + $24,000)   +$20,137

*Standard practice is to assume that there are 365 days per year.

accounts. Finally, this example assumes that an increase in inventory investment is necessary as a result of changes in the firm's credit policy. In summary, for this type of analysis to be valid and to lead to the correct decision, it must include *all* the marginal costs and benefits that result from the decision.

Credit Terms

A company's *credit terms,* or terms of sale, specify the conditions under which the customer is required to pay for the credit extended to it. These conditions include the *length of the credit period* and the *cash discount* (if any) given for prompt payment plus any special terms, such as *seasonal datings.* For example, credit terms of "net 30" mean that the customer has 30 days from the invoice date within which to pay the bill and that no discount is offered for early payment.

Credit Period. The length of a company's **credit period** (the amount of time a credit customer has to pay the account in full) is frequently determined by in-dustry customs, and thus it tends to vary among different industries. The credit period may be as short as 7 days or as long as 6 months. Variation appears to be positively related to the length of time the merchandise is in the purchaser's inventory. For example, manufacturers of goods having relatively low inventory turnover periods, such as jewelry, tend to offer retailers longer credit periods than distributors of goods having higher inventory turnover periods, such as food products.

A company's credit terms can affect its sales. For example, if the demand for a particular product depends in part on its credit terms, the company may consider lengthening the credit period to stimulate sales. For example, IBM apparently tried to stimulate declining sales of its PCjr home computer by extending the length of the credit period in which dealers had to pay for the computers. In making this type of decision, however, a company also must consider its closest competitors. If they lengthen their credit periods, too, every company in the industry may end up having about the same level of sales, a much higher level of receivables investments and costs, and a lower rate of return.

Analyzing the possible effects of an increase in a company's credit period involves comparing the profitability of the increased sales that are expected to occur with the required rate of return on the additional investment in receivables and inventories. Additional bad-debt losses must also be considered. If a company continues to accept the same quality of accounts under its lengthened credit terms, no significant change in the bad-debt loss ratio should occur.

For example, suppose that Nike, a distributor of athletic shoes and sportswear, is considering changing its credit terms from "net 30" to "net 60" in its western Michigan sales territory. The company expects sales (all on credit) to increase by about 10 percent from a current level of $2.2 million, and it expects its average collection period to increase from 35 days to 65 days. The bad-debt loss ratio should remain at 3 percent of sales. The company also estimates that an additional inventory investment of $50,000 is required for the expected sales increase. The company's variable cost ratio is 0.75, which means that its profit contribution ratio (per dollar of sales) is $1.00 - 0.75 = 0.25$. Nike's required pretax rate of return on investments in receivables and inventories is 20 percent.

Table 17-3 contains an analysis of Nike's decision. Many of the calculations in this table are similar to those in Table 17-2, which analyzed the effects of a change in credit standards. The marginal returns ($55,000) computed in Step A represent the marginal profitability of the additional sales generated by the longer credit period. The marginal costs (obtained in Steps B, C, and D) consist of the cost of the additional receivables investment ($44,000), the additional bad-debt losses ($6,600), and the cost of the additional inventory investment ($10,000). The net increase in pretax profits (Step E) that would result from the decision to lengthen the credit period is –$5,600. Therefore, the decision does not appear to be worthwhile.

Cash Discounts. A **cash discount** is a discount offered on the condition that the customer will repay the credit extended within a specified period of time. A cash discount is normally expressed as a percentage discount on the net amount of the cost of goods purchased (usually excluding freight and taxes). The length of the discount period is also specified when discount terms are offered. For example, credit terms of "2/10, net 30" mean that the customer can deduct 2 percent of the invoice amount if payment is made within 10 days from the invoice date.

TABLE 17-3
Nike's Analysis of the Decision to Change Its Credit Terms from "Net 30" to "Net 60"

Step A: Additional sales

= Percent increase × Present sales

= 0.10 × $2,200,000 $220,000

Marginal profitability of additional sales

= Profit contribution ratio × Additional sales

= 0.25 × $220,000 $55,000

Step B: Additional investment in receivables

= New average balance − Present average balance

$$= \frac{\text{New annual sales}}{365} \times \text{New average collection period}$$

$$- \frac{\text{Present annual sales}}{365} \times \text{Present average collection period}$$

$$= \frac{\$2,420,000}{365} \times 65 - \frac{\$2,200,000}{365} \times 35$$

= $430,959 − $210,959 $220,000

Cost of the additional investment in receivables

= Additional investment in receivables

× Required pretax rate of return

= $220,000 × 0.20 $44,000

Step C: Additional bad-debt loss

= Bad-debt loss ratio × Additional sales

= 0.03 × $220,000 $ 6,600

Step D: Additional investment in inventory $ 50,000

Cost of the additional investment in inventory

= Additional investment in inventory

× Required pretax rate of return

= $50,000 × 0.20 $10,000

Step E: Net change in pretax profits

= Marginal returns − Marginal costs

= A − (B + C + D)

= $55,000 − ($44,000 + $6,600 + $10,000)   −$5,600

If payment is not made by this time, the full invoice amount is due within 30 days from the invoice date. (In some cases, the discount period may begin with the date of shipment or the date of receipt by the customer.) Like the length of the credit period, the cash discount varies among different lines of business.

Cash discounts are offered (or increased) to speed up the collection of accounts receivable and, by extension, reduce a company's level of receivables investment and associated costs.[9] Offsetting these savings or benefits is the cost

---

[9]Offering a cash discount may also increase demand and sales, because some potential customers may view it as a form of price cut and be willing to purchase the product at this new "lower" price. Throughout the ensuing analysis it is assumed that the cash discount is *not* perceived as a price cut and that there is no resulting increase in demand. It is also assumed that offering cash discounts will not reduce bad-debt losses by any measurable amount.

of the discounts that are taken, which is equal to the lost dollar revenues from the existing unit sales volume.

For example, suppose that the CBS Record Company is considering instituting a cash discount. The company currently sells to record distributors on credit terms of "net 30" and wants to determine the effect on pretax profits of offering a 1 percent cash discount on terms of "1/10, net 30" to record distributors in its southwestern Ohio region. The company's average collection period is now 50 days and is estimated to decrease to 28 days with the adoption of the 1 percent cash discount policy. It also is estimated that approximately 40 percent of the company's customers will take advantage of the new cash discount. CBS's annual credit sales in their southwest region are $2.5 million, and the company's required pretax rate of return on receivables investment is 20 percent.

Table 17-4 contains an analysis of CBS's proposed cash discount policy. The marginal returns ($30,137) computed in Step A represent the earnings CBS expects to realize on the funds released by the decrease in receivables. The marginal costs ($10,000) found in Step B represent the cost of the cash discount. Subtracting the marginal costs from the marginal returns (Step C) yields a net increase in pretax profits of $20,137, indicating that CBS should offer the proposed 1 percent cash discount, if it is confident about the accuracy of the estimates used in this analysis.

Seasonal Datings. **Seasonal datings** are special credit terms that are sometimes offered to retailers when sales are highly concentrated in one or more periods during the year. Under a seasonal dating credit arrangement, the retailer is

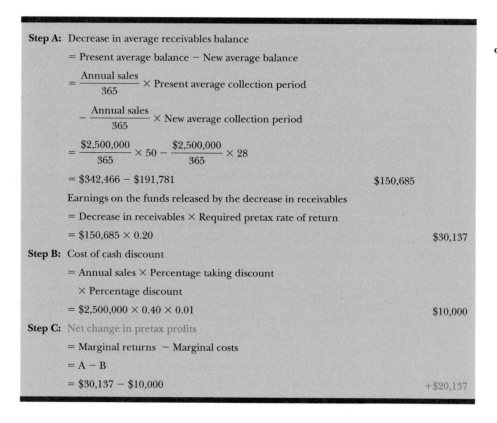

TABLE 17-4
CBS Record Company's Analysis of the Decision to Offer a 1 Percent Cash Discount

Step A: Decrease in average receivables balance

= Present average balance − New average balance

$$= \frac{\text{Annual sales}}{365} \times \text{Present average collection period}$$

$$- \frac{\text{Annual sales}}{365} \times \text{New average collection period}$$

$$= \frac{\$2,500,000}{365} \times 50 - \frac{\$2,500,000}{365} \times 28$$

= $342,466 − $191,781 $150,685

Earnings on the funds released by the decrease in receivables

= Decrease in receivables × Required pretax rate of return

= $150,685 × 0.20 $30,137

Step B: Cost of cash discount

= Annual sales × Percentage taking discount

× Percentage discount

= $2,500,000 × 0.40 × 0.01 $10,000

Step C: Net change in pretax profits

= Marginal returns − Marginal costs

= A − B

= $30,137 − $10,000   +$20,137

encouraged to order and accept delivery of the product well ahead of the peak sales period and then to remit payment shortly after the peak sales period. The primary objective of seasonal dating is to increase sales to retailers who are unable to finance the buildup of inventories in advance of the peak selling period because of a weak working capital position, limited borrowing capacity, or both.

For example, O. M. Scott and Sons, manufacturers of lawn and garden products, has used a seasonal dating plan that is tied to the growing season. Payments for winter and early spring shipments are due at the end of April and May, depending on the geographical area, and payments for shipments during the summer months are due in October or November. Payments for purchases made outside the two main selling seasons are due on the 10th of the second month following shipment. A cash discount of 0.6 percent per month is offered to encourage payments in advance of these seasonal dates. The arrangement enables and encourages dealers of lawn and garden products to be fully stocked with Scott products in advance of the peak selling periods.

Collection Effort

The collection effort consists of the methods a business employs in attempting to collect payment on past-due accounts. Some commonly used methods include the following:

- Sending notices or letters informing the customer of the past-due status of the account and requesting payment.
- Telephoning and/or visiting the customer in an effort to obtain payment.
- Employing a collection agency.
- Taking legal action against the customer.

Another approach, which is also effective in some cases, is for the firm to refuse to make new shipments to the customer until the past-due bills are paid. Although the objectives of the collection effort are to speed up past-due payments and reduce bad-debt losses, a company also must avoid antagonizing normally creditworthy customers who may be past due for some good reason; for example, because of temporary liquidity problems. A collection effort that is too aggressive may reduce future sales and profits if customers begin buying from other businesses whose collection policies are more lenient.

When determining which methods to use in its collection effort, a company has to consider the amount of funds it has available to spend for this purpose. If the firm has a relatively small amount of money available for collecting past-due accounts, it must confine itself to less costly (and less effective) methods, such as sending letters and making telephone calls. If it has a larger budget, the firm can employ more aggressive procedures, such as sending out representatives to personally contact past-due customers. In general, the larger the company's collection expenditures, the shorter its average collection period and the lower its level of bad-debt losses. The benefits of additional collection efforts, however, are likely to diminish rapidly at extremely high expenditure levels.

The marginal benefits of the decision to increase collection expenditures consist of the earnings on the funds released from the receivables investment as a result of the shorter average collection period, plus the reduction in bad-debt losses. A business should increase its collection expenditures only if these marginal benefits are expected to exceed the amount of the additional collection expenditures.

Monitoring Accounts Receivable

For a company to effectively control its receivables investment, the credit manager must monitor the status and composition of these accounts. An *aging of accounts* is a useful monitoring technique.[10] In an aging analysis, a company's accounts are classified into different categories based on the number of days they are past due. These classifications show both the aggregate amount of receivables and the percentage of the total receivables outstanding in each category. Aging of accounts receivable provides more information than such summary ratios as, for example, the average collection period. Comparing aging schedules at successive points in time (for example, monthly, quarterly, or semiannually) can help the credit manager monitor any changes in the "quality" of the company's accounts.

 EVALUATING INDIVIDUAL CREDIT APPLICANTS

Once a company has established its credit and collection policies, it can use them as a basis for evaluating individual credit applicants.[11] In general, the credit evaluation process consists of these main steps:

- Gathering relevant information on the credit applicant.
- Analyzing the information obtained to determine the applicant's creditworthiness.
- Deciding whether to extend credit to the applicant and, if so, determining the amount of the line of credit.

The credit evaluation process is limited by both time and cost. Often a business may have only a few days—or, in some cases, only a few hours—in which to evaluate a credit request. Delaying this decision too long may result in the loss of a potential customer's order.

The credit evaluation process is also limited by the amount of resources the credit department has available. The amount of time and money a company spends on evaluating a customer's request for credit should depend on the size of the losses the company would experience if it made an incorrect decision. These potential losses stem from either denying credit to a creditworthy customer or offering credit to a customer who is not creditworthy. The larger the potential losses, the more time and money a business should spend on evaluating the credit applicant.

Gathering Information on the Credit Applicant

Information for evaluating the creditworthiness of a customer is available from a variety of sources, including the following:

- Financial statements submitted by the customer.
- Credit reporting organizations.
- Banks.
- The company's own prior experience with the customer.

These sources differ with respect to their costs and the reliability of the information they provide.

[10]Aging schedules are also discussed in Chapter 3.
[11]Once these policies are established, however, they do not have to remain static over time. The credit manager should review them periodically, making appropriate modifications as dictated by changing economic conditions (for example, rising interest rates) or other circumstances.

Financial Statements. A company can ask a credit applicant to supply various kinds of financial information, such as income statements and balance sheets (preferably audited ones), and possibly even a forecasted budget. This information can be used to evaluate the applicant's financial strength—and the applicant's ability to repay credit obligations. Unwillingness on the part of the applicant to supply financial statements may indicate financial weakness and suggest the need for more detailed checking, the outright refusal to extend credit, or both.

Credit-Reporting Organizations. A number of national and local organizations collect information on the financial position and credit standing of businesses. Other companies and lending institutions that are considering extending credit to a company may obtain information about it from these organizations, usually for a fee.

The most widely known credit-reporting organization is Dun and Bradstreet Credit Services, which provides its subscribers with a credit reference book and written credit reports on individual businesses. D&B's reference book is published bimonthly and contains the names and credit ratings of over three million businesses located in the United States, including manufacturers, wholesalers, retailers, business services, and other types of businesses.

A D&B credit report provides far more detailed information about a company's financial position than the reference book does. A typical report contains a summary of trade credit payments to existing suppliers, which can be extremely valuable to companies that are considering extending credit to a particular company. Also included in a typical report are financial data from the firm's balance sheet and income statement, a review of its banking relationships, historical information about the owners, and a description of its operations, including the location of facilities and the kinds of products sold.[12]

The National Association of Credit Management also fills requests for information on the repayment patterns of specific companies. In addition, a number of other organizations collect and disseminate credit information within given industries, such as the toy and furniture industries, as well as within given geographical areas, such as Chicago and New York.

Banks. Many banks will assist their business customers in obtaining information on the creditworthiness of other businesses. Through its contacts with other banks, a customer's bank often can obtain detailed information on the payment patterns and financial status of the company under investigation and pass this information on to a customer.

Prior Experience with the Customer. A company's experience with a credit customer can be extremely useful when deciding whether to continue extending credit, increase the amount of credit it currently grants to the customer, or both. If, for example, the customer tends to remit payments well beyond the due date and/or if the company must employ expensive collection methods in obtaining payments, the credit analyst should weigh this unfavorable information in making the credit extension decision.

---

[12]The reliability and comprehensiveness of this type of report depend in part on how willing a business is to supply D&B with pertinent information.

Analyzing Creditworthiness and Making the Credit Decision

Credit analysts ideally should obtain information about an applicant from as many sources as possible, but they also should consider the time and costs involved. Specifically, analysts should weigh the expected returns to be derived from any additional information against the cost involved in obtaining it.

A good way to structure information collection is to proceed *sequentially,* beginning with the least costly and least time-consuming sources. If the results of this initial check indicate that more information is needed, the analyst can proceed to additional sources. For example, the analyst may begin by consulting the customer's past credit history with the company. If further information is needed, the analyst then can check the D&B reference book and/or ask the applicant to supply financial statements and a list of companies that have extended trade credit to it in the past. Finally, if still more information is needed, the credit analyst can request a D&B credit report on the applicant and/or request credit checks through banks and the applicant's trade creditors.

Because a great deal of information is usually available about a credit applicant, the credit manager must be able to sort through this information and extract the key elements that will enable a reliable overall assessment of the applicant's creditworthiness to be made. There are no magic formulas for making unerring credit decisions, but there are some traditional guidelines available that can serve as a framework for analysis. These guidelines are called the "five *C*s of credit":

- ■ *Character* refers to the applicant's willingness or desire to meet credit obligations. Past payment patterns are useful in gauging this aspect of creditworthiness.
- ■ *Capacity* refers to the applicant's ability to meet financial obligations. A reasonable estimate of an applicant's capacity usually can be obtained by examining its liquidity position and projected cash flows.
- ■ *Capital* refers to the applicant's financial strength, particularly with respect to net worth. Evidence about a company's capital usually can be obtained by evaluating the balance sheet using financial ratios.
- ■ *Collateral* represents the assets that the applicant may pledge as security for the credit extended to it. However, collateral often is not a critical consideration, because the primary concern for the company offering trade credit is the timely repayment of the credit, not foreclosing on the pledged assets.
- ■ *Conditions* refer to the general economic climate and its effect on the applicant's ability to pay. A good credit risk in prosperous times might be unable to make payments during a recession.

Many credit analysts feel that the first two *C*s, character and capacity, are the most important insofar as they help to ensure that the firm considering extending credit will not leave anything important out of the analysis.

Numerical credit scoring systems are another technique that has been found useful, particularly in the area of consumer credit. This technique allows the credit-granting business to quantitatively rate various financial and personal characteristics of the applicant, such as the length of the time in business, its D&B credit rating, and its current ratio. The total credit score then can be computed based on the characteristics thought to be related to creditworthiness. The applicant's credit score next is compared with those of other applicants, or with a minimally acceptable cutoff score. Although numerical

Do you think managing accounts receivable is simple—just tell your customers to "pay up!" Not hardly. Visit VisionPoint's Web site to see the many ways in which accounts receivable are classified and collected, as well as the many types of reports that AR management requires. It's no simple ordeal.
http://www.sbt.com

credit scoring systems can be beneficial in credit screening, they can be difficult and expensive to install.

Guidelines and techniques such as these can aid in the analysis of an applicant's creditworthiness; the ability to make sound credit decisions, however, ultimately depends on the decision maker's experience and judgment in evaluating the available information.

INVENTORY MANAGEMENT

Inventories serve as a buffer between the various phases in the procurement-production-sales cycle of a manufacturing firm.[13] They uncouple the various phases by giving the firm flexibility with respect to timing the purchase of raw materials, scheduling production facilities and employees, and meeting fluctuating and uncertain demand for the finished product. Inventories also serve similar purposes in the procurement-sales cycle of a wholesaling or retailing firm.

The remainder of this chapter explores the various types of inventories and their functions, along with the different categories of inventory-related costs. It also develops some models and procedures that can be used in efficiently managing a firm's level of inventory investment. Although financial managers usually do not have primary responsibility for managing a company's inventories, they are responsible for seeing that funds are invested in a manner consistent with shareholder wealth maximization. (Normally, production and/or marketing management has primary responsibility for determining the specific quantities of the various types of inventories that the firm holds.) To perform this function, financial managers must have a good working knowledge of inventory control techniques.

Like any other asset, the holding of inventories constitutes an investment of funds. Determining the optimal level of inventory investment requires that the benefits and costs, *including the opportunity cost of the funds invested,* associated with alternative levels be measured and compared. To do this, it is necessary to determine the specific benefits associated with holding the various types of inventories.

Benefits of Holding Inventories

Manufacturing firms generally hold three types of inventories:

- Raw materials inventories.
- Work-in-process inventories.
- Finished goods inventories.

Raw Materials Inventories. Raw materials inventory consists of items a business purchases for use in its production process. It may consist of basic materials (for example, iron ore for a steel-making operation), manufactured goods (for example, memory chips for a computer assembly operation), or both. Maintaining adequate raw materials inventories provides a company with advantages in both purchasing and production. Specifically, the purchasing department benefits

---

[13]Inventories are sometimes used as collateral for short-term loans. This topic is discussed in detail in Chapter 18.

by being able to buy needed items in large quantities and take advantage of *quantity discounts* offered by suppliers. In addition, if rising prices, shortages of specific items, or both are forecasted for the future, maintaining a large stock of raw materials ensures that the company will have adequate supplies at reasonable costs.

Knowing that adequate stocks of raw materials will be available when needed permits the production department to meet production schedules and make the most efficient use of its personnel and facilities. Therefore, there are a number of valid reasons why a company's purchasing and production departments will want to maintain large inventories of raw materials.

Work-in-Process Inventories. Work-in-process inventory consists of all items that presently are in the production cycle at some intermediate stage of completion. For example, they currently may be undergoing some type of operation (such as assembly or painting); they may be in transit between operations; or they may be stored somewhere, awaiting the next step in the production cycle.

Work-in-process inventories are a necessary part of modern industrial production systems, because they give each operation in the production cycle a certain degree of independence. This, in turn, aids in the efficient scheduling of the various operations and helps minimize costly delays and idle time. For these reasons, a company's production department will want to maintain reasonable work-in-process inventories. In general, the longer a firm's production cycle, the larger its work-in-process inventory.

Finished Goods Inventories. Finished goods inventory consists of those items that have completed the production cycle and are available for sale. With the exception of large-scale, specialized types of equipment—such as industrial machinery, military armaments, jet airplanes, and nuclear reactors, which normally are contracted for *before* they are produced—most consumer and industrial products are manufactured and stored in inventory to meet forecasted future sales.

Keeping enough finished goods inventories on hand provides significant benefits for both the marketing and the production departments. From marketing's perspective, large finished goods inventories enable it to fill orders promptly, minimize lost sales, and avoid shipment delays due to stockouts. From production's standpoint, maintaining a large finished goods inventory permits items to be manufactured in large production runs, which helps keep unit production costs low by spreading fixed set-up expenses over large volumes of output.

Inventory-Related Costs

At the same time that a number of benefits are to be realized from holding inventories, a number of costs also must be considered, including the following:

- Ordering costs.
- Carrying costs.
- Stockout costs.

Ordering Costs. **Ordering costs** represent all the costs of placing and receiving an order. They are stated in dollars per order. When a company is ordering from an external source, these include the costs of preparing the purchase requisition, expediting the order (for example, long-distance calls and follow-up letters), receiving and inspecting the shipment, and handling payment. Such factors as an item's price and engineering complexity also affect its ordering costs. When an order is placed for an item that is manufactured *internally* within a company, ordering costs consist primarily of *production set-up* costs, which are the expenses incurred in getting the plant and equipment ready for a production run.

In practice, the cost per order generally contains both fixed and variable components, because a portion of the cost—such as that of receiving and inspecting the order—normally varies with the quantity ordered. However, many simple inventory control models, such as the EOQ model (which is described later in this chapter), treat cost per order as fixed by assuming that these costs are independent of the number of units ordered.

Carrying Costs. Carrying costs constitute all the costs of holding items in inventory for a given period of time. They are expressed either in dollars per unit or as a percentage of the inventory value per period. Components of this cost include the following:

■ Storage and handling costs.
■ Obsolescence and deterioration costs.
■ Insurance.
■ Taxes.
■ The cost of the funds invested in inventories.

Storage and handling costs include the cost of warehouse space. If a company leases warehouse space, this cost is equal to the rent paid. If a company owns the warehouse, this cost is equal to the value of the space in its next-best alternative use (that is, the opportunity cost). These costs also include depreciation on the inventory handling equipment, such as conveyors and forklift trucks, and the wages and salaries paid to warehouse workers and supervisors.

Inventories are valuable only if they can be sold. *Obsolescence costs* represent the decline in inventory value caused by technological or style changes that make the existing product less salable. *Deterioration costs* represent the decline in value caused by changes in the physical quality of the inventory, such as spoilage and breakage.

Another element of carrying cost is the *cost of insuring* the inventory against losses due to theft, fire, and natural disaster. In addition, a company must pay any *personal property taxes* and *business taxes* required by local and state governments on the value of its inventories.

The *cost of funds invested in inventories* is measured by the *required rate of return* on these funds. Because inventory investments are likely to be of "average risk," the overall weighted cost of capital should be used to measure the cost of these funds. If it is felt that inventories constitute an investment with either an above-average or below-average risk, some adjustment in the weighted cost of capital may be necessary to account for this difference in risk.[14]

Some firms incorrectly use the rate of interest on borrowed funds as a measure of this cost. This tends to understate the true cost, because a given amount of lower-cost debt must be balanced with additional higher-cost equity financing. Inventory investment cost constitutes an opportunity cost in that it represents the return a firm forgoes as a result of deciding to invest its limited funds in inventories rather than in some other asset. Therefore, for most inventory decisions, the appropriate opportunity cost is the firm's weighted cost of capital.

---

[14]Chapters 5 and 10 discuss the determination of risk-adjusted discount rates.

The cost of carrying inventories can represent a significant cost of doing business. Table 17-5 contains some ranges on annual inventory carrying costs, expressed as a percentage of inventory value. This study found that *total* annual carrying costs were in the range of 20 to 45 percent for most of the businesses surveyed.

Like ordering costs, inventory carrying costs contain both fixed and variable components. Most carrying costs vary with the inventory level, but a certain portion of them—such as warehouse rent and depreciation on inventory handling equipment—are relatively fixed over the short run. Most of the simple inventory control models, such as the EOQ model, treat the entire carrying cost as variable.

Stockout Costs. Stockout costs are incurred whenever a business is unable to fill orders because the demand for an item is greater than the amount currently available in inventory. When a stockout in raw materials occurs, for example, stockout costs include the expenses of placing special orders (back ordering) and expediting incoming orders, in addition to the costs of any resulting production delays. A stockout in work-in-process inventory results in additional costs of rescheduling and speeding production within the plant, and it also may result in lost production costs if work stoppages occur. Finally, a stockout in finished goods inventory may result in the immediate loss of profits if customers decide to purchase the product from a competitor, and in potential long-term losses if customers decide to order from other companies in the future.

TABLE 17-5
Inventory Carrying Costs
(as a percentage of inventory value)

Source: W. E. Dollar, *Effective Purchasing and Inventory Control for Small Business* (Boston: Inc./CBI Publications, 1983): 71.

COST CATEGORY	LOW	HIGH
Storage costs	1.0%	4.0%
Obsolescence and physical loss	5.0	10.0
Insurance costs	1.0	3.0
Property taxes	1.0	3.0
Cost of money	12.0	25.0

INVENTORY CONTROL MODELS

Given the significance of the benefits and costs associated with holding inventories, it is important that the firm efficiently control the level of inventory investments. A number of inventory control models are available that can help in determining the optimal inventory level of each item. These models range from the relatively simple to the extremely complex. Their degree of complexity depends primarily on the assumptions made about the demand or use for the particular item and the lead time required to secure additional stock.

A related question involves the extent of control and the type of inventory model that should be applied to different inventory items. A technique called ABC inventory classification can be helpful in this regard. The **ABC inventory classification** method divides a company's inventory items into three groups. Group A consists of those items with a relatively large dollar value but a relatively small percentage of the total items, whereas group C contains those items with a small dollar value but a large percentage of the total items. Group B contains the items which are in between groups A and C. A typical result of an ABC analysis is that group A contains roughly 1 to 10 percent of the total number of items carried in inventory, but these items may represent as high as 80 to 90 percent of the total dollar value of the inventory. On the other hand, group C may contain about 50 percent of the total number of items, but these items may constitute less than 10 percent of the inventory's total dollar value. Group B contains the remaining items. Even though the actual cutoff between the groups is somewhat arbitrary, the ABC method provides management with information that can be used to determine how closely different inventory items should be controlled.

As an example, consider the Toro Company, which manufactures lawn mowers. It purchases gasoline motors from another company for use in these mowers. Because of their cost, the motors might be classified as group A items. As a result, Toro management might determine the inventory costs associated with the motors and use a detailed model to calculate the economic order quantity. On the other hand, Toro might classify all nuts and bolts it uses as a group C item. As a result, the company's policy on nuts and bolts might consist of little more than simply keeping an ample supply on hand.

In the "classic" inventory models, which include both the simpler *deterministic* models and the more complex *probabilistic* models, it is assumed that demand is either uniform or dispersed and *independent* over time.[15] In other words, demand is assumed either to be *constant* or to fluctuate over time due to *random* elements. These types of demand situations are common in retailing and some service operations.

The simpler deterministic inventory control models, such as the *economic order quantity* (EOQ) *model,* assume that both demand and lead times are *constant* and known with *certainty.* Thus, deterministic models eliminate the need to consider stockouts. The more complex probabilistic inventory control models assume that demand, lead time, or both are *random variables with known probability distributions.*[16]

Basic EOQ Model

In its simplest form, the EOQ model assumes that the annual demand or usage for a particular item is known with certainty. It also assumes that this demand is stationary or uniform throughout the year. In other words, seasonal fluctuations in the rate of demand are ruled out. Finally, the model assumes that orders to replenish the inventory of an item are filled instantaneously. Given a known demand and a zero lead time for replenishing inventories, there is no need for a company to maintain additional inventories, or safety stocks, to protect itself against stockouts.

The assumptions of the EOQ model yield the saw-toothed inventory pattern shown in Figure 17-1. The vertical lines at the 0, T_1, T_2, and T_3 points in time represent the instantaneous replenishment of the item by the amount of the order quantity, Q, and the negatively sloped lines between the replenishment points represent the use of the item. Because the inventory level varies between 0 and the order quantity, average inventory is equal to one-half of the order quantity, or $Q/2$.

This model assumes that the costs of placing and receiving an order are the same for each order and independent of the number of units ordered. It also assumes that the annual cost of carrying 1 unit of the item in inventory is constant, regardless of the inventory level. Total annual inventory costs, then, are the sum of ordering costs and carrying costs.[17] The primary objective of the EOQ model is to find the order quantity, Q, that minimizes total annual inventory costs.

---

[15]*Dependent* demand models, in contrast, assume that demand tends to be "lumpy," or to occur at specific points in time. Dependent demand tends to occur when products are manufactured in lots, because all the items required to produce the lot are usually withdrawn from inventory at the same time, rather than unit by unit. Dependent demand is a direct result of the demand for a "higher level" item. Material requirements planning (MRP) models have been developed to deal with the case of dependent demand. See J. Evans, D. Anderson, D. Sweeney, and T. Williams, *Applied Production and Operations Management*, 3rd ed. (St. Paul: West Publishing Co., 1990), for a discussion of MRP.

[16]Rather than survey all the various inventory control models in depth, this chapter develops the deterministic EOQ model to illustrate the cost trade-offs involved in determining the optimal inventory level. It then examines the factors that must be considered and the cost trade-offs involved in developing a probabilistic model, without using mathematical analysis or formal solution techniques.

[17]The *actual cost* of the item (that is, the price paid for items purchased externally or the production cost for items manufactured internally) is excluded from this analysis, because it is assumed to be constant regardless of the order quantity. This assumption is relaxed when quantity discounts are considered.

FIGURE 17-1
Certainty Case of the
Inventory Cycle

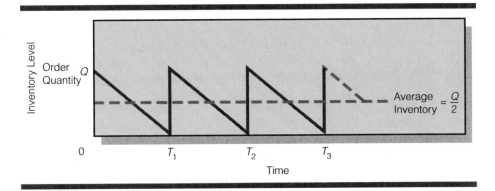

Algebraic Solution. In developing the algebraic form of the EOQ model, the following variables are defined:

Q = The order *quantity,* in units

D = The annual *demand* for the item, in units

S = The cost of placing and receiving an order, or *set-up* cost

C = The annual cost of *carrying* 1 unit of the item in inventory

Ordering costs are equal to the number of orders per year multiplied by the cost per order, S. The number of orders per year is equal to annual demand, D, divided by the order quantity, Q. Carrying costs are equal to average inventory, $Q/2$, multiplied by the annual carrying cost per unit, C.

The total annual cost equation is as follows:

$$\text{Total costs} = \text{Ordering costs} + \text{Carrying costs} \qquad (17.1)$$

By substituting the variables just defined into Equation 17.1, the following expression is obtained:

$$
\begin{aligned}
\text{Total costs} = {} & (\text{Number of orders per year} \qquad (17.2)\\
& \times \text{cost per order}) + (\text{Average inventory}\\
& \times \text{Annual carrying cost per unit})
\end{aligned}
$$

or, in algebraic terms,

$$\text{Total costs} = \left(\frac{D}{Q} \times S\right) + \left(\frac{Q}{2} \times C\right) \qquad (17.3)$$

The EOQ is the value of the Q that minimizes the total costs given in Equation 17.3. The standard procedure for finding this value of Q involves calculus.[18] The optimal solution, or EOQ, is equal to the following :

$$Q^* = \sqrt{\frac{2SD}{C}} \qquad (17.4)$$

Another item of information that is sometimes useful for planning purposes is the optimal length of one inventory cycle; that is, the time between placements

---

[18]Specifically, the first derivative of Equation 17.3 with respect to Q is set equal to 0, and the equation is solved for Q.

of orders for the item. The optimal length of one inventory cycle, T^*, measured in days, is equal to the economic order quantity, Q^*, divided by the average daily demand, $D/365$ (assuming 365 days per year), as follows:

$$T^* = \frac{Q^*}{D/365} \qquad (17.5)$$

This equation can be rewritten as follows:

$$T^* = \frac{365 \times Q^*}{D} \qquad (17.6)$$

The following example illustrates the use of the EOQ model. Suppose the Dayton Hudson Company sells Simmons mattresses through its Hudson's department stores located in the Detroit metropolitan area. All inventories are maintained at the firm's centrally located warehouse. Annual demand for the Simmons standard-sized mattress is 3,600 units and is spread evenly throughout the year. The cost of placing and receiving an order is $31.25.

Dayton Hudson's annual carrying costs are 20 percent of the inventory value. Based on a wholesale cost of $50 per mattress, the annual carrying cost per mattress is $0.20 \times \$50 = \$10$. Because Simmons maintains a large regional distribution center in Detroit, Dayton Hudson can replenish its inventory virtually instantaneously. The company wishes to determine the number of standard-sized mattresses it should periodically order from Simmons in order to minimize the total annual inventory costs. Substituting $D = 3,600$, $S = \$31.25$, and $C = \$10$ into Equation 17.4 yields the following EOQ:

$$Q^* = \sqrt{\frac{2 \times \$31.25 \times 3,600}{\$10}}$$

$$= 150 \text{ mattresses}$$

Using Equation 17.3, we can calculate the total annual inventory costs of this policy:

$$\text{Total costs}^* = \frac{3,600}{150} \times \$31.25 + \frac{150}{2} \times \$10$$

$$= \$1,500$$

Finally, Equation 17.6 can be used to determine Dayton Hudson's optimal inventory cycle for these mattresses:

$$T^* = \frac{365 \times 150}{3,600}$$

$$= 15.2 \text{ days}$$

Thus, the EOQ of 150 mattresses and the optimal inventory cycle of 15.2 days for this item indicate that Dayton Hudson should place an order for 150 mattresses every 15.2 days.

Graphic Solution. The order quantity that minimizes total annual inventory costs can be determined graphically by plotting inventory costs (vertical axis) as a function of the order quantity (horizontal axis). As we can see in Figure 17-2, annual ordering costs, DS/Q, vary *inversely* with the order quantity, Q, because the number of orders placed per year, D/Q, decreases as the size of the order quantity

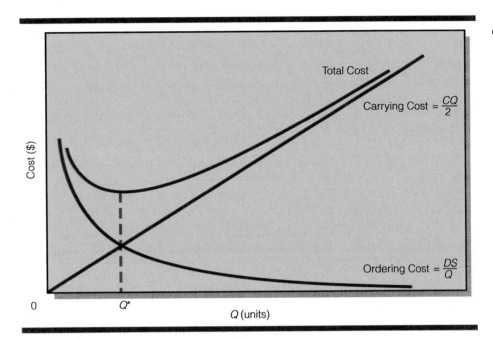

FIGURE 17-2
Graphic Solution of the EOQ Model

increases. Carrying costs, $CQ/2$, vary *directly* with the order quantity, Q, because the average inventory, $Q/2$, increases as the size of the order quantity increases.

The total inventory cost curve is found by vertically summing the heights of the ordering cost and carrying cost functions. The order quantity corresponding to the lowest point on the total cost curve is the optimal solution—that is, the economic order quantity, Q^*.

Extensions of the Basic EOQ Model

The basic EOQ model described above makes a number of simplifying assumptions, including those pertaining to replenishment lead time and demand for the item. In practical applications of inventory control models, however, some of these assumptions may not be valid. Thus, it is important to understand how different assumptions affect the analysis and the optimal order quantity. The following discussion examines what occurs when some of these assumptions are altered.

Nonzero Lead Time. The basic EOQ model assumes that orders to replenish the inventory of an item are filled instantaneously; that is, the lead time is zero. In practice, however, some time usually elapses between when a purchase order is placed and when the item actually is received in inventory. This lead time consists of the time it takes to manufacture the item, the time it takes to package and ship the item, or both.

If the lead time is *constant* and *known with certainty*, the optimal order quantity, Q^*, is not affected, although the time when an order should be placed is. Specifically, a company should not wait to reorder until the end of the inventory cycle, when the inventory level reaches zero—such as at points T_1, T_2, and T_3 in Figure 17-3. Instead, it should place an order *n days prior* to the end of each cycle, n being equal to the replenishment lead time measured in days. The **reorder point** is defined as the inventory level at which an order should be placed for replenishment of an item. Assuming that demand is constant over

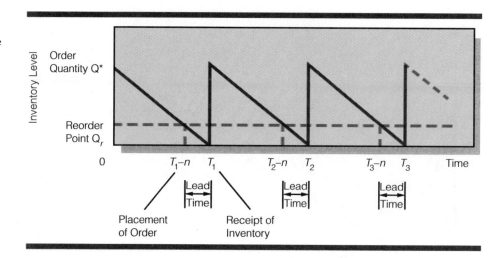

time, the reorder point, Q_r, is equal to the lead time, n (measured in days), multiplied by daily demand:

$$Q_r = n \times \frac{D}{365} \qquad (17.7)$$

where $D/365$ is daily demand (based on 365 days per year).

For example, if the lead time for standard-sized mattresses ordered by Dayton Hudson (discussed earlier in this section) is 5 days and annual demand is 3,600 mattresses, an order for 150 mattresses (that is, the economic order quantity) should be placed when the inventory level reaches the following:

$$Q_r = 5 \times \frac{3,600}{365}$$

$$= 49.3 \text{ mattresses}$$

which occurs during the 10th day of each inventory cycle. Five days later, during the 15th day of the inventory cycle—when the inventory level falls to zero—Dayton Hudson will receive the order, and the inventory level will again rise to 150.

Probabilistic Inventory Control Models. Thus far, the analysis has assumed that demand or usage is uniform throughout time and known with certainty, as well as that the lead time necessary to procure additional inventory is also a fixed, known value. However, in most practical inventory management problems either (or both) of these assumptions may not be strictly correct. Typically, demand fluctuates over time due to seasonal, cyclical, and "random" influences, and imprecise forecasts of future demands are often all that can be made. Similarly, lead times are subject to uncertainty because of such factors as transportation delays, strikes, and natural disasters. Under these conditions, the possibility of stockouts exists. To minimize the possibility of stockouts and the associated stockout costs, most companies use a standard approach of adding a *safety stock* to their inventory. A safety stock is maintained to meet unexpectedly high demand during the lead time, unanticipated delays in the lead time, or both.

Figure 17-4 shows the inventory pattern characterized by these more realistic assumptions. During the first inventory cycle ($0 - T_2$), an order to replenish the

FIGURE 17-4
Uncertainty Case of the
Inventory Cycle

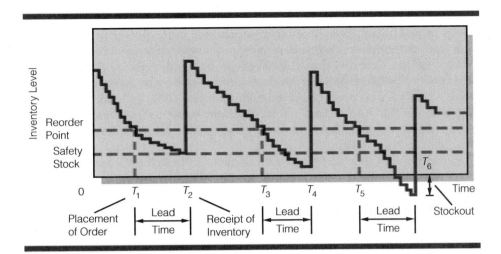

inventory is placed at T_1, when the inventory level reaches the predetermined order point. The order is then received at T_2. The second cycle $(T_2 - T_4)$ is similar to the first, except that demand exceeds the normal inventory of the item and part of the safety stock is consumed during the lead time prior to receipt of the order at T_4. During cycle 3 $(T_4 - T_6)$, demand exceeds the normal inventory plus the safety stock and, as a result, a stockout occurs during the lead time prior to receipt of the order at T_6.

Determining the optimal safety stock and order quantities under these more realistic conditions is a fairly complex process that lies beyond the scope of this text.[19] However, the factors that have to be considered in this type of analysis can be identified briefly. All other things being equal, the optimal safety stock increases as the uncertainty associated with the demand forecasts and lead times increases. Likewise, all other things being equal, the optimal safety stock increases as the cost of stockouts increases. Determining the optimal safety stock involves balancing the *expected* costs of stockouts against the cost of carrying the additional inventory.

Just-In-Time Inventory Management Systems

Just-in-time inventory management systems are part of a manufacturing approach that seeks to reduce the company's operating cycle and associated costs by eliminating wasteful procedures. Just-in-time inventory systems are based on the idea that all required inventory items should be supplied to the production process at exactly the right time and in exactly the right quantities. This approach was first developed by the Toyota Motor Company in the 1950s. In contrast, inventory models used in many plants, which rely on safety stocks, are sometimes referred to as "just-in-case" models.

The just-in-time approach works best for companies engaged in repetitive manufacturing operations. A key part of just-in-time techniques is the replacement of production in large batches with a continuous flow of smaller quantities.

[19]See any of the following books for a discussion of these more complex models: H. M. Wagner, *Principles of Operations Research: With Applications to Managerial Decision*, 2nd ed. (Englewood Cliffs, NJ: Prentice-Hall, 1975); J. Evans, D. Anderson, D. Sweeney, and T. Williams, *Applied Production and Operations Management*, 3rd ed. (St. Paul: West Publishing Co., 1990); and Richard I. Levin, Joel P. Stinson, and Everette S. Gardner, Jr., *Quantitative Approaches to Management*, 7th ed. (New York: McGraw-Hill, 1989).

The use of a just-in-time inventory system requires close coordination between a company and its suppliers, because any disruption in the flow of parts and materials from the supplier can result in costly production delays and lost sales.

Large as well as small businesses have reported reductions in production time and inventory costs resulting from the use of just-in-time techniques. One example is AT&T's Shreveport, Louisiana, plant, which produces office communication systems. The use of just-in-time manufacturing techniques reduced the production cycle from 3½ weeks to 2½ hours. Also, the U.S. Repeating Arms Company in New Haven, Connecticut, used just-in-time techniques to reduce the time required to make wooden shotgun stocks from 5 to 2 weeks. The minimum economic lot size also was lowered from 500 to 100 units.

■ SUMMARY

- For a business to extend credit to its customers, it must invest a certain amount of funds in *accounts receivable*.
- A company should change its credit extension policy only if the expected *marginal benefits* of the change will exceed the expected *marginal costs*. A more liberal credit policy normally leads to increased sales and generates marginal benefits in the form of higher gross profits. The marginal costs of this type of policy, however, include the cost of the additional funds invested in accounts receivable and inventories, any additional credit checking and collection costs, and increased bad-debt expenses.
- A financial manager can exercise control over the company's level of receivables investment through three credit policy variables: *credit standards, credit terms,* and the *collection effort.* All three variables can be used to control the average collection period and bad-debt loss ratio.
  1. Credit standards are the criteria a business uses to screen its credit applicants.
  2. Credit terms are the conditions under which customers are required to repay the credit extended to them. Credit terms specify the length of the credit period and the cash discount (if any) given for early payment.
  3. The collection effort represents the methods used in attempting to collect payment from past-due accounts.
- Evaluating individual credit applicants involves *gathering information* about the applicant, *analyzing this information* to determine the applicant's creditworthiness, and then *making the credit decision.*
- The amount of information a business can collect on a credit applicant is limited by both time and cost considerations. In deciding whether to seek more information about an applicant, the credit analyst should weigh the expected returns from more information against the cost of obtaining it.
- Possible sources of relevant information about a credit applicant include financial statements submitted by the applicant, credit reporting organizations (such as Dun and Bradstreet), banks, and the company's own prior experience with the customer.
- The five *C*s of credit, which are *character, capacity, capital, collateral,* and *conditions,* can be used as credit-screening guidelines to help ensure that a company will consider most of the relevant factors in the analysis and decision-making process.

- Inventories serve as a *buffer* between the various stages of the manufacturing firm's procurement-production-sales cycle. By uncoupling the various phases of the firm's operations, inventories provide the firm with *flexibility* in timing purchases, scheduling production, and meeting fluctuating, uncertain demand for the finished product.

- Inventory-related costs include *ordering costs, carrying costs,* and *stockout costs.* Ordering costs include all the costs of placing and receiving an order. Carrying costs include the various costs of holding items in inventory, including the cost of funds invested in inventory. Stockout costs are the costs incurred when demand exceeds available inventory, such as lost profits.

- ABC inventory classification is a method of dividing inventory items into three groups: those with a relatively large dollar value but a small percentage of the total items (A), those with a small dollar value but a large percentage of the total items (C), and items in between (B). Group A items should be controlled more closely than group B or C items.

- Inventory control models are usually classified into two types: *deterministic,* if demand and lead time are known with *certainty,* and *probabilistic,* if demand and/or lead time are *random variables* with known probability distributions.

- The objective of the deterministic *economic order quantity* (EOQ) *model* is to find the order quantity that minimizes total inventory costs.

- The economic order quantity is equal to $\sqrt{2SD/C}$, where D is the annual demand; S, the fixed cost per order; and C, the annual carrying cost per unit.

- Some of the assumptions made in the basic EOQ model do not necessarily apply in practice. In the event of a nonzero lead time, for example, the model must be modified.

- Probabilistic inventory control models require consideration of the possibility of *stockouts.* One approach used to handle this problem is to add a *safety stock* to the inventory.

- *Just-in-time inventory models* are based on the concept that required inventory items are supplied exactly as needed by production. Successful implementation of just-in-time models can reduce inventory investment.

■ QUESTIONS AND TOPICS FOR DISCUSSION

1. What are the marginal returns and costs associated with a more liberal extension of credit to a firm's customers?

2. What are the major credit policy variables a firm can use to control its level of receivables investment?

3. Define the following terms:
   a. Average collection period.
   b. Bad-debt loss ratio.
   c. Aging of accounts.

4. Discuss at least two reasons why a firm might want to offer seasonal datings to its customers.

5. Describe the marginal costs and benefits associated with each of the following changes in a firm's credit and collection policies:
   a. Increasing the credit period from 7 to 30 days.
   b. Increasing the cash discount from 1 to 2 percent.
   c. Offering a seasonal dating credit plan.
   d. Increasing collection expenditures (and effort).

6. Describe the three steps involved in evaluating credit applicants.

7. What are the primary sources of information about the creditworthiness of credit applicants?

8. Describe the five *C*s of credit used in evaluating the creditworthiness of a credit applicant.

9. How does a firm's required rate of return on investment enter into the analysis of changes in its credit and collection policies?

10. A firm is currently selling on credit terms of "net 30," and its accounts receivable average 30 days past due (that is, the firm's average collection period is 60 days). What credit policy variables might the firm consider changing to reduce its average collection period?

11. "The objective of the firm's credit and collection policies should be to minimize its bad-debt losses." Do you agree or disagree with this statement? Explain.

12. Discuss how each of the following factors would tend to affect a firm's credit extension policies:
    a. A shortage of working capital.
    b. An increase in output to the point where the firm is operating at full production capacity.
    c. An increase in the firm's profit margin (that is, its profit contribution ratio).
    d. An increase in interest rates (that is, borrowing costs).

13. Describe the benefits of holding the following:
    a. Raw materials inventories.
    b. Work-in-process inventories.
    c. Finished goods inventories.

14. Describe the components of carrying costs.

15. How do ordering costs for items purchased externally differ from ordering costs for items manufactured internally within the firm?

16. Describe the nature of stockout costs associated with a stockout in the following:
    a. Raw materials inventories.
    b. Work-in-process inventories.
    c. Finished goods inventories.

17. What is ABC inventory classification? How can this method be useful to a business?

18. Describe the assumptions underlying the basic EOQ model.

19. In general terms, describe how to deal with each of the following conditions when determining the optimal inventory level:
    a. Constant (nonzero) replenishment lead time known with certainty.
    b. Demand and replenishment lead time subject to uncertainty.

20. How does the firm's required rate of return on investment enter into inventory decisions?

21. What are just-in-time inventory models?

22. Define the following terms:
    a. Stockout.
    b. Deterministic inventory control models.
    c. Probabilistic inventory control models.
    d. Safety stock.
    e. Lead time.

■ SELF-TEST PROBLEMS

Note: **When converting from annual data to daily data or vice versa, assume there are 365 days per year.**

ST1. Taiwan Electronic Company sells on terms of "net 30." Annual credit sales are $54.75 million, and its accounts receivable average 10 days overdue.
    a. Determine Taiwan Electronic Company's investment in receivables.
    b. Suppose that, as the result of a recession, annual credit sales decline by 15 percent and customers delay their payments to an average of 25 days past due. Determine the company's new level of receivables investment.

ST2. Plant Nutrients, Inc. (PNI) sells fertilizers and pesticides to various retail hardware and nursery stores on terms of "2/10, net 30." The company currently does not grant credit to retailers with a 3 (fair) or 4 (limited) Dun and Bradstreet Composite Credit Appraisal. An estimated $5,475,000 in additional sales per year could be generated if PNI extended credit to retailers in the "fair" category. The estimated average collection period for these customers is 75 days, and the expected bad-debt loss ratio is 5 percent. The company also estimates that an additional inventory investment of $800,000 is required for the anticipated sales increase. Approximately 10 percent of these customers are expected to take the cash discount. PNI's variable cost ratio is 0.75, and its required pretax rate of return on investments in current assets is 18 percent. Determine the following:
   a. Marginal profitability of additional sales.
   b. Cost of additional investment in receivables.
   c. Additional bad-debt loss.
   d. Cost of additional investment in inventory.
   e. Additional cash discounts.
   f. Net change in pretax profits.

ST3. Blackhawk Supply Company sells $21.9 million of its products to wholesalers on credit terms of "net 30." Currently, the firm's average collection period is 55 days. Blackhawk is considering offering a 2 percent discount to customers who pay their bills within 10 days. The firm expects 50 percent of its customers to take the discount and its average collection period to decline to 35 days. Blackhawk's required pretax return on receivables investment is 18 percent. Determine the net effect on Blackhawk's pretax profits of offering a 2 percent cash discount.

ST4. SportsMart, a chain of sporting goods stores, sells 360,000 baseballs per year. (Assume that sales are uniform throughout the year.) The baseballs cost SportsMart $15 per dozen ($1.25 each). Annual inventory carrying costs are 20 percent of inventory value. The costs of placing and receiving an order are $72. Assume that inventory replenishment occurs virtually instantaneously. Determine the following:
   a. Economic order quantity.
   b. Total annual inventory costs of this policy.
   c. Optimal ordering frequency.

■ PROBLEMS*

Note: **When converting annual data to daily data or vice versa in these problems, assume there are 365 days per year.**

1. Miranda Tool Company sells to retail hardware stores on credit terms of "net 30." Annual credit sales are $18 million and are spread evenly throughout the year. The company's variable cost ratio is 0.70, and its accounts receivable average $1.9 million. Using this information, determine the following for the company:
   a. Average daily credit sales.
   b. Average collection period.
   c. Average investment in receivables.

2. Drake Paper Company sells on terms of "net 30." The firm's variable cost ratio is 0.80.
   a. If annual credit sales are $20 million and its accounts receivable average 15 days *overdue*, what is Drake's investment in receivables?
   b. Suppose that, as the result of a recession, annual credit sales decline by 10 percent to $18 million, and customers delay their payments to an average of 25 days *past the due date*. What will be Drake's new level of receivables investment?

3. Looking back at Tables 17-1 and 17-2, evaluate the impact on Bassett's pretax profits of extending full credit to the customers in Credit Risk Group 5. Assume that Bassett's pretax required rate of return on inventory investments is 20 percent and

that an additional inventory investment of $40,000 is required due to the anticipated sales increase from customers in Credit Risk Group 5.

4. Once again, consider the Bassett Furniture Industries example (Tables 17-1 and 17-2). Assume that rising labor and interest costs have increased Bassett's variable cost ratio from 0.75 to 0.80 and its required pretax rate of return on receivables and inventory investments from 20 to 25 percent. Reevaluate the effect of Bassett's pretax profits of extending full credit to the customers in Credit Risk Group 4.

e✗cel

5. Epstein Company, a wholesale distributor of jewelry, sells to retail jewelry stores on terms of "net 120." Its average collection period is 150 days. The company is considering the introduction of a 4 percent cash discount if customers pay within 30 days. Such a change in credit terms is expected to reduce the average collection period to 108 days. Epstein expects 30 percent of its customers to take the cash discount. Annual credit sales are $6 million. Epstein's variable cost ratio is 0.667, and its required pretax return on receivables investment is 15 percent. The company does not expect its inventory level to change as a result of the change in credit terms. Determine the following:
   a. The funds released by the change in credit terms.
   b. The net effect on Epstein's pretax profits.

e✗cel

6. In an effort to speed up the collection of receivables, Hill Publishing Company is considering increasing the size of its cash discount by changing its credit terms from "1/10, net 30" to "2/10, net 30." Currently, the company's collection period averages 43 days. Under the new credit terms, it is expected to decline to 28 days. Also, the percentage of customers who will take advantage of the cash discount is expected to increase from the current 50 percent to 70 percent with the new credit terms. Bad-debt losses currently average 4 percent of sales and are not expected to change significantly if Hill changes its credit policy. Annual credit sales are $3.5 million, the variable cost ratio is 60 percent, and the required pretax rate of return (that is, the opportunity cost) on receivables investment is 14 percent. The company does not expect its inventory level to change as a result of its proposed change in credit terms. Assuming that Hill does decide to increase the size of its cash discount, determine the following:
   a. The earnings on the funds released by the change in credit terms.
   b. The cost of the additional cash discounts taken.
   c. The net effect on Hill's pretax profits.

7. The North Carolina Furniture Company (NCFC) manufactures upholstered furniture, which it sells to various small retailers in the Northeast and Midwest on credit terms of "2/10, net 60." The company currently does not grant credit to retailers with a 3 (fair) or 4 (limited) Dun and Bradstreet Composite Credit Appraisal. If NCFC were to extend credit to retailers in the "fair" category, an estimated additional $1.2 million per year in sales could be generated. The estimated average collection period for these customers is 90 days, and the expected bad-debt loss ratio is 6 percent. Approximately 20 percent of these customers are expected to take the cash discount. NCFC's variable cost ratio is 0.70, and its required pretax rate of return on current assets investments is 20 percent. The company also estimates that an additional investment in inventory of $350,000 is necessary for the anticipated sales increase. Determine the net change in NCFC's pretax profits from extending credit to retailers in the "fair" category.

8. Michigan Pharmaceuticals, Inc., a wholesale distributor of ethical drugs to local pharmacies, has been experiencing a relatively long average collection period because many of its customers face liquidity problems and delay their payments well beyond the due date. In addition, its bad-debt loss ratio is high because a number of pharmacies have closed due to financial difficulties. To avoid these problems in the future, Michigan Pharmaceuticals is considering a plan to *institute more stringent credit standards* to keep the average collection period and bad-debt losses from rising beyond acceptable limits. Specifically, the firm plans to refuse to grant additional

credit to any current customers more than 15 days past due on their payments. Such a change in credit policy is expected to reduce current annual sales of $6.5 million by 20 percent, *reduce* the average collection period from 110 days to 75 days, and lower bad-debt losses from 8 to 4 percent. Due to the expected decrease in sales, the company estimates that its inventories will decrease by $250,000. The firm's variable cost ratio is 0.75, and its required pretax return on investments in receivables and inventories is 15 percent. Determine the net effect of this plan on the pretax profits of Michigan Pharmaceuticals.

9. Swenson Electric Company sells on terms of "net 30." Given the following information on its receivables, construct an aging of accounts schedule as of September 1, showing the percentage of accounts that are current, 1 to 30 days past due, 31 to 60 days past due, 61 to 90 days past due, and over 90 days past due. (Assume 30 days in each month.)

Account Number	Invoice Date	Amount Due
1311	August 15	$1,315
1773	July 14	721
1217	July 25	677
1319	August 14	1,711
1814	April 10	325
1713	August 5	917
1443	May 8	493
1144	June 28	211
1972	May 5	755
1011	April 21	377
1619	August 28	1,550
1322	August 13	275
1173	March 5	675
1856	August 12	695
1317	June 10	720

10. Creole Industries, Inc. estimates that if it spent an additional $20,000 to hire another collection agent in its credit department, it could lower its bad-debt loss ratio to 3.5 percent from a current rate of 4 percent and also reduce its average collection period from 50 to 45 days. (Assume that sales and inventory remain unchanged if the agent is hired.) Creole's annual credit sales are $5 million, and its variable cost ratio is 0.75. The firm's required pretax rate of return on receivables investment (that is, the opportunity cost) is 18 percent. Determine the net effect on Creole's pretax profits of hiring the additional collection agent.

11. Jenkins Supply Corporation sells $120 million of its products to wholesalers on terms of "net 50." Currently, the firm's average collection period is 65 days. In order to speed up the collection of receivables, Jenkins is considering offering a 1 percent cash discount if customers pay their bills within 15 days. The firm expects 40 percent of its customers to take the discount and its average collection period to decline to 40 days. The firm's required pretax return on receivables investments is 20 percent. Determine the net effect on Jenkins' pretax profits of offering a 1 percent cash discount.

eXcel

12. The Bimbo Corporation has been experiencing a decline in sales relative to its major competitors. Because Bimbo is confident about the quality of its products, it suspects that this sales loss may reflect its relatively stringent credit standards and terms. The firm currently has credit sales of $50 million annually. With current credit terms of "net 20," its average collection period is now 25 days. Bad debt losses are 2 percent of credit sales. The firm's variable cost ratio is 0.80, and its required pretax return on receivables and inventory investments is 20 percent.

eXcel

Bimbo plans to change its credit terms to "2/10, net 30." It expects 20 percent of its customers to take advantage of the cash discount. Bimbo also plans to relax credit standards and take on riskier accounts. This action is expected to increase credit sales by 30 percent. Bad-debt losses are expected to increase to 3 percent of credit sales, and the average collection period is expected to become 30 days. The company also estimates that an additional investment in inventory of $3 million is required because of the anticipated sales increase. Determine the net effect of this plan on the pretax profits of Bimbo.

13. Allied Apparel Company received a large order from Websters Department Stores, which operates a chain of approximately 300 popular-priced department stores located primarily in the New England–Middle Atlantic states. Allied is considering extending trade credit to Websters. As part of its credit check, Allied obtained Websters' balance sheets and income statements (which follow) for the last three years. A check of several of Websters' trade creditors has revealed that the firm generally takes any cash discounts when they are offered but averages about 30 days overdue on its payments to two suppliers whose credit terms are "net 30."

A Dun and Bradstreet publication entitled *Key Business Ratios* yielded the following information concerning the "average" financial ratios for firms in the same line of business as Websters:

Current assets to current liabilities	2.82
Earnings after taxes to sales	1.89%
Earnings after taxes to stockholders' equity	5.65%
Total liabilities to stockholders' equity	1.48

Websters Department Stores Balance Sheet (in thousands of dollars)

	19X1	19X2	19X3
Assets			
Current assets:			
Cash and marketable securities	$ 9,283	$ 13,785	$ 23,893
Accounts receivable (net)	162,825	179,640	140,543
Inventories	119,860	135,191	120,707
Other	1,994	2,190	1,956
Total current assets	$293,962	$330,806	$296,099
Long-term assets:			
Building and equipment (net)	$ 27,426	$ 30,295	$ 30,580
Other	11,821	14,794	16,687
Total long-term assets	$ 39,247	$ 45,089	$ 47,267
Total assets	$333,209	$375,895	$343,366
Liabilities and stockholders' equity			
Current liabilities:			
Accounts payable	$ 23,637	$ 21,861	$ 15,020
Notes payable	117,010	135,929	165,299
Other	49,273	49,229	29,653
Total current liabilities	$189,920	$207,019	$209,972
Long-term liabilities:			
Debentures	$ 38,001	$ 36,101	$ 35,201
Term loan	—	28,440	29,701
Other	4,986	853	655
Total long-term liabilities	$ 42,987	$ 65,394	$ 65,557
Stockholders' equity:			
Common stock	$ 5,576	$ 5,576	$ 5,576
Preferred stock	2,580	2,580	2,580
Retained earnings	92,146	95,326	59,681
Total stockholders' equity	$100,302	$103,482	$ 67,837
Total liabilities and stockholders' equity	$333,209	$375,895	$343,366

Websters Department Stores Income Statement (in thousands of dollars)

	19X1	19X2	19X3
Sales	$494,550	$556,132	$529,857
Cost of sales	337,580	384,899	390,980
Gross profit	$156,970	$171,233	$138,877
Selling, general and administrative expenses	133,330	155,494	187,926
Earnings before taxes	$ 23,640	$ 15,739	$-49,049
Income taxes	7,715	6,222	–14,741
Earnings after taxes	$ 15,925	$ 9,517	$-34,308
Dividends	6,343	6,337	1,337
Additions to retained earnings	$ 9,582	$ 3,180	$-35,645

In evaluating Websters' application for trade credit, answer the following questions:

a. What positive financial factors would lead Allied to decide to extend credit to Websters?

b. What negative financial factors would lead Allied to decide *not* to extend credit to Websters?

c. What additional information about Websters would be useful in performing the analysis?

14. Saccomanno Industries, Inc. is considering whether to discontinue offering credit to customers who are more than 10 days overdue on repaying the credit extended to them. Current annual credit sales are $10 million on credit terms of "net 30." Such a change in policy is expected to reduce sales by 10 percent, cut the firm's bad-debt losses from 5 to 3 percent, and reduce its average collection period from 72 days to 45 days. The firm's variable cost ratio is 0.70 and its required pretax return on receivables and inventory investments is 25 percent. Because of the anticipated decrease in sales, the company expects its inventories to decrease by $200,000. Determine the net effect of this credit-tightening policy on the pretax profits of Saccomanno Industries.

15. The Blawnox Company is concerned about its bad-debt losses and the length of time required to collect receivables. Current sales are $43.8 million per year. Bad-debt losses are currently 3.5 percent of sales, and the average collection period is 68 days (credit terms are "net 30"). One plan under consideration is to tighten credit standards by refusing to grant additional credit to any customers who are more than 15 days past due on their payments. This change in credit policy is expected to reduce sales by 10 percent but also reduce bad-debt losses to 2.5 percent of sales and reduce the average collection period to 40 days. The firm's variable cost ratio is 70 percent, and its required pretax rate of return on current assets investments is 18 percent. The company also expects its inventory investment to decrease by $1 million due to the anticipated decrease in sales. Determine the net effect of this plan on Blawnox's pretax profits.

16. Allstar Shoe Company produces a wide variety of athletic-type shoes for tennis, basketball, and running. Although sales are somewhat seasonal, production is uniform throughout the year. Allstar's production and sales average 1.92 million pairs of shoes per year. The company purchases shoelaces for its entire product line. Shoelaces are bought in lots of 10,000 pairs at a price of $800 per lot. Ordering costs are $20, including the cost of preparing the purchase order and inspecting the shipment when it arrives at the company's warehouse. Annual inventory carrying costs average 15 percent of the inventory value. Assuming that the shoelace manufacturer is located nearby and that orders are filled on the same day they are placed (that is, virtually instantaneously), determine the following:

a. The EOQ for shoelaces.

b. The total annual inventory costs of this policy.

c. The frequency with which Allstar should place its orders for shoelaces.

17. Quick-Copy Duplicating Company uses 110,000 reams of standard-sized paper a year at its various duplicating centers. Its current paper supplier charges $2.00 per ream.

Annual inventory carrying costs are 15 percent of inventory value. The cost of placing and receiving an order of paper are $41.25. Assuming that inventory replenishment occurs virtually instantaneously, determine the following:

a. The firm's EOQ.

b. The total annual inventory costs of this policy.

c. The optimal ordering frequency.

d. Compute and plot ordering costs, carrying costs, and total inventory costs for order quantities of 2,000, 4,000, 5,000, 5,500, 6,000, 7,000 and 9,000 reams. Connect the points on each function with a smooth curve, and determine the EOQ from the graph (and the table used in constructing the graph).

18. East Publishing Company employs a high-speed printing press in its operations. A typical production run of 5,000 to 50,000 copies of a textbook can be produced in less than 1 day. The manager of the business textbook division is attempting to determine the optimal number of copies of the seventh editions of its financial management and managerial economics textbooks to produce. Expected annual demand for the two books are 50,000 and 22,500 copies, respectively. Furthermore, the manager does not want to produce more than a 3-year supply of either book, because these textbooks are normally revised after the third year. Setup costs of getting the printing press (and bindery) ready for a production run of a given textbook are $2,500 and $2,000, respectively, for the two books. Annual carrying costs are $0.80 per copy (16 percent annual carrying charge times the $5.00 production cost per copy). For each textbook, determine the following:

a. The economic order quantity.

b. The total annual inventory costs.

c. The optimal ordering frequency.

19. Arizona Instruments uses integrated circuits (ICs) in its business calculators. Its annual demand for ICs is 120,000 units. The ICs cost Arizona Instruments $10 each. The company has determined that the EOQ is 20,000 units. It takes 18 days between when an order is placed and when the delivery is received. Carrying costs are 20 percent of the inventory value. Determine the following:

a. The optimal ordering frequency.

b. The average inventory and annual carrying costs.

c. The reorder point.

20. General Cereal Company purchases various grains (e.g., wheat and corn) that it processes into ready-to-eat cereals. Its annual demand for wheat is 250,000 bushels. Assume that demand is uniform throughout the year. The average price of wheat is $3.0625 per bushel (delivered). Annual inventory carrying costs are 16 percent of inventory value. The costs of placing and receiving an order are $98. Assume that inventory replenishment occurs virtually instantaneously. Determine the following:

a. Economic order quantity.

b. Total annual inventory costs of this policy.

c. Optimal ordering frequency.

21. Books, etc., a nationwide chain of bookstores, anticipates that annual demand for the paperback version of a best-selling novel will be 150,000 copies. The books cost the firm $2 each. Books, etc. has determined that the optimal order quantity (EOQ) is 30,000 copies. It takes 20 days between when an order is placed to when the delivery is received. Carrying costs are 15 percent of the inventory value. Determine the following:

a. Optimal ordering frequency.

b. Average inventory and annual carrying costs.

c. Reorder point.

Books, etc. decides that it wants to maintain a 60-day safety stock of the novel to meet unexpected demand and possible shipment delays from the publisher. Determine the following:

d. Amount of safety stock, in units.

e. Average inventory and annual carrying costs.

f. Reorder point.

22. Your boss has heard of a new company called VisionPoint that offers a complete accounts-receivable system for interested firms. Visit their Web site and then prepare a one-page memo for your boss summarizing VisionPoint's services. www.sbt.com

23. Take a look at the inventory control system maintained by RWS Information Systems. Prepare a one-page memo summarizing their system. www.rwsinfo.com/index.html

■ SOLUTIONS TO SELF-TEST PROBLEMS

ST1. a. Average collection period = 30 + 10 = 40 days

Average daily sales = Annual sales/365

$$= \$54,750,000/365$$

$$= \$150,000$$

Investment in receivables = Average daily sales × Average collection period

$$= \$150,000 \times 40 = \$6,000,000$$

b. Investment in receivables = {[\$54,750,000 × (1 − 0.15)]/365} × (30 + 25)

$$= \$7,012,500$$

ST2. a. Additional sales = \$5,475,000

Marginal profitability of additional sales = Additional sales × Profit contribution ratio

$$= \$5,475,000 \times (1 - 0.75) = \$1,368,750$$

b. Additional investment in receivables = (Additional annual sales/365) × Average collection period

$$= (\$5,475,000/365) \times 75 = \$1,125,000$$

Cost of additional investment in receivables = Additional investment in receivables × Required rate of return

$$= \$1,125,000 \times 0.18 = \$202,500$$

c. Additional bad-debt loss = Additional sales × Bad-debt loss ratio

$$= \$5,475,000 \times 0.05 = \$273,750$$

d. Cost of additional investment in inventory

= Additional investment in inventory × Required rate of return

= \$800,000 × 0.18 = \$144,000

e. Additional cash discounts = Additional sales × Percent taking discount × Cash discount percent

$$= \$5,475,000 \times 0.10 \times 0.02 = \$10,950$$

f. Net change in pretax profits = Marginal returns − Marginal costs

$$= \$1,368,750 - (\$202,500 + \$273,750 + \$10,950 + \$144,000)$$

$$= \$737,550$$

ST3. Reduction in receivables balance = Annual sales/365 × Reduction in average collection period

$$= (\$21,900,000/365) \times (55 - 35) = \$1,200,000$$

Return on reduction in receivables balance = Reduction in receivables balance × Required rate of return

$$= \$1,200,000 \times 0.18 = \$216,000$$

Cost of discount = Sales × Percent taking discount × Cash discount percent

$$= \$21,900,000 \times 0.50 \times 0.02 = \$219,000$$

Net change in pretax profits = Marginal returns − Marginal costs

$$= \$216,000 - \$219,000$$

$$= -\$3,000$$

ST4. a. S = $72; D = 360,000 baseballs;

C = 0.20 × $1.25 = $0.25/baseball

$$Q^* = \sqrt{\frac{2SD}{C}}$$

$$= \sqrt{\frac{2(\$72)(360,000)}{\$0.25}}$$

= 14,400 baseballs (1,200 dozen)

b. $$TC = \frac{D \times S}{Q^*} + \frac{Q^* \times C}{2}$$

$$= \frac{360,000 \times \$72}{14,400} + \frac{14,400 \times \$0.25}{2}$$

$$= \$3,600$$

c. $$T^* = \frac{365 \times Q^*}{D}$$

$$= \frac{365 \times 14,400}{360,000}$$

$$= 14.6 \text{ days}$$

■ GLOSSARY

ABC Inventory Classification A method of dividing inventory items into three groups—those with a relatively large dollar value but a small percentage of the total items, those with a small dollar value but a large percentage of the total items, and those items in between.

Average Collection Period The average number of days between when a credit sale is made and when the customer's payment is received.

Bad-Debt Loss Ratio The proportion of the total receivables volume that is never collected by a business.

Carrying Costs All costs associated with holding items in inventory for a given period of time.

Cash Discount A discount offered for early payment of an invoice.

Credit Period The length of time a credit customer has to pay the account in full.

Discount Period The length of time a credit customer has to pay the account and still be eligible to take any cash discount offered.

Economic Order Quantity The quantity of an inventory item that should be ordered to minimize total inventory costs.

Inventory Cycle The time between placement of successive orders of an item.

Just-in-time Inventory System An approach to inventory and production management in which required inventory items are supplied exactly as needed by production.

Lead Time The time between when an order is placed for an item and when the item actually is received in inventory.

Ordering Costs All costs associated with placing and receiving an order.

Reorder Point The inventory level at which an order should be placed for replenishment of an item.

Seasonal Datings Credit terms under which the buyer of seasonal merchandise is encouraged to take delivery well before the peak sales period. Payment on the purchase is deferred until after the peak sales period.

Stockout Costs The cost of lost sales associated with the inability to fill orders from inventory.

Variable Cost Ratio Variable production, administrative, and marketing costs per dollar of sales.

SHORT- AND INTERMEDIATE-TERM FUNDING ALTERNATIVES

18

1. *Trade credit, or accounts payable,* is the principal source of *spontaneous* short-term credit.

2. *Bank loans, commercial paper, accounts receivable loans,* and *inventory loans* are the major sources of negotiated short-term credit.

3. The cost of trade credit is dependent on the size of any cash discount offered and the lengths of the credit and discount periods.

4. The types of short-term bank credit include *single loans, lines of credit,* and *revolving credit agreements.*

5. Commercial paper is a short-term unsecured credit instrument issued by major corporations with good credit ratings.

6. A company can use its accounts receivable to obtain short-term financing. It can either *pledge* the accounts receivable as collateral for a loan or sell *(factor)* the receivables to obtain cash.

7. A company also can use its inventory as collateral for a short-term loan. The lender can either allow the borrower to hold the collateral (under a *floating lien* or *trust receipts* arrangement) or require that a third party hold the collateral (under a *terminal warehouse* or *field warehouse* arrangement).

KEY CHAPTER CONCEPTS

8. Term loans are debt obligations having an initial maturity between 1 and 10 years.

   a. The major suppliers of term loans are banks, insurance companies, pension funds, and equipment suppliers.

   b. Term loans usually are amortized over the life of the loan.

   c. The interest rate on term loans obtained from commercial banks is normally greater than the bank's prime rate.

   d. Some term loans from banks require that a compensating balance be maintained at the bank. Other term loans contain a provision that gives the lender an equity participation in the borrowing company.

   e. Most term loans are secured. The loan agreement contains affirmative, negative, and restrictive covenants. In addition, the conditions that determine when a default on the loan has occurred are detailed in the loan agreement.

9. Equipment financing loans are commonly made for equipment that is readily marketable. These loans are normally secured with a *conditional sales contract* or a *chattel mortgage.*

R. H. MACY & COMPANY AND ITS SUPPLIERS*

Many small apparel makers who supply retailers with merchandise finance their operations by selling their receivables to companies and banks known as *factors*. A factor purchases these receivables from the supplier at a discount and assumes the risk that the amount owed by the retailer will not be paid. The discount from the face value of the receivables represents the fee that the factor receives for performing the credit checking and collection functions and for bearing the default risk.

Consider the case of R. H. Macy & Company, a large retail department store chain. Approximately 15 percent of its merchandise purchases involve factoring companies. Prior to 1990, factors accepted all of Macy's receivables that suppliers wanted to sell. However, as a result of Macy's highly leveraged balance sheet and continuing losses during its 1990 and 1991 fiscal years, a number of factors attempted to reduce their risk exposure by cutting back on the amount of Macy's receivables they would purchase or guarantee. For example, in November 1991, Heller Financial (a unit of Fuji Bank of Tokyo) decided to no longer guarantee payments for new goods shipped by suppliers to Macy. Other factors limited their exposure by reducing the amount of orders they were willing to guarantee. Such actions by factors sometimes precede

a retailing firm being forced to file for bankruptcy, as was the case in the Federated Department Stores and Allied Stores bankruptcies in January 1990.

Suppliers were faced with the following decision. They could continue to do business with Macy and assume all or part of the risk that they would not be paid for the merchandise shipped to the department store chain, or they could stop shipping merchandise to Macy. However, with the latter alternative, they probably would be forced to reduce production, which would result in lower profits. Also, as the result of numerous bankruptcies in the retailing industry, these apparel makers have fewer customers to sell to, and every remaining major account (like Macy) becomes that much more significant.

As it turned out, Macy was forced to declare bankruptcy in January 1992, owing its suppliers an estimated $275 million. These suppliers expected to collect 50 percent or less of their claims against the retailer. In December 1994, Macy merged with Federated Department Stores.

This chapter considers the characteristics and costs of various sources of short- and intermediate-term credit, such as factoring receivables.

*Based on "Macy's Smaller Suppliers Forced Into Riskier Position," *Wall Street Journal* (November 2, 1990): B2; "Macy Payments Lose Guarantee of Factor Firm," *Wall Street Journal* (November 18, 1991): A6; and "Macy Files for Chapter 11, Lists Assets of $4.95 Billion, Liabilities of $5.32 Billion," *Wall Street Journal* (January 28, 1992): A3.

INTRODUCTION

A company normally employs a combination of short- and intermediate-term credit and long-term debt and equity in financing its current and fixed assets. The various sources of long-term financing have already been discussed. This chapter focuses on the major sources of short- and intermediate-term credit.

Short-term credit includes all of a company's debt obligations that originally were scheduled for repayment within one year.[1] Short-term credit may be either *unsecured* or *secured*.[2] In the case of unsecured short-term debt, a firm obtains credit from the lender without having to pledge any specific assets as collateral, and the lender depends primarily on the cash-generating ability of the firm to repay the debt. If the firm becomes insolvent and declares bankruptcy, the unsecured lender usually stands little chance of recovering all or even a significant portion of the amount owed.

In the case of secured short-term debt, the borrower pledges certain specified assets—such as accounts receivable, inventory, or fixed assets—as collateral.[3] The Uniform Commercial Code, which was adopted by all states during the 1960s, outlines the procedures that must be followed in order for a lender to establish a valid claim on a firm's collateral.

The first step in this process involves the execution of a *security agreement*, which is a contract between the lender and the firm specifying the collateral held against the loan. The security agreement then is filed at the appropriate public office within the state where the collateral is located. Future potential lenders can check with this office to determine which assets the firm has pledged and which are still free to be used as collateral. Filing this security agreement legally establishes the lender's security interest in the collateral. If the borrower defaults on the loan or otherwise fails to honor the terms of the agreement, the lender can seize and sell the collateral to recover the amount owed. Thus, the lender in a secured short-term debt agreement has *two* potential sources of loan repayment: the firm's cash-generating ability and the collateral value of the pledged assets.

Short-term lenders can be classified as either *cash-flow lenders* or *asset-based lenders,* depending upon how they view the two potential sources of loan repayment. Cash-flow lenders look upon the borrower's future cash flows as the *primary* source of loan repayment and the borrower's assets as a *secondary* source of repayment. Asset-based lenders tend to make riskier loans than cash-flow lenders, and as a result, they place much greater emphasis on the value of the borrower's collateral. Generally, large, low-leveraged companies with good expected cash flows are able to borrow from cash-flow lenders, such as commercial banks, at relatively low rates. Smaller, highly leveraged businesses with more uncertain future cash flows, often have to borrow on a secured basis from asset-based lenders, such as commercial finance companies, at relatively high rates.

[1]Short-term credit does *not* always correspond exactly to the current liabilities shown on the firm's balance sheet. Current liabilities also include that portion of long-term debt (such as term loans and mortgages) scheduled for repayment during the next year.

[2]Intermediate- and long-term debt also may be either unsecured or secured.

[3]As an alternative to pledging specific assets as collateral for a loan, a company may get a third party to *cosign,* or *guarantee,* the loan. If the borrower defaults, the third party becomes responsible for repayment. Lenders usually will accept only financially sound third parties, such as a stockholder, supplier, or customer who has a vested interest in the company's success.

In general, companies prefer to borrow funds on an unsecured basis, because the added administrative costs involved in pledging assets as security raise the cost of the loan to the borrower. In addition, secured borrowing agreements can restrict a company's future borrowing. Many companies, particularly small ones, are not able to obtain unsecured credit, however. For example, a company may be financially weak or too new to justify an unsecured loan, or it may want more credit than the lender is willing to give on an unsecured basis. In any of these circumstances, the company either must provide collateral or it will not receive the loan.

The short-term credit sources available to a company can be either *spontaneous* or *negotiated*. Spontaneous sources, which include *trade credit, accrued expenses,* and *deferred income,* are discussed in upcoming sections. Later sections of this chapter consider the various negotiated sources, such as *bank credit, commercial paper, receivables loans,* and *inventory loans.*

The primary sources of intermediate-term funding for companies are term loans and leases. Term loans are examined later in the chapter and lease financing is examined in Chapter 19.

COST OF SHORT-TERM FUNDS

Managers need a method to calculate the financing cost for the various sources of short-term financing available to a firm. Equation 4.1 from Chapter 4 gives the amount of interest paid, I, on borrowed money:

$$I = PV_0 \times i \times n \tag{18.1}$$

where I = the interest amount in dollars; PV_0 = the principal amount at time 0, or the present value; i = the interest rate per time period; and n = the number of time periods. Solving for i, we obtain

$$i = \frac{I}{PV_0} \times \frac{1}{n} \tag{18.2}$$

The interest rate, i, is equal to the fractional interest cost per period, I/PV_0, times one divided by the number of time periods, or $1/n$.

The equation we use to calculate the **annual financing cost,** AFC, for short-term financing sources is a variation of Equation 18.2:

$$\text{AFC} = \frac{\text{Interest costs} + \text{fees}}{\text{Usable funds}} \times \frac{365}{\text{Maturity (days)}} \tag{18.3}$$

Short-term financing sources may involve fees in addition to the interest costs. Also, the term *usable funds* is used in place of present value, because some of the money from a particular short-term financing source actually may not be available for a company to use. The term, 365/maturity (days), converts the financing cost to an annual rate.

The annual financing cost calculated using Equation 18.3 is only an approximation to the true (effective) **annual percentage rate,** or APR, of a loan. Equation 18.3 does not consider compounding and slightly understates the true APR. Also, Equation 18.3 is normally used for financing sources of one year or less. The following equation gives the true APR for a short-term financing source:

$$APR = \left(1 + \frac{\text{Interest costs} + \text{fees}}{\text{Usable funds}}\right)^m - 1 \qquad (18.4)$$

where m is the number of times per year compounding occurs. Equation 18.4 is a variation of Equation 4.31 from Chapter 4. In addition, the APR of a loan is the internal rate of return between the funds received and the funds paid back.

To illustrate the use of Equations 18.3 and 18.4, consider a 6-month, $10,000 loan that has $500 of interest. If we assume that principal is paid only at maturity and there are 182 days in the 6-month period, the annual financing cost is calculated, using Equation 18.3, as follows:

$$AFC = \frac{\$500}{\$10,000} \times \frac{365}{182}$$

$$= 0.1003 \text{ or } 10.03\%$$

The loan's APR is determined as follows, using Equation 18.4:

$$APR = \left(1 + \frac{\$500}{\$10,000}\right)^{365/182} - 1$$

$$= 0.1028 \text{ or } 10.28\%$$

The annual financing cost percentage closely approximates the true APR, unless the number of compounding periods is large.

Equation 18.3 is used throughout this chapter to calculate the annual financing cost of the various short-term financing sources available to a firm.

TRADE CREDIT

Whenever a business receives merchandise ordered from a supplier and then is permitted to wait a specified period of time before having to pay, it is receiving *trade credit*.[4] In the aggregate, trade credit is the most important source of short-term financing for business firms. Smaller businesses in particular usually rely heavily on trade credit to finance their operations, because they often are unable to obtain funds from banks or other lenders in the financial markets.

Most trade credit is extended on an *open account* basis. A firm sends a purchase order to a supplier, who then evaluates the firm's creditworthiness using various information sources and decision criteria.[5] If the supplier decides to extend the firm credit, it ships the ordered merchandise to the firm, along with an invoice describing the contents of the shipment, the total amount due, and the terms of sale. When the firm accepts the merchandise shipped by the supplier, it in effect agrees to pay the amount due as specified by the terms of sale on the invoice. Once it has been established, trade credit becomes almost automatic and is subject to only periodic reviews by the supplier. Open account trade credit appears on the balance sheet as *accounts payable*.

Promissory notes are sometimes used as an alternative to the open account arrangement. When a company signs a **promissory note,** which specifies the

---

[4]If the supplier does not feel the firm is creditworthy, it can require that payment be made either before the goods are shipped (cash before delivery, or CBD) or upon delivery of the merchandise (cash on delivery, or COD). These are cash sales and do not involve an extension of credit.

[5]These sources and criteria are discussed in Chapter 17.

amount to be paid and the due date, it is formally recognizing an obligation to repay the credit. A supplier may require a company to sign a promissory note if it questions the company's creditworthiness. Promissory notes usually appear on the balance sheet as *notes payable.*

Credit Terms

Credit terms, or terms of sale, specify the conditions under which a business is required to repay the credit that a supplier has extended to it. These conditions include the *length* and the *beginning date* of the credit period, the *cash discount* (if any) given for prompt repayment, and any *special terms,* such as *seasonal datings.*[6]

Cost of Trade Credit

Trade credit is considered a *spontaneous* source of financing, because it normally expands as the volume of a company's purchases increases. For example, suppose a company experiences increased demand for its products. As a result, the company increases purchases from suppliers by 20 percent from an average of $10,000 per day to an average of $12,000 per day. Assuming that these purchases are made on credit terms of "net 30" and that the company waits until the last day of the credit period to make payment, its average accounts payable outstanding (trade credit) automatically will increase by 20 percent from $300,000 ($10,000 × 30) to $360,000 ($12,000 × 30).

Because the use of trade credit is flexible, informal, and relatively easy to obtain, it is an attractive source of financing for virtually all firms, especially new and smaller firms. To make intelligent use of trade credit, however, a firm should consider the associated costs. Unlike other sources of financing, such as bank loans and bonds, which include explicit interest charges, the cost of trade credit is not always readily apparent. It may appear to be "cost-free" because of the lack of interest charges, but this reasoning can lead to incorrect financing decisions.

Obviously, someone has to bear the cost of trade credit. In extending trade credit, the supplier incurs the cost of the funds invested in accounts receivable, plus the cost of any cash discounts that are taken. Normally, the supplier passes on all or part of these costs to its customers implicitly as part of the purchase price of the merchandise, depending on market supply and demand conditions. If a company is in a position to pay cash for purchases, it may consider trying to avoid these implicit costs by negotiating lower prices with suppliers.

If the terms of sale include a cash discount, the firm must decide whether or not to take it. If the firm *takes the cash discount,* it forgoes the credit offered by the supplier beyond the end of the discount period. Assuming that the firm takes the cash discount and wants to make maximum use of the credit offered by suppliers, it should pay its bills on the last day of the discount period. Under these conditions, trade credit does represent a "cost-free" source of financing to the firm (assuming that no additional discounts are available if the firm pays cash on delivery or cash before delivery).

If a company *forgoes the cash discount* and pays bills after the end of the discount period, a definite opportunity cost of trade credit is incurred. In calculating the cost of not taking the cash discount, it is assumed that the

---

[6]This topic is discussed in Chapter 17.

company will make maximum use of extended trade credit by paying on the last day of the credit period. Paying after the end of the credit period, or *stretching accounts payable*, subjects the company to certain other costs.

The annual financing cost of forgoing a cash discount is calculated using Equation 18.5. In this application, the AFC is equal to the fractional interest cost per period times the number of borrowing periods per year:

$$\text{AFC} = \frac{\text{Percentage discount}}{100 - \text{Percentage discount}} \times \frac{365}{\text{Credit period} - \text{Discount period}} \tag{18.5}$$

For example, suppose the Benson Company has been extended $1500 of trade credit from a supplier on terms of "2/10, net 30." As shown in Figure 18-1, the company can either pay the discounted amount ($1,470) by the end of the discount period (day 10) or pay the full amount of the invoice ($1,500) by the end of the credit period (day 30).

By *not* paying on the tenth day—that is, by forgoing the cash discount—the company has the use of $1,470 (98 percent of the invoice amount) for an additional 20 days and effectively pays $30 in interest.[7] Substituting this information into Equation 18.5 yields the following:

$$\text{AFC} = \frac{2}{100 - 2} \times \frac{365}{30 - 10}$$

$$= \frac{2}{98} \times \frac{365}{20}$$

$$= 37.2\%$$

FIGURE 18-1
Benson Company's Cost of Forgoing the Cash Discount

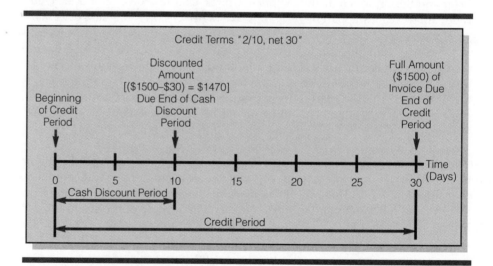

[7]If a firm does not pay by the cash discount date, it should not pay the invoice until the final date. If the invoice is paid before the final due date, the cost of this financing increases dramatically. For example, assume Benson Company pays on day 11 and does not take the cash discount. The cost of this financing is nearly 745 percent:

$$\left(\frac{2}{98} \times \frac{365}{11 - 10} \right)$$

As this example shows, the annual cost of forgoing cash discounts can be quite high. Therefore, when making financing decisions, a company should compare this cost to the costs of other sources of credit.

Also, the company that offers credit terms of "2/10, net 30" should consider the annual financing cost of having the use of funds for an additional 20 days. As the preceding calculation illustrates, the annual financing cost of offering cash discounts when the credit terms are "2/10, net 30" is about 37 percent. Accordingly, a company may want to consider other less expensive methods of encouraging prompt payment of trade credit. However, other benefits may accrue to a company that offers cash discounts. For example, a company may actually increase its sales by offering cash discounts. Or, a company may find that its bad-debt loss ratio is lowered if it offers a discount.

benefits of discount

Abuses of cash discounts also exist; for example, a purchaser may deduct the discount amount even when payment is made after the discount period has passed. As a result, the seller has to decide whether simply to accept the lower payment or attempt to collect the unearned cash discount amount. With either alternative, the seller incurs costs.

Stretching Accounts Payable

Rather than pay suppliers within the credit period specified in the terms of sale, a firm can postpone payment of the amount due to beyond the end of the credit period. *Stretching* payments in this manner generates additional short-term financing for the firm, but this credit is not cost-free. Not only does the firm incur the costs of forgoing any cash discounts, but its credit rating also may deteriorate, along with its ability to obtain future credit. Late payment penalties or interest charges also may be added to these costs, depending on specific industry practices. Although occasional stretching of payables—for example, to meet a seasonal need for funds—might be tolerated by suppliers and involve little or no cost to the firm, a firm that persistently stretches accounts payable well beyond their due dates may find its trade credit cut off by suppliers, who may adopt a cash before delivery (CBD) or a cash on delivery (COD) policy when dealing with the firm in the future. Finally, when a firm develops a reputation for being consistently slow in meeting financial obligations, banks and other lenders may refuse to loan funds on reasonable terms.

 ### ACCRUED EXPENSES AND DEFERRED INCOME

Accrued expenses and deferred income are additional spontaneous sources of unsecured short-term credit.

Accrued Expenses

Accrued expenses—such as *accrued wages, taxes,* and *interest*—represent liabilities for services rendered to the firm that have not yet been paid for by the firm. As such, they constitute an interest-free source of financing.

Accrued wages represent the money a business owes to its employees. Accrued wages build up between paydays and fall to zero again at the end of the pay period, when the employees receive their paychecks. A company can increase the average amount of accrued wages by lengthening the period between paydays. For example, changing from a 2-week pay cycle to a 4-week pay cycle would effectively double a firm's average level of accrued wages. Also, a company can increase accrued expenses by delaying the payment of sales commissions and bonuses. Legal and practical considerations, however, limit the extent to which a company can increase accrued wages in this manner.

The amounts of *accrued taxes* and *interest* a firm may accumulate is also determined by the frequency with which these expenses must be paid. For example, corporate income tax payments normally are due quarterly, and a firm can use accrued taxes as a source of funds between these payment dates. Similarly, accrued interest on a bond issue requiring semiannual interest payments can be used as a source of financing for periods as long as 6 months. Of course, a firm has no control over the frequency of these tax and interest payments, so the amount of financing provided by these sources depends solely on the amounts of the payments themselves.

Deferred Income

Deferred income consists of payments received for goods and services that the firm has agreed to deliver at some future date. Because these payments increase the firm's liquidity and assets—namely, cash—they constitute a source of funds.

Advance payments made by customers are the primary sources of deferred income. These payments are common on large, expensive products, such as jet aircraft. Because these payments are not "earned" by the firm until delivery of the goods or services to the customers, they are recognized on the balance sheet as a liability called *deferred income*.

SHORT-TERM BANK CREDIT

Commercial banks are an important source of both secured and unsecured short-term credit. In terms of the aggregate amount of short-term financing they provide to business firms, they rank second behind trade credit. Although trade credit is a primary source of *spontaneous* short-term financing, bank loans represent the major source of *negotiated* short-term funds.

A major purpose of short-term bank loans is to meet the firm's seasonal needs for funds—such as financing the buildup of inventories and receivables. Bank loans used for this purpose are regarded as self-liquidating, because sale of the inventories and collection of the receivables are expected to generate sufficient cash flows to permit the firm to repay the loan prior to the next seasonal buildup.

When a firm obtains a short-term bank loan, it normally signs a promissory note specifying the amount of the loan, the interest rate being charged, and the due date. The loan agreement may also contain various protective covenants.[8] Short-term bank loans appear on the balance sheet under *notes payable*.

The interest rate charged on a bank loan is usually related to the **prime rate,** which is the rate banks historically have charged on loans made to their most

---

[8]The section on term loans discusses these protective covenants.

creditworthy, or *prime,* business customers. The prime rate fluctuates over time with changes in the supply of and demand for loanable funds. During the past 25 years, for instance, the prime rate ranged from as low as 4.5 percent to as high as 21.5 percent. In recent years many large, highly profitable companies have been able to borrow at less than the prime rate. Subprime borrowing is partially the result of increased competition among large banks and other suppliers of short-term financing for especially creditworthy borrowers.

As an alternative to borrowing funds in the United States, large, well-established multinational corporations can borrow short-term funds in the Eurodollar market.[9] The interest rate in the Eurodollar market is usually related to the **London interbank offer rate,** or **LIBOR.** LIBOR is the interest rate at which banks in the Eurocurrency market lend to each other. For example, large, well-established multinational corporations usually can borrow at about 0.5 percentage points over LIBOR. Because LIBOR is frequently about 1.5 percentage points below U.S. bank prime rates, large companies can often borrow in the Eurodollar market at subprime rates. For example, Browning-Ferris, a large multinational corporation in the solid waste business, borrowed $30 million at a rate of LIBOR plus 0.25 percentage points from two foreign banks.[10]

Short-term bank financing is available under three different arrangements:

■ Single loans (notes).
■ Lines of credit.
■ Revolving credit agreements.

Single Loans (Notes)

Businesses frequently need funds for short time periods to finance a particular undertaking. In such a case, they may request a bank loan. This type of loan is often referred to as a *note.* The length of this type of loan can range from 30 days to 1 year, with most being for 30 to 90 days.

The interest rate a bank charges on an individual loan at a given point in time depends on a number of factors, including the borrower's creditworthiness relative to prime (lowest) credit risks. The interest rate often includes a premium of 1 to 2 or more percentage points above the prime rate, depending on how the bank officer perceives the borrower's overall business and financial risk. If the borrower is in a weak financial position and has overall risk that is thought to be too high, the bank may refuse to make an unsecured loan, regardless of the interest rate. When making the loan decision, the loan officer also considers the size of the checking account balance the company maintains at the bank, the amount of other business it does with the bank, and the rates that competitive banks are charging on similar loans.

The annual financing cost of a bank loan is also a function of when the borrower must pay the interest and whether the bank requires the borrower to maintain a compensating balance.

Interest Payments. If the interest on a note is paid at *maturity,* the annual financing cost is equal to the stated annual interest rate. In the case of a

[9]The Eurocurrency market is discussed in Chapter 2.
[10]Browning-Ferris Industries, Inc., *Annual Report* (1988): 47.

discounted loan, however, the bank deducts the interest at the time the loan is made, and thus the borrower does not receive the full loan amount. In other words, the borrower pays interest on funds it does not receive, and the annual financing cost of the loan is greater than the stated annual interest rate.[11]

For example, suppose the Edgewood Flower and Gift Shop receives a 6-month (183 day), $5,000 discounted loan at a stated annual interest rate of 8 percent. The firm pays $201 interest in advance ($0.08 \times \$5,000 \times 183/365$) and receives only $4,799 ($5,000 – $201). Using Equation 18.3, the annual financing cost is calculated as follows:

$$\text{AFC} = \frac{\$201}{\$4799} \times \frac{365}{183}$$

$$= 8.4\%$$

Discounted bank loans today are relatively uncommon; however, other securities—commercial paper and Treasury bills, for example—are sold on a discount basis.

Compensating Balances. A **compensating balance** is a certain percentage, usually 5 to 20 percent, of a loan balance that the borrower keeps on deposit with a bank as a requirement of a loan made by the bank. The compensating balance requirement is stated either in terms of an *absolute minimum* balance or an *average* balance over some stipulated period; borrowers prefer average balances to minimum balances. A compensating balance increases the return the bank earns on the loan and also provides the bank with a small measure of protection ("right of offset") in the event that the borrower defaults. Compensating balances tend to diminish in importance during periods of slack loan demand.

If the required compensating balance is *in excess* of the amount of funds that normally would be maintained in the company's checking account, the annual financing cost of the loan is greater than the stated interest rate. It can be calculated using Equation 18.3. When a compensating balance is required, the *usable funds* amount in the denominator is the *net* amount of the loan that the company can spend after taking into account the amount borrowed, any required compensating balance, and the balance normally maintained in the bank account.

For example, suppose the Cutler Company obtains a 1-year (365 day) $200,000 bank loan at 9 percent interest but is required to maintain a 20 percent average compensating balance. In other words, the company must maintain a $40,000 ($0.20 \times \$200,000$) average compensating balance to obtain the loan. If Cutler currently maintains a $30,000 average balance that can be used to meet the compensating balance requirement, it needs to keep an additional $10,000 in the account, and thus the loan generates $190,000 in usable funds. The interest charges on the loan are $18,000 ($200,000 \times 0.09$). Substituting these values into Equation 18.3 yields the following:

$$\text{AFC} = \frac{\$18,000}{\$190,000} \times \frac{365}{365}$$

$$= 9.5\%$$

[11]The process for determining the AFC (or APR) of a bank loan is a function of when the loan principal is repaid. The calculations in this section assume that the principal is repaid at maturity. In the case of *installment* loans, principal payments are made periodically (e.g., monthly) over the term of the loan.

However, if Cutler currently has no balances in its bank account that can be used to meet the average compensating balance requirement, it has to keep $40,000 of the $200,000 loan in the checking account, and the amount of usable funds is reduced to $160,000. In this case, the annual financing cost becomes significantly higher:

$$\text{AFC} = \frac{\$18,000}{\$160,000} \times \frac{365}{365}$$

$$= 11.3\%$$

Lines of Credit

A firm that needs funds periodically throughout the year for a variety of purposes may find it useful to negotiate a line of credit with its bank. A **line of credit** is an agreement that permits the firm to borrow funds up to a predetermined limit at any time during the life of the agreement. The major advantage of this type of borrowing agreement, as compared with single loans, is that the firm does not have to renegotiate with the bank every time funds are required. Instead, it can obtain funds on short notice with little or no additional justification. Another advantage to establishing a line of credit is that the firm can plan for its future short-term financing requirements without having to anticipate exactly how much it will have to borrow each month.

A line of credit is usually negotiated for a 1-year period, with renewals being subject to renegotiation each year. In determining the size of a credit line, a bank will consider a company's creditworthiness, along with its projected financing needs. As part of the application for a line of credit, the company is normally required to provide the bank with a cash budget for the next year, along with current and projected income statements and balance sheets. The interest rate on a line of credit is usually determined by adding to the prime rate a premium based on the borrower's creditworthiness. Because the prime rate normally fluctuates over time, the interest rate charged varies during the life of the agreement.

To illustrate, suppose the Bellevue Candy Company has a $500,000 line of credit at 1 percentage point above the bank's prime rate.[12] During the year, the company borrows, or "draws down," $200,000 on the line, and no compensating balances are in effect during the year. The bank's prime rate is 8.0 percent from January 1 to March 31, and on April 1, the bank raises its prime rate to 8.25 percent, where it remains for the rest of the year. The annual financing cost is calculated as follows using Equation 18.3:

Interest costs (January 1–March 31):

$$I = \$200,000 \times 0.09 \times \frac{90}{365}$$

$$= \$4,438.36$$

Interest costs (April 1–December 31):

[12]Finance professionals often refer to this rate as "prime plus one," or "one over prime." In addition, they often write it as "P + 1."

$$I = \$200,000 \times 0.0925 \times \frac{275}{365}$$

$$= \$13,938.36$$

$$\text{Total interest costs} = \$4,438.36 + \$13,938.36$$

$$= \$18,376.72$$

$$\text{AFC} = \frac{\$18,376.72}{\$200,000.00} \times \frac{365}{365}$$

$$= 9.19\%$$

A line of credit agreement normally includes certain protective covenants. In addition to possibly including a compensating balance requirement, the loan agreement usually contains an annual "clean-up" provision requiring that the company have no loans outstanding under the line of credit for a certain period of time each year, usually 30 to 90 days. This type of policy helps reassure the bank that the company is using the line of credit to finance seasonal needs for funds and not to finance permanent capital requirements. Finally, a line of credit agreement also may contain provisions (similar to those in a term loan agreement) that require the firm to maintain a minimum working capital position, limit total debt and lease financing, and restrict dividend payments.

Revolving Credit Agreements

Would you or your business like to apply over the Internet for a line of credit? Type in the term line of credit *and watch how many thousands (and thousands) of lenders will extend a line of credit to you.*

Although a line of credit agreement does not legally commit the bank to making loans to the firm under any and all conditions, the bank normally will feel morally obligated to honor the line of credit. Some banks, however, have chosen not to provide financing to a firm when the firm's financial position has deteriorated significantly or when the bank lacks sufficient loanable funds to satisfy all its commitments. If the firm desires a guaranteed line of credit, it must negotiate a revolving credit agreement.

Under a **revolving credit agreement,** or "revolver," the bank is *legally committed* to making loans to a company up to the predetermined credit limit specified in the agreement. Revolving credit agreements differ from line of credit agreements in that they require the borrower to pay a *commitment fee* on the unused portion of the funds. This fee typically is in the range of 0.25 to 0.50 percent. Revolving credit agreements frequently are made for a period of 2 to 5 years. For example, at the end of 1995, Ford Motor Company had revolving credit agreements with various banks in the United States that permitted the firm to borrow up to $8.4 billion through at least mid-2000.[13]

Calculating the annual financing cost of funds borrowed under a revolving credit agreement is slightly more complex than with either a single loan or a line of credit. In addition to the interest rate, commitment fee, compensating balance, and the firm's normal account balance, the annual financing cost of a revolving credit loan also depends on the amount borrowed and the credit limit of the agreement. The annual financing cost can be calculated based on Equation 18.3, as follows:

---

[13]Ford Motor Company, *Annual Report* (1995): 28.

$$AFC = \frac{\text{Interest costs} + \text{Commitment fee}}{\text{Usable funds}} \times \frac{365}{\text{Maturity (days)}} \qquad (18.6)$$

For example, suppose the Kalamazoo Company has a $4 million revolving credit agreement with its bank to borrow at the prime rate. The agreement requires the company to maintain a 10 percent average compensating balance on any funds borrowed under the agreement, as well as to pay a 0.5 percent commitment fee on the unused portion of the credit line. The prime rate during the year is expected to be 8 percent. Kalamazoo's average borrowing under the agreement during the year is expected to be $2 million. The company maintains an average of $100,000 in its account at the bank, which can be used to meet the compensating balance requirement.

To calculate the annual financing cost of the revolving credit agreement, Kalamazoo must determine the amount of usable funds generated by the loan, the total interest costs, and the commitment fees. Given average borrowing of $2 million during the year, Kalamazoo is required to maintain an average compensating balance of $200,000 (0.10 × $2 million). Because the company currently maintains an average balance of $100,000, $100,000 of the loan is needed to meet the compensating balance requirement. Therefore, the amount of usable funds is $1.9 million. Interest costs on the average amount borrowed are $160,000 (0.08 × $2 million), and the commitment fee on the unused portion of the credit line is $10,000 [0.005 × ($4 million – $2 million)]. Substituting these figures into Equation 18.6 yields the following annual financing cost of the loan:

$$AFC = \frac{\$160,000 + \$10,000}{\$1,900,000} \times \frac{365}{365}$$

$$= \frac{\$170,000}{\$1,900,000} \times \frac{365}{365}$$

$$= 8.95\%$$

Thus, the annual financing cost of the revolving credit agreement is higher than the stated interest rate.

Many financially sound companies view revolving credit agreements as a form of financial insurance, and, as a result, these companies frequently have little or no borrowings outstanding against the agreements. For example, in the case of the Ford Motor Company revolving credit agreement discussed earlier, the company had no loans outstanding under the agreement at the end of 1995.

COMMERCIAL PAPER

Commercial paper consists of short-term unsecured promissory notes issued by major corporations. Only companies with good credit ratings are able to borrow funds through the sale of commercial paper. Purchasers of commercial paper include corporations with excess funds to invest, banks, insurance companies, pension funds, money market mutual funds, and other types of financial institutions.

Large finance companies, such as General Motors Acceptance Corporation (GMAC) and CIT Financial Corporation, issue sizable amounts of commercial paper on a regular basis, selling it directly to investors like those just mentioned. Large industrial, utility, and transportation firms, as well as smaller finance companies, issue commercial paper less frequently and in smaller amounts; they sell it to dealers who, in turn, sell the commercial paper to investors.

Maturities on commercial paper at the time of issue range from several days to a maximum of 9 months. Companies usually do not issue commercial paper with maturities beyond 9 months, because these issues must be registered with the Securities and Exchange Commission. The size of an issue of commercial paper can range up to several hundred million dollars. It is usually sold to investors in multiples of $100,000 or more. Large issuers of commercial paper normally attempt to tailor the maturity and amounts of an issue to the needs of investors.

Commercial paper represents an attractive financing source for large, financially sound firms, because interest rates on commercial paper issues tend to be below the prime lending rate. To successfully market commercial paper (and get an acceptable rating from Moody's, Standard and Poor's, or both), however, the company normally must have unused bank lines of credit equal to the amount of the issue.

The primary disadvantage of this type of financing is that it is not always a reliable source of funds. The commercial paper market is impersonal. A firm that is suddenly faced with temporary financial difficulties may find that investors are unwilling to purchase new issues of commercial paper to replace maturing issues. In addition, the amount of loanable funds available in the commercial paper market is limited to the amount of excess liquidity of the various purchasers of commercial paper. During tight money periods, enough funds may not be available to meet the aggregate needs of corporate issuers of commercial paper at reasonable rates. As a result, a company should maintain adequate lines of bank credit and recognize the risks of relying too heavily on commercial paper. Finally, a commercial paper issue usually cannot be paid off until maturity. Even if a company no longer needs the funds from a commercial paper issue, it still must pay the interest costs.

Commercial paper is sold on a discount basis; this means that the firm receives less than the stated amount of the note at issue and then pays the investor the full face amount at maturity. The annual financing cost of commercial paper depends on the maturity date of the issue and the prevailing short-term interest rates. In addition to the interest costs, borrowers also must pay a *placement fee* to the commercial paper dealer for arranging the sale of the issue. The annual financing cost can be computed as follows, based on Equation 18.3:

$$\text{AFC} = \frac{\text{Interest costs} + \text{Placement fee}}{\text{Usable funds}} \times \frac{365}{\text{Maturity (days)}} \quad (18.7)$$

The usable funds are equal to the face amount of the issue less the interest costs and placement fee.

For example, suppose Midland Steel Company is considering issuing $10 million of commercial paper. A commercial paper dealer has indicated that Midland could sell a 90-day issue at an annual interest rate of 9.5 percent. The placement fee would be $25,000. Using Equation 18.7, the annual financing cost of this commercial paper issue is calculated as follows:

$$\text{Interest costs} = \$10,000,000 \times 0.095 \times \frac{90}{365}$$

$$= \$234,247$$

$$\text{AFC} = \frac{\$234,247 + \$25,000}{\$10,000,000 - \$234,247 - \$25,000} \times \frac{365}{90}$$

$$= 10.79\%$$

ACCOUNTS RECEIVABLE LOANS

Accounts receivable are one of the most commonly used forms of collateral for *secured* short-term borrowing. From the lender's standpoint, accounts receivable represent a desirable form of collateral, because they are relatively liquid and their value is relatively easy to recover if the borrower becomes insolvent. In addition, accounts receivable involve documents representing customer obligations rather than cumbersome physical assets. Offsetting these advantages, however, are potential difficulties. One disadvantage is that the borrower may attempt to defraud the lender by pledging nonexistent accounts. Also, the recovery process in the event of insolvency may be hampered if the customer who owes the receivables returns the merchandise or files a claim alleging that the merchandise is defective. Finally, the administrative costs of processing the receivables can be high, particularly when a firm has a large number of invoices involving small dollar amounts. Nevertheless, many companies use accounts receivable as collateral for short-term financing by either *pledging* their receivables or *factoring* them.

Pledging Accounts Receivable

The pledging process begins with a loan agreement specifying the procedures and terms under which the lender will advance funds to the firm. When accounts receivable are pledged, the firm retains title to the receivables and continues to carry them on its balance sheet. However, the pledged status of the firm's receivables should be disclosed in a footnote to the financial statements. (Pledging is an accepted business practice, particularly with smaller businesses.) A firm that has pledged receivables as collateral is required to repay the loan, even if it is unable to collect the pledged receivables. In other words, the borrower assumes the default risk, and the lender has *recourse* back to the borrower. Both commercial banks and finance companies make loans secured by accounts receivable.

Once the pledging agreement has been established, the firm periodically sends the lender a group of invoices along with the loan request. Upon receipt of the customer invoices, the lender investigates the creditworthiness of the accounts to determine which are acceptable as collateral. The percentage of funds that the lender will advance against the collateral depends on the quality of the receivables and the company's financial position. The percentage normally ranges from 50 to 80 percent of the face amount of the receivables pledged. The company then is required to sign a promissory note and a security agreement, after which it receives the funds from the lender.

Most receivables loans are made on a *nonnotification basis,* which means the customer is not notified that the receivable has been pledged by the firm. The customer continues to make payments directly to the firm. To protect itself against possible fraud, the lender usually requires the firm to forward all customer payments in the form in which they are received. In addition, the borrower is usually subject to a periodic audit to ensure the integrity of its receivables and payments. Receivables that remain unpaid for 60 days or so usually must be replaced by the borrower.

The customer payments are used to reduce the loan balance and eventually repay the loan. Receivables loans can be a continuous source of financing for a company, however, provided that new receivables are pledged to the lender as existing accounts are collected. By periodically sending the lender new receivables, the company can maintain its collateral base and obtain a relatively constant amount of financing.

Receivables loans can be an attractive source of financing for a company that does not have access to unsecured credit. As the company grows and its level of receivables increases, it can normally obtain larger receivables loans fairly easily. And, unlike line of credit agreements, receivables loans usually do not have compensating balance or "clean-up" provisions.

The annual financing cost of a loan in which receivables are pledged as collateral includes both the interest expense on the unpaid balance of the loan and the service fees charged for processing the receivables. Typically, the interest rate ranges from 2 to 5 percentage points over the prime rate, and service fees are approximately 1 to 2 percent of the amount of the pledged receivables. The services performed by the lender under a pledging agreement can include credit checking, keeping records of the pledged accounts and collections, and monitoring the agreement. This type of financing can be quite expensive for the firm.

The following example illustrates the calculation of the annual financing cost of an accounts receivable loan: Port City Plastics Corporation is considering pledging its receivables to finance a needed increase in working capital. Its commercial bank will lend 75 percent of the pledged receivables at 2 percentage points above the prime rate, which is currently 10 percent. In addition, the bank charges a service fee equal to 1 percent of the pledged receivables. Both interest

TABLE 18-1
Cost of Pledging Receivables for Port City Plastics Corporation

$$\text{Usable funds} = 0.75 \times \text{Pledgeable receivables}$$

$$= 0.75 \times \$2,000,000$$

$$= \$1,500,000$$

$$\text{Interest costs} = \$1,500,000 \times 0.12 \times \frac{45}{365}$$

$$= \$22,192$$

$$\text{Service fee} = \$2,000,000 \times 0.01$$

$$= \$20,000$$

$$\text{AFC} = \frac{\$22,192 + \$20,000}{\$1,500,000} \times \frac{365}{45}$$

$$= 22.8\%$$

payments and the service fee are payable at the end of each borrowing period. Port City's average collection period is 45 days, and it has receivables totaling $2 million that the bank has indicated are acceptable as collateral. As shown in Table 18-1, the annual financing cost for the pledged receivables is 22.8 percent.

Factoring Accounts Receivable

Factoring receivables involves the outright sale of the firm's receivables to a financial institution known as a *factor*. A number of so-called old-line factors, in addition to some commercial banks and finance companies (asset-based lenders), are engaged in factoring receivables. When receivables are factored, title to them is transferred to the factor, and the receivables no longer appear on the firm's balance sheet.

Traditionally, the use of factoring was confined primarily to the apparel, furniture, and textile industries. (The importance of factoring in the retail apparel industry is illustrated in the Financial Challenge at the beginning of the chapter.) In other industries, the factoring of receivables was considered an indication of poor financial health. Today, factoring seems to be gaining increased acceptance in other industries.

The factoring process begins with an agreement that specifies the procedures for factoring the receivables and the terms under which the factor will advance funds to the firm. Under the normal factoring arrangement, the firm sends the customer order to the factor for credit checking and approval *before* filling it. The factor maintains a credit department to perform the credit checking and collection functions. Once the factor decides that the customer is an acceptable risk and agrees to purchase the receivable, the firm ships the order to the customer. The customer is usually notified that its account has been sold and is instructed to make payments directly to the factor.

Most factoring of receivables is done on a *nonrecourse* basis; in other words, the factor assumes the risk of default.[14] If the factor refuses to purchase a given receivable, the firm still can ship the order to the customer and assume the default risk itself, but this receivable does not provide any collateral for additional credit.

In the typical factoring agreement, the firm receives payment from the factor at the normal collection or due date of the factored accounts; this is called *maturity factoring*. If the firm wants to receive the funds prior to this date, it usually can obtain an advance from the factor; this is referred to as *advance factoring*. Therefore, in addition to credit checking, collecting receivables, and bearing default risk, the factor also performs a lending function and assesses specific charges for each service provided. The maximum advance the firm can obtain from the factor is limited to the amount of factored receivables *less* the factoring commission, interest expense, and reserve that the factor withholds to cover any returns or allowances by customers. The reserve is usually 5 to 10 percent of the factored receivables and is paid to the firm after the factor collects the receivables.

The factor charges a factoring commission, or service fee, of 1 to 3 percent of the factored receivables to cover the costs of credit checking, collection, and bad-debt losses. The rate charged depends on the total volume of the receiv-

---

[14]If the receivables are sold to the factor on a *recourse* basis, the firm is liable for losses on any receivables that are not collected by the factor.

Savings by factoring

ables, the size of the individual receivables, and the default risk involved. The factor normally charges an interest rate of 2 to 5 percentage points over the prime rate on advances to the firm. These costs are somewhat offset by a number of internal savings that a business can realize through factoring its receivables. A company that factors all its receivables does not need a credit department and does not have to incur the administrative and clerical costs of credit investigation and collection or the losses on uncollected accounts. In addition, the factor may be able to control losses better than a credit department in a small or medium-sized company due to its greater experience in credit evaluation. Thus, although factoring receivables may be a more costly form of credit than unsecured borrowing, the net cost may be below the stated factoring commission and interest rates because of credit department and bad-debt loss savings.

For example, the Masterson Apparel Company is considering an advance factoring agreement because of its weak financial position and because of the large degree of credit risk inherent in its business. The company primarily sells large quantities of apparel to a relatively small number of retailers, and if even one retailer does not pay, the company could experience severe cash flow problems. By factoring, Masterson transfers the credit risk to the factor, Partners Credit Corporation, an asset-based lender. Partners requires a 10 percent reserve for returns and allowances, charges a 2 percent factoring commission, and will advance Masterson funds at an annual interest rate of 4 percentage points over prime.[15] Assume the prime rate is 10 percent. Factoring receivables will allow the company to eliminate its credit department and save about $2,000 a month in administrative and clerical costs. Factoring also will eliminate bad-debt losses, which average about $6,000 a month. Masterson's average collection period is 60 days, and its average level of receivables is $1 million.

In Table 18-2, the amount of funds Masterson can borrow from the factor and the annual financing cost of these funds are calculated. As the table shows, Masterson can obtain an advance of $859,748, and the annual financing cost is 28.5 percent *before* considering cost savings and elimination of bad-debt losses. *After* considering savings and loss eliminations, the annual financing cost drops to 17.2 percent. Masterson can compare the cost of this factoring arrangement with the cost of other sources of funds in deciding whether or not to factor its receivables. This example calculates the factoring cost for a single 60-day period. In practice, if Masterson did enter into a factoring agreement, the agreement most likely would become a continuous procedure.

What won't they think of next? Now you can take a course at home from the 1st Factoring Academy and become a factoring specialist/broker in the $60 billion factoring industry.
http://home.earthlink.net:80/
~factor

INTERNATIONAL ISSUES
FOREIGN RECEIVABLES FINANCING[16]

Small and medium-size U.S. businesses that sell on credit to customers in foreign countries are faced with additional problems in obtaining loans on

[15]Although the reserve for returns is deducted when figuring the amount of usable funds advanced by the factor, it is not part of the cost of factoring, because the factor will return it to Masterson provided that the company's customers make no returns or adjustments.

[16]See Bill Holstein, "Exporting: Congratulations Exporter! Now About Getting Paid . . ." *Business Week* (January 17, 1994): 98.

TABLE 18-2
Cost of Factoring Receivables for Masterson Apparel Company

Calculation of usable funds:

Average level of receivables		$1,000,000
Less Factoring commission	0.02 × $1,000,000	−20,000
Less Reserve for returns	0.10 × $1,000,000	−100,000
Amount available for advance before interest is deducted		$ 880,000
Less Interest on advance	(0.14× $880,000 × 60/365)	−20,252
Amount of funds advanced by factor, or *usable funds*		$ 859,748

Interest costs and fees:

Interest costs		$ 20,252
Fee, or factoring commission		20,000
Total		$ 40,252

Calculation of annual financing cost, *before* considering cost savings and bad-debt losses:

$$AFC = \frac{\$40,252}{\$859,748} \times \frac{365}{60}$$

$$= 28.5\%$$

Calculation of annual financing cost, *after* considering cost savings and bad-debt losses:

Credit department savings, per 60-day period	$ 4,000
Average bad-debt losses, per 60-day period	12,000
Total	$ 16,000

$$AFC = \frac{\$40,252 - \$16,000}{\$859,748} \times \frac{365}{60}$$

$$= 17.2\%$$

these receivables. Because of low profit margins and unfamiliarity with international markets, bank financing of these receivables is often difficult. For example, if a commercial bank does advance funds on the foreign receivables, it may want the seller to use its U.S. assets as additional collateral for the loan.

Alternatively, factors will finance foreign receivables that are insured by the Export-Import Bank. The factor will advance about 85 percent of the amount of the receivables and then remit the remainder, less fees of 1.5 to 3 percent, after the foreign customer's payment is received. Another alternative source of receivables financing is a forfait company, such as London Forfaiting, which will advance funds to the seller before they collect from the buyer. Forfaiters usually want the sales contract guaranteed by a foreign bank or government.

Finally, a trading company can be used to obtain financing. The trading company will take title to the goods and arrange shipment to the foreign buyer. Such companies work with sales contracts that are guaranteed or insured by programs of U.S. and foreign governments. Generally, U.S. exporters that require receivables financing should expect to pay in the range of 2 to 3 percent of the amount of the transaction.

INVENTORY LOANS

Inventories are another commonly used form of collateral for secured short-term loans. They represent a flexible source of financing since additional funds can be obtained as the firm's sales and inventories expand. Like receivables, many types of inventories are fairly liquid. Therefore, lenders consider them a desirable form of collateral. When judging whether a firm's inventory would be suitable collateral for a loan, the primary considerations of the lender are the type, physical characteristics, identifiability, liquidity, and marketability of the inventory.

Firms hold three types of inventories: *raw materials, work-in-process,* and *finished goods*. Normally, only raw materials and finished goods are considered acceptable as security for a loan. The physical characteristic with which lenders are most concerned is the item's *perishability*. Inventory subject to significant physical deterioration over time is usually not suitable as collateral.

Inventory items also should be *easily identifiable* by means of serial numbers or inventory control numbers; this helps protect the lender against possible fraud and also aids the lender in establishing a valid title claim to the collateral if the borrower becomes insolvent and defaults on the loan. The ease with which the inventory can be *liquidated* and the stability of its *market price* are other important considerations. In the event that the borrower defaults, the lender wants to be able to take possession, sell the collateral, and recover the full amount owed with minimal expense and difficulty.

Both commercial banks and asset-based lenders make inventory loans. The percentage of funds that the lender will advance against the inventory's book value ranges from about 50 to 80 percent and depends on the inventory's characteristics. Advances near the upper end of this range are normally made only for inventories that are standardized, nonperishable, easily identified, and readily marketable. To receive an inventory loan, the borrower must sign both a promissory note and a security agreement describing the inventory that will serve as collateral.

In making a loan secured with inventories, the lender can either allow the borrower to hold the collateral or require that it be held by a third party. If the borrower holds the collateral, the loan may be made under a *floating lien* or *trust receipt* arrangement. If a third party is employed to hold the collateral, either a *terminal warehouse* or a *field warehouse* financing arrangement can be used.

Floating Liens

Under a **floating lien** arrangement, the lender receives a security interest or general claim on *all* of the firm's inventory; this may include both present and future inventory. This type of agreement is often employed when the average value of the inventory items is small, the inventory turns over frequently, or both. Specific items are not identified. Thus, a floating lien does not offer the lender much protection against losses from fraud or bankruptcy. As a result, most lenders will not advance a very high percentage of funds against the book value of the borrower's inventory.

Trust Receipts

A **trust receipt** is a security agreement under which the firm holds the inventory and proceeds from the sale in trust for the lender. Whenever a portion of the inventory is sold, the firm is required to immediately forward the proceeds to the lender; these then are used to reduce the loan balance.

Some companies engage in inventory financing on a continuing basis. In these cases, a new security agreement is drawn up periodically, and the lender advances the company additional funds using recently purchased inventories as collateral.

All inventory items under a trust receipt arrangement must be readily identified by serial number or inventory code number. The lender makes periodic, unannounced inspections of the inventory to make sure that the firm has the collateral and has not withheld payment for inventory that has been sold.

Businesses that must have their inventories available for sale on their premises, such as automobile and appliance dealers, frequently engage in trust receipt financing, also known as *floor planning*. Many "captive" finance companies that are subsidiaries of manufacturers, such as General Motors Acceptance Corporation (GMAC), engage in floor planning for their dealers.

Terminal Warehouse and Field Warehouse Financing Arrangements

Under a **terminal warehouse financing arrangement,** the inventory being used as loan collateral is stored in a bonded warehouse operated by a public warehousing company. When the inventory is delivered to the warehouse, the warehouse company issues a warehouse receipt listing the specific items received by serial or lot number. The warehouse receipt is forwarded to the lender, who then advances funds to the borrower.

Holding the warehouse receipt gives the lender a security interest in the inventory. Because the warehouse company will release the stored inventory to the firm only when authorized to do so by the holder of the warehouse receipt, the lender is able to exercise control over the collateral. As the firm repays the loan, the lender authorizes the warehouse company to release appropriate amounts of the inventory to the firm.

Under a **field warehouse financing agreement,** the inventory that serves as collateral for a loan is segregated from the firm's other inventory and stored on its premises under the control of a field warehouse company. The field warehouse company issues a warehouse receipt, and the lender advances funds to the firm. The field warehouse releases inventory to the firm only when authorized to do so by the lender.

Although terminal warehouse and field warehouse financing arrangements provide the lender with more control over the collateral than it has when the borrower holds the inventory, fraud or negligence on the part of the warehouse company can result in losses for the lender. The fees charged by the warehouse company make this type of financing more expensive than floating lien or trust receipt loans. In a terminal warehouse arrangement, the firm incurs storage charges, in addition to fees for transporting the inventory to and from the public warehouse. In a field warehouse arrangement, the firm normally has to pay an installation charge, a fixed operating charge based on the overall size of the warehousing operation, and a monthly storage charge based on the value of the inventory in the field warehouse.

Overall warehousing fees are generally 1 to 3 percent of the inventory value. The total cost of an inventory loan includes the service fee charged by the lender and the warehousing fee charged by the warehousing company, plus the interest on the funds advanced by the lender. Any internal savings in inventory handling and storage costs that result when the inventory is held by a warehouse company are deducted in computing the cost of the loan.

TERM LOANS

A **term loan,** or *intermediate-term credit,* is defined as any debt obligation having an initial maturity between 1 and 10 years. It lacks the permanency characteristic of long-term debt. Term loans are well suited for financing small additions to plant facilities and equipment, such as a new piece of machinery. These loans can also be used to finance a moderate increase in working capital when

■ The cost of a public offering of bonds or stock is too high.
■ The firm intends to use the term debt only until its earnings are sufficient to amortize the loan.
■ The desired increase is relatively long-term but not permanent.

Term loans often are preferable to short-term loans, because they provide the borrower with a certain degree of security. Rather than having to be concerned about whether a short-term loan will be renewed, the borrower can have a term loan structured in such a way that the maturity coincides with the economic life of the asset being financed. Thus, the cash flows generated by the asset can service the loan without putting any additional financial strain on the borrower.

Term loans also offer potential cost advantages over long-term sources of financing. Because term loans are privately negotiated between the borrowing firm and the lending institution, they are less expensive than public offerings of common stock or bonds. The issuing firm in a public offering must pay the registration and issue expenses necessary to sell the securities. For small- to moderate-sized offerings, these expenses can be large in relation to the funds raised.[17]

Repayment Provisions

A term loan agreement usually requires that the principal be **amortized** over the life of the loan, which means that the firm is required to pay off the loan in installments, rather than in one lump sum. Amortizing has the effect of reducing the risk to the lender that the borrower will be unable to retire the loan in one lump sum when it comes due. Amortization of principal also is consistent with the idea that term loans are not a permanent part of a firm's capital structure.

The **amortization schedule** of a term loan might require the firm to make equal quarterly, semiannual, or annual payments of principal and interest. For example, assume that Arrow Envelope Company borrows $250,000 payable over 5 years, with an interest rate of 10 percent per annum on the unpaid balance. The repayment schedule calls for five equal annual payments, the first occurring at the end of year 1.

Recall from Chapter 4 that the annual payment (*PMT*) required to pay off a loan can be computed using Equation 4.22:

$$\text{PVAN}_0 = PMT(\text{PVIFA}_{i,n}) \tag{18.8}$$

or

[17]For example, one study indicated that the total issuance cost as a percentage of the gross proceeds for a $500,000 debt issue was 8 percent; for a $500,000 common stock issue, it was about 16 percent. These costs dropped to 1.4 percent for a $10 million debt issue and 6.9 percent for a $10 million common stock issue. For further information on issue costs, see Securities and Exchange Commission, *Cost of Flotation of Registered Equity Issues, 1963–1965* (Washington, DC: GPO, 1979); and Irwin Friend, *Investment Banking and the New Issues Market* (Cleveland: World Publishing, 1967). See also Chapter 7 of this text.

$$PMT = \frac{PVAN_0}{PVIFA_{i,n}}$$

In this example, substituting the present value of the annuity ($PVAN_0$) = $250,000, the number of time periods (n) = 5, the interest rate (i) = 10 percent, and the $PVIFA_{0.10,5}$ = 3.791 from Table IV into this equation yields an approximate annual payment of $65,945.66. A more accurate solution, obtained with a financial calculator, is $65,949.37.

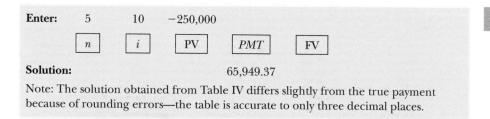

CALCULATOR SOLUTION

Enter: 5 10 −250,000

n i PV PMT FV

Solution: 65,949.37

Note: The solution obtained from Table IV differs slightly from the true payment because of rounding errors—the table is accurate to only three decimal places.

By making five annual payments of $65,949.37 to the lender, Arrow will just pay off the loan and provide the lender with a 10 percent return. Panel (a) of Table 18-3 shows the amortization schedule for this term loan.

Over the life of this loan, Arrow will make total payments of $329,746.85. Of this amount, $250,000 is the repayment of the principal, and the other $79,746.85 is interest. It is important to know what proportions of a loan payment are principal and interest, because interest payments are tax deductible.

In this example, the repayment schedule calls for equal periodic payments to the lender consisting of both principal and interest. Other types of repayment schedules also are possible, including the following:

- The borrower might be required to make equal reductions in the principal outstanding each period, with the interest being computed on the remaining balance for each period. Panel (b) of Table 18-3 illustrates such a repayment schedule, where Arrow is required to repay $50,000 of the principal each year.
- The borrower might be required to make equal periodic payments over the life of the loan that only partially amortize the loan, leaving a lump sum payment that falls due at the termination of the loan period, called a **balloon loan.** Panel (c) of Table 18-3 shows a repayment schedule requiring Arrow to repay one-half ($125,000) of the term loan over the first four years with the balance ($125,000) due at the end of the fifth year.
- The borrower might be required to make a single principal payment at maturity while making periodic (usually quarterly) interest payments only over the life of the loan, called a **bullet loan.** Panel (d) of Table 18-3 lists the payments required to pay off this loan, given that Arrow is required to make only annual interest payments over the first four years of the loan with the principal ($250,000) plus an annual interest payment due at maturity.

Interest Costs

The interest rate charged on a term loan depends on a number of factors, including the general level of interest rates in the economy, the size of the loan, the maturity of the loan, and the borrower's credit standing. Generally, interest rates on intermediate-term loans tend to be slightly higher than interest rates on

	END OF YEAR (1)	ANNUAL PAYMENT (2)	INTEREST* (3)	PRINCIPAL REDUCTION** (4)	REMAINING BALANCE† (5)
(a) Equal Annual Payments	0	$ —	$ —	$ —	$250,000.00
	1	65,949.37††	25,000.00	40,949.37	209,050.63
	2	65,949.37	20,905.06	45,044.31	164,006.32
	3	65,949.37	16,400.63	49,548.74	114,457.58
	4	65,949.37	11,445.76	54,503.61	59,953.97
	5	65,949.37	5,995.40	59,953.47	0.00
	Total	$329,746.85	$ 79,746.85	$250,000.00	
(b) Equal Annual Reductions in Principal ($50,000 each year)	0	$ —	$ —	$ —	$250,000
	1	75,000	25,000	50,000	200,000
	2	70,000	20,000	50,000	150,000
	3	65,000	15,000	50,000	100,000
	4	60,000	10,000	50,000	50,000
	5	55,000	5,000	50,000	0
	Total	$325,000	$ 75,000	$250,000	
(c) Balloon Loan ($125,000 due at maturity)	0	$ —	$ —	$ —	$250,000.00
	1	51,933.85‡	25,000.00	26,933.85	223,066.15
	2	51,933.85	22,306.62	29,627.23	193,438.91
	3	51,933.85	19,343.89	32,589.96	160,848.95
	4	51,933.85	16,084.90	35,848.95	125,000.00
	5	137,500.00	12,500.00	125,000.00	0.00
	Total	$345,235.40	$ 95,235.41	$249,999.99‡‡	
(d) Bullet Loan ($250,000 due at maturity)	0	$ —	$ —	$ 0	$250,000
	1	25,000	25,000	0	250,000
	2	25,000	25,000	0	250,000
	3	25,000	25,000	0	250,000
	4	25,000	25,000	0	250,000
	5	275,000	25,000	250,000	0
	Total	$375,000	$125,000	$250,000	

*Interest each year is equal to 0.10 times the remaining balance from the previous year.
**Principal reduction each year equals the annual payment minus interest.
†Remaining balance each year is equal to the previous year's remaining balance minus principal reduction.
††$PMT = \$250,000/3.790786769 = \$65,949.37$.
‡$PMT = \$125,000/3.169865446 + \$125,000 \times 0.10 = \$51,933.85$.
‡‡Differs from $250,000 because of rounding error. If fractional cents were used, no rounding would be necessary.

TABLE 18-3
**Loan Amortization Schedules
for Arrow Envelope Company**

short-term loans because of the higher risk assumed by the lender. Also, large term loans tend to have lower rates than small term loans, because the fixed costs associated with granting and administering a loan do not vary proportionately with the size of the loan. In addition, large borrowers often have better credit standings than small borrowers. An interest rate between 0.25 and 2.5 percentage points above the prime rate is common for term loans obtained from banks.

The interest rate on a small term loan is sometimes the same throughout the loan's lifetime. In contrast, most larger term loans specify a *variable* interest rate, which depends on the bank's prime lending rate. For example, if a loan is initially made at 0.5 percentage points above the prime rate, the loan agreement might specify that the interest charged on the remaining balance will continue to be 0.5 percentage points above the prevailing rate. Thus, whenever the prime rate is increased, the loan rate also increases; if the prime rate declines, so does the interest rate on the loan.

Compensating Balances. It is not uncommon for a bank to require a borrowing firm to keep a percentage of its loan balance—for example, 10 percent—on deposit as a compensating balance. If this balance is greater than the amount the firm would normally keep on deposit with the bank, this requirement effectively increases the firm's cost of the loan. Compensating balance requirements and their effect on the cost of a loan are discussed earlier in this chapter.

Equity Participations. The interest rate charged on a term loan also may be influenced by a desire on the part of the lending institution to take an equity position (often called a "kicker") in the company as an additional form of compensation. This is usually accomplished through the issuance of a *warrant* by the borrower to the lender. A **warrant** is an option to purchase a stated number of shares of a company's common stock at a specified price sometime in the future. If the company prospers, the lending institution shares in this prosperity on an equity basis. The issuance of warrants in conjunction with a term loan is common when the loan has an above-normal level of risk but the lending institution feels the borrower has promising growth potential. Alternatively, the borrower may issue warrants to secure a more favorable lending rate. Warrants are discussed in detail in Chapter 20.

SECURITY PROVISIONS AND PROTECTIVE COVENANTS

The security provisions and protective covenants specified by a term loan agreement often are determined by the borrower's credit standing: the weaker the credit standing, the more restrictive the protective covenants.

Security Provisions

In general, security requirements apply more often to intermediate-term loans than to short-term loans, due to the fact that longer-term loan contracts tend to have more default risk. Security provisions are also dependent on the size of the borrowing firm. For example, term loans to small firms tend to be secured more often than term loans to large firms, although there is an increasing tendency for all bank-oriented term loans to be secured.

The sources of security for a term loan include the following:

- An assignment of payments due under a specific contract.
- An assignment of a portion of the receivables or inventories.
- The use of a floating lien on inventories and receivables.
- A pledge of marketable securities held by the borrower.
- A mortgage on property, plant, or equipment held by the borrower.
- An assignment of the cash surrender value of a life insurance policy held by the borrower for its key executives.

Affirmative Covenants

An **affirmative loan covenant** is a portion of a loan agreement that outlines actions the borrowing firm *agrees to take* during the term of the loan. Typical affirmative covenants include the following:

- The borrower agrees to furnish periodic financial statements to the lender, including a balance sheet, income statement, and a statement of cash flows. These may be furnished monthly, quarterly, or annually and frequently are required to be audited. Pro forma cash budgets and projections of the costs needed to complete contracts on hand also may be required.
- The borrower agrees to carry sufficient insurance to cover insurable business risk.
- The borrower agrees to maintain a minimum amount of net working capital (current assets less current liabilities).
- The borrower agrees to maintain management personnel who are acceptable to the financing institution.

Negative Covenants

A **negative loan covenant** outlines actions that the borrowing firm's management *agrees not to take* without prior written consent of the lender. Typical negative covenants include the following:

- The borrowing firm agrees not to pledge any of its assets as security to other lenders, as well as not to factor (sell) its receivables. This type of agreement, called a *negative pledge clause,* is found in nearly all unsecured loans. It is designed to keep other lenders from interfering with the immediate lender's claims on the assets of the firm.
- The borrower is prohibited from making mergers or consolidations without the lender's approval. In addition, the borrower may not sell or lease a major portion of its assets without written approval of the lender.
- The borrower is prohibited from making or guaranteeing loans to others that would impair the lender's security.

Restrictive Covenants

Rather than requiring or prohibiting certain actions on the part of the borrower, **restrictive loan covenants** merely *limit their scope.* These are typical restrictive covenants:

- Limitations on the amount of dividends a firm may pay.
- Limitations on the level of salaries, bonuses, and advances a firm may give to employees.

These restrictions, in essence, force the firm to increase its equity capital base, thereby increasing the security for the loan.

Other restrictive covenants might include the following:

- Limitations on the total amount of short- and long-term borrowing the firm may engage in during the period of the term loan.
- Limitations on the amount of funds the firm may invest in new property, plant, and equipment. (This restriction usually applies only to those investments that cannot be financed from internally generated funds.)

And, finally, a firm that has outstanding long-term debt may be restricted as to the amount of debt it can retire without also retiring a portion of the term loan.

These restrictions are quite common, but the list is not all-inclusive. For example, a standard loan agreement checklist published by a large New York City bank lists thirty-four commonly used covenants. In general, covenants included in a loan agreement are determined by the particular conditions surrounding the granting of the term loan, including the credit record of the borrower and the maturity and security provisions of the loan.

Default Provisions

All term loans have *default provisions* that permit the lender to insist that the borrower repay the entire loan immediately under certain conditions. The following are examples:

- The borrower fails to pay interest, principal, or both as specified by the terms of the loan.
- The borrower materially misrepresents any information on the financial statements required under the loan's affirmative covenants.
- The borrower fails to observe any of the affirmative, negative, or restrictive covenants specified within the loan.

A borrower who commits any of these common acts of default will not necessarily be called on to repay a loan immediately, however. Basically, a lender will use a default provision only as a last resort, seeking in the meantime to make some agreement with the borrower, such as working out an acceptable modified lending plan with which the borrower is more able to comply. Normally, a lender will call a loan due only if no reasonable alternative is available or if the borrower is facing near-certain failure.

 ## SUPPLIERS OF TERM LOANS

There are numerous sources of term loans, including commercial banks, insurance companies, pension funds, commercial finance companies, government agencies, and equipment suppliers. Many of these sources are discussed in the following subsections.

Commercial Banks and Savings and Loan Associations

Many commercial banks and some savings and loan associations are actively involved in term lending. For example, about one-third of all commercial and industrial loans made by commercial banks are term loans. However, the market share of commercial banks has declined as more firms have issued "junk" bonds, either publicly or in private placements.

In spite of this level of activity, banks generally tend to favor loans having relatively short maturities—that is, less than 5 years—although some banks will make loans having maturities as long as 10 years or more. In addition, some banks limit their term lending to existing customers. Often banks will form *syndicates* to share larger term loans; this not only limits the risk exposure for any one bank but also complies with regulations that limit the size of *unsecured* loans made to single customers.

Life Insurance Companies and Pension Funds

Whereas commercial banks tend to prefer shorter-term loans, insurance companies and pension funds are more interested in longer-term commitments, for example, 10 to 20 years. As a result, it is common for a bank and an insurance company to share a term loan commitment. Under this type of arrangement, the bank might agree to finance the first 5 years of a loan with the insurance company financing the loan for the remaining years. This arrangement also can be advantageous to the borrower, because banks generally can charge a lower rate of interest for loans having shorter maturities.

From the borrowing firm's perspective, term loan agreements with pension funds and insurance companies have one significant limitation. If a firm decides to retire a term loan with a bank, it usually may do so without penalty. Because insurance companies are interested in having their funds invested for longer periods of time, however, prepayment of an insurance company term loan may involve some penalties.

Term loans from insurance companies and pension funds usually are secured, often with a mortgage on an asset, such as a building. These mortgage-secured loans are rarely made for amounts greater than 65 to 75 percent of the value of the collateral, however.

And, finally, term loans from life insurance companies and pension funds tend to have slightly higher stated rates of interest than bank term loans; this is because (1) they generally are made for longer maturities and (2) there are no compensating balance requirements.

Small Business Administration (SBA)

The Small Business Administration (SBA), an agency of the federal government, was established in 1953 to make credit available to small businesses that cannot reasonably obtain financing from private sources.

Normally, an SBA loan is secured by a mortgage on the firm's plant and equipment, third-party guarantees, or an assignment of accounts receivable and/or inventories.

The SBA makes three major types of loans:

- **Direct loans** are financed by the SBA, and because funds are quite limited, these loans usually are made only when the applicant firm cannot borrow from private sources at reasonable rates.
- **Participation loans** are obtained from a local bank, with the SBA guaranteeing up to 90 percent of a loan amount. The SBA prefers participation loans over direct loans. Typical SBA loans have a maximum 10-year maturity. In addition, they usually carry an interest rate that is considerably lower than the rate charged for a similar non-SBA loan. A rate about 1 percentage point higher than the U.S. Treasury bond rate is common. Like other term loans, SBA loans normally must be amortized; that is, paid off in periodic (usually monthly) installments.
- **Economic opportunity loans** have been made available since 1970 to assist economically and socially disadvantaged individuals who own their own firms.

Small Business Investment Companies (SBICs)

Small business investment companies (SBICs) are licensed by the government to make both equity and debt investments in small firms. They raise their capital by borrowing from the SBA and other sources.

The SBICs take an equity interest in the small firms they loan funds to, hoping to profit from their growth and prosperity. Unlike SBA loans, which are made to any eligible creditworthy small business, SBICs specialize in providing funds to firms that have above-average growth potential. Naturally, these firms often have above-average risk as well. Thus, the interest charge on an SBIC loan generally is somewhat higher than that on a normal bank term loan. SBIC loans have maturities as long as 10 to 20 years.

Industrial Development Authorities (IDAs)

Many states and municipalities have organized industrial development authorities (IDAs) to encourage new firms to locate in their area or to assist existing firms with expansion plans. In a typical financing plan, a local IDA sells tax-exempt municipal revenue bonds and uses the proceeds to build a firm's new facility. It then leases the plant to the firm, collecting lease payments from the firm that are large enough to pay the principal and interest on the municipal revenue bonds. Because bonds of this nature are tax exempt, the interest on them is generally lower than the interest on bonds issued directly by a private corporation. As a result, an IDA can charge a firm an attractively low lease rate.

The growing need to finance pollution control expenditures has led to the development of *pollution control revenue bonds,* which are issued by municipalities. Proceeds from these bonds are used to acquire pollution control equipment, which is then sold or leased to local industries. Because interest payments on pollution control revenue bonds are tax-free to investors, a firm's cost is much lower than it would be if these investments had to be financed with conventional debt or equity. For example, in February 1986, the troubled Public Service Company of New Hampshire sold $100 million of 30-year pollution control revenue bonds through the Industrial Development Authority of New Hampshire. The interest cost on these bonds was 10.5 percent, compared to a return requirement in excess of 12.0 percent had the bonds not been tax-exempt.

 EQUIPMENT LOANS

When a firm procures a loan to finance new equipment, it may use the equipment itself as collateral for an intermediate-term loan. These loans are called *equipment financing loans.* Equipment financing loans are commonly made for readily marketable equipment. These loans are normally made for somewhat less than the market value of the equipment, and the difference provides a margin of safety for the lender. This difference may range between 20 and 30 percent for readily marketable and mobile equipment, such as trucks or cars. The amortization schedule for an equipment financing loan is usually tied closely to the asset's economic life.

There are several potential sources of equipment financing, including commercial banks, sales finance companies, equipment sellers, insurance companies, and pension funds. Commercial banks are often the least expensive source of such financing—especially when compared with sales finance companies. The equipment seller may provide financing either directly or through a captive finance subsidiary (that is, the seller's own financing subsidiary). Although at first glance, an equipment seller may appear to charge a very modest interest rate, it often is difficult to make a meaningful comparison between the rates charged by a supplier and other financing sources, such as commercial banks. The reason is because the selling firm might price the equipment in such a way as to conceal part of the cost of carrying its credit customers; that is, noncash customers may pay relatively higher prices than cash customers.

There are two primary security instruments used in connection with equipment financing loans; the *conditional sales contract* and the *chattel mortgage*. Each of these is discussed in the following subsections.

Conditional Sales Contract

When a **conditional sales contract** (sometimes called a *purchase money mortgage*) is used in an equipment financing transaction, the seller retains title until the buyer has made all payments required by the financing contract. Conditional sales contracts are used almost exclusively by equipment sellers. At the time of purchase, the buyer normally makes a down payment to the seller and issues a promissory note for the balance of the purchase price. The buyer then agrees to make a series of periodic payments (usually monthly or quarterly) of principal and interest to the seller until the note has been paid off. When the last payment has been made, the title to the equipment passes to the buyer. In the case of default, the seller may repossess the asset.

Chattel Mortgage

A **chattel mortgage** is a lien on property other than real estate. Chattel mortgages are most common when a commercial bank or sales finance company makes a direct equipment financing loan. It involves the placement of a lien against the property by the lender. Notification of the lien is filed with a public office in the state where the equipment is located. Given a valid lien, the lender may repossess the equipment and resell it if the borrower defaults on the loan payment.

■ SUMMARY

- Short-term credit may be either *secured* or *unsecured*. In the case of secured credit, the borrower pledges certain assets (such as inventory, receivables, or fixed assets) as collateral for the loan. In general, firms prefer to borrow on an unsecured basis, because pledging assets as security generally raises the overall cost of the loan and also can reduce the firm's flexibility by restricting future borrowing.
- *Trade credit, accrued expenses,* and *deferred income* are the primary sources of spontaneous short-term credit. *Bank loans, commercial paper, accounts receivable loans,* and *inventory loans* represent the major sources of *negotiated* short-term credit.
- The *annual financing cost, AFC,* for a short-term credit source is calculated as follows:

$$AFC = \frac{\text{Interest costs} + \text{fees}}{\text{Usable funds}} \times \frac{365}{\text{Maturity (days)}}$$

- Trade credit is extended to a firm when it makes purchases from a supplier and is permitted to wait a specified period of time before paying for them. It normally is extended on an *open-account* basis, which means that once a firm accepts merchandise from a supplier, it agrees to pay the amount due as specified by the terms of sale on the invoice.

- *Stretching accounts payable,* or postponing payment beyond the end of the credit period, can be used to obtain additional short-term financing. The costs of stretching accounts payable include forgone cash discounts, penalties, and interest, as well as possible deterioration of the firm's credit rating and ability to obtain future credit.

- *Accrued expenses,* such as accrued wages, taxes, and interest, are liabilities for services provided to the firm that have not yet been paid for by the firm.

- *Deferred income* consists of payments received for goods and services a company will deliver at a future date.

- Short-term *bank credit* can be extended to the firm under a *single loan,* a *line of credit,* or a *revolving credit agreement.* A line of credit permits the firm to borrow funds up to a predetermined limit at any time during the life of the agreement. A revolving credit agreement legally commits the bank to provide the funds when the firm requests them.

- *Commercial paper* consists of short-term unsecured promissory notes issued by major corporations with good credit ratings.

- *Accounts receivable loans* can be obtained by either *pledging* or *factoring* receivables. In the case of a pledging arrangement, the firm retains title to the receivables, and the lender advances funds to the firm based on the amount and quality of the receivables. With factoring, receivables are sold to a factor, who takes the responsibility for credit checking and collection of the accounts. With pledging, the lender does not assume credit risk and has *recourse* back to the borrower if payment is not made, whereas factoring is normally a nonrecourse form of financing.

- Several types of *inventory loans* are available. In a *floating lien* or *trust receipt* arrangement, the borrower holds the collateral. In a floating lien arrangement, the lender has a general claim on all of the firm's inventory. In a trust receipt arrangement, the inventory being used as collateral is specifically identified by serial or inventory code numbers. In a *terminal warehouse* and a *field warehouse* arrangement, a third party holds the collateral; in the case of a terminal warehouse arrangement, collateral is stored in a public warehouse, whereas in a field warehouse arrangement, collateral is stored in a field warehouse located on the borrower's premises.

- No one source (or combination of sources) of short-term financing is necessarily optimal for all firms. Many other factors, in addition to the cost of financing, need to be considered when choosing the optimal source or sources of short-term financing. Some of these factors include the availability of funds during periods of financial crisis or tight money, restrictive covenants imposed on the firm, and the nature of the firm's operations and funds requirements. The advantages and disadvantages of the various sources of short-term credit are summarized in Table 18-4.

- *Term loans,* or *intermediate-term credit,* include any debt obligation having an initial maturity between 1 and 10 years.

TABLE 18-4
**Advantages and Disadvantages
of Various Sources of
Short-term Credit**

CREDIT SOURCE	ADVANTAGES	DISADVANTAGES
Trade credit	Flexible source of financing—Expands as firm's purchases increase Relatively easy to obtain	Opportunity cost of forgoing cash discounts can be quite high
Accrued expenses and deferred income	Interest-free source of financing	Limited by legal, contractual, and practical considerations
Short-term bank credit	Flexible source of financing—Credit line can be used to meet seasonal needs for funds	May require compensating balance in excess of firm's normal checking-account balance Commitment fees required for guaranteed credit May require "clean up" provision and other protective covenants that limit firm's financing activities
Commercial paper	Interest rate is often below bank prime rate	Requires unused bank line of credit to issue commercial paper Not always a reliable source of funds—Tight credit market conditions or temporary financial difficulties may limit firm's access to this source of funds
Accounts receivable loans	Flexible source of financing—Additional financing available as sales and accounts receivable increase Possible credit department and bad-debt loss savings Does not require compensating balance or "clean up" provisions like line of credit borrowing	Service fees can make this source of financing more expensive than unsecured sources Pledging or selling of accounts receivables may weaken firm's financial strength and limit its access to unsecured credit
Inventory loans	Flexible source of financing—Additional financing is available as sales and inventories increase Possible savings in inventory handling and storage costs under field warehouse or terminal warehouse agreement Does not require compensating balance or "clean-up" provisions like line-of-credit borrowing	Service fees (fixed and variable costs) for a field warehouse or terminal warehouse agreement can make this source of financing more expensive than unsecured sources

■ Term loans, being privately negotiated between the borrower and the lender, tend to be cheaper than public security offerings, because issuance costs on small to medium-sized public offerings are high. Therefore, term loans are a good source of funds for financing small and medium-sized increases in working capital or for financing the acquisition of equipment.

■ Term loans are usually amortized by a series of installments. The interest rate normally ranges between 0.25 and 2.5 percent above the prime rate. Many term loan agreements require that some specific asset be pledged as *security*. In addition, the borrowing firm may have to agree to certain *affirmative*, *negative*, and *restrictive covenants* governing its actions during the loan period.

■ Term loans are supplied by several institutions, including commercial banks (frequently the cheapest supplier of term funds), life insurance companies and pension funds (who prefer making loans having longer maturities), the Small Business Administration, small business investment companies, municipal or state industrial development authorities, and equipment suppliers.

■ Term loans that are secured by a lien on a piece of equipment are called *equipment financing loans*. They are made by the lending institutions previously named, as well as by equipment sellers or their *captive finance subsidiaries*. The two primary security instruments used in equipment financing are the *conditional sales contract* and the *chattel mortgage*.

■ QUESTIONS AND TOPICS FOR DISCUSSION

1. Define and discuss the function of *collateral* in short-term credit arrangements.
2. How is the annual financing cost for a short-term financing source calculated? How does the annual financing cost differ from the true annual percentage rate?
3. Explain the difference between *spontaneous* and *negotiated* sources of short-term credit.
4. Under what condition or conditions is trade credit *not* a "cost-free" source of funds to the firm?
5. Define the following:
   a. Accrued expenses.
   b. Deferred income.
   c. Prime rate.
   d. Compensating balance.
   e. Discounted loan.
   f. Commitment fee.
6. Explain the differences between a line of credit and a revolving credit agreement.
7. What are some of the disadvantages of relying too heavily on commercial paper as a source of short-term credit?
8. Explain the differences between pledging and factoring receivables.
9. Explain the difference between a floating lien and a trust receipts arrangement.
10. Explain why the annual financing cost of secured credit is frequently higher than that of unsecured credit.
11. Explain why banks normally include a "clean-up" provision in a line of credit agreement.
12. What savings are realized when accounts receivable are factored rather than pledged?
13. Determine the effect of each of the following conditions on the annual financing cost for a line of credit arrangement (assuming that all other factors remain constant):
    a. The bank raises the prime rate.
    b. The bank lowers its compensating balance requirements.
    c. The firm's average bank balance increases as the result of its instituting more stringent credit and collection policies.
14. Under what condition or conditions, if any, might a firm find it desirable to borrow funds from a bank or other lending institution in order to take a cash discount?

15. Under what circumstances might a firm prefer intermediate-term borrowing to either long- or short-term borrowing?

16. Discuss the advantages and disadvantages of the following types of term loans:
    a. Those that require equal periodic payments.
    b. Those that require equal periodic reductions in outstanding principal.
    c. Balloon loans.
    d. Bullet loans.

17. What are the major factors that influence the effective cost of a term loan?

18. Define the following and give an example of each:
    a. Affirmative covenants.
    b. Negative covenants.
    c. Restrictive covenants.

19. What institutions are the primary suppliers of business term loans?

20. Define the following:
    a. A conditional sales contract.
    b. A chattel mortgage.

21. Under what conditions would a firm prefer the following:
    a. A "fixed-rate" term loan from a bank?
    b. A "floating-rate" term loan, with the rate tied to the bank's prime rate?

■ SELF-TEST PROBLEMS

Note: **Assume that there are 365 days per year when converting from annual to daily amounts or vice versa.**

ST1. Determine the annual financing cost of forgoing the cash discount under each of the following credit terms:
    a. 2/10, net 120.
    b. 2/30, net 4 months (assume 122 days).

ST2. Determine the annual financing cost of a 9-month (274 day), $25,000 discounted bank loan at a stated interest rate of 10.5 percent, assuming that no compensating balance is required.

ST3. Tarentum Industries, Inc. has a revolving credit agreement with its bank under which the company can borrow up to $10 million at an interest rate of 1.5 percentage points above the prime rate (currently 9.5 percent). Tarentum is required to maintain a 10 percent compensating balance on any funds borrowed under the agreement and to pay a 0.50 percent commitment fee on the unused portion of the credit line. Assume that the company has no funds in its account at the bank that can be used to meet the compensating balance requirement. Determine the annual financing cost of borrowing each of the following amounts under the credit agreement:
    a. $2 million.
    b. $7 million.

ST4. The Chalfant Company is considering the use of commercial paper to finance a seasonal need for funds. A commercial paper dealer will sell a $25 million issue maturing in 91 days at an annual interest rate of 8.5 percent (deducted in advance). The fee to the dealer for selling the issue is $75,000. Determine Chalfant's annual financing cost of this commercial paper issue.

ST5. The Boone Furniture Company is considering factoring its receivables. Its average level of receivables is $4 million, and its average collection period is 70 days. Boone's bad-debt losses average $9,000 per month. (Assume 30 days per month.) Factoring receivables will save the company $3,000 per month through the elimination of its credit department. The factor charges a 2 percent commission and requires a 10 percent reserve for returns and allowances. Boone can borrow funds from the factor at 3 percentage points over the prime rate, which is currently 9 percent.

    a. Determine the amount of usable funds Boone can obtain by factoring its receivables.

    b. Calculate the annual financing cost of this arrangement.

ST6. Deseret Resources has received approval for a 5-year term loan from a commercial bank for $2 million at a stated interest rate of 8 percent. The loan requires that interest be paid at the end of each year on the balance remaining at the beginning of each year. In addition, a principal payment of $250,000 must be paid at the end of each of the first four years, with the remaining balance being paid off at the end of five years. The bank will charge Deseret a $50,000 loan-processing fee.

    a. What payments are required at the end of each of the five years?

    b. What is the effective, pretax cost of this loan?

■ PROBLEMS*

Note: **Assume that there are 365 days per year when converting from annual to daily amounts or vice versa.**

1. The Milton Company currently purchases an average of $22,000 per day in raw materials on credit terms of "net 30." The company expects sales to increase substantially next year and anticipates that its raw material purchases will increase to an average of $25,000 per day. Milton feels that it may need to finance part of this sales expansion by *stretching* accounts payable.

    a. Assuming that Milton currently waits until the end of the credit period to pay its raw material suppliers, what is its current level of trade credit?

    b. If Milton stretches its accounts payable an extra 10 days beyond the due date next year, how much *additional* short-term funds (that is, trade credit) will be generated?

2. Van Buren Resources, Inc. is considering borrowing $100,000 for 182 days from its bank. Van Buren will pay $6,000 of interest at maturity, and it will repay the $100,000 of principal at maturity.

    a. Calculate the loan's annual financing cost.

    b. Calculate the loan's annual percentage rate.

    c. What is the reason for the difference in your answers to Parts a and b?

3. Determine the *annual financing cost* of forgoing the cash discount under each of the following credit terms:

    a. 2/10, net 60.

    b. 1½/10, net 60.

    c. 2/30, net 60.

    d. 5/30, net 4 months (assume 122 days).

    e. 1/10, net 30.

4. Calculate the *annual percentage rate* of forgoing the cash discount under each of the following credit terms:

    a. 2/10, net 60.

    b. 2/10, net 30.

5. Determine the *annual financing cost* of forgoing the cash discount if the credit terms are "1/10, net 30" and the invoice is not paid until it is 20 days past due.

6. Determine the annual financing cost of a 1-year (365 day), $10,000 discounted bank loan at a stated annual interest rate of 9.5 percent. Assume that no compensating balance is required.

7. The Pulaski Company has a line of credit with a bank under which it can borrow funds at an 8 percent interest rate. The company plans to borrow $100,000 and is required by the bank to maintain a 15 percent compensating balance. Determine the annual financing cost of the loan under each of the following conditions:

    a. The company currently maintains $7,000 in its account at the bank that can be used to meet the compensating balance requirement.

*Colored numbers denote problems that have check answers provided at the end of the book.

b. The company currently has no funds in its account at the bank that can be used to meet the compensating balance requirement.

8. Determine the annual financing cost of a 6-month (182 day), $20,000 discounted bank loan at a stated annual interest rate of 10 percent. Assume that no compensating balance is required.

9. Pyramid Products Company has a revolving credit agreement with its bank. The company can borrow up to $1 million under the agreement at an annual interest rate of 9 percent. Pyramid is required to maintain a 10 percent compensating balance on any funds borrowed under the agreement and to pay a 0.5 percent commitment fee on the unused portion of the credit line. Assume that Pyramid has no funds in the account at the bank that can be used to meet the compensating balance requirement. Determine the annual financing cost of borrowing each of the following amounts under the credit agreement:
   a. $250,000.
   b. $500,000.
   c. $1,000,000.

10. Wellsley Manufacturing Company has been approached by a commercial paper dealer offering to sell an issue of commercial paper for the firm. The dealer indicates that Wellsley could sell a $5 million issue maturing in 182 days at an interest rate of 8.5 percent per annum (deducted in advance). The fee to the dealer for selling the issue would be $8,000. Determine Wellsley's annual financing cost of this commercial paper financing.

11. The Brandt Company has been approached by two different commercial paper dealers offering to sell an issue of commercial paper for the company. Dealer A offered to market an $8 million issue maturing in 90 days at an interest cost of 8.5 percent per annum (deducted in advance). The fee to Dealer A would be $12,000. Dealer B has offered to sell a $10 million issue maturing in 120 days at an interest rate of 8.75 percent per annum (deducted in advance). The fee to Dealer B would be $15,000. Assuming that Brandt wishes to minimize the annual financing cost of issuing commercial paper, which dealer should it choose?

12. Ranger Enterprises is considering pledging its receivables to finance a needed increase in working capital. Its commercial bank will lend 75 percent of the pledged receivables at 1.5 percentage points above the prime rate, which is currently 12 percent. In addition, the bank charges a service fee equal to 1 percent of the pledged receivables. Both interest and the service fee are payable at the end of the borrowing period. Ranger's average collection period is 50 days, and it has receivables totaling $5 million that the bank has indicated are acceptable as collateral. Calculate the annual financing cost for the pledged receivables.

13. Designer Textiles, Inc. is considering factoring its receivables. The company's average collection period is 60 days, and its average level of receivables is $2.5 million. Designer's bad-debt losses average $15,000 a month. If the company factors its receivables, it will save $4,000 a month by eliminating its credit department. The factor has indicated that it requires a 10 percent reserve for returns and allowances and charges a 2.5 percent factoring commission. The factor will advance Designer funds at 4 percentage points over prime, which is currently 8 percent.
   a. Determine the annual financing cost, *before* considering cost savings and bad-debt losses.
   b. Determine the annual financing cost, *after* considering cost savings and bad-debt losses.

14. The Eaton Company needs to raise $250,000 to expand its working capital and has been unsuccessful in attempting to obtain an unsecured line of credit with its bank. The firm is considering *stretching* its accounts payable. Eaton's suppliers extend credit on terms of "2/10, net 30." Payments beyond the credit period are subject to a 1½ percent per month penalty. Eaton purchases $100,000 per month from its suppliers and currently takes cash discounts. For this problem, assume that a year consists of

twelve 30-day months. Assuming that Eaton is able to raise the $250,000 it needs by stretching its accounts payable, determine the following:

a. The firm's annual lost cash discounts.

b. Annual penalties.

c. The annual financing cost of this source of financing.

15. Which of the following credit terms would you prefer as a customer?

a. 2/10, net 30.

b. 1/10, net 40.

c. 2/10, net 40.

d. 1/10, net 25.

e. Indifferent among all options.

Explain your choice.

16. The Odessa Supply Company is considering obtaining a loan from a sales finance company secured by inventories under a field warehousing arrangement. Odessa would be permitted to borrow up to $300,000 under such an arrangement at an annual interest rate of 10 percent. The additional cost of maintaining a field warehouse is $16,000 per year. Determine the annual financing cost of a loan under this arrangement if Odessa borrows the following amounts:

a. $300,000.

b. $250,000.

17. Harpo Music Mart needs to raise $300,000 to increase its working capital. The bank, mindful of Harpo's strained financial condition, has refused to loan the firm the needed funds. Harpo is considering *stretching* its accounts payable in order to raise the funds. Current credit terms are "3/10, net 30." Payments beyond the credit period are subject to a 1 percent per month penalty. Harpo purchases $125,000 per month from its suppliers and currently takes cash discounts. If Harpo is able to raise the $300,000 it needs by stretching its accounts payable, determine the annual financing cost of this source of financing. For this problem, assume that a year consists of twelve 30-day months.

18. The Kittanning Company has a $2 million line of credit with First Interstate Bank under which it can borrow funds at 1.5 percentage points above the prime rate (currently 9 percent). The company plans to borrow $1.5 million and is required by First Interstate to maintain a 10 percent compensating balance. Determine the annual financing cost of the loan under each of the following conditions:

a. Kittanning currently maintains $100,000 in its account at the bank that can be used to meet the compensating balance requirement.

b. The company currently has no funds in its account at the bank that can be used to meet the compensating balance requirement.

19. The Vandergrift Company has a revolving credit agreement with Commerce Bank under which the company can borrow up to $5 million at an annual interest rate of 1 percentage point above the prime rate (currently 9 percent). The company is required to maintain a 10 percent compensating balance on any funds borrowed under the agreement and to pay a 0.4 percent commitment fee on the unused portion of the credit line. Assume that Vandergrift has no funds in its account at Commerce Bank that can be used to meet the compensating balance requirement. Determine the annual financing cost of borrowing each of the following amounts under the credit agreement:

a. $1 million.

b. $4 million.

20. Titusville Petroleum Company is considering pledging its receivables to finance an increase in working capital. Citizens National Bank will lend the company 80 percent of the pledged receivables at 2 percentage points above the prime rate (currently 10 percent). The bank charges a service fee equal to 1.5 percent of the pledged receivables. The interest costs and the service fee are payable at the end of the borrowing period. Titusville has $2 million in receivables that can be pledged as

collateral. The average collection period is 45 days. Determine the annual financing cost to Titusville of this receivables-backed loan.

21. DuBois Apparel Company is considering factoring its receivables. The company's average level of receivables is $1.5 million, and its average collection period is 45 days. DuBois's bad-debt losses average $8,000 per month, which it would not incur if it factored its receivables. (Assume 30 days per month.) Also, the company would save $4,000 per month in credit department costs if it factored its receivables. The factor requires a 10 percent reserve for returns and allowances and charges a 2 percent factoring commission. DuBois can borrow funds from the factor at 3 percentage points over the prime rate (currently 9 percent). Determine the *net* annual financing cost of this factoring arrangement.

22. The Clearfield Company would be permitted to borrow up to $750,000 secured by inventories under a field warehouse arrangement with a sales finance company. The annual interest rate would be 12 percent. The additional cost of establishing a field warehouse would be $35,000 per year. Determine the annual financing cost to Clearfield under this arrangement if Clearfield borrows
   a. $750,000.
   b. $500,000.

 23. Lobo Banks normally provides term loans that require repayment in a series of equal annual installments. If a $10 million loan is made, what would be the annual end-of-year payments, assuming the following?
   a. A 10 percent loan for 12 years.
   b. A 10 percent loan for 9 years.
   c. A 6 percent loan for 8 years.

 24. Set up the amortization schedule for a 5-year, $1 million, 9 percent term loan that requires equal annual end-of-year payments. Be sure to distinguish between the *interest* and the *principal* portion of each payment. What is the *effective* interest cost of this loan?

 25. Set up the amortization schedule for a 5-year, $1 million, 9 percent loan that requires equal annual end-of-year *principal* payments plus interest on the unamortized loan balance. What is the *effective* interest cost of this loan?

26. Set up the amortization schedule for a 5-year, $1 million, 9 percent bullet loan. How is the principal repaid in this type of loan? What is the *effective* interest cost of this loan?

27. A firm receives a $1 million, 5-year loan at a 10 percent interest rate. The loan requires annual payments of $125,000 per year (at the end of each year) for years 1 to 4.
   a. What payment is required at the end of year 5?
   b. What would you call this type of loan?
   c. How does it differ from the loan in Problem 24?
   d. What is the *effective* interest cost of this loan?

 28. A $10 million, 5-year loan bears an interest rate of 7 percent. The loan repayment plan calls for five annual end-of-year payments. Each payment is to include an equal amount of principal repayment ($2 million per year) plus accrued interest. Set up the amortization schedule for this loan. Be sure to distinguish between the *interest* and the *principal* portions of each annual payment. What is the *effective* interest cost of this loan?

29. Huskie Bank has provided the Mucklup Manufacturing Company with a 2-year term loan for $200,000 at a stated annual rate of interest of 10 percent. Interest for the entire 2-year period must be prepaid; that is, the loan's total interest payments must be made at the same time the loan is granted. Mucklup is required to repay the entire $200,000 principal balance at the end of the 2-year period. Compute the *effective* annual percentage rate of the loan.

30. The James Company has been offered a 4-year loan from its bank in the amount of $100,000 at a stated interest rate of 10 percent per year. The loan will require four

equal end-of-year payments of principal and interest plus a $30,000 balloon payment at the end of the fourth year.

   a. Compute the amount of each of the end-of-year payments.

   b. Prepare a loan amortization schedule detailing the amount of principal and interest in each year's payment.

   c. What is the *effective* interest rate on this loan? Prove your answer.

31. A $1 million loan requires five end-of-year equal payments of $284,333.

   a. Calculate the *effective* interest rate on this loan.

   b. How much interest (in dollars) is paid over the life of this loan?

32. U.S. Fax has been granted a loan from a commercial finance company for $1 million at a stated interest rate of 10 percent. The loan requires that interest payments be made at the end of each of the next 5 years. At the end of 5 years, the entire loan balance must be repaid. The finance company requires U.S. Fax to pay a $25,000 loan-processing fee at the time the loan is approved. What is the *effective* cost of this loan?

33. A $10 million principal amount, 3-year, term loan carries an interest rate of 10 percent. All interest payments (which would normally be due at the end of each year) are deferred until the end of 3 years. The unpaid interest amount compounds at a 10 percent annual rate during the period(s) it remains unpaid. At the end of 3 years, the borrower must repay the principal amount, the deferred interest, plus interest on the deferred interest. The lender also charges a front-end loan origination fee on this loan of $100,000. Compute the *effective* cost of this loan.

34. Visit the following Small Business Workshop and complete the tutorials in short-term and long-term financing. Prepare a one-page business memo summarizing what you found.

www.sb.gov.bc.ca

35. Read, at the following Web site, about how to best finance your business. Then study the example of how your loan privileges can be abused by using your line of credit as a term loan. Prepare a one-page business memo explaining why abuse such as this would jeopardize the viability of your business.

www.sb.gov.bc.ca

36. Use the credit-card calculator at the following Web site to analyze your credit card situation. Based on what you found, what changes (if any) should you make in your usage of credit cards?

www.moneyadvisor.com

■ SOLUTIONS TO SELF-TEST PROBLEMS

ST1. a. $\text{AFC} = \dfrac{\text{Percentage discount}}{100 - \text{Percentage discount}} \times \dfrac{365}{\text{Credit period} - \text{Discount period}}$

$$= \frac{2}{100 - 2} \times \frac{365}{120 - 10}$$

$$= 6.77\%$$

b. $\text{AFC} = \dfrac{2}{100 - 2} \times \dfrac{365}{122 - 30} = 8.10\%$

ST2. $\text{AFC} = \dfrac{\text{Interest cost}}{\text{Usable funds}} \times \dfrac{365}{\text{Maturity (days)}}$

$$\text{Interest cost} = 0.105\,(\$25,000) \times \frac{274}{365}$$

$$= \$1,971$$

$$AFC = \frac{\$1,971}{\$25,000 - \$1,971} \times \frac{365}{274}$$

$$= 11.4\%$$

ST3. a.
$$AFC = \frac{\text{Interest costs} + \text{Commitment fee}}{\text{Usable funds}} \times \frac{365}{\text{Maturity (days)}}$$

Interest cost $= 0.11 \, (\$2,000,000) = \$220,000$

Commitment fee $= 0.005 \, (\$8,000,000) = \$40,000$

Usable funds $= 0.90 \, (\$2,000,000) = \$1,800,000$

$$AFC = \frac{\$220,000 + \$40,000}{\$1,800,000} \times \frac{365}{365}$$
$$= 14.4\%$$

b. Interest cost $= 0.11 \, (\$7,000,000) = \$770,000$

Commitment fee $= 0.005 \, (\$3,000,000) = \$15,000$

Usable funds $= 0.90 \, (\$7,000,000) = \$6,300,000$

$$AFC = \frac{\$770,000 + \$15,000}{\$6,300,000} \times \frac{365}{365}$$
$$= 12.5\%$$

ST4.
$$AFC = \frac{\text{Interest costs} + \text{Placement fee}}{\text{Usable funds}} \times \frac{365}{\text{Maturity date (days)}}$$

Interest costs $= 0.085 \, (\$25,000,000) \left(\frac{91}{365}\right) = \$529,795$

Usable funds $= \$25,000,000 - \$529,795 - \$75,000 = \$24,395,205$

$$AFC = \frac{\$529,795 + \$75,000}{\$24,395,205} \times \frac{365}{91} = 9.94\%$$

ST5. a. Average level of receivables $4,000,000
Less Factoring commission

$0.02 \times \$4,000,000 =$	−80,000
Less Reserve for returns	
$0.10 \times \$4,000,000 =$	−400,000
Amount available for advance before interest is deducted	$3,520,000
Less Interest on advance	
$0.12 \times \$3,520,000 \times \frac{70}{365} =$	−81,008
Amount of funds advanced by factor (Usable funds)	$3,438,992

b. Interest costs $ 81,008

    Factoring commission   80,000

    Total interest and factoring costs $161,008

    Less Credit department savings per 70-day period

$$\$3{,}000 \times \frac{70}{30} =$$ $-7{,}000$

    Less Average bad-debt losses per 70-day period

$$\$9{,}000 \times \frac{70}{30} =$$ $\underline{-21{,}000}$

    Net financing cost per 70 days $ 133,008

$$AFC = \frac{\$133{,}008}{\$3{,}438{,}992} \times \frac{365}{70}$$

$$= 20.2\%$$

ST6. a.

End of Year	Principal Payment	Interest Payment	Total Payment	Remaining Balance
0	—	—	—	$2,000,000
1	$ 250,000	$160,000	$ 410,000	1,750,000
2	250,000	140,000	390,000	1,500,000
3	250,000	120,000	370,000	1,250,000
4	250,000	100,000	350,000	1,000,000
5	1,000,000	80,000	1,080,000	0

b. Funds available for use:

$2,000,000 − $50,000 processing fee = $1,950,000

$$\$1{,}950{,}000 = \$410{,}000(PVIF_{i,1}) + \$390{,}000(PVIF_{i,2})$$

$$+ \$370{,}000(PVIF_{i,3}) + \$350{,}000(PVIF_{i,4})$$

$$+ \$1{,}080{,}000(PVIF_{i,5})$$

$$i = 8.83\% \text{ (by calculator)}$$

■ GLOSSARY

Affirmative Loan Covenant A portion of a loan agreement that outlines actions a firm's management *agrees to take* as conditions for receiving the loan.

Amortization Schedule A schedule of periodic payments of interest and principal owed on a debt obligation.

Annual Financing Cost (AFC) The simple, annual interest rate for a short-term credit source.

Annual Percentage Rate (APR) The true annual interest rate paid on a loan. Also called the *effective rate* of a loan.

Balloon Loan A loan that requires a large final payment greater than each of the periodic (principal and interest) payments.

Bullet Loan A loan that requires only the periodic payment of interest during the term of the loan, with a final single repayment of principal at maturity.

Chattel Mortgage A lien on personal property, such as machinery, as security for the repayment of a loan.

Commercial Paper Short-term unsecured promissory notes issued by major corporations with good credit ratings.

Compensating Balance A certain percentage of a loan balance that the borrower keeps on deposit with a bank as a requirement of a loan provided by the bank.

Conditional Sales Contract A financing agreement in which the seller of a piece of equipment retains title until all payments have been made.

Discounted Loan A loan in which the bank deducts the interest in advance at the time the loan is made.

Factoring The sale of a firm's accounts receivable to a financial institution known as a *factor.*

Field Warehouse Financing Agreement A loan agreement in which the inventory being pledged as collateral is segregated from the company's other inventories and stored on its premises under the control of a field warehouse company.

Floating Lien An inventory loan in which the lender receives a security interest or general claim on all of a company's inventory.

Line of Credit An agreement that permits a firm to borrow funds up to a predetermined limit at any time during the life of the agreement.

London Interbank Offer Rate (LIBOR) Interest rate at which banks in the Eurocurrency market lend to each other.

Negative Loan Covenant A portion of a loan agreement that outlines actions a firm's management *agrees not to take* during the term of the loan.

Pledging of Accounts Receivable A short-term borrowing arrangement with a financial institution in which a loan is secured by the borrower's accounts receivable.

Prime Rate The lowest rate normally charged by banks on loans made to their most creditworthy business customers.

Promissory Note A formal short-term credit obligation that states the amount to be paid and the due date.

Restrictive Loan Covenant A portion of a loan agreement that limits the scope of certain actions a firm may take during the term of the loan.

Revolving Credit Agreement A binding agreement that commits a bank to make loans to a company up to a predetermined credit limit. To obtain this type of commitment from a bank, a company usually pays a *commitment fee* based on the unused portion of the pledged funds.

Term Loan Any debt obligation having an initial maturity between 1 and 10 years. This often is referred to as *intermediate-term credit.*

Terminal Warehouse Financing Agreement A loan agreement in which the inventory being pledged as collateral is stored in a bonded warehouse operated by a public warehousing company.

Trust Receipt A security agreement under which the borrower holds the inventory and proceeds from the sale of the inventory in trust for the lender. This is also known as *floor planning.*

AN INTEGRATIVE CASE PROBLEM
WORKING CAPITAL MANAGEMENT

Anderson Furniture Company manufactures furniture and sells its products to department stores, retail furniture stores, hotels, and motels throughout the United States and Canada. The firm has nine manufacturing plants located in Virginia, North Carolina, and Georgia. The company was founded by Edward G. Anderson in 1906 and has been managed by members of the Anderson family since that time. E. G. Anderson III is currently chairman and president of the company. The treasurer and controller of the company is Claire White, who was hired away from a competing furniture company a few years ago. Anderson owns 35 percent of the common stock of the company and (along with the shares of the firm owned by relatives and employees) has effective control over all of the firm's decisions.

Financial data relating to last year's (19X1) operations, along with relevant industry comparisons, are shown in Table 18C-1. The firm's overall rates of return on equity and total assets have been around the industry average over the past several years—sometimes slightly above average and sometimes slightly below average. The company is currently operating its plants near full capacity and would like to build a new plant in Georgia at a cost of approximately $7.5 million. White has been exploring various alternative methods of financing this expansion and has been unsuccessful thus far in developing an acceptable plan. The sale of new common stock is not feasible at this time because of depressed stock market prices. Likewise, Anderson's banker has advised the firm that the use of additional long-term debt or lease financing is not possible at this time, given the firm's large amount of long-term debt currently outstanding and its relatively low times interest earned ratio. Anderson has ruled out a cut in the firm's dividend as a means of accumulating the required financing. The only other possible sources of financing available to the firm at this time, according to White, appear to be a reduction in working capital (current assets), an increase in short-term liabilities, or both.

Upon learning of these proposed financing methods, Anderson expressed concern about the effect these plans might have on the liquidity and risk of the firm. White replied that the firm currently follows a very conservative working capital policy and that these financing methods would not increase shareholder risk significantly. As evidence, she cited the firm's relatively high current and quick ratios. Anderson was unconvinced and asked White to provide additional information on the effects of these financing plans on the firm's financial status.

1. Anderson's bank requires a compensating balance of $3 million. How much additional funds can be freed up for investment in fixed assets if the firm reduces its cash balance to the minimum required by the bank?
2. How much additional financing can be obtained from receivables if Anderson institutes more stringent credit and collection policies and is able to reduce its average collection period to the industry average? (Assume that credit sales remain constant at $75 million.)

TABLE 18C-1
Anderson Furniture
Company's Financial Data
(in thousands of dollars)

			INDUSTRY AVERAGE
BALANCE SHEET AS OF DECEMBER 31, 19X1			
Assets			
Cash	$ 3,690	6.5%	5.0%
Receivables, net	15,000	26.3	21.6
Inventories	20,250	35.5	33.4
Total current assets	$38,940	68.3%	60.0%
Net fixed assets	18,060	31.7	40.0
Total assets	$57,000	100.0%	100.0%
Liabilities and stockholders' equity			
Accounts payable	$ 3,000	5.3%	7.0%
Notes payable (8%)	3,750	6.6	10.0
Total current liabilities	$ 6,750	11.8%	17.0%
Long-term debt (10%)	18,000	31.6	28.0
Stockholders' equity	32,250	56.6	55.0
Total liabilities and equity	$57,000	100.0%	100.0%
INCOME STATEMENT FOR THE YEAR ENDED DECEMBER 31, 19X1			
Net sales (all on credit)	$75,000	100.0%	
Cost of sales	60,750	81.0	
Gross profit	$14,250	19.0	
Selling and administrative expenses	7,500	10.0	
Earnings before interest and taxes	$ 6,750	9.0	
Interest expense	2,100	2.8	
Earnings before taxes	$ 4,650	6.2	
Income taxes (45.16%)	2,100	2.8	
Earnings after taxes	$ 2,550	3.4%	

Significant Ratios	Anderson	Industry Average
Current	5.76	3.50
Quick	2.77	1.60
Average collection period (days)	73.00	58.803
Inventory turnover (Cost of sales/inventory)	3.00	3.50
Sales to total assets	1.30	1.60
Debt to equity	0.80	0.90
Times interest earned	3.20	4.70
Earnings after tax/sales	3.40%	2.40%
Earnings after tax/equity	7.90%	7.90%

3. How much additional financing can be obtained for fixed-asset expansion if Anderson is able to increase its inventory turnover ratio to the industry average through tighter control of its raw materials, work-in-process, and finished goods inventories? (Assume that the cost of sales remains constant at $60.75 million.)

4. Anderson's suppliers extend credit to the firm on terms of "net 30." Anderson normally pays its bills on the last day of the credit period. How much additional financing could be generated if Anderson were to *stretch* its payables 10 days beyond the due date?

5. Prepare a pro forma balance sheet (dollars and percentages) as of December 31, 19X2, assuming that Anderson has instituted *all* actions

described in Questions 1, 2, 3, and 4, and that the funds generated have been used to build a new plant. (Assume that long-term debt and stockholders' equity at the end of 19X2 remain the same as at the end of 19X1. In other words, no new long-term debt is issued or old long-term debt retired, and all net income after taxes is paid out in common stock dividends. Also assume that net fixed assets, *except for the new plant,* remain unchanged during 19X2. Finally assume that notes payable remain unchanged during 19X2.) Hint: The *total* amount of funds generated from the reduction of current assets and the increase in current liabilities determined in Questions 1, 2, 3, and 4 is $7.5 million (rounded to the nearest $1,000). Round all figures to the nearest $1,000.

6. Prepare a pro forma income statement for 19X2. Assume that sales increase to $87 million as a result of the plant expansion. Also assume that the cost of sales and selling and administrative expense ratios (as a percentage of sales) remain constant. Finally, assume that interest expense and the firm's tax rate remain the same in 19X2.

7. Calculate the firm's current, quick, times interest earned, and rate of return on equity ratios based on the pro forma statements determined in Questions 5 and 6. How do these ratios compare with the actual values for 19X1 and the industry averages?

8. What considerations might lead Anderson and White to disagree about the desirability of using short-term sources of funds to finance the plant expansion?

9. What other sources of short-term funds might the firm consider using to finance the plant expansion?

ADVANCED TOPICS IN CONTEMPORARY FINANCIAL MANAGEMENT

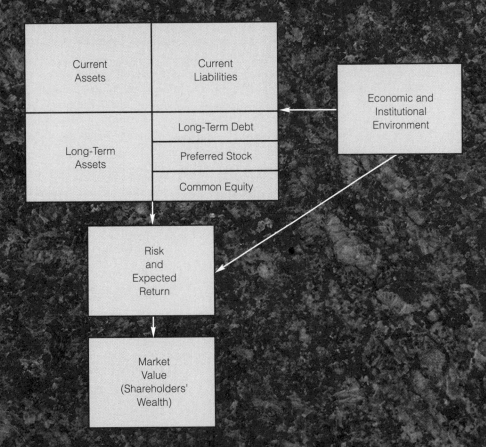

Part 6 looks at a number of advanced topics that are important for financial managers. Chapter 19 deals with leasing as another financing alternative. Chapter 20 discusses *derivative* financial instruments including options and option-related financing instruments and strategies. Puts, calls, convertible securities, warrants, rights, and swaps are all discussed.

Chapter 21 covers advanced international finance topics including parity conditions and international risk hedging. Chapter 22 focuses on corporate restructuring, with emphasis on mergers, liquidations, spinoffs, and failure and reorganization. Each of the decision areas covered in this part offers significant opportunities for adding to shareholders' wealth.

LEASE FINANCING
19

1. A *lease* is a contract that allows an individual or a firm to make economic use of an asset for a stated period of time without obtaining an ownership interest in the asset.

2. The major parties to a lease are the *lessor* and the *lessee*.

   a. The lessor is the owner of the asset and the party who receives the lease payments.

   b. The lessee is the user of the asset and the party who makes the lease payments.

3. There are several different classifications of leases.

   a. *Operating leases* are cancelable, period-by-period leases.

   b. *Financial* or *capital leases* are not cancelable. The lease payments under a financial lease are sufficient to fully amortize the cost of the asset plus provide a return to the lessor.

   c. *Leveraged leases* are special financial leases involving three parties: the lessor, the lessee, and a group of lenders. Leveraged leases are especially important to firms that cannot take advantage of the tax benefits of ownership.

4. Leasing decisions are often influenced by the tax and accounting treatment of the transaction.

5. An asset should be leased rather than owned if the present value cost of leasing is less than the present value cost of owning.

RYDER'S AIRLINE LEASING BUSINESS CRASH LANDS*

In 1984, Ryder System, Inc., entered the aircraft leasing business, attracted by the high returns and expected low risk. Airlines were expanding their fleets and the demand for aircraft was high. Ryder bought a fleet of 47 aircraft by 1989 and leased them to Continental, Midway, and America West. By early 1991, Ryder wrote off its aircraft leasing business and took a $25 million loss. Ryder completed a spinoff of its Aviation Services division in 1993.

Higher fuel prices, the recession of 1990–1991, and travel fears arising from the Persian Gulf War caused Midway Airlines and bankrupt Continental Airlines to stop making lease payments to Ryder. Ryder was losing nearly $1 million a month. In addition, the market for used aircraft was glutted, partially due to the liquidation of failed Eastern Air Lines.

Ryder is not alone in facing the woes of aircraft leasing. In the early 1990s over 700 aircraft were leased to the airlines in the most serious financial difficulties. Individual investors put more than $1.8 billion into public limited partnerships formed to lease aircraft. Commercial banks provided an additional $4 billion in direct loans for aircraft to troubled airlines. But by February 1991, 837 used aircraft were for sale, up from 200 in 1989. The price of a Boeing 727-200 declined by nearly 20 percent in just 6 months.

Normally, troubled airlines find it easier to finance the acquisition of aircraft through financial leases than through direct borrowing, because the lessor retains title to the plane. If the airline ceases to make lease payments, the lessor normally can sell the plane or lease it to someone else. The attractiveness of these leases to the leasing company depends on the existence of a market for the used aircraft, either for sale or for lease. When the market value of used aircraft declines because of a glutted market or a depressed airline industry, lessors are exposed to high risk and large potential losses.

In this chapter we will explore the reasons a firm, such as Continental Air Lines, might choose to lease rather than buy some of its assets. Specifically, we will examine the type of analysis that should go into a lease versus purchase decision if the firm wishes to maximize shareholder wealth. We also will examine the reasons a leasing company, such as Ryder, would want to enter this high risk business.

*Based on "All the Trouble Isn't in the Sky," *Business Week* (March 11, 1991): 84–85.

INTRODUCTION

A promotional brochure from the Warner and Swasey Financial Corporation states, "The value of a machine is in the use, not its ownership." This is true in the sense that a firm may wish to acquire the *use* of an asset needed in the production of goods and the providing of services, but finds it unnecessary to acquire legal title to the asset. Leasing is a means of obtaining economic use of an asset for a specific period of time without obtaining an ownership interest in the asset. In the lease contract, the property owner (*lessor*) agrees to permit the property user (*lessee*) to make use of the property for a stated time. In return, the lessee agrees to make a series of periodic payments to the lessor.

Leasing as a source of intermediate- and long-term financing has become increasingly popular since World War II. Prior to that time, most lease contracts were written for real estate and farm property. Today, few major firms are not involved in leasing. Leased assets range from transportation equipment (such as railroad rolling stock, trucks, automobiles, airplanes, and ships) to computers, medical equipment, specialized industrial equipment, energy transmission equipment, and mining equipment. Some firms lease entire power-generating plants and aluminum reduction mills. In the hotel and motel industry, leases may even include bathroom fixtures, paintings, furniture, and bedding.

The volume of leasing activity expanded greatly during the 1980s—growing at an estimated rate of 16 percent per year. Equipment leasing by companies rose to more than $147 billion per year by 1995. Leasing accounts for more than 30 percent of all business investment in equipment.

Many types of firms originate leases: commercial banks, savings and loan institutions, finance companies, insurance companies, investment banks, equipment manufacturing companies (often through captive leasing subsidiaries), and independent leasing companies. Leasing companies account for over 60 percent of all leases. Manufacturers provide about 36 percent of lease financing, and banks account for about 17 percent.[1]

Because of the growing importance and widespread acceptance of lease financing, the contemporary financial manager should have a good understanding of this financing method. The following sections discuss the characteristics of various types of leases and develop a lease analysis model from the perspective of the lessor. Later sections consider the tax and accounting treatment of leases and the advantages and disadvantages of leases. Finally, a lease analysis model is developed from the perspective of the lessee.

TYPES OF LEASES

Leases are classified in a number of ways. "True leases," which are the primary focus of this chapter, are traditional leases in which the lessor is considered to hold the legal title to the leased asset. The asset user, the lessee, has no ownership interest in the asset. *Operating leases* and various types of *financial,* or *capital, leases* are subcategories of true leases.

---

[1]"Understanding the Equipment Leasing Marketplace" (New York: Foundation for Leasing Education and Dun & Bradstreet Information Services, 1995).

Operating Leases

An **operating lease,** sometimes called a *service* or *maintenance lease,* is an agreement that provides the lessee with use of an asset on a period-by-period basis. Normally, the payments under an operating lease contract are insufficient to recover the full cost of the asset for the lessor. As a result, the contract period in an operating lease tends to be somewhat less than the usable economic life of the asset, and the lessor expects to recover the costs (plus a return) from renewal rental payments, the sale of the asset at the end of the lease period, or both.

The most important characteristic of an operating lease is that it may be canceled at the option of the lessee as long as the lessor is given sufficient notice. Even though the lessee may be required to pay a penalty to the lessor upon cancellation, this is preferable to being compelled to keep an asset that is expected to become obsolete in the near future. For example, many firms lease their computers under an operating lease arrangement. (Of course, the lessor charges a rental fee that is consistent with expectations of the asset's economic life.)

Most operating leases require the lessor to maintain the leased asset. In addition, the lessor normally is responsible for any property taxes owed on the asset and for providing appropriate insurance coverage. The costs of these services are built into the lease rate.

Financial or Capital Leases

A **financial lease,** also termed a *capital lease,* is a noncancelable agreement.[2] The lessee is required to make payments throughout the lease period, whether or not the asset continues to generate economic benefits. Failure to make payments has serious financial consequences and eventually could force the lessee into bankruptcy.

With financial leases, the lessee generally is responsible for maintenance of the asset. The lessee also may have to pay insurance and property taxes. The total payments over the lease period are sufficient to amortize the original cost of the asset and provide a return to the lessor. Some financial leases provide for a renewal or repurchase option at the end of the lease; these renewal and repurchase options are subject to IRS regulations.

A financial lease may originate either as a *sale and leaseback* or as a *direct lease.*

Sale and Leaseback. A sale and leaseback occurs when a company sells an asset to another firm and immediately leases it back for its own use. In this transaction, the lessor normally pays a price close to the asset's fair market value. The lease payments are set at a level that will return the full purchase price of the asset to the lessor, plus provide a reasonable rate of return. The sale and leaseback is advantageous to the lessee for the following reasons:

■ The lessee receives cash from the sale of the asset, which may be reinvested elsewhere in the firm or used to increase the firm's liquidity.

■ The lessee can continue using the asset, even though it is owned by someone else.

Visit the Web site of one of the thousands of lessors who advertise their leasing services over the Internet. For example, Advanced Leasing Concepts, Inc., is a typical lessor that leases machinery, computers, software, vehicles, audio/visual equipment, and virtually anything else you and/or your firm could need. ACLI also has a nice tutorial on leasing and its advantages.
http://www.alci.com

---

[2]This chapter focuses primarily on financial leases, rather than operating leases, because financial leases represent more permanent obligations. The analysis techniques discussed at the end of this chapter, however, are equally applicable to both operating and financial leases.

A good illustration of a sale and leaseback transaction was Public Service of New Mexico's decision to sell and lease back its partial interest in Palo Verde Nuclear Plant Unit 1 for $325 million. This transaction reduced its annual mortgage payments by one-half, to $40 million per year for the next 15 years, and its total cost by $375 million.

Sale and leaseback financing has been popular among financial institutions (e.g., banks and insurance companies). The institutions are subject to regulation concerning their financial condition (capital position and asset quality). Financial institutions with weak capital positions have sold headquarters buildings for a price greater than their book value, recorded a gain on the sale, thereby bolstering the capital account, and leased back the building under a long-term, generally noncancelable lease. The resulting increase in the institution's capital accounts reduces regulatory pressure to increase capital via the sale of new equity (common stock). First Republic Corporation, a Dallas-based bank holding company, engaged in this type of transaction. In early 1994, Integon Life Insurance Company also undertook similar action in the face of a weak capital position.

These types of transactions are poorly motivated and do not change the fundamental value or risk of the firm. They are primarily accounting manipulations. To be sure, many of the banks that have engaged in these transactions have subsequently failed or been forced to merge with financially stronger firms.

Direct Lease. A direct lease is initiated when a firm acquires the use of an asset that it previously did not own. The lessor may be the manufacturer of the asset or a financial institution. In the latter instance, the user-lessee first determines the following:

- What equipment will be leased.
- Which manufacturer will supply the equipment.
- What options, warranties, terms of delivery, installment agreements, and service agreements will have to be made.
- What price will be paid for the asset.

The lessee then contacts a financial institution and works out the terms of the lease, after which the institution (which then becomes the lessor) acquires the asset for the lessee and the lessee starts making the lease payments. Under this arrangement, the lessee is usually responsible for taxes, insurance, and maintenance.

Leveraged Leases

A large proportion of all financial leases currently written in the United States are leveraged leases. Also known as *third-party equity leases* and *tax leases,* leveraged leases are designed to provide financing for assets that require large capital outlays (generally greater than $300,000) and have economic lives of 5 years or more. Leveraged leases are usually tax motivated because the asset-user (lessee) is not in a tax position where it can make use of the accelerated depreciation tax shields if the asset is owned instead of leased.

A **leveraged lease** is a three-sided agreement among the lessee, the lessor, and the lenders. The *lessee* selects the leased asset, receives all the income generated from its use, and makes the periodic lease payments. The *lessor* (normally a financial institution, such as a leasing company or a commercial bank) acts either for itself or as a trustee for an individual or a group of individuals to provide the equity funds needed to purchase the asset. The *lenders* (usually banks, insurance companies, trusts, pension funds, or foundations) lend the funds needed to make up the asset's full purchase price. Specifically, the lessor normally supplies 20 to 40 percent of the purchase price, and the lenders provide the remaining 60 to 80 percent. For example, in the Public Service Company of New Mexico sale and leaseback of the Palo Verde Nuclear Plant discussed earlier, the lessors (Chrysler Capital, Drexel Burnham Leasing, and Mellon Financial Services) borrowed approximately 80 percent of the purchase price of the facilities.

Figure 19-1 is an announcement of a leveraged lease that was arranged by Salomon Brothers for Kansas City Southern Lines. In this case, the Ford Motor Credit Company acted as the lessor and provided equity funds of $4,728,974 to acquire 450 boxcars, which were leased to Kansas City Southern Lines. Debt funds of $10,072,198 were provided by a number of institutional lenders.

In a leveraged lease, the long-term money is supplied to the lessor by the lenders on a nonrecourse basis; that is, the lenders cannot turn to the lessor for repayment of the debt in the event of default. Normally, the lender receives mortgage bonds secured by the following:

- A first lien on the asset.
- An assignment of the lease.
- An assignment of the lease rental payments.
- Occasionally, a direct guarantee from the lessee or a third party (such as the government, in the case of merchant vessel financing).

FIGURE 19-1
Announcement of a Leveraged Lease Financing Arrangement

Referring again to the Public Service Company of New Mexico nuclear plant sale and leaseback example, the public debt used to finance the transaction was indirectly secured by the facilities and was payable from rental payments due by the utility under the leases. The debt was structured to have principal and interest payments that correspond to the receipt of rental payments. Because the lenders do not have recourse to the lessor in the event of default, the lessor's risk is limited to the 20 to 40 percent equity contribution.

As the owner of the asset, the lessor reports the lease payments as gross income. The lessor receives benefits from the tax-deductible interest and accelerated depreciation. As a result, the lessor incurs large tax losses and receives large cash inflows during the early years of the lease.

Because the lessor receives the entire accelerated depreciation tax shield although making a relatively small equity investment, the lessor can provide an attractive lease rate to the lessee. Lease rates of 4 to 6 percent are not uncommon when AAA-rated bonds are yielding from 9 to 10 percent. Figure 19-2 is a diagram of a typical leveraged lease arrangement.

Lessees who anticipate that their taxable income will not be sufficient to allow them to take advantage of the tax benefits of ownership are most likely to use leveraged leases for large transactions. These include firms with low profit levels, large tax-loss carryforwards, or large amounts of tax-exempt income. The lessee effectively gives up the tax benefits of ownership in exchange for more favorable lease rates.

FIGURE 19-2
Diagram of a Typical Leveraged Lease

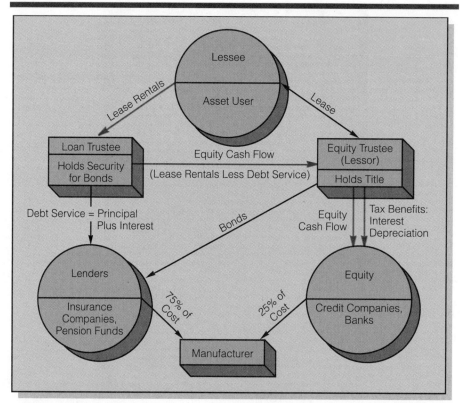

ADVANTAGES AND DISADVANTAGES OF LEASING

Leasing offers a number of potential advantages. However, the prudent financial manager also should be aware of the disadvantages.

Advantages

Perhaps the major advantage of leasing is that it provides *flexible financing.* Most lease arrangements tend to have fewer restrictive covenants than loan agreements. In addition, leasing is well suited to piecemeal financing. A firm that is acquiring assets over time may find it more convenient to lease them than to negotiate term loans or sell securities each time it makes a new capital outlay.

In the case of real estate leasing, the lessee may *effectively be able to depreciate land.* Because the lease payments will reflect both the lessor's investment in any buildings *and* the cost of the land, the lessee is able to effectively depreciate the land by deducting the full amount of the lease payment for tax purposes. To keep this benefit in perspective, however, it should be noted that the lessee also loses any salvage value associated with the property at the end of the lease.

The lessee also may be able to make *lower payments* because of the tax benefits enjoyed by the lessor. This is especially important in the case of a leveraged lease, when the lessee is a firm with insufficient taxable income to take advantage of the tax benefits of ownership. In fact, the majority of lease transactions made are tax motivated.

In addition, it *may* be possible for the lessee to *avoid some of the risks of obsolescence* associated with ownership. This is the second most cited reason why lessees choose lease financing. The lessor will charge a lease rate intended to provide a specified return on the required net investment. The net investment is equal to the cost of the asset minus the present value of the expected salvage value at the end of the lease. If the actual salvage is less than originally expected, the lessor bears the loss.

For the small or marginally profitable firm, *leasing is often the only available source of financing,* because the title to leased property remains with the lessor and reduces the lessor's risk in the event of failure. If the lessee does fail, the lessor can recover the leased property more quickly than a secured lender.[3]

Leasing tends to *smooth out expenses* for the lessee. Because lease payments are a constant annual outlay, whereas MACRS depreciation expenses are large in the early years of ownership and less in later years, earnings tend to appear more stable when assets are leased rather than owned. In addition, reported earnings per share normally may be higher in the early years of a lease, compared with ownership, because of the use of MACRS depreciation when the asset is owned.

Leasing is said to provide *100 percent financing,* whereas most borrowing requires a down payment. This is the major reason cited by lessees for why they choose lease financing. However, because lease payments normally are made in advance of each period, this 100 percent financing benefit is diminished by the amount of the first required lease payment.

From the lessee's perspective, leases can *increase a firm's liquidity.* For example, a sale and leaseback transforms some of a firm's fixed assets into cash in

---

[3]For a more complete discussion of the bankruptcy implications of leasing see V. S. Krishnan and R. C. Moyer, "Bankruptcy Costs and the Financial Leasing Decision," *Financial Management* (Summer 1994).

exchange for an obligation to make a series of fixed future payments. This has been the primary motivation for sale and leaseback transactions undertaken by several troubled airlines.

(9) And, finally, leasing gives some plant or divisional managers additional *flexibility in acquiring assets* if lease agreements are not subject to internal capital expenditure constraints. In recent years, local school districts, municipalities, and the U.S. Navy, among other organizations, have used leasing to circumvent capital outlay restrictions.

Disadvantages

(1) The primary disadvantage of leasing is *cost*. For a firm with a strong earnings record, good access to the credit markets, and the ability to take advantage of the tax benefits of ownership, leasing is often a more expensive alternative. Of course, the actual cost difference between ownership and leasing depends on a number of factors and varies from case to case.

(2) Another disadvantage of leasing is the *loss of the asset's salvage value*. In real estate, this loss can be substantial. A lessee may also have *difficulty getting approval to make property improvements* on leased real estate. If the improvements substantially alter the property or reduce its potential range of uses, the lessor may be reluctant to permit them.

(3) In addition, if a leased asset (with a financial lease) becomes obsolete or if the capital project financed by the lease becomes uneconomical, the *lessee may not cancel the lease without paying a substantial penalty.*

(4) Also, in bankruptcy, lease payments normally must be made, whereas interest and principal payments are suspended.

TAX AND ACCOUNTING ASPECTS OF LEASES

Leasing assets involves a number of tax and accounting considerations, which are examined in this section.

Tax Status of True Leases

Annual lease payments are tax deductible for the lessee if one crucial criterion is met; namely, the IRS must agree that a contract truly is a lease and not just an installment loan called a lease. Before embarking on a lease transaction, all involved parties should obtain an opinion from the IRS regarding the tax status of the proposed lease. The opinion of the IRS normally revolves primarily around the following general rules:

- The remaining useful life of the equipment at the end of the lease term must be the greater of 1 year or 20 percent of its originally estimated useful life.
- Leases in excess of 30 years are *not* considered to be leases for tax purposes.
- The lease payments must provide the lessor with a reasonable return on the investment. At this point in time, a range of 8 to 16 percent probably would be viewed as reasonable. This profit potential must exist apart from the transaction's tax benefits.
- Renewal options must be reasonable; that is, the renewal rate must be closely related to the economic value of the asset for the renewal period.

- If the lease agreement specifies a purchase option at the end of the lease period, the purchase price must be based on the asset's fair market value at that time.
- In the case of a leveraged lease, the lessor must provide a minimum of 20 percent equity.
- Limited-use property (valuable only to the lessee) may not be leased.

If the IRS does not agree that a contract is truly a lease, taxes are applied as if the property had been sold to the lessee and pledged to the lessor as security for a loan. The reason for the IRS restrictions previously cited is that the IRS wants to prohibit lease transactions set up purely to speed up tax deductions. For example, a building normally would be depreciated over 39 years under MACRS depreciation rules. It would be possible to set up a lease over a 3-year period that allowed the lessee to effectively write off the cost of the building for tax purposes over 3 years. This would increase tax deductions for the lessee at the expense of tax receipts to the U.S. Treasury. These IRS guidelines are designed to prevent this type of abuse.

Leases and Accounting Practices

In recent years, firms have tended to disclose more information regarding lease obligations.

In November 1976, the Financial Accounting Standards Board (FASB) issued *Standard No. 13,* which *requires* lessees to capitalize certain types of leases, primarily financial or capital leases. The capitalized value of a lease is determined by computing the present value of all required lease payments, discounted at a rate equal to the lessee's incremental borrowing rate for a secured loan over a term similar to the lease.[4] Table 19-1 illustrates this procedure.

In addition to making these balance sheet adjustments, a firm must show the following in the footnotes to the financial statements:[5]

- For financial leases:
    1. The gross amount of assets by major classes according to nature or use reported under financial leases as of the date of the balance sheet.
    2. The amount of accumulated lease amortization.
    3. Future minimum lease payments as of the date of the latest balance sheet presented, in total and for each of the next five fiscal years.

TABLE 19-1
Accounting Treatment of Leases

ASSETS		LIABILITIES	
Leased property under capital leases less accumulated amortization		Current:	
		Obligations under capital leases*	$150
	$1,500	Long term:	
	$1,500	Obligations under capital leases*	$1,350
			$1,500

*The $150 represents lease payments due during the next year. The $1,350 represents the present value of lease payments due beyond one year in the future.

[4]In certain circumstances, it is possible for a firm to use a lower rate. See FASB *Standard No. 13* for a more detailed discussion.
[5]The requirements presented here are not inclusive; they merely summarize the most significant disclosures.

■ For operating leases:
1. Future minimum rental payments required as of the date of the latest balance sheet presented, in total and for each of the following five fiscal years.
2. The rental expense for each period for which an income statement is presented.

The lessee must also indicate in the notes to the financial statements the existence and terms of renewal or repurchase options and escalation clauses, any restrictions imposed by leases (such as restrictions on dividends, additional debt, or further leasing), and any contingent rental obligations. Figure 19-3 illustrates how these lease disclosure requirements affected The Limited, Inc., as reported in their annual report.

The effect of these disclosure requirements is to lower a firm's reported return on investment and to increase the reported debt-to-equity ratios of a firm that has acquired a portion of its assets through leasing. In the past, some analysts argued that one of the advantages of leasing was that it provided "off-balance sheet" financing and tended to increase a firm's capacity to borrow. Whether or not this was true, the lease-reporting requirements help to eliminate this distortion, facilitate clearer analysis of a firm's financial condition, and make it easier to make comparisons among firms.

 ENTREPRENEURIAL FINANCE ISSUES
LEASING BY SMALL BUSINESSES[6]

During the recession of the late 1980s and early 1990s, many small businesses found it increasingly difficult to get small business loans from banks. For exam-

FIGURE 19-3
Lease Disclosure for The Limited, Inc., 1995 Annual Report

5. Leased Facilities and Commitments

Annual store rent is comprised of a fixed minimum amount, plus contingent rent based upon a percentage of sales exceeding a stipulated amount. Store lease terms generally require additional payments covering taxes, common area costs, and certain other expenses.

A summary of rent expense for 1995, 1994, and 1993 follows (thousands):

	1995	1994	1993
Store Rent:			
Fixed Minimum	$643,200	$586,437	$540,381
Contingent	18,812	17,522	19,727
Total Store Rent	662,012	603,959	560,108
Equipment and Other	26,101	27,710	31,897
Total Rent Expense	$688,113	$631,669	$592,005

At February 3, 1996, the Company was committed to noncancelable leases with remaining terms of one to forty years. A substantial portion of these commitments are store leases with initial terms ranging from ten to twenty years, with options to renew at varying terms. Accrued rent expense was $102.2 million and $116.5 million at February 3, 1996 and January 28, 1995.

A summary of minimum rent commitments under noncancelable leases follows (thousands):

1996	$ 659,259
1997	642,450
1998	620,372
1999	596,387
2000	578,913
Thereafter	$2,878,037

[6]Based on "Many Small Businesses Are Sold on Leasing," *Wall Street Journal* (October 27, 1993): B2.

ple, when Nun-Lo Corporation of Ballwin, Missouri, sought bank financing to acquire a new $20,000 printing press, its bankers said no because of the firm's $60,000 in outstanding debt. Nun-Lo ended up leasing the press instead, for $550 per month over a 36-month period.

Many firms are in the same position as Nun-Lo, and they have sought lease financing as an alternative to traditional bank financing. Equipment financed through leasing amounts to more than $147 billion per year.

In addition to its greater availability, firms that have made use of lease financing cite the following advantages:

1. Less cash required upfront.
2. Better protection against obsolescence at the end of the lease term.
3. Quicker approvals from lessors than from lenders.
4. Fewer restrictive covenants from lessors than from lenders.

advantages to lease

However, these advantages do not come cheap. Lease financing often entails high effective interest costs relative to borrowing. One firm that chose to lease an asset rather than borrow to buy it found that the effective interest cost on the lease was 15.4 percent, nearly double the bank's loan rate. In addition, the lessee had to give up all of the tax benefits of ownership—notably the depreciation tax shields arising from the new equipment.

Thus, while leasing has gained favor among small firms as a quick and flexible financing alternative, these benefits typically have come at a high cost.

DETERMINING LEASE PAYMENTS: THE LESSOR'S PERSPECTIVE

Suppose that the Dole Company (lessee) desires to lease a piece of farm equipment valued at $100,000 from Deere & Company (lessor) for a period of 5 years. Under the terms of the lease, payments are to be made at the beginning of each of the 5 years. Deere expects to depreciate the asset on a straight-line basis of $20,000 per year down to a book salvage value of $0. Actual salvage value is expected to be $10,000 at the end of 5 years. This salvage value will be treated as a recapture of depreciation and taxed at Deere's marginal tax rate of 40 percent. Thus, the after-tax salvage value will be $6,000 ($10,000 actual salvage less $4,000 tax on depreciation recapture). If Deere requires an 11 percent after-tax rate of return on the lease, what will be the annual lease payments?

■ **Step 1: Compute the lessor's amount to be amortized.** In this case, it is the $100,000 initial outlay minus the present value of the after-tax salvage at the end of year 5 minus the present value of the after-tax depreciation tax shield for each year. (Recall that depreciation reduces taxable income by the amount of the depreciation and thus reduces a firm's cash outflow for tax payments by an amount equal to the depreciation times the company's marginal ordinary tax rate.)

Initial outlay	$100,000
Less Present value of $6,000 after-tax salvage at 11% ($6,000 × 0.593)	3,558
Less Present value of annual depreciation tax shield ($20,000 × 0.4 × $PVIFA_{0.11,5}$) = $8,000 × 3.696	29,568
Amount to be amortized	$ 66,874

(If an accelerated depreciation method, such as MACRS, was used by the lessor, the present value of the annual depreciation tax shield would have to be done using a series of Table II PVIF factors, because the annual depreciation tax shield normally will change most years under accelerated depreciation methods.)

■ **Step 2: Compute the annual *after-tax* lease income.** This is the income that the lessor must receive in order to earn the needed 11 percent return. Remember that lease payments received by a lessor are treated as taxable, ordinary income. These payments can be computed using the appropriate interest factor for the present value of an annuity (PVIFA from Table IV). Because lease payments normally are made at the beginning of each year, they constitute an *annuity due*. Thus, the last four payments, which occur at the ends of years 1 through 4, are discounted, whereas the present value of the first payment, made at the *beginning* of year 1, is not discounted. Recall from Chapter 4 that taking the PVIFA for 11 percent and 5 years and multiplying by $(1 + 0.11)$ gives the required PVIFA for an annuity due. If *PMT* is the annual after-tax lease income to the lessor, the present value of the lease income may be set equal to the amount to be amortized to determine the required *PMT,* as follows:

$$\text{Amount to be amortized} = PMT(\text{PVIFA}_{0.11,5})\,(1 + 0.11)$$

$$\$66{,}874 = PMT(3.696)\,(1.11)$$

$$\$66{,}874 = PMT(4.103)$$

$$PMT = \$16{,}299$$

CALCULATOR SOLUTION

This problem must be solved with the calculator in the beginning of period payment mode.

Enter: 5   11   −66,874

        | n | | i | | PV | | PMT | | FV |

Solution: 16,301

Note: The difference between the interest table solution and the calculator solution is due to rounding.

■ Therefore, Deere & Company needs to receive five beginning-of-the-year, after-tax lease income amounts of $16,301 in order to earn an 11 percent after-tax return on the lease.

■ **Step 3: Convert the lease income requirement of the lessor to a lease payment requirement of the lessee.** Recalling that lease payments received by the lessor from the lessee are taxed as ordinary income, we can convert the after-tax lease income requirement of the lessor into a lease payment requirement for the lessee as follows:

$$\begin{array}{l}\text{Lease payment required} \\ \text{from the lessee}\end{array} = \dfrac{\begin{array}{c}\text{Lease income required} \\ \text{by lessor (after-tax)}\end{array}}{\begin{array}{c}1 \text{ minus lessor's marginal} \\ \text{tax rate}\end{array}}$$

$$= \frac{\$16{,}301}{1 - 0.4}$$

$$= \$27{,}168$$

■ Therefore, the Dole Company will have to make an annual lease payment of $27,168 to Deere & Company at the beginning of each year.

 ## LEASE–BUY ANALYSIS: THE LESSEE'S PERSPECTIVE

Financial theorists and model builders have devoted a substantial amount of time and effort to developing an analytical framework within which the differential costs associated with leasing versus buying can be compared. At least fifteen different approaches to the problem have been suggested, and there is considerable disagreement as to which one is the best.[7] In spite of this abundance of models, the perplexed financial manager can take some comfort in the fact that the practical effects resulting from the differences in the models tend to be small, because few real-world decisions are changed as a result of which lease–buy model is chosen.[8]

One of the most commonly used approaches to the analysis of a lease versus purchase decision assumes that the appropriate comparison should be between *leasing* and *borrowing to buy.* Advocates of this approach argue that a financial lease is much like a loan in that it requires a series of fixed payments. Failure to make lease payments, like failure to make loan payments, may result in bankruptcy.

The basic approach of the lease–buy analysis model is to compute the *net advantage to leasing* (NAL). The net advantage to leasing compares the present value cost of leasing with the present value cost of owning the asset. If the cost of owning the asset is greater than the cost of leasing the asset, the NAL is positive and the model indicates that the asset should be leased.

The *net advantage to leasing* calculation is as follows:

	Installed cost of the asset
Less	Present value of the after-tax lease payments
Less	Present value of depreciation tax shield
Plus	Present value of after-tax operating costs incurred if owned but not if leased
Less	Present value of the after-tax salvage value
Equals	Net advantage to leasing

The installed cost of the asset equals the purchase price plus installation and shipping charges. The installed cost forms the basis on which depreciation is computed.

The present value of the after-tax lease payments that are made if the asset is leased reduce the NAL; hence, they are subtracted when computing the NAL. These lease payments are discounted at the firm's after-tax marginal cost of borrowing to reflect the fact that lease payments are contractually known in advance and thus are not subject to much uncertainty. The present value of the depreciation tax shield is equal to the depreciation claimed each year if the asset is owned times the firm's marginal tax rate. The depreciation tax shield reduces the cost of ownership and hence is subtracted when computing the NAL.

---

[7]Basically, the various models differ as to which discount rate should be used to evaluate various components of the cash flows and which cash flows should be considered.

[8]Evidence of this is presented in a paper by Arthur Gudikunst and Gordon Roberts, "Empirical Analysis of Lease–Buy Decisions," presented at the 1975 Meeting of the Eastern Finance Association.

Because the depreciation amounts also are known with relative certainty, they also are discounted at the firm's after-tax marginal cost of borrowing.[9]

Sometimes operating costs are incurred if the asset is owned but not if it is leased. These may include property tax payments, insurance, or some maintenance expenses. If these do exist, they represent a benefit of leasing and increase the NAL. Hence, the after-tax amount of these costs is added in the NAL calculation. These operating cost savings also are discounted at the after-tax marginal cost of borrowing, reflecting their relative certainty. Finally, if the asset is owned, the owner will receive the after-tax salvage value. This is lost if the asset is leased. Hence the after-tax salvage reduces the NAL and must be subtracted when calculating the NAL. Because asset salvage values generally are subject to substantial uncertainty, they normally are discounted at a rate equal to the firm's weighted (marginal) cost of capital.

Example of Lease–Buy Analysis

Consider the following example to illustrate the lease–buy analysis procedure just described. Suppose that the Alcoa Corporation is trying to decide whether it should purchase or lease a new heavy duty GMC truck. (The firm already has computed the net present value of this proposed asset acquisition and found the project to be acceptable.) The truck can be purchased for $50,000, including delivery. Alternatively, the truck can be leased from General Motors Acceptance Corporation for a 6-year period at a beginning-of-the-year lease payment of $10,000. If purchased, Alcoa could borrow the needed funds from Mellon Bank at an annual interest rate of 10 percent. If the truck is purchased, Alcoa estimates that it will incur $750 per year of expenses to cover insurance and a maintenance contract. These expenses would not be incurred if the truck is leased. The truck will be depreciated under MACRS guidelines as a 5-year asset. Alcoa expects the actual salvage value to be $20,000 at the end of 6 years. Alcoa's marginal tax rate is 40 percent, and its weighted after-tax cost of capital is 15 percent. Which alternative—leasing or buying—should be chosen? In order to answer this question, we need to compute the NAL. This is shown in Table 19-2. The calculation in Table 19-2 indicates a net advantage to leasing of –$1,296. Because the NAL is negative, the asset should be owned rather than leased.[10]

This procedure can be used to evaluate any lease versus buy decision only after it has been determined by standard capital budgeting techniques that an asset should be acquired, i.e., it has a positive net present value.

 ETHICAL ISSUES
CONTINENTAL AIRLINES' LEASES IN BANKRUPTCY

In December 1990, Continental Airlines, faced with poor operating cash flow, declared bankruptcy because of its inability to meet its financial obligations,

---

[9]The depreciation amounts are known with certainty, but the tax shield from depreciation may not be certain. For example, in 1986, Congress passed a major tax reform plan that lowered the marginal corporate tax rate, thereby reducing the value of the tax shield. Also, there always is the chance that a company will not have sufficient taxable income to take advantage of the depreciation tax shield.

[10]The lease–buy analysis procedure used here implicitly assumes that the leasing alternative and the borrowing-to-buy alternative have the same impact on the company's debt capacity. This is desirable because leasing and borrowing both represent fixed obligations that are treated by financial analysts as equivalent to debt. Lease–buy analysis also assumes that the asset satisfies the lessee's normal capital investment criteria, such as NPV.

END OF YEAR (1)	INSTALLED ASSET COST (2)	LEASE PAYMENT AFTER-TAX* (3)	DEPRECIATION** (4)	DEPRECIATION TAX SHIELD† (5)	ADDITIONAL OPERATING COSTS IF OWNED AFTER-TAX†† (6)	NAL CASH FLOWS EXCEPT SALVAGE‡ (7) = (2) − (3) − (5) + (6)
0	$50,000	$6,000	—	—	—	$ 44,000
1	—	6,000	$10,000	$4,000	$450	−9,550
2	—	6,000	16,000	6,400	450	−11,950
3	—	6,000	9,600	3,840	450	−9,390
4	—	6,000	5,760	2,304	450	−7,854
5	—	6,000	5,760	2,304	450	−7,854
6	—	—	2,880	1,152	450	−702

PVIF @ 6%‡‡ (8)	PRESENT VALUE§ (9) = (7) × (8)	AFTER-TAX SALVAGE§§ (10)	PVIF @15% (11)	PRESENT VALUE SALVAGE¶ (12) = (10) × (11)	NAL¶¶ (13) = (9) − (12)
1.000	$ 44,000	—	—	—	$ 44,000
0.943	−9,006	—	—	—	−9,006
0.890	−10,636	—	—	—	−10,636
0.840	−7,888	—	—	—	−7,888
0.792	−6,220	—	—	—	−6,220
0.747	−5,867	—	—	—	−5,867
0.705	−495	$12,000	0.432	$5,184	−5,679

Net Advantage to Leasing = −$1,296

*The after-tax lease payment equals the total lease payment ($10,000) times 1 minus Alcoa's marginal tax rate (40 percent). The benefit of the tax deductibility of lease payments is assumed to be received at approximately the same time the lease payments are made, reflecting the quarterly payment of taxes.
**MACRS depreciation is computed using the 5-year MACRS rates times the asset cost. The MACRS rates are 20%, 32%, 19.2%, 11.52%, 11.52% and 5.76%, respectively over the 6 years.
†The depreciation tax shield is equal to the depreciation in column (4) times Alcoa's marginal tax rate (40 percent).
††Column (6) is equal to $750 pretax cost times 1 minus Alcoa's marginal tax rate (40 percent).
‡Column (7) is the total of the cash flows needed to compute the NAL that are discounted at the after-tax cost of debt for Alcoa. It is equal to the asset cost (2), less the after-tax lease payments (3), less the depreciation tax shield (5), plus the additional after-tax operating costs incurred if the asset is owned (6).
‡‡The after-tax cost of debt is 6 percent [10 percent pretax cost times 1 minus Alcoa's marginal tax rate (40 percent)].
§The present value of column (9) is equal to the cash flows in column (7) times the PVIF factors in column (8).
§§The after-tax salvage is equal to the pretax salvage ($20,000) times 1 minus Alcoa's marginal tax rate (40 percent).
¶The present value of the salvage is equal to the after-tax salvage times the PVIF for 15 percent and 6 years, where the 15 percent represents Alcoa's weighted cost of capital.
¶¶The NAL is equal to the sum of the present value cash flows from column (9) minus the present value of the after-tax salvage from column (12).

TABLE 19-2
Calculation of the Net Advantage to Leasing for Alcoa

such as debt payments and lease payments. Normally, when a firm operates under the protection of a bankruptcy court, it is able to suspend payments to its creditors, pending a reorganization of the firm. However, lease payments normally must continue to be paid to the lessors, usually within 60 days of the bankruptcy filing, because the lessors hold title to the leased assets. If lease payments are suspended, the lessors can seize their assets, under most circumstances, and lease them to other parties.

In its bankruptcy case, Continental argued that some of its leases were not truly leases but rather were, in reality, debt instruments that did not have to be paid while the firm was in bankruptcy. A Delaware bankruptcy judge ruled in favor of the company in early February 1991. This ruling sent shockwaves through the aircraft leasing business because of the implications about the security position of lessors of billions of dollars of aircraft leases. Not surprisingly, the lessors appealed this ruling. On April 1, a U.S. district judge ruled that the aircraft leases were indeed leases and had to be paid within 60 days of the bankruptcy filing, thus reaffirming the security position of the lessors. It was not clear, however, whether Continental had the cash needed to make the payments. Continental appealed this ruling, thus deferring the payments further.

What implications do you feel a ruling in favor of Continental would have had on the leasing industry and on other firms facing financial difficulty? Do you believe that Continental's actions in this case were ethically appropriate, in light of the contracts that it had entered into with the lessors and in light of its own circumstances? If Continental had been successful in this suit, who would be the net winners and the net losers? Are there any potential benefits to the lessors if Continental wins this suit?

■ SUMMARY

- A *lease* is a written agreement that permits the *lessee* to use a piece of property owned by the *lessor* in exchange for a series of periodic lease or rental payments.
- An *operating lease* provides the lessee with the use of an asset on a period-by-period basis. An operating lease *may be canceled* at the lessee's option. Most operating leases are written for a relatively short period of time, normally less than 5 years.
- A *financial lease* is a *noncancelable* agreement that obligates the lessee to make payments to the lessor for a predetermined period of time. There are two major types of financial leases: *sale and leaseback* agreements and *direct leases. Leveraged leases,* also called *tax leases,* have become increasingly common. Approximately 85 percent of the financial leases written today are leveraged leases.
- Subject to a series of IRS guidelines, firms that lease a portion of their assets may deduct the full amount of the lease payment for tax purposes.
- Decisions by the Financial Accounting Standards Board (FASB) require that many financial leases be capitalized and shown on the lessee's balance sheet.
- Leasing offers a number of potential advantages, including flexibility, the effective depreciation of land, and tax benefits (in some cases). It also may be the only source of financing available to many marginally profitable firms. It has a number of potential disadvantages, too. For example, leasing tends to be more costly than ownership for a firm with a good earnings record and good access to the capital markets.
- A number of analytical models are available to assist the lessor in determining what lease payments to charge. Other models are available to assist the lessee in determining which is the less expensive source of financing—leasing or borrowing to buy.

■ QUESTIONS AND TOPICS FOR DISCUSSION

1. What are the primary differences between operating leases and financial leases?
2. How does a leveraged lease differ from a nonleveraged financial lease? What type of firm or organization is most likely to take advantage of the leveraged lease financing option? What type of individual or financial institution is most likely to act as the lessor in a leveraged lease?

3. From a tax perspective, what primary requirements in a lease transaction must be met in order for the IRS to consider the transaction a genuine lease? Why is a favorable IRS ruling regarding the tax status of a lease important to both the lessor and the lessee?

4. One advantage that often has been claimed of lease financing is that it creates "off-balance sheet" financing. Evaluate this benefit in light of FASB *Standard No. 13*.

5. How can leasing allow a firm to effectively "depreciate" land?

6. What effect does leasing have on the stability of a firm's reported earnings?

7. It has been argued that leasing is almost always more expensive than borrowing and owning. Do you think this is true? Why or why not? Under what circumstances is leasing likely to be more desirable than direct ownership?

8. Why do you think it is easier for firms with weak credit positions to obtain lease financing than bank loan financing?

■ SELF-TEST PROBLEM

ST1. Pepsico is planning to acquire a fleet of trucks to support its new Pepsi Express distribution system in the Omaha area. The installed cost of the trucks is $777,000. The salvage value at the end of five years is expected to be $75,000 after-tax. The present value of the expected salvage is $42,600, after discounting at Pepsico's cost of capital. The present value (using Pepsico's after-tax cost of debt as the discount rate) of the depreciation tax shield from this project is $210,000. The present value of the after-tax lease payments (also using Pepsico's after-tax cost of debt as the discount rate) is $575,000. Pepsico will incur (in present value terms) operating costs of $140,000 more, after-tax, if the trucks are owned than if they are leased.

What is the net advantage to leasing in this case? What should Pepsico do?

■ PROBLEMS*

1. MacKenzie Corporation is considering leasing a new asset. The lease would run for 8 years and require 8 *beginning-of-year* payments of $100,000 each. If MacKenzie capitalizes this lease for financial reporting purposes at a 10 percent rate, what asset amount will be reported initially on its balance sheet? What liability amount will be reported on its balance sheet? (Remember, lease payments are made at the beginning of each year, making them an annuity due.)

2. Ajax Leasing Services has been approached by Gamma Tools to provide lease financing for a new automated screw machine. The machine will cost $220,000 and will be leased by Gamma for 5 years. Lease payments will be made at the *beginning* of each year. Ajax will depreciate the machine on a straight-line basis of $44,000 per year down to a book salvage value of $0. Actual salvage value is estimated to be $30,000 at the end of 5 years. Ajax's marginal tax rate is 40 percent. Ajax desires to earn a 12 percent, after-tax rate of return on this lease. What are the required annual beginning-of-year lease payments?

3. The First National Bank of Springer has established a leasing subsidiary. A local firm, Allied Business Machines, has approached the bank to arrange lease financing for $10 million in new machinery. The economic life of the machinery is estimated to be 20 years. The estimated salvage value at the end of the 20-year period is $0. Allied Business Machines has indicated a willingness to pay the bank $1 million per year at the *end* of each year for 20 years under the terms of a financial lease.

   a. If the bank depreciates the machinery on a straight-line basis over 20 years to a $0 estimated salvage value and has a 40 percent marginal tax rate, what *after-tax* rate of return will the bank earn on the lease? 4.96

   b. In general, what effect would the use of MACRS depreciation by the bank have on the rate of return it earns from the lease?

*Colored numbers denote problems that have check answers provided at the end of the book.

4. Jenkins Corporation wants to acquire a $200,000 computer. Jenkins has a 40 percent marginal tax rate. If owned, the computer would be depreciated on a straight-line basis to a *book* salvage value of $0. The actual cash salvage value is expected to be $20,000 at the end of 10 years. If the computer is purchased, Jenkins could borrow the needed funds at an annual pretax interest rate of 10 percent. If purchased, Jenkins will incur annual maintenance expenses of $1,000. These expenses would not be incurred if the computer is leased. The lease rate would be $28,000 per year, payable at the beginning of each year. Jenkins' weighted after-tax cost of capital is 12 percent.
   a. Compute the *net advantage* to leasing.
   b. In general, what effect would the use of accelerated depreciation, such as MACRS, have on the answer to Part a?
   c. What alternative, leasing or owning, should be chosen?

5. The following stream of after-tax cash flows are available to you as a potential equity investor in a leveraged lease:

End of Year	Cash Flow (after-tax)	End of Year	Cash Flow (after-tax)
0	$-50	6	$ 0
1	+30	7	-5
2	+20	8	-10
3	+15	9	-15
4	+10	10	+10
5	+5		

   The cash flow in year 0 represents the initial equity investment. The positive cash flows in years 1 to 5 result from the tax shield benefits from accelerated depreciation and interest deductibility on the nonrecourse debt. The negative cash flows in years 7 to 9 are indicative of the cash flows generated in a leveraged lease after the earlier-period tax shields have been utilized. The positive cash flow occurring in year 10 is the result of the asset's salvage value.
   a. What problems would you encounter in computing the equity investor's rate of return on this investment?
   b. If, as a potential equity investor, you require an 8 percent after-tax rate of return on investments of this type, should you make this investment?

6. The Jacobs Company desires to lease a numerically controlled milling machine costing $200,000. Jacobs has asked both First Manufacturers Bank Leasing Corporation and Commercial Associates, Inc. (a commercial finance company) to quote an annual lease rate. Both leasing companies now require a 20 percent *pretax* rate of return on this type of lease. Suppose First Manufacturers estimates the machine's salvage value at the end of the lease to be $30,000 and Commercial Associates estimates salvage to be $80,000. Based on this information, what annual (beginning-of-year) lease payments will each leasing company require, if the lease term is 5 years? (Note: Because the required rate of return of both the bank and the finance company is stated on a pretax basis, you need not consider depreciation or the tax effects of salvage.)

7. The First National Bank of Great Falls is considering a leveraged lease agreement involving some mining equipment with the Big Sky Mining Corporation. The bank (40 percent tax bracket) will be the lessor; the mining company, the lessee (0 percent tax bracket); and a large California pension fund, the lender. Big Sky is seeking $50 million, and the pension fund has agreed to lend the bank $40 million at 10 percent. The bank has agreed to repay the pension fund $4 million of principal each year plus interest. (The remaining balance will be repaid in a balloon payment at the end of the fifth year.) The equipment will be depreciated on a straight-line basis over a

5-year estimated useful life with no expected salvage value. Assuming Big Sky has agreed to annual lease payments of $10 million, calculate the bank's initial cash outflow and its first 2 years of cash inflows.

8. As a financial analyst for Muffin Construction, you have been asked to recommend the method of financing the acquisition of new equipment needed by the firm. The equipment has a useful life of 8 years. If purchased, the equipment, which costs $700,000, will be depreciated under MACRS rules for 7-year class assets. If purchased, the needed funds can be borrowed at a 10 percent pretax annual rate. Muffin's weighted after-tax rate of capital is 12 percent. The *actual* salvage value at the end of 8 years is expected to be $50,000. Muffin's marginal ordinary tax rate is 40 percent. Annual, beginning-of-year lease payments would be $160,000.

   a. Compute the net advantage to leasing.
   b. Should Muffin lease or own the equipment?

9. Darling Leasing is considering the lease to Major State University of a piece of equipment costing $100,000. The period of the lease will be 8 years. The equipment will be depreciated under MACRS rules for 7-year class assets. Darling's marginal tax rate is 40 percent. Annual (end-of-year) lease payments will be $20,000. Estimated salvage is $10,000. If Darling requires a 20 percent after-tax return on equipment it leases, should the lease be made?

10. Use the lease-versus-buy calculator at the following Web site to determine whether to lease or buy your next car. Hand in a printout of the screen on which your average cost per year is calculated.
    www.moneyadvisor.com

11. Suppose your firm has decided to build a 10-story office building and, just like Sears leases the Sears Tower in Chicago, your firm has decided to contract a professional lessor to build the building and then lease it to you on a 30-year lease. Using a major search engine, find three leasing companies that provide such real estate leasing.

■ SOLUTION TO SELF-TEST PROBLEM

ST1. NAL = Installed cost ($777,000), *less* Present value of after-tax lease payments ($575,000), *less* Present value of depreciation tax shield ($210,000), *plus* Present value of after-tax operating costs if owned but not if leased ($140,000), *less* Present value of the after-tax salvage value ($42,600)

= $89,400

Based on the numerical analysis, Pepsico should lease. It would be a good idea to test the sensitivity of this conclusion with alternative estimates of the salvage value and the operating cost differential between leasing and owning.

■ GLOSSARY

Direct Lease A lease that is initiated when a firm acquires the use of an asset that it did not previously own.

Financial Lease A *noncancelable* agreement that obligates the lessee to make payments to the lessor for a predetermined period of time. These payments usually are sufficient to amortize the full cost of the asset plus provide the lessor with a reasonable rate of return on the investment in the asset.

Lease A contract that allows an individual or a firm to make economic use of an asset for a stated period of time without obtaining an ownership interest in it.

Lessee The user and renter of the property in a lease transaction.

Lessor The property owner who collects rental payments from the lessee in a lease transaction.

Leveraged Lease A type of financial lease in which the lessor borrows up to 80 percent of the cost of the leased asset on a nonrecourse basis from a group of lenders. The lessor receives the full tax benefits of ownership. This is also sometimes called a *third-party equity lease* or a *tax lease*.

Operating Lease A *cancelable* lease agreement that provides the lessee with the use of an asset on a period-by-period basis. This sometimes is called a *service* or *maintenance lease*, especially if the lessor provides maintenance services as part of the lease contract.

Sale and Leaseback A lease that is initiated when a firm sells an asset it owns to another firm and simultaneously leases the asset back for its own use.

AN INTEGRATIVE CASE PROBLEM
LEASE AND TERM LOAN ANALYSIS

Suppose that Kinko's Copy Centers has decided to install personal computers and printers in its Pittsburgh store that will be rented to customers on an hourly basis. Kinko's management has called in consultants from a number of computer suppliers to assist it in designing a system. After considering a number of alternatives, Kinko's decided that an Apple Computer system consisting of eight Macintosh Quadra computers and two Laser Writer printers best meets its current and projected future needs. Kinko's evaluated the desirability of the acquisition of the Apple computer system using its normal capital budgeting procedures. It found that the computer system has a large positive expected net present value.

Jim Horn, a new management trainee in the financial planning office, has recently been reading about the boom in the leasing industry. He feels that if leasing is growing as rapidly as it seems, there must be some significant advantages of the leasing alternative compared to ownership.

If purchased, the new computer system will cost $50,000 installed. The computer system has an estimated economic life of 6 years. Kinko's would depreciate the computer system as a 5-year class asset under MACRS rules to a $0 estimated salvage value. If purchased, Kinko's could borrow the needed funds from Pittsburgh National Bank (PNB) at a 10 percent pretax annual percentage rate of interest.

If Kinko's decides to lease the computer system, it will be required to make six beginning-of-year lease payments of $11,000 each. Kinko's weighted cost of capital is 12 percent (after-tax). Kinko's marginal tax rate is 40 percent.

Under both the lease alternative and the borrow-and-buy alternative, Kinko's will contract with a computer service company to handle the estimated annual service and maintenance costs.

1. Compute the net advantage to leasing.
2. Which alternative should Kinko's accept? What other factors might be considered?
3. If the computer system is owned and Kinko's borrows the needed funds from PNB in the form of a bullet loan carrying a 10 percent interest rate instead of an equal payment loan at 10 percent, what effect would this have on the decision to lease or buy? (Bullet loans are discussed in Chapter 18.)
4. What effect would the use of straight-line depreciation have on the lease–buy decision? (Answer verbally; no calculations are needed. Ignore the bullet loan assumption in Question 3.)
5. If, at the end of 6 years, the computer system is expected to have an actual salvage value of $5,000, what would be the impact on the net advantage to leasing?

FINANCING WITH DERIVATIVES

20

1. To manage long-term funding sources effectively, financial managers must understand the different types of securities the firm can issue.

2. An *option* is one type of *derivative* security giving the right to buy or sell an asset at a set price during a specified time period.

   a. A *call* option is an option to *buy* an asset at a set price.

   b. A *put* option is an option to *sell* an asset at a set price.

3. The value of a call option is dependent upon four variables:

   a. The relationship between the option's exercise price and the price of an underlying stock.

   b. The time remaining until the option expires.

   c. The level of interest rates.

KEY CHAPTER CONCEPTS

   d. The expected volatility of the underlying stock's price.

4. A convertible security is a fixed-income security, such as a debenture or a share of preferred stock, that may be exchanged for the company's common stock at the holder's option.

5. A warrant is an option issued by a company to purchase shares of the company's common stock for a particular price during a specified period of time.

6. In a rights offering, common stockholders receive an option to purchase additional shares of the company's common stock, in proportion to the shares they currently own, at a price below the market value.

7. *Swaps* can be used to manage certain types of financial risk.

BARING BROTHERS BANK*

By early 1995, the Baring Brothers Bank had a distinguished 233 year history as the original blue-blooded investment bank of England. The bank was headed by Peter Baring, the last of a long line of family members who had headed the bank during its long and distinguished history. The bank served as the bank to the House of Windsor. In 1803 it financed the Louisiana Purchase for the United States. During the Napoleonic Wars, money from the bank helped to support Britain's troops.

Nicholas Leeson joined the Singapore office of Baring in 1992. He served as the chief trader in the Singapore office of Baring Futures, a unit of Baring Bank. Leeson started trading conservatively, engaging in futures arbitrage trading on contracts for the Nikkei 225, a major Japanese stock index. His trading initially focused on taking advantage of small price differences for the Nikkei contract trading in two different markets—Singapore and Osaka. This type of trade has very low risk, but also low return possibilities.

During 1994 Leeson changed his trading strategy. He began to sell futures options in a market bet that the Nikkei average would remain in a cer-

tain price range. Essentially, he was betting that the average would neither rise nor fall by a large amount. In January 1995, the Kobe earthquake precipitated a 1,000 point decline in the Nikkei average—leading to large losses for Baring.

At this time Leeson could (should) have withdrawn from the market and cut his losses. Instead, he purchased large amounts of the March 1995 Nikkei futures contract, betting that the Nikkei would rebound from its post-earthquake plunge. In addition, he sold (shorted) futures contracts on Japanese interest rates and government bonds. These shorted contracts were "naked"

in that he was selling contracts not owned by Barings. Leeson was hoping that if the Nikkei fell, the value of his shorted futures would rise, thus providing a partial hedge against the risks he had taken.

The Nikkei average kept declining through February and into March. Barings had to put up about $900 million to meet "margin" calls on the contracts. On February 26, 1995, Barings Bank failed. At that time it was holding over $6 billion of March Nikkei futures contracts and was short approximately $20 billion in interest rate futures. Total losses exceeded $1 billion.

The use of derivative contracts such as options and futures contracts can be a very effective way to manage risk. However, in the hands of a naïve and greedy manager, derivatives also have the potential to greatly increase the financial risk of an individual investor, a corporation, or an investment bank. Hence, it is important that financial managers gain an understanding of the potential and limitations of the use of these instruments. We discuss these issues in this chapter.

*Based on "Busted," *Newsweek* (March 13, 1995): 37–50.

INTRODUCTION

Options and option-related financing play an important role in the management of a firm's assets and liabilities. Options are one of two important classes of so-called **derivative** securities—that is, securities whose value is derived from another asset. The other important class of derivative securities is forward-type contracts, such as futures contracts and forward contracts. Swaps are another important class of derivative securities. A wide array of securities contain option features, including

1. *Short-term options* on common stocks, stock market indexes (e.g., Standard & Poor's 500 index), 30-year Treasury bonds (e.g., interest rate options), and foreign currency options (e.g., on the British pound and Japanese yen). These options are traded on organized exchanges, such as the Chicago Mercantile Exchange and the Chicago Board Options Exchange.[1]

2. *Convertible fixed-income securities,* such as debentures or preferred stocks, that may be exchanged for the company's common stock at the holder's option. By giving the fixed-income security holder an opportunity to share in any increase in its common stock value, the firm is able to reduce potential conflicts between the fixed-income security holders and stockholders, resulting in lower agency costs.

3. *Warrants,* which are options issued by a company to purchase shares of the company's common stock at a particular price during a specified period of time. Warrants are frequently sold to investors as part of a *unit* that consists of a fixed-income security with a warrant attached. As a result, warrants are issued by firms for similar reasons as convertible securities.

4. *Bond refunding* is an action that may be taken by a firm when it issues debt securities that include a call feature in the indenture, which gives the company the option to buy back the debt issue from the holders should a decline in interest rates make this action worthwhile. Some bonds also contain a *put option,* which gives the holder of the bond the right to sell it back to the issuer (usually at face value) under certain conditions.

5. A *rights offering* occurs when common stockholders are given an option to purchase additional shares of the company's common stock, in proportion to the fraction they currently own, at a price below the market value.

Also, as we will see in the next section, a firm's common stock can be understood more fully using an options framework.

This chapter examines the characteristics and valuation of options and option-related financing. An understanding of these concepts is necessary to evaluate the impact that decisions to issue or purchase these types of securities have on shareholder wealth.

OPTIONS

An **option** is a security that gives its holder the right, but not the obligation, to buy or sell an asset at a set price during a specified time period. Options are clas-

---

[1]See, for example, Tim S. Campbell and William A. Kracow, *Financial Risk Management* (New York: Harper Collins, 1993) for a discussion of many of these instruments. See also Robert Jarrow and Stuart Turnbull, *Derivative Securities* (Cincinnati: South-Western, 1996).

sified as either *call* or *put* options. A **call** is an option to *buy* a particular asset, whereas a **put** is an option to *sell* it.

Call = buy
put = sell

Option Valuation Concepts

Suppose an investor is offered an opportunity to purchase a call option on one share of McKean Company stock. Consider the following sets of conditions:

1. The option's exercise price is $25; the McKean stock price is $30 a share; and the option's expiration date is today. Under these conditions, the investor is willing to pay $5 for the option. In other words, the value of a call option is equal to the stock price minus the exercise price, or

$$\text{Value of a call option at expiration} = \text{Stock price} - \text{Exercise price} \qquad (20.1)$$

2. The option's exercise price is $25; the McKean stock price is $30 a share; and the option expires in 6 months. Given these conditions, the investor is willing to pay more than $5 for the option because of the chance that the stock price will increase, thereby also causing the option to increase in value. Therefore,

$$\text{Value of a call option prior to expiration} > \text{Stock price} - \text{Exercise price} \qquad (20.2)$$

3. The option's exercise price is $0.01; the McKean stock price is $30; and the option expires in 6 months. Under these somewhat unusual conditions, the option investor is willing to pay *almost as much as the stock price*. However, under no conditions should the investor be willing to pay more than the stock price. Therefore,

$$\text{Maximum value of a call option} = \text{Stock price} \qquad (20.3)$$

4. The option's exercise price is $25; the McKean stock price is $0.01; and the option expires today. The investor most likely is willing to pay nothing for the option given these conditions, but the investor also is not willing to pay someone to take the option "off his hands," because it is an option and can be allowed to expire with no additional cost. Therefore,

$$\text{Minimum value of a call option} = 0 \qquad (20.4)$$

The results of these sets of conditions are shown in Figure 20-1.[2]

Variables Affecting Call Option Valuation

The examples in the previous section illustrate that the value of a call option is dependent on the relationship between the option's exercise price and the price of the underlying stock and the length of time before the option's expiration date. Two other variables that influence the value of a call option are the level of

---

[2]Figure 20-1 shows a $25 exercise price. Technically, Figure 20-1 shows only the results of conditions 1, 2, and 4.

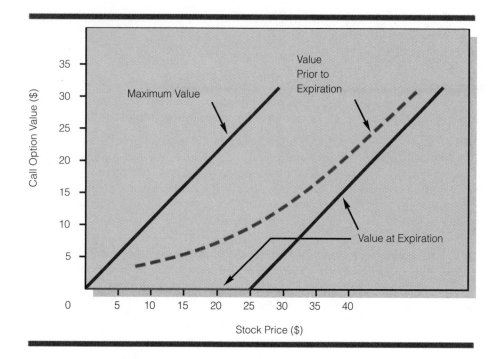

interest rates and the expected volatility of the underlying stock's price. A discussion of these four variables follows.[3]

Relationship Between the Exercise Price and the Stock Price. The effect of the exercise, or strike price, on option value is seen by examining Table 20-1, which lists a number of options quotations for Apple Computer. At the time, Apple's stock was selling at $16⅝ a share. For options expiring in April, the call option with a $17½ exercise price sold at a higher price than the option with a $20 exercise price, because buyers have to pay more money to exercise options with higher exercise prices. Thus, these options have less value to potential buyers. Therefore, *the higher the exercise price, given the stock price, the lower is the call option value,* all other things being equal.

Because an option's value (payoff) is dependent, or *contingent,* on the value of another security (in this case, the underlying stock), an option is said to be a **contingent claim.**

Time Remaining Until Expiration Date. The figures in Table 20-1 show that an option expiring in July has a higher value than an option with an April expiration date, because investors realize that Apple's stock has a greater chance to increase in value with three additional months before expiration. Thus, *the longer the time remaining before the option expires, the higher the option value,* all other things being equal. Because of this, an option is sometimes referred to as a "wasting asset."

TABLE 20-1
Selected Call Option Prices for
Apple Computer

EXERCISE PRICE	EXPIRATION MONTH	
	April	*July*
17½	⅝	—
20	3⁄16	1 1⁄16

Note: Apple's stock was selling at 16⅝ a share. The date of the option prices is March 24, 1997.

[3]A model for determining the equilibrium value of an option as a function of these variables is developed in Fischer Black and Myron Scholes, "The Pricing of Options and Corporate Liabilities," *Journal of Political Economy* 81 (May–June 1973): 637–654. The Excel templates available with the text include a Black-Scholes option pricing model.

Interest Rates. The buyer of common stock incurs either interest expense (explicit cost) if the purchase funds are borrowed or lost interest income (implicit cost) if existing funds are used for purchase. In either case, an interest cost is incurred.[4]

Buying a call option is an alternative to buying stock, and by buying an option, the interest cost associated with stock is avoided. Because options are an alternative to ownership, option values are affected by the stock ownership interest costs. As a result, *the higher the level of interest rates* (and, hence, the interest cost of stock ownership), *the higher the call option's value is,* all other things being equal.

Expected Stock Price Volatility. Suppose an investor has a choice of buying a call option on either stock S or stock V. Both stocks currently sell at $50 a share, and the exercise price of both options is $50. Stock S is expected to be the more stable of the two—its value at the time the option expires has a 50 percent chance of being $45 and a 50 percent chance of being $55 a share. In valuing the call option on stock S, the investor considers only the $55 price and its probability, because if the stock goes to $45 a share, the call option with a $50 exercise price becomes worthless.

Stock V is expected to be more volatile—its expected value at the time of option expiration has a 50 percent probability of being $30 and a 50 percent probability of being $70 a share. Similarly, in valuing the call option on stock V, the investor considers only the $70 price and its probability.

The investor now has sufficient information to conclude that the call option on stock V is more valuable than the call option on stock S because a greater return can be earned by investing in an option that has a 50 percent chance of being worth $20 (stock price – exercise price = $70 – $50 = $20) at expiration than an option that has a 50 percent probability of being worth $5 (stock price – exercise price = $55 – $50 = $5) at expiration. Therefore, the *greater the expected stock price volatility, the higher the call option value is,* all other things being equal.

Common Stock in an Options Framework

Any firm with debt can be analyzed in an options framework.[5] Suppose a start-up firm raises equity capital and also borrows $7 million, due two years from now. Then, suppose further that the firm undertakes a risky project to develop new computer parts. In two years, the firm must decide whether or not to default on its debt repayment obligation.

Consider this example in an options context. The stockholders can be viewed as having sold this firm to the debtholders for $7 million when they borrowed the $7 million. But the stockholders retained an option to buy back the firm. The stockholders have the right to exercise their option by paying off the debt claim at maturity. Whether they do depends on the value of the firm at the time the debt is due. If the value of the firm is greater than the debt claim, the stockholders will exercise their option by paying off the debt. But if the value of the firm is less than the debt claim, the stockholders will let their option expire by not repaying the debt.

---

[4]The interest cost is offset by any dividends received.

[5]The following discussion is based on Scott P. Mason and Robert C. Merton, "The Role of Contingent Claims Analysis in Corporate Finance," in *Recent Advances in Corporate Finance,* Edward I. Altman and Marti G. Subrahmanyam, eds. (Homewood, IL: Richard D. Irwin, 1985).

This simplified example has interesting implications. Earlier in the options discussion, we showed that the greater the expected stock price volatility, the higher will be the call option value. Therefore, if the stockholders choose high-risk projects with a chance of very large payoffs, they increase the value of their option. But, at the same time, they also increase the likelihood of defaulting on the debt, thereby decreasing its value. Thus, it is easy to see how potential conflicts between stockholders and debtholders can occur. These potential conflicts are discussed further in the next section on convertible securities. In fact, we shall see that giving the bondholders an equity stake in the firm decreases the potential for conflicts between stockholders and debtholders.

 ## CONVERTIBLE SECURITIES

Both debentures and preferred stock can have convertibility or conversion features. When a company issues convertible securities, its usual intention is the future issuance of common stock. To illustrate, suppose the Beloit Corporation issues 2 million shares of convertible preferred stock at a price of $50 a share. After the sale, the company receives gross proceeds of $100 million. Because of the convertibility feature, the company can expect to issue shares of common stock in exchange for the redemption of the convertible preferred stock over some future time period. As a result, convertibles sometimes are described as a deferred equity offering. In the case of Beloit's convertible preferred, each $50 preferred share can be exchanged for two shares of common stock; that is, the holder has a call option to buy two shares of the company's common stock at an exercise price of $25 a share. Therefore, if all the preferred shares are converted, the company in effect will have issued 4 million new common shares, and the preferred shares no longer will appear on Beloit's balance sheet. No additional funds are raised by the company at the time of conversion.

Features of Convertible Securities

As an introduction to the terminology and features of convertible securities, consider the $115 million, 25-year issue of 6⅛ percent convertible subordinated debentures sold by Cray Research, Inc., a computer manufacturer. **Convertible securities** are exchangeable for common stock at a stated **conversion price.** In the case of the Cray issue, the conversion price at the time of issue was $84. This means that each $1,000 debenture was convertible into common stock at $84 a share. (As the result of a spin-off to shareholders of its operations based in Colorado Springs as a separate company, the conversion price of the Cray Research bonds was reduced—three years after the initial issue—to $78, and the conversion ratio was increased to 12.82.)

The number of common shares that can be obtained when a convertible security is exchanged is determined by the conversion ratio, which is calculated as follows:

$$\text{Conversion ratio} = \frac{\text{Par value of security}}{\text{Conversion price}} \qquad (20.5)$$

In the case of Cray Research's convertible subordinated debentures, the conversion ratio at the time of issue was the following:

$$\text{Conversion ratio} = \frac{\$1,000}{\$84}$$

$$= 11.9$$

Thus, each $1,000 Cray debenture could be exchanged for 11.9 shares of common stock. Although the conversion ratio may change one or more times during the life of the conversion option (as it did for the Cray Research bonds), it is more common for it to remain constant.

Normally, the conversion price is set about 15 to 30 percent above the common stock's market price prevailing at the time of issue. For example, at the time Cray issued its convertible debentures, the market price of its common stock was about $65 a share. The $19 difference between the conversion price and the market price represents a 29 percent premium.

Holders of convertible securities are protected against dilution by the company. For example, suppose Cray were to split its common stock two for one. The conversion price (and therefore the conversion ratio) would be adjusted so that the holders would not be disadvantaged by the split. Specifically, in the Cray case, the new conversion price would be $39, and the new conversion ratio would be 25.64.

Managing Long-Term Funding with Convertibles

As a general rule, relatively small, risky companies whose common stock is publicly traded are the principal issuers of convertibles. These companies, for the most part, are rapidly growing and in need of funds to finance their growth. Investors, on the other hand, are frequently reluctant to lend money to small, risky companies without promises of high interest payments and assurances from the company that it will properly manage the debt.

Recall that in Chapter 1 we introduced agency problems and discussed the conflicts that can occur between a firm's stockholders and its creditors. We said that creditors, to protect their interests, often insist on certain protective covenants in the company's bond indentures. The agency costs to properly implement and monitor the covenants can be high, particularly for small, risky companies. As a result, because of potential conflicts between shareholders and bondholders and the associated agency costs, it usually is easier and cheaper to offer the bondholders an equity stake in the company—that is, a convertible security. With an equity stake, the bondholders are less concerned about any company attempts to increase the returns to the shareholders by means of risky projects.

In addition to agency costs, there are several other reasons for issuing convertibles. One is that cash flow benefits accrue to the issuing company in the form of lower interest payments or dividends; this occurs because investors are willing to accept the conversion privilege as part of their overall return. As an example, consider again the Cray Research 6⅛ percent convertible subordinated debentures. At the time Cray sold those convertibles, the company would have had to pay about 9 percent interest on any nonconvertible debt it issued. Thus, the convertibility feature is saving Cray about $2.9 million a year ([0.09 − 0.06125] × $100 million) in interest expense. Typically, firms can issue convertible securities with interest rates or dividend yields about 3 percentage points below similar, nonconvertible issues, that is, issues without convertibility features.

Another reason firms issue convertible securities is to sell common stock at a higher price than the prevailing market price at the time of issue. Suppose a company needs additional equity financing because of a relatively high proportion of fixed-income securities in its capital structure. If the company's management feels the price of its common stock is temporarily depressed, one alternative is to consider issuing a convertible security. With the conversion price typically set about 15 to 30 percent above the market price at the time of issue, the use of a convertible security effectively gives the issuing company the potential for selling common stock above the existing market price. However, for the sale to be successful, conditions in the future must be such that investors will want to exercise their conversion option. Also, if the market price rises considerably above the conversion price, it may turn out that the company would have been better off to wait and sell common stock directly, rather than sell the convertible issue at all.

A final reason for issuing convertible securities centers around the fact that the earnings resulting from projects funded by a particular external financing issue may not begin for some time after financing occurs. For example, the construction and start-up period for a major expansion may be several years. During this period, the company may desire debt or preferred stock financing. Eventually, once the expansion is fully operational and producing income, the company may want to achieve its original goal of additional common stock financing. The deferred issue of common stock minimizes the dilution in earnings per share that results from the immediate issuance of common stock.

Valuation of Convertible Securities

Because convertible securities possess certain characteristics of both common stock and fixed-income securities, their valuation is more complex than that of ordinary nonconvertible securities. The actual market value of a convertible security depends on both the *common stock value,* or *conversion value,* and the value of a fixed-income security, or *straight-bond* or *investment value.* Each of these is discussed here.[6]

Conversion Value. The **conversion value,** or stock value, of a convertible bond is defined as the conversion ratio times the common stock's market price:

$$\text{Conversion value} = \text{Conversion ratio} \times \text{Stock price} \qquad (20.6)$$

To illustrate, assume a firm offers a convertible bond that can be exchanged for 40 shares of common stock. If the market price of the firm's common stock is $20 per share, the conversion value is $800. If the market price of the common stock rises to $25 per share, the conversion value becomes $1,000. And if the stock price rises to $30 per share, the conversion value becomes $1,200. In the case of Cray's convertible bonds, the conversion value was 11.9 × $65 (the price per common share at the time of issue), or $774.

Straight-Bond Value. The **straight-bond value,** or investment value, of a convertible debt issue is the value it would have if it did not possess the conversion feature (option). Thus, it is equal to the sum of the present value of the interest annuity plus the present value of the expected principal repayment:

---

[6]For simplicity, only convertible debt is considered in this discussion, although the principles apply to convertible preferred stock as well.

$$\text{Straight-bond value} = \sum_{t=1}^{n} \frac{\text{Interest}}{(1 + k_\text{d})^t} + \frac{\text{Principal}}{(1 + k_\text{d})^n} \qquad (20.7)$$

where k_d is the current yield to maturity for *nonconvertible* debt issues of similar quality and maturity; t, the number of years; and n, the time to maturity.

Considering again Cray Research's 6⅛ percent, 25-year convertible debentures, the bond value at the time of issue is calculated as follows, assuming that 9 percent is the appropriate discount rate (and that interest is paid annually):

$$\text{Straight-bond value} = \sum_{t=1}^{25} \frac{\$61.25}{(1.09)^t} + \frac{\$1,000}{(1.09)^{25}}$$

$$= \$61.25(\text{PVIFA}_{0.09,25}) + \$1,000(\text{PVIF}_{0.09,25})$$

$$= \$61.25(9.823) + \$1,000(0.116)$$

$$= \$601.66 + \$116$$

$$= \$717.66$$

Market Value. The market value of a convertible debt issue is usually somewhat above the higher of the conversion or the straight-bond value; this is illustrated in Figure 20-2.

The difference between the market value and the higher of the conversion or the straight-bond value is the **conversion premium** for which the issue sells. This premium tends to be largest when the conversion value and the straight-bond value are nearly identical. This set of circumstances allows investors to participate in any common stock appreciation while having some degree of downside protection, because the straight-bond value can represent a "floor" below which the market value will not fall.[7] The Cray convertible debentures described in this section were offered to the public at $1,000 per bond and quickly were bought up by investors. In this case, investors were willing to pay $1,000 for an issue having a conversion value of approximately $774 and a bond value of about $718. The $1,000 market value contained a premium of $226 over the conversion value (which was higher than the bond value). This premium can be thought of as the value of the implicit call option on a firm's common stock associated with this convertible security. In practice, convertible securities are valued by adding the straight-bond value to the value of the conversion options to buy common stock. These conversion options can be valued using a variant of the Black-Scholes option pricing model (see Footnote 3).

Converting Convertible Securities

Conversion can occur in one of two ways:

- It may be *voluntary* on the part of the investor.
- It can be effectively *forced* by the issuing company.

Whereas voluntary conversions can occur at any time prior to the expiration of a conversion feature, forced conversions occur at specific points in time.

---

[7]The straight-bond value may fall if long-term interest rates rise or if the perceived risk of the firm increases.

FIGURE 20-2
Cray Research: Convertible Debenture Valuation at Different Stock Prices*

*Conversion ratio = 11.9
Straight-bond value = $718

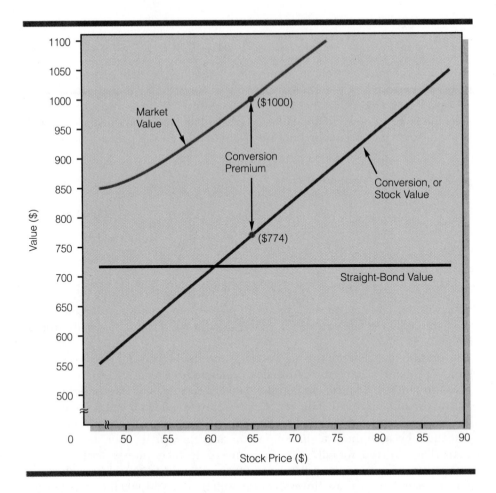

The method most commonly used by companies to force conversion is the exercise of the *call* privilege on the convertible security. For example, consider the Compaq Computer convertible bonds maturing in 2012, which the company decided to call for redemption in 1988. The bonds had a conversion ratio of 25.22, and the market price of the Compaq common stock at the time of the call was $61.25 per share. Therefore, the conversion value was approximately $1,545 per bond. The call price—which was set and agreed upon by both the borrower and the lender at the time of the original issue—was $1,047.25 per bond.

Holders of the Compaq convertibles had two alternatives under these circumstances:

- Conversion, in which case the holder would receive common stock having a market value of $1,545 per bond.
- Redemption, in which case the holder would receive $1,047.25 in cash for each bond.

The conversion alternative was the obvious choice, because even those investors who did not wish to hold the common stock could sell it upon conversion for more money than they would receive from redemption. By calling the bonds, Compaq was able to remove $150 million in long-term debt from its balance sheet without having to redeem the bonds for cash and to save $7.9 million a year in interest expense.

Another way in which a company can encourage conversion is by raising its dividend on common stock to a high enough level that holders of convertible securities are better off converting them and receiving the higher dividend.

[handwritten: Carrot + stick method]

Convertible Securities and Earnings Dilution

If a convertible security (or warrant) issue is ultimately exchanged for common stock, the number of common shares will increase and earnings per share will be reduced (i.e., diluted), all other things being equal. Companies are required (by Accounting Principles Board Opinion 15) to disclose this potential dilution by reporting both primary and fully diluted earnings per share. Primary earnings per share are calculated based on the number of common shares outstanding plus common stock equivalents. A common stock equivalent must meet certain tests, but it basically includes any convertible security that derives its value primarily from the common stock into which it can be converted. Fully diluted earnings per share are calculated based on the assumption that *all* dilutive securities are converted into common shares. In calculating primary or fully diluted earnings per share, earnings must be adjusted for the interest or preferred dividends saved as the result of conversion.

WARRANTS

As mentioned earlier in this chapter, a **warrant** is a company-issued option to purchase a specific number of shares of the issuing company's common stock at a particular price during a specified time period. Warrants are frequently issued in conjunction with an offering of debentures or preferred stock. In these instances, like convertibles, warrants tend to lower agency costs.

In addition, during the 1980s, the various ways in which warrants were used as a financing device seemed to expand. For example, warrants were used in conjunction with bond swaps, equity offerings, and debt restructurings. In the 1987 bankruptcy reorganization of Global-Marine, an off-shore operator of oil and gas drilling rigs, warrants were issued to preferred and common stock-holders (along with a small percentage of the new common stock). Also, small, high-risk companies in need of additional financing may offer warrants to prospective lenders in order to give the potential for high expected returns as compensation for the loan's high risk.

Features of Warrants

To illustrate some of the features of financing with warrants, consider the Federal National Mortgage Association ("Fannie Mae"), which in 1986 sold 500,000 units, consisting of a $1,000 debenture and 23, 5-year warrants (expiration date February 25, 1991), to raise approximately $500 million (less issuance costs). Each warrant allowed the purchase of one common share at $44.25.

The (exercise price) of a warrant is the price at which the holder can purchase common stock of the issuing company. The exercise price is usually between 10 and 35 percent above the market price of the common stock prevailing at the time of issue. The exercise price of the Fannie Mae warrants was $44.25, approximately 34 percent above the $33 per-share market price of the common stock at

[handwritten: 44.25 − 33 = 11.25   11.25/33 = 34%]

(handwritten marginal note: Except for Split Stock)

the time of issue. The exercise price normally remains constant over the life of the warrant. One exception is the case of a stock split. When this occurs, the exercise price of the warrant is adjusted to reflect the new number of shares and share price. For example, in October 1989, Fannie Mae's common stock was split 3 for 1. Accordingly, the exercise price of the warrants was reduced from $44.25 to $14.75 per share. Typically, the life of a warrant is between 5 and 10 years, although on occasion the life can be longer or even perpetual.

When the management of Fannie Mae issued the warrants, they hoped that the common share price would rise above the $44.25 level and remain there, especially until after the warrants expired, because this would mean that the company could reasonably expect holders to exercise their warrants. If this happened, Fannie Mae would realize its goal of raising additional capital totaling approximately $509 million (500,000 units times 23 warrants per unit times $44.25 per warrant) at expiration. In 1991 when the warrants expired, Fannie Mae's stock price was well above the post-split exercise price of $14.75, and the warrants were exercised. In contrast, with convertible securities such as convertible bonds or preferred stock, the company does not receive additional funds at the time of conversion.

If a warrant is issued as part of a "unit" with a fixed-income security, the warrant is usually *detachable* from the debenture or preferred stock; this means that purchasers of the units have the option of selling the warrants separately and continuing to hold the debenture or preferred stock. As a result, other investors can purchase and trade warrants.

Prior to 1970, warrants usually were not used as a financing vehicle by large, established firms. In April of that year, however, AT&T sold $1.6 billion of 30-year debentures with warrants to buy 31.4 million common shares at $52 each through May 15, 1975. The use of warrant financing by AT&T undoubtedly caused other large, established firms to consider warrants. Also, before 1970, warrants normally were listed either on the American Stock Exchange or traded over the counter, because the New York Stock Exchange would not list them. However, with the AT&T warrants, the NYSE changed its policy and began to list warrants of NYSE companies if the warrants met certain requirements, including a life greater than 5 years. For example, Fleet Financial, LTV Corp., Travelers, and Zale, among others, now have warrants that are traded on the NYSE.

Holders of warrants do not have the rights of common stockholders, such as the right to vote for directors or receive dividends, until they exercise their warrants.

Reasons for Issuing Warrants

The primary reason for issuing warrants with a fixed-income security offering is to lower agency costs. In addition, just as with convertible securities, warrants can permit a company to sell common stock at a price above the price prevailing at the time of original issue. Warrants also allow a company to sell common stock in the future without incurring significant issuance costs at the time of sale.

Valuation of Warrants

In general, the value of a warrant depends upon the same variables that affect call option valuation. Because a warrant's value depends upon the price of the issuing company's stock, it is a contingent claim, just like an option. In this connection, the formula value of a warrant (also called "the value at expiration") is defined by the following equation:

$$\begin{matrix} \text{Formula} \\ \text{value} \\ \text{of a} \\ \text{warrant} \end{matrix} = \text{Max} \left\{ \$0; \left(\begin{matrix} \text{Common stock} \\ \text{market price} \\ \text{per share} \end{matrix} - \begin{matrix} \text{Exercise} \\ \text{price} \\ \text{per share} \end{matrix} \right) \times \begin{matrix} \text{Number of shares} \\ \text{obtainable with} \\ \text{each warrant} \end{matrix} \right\} \quad (20.8)$$

At the time of issue, a warrant's exercise price is normally greater than the common stock price. Even though the calculated formula value may be negative, it is considered to be zero, because securities cannot sell for negative amounts. For example, at the time of issue, the Fannie Mae warrants had an exercise price of $44.25 and the firm's common stock price was $33 per share. Each warrant entitled the holder to 1 share, and the formula value was zero:

$$\text{Formula value} = \text{Max} \{\$0; (\$33 - \$44.25)(1)\}$$

$$= \$0$$

Once the stock price rises above the exercise price of the warrant, the formula value will be greater than zero. For example, on February 24, 1989 (approximately two years prior to expiration of the warrant), Fannie Mae's stock price was $59 and the warrant price was $19.375. At this point, the formula value of the warrant was

$$\text{Formula value} = \text{Max} \{\$0; (\$59 - \$44.25)(1)\}$$

$$= \$14.75$$

and the warrant was selling for about 31 percent above the formula value. Prior to the warrant's expiration, we see that the market price of the warrant is greater than the formula value, just as we discussed in the case of options.

On the expiration date of a warrant, the market price of the warrant should be equal to the formula value, as was the case for options discussed earlier. For the Fannie Mae warrants, which expired on February 25, 1991, the market price of the stock (after the 3-for-1 stock split) was $45.375, and the market price of the warrants was $30.625. As we see, the market price of the warrants was equal to the formula value:[8]

$$\text{Formula value} = \text{Max} \{\$0; (\$45.375 - \$14.75)(1)\}$$

$$= \$30.625$$

Comparison of Convertible Securities and Warrants

Having covered the characteristics and valuation of convertible securities and warrants, we now summarize the similarities of and differences between these types of securities. In this comparison, we are assuming that the warrants are issued as part of a fixed-income security offering, such as the Fannie Mae warrants discussed above. The similarities include the following:

1. Both convertibles and warrants tend to lessen potential conflicts between fixed-income security holders and stockholders, thereby reducing agency costs.

---

[8]Recall that the exercise price of the warrants was lowered from $44.25 to $14.75 as a result of the 3-for-1 stock split in October 1989.

2. The intention is the deferred issuance of common stock at a price higher than that prevailing at the time of the convertible or warrant issue.

3. Both the convertibility option and the attachment of warrants result in interest expense or preferred dividend savings for the issuing company, thereby easing potential cash flow problems.

Some of the differences include the following:

1. The company receives additional funds at the time warrants are exercised, whereas no additional funds are received at the time convertibles are converted.

2. The fixed-income security remains on the company's books after the exercise of warrants; in the case of convertibles, the fixed-income security is exchanged for common stock and taken off the company's books.

3. Because of the call feature, convertible securities potentially give the company more control than warrants over when the common stock is issued.

ANALYSIS OF RIGHTS OFFERINGS

In addition to the sale of new common stock through underwriters, new equity capital can be raised using another option-based financing approach called a *rights offering*. In a **rights offering** the firm's existing stockholders are given an *option* to purchase a fraction of the new shares equal to the fraction they currently own, thereby maintaining their original ownership percentage.

Hence, rights offerings are used in equity financing by companies whose charters contain the *preemptive right*. In addition, rights offerings *may* be used as a means of selling common stock in companies in which preemptive rights do not exist. The number of rights offerings has gradually declined over the years.

The following example illustrates what a rights offering involves. The Miller Company has 10 million shares outstanding and plans to sell an additional 1 million shares via a rights offering. In this case, each right entitles the holder to purchase 0.1 share, and it takes ten rights to purchase one share. (The **rights** themselves really are the documents describing the offer. Each stockholder receives one right for each share currently held.) The company has to decide on a *subscription price,* which is the price the rightholder will have to pay per new share. The subscription price has to be less than the market price, or rightholders will have no incentive to subscribe to the new issue. As a general rule, subscription prices are 5 to 20 percent below market prices. If the Miller Company's stock is selling at $40 per share, a reasonable subscription price might be $35 per share.

Valuation of Rights

Because a right represents an opportunity to purchase stock below its current market value, the right itself has a certain value, which is calculated under two sets of circumstances:

■ The *rights-on* case.
■ The *ex-rights* case.

A stock is said to "trade with **rights-on**" when the purchasers receive the rights along with the shares they purchase. In contrast, a stock is said to "trade **ex-rights**" when the stock purchasers no longer receive the rights.

For example, suppose the Miller Company announced on May 15 that shareholders of record as of Friday, June 20, will receive the rights. This means that anyone who purchased stock on or before Monday, June 16, will receive the rights, and anyone who purchased stock on or later than June 17 will not.[9] The stock trades with rights up to and including June 16 and goes ex-rights on June 17, the *ex-rights date*. On that date, the stock's market value falls by the value of the right, all other things being equal.

The theoretical, or formula, value of a right for the rights-on case can be calculated using the following equation:

$$R = \frac{M_o - S}{N + 1} \tag{20.9}$$

where R is the theoretical value for the right; M_o, the rights-on market price of the stock; S, the subscription price of the right; and N, the number of rights necessary to purchase one new share. In the Miller Company example, the right's theoretical value is

$$R = \frac{\$40 - \$35}{10 + 1}$$

$$= \$0.455$$

The theoretical value of a right when the stock is trading ex-rights can be calculated by using the following equation:

$$R = \frac{M_e - S}{N} \tag{20.10}$$

where M_e is the ex-rights market price of the stock; S, the subscription price of the right; and N, the number of rights necessary to purchase one new share. If the Miller stock were trading ex-rights, the theoretical value of a right would be as follows:

$$R = \frac{\$39.545 - \$35}{10}$$

$$= \$0.455$$

(Note that M_e is lower than M_o by the amount of the right; that is, $40 versus $39.545.)

Some shareholders may decide not to use their rights because of lack of funds or some other reason. These stockholders can sell their rights to other investors who wish to purchase them. Thus, a market exists for the rights, and a market price is established for them. Generally, the market price is higher than the theoretical value until the time of expiration. The same factors discussed previously, which determine the value of a call option, also determine the value of a right, since a right is simply a short-term call option on the stock. As with call options, investors can earn a higher return by purchasing the rights than by purchasing

---

[9]A stock purchaser becomes a "shareholder of record" 4 *trading* days after purchase.

the stock because of the leverage rights provide. In general, the premium of market value over theoretical value decreases as the rights expiration date approaches. A right is worthless after its expiration date.

One can demonstrate that there is no net gain or loss to shareholders either from exercising the rights or from selling the right at the theoretical formula value.[10] For example, suppose an investor owns 100 shares of the Miller Company common stock discussed earlier. The investor is entitled to purchase 10 (0.1×100) additional shares at $35 per share. Prior to the rights offering, the 100 shares of Miller Company are valued at $4,000 (100 shares $\times$ $40 per share). *Exercise* of the rights will give the investor 10 additional shares at a cost of $35 per share, or a total of $350. These 110 shares will be valued at $4,350 (110 $\times$ $39.545). Deducting the cost of these additional shares ($350) from the total value of the shares ($4,350), one obtains the same value ($4,000) as before the rights offering. *Sale* of the rights will yield $45.50 (100 $\times$ $0.455) to the investor. Combining this value with the $3,954.50 (100 $\times$ $39.545) value of the 100 shares still owned, one also obtains the same value ($4,000) as before the rights offering.

INTEREST RATE SWAPS[11]

A swap is another type of financial derivative that can be used in the financing activities of a firm. A financial swap is a contractual agreement between two parties (financial institutions or businesses) to make periodic payments to each other. There are two major types of swaps: *interest rate swaps* and *currency swaps*. This section will focus on interest rate swaps. The over-the-counter swaps market, which consists of about 130 banks and securities firms, is largely unregulated. Over $5 *trillion* worth of interest rate swaps are outstanding worldwide.

Interest rate swaps can be used to protect financial institutions and businesses against fluctuations in interest rates. Like futures contracts,[12] swaps can be used to hedge against interest rate risk. Even though futures contracts are more effective in hedging against short-term risks (less than one year), swaps are more effective in hedging against longer-term risks (up to ten years or more).

Of the many and various types of **interest rate swaps,** the most basic is one in which a party is seeking to exchange floating rate interest payments for fixed rate interest payments, or vice versa. Consider the case of a finance company (e.g., Chrysler Financial) with floating rate debt (e.g., floating rate bonds) and fixed rate loans (e.g., automobile installment loans) that wants to protect itself against an increase in interest rates. The finance company can enter into a swap contract with another party who agrees to pay the interest costs in excess of a specified rate (e.g., 7.5 percent) for a given period of time (e.g., 3 years). Should interest rates increase in the future, the finance company will receive rising payments from the other party to the swap agreement to cover its losses.

The other party to the swap agreement could be a bank, which borrows at fixed interest rates (e.g., certificates of deposit) and lends money to corporations at floating rates. The bank may desire to protect itself against a decline in interest rates. Should interest rates decline in the future, the bank will continue

---

[10]This analysis ignores any brokerage fees incurred in the sale of the rights.
[11]See John F. Marshall and Kenneth R. Kapnes, *Understanding Swap Finance* (Cincinnati, OH: South-Western, 1990) for a more detailed discussion of interest rate swaps.
[12]Futures contracts are discussed in Chapter 2.

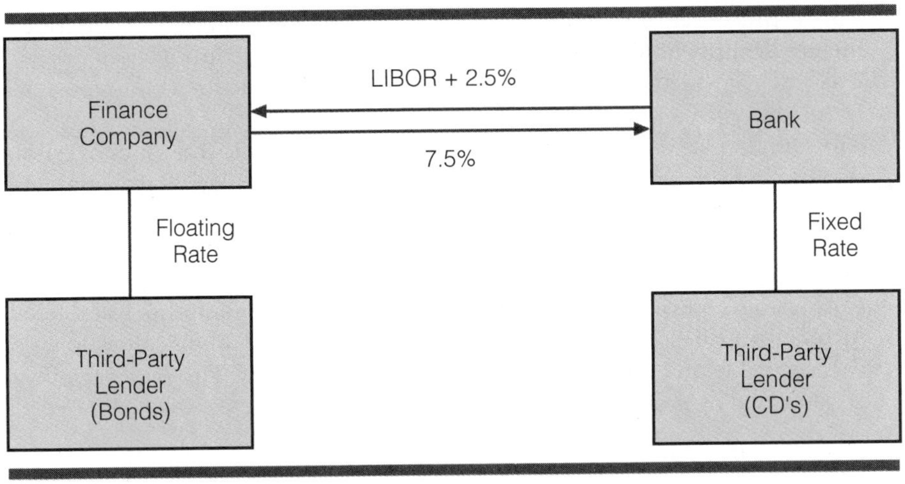

FIGURE 20-3
Interest Rate Swap

receiving fixed interest payments from the other party to the swap agreement. This swap is illustrated in Figure 20-3. In most interest rate swaps, the floating rate used in computing the payments between the parties to the swap is tied to the London Interbank Offer Rate (LIBOR). (LIBOR is discussed in Chapter 2.) In this example it is 2.5 percentage points above LIBOR. Generally, in a swap agreement, the parties exchange only the interest differential, not the principal or actual interest payments.

Many financial institutions, such as investment banks, commercial banks, and nonfinancial companies, act as intermediaries in arranging swaps. Some intermediaries act as brokers and receive commissions for finding parties with matching needs. Other intermediaries act as dealers or market makers by offering themselves as a party to the swap until such time as they can arrange a match with another party.

■ SUMMARY

Options

- An *option* is a derivative security that gives its holder the right to buy or sell an asset at a set *exercise price* until a specified *expiration date*. A *call* is an option to *buy;* and a *put* is an option to *sell.*
- The value of a call option is dependent upon four variables:
  1. The relationship between the exercise price and the stock price.
  2. The time remaining until the option's expiration date.
  3. The level of interest rates.
  4. The expected stock price volatility.
- An option is a *contingent claim;* that is, its value depends upon the value of another security.

Convertible Securities

- *Convertible* debt or preferred stock securities are exchangeable for a company's common stock at the option of the holder.

■ Convertible securities tend to reduce potential conflicts between fixed-income security holders and stockholders, resulting in reduced agency costs.

■ The price at which a convertible security is exchangeable for a common stock is the *conversion price.*

■ The number of common shares that can be obtained when a convertible security is exchanged is the *conversion ratio,* which is calculated by dividing the par value of the security by the conversion price.

■ At the time of issue, the conversion price normally exceeds the market price of the common stock by about 15 to 30 percent.

■ Convertible securities possess characteristics of both common stock and fixed-income securities. Their market value is a function of both their stock, or conversion, value and their value as a fixed-income security. The *conversion value* is calculated by multiplying the conversion ratio by the current stock price.

Warrants

■ A *warrant* is an option issued by a company to purchase shares of the company's common stock at a particular price during a specific time period. Warrants frequently are issued as part of a fixed-income security offering.

■ The *exercise price* of a warrant is the price at which the holder can purchase common stock of the issuing company.

■ The primary reason for issuing a warrant with a fixed-income security offering is that warrants tend to lower agency costs.

■ The *formula value* of a warrant depends on the number of common shares each warrant is entitled to receive when exercised and the difference between the common stock market price and the warrant exercise price. Warrants normally sell at a premium over their formula value.

Rights Offering

■ In a *rights offering,* common stockholders receive stock purchase rights, which entitle them to purchase additional shares of the company's common stock, in proportion to the shares they currently own, at a price below the market value.

■ In a rights offering, there is no gain or loss to shareholders either from exercising the rights or selling the rights at the theoretical formula value.

■ QUESTIONS AND TOPICS FOR DISCUSSION

1. Define the following terms:
   a. Option.
   b. Call.
   c. Put.
   d. Contingent claim.
2. What are the similarities and differences between options and warrants?
3. What variables are important in determining call option prices?
4. Will call option values generally be higher at a time when interest rates are relatively high, compared with a time when interest rates are relatively low, all other things being equal?
5. How does a stock's expected price volatility affect the value of a call option on it?
6. In what ways are convertible securities and warrants similar? Dissimilar?
7. Why do companies issue convertible securities?

8. What is the relationship between conversion value, bond value, and market value for a convertible security?
9. How can a company effectively force conversion of a convertible security?
10. What is the *preemptive right* of common stockholders? In what type of company is the preemptive right important? Unimportant?
11. Why would a firm use an interest rate swap as part of its financing strategy?

■ SELF-TEST PROBLEMS

ST1. The Bradford Company has debentures outstanding (par value = $1,000) that are convertible into common stock at a price of $40 per share. The convertible bonds have a coupon interest rate of 8 percent and mature in 20 years. The convertible bonds are callable at 102 percent of par value. The company has a marginal tax rate of 40 percent.
  a. Calculate the conversion value of the bonds if Bradford's common stock is selling for $35 per share.
  b. Calculate the straight-bond value, assuming that straight debt of equivalent risk and maturity is yielding 11 percent.
  c. Determine the conversion premium if the market value of the bonds is $925.
  d. Determine the conversion value of the bonds if the company's common stock price increases to $55 per share.
  e. Given the information in Part d, what is a realistic estimate of the market price of the convertible bond issue? (No numerical calculations are necessary for this part of the problem.)

ST2. The Somerset Company has warrants outstanding that expire in 3 years. Each warrant entitles the holder to purchase one share of common stock at an exercise price of $40 per share. Determine the formula value and premium over the formula value if the respective prices of common stock and warrants are:
  a. $32 per share and $1.50 per warrant.
  b. $40 per share and $3.50 per warrant.
  c. $48 per share and $10 per warrant.

ST3. The Seven Springs Company plans to sell an additional 2 million shares of common stock through a rights offering. The company currently has 20 million shares outstanding. Each shareholder will receive one right for each share currently held. Therefore, each right will enable shareholders to purchase 0.10 shares. Seven Springs common stock currently is selling for $25 per share and the subscription price of the rights will be $22 per share.
  a. Calculate the theoretical value of the right for both the *rights-on* and *ex-rights* cases.
  b. Determine the amount that the market price of the company's stock is expected to drop on the ex-rights date, assuming all other things are equal.
  c. If the market price of Seven Springs common stock increases to $30 per share, determine the theoretical value of the rights (*rights-on* case).

■ PROBLEMS*

1. The BWS Corporation stock is selling at $50 a share today.
  a. Calculate the value of a BWS call option if its exercise price is $40 and it expires today.
  b. What can you say about the value of a BWS call option if its exercise price is $40 and it expires in 6 months?
  c. Calculate the value of a BWS call option if its exercise price is $60 and it expires today.

*Colored numbers denote problems that have check answers provided at the end of the book.

d. What can you say about the value of a BWS call option if its exercise price is $60 and it expires in 6 months?

2. The BWS Corporation stock is selling at $50 a share today.

   a. Calculate the value of a BWS put option if its exercise price is $40 and it expires today.

   b. What can you say about the value of a BWS put option if its exercise price is $40 and it expires in 6 months?

   c. Calculate the value of a BWS put option if its exercise price is $60 and it expires today.

   d. What can you say about the value of a BWS put option if its exercise price is $60 and it expires in 6 months?

3. The LeMonde Corporation has debentures outstanding (par value = $1,000) that are convertible into the company's common stock at a price of $25 per share. The convertibles have a coupon interest rate of 6 percent and mature 20 years from now. In addition, the convertible debenture is callable at 107 percent of par value. The company has a marginal tax rate of 40 percent.

   a. Calculate the conversion value if LeMonde's common stock is selling at $25 a share.

   b. Calculate the bond value, assuming that straight debt of equivalent risk and maturity is yielding 9 percent.

   c. Using the answers from Parts a and b, what is a realistic estimate of the market value of the convertible debentures? (No calculation is necessary for this part of the problem.)

   d. What is the conversion value if the company's common stock price increases to $35 a share?

   e. Given the situation presented in Part d, what is a realistic estimate of the market value of the convertible debenture? (No calculation is necessary for this part of the problem.)

   f. What is the minimum common stock price that will allow the LeMonde management to use the call feature of the debentures to effectively force conversion?

   g. Suppose that increased expectations concerning inflation cause the yield on straight debt of equivalent risk and maturity to reach 10 percent. How will this affect the bond value of the convertible?

4. Automatic Data Processing recently issued $150 million of 6½ percent convertible debentures maturing in 2011. The debentures are convertible into common stock at $83.45 a share. The company's common stock was trading at about $67 a share at the time the convertibles were issued.

   a. How many shares of common stock can be obtained by converting one $1,000 par value debenture; that is, what is the conversion ratio?

   b. What was the conversion value of this issue at the time these debentures were originally issued?

   c. By what percentage was the conversion price above the stock price at the time these debentures were originally issued?

5. The Manchester Corporation has warrants presently outstanding, and each warrant entitles the holder to purchase one share of the company's common stock at an exercise price of $20 a share. If the market price of the warrants is $8 and the common stock price is $24 a share, what is the premium over the formula value for the warrants?

6. Horizon Corporation has warrants to purchase common stock outstanding. Each warrant entitles the holder to purchase one share of the company's common stock at an exercise price of $20 a share. Suppose the warrants expire on September 1, 2001. One month ago, when the company's common stock was trading at about $21.50 a share, the warrants were trading at $5 each.

   a. What was the formula value of the warrants one month ago?

   b. What was the premium over the formula value one month ago?

c. What are the reasons investors were willing to pay more than the formula value for these warrants one month ago?

d. Suppose that in August 2001, the Horizon common stock is still trading at $21.50 a share. What do you think the warrant price would be then? Why?

e. Horizon paid an annual dividend of $1 a share, as of one month ago, to its common shareholders. Do warrant holders receive dividends?

7. Shaw Products Company, whose present balance sheet is summarized here, is considering issuing $100 million of 6 percent subordinated debentures (par value = $1,000), which are convertible into common stock at a price of $40.

Balance Sheet
(in millions of dollars)

Current assets	$200	Current liabilities	$100
Fixed assets, net	300	Long-term debt	150
Total assets	$500	Common equity	250
		Total liabilities and equity	$500

a. Show the pro forma balance sheet for the issuance of the convertibles prior to conversion. Assume the proceeds are invested in new plant and equipment, and disregard issuance costs.

b. Show the pro forma balance sheet, assuming conversion of the entire issue.

c. How much additional money will the company raise at the time of conversion? $0

8. The capital structure of Whitefield Mills, Inc. is as follows:

Long-term debt	$250 million
Common stock, $1 par	25 million
Contributed capital in excess of par value	150 million
Retained earnings	350 million
	$775 million

The company has decided to raise additional capital by selling $75 million of 8 percent debentures with warrants attached. Each $1,000 debenture will have 25 warrants attached, and each warrant will entitle the holder to purchase one share of common stock at $30.

a. Show the company's new capital structure after the sale of debentures and the exercise of all the warrants. Assume that no other changes in capital structure occur between now and the time the warrants are exercised.

b. What condition is necessary in order for the warrants to be exercised?

c. How much total money will the company raise as a result of this security issue, if all warrants are exercised?

9. You own 10 Bitterroot Industries, Inc., 8-percent convertible debentures maturing in 2020. The conversion ratio of the debentures is 30, and the debentures are callable at $1,070 each. You bought the debentures when they were originally issued in 1990 for $1,000 each. At that time, Bitterroot common stock was selling at $28.50 a share, and now it is up to $44 a share. The convertible debentures are now selling at $1,320 each. Last week, you received a notice from Bitterroot Industries stating that the company is calling the debentures.

a. What are your alternatives?

b. Which alternative should you choose?

10. Calculate the after-tax component cost of capital, k_c, for a 7.5 percent convertible debenture sold at par and due to mature in 25 years. The conversion ratio is 25, and conversion is expected to occur at the end of 10 years, when the common stock price is expected to be $54 a share. The company has a 40 percent marginal tax rate. Is there any reason for you to believe that this estimate may be biased up or down?

11. Oswego Manufacturing Company has decided to sell additional common stock through a rights offering. The company has 50 million shares outstanding and plans to sell an additional 5 million shares through the rights offering. Each shareholder

will receive one right for each share currently held, and thus each right will entitle shareholders to purchase 0.1 share. Oswego's common stock is currently selling at $50 a share, and the subscription price of the rights will be $45 a share.

   a. Calculate the theoretical value of the right for both the *rights-on* and the *ex-rights* cases.
   b. How much is the market price of the company's stock expected to drop on the ex-rights date, all other things being equal? Why?
   c. If the market price of Oswego's common stock increases to $52 a share, what will the theoretical value of the right be (*rights-on* case)?
   d. Discuss the trend of the right's market price over its life, assuming the company's common stock continues to trade in the $50 range. (No numerical calculations are necessary for this part of the problem.)

12. The Oil City Company plans to sell an additional 1 million shares of common stock through a rights offering. The company currently has 12 million shares outstanding. Each shareholder will receive one right for each share currently held. Therefore, each right will enable shareholders to purchase 0.0833 shares. Oil City's common stock is currently selling for $30 per share, and the subscription price of the rights will be $25 per share.

   a. Calculate the theoretical value of the right for both the *rights-on* and *ex-rights* cases.
   b. Determine the amount that the market price of the company's stock is expected to drop on the ex-rights date, assuming all other things being equal.
   c. If the market price of Oil City's common stock increases to $40 per share, what is the theoretical value of the rights (rights-on case)?

13. The Monroeville Company has warrants outstanding that expire in 5 years. Each warrant entitles the holder to purchase 0.5 shares of common stock at an exercise price of $32 per share. Determine the formula value and premium over the formula value if the respective prices of common stock and warrants are

   a. $30 per share and $1 per warrant.
   b. $32 per share and $2 per warrant.
   c. $38 per share and $3.50 per warrant.

14. The Findlay Company has debentures outstanding (par value = $1,000) that are convertible into common stock at a price of $50 per share. The convertible bonds have a coupon interest rate of 9 percent and mature in 18 years. The convertible bonds are callable at 103 percent of par value. The company has a marginal tax rate of 40 percent.

   a. Calculate the conversion value of the bonds if Findlay's common stock is selling for $45 per share.
   b. Calculate the straight-bond value, assuming that straight debt of equivalent risk and maturity is yielding 12 percent.
   c. Determine the conversion premium if the market value of the bonds is $935.
   d. Determine the conversion value of the bonds if the company's common stock price increases to $65 per share.
   e. Given the information in Part d, what is a realistic estimate of the market price of the convertible bond issue? (No calculations are required for this part of the problem.)

15. The Wolverine Corporation has a convertible preferred stock outstanding. The par value of this preferred stock is $100, and it pays a $10 dividend. The preferred stock is callable at 103 percent of par value. The preferred stock has 10 years remaining until maturity. The preferred stock is convertible into 2.5 shares of common stock. The current common stock price is $42. Similar (quality and maturity) nonconvertible preferred stock sells at a price to yield 9 percent.

   a. What is the conversion value of this preferred stock?
   b. What is the straight (nonconvertible) preferred stock value of this security?
   c. If interest rates decline such that similar (quality and maturity) nonconvertible preferred stock sells at a price to yield 7 percent and the price of Wolverine's common stock increases to $44, for how much will this convertible security sell?

16. Five years ago, in conjunction with a financial restructuring, Laurenberg Electric sold a $100 million issue of bonds at a coupon interest rate of 12 percent. Each bond came with 30 detachable warrants. Each warrant entitled the holder to purchase one share of Laurenberg's common stock at $15 per share. The warrants were set to expire 25 years from the date of issue. When Laurenberg's stock sold for $7 per share, the value of a warrant in the marketplace was $0.50.

   a. What is the theoretical value of each warrant under these conditions?

   b. What factors influence this value?

   At a stock price of $15, the market price of each warrant was $3. At a stock price of $20, the market price of each warrant was $6.50. At a stock price of $25, the market price of each warrant was $10.50.

   c. If an investor purchases the stock and the warrant when the stock price is $15, what rate of return will be earned on both, assuming the stock and the warrant are sold when the stock price reaches $20?

   d. If an investor purchases the stock and the warrant when the stock price is $20, what rate of return will be earned on both, assuming the stock and the warrant are sold when the stock price reaches $25?

   e. What happens to the rate of return from the warrant as the stock price rises? Why do you think this happens?

17. Take the virtual tour of the Chicago Board Options Exchange at the following Web site. Then describe in a one-page memo, for someone who has never visited an options exchange, what you "saw."
www.cboe.com/index.html

18. Overall, are derivatives good for our economy, or are they bad? Visit the following Web site and then prepare a one-page memo, using their figures, documenting why derivatives are "good" for our markets.
www.fortitude.com/volatil.htm

■ SOLUTIONS TO SELF-TEST PROBLEMS

ST1. a. Conversion value = Conversion ratio × Stock price

$$= \left(\frac{\$1,000}{\$40}\right)(\$35)$$

$$= \$875$$

   b. Straight-bond value $= \sum_{t=1}^{n} \frac{\text{Interest}}{(1+k_d)^t} + \frac{\text{Principal}}{(1+k_d)^n}$

$$= \sum_{t=1}^{20} \frac{\$80}{(1+0.11)^t} + \frac{\$1000}{(1+0.11)^{20}}$$

$$= \$80(\text{PVIFA}_{0.11,20}) + \$1000(\text{PVIF}_{0.11,20})$$

$$= \$80(7.963) + \$1000(0.124)$$

$$= \$761$$

   c. Conversion premium = $925 − Max {$875; $761}

$$= \$50$$

   d. Conversion value = Conversion ratio × Stock price

$$= \left(\frac{\$1000}{\$40}\right)(\$55)$$

$$= \$1,375$$

e. $1,375. At this price, the bond issue is likely to be called, effectively forcing conversion. Therefore, the debenture cannot be expected to sell at a premium above the conversion value.

ST2. a. Formula value = Max { $0;(Common stock price − Exercise price)
$\times$ Number of shares per warrant}

$$= \text{Max } \{\$0;(\$32 - \$40)(1)\}$$

$$= \$0$$

Premium = $1.50 − $0 = $1.50

b. Formula value = Max {$0; ($40 − $40)(1)}

$$= \$0$$

Premium = $3.50 − $0 = $3.50

c. Formula value = Max {$0; ($48 − $40)(1)}

$$= \$8$$

Premium = $10.00 − $8.00 = $2.00

ST3. a. Rights-on case

$$R = \frac{M_o - S}{N + 1}$$

$$= \frac{\$25 - \$22}{10 + 1}$$

$$= \$0.27$$

Ex-rights case

$$R = \frac{M_e - S}{N}$$

$$= \frac{\$24.73 - \$22}{10}$$

$$= \$0.27$$

b. $0.27

c. $R = \frac{M_o - S}{N + 1}$

$$= \frac{\$30 - \$22}{10 + 1}$$

$$= \$0.73$$

■ GLOSSARY

Call Option An option to *buy* an asset at a set price. Also referred to as a *call*.

Contingent Claim A security whose payoffs depend on the value of another security.

Conversion Premium The amount by which the market value of a convertible security exceeds the higher of its conversion value or straight-bond (preferred) value.

Conversion Price The effective price an investor pays for common stock when the stock is obtained by converting a convertible security.

Conversion Ratio The number of common shares an investor obtains by converting a convertible security.

Conversion (Stock) Value The value of a convertible security, based on the value of the underlying shares of common stock.

Convertible Security A fixed-income security that may be exchanged for a firm's common stock at the holder's option. The two most common types of convertible securities are *convertible preferred stock* and *convertible debentures*.

Derivative A financial contract that derives its value from some other security or asset, such as stocks, bonds, currencies, commodities, or interest rates. The two broadest categories of derivatives are options, and forward-type contracts.

Exercise Price The price at which an option holder can purchase or sell a company's stock. This also is termed the *strike price*.

Ex-rights A stock sells ex-rights when stock purchasers no longer receive the *rights* along with the shares purchased.

Hedge A transaction in which a position is taken in another market, such as the forward or futures market, to offset the risk associated with a position in the current cash (spot) market.

Interest Rate Swap The exchange of floating rate interest payments for fixed rate interest payments, or vice versa.

Option A contract (often in the form of a security) that gives its holder the right to buy or sell an asset at a set price during a specified time period.

Put Option An option to *sell* an asset at a set price. Also referred to as a *put*.

Right A short-term option issued by a firm that permits an existing stockholder to buy a specified number of shares of common stock at a specified price (the subscription price), which is below the current market price.

Rights Offering The sale of new shares of common stock by distributing stock purchase rights to a firm's existing shareholders. This also is termed a *privileged subscription*.

Rights-On A stock sells rights-on when purchasers receive the *rights* along with the shares purchased.

Straight-Bond Value The value a convertible debt security would have if it did not possess the conversion feature. Also referred to as the *investment* value.

Warrant A company-issued long-term option to purchase a specified number of shares of the firm's stock at a particular price during a specified time period.

INTERNATIONAL FINANCIAL MANAGEMENT

21

KEY CHAPTER CONCEPTS

1. The theory of *interest rate parity* states that the percentage differential between the spot and the forward rate for a currency is equal to the approximate difference in interest rates in the two countries over the same time horizon.

2. The theory of *relative purchasing power parity* states that in comparison to a period when exchange rates between two countries are in equilibrium, changes in differential rates of inflation between the countries will be offset by equal, but opposite changes in the future spot currency rate.

3. The forward rate is often considered to be an unbiased estimator of the future spot currency rate.

4. The *Fisher effect* states that nominal interest rates are approximately equal to the sum of the real interest rate and the expected inflation rate.

5. The *international Fisher effect* theory states that differences in interest rates between two countries should be offset by equal, but opposite changes in the future spot rate.

6. Three important categories of foreign exchange risk are (1) transaction exposure, (2) economic exposure, and (3) translation exposure.

7. A hedge is an offsetting transaction designed to reduce or avoid risk. Forward and futures exchange hedges and money market hedges are used to reduce transaction exposure. Financing with debt denominated in the same currency as foreign assets is a means of hedging against translation and economic exposure.

PANIC IN JAPAN AND GERMANY OVER THE VALUE OF THE DOLLAR*

In April 1995, economic officials in Japan and Germany were in a panic over the plunging value of the dollar relative to the yen and the mark. In both Germany and Japan, trade accounts for a very large portion of total economic activity. For example, in Germany nearly 25 percent of economic activity is closely tied to trade, compared with only 11 percent in the United States. The rising value of the mark and the yen had a major impact on U.S., German, and Japanese firms.

From early January of 1995 until mid-April of 1995, the yen increased in value relative to the dollar by 16 percent. This appreciation of the yen effectively added 16 percent to the cost of every product produced in Japan for export to the United States. Most Japanese auto makers were finding the manufacture of cars in Japan for export to the United States to be unprofitable at current price levels. The potential for price increases to offset the appreciation in the value of the yen was limited by the prices of American-made vehicles. In contrast, for American firms selling in Japan, the depreciating dollar was good news. For example, the yen price of Chrysler's Jeep Cherokee declined from ¥3,655,000 to ¥3,290,000 during early 1995.

Another worry arising from the increasing value of the yen and the mark relative to the dollar was the fear that both the German and the Japanese economies would stagnate further due to the high cost of their exported goods, and hence lower worldwide demand for these products. Faced with this dilemma, what options were open to Japanese and German firms?

With increasingly unprofitable sales in the U.S. due to the rising value of the yen and the mark, one option was to cease doing business in the U.S. to avoid

running up larger losses. This alternative was deemed undesirable by most firms because the U.S. is the world's largest and richest market. In real option terms, these companies had paid large sums over many years to set up business in the U.S. (option premiums) and to develop brand recognition. To leave the U.S. market now, in the face of short-term losses, would mean letting the option to do business in the U.S. expire prior to any mandated expiration date. Companies were unlikely to give up their brand equity because of unfa-

vorable currency value moves. What many of these firms did was to rapidly embark on a program of cost reduction, product re-engineering, and the movement of plants from high-cost Germany and Japan to the lower-cost U.S. By late 1996 these plans were paying dividends. Toyota, for example, introduced an improved Toyota Camry car model at a price that was lower than the price being charged for the old Camry model it replaced. With these new efficiency efforts, Toyota's profits increased, and its U.S. market share also increased, at the expense of many domestic auto manufacturers. By March 1997, the value of the dollar had also increased dramatically relative to the yen and the mark. For example, on March 20, 1997 one dollar was worth over 123 yen. Thus, Japanese firms that remained in the U.S. market reaped a dual benefit. First, their attention to cost control made them more competitive with U.S. firms. Second, the dollar increased in value by over 48 percent between early 1995 and early 1997, making Japanese export goods increasingly good values in the world marketplace.

This chapter looks at the determinants of foreign currency exchange rates and considers options open to multinational firms who must compete globally in a currency marketplace characterized by rapid changes in relative values.

*Based, in part, on "They're Mad About Money," *Newsweek* (April 17, 1995): 61.

INTRODUCTION

As the world economy has become more globally integrated, virtually every firm and individual is affected by developments in the economies of countries other than their own. The debate over the North American Free Trade Agreement (NAFTA) has brought many of these relationships to the fore. Individuals are affected by global economic conditions as multinational firms seek the cheapest place to produce their products—resulting in employment winners and losers. A textile firm may move to Mexico from North Carolina at the same time Audi considers the construction of a new plant in the southeastern U.S. In making plant location decisions, managers consider wage costs, the quality of the workforce, transportation costs, the cost of raw materials, exchange rate levels and risks, and political risk (such as the risk of expropriation or the blocking of funds). In addition, firms may decide to locate in multiple countries to gain quicker access to new technologies as they develop. Some international plant location decisions are designed, at least in part, to avoid political and regulatory barriers. For example, Japanese auto firms, including Toyota, Nissan, and Honda, have built large assembly plants in the United States, partly in response to auto import quotas and to reduce the pressure for greater future import restrictions.

Financial managers willing to venture into the global financial marketplace may find lower-cost financing alternatives than are available in their home country. With trade barriers being lowered around the world, the managers of tomorrow cannot limit their knowledge to "Island America." Rather, these managers will find that understanding the functioning of the global financial marketplace is a key element of their knowledge and skill base.

This chapter continues the discussion of international finance that was begun in Chapter 2. Here we explore the factors that determine exchange rates, look at ways to forecast future exchange rates, and consider various aspects of foreign exchange risk and ways of managing that risk.

FACTORS THAT AFFECT EXCHANGE RATES

Check out Michigan State University's web site for business resources with links related to international finance.
http://ciber.bus.msu.edu/busres.htm

Exchange rates between currencies vary over time, reflecting supply and demand considerations for each currency. For example, the demand for British pounds comes from a number of sources, which include foreign buyers of British exports who must pay for their purchases in pounds, foreign investors who desire to make investments in physical or financial assets in Britain, and speculators who expect British pounds to increase in value relative to other currencies. The British government may also be a source of demand if it attempts to keep the value of the pound (relative to other currencies) from falling by using its supply of foreign currencies or gold to purchase pounds in the market.

Sources of supply include British importers who need to convert their pounds into foreign currency to pay for purchases, British investors who desire to make investments in foreign countries, and speculators who expect British pounds to decrease in value relative to other currencies.

Exchange rates also are affected by economic and political conditions that influence the supply of, or demand for a country's currency. Some of these conditions include differential inflation and interest rates among countries, the government's trade policies, and the government's political stability. A high rate of inflation within a country tends to lower the value of its currency with respect to the currencies of other countries experiencing lower rates of inflation. The exchange rate will tend to decline as holders sell or exchange the country's currency for other currencies whose purchasing power is not declining at as high a rate. In contrast, relatively high interest rates within a country tend to increase the exchange rate as foreign investors seek to convert their currencies and purchase these higher-yielding securities.

Government trade policies that limit imports—such as the imposition of tariffs, import quotas, and restrictions on foreign exchange transactions—reduce the supply of the country's currency in the foreign exchange market. This, in turn, tends to increase the value of the country's currency with respect to other currencies and thus increase exchange rates.

Finally, the political stability of the government affects the risks perceived by foreign investors and companies doing business in the country. These risks include the possible expropriation of investments or restrictions on the amount of funds (such as returns from investments) that may be taken out of the country.

In the following sections we develop the important relationships between spot rates, forward rates, interest rates, and inflation rates as they impact foreign currency exchange rates.

Covered Interest Arbitrage and Interest Rate Parity

There is a close relationship between the interest rates in two countries and the forward exchange rate premium or discount. Consider a U.S. investor with $1.2 million to invest who notes that the interest rate on 90-day certificates of deposit (CDs) available at German banks is 4 percent for 90 days. At the same time, the 90-day CD rate in the U.S. is only 2 percent. The spot rate of the Deutsche mark (DM) is $0.60/DM and the 90-day forward rate is also $0.60. As an investor, you know that you can immediately convert $1.2 million into DM2 million at today's spot rate of $0.60 with no risk. You can also lock in the 4 percent German interest rate for 90 days by purchasing a German CD with your DM2 million. However, there is risk regarding the exchange rate at which you will be able to convert DM back to dollars at the end of 90 days. You can guarantee this rate by selling 2 million DM (plus the interest you will receive on your German CD) in the 90-day forward market at today's forward rate of $0.60. This transaction will guarantee you a risk-free profit. Consider the following steps in this transaction:

1. Convert $1.2 million into DM2 million at today's spot rate of $0.60/DM.
2. Buy a 90-day CD at a German bank yielding 4 percent every 90 days.
3. Simultaneously sell DM2.08 million forward (original DM2 million plus DM 80,000 in interest) at $0.60 to net you $1,248,000.
4. This compares favorably with the $1,224,000 ($1.2 million plus interest at 2 percent) you could have received from investing in a U.S. CD.

This risk-free transaction enabled you to earn an additional return of $24,000 over what would be available by investing in the United States. Because there are virtually no barriers to prevent individuals from engaging in this transaction called **covered interest arbitrage,** it can be expected that opportunities to earn risk-free additional returns such as these will not persist very long. The demand by American investors for DM will put upward pressure on the spot price of DM,

Foreign exchange actually comes in all sorts of different flavors and shapes: spot contracts, forward contracts, variable-delivery contracts, futures, options, swaps, foreign-currency loans/deposits, etc. Visit Fleet Bank's Web site for a listing (and some very good definitions) of the different kinds of foreign exchange.
http://www.fleet.com

to a price greater than \$0.60/DM. At the same time, as American investors sell DM forward to cover their position, this will put downward pressure on forward rate of the DM to a price less than \$0.60. Furthermore, as funds leave the United States for Germany, the reduced supply of funds will tend to increase U.S. interest rates. The increased supply of funds in Germany, on the other hand, will tend to lower German interest rates.

The net effect of these transactions and market pressures will be an equilibrium condition where covered interest arbitrage transactions are not possible. This relationship is called **interest rate parity** (IRP). When IRP exists, the forward rate will differ from the spot rate by just enough to offset the interest rate differential between the two currencies. The IRP condition states that the home (or domestic) interest rate must be higher (lower) than the foreign interest rate by an amount equal to the forward discount (premium) on the home currency. In other words, the forward premium or discount for a currency quoted in terms of another currency is approximately equal to the difference in interest rates prevailing between the two countries. Thus, if interest rates in Germany are higher than interest rates in the United States, then the IRP condition indicates that the dollar can be expected to increase in value relative to the DM. The exact IRP relationship is

$$\text{IRP:} \qquad \left(\frac{F - S_0}{S_0}\right) = \left(\frac{i_h - i_f}{1 + i_f}\right) \qquad (21.1)$$

where i_h is the home (U.S.) interest rate, i_f is the comparable foreign (German) interest rate, F is the *direct quote* forward rate, and S_0 is the *direct quote* spot rate.[1] (Note that the interest rates in Equation 21.1 are the interest rates for the same period of time as the number of days in the forward price, not necessarily annualized interest rates.) The relationship in Equation 21.1 can be simplified to

$$\text{IRP:} \qquad \frac{F}{S_0} = \frac{1 + i_h}{1 + i_f} \qquad (21.2)$$

An approximation of the IRP relationship is

$$\text{Approximate IRP:} \qquad \left(\frac{F - S_0}{S_0}\right) \approx (i_h - i_f) \qquad (21.3)$$

Equation 21.3 indicates that when interest rate parity exists, differences in interest rates between two countries will be (approximately) offset by changes in the relative value of the two currencies.

To illustrate, assume that the 90-day interest rate is 1.5 percent in the United States and 2.5 percent in Germany, and the current spot exchange rate between dollars and Deutsche marks is \$0.60. If IRP holds, what will the 90-day forward rate be (using the exact relationship in Equation 21.2)?

$$(F/\$0.60) = (1 + 0.015) / (1 + 0.025)$$

$$F = \$0.5941$$

In this case, the dollar has increased in value relative to the DM (i.e., it takes fewer dollars to buy each DM). Why do you think this should occur?

---

[1]Recall that a *direct quote* is the home currency price of a unit of foreign currency, such as \$/DM (from the perspective of an American).

Purchasing Power Parity

When there are no significant costs or other barriers associated with moving goods or services between markets, then the price of each product should be the same in each market. In economics, this is known as the *law of one price*. When the different markets represent different countries, the law of one price says that prices will be the same in each country after making the appropriate conversion from one currency to another. Alternatively one can say that exchange rates between two currencies will equal the ratio of the price indexes between the countries. In international finance and trade, this relationship is known as the absolute version of *purchasing power parity*.

In reality, we know that this relationship does not hold because of the costs of moving goods and services and the existence of tariffs and other trade barriers. For example, *The Economist* newspaper, in a lighthearted look at the law of one price, regularly reports on the price of Big Mac hamburgers in various countries. In 1991, a Big Mac cost \$2.20 in the United States, \$2.56 in Germany, \$1.36 in Yugoslavia, \$1.10 in Hong Kong, \$6.25 in Russia, and \$2.32 in Japan.[2] It is obviously not possible to buy Big Macs in Hong Kong and ship them to New York for sale, for example. Hence the law of one price does not hold for Big Macs. On the other hand, for goods that are standardized and somewhat easier to move and store, such as gold or crude oil, one would expect only minor violations of the law of one price.

A less restrictive form of the law of one price is known as **relative purchasing power parity (PPP)**. The relative PPP principle states that in comparison to a period when exchange rates between two countries are in equilibrium, changes in the differential rates of inflation between two countries will be offset by equal, but opposite changes in the future spot exchange rate. For example, if prices in the United States rise by 4 percent per year and prices in Germany rise by 6 percent per year, then relative PPP holds if the German Mark (DM) weakens relative to the U.S. dollar by approximately 2 percent.

The exact relative purchasing power parity relationship is

$$\text{Relative PPP:} \qquad \left(\frac{S_1 - S_0}{S_0} \right) = \left(\frac{\pi_h - \pi_f}{1 + \pi_f} \right) \qquad (21.4)$$

where S_1 is the expected future (direct quote) spot rate at time period 1, S_0 is the current (direct quote) spot rate, π_h is the expected home country (U.S.) inflation rate, and π_f is the expected foreign country inflation rate.[3] This relationship can be simplified to

$$\text{Relative PPP:} \qquad \left(\frac{S_1}{S_0} \right) = \left(\frac{1 + \pi_h}{1 + \pi_f} \right) \qquad (21.5)$$

Using the previous example, if U.S. prices are expected to rise by 4 percent over the coming year, prices in Germany are expected to rise by 6 percent during the same time, and the current spot exchange rate (S_0), is \$0.60/DM, then the expected spot rate in one year (S_1), will be

---

[2] *The Economist* (April 13, 1991): 78.

[3] The relationship in Equation 21.4 can be approximated as

$$\frac{S_1 - S_0}{S_0} \approx \pi_h - \pi_f$$

$$S_1/\$0.60 = (1 + 0.04)/(1 + 0.06)$$

$$S_1 = \$0.5887$$

The higher German inflation rate can be expected to result in a decline in the future spot value of the DM relative to the dollar by 1.89 percent.

The market forces that support the relative PPP relationship operate in the following way. If one nation has a higher inflation rate than another, its goods and services will become relatively more expensive, making its exports less price competitive and imports more price competitive. The resulting deficit in foreign trade will place downward pressure on the currency value of the high inflation country until a new, lower equilibrium value is established. The opposite will be true for the country with the lower inflation rate. For example, if the United States has a lower inflation rate than its major trading partners, relative PPP indicates that the value of the dollar can be expected to increase relative to the value of the currencies of these other trading partners.

Tests of relative PPP indicate that the relationship holds up reasonably well over long periods, but it is a less accurate indicator of short-term currency value changes. Also, the relative PPP relationship is stronger for those countries experiencing high rates of inflation. Tests of the strength of the PPP relationship are hampered by the use of noncomparable price indexes between countries and government interference in commodity and currency markets. Nevertheless, the general relationship between inflation rates and currency values is widely accepted, even if it is difficult to measure properly.

Expectations Theory and Forward Exchange Rates

If foreign currency markets are efficient, the forward rate should reflect what market participants expect the future spot rate for a currency to be. For example, if market participants expected the one-year future spot rate (S_1) for DM to be $0.58, then what would the one-year forward rate (F_1), have to be? It would also have to be $0.58. If the forward rate were lower than this amount, market participants would want to buy DM forward, thereby placing upward price pressure on the DM until an equilibrium is reached where the forward rate equals the expected future spot rate.

If the expected future spot rate is equivalent to the forward rate, we can say that the forward rate is an *unbiased* estimator of the future spot rate. It is important to recognize that this does not mean that the forward rate will always be equal to the actual future spot rate. Rather it means that the estimates of the future spot rate provided by the forward rate will not systematically overshoot or undershoot the actual future spot rate, but will equal it *on average*.

Evidence regarding the expectations theory of forward exchange rates indicates that, in general, the forward rate is an unbiased estimate of expected future spot rates, if risk in the currency markets is ignored. There is some evidence, however, that when the forward rate implies a large change from the current spot rate, these forecasts tend to overshoot the actual future spot rate.

Forward rates as unbiased estimates of expected future spot rates have important implications for managers. First, managers should not spend the firm's resources to buy forecasts of future exchange rates since unbiased forecasts are provided free in the marketplace. Second, managers will find that hedging their future foreign currency risk by making use of the forward market should be a cost-effective way of limiting this risk exposure. In the following sections, some of these hedging techniques are considered.

Hedging Techniques

The International Fisher Effect

The final piece in the international currency market puzzle is the relationship between interest rates and future spot currency rates. In his 1930 book, *The Theory of Interest,* Irving Fisher established that in equilibrium lenders will receive a nominal rate of interest equal to a real interest rate plus an amount sufficient to offset the effects of expected inflation. *Nominal interest rates* are market rates stated in current, not real terms, such as the rates quoted in financial publications like the *Wall Street Journal.* Real rates of return are not directly observable. The real rate of return is the rate at which borrowing and lending in the financial markets are in equilibrium. The real rate of return is equal to the real rate of growth in the economy, and it reflects the time preference of market participants between present and future consumption. The relationship between nominal (risk-free) rates of return, real rates of return, and expected inflation is

$$(1 + i) = (1 + i_R)(1 + \pi)$$

or

$$i = i_R + \pi + i_R\pi \qquad (21.6)$$

where i is the nominal (and risk-free) rate of interest, i_R is the real rate of return, and π is the expected inflation rate. This relationship is often referred to as the *Fisher effect.*[4] For example, if the annual real rate of return in France was 3 percent and the expected annual inflation rate was 8 percent, the nominal interest rate would be

$$i = 0.03 + 0.08 + (0.03)(0.08) = 0.1124 \text{ or } 11.24\%$$

Fisher argues that in the absence of government interference and holding risk constant, real rates of return across countries will be equalized through a process of arbitrage. If real rates of return are higher in the United States than in Japan, capital will flow to the United States from Japan until an equilibrium is reached. The assumption of equal real rates of return across countries ignores differences in risk and attitudes toward risk that may exist in different cultures. Also, to the extent that there are barriers to the movement of capital between countries, real rates of return may be different between countries. In spite of these limitations, the assumption of equal real returns is useful because (1) it is a reasonable representation of reality among the major industrialized countries; and (2) as capital markets become increasingly internationalized and barriers to capital flows fall, differences in real rates of return can be expected to decrease.

If real rates of return tend to be equalized across countries, it follows that differences in observed nominal rates between countries must be due primarily to different inflation expectations. Incorporating the equilibrium condition for real interest rates with relative PPP leads to what has been called the *international Fisher effect (IFE).* The IFE states that differences in interest rates between two countries should be offset by equal, but opposite changes in the future spot

---

[4]This relationship can be approximated as

$$i \approx i_R + \pi$$

exchange rate. For example, if one-year nominal interest rates are 10 percent in the United States and 7 percent in France, then IFE predicts that the French franc (FF) should increase in value relative to the U.S. dollar by approximately 3 percent.

The exact IFE relationship is

$$\text{IFE:} \qquad \left(\frac{S_1 - S_0}{S_0}\right) = \left(\frac{i_h - i_f}{1 + i_f}\right) \qquad (21.7)$$

where S_1 is the expected future (direct quote) spot rate at time period 1, S_0 is the current (direct quote) spot rate, i_h is the home country (U.S.) nominal interest rate, and i_f is the foreign country nominal interest rate.[5] This relationship can be simplified to

$$\text{IFE:} \qquad \left(\frac{S_1}{S_0}\right) = \left(\frac{1 + i_h}{1 + i_f}\right) \qquad (21.8)$$

Using the previous example, if one-year U.S. nominal interest rates are 10 percent, one-year French nominal interest rates are 7 percent, and the current spot exchange rate, S_0, is \$0.16/FF, then the expected spot rate in one year, S_1, will be

$$S_1/\$0.16 = (1 + 0.10)/(1 + 0.07)$$

$$S_1 = \$0.1645$$

The lower nominal French interest rate results in an expected increase in the value of the FF (decrease in the value of the \$) of 2.80 percent.

An Integrative Look at International Parity Relationships

Figure 21-1 provides an integrative look at international parity relationships. Beginning with the lower box in the figure, suppose one observes that the one-year nominal interest rate is 10 percent in the United States and 5 percent in Germany. This implies, according to the Fisher effect, that the difference in expected inflation rates between the United States and Germany is also 5 percent, because real rates of return are assumed to be equal between the United States and Germany. The 5 percent inflation differential means that the one-year future spot rate of exchange between dollars and DM can be expected to change such that the dollar will weaken by 5 percent relative to the DM. This condition is expected from the purchasing power parity relationship.

The 5 percent differential in interest rates also implies that the dollar will sell at a 5 percent discount in the one-year forward market relative to the DM. This expectation arises from the interest rate parity relationship. If the forward rate is an unbiased estimator of future spot rates, then the one-year future spot rate of exchange between dollars and DM can be expected to change such that the dollar will weaken by 5 percent relative to the DM.

Finally, the international Fisher effect implies that if one-year nominal interest rates are 5 percent higher in the United States than in Germany, then the one-year future spot rate of exchange between the dollar and the DM will change such that the dollar will weaken by 5 percent relative to the DM.

---

[5]This relationship can be approximated as

$$\frac{S_1 - S_0}{S_0} \approx i_h - i_f$$

FIGURE 21-1
International Parity Conditions:
An Integrative Look

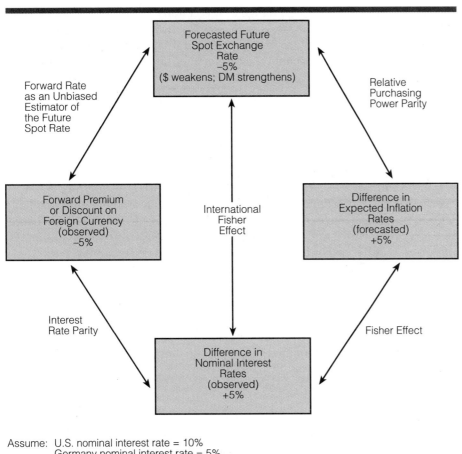

Assume: U.S. nominal interest rate = 10%
Germany nominal interest rate = 5%
Time horizon = 1 year

 ## FORECASTING FUTURE EXCHANGE RATES

The equilibrium relationships discussed in the previous sections can be very useful to managers who need forecasts of future spot exchange rates. Although empirical evidence indicates that these relationships are not perfect, the financial markets in developed countries operate in a way that efficiently incorporates the effect of interest rate differentials in the forward market and the future spot exchange market. Therefore managers can use the information contained in forward rates and interest rates to make forecasts of the future spot exchange rates. These forecasts are useful, for example, when pricing products for sale in international markets, when making international capital investment decisions, and when deciding whether to hedge foreign currency risks.

Using Forward Rates

The simplest forecast of future spot exchange rates can be derived from current forward rates. If the one-year forward rate of exchange between dollars and yen is 110 yen/dollar, then this can be used as an unbiased estimate of the expected one-year future spot rate of exchange between dollars and yen. For example, if Boeing were negotiating the sale of a Boeing 737 airliner to Japan Air with delivery and payment to take place in one year, and if Japan Air insisted on a price quoted in yen, then Boeing could use this forward rate to convert its desired dollar proceeds from the transaction into yen. As we will see in a later section, Boeing may want to hedge against the risk of a change in this exchange rate between the time the contract is signed and the time the plane is delivered and payment is received.

Using Interest Rates

Forward rates provide a direct and convenient forecast of future spot currency exchange rates. Unfortunately, forward quotes normally are not readily available beyond one year. Hence, if a manager needs a longer-term currency exchange rate forecast, forward rates are of little help. Fortunately, one can use observed interest rate differentials between two countries and the general international Fisher effect (IFE) relationship to make longer-term exchange rate forecasts. Recall from Equation 21.8 that the IFE relationship is given as

$$\left(\frac{S_1}{S_0}\right) = \left(\frac{1 + i_h}{1 + i_f}\right)$$

This relationship can be modified to cover more than one period into the future as follows:

$$\left(\frac{S_n}{S_0}\right) = \frac{(1 + i_h)^n}{(1 + i_f)^n} \tag{21.9}$$

For example, assume that the annual nominal interest rate on five-year U.S. Treasury bonds is 6 percent, and the annual nominal interest rate on five-year Swiss government bonds is 4.5 percent. Also, assume that the current spot exchange rate between dollars and Swiss francs (SFr) is \$0.6955/SFr. What is the expected future spot rate in five years? It can be calculated using Equation 21.9 as follows:

$$S_5/\$0.6955 = (1 + 0.06)^5/(1 + 0.045)^5$$

$$S_5 = \$0.7469$$

The IFE relationship predicts that the dollar will lose value relative to the SFr. The expected spot exchange rate in five years is \$0.7469/SFr.

One could also use the PPP relationship to forecast future exchange rates. However, the advantage of the IFE relationship is that interest rates between two countries are readily observable for almost any maturity, whereas differential levels of future inflation are not. In order to use PPP to make exchange rate forecasts, one would first have to forecast the inflation rates in both countries. Hence it is normally desirable to use the IFE relationship when making longer-term exchange rate forecasts, such as might be needed when evaluating foreign long-term investment projects with cash flows extending several years into the future.

FOREIGN EXCHANGE RISK

Foreign exchange risk is said to exist when a portion of the cash flows expected to be received by a firm are denominated in foreign currencies. As exchange rates change, there is uncertainty about the amount of domestic currency that will be received from a transaction denominated in a foreign currency. There are three primary categories of foreign exchange risk that multinational firms must consider:

1. Transaction exposure (short-term)
2. Economic (operating) exposure (long-term)
3. Translation (accounting) exposure

Transaction Exposure

Most firms have contracts to buy and sell goods and services, with delivery and payment to occur at some time in the future. If payments under the contract involve the use of foreign currency, additional risk is involved. The potential for change in value of a foreign-currency denominated transaction due to an exchange rate change is called **transaction exposure.**

For example, General Electric is a major producer of locomotives. Suppose that General Electric contracts with the Mexican government to sell 100 locomotives for delivery one year from now. General Electric wants to realize $400 million from this sale. The Mexican government has indicated that it will only enter into the contract if the price is stated in Mexican pesos (Ps). The one-year forward rate is Ps3.11/$. Hence General Electric quotes a price of Ps1,244,000,000. Once the contract has been signed, General Electric faces a significant transaction exposure. Unless General Electric takes actions to guarantee its future dollar proceeds from the sale—that is, unless it hedges its position, for example, by selling Ps1,244,000,000 in the one-year forward market—it stands to lose on the transaction if the value of the peso weakens. Suppose that over the coming year the inflation rate in Mexico rises significantly beyond what was expected at the time the deal was signed. According to relative PPP, the value of the peso can be expected to decline, say to Ps4/$. If this happens, General Electric will receive only $311 million (Ps1,244,000,000/Ps4/$) rather than the $400 million it was expecting.

One well-documented example of the potential consequences of transaction exposure is the case of Laker Airlines. In the late 1970s, in the face of growing demand from British tourists traveling to the United States, Laker purchased several DC-10 aircraft and financed them in U.S. dollars. This transaction ultimately led to Laker's bankruptcy because Laker's primary source of revenue was pounds sterling, whereas its debt costs were denominated in dollars. Over the period from the late 1970s to 1982, when Laker failed, the dollar strengthened relative to the pound sterling. This had a devastating effect because (1) the strong dollar discouraged British travel to the United States, and (2) the pound sterling cost of principal and interest payments on the dollar-denominated debt increased.

Managing Transaction Exposure. A number of alternatives are available to a firm faced with transaction exposure. First, the firm may choose to do nothing, and simply accept the risk associated with the transaction. Doing nothing works well for firms with extensive international transactions that may tend to cancel each other out. For example, if General Electric has purchased goods or services from Mexican firms that require the payment in approximately the same number of pesos as it expects to receive from the sale of the locomotives, then it is not necessary to do anything to counter the risk arising from a loss in value of the peso relative to the dollar.

A second alternative is to invoice all transactions in dollars (for a U.S.-based firm). This avoids any transaction risk for the U.S. firm, but shifts this risk to the other party. For example, in September 1992, in a period of extreme volatility of European currencies, Dow Chemical announced that it would use the German mark as the common currency for all of its European business transactions. This action shifts currency risks from Dow to its customers who do business in other currencies. When a firm is considering this alternative, it needs to determine whether this strategy is competitively possible, or whether parties on the other side of the transaction may resist or perhaps insist on a lower price if they are forced to bear all of the transaction risk. In Dow's case, analysts and competitors doubted that customers would be willing to bear all of the exchange rate risk and felt that Dow would ultimately abandon this strategy.

Two hedging techniques that are possible for a U.S. company to protect itself against transaction exposure are

- Execute a contract in the forward exchange market or in the foreign exchange futures market.
- Execute a *money market hedge*.

Consider a situation in which Westinghouse purchases materials from a British supplier, Commonwealth Resources, Ltd. Because the amount of the transaction (£2 million) is stated in pounds, Westinghouse bears the exchange risk. This example of transaction exposure is illustrated in Table 21-1. Assume that Commonwealth Resources extends 90-day trade credit to Westinghouse and that the value of the pound unexpectedly increases from $1.69/pound on the purchase date to $1.74/pound on the payment date. If Westinghouse takes the trade credit extended to it, the cost of the purchase effectively increases from $3.38 million to $3.48 million (that is, £2,000,000 × $1.74/pound).

First, Westinghouse could execute a contract in the forward exchange market to buy £2 million at the *known* 90-day forward rate, rather than at the *uncertain* spot rate prevailing on the payment date. This is referred to as a *forward market hedge.* Assume, for example, that the 90-day forward rate is $1.70/pound. Based on this rate, Westinghouse effectively would be able to exchange $3.4 million (that is, £2,000,000 × $1.70/pound) 90 days later on the payment date when it is required to pay for the materials. Thus, Westinghouse would be able to take advantage of the trade credit and, at the same time, hedge against foreign exchange risk.

A second hedging technique, called a *money market hedge,* involves Westinghouse borrowing funds from its bank, exchanging them for pounds at the spot rate, and investing them in interest-bearing British securities to yield £2 million in 90 days. By investing in securities that mature on the same date the payment is due to Commonwealth Resources (that is, 90 days after the purchase date), Westinghouse will have the necessary amount of pounds available to pay for the

TABLE 21-1
Example of Transaction Exchange Rate Risk

DATE	EXCHANGE RATE	AMOUNT OF TRANSACTION U.S. Dollars	British Pounds
Purchase date	$1.69/pound	$3,380,000	£2,000,000
Payment date	$1.74/pound	$3,480,000	£2,000,000

materials. The net cost of this money market hedge to Westinghouse will depend on the interest rate on the funds it borrows from its bank relative to the interest rate on the funds it invests in securities. If the conditions of interest rate parity are satisfied, these two hedging techniques are equivalent.

Other transaction risk reduction strategies include the use of options on foreign currencies (discussed in Chapter 20) and negotiating a risk-sharing contract between the two parties to a transaction in which both parties agree in advance to share in some way the financial consequences of changes in value between the affected currencies.

For large multinational companies, there will be many international transactions involving many different currencies. Attempting to hedge separately the transaction exposure for each international transaction would be time consuming and inefficient. For example, consider Sara Lee Corporation, which has operations both in Italy and France. The Italian subsidiary makes purchases in France that require French francs. At the same time the French subsidiary makes purchases in Italy that require Italian lira. To the extent that these transactions offset, no hedge is necessary. Multinational firms often make thousands of overlapping transactions using different currencies. Thus it is a complex matter to keep track of *net* currency exposures and avoid hedging against risks that do not really exist when one takes the consolidated corporate view, rather than the narrow subsidiary view of exchange risk.

Economic Exposure

Economic (or operating) **exposure** refers to changes in a firm's operating cash flows (and hence the firm's value) that come about because of *real* rather than *nominal* changes in exchange rates. Real exchange rate changes occur when there are deviations from purchasing power parity (PPP). Under relative PPP, exchange rates should vary to reflect changes in the price level of goods and services in one country relative to another. For example, if the inflation rate in Mexico is 5 percent higher per year than in the United States, relative PPP says that the value of the Mexican peso can be expected to decline by about 5 percent relative to the dollar. Thus goods purchased in the United States from Mexico will cost the same as they did before the increase in Mexican inflation, after adjusting for the decline in the value of the peso.

Real exchange rate changes can affect the way competing companies in two countries do business and can impact the business conditions in the countries. In April 1995, $1 equaled about ¥83. In March 1997, $1 equaled about ¥123. In relative terms, the dollar was "weak" and the yen was "strong" in April 1995, whereas in March 1997, the dollar was "strong" and the yen was "weak."

The weakening of the dollar and the strengthening of the yen can have a dramatic impact on firms doing business in the United States and Japan. The showcase example of these effects is the relative performance of the Japanese and American automobile industries. In the mid-1980s, Japanese products were generally cheaper (and of better quality) than their American counterparts. The Japanese share of the U.S. auto market was growing, restrained only by voluntary import restrictions agreed to by the Japanese. By 1995, the increased value of the yen relative to the dollar had reversed the fortunes of auto makers in both countries. Japanese autos were selling for several thousand dollars more in 1995 than comparable U.S. products. American firms reported significant increases in U.S. market share at the expense of the Japanese. Japanese auto firms were

Global Investor maintains a comprehensive Web site for international investors. They track the world's major markets (Hong Kong, Tokyo, the United Kingdom, etc.), provide a Global Investor Directory, and provide links to international financial Web sites. They also maintain FINANCEnetWATCH, which tracks financial developments in cyberspace.
http://www.numa.com/index.htm

experiencing significant financial difficulties at a time when U.S. auto firms were reporting substantial increases in profit. U.S. firms also had begun exporting vehicles to Japan.

In an attempt to offset the impact of their significant economic exposure in the United States, Japanese firms have aggressively moved to establish manufacturing and assembly operations in the United States and some European countries, so that many of their costs will be denominated in the same currency as their revenues. Also, by locating plants in many different countries, multinational firms have the flexibility to shift production from one location to another, in order to offset unfavorable economic exposure.

Managing Economic Exposure. Economic exposure is much more difficult and expensive to manage than the shorter-term transactions exposure already discussed. Strategies to manage the impact of real changes in exchange rates in countries where a multinational firm operates include

1. *Shift production from high-cost (exchange-rate adjusted) plants to lower-cost plants*—for example, moving labor-intensive sewing operations from U.S. textile plants to plants in Mexico.
2. *Increase productivity*—adopt labor-saving technologies, implement flexible manufacturing systems, reduce product cycles, make use of benchmarking, i.e., copy your strongest competitors.
3. *"Outsource" the supply of many of the components needed to produce a product to lower-cost locations*—for example, some U.S. publishing houses have outsourced typesetting to areas in the Far East with lower labor costs.
4. *Increase product differentiation to reduce the price sensitivity in the market*—for example, the Japanese have moved more to the luxury car market as the yen has strengthened because of the greater price flexibility the luxury market provides relative to the economy car market.
5. *Enter markets with strong currencies and reduce involvement in competitive markets with weak currencies*—U.S. firms have become increasingly aggressive in entering the Japanese market as the yen has increased in value relative to the dollar.

Translation Exposure

When a multinational firm has one or more foreign subsidiaries with assets and liabilities denominated in a foreign currency, it faces **translation exposure.** For example, if a U.S.-based multinational firm operates a subsidiary in Spain, the peseta (Ptas.) value of the subsidiary's assets and liabilities must be translated into the home (U.S. $) currency when the parent firm prepares its consolidated financial statements. When the translation occurs, there can be gains or losses, which must be recognized in the financial statements of the parent.

Current accounting standards are set forth in *Statement of Financial Accounting Standards Number 52.* The major provisions of this standard are

■ Current assets, unless covered by forward exchange contracts, and fixed assets are translated into dollars at the rate of exchange prevailing on the date of the balance sheet.

■ Current and long-term liabilities payable in foreign currency are translated into dollars at the rate of exchange prevailing on the date of the balance sheet.

- Income statement items are translated either at the rate on the date of a particular transaction or at a weighted average of the exchange rates for the period of the income statement.
- Dividends are translated at the exchange rate on the date the dividend is paid.
- Equity accounts, including common stock and contributed capital in excess of par value, are translated at historical rates.
- Gains and losses to the parent from translation are not included in the parent's calculation of net income, nor are they included in the parent's retained earnings. Rather they are reported in a separate equity account named "Cumulative foreign currency translation adjustments" or a similar title. Gains or losses in this account are not recognized in the income statement until the parent's investment in the foreign subsidiary is sold or liquidated.

A decline in the value of a foreign currency relative to the U.S. dollar reduces the conversion value of the foreign subsidiary's liabilities, as well as its assets. Therefore, the parent company's risk exposure depends on the foreign subsidiary's net equity position (that is, assets minus liabilities). Thus, on the books of the parent company, the subsidiary's creditors in effect bear part of the decline in the value of the subsidiary's assets.

The impact of a decrease in the exchange rate on the firm's balance sheet can be illustrated with the following example. American Products has a subsidiary, Canadian Products, with total assets of $12 million (Canadian) and total liabilities of $8 million (Canadian). Based on an exchange rate of $0.80 (U.S.) per dollar (Canadian), the net equity position of the Canadian subsidiary on American Products' balance sheet as shown in Table 21-2 is $3.2 million (U.S.). Suppose now that the exchange rate declines to $0.75 (U.S.) per dollar (Canadian) and all other things remain the same. As can be seen in the table, the net equity position of the Canadian subsidiary on American Products' balance sheet declines to $3 million (U.S.), resulting in a $200,000 currency exchange loss.

Managing Translation Exposure. In general, when a foreign subsidiary's assets are greater than its liabilities, currency exchange losses will occur when the exchange rate decreases. The opposite effects are true for increases in the exchange rate. A company can hedge and manage its balance sheet translation exposure by financing its foreign assets with debt denominated in the same currency.

For example, in March 1985, Hercules Inc., a Wilmington, Delaware–based chemicals and plastics manufacturer, issued 10.125 percent 7-year notes. Instead

TABLE 21-2
Effect of a Decrease in the Exchange Rate on American Products' Balance Sheet

	EXCHANGE RATE			
	$0.80 (U.S.) = $1.00 (Canadian)		$0.75 (U.S.) = $1.00 (Canadian)	
	$(Canadian)	$(U.S.)	$(Canadian)	$(U.S.)
Assets	$12,000,000	$9,600,000	$12,000,000	$9,000,000
Liabilities	8,000,000	6,400,000	8,000,000	6,000,000
Net equity position	$ 4,000,000	$3,200,000	$ 4,000,000	$3,000,000

of being denominated in U.S. dollars, as is usual for securities of U.S. companies, these notes are denominated in European Currency Units (ECU). The ECU is a composite currency whose value is based on the weighted value of ten European currencies. The Hercules debt issue totaled ECU 50 million, or about $33 million, based on the exchange rate between the U.S. dollar and the ECU at the time of issuance.

The Hercules financial managers apparently had a choice between whether to issue ECU-denominated or U.S. dollar-denominated debt. They chose the ECU-denominated debt in order to hedge the company's European assets. For example, if the value of the ECU drops compared to the U.S. dollar value, presumably the U.S. dollar value of Hercules's European assets also decreases. However, if this happens the U.S. dollar amount of both the interest and principal that Hercules has to pay decreases. The Hercules management stated that although the weight of the various currencies in the ECU did not exactly match the relationship of Hercules's European assets, the ECU-denominated debt issue did make a reasonably good hedge overall.

A multinational company can also minimize its exchange rate risk, as well as the risk of expropriation or nationalization of its assets by a foreign government, by developing a *portfolio* of foreign investments. Rather than making all its direct investments in foreign subsidiaries that are located in one particular country, the firm can spread its foreign investments among a number of different countries, thus limiting the risk of incurring large losses within any one country.

ETHICAL ISSUES
PAYMENT OF BRIBES ABROAD[6]

Managers of multinational firms often must deal with the problem of making bribes or "grease" payments abroad in order to facilitate a transaction. Customs with respect to the acceptability and need for such payments vary greatly in different countries. The issue of questionable payments is especially important to managers of U.S. firms because of the Foreign Corrupt Practices Act (FCPA) as amended in the Omnibus Trade and Competitiveness Act of 1988. The provisions of this act declare payments in the form of phony discounts, fake invoices, and inflated expense accounts illegal.

A study of 400 firms by the Securities and Exchange Commission (SEC) in the mid-1970s revealed that these firms had made over $300 million in questionable payments to officials of foreign governments, politicians, agents, and others to secure business abroad. Exxon, for example, disclosed that it had made nearly $60 million in such payments. These payments have been most common in capital-intensive industries such as aerospace, construction, and energy, which deal with large projects or contracts.

In spite of the FCPA, U.S.-based firms have continued to make grease payments abroad. Many times these payments have been cleverly disguised. For example, in April 1980, Ashland Oil paid about $29 million to acquire a mining operation in Zimbabwe that had been controlled by an official of the

---

[6]This ethical issue is based largely on Charles R. Kennedy, Jr., *Managing the International Business Environment: Cases in Political and Country Risk* (Englewood Cliffs, NJ: Prentice-Hall, 1991).

Omani government. The mining operation proved to be unprofitable and was written off its books by Ashland two years later. In September 1980, the Omani government awarded Ashland a 20,000 barrel-per-day crude oil contract at a price $3 below the regular selling price for crude oil. In 1986 the SEC brought an action against Ashland and its former chairman, charging violations of the FCPA. Ashland agreed to an SEC consent injunction barring these types of corrupt practices.

Both ethical standards and U.S. law prohibit the payment of bribes to obtain business abroad. However, in many countries the receipt of bribes is not only permitted, it is expected. How can managers reconcile this conflict between domestic ethical standards and traditional foreign business practice?

■ SUMMARY

- The theory of *interest rate parity* states that the percentage differential between the spot and the forward rate for a currency quoted in terms of another currency is equal to the approximate difference in interest rates in the two countries over the same time horizon.
- The theory of *relative purchasing power parity* states that in comparison to a period when exchange rates between two countries are in equilibrium, changes in differential rates of inflation between two countries will be offset by equal, but opposite changes in the future spot currency rate.
- The forward rate is often taken as an *unbiased estimator* of the future spot currency rate.
- The nominal rate of interest is approximately equal to the sum of the real rate of interest and the expected inflation rate. This relationship is known as the *Fisher effect.*
- The *international Fisher effect* theory states that differences in interest rates between two countries will be offset by equal, but opposite changes in the future spot rate.
- Forecasts of future spot exchange rates can be derived from forward rates, if available, or from observed interest rates between two countries in conjunction with the international Fisher effect theory.
- Firms that compete in a global economy face three categories of foreign exchange risk:
  1. Transaction or short-term exposure.
  2. Economic (operating) or long-term exposure.
  3. Translation (accounting) exposure.
- Many risk-reducing strategies are available to firms facing these risks, including the use of various hedges, such as a forward hedge and a money market hedge.

■ QUESTIONS AND TOPICS FOR DISCUSSION

1. What is the theory of interest rate parity?
2. What is covered interest arbitrage?
3. Describe two techniques that a company can use to hedge against transaction exchange risk.
4. Describe the factors that cause exchange rates to change over time.

5. What are the advantages to a U.S. firm of financing its foreign investments with funds raised abroad?

6. Describe how the concepts of relative purchasing power parity, interest rate parity, and international Fisher effect are related.

■ SELF-TEST PROBLEMS

ST1. Assume that the annualized discount on forward Canadian dollars is 3 percent. The annualized U.S. interest rate is 8 percent, and the comparable Canadian interest rate is 12 percent. How can a U.S. trader use covered interest arbitrage to take advantage of this situation?

ST2. Chrysler is planning to sell its new minivan in Japan. Chrysler receives $12,000 for each van sold in the United States and wants to get the same net proceeds from its export sales.

    a. If the exchange rate of Japanese yen for U.S. dollars is ¥140 = $1, what price must Chrysler charge in Japan (in yen)?

    b. What price will Chrysler have to charge in Japan if the value of the dollar falls to 120 yen?

ST3. The annualized yield on three-year maturity U.S. government bonds is 4 percent, while the yield on similar maturity Italian bonds is 9 percent. The current spot exchange rate between the dollar and the lira is $0.000592/lira. What is the expected future spot rate for the lira in three years?

■ PROBLEMS*

1. If the 1-year U.S. Treasury bill rate is 7.0 percent, the spot rate between U.S. dollars and British pounds is £1 = $1.69, and the 90-day forward rate is £1 = $1.68, what rate of interest is expected on British Treasury bills, assuming interest rate parity between the dollar and pound exists?

2. Suppose the British short-term interest rates are 13 percent and the corresponding U.S. rate is 8 percent. Suppose at the same time that the discount on forward pounds is 3 percent per year. Do these conditions present an opportunity for covered interest arbitrage? If so, what steps should a trader in New York take? What annual rate will the trader earn?

3. Mammouth Mutual Fund of New York has $5 million to invest in certificates of deposit (CDs) for the next six months (180 days). It can buy either a Philadelphia National Bank (PNB) CD with an annual yield of 10 percent or a Cologne (Germany) Bank CD with a yield of 12.5 percent. Assume that the CDs are of comparable default risk. The analysts of the mutual fund are concerned about exchange rate risk. They were quoted the following exchange rates by the international department of a New York City bank:

Germany (Deutsche mark)

Spot	$0.4200
30-day forward	0.4190
90-day forward	0.4170
180-day forward	0.4155

    a. If the Cologne Bank CD is purchased and held to maturity, determine the net gain (loss) in U.S. dollars relative to the PNB CD, assuming that the exchange rate in 180 days equals today's spot rate.

    b. Suppose the German mark declines in value by 5 percent relative to the U.S. dollar over the next 180 days. Determine the net gain (loss) of the Cologne Bank CD in U.S. dollars relative to the PNB CD for an uncovered position.

*Colored numbers denote problems that have check answers at the end of the book.

c. Determine the net gain (loss) from a covered position.

d. What other factor or factors should be considered in the decision to purchase the Cologne Bank CD?

4. Last year, the French marketing subsidiary of International Pharmaceuticals Corporation (IPC), a New Jersey–based drug manufacturer, earned 700,000 French francs. This year, partly due to a weaker U.S. dollar, the French subsidiary will earn 900,000 French francs. Last year, the exchange rate was 10 francs per dollar, and this year, it is 7 francs per dollar. Calculate how many U.S. dollars the French subsidiary contributes to IPC's earnings in each year.

5. As of today, the following information is available:

	United States	France
Real rate of interest required by investors	2.0%	2.0%
Nominal interest rate	11.0	15.0
Spot rate	$0.20/FF	
One-year forward rate	$0.19/FF	
Call option premium at a strike price of $0.20	2%	

Using this information, make three *independent* forecasts of the one-year future spot rate for FF. (Use exact, not approximation, relationships.)

6. Shoesmith Wave, Inc., a new and largely unproven economic forecasting service, expects the inflation rate in Italy to average 9 percent per year over the next five years. In comparison, Shoesmith expects a U.S. inflation rate over this same period to be 3 percent per year. The yield on five-year U.S. government bonds is 6 percent per year. The yield on five-year Italian government bonds is 11 percent per year. One percentage point of this yield differential can be accounted for by political risk differences between the United States and Italy, with the United States perceived as having the lower political risk. The current exchange rate is 1220 lira per dollar.

Forecast the future five-year spot rate for the lira (versus the dollar) using the Shoesmith Wave forecast and the forecast from the financial markets.

7. The Jennette Corporation, a firm based in Mt. Pleasant, South Carolina, has an account payable with a British firm coming due in 180 days. The payable requires Jennette to pay £200,000. Winthrop Jennette, the firm's founder and CEO, is an astute manager. He has asked his CFO, Artis Montgomery, to advise him on the various options for dealing with the exchange risk inherent in this payable. He wishes to know the expected dollar cost of (1) a forward hedge, (2) a money market hedge, and (3) remaining unhedged.

The following information is available to Artis. The spot rate of the pound today is $1.50. The current 180-day forward rate of the pound is $1.47. Interest rates are as follows:

	United Kingdom	United States
180-day deposit rate	4.5%	4.5%
180-day borrowing rate	5.0%	5.0%

a. What is the expected dollar cost of the forward hedge?

b. What is the expected dollar cost of the money market hedge?

c. What is the expected dollar cost of remaining unhedged?

d. Which alternative do you recommend? What are the risks associated with this recommendation?

8. On January 1, the cost of borrowing French francs for one year was 18 percent. During the year the U.S. inflation rate was 2 percent and the French inflation rate was 9 percent. The exchange rate on January 1 was FF7/$. On December 31 the exchange rate was FF8/$. If you borrowed FF100,000 on January 1, converted this to dollars and used these funds for one year, and then paid off the FF loan on December 31, what was the *real* cost of borrowing FF for one year?

9. The Vaderson Forecasting Associates sells a broad range of economic forecasting services to businesses and government agencies. One of its primary products is the Vaderson Exchange Rate Seer, a model that forecasts future spot exchange rates.

   Finley, Incorporated, a maker and exporter of Fightin Blue Hen paraphernalia, has just received a large order from Kruse, AG, a large German retailing chain. Delivery of the merchandise would occur in two years and Finley wishes to determine the price in Deutschmarks (DM) to charge for the order. If the items were being sold for delivery today, Finley would want to receive $1.4 million, an amount that would recover all variable costs and make an acceptable contribution to overhead and profit. The current exchange rate between the $ and the DM is $0.66/DM. Finley expects that its (dollar) costs will rise at about 3 percent per year over the coming two years and would like to recover these cost increases in proportional increases in the contract price. The annual yield on two-year Treasury bonds is 5.5 percent in the United States. Similar risk bonds sell to yield 4.5 percent annually in Germany. Vaderson forecasts that the spot rate of exchange between the $ and the DM will be $0.64/DM.

   If you had to make a recommendation regarding the pricing of this order, what is the *best* estimate of the price (in DM) you can recommend that management charge if it wants to just cover its costs and profit objectives?

10. The German mark (DM) is currently trading in the spot market at $0.5800/DM. The 180-day forward rate is $0.5743/DM. The U.S. Treasury Bill rate for 180 days is 3.1 percent in the United States. What do you expect is the 180-day German government security rate? Why?

11. Using the currency calculator at the following Web site, calculate the foreign currency equivalent of $100 (U.S.) in terms of British pounds, French francs, German marks, and Japanese yen. Print out the computer screen with the conversions and turn in your answers to your instructor.
    www.moneyadvisor.com

■ SOLUTIONS TO SELF-TEST PROBLEMS

ST1. A U.S. trader could sell U.S. dollars, buy spot Canadian dollars, and invest in Canadian securities to earn 12 percent. Simultaneously, the trader could sell Canadian dollars forward at a 3 percent annual discount. At the end of the forward period, the trader could convert Canadian dollars back to U.S. dollars. The net effect of these transactions is the trader earns 9 percent (12 percent interest less 3 percent depreciation in value) compared with the 8 percent return available in the U.S. market.

ST2. **a.** Yen price = 140 yen/dollar × $12,000 = 1,680,000 yen.
   b. Yen price = 120 yen/dollar × $12,000 = 1,440,000 yen.
   A decline in the value of the dollar relative to the yen makes U.S. goods more attractive abroad.

ST3.
$$\frac{S_n}{S_0} = \frac{(1 + i_h)^n}{(1 + i_f)^n}$$

$$\frac{S_3}{\$.000592/lira} = \frac{(1 + .04)^3}{(1 + .09)^3}$$

$$S_3 = \$0.000514/lira$$

The higher Italian interest rate relative to the U.S. rate implies (using IFE) that the lira should decline in value relative to the dollar, as this computation verifies.

■ GLOSSARY

Covered Interest Arbitrage A risk-free transaction in which short-term funds are moved between two currencies to take advantage of interest rate differentials. Exchange rate risk is eliminated through the use of forward contracts.

Economic Exposure The extent to which changes in *real* exchange rates lead to a change in the value of a firm's operating cash flows, and hence its value. Also known as operating exposure.

Hedge A transaction in which a position is taken in another market, such as the forward or futures market, to offset the risk associated with a position in the current cash (spot) market.

Interest Rate Parity The theory that the percentage differential between the spot and the forward rate for a currency quoted in terms of another currency is equal to the approximate difference in interest rates in the two countries over the same time horizon.

Relative Purchasing Power Parity The theory that the spot exchange rate between two currencies should change by an amount approximately equal to the difference in expected inflation rates in the two countries.

Transaction Exposure The potential for a change in the value of a foreign-currency denominated transaction due to a change in the exchange rate after the transaction is entered into but before it is settled.

Translation Exposure The change in owners' (accounting) equity because of a change in exchange rates that affects the "converted" value of foreign assets and liabilities.

CORPORATE RESTRUCTURING

22

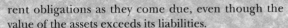
1. Reasons a company may choose external growth by merger over internal growth can include the following:
   a. The availability of lower-cost assets.
   b. Greater economies of scale.
   c. The availability of more secure raw material supplies and additional end-product markets.
   d. The possibility of more rapid growth.
   e. Greater diversification.
   f. Tax considerations.

2. The valuation of merger candidates involves application of capital budgeting principles. A merger is an acceptable project if the present value of its expected free cash inflows exceeds the acquisition cost.

3. The acquisition of a company with a higher P/E ratio causes the earnings per share figure of the acquiring company to decrease if the exchange ratio is based on current stock market prices and no synergy exists. Similarly, the acquisition of a company with a lower P/E ratio causes the earnings per share figure of the acquiring company to increase.

4. In the pooling of interests method of accounting for mergers, the acquired assets are recorded at their original cost. In the purchase method, acquired assets are recorded at their fair market values, and any additional amount paid is listed as goodwill, which then must be amortized.

5. In a financial context, a firm is
   a. *Technically insolvent* when it is unable to meet its current obligations as they come due, even though the value of the assets exceeds its liabilities.
   b. *Legally insolvent* if the recorded value of its assets is less than the recorded value of its liabilities.
   c. *Bankrupt* if it is unable to pay its debts and it files a bankruptcy petition in accordance with the federal bankruptcy laws.

6. The primary causes of business failures are economic factors and lack of experience on the part of the owners of the business.

7. A failing company can either
   a. Attempt to resolve its difficulties with its creditors on a voluntary, or informal, basis; or
   b. Petition the courts for assistance and formally declare bankruptcy.

8. In a bankruptcy proceeding, if the going-concern value of the firm is greater than its liquidation value, it is reorganized; otherwise, it is liquidated.
   a. A reorganization plan is carried out under Chapter 11 of the Bankruptcy Reform Act.
   b. A liquidation is carried out under Chapter 7 of the Bankruptcy Reform Act.

9. Other important topics include
   a. Leveraged buyouts.
   b. Divestitures and restructuring.
   c. Antitakeover measures.

THE SNAPPLE DEBACLE AT QUAKER OATS*

Quaker Oats purchased the Snapple Beverage Company for $1.7 billion in November 1994. At the time of the acquisition, many financial analysts felt that the price was much too high for the beverage company. Combined with its Gatorade sports drink business, the acquisition made Quaker the third largest beverage company in the United States after Coca-Cola and Pepsi. However, the acquisition failed to meet Quaker's expectations and, less than 2½ years later in April 1997, the company agreed to sell Snapple for $300 million to Triarc Company—owner of RC Cola and Mistie beverages and Arby's restaurants. In addition to the pretax loss of $1.4 billion, Quaker also incurred over $100 million in operating losses and charges related to Snapple.

The acquisition and subsequent sale of Snapple damaged Quaker's balance sheet, lowered its credit rating, and raised its cost of capital. Also, over the 2½ years that Quaker Oats owned Snapple, Quaker's stock price remained virtually unchanged, while the stock market rose approximately 70 percent during this period.

A number of possible factors may have contributed to the failure of the Snapple acquisition to meet Quaker's expectations. A few of them are examined below.

Demand forecasts. The rate of growth of industry sales of so-called "New Age" drinks (i.e., uncarbonated beverages

such as water, juices, and teas) had peaked and begun to decline around the time of the Snapple acquisition. Overly optimistic forecasts of the growth in future demand may have led Quaker to misjudge the future profits from Snapple.

Synergies. Quaker may have overestimated the benefits, or *synergies*, of combining Snapple with its existing bev-

erage business. The attempt to generate significant cost savings from integrating the Snapple distribution network into the existing Gatorade distribution network was unsuccessful.

Increased competition. Rather than concede the iced tea market to competitors, such as Snapple, Coca-Cola and Pepsi began to aggressively market similar drinks under the Lipton and Nestea labels. As a result of these actions, the market share of Snapple's line of iced teas fell to 13 percent, compared with Lipton's 33 percent share and Nestea's 18 percent share. Coca-Cola also introduced a line of fruit-flavored drinks under the Fruitopia brand to compete with similar beverages offered by Snapple.

In summary, this example illustrates some of the factors that may cause the potential benefits of an acquisition to fall short of expectations. Techniques that can be used in the valuation of merger candidates are examined in this chapter.

*Based on Michael J. McCarthy, Richard Gibson, and Nikhil Deagon, "Quaker to Sell Snapple for $300 Million," *Wall Street Journal* (March 28, 1997): A3; and Greg Burns, "What Price the Snapple Debacle," *Business Week* (April 14, 1997): 42.

INTRODUCTION

Corporate restructuring encompasses a broad array of activities that include changes in the ownership, asset structure, and/or capital structure of a company. The goal of any corporate restructuring should be to maximize shareholder wealth. Some aspects of corporate restructuring have already been examined, such as share repurchases discussed in Chapter 7. This chapter focuses on a number of other forms of corporate restructuring, including external expansion (mergers) and business failure (bankruptcy). The next three sections examine mergers, and the final two sections discuss bankruptcy.

MERGERS

Businesses grow *externally* by acquiring, or combining with, other ongoing businesses; this is in contrast to *internal* growth, which is achieved by purchasing individual assets, such as those evaluated in the discussion of capital expenditures in Chapters 8 through 10. When two companies combine, generally the acquiring company pays for the acquired business either with cash or with its own securities, and the acquired company's liabilities and assets are transferred to the acquiring company.

Mergers Defined

A **merger** technically is a combination of two or more companies in which all but one of the combining companies legally cease to exist and the surviving company continues in operation under its original name. A **consolidation** is a combination in which all of the combining companies are dissolved and a new firm is formed. The term *merger* is generally used to describe both of these types of business combinations. *Acquisition* is also used interchangeably with *merger* to describe a business combination. In the following discussion, the term *merger* is used, and it is assumed that only two companies are involved—the acquiring company and the merger candidate.[1]

Merger Statistics

Merger activity expanded greatly during the late 1980s, reaching a high in 1989. In that year there were more than 3,800 merger transactions valued at $5 million or more involving U.S. corporations, with the aggregate value of these transactions being over $311 billion.[2] During the recession of the early 1990s, the aggregate value of mergers declined to a low of $125 billion in 1992. More recently, merger activity has been increasing—reaching a record of over 5,800 transactions and an aggregate value of about $388 billion in 1995. Approximately one-fourth of these transactions were international in scope—that is, involving both U.S. and foreign companies. Table 22-1 contains a listing of the largest mergers involving U.S. companies. Five of the acquisitions involved the purchase of U.S. companies by foreign companies, namely, Beecham Group, British Petroleum, Campeau, Matsushita Electric, and Hoechst.

---

[1]In some instances, merger candidates may be referred to as *takeover candidates, to-be-acquired companies, acquired companies,* or *target companies.*
[2]*Mergers and Acquisitions* (March–April, 1996): 37.

TABLE 22-1
**Largest Mergers and Acquisitions
Involving U.S. Companies***

Sources: *Mergers and Acquisitions*, various issues.

PURCHASER	COMPANY ACQUIRED	PURCHASE PRICE (IN BILLIONS OF DOLLARS)	YEAR
Kohlberg Kravis Roberts (LBO)**	RJR Nabisco	$24.7	1989
AT&T	McCaw Cellular	18.9	1994
Walt Disney	Capital Cities/ABC	18.9	1996
AirTouch Communications	U.S. West (cellular)	13.5	1995
Chevron	Gulf Oil	13.3	1984
Bell Atlantic (cellular)	NYNEX (cellular)	13.0	1995
Philip Morris	Kraft	12.6	1988
Time, Inc.	Warner Communications	12.6	1990
Bristol-Myers	Squibb	12.5	1989
Texaco	Getty Oil	10.1	1984
Lockheed	Martin Marietta	10.0	1995
Viacom	Paramount	9.6	1994
American Home Products	American Cyanamid	9.6	1994
Lockheed Martin	Loral	8.8	1995
Beecham Group	SmithKline Beckman	8.3	1989
Viacom	Blockbuster Entertainment	8.0	1994
Dupont	Conoco	6.9	1981
British Petroleum	Standard Oil Ohio (remaining 45% interest)	7.6	1987
AT&T	NCR	7.5	1991
Dow Chemical	Marion Laboratories (67%)	7.1	1989
Hoechst, AG	Marion Merrill Dow	7.1	1995
Matsushita Electric	MCA, Inc.	6.9	1991
Upjohn	Pharmacia, AB	6.9	1995
GTE	Contel	6.8	1991
Kimberly-Clark	Scott Paper	6.8	1995
Campeau**	Federated Department Stores	6.5	1988

*Excludes companies whose primary businesses are banking, insurance, brokerage, or similar financial services.
**LBO = leveraged buyout

Types of Mergers

Mergers are generally classified according to whether they are *horizontal, vertical,* or *conglomerate*. A **horizontal merger** is a combination of two or more companies that compete directly with one another: for example, the acquisition of American Hospital Supply by Baxter Travenol Laboratories, both large health care products companies, was a horizontal merger. The U.S. government has vigorously enforced antitrust legislation in an attempt to stop large horizontal combinations, and this effort has been effective. However, horizontal combinations in which one of the firms is failing are often viewed more favorably. Also, mergers that allow the companies to compete effectively in world markets are viewed more favorably—the acquisition of RCA by General Electric for $6 billion was an example of this type of horizontal merger.

A **vertical merger** is a combination of companies that may have a buyer-seller relationship with one another. For example, if Sears were to acquire one of its appliance suppliers, this would constitute a vertical merger. This type of business combination has gradually declined in importance in recent years.

A **conglomerate merger** is a combination of two or more companies in which neither competes directly with the other and no buyer-seller relationship exists.

For example, the Philip Morris acquisition of General Foods in 1985 for $5.6 billion in cash was a conglomerate merger.

Form of Merger Transactions

A merger transaction may be a stock purchase or an asset purchase. In a *stock purchase,* the acquiring company buys the stock of the to-be-acquired company and assumes its liabilities. In an *asset purchase,* the acquiring company buys only the assets (some or all) of the to-be-acquired company and does not assume any of its liabilities.

Normally, the buyer of a business prefers an asset purchase rather than a stock purchase, because unknown liabilities, such as any future lawsuits against the company, are not incurred. In addition, an asset purchase frequently allows the acquiring company to depreciate its new assets from a higher basis than is possible in a stock purchase. As a result of the unknown liability question, many large companies that acquire small companies refuse to negotiate on any terms other than an asset purchase.

Holding Companies

One form of business combination is the **holding company,** in which the acquiring company simply purchases all or a controlling block of another company's common shares. The two companies then become *affiliated,* and the acquiring company becomes the holding company in this *parent-subsidiary* relationship. For example, General Foods USA and Kraft USA are subsidiaries of Philip Morris.

Joint Ventures

Another form of business combination is a **joint venture,** in which two (unaffiliated) companies contribute financial and/or physical assets, as well as personnel, to a new company formed to engage in some economic activity, such as the production or marketing of a product. The Dow Corning Company is an example of a joint venture established by Dow Chemical and Corning in 1943. Dow Chemical and Corning each have a 50 percent interest in the company. Joint ventures are often international in scope, such as the agreement among IBM (United States), Toshiba (Japan), and Siemens (Germany) to form a company to develop and produce computer memory chips.

Leveraged Buyouts

One frequently used method to buy a company or a division of a large company is a **leveraged buyout,** or LBO. In a typical LBO, the buyer borrows a large amount of the purchase price, using the purchased assets as collateral for a large portion of the borrowings. The buyers frequently are the managers of the division or company being sold. It is anticipated that the earnings (and cash flows) of the new company will be sufficient to service the debt and permit the new owners to earn a reasonable return on their investment. In some cases, sales of assets are used to help pay off the debt. The LBO of a publicly held company is sometimes referred to as *going private,* because the entire equity in the company is purchased by a small group of investors and is no longer publicly traded.

The majority of LBOs involve relatively small companies. However, a number of LBOs involving large companies have occurred. For example, in the largest merger or acquisition ever undertaken up to that time, the investment firm of Kohlberg Kravis Roberts used an LBO to purchase RJR Nabisco for $24.7 billion in 1989. However, by the early 1990s, the number of LBO transactions had declined sharply, partly because many existing LBOs were experiencing difficulties servicing their large debt loads.

In addition to LBOs undertaken by investment bankers and managers, workers sometimes take over their division or company through an Employee Stock Ownership Plan (ESOP). Significant tax advantages make ESOPs a useful instrument for financing LBOs. In an ESOP transaction, lenders can offer below-market interest rates because 50 percent of the interest income they receive from these loans is excluded from taxable income; this often allows employees to pay more than other bidders that do not qualify for these tax breaks. In the past, ESOPs were used to buy either larger companies faced with financial difficulties or smaller companies. However, ESOPs have also been used to finance (either in whole or in part) large, healthy companies, such as Avis and J.C. Penney.

Divestitures and Restructurings

Divestitures and *restructurings* can be an important part of a company's merger and acquisition strategy. After an acquiring company completes an acquisition, it frequently examines the various assets and divisions of the recently acquired company to determine whether all the acquired company's pieces "fit" into the acquiring company's future plans. If not, the acquiring company may sell off, or *divest,* a portion of the acquired company. In so doing, the acquiring company is said to be *restructuring* itself.

Divestitures and restructurings, however, frequently are not associated directly with a company's acquisitions. A company may divest itself of certain assets because of a change in overall corporate strategy. For example, Warner-Lambert, a drug and consumer products manufacturer, decided to get out of the hospital supply business. The company used the proceeds from the sale of its hospital supply assets to buy back some of its stock. As a result, Warner-Lambert changed, or restructured, the asset side of its balance sheet; this is called an *operational restructuring*. In addition, the company changed its capital structure and thereby carried out a *financial restructuring*.

Instead of selling a part of the company for cash, divestures can be accomplished through a *spinoff* or an *equity carve-out*. In a spinoff, common stock in a division or subsidiary is distributed to shareholders of the parent company on a pro rata basis. The subsidiary or division becomes a separate company. Owners of the parent company who receive common stock in the new company can keep the shares or sell them to other investors. An example of such a divestiture was the recent breakup of AT&T, where AT&T shareholders received stock in two new companies—Lucent Technologies (network equipment) and NCR (global information systems). Another example, discussed in the Financial Challenge of Chapter 6, was the breakup of Marriott into two companies—an operating unit, Marriott International, and a real estate unit, Host Marriott. In an equity carve-out, or partial public offering, common stock in the subsidiary or division is sold directly to the public, with the parent company usually retaining a controlling interest in the shares outstanding. For example, Sears sold a 20 percent stake in its Allstate insurance subsidiary through an initial public offering, while retaining an 80 percent interest in the unit.

Spinoffs and equity carve-outs can be used by large, diversified companies to remove either an underperforming unit (e.g., Marriott's real estate operations) that is hurting the overall firm or a healthy subsidiary (e.g., Sears' Allstate insurance unit) that is buried among underperforming units. In the 1990s, spinoffs may achieve the same results that leveraged buyouts did in the 1980s, namely, more focused and efficient companies.

Tender Offers

Although many mergers are the result of a friendly agreement between the two companies, a company may wish to acquire another company even when the combination is opposed by the management or board of directors of the merger candidate company. In such a case, the acquiring company makes a *tender offer* for common shares of the merger candidate. In a **tender offer,** the acquiring company effectively announces that it will pay a certain price above the then-existing market price for any of the merger candidate's shares that are "tendered" (that is, offered to it) before a particular date.

Rationale for Restructuring

A number of reasons have been suggested for the increased corporate restructuring activity during the 1980s and 1990s. According to Jensen, the most important reason was the failure of internal control mechanisms to prevent unproductive capital investment (that is, overinvestment) and organizational inefficiencies (overstaffing) by many large U.S. corporations.[3] He claims that this control system—the internal management supervised by a board of directors—breaks down in mature companies with large cash flows and few good investment opportunities. Firms in the oil, tobacco, food processing, and retailing industries have been notable in this regard. These inefficiencies allow acquirers to pay a large premium over the pretakeover market value of the company and earn high returns on their investment by using the acquired company's resources more efficiently.

A second reason cited is the emergence of investors, such as Kohlberg, Kravis Roberts & Company, Warren Buffett, and the Bass brothers, who hold large equity (and/or debt) positions in the companies. Unlike more passive institutional investors, such as pension funds, these investors take an active role in setting the strategic direction and monitoring the performance of the companies. Often these investors give managers significant equity positions in the companies as incentives to operate efficiently and increase shareholder value. Also, in the case of highly leveraged transactions, such as LBOs, large debt service payments put pressure on managers to reduce costs and make better capital investment decisions.

A third reason for the corporate restructuring boom of the 1980s was the ready availability of credit to finance these transactions. Junk bond financing, underwritten by Drexel Burnham Lambert and other investment banks, as well as financing provided by commercial banks, insurance companies, and pension funds, provided debt capital that permitted acquirers to leverage their purchases.

---

[3]Michael C. Jensen, "Corporate Control and the Politics of Finance," *Journal of Applied Corporate Finance* (Summer 1991): 13–33.

Finally, the inflationary environment and long economic expansion of the 1980s increased the revenues and asset values of the acquired companies. This allowed acquirers to sell off unwanted corporate assets and to meet their debt obligations.

Antitakeover Measures

In response to the merger and acquisitions boom of the late 1980s, many companies adopted various measures designed to discourage unfriendly takeover attempts. These antitakeover measures, sometimes referred to as *shark repellants,* include

1. *Staggered board.* Stagger the terms of the board of directors over several years instead of having the entire board come up for election at one time. Thus, the acquiring firm will have difficulty electing its own board of directors to gain control.
2. *Golden parachute contracts.* Give key executives employment contracts under which the executives will receive large benefits if they are terminated without sufficient cause after a merger. Corporate takeovers often raise serious agency problems between stockholders and managers. A takeover at a large premium over the current market price of the firm's stock is beneficial to stockholders. At the same time, the offer may be detrimental to managers because they may lose their jobs if the takeover is successful and the new owners replace them. Golden parachute contracts are used to encourage management to act in the interests of stockholders in any takeover attempt.
3. *Supermajority voting rules.* Insert in the corporate charter voting rules that require a supermajority of shares (e.g., 80 percent) to approve any takeover proposals.
4. Use *poison pills*—Issue securities that become valuable only when an unfriendly bidder obtains control of a certain percentage of a company's shares. One example is a bond that contains a put option (called a "poison put") that can be exercised only if an unfriendly takeover occurs. The issuing company hopes that the cashing in by bondholders of a portion of its debt will make the takeover unattractive.

Once an unfriendly takeover attempt has been initiated, the target company's management has various other antitakeover measures that it can employ to deter a takeover, including

1. *White knight.* The target company's management can try to find another, more friendly acquiring company that is willing to enter into a bidding war with the company making the first offer.
2. *Standstill agreement.* The target company's management can attempt to negotiate an agreement with the bidder, whereby the bidder agrees to limit its holdings in the target company.
3. *Pacman defense.* Named after the video game, the target company can make a takeover bid for the stock of the bidder.
4. *Litigation.* Legal action (i.e., suits and appeals in state and federal courts) can be used to delay a takeover attempt.
5. *Asset and/or liability restructuring.* A target company can sell assets that the bidder wants to another company, or it can issue larger amounts of debt

and use the proceeds to repurchase its common stock. These actions make the target company less desirable to the bidder.

6. *Greenmail.* The takeover candidate can attempt to buy back its shares, at a premium over the shares' market price, from the company or investor who initiated the unfriendly takeover attempt. The amount of the premium is referred to as "greenmail."

More recently, institutional investors, who often control a significant block of a company's stock, have become increasingly active participants in battles for control in many firms. Some institutional investors have used what is called "boardmail" to fight antitakeover devices, such as poison pills and staggered elections of board members. Boardmail consists of requiring the board of directors to adopt weaker antitakeover measures in exchange for voting support from the institutional owners. In some cases, institutions have been successful in placing sympathetic members on boards of companies in which the institution has a significant ownership interest. A number of companies, such as Abbott Labs and Westinghouse Electric, recently have dismantled some of the antitakeover defenses instituted during the 1980s.

Reasons for Mergers

The following are some of the reasons why a firm might consider acquiring another firm, rather than choosing to grow internally:

■ A firm may be able to acquire certain desirable assets at a lower cost by combining with another firm than it could if it purchased the assets directly. In this context, when the *market* value of a company's common stock is below its *book* value (or, more important, below the replacement value of the firm's net assets), this company frequently is considered a possible "takeover candidate."

■ A firm may be able to achieve greater economies of scale by merging with another firm; this is particularly true in the case of a horizontal merger. When the net income for the combined companies after merger exceeds the sum of the net incomes prior to the merger, *synergy* is said to exist. For example, in the merger proposed between Manufacturers Hanover and Chemical Bank in July 1991, the banks expected to be able to reduce their combined workforce by about 6,200 employees and eliminate other duplicated costs, resulting in savings of up to $650 million per year.

■ A firm that is concerned about its sources of raw materials or end-product markets might acquire other firms at different stages of its production or distribution processes. These are vertical mergers. For example, in 1984 Mobil Corporation, a major international oil company considered strong in refining and marketing but somewhat "crude poor," acquired Superior Oil Company, which owned large oil and gas reserves and had no refining and marketing operations. The acquisition resulted in Mobil becoming a better-balanced oil company.

■ A firm may wish to grow more rapidly than is possible through internal expansion. Acquiring another company may allow a growing firm to move more rapidly into a geographic or product area in which the acquired firm already has established markets, sales personnel, management capability, warehouse facilities, and so on, than would be possible by starting from scratch.

- A firm may desire to diversify its product lines and businesses in an attempt to reduce its business risk by smoothing out cyclical movements in its earnings. For example, a capital equipment manufacturer might achieve steadier earnings by expanding into the replacement parts business. During a recession, expenditures for capital equipment may slow down, but expenditures on maintenance and replacement parts may increase. This reason is of questionable benefit to the company's shareholders because most investors can diversify their holdings (through the securities markets) more easily and at a lower cost than the company can.

- A firm that has suffered losses and has a tax-loss carryforward may be a valuable merger candidate to a company that is generating taxable income. If the two companies merge, the losses may be deductible from the profitable company's taxable income and hence lower the combined company's income tax payments. This was a major factor in NCNB's acquisition of the failed First Republic Bank in Texas.

This list, although not exhaustive, does indicate the principal reasons why a firm may choose external expansion over internal growth.

If one firm wishes to acquire all or a portion of another firm, it is important to question whether the acquisition will be anything more than a zero net present value project in an efficient capital market. If it is, this excess value must result from the acquiring firm's access to superior managerial and labor talents at costs not fully reflective of their marginal value, access to raw material and other necessary inputs at lower costs, an ability to price the product in a more profitable way (perhaps because of an established brand name), operating synergies in the production and/or distribution areas, access to capital at a lower cost, generally more efficient operations due to lower agency costs in the acquiring firm compared to those in the acquired firm, or some other reason. Each of these possible reasons is suggestive of an inefficiency in a factor, product, or portion of the capital markets.

A number of empirical studies have examined the returns to the stockholders of the merger candidate and the acquiring company in a takeover.[4] Because the acquiring company must pay a premium over the current market price to obtain the merger candidate, one would expect to see positive returns to the acquired firm's shareholders. This is the case, with average returns of 20 percent or more in successful mergers.[5] For the acquiring company's shareholders, the returns are not as good—averaging 5 percent or less in successful mergers.[6]

Accounting Aspects of Mergers

Two basic methods can be used to account for mergers: the *purchase method* or the *pooling of interests method*. In the **purchase method,** the total value paid or exchanged for the acquired firm's assets is recorded on the acquiring company's books. The tangible assets acquired are recorded at their fair market values, which may or may not be more than the amount at which they were carried on the acquired firm's balance sheet prior to the merger.

---

[4]See J. Fred Weston, Kwang S. Chung and Susan E. Hoag, *Mergers, Restructuring, and Corporate Control* (Englewood Cliffs, NJ: Prentice-Hall, 1990), Chapter 10, for a summary of the empirical studies relating to the returns associated with corporate restructuring. See also Steven Kaplan, "The Effects of Management Buyouts on Operating Performance and Value," *Journal of Financial Economics* (October 1989): 217–254.

[5]*Mergers, Restructuring, and Corporate Control:* 257.

[6]*Mergers, Restructuring, and Corporate Control:* 259.

The excess of the total value paid over the fair market value of the acquired assets is an intangible asset termed **goodwill.**[7] The intangible asset of goodwill can be quite significant for many companies. For example, when Philip Morris purchased Kraft, Inc. in 1988 for $12.9 billion, the fair market value of Kraft's physical assets was about $1.3 billion—the difference of $11.6 billion, or 90 percent of the purchase price, represented the intangible asset of goodwill (i.e., Kraft brands and consumer loyalty).

In the **pooling of interests method,** the acquired company's assets are recorded on the acquiring company's books at their cost (net of depreciation) when originally acquired. Thus, any difference between the purchase price and the book value is not recorded on the acquiring company's books, and no goodwill account is created.

The pooling of interests method has certain advantages over the purchase method. All other things being equal, reported earnings will be higher under the pooling method, primarily because depreciation will not be more than the sum of the depreciation charges prior to the merger. In addition, because goodwill is not created on the balance sheet in a pooling, it cannot appear as an amortization charge on the acquiring firm's income statement.

For example, suppose that Company B acquires Company A's outstanding common stock for $10 million. The book value of the acquired shares is $7 million. Table 22-2 shows the results of this merger, according to both the purchase and pooling of interests methods.

In the pooling of interests method, the two balance sheets are combined, and the $3 million difference between the purchase price and the book value of Company A's stock is not considered. In the purchase method, in contrast, the $3 million difference between the purchase price and the book value is recorded on both sides of Company B's postmerger balance sheet as an increase in total assets and as stockholders' equity.

The book value of Company A's *assets* is $10 million. Suppose that the market value of Company A's assets at the date of acquisition is $11 million. Company B paid $3 million above the book value of *stockholders' equity.* Of this $3 million, the $1 million difference between the assets' market value and book value is recorded on the balance sheet in the appropriate tangible assets accounts. The other $2 million is recorded as goodwill.

The present accounting rules pertaining to mergers limit use of the pooling of interests method to mergers that essentially combine the entire existing interests of *common* stockholders in independent companies. Otherwise, the purchase method must be used. As a result, most mergers are accounted for using the purchase method.

Tax Aspects of Mergers

Taxes can play an important role in determining how an acquired company's shareholders receive compensation for their shares. Merger transactions that are effected through the use of voting equity securities (either common stock or *vot-*

---

[7]The expression *goodwill* rarely appears on the balance sheet; instead, we often find "investment in consolidated subsidiaries in excess of net assets at date of acquisition, less amortization." Under U.S. tax laws, amortization of goodwill acquired after August 10, 1993 and held in connection with a business or income-producing activity occurs over a 15-year period and is a tax-deductible expense in computing corporate income taxes.

TABLE 22-2
Comparison of the Purchase and
the Pooling of Interests Methods
of Accounting for Mergers*

	BEFORE ACQUISITION		COMPANY B (AFTER ACQUISITION OF COMPANY A)	
	Company A	*Company B*	*Purchase Method*	*Pooling of Interests Method*
Total assets, book value	$10	$50	$63	$60
Liabilities, book value	3	15	18	18
Stockholders' equity, book value	7	35	45	42

*Terms of merger: Company B acquires common stock of Company A for $10 million.

ing preferred stock) are tax-free. For example, if an acquired company's stockholders have a gain on the value of their shares at the time of the merger, the gain is not recognized for tax purposes if these shareholders receive voting equity securities of the acquiring company; any gains are not recognized until the newly acquired shares are sold.

In contrast, if the acquired company's shareholders receive cash or *nonvoting* securities (such as debt securities, *nonvoting* preferred stock, or warrants) in exchange for their shares, any gains are taxable at the time of the merger. When a partial cash down payment is made, however, the exchange can be treated as an installment purchase, and the seller can spread the tax liability that is created over the payment period.

 ## VALUATION OF MERGER CANDIDATES

In principle, the valuation of merger candidates is an application of the capital budgeting techniques described in Chapters 8 through 10. The purchase price of a proposed acquisition is compared to the present value of the expected future cash inflows from the merger candidate. If the present value of the cash inflows exceeds the purchase price, the merger project has a positive net present value and is acceptable.

In the case of an acquisition candidate whose common stock is actively traded, the market value of the stock is a key factor in the valuation process. To induce the stockholders of the acquisition candidate to give up their shares for the cash and/or securities of the acquiring firm, they have to be offered a premium over the market value of the stock prior to the merger announcement. Generally, a 10 to 20 percent premium is considered a minimum offer. Even then, in many situations, stockholders may hold out for much better offers—either from the company making the initial offer or from other interested companies.

Valuation Techniques

Three major methods are typically used to value merger candidates: the comparative price-earnings ratio method, the adjusted book value method, and the discounted cash flow method.

The *comparative price-earnings ratio method* examines the recent prices and price-earnings (P/E) ratios paid for other merger candidates that are comparable to the company being valued. For example, if two companies in a specific industry recently were acquired at P/E ratios of 10, the comparative P/E ratio method suggests that a P/E ratio of 10 may be reasonable for other, similar companies. Financial analysts who use this method should exercise caution and determine whether the companies being compared really are similar. This method, which focuses on the current income statement, may not be useful if the P/E ratios of recent, similar mergers vary widely.

The *adjusted book value method* involves determining the market value of the company's underlying assets. For example, suppose a company has equipment fully depreciated on its books but still in use. The market value of this equipment is determined, and the company's shareholders' equity (book value) is adjusted by the difference between the asset's book value and its market value. Financial analysts who use this method should exercise caution, because the determination of the market value of the merger candidate's assets may be difficult.

The *discounted cash flow method* for valuing merger candidates calculates the present value of the company's expected future *free cash flows* and compares this figure to the proposed purchase price to determine the proposed acquisition's net present value. The free cash flow (FCF) concept is particularly important in long-range corporate financial planning and when evaluating the acquisition of a firm or a portion of a firm. FCF recognizes that part of the funds generated by an ongoing enterprise must be set aside for reinvestment in the firm. Therefore, these funds are not available for distribution to the firm's owners.

Free cash flow can be computed as

$$FCF = CF - I(1 - T) - D_p - P_f - B - Y \tag{22.1}$$

where CF is the after-tax operating cash flow, I is the before-tax interest payments, D_p is the preferred stock dividend payments, P_f is the required redemption of preferred stock, B is the required redemption of debt, and Y is the investment in property, plant, and equipment required to maintain cash flows at their current levels. (If a firm has interest income, this is netted out against interest expense. If interest income exceeds interest expense, FCF will increase by the amount of the net after-tax interest income.) FCF represents the portion of a firm's total cash flow available to service additional debt, to make dividend payments to common stockholders, and to invest in other projects.

When valuing a takeover prospect, it is important to recognize that explicit cash outlays normally are required to sustain or increase the current cash flows of the firm. For example, in considering the acquisition of an oil production company, it is not correct to project current cash flows into an indefinite future without explicitly recognizing that crude oil reserves are a depleting resource that require continual, significant investment to assure future cash flow streams. Also, the free cash flows from a merger should include any effects of synergy because the marginal impact of the merger on the acquiring firm is of interest to us.

Consider the following example. Suppose the annual after-tax free cash flow from a merger candidate is calculated to be $2 million and is expected to continue for fifteen years, at which time the business can be sold for $10 million. If the appropriate risk-adjusted discount rate is 14 percent, for example, the present value of the expected cash inflows is as follows:

Present value of an annuity of $2 million for 15 years at 14%

+ Present value of $10 million in 15 years at 14%

$$= \$2,000,000 \, (\text{PVIFA}_{0.14,15}) + \$10,000,000 \, (\text{PVIF}_{0.14,15})$$

$$= \$2,000,000 \, (6.142) + \$10,000,000 \, (0.140)$$

$$= \$12,284,000 + \$1,400,000$$

$$= \$13,684,000$$

Therefore, if the merger candidate's purchase price is less than $13,684,000, the proposed merger has a positive net present value and is an acceptable "project."

In principle, the discounted cash flow method is the most correct of the three methods discussed in this section, because this method compares the present value of the cash flow benefits from the merger with the present value of the merger costs. However, in practice, the future cash inflows from a merger can be quite difficult to estimate.

Most financial analysts who work on proposed mergers use all of these methods to attempt to value merger candidates. In addition, they consider a large number of other factors in valuing merger candidates. These factors include the merger candidate's management, products, markets, distribution channels, production costs, expected growth rate, debt capacity, and reputation.

Analysis of a Merger

The following merger examples illustrate some of the steps and considerations involved in typical mergers. Diversified Industries, Inc. is considering acquiring either High-Tech Products, Inc. or Stable Products, Inc. High-Tech Products has a high expected growth rate and sells at a higher P/E ratio than Diversified. Stable Products, on the other hand, has a low expected growth rate and sells at a lower P/E ratio than Diversified. Table 22-3 contains financial statistics on Diversified and the two merger candidates.

The possible merger of Diversified with Stable Products is considered first. To entice Stable Products' present stockholders to tender their shares, Diversified probably would have to offer them a premium of at least 10 to 20 percent over Stable Products' present stock price. Suppose Diversified decides to offer a price of $24 per share and Stable Products accepts. The exchange is on a stock-for-stock basis. As a result, because Diversified's stock price is $30 a share, Stable Products' shareholders receive 0.8 shares of Diversified common stock for every share of Stable Products stock they hold; in other words, the *exchange ratio* is 0.8.

TABLE 22-3
Selected Financial Data:
Diversified Industries and Two Merger Candidates

	DIVERSIFIED INDUSTRIES	STABLE PRODUCTS	HIGH-TECH PRODUCTS
Sales	$1,200 million	$130 million	$100 million
Net earnings, E	$120 million	$12 million	$16 million
Number of shares outstanding, NS	40 million	4 million	4 million
Earnings per share, EPS	$3.00	$3.00	$4.00
Dividends per share, D_0	$1.65	$1.50	$0.80
Common stock market price	$30.00	$21.00	$52.00
Price-earnings (P/E) ratio	10.0	7.0	13.0
Expected annual growth rate, g	7%	5%	14%

TABLE 22-4
Diversified Industries: Pro Forma Financial Statement Summary Assuming Separate Mergers*

	BEFORE MERGER	AFTER MERGER WITH STABLE PRODUCTS	AFTER MERGER WITH HIGH-TECH PRODUCTS
Sales	$1,200 million	$1,330 million	$1,300 million
Net earnings	$120 million	$132 million	$136 million
Common shares outstanding	40 million	43.2 million	48 million
Earnings per share	$3.00	$3.06	$2.83

*The exchange ratio is 0.8 shares of Diversified common stock for each 1.0 share of Stable Products and 2.0 shares of Diversified for each 1.0 share of High-Tech Products. The net income figure for Diversified Industries (after merger) assumes that no economies of scale or synergistic benefits are realized as a result of either proposed merger.

The **exchange ratio,** *ER,* is the number of acquiring company shares received per share of acquired company stock owned.

Next, the possible merger of Diversified with High-Tech Products is considered. If Diversified decides to offer $60 a share and High-Tech Products accepts, the High-Tech Products' shareholders would receive two shares of Diversified common stock for every share of High-Tech Products stock they hold; in other words, the exchange ratio would be 2.0.

Table 22-4 shows the pro forma financial statement summary for Diversified, assuming separate mergers with each of the merger candidates. The following equation is used to calculate the postmerger earnings per share for the combined companies, EPS_c:

$$EPS_c = \frac{E_1 + E_2 + E_{1,2}}{NS_1 + NS_2(ER)} \qquad (22.2)$$

where E_1 and E_2 are the net earnings of the acquiring and acquired companies respectively, $E_{1,2}$ is the immediate synergistic earnings from the merger, and NS_1 and NS_2 are the number of shares outstanding of the acquiring and acquired companies respectively. For the acquisition of Stable Products by Diversified, EPS_c is calculated as follows:

$$EPS_c = \frac{\$120 \text{ million} + \$12 \text{ million} + 0}{40 \text{ million} + [(4 \text{ million})(0.8)]}$$

$$= \$3.06$$

As a result of a merger with Stable Products, Diversified has earnings per share of $3.06, as compared with $3.00 without the merger. In other words, the merger transaction can cause Diversified's earnings to change, due to P/E differences between merging companies. Specifically, if the exchange ratio is based on current stock market prices and no synergy exists, *the acquisition of a company with a lower P/E ratio causes the earnings per share figure of the acquiring company to increase.* Similarly, *the acquisition of a company with a higher P/E ratio causes the earnings per share figure to decrease.* This short-term earnings per share change is caused solely by the merger transaction, and a rational stock market does not perceive this change to be *real* growth or *real* decline.

A more important question remains: What will happen to the price and the P/E ratio of Diversified's stock after a merger has been accomplished? Obviously, it can go up, stay the same, or go down. Normally, the stock market seems to view mergers rationally, recognizing that the postmerger P/E ratio is a weighted average of the two premerger P/E ratios. As a result, the postmerger share price of the acquiring company is usually in the same range as prior to the merger, unless significant economies of scale or synergistic benefits are achieved in the merger.

With regard to a possible merger with Stable Products, suppose Diversified's management is not willing to incur an initial dilution in its earnings per share. What is the maximum price and exchange ratio Diversified should agree to under this criterion? The maximum price is calculated using the following equation:

$$P_{max} = (P/E)_1 (EPS_2) \qquad (22.3)$$

where P_{max} is the maximum offering price without incurring an initial *EPS* dilution, $(P/E)_1$ is the price to earnings ratio of the acquiring company, and EPS_2 is the earnings per share for the to-be-acquired company. Diversified can offer up to $30 a share for Stable Products without diluting its *EPS*:

$$P_{max} = (10)(\$3.00)$$
$$= \$30$$

A price of $30 a share in this example results in an exchange ratio of 1.0, because Diversified's stock is also selling at $30 a share.

Suppose Diversified Industries merges with High-Tech Products and initially dilutes its *EPS* to $2.83 from its present $3.00 level, assuming no immediate synergy. Diversified's managers may want to know how long it will take the expected *EPS* of the combined companies to equal the expected *EPS* of Diversified without the acquisition. To answer this question, we have to consider the expected growth rates of the individual companies given in Table 22-3. Without a merger, Diversified's earnings, dividends, and assets are expected to grow at an annual rate of 7 percent, and High-Tech Products' earnings are expected to grow at 14 percent a year. Assume that the combined companies grow at 9 percent a year. The expected *EPS* growth for Diversified with and without merger is shown in Figure 22-1. Based on expected growth rates, the *EPS* of Diversified with the merger will be equal to its *EPS* without the merger in about 3 years.[8] This information will be used by the Diversified management in its decision whether to acquire High-Tech Products.

ANALYSIS OF A LEVERAGED BUYOUT

The following example illustrates some of the steps and considerations involved in typical LBOs. Suppose that, as part of a corporate restructuring, Universal Industries, Inc. recently has decided to sell its Gray Manufacturing Division, a manufacturer of industrial products. The Gray division's top management, together with several private investors, are considering buying Gray and operating it

---

[8]The number of years, *n*, for the two alternatives to produce equal *EPS* levels is calculated using the following equation:

$$EPS_1 (1 + g_1)^n = EPS_2 (1 + g_2)^n$$

where EPS_1 and EPS_2 are the initial *EPS* values for each alternative, and g_1 and g_2 are the expected annual growth rates for each alternative.

FIGURE 22-1
Diversified Industries' Expected EPS Growth with and without the High-Tech Products Acquisition

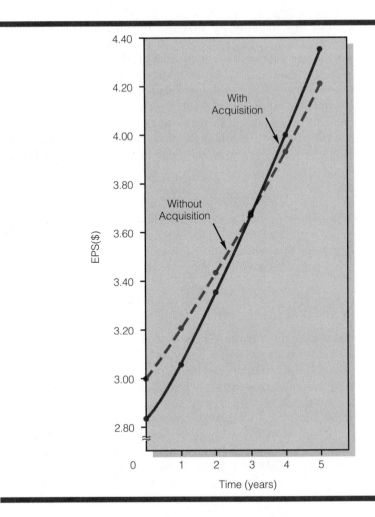

as a separate company. As is fairly typical of LBO candidates, Gray is in a mature industry and its products have a low probability of becoming obsolete. In addition, Gray's fixed assets have a present market value greater than their book value.

The Gray division's financial statements listed in Table 22-5 show that the division presently has an annual pretax loss of $1 million, and therefore, its return on stockholders' equity is negative. The Gray management group intends to return Gray to profitability by various cost-cutting and other measures. Gray's parent company, Universal Industries, also could have initiated cost-cutting measures to attempt to return Gray to profitability. However, partly because of Universal's new corporate strategy to get out of the industrial products business, it has chosen instead to sell Gray. Following negotiations between the Gray management group and Universal Industries, the management group agreed to purchase all of the assets of the Gray division for $30 million.

The Gray management group plans to take the following steps to complete the LBO transaction.

1. The management group has put together equity totaling $5 million. Some of these funds will come from liquidated Universal Industries retirement and employee benefit plans. In LBO terminology, equity is sometimes referred to as "ground floor financing."

TABLE 22-5
Leveraged Buyout of Gray
Manufacturing Division

**BALANCE SHEET
(IN MILLIONS OF DOLLARS)**

	Before LBO	Pro Forma After LBO
Current assets	$22	$22
Fixed assets, net	8	16
Total assets	$30	$38
Current liabilities	$15	$15
Long-term debt	—	18
Stockholders' equity	15	5
Total liabilities and equity	$30	$38

**ANNUAL INCOME STATEMENT
(IN MILLIONS OF DOLLARS)**

	Before LBO	Pro Forma After LBO
Revenues	$30	$30
Cash operating expenses	29	21
Interest expense	1	5
Depreciation	1	3
Earnings before tax	$−1	$ 1

2. The management group has arranged for short-term commercial bank financing, agreeing to pledge Gray's accounts receivable and inventory as collateral. This level of financing is called either "second floor" or "top floor" financing.

3. The management group has also arranged to finance the remaining portion of the buyout with subordinated long-term debt financing from an investment banking firm specializing in providing financing for LBOs. This subordinated debt is called "mezzanine" financing because of its position between the ground floor and the second floor financing. Mezzanine financing is high-risk capital because the company's fixed assets do not provide sufficient collateral for the debt. In addition, Gray's cash flow forecast for its early years as a separate entity indicates that it may experience some difficulty in servicing its debt obligations. As a result, the investment bankers providing the mezzanine financing have insisted that the debentures include attached warrants to provide additional opportunities for return other than the debt's interest payments. Because these debentures are highly risky, they are referred to as "junk bonds." (Recall from Chapter 6 that the term *junk bond* is frequently applied to a debt issue rated Ba or lower by Moody's or BB or lower by Standard & Poor's.)[9]

4. The management group intends to initiate a major cost-cutting program as soon as Gray becomes a separate company. They plan to cut unnecessary personnel at all levels, and for the remaining employees, they plan to cut salaries and employee benefits. In return, however, they do plan to

[9]In the case of privately placed debt, a *junk bond* is a debt issue whose characteristics would cause it to be rated Ba, BB, or lower, if it were rated.

offer key employees stock options, and all employees will participate in a bonus plan. In addition, Gray personnel no longer will have to provide reports to Universal, which in turn reports to its stockholders and the Securities and Exchange Commission. Also, the Gray managers themselves will no longer be spending time talking to security analysts.

5. The management group has determined that Gray's fixed assets (real estate and equipment) have a market value of approximately $16 million, or about twice their present book value. As a result of the LBO, the fixed assets will be written up to their market value and depreciated on the basis of the higher value. The increased depreciation charge will shelter a greater portion of Gray's cash flow from federal income taxes, all other things being equal.

This example illustrates many of the steps a buyer usually takes in an LBO.

 ## BUSINESS FAILURE

The remainder of this chapter considers what happens when businesses experience severe and extended problems that might cause failure. The purpose is to present an overview of business failure and the alternatives available to the failing firm. In this section, we define business failure and discuss its frequency and causes. The following section examines the various alternatives available to failing firms including the procedures involving the federal bankruptcy laws.

Definitions of Business Failure

Business failure can be considered from both an *economic* and a *financial* viewpoint. In an economic sense, *business success* is associated with firms that earn an adequate return (equal to or greater than the cost of capital) on their investments. Similarly, *business failure* is associated with firms that earn an inadequate return on their investments. An important aspect of business failure involves the question of whether the failure is *permanent* or *temporary*. For example, suppose a company has $1 million invested in assets and only generates operating earnings of $10,000. Obviously, this 1 percent return on investment is inadequate. However, the appropriate course of action depends to some extent on whether this business failure is judged to be permanent or temporary. If it is permanent, the company probably should be liquidated. If failure is temporary, the company probably should attempt "to ride out the storm," especially if steps can be taken to speed the company's return to business success. From an economic standpoint, business failure is also said to exist when a firm's revenues are not sufficient to cover the costs of doing business.

It is more common, however, for business failure to be viewed in a *financial context*, as a *technical insolvency*, a *legal insolvency*, or a *bankruptcy*. A firm is said to be **technically insolvent** if it is unable to meet its current obligations as they come due, even though the value of its assets exceeds the value of its liabilities.[10] A firm is **legally insolvent** if the recorded value of its assets is less than the recorded value of its liabilities. A firm is **bankrupt** if it is unable to pay its debts and files a bankruptcy petition in accordance with the federal bankruptcy laws.

[10]A firm that is *technically insolvent* can also be said to be *illiquid*.

One year or less	9.0%	
Two years	11.2	
Three years	11.2	
Total Three Years or Less	31.4%	
Four Years	10.0	
Five Years	8.4	
Total Five Years or Less	49.8%	
Total Six to Ten Years	24.3	
Total Over Ten Years	25.9	
	100.0%	

TABLE 22-6
Failures by Age of Business

Source: The Dun and Bradstreet Corporation, Economic Analysis Department, March 1991.

Business Failure Statistics

During the 1990s, approximately 72,000 businesses failed each year in the United States—a failure rate of about 1 percent of all listed businesses. About 43 percent of the businesses that failed in those years had liabilities over $100,000.[11]

Another interesting characteristic involves the ages of failed businesses. As shown in Table 22-6, about 30 percent of all the companies that failed had been in business 3 years or less and about 50 percent had been in business 5 years or less. Only about one-quarter had been in business more than 10 years.

Table 22-7 lists some large bankruptcy filings through 1995. A number of these companies, such as Federated Department Stores and Continental Airlines, have successfully reorganized themselves while in bankruptcy and have emerged to become profitable again. Other companies, such as Eastern Airlines and Pan Am, were liquidated and ceased to exist. For a number of companies the outcome is pending and may not be known for some time. In the case of Penn Central (the largest U.S. railroad), it took more than 8 years for the company to emerge from bankruptcy.

Causes of Business Failure

Table 22-8 shows the causes of business failure for companies that have failed. Although there are a number of reasons why businesses fail, most failures seem to be due at least in part to economic factors, financial causes, and lack of experience on the part of the owners of the businesses.

When businesses experience problems such as inadequate sales and heavy operating expenses, they frequently encounter cash flow problems as well. As a result of the cash flow problems, these businesses often increase their short-term borrowings. If the problems persist, the cash flow difficulties can become more acute, and the business may not be able to meet its obligations to its creditors on a timely basis.

Many of these characteristics of failing firms were measured by the financial ratios used in the Altman bankruptcy prediction model discussed in Chapter 15. Such financial variables as sales, operating expenses (through its effect on EBIT), short-term borrowings (debt), and cash flow (through its effect on net working capital) were all components of one or more of the ratios used to forecast failure.

---

[11]*Economic Report of the President* (1997): 407.

TABLE 22-7
Some Large
Corporate Bankruptcies*

Sources: Christopher M. McHugh, ed., *The 1993 Bankruptcy Yearbook and Almanac* (Boston: New Generation Research, 1993): 60; *The 1995 Bankruptcy Yearbook and Almanac* (Boston: New Generation Research, 1995): 62; *Turnarounds and Workouts,* Washington, DC; *Value Line,* various issues.

COMPANY	TOTAL ASSETS ($ BILLION)	DATE FILED	OUTCOME
Texaco	$35.9	April 1987	Emerged April 1988
Federated Dept. Stores	7.9	January 1990	Emerged January 1992
Continental Airlines	7.7	December 1990	Emerged April 1993
Olympia & York Development	7.0	May 1992	Pending
Penn Central	6.9	June 1970	Emerged October 1978
Maxwell Communication	6.4	December 1991	Pending
LTV	6.3	July 1986	Emerged June 1993
Columbia Gas Systems	6.2	July 1991	Pending
R. H. Macy & Co.	4.8	January 1992	Merged with Federated Department Stores, December 1994
Dow Corning	4.1	May 1995	Pending
Eastern Airlines	4.0	March 1989	Liquidated
Allied Stores	3.5	January 1990	Emerged January 1992
Walter Industries	3.5	December 1989	Emerged March 1995
Southland	3.4	October 1990	Emerged March 1991
Trans World Airlines	3.3	January 1992	Emerged November 1993
Public Service of New Hampshire	2.6	January 1988	Emerged May 1991
Pan Am	2.4	January 1991	Liquidated
Farley	2.4	September 1991	Emerged December 1992
Manville	2.3	August 1982	Emerged November 1988
E-II Holdings	2.1	July 1992	Emerged May 1993
Ames Dept. Stores	2.1	April 1990	Emerged December 1992

*Excludes companies whose primary businesses are banking, insurance, brokerage, or similar financial services.

ALTERNATIVES FOR FAILING BUSINESSES

Once a firm begins encountering these difficulties, the firm's owners and management have to consider the alternatives available to failing businesses. In general, a failing company has two alternatives:

1. It can attempt to resolve its difficulties with its creditors on a *voluntary,* or *informal,* basis.
2. It can petition the courts for assistance and *formally* declare *bankruptcy.*

A company's creditors may also petition the courts, and this may result in the company's being involuntarily declared bankrupt.

Regardless of whether a business chooses informal or formal methods to deal with its difficulties, eventually the decision has to be made whether to *reorganize* or *liquidate* the business. Before this decision can be made, both the business's liquidation value and its going-concern value have to be determined. *Liquidation value* equals the proceeds that would be received from the sale of the business assets minus liabilities. *Going-concern value* equals the capitalized value of the company's operating earnings minus its liabilities. Basically, if the going-concern value exceeds the liquidation value, the business should be reorganized; otherwise, it should be liquidated. However, in practice, the determination of the going-concern and

UNDERLYING CAUSES	PERCENTAGE*
Economic factors (e.g., industry weakness, insufficient profits)	41.0%
Finance factors (e.g., heavy operating expenses, insufficient capital)	32.5
Experience factors (e.g., lack of business knowledge, lack of line experience, lack of management experience)	20.6
Neglect (e.g., poor work habits, business conflicts)	2.5
Fraud	1.2
Disaster	1.1
Strategy factors (e.g., receivables difficulties, overexpansion)	1.1
	100.0%

*Results are based on primary reason for failure.

TABLE 22-8
Causes of Business Failures

Source: The Dun and Bradstreet Corporation, Economic Analysis Department, March 1991.

liquidation values is not an easy matter. For example, problems may exist in estimating the price the company's assets will bring at auction. In addition, the company's future operating earnings and the appropriate discount rate at which to capitalize the earnings may be difficult to determine. Also, management understandably is not in a position to be completely objective about these values.

Informal Alternatives for Failing Businesses

Regardless of the exact reasons why a business begins to experience difficulties, the result is often the same: namely, cash flow problems.

Frequently, the first steps taken by the troubled company involve stretching its payables. In some cases, this action can buy the troubled company up to several weeks of needed time before creditors take action.

If the difficulties are more than just minor and temporary, the company may next turn to its bankers and request additional working capital loans. In some situations, the bankers may make the additional loans, especially if they perceive the situation to be temporary. Another possible action the company's bankers and creditors may take is to restructure the company's debt.

Debt restructuring by bankers and other creditors can be quite complex. However, debt restructuring basically involves either extension, composition, or a combination of the two. In an **extension,** the failing company tries to reach an agreement with its creditors that will permit it to lengthen the time it has to meet its obligations. In a **composition,** the firm's creditors accept some percentage amount less than their actual original claims, and the company is permitted to discharge its debt obligations by paying less than the full amounts owed. The percentage a company's creditors will agree to in the event of a composition is usually greater than the percentage they could net if the company had to sell its assets to satisfy their claims. If a company's creditors feel that the company can overcome its financial difficulties and become a valuable customer over the long run, they may be willing to accept some form of composition.

Debt restructuring by lenders can involve deferment of both interest and principal payments for a time. Before lenders will agree to these deferments, they often require the troubled company's suppliers to make various concessions as well. In addition, the lenders frequently demand and receive *warrants* in return for making their deferment concessions.

Large companies that experience cash flow difficulties often sell off real estate, various operating divisions, or both to raise needed cash. For example, Pan American Airlines, which incurred over $1 billion in losses during the 1980s, sold its New York headquarters building, Intercontinental Hotels subsidiary, Pacific route system, and various aircraft during this period to raise the cash needed to stay in business. These asset sales continued into 1991 when the company essentially liquidated itself.

Another method often used by failing companies to raise needed cash involves the sale and leaseback of its land and buildings. Some companies also resort to more unusual methods of conserving cash, such as offering preferred stock to certain employees in exchange for a portion of their salary.

Frequently, failing companies voluntarily form a *creditors' committee* that meets regularly and attempts to help the company out of its predicament. The creditors are usually requested to accept deferred payments, and in return, the creditors usually request that the company cut various expenditures. If the company and its creditors are able to reach an agreement on the appropriate actions to take, the legal and administrative expenses associated with formal bankruptcy procedures are not incurred. Accordingly, both the company and creditors may be better off as a result.

Liquidation can also occur outside the bankruptcy courts. The process is called an **assignment.** Usually a trustee, who is probably one of the major creditors, is assigned the assets. The trustee then has the responsibility of selling the assets and distributing the proceeds in the best interest of the creditors.

Formal Alternatives for Failing Businesses under the Bankruptcy Laws

The **Bankruptcy Reform Act of 1978** states the basic mechanics of the bankruptcy procedure.[12] Either the failing company or its unsecured creditors may initiate bankruptcy procedures by filing a claim in bankruptcy court. When the debtor company files for bankruptcy, it is termed a *voluntary* petition. A bankruptcy proceeding may also be initiated by a group of three or more of the company's unsecured creditors that have aggregate claims of at least $500. The unsecured creditors filing the claim must assert that the debtor company is not paying its present debts as they come due. Such a claim is termed an *involuntary* petition.

After the initial bankruptcy petition has been filed, both the failing company and its creditors receive protection from the courts. The company itself is protected from any further actions on the part of the creditors while it attempts to work out a *plan of reorganization*. The debtor company has 120 days to work out a plan of reorganization. After that, the creditors may file a plan of their own. The court has considerable latitude in a bankruptcy case. For example, depending on the nature of the case, it may decide to appoint a *trustee* who will be responsible for running the business and protecting the creditors' interests. Normally, the troubled company is allowed to continue operations. If there is reason to believe that continuing operations will result in further deterioration of the creditors' position, however, the court can order the firm to cease operating.

A new development and alternative for firms considering bankruptcy is the "prepackaged bankruptcy." Prepackaged bankruptcy filings must be agreed to by 51 percent of the creditors who hold at least two-thirds of the debt before filing for bankruptcy. Prepackaged filings can speed a firm through the process in a few months (e.g., 4 months for Southland, owner of the 7-Eleven chain) compared to the many years traditional filings last. For example, Revco Drug Stores

---

[12]The Bankruptcy Reform Act of 1978, in general, streamlined the U.S. bankruptcy procedures and increased the number of bankruptcy courts. The Reform Act contains eight odd-numbered chapters, 1 through 15, which are labeled with Arabic numerals instead of the roman numerals used in the old Bankruptcy Act.

declared bankruptcy in 1988, and did not emerge from bankruptcy until 1992. Revco incurred over $40 million in legal and accounting fees associated with resolving its bankruptcy.

An important aspect of the bankruptcy procedures involves what to do with the failing firm. Just as in the case of the informal alternatives, a decision has to be made about whether a firm's value as a *going concern* is greater than its *liquidation* value. Generally, if this is the case and a suitable plan of reorganization can be formulated, the firm is reorganized; otherwise, it is liquidated.

Reorganization

During **Chapter 11** proceedings, the failing company presents its current financial status and its proposed plan of reorganization. This plan of reorganization is normally similar to either composition or extension.

The bankruptcy court and the Securities and Exchange Commission (SEC) review the plan of reorganization for fairness and feasibility. The term *fairness* means that the claims are to be settled in the order of their priority. The priority of claims is discussed in detail in the next section on liquidation. A *feasible* plan of reorganization is one that gives the business a good chance of reestablishing successful operations. For example, the plan must provide an adequate level of working capital, a reasonable capital structure and debt-to-equity ratio, and an earning power sufficient to reasonably cover interest and dividend requirements. Often a recapitalization may result in fewer fixed charges for the reorganized company and thereby afford it a better chance of succeeding. The reorganization also may involve an extension of the debt maturities, which would help the company's cash flow by causing the debt's principal retirement to occur at later dates.

After the bankruptcy court and the SEC have reviewed the reorganization plan, it is submitted to the firm's creditors for approval. Creditors vote by class (e.g., unsecured creditors, secured creditors, common stockholders) on the reorganization plan (or plans in the case where more than one plan is submitted for approval). The plan must be approved by a simple majority (i.e., 50 percent) of the creditors voting in each class and by creditors representing two-thirds (i.e., 66.7 percent) of the total amount of claims voting in each class. Once the bankrupt company obtains approval from the bankruptcy court and its creditors, it can leave Chapter 11. At this point, the court-appointed trustee's task is to implement the plan.

A recent example of a company that went through a Chapter 11 reorganization is Global Marine, an offshore oil drilling company.[13] Faced with reduced revenues because of the decline in oil prices and with $1.3 billion in debt, the company filed for bankruptcy in January 1986. Over the next 3 years, under the supervision of the bankruptcy court, Global cut its workforce from a high of 3,047 to 1,506 employees. It reduced its yearly overhead from $59 million to $25 million. In February 1989, Global Marine emerged from bankruptcy. Between 1984 and 1988 the company lost $874 million. Over the next five years (1989 to 1993), after it emerged from bankruptcy, its losses narrowed to $161 million. During 1994 and 1995 GlobalMarine had positive net income of $1.3 million and $51.9 million respectively.

The reorganization plan is shown in Table 22-9. About 40 senior creditors received a combination of cash, debt securities, and 90 percent of the common stock of the reorganized company. Subordinated debtholders received 7.5 percent of the common stock. Global's negative net worth of $116 million virtually wiped out preferred and common shareholders. They received only 2.5 percent

---

[13]*Business Week* (March 13, 1989): 44.

TABLE 22-9
Reorganization of Global-Marine, Inc.

Source: Reprinted from the March 13, 1989, issue of *Business Week* by special permission, copyright © 1989 by the McGraw-Hill Companies.

CREDITOR GROUP	AMOUNT OWED	AMOUNT RECEIVED
Secured creditors	$700 million	$95 million in cash $400 million in debt 60% of the common stock
Senior unsecured creditors	$154 million	$17 million in debt 30% of the common stock
Subordinated bondholders	$400 million	7.5% of the common stock
Preferred shareholders	—	0.7% of the common stock
Common shareholders	—	1.8% of the common stock

of the common stock of the reorganized company, valued at about $3.7 million, plus warrants.

Liquidation

If for some reason reorganization is judged unfeasible, a legally declared bankrupt company may be liquidated. The liquidation procedures are described in **Chapter 7** of the Bankruptcy Reform Act. In the liquidation procedure, a *referee* is normally appointed to handle the administrative aspects of the bankruptcy procedure. The referee then arranges for a meeting of the creditors, and they in turn select a *trustee,* who liquidates the business and pays the creditors' claims according to the priority of claims set forth in Chapter 7.

The **absolute priority rule** states that, in general, secured debts are satisfied first from the sale of the secured assets and that all claims of creditors must be satisfied before any claims by stockholders. The following list specifies the order of priority in which unsecured debts must be paid:

1. The expenses involved in the administration of the bankruptcy.
2. Business expenses incurred after an involuntary petition has been filed but before a trustee has been appointed.
3. Wages owed for services performed during the three months prior to the bankruptcy proceedings, not to exceed $2,000 per employee.
4. Certain unpaid contributions to employee benefit plans (limited to $2,000 per employee).
5. Certain customer layaway deposits, not to exceed $900 per individual.
6. Taxes owed to federal, state, and local governments.
7. Claims of general and unsecured creditors.
8. Preferred stockholders—they receive an amount up to the par value or stated value of the preferred stock.
9. Common stockholders—they share any remaining funds equally on a per-share basis.

To illustrate the absolute priority rule in a liquidation, consider the balance sheet prior to the liquidation of Failures Galore, Inc., shown in Table 22-10.[14] Suppose the total proceeds of the liquidation are $6.8 million. The distribution of these proceeds is shown in Table 22-11. The proceeds have been distributed in accordance with the absolute priority rule. Each general and unsecured cred-

[14]Assume that this liquidation is a voluntary petition, that no unpaid contributions to employee benefit plans exist, and that no customer layaway deposits are involved. In other words, items 2, 4, and 5 in the priority of claims do not apply to this example.

TABLE 22-10
Balance Sheet, Failures
Galore, Inc.*

ASSETS		LIABILITIES AND EQUITY	
Current assets	$ 6,000,000	Accounts payable	$ 2,000,000
Fixed assets, net	6,500,000	Bank notes payable	2,000,000
		Accrued wages	200,000
		Accrued taxes	300,000
		Mortgage bonds	2,000,000
		Debentures	2,000,000
		Subordinated debentures	2,000,000
		Preferred stock	1,000,000
		Common equity	1,000,000
Total assets	$12,500,000	Liabilities and equity	$12,500,000

*The subordinated debentures are subordinate to the bank notes payable. Assume that all the accrued wages can be paid out of the liquidation proceeds.

itor receives a settlement percentage of the funds owed after priority claims have been settled. As shown in Table 22-11, these priority claims are bankruptcy administration expenses, wages, and taxes owed. In addition, mortgage bond-holders receive $1.5 million from the sale of secured assets; this leaves the mortgage bondholders as general creditors for the balance of their claim ($500,000). After these priority claims have been met, there is $4.25 million in assets remaining to meet the remaining creditor claims of $8.5 million. Each general creditor

TABLE 22-11
Distribution of the Proceeds
from the Liquidation of Failures
Galore, Inc.

Total liquidation proceeds	$6,800,000
1. Bankruptcy administration expenses	$ 550,000
2. Wages owed to employees	200,000
3. Taxes owed to governments	300,000
Total priority claims	$1,050,000
Funds available for claims of creditors	$5,750,000
4. Payment to mortgage bondholders (proceeds from sale of secured assets)	1,500,000
Funds available for claims of general and unsecured creditors	$4,250,000

$$\text{Settlement percentage for general and unsecured creditors} = \frac{\text{Funds available for general and unsecured creditors}}{\text{Total claims of general and unsecured creditors}}$$

$$= \frac{\$4,250,000}{\$8,500,000}$$

$$= 50\%$$

	TOTAL CLAIM	SETTLEMENT, 50% OF CLAIM (BEFORE SUBORDINATION ADJUSTMENT)	SETTLEMENT, 50% OF CLAIM (AFTER SUBORDINATION ADJUSTMENT)
Accounts payable	$2,000,000	$1,000,000	$1,000,000
Bank notes payable	2,000,000	1,000,000	2,000,000
Mortgage bonds	500,000	250,000	250,000
Debentures	2,000,000	1,000,000	1,000,000
Subordinated debentures	2,000,000	1,000,000	0
	$8,500,000	$4,250,000	$4,250,000
Funds available for preferred and common stockholders	$0		

receives 50 percent of the claim, except bank notes. Because the subordinated debentures are subordinate to bank notes, the bank notes receive the proportionate claim of the subordinated holders ($1 million in this case) in addition to the $1 million directly due the bank notes. Hence, because of the subordination provision in the debentures, the bank notes are paid off in full.

The absolute priority rule is also used in bankruptcy reorganizations. However, in reorganization proceedings, deviations from the absolute priority rule by the courts have been observed. In a detailed study of 30 bankruptcy cases filed subsequent to the effective date of the 1978 Bankruptcy Reform Act, 23 cases resulted in shareholders being awarded more than they were entitled to under strict adherence to the absolute priority rule.[15] The excess amount received by the shareholders averaged 7.6 percent for the 30 cases. Two of the major reasons for the deviations are that the creditors may lack adequate information about the firm's value or that they may be willing to compromise because of the potential cost of a lengthy reorganization.

■ SUMMARY

- Technically, a *merger* is a combination of two or more companies in which all but one of the companies legally cease to exist and the surviving company continues operation under its original name. A *consolidation* is a combination in which all the companies are dissolved and a new company is formed. The term *merger* is used to describe both of these types of business combinations.
- Mergers are classified according to whether they are *horizontal, vertical,* or *conglomerate.* In a horizontal merger, the combining companies are direct competitors. In a vertical merger, the companies have a buyer-seller relationship. In a conglomerate merger, neither company competes directly with the other, and no buyer-seller relationship exists.
- A *holding company* owns controlling interest in another legally separate company, and the relationship between these affiliated companies is called a *parent-subsidiary* relationship.
- In a *leveraged buyout,* the buyer of a company borrows a large portion of the purchase price, using the purchased assets as partial collateral for the loans.
- There are a number of reasons companies choose external growth over internal growth, including the following:
  1. The availability of lower-cost assets.
  2. Greater economies of scale.
  3. The availability of more secure raw material supplies and additional end-product markets.
  4. The possibility of more rapid growth.
  5. Greater diversification.
  6. Tax considerations.
- In the *pooling of interests* method of accounting for mergers, the acquired assets are recorded at their cost when acquired. In the *purchase* method, acquired assets are recorded at their fair market values, and any additional amount paid is listed as *goodwill,* which then must be amortized.

[15]Allan C. Eberhart, William T. Moore, and Rodney L. Roenfeldt, "Security Pricing and Deviations from the Absolute Priority Rule in Bankruptcy Proceedings," *Journal of Finance* (December 1990): 1457–1469.

■ Three major methods are used to value merger candidates: the *comparative price-earnings ratio method,* the *adjusted book value method,* and the *discounted cash flow method.* The discounted cash flow method, which is an application of capital budgeting techniques, is the most theoretically correct valuation method.

■ The acquisition of a company with a higher P/E ratio causes the earnings per share figure of the acquiring company to decrease if the exchange ratio is based on current stock market prices and no synergy exists. Similarly, the acquisition of a company with a lower P/E ratio causes the earnings per share figure of the acquiring company to increase.

■ A firm is *bankrupt* if its total liabilities exceed the value of its total assets. A firm is *technically insolvent* if it cannot meet its current obligations as they come due, even though the value of its assets exceeds its liabilities.

■ Economic factors and lack of experience on the part of business owners are generally considered to be the primary causes of most business failures.

■ Failing firms have two basic alternatives:
  1. They can attempt to resolve the difficulties with their creditors on an *informal,* voluntary basis.
  2. They can petition the courts for assistance and *formally* declare *bankruptcy.* In addition, the creditors may petition the courts, and the firm involuntarily may be declared bankrupt.

■ Legal bankruptcy proceedings focus on the decision of whether the failing firm should be *reorganized* or *liquidated.* If its going-concern value is greater than its liquidation value, the business will usually be reorganized; otherwise, it will be liquidated.

■ The Bankruptcy Reform Act contains two chapters that outline different bankruptcy procedures. In a Chapter 11 proceeding, the troubled company seeks court protection from its creditors while it works out a *reorganization plan.* If reorganization is judged not feasible, the bankrupt company is liquidated. The liquidation procedures are set forth in Chapter 7 of the act.

■ QUESTIONS AND TOPICS FOR DISCUSSION

1. Define the following terms:
   a. Merger.
   b. Consolidation.
   c. Holding company.
2. Describe some of the measures used by companies to discourage unfriendly takeover attempts.
3. What is the difference between an asset purchase and a stock purchase?
4. What is the difference between an operational restructuring and a financial restructuring?
5. Discuss the differences between the following types of mergers:
   a. Horizontal mergers.
   b. Vertical mergers.
   c. Conglomerate mergers.
6. What are some of the reasons why firms merge with other firms?
7. What methods do financial analysts use to value merger candidates? What are the limitations of each method?
8. Explain what happens to the postmerger earnings per share figure when a company with a relatively high P/E ratio acquires a company with a lower P/E ratio, assuming the exchange ratio is based on current stock market prices and no synergy exists.
9. What are the differences between the *purchase* method and the *pooling of interests* method of accounting for mergers?

10. What is a *leveraged buyout*? What is *mezzanine financing*?
11. What is a *tax-free merger*?
12. Explain the difference between the economic and financial definitions of business failure.
13. Explain the differences among the following terms related to financial failure:
    a. Technical insolvency.
    b. Legal insolvency.
    c. Bankruptcy.
14. What alternatives are available to the failing firm?
15. Basically, what determines whether a bankrupt company is reorganized or liquidated?
16. In a debt reorganization, explain the difference between a *composition* and an *extension*.
17. Explain why an informal settlement may be preferable to declaring bankruptcy for both the failing firm and its creditors.
18. What are the differences between Chapter 7 and Chapter 11 of the Bankruptcy Reform Act?
19. In connection with reorganization plans, what do *fairness* and *feasibility* mean?
20. Explain how a firm that has failed can be reorganized to operate successfully.
21. Rank in order of priority (highest to lowest) the following claims on the proceeds from the liquidation of a bankrupt firm:
    ■ Taxes owed to federal, state, and local governments.
    ■ Preferred stockholders.
    ■ Common stockholders.
    ■ Expenses of administering the bankruptcy.
    ■ Secured creditors.
    ■ Unsecured creditors.
    ■ Wages in 3 months before bankruptcy (up to $2,000 per employee).
    ■ Customer deposits (up to $900 each).
    ■ Expenses incurred after the bankruptcy petition is filed and before a trustee is appointed.
    ■ Contributions to employee benefit plans (up to $2,000 per employee).

■ SELF-TEST PROBLEM

ST1. Zenith Industries is considering acquisition of the Nadir Corporation in a stock-for-stock exchange. (The expression *stock-for-stock exchange* means that the common stock of one company is exchanged for the common stock of another company.) Assume that no immediate synergistic benefits are expected. Selected financial data on the two companies are shown here:

	Zenith	Nadir
Sales, millions	$500	$100
Net earnings, millions	$ 30	$ 12
Common shares outstanding, millions	6	2
Earnings per share	$ 5	$ 6
Common stock price, per share	$ 50	$ 40
Dividends per share	$ 2	$ 1.50

a. If Zenith is not willing to incur an initial dilution in its earnings per share—that is, not have the postmerger earnings per share be below $5 per share—and if Zenith also feels that it will have to offer the Nadir shareholders a minimum of 25 percent over Nadir's current market price, what is the relevant range of Nadir per-share stock prices with which Zenith is working?

b. Calculate Zenith's postmerger earnings per share if the Nadir stockholders accept an offer by Zenith of $50 a share in a stock-for-stock exchange.

■ PROBLEMS*

1. The Blue Oil Corporation and the Grey Plastics Company have agreed to a merger. The Grey Plastics stockholders will receive 0.75 shares of Blue for each share of Grey held. Assume that no synergistic benefits are expected.

   a. Complete the following table:

	Blue Oil	Grey Plastics	Combined Companies
Sales (millions)	$500	$125	_____
Net earnings (millions)	$ 60	$ 13	_____
Common shares outstanding (millions)	16	4	_____
Earnings per share	$ 3.75	$ 3.25	_____
Common stock (price per share)	$ 41.25	$ 26	_____
Price-earnings ratio	_____	_____	10.0

   b. Calculate the premium percentage received by the Grey stockholders. Assume *both* that immediate synergistic earnings of $3 million per year will occur as a result of the merger and that the P/E ratio of the combined companies is 10.5.

   c. Rework Part a.

   d. Rework Part b.

2. The McPherson Company is considering acquiring the McAlester Company. Selected financial data for the two companies are shown here:

	McPherson	McAlester
Sales (millions)	$250	$30
Net earnings (millions)	$ 20	$ 2.25
Common shares outstanding (millions)	5	1
Earnings per share	$ 4.00	$ 2.25
Dividends per share	$ 1.20	$ 0.40
Common stock (price per share)	$ 40	$18

   Both companies have 40 percent marginal tax rates. Assume that no synergistic benefits are expected.

   a. Calculate the McPherson Company's postmerger earnings per share if the McAlester stockholders accept an offer of $20 a share in a stock-for-stock exchange. (The expression *stock-for-stock exchange* means that the common stock of one company is exchanged for the common stock of another company.)

   b. Recalculate Part a, assuming that the McPherson common stock price is $42 a share. (All other figures remain constant.)

   c. Calculate McPherson's earnings per share if the McAlester stockholders accept one $6 convertible preferred share (stated value, $100) for each five shares of McAlester stock held.

   d. Calculate McPherson's earnings per share if each group of 50 shares of McAlester stock is exchanged for one 8-percent, $1,000 debenture.

   e. Compare the premerger expected dividend return on the McAlester stock with the expected postmerger dividends or interest available with the exchanges described in Parts a, c, and d. (Undoubtedly, at the time of acquisition, McPherson would have pointed out these expected increases in yield to the McAlester stockholders.) Assume that an investor initially holds 100 shares of McAlester stock.

   f. What can be said about comparing the expected total postmerger return (dividends plus price appreciation) on the McAlester stock versus the expected total postmerger return on the McPherson securities?

3. Ball Industries is considering acquiring the Keyes Corporation in a stock-for-stock exchange. Selected financial data on the two companies follow:

*Colored numbers denote problems that have check answers provided at the end of the book.

	Ball	**Keyes**
Sales (millions)	$600	$75
Net earnings (millions)	$ 30	$10
Common shares outstanding (millions)	6	4
Earnings per share	$ 5	$ 2.50
Common stock (price per share)	$ 50	$20

Assume that no synergistic benefits are expected.

a. What is the maximum exchange ratio Ball should agree to if one of its acquisition criteria is no initial dilution in earnings per share?

b. Suppose an investor had purchased 100 shares of Keyes common stock 5 years ago at $12 a share. If the Keyes stockholders accept an offer of $24 a share in a stock-for-stock exchange, how much capital gains tax would this investor have to pay at the time the Keyes shares are exchanged for the Ball shares? (Assume a capital gains tax rate of 28 percent for this investor.)

c. Calculate the postmerger earnings per share if the Keyes stockholders accept an offer by Ball of $24 a share in a stock-for-stock exchange. Assume that immediate synergistic earnings of $4 million will occur as a result of the acquisition.

4. Looking back at Tables 22-3 and 22-4, assume that Diversified Industries acquires High-Tech Products in a stock-for-stock transaction and no immediate synergistic benefits are expected. How long will it take the expected *EPS* of the combined companies to equal the expected *EPS* of Diversified without the merger if Diversified is expected to grow at an annual rate of 7 percent without the merger and the combined companies are expected to grow at 8 percent a year?

5. Consider Failures Galore, Inc. (Tables 22-10 and 22-11), discussed in this chapter.

   a. If total liquidation proceeds are $5.95 million, what is the distribution of these proceeds among the various creditors of Failures Galore?

   b. If total liquidation proceeds are $7.65 million, what is the distribution of these proceeds among the various creditors of Failures Galore?

6. Go-for-Broke Company is being liquidated under Chapter 7 of the bankruptcy code. When it filed for bankruptcy, its balance sheet was as follows:

Assets		**Liabilities and Equity**	
Current assets	$14,500,000	Accounts payable	$12,145,000
Fixed assets		Accrued wages*	2,030,000
Land and buildings (net)	6,525,000	Accrued taxes	1,160,000
Equipment	7,975,000	Notes payable (bank)**	1,350,000
Total assets	$29,000,000	Total current liabilities	$16,685,000
		Mortgage bonds†	4,775,000
		Debentures	2,450,000
		Stockholders' equity	5,090,000
		Total liabilities and equity	$29,000,000

*All accrued wages must be paid out of the liquidation proceeds.
**The bank loan is unsecured.
†Mortgage bonds are secured by land and buildings.

Assume that the liquidation is a voluntary petition, that no unpaid contributions to employee benefit plans exist, and that no customer layaway deposits are involved. The proceeds from the liquidation of the company's assets are as follows:

Current assets	$ 9,425,000
Land and buildings	3,045,000
Equipment	4,130,000
Total	$16,600,000

Bankruptcy administration charges are $643,750.

a. Determine the distribution (dollar amount and percentage) of the liquidation proceeds among the various creditors of Go-For-Broke.

b. Assume that the debentures ($2.45 million) are subordinated to bank notes payable. Determine the distribution (dollar amount and percentage) of the liquidation proceeds among the various creditors of Go-for-Broke.

7. Wilson Industries is considering the acquisition of the Blanchard Company in a stock-for-stock exchange. Selected financial data for the two companies is shown next. An immediate synergistic earnings benefit of $1 million is expected in this merger, due to cost savings.

	Wilson	**Blanchard**
Sales (millions)	$150	$30
Net earnings (millions)	$ 25	$ 3.5
Common shares outstanding (millions)	8	2
Earnings per share	$ 3.125	$ 1.75
Dividends per share	$ 1.50	$ 0.75
Common stock price per share	$ 40	$19.50

Calculate the postmerger earnings per share if the Blanchard shareholders accept an offer of $22 per share in a stock-for-stock exchange.

8. A financial analyst with MTC International has estimated the annual after-tax free cash flow from a proposed merger to be $1.5 million. This cash flow is expected to continue for 10 years. For the following 5 years, the free cash flow is estimated to be $0.7 million per year. MTC International feels that the appropriate risk-adjusted discount rate is 16 percent. Calculate the present value of the expected free cash flows from the proposed merger through year 15.

9. Using a search engine, find out how many business bankruptcies occurred in the United States last calendar year. Then try to break down these bankruptcies by type (retail, restaurant, etc.). Finally, find out whether the trend for bankruptcies (both in absolute number and as a percent of businesses in existence) is up or down.

http://

10. Using the M&A Marketplace at the following Web site, find a business for sale in each of three major industries of your choice. Then, using their M&A search engine, find the "dream" business you'd love to own (consulting? restaurant? manufacturing? . . .).
http://www.mergernetwork.com/default.htm

http://

◼ SOLUTION TO SELF-TEST PROBLEM

ST1. a. Low end of range:

$40 \times 1.25 = $50

High end of range:

$P_{max} = (P/E)_1 (EPS_2)$

$= (10)($6.00)$

$= 60

b. $EPS_c = \dfrac{E_1 + E_2 + E_{1,2}}{NS_1 + NS_2 (ER)}$

$= \dfrac{$30 \text{ million} + $12 \text{ million} + 0}{6 \text{ million} + 2 \text{ million} (1.0)}$

$= 5.25

■ GLOSSARY

Absolute Priority Rule A rule used in bankruptcy proceedings that states that the claims of creditors are satisfied before the claims of stockholders.

Assignment The process of informally liquidating a business. Assignment occurs outside the jurisdiction of the bankruptcy courts.

Bankruptcy A situation in which a firm is unable to pay its debts and its assets are turned over to the court for administration.

Bankruptcy Reform Act of 1978 A U.S. bankruptcy act that significantly changed certain aspects of the federal bankruptcy laws.

Chapter 7 The liquidation chapter of the Bankruptcy Reform Act. Under Chapter 7, a company's assets are sold off, and the proceeds are distributed to creditors.

Chapter 11 The reorganization chapter of the Bankruptcy Reform Act. Under Chapter 11, a company continues to operate while it attempts to work out a reorganization plan.

Composition A situation in which a failing business is permitted to discharge its debt obligations by paying less than the full amounts owed to creditors.

Conglomerate Merger A combination of two or more companies in which neither competes directly with the other and no buyer-seller relationship exists.

Exchange Ratio The number of shares an acquiring company must give, or *exchange*, for each share of an acquired company in a merger.

Extension A situation in which a failing business is permitted to lengthen the amount of time it has to meet its obligations with creditors.

Goodwill An intangible asset equal to the premium over fair market value of the acquired assets that is paid for a company in a merger.

Holding Company A corporation that controls the voting power of one or more other companies.

Horizontal Merger A combination of two or more companies that compete directly with each other.

Legal Insolvency A situation in which the recorded value of a firm's assets is less than its liabilities.

Leveraged Buyout A transaction in which the buyer of a company borrows a large portion of the purchase price, using the purchased assets as partial collateral for the loans.

Merger A combination of two or more companies into one surviving company. Mergers also are called *acquisitions* or *consolidations*.

Pooling of Interests Method A method of accounting for mergers in which the acquired company's assets are recorded on the acquiring company's books at their cost when originally acquired. No goodwill account is created under the pooling method.

Purchase Method A method of accounting for mergers in which the total value paid or exchanged for the acquired firm's assets is recorded on the acquiring firm's books. Any difference between the acquired assets' fair market value and their purchase price is recorded as goodwill.

Technical Insolvency A situation in which a firm is unable to meet its current obligations as they come due, even though the value of its assets may exceed its liabilities.

Tender Offer A public announcement by a company or individual indicating that it will pay a price above the current market price for the shares "tendered" of a company it wishes to acquire.

Vertical Merger A combination of two or more companies that have a buyer-seller relationship with one another.

AN INTEGRATIVE CASE PROBLEM
MERGERS AND ACQUISITIONS

Admiral Foods Corporation is a diversified food processing and distributing company that has shown excellent growth over the past 10 years as a result of a balanced program of acquisitions and internal growth.

One segment of the food business in which Admiral only recently has begun to compete, however, is the fast-food business. The present top management of Admiral Foods feels that good future growth in the fast-food business is still possible, regardless of the rapid expansion of the 1980s. During the past year, members of the Admiral staff have examined and analyzed a number of independent fast-food firms. One company that the analysis indicated as potentially suitable for acquisition by Admiral is Favorite Food Systems, Inc.

Favorite Food Systems, Inc., which was founded by John Favorite in 1974, is a West Coast chain with current annual sales of approximately $75 million. Favorite's history can best be described as up and down, with the general trend up. The company survived several brief shaky periods during the late 1970s. In 1983, the company went public. (The Favorite family now controls about 57 percent of the common stock.) By 1986, Favorite Foods was recommended by two brokerage firms and was touted by one investment service as "another potential McDonald's." This and other predictions never came true. In fact, Favorite Food Systems' growth rate has slowed appreciably during the past 5 years. One reason frequently given in the trade for Favorite's growth slowdown is Mr. Favorite's apparent indecision regarding expansion. As a result, the competition increasingly has gotten the jump on Favorite with the best locations in new residential growth areas.

The following table shows last year's balance sheets and income statements for both Admiral and Favorite.

Admiral Foods Corporation Balance Sheet
(in millions of dollars)

Current assets	$225	Current liabilities	$101
Fixed assets, net	307	Long-term debt	106
		Common equity	
		(10,000,000 shares)	325
Total assets	$532	Total liabilities and equity	$532

Admiral Foods Corporation Income Statement
(in millions of dollars)

Sales	$1261.0
Less Expenses, excluding depreciation	1118.2
Less Depreciation	36.0
Earnings before interest and taxes	$ 106.8
Less Interest	12.8
Earnings before taxes	$ 94.0
Less Taxes (40%)	37.6
Earnings after taxes	$ 56.4

**Favorite Food Systems, Inc. Balance Sheet
(in millions of dollars)**

Current assets	$10.6	Current liabilities	$ 6.5
Fixed assets, net	12.1	Long-term debt	2.2
		Common equity (2,000,000 shares)	14.0
Total assets	$22.7	Total liabilities and equity	$22.7

**Favorite Food Systems, Inc., Income Statement
(in millions of dollars)**

Sales	$75.2
Less Expenses, excluding depreciation	65.4
Less Depreciation	1.4
Earnings before interest and taxes	$ 8.4
Less Interest	0.4
Earnings before taxes	$ 8.0
Less Taxes (40%)	3.2
Earnings after taxes	$ 4.8

Additional Information

	Admiral Foods Corporation	Favorite Food Systems
Dividends per share	$ 2.50	$ 0.60
Common stock (price per share)	$50	$15

Marie Harrington received her B.B.A. degree in finance 3 years ago and went to work for Admiral Foods as a financial analyst in the corporate budget department. Recently, she became a senior financial analyst responsible for analyzing mergers and major capital expenditures. One of her first assignments is to prepare a financial analysis of the proposed Favorite acquisition. It is the conservative policy of Admiral Foods to analyze acquisitions assuming that no synergistic benefits will occur. Admiral Foods has found that the amount of synergy in a merger is relatively difficult to forecast. During Harrington's discussions with her supervisor, they decided the analysis should contain the following items:

1. Calculate the exchange ratios, based on the common stock market value and earnings per share.
2. Mr. Favorite has suggested an exchange ratio based on a 25 percent increase over Favorite's current market price. Calculate this exchange ratio.
3. What is the maximum exchange ratio Admiral Foods should agree to if one of its acquisition criteria specifies no initial dilution in earnings per share? What per-share price for Favorite Food Systems does this exchange ratio represent?
4. Even though Harrington's assignment is primarily financial in nature, what other considerations are important in a merger such as this?
5. Calculate the Admiral Foods postmerger earnings per share assuming each share of Favorite stock is exchanged for 0.40 shares of Admiral stock.
6. In discussions with Admiral, Mr. Favorite has stated that he would prefer to exchange his Favorite shares for either Admiral common stock or a convertible preferred rather than cash or debentures. Why?
7. If Admiral Foods is concerned about the possibility that Mr. Favorite will sell his new Admiral shares relatively soon after the merger (and thereby

put downward pressure on the price of Admiral's stock), what can Admiral do to effectively prevent such a sale?

8. If Mr. Favorite is unsuccessful in his negotiations with Admiral, two of his key managers, together with a group of private investors, have expressed a willingness to take the company private in a leveraged buyout transaction. How do you think such a transaction would be structured?

9. Based on the information given in the case and your analysis, what do you feel is a fair exchange ratio?

APPENDIX A
TAXES AND DEPRECIATION

GLOSSARY OF NEW TERMS

Capital Gain   Profit on the sale of a capital asset.

Capital Loss   Loss on the sale of a capital asset.

Marginal Tax Rate   The tax rate on the next dollar of taxable income earned by an individual or firm.

S Corporation   A small business that takes advantage of the corporate form of organization while having its income taxed directly to the stockholders at their individual personal income tax rates.

Tax Deduction   An amount subtracted from taxable income. For a corporation with a 35 percent marginal tax rate, a $100 tax deduction reduces taxable income by $100 and reduces taxes owed by $35.

INTRODUCTION

Both individuals and businesses must pay taxes on their incomes. The type and rates of taxation that businesses must pay depends on how they are organized. Generally, when organized as a corporation, business income is taxed at corporate rates, whereas business income of sole proprietorships and partnerships is taxed at the rates of the individual owners or partners.[1] Since corporations are the dominant form of business organization (in terms of sales), this appendix focuses on corporate income taxes.

Federal income tax laws were first enacted by the government in 1913 and have been changed numerous times since then. The most recent major changes occurred with the passage of the Revenue Reconciliation Act of 1993. The act raised both individual and corporate income tax rates and decreased the tax deductions that may be taken. This appendix contains a brief introduction to some tax law concepts and provides the background needed for understanding tax issues discussed in the book.

CORPORATE INCOME TAXES

In general, the taxable income of a corporation is calculated by subtracting business expenses from revenues. Tax-deductible[2] business expenses normally include the cost of goods sold, selling and administrative expenses, depreciation

---

[1]One exception is the S corporation, which is discussed later in this appendix.

[2]A *tax deduction* differs from a *tax credit*. A tax deduction is subtracted from a firm's revenues in calculating taxable income, whereas a tax credit is a direct deduction from the firm's tax liability.

TAXABLE INCOME	MARGINAL TAX RATE	TAX CALCULATION BASE TAX + (MARGINAL TAX RATE × AMOUNT OVER BASE INCOME)
Up to $50,000	15%	$0 + (15% × Amount over $0)
$50,001–$75,000	25%	$7,500 + (25% × Amount over $50,000)
$75,001–$100,000	34%	$13,750 + (34% × Amount over $75,000)
$100,001–$335,000	39%*	$22,250 + (39% × Amount over $100,000)
$335,001–$10,000,000	34%	$113,900 + (34% × Amount over $335,000)
$10,000,001–$15,000,000	35%	$3,400,000 + (35% × Amount over $10,000,000)
$15,000,001–$18,333,333	38%**	$5,150,000 + (38% × Amount over $15,000,000)
Over $18,333,333	35%	35% × Taxable Income

*Includes additional 5% "recapture" tax under the Tax Reform Act of 1986.
**Includes additional 3% "recapture" tax under the Revenue Reconciliation Act of 1993.

TABLE A-1
Corporate Tax Rates under Revenue Reconciliation Act of 1993

allowances,[3] and interest expenses. Federal income taxes are computed on the resulting taxable income. For tax years beginning on or after December 31, 1992, the tax rates imposed on corporations are shown in Table A-1.

The benefits of the 15 percent and 25 percent rates are phased out (or "recaptured") by imposing an additional 5 percent tax (i.e., 39 percent instead of 34 percent) on taxable income between $100,001 and $335,000. The benefit of the 34 percent rate on taxable income between $335,000 and $10,000,000 is phased out by imposing an additional 3 percent tax (i.e., 38 percent instead of 35 percent) on taxable income between $15,000,001 and $18,333,333. The effect of these provisions is that corporations with taxable incomes in excess of $18,333,333 pay a flat rate of 35 percent on all taxable income.

The calculation of the total tax for various levels of taxable income is shown in Table A-2. The *average tax rate* of a corporation is calculated by dividing the total tax by taxable income. The *marginal tax rate* of a corporation is defined as the tax rate on the next dollar of taxable income. For large corporations with taxable incomes exceeding $18,333,333, the effective marginal and average tax rates will be equal to 35 percent.

In addition to paying taxes on *operating* or *ordinary income,* corporations must also pay taxes on *capital gains income* and *dividend income.*

TABLE A-2
Computation of Corporate Income Taxes

TAXABLE INCOME	MARGINAL TAX RATE	TAX CALCULATION	AVERAGE TAX RATE
$ 25,000	15%	$0 + (.15 × $25,000) = $3,750	15%
75,000	25	$7,500 + (.25 × $25,000) = $13,750	18.33
100,000	34	$13,750 + (.34 × $25,000) = $22,250	22.25
250,000	39	$22,250 + (.39 × $150,000) = $80,750	32.3
1,250,000	34	$113,900 + (.34 × $915,000) = $425,000	34.0
2,500,000	34	$113,900 + (.34 × $2,165,000) = $850,000	34.0
12,500,000	35	$3,400,000 + (.35 × $2,500,000) = $4,275,000	34.2
17,500,000	38	$5,150,000 + (.38 × $2,500,000) = $6,100,000	34.86
25,000,000	35	.35 × $25,000,000 = $8,750,000	35.0
125,000,000	35	.35 × $125,000,000 = $43,750,000	35.0

[3]This appendix contains a detailed discussion of depreciation methods.

Capital Gains Income

Corporate capital gains income currently (1997) is taxed at the same marginal tax rate as ordinary income. Prior to the enactment of the Tax Reform Act of 1986, capital gains income for most large U.S. corporations was taxed at a lower rate than ordinary income. Corporate capital losses are deductible only against capital gains. Net capital losses may be carried back and applied against net gains in the prior three years. Any remaining net capital loss may be carried forward for five years and applied against capital gains in those years.

Dividend Income

Dividends received by a corporation are normally entitled to a 70 percent exclusion from federal income taxes. To illustrate, suppose that the Hastings Corporation owns stock in the Fremont Corporation and that Fremont pays $100,000 in dividends to Hastings during 1993. Hastings has to pay taxes on only 30 percent of the $100,000, or $30,000. (The other 70 percent, or $70,000, is excluded; that is, received tax-free. However, Fremont has to pay taxes on its income before paying the $100,000 to Hastings, because *dividends paid by a firm are not considered tax-deductible expenses.*) The $30,000 of taxable dividend income is taxed at ordinary income tax rates.[4] Assuming that Hastings is large enough to have a marginal tax rate of 35 percent, the tax on the dividends is $30,000 × 0.35 = $10,500. For corporations having a marginal tax rate of 35 percent, intercompany dividends are taxed at an effective rate of 10.5 percent; that is, $(1 - 0.7) \times 35\%$.

Loss Carrybacks and Carryforwards

Corporations that sustain net operating losses during a particular year are permitted by tax laws to apply the losses against any taxable income in other years, thereby lowering the taxes owed in those years. If such a loss is applied against a previous year, it is called a *loss carryback;* if it is applied against a succeeding year, it is called a *loss carryforward.*

The tax laws specify that a corporation's net operating loss may be carried back three years and forward fifteen years to offset taxable income in those years. For example, suppose the NOL Corporation incurs a net operating loss totaling $200,000 in 19X6. This loss may be carried back three years to 19X3. If the NOL Corporation had 19X3 taxable income of $125,000, for example, it could receive a tax refund equal to the taxes it paid for that year. The remaining $75,000 portion of the 19X6 net operating loss next could be carried back to 19X4.

 ENTREPRENEURIAL FINANCE
S CORPORATIONS

The Internal Revenue Code allows certain small businesses to take advantage of the corporate form of organization while having their business income taxed directly to their shareholders at individual income tax rates. To qualify for S corporation status, a firm may not have more than 35 shareholders.

---

[4]For corporate shareholders that own between 20 percent and 80 percent of the voting power and value of the stock of a dividend-paying corporation, there is an 80 percent dividends-received exclusion. There is a 100 percent dividends-received exclusion if a corporation owns more than 80 percent of the stock of a dividend-paying corporation.

The primary benefit of S corporations is the avoidance of the *double taxation of dividends*. With a regular corporation, earnings are taxed twice—once at the corporate level and a second time as dividends at the individual level. With an **S corporation,** the company's earnings are passed (tax-free) to the shareholders and taxed only once as personal income. Despite the fact that the top personal tax rate of 39.6 percent is higher than the top corporate rate of 34 percent for companies with less than $10 million in income, the combination of the corporate and personal taxes usually is greater than the single personal tax paid by S corporation shareholders on an equivalent amount of income.

A further advantage of the S corporation form of organization is that the company often can pass losses (deductible backward or forward for three years) to shareholders who can then use these losses to offset other income and thus reduce their tax liability.

 INTRODUCTION TO DEPRECIATION

Prior to the establishment of the Modified Accelerated Cost Recovery System (MACRS) of depreciation, a number of alternative methods of depreciation were permitted by the IRS. These methods included straight-line depreciation and various accelerated methods, such as the sum-of-the-years'-digits. Although tax law changes have rendered these techniques out of date for tax purposes, it is still useful to understand them for the following reasons:

1. Most firms continue to own assets acquired prior to these tax law changes. These assets are being depreciated using one of the alternative depreciation methods.
2. Some firms continue to use these alternative methods for financial reporting purposes.

Details also are provided about the calculation of depreciation amounts under the Modified ACRS (MACRS) system of depreciation, which is used for assets placed in service after December 31, 1986.

 STRAIGHT-LINE DEPRECIATION

Under the pre-ACRS straight-line depreciation method, the annual amount of an asset's depreciation is calculated as follows:[5]

$$\text{Annual depreciation amount} = \frac{\text{Cost} - \text{Estimated salvage value}}{\text{Estimated economic life (years)}} \quad \text{(A.1)}$$

For example, if a company purchases a machine that costs $12,000 and has an estimated salvage value of $2,000 at the end of a 5-year economic life, the annual depreciation amount is ($12,000 – $2,000)/5 = $2,000.

---

[5]Note that under pre-ACRS depreciation rules, the annual depreciation amount was determined as the cost of the asset less its estimated salvage value divided by the estimated economic life. In comparison, under the Accelerated Cost Recovery System provisions of the 1986 Tax Reform Act, no consideration is given to estimated salvage value in determining the annual depreciation amount. See Steven C. Dilley and James C. Young, *The Tax Reform Act of 1986: The New ACRS Rules* (Paramus, NJ: Prentice-Hall, 1986) for a discussion of the Accelerated Cost Recovery System and additional detail on the MACRS system.

Straight-line depreciation is an appropriate method to employ when an asset is being used up fairly evenly over its lifetime. Many companies use straight-line depreciation for financial accounting purposes—that is, in their reports to stockholders, because it usually results in a greater reported net income—and an accelerated depreciation method for federal income tax purposes, because accelerated depreciation can result in the deferment of tax payments.

 ## SUM-OF-THE-YEARS'-DIGITS METHOD

In the sum-of-the-years'-digit method, annual depreciation charges are computed by multiplying a decreasing fraction by the asset's original cost (less salvage value). The fraction's denominator is the sum of the digits that represent each year of the asset's expected economic life. For example, the sum-of-the-years'-digits for an asset with an expected 5-year lifetime is $5 + 4 + 3 + 2 + 1$, or 15.[6] The numerator of the fraction for the first year is the highest digit—in this case, 5. The second year's numerator is the next highest digit—in this case, 4—and so on.

For example, suppose the company mentioned earlier decides to depreciate its $12,000 asset according to the sum-of-the-years'-digits method. Recall that the asset has a $2,000 expected salvage value and a 5-year expected useful life. The calculations are shown in Table A-3.

 ## DECLINING BALANCE METHOD

The declining balance method allows a firm to take a percentage of the depreciation amount greater than the straight-line amount during the first year of an asset's life. During subsequent years, the book value, or undepreciated amount, of the asset is multiplied by this percentage to calculate annual depreciation costs.

Two commonly used variations of the declining balance method include the 200 percent declining balance, often termed *double declining balance,* and the 150 percent declining balance. The MACRS tax laws specify which variation is to be used for each asset class.

TABLE A-3
Sample Sum-of-the-Years'-Digits Depreciation Calculations

YEAR (1)	DEPRECIABLE BASE (2)	FRACTION (3)	DEPRECIATION AMOUNT (4) = (2) × (3)
1	$10,000	5/15	$ 3,333
2	10,000	4/15	2,667
3	10,000	3/15	2,000
4	10,000	2/15	1,333
5	10,000	1/15	667
			$10,000

[6]In general, the sum of the years' digits is equal to $n(n + 1)/2$, where n is the number of years.

In the declining balance method, the annual depreciation amount of an asset is calculated by multiplying the straight-line rate by the declining balance percentage figure to get an accelerated rate. The accelerated rate then is multiplied by the asset's book value at the end of each previous year. As each year's depreciation amount is subtracted from the cost of the asset, the resulting *balance* in the asset's book value *declines*. Thus, the depreciation amount *decreases* as the years pass.

 ## MODIFIED ACCELERATED COST RECOVERY SYSTEM

The Tax Reform Act of 1986 created the Modified Accelerated Cost Recovery System of depreciation. Under this depreciation system, six classes of assets are established. All depreciable assets (new and used), except real estate, are assigned to one of these six classes. Regardless of the expected useful life of an asset, its annual depreciation is computed according to the rules for the class of assets to which it has been assigned.

Table A-4 summarizes the MACRS classes and depreciable lives that must be used under the 1986 Tax Act. The vast majority of business equipment, from office furnishings to machinery, is found in the 7-year class.

Depreciation Rate

Annual depreciation charges for each asset class must be computed using the declining balance method of depreciation, switching to straight-line at the optimal time. For the 3-, 5-, 7- and 10-year asset classes, a 200 percent declining balance method is used. A 150 percent declining balance method is used for the 15- and 20-year asset classes. The full installed cost of each asset forms the basis

TABLE A-4
MACRS Recovery Periods

RECOVERY PERIOD AND ASSET CLASS*	PROPERTY INCLUDED IN CLASS
3-Year	A small class of short-lived assets, including some special tools, some tractors, and race horses (over 2 years old)
5-Year	Automobiles, light trucks, heavy general purpose trucks, buses, oil drilling equipment, information systems, certain semiconductor, textile, chemical, electronic, and manufacturing equipment, and dairy and breeder cattle
7-Year	Most manufacturing equipment, railroad track, office furniture and equipment, railroad cars and locomotives, airplanes, amusement parks, and mining equipment
10-Year	Vessels, barges, petroleum refining equipment, railroad tank cars, and some manufacturing equipment
15-Year	Electric generation and distribution systems, cement manufacturing equipment, nuclear power plants, natural gas pipelines, billboards, sewage treatment plants, and telephone distribution plants
20-Year	Most public utility property, sewer pipes, and railroad structures

*Most equipment is contained in the 7-year class.

upon which depreciation is computed and charged. *Expected salvage value is not considered* in the depreciation calculations under MACRS.

Table A-5 provides the annual depreciation percentages. These percentages are multiplied by the installed cost of the asset when computing annual depreciation for any asset in the six classes. Note that the number of years of depreciation is always one greater than the number indicated in the asset class; for example, for a 5-year class asset, depreciation is spread over a total of 6 years. The reason for this is that the 1986 Tax Reform Act requires that the half-year convention be followed. The half-year convention treats any asset placed in service during year 1 as being placed in service in the middle of the year. Consequently, the asset only receives one-half of the first year's depreciation. The half-year convention also applies to the last year of depreciation, thus making the number of years of depreciation 1 year longer than is indicated in the asset class name.

For example, assume General Electric acquires a $9,000 piece of machinery, which requires $1,000 for shipping and installation. Under MACRS, this asset would be in the 7-year class. The depreciable basis for the asset is

Asset cost	$ 9,000
Plus Installation and shipping	1,000
Equals Depreciable basis	$10,000

Table A-5 provides the depreciation rates applied to this 7-year asset that General Electric has acquired. The annual MACRS depreciation for this asset is computed as follows:

TABLE A-5
Depreciation Rates for MACRS Property Other than Real Property*

RECOVERY YEAR	3-YEAR	5-YEAR	7-YEAR	10-YEAR	15-YEAR	20-YEAR
1	33.33%	20.00%	14.29%	10.00%	5.00%	3.750%
2	44.45	32.00	24.49	18.00	9.50	7.219
3	14.81	19.20	17.49	14.40	8.55	6.677
4	7.41	11.52**	12.49	11.52	7.70	6.177
5		11.52	8.93**	9.22	6.93	5.713
6		5.76	8.92	7.37	6.23	5.285
7			8.93	6.55**	5.90**	4.888
8			4.46	6.55	5.90	4.522
9				6.56	5.91	4.462**
10				6.55	5.90	4.461
11				3.28	5.91	4.462
12					5.90	4.461
13					5.91	4.462
14					5.90	4.461
15					5.91	4.462
16					2.95	4.461
17						4.462
18						4.461
19						4.462
20						4.461
21						2.231

*Assumes the half-year convention applies.
**Switchover to straight-line depreciation over the remaining useful life.

Year	MACRS Depreciation Rate	Amount of Depreciation (MACRS Rate × $10,000)
1	14.29%	$ 1,429
2	24.49	2,449
3	17.49	1,749
4	12.49	1,249
5	8.93	893
6	8.92	892
7	8.93	893
8	4.46	446
	100.00%	$10,000

MACRS Recovery Periods and Economic Life of an Asset

With the adoption of the MACRS recovery periods for all assets, there no longer is any direct relationship between the period over which depreciation is taken on an asset and that asset's economic life. Consequently, when estimating the cash flows from a project, there normally will be several years beyond the MACRS recovery period when no depreciation expense will be recorded. It is important to remember that cash flows for all projects (assets) should be projected over the full economic life of the project, not just the MACRS recovery period.

REAL PROPERTY

The Tax Reform Act of 1986 establishes two classes of real property for depreciation purposes. The 27.5-Year Straight-Line Class includes residential rental property. The second class includes all nonresidential real property, such as office buildings. The recovery period for nonresidential real property was originally 31.5 years, but it was changed to 39 years in 1993 for property placed in service after May 12, 1993.

Depreciation for real property is computed on a straight-line basis. The amount of depreciation taken during the first year depends upon the month property is placed in service. Furthermore, a mid-month convention is used; that is, it is assumed that a building is placed in service in the middle of the first month and is therefore eligible for only one-half month's depreciation during month one. For example, consider a $100,000 building placed in service during April 1994. The straight-line rate is 2.564 percent (1/39), and the depreciation on a $100,000 building for a full year is $2,564. Under the mid-month convention, April, the month the property is placed in service, is considered half a month. Thus, for 1994, the building owner gets 8.5 months (8.5/12) or 70.83 percent of a full year's depreciation; this amounts to $1,816 (70.83 percent × $2,564) in 1994 for the $100,000 building.

■ QUESTIONS AND TOPICS FOR DISCUSSION

1. What are the differences between the operating income, capital gains income, and dividend income of a corporation? At approximately what rates are these different types of income taxed?

2. What is an *S corporation?*

3. What do you think is the reason for the 70 percent corporate-dividend exclusion?

4. What method of depreciation would you prefer, MACRS or straight-line, if your objective is to maximize the present value of your firm's cash flows?

■ SELF-TEST PROBLEMS

ST1. During the past year, Alcore Enterprises, Inc. had sales of $3 million, cost of goods sold of $1.8 million, operating expenses of $800,000, and interest expenses of $200,000. Alcore paid preferred stock dividends of $100,000 and common stock dividends of $200,000 during the year. Alcore also retired maturing debt totaling $1.5 million during the year. Using the U.S. federal corporate tax rates shown in Table A-1, what was Alcore's taxable income and its total tax liability for the year? What are Alcore's average and marginal tax rates?

ST2. Jenkins Products, Inc. had sales of $5 million, cost of goods sold of $3 million, other operating expenses of $1 million, and interest expenses of $200,000 last year. During the year, Jenkins sold a plant and its associated equipment for $1.2 million. The book value of the plant and equipment was $500,000. What is Jenkins's taxable income and what taxes are due?

ST3. Calculate the MACRS depreciation schedule for a milling machine that costs $47,500 and has installation and shipping costs of $2,500. The milling machine is classified as a 7-year MACRS asset. The milling machine is estimated to have a salvage value of $15,000 at the end of its 15-year economic life.

■ PROBLEMS*

1. Last year, Idaho Steel Corporation had taxable ordinary income of $2 million and capital gains income of $500,000. The company also had $50,000 in dividend income and paid its stockholders $150,000 in dividends. Calculate the Idaho Steel Corporation's tax bill.

2. Last year the Selling Corporation had earnings before interest and taxes (operating income) equal to $1 million. It paid $200,000 in dividends to its stockholders and $100,000 in interest to its creditors. During the year the company also repaid a bank loan of $150,000. Assuming a corporate income tax rate of 40 percent on all taxable income, calculate the Selling Corporation's tax bill.

3. Clapper Industries reported taxable income of $290,000.
   a. What is Clapper's marginal tax rate based on the corporate tax rate table in this appendix?
   b. What is Clapper's average tax rate?
   c. If Clapper's taxable income increases to $410,000, what will be Clapper's marginal and average tax rates?

4. Using the tax rates shown in Table A-1, determine the expected annual tax liability of Kaiser Enterprises (a new firm formed in 1996), if the firm anticipates the following stream of taxable income:

Year	Taxable Income
1996	$30,000
1997	80,000
1998	(150,000)
1999	125,000
2000	150,000
2001	(75,000)

*Colored numbers denote problems that have check answers provided at the end of the book.

5. The CIG Power Corporation expects to report earnings before interest and taxes of $25 million this year. Management has determined that the firm needs $10 million of new capital this year to fund its anticipated capital investments. One alternative is to borrow the funds from a syndicate of banks at a 15 percent rate of interest. Alternatively, CIG could sell $10 million of a new preferred stock that pays annual dividends of $1.4 million. The marginal tax rate for CIG is 40 percent.

   a. What will be the "earnings after tax and available for common stockholders" if the money is borrowed?

   b. What will be the "earnings after tax and available for common stockholders" if preferred stock is sold?

6. Canon Corporation expects to receive $3 million of dividend income from the shares of stock it holds in Fuji Enterprises. Canon currently owns 15 percent of Fuji's outstanding stock. Canon's marginal tax rate is 40 percent and its average tax rate is 37 percent. What after-tax amount of cash will Canon receive from Fuji?

7. Patriot Industries recently sold its fin fabrication machine for $150,000. The machine originally cost $500,000 and has a current book value of $100,000. Patriot's marginal tax rate is 35 percent for ordinary income and 35 percent for capital gains income.

   a. What amount of gain has Patriot received from this transaction?

   b. Is this a capital or ordinary gain?

   c. How much tax must Patriot pay on this transaction?

8. Amexicorp, Inc., a producer of security systems, had sales of $400 million, cost of goods sold of $150 million, operating expenses of $100 million, and interest expense of $100 million. Amexicorp also received $10 million in dividends from other corporations in which it had less than a 20 percent ownership stake. During the year, Amexicorp also sold $20 million of assets that it carried on its books at a book value of $17 million. Amexicorp paid preferred stock dividends totaling $10 million during the year. Common stock dividends paid were $5 million. Use the tax rates shown in Table A-1.

   a. What is Amexicorp's after-tax net income available to common stockholders?

   b. What would have been Amexicorp's after-tax net income available to common stockholders if the assets that were sold had a book value of $25 million?

9. Using the following methods, calculate the depreciation schedule for an asset that has a $15,000 original cost, an expected useful life of 5 years, and no expected salvage value:

   a. Straight-line depreciation.

   b. Sum-of-the-years'-digits depreciation.

10. a. Calculate the annual MACRS depreciation for a machine in the 7-year MACRS asset class, assuming that the asset costs $20,000.

    b. If you knew that the asset had an expected salvage value of $2,000 at the end of its 12-year economic life, would your answer to Part a change?

11. Calculate the annual MACRS depreciation for a $20,000 truck that qualifies as a 5-year MACRS asset. The truck is estimated to have a $7,000 salvage value 6 years from now.

12. Calculate the MACRS depreciation schedule for a drill press that costs $148,000 and has installation and shipping costs of $2,000. The drill press is classified as a 7-year MACRS asset.

13. Calculate the depreciation schedule for a $100,000 office building placed in service in October 1996.

■ SOLUTIONS TO SELF-TEST PROBLEMS

ST1.

Sales	$3,000,000
Less: Cost of goods sold	1,800,000
Gross profit margin	$1,200,000

Less: Operating expenses	800,000
Operating earnings before interest and taxes	$ 400,000
Less: Interest expense	200,000
Earnings before tax (taxable income)	$ 200,000

Tax calculation:

$$Total\ tax = \$22,250 + .39\ (\$200,000 - \$100,000)$$

$$= \$61,250$$

The marginal tax rate is 39 percent (34 percent bracket plus 5 percent surcharge). The average tax rate is 30.63 percent ($61,250 ÷ $200,000).

Note that there are no tax consequences associated with the retirement of maturing debt or the payment of common and preferred stock dividends. None of those outlays is tax deductible.

ST2.

Sales		$5,000,000
Less: Cost of goods sold		3,000,000
Gross profit margin		$2,000,000
Less: Operating expenses		1,000,000
Operating earnings before interest and taxes		$1,000,000
Less: Interest expense		200,000
Earnings before tax and gains from asset sales		$ 800,000
Plus: Gain on sale of plant and equipment		
Sale price	$1,200,000	
Book value	500,000	700,000
Earnings before tax (taxable income)		$1,500,000

$$Total\ tax = \$113,900 + .34(\$1,500,000 - \$335,000)$$

$$= \$510,000$$

Note that a portion of the gain on the sale of the plant and equipment might have been classified as a capital gain if the sales price had exceeded the original cost of the asset. However, because the corporate capital gain and ordinary tax rates are currently (1997) the same, this distinction is unimportant.

ST3. Basis for depreciation = $50,000. (Expected salvage value is not considered under the MACRS system of depreciation.)

Year	MACRS Rate	Depreciation
1	14.29%	$ 7,145
2	24.49	12,245
3	17.49	8,745
4	12.49	6,245
5	8.93	4,465
6	8.92	4,460
7	8.93	4,465
8	4.46	2,230

APPENDIX B
AN OVERVIEW OF THE
CFM EXCEL DISK

The seventh edition of *Contemporary Financial Management* has a diskette available, the *CFM* Excel Disk, with a set of financial templates that can be used to solve a large number of selected problems and cases in the book. These problems are identified with a computer diskette logo in the margin. The templates are designed to be used in conjunction with the popular spreadsheet program Excel. *The templates are extremely user-friendly, and require no prior knowledge of Excel.* Excel is available in most microcomputer labs. Excel and the accompanying templates run on any DOS-based machine and on Macintosh machines. The diskette includes a user's manual.

The following 20 templates are available:

1.	Bondref:	Bond refunding analysis
2.	Bonval:	Bond valuation analysis
3.	Capbudg:	Capital budgeting analysis
4.	Cashbudg:	Cash budgeting analysis
5.	Compaper:	Commercial paper financing analysis
6.	Compbal:	Compensating balance loan analysis
7.	Convsec:	Convertible security valuation
8.	Costcap:	Weighted cost of capital analysis
9.	Credstd:	Credit standards analysis
10.	Credterm:	Credit terms analysis
11.	Cstockvl:	Common stock valuation
12.	Factorar:	Factoring accounts receivable analysis
13.	Finstmta:	Financial statement analysis
14.	Indiffpt:	Indifference point analysis
15.	Levb-e:	Leverage (operating, financial, and combined) and breakeven analysis
16.	Loanamor:	Loan amortization
17.	Lockbox:	Lockbox analysis
18.	Option:	Black-Scholes option pricing analysis
19.	Pfdstk:	Preferred stock valuation
20.	Revcredit:	Revolving credit analysis

APPENDIX C
AN INTRODUCTION TO THE INTERNET
WITH APPLICATIONS IN FINANCE

WHAT IS THE INTERNET?

The Internet is a worldwide system of computers that electronically share information with each other. More exactly, the "Net" is composed of several million computers (mainframes, personal computers, laptops, and so on) that are linked by cable, telephone wire, satellite signal, and other electronic means. Every day, literally thousands of newcomers plug into the net and become part of this ever-expanding "Information Highway."

THE ORIGIN OF THE INTERNET

The Internet began as a military project in the 1960s. The U.S. Defense Department, seeking an information-exchange system immune to nuclear attack, leased a network of telephone lines that could automatically route data around failed circuits, thereby linking together key government agencies, military bases, and other entities deemed vital to nuclear survival. In the 1970s numerous universities began tapping into this information-exchange system and found it to be a highly convenient means of sharing research data. In the last decade (and especially within the last several years), commercial enterprises have also begun to use (and, within the past year, dominate) this rapidly growing phenomenon.

HOW INFORMATION IS RELAYED OVER THE INTERNET

Information is shared over the Net using various conventions and standards ("rules of the game") that have evolved over the last several decades. For example, files are transferred from one computer to another by a system known as **FTP** (File Transfer Protocol). Other conventions include the Web (where various entities maintain information for others to see) and a standardized Web address format known as **URL** (Uniform Resource Locator). Other common Internet terms are included in a glossary at the end of this appendix.

Because it is largely unregulated, the Internet offers no guarantee as to the validity or accuracy of its information. However, major users (government agencies, Fortune 500 firms, and others) generally stand behind the integrity of the information/data that they make available through the Net.

ACCESSING THE INTERNET

Anyone can access the Internet in one of three ways. A "direct" connection requires laying cable to connect to the Net, and is—needless to say—very expensive. Generally, only major organizations, such as large universities or Fortune 500 firms, can afford a direct connection.

Internet Service Providers (ISPs, or just "service providers") are a second means of tapping into the Net. These are commercial enterprises (such as AT&T, MCI, and Earthlink) that have a direct connection to the Net and sell Internet access to others (mostly businesses) that connect to the service provider mostly through standard phone wires.

On-line services are the third (and most popular) avenue to the Information Highway. These are essentially giant service providers that primarily target private individuals who tap into the on-line service via their home phones. Anyone with a personal computer, a home phone, and a modem can tap into an on-line service. Some of the more popular on-line services include America Online, Compuserve, and Prodigy.

Once users are connected to the Net, they are able to take advantage of a vast array of services. Besides e-mail, these services include free information and data, free software and games, entertainment, shopping, travel arrangements, and hundreds of major newspapers, journals, and full-color magazines. Another popular on-line service is the "chat group," where people from all walks of life "talk" with each other in real time.

FINANCIAL INFORMATION AVAILABLE ON THE INTERNET

The amount of financial information available on the Net is simply staggering (Figure C-1). Besides a vast array of current financial news, the Net provides access to: thousands of reference sources, including entire encyclopedias; financial/economic databases; professional journals of every sort; scores of financial newspapers and magazines (Figure C-2); electronic discussions on any financial topic; think-tank studies; speeches; articles; announcements; reports; tutorials; and more.

Without a doubt, the Internet is a researcher's dream come true. Sitting at your computer, you can quickly research any financial or economic topic.

FIGURE C-1
Financial Uses of the Internet

- News/information/research
- Financial planning
- Discussion groups
- Financial services (see Figure C-11)
- Financial software (see Figure C-12)
- Education (see Figure C-13)

FIGURE C-2
**Selected Financial Publications
Available on the Net***

- *Economist*
- *Business Week*
- *Wall Street Journal*
- *Financial Times*
- *New York Times*
- *Worth* Magazine
- *Investors Business Daily*
- *Consumer Reports on Money*
- *Inc.* Magazine
- *Dow Jones Newsletters*

*Note: These publications comprise only a small fraction of the financial publications currently available on the Net; moreover, additional publications are constantly being added. All publications are available by accessing the publisher's Web site directly or indirectly through an on-line service (such as America Online). For example, the Web address of the *Wall Street Journal* is http://www.wsj.com; alternatively, many on-line services will provide a link to this Web site.

Facilitating this process are a number of **search engines,** which conduct searches in the keywords you designate. (Figure C-3 lists a few of the more common search engines available to researchers, along with instructions on how to use Yahoo, one of the most popular search engines.)

WHAT IS THE WEB?

The **World Wide Web** (WWW, or the Web) is the portion of the Internet containing highly colorful and graphical information on every topic and is a wealth of information and data. Thousands of organizations (and thousands of individuals) maintain **Web sites** where they park mountains of multimedia information about themselves, their products, their services, their histories, their favorite subjects, and so on.

FIGURE C-3
Common Search Engines

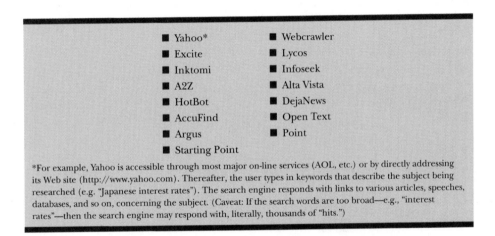

- Yahoo*
- Excite
- Inktomi
- A2Z
- HotBot
- AccuFind
- Argus
- Starting Point
- Webcrawler
- Lycos
- Infoseek
- Alta Vista
- DejaNews
- Open Text
- Point

*For example, Yahoo is accessible through most major on-line services (AOL, etc.) or by directly addressing its Web site (http://www.yahoo.com). Thereafter, the user types in keywords that describe the subject being researched (e.g. "Japanese interest rates"). The search engine responds with links to various articles, speeches, databases, and so on, concerning the subject. (Caveat: If the search words are too broad—e.g., "interest rates"—then the search engine may respond with, literally, thousands of "hits.")

With respect to finance, Web sites provide practically any piece of financial information imaginable—stock prices, commodity prices, currency exchange rates, bond ratings, and so on (Figure C-4). Also, the Net provides a wealth of company-specific information, from detailed financial statements to analysts' earnings predictions (Figure C-5). Literally, almost any publicly available piece of information can be obtained through the Internet: information on financial/economic databases, financial services, search engines, educational resources, electronic journals (Figure C-6), electronic working papers (Figure C-7), and much more. You can even tour the Finance Virtual Library (Figure C-8).

FIGURE C-4
Selected Financial Web Sites

SERVICE ORGANIZATIONS	WEB ADDRESS
Thomson Investors Network[1]	http://www.thomsoninvest.net
Hoovers[2]	http://www.hoovers.com
PC Quote	http://www.pcquote.com
Corporate Financials Online[3]	http://cfonews.com
FinanCenter	http://www.financenter.com
EDGAR[4]	http://www.sec.gov/
CorpFiNet	http://www.corpfinet.com
National Financial Services Network	http://www.nfsn.com
Investors Edge	http://www.irnet.com
Money Magazine	http://www.pathfinder.com/money
Financial Economics Network	http://www.ssrn.com
National Corporate Services[5]	http://www.natcorp.com

[1]A comprehensive financial information/services Web site.
[2]Financial information on 10,000+ companies.
[3]Financial information on thousands of U.S. and foreign companies.
[4]Complete SEC information (10-Ks, etc.) on every publicly traded U.S. company.
[5]A cornucopia of financial information, including the Web addresses of major corporations.
Note: Most search engines (such as Yahoo) provide excellent links to major financial Web sites.

FIGURE C-5
Selected Company Information Available on the Net*

■ Company histories

■ Balance sheets

■ Income statements

■ Cash-flow statements

■ Ratio analyses

■ Earnings predictions

■ 10Ks

■ 10Qs

■ Industry comparisons

*For example, information about Ford Motor Company could be obtained in several ways: 1. access the firm's Web page (http://www.ford.com) and then follow the links to Ford's history, products, financial statements, etc.; 2. utilizing an on-line service (such as America Online), choose the "Finance" option from its main menu and then follow the appropriate submenus to arrive at exhaustive financial information on any major firm and/or industry; or 3. access the Web site of a major financial services firm (such as Hoovers) and then follow the links to its analysis of the particular company.

FIGURE C-6
Selected Finance Journals
on the Internet

- *Journal of Finance**
- *Journal of Financial and Quantitative Analysis*
- *Journal of Financial Economics**
- *Journal of Financial Research*
- *Journal of Applied Corporate Finance**
- *Financial Analysts Journal*
- *Applied Mathematical Finance**
- *Review of Financial Studies*

*Note: All of these journals are available through FEN (whose Web address is given in Figure C-4), and most are available by directly accessing the Web site of the sponsoring institution. For example, the *Journal of Finance* can be accessed through FEN or by directly accessing the home page of Ohio State University's Finance Department (whose Web address is given in Figure C-8).

FIGURE C-7
Selected Working Paper Series*

- Washington University
- Georgetown University
- University of Georgia
- University of Maryland
- UCLA
- McGill University
- Ohio State University
- USC
- Harvard University
- University of Texas
- Salomon Center
- New York University
- Federal Reserve Banks
- University of Western Australia
- Price Waterhouse
- IFCI Geneva Papers
- Berkeley University
- University of Edinburgh

*Note: Some working paper series are currently available in abstract and/or list form only. All working papers are accessible through Internet financial services (such as FEN), or by directly accessing the sponsoring organization's Web site.

FIGURE C-8
Finance Virtual Library*
(Selected Holdings)

- Financial Data (including price quotes)
- Commercial Banks
- Investment Banks
- Jobs in Finance
- Web Pages of Finance Faculty
- The Detective's Guide to Financial Information
- Sites of interest to Investors
- Sites of interest to Finance Researchers
- Sites of interest to Finance Students
- Sites of interest to Finance Executives
- Sites of interest to Investment Bankers
- Sites of interest to Finance Educators

*Web site address: http://www.cob.ohio-state.edu/dept/fin/overview.htm

For experienced Net users, a lot of not-so-public information is also available. Currently, there exist millions of Web sites, and thousands more are being created every day as more and more users crowd the Information Highway.

The various departments and agencies of the U.S. federal government also maintain Web sites, as do the governments of other major industrialized countries. These Web sites are excellent sources for instant price information, monetary data, trade statistics, and other data normally maintained by the federal government (Figure C-9).

Finally, stock exchanges, multilateral organizations, media services, and numerous private firms also offer a cornucopia of financial information at their respective Web sites (Figure C-10). Like most other Web sites, these also offer links to thousands of other resources.

 NEWSGROUPS

Besides sending and receiving e-mail, the Net can be used for discussions on any subject. You can join **newsgroups** to discuss any subject that interests you—corpo-

FIGURE C-9
Selected U.S. Government Web Sites

DEPARTMENT/AGENCY	WEB ADDRESS
U.S. Treasury	http://www.ustreas.gov/
Federal Reserve	http://www.bog.frb.fed.us/
Bureau of Labor Statistics	gopher://stats.bls.gov:70/1/
FDIC	http://www.fdic.gov/
OCC	http://www.occ.treas.gov
Securities and Exchange Commission	http://www.sec.gov/
Library of Congress	http://lcweb.loc.gov/
Fed World*	http://www.fedworld.gov/

*One-stop shopping for 130 government Web sites, with over 15,000 files on financial, business, health, environmental, and numerous other issues.

FIGURE C-10
Selected Sites of General Financial Interest

ORGANIZATION	WEB ADDRESS
New York Stock Exchange	http://www.nyse.com/
American Stock Exchange	http://www.amex.com
NASDAQ	http://.www.nasdaq.com/
World Bank (IMF)	http://www.worldbank.org/
American Journal Review[1]	http://www.newslink.org
Financial Pipeline	http://www.finpipe.com
Money Page	http://www.moneypage.com
Finance Hub	http://www.financehub.com
CNN Financial	http://cnnfn.com/
Bloomberg[2]	http://www.bloomberg.com/
Financial Executives Institute	http://www.fei.org
Investor Web	http://www.investorweb.com

[1]Provides links to over 3,700 on-line newspapers, magazines, and news services worldwide—including many financial Web sites.
[2]Provides extensive financial data both domestically and internationally.

rate mergers, black holes, cooking, jogging, witchcraft, higher mathematics, and any other topic that at least two people want to discuss. Just park your opinion on a "bulletin board" and you will receive feedback from all over the world. Many of these newsgroups have **distribution lists** which automatically distribute new bulletin-board notices and information (via e-mail) to the people comprising the newsgroups.

FINANCIAL SERVICES AVAILABLE ON THE NET

A multitude of financial services exist on the Internet, from banking and trading on-line to free financial software (Figure C-11). Many major banks allow routine banking transactions to be conducted over the Net, and most on-line services provide real-time trading of most financial securities (after you set up an on-line account with their respective brokers).

Also, financial software (and, in fact, software of every type) is available on either a "freeware" or "shareware" basis. **Freeware** is software that is literally free to download; **shareware** is software that can be downloaded on a trial basis and purchased later if the user likes it. On-line services typically offer freeware and software, as do many major universities and large corporations. For finance, such software includes stock analyses (both technical and fundamental), retirement planning, loan amortizations, and even balance-sheet construction (Figure C-12). Upgrades and patches of freeware and software are also available. To download a particular software program (or any other data), the user simply chooses the "download" option from the menu bar, and then follows instructions from there.

A number of financial "short courses" exist on the Net, from how to pick stocks to how to analyze a company. The on-line services offer such courses, as do many Web sites (Figure C-13).

FIGURE C-11
Financial Services Available on the Net*

- Brokerage services
- Banking services
- Insurance services
- Accounting services
- Financial analyses
- Retirement planning
- Portfolio management
- Tax planning
- Loan amortizations
- Mutual funds
- Stock quotes
- Financial news
- Financial research
- Financial discussion groups

*Primarily available in three ways: 1. via the major on-line services (American Online, Compuserve, etc.) by choosing the "Finance" option from the main menu and thereafter choosing submenu choices until the user arrives at the service desired; 2. by accessing the Web sites of major financial services firms (banks, brokers, mutual funds, etc.) and thereafter following the links to the service desired; or 3. by accessing a search engine (such as Alta Vista) and following its links to the service desired.

FIGURE C-12
Financial Software Available on the Net*

- Financial statement construction
- Financial forecasting
- Retirement planning
- Tax planning
- Investment programs
- Portfolio management
- Real-estate analyses
- Loan amortizations

*Primarily available through the major on-line services, as well as through various Web sites related to finance. For example, by accessing Microsoft's Web page (http://www.microsoft.com), a user could download an upgrade to one of Microsoft's software programs.

FIGURE C-13
Financial Education Available on the Net*

- Financial information/research
- Stock trading simulations
- Financial short courses
    - How to pick stocks
    - How to plan for retirement
    - How to analyze a company
    - How to invest in mutual funds
    - How to choose insurance
    - How to manage a portfolio
- Financial discussion groups
- Free financial software

*Available through the major on-line services, or through the Web sites of major financial organizations.

Simulations are also available on the Internet. Although the most popular simulation in finance is stock trading, other simulations include commodities trading, risk analysis, economic scenarios, and much more. Charts, graphs, and numerous graphical aids are also available.

Students can also benefit from the free financial software available on the Net (Figure C-12). You can download such software and thereafter use it to amortize a loan, plan your retirement, calculate your taxes, make a lease-or-buy decision, analyze financial statements, predict cash flows, set up a college-savings plan, and so on.

HOW DO I GET STARTED?

Getting started on the Internet is basically a matter of getting connected (by direct cable, telephone line, or electronic signal). After connection, if you can point and click, then you can "surf the Net."

If your organization is directly wired to the Net (the best of all worlds, due primarily to the high speed of data transmission), then your system administrator should have set up a mechanism for accessing the Net. (Usually there is an Internet icon on your main screen.) Most likely, your organization will also utilize a **Web browser,** such as Netscape, which will allow you to view the many thousands of Web sites maintained by various entities (firms, government agencies, universities, individuals, and so on).

If you utilize an Internet service provider (such as AT&T), your provider will have set up a mechanism by which you can access the Net. The procedure is the same—simply point and click to explore the icons of your choice.

If you subscribe to one of the major on-line services (such as America Online, Compuserve, or Prodigy), then you will have an Internet icon as part of your main menu of choices. Again, simply point and click to open up the usual array of Internet services.

A good analogy is that the Internet is a lot like being in a foreign country. No matter where you are or how lost you might become, if you keep looking and asking, you will eventually reach your destination—in addition to taking in a lot of sightseeing along the way. Fortunately, the majority of the standard avenues to and through the Net are extremely user friendly.

Not surprisingly, there exist scores of new books about the Internet, many of which are targeted toward the "newbie" who wants to get started. Since cyberspace changes so quickly, it's generally best to access a book with the latest possible copyright.

After you learn the basics, one of the monthly publications devoted to the Net (such as *Netguide*) should provide you with an easy-to-read road map with which to navigate the Information Highway. A half- or full-day Internet seminar is an excellent hands-on means of learning how to use this powerful tool.

Finally, after learning the basics, you may even want to set up your own Web page. Many how-to short courses exist on this subject (both on the Net and in seminars), and numerous software programs are available to guide you step-by-step through this process. Having your own Web page is almost becoming a necessity in the faster lanes of the Information Highway.

■ SUMMARY

The Internet is an ever-growing electronic phenomenon. Besides providing access to up-to-the-minute news, the Net allows users to view mountains of information on every topic imaginable, at lightning speed and with unprecedented convenience. Financial uses include: financial research, financial services, financial planning, free financial software, and electronic discussions on any financial topic. Finally, the pedagogical uses of the Internet include simulations of all kinds, and how-to short courses on most major financial subjects.

Access to the Information Highway is easy. If you can point and click, you can surf the Net.

■ GLOSSARY

Bookmark Saving favorite Web site addresses into hard-disk memory for easy access later.

Download Transferring information found on the Net to your computer's memory (and then, usually, to a disk for storage).

FAQs Frequently Asked Questions (pronounced "Fax"); this is a list of common questions (with answers) that new users often have.

FTP File Transfer Protocol—the system (i.e., protocol) by which files are transferred between computers.

Hit A find, by a search engine, of a Web site containing the designated key words.

Home Page The first page of a particular Web site.

html Hypertext markup language; this is the computer language in which Web sites are written.

http Hypertext transfer protocol. The means (i.e., protocol) by which hypertext is transferred from one computer to another.

Hypertext Multicolor information and graphics appearing in a Web page, with "links" to other Web sites.

Internet The Net—a worldwide network of computers that electronically share information with one another.

ISP Internet Service Provider, or just "service provider." A company providing, for a fee, access to the Internet.

Link A highlighted word or icon appearing on a Web page that when clicked "on" with a mouse, takes the user to another Web site.

List Server Automated group mailing lists; commonly used by newsgroups.

Newbie A newcomer on the Net.

Newsgroups An ongoing discussion of a particular topic occurring at a particular Web site called a "bulletin board."

On-Line Service A giant service provider (such as America Online) that primarily targets home users and provides a full range of educational and entertainment services.

Search Engine A software program that finds Web sites containing designated key words. See Figure C-3 for a listing of the more popular search engines.

Surfing As in "surfing the Net," refers to the process of meandering from one place to another on the Internet.

URL Uniform Resource Locator—the access address of a Web site. For example, the Web site address of the *Wall Street Journal* is http://www.wsj.com. The three letters following the organization's name/abbreviation specify its type: "com" is commercial; "edu" is educational; "org" is organization, such as a nonprofit; "gov" is government organization; and "net" refers to an internet-related organization, such as Netscape. (Note: URL is sometimes defined as the *Universal* Resource Locator.)

Web Browser A software program enabling the user to "browse" (i.e., navigate through) the Web; some popular browsers include Netscape and Microsoft's Internet Explorer. Browsers translate html language into the graphics and information seen on the screen.

Web Page/Site A place on the Web maintained by an organization, individual, or interest group, usually consisting of numerous "pages" (i.e., screens) of information.

World Wide Web The Web—the part of the Net where users place multimedia information for others to see.

REFERENCE MATERIALS

PERIOD, n	1%	2%	3%	4%	5%	6%	7%	8%	9%	10%	11%	12%	13%
0	1.000	1.000	1.000	1.000	1.000	1.000	1.000	1.000	1.000	1.000	1.000	1.000	1.000
1	1.010	1.020	1.030	1.040	1.050	1.060	1.070	1.080	1.090	1.100	1.110	1.120	1.130
2	1.020	1.040	1.061	1.082	1.102	1.124	1.145	1.166	1.188	1.210	1.232	1.254	1.277
3	1.030	1.061	1.093	1.125	1.158	1.191	1.225	1.260	1.295	1.331	1.368	1.405	1.443
4	1.041	1.082	1.126	1.170	1.216	1.262	1.311	1.360	1.412	1.464	1.518	1.574	1.630
5	1.051	1.104	1.159	1.217	1.276	1.338	1.403	1.469	1.539	1.611	1.685	1.762	1.842
6	1.062	1.126	1.194	1.265	1.340	1.419	1.501	1.587	1.677	1.772	1.870	1.974	2.082
7	1.072	1.149	1.230	1.316	1.407	1.504	1.606	1.714	1.828	1.949	2.076	2.211	2.353
8	1.083	1.172	1.267	1.369	1.477	1.594	1.718	1.851	1.993	2.144	2.305	2.476	2.658
9	1.094	1.195	1.305	1.423	1.551	1.689	1.838	1.999	2.172	2.358	2.558	2.773	3.004
10	1.105	1.219	1.344	1.480	1.629	1.791	1.967	2.159	2.367	2.594	2.839	3.106	3.395
11	1.116	1.243	1.384	1.539	1.710	1.898	2.105	2.332	2.580	2.853	3.152	3.479	3.836
12	1.127	1.268	1.426	1.601	1.796	2.012	2.252	2.518	2.813	3.138	3.498	3.896	4.335
13	1.138	1.294	1.469	1.665	1.886	2.133	2.410	2.720	3.066	3.452	3.883	4.363	4.898
14	1.149	1.319	1.513	1.732	1.980	2.261	2.579	2.937	3.342	3.797	4.310	4.887	5.535
15	1.161	1.346	1.558	1.801	2.079	2.397	2.759	3.172	3.642	4.177	4.785	5.474	6.254
16	1.173	1.373	1.605	1.873	2.183	2.540	2.952	3.426	3.970	4.595	5.311	6.130	7.067
17	1.184	1.400	1.653	1.948	2.292	2.693	3.159	3.700	4.328	5.054	5.895	6.866	7.986
18	1.196	1.428	1.702	2.026	2.407	2.854	3.380	3.996	4.717	5.560	6.544	7.690	9.024
19	1.208	1.457	1.754	2.107	2.527	3.026	3.617	4.316	5.142	6.116	7.263	8.613	10.197
20	1.220	1.486	1.806	2.191	2.653	3.207	3.870	4.661	5.604	6.728	8.062	9.646	11.523
24	1.270	1.608	2.033	2.563	3.225	4.049	5.072	6.341	7.911	9.850	12.239	15.179	18.790
25	1.282	1.641	2.094	2.666	3.386	4.292	5.427	6.848	8.623	10.835	13.585	17.000	21.231
30	1.348	1.811	2.427	3.243	4.322	5.743	7.612	10.063	13.268	17.449	22.892	29.960	39.116
40	1.489	2.208	3.262	4.801	7.040	10.286	14.974	21.725	31.409	45.259	65.001	93.051	132.782
50	1.645	2.692	4.384	7.107	11.467	18.420	29.457	46.902	74.358	117.391	184.565	289.002	450.736
60	1.817	3.281	5.892	10.520	18.679	32.988	57.946	101.257	176.031	304.482	524.057	897.597	1,530.05

TABLE I
**Future Value Interest Factor
(FVIF) ($1 at i% per period
for n periods);**

$$FVIF = (1 + i)^n; \quad FV_n = PV_0(FVIF_{i,n})$$

PERIOD, n	14%	15%	16%	17%	18%	19%	20%	24%	28%	32%	36%	40%
0	1.000	1.000	1.000	1.000	1.000	1.000	1.000	1.000	1.000	1.000	1.000	1.000
1	1.140	1.150	1.160	1.170	1.180	1.190	1.200	1.240	1.280	1.320	1.360	1.400
2	1.300	1.322	1.346	1.369	1.392	1.416	1.440	1.538	1.638	1.742	1.850	1.960
3	1.482	1.521	1.561	1.602	1.643	1.685	1.728	1.907	2.067	2.300	2.515	2.744
4	1.689	1.749	1.811	1.874	1.939	2.005	2.074	2.364	2.684	3.036	3.421	3.842
5	1.925	2.011	2.100	2.192	2.288	2.386	2.488	2.932	3.436	4.007	4.653	5.378
6	2.195	2.313	2.436	2.565	2.700	2.840	2.986	3.635	4.398	5.290	6.328	7.530
7	2.502	2.660	2.826	3.001	3.185	3.379	3.583	4.508	5.629	6.983	8.605	10.541
8	2.853	3.059	3.278	3.511	3.759	4.021	4.300	5.590	7.206	9.217	11.703	14.758
9	3.252	3.518	3.803	4.108	4.435	4.785	5.160	6.931	9.223	12.166	15.917	20.661
10	3.707	4.046	4.411	4.807	5.234	5.695	6.192	8.594	11.806	16.060	21.647	28.925
11	4.226	4.652	5.117	5.624	6.176	6.777	7.430	10.657	15.112	21.199	29.439	40.496
12	4.818	5.350	5.926	6.580	7.288	8.064	8.916	13.215	19.343	27.983	40.037	56.694
13	5.492	6.153	6.886	7.699	8.599	9.596	10.699	16.386	24.759	36.937	54.451	79.372
14	6.261	7.076	7.988	9.007	10.147	11.420	12.839	20.319	31.961	48.757	74.053	111.120
15	7.138	8.137	9.266	10.539	11.974	13.590	15.407	25.196	40.565	64.359	100.712	155.568
16	8.137	9.358	10.748	12.330	14.129	16.172	18.488	31.243	51.923	84.954	136.969	217.795
17	9.276	10.761	12.468	14.426	16.672	19.244	22.186	38.741	66.461	112.139	186.278	304.914
18	10.575	12.375	14.463	16.879	19.673	22.901	26.623	48.039	85.071	148.023	253.338	426.879
19	12.056	14.232	16.777	19.748	23.214	27.252	31.948	59.568	108.890	195.391	344.540	597.630
20	13.743	16.367	19.461	23.106	27.393	32.429	38.338	73.864	139.380	257.916	468.574	836.683
24	23.212	28.625	35.236	43.297	53.109	65.032	79.497	174.631	374.144	783.023	1,603.00	3,214.20
25	26.462	32.919	40.874	50.658	62.669	77.388	95.396	216.542	478.905	1,033.59	2,180.08	4,499.88
30	50.950	66.212	85.850	111.065	143.371	184.675	237.376	634.820	1,645.50	4,142.07	10,143.0	24,201.4
40	188.884	267.864	378.721	533.869	750.378	1,051.67	1,469.77	5,455.91	19,426.7	66,520.8	219,562	700,038
50	700.233	1,083.66	1,670.70	2,566.22	3,927.36	5,988.91	9,100.44	46,890.4	229,350	*	*	*
60	2,595.92	4,384.00	7,370.20	12,335.4	20,555.1	34,105.0	56,347.5	402,996	*	*	*	*

*These interest factors exceed 1,000,000

TABLE I
continued

PERIOD, n	1%	2%	3%	4%	5%	6%	7%	8%	9%	10%	11%	12%	13%
0	1.000	1.000	1.000	1.000	1.000	1.000	1.000	1.000	1.000	1.000	1.000	1.000	1.000
1	0.990	0.980	0.971	0.962	0.952	0.943	0.935	0.926	0.917	0.909	0.901	0.893	0.885
2	0.980	0.961	0.943	0.925	0.907	0.890	0.873	0.857	0.842	0.826	0.812	0.797	0.783
3	0.971	0.942	0.915	0.889	0.864	0.840	0.816	0.794	0.772	0.751	0.731	0.712	0.693
4	0.961	0.924	0.889	0.855	0.823	0.792	0.763	0.735	0.708	0.683	0.659	0.636	0.613
5	0.951	0.906	0.863	0.822	0.784	0.747	0.713	0.681	0.650	0.621	0.593	0.567	0.543
6	0.942	0.888	0.838	0.790	0.746	0.705	0.666	0.630	0.596	0.564	0.535	0.507	0.480
7	0.933	0.871	0.813	0.760	0.711	0.665	0.623	0.583	0.547	0.513	0.482	0.452	0.425
8	0.923	0.853	0.789	0.731	0.677	0.627	0.582	0.540	0.502	0.467	0.434	0.404	0.376
9	0.914	0.837	0.766	0.703	0.645	0.592	0.544	0.500	0.460	0.424	0.391	0.361	0.333
10	0.905	0.820	0.744	0.676	0.614	0.558	0.508	0.463	0.422	0.386	0.352	0.322	0.295
11	0.896	0.804	0.722	0.650	0.585	0.527	0.475	0.429	0.388	0.350	0.317	0.287	0.261
12	0.887	0.788	0.701	0.625	0.557	0.497	0.444	0.397	0.356	0.319	0.286	0.257	0.231
13	0.879	0.773	0.681	0.601	0.530	0.469	0.415	0.368	0.326	0.290	0.258	0.229	0.204
14	0.870	0.758	0.661	0.577	0.505	0.442	0.388	0.340	0.299	0.263	0.232	0.205	0.181
15	0.861	0.743	0.642	0.555	0.481	0.417	0.362	0.315	0.275	0.239	0.209	0.183	0.160
16	0.853	0.728	0.623	0.534	0.458	0.394	0.339	0.292	0.252	0.218	0.188	0.163	0.141
17	0.844	0.714	0.605	0.513	0.436	0.371	0.317	0.270	0.231	0.198	0.170	0.146	0.125
18	0.836	0.700	0.587	0.494	0.416	0.350	0.296	0.250	0.212	0.180	0.153	0.130	0.111
19	0.828	0.686	0.570	0.475	0.396	0.331	0.276	0.232	0.194	0.164	0.138	0.116	0.098
20	0.820	0.673	0.554	0.456	0.377	0.312	0.258	0.215	0.178	0.149	0.124	0.104	0.087
24	0.788	0.622	0.492	0.390	0.310	0.247	0.197	0.158	0.126	0.102	0.082	0.066	0.053
25	0.780	0.610	0.478	0.375	0.295	0.233	0.184	0.146	0.116	0.092	0.074	0.059	0.047
30	0.742	0.552	0.412	0.308	0.231	0.174	0.131	0.099	0.075	0.057	0.044	0.033	0.026
40	0.672	0.453	0.307	0.208	0.142	0.097	0.067	0.046	0.032	0.022	0.015	0.011	0.008
50	0.608	0.372	0.228	0.141	0.087	0.054	0.034	0.021	0.013	0.009	0.005	0.003	0.002
60	0.550	0.305	0.170	0.095	0.054	0.030	0.017	0.010	0.006	0.003	0.002	0.001	0.001

TABLE II
Present Value Interest Factor
(PVIF) ($1 at i% per period
for n periods);

$$\text{PVIF} = \frac{1}{(1 + i)^n} \; ; \; PV_0 = FV_n(\text{PVIF}_{i,n})$$

PERIOD, n	14%	15%	16%	17%	18%	19%	20%	24%	28%	32%	36%	40%
0	1.000	1.000	1.000	1.000	1.000	1.000	1.000	1.000	1.000	1.000	1.000	1.000
1	0.877	0.870	0.862	0.855	0.847	0.840	0.833	0.806	0.781	0.758	0.735	0.714
2	0.769	0.756	0.743	0.731	0.718	0.706	0.694	0.650	0.610	0.574	0.541	0.510
3	0.675	0.658	0.641	0.624	0.609	0.593	0.579	0.524	0.477	0.435	0.398	0.364
4	0.592	0.572	0.552	0.534	0.516	0.499	0.482	0.423	0.373	0.329	0.292	0.260
5	0.519	0.497	0.476	0.456	0.437	0.419	0.402	0.341	0.291	0.250	0.215	0.186
6	0.456	0.432	0.410	0.390	0.370	0.352	0.335	0.275	0.227	0.189	0.158	0.133
7	0.400	0.376	0.354	0.333	0.314	0.296	0.279	0.222	0.178	0.143	0.116	0.095
8	0.351	0.327	0.305	0.285	0.266	0.249	0.233	0.179	0.139	0.108	0.085	0.068
9	0.308	0.284	0.263	0.243	0.225	0.209	0.194	0.144	0.108	0.082	0.063	0.048
10	0.270	0.247	0.227	0.208	0.191	0.176	0.162	0.116	0.085	0.062	0.046	0.035
11	0.237	0.215	0.195	0.178	0.162	0.148	0.135	0.094	0.066	0.047	0.034	0.025
12	0.208	0.187	0.168	0.152	0.137	0.124	0.112	0.076	0.052	0.036	0.025	0.018
13	0.182	0.163	0.145	0.130	0.116	0.104	0.093	0.061	0.040	0.027	0.018	0.013
14	0.160	0.141	0.125	0.111	0.099	0.088	0.078	0.049	0.032	0.021	0.014	0.009
15	0.140	0.123	0.108	0.095	0.084	0.074	0.065	0.040	0.025	0.016	0.010	0.006
16	0.123	0.107	0.093	0.081	0.071	0.062	0.054	0.032	0.019	0.012	0.007	0.005
17	0.108	0.093	0.080	0.069	0.060	0.052	0.045	0.026	0.015	0.009	0.005	0.003
18	0.095	0.081	0.069	0.059	0.051	0.044	0.038	0.021	0.012	0.007	0.004	0.002
19	0.083	0.070	0.060	0.051	0.043	0.037	0.031	0.017	0.009	0.005	0.003	0.002
20	0.073	0.061	0.051	0.043	0.037	0.031	0.026	0.014	0.007	0.004	0.002	0.001
24	0.043	0.035	0.028	0.023	0.019	0.015	0.013	0.006	0.003	0.001	0.001	0.000
25	0.038	0.030	0.024	0.020	0.016	0.013	0.010	0.005	0.002	0.001	0.000	0.000
30	0.020	0.015	0.012	0.009	0.007	0.005	0.004	0.002	0.001	0.000	0.000	0.000
40	0.005	0.004	0.003	0.002	0.001	0.001	0.001	0.000	0.000	0.000	0.000	0.000
50	0.001	0.001	0.001	0.000	0.000	0.000	0.000	0.000	0.000	0.000	0.000	0.000
60	0.000	0.000	0.000	0.000	0.000	0.000	0.000	0.000	0.000	0.000	0.000	0.000

TABLE II
continued

PERIOD, n	1%	2%	3%	4%	5%	6%	7%	8%	9%	10%	11%	12%	13%
1	1.000	1.000	1.000	1.000	1.000	1.000	1.000	1.000	1.000	1.000	1.000	1.000	1.000
2	2.010	2.020	2.030	2.040	2.050	2.060	2.070	2.080	2.090	2.100	2.110	2.120	2.130
3	3.030	3.060	3.091	3.122	3.152	3.184	3.215	3.246	3.278	3.310	3.342	3.374	3.407
4	4.060	4.122	4.184	4.246	4.310	4.375	4.440	4.506	4.573	4.641	4.710	4.779	4.850
5	5.101	5.204	5.309	5.416	5.526	5.637	5.751	5.867	5.985	6.105	6.228	6.353	6.480
6	6.152	6.308	6.468	6.633	6.802	6.975	7.153	7.336	7.523	7.716	7.913	8.115	8.323
7	7.214	7.434	7.662	7.898	8.142	8.394	8.654	8.923	9.200	9.487	9.783	10.089	10.405
8	8.286	8.583	8.892	9.214	9.549	9.897	10.260	10.637	11.028	11.436	11.859	12.300	12.757
9	9.369	9.755	10.159	10.583	11.027	11.491	11.978	12.488	13.021	13.579	14.164	14.776	15.416
10	10.462	10.950	11.464	12.006	12.578	13.181	13.816	14.487	15.193	15.937	16.722	17.549	18.420
11	11.567	12.169	12.808	13.486	14.207	14.972	15.784	16.645	17.560	18.531	19.561	20.655	21.814
12	12.683	13.412	14.192	15.026	15.917	16.870	17.888	18.977	20.141	21.384	22.713	24.133	25.650
13	13.809	14.680	15.618	16.627	17.713	18.882	20.141	21.495	22.953	24.523	26.212	28.029	29.985
14	14.947	15.974	17.086	18.292	19.599	21.051	22.550	24.215	26.019	27.975	30.095	32.393	34.883
15	16.097	17.293	18.599	20.024	21.579	23.276	25.129	27.152	29.361	31.772	34.405	37.280	40.417
16	17.258	18.639	20.157	21.825	23.657	25.673	27.888	30.324	33.003	35.950	39.190	42.753	46.672
17	18.430	20.012	21.762	23.698	25.840	28.213	30.840	33.750	36.974	40.545	44.501	48.884	53.739
18	19.615	21.412	23.414	25.645	28.132	30.906	33.999	37.450	41.301	45.599	50.396	55.750	61.725
19	20.811	22.841	25.117	27.671	30.539	33.760	37.379	41.446	46.018	51.159	56.939	63.440	70.749
20	22.019	24.297	26.870	29.778	33.066	36.786	40.995	45.762	51.160	57.275	64.203	72.052	80.947
24	26.973	30.422	34.426	39.083	44.502	50.816	58.117	66.765	76.790	88.497	102.174	118.155	136.831
25	28.243	32.030	36.459	41.646	47.727	54.865	63.249	73.106	84.701	98.347	114.413	133.334	155.620
30	34.785	40.568	47.575	56.085	66.439	79.058	94.461	113.283	136.308	164.494	199.021	241.333	293.199
40	48.886	60.402	75.401	95.026	120.080	154.762	199.635	259.057	337.882	442.593	581.826	767.091	1,013.70
50	64.463	84.572	112.797	152.667	209.348	290.336	406.529	573.770	815.084	1,163.91	1,668.77	2,400.02	3,459.51
60	81.670	114.052	163.053	237.991	353.584	533.128	813.520	1,253.21	1,944.79	3,034.82	4,755.07	7,471.64	11,761.9

TABLE III
Future Value of an Annuity Interest Factor (FVIFA) ($1 per period at $i\%$ per period for n periods);

$$\text{FVIFA} = \frac{(1 + i)^n - 1}{i};$$

$$\text{FVAN}_n = PMT(\text{FVIFA}_{i,n})$$

PERIOD, n	14%	15%	16%	17%	18%	19%	20%	24%	28%	32%	36%	40%
1	1.000	1.000	1.000	1.000	1.000	1.000	1.000	1.000	1.000	1.000	1.000	1.000
2	2.140	2.150	2.160	2.170	2.180	2.190	2.200	2.240	2.280	2.320	2.360	2.400
3	3.440	3.473	3.506	3.539	3.572	3.606	3.640	3.778	3.918	4.062	4.210	4.360
4	4.921	4.993	5.066	5.141	5.215	5.291	5.368	5.684	6.016	6.362	6.725	7.104
5	6.610	6.742	6.877	7.014	7.154	7.297	7.442	8.048	8.700	9.398	10.146	10.846
6	8.536	8.754	8.977	9.207	9.442	9.683	9.930	10.980	12.136	13.406	14.799	16.324
7	10.730	11.067	11.414	11.772	12.142	12.523	12.916	14.615	16.534	18.696	21.126	23.853
8	13.233	13.727	14.240	14.773	15.327	15.902	16.499	19.123	22.163	25.678	29.732	34.395
9	16.085	16.786	17.518	18.285	19.086	19.923	20.799	24.712	29.369	34.895	41.435	49.153
10	19.337	20.304	21.321	22.393	23.521	24.709	25.959	31.643	38.592	47.062	57.352	69.814
11	23.044	24.349	25.733	27.200	28.755	30.404	32.150	40.238	50.399	63.122	78.998	98.739
12	27.271	29.002	30.850	32.824	34.931	37.180	39.580	50.985	65.510	84.320	108.437	139.235
13	32.089	34.352	36.786	39.404	42.219	45.244	48.497	64.110	84.853	112.303	148.475	195.929
14	37.581	40.505	43.672	47.103	50.818	54.841	59.196	80.496	109.612	149.240	202.926	275.300
15	43.842	47.580	51.660	56.110	60.965	66.261	72.035	100.815	141.303	197.997	276.979	386.420
16	50.980	55.717	60.925	66.649	72.939	79.850	87.442	126.011	181.868	262.356	377.692	541.988
17	59.118	65.075	71.673	78.979	87.068	96.022	105.931	157.253	233.791	347.310	514.661	759.784
18	68.394	75.836	84.141	93.406	103.740	115.266	128.117	195.994	300.252	459.449	700.939	1,064.70
19	78.969	88.212	98.603	110.285	123.414	138.166	154.740	244.033	385.323	607.472	954.277	1,491.58
20	91.025	102.444	115.380	130.033	146.628	165.418	186.688	303.601	494.213	802.863	1,298.82	2,089.21
24	158.659	184.168	213.978	248.808	289.494	337.010	392.484	723.461	1,322.66	2,443.82	4,450.00	8,033.00
25	181.871	212.793	249.214	292.105	342.603	402.042	471.981	898.092	1,706.80	3,226.84	6,053.00	11,247.2
30	356.787	434.745	530.321	647.439	790.948	966.712	1,181.88	2,640.92	5,873.23	12,940.9	28,172.3	60,501.1
40	1,342.03	1,779.09	2,360.76	3,134.52	4,163.21	5,529.83	7,343.86	22,728.8	69,377.5	207,874	609,890	*
50	4,994.52	7,217.72	10,435.6	15,089.5	21,813.1	31,515.3	45,497.2	195,373	819,103	*	*	*
60	18,535.1	29,220.0	46,057.5	72,555.0	114,190	179,495	281,733	*	*	*	*	*

*These interest factors exceed 1,000,000

TABLE III
continued

PERIOD, n	1%	2%	3%	4%	5%	6%	7%	8%	9%	10%	11%	12%	13%
1	0.990	0.980	0.971	0.962	0.952	0.943	0.935	0.926	0.917	0.909	0.901	0.893	0.885
2	1.970	1.942	1.913	1.886	1.859	1.833	1.808	1.783	1.759	1.736	1.713	1.690	1.668
3	2.941	2.884	2.829	2.775	2.723	2.673	2.624	2.577	2.531	2.487	2.444	2.402	2.361
4	3.902	3.808	3.717	3.630	3.546	3.465	3.387	3.312	3.240	3.170	3.102	3.037	2.974
5	4.853	4.713	4.580	4.452	4.329	4.212	4.100	3.993	3.890	3.791	3.696	3.605	3.517
6	5.795	5.601	5.417	5.242	5.076	4.917	4.766	4.623	4.486	4.355	4.231	4.111	3.998
7	6.728	6.472	6.230	6.002	5.786	5.582	5.389	5.206	5.033	4.868	4.712	4.564	4.423
8	7.652	7.325	7.020	6.733	6.463	6.210	5.971	5.747	5.535	5.335	5.146	4.968	4.799
9	8.566	8.162	7.786	7.435	7.108	6.802	6.515	6.247	5.995	5.759	5.537	5.328	5.132
10	9.471	8.983	8.530	8.111	7.722	7.360	7.024	6.710	6.418	6.145	5.889	5.650	5.426
11	10.368	9.787	9.253	8.760	8.306	7.887	7.499	7.139	6.805	6.495	6.207	5.938	5.687
12	11.255	10.575	9.954	9.385	8.863	8.384	7.943	7.536	7.161	6.814	6.492	6.194	5.918
13	12.134	11.348	10.635	9.986	9.394	8.853	8.358	7.904	7.487	7.103	6.750	6.424	6.122
14	13.004	12.106	11.296	10.563	9.899	9.295	8.745	8.244	7.786	7.367	6.982	6.628	6.302
15	13.865	12.849	11.938	11.118	10.380	9.712	9.108	8.559	8.061	7.606	7.191	6.811	6.462
16	14.718	13.578	12.561	11.652	10.838	10.106	9.447	8.851	8.312	7.824	7.379	6.974	6.604
17	15.562	14.292	13.166	12.166	11.274	10.477	9.763	9.122	8.544	8.022	7.549	7.120	6.729
18	16.398	14.992	13.754	12.659	11.690	10.828	10.059	9.372	8.756	8.201	7.702	7.250	6.840
19	17.226	15.678	14.324	13.134	12.085	11.158	10.336	9.604	8.950	8.365	7.839	7.366	6.938
20	18.046	16.351	14.877	13.590	12.462	11.470	10.594	9.818	9.128	8.514	7.963	7.469	7.025
24	21.243	18.914	16.936	15.247	13.799	12.550	11.469	10.529	9.707	8.985	8.348	7.784	7.283
25	22.023	19.523	17.413	15.622	14.094	12.783	11.654	10.675	9.823	9.077	8.422	7.843	7.330
30	25.808	22.397	19.600	17.292	15.373	13.765	12.409	11.258	10.274	9.427	8.694	8.055	7.496
40	32.835	27.355	23.115	19.793	17.159	15.046	13.332	11.925	10.757	9.779	8.951	8.244	7.634
50	39.196	31.424	25.730	21.482	18.256	15.762	13.801	12.233	10.962	9.915	9.042	8.304	7.675
60	44.955	34.761	27.676	22.623	18.929	16.161	14.039	12.377	11.048	9.967	9.074	8.324	7.687

TABLE IV
Present Value of an Annuity Interest
Factor (PVIFA) ($1 per period at i%
per period for n periods);

$$\text{PVIFA} = \frac{1 - \frac{1}{(1+i)^n}}{i} \; ;$$

$$\text{PVAN}_0 = PMT(\text{PVIFA}_{i,n})$$

PERIOD, n	14%	15%	16%	17%	18%	19%	20%	24%	28%	32%	36%	40%
1	0.877	0.870	0.862	0.855	0.847	0.840	0.833	0.806	0.781	0.758	0.735	0.714
2	1.647	1.626	1.605	1.585	1.566	1.547	1.528	1.457	1.392	1.332	1.276	1.224
3	2.322	2.283	2.246	2.210	2.174	2.140	2.106	1.981	1.868	1.766	1.674	1.589
4	2.914	2.855	2.798	2.743	2.690	2.639	2.589	2.404	2.241	2.096	1.966	1.849
5	3.433	3.352	3.274	3.199	3.127	3.058	2.991	2.745	2.532	2.345	2.181	2.035
6	3.889	3.784	3.685	3.589	3.498	3.410	3.326	3.020	2.759	2.534	2.399	2.168
7	4.288	4.160	4.039	3.922	3.812	3.706	3.605	3.242	2.937	2.678	2.455	2.263
8	4.639	4.487	4.344	4.207	4.078	3.954	3.837	3.421	3.076	2.786	2.540	2.331
9	4.946	4.772	4.607	4.451	4.303	4.163	4.031	3.566	3.184	2.868	2.603	2.379
10	5.216	5.019	4.833	4.659	4.494	4.339	4.193	3.682	3.269	2.930	2.650	2.414
11	5.453	5.234	5.029	4.836	4.656	4.486	4.327	3.776	3.335	2.978	2.683	2.438
12	5.660	5.421	5.197	4.988	4.793	4.611	4.439	3.851	3.387	3.013	2.708	2.456
13	5.842	5.583	5.342	5.118	4.910	4.715	4.533	3.912	3.427	3.040	2.727	2.469
14	6.002	5.724	5.468	5.229	5.008	4.802	4.611	3.962	3.459	3.061	2.740	2.478
15	6.142	5.847	5.575	5.324	5.092	4.876	4.675	4.001	3.483	3.076	2.750	2.484
16	6.265	5.954	5.669	5.405	5.162	4.938	4.730	4.033	3.503	3.088	2.758	2.489
17	6.373	6.047	5.749	5.475	5.222	4.990	4.775	4.059	3.518	3.097	2.763	2.492
18	6.467	6.128	5.818	5.534	5.273	5.033	4.812	4.080	3.529	3.104	2.767	2.494
19	6.550	6.198	5.877	5.584	5.316	5.070	4.844	4.097	3.539	3.109	2.770	2.496
20	6.623	6.259	5.929	5.628	5.353	5.101	4.870	4.110	3.546	3.113	2.772	2.497
24	6.835	6.434	6.073	5.746	5.451	5.182	4.937	4.143	3.562	3.121	2.776	2.499
25	6.873	6.464	6.097	5.766	5.467	5.195	4.948	4.147	3.564	3.122	2.776	2.499
30	7.003	6.566	6.177	5.829	5.517	5.235	4.979	4.160	3.569	3.124	2.778	2.500
40	7.105	6.642	6.233	5.871	5.548	5.258	4.997	4.166	3.571	3.125	2.778	2.500
50	7.133	6.661	6.246	5.880	5.554	5.262	4.999	4.167	3.571	3.125	2.778	2.500
60	7.140	6.665	6.249	5.882	5.555	5.263	5.000	4.167	3.571	3.125	2.778	2.500

TABLE IV
continued

TABLE V
Normal Distribution (Area of the Normal Distribution That Is to the Right of +z _or_ the Left of –z Standard Deviations from the Mean)

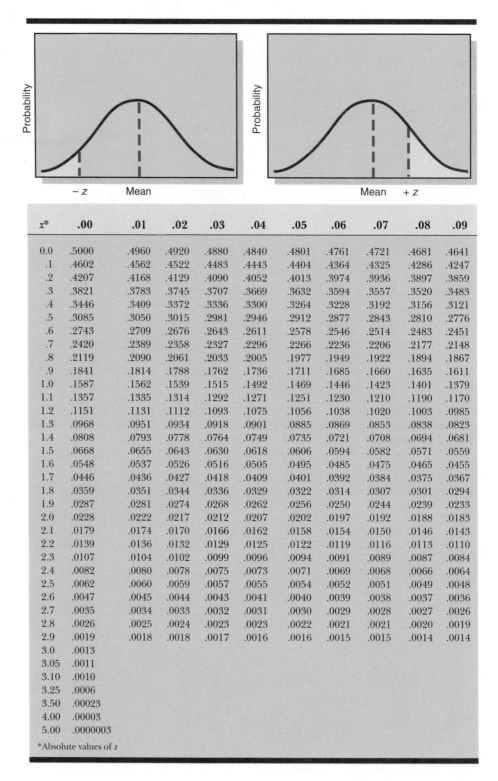

z*	.00	.01	.02	.03	.04	.05	.06	.07	.08	.09
0.0	.5000	.4960	.4920	.4880	.4840	.4801	.4761	.4721	.4681	.4641
.1	.4602	.4562	.4522	.4483	.4443	.4404	.4364	.4325	.4286	.4247
.2	.4207	.4168	.4129	.4090	.4052	.4013	.3974	.3936	.3897	.3859
.3	.3821	.3783	.3745	.3707	.3669	.3632	.3594	.3557	.3520	.3483
.4	.3446	.3409	.3372	.3336	.3300	.3264	.3228	.3192	.3156	.3121
.5	.3085	.3050	.3015	.2981	.2946	.2912	.2877	.2843	.2810	.2776
.6	.2743	.2709	.2676	.2643	.2611	.2578	.2546	.2514	.2483	.2451
.7	.2420	.2389	.2358	.2327	.2296	.2266	.2236	.2206	.2177	.2148
.8	.2119	.2090	.2061	.2033	.2005	.1977	.1949	.1922	.1894	.1867
.9	.1841	.1814	.1788	.1762	.1736	.1711	.1685	.1660	.1635	.1611
1.0	.1587	.1562	.1539	.1515	.1492	.1469	.1446	.1423	.1401	.1379
1.1	.1357	.1335	.1314	.1292	.1271	.1251	.1230	.1210	.1190	.1170
1.2	.1151	.1131	.1112	.1093	.1075	.1056	.1038	.1020	.1003	.0985
1.3	.0968	.0951	.0934	.0918	.0901	.0885	.0869	.0853	.0838	.0823
1.4	.0808	.0793	.0778	.0764	.0749	.0735	.0721	.0708	.0694	.0681
1.5	.0668	.0655	.0643	.0630	.0618	.0606	.0594	.0582	.0571	.0559
1.6	.0548	.0537	.0526	.0516	.0505	.0495	.0485	.0475	.0465	.0455
1.7	.0446	.0436	.0427	.0418	.0409	.0401	.0392	.0384	.0375	.0367
1.8	.0359	.0351	.0344	.0336	.0329	.0322	.0314	.0307	.0301	.0294
1.9	.0287	.0281	.0274	.0268	.0262	.0256	.0250	.0244	.0239	.0233
2.0	.0228	.0222	.0217	.0212	.0207	.0202	.0197	.0192	.0188	.0183
2.1	.0179	.0174	.0170	.0166	.0162	.0158	.0154	.0150	.0146	.0143
2.2	.0139	.0136	.0132	.0129	.0125	.0122	.0119	.0116	.0113	.0110
2.3	.0107	.0104	.0102	.0099	.0096	.0094	.0091	.0089	.0087	.0084
2.4	.0082	.0080	.0078	.0075	.0073	.0071	.0069	.0068	.0066	.0064
2.5	.0062	.0060	.0059	.0057	.0055	.0054	.0052	.0051	.0049	.0048
2.6	.0047	.0045	.0044	.0043	.0041	.0040	.0039	.0038	.0037	.0036
2.7	.0035	.0034	.0033	.0032	.0031	.0030	.0029	.0028	.0027	.0026
2.8	.0026	.0025	.0024	.0023	.0023	.0022	.0021	.0021	.0020	.0019
2.9	.0019	.0018	.0018	.0017	.0016	.0016	.0015	.0015	.0014	.0014
3.0	.0013									
3.05	.0011									
3.10	.0010									
3.25	.0006									
3.50	.00023									
4.00	.00003									
5.00	.0000003									

*Absolute values of z

INDEX TO GLOSSARY TERMS

INDEX

FINANCIAL CHALLENGE PHOTO CREDITS

35 Lara Jo Regan/ SABA; 67 © John Madere; 125 © The Stock Market/ Robert Essel 1997; 177 © Frank Herholdt/ Tony Stone Images; 227 Ann States/ SABA; 273 © John S. Abbott; 311 © Kevin Horan/ Tony Stone Images; 343 © The Stock Market/ Chromosohm/ Sohm 1997; 385 Courtesy of The Boeing Company; 415 © Walter Hodges/ Tony Stone Images; 455 Ed Quinn/ SABA; 485 © PhotoDisc, Inc. 1996; 533 © Andy Sacks/ Tony Stone Images; 569 Photograph by Joe Higgins; 611 Peter Yates/ SABA; 643 © Michael L. Abramson; 679 Luv Novovitch/ Gamma Liaison; 727 © PhotoDisc, Inc. 1996; 749 Vincent Yu/ AP/ Wide World Photos; 775 © Tim Flach/ Tony Stone Images; 797 Photonics 1995

Check Answers to Selected Problems

2

1. a. +24.52%
5. 8.72%
6. a. 15%
10. 8,964
11. a. Total cost = $838,908
    Cost per watch = $83.89
12. a. 10.58% discount

3

1. a. $219,178
2. a. 15%
3. $3,945,205
5. a. Firm A: ROE = 30%
    Equity multiplier = 1.5
8. b. Current ratio = 2.2x
13. a. ROE = 25%
14. a. ROE = 28.57%
19. a. 5.0 times
20. c. $16
22. $66.7 million
24. $2,700,000
26. $1,150,000
27. $200
29. b. $2.6 million

4

1. a. $1,191
3. $240,410.40
5. $1,343.72
6. 13%
7. a. 9 years
9. a. $584.80
11. 20%
14. a. $1,281.58
17. $13,018.71
20. a. $29,806
22. $3,386
24. $51,354
26. $30,807
27. $690,274
30. $111,031
31. a. $31,401
34. $51,980.44
36. $94,337
37. a. $12,653
38. 3.6%
41. $21,879
43. $5,907.83

48. $3,890
51. $84,573
55. $10,075
57. $0.95
59. $108,151
61. $7,642
63. $16,333
65. $3,386,465
67. a. 7.2%

4A

2. $2,744
4. d. 22.14%
6. $123.13

5

1. a. $r_x = 15\%$
   b. $\sigma_x = 11.62\%$
2. p(Loss) = 2.28%
5. a. 11.6%
6. a. i. $r_p = 8.2\%$
   ii. $\sigma_p = 4.87\%$
7. b. $r_p = 13.05\%$
   c. $\sigma_p = 3.64\%$
12. b. Before: $k_j = 17.0\%$
    After: $k_j = 18.5\%$
13. b. Rate of return = 9.74%
17. a. $w_a = 61.54\%$
18. b. i. $\sigma_p = 7.8\%$
    ii. $\sigma_p = 6.18\%$
21. 47%
25. a. p(Loss) = 4.75%
30. b. 90.82%
34. 82.89%

6

1. b. $P_0 = \$800$
3. a. $P_0 = \$1,137$
4. $P_0 = \$964$
7. a. $k_d = 13.6\%$
10. a. $P_0 = \$22.22$
13. b. YTM = 7.60%
15. a. $P_0 = \$768$
18. $10.97

6A

1. $8,486,832
2. $14,812,741

7

2. a. $88.33
4. $57.36
8. $21.34
9. $16.21
14. a. $40.36
16. a. 300,001
19. $12.10
21. b. $30.97
23. $16.80
25. $20.25

8

2. $5,100
4. a. $122,500
8. $402,000
11. $144,730
13. $NCF_1 = \$14,716$
    $NCF_2 = \$18,796$
16. $8,850,000
18. $2,780,000
19. $NCF_2 = \$347,960$
20. $148,000

9

1. NPV = $-3,050
2. a. $158
3. 9.11%
5. $364.53
9. $13,844
10. 8%
12. $4,245
14. a. NPV = $19,031
17. $n \approx 19$
19. a. $-250,800
21. b. $NCF_1 = \$2,537,400$
    $NCF_3 = \$2,729,400$

9A

1. a. $NPV_A = \$1,888.50$
    $NPV_B = \$2,292$
2. Alternative P

10

2. a. 5.48%
6. a. 17%
9. a. $703,600
11. b. $-0.1795 million

13. a. $230,250
15. c. $29,599
19. 19.8%
22. 12.6%
23. 14.2%

11

2. 7.2%
4. b. 13%
5. a. 12.5%
8. a. 13.4%
9. 17.3%
12. First break: $33.33 million
$k_a = 13.1\%$ (for first block)
14. First break: $60 million
$k_a = 13.19\%$ (for first block)
20. a. $27.65
21. a. 1.4
24. a. $10.10

12

1. $10,000
3. a. $600,000
5. a. i. 45% debt + 55% equity

13

1. a. EPS (Sales = $6 million) = $5.40
d. i. DCL = 2.778
2. b. i. DOL = 1.875
ii. DFL = 1.67
iii. DCL = 3.13
5. a. DOL = 10.67
b. DFL = 1.765
9. 9.18%
12. b. DFL = 1.6
d. EPS = $2.46
15. EPS = $3.36
16. 24.51%
17. 2.28%
19. a. EBIT = $15 million
21. a. EBIT = $2.4 million
22. a. EBIT = $170,000
23. a. EBIT = $133.2 million
26. a. Approximately 26%
27. a. EBIT = $17.5 million
29. a. 2.28%
31. a. 9.68%
32. a. 4.01%
33. a. $47 million

13A

1. a. i. $Q_b = 5,000$
d. ii. Profit = $0
4. $250,000
6. a. $2,300,000

14

1. b. $0.50
3. 16.7%
4. $1,425,000
7. b. $1.60
15. Wednesday, August 18th

15

1. b. $50,703,000
2. Aggressive: ROE = 14.55%
3. c. 124.1 days
e. 69.35 days
4. a. i. Aggressive: ROA = 12.29%
5. a. iii. Aggressive: CA/CL = 1.25
6. a. i. Aggressive: 10.85%
7. c. ii. Interest = $7.79 million
8. a. $889,980
12. a. 46.7 days
13. b. $500,000 additional financing
14. Cash loans needed at the end of
January = $40,000
16. $108 million
18. b. $300,000

16

1. a. $7,500,000
2. b. $177,534
3. d. $-18,424
4. $411,044
5. c. $90,959
7. a. $10,471.50
9. a. $257,849
12. a. $-1,562

17

1. b. 38.5 days
3. $-932
6. c. -$11,363
8. $158,062
10. $17,329
11. $1,163,836
15. $104,700
16. a. 80,000 units
18. a. 17,678; 10,607
20. c. 14.6 days
21. d. 24,658

18

1. b. $340,000
2. b. APR = 12.40%
3. a. AFC = 14.9%
7. a. AFC = 8.7%
9. a. AFC = 11.67%
12. AFC = 23.23%
14. c. AFC = 20.4%

17. AFC = 22%
19. a. AFC = 12.89%
21. AFC = 19.66%
23. a. PMT = $1,467,567
27. a. $972,373
29. 11.8% (calculator accuracy)
30. a. Year 1 = $25,082
31. a. 13%

19

3. a. 4.96%
4. a. $10,624
7. Year 1 cash flow = $3.6 million

20

1. c. $0
2. c. $10
3. a. $1,000
b. $726
4. a. 11.98 shares
6. a. $1.50
b. $3.50
7. c. $0
8. c. $131.25 million
12. c. $1.15
13. a. Formula value = $0
Premium = $1
14. b. $783
16. c. Stock: 33.33%
Warrant: 116.67%

22

1. b. 19%
2. a. EPS = $4.045
d. EPS = $4.258
3. a. 0.5 shares of Ball for 1 share of Keyes
7. $EPS_c = $3.24

Appendix A

1. $855,100
5. a. $14,100,000
6. $2,640,000
8. a. $33,400,000
11. Year 4 depreciation = $2,304

MACRS	Modified accelerated cost recovery system of depreciation
MC	Marginal cost
MR	Marginal revenue
MVA	Market value added
n	Number of time periods
N	Number of rights required to purchase one share of stock
NAL	Net advantage to leasing
NCF	Net cash flow
NINV	Net investment
NPV	Net present value
NWC	Net working capital
O	Operating costs
p	(1) Probability of occurrence of a specific rate of return
	(2) Price per unit
P_{net}	Net proceeds to firm from the sale of a security
P_t	Price of a security at time period t
PB	Payback period
P/BV	Market price per share; book value per share
P/E	Market price per share; current earnings per share
P_f	(1) Preferred stock in a firm's capital structure
	(2) Market value of a firm's preferred stock
PI	Profitability index
PMT	Annuity payment
PPP	Purchasing power parity
PV	Present value
PVAN	Present value of an annuity
PVAND	Present value of an annuity due
PVIF	Present value interest factor
PVIFA	Present value interest factor of an annuity
PVPER	Present value of a perpetuity
PVPERD	Present value of a perpetuity due
π_f	Expected foreign country inflation rate
π_h	Expected home country inflation rate